# FUND ACCOUNTING
## Theory and Practice

EDWARD S. LYNN, Ph.D., CPA
Professor of Accounting, University of Arizona

ROBERT J. FREEMAN, Ph.D., CPA
Professor of Accounting, University of Alabama

PRENTICE-HALL, INC., Englewood Cliffs, New Jersey

ISBN: 0-13-332379-X

Library of Congress Catalog Card Number: 74-4917

Printed in the United States of America

10 9 8 7 6 5 4 3 2 1

PRENTICE-HALL INTERNATIONAL, INC., *London*
PRENTICE-HALL OF AUSTRALIA, PTY., LTD., *Sydney*
PRENTICE-HALL OF CANADA, LTD., *Toronto*
PRENTICE-HALL OF INDIA PRIVATE LIMITED, *New Delhi*
PRENTICE-HALL OF JAPAN, INC., *Tokyo*

# Contents

# 5

# General and Special Revenue Funds:
# Balance Sheets and Fund Balance Statements    159

BALANCE SHEETS
ANALYSIS OF CHANGES IN FUND BALANCE

# 6

# Revenue Accounting    176

CLASSIFICATION OF REVENUE ACCOUNTS
TAXES
General Property Taxes / General Property Tax Statements
LICENSES AND PERMITS
INTERGOVERNMENTAL REVENUE
CHARGES FOR SERVICES
FINES AND FORFEITS
MISCELLANEOUS REVENUE
REVENUE LEDGER
REVENUE STATEMENTS

# 7

# Expenditure Accounting    220

ACCOUNTING CONTROLS
EXPENDITURE ACCOUNTING PROCEDURES
Personal Services / Supplies / Other Services and Charges
CLASSIFICATION OF EXPENDITURES
Coding Expenditure Accounts
SUBSIDIARY ACCOUNTS FOR EXPENDITURES
Entries in Subsidiary Ledger / Closing Entries /
Reserve for Encumbrances of Prior Years
EXPENDITURE STATEMENTS

# 10

## Debt Service Funds 379

Types of Long-Term Debt / Timing of Debt Service Payments /
Sources of Financing / Debt Service Fund for a Refunding Issue /
Debt Service Fund for a Serial Issue / Sinking Fund Requirements /
Debt Service Fund for a Term Issue / Accrual of Interest Payable /
Balance Sheet Prior to Maturity / Balance Sheet at Maturity / Statements
of Operation / Single Debt Service Fund for Several Bond Issues /
Pooling of Assets

# 11

## General Fixed Assets; General Long-Term Debt; Introduction to Interfund Transactions and Relationships 401

### GENERAL FIXED ASSETS

"General" Fixed Assets Defined / Acquisition and Initial Valuation /
Classification / Recording Fixed Assets Acquisitions /
Establishing Property Records / Classifying Individual Property Records /
Additions, Betterments, and Renewals / Depreciation Not Recorded /
Sale, Retirement, or Replacement / Transfer of Fixed Assets /
Statement of General Fixed Assets / Property Damaged or Destroyed /
Inventory of Fixed Assets

### GENERAL LONG-TERM DEBT

"General" Long-Term Debt Defined / Overview of General Long-Term
Debt Accounting / Relation to Term Debt / Relation to Serial Debt /
Relation to Non-GLTD Issuances / Premiums and Discounts /
Establishing GLTD Records / GLTD Statements, Schedules,
and Statistical Tables

### INTERFUND RELATIONSHIPS

# 12

## Trust and Agency Funds 475

Budgetary Considerations / The Accountability Focus /
Financial Statements Required

**TRUST FUNDS**
Expendable Trust Funds / Nonexpendable Trust Funds
**AGENCY FUNDS**
Simpler Agency Funds / More Complex Agency Funds

# 13
# Intragovernmental Service Funds   530

Overview of Accounting Principles / Cost Accounting in the IGS Fund /
Creation of the IGS Fund / Pricing Policies / Pricing Methods /
Relation to the Budget
**IGS FUND ACCOUNTING ILLUSTRATED**
A Central Automotive Equipment Unit / A Central Stores Fund /
Disposition of Under- or Over-Applied Overhead /
Disposition of Retained Earnings / Dissolution of an IGS Fund /
Accounting for Budgetary Operations
**IGS FUND STATEMENTS**

# 14
# Enterprise Funds;
# Summary of Interfund Accounting   577

**ENTERPRISE FUND ACCOUNTING**
Characteristics of Enterprise Fund Accounting /
Enterprise Fund Accounting Illustrated
**SUMMARY OF INTERFUND ACCOUNTING**

# 15
# Cost Accounting, Finding, and Analysis   644

**COST CONCEPTS, TERMINOLOGY, AND BEHAVIOR**
Cost Concepts / Cost Elements / Cost Behavior
**COST ACCOUNTING—OVERVIEW**
Cost Centers / Basic Cost Accounting Approaches /
Reconciliation of Cost and General Accounts

**COST ACCOUNTING—APPLICATIONS**
Equipment Operation Costs / Maintenance Activity Costs /
Construction Costs / Cost Accounting as Applied to Enterprises /
Cost Standards and Variance Analyses
**COST FINDING**
Cost Finding Approaches / A Hospital Cost Finding Example

The Treasurer / Accounting for Cash Receipts / Recording Collections /
Accounting for Cash Disbursements / Cash Statements /
Funds and Bank Accounts / Interfund Settlements / Reconciliations /
Concluding Comment

**THE ANNUAL FINANCIAL REPORT**
The Principle of Full Disclosure /
Content of the Annual Financial Report
**INTERIM STATEMENTS**
**POPULAR REPORTS**

**AUDITING STANDARDS**
**THE FISCAL (FINANCIAL AND COMPLIANCE) AUDIT ELEMENTS**
Auditing Standards / Audit Procedures / The Audit Report
**THE OPERATIONAL (PERFORMANCE) AUDIT ELEMENTS**
Standards of Managerial Performance / Auditing Standards /
Audit Procedures / Reporting
**CONCLUDING COMMENT**

# PART II
# FEDERAL AND INSTITUTIONAL
# ACCOUNTING AND REPORTING   795

## 19
## Federal Government Accounting   797

**OVERVIEW OF THE FEDERAL
FINANCIAL MANAGEMENT ENVIRONMENT**
Landmark Legislation / Financial Management
Roles and Responsibilities / Fund Structure
**OVERVIEW OF THE BUDGETARY PROCESS**
The Budget Cycle / An Evolutionary Process
**ACCOUNTING PRINCIPLES AND STANDARDS FOR
FEDERAL AGENCIES**
Purposes and Objectives / Standards for Internal Management Control /
Standards for Accounting Systems / The Accrual Basis of Accounting /
Fund Control / Accounting Entity and Account Structure /
Financial Reporting
**FEDERAL AGENCY ACCOUNTING AND
REPORTING ILLUSTRATED**
Overview of the Federal Agency Accounting Equation /
A Case Illustration / Reporting

## 20
## Accounting for Hospitals   848

**AN OVERVIEW OF HOSPITAL ACCOUNTING**
Funds / Unique Income Determination and Asset Valuation Features
**ILLUSTRATIVE TRANSACTIONS, ENTRIES,
AND FINANCIAL STATEMENTS**
Illustrative Transactions and Entries / Financial Statements
**UNSETTLED ISSUES/CONCLUDING COMMENTS**
AICPA Audit Guide / Other Issues and Concluding Comments

**21**

## Accounting for Colleges and Universities 926

# Preface

This *should* have been the fifth edition of *Municipal and Govern-mental Accounting*. However, the publication of *Governmental Accounting, Auditing, and Financial Reporting* in 1968, the acquisition of a co-author, and the passage of time have required and at the same time facilitated so complete a revision of that text that we in fact came up with a new book. This first edition of *Fund Accounting: Theory and Practice* includes, hope-fully, everything from *Municipal and Governmental Accounting* that met with favorable response.

The text's teachability has been strengthened by a number of innova-tions. Graphic illustrations have been added to assist the student in under-standing fund purposes, the life cycles of funds, budgetary accounting, budget processes and procedures, adaptations of the accounting equation, forms design, and the like. Early in the text a "primer" provides an overview of fund accounting before the student plunges into the details of the theory and practice of fund accounting. Many illustrative examples are summarized in worksheet format to facilitate student comprehension and review. We have provided expanded coverage, as compared with the predecessor text, of the environment of fund accounting, its evolution, alternative accounting and budgetary approaches and techniques, auditing, and other important topics.

We introduce the interfund entry problem before all the funds and account groups have been discussed. The reader is by this device encouraged to recognize interfund relationships at an early point. He is thus spared, to some extent, the shock that interfund transactions bring when he has gone through the accounting for ten funds and account groups and suddenly has to integrate the several kinds of accounting.

This text is designed to be sufficiently adaptable to meet the needs of a variety of course types and instructor preferences. Its breadth and depth of coverage, the balanced treatment of theory and practice, and the wealth of assignment material provide ample basis for the graduate level or two-term undergraduate level course. It is equally suited for use in the more traditional one-term course, affording the instructor wide latitude in selecting those topics, approaches, and emphases that best fit the objectives of the course, and for use as a practitioner reference text.

We thank the many users of the editions of the previous text, who over the years have offered numerous helpful suggestions for improvement, and solicit comment and constructive criticism with regard to this volume. Our special thanks go to Lennis M. Knighton, Professor of Accounting and Public Administration, Brigham Young University, for his review of this manuscript and to our wives, Marcille and Beverly, for their assistance and encouragement throughout the course of its preparation.

ESL
RJF

# Governmental and Institutional Accounting:
# Its Environment and Characteristics

Accounting is the art of analyzing, recording, summarizing, evaluating, and interpreting an organization's financial activities and position, and communicating the results to those who are interested. This book deals with accounting and reporting principles, standards, and procedures applicable to (1) state and local governments, including counties, cities, townships, and villages, (2) the Federal government, and (3) other not-for-profit institutions such as universities and hospitals. Financial management considerations and problems peculiar to the not-for-profit (NFP) sector receive emphasis throughout. In addition, unique aspects of auditing in this environment are discussed from the standpoint of both organization management and the independent auditor.

## CHARACTERISTICS AND TYPES OF NFP ORGANIZATIONS

Governments and other not-for-profit organizations are unique in that:

1. The profit motive is not inherent in their inception or operation.
2. They are usually owned collectively by their constituents; i.e., ownership is not normally evidenced by individually owned equity shares which may be sold or exchanged.
3. Those contributing financial resources to the organization do not necessarily receive a direct or proportionate share of its goods or services; e.g.,

the welfare recipient most likely did not pay the taxes from which his benefits are paid.

A not-for-profit organization exists, therefore, because a community or society considers it necessary or desirable to provide certain goods or services to its group as a whole, often without reference to whether costs incurred will be recovered through charges for the goods or services or whether those paying for the goods or services are those benefiting from them. In most instances NFP organizations provide goods or services which are not commercially feasible to produce through private enterprise and/or which are deemed so vital to the public well-being that it is felt that their provision should be supervised by elected or appointed representatives of the populace.

The major types of not-for-profit organizations may be classified as follows.

1. *Governmental:* Federal, state, county, municipal, township, village, and other local governmental authorities, including special districts.
2. *Educational:* including kindergartens, elementary and secondary schools, colleges and universities.
3. *Health and welfare:* such as hospitals, nursing homes, orphanages, penal and correctional institutions, the American Red Cross, and the USO.
4. *Religious:* churches, YMCA, Salvation Army, and other church-related organizations.
5. *Charitable:* Community Chests, United Appeals, United Funds, and other charitable organizations.
6. *Foundations:* private trusts and corporations organized for educational, religious, or charitable purposes.

The above is a general classification scheme, of course, and much overlap occurs. There are many church-related charitable organizations, for example, and governments are deeply involved in education, health, and welfare activities.

## GROWTH AND IMPORTANCE OF THE NFP SECTOR

Governments and other not-for-profit organizations have experienced dramatic growth in recent years and have emerged—individually and collectively—as major economic, political and social forces in our society. Of rather minor consequence thirty or forty years ago, the NFP sector now generates approximately *one-third* (1/3) of all expenditures within our economy, and many "growth industries" may be found within it. The total value of resources devoted to this sector is gigantic, both absolutely and relatively.

Governments have experienced particularly dynamic growth in recent years, both in the scope and in the magnitude of their activities. Over 13,000,000 people work in government positions—about 20 percent of the employed civilian labor force—and both total and per capita expenditures of governments have increased dramatically in the past decade. Governments spend over $400 billion annually, some $2,000 per citizen per year. The Federal government alone spends about $2.5 billion each year—more than twice as much as in 1960 and over four times its 1950 expenditure level. In addition, total governmental debt exceeds $600 billion at this writing, approximately $3,000 per capita.

Sound financial management—including thoughtful budgeting, appropriate accounting, meaningful financial reporting, and timely audits by qualified auditors—is at least as important in the not-for-profit sector as in the private sector. Furthermore, because of the scope and diversity of its activities, proper management of the financial affairs of a city or town, for example, may be far more complex than that of a private business with comparable assets or annual expenditures.

## THE NFP ENVIRONMENT

Not-for-profit organizations are in many ways similar to profit-seeking enterprises. For example:

1. They are integral parts of the same economic system and utilize similar resources in accomplishing their purposes.
2. Both must acquire and convert scarce resources into their respective goods or services.
3. Financial management processes are essentially similar in both and each must have a viable information system—of which the accounting system is an integral component—if its managers and other interested persons or groups are to receive relevant and timely data for planning, directing, controlling, and evaluating the use of its scarce resources.
4. Inasmuch as their resources are relatively scarce—whether donated, received from customers or consumers, acquired from investors or creditors, or secured through taxation—least-cost analysis and other control and evaluation techniques are essential to assuring that resources are utilized economically, effectively, and efficiently.
5. In some cases, both produce similar products, e.g., both governments and private enterprise may own and operate transportation systems, sanitation services, and electric or gas utilities.

There are, of course, major differences between profit-seeking and not-for-profit organizations. Although there are many types of NFP organizations and broad generalizations about such a diversified group are difficult, the major differences may be classified for discussion purposes as arising from differing organizational objectives, sources of resources, and regulation and control.

ORGANIZATIONAL OBJECTIVES. Expectation of income or gain is the principal factor motivating investors to provide resources to profit-seeking enterprises. On the other hand, as has been noted, a not-for-profit organization exists to provide certain goods or services to a community or society as a whole, often without reference to whether costs incurred are recouped through charges levied on those receiving them and without regard to whether those receiving the goods or services are those paying for them. There is no profit motive; there are no individual shareholders to whom dividends are paid.

The objective of most not-for-profit organizations is to acquire resources and provide as many goods or as much service as these resources permit. Not only is there no desire to increase the organization's capital, as is common in private enterprise, there is not necessarily a desire to maintain its capital. On the contrary, the intent at times may be to deplete the entity's capital. Emphasis in this environment is, therefore, upon acquiring and using resources—upon cash flow, sources and uses of working capital and budgetary position—as opposed to the determination of net income or earnings per share.

SOURCES OF RESOURCES.    The sources of resources vary widely among not-for-profit organizations. And, in the absence of a net income determination emphasis, no distinction is generally made between invested capital and revenue. A dollar is a resource whether acquired through donation, user charge, sale of assets, loan or in some other manner.

Governments are unique in that they may force resource contributions through taxation. All levels rely heavily upon this power, and total tax revenues of governments exceed $300 billion at this writing—providing governments over $1,500 per citizen annually. Grants and shared revenue from other governments also are important state and local government revenue sources—those from the Federal government exceed $40 billion per year—as are charges levied for goods or services provided, such as those of utilities.

Other not-for-profit organizations also derive resources from a variety of sources. Religious groups and charitable organizations usually rely heavily on donations, though they may have other revenue sources. Some colleges and universities rely heavily upon donations and income from trust funds; others depend upon state appropriations or tuition charges for support. Finally, hospitals generally charge their clientele, though few select their patients on the basis of ability to pay, and many rely heavily upon gifts and bequests.

There are other, more subtle differences in sources of resources as compared with profit-seeking businesses. It is important to note, for example, that:

1. User charges, where levied, are usually based on the cost of the goods or services rendered rather than upon supply-and-demand-related pricing policies common to private enterprise.
2. Many services or goods provided by these organizations are unique, or relatively unique, to the extent that there is no open market in which their value may be objectively appraised or evaluated.
3. Charges levied for goods or services may cover only part of the costs in-

curred in their provision, e.g., tuition generally covers only a fraction of the cost of operating state or local colleges or universities, and token charges may be made to indigent hospital patients more to allow them to retain their self-respect than to recover costs incurred or to maximize profit.

REGULATION AND CONTROL.   The goods or services offered the consuming public by unregulated profit-seeking enterprises will be modified or withdrawn if they are not profitable. There is a direct relationship between the producer and the consumer and every consumer is free to cast his dollar vote for that firm whose goods or services are most suitable to him. In this situation a firm whose management is inept or unresponsive to the desires of the consuming public will not be profitable and will ultimately be forced out of business. Therefore the profit motive and profit measurement constitute an automatic regulating device in our free enterprise economy.

Inasmuch as this profit test/regulator device is not present in the usual not-for-profit situation, NFP organizations must strive to attain their objectives without its benefits. In addition, as has been noted, many not-for-profit organizations provide goods or services for which there is no open market value measurement by which to test consumer satisfaction because (1) the goods and services are unique, or (2) the consumers are receiving "free" (to them) goods or services for which the community or society as a whole is paying, i.e., the consumers have no "dollar vote" to cast.

Unless alternative controls are employed, (1) the absence of the need to operate profitably, (2) the lack of an open market test of the value of the organization's output, (3) the remote and indirect relationship, if any, between the resource contributor and the goods or services recipient, and (4) in the case of governments, the ability to force resource contributions via taxation, might make it possible for an inefficient, uneconomical, or even ineffective not-for-profit organization to continue operating indefinitely. Not-for-profit organizations, particularly governments, are therefore subject to more stringent legal, regulatory, and other controls than are private businesses.

All facets of a NFP organization's operations may be affected by legal or quasi-legal requirements that are (1) imposed externally, as by Federal or state statute, ruling, grant stipulation, or judicial decree, or (2) imposed internally by charter, by-law, ordinance, trust agreement, donor stipulation, or contract. Furthermore, operational and administrative controls may be more stringent than in private enterprise because of the need to assure compliance with legal and other requirements. Among the aspects of a NFP organization's operations that may be regulated or otherwise controlled are:

1. *Organization Structure.* Form; composition of its directing board or similar body; the number and duties of its personnel; lines of authority and responsibility; which officials or employees are to be elected, appointed, or hired from among applicants.

2. *Personnel Policies and Procedures.* Who will appoint or hire personnel; tenure of personnel; policies and procedures upon termination; extent of minority group representation on the staff; levels of compensation; promotion policies; and types and amounts of compensation increments permissible.

3. *Sources of Resources.* The types and amounts of taxes, licenses, fines, or fees a government may levy; the manner in which users charges are to be set; tuition rates; debt limits; the purposes for which debt may be incurred.

4. *Use of Resources.* The purpose for which resources may be used, including "earmarking" of certain resources for use only for specific purposes; purchasing procedures to be followed, budgeting methods, forms, or procedures used.

5. *Accounting.* Any or all phases of the accounting systems, e.g., charts of accounts, bases of accounting, forms, procedures.

6. *Reporting.* Type and frequency of reports; report format and content; to whom reports are to be furnished.

7. *Auditing.* Frequency of audit; who is to perform the audit; the scope and type of audit to be performed; the time and place for filing the audit report; who is to receive or have access to the audit report; the wording of the auditor's report.

Thus, managers of NFP organizations may have limited discretion compared with managers of business enterprises. It may be difficult to (1) modify an organization's structure, no matter how archaic, awkward, or ineffective; (2) attract qualified employees at prescribed pay rates, discharge or demote incompetent employees, or reward outstanding employees; (3) acquire sufficient resources or use available resources as management deems most appropriate; or (4) improve the existing budgeting, accounting, reporting, or auditing arrangements. The role and emphasis of financial accounting and reporting may be correspondingly altered, therefore, as compared with the profit-seeking enterprise environment.

## ROLE AND CHARACTERISTICS OF NFP ACCOUNTING

According to a major committee of the American Accounting Association, the objectives of accounting are to provide information for:

1. Making decisions concerning the use of limited resources, including the identification of crucial decision areas and determination of objectives and goals.

2. Effectively directing and controlling an organization's human and material resources.

3. Maintaining and reporting on the custodianship of resources.

4. Contributing to the effectiveness of all organizations, whether profit-oriented or not, in fulfilling the desires and demands of all society for social control of their functions.[1]

One finds many similarities in the accounting for profit-seeking and not-for-profit organizations. A double-entry system of accounts is universally recommended for both. The general mechanics of record-keeping are the same: documents form the basic record, books of original entry (journals) are kept and posted to general ledgers and subsidiary ledgers, trial balances are drawn to prove the equality of debits and credits, a chart of accounts properly classified and properly fitted to the organization's structure is essential to good accounting, and, of course, uniform terminology is highly desirable in both fields.

Some NFP organization activities (such as utilities, public transportation, and parking facilities) parallel those of some profit-seeking enterprises. In such cases the accounting parallels that of their privately-owned counterparts. In most of their operations, however, governments and other not-for-profit institutions are not concerned with profit measurement. (In even the cited activities the NFP organization may not seek to maximize profits, but only to assure continuity and/or improvement of service.)

Accounting is a service function. It does not operate in a vacuum but must evolve to meet the information demands in a given environment. In the NFP environment decisions concerning resource acquisition and allocation, managerial direction and control of resource utilization, and custodianship for resources have traditionally been framed in terms of social and political objectives and constraints rather than profitability. Legal and administrative constraints have been used as society's methods of directing its NFP institutions in achieving those objectives. Thus, NFP organization accounting and reporting have correspondingly evolved with a distinctive "control" flavor and expendable resource emphasis. The two most important types of legal and administrative control provisions affecting accounting in this environment are the use of funds and the distinctive role of the budget.

FUNDS AND FUND ACCOUNTING. It has been observed that the resources made available to a not-for-profit organization may be restricted, that is, they may be usable only for certain purposes or specific activities. For example, a church may receive donations for a building addition; a hospital may receive a grant for adding an intensive care facility; a city may borrow money to construct a sewage treatment plant or receive state gasoline tax "shared revenues" that are earmarked for local road improvement; a university may receive a Federal grant for research purposes or may be the custodian of resources to be used only for making student loans. There may also be instances in which the management

[1] American Accounting Association, Committee to Prepare a Statement of Basic Accounting Theory, *A Statement of Basic Accounting Theory* (Evanston, Ill.: The Association, 1966), p. 4.

decides to designate specific purposes for which certain resources must be used, e.g., they may wish to accumulate resources for equipment replacement or facility enlargement. An essential custodianship obligation in such situations is to use the resources in accordance with stipulations inherent in their receipt and report upon this compliance to others.

In order to control earmarked resources and both ensure and demonstrate compliance with legal or administrative requirements, not-for-profit organizations establish funds. In the early days of fund accounting, "funds" meant "cash funds." Each might be housed in a separate cash drawer or cigar box; some bills would be paid from one drawer and others from another drawer, in accordance with the use to which the cash in each could be put. Today "funds" are separate fiscal and accounting entities, and noncash resources as well as related liabilities and reserves are accounted for therein. A fund is

> An independent fiscal and accounting entity with a self-balancing set of accounts recording cash and/or other resources together with all related liabilities, obligations, reserves, and equities which are segregated for the purpose of carrying on specific activities or attaining certain objectives in accordance with special regulations, restrictions, or limitations[2]

Two types of fund accounting entities are used by NFP organizations:

1. *Expendable funds.* To account for the current assets, related liabilities and changes in net assets that may be expended in its not-for-profit activities (e.g., for fire and police protection).
2. *Nonexpendable funds.* To account for the revenues, expenses, assets, liabilities and equity of its "business-type" activities (e.g., utilities, cafeterias, or transportation systems), and some trust funds.

It is important to note that the fund concept involves an accounting segregation, not necessarily the physical separation of resources; however, resources are often also physically segregated—for example, through use of separate checking accounts for cash resources of various funds.

Usage of the term "fund" in not-for-profit situations should be sharply distinguished from its usage in private enterprise. A fund of a commercial enterprise is simply a portion of its assets that has been restricted to specific uses. It is not a separate and distinct accounting entity. Revenue and expense related to such funds are part of enterprise operations, i.e. fund revenue and expense accounts appear side-by-side in the general ledger with other enterprise revenue or expense accounts. On the other hand, a fund in the not-for-profit sense is a self-contained accounting entity with its own asset, liability, revenue, expenditure or expense, and fund balance or other equity accounts—and with its own ledger(s). (See Figure 1-1.)

---

[2] The National Committee on Governmental Accounting, *Governmental Accounting, Auditing, and Financial Reporting* (Chicago: The Municipal Finance Officers Association of the United States and Canada, 1968), p. 161.

Figure 1-1

## SINGLE ENTITY VERSUS MULTIPLE ENTITY ACCOUNTING

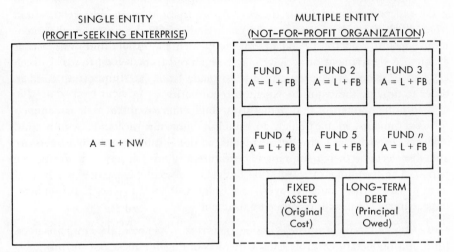

Legend:

A  = Assets
L  = Liabilities
NW = Net Worth (of the enterprise)
FB = Fund Balance (of the individual fund)
− − − = The not-for-profit organization as a whole — for which statements are generally not prepared

Though there is agreement among authorities that the fund device is essential to financial management of not-for-profit organizations generally, its use has an unfortunate fragmenting effect upon their accounting and reporting. The statements of a profit-seeking enterprise present in one place the information regarding that enterprise. It is possible, by looking at its balance sheet, to determine the nature and valuation of its assets, liabilities and net worth. The nature and amounts of the components of change in net worth occasioned by enterprise operations are presented in its periodic operating statements.

The financial reports of most not-for-profit organizations, however, consist of a series of independent fund entity balance sheets and operating statements. Combined or consolidated statements are not in widespread use in the not-for-profit sector. Thus, there is usually no balance sheet or operating statement for the organization as a whole.

BUDGETS AND APPROPRIATIONS.    The creation of an expendable fund ordinarily does not carry with it the authority to expend its resources. In most not-for-profit organizations, especially governments, expenditures may be made only within the authority of appropriations, which are authorizations to make expenditures for specified purposes.

A fixed-dollar budget is commonly prepared for each expendable fund. When approved by the directing board or enacted by the legislature, the budgetary expenditure estimates become binding appropriations—both authority to make expenditures and limits thereon. Appropriations must indicate the fund from which the expenditure may be made and specify the purposes, the maximum amount, and the period of time for which the expenditure authority is granted. A department or activity may be financed from several funds. In such cases at least one appropriation must be made from each supporting fund in order to provide the requisite expenditure authority.

In order to control and demonstrate budgetary compliance, it is common for governments, in particular, to establish budgetary accounts within fund ledgers. Through this technique, explained in detail subsequently, managers are able to determine their remaining expenditure authority at any time during the period. The technique of integrating budgetary accounts is particularly helpful in those cases where budget "over runs" subject officials to fine, imprisonment, impeachment, dismissal, or other punishment.

Some Other Distinguishing Characteristics.    As noted, the emphasis upon fund and budgetary controls causes the accounting for most not-for-profit organizations to more closely resemble cash flow or working capital analysis than commercial accounting, in which net income determination is a paramount consideration. Expendable resources, accounted for in expendable fund entities and allocated by the budget and appropriation process, are the focal point of most not-for-profit accounting and reporting. (Correspondingly, less attention is directed to inventories, fixed assets, and long-term debt in NFP organizations as compared with profit-seeking organizations.) "Expenditures" are defined as "the cost of goods delivered or services rendered, whether paid or unpaid, including [current] expenses, provision for debt retirement not reported as a liability of the fund from which retired, and capital outlays."[3] Thus the term "expenditures"—the term that is significant in expendable fund accounting—should not be confused with "expenses" as defined for accounting for profit-seeking enterprises.

Fixed assets are not normally appropriable resources and are commonly listed and accounted for separately from the expendable fund accounting entities. Similarly, long-term debt that is not a liability of a particular fund (but of the unit as a whole) may be listed in a separate nonfund accounting entity. Furthermore, since net income determination is not a consideration in most NFP organizations, (1) inventory valuation may receive only passing attention, and (2) depreciation of fixed assets is not usually accounted for, even though it is an expense, inasmuch as it did not require the use of appropriable resources during the current period. Contrariwise, a fixed asset acquisition is considered an

3 *GAAFR,* p. 160.

"expenditure" (use of current resources) in the period in which it occurs, since it reduces the net assets of an expendable fund at that time.

## Summary Comparison with Commercial Accounting

Though commercial-type accounting is employed where NFP organizations are engaged in commercial-type activities (e.g. electric utilities), accounting and reporting for not-for-profit endeavors have evolved largely in view of these key differences from profit-seeking enterprises:

1. *Objectives:* acquiring resources and expending them in a legal and appropriate manner, as opposed to seeking to increase—or even maintain—its capital.
2. *Control:* substitution of statutory, fund and budgetary controls in the absence of the profit regulator/control device inherent in profit-seeking endeavors.

These factors—objectives and control—underpin the major differences between commercial and not-for-profit accounting. The primary consideration in this environment is upon compliance—and accounting, reporting, and auditing have developed principally as tools of compliance control and demonstration.

The student should constantly take note of the similarities and differences between commercial and not-for-profit accounting in concept, approach, and terminology. He should be particularly cautious and observant in those cases where the same concepts and terms are used in both, but with different connotations. In not-for-profit accounting, for example:

1. The *entity* concept relates to the separate fund entities, not the organization as a whole; there is usually no unified accounting or reporting entity for the organization in its entirety.
2. The *periodicity* concept relates to the flow of funds during the budgetary period and to budgetary comparisons, rather than to income determination.
3. The *matching* concept as understood in commercial accounting is used similarly for commercial-type activities undertaken by NFP organizations. In all other cases reference is to matching revenue and expenditures—current, capital outlay, and debt retirement—against budgetary authorizations. *Expendable fund accounting emphasizes the inflows, outflows, and balances of expendable resources rather than the determination of revenue, expense, and net income.*
4. The *going concern* concept has relevance only when commercial type or self-supporting activities are involved in NFP organizations. Expendable resource funds exist on a year-by-year or project-by-project basis and may be intentionally exhausted and "go out of business."

## AUTHORITATIVE SOURCES OF NFP ACCOUNTING PRINCIPLES

NFP accounting and reporting principles (standards) have evolved more or less independently in several types of organizations. Thus, the American Hospital Association has fostered their development for hospitals, the National Committee on Governmental Accounting has led their formulation insofar as state and local governments are concerned, and the U.S. General Accounting Office has been at the forefront at the Federal government level. In addition, each field has its own journals, newsletters, and professional societies.

The American Institute of Certified Public Accountants (AICPA), whose Accounting Principles Board (APB) was a leading source of authoritative support for accounting principles for profit-seeking enterprises, has not played a comparable role in the not-for-profit field. Though the AICPA has assisted the various NFP associations or groups engaged in the development of accounting and reporting principles—and some APB pronouncements are applicable to NFP organizations—its pronouncements are subject to this general disclaimer:

> The committee has not directed its attention to accounting problems or procedures of religious, charitable, scientific, educational and similar non-profit institutions, municipalities, professional firms, and the like. Accordingly... its opinions and recommendations are directed primarily to business enterprises organized for profit.[4]

Likewise, the American Accounting Association (AAA), while not excluding not-for-profit organizations from its purview, has traditionally focused its efforts and pronouncements upon problems in the profit-seeking environment.

It is encouraging to note, however, that both the AICPA and the AAA have recently increased their efforts insofar as NFP accounting and reporting are concerned. The AICPA has developed audit guides for hospitals, colleges and universities, state and local governments, and voluntary health and welfare organizations, for example, and several recent AAA committees have been concerned with the NFP sector. In addition, the rules of procedure governing the Financial Accounting Standards Board (FASB), the independent public sector body formed in 1973 to succeed the APB, indicate that the FASB is to develop and issue accounting and reporting standards for both not-for-profit and profit-seeking organizations.[5]

This text is based on the pronouncements of the most authoritative group in each not-for-profit area. Sources of authoritative support are discussed in detail within the relevant text material.

---

[4] American Institute of Certified Public Accountants, *Accounting Research and Terminology Bulletins,* final ed. (New York: The Institute, 1961), p. 8.

[5] At this writing the FASB had issued no statements directed to NFP organizations, and the topics on its agenda primarily concerned profit-seeking organizations.

**Question 1-1.** What characteristics differentiate not-for-profit organizations from profit-seeking organizations?

**Question 1-2.** How does society determine which goods or services will be provided by not-for-profit organizations?

**Question 1-3.** List four factors that cause society to subject NFP organizations to more stringent legal, regulatory, and other controls than it imposes on private businesses.

**Question 1-4.** Define "fund" as used in not-for-profit organizations. Contrast that definition with the same term as used in a profit-seeking organization.

**Question 1-5.** Discuss the funds-flow concept as it applies to the operations of not-for-profit organizations.

**Question 1-6.** Contrast the terms "expense" and "expenditure."

**Question 1-7.** Contrast the following concepts as they are used in financial and fund accounting: (a) entity (b) periodicity (c) matching (d) going concern.

**Question 1-8.** Distinguish between use of the term "fund" in accounting for not-for-profit organizations from its use in accounting for profit-seeking organizations.

**Question 1-9.** Some accountants feel that supplementary consolidated statements should be prepared for not-for-profit organizations in which activities are financed through numerous funds. Assess the merits of this suggestion.

**Question 1-10.** Does the creation of a fund constitute authority to spend or obligate its resources? Explain.

**Question 1-11.** It was noted in Chapter 1 that most of the differences between commercial accounting and that for not-for-profit organizations result from differences in (1) organizational objectives and (2) methods of fiscal control employed. Explain.

**Question 1-12.** Which professional association or other agency or group has played the major role in the development of accounting and reporting practices of (1) municipalities? (2) hospitals? (3) the Federal government?

# I

# MUNICIPAL ACCOUNTING, REPORTING, AND AUDITING

# 2

# State and Local Government: Organization and Accounting Principles

State and local government is truly "big business." The fifty states and over 78,000 local governments within these United States employ over 10 million persons—two-thirds more than in 1960 and well over three times as many as are employed by the Federal government—and spend approximately $150 billion annually. Although the Federal government accounts for over half of all government expenditures, state and local governments spend substantially more than the Federal government for nondefense purposes. Furthermore, state and local government revenue, expenditures, debt, and employment—both in total and

Figure 2-1

TYPES OF LOCAL GOVERNMENTS: 1972

| | |
|---|---|
| Counties | 3,044 |
| Municipalities | 18,517 |
| Townships | 16,991 |
| School districts | 15,781 |
| Special districts | 23,885 |
| Total | 78,218 |

Source: 1972 Census of Governments, *Governmental Organization*, Vol. 1, p. 1.

per capita—have all been increasing at higher rates than those of the Federal complex in recent years. Today it is the rule, rather than the exception, to discover that the state government is the largest industry within a state or that city hall houses the biggest business in a town.

The types and numbers of local governments, by state, are shown in Figure 2-1. Not obvious from this table, however, is the extent of local government jurisdictional overlap. It is common for a given geographical area to be served by a municipality, a school district, a county, and one or more special districts. In fact, many metropolitan areas have 100 or more separate and distinct local government units. This overlap, which frequently results in jurisdictional disputes and administrative complexities, is graphically illustrated in Figure 2-2.

State and local governments have increased both the types and levels of goods and services provided their citizens in recent years and many have become among the most complex and diversified organizations in existence today. There seems little doubt that the scope and diversity of their activities, the financial management and accounting complexities involved, their total and per capita expenditures, and their relative importance in our economy and society will continue to grow as our society becomes increasingly urban and governments at all levels attempt to meet the apparently insatiable demands of their constituencies for more and better goods and services.

## ORGANIZATIONAL STRUCTURES AND FORMS

In the United States, governments traditionally have been organized in such a manner that power is divided among three distinct functional branches: legislative, executive, and judicial. Each has specified roles and duties and each is an integral part of a delicate "checks and balances" decision-making and control system designed to prevent any branch from overstepping its bounds or abusing the powers vested in it. Members of the legislative branch are invariably elected in our representative form of government. The chief executive and members of the judiciary in state and local governments may be either elected or appointed. Simply stated, the functions assigned to these branches which bear most directly on governmental accounting and reporting include:

1. *Legislative*—To establish taxation and expenditure policies, levy taxes, authorize expenditures through approval of a budget, give general direction to the executive branch, and require an accounting by the executive branch of its stewardship.

2. *Executive*—To prepare an appropriate budget(s) for approval or amendment by the legislative branch, carry out the programs established or approved by the legislature in an effective and economical manner, and account for its stewardship for the resources entrusted to it.

3. *Judicial*—To interpret laws passed by the legislature and administrative decisions of the executive branch both as to constitutionality and intent.

Figure 2-2

## LAYERS OF GOVERNMENT, FRIDLEY, MINNESOTA

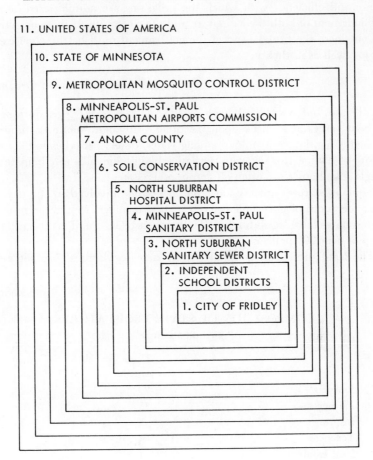

11. UNITED STATES OF AMERICA

10. STATE OF MINNESOTA

9. METROPOLITAN MOSQUITO CONTROL DISTRICT

8. MINNEAPOLIS–ST. PAUL METROPOLITAN AIRPORTS COMMISSION

7. ANOKA COUNTY

6. SOIL CONSERVATION DISTRICT

5. NORTH SUBURBAN HOSPITAL DISTRICT

4. MINNEAPOLIS–ST. PAUL SANITARY DISTRICT

3. NORTH SUBURBAN SANITARY SEWER DISTRICT

2. INDEPENDENT SCHOOL DISTRICTS

1. CITY OF FRIDLEY

Believe it or not: A citizen of Fridley, Minnesota, is expected to exercise an informed control, through the electoral franchise, over 11 separate superimposed governments, and is taxed for their support.

Source: Adapted from Committee for Economic Development, *Modernizing Local Government* (New York: The Committee, 1967), p. 12.

Both the legislative and executive branches therefore play key roles relative to governmental accounting and reporting. Accounting per se is a responsibility of the executive branch, but the legislative branch holds the all-pervasive power of the pursestring. Where duties and responsibilities are thus divided, it is mandatory that: (1) the executive branch be so organized as to be able to perform its legally assigned duties effectively and efficiently, and (2) the legality, effectiveness, and efficiency with which the programs are administered be subject to the judgment of both the legislature and the electorate. If these objectives are to be obtained, the titular head of the government must be the chief executive in fact as well as in theory.

### State Government Organization

All states but Nebraska have a bicameral (two body) legislature in which each body serves as a check upon the other. Although Nebraska's unicameral (one body) legislature is unique among states, others periodically question the necessity of having two separate legislative bodies and bills to eliminate one of the legislative houses are often offered in other states.

Most legislatures are far too large to become involved in the day to day business decisions of government, even if their members should desire to do so. Only ten states have legislatures of 100 members or less; and eight have a membership of over 200 persons.

The legal profession dominates most state legislatures (see Figure 2-3),

**Figure 2-3**

### COMPOSITION OF STATE LEGISLATURES
(based on a sample)

|  | House | Senate |
|---|---|---|
| Lawyers | 29% | 42% |
| Farmers | 13 | 10 |
| Insurance | 7 | 5 |
| Teachers | 4 | 3 |
| Real Estate | 4 | 2 |
| Laborers | 4 | 1 |
| Merchants | 3 | 3 |
| Retired | 3 | 2 |
| Housewives | 3 | 1 |
| Doctors and Engineers | 2 | 3 |
| Bank and Trusts | 2 | 1 |
| All Others | 26 | 27 |

Source: Committee for Economic Development, *Modernizing State Government.* (New York: The Committee, 1967), p. 33.

though members come from all walks of life. The typical legislator is severely underpaid. Thus, as the personal sacrifices necessary to be a legislator and the time which must be devoted to legislative business have increased as state governments have become more complex, it has become more and more difficult to attract qualified candidates for legislative races.

The executive branch of state governments is typically complicated administratively because (1) some or all department heads are popularly elected, and (2) numerous administrative boards are usually appointed by the governor, with or without the approval of the legislative branch,[1] for multiple-year overlapping terms. Such elected or appointed officials in some cases owe political allegiance to the chief executive, but they are not subject to his administrative control. The elected officials are, in their own minds, responsible to the public. The administrative boards frequently feel the same way or feel that their responsibility is to the legislature, which controls their operations through the general laws and through its appropriation authority. Although the chief executive often lacks real authority over such agencies and boards, the public may consider him responsible for their performance.

Reorganizations of state governments within recent decades have evidenced a tendency to form an administrative hierarchy in which the executive power of the governor is strengthened. The number of elected officials, for example, has been reduced, and the governor has been given basic authority to direct the operations of agencies through his power to appoint and discharge their heads. Similarly, the number of units reporting to the governor has been reduced by eliminating duplications of activities and by combining similar programs into a single agency. Further, some states have grouped many executive agencies within a single "super department" in order to reduce the span of control and permit more effective supervision by the chief executive.

Typical reorganizations have also provided the governor with staff agencies designed to assist him in planning, directing, and controlling state activities. Staff agencies of this type may include a personal office staff, a central budget office, and centralized purchasing, personnel administration, or data processing. Among the assignments typically given a governor's personal staff are: (1) developing policy recommendations for legislative presentation, (2) maintaining liaison with Federal, state and local agencies, (3) planning and coordinating programs, (4) managing press and public relations, (5) responding to mail, (6) scheduling appointments, (7) receiving callers, (8) writing speeches, (9) counseling with legislators concerning proposed legislation, and (10) keeping in touch with party officials.

Finally, such reorganizations have often provided for an independent auditor who reports to and is responsible to the legislature—not the governor—and has no powers or duties other than those of postaudit. The objective is to give the legislature an effective tool for evaluating the governor's discharge of the

---

[1] According to a recent study the states have an average of eighty-five separate state agencies and five independently elected department heads.

duties assigned to the executive branch of government. When such reports are made available to the public, the executive branch also becomes more accountable to the electorate.

## City Government Organization

The organizational structures of American cities vary widely in arrangements for achieving their objectives and maintaining checks and balances among the functional areas of government. However, one (or a variation) of three distinct organizational types—mayor-council, commission, and council-manager —will be found in virtually every city or town within the United States. (See Figure 2-4.)

**Figure 2-4**

### FORM OF GOVERNMENT IN CITIES OVER 5,000 POPULATION

| Population Group | Total Number of Cities | Mayor-Council Number | Percent | Council-Manager Number | Percent | Commission Number | Percent |
|---|---|---|---|---|---|---|---|
| Over 500,000 | 27 | 22 | 82 | 5 | 18 | — | — |
| 250,000 to 500,000 | 27 | 11 | 41 | 13 | 48 | 3 | 11 |
| 100,000 to 250,000 | 93 | 33 | 35 | 50 | 54 | 10 | 11 |
| 50,000 to 100,000 | 215 | 83 | 39 | 116 | 54 | 16 | 7 |
| 25,000 to 50,000 | 439 | 166 | 38 | 233 | 53 | 40 | 9 |
| 10,000 to 25,000 | 1,072 | 511 | 48 | 488 | 45 | 73 | 7 |
| 5,000 to 10,000 | 1,112 | 686 | 62 | 378 | 34 | 48 | 4 |
| All cities over 5,000 | 2,985* | 1,512† | 51 | 1,283 | 43 | 190 | 6 |
| Change since 1957 survey: | | | | | | | |
| Number | + 510 | + 260 | | + 372 | | — 122 | |
| Percent | +21% | +21% | | +41% | | −39% | |

\* Not included are 89 places with town meeting government and 38 with representative town meeting government.

† Includes the District of Columbia.

Source: This table is based on a late 1967 survey. Adapted from Mark E. Keane and David S. Arnold, eds., *The Municipal Year Book, 1968* (Washington, D.C.: The International City Managers' Association, 1968), p. 54.

MAYOR-COUNCIL. The mayor-council form follows traditional American ideas concerning the separation of the executive and legislative branches of government. The typical council has from six to twelve elected members—although some are as small as two and others as large as fifty—and is the legislative branch of the local government. The mayor is elected by popular vote and occupies a conspicuous, prestigious, and powerful position. Just how powerful depends on personalities, as well as state laws and local charters and ordinances. For there truly to be an executive branch, the mayor should have power to appoint and remove department heads without reference of any sort to the council, to manage the routine affairs of the government, and to prepare a detailed budget within broad appropriation limits—but these practices are by no means universally accepted. Another sign of his effectiveness in this sense is whether he can veto ordinances of the council.

In practice, both legislative and administrative authority in mayor-council cities have tended to be divided between mayor and council. The council in many cases is required by law to participate in the selection and removal of department heads, and it is virtually impossible for the body which ultimately provides the money for departmental activities to refrain from becoming involved in the day-to-day management of departmental affairs. Thus there is likely to be friction between mayor and council, and the public seldom is able to determine who is responsible for the quality of services it receives. Despite such defects, the mayor-council form is used by over three-fourths of those cities having populations in excess of 500,000 and by over half of those of over 5,000 population. It is a particularly popular form of organization in both very large and in very small cities.

COMMISSION. The frailties of the mayor-council arrangement have led almost half the cities having a population in excess of 5,000 to institute either the commission or council-manager form of government. The typical commission is composed of three to five members elected by the public. The commissioners are the administrative heads of the departments into which the government has been grouped, and collectively they constitute both the legislature and the chief executive of the city. Thus, legislative and executive powers are merged under this form. The law may provide for the appointment of subordinates either individually or collectively, or a separate and distinct personnel or merit board may be utilized. One of the commissioners is usually designated mayor by vote of the electorate or by his fellow commissioners; but if his ceremonial duties be excepted, he has the same authority and responsibility as the other commissioners.

The charters of commission-governed cities tend to emphasize the political features of city government—for example, nominations, elections, the initiative, referendum and recall—rather than the administrative activities to which the commissioners must devote the major portions of their time. Such charters may not indicate, for example, whether the commissioners should become active supervisors of their assigned functions or should supervise the functions only in a rather general manner. Charter provisions dealing with budgeting, accounting, purchasing, and similar business details are frequently inadequate.

Basic organizational flaws of the commission form include: (1) merger of the legislative and executive functions with the concomitant loss of traditional checks and balances, and (2) the absence of a chief executive and the centering of his duties in the hands of a committee—the commission. The resulting lack of clear-cut lines of authority and responsibility typically leads to friction between the commissioners and to diversity of policies in the several areas of jurisdiction. No final authority providing decisiveness, leadership, and uniformity is provided by the organization structure; hence the existence of these qualities in the commission of a specific city is the result of fortunate circumstances rather than of the organizational form itself.

Another criticism often made of the commission form is that major decisions with far-reaching consequences may be made over the telephone or in executive session rather than in public session. Also, it is often contended that commissioners tend to become concerned only with their own realm of authority and do not keep abreast of activities under the jurisdiction of other commissioners. Finally, when the number of commissioners is small, it is contended that this form of government lends itself to collusion among commissioners for personal gain or at least to unwarranted "trade-offs" in which questionable expenditure requests by other commissioners are approved by a commissioner in order to gain approval of his own requests.

The commission plan has been rather successful in a few instances despite its obvious weaknesses. Its measure of success is probably due to the small number of commissioners, who can be assembled readily and held responsible by the electorate more easily than can the larger number of councilmen typical of the mayor-council form. Too, a small commission can usually make and implement decisions more rapidly than can a large, dual-branch organization. Because of its limitations, however, use of the commission form has declined substantially in recent years. Only 6 percent of the cities of over 5,000 population are presently organized under the commission form.

COUNCIL-MANAGER. The council-manager form of city government first appeared in the United States in the second decade of this century. Its use spread quite rapidly, and today it is second only to the mayor-council form in popularity. The popularity of the manager form is continually increasing, particularly in medium-size cities, and it is now used by over half of all cities of 25,000–500,000 population.

City manager cities ordinarily have a small council which is elected at large or by districts. They may also have a mayor, either elected by popular vote or selected from the council membership, but his role is usually more ceremonial than managerial. The functions of the council or board include legislation and policymaking, and it has authority to hire and fire the manager. The latter is responsible for submitting both broad-gauge and detailed plans to the council for approval, for administering city government and executing the plans approved by the council, and for reporting upon city activities. To be effective, he must have the power of appointment and removal of employees within limitations imposed by civil service or merit board rules.

Such an arrangement is comparable to the organization of a typical large business corporation. The council has a basic trusteeship function and in theory does not participate in administrative matters. The chief executive is subject to policy direction but is not faced with the necessity of answering politically for city policy, that is, trying to get re-elected on the basis of his record. The council is free to employ an expert in administration as chief executive, a qualification often not possessed by an elected mayor. In practice, a distinctive strength of this form has been that the manager has almost invariably been a competitively paid, full-time employee. (With the exception of larger cities, mayors and commissioners almost invariably serve part-time, often for token compensation.)

A form of government cannot guarantee effective administration; it can only create conditions conducive to such operations. Under the council-manager form of government, councilmen can and frequently do participate in and interfere with administrative matters; and city managers may not be effective or may not be protected by the council and/or the mayor from political pressures. It has also been argued that since the manager, by definition of his position, is not to participate in politics, political leadership may be lacking in the council-manager form. None of these arguments has sufficient merit, however, to outweigh the numerous advantages of this system.

## EVOLUTION OF ACCOUNTING PRINCIPLES

Although the origin of the profession of accountancy is sometimes traced to ancient governments, modern municipal accounting is a development of the twentieth century—its beginning inseparably woven within the municipal reform movement which peaked near the turn of the century. About that time attention was focused on scandalous practices in the financial administration of many cities, the National Municipal League had suggested uniform municipal reporting formats, and the Census Bureau was working toward building interest in obtaining uniformity in city accounts and reports.

There was a flurry of change in accounting and reporting practices during this first decade. In 1901 the firm of Haskins and Sells, Certified Public Accountants, made an investigation into the affairs of the City of Chicago at the request of the Merchants' Club, and subsequently installed a completely new system of accounting for that city. The cities of Newton, Massachusetts, and Baltimore, Maryland, published annual reports during 1901 and 1902 along lines suggested by the National Municipal League, and the States of New York and Massachusetts passed legislation in the areas of uniform accounting and reporting in 1904 and 1906, respectively. There were many examples of progress during this period as other cities and states followed suit.

It was during this era that Herman A. Metz was elected Comptroller of the City of New York on a "business man for the head of the city's business office" slogan. When Metz assumed office it was estimated that one-fourth of New York's eighty-million dollar personal services budget was being lost through collusion, idleness, or inefficiency; and city departments commonly issued bonds to finance their current operating expenditures.

Although his work as New York City's comptroller was said to have been outstanding, Metz's most important contribution was the formation of the Bureau of Municipal Research, which was commonly known as the Metz Fund. One of its purposes was "...to promote the adoption of scientific methods of accounting and of reporting the details of municipal business...."[2]

The *Handbook of Municipal Accounting,* commonly referred to as "The Metz Fund Handbook," was called

> ...the most significant contribution of the 1910 decade...(because) it brought together for the first time many of the basic characteristics and requirements of municipal accounting and outlined methods of appropriate treatment.[3]

Likewise, the Bureau's publications were referred to as the "first organized materials that could be called a treatise in Municipal Accounting."[4]

As others became more interested in the subject, pamphlets, articles, and a few textbooks appeared. Municipal leagues were formed in various states and, as Newton expressed it, "we soon began a very serious ·development of the specialized field of Municipal Accounting."[5]

Although some work continued, interest waned during the 1920's and early 1930's. In a study of Illinois cities during 1931 and 1932, W. E. Karrenbrock found that few had adequate accounting systems to segregate transactions of different activities and none had budgetary accounts coordinated within the regular accounting system.[6]

Writing in 1933, R. P. Hackett observed that:

> The first fact that we are confronted with when searching for recent developments, or any developments, in governmental accounting, particularly that of municipal governments, is the marked absence of any general improvement

2 Bureau of Municipal Research, *Making a Municipal Budget: Functional Accounts and Operative Statistics for the Department of Greater New York* (New York: Bureau of Municipal Research, 1907), p. 5.

3 Lloyd Morey, "Trends in Governmental Accounting," *The Accounting Review,* 23 (July, 1948), p. 224.

4 W. K. Newton, "New Developments and Simplified Approaches to Municipal Accounting," *The Accounting Review,* 29 (October, 1954), p. 656.

5 *Ibid.*

6 R. P. Hackett, "Recent Developments in Governmental and Institutional Accounting," *The Accounting Review,* 8 (June, 1933), p. 122.

...it must be admitted that there is very little development in the actual practice of governmental and institutional accounting.[7]

The National Committee on Municipal Accounting was organized in 1934 under the auspices of the Municipal Finance Officers Association of the United States and Canada in order to bring together representatives of various groups concerned with municipal accounting and to put into effect sound principles of accounting, budgeting, and reporting. Its membership included representatives of the American Association of University Instructors in Accounting; the American Institute of Accountants; the American Municipal Association; the American Society of Certified Public Accountants; the International City Managers' Association; the Municipal Finance Officers' Association; the National Association of Cost Accountants; the National Association of State Auditors, Controllers, and Treasurers; the National Municipal League; and the Bureau of the Census.[8] Each group represented was also to have a subcommittee on municipal or governmental accounting within its own ranks.

At its organizational meeting the Committee tentatively adopted certain principles as a guide to its activities and set out a fourteen point program of research into areas of municipal accounting. The Committee's formation was immediately hailed as "the first effort on a national scale to establish principles and standards for municipal accounting and actively promote their use."[9] No doubt it was indeed the major event in the area of municipal accounting until that time.

Numerous publications defining proper or improved practice in municipal accounting and other areas of financial administration have come from the Committee and the Municipal Finance Officers Association (MFOA) since 1934. In 1948, Morey stated:

There is no longer any doubt as to what constitutes good accounting, reporting, and auditing for public bodies. The work of the National Committee on Municipal Accounting in particular, in establishing standards and models in these subjects, provides an authority to which officials, accountants, and public may turn with confidence.[10]

In 1951, the Committee, then and since known as the National Committee on Governmental Accounting (NCGA), issued *Municipal Accounting and Auditing*. This book combined and revised the major publications of the Committee and became the basis for the major modern textbooks in the area as well as for many state laws and guides relating to municipal accounting, auditing, and

[7] *Ibid.*, pp. 122, 127.
[8] Carl H. Chatters, "Municipal Accounting Progresses," *Certified Public Accountant,* 14 (February, 1934), p. 101.
[9] *Ibid.*
[10] Morey, *op. cit.,* p. 231.

reporting. This "Bible of municipal accounting," as it came to be called, was succeeded in 1968 by *Governmental Accounting, Auditing, and Financial Reporting (GAAFR)*,[11] often referred to as "the blue book."

The National Committee on Governmental Accounting is not a staff-supported, permanent body which meets regularly. Rather, a new NCGA is formed of appointees of various government agencies, public administration groups, and accounting organizations whenever deemed necessary—historically about every ten years—and serves in an advisory and review capacity with respect to revisions proposed by consultants it engages.[12]

NCGA pronouncements have typically presented what it considers to be the better existing accounting and reporting practices rather than being highly conceptual or innovative. Although NCGA pronouncements have been neither endorsed nor rejected by either the AICPA or the FASB, they constitute the most authoritative and widely accepted statements of municipal accounting and reporting principles. Further, *GAAFR* is referred to as "a useful and authoritative publication" in the AICPA governmental audit guide.[13] Hence, though the AICPA is considered the superior auditing authority and the FASB is clearly the higher accounting principles or standards authority, the chapters of this text dealing with state and local government accounting and reporting are (unless otherwise noted) based upon and consistent with the recommendations of the National Committee on Governmental Accounting contained in *Governmental Accounting, Auditing, and Financial Reporting*.

## THE NCGA PRINCIPLES

The National Committee on Governmental Accounting has defined accounting principles as:

> ...specific fundamental tenets which, on the basis of reason, demonstrated performance, and general acceptance...are generally recognized as being

---

11 Published by the Municipal Finance Officers Association of the United States and Canada, 1313 East 60th Street, Chicago, Illinois 60637. Hereafter this publication is referenced as *GAAFR*. © Chicago: Municipal Finance Officers Association of the United States and Canada.

12 During 1973, a MFOA task force circulated a proposal under which the NCGA would be reorganized as a permanent, quasi-independent body; its name would be changed to the National *Council* on Governmental Accounting; and it would conduct and sponsor research, hold public hearings, and issue formal statements and interpretations with respect to principles and standards of governmental budgeting, accounting, reporting, and auditing. At this writing, the MFOA staff is actively engaged in efforts to implement these recommendations.

13 Committee on Governmental Accounting and Auditing, American Institute of Certified Public Accountants, *Audits of State & Local Governmental Units*, Exposure Draft of April, 1973 (New York: The Institute, 1973), p. v. Publication of this AICPA guide was imminent as this text went to press.

essential to correct analysis of financial operations and to the proper preparation and presentation of required financial statements and reports.[14]

The 1968 Committee, as did its predecessors since the 1930's, set forth what it considered to be the basic accounting and reporting principles applicable to state and local governments. Its thirteen principles, which have been significantly influenced by the typical legal compliance-control environment of government, may be conveniently divided into the following seven groups for ease of discussion: (1) Legal compliance, (2) Budgetary planning and control, (3) Funds and account groups, (4) General fixed assets and depreciation, (5) Basis of accounting, (6) Terminology and account classification, and (7) Financial reporting.

### Legal Compliance

Governments must comply with the many and varied legal requirements, regulations, restrictions, and agreements that affect their financial management and accounting; and such compliance must be demonstrable and reported upon regularly. Compliance is necessary even though legal requirements may be archaic, useless, or even detrimental to sound financial management.

That laws take precedence over accounting principles (if they are in conflict) is recognized in these first two principles:

*Legal Compliance and Financial Operations*
1. A government accounting system must make it possible: (a) to show that all applicable legal provisions have been complied with; and. (b) to determine fairly and with full disclosure the financial position and results of financial operations of the constituent funds and self-balancing account groups of the governmental unit.

*Conflict between Accounting Principles and Legal Compliance*
2. If there is a conflict between legal provisions and generally accepted accounting principles applicable to governmental units, legal provisions must take precedence. Insofar as possible, however, the governmental accounting system should make possible full disclosure and fair presentation of financial position and operating results in accordance with generally accepted principles of accounting applicable to governmental units.

If financial statements prepared in compliance with legal requirements are not in accordance with appropriate accounting and reporting principles and might therefore be misleading, (1) that fact should be disclosed in notes to the financial statements, and (2) supplemental financial statements should be pre-

---

[14] *GAAFR*, p. 1. The NCGA principles cited in this section of the chapter are discussed in Chapter 1 of *GAAFR*.

pared that are in accordance with sound accounting and reporting principles.[15] Governmental accountants and auditors should, of course, strive to eliminate unnecessary legal provisions, especially those that are detrimental to sound financial management, accounting, or reporting.

## Budgetary Planning and Control

The need to plan the complex activities of government, the fact that the expenditure estimates of budgets become legally binding appropriations upon receiving legislative approval, and the necessity for operating controls to help managers avoid exceeding their budgetary authority are recognized in the third NCGA principle:

*The Budget and Budgetary Accounting*
3. An annual budget should be adopted by every governmental unit, whether required by law or not, and the accounting system should provide budgetary control over general government revenues and expenditures.

The states and most medium-size and larger cities and counties comply with this principle. On the other hand, many smaller units fail to realize the advantages and necessity of budgetary planning and preparation and to provide operational budgetary control through integration of budgetary accounts in the general and subsidiary ledger structures. (Budgeting is considered in depth in Chapter 3.)

## Funds and Account Groups

The significance attributed by the NCGA to fund accounting, probably the most distinctive feature of governmental accounting, is evidenced by the fact that four of its thirteen principles are directly concerned with this topic. These four principles deal with: (1) the need for fund accounting and definition of the term "fund," (2) the types of funds recommended for state and local government use, (3) the need to limit the number of fund entities employed in order to avoid undue accounting, reporting and analytical complexities, and (4) the autonomy of the separate fund entities and the necessity of maintaining accountability for general fixed assets and general long-term debt, which are not accounted for through fund entities.

*Fund Accounting*
4. Government accounting systems should be organized and operated on a fund basis. A fund is defined as an independent fiscal and accounting

15 The AICPA Committee on Governmental Accounting and Auditing has suggested that this emphasis be transposed. Its view is that general purpose reports should be prepared in accordance with generally accepted accounting principles, where these conflict with local legal requirements, and supplemental reports should be prepared to demonstrate legal compliance. See *Audits of State & Local Governmental Units,* Exposure Draft of April, 1973, pp. 14–15.

entity with a self-balancing set of accounts recording cash and/or other resources together with all related liabilities, obligations, reserves, and equities which are segregated for the purpose of carrying on specific activities or attaining certain objectives in accordance with special regulations, restrictions or limitations.

*Types of Funds*

5. The following types of funds are recognized and should be used in accounting for governmental financial operations as indicated.

   (1) *The General Fund* to account for all financial transactions not properly accounted for in another fund;

   (2) *Special Revenue Funds* to account for the proceeds of specific revenue sources (other than special assessments) or to finance specified activities as required by law or administrative regulation;

   (3) *Debt Service Funds* to account for the payment of interest and principal on long term debt other than special assessment and revenue bonds;

   (4) *Capital Projects Funds* to account for the receipt and disbursement of moneys used for the acquisition of capital facilities other than those financed by special assessment and enterprise funds;

   (5) *Enterprise Funds* to account for the financing of services to the general public where all or most of the costs involved are paid in the form of charges by users of such services;

   (6) *Trust and Agency Funds* to account for assets held by a governmental unit as trustee or agent for individuals, private organizations, and other governmental units;

   (7) *Intergovernmental Service Funds* to account for the financing of special activities and services performed by a designated organization unit within a governmental jurisdiction for other organization units within the same governmental jurisdiction;

   (8) *Special Assessment Funds* to account for special assessments levied to finance public improvements or services deemed to benefit the properties against which the assessments are levied.

*Number of Funds*

6. Every governmental unit should establish and maintain those funds required by law and sound financial administration. Since numerous funds make for inflexibility, undue complexity, and unnecessary expense in both the accounting system and the over-all financial administration, however, only the minimum number of funds consistent with legal and operating requirements should be established.

*Fund Accounts*

7. A complete self-balancing group of accounts should be established and maintained for each fund. This group should include all general ledger accounts and subsidiary records necessary to reflect compliance with legal provisions and to set forth the financial position and the results of financial operations of the fund. A clear distinction should be made between the accounts relating to current assets and liabilities and those relating to fixed assets and liabilities. With the exception of Intragovernmental Service Funds, Enterprise Funds, and certain Trust Funds, fixed assets should not be accounted for in the same fund with the current assets, but should be set up in a separate, self-balancing group of accounts called the *General Fixed Asset Group of Accounts*. Similarly, except in

Special Assessment, Enterprise, and certain Trust Funds, long term liabilities should not be carried with the current liabilities of any fund, but should be set up in a separate, self-balancing group of accounts known as the *General Long-Term Debt Group of Accounts.*

As noted earlier, fund accounting evolved because portions of a government's resources may be restricted as to use because of grantor or donor stipulation, by law, by contractual agreement, through action by the legislature or council, or for some other reason. The several fund types recommended in *GAAFR* vary primarily in accordance with (1) the extent of budgetary control normally employed and (2) whether the resources of the fund may be expended or are to be maintained on a self-sustaining basis. Furthermore, the various types of *expendable* funds suggested differ principally according to the uses to which the resources accounted for therein may be put: (1) general operating, (2) special purpose or project, or (3) merely transferred to those for whom the government is acting as a trustee or agent. The types of fund and nonfund accounting entities recommended in *GAAFR* are summarized in Figure 2-5; typical expendable fund resource flow patterns are indicated in Figure 2-6. Note that a state or local government will only have *one* General fund, *one* General Fixed Asset group

**Figure 2-5**

### TYPES OF STATE AND LOCAL GOVERNMENT FUNDS AND ACCOUNT GROUPS (NCGA RECOMMENDATIONS)

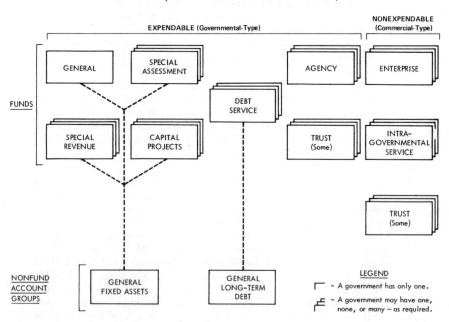

Figure 2-6

TYPICAL RESOURCE FLOW PATTERN—EXPENDABLE FUNDS*

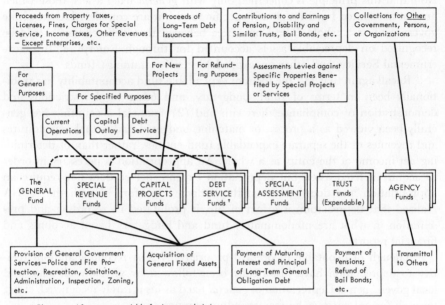

* Flows to and from nonexpendable funds are excluded.

† As indicated by ----, resources may be transferred to the Debt Service Fund from other funds; also, General Long-term Debt may be serviced directly from other expendable funds.

of accounts, and *one* General Long-Term Debt group of accounts. It may have one, none, or a multitude of the other types of funds.

### Fixed Assets and Depreciation

The eighth principle sets forth the application of the cost (or "original cost") concept to fixed asset valuation in governments:

*Valuation of Fixed Assets*
8. The fixed asset accounts should be maintained on the basis of original cost, or the estimated cost if the original cost is not available, or, in the case of gifts, the appraised value at the time received.

This principle also sets the stage for, and relates to, the ninth NCGA principle, one of the more controversial promulgated by the NCGA:

*Depreciation*
9. Depreciation on general fixed assets should not be recorded in the general accounting records. Depreciation charges on such assets may be

computed for unit cost purposes, provided such charges are recorded
only in memorandum form and do not appear in the fund accounts.

Note that this principle is concerned only with *general* fixed assets, those which
are not accounted for through any specific fund but are considered assets of the
government as a whole. The Committee believed that depreciation *should* be
recognized on depreciable assets accounted for through Enterprise, Intragovernmental Service, and other nonexpendable (self-sustaining) funds.

Recall again that (1) the focus of expendable fund accountability has traditionally been in terms of fund, budgetary, and other legal restrictions and
demonstration of compliance therewith and (2) financial accounting has generally been viewed as a process of matching budgeted and actual expenditures
and revenues of the separate expendable fund entities, rather than of determining net income of the entity as a whole. An appropriation is necessary in order
to acquire a fixed asset, but depreciation expense per se does not require an
appropriation and does not affect the budget. Therefore, though the NCGA
realized that depreciation is a fact of life, it prohibited its recording and presentation in what are predominately fund and budgetary based accounts and
financial reports.

Though of debatable theoretical propriety, NCGA recommendations relative to depreciation have historically been followed by virtually all state and
local governments. Depreciation of *general* fixed assets is rarely recognized, either
through formal entry or by memorandum computation.

## Basis of Accounting

The all-pervasive focus in state and local government accounting upon
matching *estimated* revenues and expenditures against *actual* revenues and expenditures of the various budgeted funds means, in effect, that the basis upon
which the budget is prepared determines the basis of accounting. Obviously, the
basis of the budget must be the basis of accounting and reporting if budgetary
comparisons are to be valid.

*Basis of Accounting*
10.  The accrual basis of accounting is recommended for Enterprise, Trust,
     Capital Projects, Special Assessment, and Intragovernmental Service
     Funds. For the General, Special Revenue, and Debt Service Funds, the
     modified accrual basis of accounting is recommended. The modified
     accrual basis of accounting is defined as that method of accounting in
     which expenditures other than accrued interest on general long-term
     debt are recorded at the time liabilities are incurred and revenues are
     recorded when received in cash, except for material or available revenues
     which should be accrued to reflect properly the taxes levied and the
     revenues earned.

The accrual basis of accounting was formerly recommended for all funds. The 1968 Committee recommended the accrual basis for most funds, but suggested that the "modified accrual" basis be used for funds which are typically subjected to stringent budgetary control. The funds for which the modified accrual basis is recommended—the General, Special Revenue and Debt Service Funds—often have revenue sources (such as self-assessed income taxes) whose yields are not susceptible to reasonably accurate estimation prior to collection. Given the NCGA's definitions of fund revenues and expenditures, the modified accrual basis is substantially the same as the accrual basis, because: (1) the treatment recommended for revenues is, in substance, the accrual basis; and (2) the modified accrual basis differs from the accrual basis insofar as expenditures are concerned only in that interest on General Long-Term Debt, which is normally appropriated for in the year in which it must be paid, is not recognized until appropriated for, regardless of its due date.

## Terminology and Account Classification

Consistent classification and terminology among the budget, the accounts, and the budgetary reports is a prerequisite to valid comparisons. In addition, effective budgetary control and accountability require that the accounts and budgetary reports, particularly those related to appropriations and expenditures, be in at least as much detail as appropriation control points. The NCGA has recognized the necessity of such consistency and comparability and, in addition, recommends classification of expenditures in several ways: (1) to facilitate assembling data in a manner that crosses fund and departmental lines in order that intragovernmental analyses may be prepared, and (2) so that data required for various intergovernmental comparisons and analyses will be available.

*Classification of Accounts*
11.  Governmental revenues should be classified by fund and source. Expenditures should be classified by fund, function, organization unit, activity, character, and principal classes of objects in accordance with standard recognized classification.[16]

*Common Terminology and Classification*
12.  A common terminology and classification should be used consistently throughout the budget, the accounts, and the financial reports.

Revenue and expenditure classification and account structures will be con-

---

16 Principle 11 is not relevant to (1) commercial-type activities of a government, which should be accounted for in a manner similar to that of commercial organizations, or (2) government-operated hospitals, libraries, schools, airports, transit authorities, or other facilities for which account classifications have been developed by organizations other than the National Committee on Governmental Accounting.

sidered in depth in Chapters 6 and 7. It may be observed at this point, however, that multiple revenue and expenditure classification—a rather simple matter for those governments having computerized accounting systems—can be difficult to implement in manual or slightly automated systems. Many smaller governments therefore limit their account classifications to two or three categories.

## Financial Reporting

This final principle stresses the importance of both interim and annual financial reports for operational control during the year and for reporting on the stewardship of government officials to the public.

*Financial Reporting*
13.  Financial statements and reports showing the current condition of budgetary and proprietary accounts should be prepared periodically to control financial operations. At the close of each fiscal year, a comprehensive annual report covering all funds and financial operations of the governmental unit should be prepared and published.

## SUMMARY AND OVERVIEW

Orienting oneself to state and local government accounting and reporting requires that particular attention be given to terminology, fund types, and budgetary control techniques.

New and unique terms should be noted carefully. Familiar terminology also deserves analysis as it may be used with either usual or unique connotations. Definitions of pertinent terms may be found both within the chapters and in the glossary (Appendix B).

Adapting to a situation in which there are many accounting entities will be found to require both concentration and practice. The nature, role, and distinguishing characteristics of each of the eight types of funds and the two nonfund account groups recommended by the NCGA must be understood thoroughly. This is made easier when one realizes that these ten separate types of accounting entities have many common characteristics and may be classified as either:

1.  *Expendable funds*—which are employed to account for the acquisition, use, and balances of expendable resources. Only the General Fund is unrestricted as to use; restricted expendable fund types include Special Revenue, Capital Projects, Special Assessment, Debt Service, *expendable* Trust, and Agency funds.
2.  *Nonfund account groups*—used to establish accountability for General Fixed Assets and General Long-Term Debt.
3.  *Nonexpendable funds*—which are used to account for self-sustaining or

self-supporting activities. Commercial-type accounting and reporting is appropriate for these, which include Enterprise, Intragovernmental Service, and *nonexpendable* Trust Funds.

This three-way classification of entities—and the related accounting equation adaptations—is illustrated more fully in the appendix to this chapter.

A peculiarity of the multiple entity approach of fund accounting is that a single transaction may require entries in more than one accounting entity, e.g., the purchase of a *general* fixed asset necessitates entries to record both the expenditure in the accounts of the acquiring fund and the asset in the General Fixed Assets group of accounts. Furthermore, one must also both accept and adapt to virtual personification of the fund accounting entities and the definition of "revenue" and "expenditure" in a fund accounting context. Organizational units financed from different funds may buy from and sell to one another (interfund transactions) and resources of one fund may be owed to another (interfund relationships). A fund generally is deemed to have revenue whenever its net assets are increased, and most net asset decreases are considered expenditures. Therefore, a fund may have revenues or incur expenditures that are not revenues or expenditures of the government as a whole. For example, proceeds of a loan are considered revenues of an expendable fund if the loan liability is established elsewhere, and a fund may have interfund revenue that is not revenue from the standpoint of the organization as a whole. Likewise, payment from the General Fund to the fund through which the government's central repair shop is financed would constitute a General Fund expenditure, though not an expenditure of the government as a whole.

Finally, the budget is of such importance in governments that governmental accounting is often referred to as "budgetary" accounting. It is appropriate, therefore to examine the role of the budget and major budgetary approaches before delving into the details of fund accounting technique.

**Question 2-1.** The terms "fund" and "funds" are used with varying connotations. For example, a college student may consider his cash and checking account balance to be his "funds" and his savings account his "fund." Indicate (1) the various meanings associated with these terms in business and (2) the principal manner in which these terms are used in state and local government accounting.

**Question 2-2.** A state or local government may employ only one of certain fund or non-fund account group entities but one, none, or many of other types. Of which would you expect a government to have only one? One, none, or many?

**Question 2-3.** The following are names of funds encountered in governmental reports and the purposes for which these funds have been established. You are required to indicate the corresponding fund type recommended by the National Committee on Governmental Accounting.

1. School Fund (to account for special taxes levied to finance the operation of schools).

2. Bond Redemption Fund (to account for taxes and other revenues to be used in retiring sinking fund bonds).

3. Bridge Construction Fund (to account for the proceeds from the sale of bonds).

4. Park Fund (to account for special taxes levied to finance the operation of parks).

5. Street Improvement Trust Fund (to account for the expenditure of money raised by special assessments on property deemed to be benefited by an improvement).

6. Interdepartment Printing Shop Fund (to account for revenues received from departments for printing done for them by the interdepartmental printing shop).

7. City Bus Line Fund (to account for revenues received from the public for transportation services).

8. Money Collected For The State Fund (to account for money collected as agent for the state).

9. Operating Fund (to account for revenues not handled through any other fund).

10. Electric Fund (to account for revenues received from the sale of electricity to the public).

11. Federal Fund (to account for federal construction grant proceeds).

12. Bond Redemption Fund (to account for proceeds of bond refunding issue).

13. Federal Fund (to account for shared revenue which may be used for any of several broad purpose categories).

14. Bond Proceeds Fund (to account for proceeds of bonds issued to finance street construction).

15. Employees' Pension and Relief Fund (to provide retirement and disability benefits to employees).

**Question 2-4.** Why are a municipality's general fixed assets and general long-term debt accounted for through non-fund account groups rather than within one of its funds, such as the General Fund?

**Question 2-5.** What differences would you expect to find between the accounting principles for the General Fund and for Special Revenue funds?

**Question 2-6.** Revenues or expenditures of a specific fund may not be revenues or expenditures of the government as a whole. Why is this true?

**Question 2-7.** It has been asserted that terms such as "sources" and "uses" should be substituted for "revenues" and "expenditures," respectively, in the accounting and reporting for a government's expendable funds. Do you agree? Why or why not?

**Question 2-8.** It is said that one of the differences between government and business is that business expenditures create revenues, whereas governmental expenditures do not. Is this statement true, or are there any governmental expenditures which create revenues?

**Question 2-9.** It is not uncommon to find the terms "expenditures" and "expenses" erroneously used as synonyms. How do "expenditures" differ from "expenses"?

**Question 2-10.** What is the difference, if any, between a revenue and expenditure statement prepared on a cash basis and a statement of receipts and disbursements?

**Question 2-11.** A governmental unit has a choice of adopting either a cash basis or a modified accrual basis of accounting. Which method should it adopt and why?

**Question 2-12.** NCGA Principle 12 states that "A common terminology and classification should be used consistently throughout the budget, the accounts, and the financial reports." Why is this important?

**Question 2-13.** Cite at least two examples of financial management or accounting-related procedures which may not be required by law but are nevertheless required to achieve sound financial control and accountability.

**Question 2-14.** The principal financial statements of business enterprises are the Balance Sheet, Statement of Net Income, and Statement of Changes in Financial Position (funds flow). What *similarities* are there, if any, between these statements and the operating and position statements of a nonexpendable fund? An expendable fund?

**Question 2-15.** Fund accounting and budgetary control were deemed of such importance by the NCGA that 4 of its 13 "principles" deal directly with these topics and most of the others relate to them at least indirectly. Why?

**Problem 2-1.** Select the lettered response which best completes the numbered statements.

## ITEMS TO BE ANSWERED

1. The operations of a public library receiving the majority of its support from property taxes for that purpose should be accounted for in
   a. The General Fund.
   b. A Special Revenue Fund.
   c. An Enterprise Fund.
   d. An Intragovernmental Service Fund.
   e. None of the above.
2. The proceeds of a Federal grant made to assist in financing the future construction of an adult training center should be recorded in
   a. The General Fund.
   b. A Special Revenue Fund.
   c. A Capital Projects Fund.
   b. A Special Assessment Fund.
   e. None of the above.
3. The receipts from a special tax levy to retire and pay interest on general obligation bonds issued to finance the construction of a new city hall should be recorded in a
   a. Debt Service Fund.
   b. Capital Projects Fund.
   c. Revolving Interest Fund.
   d. Special Revenue Fund.
   e. None of the above.
4. The operations of a municipal swimming pool receiving the majority of its support from charges to users should be accounted for in
   a. A Special Revenue Fund.
   b. The General Fund.
   c. An Intragovernmental Service Fund.
   d. An Enterprise Fund.
   e. None of the above.
5. The monthly remittance to an insurance company of the lump sum of hospital-surgical insurance premiums collected as payroll deductions from employees should be recorded in
   a. The General Fund.
   b. An Agency Fund
   c. A Special Revenue Fund.
   d. An Intragovernmental Service Fund.
   e. None of the above.

6. A transaction in which a municipality issued general obligation serial bonds to finance the construction of a fire station requires accounting recognition in the
   a. General Fund.
   b. Capital Projects and General Funds.
   c. Capital Projects Fund and the General Long-Term Debt Group of Accounts.
   d. General Fund and the General Long-Term Debt Group of Accounts.
   e. None of the above.

7. Expenditures of $200,000 were made during the year on the fire station in item 6. This transaction requires accounting recognition in the
   a. General Fund.
   b. Capital Projects Fund and the General Fixed Assets Group of Accounts.
   c. Capital Projects Fund and the General Long-Term Debt Group of Accounts.
   d. General Fund and the General Fixed Assets Group of Accounts.
   e. None of the above.

8. The activities of a central motor pool which provides and services vehicles for the use of municipal employees on official business should be accounted for in
   a. An Agency Fund.
   b. The General Fund.
   c. An Intragovernmental Service Fund.
   d. A Special Revenue Fund.
   e. None of the above.

9. A transaction in which a municipal electric utility paid $150,000 out of its earnings for new equipment requires accounting recognition in
   a. An Enterprise Fund.
   b. The General Fund.
   c. The General Fund and the General Fixed Assets Group of Accounts
   d. An Enterprise Fund and the General Fixed Assets Group of Accounts.
   e. None of the above.

10. The activities of a municipal employee retirement plan which is financed by equal employer and employee contributions should be accounted for in
    a. An Agency Fund.
    b. An Intragovernmental Service Fund.
    c. A Special Assessment Fund.
    d. A Trust Fund.
    e. None of the above.

11. A city collects property taxes for the benefit of the local sanitary, park and school districts and periodically remits collections to these units. This activity should be accounted for in
    a. An Agency Fund.
    b. The General Fund.
    c. An Intragovernmental Service Fund.
    d. A Special Assessment Fund.
    e. None of the above.

12. A transaction in which a municipal electric utility issues bonds (to be repaid from its own operations) requires accounting recognition in
    a. The General Fund.
    b. A Debt Service Fund.
    c. Enterprise and Debt Service Funds.
    d. An Enterprise Fund, a Debt Service Fund and the General Long-Term Debt Group of Accounts.
    e. None of the above.

(AICPA, adapted.)

**Problem 2-2.** The following balance sheet is prepared on a cash basis:

CITY OF *X*

General Fund

Balance Sheet

at Close of Fiscal Year

*Assets*

| | | |
|---|---:|---:|
| Cash ............................................... | | $150,000 |
| Taxes Receivable ............................ | $300,000 | |
| Less: Reserve for Uncollected Taxes ............. | 300,000 | |
| | | $150,000 |

*Fund Balance*

| | |
|---|---:|
| Fund Balance ......................................... | $150,000 |

Additional facts:

| | |
|---|---:|
| Estimated uncollectible taxes ................. | $ 10,000 |
| Accounts payable    ......................... | 65,000 |

Required:

Recast the foregoing balance sheet (a) on an accrual basis and (b) on a modified accrual basis.

**Problem 2-3.** The following revenue and expense statement was prepared by a municipality's bookkeeper:

CITY OF *B*

Intragovernmental Service Fund

Revenue and Expense Statement

for Fiscal Year Ended December 31, 19xx

| | | |
|---|---:|---:|
| Sales to departments ........................... | $ 85,000 | |
| Borrowed from other funds .................... | 17,500 | $102,500 |
| Less-cost of operating: | | |
| Materials .................................... | $ 58,000 | |
| Labor ....................................... | 5,000 | |
| Heat ....................................... | 2,000 | |
| Light and power .......................... | 2,000 | |
| Superintendent's salary ...................... | 3,000 | |
| Purchase of machinery ....................... | 11,000 | |
| Payment of liability to other fund ............. | 15,000 | |
| Total cost of operating ..................... | | 96,000 |
| Net income ............................. | | $ 6,500 |

The following are additional facts concerning this statement:

1.    The cost of materials shown in this statement is the total amount paid for materials during the year. An inventory of $10,000 was carried over from last year; $5,000 was paid for materials purchased during the preceding year; materials costing $20,000 were purchased during the year but have not yet been paid for; the closing inventory is $24,000.

2.    The amounts shown for labor, heat, light and power, and superintendent's salary represent actual payments. Charges incurred last year but not paid until this year include the following: labor, $450; heat, $100; light and power, $225; superintendent's salary, $190. Charges incurred but not yet paid include the following: labor, $750; heat, $150; light and power, $300; superintendent's salary, $150.

3.    The amount shown for sales represents actual receipts of cash from other funds; only $75,000 of the total collections is applicable to sales made this year; $20,000 is still due from other funds on account of sales made this year.

Required:

Prepare a correct revenue and expense statement for the Intragovernmental Service Fund on (1) a cash basis, and (2) the accrual basis.

**Problem 2-4.**    From the data in Problem 2-3, prepare a revenue and expense statement on a modified accrual basis. Assume the modified accrual basis has been used since the inception of the fund because charges to departments are not calculated frequently, but through semi-annual analyses each March and September.

**Problem 2-5.**    The following is the trial balance at December 31, 19X3, of an employee coffee shop operated by the City of *J*:

| | | |
|---|---:|---:|
| Cash | $  2,150 | |
| Inventory | 12,900 | |
| Equipment | 16,850 | |
| Allowance for depreciation | | $  3,500 |
| Accounts payable | | 200 |
| Capital | | 10,000 |
| Retained earnings | | 7,000 |
| Sales | | 97,000 |
| Purchases | 42,000 | |
| Personal services | 40,000 | |
| Laundry | 500 | |
| Equipment repairs | 400 | |
| Heat, light, and gas | 2,100 | |
| Telephone and telegraph | 600 | |
| Miscellaneous | 200 | |
| | $117,700 | $117,700 |

Adjustment data:
(1)    Depreciation, 10 per cent of original cost
(2)    Closing inventory, $11,500
(3)    Prepaid miscellaneous expense, $40
(4)    Accrued wages, $800

Required:

Prepare working papers from which a balance sheet and a revenue and expense statement on an accrual basis could be readily prepared.

**Problem 2-6.** In order to assure continuous and dependable bus service to its citizens "from now on," Mobiline County acquired the following assets of Mobiline Transit, Inc., a privately owned bus line in financial difficulty:

| *Assets* | *Amount Paid by County* |
|---|---|
| Land......................................... | $ 10,000 |
| Garage and office building ...................... | 30,000 |
| Inventory of tires and parts ..................... | 15,000 |
| Shop equipment .............................. | 5,000 |
| Buses........................................ | 140,000 |
| Total paid—February 1, 19X3................ | $200,000 |

The purchase was financed through the issue of 6% general obligation notes payable, scheduled to mature in amounts of $20,000 each February 1 for 10 years. Interest is payable annually each February 1.

Bus line revenues and expenditures are accounted for through the General Fund. The fixed assets acquired were recorded in the General Fixed Assets Group of Accounts; and the notes payable were entered in the General Long-Term Debt Group of Accounts. In November of 19X3, following the close of the county's fiscal year on October 31, the Mobiline *Daily Banner* published a feature story about the county-owned bus line under the heading "Bus Line Prospers Under County Management." The following Operating Statement, prepared by the county clerk from the General Fund records, appeared within the newspaper article:

MOBILINE COUNTY BUS LINES

Operating Statement

For the Nine-Month Period Ending October 31, 19X3

| | | |
|---|---:|---:|
| Revenues: | | |
| Passenger fares-routine route service ............ | $ 77,000 | |
| Special charter fees........................... | 3,000 | $ 80,000 |
| Expenditures: | | |
| Salaries (superintendent, drivers, mechanics) .... | $ 52,000 | |
| Fuel and lubrication ......................... | 12,000 | |
| Tires and parts ............................. | 1,000 | |
| Contracted repairs and maintenance ........... | 8,000 | |
| Miscellaneous ............................... | 1,000 | 74,000 |
| Net profit ..................................... | | $ 6,000 |

The story quoted a county commissioner as saying:

"We are extremely pleased with our bus line operating results to date. Through sound management, we have turned a losing operation into a profitable one—and we expect an even greater profit next year. When we got into the bus line business we determined that the buses would last five years and the building and shop equipment would suffice for ten years—so we do not anticipate any capital outlay expense for some time. In addition, we have $3,000 worth of tires and parts on hand which do not appear in the Operating Statement but will help us hold down our expenses during the next few months, and we should collect another $500 fee for an October charter this week."

Required:
(1)   Prepare an accrual basis Statement of Revenues and Expenses (Income State-ment) for Mobiline County Bus Lines for the nine month period ending October 31, 19X3.
(2)   Evaluate the propriety of the information contained within the *Daily Banner* feature story.

# STATE AND LOCAL GOVERNMENT FUND ACCOUNTING EQUATIONS AND TECHNIQUES: A PRIMER

The use of many separate accounting entities to account for the financial activities and status of a single organization is usually a bit awkward and con-fusing to the newcomer to governmental accounting. Some users of this text may therefore find it helpful to *preview* the uses and variations of the accounting equation in this setting by considering an extremely simplified example prior to examining the details of accounting for the various funds and account groups in Chapters 3-14.

This discussion is built around the broad classification of fund and account group types noted in Chapter 2:

1. *Nonexpendable ("Commercial-type") Funds*—used to account for self-supporting or self-sustaining activities, most of which are similar to activities of some organizations in the "for-profit" sector. (Enterprise, Intragovernmental Service, and nonexpendable Trust Funds.)

2. *Expendable ("Government-type") Funds*—through which the acquisition, use, and balances of all other expendable (current) resources are ac-counted for. (General, Special Revenue, Capital Projects, Special Assess-ment, Debt Service, expendable Trust, and Agency Funds.)

3. *Nonfund Account Groups*—used to establish accountability for nonappro-priable assets and unmatured general obligation long-term debt of the government as a whole that is not associated with any particular fund. (General Fixed Assets and General Long-Term Debt Groups of Accounts.)

Transactions of the Simplified City example that follows may be viewed as summaries of many transactions. Small, whole-dollar amounts are used for illustrative simplicity and clarity; a calendar year accounting period is assumed in all cases.

### Nonexpendable Funds

Activities accounted for through these funds are usually more common to the business world than to governments, and Nonexpendable Fund accounting parallels that of business organizations. The accounting equation applicable to Nonexpendable Fund activities—such as electricity or natural gas utilities and central repair or printing shops—is the familiar one of Assets equal Liabilities plus Net Worth $(A = L + NW \text{ or } A - L = NW)$. Only general ledger accounts are illustrated in the following example, though subsidiary accounts for items such as receivables, fixed assets, inventories, and payables might be used in practice. Furthermore, the balance sheet accounts used are for groups of assets and liabilities in order that attention may be focused upon the accounting equation rather than upon procedural details.

The following transactions and events are illustrated in Figure A-1:

| Legend | Description |
|--------|-------------|
| (1/1) | Beginning balances. |
| (1) | Operating revenues for the period were $5,000, of which $100 resulted from forgiveness of current debt. |
| (2) | Operating expenses for the period were $4,500; of this amount, $300 has not been paid and $200 represents depreciation and amortization of noncurrent assets. |
| (3) | Acquired a truck for $600, paying $200 cash and promising to pay the balance within a year. |
| (4) | Sold equipment, book value $400, for $500. |
| (5) | Paid a loss claim resulting from an unusual accident, $300. |
| (6) | Received an additional capital contribution from another fund, $700. |
| (7) | Retired noncurrent debt of $200. |
| (C) | Closing entries at 12/31. |
| (12/31) | Ending balances. |

Notice in studying the example that (1) *all* assets and liabilities—both current and noncurrent—associated with the Nonexpendable Fund activities are accounted for therein, (2) the *accrual* basis for the timing of revenue and expense recognition is employed, i.e., receivables and payables are recorded, as are depreciation and amortization, (3) *expenses* are accounted for, rather than expenditures, (4) *gain or loss* is recognized upon sale of fixed assets, (5) *net income*

SIMPLIFIED CITY

A Nonexpendable ("Commercial-type") Fund

the Accounting Equation Illustrated

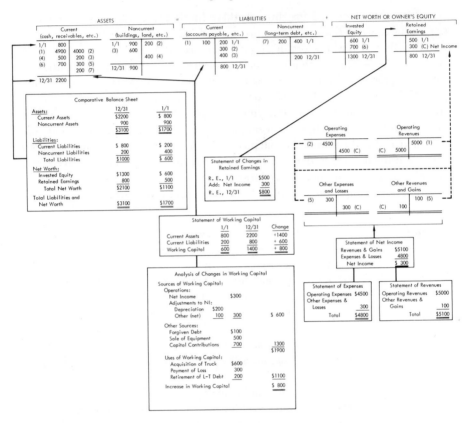

*or loss* is determined as in commercial accounting, (6) *invested capital or equity* is accounted for separately from *earned equity or retained earnings,* and (7) the primary financial statements prepared correspond to those for private businesses.

## Expendable Funds

Expendable Funds are employed to account for the relatively liquid portion of the government's assets that are not accounted for through Nonexpendable Funds, the debt pertaining thereto, and the balance of these resources, if any, available for subsequent appropriation and expenditure. In this situation (1) the assets and liabilities pertaining to a given activity may be accounted for through several different Expendable Funds—and some may be recorded in the Nonfund Account Groups—as only *current* assets and *current* liabilities are normally accounted for in Expendable Funds, (2) a modified accrual basis of accounting is generally employed, (3) *expenditures* are accounted for rather than expenses, that is, operating expenses, capital outlay, and debt retirement all reduce the Expendable Fund balance and are "expensed," (4) gain or loss on sales of fixed assets, forgiveness of long-term debt, etc., are not recognized, (5) net income or loss is *not* determined—rather, the accounting focus is upon sources, uses, and balances of net current assets, (6) no distinction between invested and earned equity is maintained, and (7) the principal statements differ somewhat from those of private businesses.

No BUDGETARY CONTROL. It is assumed in the next example that no budget is prepared or that formal budgetary control is not exercised through the account structure. Using data similar to that of the preceding example, note the treatment (see Figure A-2) of the following transactions and events in the account structure of an Expendable Fund:

| *Legend* | *Description* |
|---|---|
| (1/1) | Beginning balances (exclude noncurrent items). |
| (1) | Operating revenues for the period were $5,000, including $100 forgiveness of *current* debt. |
| (2) | Operating expenditures for the period were $4,300, of which $300 has not been paid. (Depreciation is not recognized; noncurrent assets are not accounted for in the fund.) |
| (3) | Acquired a truck for $600, paying $200 cash and promising to pay the balance within two years. (The truck is not capitalized here, but in the General Fixed Assets Group of Accounts; assume that the $400 balance is not a liability of any particular fund and is therefore recorded in the General Long-term Debt Group of Accounts.) |
| (4) | Sold equipment, carrying value $400, for $500. (The sale proceeds considered "revenue" as equipment is accounted for through the GFA Group of Accounts; no gain or loss is determined.) |
| (5) | Paid a loss claim resulting from an unusual accident, $300. |
| (6) | Received a transfer from another fund, $700. (No separation of invested and earned equity; no income determination.) |
| (7) | Retired non-current debt of $200. (Noncurrent debt is carried in the GLTD Group of Accounts; payment reduces the Expendable Fund balance.) |
| (C) | Closing entries at 12/31. |
| (12/31) | Ending balances. |

### SIMPLIFIED CITY

An Expendable ("Government-type") Fund
The Accounting Equation Illustrated—
No Integrated Budgetary Control
(General Ledger)

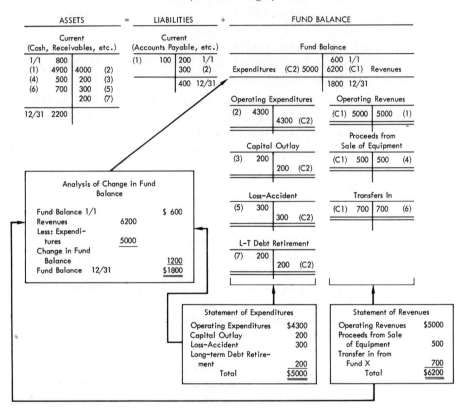

Subsidiary ledgers are widely used in governmental bookkeeping systems (1) to permit division of posting duties between or among employees in order to achieve bookkeeping economies and enhance the system of internal controls, (2) to make both total and detailed data readily available continually, and (3) to keep the general ledger (and other ledgers) to a manageable weight and/or number of pages. The general and subsidiary ledger accounts of Simplified City's Expendable Fund, using separate Revenue and Expenditure subsidiary ledgers, appears in Figure A-3. The results are the same, of course, only the bookkeeping technique is changed.

WITH BUDGETARY CONTROL. Several types of Expendable Funds, particularly

**Figure A-3**

## SIMPLIFIED CITY
### An Expendable ("Government-type") Fund
### The Accounting Equation Illustrated—No Integrated Budgetary Control
### (Using Revenue and Expenditure Ledgers)

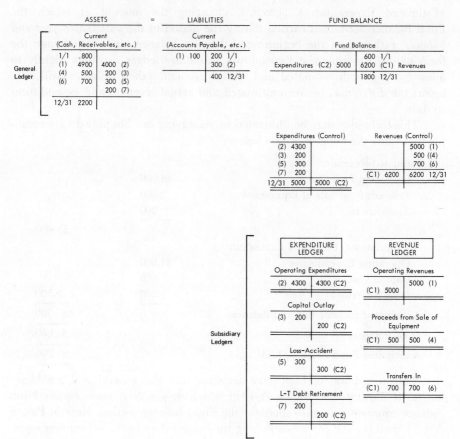

General and Special Revenue Funds, must be operated within budgetary plans and constraints. After-the-fact accountability may be achieved, of course, by exercising little or no budgetary accounting control during the period and merely inserting budget data comparison columns in the operating statements. Such an approach fails, however, to afford *continuous* comparative data on budgeted versus actual results in order to highlight potential or actual deviations from the budgetary plan early enough to avoid overexpenditure or to make any necessary budgetary adjustments on a timely basis. In other words, this approach provides information at a point in time at which it may well be too late to take corrective action.

Introducing budgetary accounts—a type of temporary account peculiar to fund accounting—into the account structure and thereby obtaining the valuable fiscal management tool of continuous budgetary control is a relatively simple task. To do so we need only (1) insert Estimated Revenues and Appropriations (Estimated Expenditures) accounts, changing the amount at which the Fund Balance account is carried during the period to the *anticipated year-end balance,* rather than the beginning-of-the-year balance, and (2) change the form of the Revenue and Expenditure subsidiary ledger accounts slightly to allow posting both estimated and actual amounts—their balances will now report the *differences* between estimated and actual revenues and expenditures to date.

This technique may be illustrated by modifying our Simplified City example by adding the budgetary data below:

|  |  |  |
|---|---:|---:|
| Estimated Revenues |  |  |
|    Operating Revenues | $4,900 |  |
|    Proceeds from Sale of Equipment | 600 |  |
|    Transfers In | 300 |  |
|  |  | $5,800 |
| Appropriations (Estimated Expenditures) |  |  |
|    Operating Expenditures | $4,500 |  |
|    Capital Outlay | 800 |  |
|    Debt Retirement | 200 | 5,500 |
| Anticipated Increase in Fund Balance |  | $ 300 |
| Fund Balance, 1/1 |  | $ 600 |
| Anticipated Fund Balance, 12/31 |  | $ 900 |

The integration of budgetary accounts into the general and subsidiary ledgers is illustrated in Figure A-4, in which only a Net Assets equals Fund Balance equation is used to spotlight the Fund Balance section. Note in Figure A-4(I) that (1) the entry establishing the budget data in the accounting equation closely resembles the *closing* entries that would be posted to the "actual" revenue and expenditure accounts, that is, the Appropriations account has a credit balance and the Estimated Revenues account has a debit balance, (2) the Fund Balance account now has a balance of $900, the amount that it would be at year end, after closing, if actual transactions equal those estimated during this period or if differences between planned and actual exactly cancel out, and (3) the Revenue subsidiary ledger is now controlled jointly by both the Revenues and Estimated Revenues control accounts in the general ledger and the Expenditure subsidiary ledger is controlled jointly by both the Appropriations (Estimated Expenditures) and Expenditures accounts—that is, the sum of the net balances of the subsidiary ledger accounts should at all times equal the *difference* between the balances of their control accounts. Budgetary entries are Keyed "B" in this example.

The management value of continuous budgetary control (See Figure A-4 (II).) may not be readily apparent from such a simplified example. However, visualize a typical situation in which scores or hundreds of accounts are in use and in which many transactions occur daily. By having information as to the

**Figure A-4(I)**

SIMPLIFIED CITY
An Expendable Fund
Establishing Integrated Budgetary Control

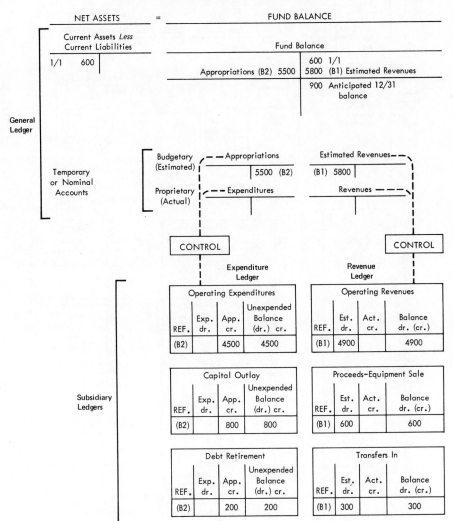

budget status available to him at any time—in total and by subsidiary account—a government manager is certainly better prepared to decide whether to permit, postpone or refuse specific expenditures, increase enforcement of a tax whose collections are lagging, or request budget revisions on a timely basis.

**Figure A-4(II)**

### SIMPLIFIED CITY
### An Expendable Fund
### Establishing Integrated Budgetary Control

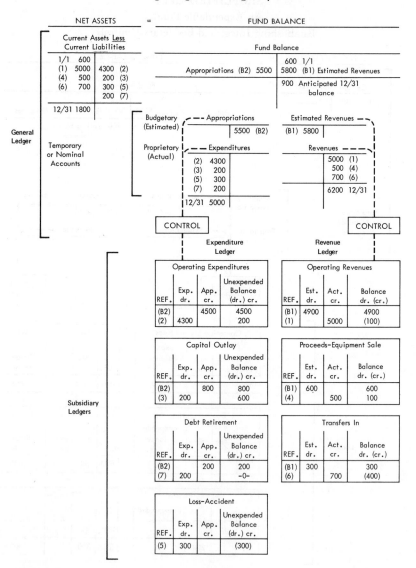

Assuming all appropriations lapse at the end of the period, the accounts may be closed at 12/31 by:

1. Reversing the budgetary entries in the general ledger and returning the Fund Balance account to its actual preclosing balance. The budgetary accounts have now served their purpose—they have afforded continuous budgetary control during the period—and are no longer needed;
2. Closing general ledger Revenues and Expenditures (actual) account balances to the Fund Balance account as in earlier examples.
3. "Erasing" the net balances in the subsidiary ledger accounts by offsetting their pre-closing balances.

This may be achieved (see Figure A-5) by posting the following entries:

| | | Subsidiary Ledger | | General Ledger | |
| --- | --- | --- | --- | --- | --- |
| | | Dr. | Cr. | Dr. | Cr. |
| (C1) | Appropriations | | | 5500 | |
| | Fund Balance | | | 300 | |
| | Estimated Revenues | | | | 5800 |
| | To reverse budgetary entry effect and return Fund Balance account to actual preclosing balance. | | | | |
| (C2) | Revenues | | | 6200 | |
| | Expenditures | | | | 5000 |
| | Fund Balance | | | | 1200 |
| | To close actual Revenues and Expenditures to Fund Balance, bringing that account up to date at 12/31 | | | | |
| (C3) | *Revenue Ledger:* | | | | |
| | Operating Revenues | 100 | | | |
| | Proceeds—Equipment Sale | | 100 | | |
| | Transfers In | 400 | | | |
| | Total (not posted) | 500 | 100 | | |
| | | |⌐ 400 ⌐| | | |
| | *Expenditure Ledger:* | | | | |
| | Operating Expenditures | 200 | | | |
| | Capital Outlay | 600 | | | |
| | Loss—Accident | | 300 | | |
| | Total (not posted) | 800 | 300 | | |
| | | |⌐ 500 ⌐| | | |

# SIMPLIFIED CITY
An Expendable Fund
Closing Entries—With Budgetary Control

SIMPLIFIED CITY — An Expendable Fund — Closing Entries—With Budgetary Control

NET ASSETS = FUND BALANCE

**Current Assets Less Current Liabilities**

| 1/1 | 600 |
| 12/31 | 1800 |

**Fund Balance**

Appropriations (B2) 5500 | 600 1/1
| 5800 (B1) Estimated Revenues
Reverse Budgetary Effect (C1) 300 | 900 Anticipated 12/31 Balance
| 600
| 1200 (C2) Revenues less Expenditures
| 1800 12/31

**Appropriations**

(C1) 5500 | 5500 (B2)

**Estimated Revenues**

(B1) 5800 | 5800 (C1)

**Expenditures**

12/31 5000 | 5000 (C2)

**Revenues**

(C2) 6200 | 6200 12/31

General Ledger

Subsidiary Ledgers

**Operating Expenditures**

| REF. | Exp. dr. | App. cr. | Unexpen. Bal. (dr.) cr. |
|---|---|---|---|
| (B2) | | 4500 | 4500 |
| (2) | 4300 | | 200 |
| (C3) | 200 | | -0- |

**Operating Revenues**

| REF. | Est. dr. | Act. cr. | Bal. dr. (cr.) |
|---|---|---|---|
| (B1) | 4900 | | 4900 |
| (1) | | 5000 | (100) |
| (C3) | 100 | | -0- |

**Capital Outlay**

| REF. | Exp. dr. | App. cr. | Unexpen. Bal. (dr.) cr. |
|---|---|---|---|
| (B2) | | 800 | 800 |
| (3) | 200 | | 600 |
| (C3) | 600 | | -0- |

**Proceeds-Equipment Sale**

| REF. | Est. dr. | Act. cr. | Bal. dr. (cr.) |
|---|---|---|---|
| (B1) | 600 | | 600 |
| (4) | | 500 | 100 |
| (C3) | | 100 | -0- |

**Debt Retirement**

| REF. | Exp. dr. | App. cr. | Unexpen. Bal. (dr.) cr. |
|---|---|---|---|
| (B2) | | 200 | 200 |
| (7) | 200 | | -0- |

**Transfers In**

| REF. | Est. dr. | Act. cr. | Bal. dr. (cr.) |
|---|---|---|---|
| (B1) | 300 | | 300 |
| (6) | | 700 | (400) |
| (C3) | 400 | | -0- |

**Loss-Accident**

| REF. | Exp. dr. | App. cr. | Unexpen. Bal. (dr.) cr. |
|---|---|---|---|
| (5) | 300 | | (300) |
| (C3) | | 300 | -0- |

Observe in the example that (1) the subsidiary ledger entries need not balance —these accounts merely support those in the general ledger, and their closing does not affect the Fund Balance or other general ledger accounts, (2) the difference between the total debits and credits in the subsidiary ledger closing process may be reconciled with the general ledger closing entries, e.g., the $400 net debits ($500 − $100) required to close the Revenue Ledger accounts equals the difference between the Revenues and Estimated Revenues accounts ($6,200 − $5,800) in the general ledger, and (3) in those cases where estimated equalled actual results—for example, the Debt Retirement account in this illustration— the subsidiary ledger has a zero balance and no closing entry is required. Other approaches to closing entries, and differing conditions that may affect them, are discussed in Chapter 4-10.

ENCUMBRANCES. The earliest point at which expenditures for goods or services may be controlled from the standpoint of avoiding overspending budgetary authority is at the point of order placement. As a matter of routine, the expenditure account (subsidiary ledger) to be charged for a proposed expenditure should be examined prior to issuing a purchase order to be sure that sufficient expenditure authority remains. Where several officials may place orders chargeable to a particular account, or in situations in which several orders to be charged to one account upon delivery may be outstanding simultaneously, both expenditures to date and orders already outstanding against the account— termed "encumbrances"—must be considered prior to approving an additional purchase order. Failure to consider outstanding orders—looking only at expenditures to date—could lead to issuance of purchase orders in excess of remaining expenditure authority and, upon delivery and billing, to budget "overruns".

In order to have data on "unencumbered appropriations" (Appropriations less the sum of Expenditures and Encumbrances) readily available to the manager in such cases, it is necessary to record encumbrances in the expenditure subsidiary accounts and "reserve" sufficient expenditure authority to cover their cost upon delivery and billing. Encumbrance accounting necessitates:

1. Inserting off-setting Encumbrances and Reserve for Encumbrances accounts in the *general* ledger (the order outstanding is not yet an expenditure and does not affect the fund's balance);
2. Modification of the expenditure *subsidiary* ledger accounts to provide for recording encumbrances in a manner similar to expenditures and heading the balance column "Unencumbered Balance" rather than "Unexpended Balance";
3. Recording the encumbrance at the estimated amount of the expenditure likely to result therefrom;
4. Upon delivery and billing of the goods or services (a) reversing the encumbrance entry, and (b) recording the expenditure in the usual manner; and,

5.    Modifying the closing entries, as appropriate, to compensate for the effect of any encumbrances outstanding at period-end.

Note that the expenditure *subsidiary* ledger is now controlled severally by the Appropriations, Expenditures, and Encumbrances accounts in the *general* ledger.

In order to illustrate the basics of encumbrance accounting, let us assume that one of the orders resulting in the operating expenditures of $4,300 was for $1,050, $100 of which has not been delivered at year-end. Assume further that the goods or services expected to cost $950, only cost $900 upon delivery. (This order, then, resulted in only $900 of the $4,300 expenditures recorded.) The following entries differing from those earlier are reflected in Figure A-6, in

**Figure A-6**

## SIMPLIFIED CITY
### An Expendable Fund
### Encumbrance Accounting Illustrated

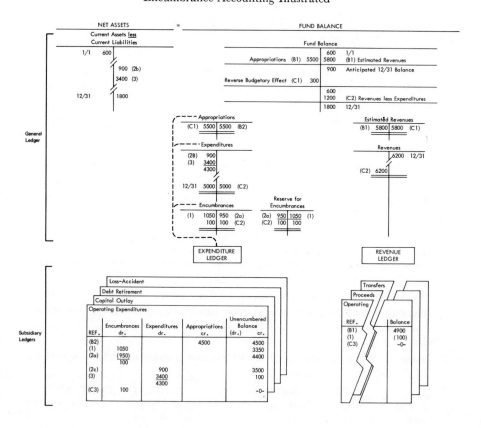

which the appropriation-expenditure-encumbrance related accounts are highlighted:

(1) The $1,050 purchase order is issued.
(2) Goods or services expected to cost $950 were delivered at a cost of only $900.
(3) The remaining portion of the $4,300 of operating expenditures, $3,400, is recorded in summary form.
(C) The accounts are closed. (It is assumed here that all appropriations lapse at year-end, i.e., if the goods or services on order are delivered in the subsequent period they must be refused or charged to an appropriation of that year. Other assumptions are discussed in Chapter 4.)

Observe in the example that (1) the expenditure subsidiary ledger is controlled severally by the Appropriations, Expenditures, and Encumbrances general ledger accounts, (2) the Encumbrances and Reserve for Encumbrances general ledger accounts off-set one another, neither their "transaction" nor closing entries (in this case) affect Fund Balance, (3) the unencumbered balance of the expenditure subsidiary ledger accounts always equals the difference between the appropriations and the total of encumbrances outstanding at the time and expenditures to date, and (4) as in previous examples, the necessary expenditure subsidiary ledger closing entries may be determined simply by observing their preclosing balances.

### Nonfund Account Groups

Dollar and item accountability for General Fixed Assets and General Long-Term Debt, which are not accounted for in either Expendable or Nonexpendable Funds, is achieved through a "list and off-set" procedure. General Fixed Assets are recorded at cost upon acquisition with an off-setting entry to an "Investment in General Fixed Assets" account; the acquisition entry is reversed upon their disposal. Similarly, in the General Long-Term Debt Group (1) the principal of general obligation long-term debt is established as a liability upon its incurrence, off-set by an "Amount to be Provided for Debt Retirement" account; (2) as amounts are accumulated in an Expendable Fund(s) for subsequent retirement of the debt, this is indicated by reclassifying a portion of the "Amount to be Provided..." account to an "Amount Provided (or Available) ..." account; and (3) upon the liability being assigned to and recorded in a specific Expendable Fund, the liability account and the "Amount to be Provided ..." and "Amount Provided (or Available) ..." accounts are correspondingly reduced. The basic technique of Nonfund Account Group bookkeeping technique is illustrated in Figure A-7.

In practice, separate accounts would be used for each General Fixed Asset or asset type (Land, Building, etc.) and separate "Investment in GFA" ac-

## NONFUND ACCOUNT GROUP ACCOUNTING EQUATIONS

### General Fixed Assets

| GENERAL FIXED ASSETS | | = | INVESTMENT IN GENERAL FIXED ASSETS | |
|---|---|---|---|---|
| (1) Cost of GFA Acquired | | | | Cost of GFA Acquired (1) |
| | Cost of GFA Disposed of (2) | | (2) Cost of GFA Disposed of | |
| Balance | | | | Balance |

### General Long-Term Debt

AMOUNT ACCUMULATED PLUS THAT WHICH MUST BE PROVIDED IN THE FUTURE = LIABILITY

| Amount Provided (Accumulated) | | Amount To Be Provided | | General Long-Term Debt | |
|---|---|---|---|---|---|
| | | (1) Principal of Debt Incurred | | | (1) Principal of Debt Incurred |
| (2) The Amount of Resources accumulated in Funds for Debt Retirement | | | (2) The amount of Resources accumulated in Funds for Debt Retirement | (3) Principal of Debt which has now been assumed by a specific fund | |
| | (3) Remove an appropriate amount— See contra | | (3) Remove an appropriate amount— See contra | | |
| Balance | | Balance | | | Balance |

counts might be used to indicate the source of these assets, e.g., Federal Grants, Fund X, etc. Similarly, separate liability accounts for each major item of General Long-Term Debt would likely be employed, as would distinctly labeled "Amount to be Provided..." and "Amount Provided (or Available)..." accounts, indicating the debt issue or the fund in which debt service resources have been accumulated. Finally, subsidiary ledgers frequently prove useful in maintaining detailed information as to the specific fixed assets owned, the sources of these assets, the debt owed, and the amounts accumulated or required to be accumulated in the future for debt principal retirement.

**3**

# Accounting and
# the Budget Process

Budgeting may be described as the process of allocating scarce resources to unlimited demands. Simply stated, a budget is a dollars and cents plan of operation for a specific period of time. As a minimum, such a plan should contain information about the types and amounts of proposed expenditures, the purposes for which they are to be made, and the proposed means of financing them.

Although practices are by no means uniform, budgeting and budgets typically play a far greater role in the planning, conduct and evaluation of governmental endeavors than in privately owned businesses. The NCGA, it will be recalled from Chapter 2, considered the budget of such import that its third principle is concerned with this subject:

*The Budget and Budgetary Accounting*
3. An annual budget should be adopted by every governmental unit, whether required by law or not, and the accounting system should provide budgetary control over general government revenues and expenditures.[1]

The prominence to which the budgetary process has risen in government is a natural outgrowth of its environment. *Planning* is a special concern here since, as noted previously, (1) neither the type, quantity, nor quality of governmental goods and services provided are normally evaluated and adjusted

[1] *GAAFR,* p. 5.

59

through the open market mechanism; (2) these goods and services are often considered among the most critical to the public interest and well-being, e.g., education, police and fire protection, and sanitation; (3) the scope and diversity of modern government activities have become so great that comprehensive, thoughtful, and systematic planning is a prerequisite to orderly decision-making in this complex environment; and (4) governments are "owned" by their citizens; and planning and decision-making are therefore generally a joint process participated in by citizens, either individually or in groups, by their elected representatives within the legislative branch, and by the members of the executive branch. The legislative-executive division of powers, the so-called "checks-and-balances" device, is operative in all states and in most local governments. In these, and in most manager-council forms of organization, "the executive proposes, the legislature disposes," i.e., the executive is responsible for drafting tentative plans, but final plans are made by the legislative body—often after public hearings in which interested citizens or groups are able to participate. Written budget proposals are obviously essential to communication, discussion, revision, and documentation of plans by those concerned with and responsible for planning.

Budgets are also widely used as devices of *control* in governments, both in regard to (1) control of the legislative branch over the executive branch, and (2) control of the chief executive over subordinate executive agencies or departments. As observed earlier, when a budget is enacted by the legislative branch, the expenditure estimates become appropriations—both authorizations to and limitations upon the executive branch. Appropriations may be enacted in very broad categorical terms or in minute detail. In the former case, the legislature exercises general or policy-level control only and the executive is given much managerial discretion in the conduct of government business; in the latter case, the chief executive may have almost no discretion, his role being restricted to that of carrying out various specific, detailed orders from the legislature. Similarly, the chief executive may restrict his subordinates by granting agency or departmental expenditure authority in more detailed or specific categories (allocations) than those approved by the legislature and/or by rationing expenditure authority to subordinate agencies or departments in terms of monthly or quarterly expenditure ceilings, referred to as "allotments." When allocations or allotments have been made, it is essential that the accounting system provide information that will enable (1) agencies or departments to keep their expenditures within limitations imposed by the chief executive and demonstrate compliance therewith and (2) the chief executive to keep the expenditures of the government as a whole within limitations imposed by the legislative branch and demonstrate such compliance. The budgetary authority extended one branch or level of government by another therefore becomes a standard for measurement of compliance or noncompliance. Appropriate financial reports serve as a basis for *evaluating* the extent of compliance with the standards established by the various "dollar stewardship" relationships in this environment.

## BASIC BUDGETARY TERMINOLOGY

Although the operating budget of each year stands alone from a legal stand-point, budgeting is a continuous process. Budget officials will be engaged during any given year in assuring that the prior year's budgetary reports are properly audited and appropriately distributed, in administering the budget of the current year, and in preparing the budget for the upcoming year(s). This is illustrated in Figure 3-2. The budget for any year (see Figure 3-1) goes through five phases: (1) preparation, (2) legislative enactment, (3) administration, (4) reporting and (5) postaudit.

Figure 3-1

A GOVERNMENTAL UNIT
The Budget Cycle

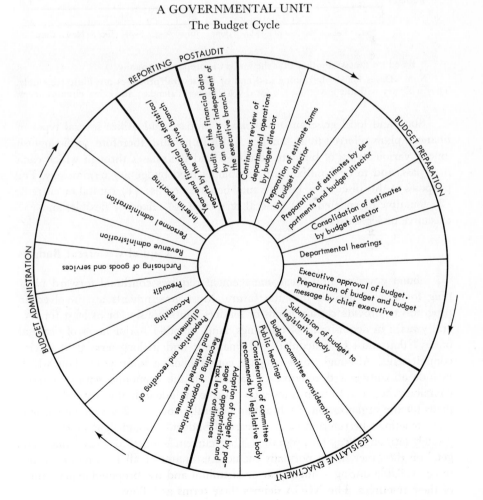

Figure 3-2

A GOVERNMENTAL UNIT
Budgetary Processes
During a Fiscal Year*

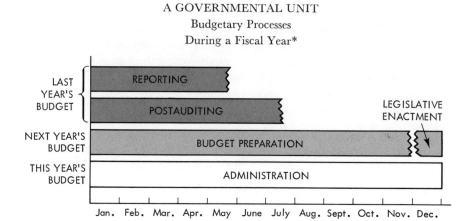

\* Based on the assumption that the budget is prepared annually.

Note: Dates for the beginning and end of the several processes are illustrative only. They will vary with the government's fiscal year, budget calendar, and other circumstances.

State and local governments typically prepare and utilize several types of financial plans referred to as "budgets." It is important, therefore, to distinguish among various types of budgets, to understand the phases through which each may pass, and to be familiar with commonly used budgetary terminology. For purposes of this discussion, budgets may be classified as: (1) capital or current, (2) tentative or enacted, (3) general or special, (4) fixed or flexible, and (5) executive or legislative.

**Capital v. Current Budgets**

Sound governmental fiscal management requires continual forward planning for several periods into the future. Most governments are involved in programs to provide certain goods or services continuously (or at least for several years); in acquisitions of buildings, land, or other major items of "capital outlay" that must be scheduled and financed; and in long-term debt service commitments. Although some prepare comprehensive multi-year plans which include all anticipated resources ("capital" in the economic sense), a more common practice at present is for such plans to include only the "capital outlay" plans for the organization. Such a plan generally covers a 2–6 year period and may sometimes be referred to as a "capital budget," though it is more appropriately termed a "capital program." The "current budget" or "operating budget," on the other hand, normally includes estimates of all resources expected to be available during a single year or biennium and the proposed expenditures of these resources. The NCGA defines these terms as follows:

*Capital Program.* A plan for capital expenditures to be incurred each year over a fixed period of years.... It sets forth each project or contemplated expenditure in which the government is to have a part and specifies the full resources estimated to be available to finance the projected expenditures.

*Capital Budget.* A plan of proposed capital outlays and the means of financing them for the current fiscal period. It is usually a part of the current budget. If a Capital Program is in operation, it will be the first year thereof.

*Current Budget.* The annual budget prepared for and effective during the present fiscal year; or, in the case of some state governments, the budget for the present biennium.[2]

The typical interrelationships of a capital program, capital budget, and current budget are illustrated in Figure 3-3. The remainder of this chapter is concerned primarily with current or operating budgets.

**Figure 3-3**

### INTERRELATIONSHIP OF
### CAPITAL PROGRAM—CAPITAL BUDGET—OPERATING BUDGET

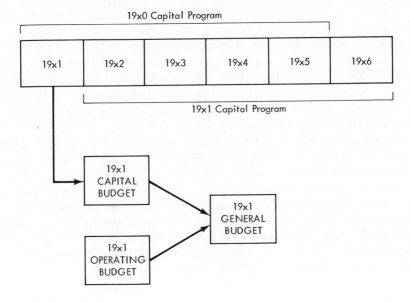

**Tentative v. Enacted Budgets**

One of the most important distinctions between budgets is in regard to their legal status. Preliminary or tentative budgets are merely plans which may later become requests and might, if approved, become "enacted." Since proposed budgets serve mainly as a basis for discussion and negotiation, and are

[2] *GAAFR,* pp. 155, 157.

primarily for internal use, they need not be as precise as enacted ones. Capital programs, for example, do not represent requests, and are not normally enacted into law, though the legislature may review them prior to enacting the current budget and may also indicate its general approval or disapproval of their content and direction. Similarly, a departmental budget request for the upcoming year may be termed a "budget," but normally it is a request that the chief executive include certain amounts for a given department in the current budget for the organization. Further, a proposed current budget may go through several revisions prior to being submitted for legislative approval and may be revised substantially before that approval is granted. Only the final legislatively-approved budget, the appropriations portion of which is enacted into law, is legally binding upon the executive. This final budget, whatever its content or form, constitutes the basis of legislative control over the executive branch and is the budget which the chief executive may further refine in order to control and evaluate the activities of his subordinates. Only the legislature may revise the terms or conditions set forth in this final budget, though the chief executive may revise terms he has imposed upon his subordinates.

### General v. Special Budgets

Budget requests, executive budgets, and appropriation bills must clearly specify the funds from which expenditures are to be made. The budgets of the various funds are frequently compiled into a single booklet or document which may be referred to as "the budget." The usual type and extent of budgetary planning and control techniques employed in managing the various fund types is discussed in detail within the chapters devoted to each.

As a matter of nomenclature, it may be observed that the budgets of general governmental activities, commonly financed through the General, Special Revenue and Debt Service Funds, are referred to as "general" budgets. A budget prepared for any other fund is referred to as a "special" budget. Appropriations are not normally required for Trust and Agency Funds since the government is acting merely as a fiduciary in such situations; consequently, formal budgets are rarely prepared for these types of funds. Special budgets are therefore commonly limited to those for (1) Capital Projects, (2) Special Assessment, (3) Intragovernmental Service, and (4) Enterprise Funds.

### Fixed v. Flexible Budgets

Fixed budgets are those in which appropriations are for a specific (fixed) dollar amount and may not be exceeded because of changes in demand for governmental goods or services. On the other hand, expenditures authorized by flexible budgets are fixed *per unit* of goods or services, but are variable in total according to demand for either production or delivery of the goods or services.

Fixed budgets are relatively simple to prepare and administer, are more easily understood than flexible ones, lend themselves to the desire of "strong" legislatures to limit the discretion of the executive (or the executive of his subordinates), are more readily adaptable to integrating budgetary control techniques into accounting systems, and are in harmony with the intent of allocating a fixed amount of resources among various departments or programs. Expendable fund budgets of governments are almost invariably of the fixed variety. Flexible budgets are more realistic when changes in the quantities of goods or services provided directly affect resource availability and expenditure requirements—as is the case with Enterprise and Intragovernmental Service Funds—and when formal budgetary control (in the account structure) is not deemed essential.

### Executive v. Legislative Budgets

Budgets are also sometimes categorized by preparer. As noted earlier, budget preparation is usually considered an executive function, though the legislature may revise the budget prior to approval. In some instances, however, the legislative branch prepares the budget, possibly subject to executive veto; in other instances, the budget may originate with a joint legislative-executive committee (possibly with citizen representatives) or with a committee comprised solely of citizens or constituents. Such budgets are frequently referred to by terms such as "executive budget," "legislative budget," "joint budget," or "committee budget."

## BUDGETARY APPROACHES AND EMPHASES

Viable budget systems do not come neatly wrapped as standardized packages of universal applicability. Rather, a government's budgetary system ideally should be designed to fit the many environmental factors[3] unique to that organization (as well as those of governments generally) and provide a planning-control-evaluation balance appropriate to the circumstances. Rarely does one find two governments with identical budgetary approaches and procedures.

Any budgetary system, rudimentary or complex, includes *planning, control,* and *evaluation* processes, but they are seldom given equal emphasis. Indeed, the major differences among the three most common general approaches to budgeting governmental operations arise principally from differing relative emphasis being placed upon these important management functions.

The most common approaches to operating expenditure budgeting may be classified as (1) the object-of-expenditure approach, (2) the performance approach, and (3) the program and planning-programming-budgeting (PPB)

[3] For an excellent discussion of these environmental factors or "bases," see Lennox L. Moak and Kathryn W. Killian, *Operating Budget Manual,* (Chicago: Municipal Finance Officers Association, 1963), pp. 21–55.

approach. A complete discussion of each approach—or possible combinations of approaches—is beyond the scope of this text. In the discussion of each that follows, one should bear in mind that budgetary nomenclature is far from standardized, that each approach may be implemented to varying degrees, that these approaches overlap significantly, and that elements of all three are often found in a single budget system. Furthermore, one must always look to the substance of a system rather than to the terminology used in reference to it, e.g., an object-of-expenditure budget may be referred to publicly as a performance or program budget, since these have been considered the more modern approaches in recent years.

### The Object-of-Expenditure Approach

The object-of-expenditure approach to budgeting, often referred to as the "traditional" or "line-item" approach, is the simplest of the three tacks. This method, which has an expenditure *control* orientation, became popular as the basis for legislative control over the executive branch. It continues to be the most widely used, though elements of newer approaches are often added.

Simply described, this method involves (1) subordinate agencies submitting budget requests to the chief executive in terms of the type of expenditures to be made, that is, the number of people to be hired in each specified position and salary level and the specific goods or services (objects) to be purchased during the upcoming period; (2) the chief executive compiling, modifying and submitting an overall request for the organization to the legislature in the same object-of-expenditure terms; and, frequently (3) the legislature making "line-item" appropriations, possibly after revising the requests, along object-of-expenditure "input" lines. Performance or program data may be included within the budget document, but they are used only to supplement or support the object-of-expenditure requests. The basic elements of this approach are illustrated in Figure 3-4.

Various degrees of appropriation control that might be exercised by a legislature through object-of-expenditure budgets may be illustrated by identifying the possible "control points" in the example in Figure 3-4. A great degree of legislative control will be typified if appropriations are stated in terms of the most detailed level. For example, the police department appropriation might be in terms of: one chief, $12,000; two captains, $19,000; etc. Alternatively, a lesser amount of control would result if appropriations are stated in terms of object classes, that is, Salaries and Wages, $165,000; Supplies, $6,000; Other Services and Charges, $3,000; and Capital Outlay, $6,000. In this case the detailed objects listed would be indicative of the types of goods and services to be secured, but the executive branch would have discretion as to an appropriate "input mix" so long as these expenditure category subtotals were not exceeded.

Figure 3-4

## SIMPLIFIED OBJECT-OF-EXPENDITURE BUDGET
(Classified by Organizational Unit and Object of Expenditure)

**Mayor's Office**

**Police Department**

| | Rate | | |
|---|---|---|---|
| Salaries and Wages: | *Rate* | | |
| 1—Chief | $12,000 | $12,000 | |
| 2—Captains | 9,500 | 19,000 | |
| 2—Sergeants | 8,500 | 17,000 | |
| 12—Patrolmen | 7,000 | 84,000 | |
| 3—Radio operators | 5,000 | 15,000 | |
| 10—School guards (part time) | 1,800 | 18,000 | $165,000 |
| Supplies: | | | |
| Stationery and other office supplies | | $   200 | |
| Janitorial supplies | | 100 | |
| Gasoline and oil | | 3,000 | |
| Uniforms | | 2,200 | |
| Other | | 500 | 6,000 |
| Other Services and Charges: | | | |
| Telephone | | $   400 | |
| Out-of-town travel | | 800 | |
| Parking tickets | | 600 | |
| Utilities | | 1,000 | |
| Other | | 200 | 3,000 |
| Capital Outlay: | | | |
| 1—Motorcyle (net) | | $ 1,600 | |
| 2—Patrol car (net) | | 4,400 | 6,000 |
| Total Police Department | | | $180,000 |

**Fire Department**
Salaries and Wages:

| | | |
|---|---|---|
| Total Budget | | $1,801,720 |

Next, an even greater degree of executive discretion would be granted if appropriations are stated in "lump sum" at the departmental level, e.g., Police Department, $180,000. Only departmental totals would be legally binding upon the executive in such a situation. Finally, it is conceivable that the legislative branch would appropriate a "lump-sum" total, $1,801,720, for operation of the entire city. Again, the chief executive may further refine the level of legislative control in order to achieve the degree of fiscal control he desires to exercise over his subordinates.

Despite its widespread use, the object-of-expenditure approach has been widely criticized. Some feel, for example, that it is overly control-centered, to the detriment of the planning and evaluation processes. Critics assert that in practice a disproportionate amount of attention is focused upon short-term dollar inputs of specific departments (personnel, supplies, etc.) ; and, consequently, that both long-run considerations and those relevent to the programs of the organization as a whole usually receive inadequate attention. Too, they argue that crucial planning decisions tend to originate at the lowest levels of the organization and flow upward; whereas broad goals, objectives, and policies should originate in the upper echelon and flow downward to be implemented by subordinates. As a result, governmental goals tend to be stated in terms of uncoordinated aggregations of goals of the various department heads. It is also asserted that planning may be neglected, budgets being based upon hastily made requests based merely on present expenditure levels and patterns. This "budgeting by default" leads to perpetuation of past activities, whether or not appropriate, failure to set definite goals and objectives, and failure to consider all possible alternatives available to the organization in striving to accomplish its purposes. Further, it is asserted that the legislative branch is given so much object-of-expenditure detail that it cannot possibly assimilate it, yet it is not given data pertaining to the functions, programs, activities and outputs of executive branch agencies. Consequently, the legislative branch tends to exercise control over such items as the number of telephones to be permitted or the salary of a particular individual, rather than focusing its attention upon broad programs and policies of the organization. For example, it has been observed that:

> ...the traditional budgetary structure does *not* provide either the elected official or the executive administrator with the kind of information needed to effectively plan and allocate resources, or to accomplish the day-to-day job of managing the complex business of state or local government. In fact, the traditional line-item budget only *appears* to provide an orderly and seemingly objective approach to financial planning and control. In too many instances, all it really provides is a uniform framework for establishing and maintaining a set of orderly records which comply with legal requirements, but which provide very little in the way of useful management information.[4]

4 Ernst and Ernst, *Planning-Program-Budgeting Systems for State and Local Governments* (Olympia, Wash.: State of Washington, 1968), p .22.

This approach is also criticized as being archaic. Along these lines, it is contended that the line-item approach was a necessary reaction to the "boss rule" and "invisible government" scandals around the turn of the century, that it served its purpose well at a time when governments generally lacked internal control systems and/or competent employees and the legislature could indeed control the relatively simple activities of government. However, they assert, an object of expenditure budget and line-item appropriations are anachronisms in today's governmental environment because the executive branch must have reasonable discretion and flexibility as it attempts to manage diverse and complex governmental programs. Finally, it is contended that this method encourages spending rather than economizing, and that department heads feel compelled to expend their full appropriations—whether or not needed—as (1) performance evaluation tends to be focused upon spending, and the manager is assumed to be "good" as long as he keeps his spending within budgetary limitations, and (2) a manager's subsequent budgets may be reduced if he spends less than he requests for a given year, as legislators often base appropriations on prior expenditures and also may consider the fact that a manager did not spend as much as he requested in one year indicative of budget request "padding."

Defenders of the object-of-expenditure approach note its longstanding use, its simplicity, and its ease of preparation and understanding by all concerned. Too, they note that budgeting by organizational units and objects-of-expenditure closely fits patterns of responsibility accounting, that this method facilitates accounting control in the budget execution process, and that comparable data may be accumulated for a series of years in order to facilitate trend comparison. In addition, they contend that (1) most programs are of an ongoing nature, (2) most expenditures are relatively unavoidable, (3) decisions must, in the real world, be based on *changes* in programs, and attention can most readily be given to changes proposed, compared with prior year data, and (4) the object-of-expenditure approach does not preclude supplementing object-of-expenditure data with planning and evaluation information commonly associated with other budgetary approaches.

## The Performance Approach

Though the performance approach originated near the turn of the century, it received its biggest impetus from the report of the first Hoover Commission in 1949 and came into popular usage in the fifties. The Hoover Commission report included the statement that:

> We recommend that the whole budgetary concept of the federal government should be refashioned by the adoption of a budget based on functions, activities, and projects: this we designate a "performance budget."[5]

5 Commission on Organization of the Executive Branch of the Government, *Budgeting and Accounting* (Washington, D.C.: USGPO, 1949), p. 8.

Terminology confusion accompanied the report of the Commission's Task Force, however, as it used the terms "performance" and "program" synonymously:

> A program or performance budget should be substituted for the present budget, thus presenting a document. . . in terms of services, activities, and work projects rather than in terms of the things bought.[6]

Although these terms have been used synonymously by many eminent authorities, the term "program budgeting" has recently taken on different connotations from that of "performance budgeting" and these terms will be distinguished here.[7]

The NCGA defines a performance budget as:

> A budget wherein expenditures are based primarily upon measurable performance of activities and work programs. A performance budget may also incorporate other bases of expenditure classification, such as character and object, but these are given a subordinate status to activity performance.[8]

This approach embodies a shifting of emphasis from objects of expenditure to "measurable performance of activities and work programs." The primary focus is on *evaluation* of the efficiency with which existing activities are being carried out; its primary tools are cost accounting and work measurement. The gist of this method may be summarized as (1) classifying budgetary accounts by function and activity, as well as by organization unit and object of expenditure, (2) investigating and measuring existing activities in order to obtain maximum efficiency and to establish cost standards, and (3) basing the budget of the succeeding period upon unit cost standards multiplied by the expected number of units of the activity estimated to be required in that period. The total budget for an agency would be the sum of the products of its unit cost standards multiplied by the expected units of activity in the upcoming period. The enacted budget is viewed somewhat as a performance contract between the legislative branch and the chief executive.

Probably the most important contributions of the performance approach have been (1) its emphasis upon the inclusion within the proposed budget of a narrative description of each proposed activity, and (2) organization of the budget by activities, with requests supported by estimates of costs and accom-

---

[6] Task Force Report, *Fiscal, Budgeting, and Accounting Activities* (Washington, D.C.: USGPO, 1949), p. 43.

[7] The confusion has arisen primarily over differing uses of the term "program." In performance budgeting the term has been applied generally to specific activities within a single department (street sweeping, police patrol, etc.), whereas in program or planning-programming-budgeting (PPB) the term usually has a broader connotation (preservation of life and property, alleviation of pain and suffering, etc.) which may include activities of many departments of a government.

[8] *GAAFR,* p. 166.

plishments in quantitative terms, and (3) its emphasis on the need to measure output as well as input. The performance budget emphasizes the activities for which funds are requested, therefore, rather than merely how much will be spent, and requires answers to questions such as these:

1. What are the agency's objectives; for what reason does the agency ask for appropriations; what services does the agency render to justify its existence?
2. What programs or activities does the agency use to achieve its objective?
3. What volume of work is required in each of the activities?
4. What levels of services have past appropriations provided?
5. What level of activity or service may legislators and the taxpayers expect if the requested amounts are appropriated?

To provide the legislative body with a reasonable program, each department must do some clear thinking about what it is trying to do and how it can do it best. In addition, when the legislators fully understand the department's work, its objectives, and its problems, the appropriation ordinance achieves its full meaning as a contract between the executive and legislative branches.

In addition to assisting both the legislature and the public in understanding the nature of the activities undertaken by the executive branch, performance data also provide legislators additional freedom to reduce or expand the amounts requested for particular functions or activities. This additional freedom may be illustrated by contrasting the legislative position under the performance approach with that when an object-of-expenditure budget is used. The detailed listings of positions to be filled and things to be bought in object-of-expenditure budgets provide the legislative group with a wealth of detail. And, in the usual case, the appropriations are made in almost as great detail, so that any attempt to change the budget requests requires that the detailed items making up the budget be changed by the legislature. Decisions as to such changes are administrative, not legislative, in nature. The legislative body should make decisions concerning the distribution of limited resources in accordance with the relative importance of the several functions and activities for which funds are needed. Where information is available as to particular functions and activities, these may be readily expanded or contracted at the will of legislature; where only object-of-expenditure data are available, the legislature must deal with minutiae; it may be tempted to make changes arbitrarily, such as slashing all requests a given percentage. If the final appropriation under the performance approach provides more or less than was budgeted for a function or activity, the executive branch must, of course, revise its plans in order to make the most effective use of amounts appropriated.

The performance approach also provides the chief executive with an additional avenue of control over his subordinates. Rather than being restricted merely to how much his subordinates spend, he may evaluate the performance of activities in terms of both dollar and activity unit standards.

Though much has been written about the performance approach, it does not appear to have often been adopted in its "pure state," though performance data are frequently used to supplement or support object-of-expenditure requests and are essential to program budgeting. Although the approach is fundamentally sound, (1) few state and local governments have sufficient budgetary or accounting staffs to identify units of measurement, perform cost analyses, etc.; (2) many services and activities of governments do not appear readily measurable in meaningful output units or unit cost terms; and (3) accounts of governments have typically been maintained on a budgetary expenditure basis, rather than on a full cost basis, making data gathering difficult if not impossible. In practice, expenditure data often have been substituted indiscriminately for cost (expense) data; and input measures have been used in place of output measures. In addition, activities sometimes have been costed and measured in great detail without sufficient consideration being given to the necessity or desirability of the activities themselves—that is, without concern for whether the activity contributed to achievement of the government's goals or, if the activity was necessary, whether it could be accomplished in a better way. For these and other reasons, most attempts to install comprehensive performance budgeting systems were disappointing and the adverse publicity received by some attempts no doubt discouraged others from experimenting with the approach. Advocates of the performance approach feel that it has been successful in instilling an attitude of cost consciousness in government, however, and note the many governmental activities now being measured objectively. The approach has therefore proved extremely helpful, especially when its application has been limited to discrete, tangible, routine types of activities such as street sweeping, police patrol, and garbage collection.

### The Program and Planning-Programming-Budgeting (PPB) Approaches

Another reason for the apparent demise of the performance budget (as such) was the shift in emphasis in the late fifties and early sixties to the program approach and then, in the mid-sixties, to what has come to be known as the Planning-Programming-Budgeting System, often referred to as PPB or PPBS. Here again, terminology is a problem. The term "program budget" is sometimes used to refer to PPB systems or approaches and at other times is used in distinctly different ways. The NCGA, for example, defines a program budget as:

> A budget wherein expenditures are based primarily on programs of work and secondarily on character and object...a transitional type of budget between the traditional character and object budget, on the one hand, and the performance budget, on the other.[9]

9 *GAAFR*, p. 166.

Others distinguish between "full program" and "modified program" budgetary approaches, the latter being essentially a performance approach in which unit cost measurement is attempted only selectively. The following definition is preferred by the authors:

> Program budgets deal principally with broad planning and the costs of functions or activities. A *full* program approach to budgeting would require that the full cost of a function, e.g., juvenile delinquency control, would be set forth under the *program* regardless of the organizational units that may be involved in carrying such programs into execution. Thus, in the juvenile delinquency "program," certain activities of the welfare agency, the police department, the juvenile courts, the law department, and the district attorney would be included. . . .
> A *modified* program budget approach would be organized solely within major organizational units, e.g., departments.[10]

As the term is used here, "program budgeting" refers to a *planning-oriented* approach which emphasizes programs, functions and activities—with lesser emphasis upon evaluation or control. Performance measurement is not, therefore, a prerequisite to program budgeting, though it may be a useful adjunct. Too, the program approach is *communication-oriented,* with budgetary requests and reports summarized in terms of a few broad programs rather than in a myriad of object-of-expenditure or departmental activity detail—though such details may be provided in the executive budget and the final appropriation may be on a line-item basis.

The most elaborate version of program budgeting, of rather recent origin and still in the developmental stage, has come to be known as the Planning-Programming-Budgeting system (PPB or PPBS). As was the case with performance budgeting, PPB emphasis originated with the Federal government when concepts developed in the early part of this century were refined by the Rand Corporation in the late fifties and experimented with in the Department of Defense in the early sixties. The movement to PPB received its greatest impetus in 1965 when President Johnson instructed most Federal departments and agencies to apply this approach to their program planning and budgeting. Several state and local governments began experimenting with PPB immediately and many are today in the process of implementing this approach. (See Figure 3-5.)

PPB or PPBS is not so much a new system or approach as a re-ordered synthesis of time-honored budgetary concepts and techniques, with additional emphasis on long-run considerations, systems analyses, and cost-benefit analyses of alternative courses of action. As Hatry observed:

> Its essence is development and presentation of information as to the full implications, the costs and benefits, of the major alternative courses of action relevant to major resource allocation decisions.

[10] Moak and Killian, *op. cit.,* pp. 11–12. (Emphasis added.)

Figure 3-5

## COUNTY PROGRAM BUDGET—19X1–X2 APPROPRIATIONS

| Programs and Program Elements | Salaries and Employee benefits | Services and Supplies | Other Charges | Fixed Assets | Capital Projects | Total | Percent |
|---|---|---|---|---|---|---|---|
| I. Personal safety: | | | | | | | |
| (A) Law enforcement | $81.1 | $10.4 | $1.9 | $1.3 | $2.6 | $97.3 | |
| (B) Judicial | 57.8 | 13.6 | * | .4 | 2.0 | 73.8 | |
| (C) Traffic safety | 5.7 | 7.1 | 9.0 | .2 | .4 | 22.4 | |
| (D) Fire prevention and control | 29.6 | 8.5 | .1 | 1.8 | .8 | 40.8 | |
| (E) Safety from animals | 1.7 | .1 | * | * | .2 | 2.0 | |
| (F) Protection of and control of the natural and manmade disasters | .1 | 23.0 | 35.3 | 31.8 | | 90.2 | |
| (G) Prevention of food and drug hazards, non-motor-vehicle accidents and occupational hazards | 4.6 | 1.0 | | * | .3 | 5.9 | |
| (H) Unassignable research and planning | | | | | | | |
| (I) Unassignable support | | | | | | | |
| Total personal safety | 180.6 | 63.7 | 46.3 | 35.5 | 6.3 | 332.4 | (22.0) |

II. Health:

| | | | | | | | |
|---|---|---|---|---|---|---|---|
| (A) Physical health | 145.5 | 133.0 | 5.4 | 2.1 | 5.5 | 291.5 | |
| (B) Mental health | 9.0 | 14.8 | | .2 | .1 | 24.1 | |
| (C) Drug addiction prevention and control | 9.3 | 2.0 | | .2 | .4 | 11.9 | |
| (D) Environmental health, included under IV, D-H. | | | | | | | |
| (E) Other | | | | | | | |
| (F) Unassignable research and planning | | | | | | | |
| (G) Unassignable support | | | | | | | |
| Total health | 163.8 | 149.8 | 5.4 | 2.5 | 6.0 | 327.5 | (21.8) |

VII. Transportation, communication, location:

| | | | | | | | |
|---|---|---|---|---|---|---|---|
| (A) Motor vehicle transportation | | 17.5 | 65.3 | 1.9 | | 84.6 | |
| (B) Urban transit system | | | | | | | |
| (C) Pedestrian | | | | | | | |
| (D) Water transport | | | | | | | |
| (E) Air transport | .5 | .1 | | * | 2.9 | 3.6 | |
| (F) Location programs | | | | | | | |
| (G) Communications substitutes for transportation | | | | | | | |
| (H) Unassignable research and planning | | | | | | | |
| (I) Unassignable support | | | | | | | |
| Total transportation, communication, location | .5 | 17.6 | 65.3 | 1.9 | 2.9 | 88.2 | (5.9) |

## Figure 3-5 (cont.)

| Programs and Program Elements | Salaries and Employee Benefits | Services and Supplies | Other Charges | Fixed Assets | Capital Projects | Total | Percent |
|---|---|---|---|---|---|---|---|
| VIII. General administration and government: | | | | | | | |
| (A) General government management | 2.3 | .4 | | .1 | | 2.8 | |
| (B) Financial | 23.1 | 4.2 | | .1 | * | 27.4 | |
| (C) Unassignable purchasing and property management | 11.6 | 6.9 | .1 | .2 | .1 | 18.9 | |
| (D) Personnel services for the government | 3.4 | .4 | | * | .1 | 3.9 | |
| (E) Unassignable EDP | .1 | * | | * | .2 | .3 | |
| (F) Legislature | 2.2 | .4 | | .1 | | 2.7 | |
| (G) Legal | 2.6 | .2 | | * | * | 2.8 | |
| (H) Elections | 2.9 | 2.5 | | * | * | 5.4 | |
| (I) Other | 14.5 | 20.6 | .9 | .8 | 14.3 | 51.1 | |
| Total general administration and government | 62.7 | 35.6 | 1.0 | 1.3 | 14.7 | 115.3 | (7.6) |

| | | | | | | | |
|---|---|---|---|---|---|---|---|
| Subtotal all programs | 544.7 | 754.5 | 119.1 | 44.6 | 45.3 | 1,508.2 | (100.0) |
| Less costs applied | | | | | | 33.3 | |
| Total all programs | | | | | | 1,474.9 | |
| Appropriation for deficiencies | | | | | | 1.7 | |
| Reserves | | | | | | 21.8 | |
| Estimated delinquencies | | | | | | 14.0 | |
| Grand total, requirements | | | | | | 1,512.4 | |

\* Denotes figure less than $50,000.

(Includes general county, special county, and special district funds under control of Board; dollar amounts in millions)

Source: Adapted from L. S. Hollinger, "Changing Rules of the Budget Game: The Development of a Planning-Programming-Budgeting System for Los Angeles County," in *Innovations In Planning, Programming, and Budgeting In State and Local Governments* (USGPO, 1969), pp. 82–84.

The main contribution of PPBS lies in the *planning* process, i.e., the process of making program policy decisions that lead to a specific budget and specific multi-year plans. The *budget* is a detailed short term resource plan for implementing the program decisions. PPBS does not replace the need for careful budget analysis to assure that approved programs will be carried out in an efficient and cost-conscious manner, nor does it remove the need for the preparation of the detailed, line-item type of information to *support* budget submission.[11]

The major distinctive characteristics of PPB, as described by Hatry, are:

1. It focuses on identifying the fundamental objectives of the government and then relating all activities to these (regardless of organizational placement).
2. Future year implications are explicitly identified.
3. All pertinent costs are considered.
4. Systematic analysis of alternatives is performed.[12]

Among the benefits to states and localities attributed to the PPB approach are these:

1. *Long range fiscal planning becomes routine.* All government programs have to be viewed in a perspective that considers not only the expenditures in the immediate budget period but for the years ahead.
2. *Plans and programs are reviewed continuously.* Under the system progress on each program will have to be reviewed each year, and the program revised, when new, previously unknown factors come into play, or when previous judgments have to be corrected. The periodic review helps to ascertain whether existing and proposed programs are the most effective ways of accomplishing a particular government mission. The most effective way is to be determined in terms of budgetary costs, the extent to which ample or scarce resources (for instance, highly skilled labor) are to be utilized, and whether a program has a positive or negative effect with respect not only to the primary but also to the secondary goals.
3. *Government activities are classified in terms of programs and their purposes.* Budgeting by programs rather than by administrative units, by budgeted positions, and by object expenditures has long been advocated. It permits a better understanding of the role of individual activities in meeting governmental objectives.
4. *Interagency coordination of programs is strengthened.* The system requires

11 Harry P. Hatry and John F. Cotton, *Program Planning for State, County, City* (Washington, D. C.: George Washington University, 1967), pp. 14–15. (Emphasis added.)

12 *Ibid.*, p. 15.

that each agency of the government engage periodically in meaningful self-examination both in terms of the specific function of the agency, and of the relation of this function to the activities of other agencies of the government. The latter requires interagency discussion and clarification, even prior to review in any office for program coordination.

5. *Intergovernmental planning is improved.* Federal aid programs will be viewed in the context of the jurisdictions' own program plans. The system will strengthen the federal effort toward improving budgeting and decision making by a counterpart effort in the state and local governments where the major portion of civilian public services are provided.

6. *A program evaluation cycle of program formulation, progress reporting, and program revision is established.* Planning will be linked to budget decisions and program evaluation to planning. The budget process becomes a more meaningful tool of government.

7. *Each program is to be evaluated in terms of national goals.* This requires not only consideration of the appropriate functions of the various levels of government but also the relationship of government to private activities in the same field; activities which may either support these goals, or be in conflict with them.[13]

Those closely associated with PPB do not claim it to be a panacea. But this approach is designed to overcome criticisms that have been made of object-of-expenditure and performance budgeting. Both of these other approaches are based principally upon historical data and focus upon a single period, whereas PPB emphasizes long-range planning in which (1) ultimate goals and intermediate objectives must be explicitly stated, and (2) the costs and benefits of major alternative courses to achieve these goals and objectives are to be explicitly evaluated—in quantitative terms where practicable and narratively in all cases. PPB theory assumes that all programs are to be evaluated annually, so that poor ones may be weeded out and new ones added. Changes in existing programs are evaluated in terms of discounted marginal costs (and benefits), whereas object-of-expenditure budgets focus upon total expenditures and performance budgets are based upon an average cost or average expenditure concept. Program decisions are to be formulated at upper management levels under PPB, as illustrated in Figure 3-6, and department or agency heads are expected to gear their activities to fulfilling those agreed-upon objectives and goals. Finally, though PPB can be adapted to any level of appropriation specificity, many of its advocates hope to encourage (1) decision-making and appropriations by legislatures in broader policy terms, and (2) increased executive powers by use of "lump-sum" appropriations.

---

[13] *Ibid.,* p. 7. (Emphasis added.)

Figure 3-6

PPBS CYCLE

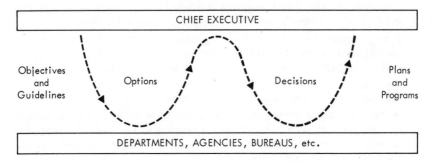

Source: Harry P. Hatry and John F. Cotton, *Program Planning For State, County, City,* (Washington, D.C.: George Washington University, 1967), p. 38.

Figure 3-7

ILLUSTRATIVE PPBS PROGRAM STRUCTURE

I. *Personal Safety*
  A. Law Enforcement
  B. Traffic Safety
  C. Fire Prevention and Control
  D. Safety From Animals
  E. Protection and Control of Disasters,
    Natural and Man-made
  F. Prevention of Other
    Accidents

II. *Health*
  A. Physical Health
  B. Mental Health
  C. Drug and Alcohol Addiction,
    Prevention and Control

III. *Intellectual Development and Personal Enrichment*
  A. Preschool Education
  B. Primary Education
  C. Secondary Education
  D. Higher Education
  E. Adult Education

IV. *Satisfactory Home/Community Environment*
  A. Comprehensive Community Planning
  B. Homes for the Dependent
  C. Housing (other than that in A and B)
  D. Water Supply

Source: Harry P. Hatry and John F. Cotton, "Individual PPBS Characteristics," *Program Planning for State, County, City* (Washington, D.C.: George Washington University, 1967), p. 17.

**Figure 3-7** (cont.)

E. Solid Waste Disposal
F. Air Pollution Control
G. Pest Control
H. Noise Abatement
I. Local Beautification
J. Intra-Community Relations
K. Homemaking
   Aid/Information

D. Aid to the Individual as a
   Businessman
E. Protection of the Individual
   as a Consumer of Goods and
   Services
F. Judicial Activities for
   Protection of Consumers and
   Businessmen, alike

V. *Economic Satisfaction &*
   *Satisfactory Work Opportunities*
   *for the Individual*
   A. Financial Assistance to the
      Needy
   B. Increased Job Opportunity
   C. Protection of an Individual as
      an Employee

VI. *Leisure-Time Opportunities*
   A. Outdoor
   B. Indoor
   C. Recreational Activities for
      Senior Citizens
   D. Cultural Activities

---

The focus of this categorization is the individual citizen—his needs and wants. Two category levels are shown (one represented by the roman numerals, the other by the capital letters. For a complete program structure, however, more levels are needed to display the applicable individual government activities.

Furthermore, the description of each category (not shown here), including statements of major objectives, are an indispensable part of program structure preparation. The categories "Unassignable Research" and "Unassignable Support" might also be included for each of the eight program areas. These categories would contain activities directly related to the program area but which could not be related to individual categories within the program area.

The broadened concept of a "program" under program type budgeting is illustrated in Figure 3-7; the typical relationships between programs, subprograms (functions) and program elements (facilities) are shown in Figures 3-8 and 3-9; a multi-year program and fiscal plan format is illustrated in Figure 3-10; and a typical program, subprogram, or element analysis form comprises Figure 3-11.

It is too early to assess fully the impact of PPB upon state and local budgeting. As one observer noted:

Figure 3-8

EXAMPLE OF A PROGRAM STRUCTURE FORMAT

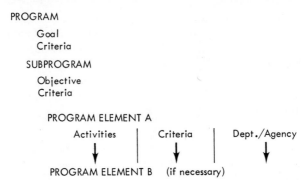

PROGRAM
    Goal
    Criteria
  SUBPROGRAM
    Objective
    Criteria

    PROGRAM ELEMENT A
       Activities   |   Criteria   |   Dept./Agency
         ↓          ↓         ↓
    PROGRAM ELEMENT B   (if necessary)

Source: H. Sternberger, J. Renz, and G. Fasolina, "Planning-Programming-Budgeting Systems (PPBS) in Nassau County, N. Y.," in *Innovations In Planning, Programming, and Budgeting Systems In State And Local Governments* (USGPO, 1969), p. 145.

Figure 3-9

PPB SYSTEMS: TYPICAL RELATIONSHIPS OF PROGRAMS,
SUBPROGRAMS, AND PROGRAM ELEMENTS

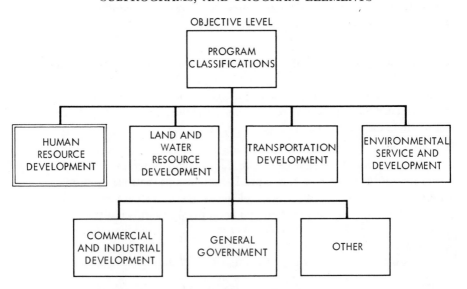

Source: Ernst and Ernst, *Planning-Programming-Budgeting Systems for State and Local Governments* (Olympia, Washington: State of Washington, 1968), pp. 34–37.

**Figure 3-9 (cont.)**

MAJOR PROGRAM AREA LEVEL

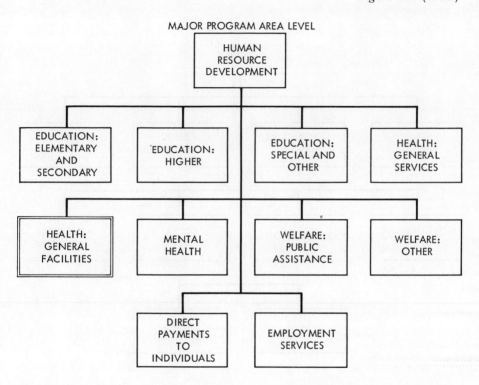

**Figure 3-9 (cont.)**

PROGRAM [SUBPROGRAM] LEVEL

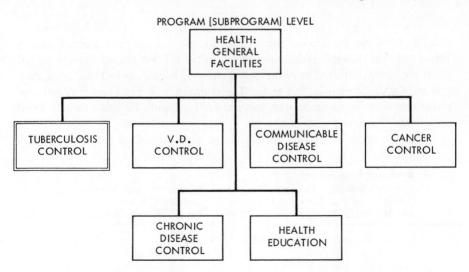

**Figure 3-9 (cont.)**

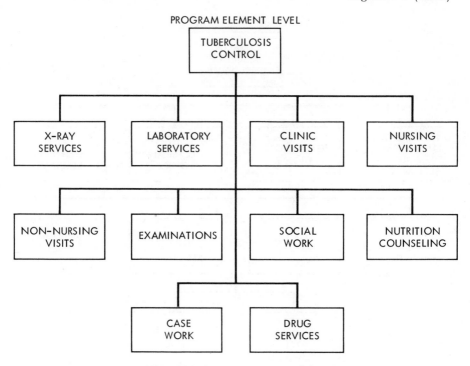

PROGRAM ELEMENT LEVEL

PPBS has generated more hopes, fears and mechanistic nonsense in a few short years than all the budgetary, economic and planning jargon of the last thirty.[14]

The most extensive experimentation with PPB at the state and local level to date has been that carried out through the auspices of the State-Local Finances Project of The George Washington University, a Ford Foundation-supported effort commonly referred to as the 5–5–5 project. Beginning in 1966, pilot projects were set in motion in five states, five counties, and five cities.[15] A series of reports issued in conjunction with this project highlights the lessons learned and the pitfalls discovered to date.

Though the logic of PPB is convincing, there are many barriers to imple-

14 Ernst and Ernst, *op. cit.,* p. 65.

15 States: California, Michigan, New York, Wisconsin, and Vermont; Counties: Dade (Florida), Nashville-Davidson (Tennessee), Los Angeles (California), Nassau (New York), and Wayne (Michigan); Cities: Dayton, Denver, Detroit, New Haven, and San Diego.

mentation of a complete PPB system. (1) It is quite difficult to formulate a meaningful, explicit statement of a government's goals and objectives that can be agreed upon by all concerned—regardless of how worthwhile such a statement may be. (2) Not only do goals change, but elected officials, in particular, often prefer not to commit themselves to more than very general statements lest they be precluded from changing their positions when politics dictates. (3) The time period considered relevant by an elected official may be limited to that remaining prior to the expiration of his current term of office; he may, at least subconsciously, be more interested in short run costs and results than in long run results or costs. (4) PPB, like performance budgeting, assumes both adequate computer capability and a high level of analytical ability to be readily available to the government. Though governmental computer capability is steadily increasing, staff analysts are a luxury few state or local governments have acquired to date. (5) Finally, it should be noted that objective measurement is even more of a problem here than in the performance approach, as both costs and benefits, over a period of several years, must be estimated. Both are often quite difficult to measure and the ratio or relationship between two such estimates is apt to imply far more precision than is actually present.

Both the habits of years of object-of-expenditure budgeting and a jealously guarded legislative power of the pursestring have necessitated creation of crosswalks (see Figure 3-12) between PPB plans and the object-of-expenditure or departmental appropriations that most legislative bodies continue to insist upon. These "traditional" appropriations may not be so unwise or archaic as some critics might claim, as program categories that cross departmental lines and are based on many allocations are not well suited to responsibility accounting or to control purposes. The implications here are at least two-fold: (1) PPB data appear to be used in practice more to supplement and support line-item appropriations than vice versa, and (2) there seems to be little or no accounting follow-up for comparisons of PPB plans versus actual results, as governmental accounting systems must be geared first to budgetary accounting and only secondarily, if time and capacity permit, to supplemental data. Progress in implementing PPB at the Federal level, where there are more of the requisite resources than in any state or local government, has been limited; and at least one state has modified earlier plans and adopted a policy of evolving slowly into a modified PPB system.

It is clear that implementation of a PPB-based system requires several years at best. Early disappointments are to be expected, of course, particularly since some have oversold the value of PPB—thereby virtually guaranteeing disappointment to the most optimistic advocates. Only time will tell to what extent PPB or similar systems (or "nonsystems") will replace the other approaches or will become supplementary to them.

Figure 3-10

MULTI-YEAR PROGRAM AND FINANCIAL PLAN

From Year 19X3 to 19X7 in millions of dollars

| Level | | Program Categories* | FY 19X1 Actual | FY 19X2 Current Estimate | FY 19X3 Budget Year Estimate | FY 19X4 Program Estimate | FY 19X5 Program Estimate | FY 19X6 Program Estimate | FY 19X7 Program Estimate | Total Costs 19X3–X7 |
| 1st | 2nd | | | | | | | | | |
|---|---|---|---|---|---|---|---|---|---|---|
| I | | Personal Safety | | | | | | | | |
| | A | Law Enforcement | | | | | | | | |
| | B | Traffic Safety | | | | | | | | |
| | C | Fire Prevention and Control | | | | | | | | |
| | D | Safety From Animals | | | | | | | | |
| | E | Protection and Control of Natural and Man-Made Disasters | | | | | | | | |
| | F | Prevention of Other Accidents | | | | | | | | |
| | | Total Program Area I | | | | | | | | |
| II | | Health | | | | | | | | |
| | A | Physical Health | | | | | | | | |
| | B | Mental Health | | | | | | | | |
| | C | Drug and Alcohol Addiction— Prevention and Control | | | | | | | | |
| | | Total Program Area II | | | | | | | | |

* In practice, more category levels would be needed to display the individual government activities/programs.

Source: Adapted from Harry P. Hatry and John F. Cotton, "Individual PPBS Characteristics," *Program Planning for State, County, City* (Washington, D.C.: George Washington University, 1967), pp. 20–21.

ILLUSTRATIVE PROGRAM ANALYSIS WORKSHEET FORM FOR BUDGETARY REQUESTS **Figure 3-11**

| PROGRAM ANALYSIS WORKSHEET FORM | PAGE ____ ⌐ | PROGRAM FUND SOURCE SUMMARY | | PROGRAM EXPENDITURE TYPE SUMMARY | |
|---|---|---|---|---|---|
| | | TYPE | AMOUNT | TYPE | AMOUNT |

DEPARTMENT:    NUMBER:

MAJOR PROGRAM AREA:    NUMBER:

PROGRAM:    NUMBER:

PROGRAM GOALS AND OBJECTIVES:

SPECIAL REMARKS

DATE:     FILED BY:     APPROVED BY:

| NO. | PROGRAM ELEMENT | UNIT OF MEASURE | | CURRENT QUARTER | | CURRENT YEAR | | BUDGET YEAR | | | FUTURE YEARS | | | |
|---|---|---|---|---|---|---|---|---|---|---|---|---|---|---|
| | | | | ACTUAL | BUDGET | ACTUAL | BUDGET | CONTINUE PROGRAM | CHANGE UP(DOWN) | TOTAL | TWO | THREE | FOUR | FIVE |
| | | UNITS | | | | | | | | | | | | |
| | | COST | CODE | | | | | | | | | | | |
| | | UNITS | | | | | | | | | | | | |
| | | COST | CODE | | | | | | | | | | | |
| | | UNITS | | | | | | | | | | | | |
| | | COST | CODE | | | | | | | | | | | |
| | | UNITS | | | | | | | | | | | | |
| | | COST | CODE | | | | | | | | | | | |
| | | UNITS | | | | | | | | | | | | |
| | | COST | CODE | | | | | | | | | | | |

| ELEM. NO. | PROJECTS SUPPORTING PROGRAM ELEMENTS | | | | | | | | | | | | | |
|---|---|---|---|---|---|---|---|---|---|---|---|---|---|---|
| | | COST | | | | | | | | | | | | |
| | | CODE | | | | | | | | | | | | |

*Note:* This same form would be used for program elements, subprograms, and program data, the data being increasingly summarized.

Source: Ernst and Ernst, *Planning-Programming-Budgeting Systems for State and Local Governments* (Olympia, Washington: State of Washington, 1968), p. 40.

87

## PPB/LINE ITEM "CROSSWALK":
## 19X1 RECOMMENDED PROGRAM BUDGET-ALL DEPARTMENTS
### ($ thousands)

| Agency and/or Object-of-Expenditure Budget (Appropriations) Department/Agency | Protection Services | Health | Education | Community Development |
|---|---|---|---|---|
| 1 Board of Assessors | | | | |
| 2 Board of Elections | | | | |
| 3 Board of Supervisors | | | | |
| 4 Budget Office | | | | |
| 5 Civil Defense | $ 235 | | | |
| 34 Office for the Aging | | $ 28 | | $ 14 |
| 35 Planning Department | | | | 431 |
| 36 Police Headquarters & Districts | 35,674 | | | |
| 37 Probation Department | 3,791 | | | |
| 38 Public Administrator | 63 | | | |
| 39 Public Works Department | | 9,241 | | |
| 40 Sheriff/Corrections Department | 2,517 | | | |
| 41 Social Services | | 4,143 | | |
| 42 Sole Supervisory District | | | 91 | |
| 54 Nassau Community College | | | 7,900 | |
| Total Program Budget Operating Expenditures | $51,941 | $43,293 | $ 9,821 | $ 984 |
| Total Program Budget Revenues | $ 3,023 | $24,729 | $ 9,684 | $ 105 |

* Primarily for intragovernmental and/or interfund items.
Source: Adapted from H. Sternberger, J. Renz, and G. Fasolina, "Planning-Program-ming-Budgeting Systems (PPBS) In Nassau County, N. Y.," in *Innovations In Planning, Programming, and Budgetary Systems In State And Local Governments* (USGPO, 1969), p. 187.

Figure 3-12

Program Budget
(Request Support,
Communication)

| Trans-portation | Recreation & Cultural | Social Services | Legal, Fiscal Man-agement | Support Services | Non-Program Items | Total | Line No. |
|---|---|---|---|---|---|---|---|
| | | | $ 1,622 | $ 201 | | $1,823 | 1 |
| | | | 2,352 | | | 2,352 | 2 |
| | | | 218 | 237 | | 455 | 3 |
| | | | 103 | 54 | | 157 | 4 |
| | | | | 204 | | 439 | 5 |
| | | $ 14 | | | | 56 | 34 |
| $ 63 | $ 16 | | 45 | 104 | | 659 | 35 |
| 3,531 | | 1,686 | | 9,871 | | 50,762 | 36 |
| | | 54 | | 679 | | 4,524 | 37 |
| | | | | | | 63 | 38 |
| $10,142 | 7,931 | | | 8,660 | | 35,974 | 39 |
| | | | | 2,500 | | 5,107 | 40 |
| | | 94,616 | | 6,952 | | 105,711 | 41 |
| | | | | | | 91 | 42 |
| | | | | 3,567 | | 11,467 | 54 |
| $14,587 | $ 8,155 | $98,181 | $ 9,777 | $57,817 | $43,216 | $337,772 | |
| | | | | | | (60,292) | Adjustments* |
| | | | | | | $277,480 | |
| $22,549 | $ 1,013 | $70,083 | $ 6,708 | $14,487 | $ 5,114 | $157,495 | |
| | | | | | | (34,960) | Adjustments* |
| | | | | | | $122,535 | |

### Selecting an Appropriate Approach

In summary, designing an appropriate approach to expenditure budgeting for a specific government requires (1) a knowledge of the various general approaches that have been developed, (2) insight into the history and activities of the organization in question and the attitudes and capabilities of its personnel, in order to assess the proper planning-control-evaluation balance to be sought, (3) originality in combining the strengths of the object-of-expenditure, performance, and program approaches, while avoiding their weaknesses, and (4) patience in system design and implementation and the ability to adapt the system to changed circumstances. Larger governments should certainly consider a PPB-based approach; smaller ones should find its concepts useful and might do well to experiment (at least informally) with PPB-type analysis, possibly in conjunction with proposed new programs or when major changes in the existing ones are contemplated. Slavish ties to any one of these three approaches should be avoided, however, lest the budget become an end in itself rather than a means to an end.

Because of its widespread use and adaptability to budgetary accounting, illustrations in the remainder of this text generally assume an object-of-expenditure type budget to be in use. This is done for consistency and ease of illustration only and should not be construed as being indicative of author preference for any particular approach. The concepts and procedures illustrated apply generally to all budgetary systems; only the expenditure account classifications need be changed, and additional performance or other data gathered, to achieve performance or program budget accountability. A comprehensive PPB system would require also that expense data be collected or derived analytically.

## BUDGET PREPARATION

Sound financial planning requires that preparation of the budget be started in time for its adoption before the beginning of the period to which it applies. To insure that adequate time will be allowed, a budget calendar (see Figure 3-13)

### Figure 3-13

A GOVERNMENTAL UNIT
Budget Calendar
For Year Beginning January 1, 19X7

| *Date* | *Steps in Budget Procedure* |
| --- | --- |
| Prior to October 1, 19X6 ........ | Budget officer prepares estimate forms and instructions. |
| October 1 ..................... | Budget officer distributes estimate forms and instructions among departments. |

Figure 3-13 (cont.)

| | |
|---|---|
| October 1 to October 21 ........ | Departments prepare estimates. |
| | Budget officer prepares estimates of fixed charges and other nondepartmental items. Budget officer also prepares estimates of taxes and other nondepartmental revenues. Completed departmental estimate forms are returned to the budget officer by departments. |
| October 22 to November 1 ...... | Budget officer consolidates estimates. |
| November 2 to November 30 .... | Budget officer conducts departmental hearings. Budget officer confers with chief executive, and the latter determines amounts to be finally recommended to the legislative body. Chief executive also determines amounts to be adopted as the official revenue estimates of the municipality for the budget year. Chief executive prepares budget message. Budget officer prepares final budget document for submission to legislative body. |
| December 1 ................. | Budget document, including message of chief executive, is turned over to legislative body. |
| December 2 ................. | Legislative body turns budget document over to its budget committee. |
| December 2 to December 15...... | Budget committee conducts public hearings and makes recommendations concerning the amounts to be appropriated. |
| December 16 ................. | Budget committee turns its recommendations over to the legislative body. |
| December 16 to December 23 .... | Legislative body considers the committee's recommendations. |
| December 23 ................. | Legislative body adopts the budget by passing an appropriation ordinance. Legislative body levies taxes by passing a tax levy ordinance(s). |
| December 27 ................. | Request for allotments is sent out by chief executive through budget officer. |
| January 2, 19X7................ | Adopted budget is recorded on the books. |
| January 6..................... | Departments submit work programs and allotment schedules to budget officer. |
| January 6 to January 15 ........ | Budget officer consolidates allotment schedules and presents them with recommendations to chief executive. |

**Figure 3-13 (cont.)**

January 15 ................... Chief executive makes final revisions.

January 16 ................... Department heads are informed of the amounts
alloted to them. Allotments are recorded on the
books.

**Figure 3-14**

TRADITIONAL INFORMATION FLOW—BUDGET PREPARATION

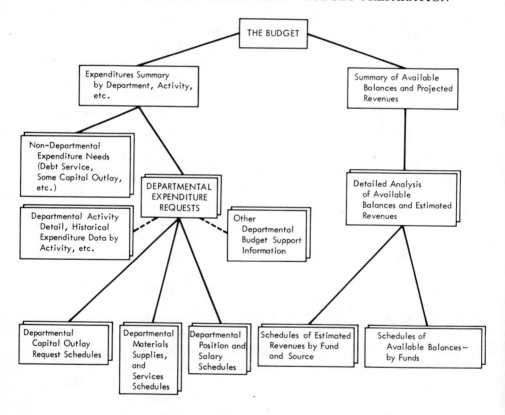

listing each step in the budgetary procedure and the time allowed for its completion should be prepared. The budget preparation then proceeds in a manner similar to that shown in Figure 3-14.

Budgeting has been described as the process of allocating scarce resources to unlimited demands. Certainly the budget officer must have an accurate idea of the resources which taxes and other revenue sources currently provided by law will yield at current rates. Having produced such an estimate, the budget officer and the chief executive can compare it with revenues and expenditures of prior years and with their knowledge of changes in demands on the government and in its programs. Such a comparison should provide an impression of the adequacy of estimated revenues to meet the needs for expenditures.

### Revenue Estimates

The process of estimating revenues has almost as many facets as there are types of revenue. The general property tax, the chief reliance of most municipalities, is described in detail in Chapter 6. The revenue from the property tax is computed by applying a rate determined by the legislative body to a tax base of assessed property values. The latter may be expected to increase with building activity and, to some extent, with inflation and economic development. Since most assessments do not equal market value, property tax revenue may also be changed by changing the percentage of market value at which property is assessed. Thus the general property tax has a number of variables which must be considered in estimating revenues.

Nearly all revenues are determined by applying a rate to some base. Many municipalities now depend on an income tax, a tax form which has become an increasingly important revenue source of non-Federal governments in recent years. Here the rates expected to be in effect must be used to estimate expected revenue, which will be directly related to levels of economic activity and wage and salary rates. Licenses and permits, important revenue sources in many municipalities, require evaluation of the number of such licenses or permits to be issued and any rate changes contemplated. Other revenues, such as from fines and forfeitures, intergovernmental grants or shared revenue, and fees must be estimated on the best available basis.

After all of these estimates have been made, they are tabulated in a Statement of Actual and Estimated Revenues (Figure 3-15). This statement provides for the computation of total estimated revenues for the new year and for comparisons with prior years. If the governmental unit expects to have fund balances available at the end of the year that are not designated for nonoperating purposes, these may be taken into account in estimating the resources available to finance operating expenditures of the coming year.

Figure 3-15

A GOVERNMENTAL UNIT

General Fund

Statement of Actual and Estimated Revenues

| | Actual 19X5 | Actual First Nine Months of 19X6 | Estimated Remainder of 19X6 | Total Columns 2 and 3 | Estimated 19X7 |
|---|---|---|---|---|---|
| **Taxes:** | | | | | |
| General property taxes ...... | $294,000 | $291,000 | — | $291,000 | $288,000 |
| Penalties and interest on delinquent taxes .......... | 1,100 | 800 | $ 250 | 1,050 | 1,000 |
| Total taxes ........... | $295,100 | $291,800 | $ 250 | $292,050 | $289,000 |
| **Licenses and Permits:** | | | | | |
| Motor vehicles .............. | $ 31,000 | $ 25,500 | $ 7,000 | $ 32,500 | $ 34,000 |
| Building structures and equipment ................ | 1,500 | 1,450 | 450 | 1,900 | 2,000 |
| Alcoholic beverages .......... | 11,000 | 9,000 | 3,000 | 12,000 | 13,000 |
| Professional and occupational .. | 6,200 | 4,650 | 1,225 | 5,875 | 6,000 |
| Amusements ............ | 1,350 | 990 | 300 | 1,290 | 1,300 |
| Total licenses and permits | $ 51,050 | $ 41,590 | $11,975 | $ 53,565 | $ 56,300 |
| **Intergovernmental Revenues:** | | | | | |

~~~~~~~~~~~~~~~~~~~~~~~~~~~~~~~~~~~~~~~~~~~~~~~

| | | | | | |
|---|---|---|---|---|---|
| **Charges for Services:** | | | | | |
| Court costs, fees and charges .. | $ 1,100 | $ 1,000 | $ 200 | $ 1,200 | $ 1,000 |
| Sale of ordinances parking meters .................... | 1,200 | 925 | 250 | 1,175 | 1,000 |
| Special police services ........ | 5,100 | 3,000 | 1,050 | 4,050 | 4,000 |
| Health inspection ............ | 375 | 465 | 135 | 600 | 800 |
| Total charges for services .. | $ 7,775 | $ 5,390 | ¢ 1,635 | $ 7,025 | $ 6,800 |
| **Fines and Forfeits** ............ | $ 6,000 | $ 4,000 | $ 500 | $ 4,500 | $ 5,100 |
| **Miscellaneous Revenue** ...... | 4,000 | 3,000 | 1,200 | 4,200 | 4,300 |
| Grand Total ............ | $437,000 | $397,000 | $36,000 | $433,000 | $431,000 |

### Expenditure Planning

In organizations the size of a state government or a large municipality, expenditure planning should be considered a year-round activity. The budget director and his budget examiners should be continually in the process of becoming acquainted with the agencies with whose budgets they will work, as analyses of agency operations, including both what the agency does and how it does it, are essential if the budget office is to give proper consideration to agency requests. In many jurisdictions the budget office has been assigned responsibilities for doing work best described as that of an "efficiency expert." This assignment has come in many cases because of the qualifications of budget personnel; in other cases it has been a natural outgrowth of the intimate, yet independent, knowledge and viewpoint of the budget examiners. The budget office should also utilize relevant reports of the internal audit staff, independent auditors, management consultants, or others in familiarizing itself with agency operations.

The review of agency operations becomes a secondary (but still important) operation when the actual production of an expenditure budget begins. The first move in the latter process is to design forms that will make feasible the handling of the volume of work. The process continues as outlined in the budget calendar, Figure 3-13, and in Figure 3-14.

BUDGET INSTRUCTIONS.   The instructions the budget officer sends to the agencies should include: (1) the budget calendar, (2) a statement of executive goals, policies, and expectations relative to the upcoming budget period, (3) other appropriate comments or instructions explaining how decisions regarding amounts to be requested should be made, necessary supporting data, etc., and (4) an explanation of how to perform the mechanics of filling out the budget estimate forms, with emphasis upon any changes from prior years. Policy statements to aid the heads of agencies or departments in deciding amounts of budget requests will include such matters as the following:

1. The type of budget to be prepared (see the "Budgetary Approaches and Emphases" section earlier in this chapter) and the character and quantity of explanatory material.
2. The general level of revenue and expenditures anticipated for the period and the attitude of the chief executive toward improved or expanded services, i.e., the major program thrusts and their approximate magnitude.
3. The application of legal or administrative requirements to the departments. For example, new personnel regulations may drastically change the pattern for staffing the departments.
4. Relevant economic and other data bearing on subjects such as the expected state of the economy and its effect on commodity and labor prices and

levels of business activity. For example, an estimate of the level and type of construction activity in a community will determine the number of building permits to be issued and the number of inspections that the government will have to make in the succeeding period. City-owned utilities will also obtain from such data their estimates of new connections.

IDENTITY OF ORGANIZATIONAL, BUDGETARY, AND ACCOUNTING UNITS. In the process of organizing the agencies or departments of a governmental unit the programs and activities of the organization should be the controlling factor. From the standpoint of managerial control through budgeting and accounting, it would be desirable for each program and activity to be within a single organizational unit. (At the lowest organization level, no more than one activity or subactivity should be assigned to each unit.) This is not to say that the city organization would have hundreds of small departments, or only a few large ones, but simply that the major functions should be assigned to departments and that activities and subactivities under each function should be charged to the organization subunits of the departments on the basis indicated. For example, the business office of the city should be broken down into such units as general ledger, accounts payable, accounts receivable, purchasing, and the like. There will be instances in which organizational patterns will have to be determined by technical skills rather than by functions and activities, but these cases should be relatively few.

Organizational units are also budgetary planning units, budgetary accounting units, and, if cost accounting is used, cost accounting units. The concept of identical units for these several purposes is essential to the smooth operation of the financial affairs of the city. The accumulation of accurate past and current costs for a unit and its activity is necessary for the adequate and accurate calculation of future costs for that unit and its activity.

CALL FOR DEPARTMENTAL ESTIMATES. The chief executive's call for departmental estimates is one of the first steps in the preparation of the budget. Following the object-of-expenditure/performance combination approach illustrated here, a department's first move in preparing its estimate would be to accumulate and schedule workload data. A work program for the Bureau of Sanitation of the Department of Public Works is presented in Figure 3-16. Actual and estimated workload and unit cost[16] figures are compiled and used both to produce and support the budget request. Note that there are slight changes in the unit cost figures used for estimating 19X7 expenditures. Such changes may be due to expected changes in the cost of labor, materials, or equipment. Unit cost figures will also fluctuate with volume as fixed costs are spread over a greater or lesser volume of work. (Capital outlay is treated separately to avoid distortion

---

[16] The term "cost" and "unit cost," when used with reference to expendable funds, usually connotes *expenditure* rather than expense.

of year-to-year comparisons.) To avoid the influence of price level vagaries upon the measurement of efficiency, some cities use man-hours or other work measurement units rather than total cost as the measure, or indicator, of performance.

Many activities of a city or state are not susceptible to such exact costing as are those of the Bureau of Sanitation. Organizations responsible for such activities should nonetheless attempt to describe their activities in meaningful units. For example, the Patrol Division of a Police Department might provide comparative data by years for such significant activities as those indicated in Figure 3-17. Note also the information on the change from two-man to one-man prowl cars and the resulting improvement of service as indicated by (1) estimates of prowl car average response time and (2) the increase in the number of patrol beats. Progress is continually being made in relating such activity information to the cost of operations; activities previously considered unmeasurable are steadily subjected to analysis and control through newly devised criteria indicative of performance.

A series of several performance measures or indicators often proves superior to the use of a single compromise measure. It is essential in all cases to remember that such measures are merely *indicators* to guide management decisions, not substitutes therefor, and that such indicators must actually relate directly to either (or both) the *quality* or *quantity* of work performed in terms of organizational goals. This latter point is of particular importance because poorly selected indicators or failure to specify and control performance quality may lead to a decline in efficiency. To illustrate, should the purchasing department's performance be measured only in terms of the number of purchase orders issued one might find its performance "dressed up" through such tactics as making many unnecessarily small orders, e.g., ordering supplies in uneconomically small quantities in order to generate many purchase order "performance measures."

After work load and unit cost information for an organizational unit have been accumulated to the extent deemed practicable, this information should be converted into estimates of total costs for the upcoming budget period. Estimates should be made for each organizational unit and subunit (remember that insofar as possible organizational lines should be based on activities). Estimates for the supervisory activity of the Police Department are set out in Figure 3-18. The first eight columns are filled in by the finance officer; columns 9–11 are filled in by the chief of police. In some jurisdictions columns are provided following column nine in which the chief executive places his recommendation as to the number of employees, their rates of pay, and the total amount. If these latter columns are provided, and if the chief executive's recommendations differ from departmental requests, the city council will be presented with conflicting information. Some feel that since the chief executive is responsible for planning and administration, it is better for the council to receive only his recommenda-

Figure 3-16

## A GOVERNMENTAL UNIT
### Work Program—19X7

Departmental Code: 4000

Fund: General
Function: Sanitation and Waste Removal
Department: Public Works
Bureau: Sanitation
Submitted by: M. A. Downs, Chief
Date: October 10, 19X6

| Operation | Work Unit | Actual 19X5 | | | Estimated 19X6 | | | Estimated 19X7 | | |
|---|---|---|---|---|---|---|---|---|---|---|
| | | No. of Units | Unit Cost | Total | No. of Units | Unit Cost | Total | No. of Units | Unit Cost | Total |
| Garbage Collection | Tons | 158,319 | $1.45 | $229,562.22 | 168,000 | $1.46 | $245,280.00 | 170,000 | $1.44 | $244,800.00 |
| Incineration | Tons | 170,350 | 1.18 | 201,013.00 | 180,000 | 1.18 | 212,400.00 | 182,000 | 1.19 | 216,580.00 |

**Figure 3-17**

| | Actual 19X4 | Actual 19X5 | Estimated 19X6 | Estimated 19X7 |
|---|---|---|---|---|
| **A GOVERNMENTAL UNIT—POLICE DEPARTMENT** Patrol Division Work Load Information | | | | |
| Prowl car average response time | 3.4 | 3.4 | 3.4 | 3.4—2.0 |
| Mileage | 1,763,900 | 1,837,000 | 1,936,000 | 2,800,000 |
| Arrests | 25,625 | 28,832 | 32,725 | 35,000 |
| Citations | 103,319 | 94,741 | 106,316 | 114,000 |
| Investigations | 9,078 | 10,604 | 11,600 | 12,650 |
| Shakedowns | 69,460 | 77,116 | 90,750 | 98,000 |

The prowl car is one of the basic elements in a modern police system, and the field operations of the Patrol Division during the coming year are scheduled for conversion to one-man prowl cars on all watches. The number of patrol beats during the two evening watches also will be increased from 24 to 48. This major change in operations will result in a higher utilization of existing manpower, and prowl car response time to radio calls should be reduced from 3.4 to 2 minutes. An improved level of crime prevention and traffic control is anticipated.

Conversion to one-man patrol car operations will require three additional positions of Sergeant to provide adequate field supervision. Also required is one position of Intermediate Stenographer Clerk, which would relieve the Patrol Division staff of a considerable volume of clerical work.

*16 7013*

tions. Where this view prevails, the chief of police will fill out columns 9–11; but when the estimate is presented to the council, these columns will have been revised to contain the chief executive's recommendations, which may or may not be the same as those of the chief of police. Others feel that the council should have knowledge of departmental requests as well as executive proposals (where these differ) and include such information in the budget document or in notes thereto.

Column 12 contains the appropriation granted by the council. Note that in this case a lump sum of $27,400 was granted for personal services. The council could have made an appropriation for each line; in doing so it would have secured detailed control of expenditures, but would have sacrificed the advantages of executive flexibility.

Figures 3-19 and 3-20 illustrate forms used for estimating supervisory expenditures other than personal services. Figure 3-21 summarizes the estimates of the department's supervisory activity.

Figure 3-22 presents the departmental summary. Notice that the summary

Figure 3-18

# A GOVERNMENTAL UNIT
## Departmental Estimate Personal Services—19X7

Departmental Code: 2000

Fund: General
Function: Public Safety
Department: Police
Activity: Supervision
Submitted by: A. Johnson, Chief
Date: October 10, 19X6

| Code No. | Classification | Actual January 1, 19X6 | | | Actual October 1, 19X6 | | | Proposed, 19X7 | | | Appropriation by Legislative Body |
|---|---|---|---|---|---|---|---|---|---|---|---|
| | | No. | Rate | Amount | No. | Rate | Amount | No. | Rate | Amount | Amount |
| 1 | 2 | 3 | 4 | 5 | 6 | 7 | 8 | 9 | 10 | 11 | 12 |
| 01 | Chief of Police | 1 | $8,500 | $8,500 | 1 | $8,500 | $8,500 | 1 | $8,500 | $8,500 | |
| 01 | Deputy Chief | 1 | 7,500 | 7,500 | 1 | 7,500 | 7,500 | 1 | 7,500 | 7,500 | |
| 01 | Clerk-Typist | 2 | 3,600 | 7,200 | 2 | 3,600 | 7,200 | 2 | 3,800 | 7,600 | |
| 01 | Policewoman | 1 | 3,800 | 3,800 | 1 | 3,800 | 3,800 | 1 | 3,800 | 3,800 | |
| | Total | 5 | ..... | $27,000 | 5 | ..... | $27,000 | 5 | ..... | $27,400 | $27,400 |

in this example is by object-of-expenditure and by organizational subunit. In the object-of-expenditure summary the identity of the estimates of the supervisory activity has been lost, but in the summary by organizational subunit the estimate of supervisory activity appears as an identifiable figure. Appropriations could be made by granting the amounts shown in either summary. As observed previously, if the appropriation ordinance is drawn to appropriate a lump sum for each activity, the legislative body can very easily change the requested amounts; that is, the legislators can say, by increasing or decreasing amounts requested by the several activities, that they believe an activity should be stepped up or reduced. Such a decision gives the executive branch the responsibility of scaling operations to the level indicated as desirable by the legislative group.

ESTIMATING OTHER CHARGES.   Some expenditures are ordinarily not allocated to any program or activity of an organizational unit. Examples are interest, contributions to pension funds, retirement of serial bonds, and contributions to sinking funds. These expenditure estimates are therefore prepared by the budget officer. However, refinements of accounting and budgeting are continually reducing the number of unallocated expenditures. For example, contributions to pension funds may properly be charged to activities on the basis of the employees whose salaries caused the contributions.

REVISION OF DEPARTMENTAL ESTIMATES.   As soon as department heads have filled out the budget estimate forms, and at any rate not later than the date designated in the budget calendar, they transmit the forms, together with work programs and other supporting data, to the budget officer. The latter notes whether the estimates have been properly prepared, summarizes the information received, and presents the schedules, together with the summaries and revenue estimates, to the chief executive, who must analyze all the data in order to prepare his recommendations to the legislative body.

Both the departmental estimate schedules and the work programs are of great help to the chief executive in preparing his recommendations. In addition, he confers with the budget officer and with department heads, whom he may ask to justify estimates of expenditures. In larger governmental units the chief executive may employ efficiency engineers, program consultants, or other specialists to make special investigations to determine whether departmental requests are justified.

The chief executive pays careful attention also to the revenue estimates. Whereas no single operating department head knows the relationship between total estimated expenditures and total estimated revenues, the chief executive has these data. If estimated expenditures exceed appropriable resources first estimated to be available during the budget period, (1) reductions may be made in the expenditure amounts requested, (2) additional revenues may be secured, or (3) a decision may be made to incur a deficit. A chief executive should not make arbitrary adjustments of expenditure requests at some fixed percentage.

Figure 3-19

## A GOVERNMENTAL UNIT
### Departmental Estimate
Current Expenses—Other than Personal Services
19X7

Departmental Code: 2000

Fund: General
Function: Public Safety
Department: Police
Activity: Supervision
Submitted by: A. Johnson, Chief
Date: October 10, 19X6

| Code No. | Classification | Actual 19X4 | Actual 19X5 | Actual First Nine Months of 19X6 | Estimated Remainder of 19X6 | Total Columns 5 and 6 | Proposed 19X7 | Appropriation by Legislative Body |
|---|---|---|---|---|---|---|---|---|
| 1 | 2 | 3 | 4 | 5 | 6 | 7 | 8 | 9 |
| | **Supplies:** | | | | | | | |
| 02 | Janitor Supplies | $ 95 | $ 96 | $ 77 | $ 25 | $ 102 | $ 120 | |
| 02 | Clothing | 1,011 | 1,200 | 785 | 260 | 1,045 | 1,300 | |
| 02 | Record Supplies | 100 | 115 | 95 | 30 | 125 | 150 | |
| 02 | Ammunition | 427 | 431 | 335 | 115 | 450 | 500 | |
| | Total | $1,633 | $1,842 | $1,292 | $ 430 | $1,722 | $2,070 | $2,000 |

| | Other Services and Charges: | | | | | | | |
|---|---|---|---|---|---|---|---|---|
| 03 | Printing | $ 247 | $ 255 | $ 195 | $ 65 | $ 260 | $ 280 | |
| 03 | Gas | 74 | 73 | 55 | 20 | 75 | 80 | |
| 03 | Electricity | 158 | 161 | 126 | 43 | 169 | 177 | |
| 03 | Water | 56 | 53 | 41 | 14 | 55 | 60 | |
| 03 | Repairs to Office Equipment | 293 | 300 | 235 | 80 | 315 | 363 | |
| 03 | Rent | 1,800 | 1,800 | 1,405 | 470 | 1,875 | 1,900 | |
| 03 | Surety Bond Premiums | 80 | 80 | 60 | 20 | 80 | 100 | |
| | Total | $2,708 | $2,722 | $2,117 | $ 712 | $2,829 | $2,960 | $2,900 |
| | Grand Total | $4,341 | $4,564 | $3,409 | $1,142 | $4,551 | $5,030 | $4,900 |

Figure 3-20

A GOVERNMENTAL UNIT
Departmental Estimate
Capital Outlays
19X7

Departmental Code:  2000

Fund: General
Function: Public Safety
Department: Police
Activity: Supervision
Submitted by: A. Johnson, Chief
Date: October 10, 19X6

| Code No. | Classification | Explanation | Proposed 19X7 | | | Appropriation by Legislative Body |
| | | | Quantity | Unit Price | Cost | |
| 1 | 2 | 3 | 4 | 5 | 6 | 7 |
| 04 | Office Equipment | Desks | 1 | $ 90 | $ 90 | |
| | | Total | — | — | $ 90 | $ 90 |

For example, if estimated expenditures exceed estimated revenues by 10 percent, he will not automatically reduce each department's request by this percentage but will consider each department individually. If he believes that a department's request is proper in the light of the number, volume, and quality of services projected for the budget year, his decision to increase, decrease, or approve the department's estimates will depend on his evaluation of the community's needs for the services and of the political effects of curtailing them.

THE BUDGET DOCUMENT.    After the chief executive has considered the requests of the various departments and taken action on them, he is in a position to prepare the budget document to be submitted to the legislative body for consideration and adoption. The budget document may consist of the following:

1. A budget message, in which the principal budget items are explained, the governmental unit's experience during the past year and its financial status at the present time are outlined, and recommendations regarding the programs and financial policy for the coming year are made.

2. A budget summary showing total estimated resources and expenditures by

Figure 3-21

## A GOVERNMENTAL UNIT
### Departmental Estimate
### Activity Summary—Supervision
### 19X7

Departmental Code: 421

Fund: General
Function: Public Safety
Department: Police
Activity: Supervision
Submitted by: A. Johnson, Chief
Date: October 10, 19X6

| Code No. | Classification | Actual 19X4 | Actual 19X5 | Actual First Nine Months of 19X6 | Estimated Remainder of 19X6 | Total Columns 5 and 6 | Proposed 19X7 | Appropriation by Legislative Body |
|---|---|---|---|---|---|---|---|---|
| 1 | 2 | 3 | 4 | 5 | 6 | 7 | 8 | 9 |
| 01 | Personal Services | $22,000 | $24,000 | $19,000 | $ 8,000 | $27,000 | $27,400 | $27,400 |
| 02 | Supplies | 1,633 | 1,842 | 1,292 | 430 | 1,722 | 2,070 | 2,000 |
| 03 | Other Services and Charges | 2,708 | 2,722 | 2,117 | 712 | 2,829 | 2,960 | 2,900 |
|  | Total Current Expenses | $26,341 | $28,564 | $22,409 | $ 9,142 | $31,551 | $32,430 | $32,300 |
| 06 | Capital Outlays | $ 150 | $ 200 | $ 100 | $ 40 | $ 140 | $ 90 | $ 90 |
|  | Total | $26,491 | $28,764 | $22,509 | $ 9,182 | $31,691 | $32,520 | $32,390 |

Figure 3-22

A GOVERNMENTAL UNIT
Departmental Estimate
Summary
19X7

Departmental Code: 2000

Fund: General
Function: Public Safety
Department: Police
Submitted by: A. Johnson, Chief
Date: October 10, 19X6

| Code No. | Classification | 19X4 | 19X5 | First Nine Months of 19X6 | Estimated Remainder of 19X6 | Total Columns 5 and 6 | Proposed 19X7 | Appropriation by Legislative Body |
|---|---|---|---|---|---|---|---|---|
| 1 | 2 | 3 | 4 | 5 | 6 | 7 | 8 | 9 |
| | **By Object of Expenditure:** | | | | | | | |
| 01 | Personal Services | $549,248 | $660,299 | $560,205 | $168,110 | $728,315 | $730,850 | $730,850 |
| 02 | Supplies | 43,831 | 45,941 | 39,795 | 8,925 | 48,720 | 50,100 | 50,100 |
| 03 | Other Services and Charges | 34,046 | 34,932 | 26,137 | 11,668 | 37,805 | 38,250 | 37,500 |
| | Total Current Expenses | $627,125 | $741,172 | $626,137 | $188,703 | $814,840 | $819,200 | $818,450 |
| 04–07 | Capital Outlays | $ 21,590 | $ 28,900 | $ 26,148 | $ 3,952 | $ 30,100 | $ 24,250 | $ 24,250 |
| | Total | $648,715 | $770,072 | $652,285 | $192,655 | $844,940 | $843,450 | $842,700 |

## By Organizational Subunits:

| | | | | | | | |
|---|---|---|---|---|---|---|---|
| Supervision | $ 26,491 | $ 28,764 | $ 22,509 | $ 9,182 | $ 31,691 | $ 32,520 | $ 32,390 |
| Training | 4,675 | 5,560 | 4,723 | 1,376 | 6,099 | 7,000 | 7,000 |
| General and Criminal Records | 12,444 | 14,826 | 12,596 | 3,661 | 16,257 | 16,257 | 16,257 |
| Identification Records | 7,775 | 9,266 | 7,872 | 2,293 | 10,165 | 10,165 | 10,165 |
| Custody of Recovered Property | 3,111 | 3,707 | 3,149 | 917 | 4,066 | 4,075 | 4,075 |
| Communications Systems | 34,222 | 40,772 | 34,638 | 10,091 | 44,729 | 44,700 | 44,500 |
| Detention and Custody of Prisoners | 40,445 | 48,185 | 40,935 | 11,926 | 52,861 | 52,861 | 52,861 |
| Motor Vehicle Inspection and Regulation | 15,556 | 18,533 | 15,744 | 4,587 | 20,331 | 20,331 | 20,331 |
| Criminal Investigation | 49,778 | 59,305 | 50,382 | 14,678 | 65,060 | 65,000 | 65,060 |
| Uniformed Patrol | 224,000 | 266,871 | 226,719 | 66,050 | 292,769 | 289,731 | 289,525 |
| Vice and Morals Control | 21,779 | 25,946 | 22,042 | 6,422 | 28,464 | 28,464 | 28,350 |
| Crime Prevention | 28,000 | 33,359 | 28,340 | 8,256 | 36,596 | 36,500 | 36,500 |
| Traffic Control | 118,223 | 140,849 | 119,657 | 34,868 | 154,525 | 154,525 | 154,525 |
| Special Detail Services | 20,222 | 24,093 | 20,468 | 5,963 | 26,431 | 26,431 | 26,431 |
| Auxiliary Services | 24,889 | 29,652 | 25,191 | 7,339 | 32,530 | 32,530 | 32,530 |
| Police Stations and Buildings | 17,105 | 20,384 | 17,320 | 5,046 | 22,366 | 22,300 | 22,200 |
| Total | $648,715 | $770,072 | $652,285 | $192,655 | $844,940 | $843,450 | $842,700 |

funds. Revenues are generally classified here by main sources; expenditures by organizational unit, character, and object (Figure 3-23) and/or broad programs.

Figure 3-23

A GOVERNMENTAL UNIT
Budget Summary
General Budget—19X7

| *Estimated Revenues* | | *Estimated Expenditures* | |
|---|---|---|---|
| | | General Fund | |
| Taxes | $289,000 | Personal Services | $219,000 |
| Other Revenues | 142,000 | Other Current Expenses | 63,600 |
| | | Capital Outlays | 109,400 |
| | | Debt Service | 34,000 |
| | | Excess of Resources over | |
| | | Expenditures | 5,000 |
| Total General Fund | $431,000 | Total General Fund | $431,000 |
| | | *Special Revenue Fund* | |
| Taxes | $100,000 | Personal Services | $ 75,000 |
| Other Revenues | 25,000 | Other Current Expenses | 30,000 |
| | | Capital Outlays | 20,000 |
| Total Special Revenue Fund | $125,000 | Total Special Revenue Fund | $125,000 |
| Total General Budget | $556,000 | Total General Budget | $556,000 |

Note: The estimated amount of Fund Balance at the beginning of the budget year, if any, would be added to the estimated revenues.

3.  A schedule of actual and estimated revenues classified by source (Figure 3-15).
4.  The departmental activity or work programs, request forms, and comments (Figures 3-16 through 3-22).
5.  Schedules showing charges not applicable to any particular departments, including such items as judgments and costs, interest on notes and bonds, maturing general serial bonds, contributions to debt service funds, contributions to pension funds, the governmental unit's share of special assessment costs, and estimated fund deficits.
6.  Fund balance sheets showing estimated assets, liabilities, reserves, and available fund balances or deficits as of the close of the current fiscal year.
7.  A statement of actual and estimated cash receipts, disbursements, and balances (Figure 3-24). Note that this statement is prepared in addition to

the revenue statement. The revenue statement shows merely the revenues estimated to be earned; some of these may not be collected during the year. On the other hand, the governmental unit will collect delinquent taxes and other receivables of the preceding years. Through a comparison of estimated total receipts with estimated total disbursements, it is possible to determine whether short-term borrowing will be necessary. An additional statement, showing both actual and estimated receipts and disbursements by months, would also be helpful.

8. If short-term borrowing is contemplated, a schedule showing short-term borrowing transactions during the past two years and the current year and the proposed short-term borrowing for the coming year.

9. A statement showing bonded debt outstanding (Figure 18-5).

10. Statements of tax collections (Figures 6-8 and 6-9).

11. A draft for an appropriation ordinance (Figure 3-25).

12. A draft for a tax levy ordinance (discussed in Chapter 6).

## LEGISLATIVE CONSIDERATION AND ACTION

After receiving the executive budget document, the legislative body takes steps to adopt an official, final budget. Frequently the budget document is turned over to a legislative finance committee, often called the "ways and means" committee. This committee makes any investigations it deems necessary, calls on department heads to justify their requests and on the chief executive to explain his recommendations, and conducts public hearings on the proposed budget. The committee then makes its recommendations to the legislative body. (Alternatively, the legislature may act as a committee of the whole to perform the duties necessary before adoption of the budget.)

After completing the budget hearings and investigations, the legislative body proceeds to adopt the budget through the passage of an appropriation ordinance (or appropriation act, as it is known in the case of a state). Part of an appropriation ordinance is illustrated in Figure 3-25. Note that summary objects-of-expenditure form the basis of the ordinance. The budget document itself contains detailed objects-of-expenditure, and, as noted, the appropriation ordinance sometimes contains each of the detailed objects. If proper internal control, accounting, reporting, and postauditing procedures are used, the legislative body can retain control of operations without recourse to minutely detailed appropriations and may make lump-sum appropriations by department or even by activity.

The appropriation act or ordinance merely authorizes expenditures. It is also necessary to provide the means of financing them. Some revenues (for example, profits on the sale of investments) will accrue to the governmental unit without any legal action on its part. Other revenues will come as a result of legal action taken in the past. Examples of these are licenses and fees, income

Figure 3-24

# A GOVERNMENTAL UNIT
## General Fund
### Statement of Actual and Estimated Cash Receipts, Disbursements, and Balances

| | Actual 19X5 | Actual First Nine Months of 19X6 | Estimated Balance of 19X6 | Total Columns 2 and 3† | Estimated 19X7 |
|---|---|---|---|---|---|
| Opening Cash Balance | $ 18,375 | $ 10,340 | $ 64,415 | $ 10,340* | $ 36,200 |
| **Receipts:** | | | | | |
| Taxes | $295,100 | $240,925 | $ 49,575 | $290,500 | $291,750 |
| Licenses and Permits | 51,050 | 42,100 | 11,465 | 53,565 | 56,300 |
| Intergovernmental Revenue | 38,730 | 59,130 | 19,070 | 78,200 | 78,900 |
| Charges for Services | 7,775 | 5,225 | 1,800 | 7,025 | 6,800 |
| Collections of Accounts Receivable | 8,100 | 6,070 | 1,800 | 7,870 | 5,200 |
| Fines and Forfeits | 6,000 | 4,000 | 500 | 4,500 | 5,100 |
| Miscellaneous Revenue | 4,000 | 3,000 | 1,200 | 4,200 | 4,300 |
| Total Receipts | $403,955 | $360,450 | $ 85,410 | $445,860 | $448,350 |
| Total Receipts and Balance | $422,330 | $370,790 | $149,825 | $456,200* | $484,550 |

**Disbursements:**

| | | | | | |
|---|---|---|---|---|---|
| Personal Services | $220,000 | $165,000 | $ 56,000 | $221,000 | $219,000 |
| Contractual Services | 7,800 | 5,000 | 3,000 | 8,000 | 8,165 |
| Materials and Supplies | 14,700 | 10,900 | 4,100 | 15,000 | 14,300 |
| Other Charges | 25,350 | 18,850 | 7,150 | 26,000 | 26,120 |
| Capital Outlays | 105,000 | 76,000 | 34,000 | 110,000 | 109,400 |
| Retirement of Bonds | 25,000 | 19,000 | 6,000 | 25,000 | 20,000 |
| Retirement of Notes | 8,000 | 7,825 | 2,175 | 10,000 | 14,000 |
| Payment of Vouchers Payable | 6,140 | 3,800 | 1,200 | 5,000 | 7,100 |
| Total Disbursements | $411,990 | $306,375 | $113,625 | $420,000 | $418,085 |
| Closing Cash Balance | $ 10,340 | $ 64,415 | $ 36,200 | $ 36,200* | $ 66,465 |

† With exception of items starred.

Figure 3-25

---

CITY OF *X*

Appropriation Ordinance
An Ordinance Making Appropriations for the Fiscal Year
Beginning January 1, 19X7, and Ending December 31, 19X7,
in the Sum of Five Hundred Fifty-Six Thousand Dollars
($556,000) and Regulating the Payment of Money Out of
the City Treasury.

BE IT ORDAINED by the Council of the City of *X:*
Sec. 1: That the amounts herein named, aggregating Five Hundred Fifty-Six
Thousand Dollars ($556,000), or so much thereof as may be necessary, divided
respectively as follows: (1) for the general fund Four Hundred Thirty-One
Thousand Dollars ($431,000) and (2) for a special revenue fund One Hundred
Twenty-Five Thousand Dollars ($125,000), are hereby appropriated, subject
to the conditions hereinafter set forth in this ordinance, from current revenue
for the use of the several departments of the city government, and for the
purposes hereinafter mentioned for the fiscal year beginning January 1, 19X7,
and ending December 31, 19X7, as follows:

*General Fund*

| *Departments and Code Numbers* | | *Appropriations* | |
|---|---|---|---|
| No. 1000—Council: | | | |
| 01 Personal Services | $ 7,000 | | |
| 02 Supplies | 300 | | |
| 03 Other Services and charges | 700 | | |
| 06 Equipment | 3,000 | $11,000 | |
| No. 1100—Executive Department: | | | |
| 01 Personal Services | $10,000 | | |
| 02 Materials and supplies | 200 | | |
| 03 Other services and charges | 300 | | |
| 06 Equipment | 2,000 | 12,500 | |
| No. 1200—Courts: | | | |
| 01 Personal Services | $10,200 | | |
| 02 Materials and Supplies | 350 | | |
| 03 Other services and charges | 450 | | |
| 06 Equipment | 2,100 | 13,100 | |

---

taxes, and sales taxes, the rates for which continue until they are changed by
the legislative body. A third type of revenue—for example, the general property
tax—requires new legal action each year (every two years in most states levying

property taxes). Accordingly, as soon as the legislative body has passed the appropriation ordinance or act, it proceeds to levy general property taxes.

## BUDGET EXECUTION

Just as the budget expresses in financial terms the government's planned activities, so does the process of budget execution include every decision and transaction made during the budget period. The discussion that follows emphasizes the aspects of execution that are of primary interest to the accountant, but both the administrator and the accountant should keep in mind that accounting records are a financial summary of the actual operations of the government.

BUDGETARY ACCOUNTING.   Accounting is one of the principal devices through which control of budget execution is exercised. (Other devices and activities are personnel administration, central purchasing, training schools, operating manuals, activities reporting, conferences, and the like.) In budgetary accounting the estimated revenues and appropriations, in the amounts approved by the legislative body, are recorded in the fund accounts—where they may be compared with the actual financial activities of the period. As soon as the appropriation ordinance is passed, an entry is made setting up estimated revenues and appropriations on the records. The General Journal entry in the General Fund, for example (using simulated figures), is as follows:

| | | |
|---|---|---|
| Estimated Revenues ......................... | 431,000 | |
| Appropriations ........................ | | 426,000 |
| Fund Balance ........................ | | 5,000 |
| To record estimated revenues and appropriations. | | |

Note that (1) Estimated Revenues and Appropriations are *control* accounts in the general ledger, and (2) the Fund Balance account is now stated at its *planned end-of-period* amount rather than at the actual beginning-of-period amount.

SUBSIDIARY ACCOUNTS FOR REVENUES.   Actual revenues of the fiscal period are recorded in an account, "Revenues," which joins "Estimated Revenues" in the general ledger as *dual* control accounts over the subsidiary Revenue Ledger. Because of the large number of revenue accounts usually required, it is desirable, both from the standpoint of economy (fewer accounts are needed) and from the standpoint of ease of comparison of actual and estimated revenues, to record each estimated and actual revenue in the same *subsidiary* account. For example, the account for motor vehicle licenses will appear as illustrated in Figure 6-10. As the control account Estimated Revenues is debited, the details of the total estimate are recorded in the Debit and Balance columns of all of the accounts in the subsidiary Revenue Ledger, including Motor Vehicle Licenses. Subsequently, as revenues are recorded in the Revenues control account in the General Ledger, corresponding amounts are entered in the Credit columns of the Revenue Ledger accounts. A debit balance in an individual revenue account indicates an excess of estimated revenues over actual revenues to date; a credit balance indicates an excess of actual over estimated revenues. The operation of the subsidiary Revenue Ledger will be illustrated in Chapter 6.

SUBSIDIARY ACCOUNTS FOR APPROPRIATIONS.  The General Ledger control accounts for the subsidiary Expenditures Ledger are Appropriations, Expenditures, and Encumbrances (estimated obligations on outstanding purchase orders). In the subsidiary Expenditure accounts (see Figure 7-5) the amount appropriated appears along with the expenditures and encumbrances charged to the appropriation. All the information regarding an appropriation is recorded in one subsidiary account for two reasons. First, there is usually a large number of appropriations, and the suggested arrangement is economical because it reduces the number of accounts needed. Second, the arrangement results in better budgetary control because such an account makes it possible to tell at a glance the status of each appropriation. At any point in time the individual Expenditure Ledger account shows the following information:

Appropriations
— Expenditures
----
Unexpended balance
— Encumbrances
----
Unencumbered balance

This kind of information is invaluable to the finance officer in controlling appropriations. Regulations are set up providing that no purchase order or contract is valid unless it is approved by the finance officer. As he approves the order, he adds the amount to the total of encumbrances and thus reduces the unencumbered balance. Subsequently, as the materials are received and the actual expenditures are determined, the encumbrances are canceled and the actual expenditures are added to the total of expenditures. By referring to the unencumbered balance of the account, the finance officer can see at a glance whether a sufficient balance is available for further encumbrance or expenditure.

The finance officer is also responsible for providing the administrators with the same information regarding their appropriations. Having this information, the administrator is in a position to act as the first line of control against overspending of appropriations.

The detail (number of accounts) with which expenditures accounts are set up depends in part on the detail with which appropriations are made. If appropriations are made in the same detail that is required to provide adequate expenditure information for planning and control purposes, there will be as many expenditure accounts as there are individual appropriations. On the other hand, if appropriations are made in lump sum, more detailed information is needed for planning and control purposes and the chief executive may require additional accounts. The method of setting up such additional accounts is described in the following section.

ALLOTMENTS AND ALLOCATIONS. *Allotments* are executive limitations on the time periods during which appropriations may be spent. The appropriation ordinance or act does not normally specify the rate at which expenditures are to be made throughout the year. It is evident that the flow of revenues and expenditures is not uniform. For example, expenditures for park maintenance are likely to be greater in summer than in winter, while no expenditures for snow removal are incurred during the summer months. Accordingly, the chief executive may consider it necessary to make allotments to control the expenditures for the various departments so that they may be made as they are needed and so that they will be adapted as far as is practicable to the flow of revenue.

*Allocations* are executive assignments of lump-sum appropriations to specific functions, activities, organizations, or objects of expenditure. Allocations are made by the chief executive or the administrators of an agency for control purposes. For example, the expenditures of a fire department for which a lump-sum appropriation has been made will be chargeable to such programs as supervision, training schools, fire prevention, and fire fighting. The chief executive may feel that the expenditures would be subject to more effective control if the fire chief is required to indicate his plans for the coming year and then to comply with the plans after they have been approved by the chief executive. Planning of this type, that is, after-the-appropriation planning for the use of a lump-sum appropriation, is imperative if the appropriation is greater or smaller than the budget request.

There is a fundamental distinction, from the standoint of control, between an appropriation and an allotment or allocation. Appropriations are made by the legislative body and, in the absence of legislative authority that permits them to be changed by the executive branch, can be changed only by the legislature. On the other hand, allotments and allocations are made by an executive and can be changed by him without any action of the legislative body. Changes are more likely to be made in allotments and allocations than in appropriations, though allotments and allocations will ordinarily not be changed by the executive without good reasons, since their continual adjustment is likely to upset the budget program.

Where the chief executive wants to ration annual appropriations through the use of allotments or allocations, he calls for departmental allotment or allocation request schedules immediately after the budget is enacted. At this time each department head knows the maximum amount of expenditures his department may incur. If a lump-sum appropriation has been made, he must determine how the sum will be spread among his activities and objects of expenditure. The latter distribution will be made just as his original budgetary estimates were made, except that he will now have the appropriation limitations. Expenditure Ledger accounts must be established in at least as much detail as that of the allocations made if allocation control is to be effective.

If allotments are called for, the department head must determine how much of each appropriation is to be spent or obligated during each month, quarter, or other allotment period. Estimates as to rates of expenditure are based on statistics for past periods and on the department head's general knowledge of the rate and volume of activities carried on during various parts of the year. These estimates will be expressed in the form of work programs. An example of a work program used to support a monthly allotment schedule is given in Figure 3-26.

The departmental allotment schedules (Figure 3-27), together with any additional data supporting the request for allotments, such as work programs, are submitted to the chief executive, who in the meantime has received statements from the budget officer showing estimated receipts by months, quarters, or other periods. Upon receipt of the departmental allotment request schedules, the total allotments requested for each period during the year are tabulated and compared with anticipated receipts. Adjustments are then made, as far as possible, to bring expenditure authorizations within the resource availability constraints of each period. Work programs are helpful in this connection, and usually the chief executive will also confer with department heads if any adjustments in their allotments are necessary.

If the budget is to be effectively controlled, organization units must stay within their appropriations allocations and also within the amounts alloted to them for a particular interim period. Accordingly, as soon as the allotments are approved by the new chief executive, they are certified to the finance officer, who sets up the proper accounts for each unit so as to show both the amount appropriated (by allocation) and the allotments into which the appropriation is divided.

In some situations allotments are viewed by all concerned as general plans or guidelines rather than limitations that must be strictly and continually followed. In such cases rather informal control may prove satisfactory: (1) The total annual appropriation (by allocation) is entered in the subsidiary ledger accounts, where it constitutes the primary basis of control, (2) the allotment schedule is included on the face of the subsidiary Expenditure Ledger accounts, but it is not formally entered therein, and (3) to evaluate the allotment status of a particular account it is necessary to compare accumulative allotments with the sum of encumbrances and expenditures to date.

In other situations (as is particularly true in the case of allocations of lump-sum appropriations) departmental allotments are viewed as "mini-appropriations" and constitute the primary basis for continuous budgetary accounting control. In these cases only the cumulative allotted portion of the annual departmental appropriation (or allocation) is considered the authorized expenditure level at any point in time:

Figure 3-26

## A GOVERNMENTAL UNIT
### Work Program—19X7
### by Months

Departmental Code: 432

Fund: General
Function: Public Works
Department: Public Works
Bureau: Sanitation
Submitted by: M. A. Downs, Chief
Date: January 6, 19X7

| Operation | Work Unit | Total for Year | | | January | | February | | March | |
|---|---|---|---|---|---|---|---|---|---|---|
| | | No. of Units | Unit Cost | Total | No. of Units | Amount | No. of Units | Amount | No. of Units | Amount |
| Garbage collection | Tons | 170,000 | $1.44 | $244,800.00 | 14,175 | $20,412.00 | 14,175 | $20,412.00 | 14,175 | $20,412.00 |
| Incineration | Tons | 182,000 | 1.19 | 216,580.00 | 15,150 | 18,028.50 | 15,150 | 18,028.50 | 15,150 | 18,028.50 |

Figure 3-27

## A GOVERNMENTAL UNIT
### Allotment of Appropriation
### 19X7

Departmental Code: 421

Fund: General
Function: Public Safety
Department: Police
Submitted by: A. Johnson, Chief
Date: January 6, 19X7

| Code No. | Classification | Total Appropriated | January | February | March | April | May |
|---|---|---|---|---|---|---|---|
| 01 | Personal Services | $26,000 | $2,200 | $2,150 | $2,150 | $2,175 | $2,100 |
| 02 | Supplies | 3,800 | 300 | 270 | 300 | 250 | 275 |
| 03 | Other Services and Charges | 5,200 | 425 | 440 | 445 | 410 | 465 |
| 06 | Capital Outlays | 150 | | | | 150 | |

1. The total appropriations for the organization as a whole are credited to an "Unallotted Appropriations" or similar account; that is, an Unallotted Appropriations account is credited rather than the Appropriations account in the General Ledger entry setting up the annual budget in the accounts. No Expenditure Ledger entries are made with this General Journal entry, and Unallotted Appropriations is not a control account for the Expenditure Ledger. (At a minimum, memorandum subsidiary records would have to be maintained itemizing the individual unallotted appropriations.)

2. The first allotment total is then transferred from the Unallotted Appropriations account to an "Allotted Appropriations" or "Allotments" account —which, together with the Expenditures and Encumbrances accounts, serves to control the Expenditure Ledger—and allotments are recorded in the individual accounts in the Expenditure Ledger to control expenditures and encumbrances.

3. Procedure two would be repeated at the beginning of each allotment period. Prior to the end of the budget year the total annual departmental appropriations would probably have been allotted, and the Unallotted Appropriations account would be reduced to a zero balance. (If the control process involves allocation of lump-sum appropriations, it is likely that all of the appropriations will have been allocated at the first of the year.)

The application of these controls will be discussed further in Chapter 7 on Expenditures.

PREAUDITING. The term "preaudit" is applied to the function of approving transactions before they have taken place or before they have been recorded. Responsibility for the function is usually assigned to the chief accounting officer of a city or state, although the larger state departments have other accountants who perform some or all of the preaudit functions. For revenue transactions preaudit includes, among other things, a verification of the accuracy of rates, revenue bases, and calculations, and of the propriety of classification and coding for entry in the records. From the expenditures standpoint preaudit may be directed toward prevention of misappropriation of funds, overspending of appropriations, unreasonable expenditures, and expenditures for illegal purposes. Specific preaudit procedures for revenues and expenditures are discussed in Chapters 6 and 7.

BUDGETARY CONTROL THROUGH STATEMENTS. Most of the financial statements that are prepared for the General Fund or Special Revenue Funds aid in one way or another in controlling the budget. The two statements illustrated in Figures 6-12 and 7-10 are examples of statements that are directly helpful for budgetary control. Others include the interim Balance Sheet (Figure 5-1), the Statement of Forecast of Cash Position (Figure 16-3), and the Statements of Tax Levies and Tax Collections (Figures 6-9 and 6-10).

**Question 3-1.** Distinguish between the following terms:
  (a)   a fund and an appropriation
  (b)   a budget and an appropriation
  (c)   an appropriation and an allotment
  (d)   allocations and allotments
  (e)   an expenditure and an encumbrance

**Question 3-2.** Indicate at least three ways in which the term "budget" may be used correctly.

**Question 3-3.** Governmental budgeting and budgetary control was deemed so important by the NCGA that it devoted an entire "principle" to the subject. Why?

**Question 3-4.** Budgeting is a continuous process. Explain.

**Question 3-5.** Distinguish between the following types of budgets:
  (a)   capital and current
  (b)   tentative and enacted
  (c)   general and special
  (d)   fixed and flexible
  (e)   executive and legislative

**Question 3-6.** What are budgetary "control points"? How do they affect budgetary accounting and reporting?

**Question 3-7.** A municipality's budget is prepared on a cash basis. What basis of accounting would you recommend? Explain.

**Question 3-8.** What major strengths and weaknesses are generally associated with the (1) line-item or object-of-expenditure, (2) performance, and (3) program approaches to budgeting?

**Question 3-9.** What is a budgetary "cross walk"?

**Question 3-10.** What are the major distinctive characteristics of the PPB approach to budgeting?

**Question 3-11.** Some persons contend that an inherent limitation of the line-item departmental or object-of-expenditure budget is that it is based on a "backwards" or "reverse" decision-making process. Explain and evaluate this assertion.

**Question 3-12.** (a) Why are both estimated and actual revenues reflected in the same *subsidiary* account whereas separate accounts are provided for estimated and actual revenues in the general ledger? (b) Why are appropriations, expenditures, and encumbrances shown in the same *subsidiary* account whereas separate appropriation, expenditure, and encumbrance accounts are carried in the general ledger?

**Question 3-13.** Why are General, Special Revenue, and other expendable funds typically controlled by fixed budgets integrated within the account structure, while Enterprise and other nonexpendable funds are subject to less formal control through flexible budgets not integrated within the account structure?

**Question 3-14.** A General Fund balanced budget has been amended to increase the total appropriations. From what sources may the increase be financed?

**Question 3-15.** Time-period allotments may be made either by quarters or by month in X City. Which allotment period do you think is better and why?

**Question 3-16.** An ordinance provides that collections from the sale of dog licenses are "hereby appropriated for the maintenance of the dog pound." During the month of January, $5,000 was collected. Is another appropriation necessary to spend this money for the maintenance of the dog pound?

**Question 3-17.** What is meant by "preaudit"? What functions are involved in the preaudit of revenues and expenditures?

**Question 3-18.** Discuss the meaning and implications of the following statements pertaining to budgeting:

(a)  "A budget is just a means of getting money."

(b)  "*Never* underexpend an appropriation—the more you spend, the more you get next year."

(c)  "Budgeting is easy! You just take last year's budget and add 10%—or twice what you think you might need. The council will cut your request in half and you'll wind up getting what you wanted in the first place."

(d)  "The traditional line-item budget only appears to provide an orderly and seemingly objective approach to financial planning and control. In too many instances, all it really provides is a uniform framework for establishing and maintaining a set of orderly records which comply with legal requirements, but which provide very little in the way of useful management information."

**Question 3-19.** Revenue estimates and appropriations enacted are "standards" against which performance is subsequently measured. What implications can be drawn at year end if there are variances from these standards? If there are no variances?

**Question 3-20.** Behaviorial scientists tell us that "the measurement employed affects the performance of the person or group measured." What implications for performance and program budgeting are contained in this statement?

**Question 3-21.** Most "performance measures" (number of arrests made, tons of garbage collected, miles of street cleaned, etc.) do not adequately measure the quantity or quality of performance but are only "indicators" of certain aspects of performance. Discuss (a) the validity of this statement and (b) how "performance measures" or "indicators" may be properly and beneficially employed in evaluating performance.

**Question 3-22.** Proponents of "zero-based" budgeting contend that a government's budgetary process should begin each year with the assumption that no program or department has a vested interest—that each should comprehensively justify its existence, its activities, and its appropriation requests annually as if it were a proposed program or department not in existence previously. Evaluate the merits of this approach.

**Problem 3-1.** The following information is available from the 19X4 General Fund budget, the general ledger of the City of Epps, and calculations:

|  | General Fund | Park Fund | School Fund |
|---|---|---|---|
| Fund Balance, Estimated January 1, 19X4 | $  125,000 | $ 25,000 | $ 50,000 |
| Estimated Revenues: |  |  |  |
|    Property taxes | 1,400,000 | 100,000 | 400,000 |
|    Other revenues | 1,200,000 |  | 300,000 |
| Appropriations: |  |  |  |
|    Salaries and wages | 1,800,000 | 65,000 | 435,000 |
|    Other expense | 775,000 | 15,000 | 200,000 |
|    Capital outlay | 75,000 | 19,000 | 70,000 |

Required:

(1)   Prepare a budget summary for the 19X4 Budget of the City of Epps.

(2)   Describe other methods by which proposed expenditures could be classified. Which method do you prefer? Which method is in agreement with the performance budget concept?

(3)   Prepare the journal entry to record adoption of the General Fund budget, showing both the general and subsidiary ledger accounts..

**Problem 3-2.** The portion of the proposed 19X5 budget applicable to Titusville's Department of City Manager follows:

| Major Classification | Proposed Budget 19X5 |
|---|---|
| Personal Services | |
| Salaries and Wages: | $18,000 |
| City Manager | 10,500 |
| Administrative Assistant | 7,000 |
| Secretary | $35,500 |
| | |
| Contractual Services | |
| Travel and Training | $ 2,400 |
| Telephone and Telegraph | 600 |
| Equipment Maintenance | 100 |
| Professional Services | 800 |
| | $ 3,900 |
| | |
| Materials and Supplies | |
| Supplies | $ 1,000 |
| Gasoline and Oil | 250 |
| Tires | 150 |
| Parts for equipment | 400 |
| | $ 1,800 |
| | |
| Fixed and Sundry | |
| Taxes and Licenses | $    50 |
| Memberships and Subscriptions | 350 |
| | $   400 |
| | |
| Capital Outlay | |
| Office Machinery | $ 6,000 |
| Office Furniture | 2,000 |
| | $ 8,000 |
| Total | $49,600 |

Required:
Prepare the *subsidiary* Expenditure Ledger entry necessary to record enactment of appropriations by the council as follows: (1) By department; (2) By major object-of-expenditure categories; (3) By detailed object-of-expenditure line items.

**Problem 3-3.** The following appropriations were made for 19X4 by the City of *L*:

|  |  |
|---|---:|
| City Council | $15,000 |
| Mayor | 15,000 |
| Courts | 30,000 |
| City Clerk | 15,000 |
| Department of Finance | 30,000 |
| Department of Police | 75,000 |
| Department of Fire | 60,000 |
| Department of Public Works | 30,000 |
| Interest | 15,000 |
| Retirement of bonds | 15,000 |
|  | $300,000 |

The following transfers between appropriations were subsequently authorized:

| Transferred from | Transferred to | Amount |
|---|---|---:|
| City Council | City Clerk | $ 750 |
| City Clerk | Mayor | 1,500 |
| Department of Finance | Department of Public Works | 1,500 |
| Department of Public Works | Courts | 1,000 |
|  | Department of Police | 1,500 |
| Reserve for Contingencies | Department of Fire | 2,200 |
|  | City Council | 750 |
|  | Department of Public Works | 3,000 |

Estimated revenues are $350,000; the Council reserved $30,000 for contingencies.

Required:
(1)  Prepare the journal entry necessary to record the adoption of the budget, showing both the general ledger and the subsidiary ledger accounts.
(2)  Prepare the journal entry to record the transfers between appropriations, showing both the general ledger and the subsidiary ledger accounts involved.
(3)  Prepare a statement showing the appropriation balances after the transfers have been made effective.

**Problem 3-4.** The following appropriations and first quarter allotments for 19X4 were made by Dogwood City's council and manager, respectively:

| | 19X4 Appropriations | First Quarter Allotments |
|---|---|---|
| City Council | $ 12,000 | $ 3,000 |
| Manager | 40,000 | 11,000 |
| Courts | 30,000 | 7,000 |
| City Clerk | 20,000 | 5,000 |
| Finance Department | 35,000 | 10,000 |
| Police Department | 80,000 | 20,000 |
| Fire Department | 75,000 | 16,000 |
| Public Works Department | 45,000 | 12,000 |
| Interest | 15,000 | — |
| Retirement of Bonds | 25,000 | — |
| | $377,000 | $84,000 |

Required:

Prepare the journal entry necessary to record the appropriations and first quarter allotments, showing both the general ledger and the subsidiary ledger accounts.

**Problem 3-5.** The City of $K$ has adopted the following budget for its 19X5 fiscal year, beginning February 1, 19X4:

Estimated revenues, $790,000, consisting of the following:

| | |
|---|---|
| Real property taxes | $390,000 |
| Interest on investments | 2,000 |
| Motor vehicle licenses and fees | 20,000 |
| Portion of sales tax to be received from state | 10,000 |
| Interest on bank deposits | 500 |
| Grants-in-aid to be received from state | 5,000 |
| Other revenues | 169,500 |
| Court fines | 5,000 |
| Personal property taxes | 140,000 |
| Income taxes | 25,000 |
| Alcoholic beverage licenses | 15,000 |
| Interest and penalties on taxes | 5,000 |
| Building permits | 3,000 |
| | $790,000 |

Appropriations, $787,000, consisting of the following:

| | |
|---|---|
| Civil Service Commission | $ 5,000 |
| Department of Police—Bureau of Uniformed Patrol | 40,000 |
| Department of Fire—Bureau of Fire Fighting | 40,000 |
| Court | 20,000 |
| Department of Police—Bureau of Supervision | 20,000 |

| | |
|---|---:|
| Department of Police—Bureau of Communication System | 20,000 |
| Interest | 40,000 |
| Department of Fire—Bureau of Supervision | 15,000 |
| Board of Elections | 5,000 |
| Department of Law | 25,000 |
| Department of Fire—Bureau of Prevention | 20,000 |
| Retirement of Bonds | 100,000 |
| Department of Finance—Bureau of Administration | 10,000 |
| Department of Finance—Bureau of Purchases | 6,000 |
| City Clerk | 10,000 |
| Department of Finance—Bureau of Accounts | 15,000 |
| Mayor | 15,000 |
| Department of Finance—Bureau of Assessment | 15,000 |
| Department of Fire—Bureau of Training | 10,000 |
| Department of Police—Bureau of Criminal Investigation | 20,000 |
| Department of Police—Bureau of Police Training | 8,000 |
| Department of Finance—Bureau of Treasury | 8,000 |
| City Council | 20,000 |
| All Other Departments | 300,000 |
| | $787,000 |

Required:

(1) Prepare a journal entry to record the adoption of the budget, showing both the general ledger accounts and all of the subsidiary accounts involved, the latter properly classified.

(2) Post the general ledger accounts to "T" accounts.

(3) Post the estimated revenues for Real Property Taxes to a revenue account similar to the account illustrated in Figure 6-10.

(4) Post the appropriations for the City Clerk to an appropriation account similar to the account illustrated in Figure 7-5.

**Problem 3-6.**  You are asked as the City of $A$'s Director of Public Works, on January 5, 19X4, to submit an allotment of the appropriation for your department for 19X4 based on three-month periods. (1) Prepare such a schedule from the following data, using Figure 3-27 as a model and (2) submit the journal entry necessary to record the allotment for the first quarter.

| | Personal Services | Contractual Services | Materials & Supplies | Other Charges | Capital Outlays |
|---|---:|---:|---:|---:|---:|
| First Quarter | $7,500 | $625 | $400 | $105 | $2,300 |
| Second Quarter | 6,500 | 591 | 120 | 105 | 200 |
| Third Quarter | 6,500 | 675 | 85 | 105 | 450 |
| Fourth Quarter | 7,500 | 610 | 240 | 105 | 300 |

**Problem 3-7.**  On October 1, 19X3, you are given the following data concerning the City of $N$:

| | | 19X2 | | Estimated 19X3 | | Estimated 19X4 | |
|---|---|---|---|---|---|---|---|
| Activity | Work Unit | No. of Units | Unit Cost | No. of Units | Unit Cost | No. of Units | Unit Cost |
| Hauling sweepings | Cubic yard | 3,546 | $ .87 | 3,721 | $ .85 | 3,500 | $ .84 |
| White wing | Cleaning mile | 8,041 | 2.60 | 9,236 | 2.90 | 9,000 | 2.90 |
| Snow removal: | | | | | | | |
| Plowing | Cleaning mile | 12,200 | 2.16 | 15,306 | 2.17 | 13,000 | 2.16 |
| Loading and hauling | Cubic yard | 60,742 | 1.11 | 83,140 | 1.09 | 75,000 | 1.10 |
| Street flushing | Cleaning mile | 20,129 | .84 | 22,439 | .86 | 22,000 | .86 |

Required:

(1)   Prepare a work program to be submitted on October 1 by J. P. Abner, Chief of the Division of Street Cleaning of the Department of Public Works.

(2)   Assuming that the estimates for 19X4 were adopted by the legislative body, prepare a work program as of January 2, 19X4, dividing the appropriations into four quarterly installments as follows:

| | First Quarter | Second Quarter | Third Quarter | Fourth Quarter |
|---|---|---|---|---|
| Hauling sweepings | 15% | 40% | 30% | 15% |
| White wing | 20 | 35 | 25 | 20 |
| Snow removal: | | | | |
| Plowing | 85 | — | — | 15 |
| Loading and hauling | 85 | — | — | 15 |
| Street flushing | — | 40 | 40 | 20 |

**Problem 3-8.**   The following is a portion of a draft of the 19X5 budget for the City of Woodbridge which is being compiled by its administrator. The major programs and sub-programs are indicated by notations in brackets; the departmental responsibility for program elements is indicated in parentheses.

### CITY OF WOODBRIDGE
1975 Budget (Draft)

Public Safety [Program]

Prevent & Prosecute Crime [Sub-Program]

Community Police Surveillance (Police Department)

| | |
|---|---|
| Salaries & Wages | $399,796 |
| Materials & Supplies | 34,023 |
| Contractual Services | 41,905 |
| Permanent Property | 1,734 |
| | $477,458 |

Investigate & Prosecute Adult Crime (Police Department)
    Salaries & Wages                      $258,944
    Materials & Supplies                  7,760
    Contractual Services                 7,750
                                              $274,454

Investigate & Prosecute Juvenile Crimes (Police
Department)
    Salaries & Wages                      $207,450
    Materials & Supplies                  1,100
    Contractual Services                 2,150
                                              $210,700

Detain Accused Law Violators (Police Department)
    Materials & Supplies                 $    50
    Contractual Services                 750
                                              $   800

Cooperate With Regional Law Enforcement
Agencies (Police Department)
    Materials & Supplies                 $    50
    Total                                        $963,462

Adjudication of Crimes [Sub-Program]
  Litigate Civil Cases (Municipal Court)
    Salaries & Wages                    $  6,468
    Materials & Supplies                  200
    Contractual Services                 494
                                              $  7,162

Penalize Criminal Law Violators (Municipal Court)
    Salaries & Wages                    $ 14,325
    Materials & Supplies                  575
    Contractual Services                 644
    Permanent Property                   400
                                            $ 15,944

    Total                                        $23,106

Community Development & Environmental Control [Program]
  Community Development [Sub-Program]
    Planning Land Use (Director of Planning)
    Salaries & Wages                    $ 54,439
    Materials & Supplies                  2,422
    Contractual Services                 7,825
                                            $ 64,686

Grand Total—Public Safety [Program]                     $7,261,500

The grand total budgeted (all programs) for the object-of-expenditure classifications included above was:

| | |
|---|---:|
| Salaries & Wages | $5,126,197 |
| Materials & Supplies | 1,817,923 |
| Contractual Services | 291,060 |
| Permanent Property | 2,140,781 |
| | $9,375,961 |

Required:
 Using the data given, prepare a budget presentation in a program to object-of-expenditure cross-walk format, with sub-program and program element detail.

**Problem 3-9.** Using the information contained in Problem 3-8, prepare a cross-walk budgetary presentation relating programs, sub-programs and program elements to departments. (You need not include object-of-expenditure detail.) The grand total budgeted for the departments with which this problem deals are as follows:

| | |
|---|---:|
| Police | $1,717,476 |
| Municipal Court | 81,050 |
| Director of Planning | 124,292 |

**Problem 3-10.** From the following information prepare a departmental estimate of personal services (adapt Figure 3-18) for 19X4 for the Finance Department of the City of X. Submission date: October 1, 19X3; appropriation granted January 2, 19X4.

### INFORMATION AS OF JANUARY 1, 19X4

| Code | No. | | Rate per Annum |
|---|---|---|---:|
| 1420–A1.1 | 1 | Director of Finance | $15,000 |
| 1420–A1.2 | 1 | Cashier | 7,800 |
| 1420–A1.3 | 2 | Revenue Clerk | 6,400 |
| 1420–A1.4 | 2 | Parking Meter Collector | 5,640 |
| 1420–A1.5 | 1 | License Clerk | 5,800 |
| 1420–A1.6 | 2 | Machine Operator | 5,600 |
| 1420–A1.7 | 1 | Accountant | 8,400 |

As of September 1, 19X3, stenographer-clerk (A1.8) was added to the staff at a salary of $5,800.

The Director of Finance, Adam Smith, recommended that for 19X4 all salaries be increased by 8 percent.

The chief executive recommended that the staff be reduced by one parking meter collector, that Mr. Smith's salary be increased by $700, and that all other salaries be increased by 5 percent.

The legislative body approved the recommended staff reduction and allowed a 6 percent increase in all salaries, including the salary of the Director of Finance.

**Problem 3-11.** From the information below prepare a departmental estimate of current expenses—other than personal services (see Figure 3-19) for the Fire Department of the City of Z. Submission date: October 15, 19X3.

The following additional information is available: The expenditures for the first nine months of 19X3 are estimated to be 75 percent of the total expenditures for 19X3. Fire Chief A. C. Carr proposed that the 19X4 appropriations for his department be 105 percent of the total 19X3 expenditures, with the exception of account 2100-C41, for which he proposed that $2,000 be appropriated. City Manager Johnson made the recommendation that the amounts for 19X4 appropriations be the same as the actual (for the first nine months) plus the estimated (for the remaining three months) expenditures for 19X3, with the exceptions that only $1,000 be appropriated for clothing, that accounts 2100-B26, C22, and C52 be decreased 7, 10, and 5 percent, respectively, from the 19X3 estimated and actual expenditures, and that accounts 2100-C61 and C62 be increased 10 percent over the 19X3 expenditures. The City Council appropriated $1,000 for account 2100-B26, and for the remainder of the accounts it appropriated the amounts recommended by the City Manager.

## ACTUAL EXPENDITURES

| Code | | 19X1 | 19X2 | 19X3 (First Nine Months) |
|------|--|------|------|--------------------------|
| | Contractual Services: | | | |
| 2100–B11 | Transportation | $ 70 | $ 84 | $ 150 |
| 2100–B26 | Hospital | 230 | 1,396 | 750 |
| 2100–B31 | Light and Power | 6,138 | 5,090 | 3,876 |
| 2100–B43 | Apparatus Repair | 650 | 772 | 378 |
| 2100–B44 | Automotive Repair | 11,578 | 13,878 | 8,436 |
| | Materials & Supplies: | | | |
| 2100–C11 | Office | 432 | 530 | 420 |
| 2100–C22 | Coal | 15,066 | 11,742 | 9,750 |
| 2100–C41 | Clothing | 840 | 1,030 | 798 |
| 2100–C51 | Mechanical | 648 | 364 | 300 |
| 2100–C52 | Automotive | 4,070 | 4,534 | 3,306 |
| 2100–C61 | Chemical | 206 | 200 | 234 |
| 2100–C62 | Medical | 216 | 364 | 138 |
| 2100–C71 | Books & Reports | 30 | 36 | 24 |
| | Other Charges: | | | |
| 2100–D12 | Insurance | 900 | 950 | 750 |
| 2100–D25 | Pension Contribution | 12,274 | 12,286 | 9,240 |

**Problem 3-12.** From the following information, prepare a statement of actual and estimated revenues (see Figure 3-15) for the City of $Q$'s General Fund. The percentages apply to the first column.

| | Actual 19X3 | Actual First Nine Months of 19X4 | Estimated Remainder of 19X4 | Estimated 19X5 |
|---|---|---|---|---|
| General Property Taxes .... | $601,202 | 94% | — | 101% |
| Interest and Penalties— | | | | |
| Delinquent Taxes ...... | 13,450 | 84 | — | 110 |
| Police Fines ............. | 1,410 | 80 | 30% | 112 |
| Concessions ............. | 1,750 | 42 | 21 | 50 |
| Sewer Permits ........... | 2,500 | 75 | 25 | 105 |
| Building Permit Fees ...... | 145 | 125 | 50 | 200 |
| Vendors' Licenses ........ | 7,200 | 67 | 30 | 98 |
| Share of State-Collected | | | | |
| Franchise Taxes ........ | 18,530 | 84 | 27 | 140 |
| Fire Protection Service .... | 4,365 | 69 | 30 | 103 |
| Rent of Public Properties .. | 1,720 | 77 | 23 | 95 |

# 4

# General and Special
# Revenue Funds:
# The Accounting Cycle

Special Revenue Funds are established to account for resources allocated by law or by contractual agreement to specific purposes. The General Fund is used to account for all revenues not allocated to specific purposes. The General Fund is established at the inception of a government and may be expected to exist throughout the government's life, while the Special Revenue Funds exist as long as the government has resources dedicated to specific purposes. In the typical case the resources of both kinds of funds are expended wholly or almost wholly each year and are replenished on an annual basis.

The essential character of both kinds of funds is determined by an emphasis upon the recurring nature of their revenues and commitments and the necessity of meeting current commitments from the currently expendable (appropriable) resources. There is a substantial de-emphasis of the expense concept developed for profit-seeking organizations; the accounting principles for General and Special Revenue Funds are essentially related to the funds flow concept. For example, the purchase of fixed assets by these funds results in a decrease in the Fund Balances—the expenditures for such acquisitions have exactly the same status within the funds as expenditures for materials and supplies or salaries and wages, while the fixed assets are carried as assets of other entities within the government. Similarly, if maturing general obligation bonds of the government are to be paid from the resources of these funds, the expenditures are treated exactly the same as expenditures for materials and supplies are treated; and they have the same effect on Fund Balance.

As a result of the flow of funds concept, the balance sheet for these funds is prepared so as provide information which assists in the solution of the problem: "How shall the requirements of the succeeding period be met out of the available resources?" The balance sheet at the end of the year presents the resources on hand to meet the requirements of the following year; the Fund Balance is expected to be available, together with the revenues of the following year, to meet the needs of that year.

Additional references to this concept will be necessary as transactions and statements of the funds are discussed.

## OPERATION OF THE GENERAL FUND, 19X0

The operation of the General Fund of A Governmental Unit begins with the adoption of the budget. The appropriations that it contains, together with the revenue estimates on which the appropriations are based, provide the basis for the following general ledger entry on the first day of the new year:

| | | | |
|---|---|---|---|
| (1) | Estimated Revenues..................... | 431,000 | |
| | Appropriations ...................... | | 426,000 |
| | Fund Balance ....................... | | 5,000 |
| | To record appropriations and revenue estimates. | | |

Recall that (1) both the Estimated Revenues account and the Appropriations (estimated expenditures) account are general ledger control accounts, (2) the budgetary entry above causes the Fund Balance account to be stated at its planned end-of-period balance, (3) subsidiary ledgers are maintained in which detailed records of revenues and appropriations and expenditures are recorded, and (4) these subsidiary records provide the basis for budgetary control of the operations of the agencies of the governmental unit.

This chapter focuses upon *general ledger* accounting. Detailed discussions of the revenue and expenditure subsidiary ledgers are contained in Chapters 6 and 7.

Under the modified accrual basis, when the fund balance is increased by the acquisition of new assets, the new assets and the increase in fund balance should be recorded.[1] Taxes are in general the most important revenues of the General Funds of cities; they accrue at the time that they are formally levied

---

[1] Where revenues are accounted for on the cash basis, Revenues is credited only at the time of collection. In such circumstances Taxes Receivable do not have to be recorded. Sometimes a city which is on the cash basis wants to obtain the same control over Taxes Receivable which the accrual basis affords. The following entries meet the city's needs:

| | | |
|---|---|---|
| Taxes Receivable ........................ | 300,000 | |
| Uncollected Taxes ..................... | | 300,000 |
| To record the levy of taxes. [The two accounts in the entry are memorandum accounts in the sense that they will always offset each other.] | | |

by the legislative body of the city. (The assessment date is the date on which the value and ownership of property is determined for purposes of assigning tax liability and usually precedes the date of levy by a substantial period.) On the date that A Governmental Unit's taxes are levied, the following entry is made:

| | | | |
|---|---|---|---|
| (2) | Taxes Receivable—Current .............. | 300,000 | |
| | Estimated Uncollectible Current Taxes.. | | 3,000 |
| | Revenues ........................... | | 297,000 |
| | To record accrual of taxes. | | |

The estimated uncollectible taxes figure is the expected portion of the tax levy that will not be collected. Of course at this point in time the city does not know which specific tax bills will not be collected; as specific amounts are discovered to be uncollectible they are written off by charging the Estimated Uncollectible Taxes account and crediting Taxes Receivable. Since such taxes are a primary lien on the property, no loss is incurred until the city has gone through fore-closure proceedings that result in the sale of property for taxes. The accounting for such disposition of property is discussed in Chapter 6.

As other revenues accrue the following entries are made:

| | | | |
|---|---|---|---|
| (3) | Accounts Receivable .................... | 36,000 | |
| | Estimated Uncollectible Accounts Receivable....................... | | 1,000 |
| | Revenues ........................... | | 35,000 |
| | To record accrual of miscellaneous revenues and the setting up of an allowance for estimated losses thereon. | | |

The foregoing revenues might, for example, represent charges for services rendered. Those revenues that do not accrue, or are not deemed sufficiently measurable to be accrued in the accounts, are debited to Cash and credited to Revenues at the time of collection.

One of the primary objectives of governmental accounting is to assist the administration in controlling the expenditures, including the control of over-expenditure of appropriations. Thus, a record of expenditures chargeable to each appropriation must be kept. Provision is usually made for maintaining a record of the estimated amount of "in process" expenditures through the use of

| | | |
|---|---|---|
| Cash ..................................... | 195,000 | |
| Revenues ........................... | | 195,000 |
| To record collections of taxes. | | |
| Uncollected Taxes ........................ | 195,000 | |
| Taxes Receivable ..................... | | 195,000 |
| To reverse the memorandum entry above to the extent of taxes collected. | | |

In practice, a Reserve for Uncollected Taxes account may be used rather than an Uncollected Taxes account. Better practice is to limit usage of the term "reserve" to identi-fication of *reserved* Fund Balance accounts.

an Encumbrances account. As orders are placed, entries are made setting up encumbrances; a comparison of appropriations with expenditures and encumbrances indicates the amount of uncommitted appropriations available for expenditure. When the actual expenditure is determined, the entry setting up the encumbrances is reversed and the appropriation is reduced by the actual amount of the expenditure. Thus, if we assume that an order is placed for materials and equipment estimated to cost $30,000, the entry at the time the order is placed would be as follows:

| (4) | Encumbrances............................ | 30,000 | |
|-----|------------------------------------------|--------|--------|
| | Reserve for Encumbrances, 19X0 ....... | | 30,000 |
| | To record encumbering of appropriation. | | |

Assume, however, that when the materials and equipment and the bill are subsequently received, it is found that the materials and equipment cost $29,900. The entries will in that case be as follows:

| (5) | Reserve for Encumbrances, 19X0 ............ | 30,000 | |
|-----|---------------------------------------------|--------|--------|
| | Encumbrances ....................... | | 30,000 |
| | To reverse the entry encumbering the Appropriations account. | | |

| (6) | Expenditures ............................ | 29,900 | |
|-----|------------------------------------------|--------|--------|
| | Vouchers Payable ..................... | | 29,900 |
| | To record expenditures. | | |

These entries accomplish two things. The appropriation against which the expenditures for materials and equipment are chargeable was first reduced by the estimated amount of the expenditure. Now, however, the exact amount of the expenditure is known; accordingly, the entry setting up the encumbrances is reversed. It is necessary also to record the actual liability incurred and to reduce the appropriation by the actual expenditure. The second entry accomplishes this.

If an expenditure is controlled by devices other than encumbrances, the appropriation is not encumbered first but is reduced only at the time the expenditure is actually made. This is usually true with payrolls. Thus, if the payroll at the end of a pay period was $40,000, the entry at the time the payroll was approved for payment would be as follows:

| (7) | Expenditures ........................... | 40,000 | |
|-----|------------------------------------------|--------|--------|
| | Vouchers Payable .................. | | 40,000 |
| | To record approval of payroll. | | |

Additional entries illustrating the operation of the General Fund of A Governmental Unit follow:

| (8) | Cash ................................. | 245,000 | |
|-----|----------------------------------------|---------|--------|
| | Taxes Receivable—Current .......... | | 230,000 |
| | Accounts Receivable ............... | | 15,000 |
| | To record collection of taxes receivable and accounts receivable. | | |

| (9) | Taxes Receivable—Delinquent ........... | 120,000 | |
| | Taxes Receivable—Current ......... | | 120,000 |
| | To record taxes becoming delinquent. | | |

| (10) | Estimated Uncollectible Current Taxes..... | 12,000 | |
| | Estimated Uncollectible Delinquent | | |
| | Taxes ......................... | | 12,000 |
| | To record setting up of allowance for estimated losses on delinquent taxes. | | |

| (11) | Cash ................................. | 105,000 | |
| | Revenues ........................ | | 105,000 |
| | To record receipt of miscellaneous revenues not previously accrued. | | |

| (12) | Vouchers Payable ..................... | 40,000 | |
| | Cash ............................ | | 40,000 |
| | To record payment of payroll voucher. | | |

| (13) | Cash ................................. | 1,000 | |
| | Taxes Collected in Advance .......... | | 1,000 |
| | To record collection of taxes in advance. | | |

| (14) | Encumbrances ........................ | 20,000 | |
| | Reserve for Encumbrances, 19X0...... | | 20,000 |
| | To record reduction of appropriation by amount of estimated cost of purchase orders placed. | | |

| (15) | Tax Liens Receivable................... | 9,200 | |
| | Taxes Receivable—Delinquent ....... | | 9,000 |
| | Interest and Penalties Receivable on | | |
| | Taxes ......................... | | 200 |
| | To record the legal process of conversion of taxes, interest, and penalties into tax liens on property on which taxes seem unlikely to be paid. | | |

| (16) | Tax Liens Receivable................... | 100 | |
| | Vouchers Payable ................. | | 100 |
| | To record costs required to convert taxes, interest, and penalties into tax liens and to advertise the sales of properties. | | |

| (17) | Estimated Uncollectible Delinquent Taxes.. | 2,000 | |
| | Estimated Uncollectible Interest and Penalties Receivable on Taxes ............... | 20 | |
| | Estimated Uncollectible Tax Liens .... | | 2,020 |
| | To record the transfer of estimated uncollectible taxes, interest and penalties to estimated uncollectible tax liens. | | |

(18)  Cash .................................      3,000
      Estimated Uncollectible Tax Liens ........    1,000
          Tax Liens Receivable................              4,000
      To record sale of tax liens for $3,000 and
      the writing off of the difference as uncol-
      lectible.

(19)  Expenditures ..........................     30,000
          Due to Stores Fund ................            30,000
      To record supplies provided by an Intra-
      governmental Service Fund.

(20)  Cash .................................     50,200
          Taxes Receivable—Delinquent .......            50,000
          Revenues ........................                 200
      To record collection of delinquent taxes,
      together with interest and penalties thereon
      that had not yet been accrued.

(21)  Interest and Penalties Receivable on Taxes     550
          Estimated Uncollectible Interest and
              Penalties ......................                 50
          Revenues ........................                  500
      To record interest and penalties accrued on
      delinquent taxes outstanding and to provide
      for estimated losses.

(22)  Expenditures ..........................    300,000
          Vouchers Payable .................             300,000
      To record expenditures for which no
      encumbrances had been set up.

(23)  Vouchers Payable .....................    320,000
          Cash ............................             320,000
      To record payment of vouchers.

(24)  Due to Stores Fund ....................     22,500
          Cash ............................              22,500
      To record partial payment of amount due
      the Stores Fund.

(25)  Cash .................................     13,000
          Accounts Receivable ...............             13,000
      To record payments of accounts receivable.

The following is the trial balance of the accounts after the preceding illustrative journal entries are posted:

## A GOVERNMENTAL UNIT
### General Fund
### Preclosing Trial Balance
### December 31, 19X0

| | | |
|---|---:|---:|
| Cash .............................. | 34,700 | |
| Taxes Receivable—Delinquent........... | 11,000 | |
| Estimated Uncollectible Delinquent Taxes. | | 1,000 |
| Interest and Penalties Receivable on Taxes. | 350 | |
| Estimated Uncollectible Interest and Penalties........................... | | 30 |
| Tax Liens Receivable ................. | 5,300 | |
| Estimated Uncollectible Tax Liens ....... | | 1,020 |
| Accounts Receivable .................. | 8,000 | |
| Estimated Uncollectible Accounts Receivable ........................ | | 1,000 |
| Vouchers Payable .................... | | 10,000 |
| Due to Stores Fund ................... | | 7,500 |
| Taxes Collected in Advance ............ | | 1,000 |
| Reserve for Encumbrances, 19x0 ......... | | 20,000 |
| Fund Balance ....................... | | 5,000 |
| Estimated Revenues .................. | 431,000 | |
| Revenues ........................... | | 437,700 |
| Appropriations ...................... | | 426,000 |
| Expenditures ....................... | 399,900 | |
| Encumbrances....................... | 20,000 | |
| | 910,250 | 910,250 |

The foregoing trial balance is the basis for the closing entries discussed in the following section and for statements in the next chapter.

## CLOSING THE BOOKS, 19X0

At the end of the fiscal year, entries are made closing the accounts. The closing process summarizes in the Fund Balance account the results of operations.

CLOSING THE REVENUE ACCOUNTS. The closing entry for revenue is the following:

```
(C1)   Revenues ...........................   437,700
          Estimated Revenues ...............              431,000
          Fund Balance ....................                6,700
       To record closing of actual and estimated
       revenues.
```

The entry closes the Estimated Revenues and (actual) Revenues accounts, compares the totals of those accounts, and transfers the difference to Fund Balance —to adjust that account for the variance between planned and actual revenues. In this case actual revenues exceeded the estimate; if the converse had been true, then Fund Balance would have been debited.

CLOSING THE EXPENDITURE ACCOUNTS.   The procedure for closing Expenditures and related accounts is determined by the legal provisions of the government pertaining to the lapsing of appropriations and to related matters affecting the expenditure for an article purchased in one year but ordered in a preceding year. An appropriation is said to lapse when it terminates, that is, when it may no longer be used as authorization to make an expenditure. The illustration for A Governmental Unit will be completed on the assumption that the law states that (1) unencumbered appropriations lapse at the end of the year, (2) encumbered appropriations do not lapse, and (3) the closing entry should leave on the books a Reserve for Encumbrances account that becomes the authorization for the purchase of the encumbered article in the year or years following the year of appropriation. This assumption is in this text designated "A" for ease of reference in comparing it with further assumptions which will be introduced later in this chapter.

Under the foregoing Assumption A, the closing entry for expenditure accounts is the following:

```
(C2)   Appropriations .......................   426,000
          Expenditures......................              399,900
          Encumbrances ....................               20,000
          Fund Balance ....................                6,100
       To record closing of appropriations,
       expenditures, and encumbrances.
```

This entry (1) compares Appropriations with Expenditures and Encumbrances, (2) closes those accounts, (3) converts the Reserve for Encumbrances, 19X0, from a memorandum account to a reservation of Fund Balance, and (4) adjusts the Fund Balance account for the variance between planned and actual expenditures. Since expenditures cannot legally be made without an authorizing appropriation and therefore cannot legally exceed appropriations, the balancing element in the entry should never be a debit to Fund Balance. However, both in practice and in problems an excess of expenditures, or expenditures and encumbrances, over appropriations may occur. In problems, the excess may be

charged to Fund Balance; in practice, a supplementary appropriation should
be secured from the legislative body to cover the excess.

ALTERNATIVE CLOSING ENTRY APPROACHES. The entry sequence presented
above to close the Revenue accounts (C1) and Expenditure accounts (C2) is
logical and widely used in practice. It is by no means the only acceptable approach, however. Any reasonable entry or sequence of entries is acceptable so
long as (1) the Fund Balance account is updated to its proper balance at the
end of the period, (2) the temporary proprietary accounts that should be closed
are closed, and (3) the account balances that should be carried forward to the
succeeding period are properly carried forward.

Some accountants prefer to alter the closing entry sequence illustrated by
(1) reversing the effects of the budgetary entry or entries on the Fund Balance
account, then (2) closing (actual) Revenues, Expenditures and Encumbrances
balances to Fund Balance. This approach is illustrated in Chapter 5. Other
accountants prefer to prepare a single compound closing entry. A compound
General Fund closing entry for A Governmental Unit at December 31, 19X0,
under Assumption A, would appear as follows:

| | | |
|---|---:|---:|
| Revenues ................................. | 437,700 | |
| Appropriations ............................ | 426,000 | |
|     Estimated Revenues ...................... | | 431,000 |
|     Expenditures............................. | | 399,900 |
|     Encumbrances ........................... | | 20,000 |
|     Fund Balance .......................... | | 12,800 |
|     To record closing the budgetary and proprietary | | |
| accounts at year end. | | |

RESERVE FOR ENCUMBRANCES. At this point a review of the natures of the
Reserve for Encumbrances, 19X0, account is appropriate. It started life as an
offset to the Encumbrances account and the two contained throughout 19X0
a balance that represented the amount that should be deducted from the Appropriations account to arrive at the estimated spendable balance of appropriations. In other words, the Encumbrances and Reserve for Encumbrances, 19X0,
accounts were offsetting memorandum accounts. The closing entry for expenditure accounts closed the Encumbrances account but not the Reserve for Encumbrances, 19X0; the Reserve for Encumbrances, 19X0, was converted into a
reservation of fund balance. It and the Fund Balance account should be added
to obtain the total fund balance at year end. In 19X1 the Reserve for Encumbrances, 19X0, account will serve as an authorization for expenditure for items
that were on order at the end of 19X0. In 19X1 it will be, to all intents and
purposes, an appropriations account.

Since the Reserve for Encumbrances, 19X0, is in 19X1 an appropriations
account, those preparing the budget and the appropriation ordinance for 19X1

should keep in mind that the Reserve for Encumbrances, 19X0, is available as authorization for the purchase of items on order at the end of 19X0; if the 19X1 appropriation includes the amount of such items, dual provision will have been made for them.

POSTCLOSING TRIAL BALANCE.   Following the posting of the 19X0 closing entries, the trial balance of the General Fund appears as follows:

A GOVERNMENTAL UNIT

General Fund

Postclosing Trial Balance

December 31, 19X0

|  | Dr. | Cr. |
|---|---|---|
| Cash | 34,700 | |
| Taxes Receivable—Delinquent | 11,000 | |
| Estimated Uncollectible Delinquent Taxes | | 1,000 |
| Interest and Penalties Receivable on Taxes | 350 | |
| Estimated Uncollectible Interest and Penalties | | 30 |
| Tax Liens Receivable | 5,300 | |
| Estimated Uncollectible Tax Liens | | 1,020 |
| Accounts Receivable | 8,000 | |
| Estimated Uncollectible Accounts Receivable | | 1,000 |
| Vouchers Payable | | 10,000 |
| Due to Stores Fund | | 7,500 |
| Taxes Collected in Advance | | 1,000 |
| Reserve for Encumbrances, 19X0 | | 20,000 |
| Fund Balance | | 17,800 |
| | 59,350 | 59,350 |

A worksheet summary of the "A Governmental Unit" example for the year ended December 31, 19X0, is presented in Figure 4-5.

## OPERATION OF THE FUND, 19X1

The only new subject that must be covered for the operation of the Fund in 19X1 is the treatment of expenditures made in 19X1 under the authority of 19X0 appropriations. As expenditures that are authorized by the Reserve for Encumbrances, 19X0, are incurred in 19X1, they are debited to an account called Expenditures, 19X0. For example, assume that the items represented by the Reserve for Encumbrances, 19X0, account of the General Fund of A Governmental Unit at the end of the first year are received during 19X1 at an actual cost of $19,500. The following entry would be made to record this transaction:

| | | |
|---|---|---|
| Expenditures, 19X0 .......................... | 19,500 | |
| Vouchers Payable .......................... | | 19,500 |
| To record expenditures and the resulting liability. | | |

Note the distinction between expenditures chargeable against current appropriations and those chargeable against the reserve for encumbrances. The latter group of expenditures must be kept distinct from expenditures chargeable to 19X1 appropriations because they are not authorized by 19X1 appropriations. At the end of 19X1 they are closed out with the Reserve for Encumbrances, 19X0; the entry, in the case of the figures illustrated above, is as follows:

| | | |
|---|---|---|
| Reserve for Encumbrances, 19X0 ................. | 20,000 | |
| Expenditures, 19X0 ........................ | | 19,500 |
| Fund Balance ............................ | | 500 |
| To record closing out the reserve for encumbrances for 19X0 and the expenditures chargeable thereto. | | |

We shall assume that the preclosing trial balance of the General Fund of A Governmental Unit at December 31, 19X1 contained the following accounts, among others:

| | Dr. | Cr. |
|---|---|---|
| Estimated Revenues ................... | 450,000 | |
| Appropriations ....................... | | 444,000 |
| Reserve for Encumbrances, 19X1 ........ | | 15,000 |
| Reserve for Encumbrances, 19X0 ........ | | 20,000 |
| Revenues ............................ | | 446,000 |
| Encumbrances........................ | 15,000 | |
| Expenditures, 19X1 ................... | 418,000 | |
| Expenditures, 19X0 ................... | 19,500 | |

Orders first placed during the year totaled $220,000; of these, orders that had been expected to total $205,000 were filled during the year. Summary and closing entries relating to the foregoing information are presented in Figure 4-1, and the information is used for some of the statements in Chapter 5.

## LEGAL PROVISIONS RELATING TO THE LAPSING OF APPROPRIATIONS

As previously pointed out, closing entries and accounting for certain expenditure transactions in a subsequent year are affected by the laws governing the lapsing of appropriations and related matters. The accounting for three assumptions as to such legal provisions is illustrated in Figure 4-1. The three assumptions are summarized below; note that Assumption A has already been described and illustrated but will be repeated for the sake of comparison.

ASSUMPTION A. Encumbered appropriations do not lapse; the closing entry should leave on the books the Reserve for Encumbrances account which becomes the authorization for the purchase of the encumbered article in the year or years following the year of appropriation.

ASSUMPTION B. Unexpended appropriations lapse; the closing entry should close everything pertaining to the appropriation. If an encumbered article is to be purchased in the year or years following the year of appropriation, the appropriation for the year in which it is purchased must contain authority for the expenditure.

ASSUMPTION C. Encumbered appropriations do not lapse;[2] the closing entry should leave Appropriations, Encumbrances, and Reserve for Encumbrances account balances on the books in the amount encumbered. Expenditures made in a subsequent year or years will be identified with the appropriations that authorized them.

Figure 4-1 provides journal entries summarizing expenditure operations of the General Fund of A Governmental Unit under the three foregoing Assumptions—A, B, and C—as to the laws regulating lapsing and expenditure operations. The amounts used are provided by the Fund's Preclosing Trial Balance, December 31, 19X0, and the partial list of accounts taken from the Fund's preclosing trial balance, December 31, 19X1, both of which have been presented in this chapter.

These are not the only legal provisions that may be found, but the accounting for these three will serve as a basis for variations required by other provisions. For example, in some cases the law requires that a Reserve for Encumbrances account be left on the books at the end of the year but does not permit the reserve to serve as authorization for purchases to be made in the subsequent year. In these cases no expenditure may be made unless there is a current appropriation authorizing it. Such a law is satisfied by a closing entry of the type illustrated in Figure 4-1 under Assumption A and the operating entries for Assumption B. But the opening entry is different from that illustrated for any of the assumptions. For example, assume that A Governmental Unit had at the end of 19X0 outstanding orders of $20,000, and that the Reserve for Encumbrances was left on the books as in Assumption A. If the legislative body on

---

2 The difference between the accounting under Assumptions A and C may be due to specific legal requirements or to a decision of legal counsel or administrators as to the meaning or implementation of a specific legal provision.

Figure 4-1

# A GOVERNMENTAL UNIT

Summary of Appropriation—Expenditure Accounting

Under Three Assumptions as to the Lapsing of Appropriations

| | A | | B | | C | |
|---|---|---|---|---|---|---|
| | Dr. | Cr. | Dr. | Cr. | Dr. | Cr. |
| **December 31, 19X0:** | | | | | | |
| Appropriations, 19X0 | 426,000 | | 426,000 | | 406,000 | |
| Reserve for Encumbrances, 19X0 | | | 20,000 | | | |
| Expenditures, 19X0 | | 399,900 | | 399,900 | | 399,900 |
| Encumbrances, 19X0 | | 20,000 | | 20,000 | | |
| Fund Balance | | 6,100 | | 26,100 | | 6,100 |
| To record the closing of accounts related to appropriations. | | | | | | |
| **January 1, 19X1:** | | | | | | |
| Fund Balance | 444,000 | | 464,000 | | 444,000 | |
| Appropriations, 19X1 | | 444,000 | | 464,000 | | 444,000 |
| To record the budget for the second year. | | | | | | |
| Encumbrances, 19X1 | | | 20,000 | | | |
| Reserve for Encumbrances, 19X1 | | | | 20,000 | | |
| To record as encumbrances of the second year the orders placed but not filled in the first year. | | | | | | |

*Assumption*

Figure 4-1 (cont.)

Transactions, 19X1:

| | A | | B | | C | |
|---|---|---|---|---|---|---|
| | Dr. | Cr. | Dr. | Cr. | Dr. | Cr. |
| Encumbrances, 19X1 .......... | 220,000 | | 220,000 | | 220,000 | |
| Reserve for Encumbrances, 19X1 .......... | | 220,000 | | 220,000 | | 220,000 |
| To record reduction of Appropriations by amount of estimated cost of purchase orders placed. | | | | | | |
| Reserve for Encumbrances, 19X1 .......... | 205,000 | | 225,000 | | 205,000 | |
| Encumbrances, 19X1 .......... | | 205,000 | | 225,000 | | 205,000 |
| To reverse the entry encumbering Appropriations. | | | | | | |
| Expenditure, 19X1 .......... | 418,000 | | 437,500 | | 418,000 | |
| Vouchers Payable .......... | | 418,000 | | 437,500 | | 418,000 |
| To record expenditures and the resulting liability. | | | | | | |
| Expenditures, 19X0 .......... | 19,500 | | | | | |
| Vouchers Payable .......... | | 19,500 | | | | |
| To record expenditures and the resulting liability. | | | | | | |
| Reserve for Encumbrances, 19X0 .......... | | | | | 20,000 | |
| Encumbrances, 19X0 .......... | | | | | | 20,000 |
| To reverse the entry recording all unfilled orders placed in first year. | | | | | | |
| Expenditures, 19X0 .......... | | | | | 19,500 | |
| Vouchers Payable .......... | | | | | | 19,500 |
| To record expenditures and the resulting liability. | | | | | | |

**Figure 4-1 (cont.)**

December 31, 19X1:

| | A | | B | | C | |
|---|---|---|---|---|---|---|
| *Assumption* | Dr. | Cr. | Dr. | Cr. | Dr. | Cr. |
| Appropriations, 19X1 .................. | 444,000 | | 464,000 | | 429,000 | |
| Reserve for Encumbrances, 19X1 ....... | | | 15,000 | | | |
| Expenditures, 19X1 ................... | | 418,000 | | 437,500 | | 418,000 |
| Encumbrances, 19X1 .................. | | 15,000 | | 15,000 | | |
| Fund Balance......................... | | 11,000 | | 26,500 | | 11,000 |
| To close appropriations, expenditures and encumbrances of 19X1 | | | | | | |
| Reserve for Encumbrances, 19X0......... | 20,000 | | | | | |
| Expenditures, 19X0 ................... | | 19,500 | | | | |
| Fund Balance......................... | | 500 | | | | |
| To close accounts relating to orders first placed in 19X0. | | | | | | |
| Appropriations, 19X0 .................. | | | | | 20,000 | |
| Expenditures, 19X0 ................... | | | | | | 19,500 |
| Fund Balance......................... | | | | | | 500 |
| To close accounts relating to orders first placed in 19X0. | | | | | | |

January, 1, 19X1, authorizes the expenditure of $20,000 for those orders in 19X1, the three entries to record the authorization are as follows:

| | | |
|---|---|---|
| Reserve for Encumbrances, 19X0 ................ | 20,000 | |
| Fund Balance ........................... | | 20,000 |
| To transfer the reserve to fund balance. | | |
| Fund Balance .............................. | 20,000 | |
| Appropriations ........................... | | 20,000 |
| To record the supplementary appropriations. | | |
| Encumbrances, 19X1 ........................ | 20,000 | |
| Reserve for Encumbrances, 19X1 ............ | | 20,000 |
| To record the orders placed in 19X0 as 19X1 encumbrances. | | |

Thereafter, the transactions for 19X1 are recorded as if Assumption B were in use. For example, when the goods are received the following entries are made:

| | | |
|---|---|---|
| Reserve for Encumbrances, 19X1 ................ | 20,000 | |
| Encumbrances, 19X1 ...................... | | 20,000 |
| To cancel encumbrances. | | |
| Expenditures, 19X1......................... | 19,500 | |
| Vouchers Payable ........................ | | 19,500 |
| To record actual expenditures. | | |

RESULTS OF CLOSING ENTRIES.    Figures 4-2, 4-3, and 4-4 present partial ledgers of the General Fund of A Governmental Unit following the posting of the December 31, 19X0, closing entries presented in Figure 4-1. Their purpose is to contrast the effects of closing under the three legal assumptions illustrated in Figure 4-1. First, note that Assumptions A and C closings leave exactly the same amount in the Fund Balance account after closing. The two assumptions are, in all respects other than accounting mechanics, identical.

Second, note that the December 31, 19X0, balances in the Fund Balance accounts for Assumptions A and C are $20,000 less than the balance produced by an Assumption B closing. That $20,000 is, of course, the amount of the year-end balance of the Reserve for Encumbrances, 19X0. The latter account balance is transferred to the Fund Balance account by an Assumption B closing.

Third, note that under Assumptions A and C authorization has been carried forward to 19X1 for the purchase of goods on order at the end of 19X0. Under Assumption B the managers and city council of A Governmental Unit must provide for the purchase of those goods under 19X1 authority; and in fact the amount for Appropriations, 19X1, is larger by $20,000 than the amounts under Assumptions A and C.

Finally, the reader will undoubtedly find it useful to post all of the journal entries of Figure 4-1 to partial ledgers in order to be able to see the effects of these legal assumptions upon the planning, operation, and accounting of the General Fund.

# Figure 4-2

## A GOVERNMENTAL UNIT
### General Fund
### Partial Ledger After Closing Entries Prepared Under Assumption A
### December 31, 19X0

**Expenditures, 19X0**

| Debit | | Credit | |
|---|---|---|---|
| Transaction 6 | 29,900 | C2 | 399,900 |
| Transaction 7 | 40,000 | | |
| Transaction 19 | 30,000 | | |
| Transaction 22 | 300,000 | | |
| | 399,900 | | 399,900 |

**Encumbrances, 19X0**

| Debit | | Credit | |
|---|---|---|---|
| Transaction 4 | 30,000 | Transaction 5 | 30,000 |
| Transaction 14 | 20,000 | C2 | 20,000 |

**Reserve for Encumbrances, 19X0**

| Debit | | Credit | |
|---|---|---|---|
| Transaction 5 | 30,000 | Transaction 4 | 30,000 |
| | | Transaction 14 | 20,000 |

**Fund Balance**

| Debit | | Credit | |
|---|---|---|---|
| Forward | 17,800 | Transaction 1 | 5,000 |
| | | C1 | 6,700 |
| | | C2 | 6,100 |
| | 17,800 | | 17,800 |
| | | 12–31–X0 | 17,800 |

**Appropriations, 19X0**

| Debit | | Credit | |
|---|---|---|---|
| C2 | 426,000 | Transaction 1 | 426,000 |

The closing entries have been designated C1 (revenues) and C2 (expenditures) as in the textual material. They are the entries dated December 31, 19X0 in Figure 4-1.

147

Figure 4-3

## A GOVERNMENTAL UNIT
### General Fund
Partial Ledger After Closing Entries Prepared Under Assumption B
December 31, 19X0

**Reserve for Encumbrances, 19X0**

| | | | | |
|---|---|---:|---|---:|
| Transaction | 5 | 30,000 | Transaction 4 | 30,000 |
| C2 | | 20,000 | Transaction 14 | 20,000 |

**Fund Balance**

| | | | |
|---|---:|---|---:|
| Forward | 37,800 | Transaction 1 | 5,000 |
| | | C1 | 6,700 |
| | | C2 | 26,100 |
| | 37,800 | | 37,800 |
| | 37,800 | 12-31-X0 | 37,800 |

**Appropriations, 19X0**

| | | |
|---|---:|---:|
| C2 | 426,000 | Transaction 1   426,000 |

**Expenditures, 19X0**

| | | | | |
|---|---|---:|---|---:|
| Transaction | 6 | 29,900 | C2 | 399,900 |
| Transaction | 7 | 40,000 | | |
| Transaction | 19 | 30,000 | | |
| Transaction | 22 | 300,000 | | |
| | | 399,900 | | 399,900 |

**Encumbrances, 19X0**

| | | | | |
|---|---|---:|---|---:|
| Transaction | 4 | 30,000 | Transaction 5 | 30,000 |
| Transaction | 14 | 20,000 | C2 | 20,000 |

The closing entries have been designated C1 (revenues) and C2 (expenditures) as in the textual material. They are the entries dated December 31, 19X0 in Figure 4-1.

Figure 4-4

# A GOVERNMENTAL UNIT
## General Fund
Partial Ledger After Closing Entries Prepared Under Assumption C
December 31, 19X0

### Expenditures, 19X0

| | | | | |
|---|---|---:|---|---:|
| Transaction | 6 | 29,900 | C2 | 399,900 |
| Transaction | 7 | 40,000 | | |
| Transaction | 19 | 30,000 | | |
| Transaction | 22 | 300,000 | | |
| | | 399,900 | | 399,900 |

### Encumbrances, 19X0

| | | | | | |
|---|---|---:|---|---|---:|
| Transaction | 4 | 30,000 | Transaction | 5 | 30,000 |
| Transaction | 14 | 20,000 | | | |

### Reserve for Encumbrances, 19X0

| | | | | | |
|---|---|---:|---|---|---:|
| Transaction | 5 | 30,000 | Transaction | 4 | 30,000 |
| | | | Transaction | 14 | 20,000 |

### Fund Balance

| | | | | |
|---|---:|---|---|---:|
| Forward | 17,800 | Transaction | 1 | 5,000 |
| | | C1 | | 6,700 |
| | | C2 | | 6,100 |
| | 17,800 | | | 17,800 |
| | | 12-31-X0 | | 17,800 |

### Appropriations, 19X0

| | | | | |
|---|---:|---|---|---:|
| C2 | 406,000 | Transaction | 1 | 426,000 |
| Forward | 20,000 | | | |
| | 426,000 | | | 426,000 |
| | | 12-31-X0 | | 20,000 |

The closing entries have been designated C1 (revenues) and C2 (expenditures) as in the textual material. They are the entries dated December 31, 19X0 in Figure 4-1.

Figure 4-5

# A GOVERNMENTAL UNIT
## General Fund
### Summary of Accounting Operations*
#### For the Year Ended December 31, 19X0

| | Transactions Dr. | Transactions Cr. | Preclosing Trial Balance Dr. | Preclosing Trial Balance Cr. | Assumption A Closing Entries Dr. | Assumption A Closing Entries Cr. | Postclosing Trial Balance Dr. | Postclosing Trial Balance Cr. |
|---|---|---|---|---|---|---|---|---|
| Cash | 245,000 (8)<br>105,000 (11)<br>1,000 (13)<br>3,000 (18)<br>50,000 (20)<br>13,000 (25) | 40,000 (12)<br>320,000 (23)<br>22,500 (24) | 34,700 | | | | 34,700 | |
| Taxes Receivable—Current | 300,000 (2) | 230,000 (8)<br>70,000 (9) | | | | | | |
| Estimated Uncollectible Current Taxes | 3,000 (10) | 3,000 (2) | | | | | | |
| Taxes Receivable—Delinquent | 70,000 (9) | 9,000 (15)<br>50,000 (20) | 11,000 | | | | 11,000 | |
| Estimated Uncollectible Delinquent Taxes | 2,000 (17) | 3,000 (10) | | 1,000 | | | | 1,000 |
| Interest and Penalties Receivable on Taxes | 550 (21) | 200 (15) | 350 | | | | 350 | |
| Estimated Uncollectible Interest and Penalties | 20 (17) | 50 (21) | | 30 | | | | 30 |
| Accounts Receivable | 36,000 (3) | 15,000 (8)<br>13,000 (25) | 8,000 | | | | 8,000 | |
| Estimated Uncollectible Accounts Receivable | | 1,000 (3) | | 1,000 | | | | 1,000 |

| Account | Transactions Dr | Transactions Cr | Trial Balance Dr | Trial Balance Cr | Closing | Balance Sheet Dr | Balance Sheet Cr |
|---|---|---|---|---|---|---|---|
| Tax Liens Receivable | 9,200 (15); 100 (16) | 4,000 (18) | 5,300 | | | 5,300 | |
| Estimated Uncollectible Tax Liens | | 1,000 (18); 2,020 (17) | | 1,020 | | | 1,020 |
| Vouchers Payable | 40,000 (12); 320,000 (23) | 29,900 (6); 40,000 (7); 100 (16); 300,000 (22) | | 10,000 | | | 10,000 |
| Due to Stores Fund | 22,500 (24) | 30,000 (19) | | 7,500 | | | 7,500 |
| Taxes Collected in Advance | | 1,000 (13) | | 1,000 | | | 1,000 |
| Reserve for Encumbrances | 30,000 (5); 30,000 (4) | 20,000 (14) | | 20,000 | | | 20,000 |
| Fund Balance | 5,000 (1) | | | 5,000 | 6,700 (C1); 6,100 (C2) | | 17,800 |
| Estimated Revenues | 431,000 (1) | | 431,000 | 431,000 | 431,000 (C1) | | |
| Revenues | | 297,000 (2); 35,000 (3); 105,000 (11); 200 (20); 500 (21) | 437,700; 426,000 | 437,700; 426,000 | 437,700 (C1); 426,000 (C2) | | |
| Appropriations | | 426,000 (1) | 426,000 | 426,000 | | | |
| Expenditures | 29,900 (6); 40,000 (7); 30,000 (19); 300,000 (22) | | 399,900 | 399,900 | 399,900 (C2) | | |
| Encumbrances | 30,000 (4); 20,000 (14) | 30,000 (5) | 20,000 | 20,000 | 20,000 (C2) | | |
| | | | 431,000 / 910,250 | 431,000 / 910,250 | | 59,350 | 59,350 |

\* This worksheet is not a part of the accounting activities of A Governmental Unit. It is merely a device by which the student of governmental accounting may (1) observe in convenient form the transactions and their accounting results and (2) solve many kinds of governmental accounting problems that he may find in this or other texts or on examinations.

## DRAWING INFERENCES FROM YEAR-END BALANCES

The solution of problems in governmental accounting frequently requires that inferences be drawn from a year-end balance sheet or trial balance as to the type of closing entries that were made and hence as to the legal provisions governing such entries. For example, the presence in a year-end balance sheet of Reserve for Encumbrances, Encumbrances, and Appropriations accounts, all in the same amount, indicates that encumbered appropriations do not lapse and that expenditures incurred on account of the purchase orders represented in the Encumbrances account are to be charged to the carry-over Appropriations account in the new year. The absence of the three accounts mentioned above indicates that all appropriations lapse at the end of the year; the presence of a Reserve for Encumbrances account without an Encumbrances account is the signal that Assumption A has been used. In the absence of a clear indication of a change of legal provisions, the operating and closing entries should be prepared using the assumption as to the lapsing law that was used in the preparation of the previous year's closing entries. Similarly, the absence of accounts for current taxes from a year-end balance sheet or trial balance means that taxes become delinquent before the end of the year and that the balances of Taxes Receivable—Current and Estimated Uncollectible Current Taxes should be transferred to their delinquent counterparts before the balance sheet is prepared at the end of subsequent fiscal years.

**Question 4-1.** Why is there no chapter in this text devoted to describing operations and accounting procedures of Special Revenue Funds?

**Question 4-2.** What are the characteristics of "expenditures" that distinguish them from "expenses" in the financial accounting sense?

**Question 4-3.** What is the nature of the Fund Balance account as it appears (a) on the interim balance sheet? (b) on a postclosing trial balance?

**Question 4-4.** You are the administrator of a large department of a city in which appropriations lapse at the end of the year. Near the end of the year you find that part of your appropriation is unspent and will not be required for current operations. Under what circumstances should you

    a.  Spend all of the appropriation?

    b.  Permit a substantial part of your appropriation to lapse?

**Question 4-5.** Discuss the legal assumptions as to the lapsing of appropriations for the benefit of a committee to write the charter for a newly incorporated village.

**Question 4-6.** The postclosing trial balance of the General Fund contains, in three different cases, balances for the following accounts, among others:

    **Case 1.**  Reserve for Encumbrances
                 Fund Balance
                 Appropriations
                 Encumbrances

    **Case 2.**  Fund Balance

    **Case 3.**  Reserve for Encumbrances
                 Fund Balance

Which legal assumption has been used in making the closing entries in each case?

**Question 4-7.** The appropriations of a certain government for current expenditures lapse at the end of the fiscal year for which made, while appropriations for capital outlay lapse two years later. Discuss the desirability of this dual arrangement.

---

*Note to instructor:* All problems in the text that require recording and posting transactions, taking a preclosing trial balance, recording and posting closing entries, and taking a postclosing trial balance may be solved by the use of a worksheet like or similar to that in Figure 4-5 (essentially a bookkeeping worksheet). The authors recommend that the first problem assignment or two require journals, ledgers, and trial balances. After the students have been exposed to this cycle, worksheets may be used for as many subsequent problems as the instructor thinks desirable.

---

**Problem 4-1.** At December 31, 19X1, the City of $X$ had in certain of its accounts the following balances: Appropriations, $200,000; Expenditures, $190,000; Encumbrances, $7,500; Reserve for Encumbrances, $7,500. On February 15, 19X2, the only item represented by the $7,500 encumbrance was billed to the City at $7,350.

On the basis of the above information, prepare the closing entry, December 31, 19X1; entries required to be made January 1, 19X2, and February 15, 19X2; and the closing entry December 31, 19X2, for each of the three legal assumptions pertaining to the lapsing of appropriations.

**Problem 4-2.** The trial balance of the General Fund of the City of $W$ on January 1, 19X0, was as follows:

| | | |
|---|---:|---:|
| Cash ......................................... | $15,000 | |
| Taxes Receivable—Delinquent.................... | 20,000 | |
| Estimated Uncollectible Taxes—Delinquent ........ | | $ 3,000 |
| Interest and Penalties Receivable on Taxes ......... | 1, 000 | |
| Estimated Uncollectible Interest and Penalties ...... | | 75 |
| Accounts Receivable ........................... | 10,000 | |
| Estimated Uncollectible Accounts ................ | | 1,000 |
| Vouchers Payable ............................. | | 20,500 |
| Reserve for Encumbrances—Prior Years .......... | | 10,000 |
| Fund Balance ................................. | | 11,425 |
| | $46,000 | $46,000 |

The following are the transactions that took place during the year 19X0:

1. Revenues were estimated at $110,000; appropriations of $108,000 were made.
2. An order placed at the end of the preceding year and estimated to cost $10,000 was received; the invoice indicated an actual cost of $9,500.
3. Taxes to the amount of $110,000 accrued; an allowance of 5 per cent was made for possible losses.

4.  Collections were made as follows:

| | |
|---|---:|
| Current Taxes | $90,000 |
| Delinquent Taxes | 10,000 |
| Interest and Penalties Receivable on Taxes | 300 |
| Accounts Receivable | 5,000 |

5.  Taxes amounting to $20,000 have become delinquent; the balance of Estimated Uncollectible Taxes—Current was transferred to Estimated Uncollectible Taxes—Delinquent.

6.  Delinquent Taxes amounting to $2,000 were written off; Interest and Penalties Receivable on Taxes to the amount of $20 were also written off.

7.  An order was placed for materials estimated to cost $20,000.

8.  Delinquent Taxes amounting to $200, which were written off in preceding years, were collected with interest and penalties of $35. (Hint—credit Revenues.)

9.  Payments were made as follows:

| | |
|---|---:|
| Vouchers Payable | $15,500 |
| Payrolls | 20,000 |

10.  The materials ordered were received; a bill for $21,000 was also received.

11.  An order was placed for an automobile for the police department; the estimated cost was $3,000.

12.  Payrolls of $25,000 were paid.

13.  The automobile ordered for the police department was received; the actual cost was $3,000.

14.  Bonds to the amount of $10,000 matured.

15.  The matured bonds were paid.

16.  Interest amounting to $5,000 was paid by the General Fund.

17.  Interest of $600 accrued on Delinquent Taxes, and an allowance for uncollectible losses thereon of 5 per cent was provided.

18.  An order was placed for materials estimated to cost $19,000.

Required:

(1)  Post the opening trial balance to "T" accounts.
(2)  Prepare journal entries.
(3)  Post to "T" accounts.
(4)  Prepare closing entries.
(5)  Post to "T" accounts.
(6)  Prepare postclosing trial balance.

**Problem 4-3.**  The beginning balances of the General Fund of City Two on January 1, 19X5 were as follows:

| | | |
|---|---:|---:|
| Cash | $2,000 | |
| Taxes Receivable—Current | 2,000 | |
| Estimated Uncollectible Current Taxes | | $ 100 |
| Vouchers Payable | | 900 |
| Fund Balance | | 3,000 |
| | $4,000 | $4,000 |

In 19X5 the following transactions were made:
1. Taxes Receivable—Current that were not collected by December 31 became delinquent as of January 1.
2. Revenues were estimated at $200,000. Appropriations of $197,000 were made.
3. Property Taxes were levied in the amount of $150,000. It was estimated that 1% of these taxes will not be collected.
4. The accountant was notified that the appropriations total covered a 19X4 order for materials estimated to cost $25,200.
5. The materials were received at an actual cost of $25,000.
6. Citizens paid $130,000 of taxes, of which $1,000 was for delinquent taxes.
7. Miscellaneous revenue was received in the amount of $50,000.
8. The voucher for the materials (#5) and the beginning balance in Vouchers Payable were paid.
9. Salaries were paid in the amount of $120,000.
10. Materials and supplies were ordered at an estimated cost of $30,000.
11. The ordered materials and supplies were received at an actual cost of $31,000.
12. Office equipment was ordered at an estimated cost of $20,000.
13. The City wrote off $100 of delinquent taxes as uncollectible.
14. The office equipment ordered was received at an actual cost of $20,000.
15. Vouchers were paid in the amount of $31,000.
16. The City received $14,000 in payment of Property Taxes.
17. The City ordered $1,500 of supplies.

Required:
(1) Record the beginning balances in accounts.
(2) Journalize the transactions.
(3) Post to accounts.
(4) Prepare a trial balance.
(5) Prepare closing entries.
(6) Prepare a postclosing trial balance.

**Problem 4-4.** The following is a trial balance of the General Fund of the City of *D* as of December 31, 19X0, after closing entries (Interest and Penalties on Taxes are not accrued):

| | | |
|---|---:|---:|
| Cash | $33,600 | |
| Taxes Receivable—Delinquent | 25,400 | |
| Estimated Uncollectible Delinquent Taxes | | $ 5,900 |
| Accounts Receivable | 15,500 | |
| Estimated Uncollectible Accounts | | 2,500 |
| Vouchers Payable | | 42,000 |
| Reserve for Encumbrances | | 16,000 |
| Fund Balance | | 8,100 |
| | $74,500 | $74,500 |

The following transactions took place during 19X1:
1. The budget for the year was adopted. Revenues were estimated at $216,000; appropriations of $229,000 were made, including an appropriation of $16,000 for materials ordered in 19X0, covered by the Reserve for Encumbrances.

2. The materials ordered in 19X0 and set up as an encumbrance of that year for $16,000 were received; the actual cost was $15,000.

3. Delinquent Taxes amounting to $2,800 were declared uncollectible and written off the books.

4. Taxes to the amount of $210,000 accrued; a 3 per cent allowance for estimated losses was provided.

5. Uniforms estimated to cost $15,000 were ordered.

6. Collections were made as follows:

| | |
|---|---:|
| Current Taxes | $182,000 |
| Delinquent Taxes | 8,500 |
| Interest and Penalties on Taxes | 200 |
| Accounts Receivable | 7,300 |

7. Interest of $3,000 was paid by the City.

8. Payroll vouchers for $100,000 were approved.

9. The uniforms were received; the invoice was for $16,000.

10. Serial bonds to the amount of $35,000 matured.

11. Delinquent Taxes to the amount of $350, written off in preceding years, were collected. (Credit Revenues.)

12. Current Taxes became delinquent; the amount of Estimated Uncollectible Current Taxes was transferred to Estimated Uncollectible Delinquent Taxes.

13. The payroll vouchers were paid.

14. An order was placed for a snow plow estimated to cost $3,500.

15. Vouchers paid amounted to $60,000.

16. The snow plow was received; the invoice was for $3,800.

17. Matured serial bonds were retired.

18. Miscellaneous revenues of $5,000 were collected.

19. An order was placed for civil defense equipment at an estimated cost of $24,000.

Required:

(1) Enter the opening trial balance in accounts.
(2) Prepare journal entries.
(3) Post to accounts.
(4) Prepare a preclosing trial balance.
(5) Prepare closing entries.
(6) Post to accounts.
(7) Prepare a postclosing trial balance.

**Problem 4-5.** From the following information concerning the operations of a Municipal Expendable Revenue Fund for the fiscal year ended April 30, 19X9 prepare a worksheet summarizing the year's transactions. Debit and credit columns should be provided under the following headings: "May 1, 19X8, Trial Balance and Fiscal 19X9 Transactions"; "Closing Entries, April 30, 19X9"; "Balance Sheet, April 30, 19X9." Information concerning the Expendable Fund, for the year ended April 30, 19X9, is as follows:

| | | |
|---|---|---:|
| 1. | Fund Balance at May 1, 19X8, consisted entirely of cash.... | $ 2,350 |
| 2. | Budget estimate of revenue | 185,000 |
| 3. | Budget appropriations | 178,600 |
| 4. | Tax levy $115,620, against which a reserve of $4,000 is set for estimated losses in collection. | |

5. Tax receipts, $112,246, with penalties of $310 in addition.
6. Receipts from temporary loans $20,000, all of which were repaid during period with interest of $300.
7. Balance of encumbrances unliquidated, April 30, 19X9...... 3,250
8. Vouchers approved for expense......................... 146,421
9. Vouchers approved for capital expenditures ............. 21,000
10. Vouchers approved for payment of bonds falling due during the year, $5,000, and for interest on bonds, $2,000.
11. Miscellaneous revenue received........................ 74,319
12. Rebate of current year's taxes collected in error............ 240
13. Warrants issued and payable on demand................. 169,400
14. Refund on an expense voucher on which an excess payment was made ........................................... 116

(AICPA, adapted.)

**Problem 4-6.** The following is the trial balance of the General Fund of City Eazy as of January 1, 19X7:

| | | |
|---|---:|---:|
| Cash ............................................. | 8,000 | |
| Taxes Receivable—Delinquent...................... | 15,000 | |
| Estimated Uncollectible Delinquent Taxes | | 2,000 |
| Interest & Penalties Receivable .................... | 600 | |
| Estimated Uncollectible Interest & Penalties.......... | | 100 |
| Accounts Receivable ............................. | 12,000 | |
| Estimated Uncollectible Accounts ................... | | 1,500 |
| Vouchers Payable ................................ | | 9,000 |
| Reserve for Encumbrances of Prior Years............. | | 20,000 |
| Fund Balance .................................... | | 3,000 |
| | 35,600 | 35,600 |

The following transactions occurred during 19X7:
1. Revenues were estimated at $200,000; appropriations of $195,000 were made.
2. An order placed at the end of the preceding year and estimated to cost $20,000 was received; the invoice indicated an actual cost of $19,100.
3. Property Taxes of $200,000 accrued; an allowance of 5 percent was made for possible losses.
4. An order was placed for materials estimated to cost $15,000.
5. Collections were made as follows:

| | |
|---|---:|
| Current Taxes ........................... | $180,000 |
| Accounts Receivable ..................... | 8,000 |
| Delinquent Taxes ....................... | 12,000 |
| Interest and Penalties Receivable on Taxes .. | 500 |
| | $200,500 |

6. Taxes amounting to $20,000 have become delinquent; the balance of estimated uncollectible current taxes was transferred to estimated uncollectible delinquent taxes.

7. Delinquent taxes in the amount of $5,000 were written off; interest and penalties receivable on taxes of $100 were also written off.

8. Delinquent taxes of $2,000 were collected, as were interest and penalties of $50 on these taxes. The interest and penalties had not been previously accrued.

9. Payments were made as follows:

| | |
|---|---|
| Vouchers payable ......................... | $50,000 |
| Payrolls ................................. | 80,000 |

10. The materials ordered were received; a bill for $17,000 was also received.

11. Interest amounting to $6,000 was paid by the City.

12. An order was placed for a truck for the Street Department; the estimated cost was $20,000.

13. Payrolls of $50,000 were paid.

14. The truck (Item 12) was received; the invoice cost was $20,000.

15. Bonds to the amount of $15,000 have matured.

16. The matured bonds were paid.

17. Interest of $500 has accrued on delinquent taxes; an allowance for uncollectible losses thereon of 5% was provided.

18. An order was placed for materials estimated to cost $6,000.

Required:

(1) Record the opening trial balance in accounts.
(2) Prepare journal entries.
(3) Post to accounts.
(4) Prepare a trial balance.
(5) Prepare closing entries.
(6) Post to accounts.
(7) Prepare a postclosing trial balance.

# 5

## General and Special Revenue Funds: Balance Sheets and Fund Balance Statements

All of the General Fund statements presented in this chapter except Figure 5-1 are based upon the transactions of A Governmental Unit for the years 19X0 and 19X1 as described in Chapter 4. In addition, certain accounts that were not mentioned in the simple illustration for the General Fund of A Governmental Unit are presented, and transactions accounting for such accounts are necessarily described in the process of discussing the origin and nature of the accounts.

### BALANCE SHEETS

The essential character of the General Fund should be kept constantly in mind as balance sheets and balance sheet accounts are discussed. Though the General Fund presumably will exist as long as the governmental unit exists, the operation of the Fund is on a year-to-year basis. Each year the problem of financing a new year's operations with a new year's revenues is the central concern of those managing the finances of the Fund. The balance sheet is prepared so as to provide information that assists in the solution of the problem; thus the current nature of the General Fund has a substantial bearing on the accounts and accounting of the Fund.

THE INTERIM BALANCE SHEET. Transactions that are not in all cases the same as those in Chapter 4 have been assumed in order to prepare the balance sheet prepared *during* a fiscal year that is presented in Figure 5-1. Note that the estimated revenues figure appears on the debit side as a potential asset and is reduced by the actual revenues to date to derive the net amount expected to be earned during the balance of the year—an estimated fund "resource." Similarly, the appropriations figure appears on the credit side reduced by the expenditures and encumbrances to date; the net figure presents the net unencumbered expenditure authority (unencumbered appropriations) outstanding at the statement date—the planned or potential expenditures during the balance of the year.

An interim balance sheet presents a picture of the Fund at a point within the planned year of operations. Inclusion of both budgetary (showing the results

**Figure 5-1**

A GOVERNMENTAL UNIT
General Fund
Balance Sheet
During Fiscal Year 19X0*

*Assets*

| | | |
|---|---:|---:|
| Cash ........................................ | | $ 25,000 |
| Accounts receivable ........................... | $ 36,000 | |
| Less:  Estimated uncollectible accounts receivable ............................ | 1,000 | 35,000 |
| Estimated revenues .......................... | $431,000 | |
| Less:  Revenues ............................ | 115,000 | 316,000 |
| | | $376,000 |

*Liabilities, Appropriations, Reserves, and Fund Balance*

| | | | |
|---|---:|---:|---:|
| Liabilities: | | | |
| Vouchers payable........................... | | $120,000 | |
| Due to Stores Fund ........................ | | 11,000 | $131,000 |
| Appropriations: | | | |
| Appropriations ............................ | | $426,000 | |
| Less:  Expenditures ............. | $186,000 | | |
| Encumbrances ........... | 11,000 | 197,000 | 229,000 |
| Reserve for encumbrances ..................... | | | 11,000 |
| Fund balance ................................ | | | 5,000 |
| | | | $376,000 |

* The transactions assumed to have produced this interim balance sheet bear no necessary relationship to the transactions in Chapter 4.

of budget transactions) and proprietary (showing actual financial conditions or operations) accounts for the Fund helps the reader analyze the financial position of the Fund in a way that would not be possible without them. For example, a midyear balance sheet showing an expenditure figure that is two-thirds that of appropriations tells the reader that planned expenditures (and hence the planned incurrence of liabilities) for the last half of the year are expected to be only one-third of the appropriations figure. Similarly, a midyear balance sheet that shows an actual revenue figure only one-fourth the amount of estimated revenue tells the reader that future revenue accruals or collections are expected to occur at a much faster rate than that of the first half year. In all probability the preceding situation applies to a city that levies its annual property taxes in the last half of the year.

A reader who wants to review the position of the Fund without the Revenue and Expenditure accounts must, mentally or otherwise, transfer the balances of these accounts to Fund Balance. But he may, as he would in the cases assumed in the preceding paragraph, receive a misleading impression from the resulting Fund Balance figure. If he took the data from Figure 5-1, he would calculate the Fund Balance figure as follows:

| | | | |
|---|---|---|---|
| Fund Balance per Figure 5-1 ................... | | | $    5,000 |
| Add: | | | |
|     Appropriations ............................ | | $426,000 | |
|     Less:  Expenditures ............. | $186,000 | | |
|                Encumbrances ........... | 11,000 | 197,000 | $229,000 |
| | | | $234,000 |
| Deduct: | | | |
|     Estimated Revenues........................ | | $431,000 | |
|     Revenues ................................ | | 115,000 | 316,000 |
| Deficit ...................................... | | | $  82,000 |

The deficit is by no means an accurate indication of the General Fund's financial position. A further look at the assets reveals no taxes receivable. Evidently the tax levy has not yet been recorded, and the Fund may well be operating exactly as planned.

THE YEAR-END BALANCE SHEET.    The balance sheet of the General Fund of A Governmental Unit at December 31, 19X0 (Figure 5-2), is based on the trial balance at that date and on the closing entries that were illustrated under Assumption A in the preceding chapter. The statement is for the most part self-explanatory, but comments on some of the accounts will help to produce a clear picture of its characteristics. The comments deal with (1) the significance of the Fund Balance account, (2) the nature of several fund balance reserve

**Figure 5-2**

A GOVERNMENTAL UNIT
General Fund
Balance Sheet
December 31, 19X0

*Assets*

| | | |
|---|---:|---:|
| Cash ......................................... | | $34,700 |
| Taxes receivable—delinquent..................... | $11,000 | |
| Less: Estimated uncollectible delinquent taxes ...... | 1,000 | 10,000 |
| Interest and penalties receivable on taxes ........... | $   350 | |
| Less: Estimated uncollectible interest and penalties.. | 30 | 320 |
| Accounts receivable ............................ | $ 8,000 | |
| Less: Estimated uncollectible accounts............. | 1,000 | 7,000 |
| Tax liens receivable ........................... | $ 5,300 | |
| Less: Estimated uncollectible tax liens ............ | 1,020 | 4,280 |
| | | $56,300 |

*Liabilities, Reserves, and Fund Balance**

| | | |
|---|---:|---:|
| Liabilities: | | |
| Vouchers payable............................ | $10,000 | |
| Due to Stores Fund ......................... | 7,500 | |
| Taxes collected in advance .................... | 1,000 | $18,500 |
| Reserve for encumbrances ....................... | | 20,000 |
| Fund balance ................................. | | 17,800 |
| | | $56,300 |

\* Alternatively, this section may be headed "Liabilities and Fund Balance" and appear as follows:

| | | |
|---|---:|---:|
| Liabilities: | | |
| Vouchers payable ...................... | $10,000 | |
| Due to Stores Fund .................... | 7,500 | |
| Taxes collected in advance ............... | 1,000 | $18,500 |
| Fund balance: | | |
| Reserved for encumbrances ............... | 20,000 | |
| Unreserved .......................... | 17,800 | 37,800 |
| | | $56,300 |

accounts, and (3) the exclusion of fixed assets and long-term (noncurrent) liabilities from the General Fund accounts and its Balance Sheet.

FUND BALANCE. As previously indicated, the General Fund is a current fund.

Its fiscal operations are concerned with the current year's revenues and the current year's expenditures, and as a general rule the Fund is intended to show neither a surplus nor a deficit. A credit balance in the Fund Balance account after closing entries does not in any sense represent retained earnings. Rather it indicates an excess of the assets of the fund over its liabilities and Fund Balance reservations, if any, and would more properly be titled "unreserved, unappropriated Fund Balance." Accordingly, the legislative body is likely to use the available assets, as indicated by the credit balance, in financing the budget for the succeeding year.

During a fiscal year the balance of the Fund Balance account may be of a nature substantially different from that of the year-end balance. Suppose that the year-end Fund Balance (post-closing) is $5,000, and that in the following year budgeted revenues are $100,000 and appropriations total $97,000. The Fund Balance account will be carried at $8,000 after the recording of the budget, that is, at the planned balance at period end. The exact nature of the balance can be determined only by examining all the facts. Its balance is neither exclusively budgetary nor exclusively proprietary.

If the General Fund has a deficit, the amount of the deficit should be exhibited on the balance sheet in the same position as the Fund Balance and called a "Deficit." Typical municipal financial administration policy requires that the deficit be eliminated in the following fiscal year and that the necessary revenues for this purpose be provided in the budget.

The Analysis of Changes in Fund Balance (Account) for year ended December 31, 19X0 (Figure 5-3), will help to illustrate further the nature of the Fund Balance account. The amounts are identical with those used in the illustrative entries in Chapter 4.

FUND BALANCE RESERVES. Since assets in an amount equal to the Fund Balance account are assumed to be available to finance appropriations for expenditures of the succeeding year, it is desirable to remove therefrom any portions that are not available for the purpose. The Reserve for Encumbrances left on the books by the closing entries made under Assumption A has already been discussed as a fund balance reserve at the end of the year and as authorization for expenditures in the next year. If both the Encumbrances and Reserve for Encumbrances accounts are either closed or left on the books, the Reserve for Encumbrances is not converted into a fund balance reserve. If the closing entries are made in accordance with Assumption B, the Fund Balance account is larger, by the amount of encumbrances, than it would have been if a reserve had been created. Under Assumption C the unclosed balance of the Appropriations account is, in effect, a reservation of Fund Balance, and Encumbrances and Reserve for Encumbrances continue to be off-setting memorandum accounts.

Frequently some of the assets of a General Fund are needed as working capital. Such assets as petty cash and inventories of materials and supplies are not available for financing expenditures of a subsequent period because they must be maintained at or near the required level. The entries to account for materials and supplies and the related Reserve for Inventories are discussed in Chapter 7. Entries for petty cash are as follows:

| | | |
|---|---|---|
| Petty Cash .................................... | 2,000 | |
| Cash....................................... | | 2,000 |
| To record the creation of a petty cash fund out of general cash. | | |
| | | |
| Fund Balance.................................... | 2,000 | |
| Reserve for Petty Cash Fund................... | | 2,000 |
| To record a reservation of fund balance in the amount of the petty cash fund. | | |

Similar reservations may be made for other assets that are not expected to be available to finance current operations. Examples of such assets are advances to other funds, deposits, and accounts and claims receivable.

EXCLUSION OF FIXED ASSETS AND LONG-TERM DEBT.   Although some General Fund expenditures represent outlays that should be capitalized, fixed assets are not included in the balance sheet of the General Fund. For example, let us assume that, out of the total expenditures of $29,900 shown in the entry on page 134, the sum of $2,000 was for equipment. In commercial accounting this $2,000 would be shown in the general balance sheet as part of the assets, but not so in governmental accounting. Here, too, the expenditures are capitalized, but they are recorded in a separate nonfund group of accounts rather than as a part of the General Fund (see Chapter 11). Even if long-term debt (such as bonds) is ultimately payable out of the General Fund, and even if it has been issued to eliminate a deficit in the General Fund, unmatured long-term debt is not recorded as a liability of the General Fund but in a separate nonfund group of accounts (see Chapter 11). The only long-term debt included is that which has matured and is payable from the current resources of the General Fund (an unusual occurrence, since bonds and other long-term debts are ordinarily repaid from a Debt Service Fund).

Fixed assets are excluded from the General Fund balance sheet because they do not represent resources out of which the government intends to finance its current activities or meet its liabilities. These assets are not acquired for resale, but for the purpose of rendering service over a relatively long period of time.

Bonds and other long-term debts payable are not included as part of the liabilities of the General Fund because the existing resources of the Fund are not expected to be used for their payment. The governmental unit's future taxing power will ultimately provide resources to pay them. Taxes designated for debt service usually are treated as revenues of a Debt Service Fund and do not affect the General Fund. In specific cases, however, the taxes may be collected through the General Fund and transmitted to the Debt Service Fund. In such cases they would be accounted for as General Fund revenues and the expenditure (transfer to the Debt Service Fund) would be treated as would any other budgeted expenditure of the General Fund.

## ANALYSIS OF CHANGES IN FUND BALANCE

A second major General Fund financial statement is the Analysis of Changes in Fund Balance. This statement may present data pertaining either to the Fund Balance account or to total fund balance, including reserves. The former (Figures 5-3, 5-4, and 5-5) is customary when the Fund Balance account is shown in a balance sheet subsection separate from the Reserved Fund Balance (see Figure 5-2), as illustrated by the NCGA in *GAAFR*; the latter (Figure 5-7) is equally acceptable and is preferable where a single "Fund Balance" section is presented, as shown in the footnote to Figure 5-2. The various analyses of Fund Balance approaches and presentations are explained in the remaining pages of this chapter. The illustrations are based on the information for the General Fund of A Governmental Unit in Chapter 4 and on the use of Assumption A for closing entries.

SUMMARY ANALYSIS OF CHANGES IN THE FUND BALANCE ACCOUNT. The two summary statements analyzing changes in the Fund Balance *account* (Figures 5-3 and 5-4) provide information only about the proprietary activities that affect the Fund Balance account of the General Fund. Detailed schedules sup-

**Figure 5-3**

A GOVERNMENTAL UNIT
General Fund
Analysis of Changes in Fund Balance (Account)
For the Fiscal Year Ended December 31, 19X0

| | | |
|---|---:|---:|
| Fund balance, January 1, 19X0.............. | | –0– |
| Add: | | |
| Excess of revenues over expenditures: | | |
| Revenues ........................... | $437,700 | |
| Expenditures ........................ | 399,900 | $37,800 |
| Total balance and additions ................ | | $37,800 |
| Deduct: | | |
| Reserve for encumbrances, 19X0* .......... | | 20,000 |
| Fund balance, December 31, 19X0........... | | $17,800 |

* Alternatively, this may be referred to as "Increase in Reserve for Encumbrances, 19X0" or "Establishment of Reserve for Encumbrances, 19X0."

**Figure 5-4**

## A GOVERNMENTAL UNIT
### General Fund
Analysis of Changes in Fund Balance (Account)
For the Fiscal Year Ended December 31, 19X1

| | | |
|---|---:|---:|
| Fund balance, January 1, 19X1 .............. | | $17,800 |
| Add: | | |
| Excess of revenues over expenditures: | | |
| Revenues ........................... | $446,000 | |
| Expenditures, 19X1.................... | 418,000 | 28,000 |
| Reserve for encumbrances, 19X0, lapsed:* | | |
| Reserve for encumbrances, 19X0.......... | $ 20,000 | |
| Less, expenditures charged thereto ........ | 19,500 | 500 |
| Total balances and additions ................ | | $46,300 |
| Deduct: | | |
| Reserve for encumbrances, 19X1 ........... | | 15,000 |
| Fund balance, December 31, 19X1............ | | $31,300 |

    * Alternatively, this may be referred to as "Decrease in Reserve for Encumbrances, 19X0" or "Reserve for Encumbrances from 19X0 Cancelled."

porting the amounts shown for revenues, appropriations, expenditures, encumbrances, and expenditures chargeable to the reserve for encumbrances, 19X0, are in Chapters 6 and 7, which deal with revenues and expenditures. These detailed schedules provide for a comparison of budgetary plans and the actual operations.

As the name of the statement implies, the Analysis of Changes in Fund Balance (account) is designed to explain the reasons for the changes in the Fund Balance account during the fiscal year. A principal reason for such changes is ordinarily the difference between revenues and expenditures for the current year. Figure 5-3, for example, shows that revenues exceeded expenditures by a substantial amount. However, it should be noted that the Reserve for Encumbrances in existence at the end of 19X0 represents authorization for future expenditures that are represented by purchase orders outstanding at that date. It was created by a reduction of the Fund Balance *account,* a reduction that was made when the Encumbrances account was closed to the Fund Balance account at the same time Appropriations and Expenditures were closed.

At the beginning of the year 19X1 there was a carryover of the Reserve for Encumbrances, 19X0—a reservation of total fund balance. During 19X1 expenditures were made under the authority of that account. In the Analysis of Changes in Fund Balance (account) for the year ending December 31, 19X1, the difference between these expenditures and the authorization therefor is an addition to the Fund Balance, since the authorization has lapsed and the unexpended amount is no longer reserved.

If the city had made changes in fund balance reserves other than the Reserve for Encumbrances during the year, those changes would have been included in the Analysis of Changes in Fund Balance (account) since all such changes are made through the Fund Balance account. Decreases in reservations of fund balance result in additions to Fund Balance; increases in reservations result in decreases in Fund Balance.

An exercise that is useful in understanding the Analysis of Changes in Fund Balance (account) is to compare the actual Fund Balance account for 19X1, as prepared from data in Chapter 4, with the Analysis of Changes in Fund Balance (account) for the year ending December 31, 19X1. The closing entries sequence presented in Chapter 4 includes the budgetary accounts, of course; but there is a substantial difference between the philosophy of those closing entries and the philosophy of the Analysis of Changes in Fund Balance (account), Figures 5-3 and 5-4, which, as already explained, contain no budgetary information. The following sequence of closing entries for the General Fund of A Governmental Unit for the year ending December 31, 19X1 is more in accordance with the philosophy of the statement:

| | | | | |
|---|---|---|---|---|
| (C1) | Appropriations ......................... | 444,000 | | |
| | Fund Balance .......................... | 6,000 | | |
| | Estimated Revenues ................ | | | 450,000 |
| | To reverse the entry by which the budget was recorded at the beginning of the year. | | | |
| (C2) | Revenues ............................. | 446,000 | | |
| | Expenditures....................... | | | 418,000 |
| | Fund Balance ...................... | | | 28,000 |
| | To close the revenues and expenditures accounts. | | | |
| (C3) | Fund Balance ......................... | 15,000 | | |
| | Encumbrances ..................... | | | 15,000 |
| | To close the Encumbrances account and establish Reserve for Encumbrances, 19X1, as a reservation of fund balance. | | | |
| (C4) | Reserve for Encumbrances, 19X0 ......... | 20,000 | | |
| | Expenditures, 19X0................ | | | 19,500 |
| | Fund Balance ...................... | | | 500 |
| | To close out the accounts dealing with orders that originated in 19X0 and adjust Fund Balance accordingly. | | | |

The foregoing journal entries reverse the budget entry of January 1, 19X1, and then proceed to close the temporary proprietary accounts. If they are posted to the Fund Balance account for 19X1, they will produce an account that is directly comparable with the Analysis of Changes in Fund Balance (account) for the Year Ending December 31, 19X1 (Figure 5-4).

Finally, as noted in Chapter 4, some accountants prefer to prepare a compound closing entry at year end and obtain the data needed for the various ledger accounts. A compound closing entry for the General Fund of A Governmental Unit at December 31, 19X1 under Assumption A would be:

| | | |
|---|---|---|
| Revenues ................................... | 446,000 | |
| Appropriations ............................. | 444,000 | |
| Reserve for Encumbrances, 19X0 .............. | 20,000 | |
|     Estimated Revenues ...................... | | 450,000 |
|     Expenditures............................ | | 418,000 |
|     Encumbrances ........................... | | 15,000 |
|     Expenditures, 19X0 ...................... | | 19,500 |
|     Fund Balance ........................... | | 7,500 |

    To close the budgetary and proprietary accounts at year-end.

DETAILED ANALYSIS OF CHANGES IN THE FUND BALANCE ACCOUNT. A Detailed Analysis of Changes in Fund Balance (account) of A Governmental Unit's General Fund for the year ended December 31, 19X1 is presented in

**Figure 5-5**

A GOVERNMENTAL UNIT
General Fund
Detailed Analysis of Changes in Fund Balance (Account)
For the Fiscal Year Ended December 31, 19X1

| | Budgeted (Estimated) | Actual | Actual Fund Balance More ⟨Less⟩ Than Planned |
|---|---|---|---|
| Fund balance, January 1, 19X1.......... | $ 17,800 | $ 17,800 | $ – |
| Add: | | | |
|   Revenues ......................... | $450,000 | $446,000 | ⟨$ 4,000⟩ |
|   Reserve for encumbrances, 19X0, lapsed | 20,000 | 20,000 | – |
| | $470,000 | $466,000 | ⟨$ 4,000⟩ |
| Less: | | | |
|   Expenditures, 19X1 ................ | $444,000 | $418,000⎫ | $11,000 |
|   Encumbrances, 19X1 ............... | – | 15,000⎭ | |
|   Expenditures, 19X0 ................ | 20,000 | 19,500 | 500 |
| | $464,000 | $452,500 | 11,500 |
| Fund balance, December 31, 19X1 ...... | $ 23,800 | $ 31,300 | $ 7,500 |

Figure 5-5; an alternate format for this statement is shown in Figure 5-6. A detailed analysis adds budgetary information to the proprietary information presented in Figure 5-4 and is preferred by some accountants. The National Committee on Governmental Accounting endorses the concept of Figure 5-4— presenting only proprietary information in the analysis of changes in the Fund Balance account and presenting the budgetary data in the revenues and expenditures statements.

**Figure 5-6**

A GOVERNMENTAL UNIT
General Fund
Detailed Analysis of Changes in Fund Balance (Account)
(Alternate Format)
For the Fiscal Year Ended December 31, 19X1

| | | |
|---|---:|---:|
| Fund balance, January 1, 19X1 .............. | | $17,800 |
| Add: | | |
| Excess of estimated revenues over appropriations: | | |
|     Estimated revenues.................... | $450,000 | |
|     Appropriations ....................... | 444,000 | 6,000 |
| Excess of appropriations over expenditures and encumbrances: | | |
|     Appropriations ....................... | $444,000 | |
|     Expenditures .............. $418,000 | | |
|     Encumbrances ............ 15,000 | 433,000 | 11,000 |
| Excess of reserve for encumbrances, 19X0, over expenditures chargeable thereto: | | |
|     Reserve for encumbrances, 19X0 ......... | $ 20,000 | |
|     Expenditures chargeable thereto.......... | 19,500 | 500 |
| | | $35,300 |
| Deduct: | | |
| Excess of estimated revenues over revenues: | | |
|     Estimated revenues.................... | $450,000 | |
|     Revenues .......................... | 446,000 | 4,000 |
| Fund balance, December 31, 19X1........... | | $31,300 |

ANALYSIS OF CHANGES IN TOTAL FUND BALANCE.    Rather than limiting the analysis of changes in fund balance to the changes in the Fund Balance *account* per se, some accountants prefer to analyze *all* fund balance changes in a columnar statement such as that presented in Figure 5-7. This format permits simultaneous analyses of changes in both the total fund balance and its unreserved (Fund Balance account) and reserved components. Where budgetary data are included in the revenues and expenditures statements (rather than in the Analysis of Changes in Fund Balance), as is the customary practice, the combined analysis approach provides a simple, straightforward, and unconfusing alternative to the formats presented earlier in the chapter. Though the Analysis of Changes in Fund Balance is presented annually, whether prepared on a total fund balance or Fund Balance account basis, the statement shown in Figure 5-7 covers the two-year period ended December 31,19X1 in order that it may summarize succinctly the discussions in this chapter.

**Figure 5-7**

A GOVERNMENTAL UNIT
Analysis of Changes in Fund Balance (Total)
For the Two Fiscal Years Ended December 31, 19X1

| | | *Reserved for :\** | | |
| | *Unreserved* | *Encumbrances, 19X0* | *Encumbrances, 19X1* | *Total* |
| --- | --- | --- | --- | --- |
| Fund balance, January 1, 19X0 .... | $   – | $   – | $   – | $   – |
| Changes during 19X0: | | | | |
| Revenues ..................... | $437,700 | | | $437,700 |
| Expenditures, 19X0............ | ⟨399,900⟩ | | | ⟨399,900⟩ |
| Encumbrances, 19X0 .......... | ⟨20,000⟩ | $ 20,000 | | – |
| | $ 17,800 | $ 20,000 | $   – | $ 37,800 |
| Fund balance, December 31, 19X0 .. | $ 17,800 | $ 20,000 | $   – | $ 37,800 |
| Changes during 19X1: | | | | |
| Revenues ..................... | $446,000 | | | $446,000 |
| Expenditures, 19X1............ | ⟨418,000⟩ | | | ⟨418,000⟩ |
| Encumbrances, 19X1 .......... | ⟨15,000⟩ | | $ 15,000 | – |
| Expenditures, 19X0............ | | ⟨$19,500⟩ | | ⟨19,500⟩ |
| Reserve for Encumbrance, 19X0 Lapsed ..................... | 500 | ⟨500⟩ | | – |
| | $ 13,500 | ⟨$20,000⟩ | $ 15,000 | $  8,500 |
| Fund balance, December 31, 19X1 .. | $ 31,300 | $   – | $ 15,000 | $ 46,300 |

* A separate column is used for each reserve. Other possible General Fund reservations of Fund Balance include, among others, Reserve for Petty Cash and Reserve for Materials and Supplies Inventory.

**Question 5-1.** In your opinion, should revenues or expenditures applicable to a preceding year be credited directly to or charged directly against Fund Balance?

**Question 5-2.** (a) John Smith, a taxpayer, discovered that he had paid the same tax bill of $100 twice. He discovered the error before the end of the year, applied for a rebate, and was paid $100. How should the city record this rebate on its books? (b) Suppose he did not discover the error and was therefore not paid until the following year. How should the city record the rebate on its books?

**Question 5-3.** Included in a municipality's General Fund preclosing trial balance were the following two accounts:

> Taxes Receivable—Current ................ 5,000
> Estimated Uncollectible Current Taxes........ 6,000

It was decided to reduce the Estimated Uncollectible Current Taxes account by $1,000. Give the necessary entry or entries.

**Question 5-4.** The Ace Company rendered services on December 22,19X3 amounting to $150, but the invoice was not received until January 3, 19X4. However, the appropriation accounts had been encumbered for $160 on December 20, 19X3. Assuming the accrual basis is used, should the expenditure be reported in 19X3 or 19X4? Record the transaction in the journal.

**Question 5-5.** In a certain municipality, bonds in the amount of $10,000 and interest in the amount of $5,000 payable by the General Fund matured on May 1, 19X0. Appropriations for these items were made on January 2, 19X0. What entry should be made to record these current liabilities and when should it be made (that is, on January 2, 19X0, or on May 1, 19X0)?

**Question 5-6.** Referring to Figure 5-1, suppose that, after the balance sheet illustrated there was prepared but before the end of the year, additional revenues amounting to $5,000 were collected. Would the asset total be changed? Would the Fund Balance be affected?

**Question 5-7.** Because of legal technicalities, the tax on a certain property will not be collected until 5 years from the date of the balance sheet, December 31, 19X0. There is some certainty that it will be collected at that time. Disregarding penalties and interest, how should these taxes be handled in the balance sheet of December 31, 19X0?

**Question 5-8.** The following is the balance sheet of the General Fund of the County of X:

COUNTY OF X

General Fund

Balance Sheet

December 31, 19X3

*Assets*

| | | |
|---|---:|---:|
| Cash ................................... | | $ 50,000 |
| Taxes receivable ........................ | $200,000 | |
| Less:   Estimated uncollectible taxes ........ | 30,000 | 170,000 |
| Amount to be provided for retirement | | |
| of funding bonds ....................... | | 280,000 |
| | | $500,000 |

*Liabilities and Fund Balance*

Liabilities:

Funding Bonds of 19W7 (that is, bonds issued
to finance a deficit) .................... $280,000

Accounts payable ...................... 70,000      $350,000

Fund balance ............................                150,000

$500,000

The funding bonds (total issued, $1,000,000) were issued in 19W7 to finance accumulated deficits. They have been retired at the rate of $60,000 each January.
(a) Is the amount of Fund Balance shown in this statement correct? (b) Does the statement show the true financial condition of the General Fund? (c) If not, recast the balance sheet so as to show the true financial condition of this Fund.

**Question 5-9.** Compare the meaning of the term Fund Balance with that of the Retained Earnings of a corporation.

**Question 5-10.** (a) What is the purpose of Fund Balance reserves in the General Fund?
(b) Do you think that Fund Balance reserves for Cash, Petty Cash, Taxes Receivable, Inventories, and Due from Other Funds are desirable? Consider each separately in your answer.

**Question 5-11.** What is the nature of a Reserve for Encumbrances account in a governmental unit governed by a lapsing law like that of Assumption A in the text:
(a)   During the year in which the purchase order was placed?
(b)   In the year-end balance sheet?
(c)   During the year subsequent to that in which the purchase order was placed?

**Problem 5-1.** The schedules on page 173 list account balances from the preclosing trial balances of a number of separate General or Special Revenue Funds at December 31, 19X3. For each case the requirements are as follows:
(a)   Prepare closing entries.
(b)   Prepare an analysis of changes in Fund Balance for the year ending December 31, 19X3. Your instructor may want to specify that one or more be detailed.
(c)   Prepare a balance sheet at December 31, 19X3.
(d)   In Cases I, II, III, IV, VI and VIII prepare a detailed analysis of changes in Fund Balance as if the fund had been operated under a law like that of Assumption B in the text since its inception. Assume that management and council have operated in such a way that all transactions took place in the same way and at the same time as under Assumption A.

**Problems 5-2 through 5-6.** Using the materials prepared for the respective problems 4-2 through 4-6, prepare (a) a preclosing balance sheet, (b) a postclosing balance sheet, and (c) an analysis of changes in Fund Balance. (A preclosing balance sheet would not ordinarily be prepared by a government. You are asked to prepare one to give you practice in the preparation of *interim* balance sheets.)

**Problem 5-7.** The Sleepy Haven Township's adjusted trial balance for the General Fund as at the close of its fiscal year ending June 30, 19X2, is shown on page 174.

## DATA FOR PROBLEM 5-1

| | Case I | Case II | Case III | Case IV | Case V | Case VI | Case VII | Case VIII |
|---|---|---|---|---|---|---|---|---|
| Cash | 25,000 | 45,000 | 30,000 | 35,000 | 45,000 | 110 | 100 | 6,500 |
| Taxes Receivable—Current | 3,000 | 30,000 | 6,000 | 17,000 | 30,000 | | | |
| Estimated Uncollectible Current Taxes | 2,000 | 3,000 | 2,000 | 2,000 | 3,500 | | | |
| Taxes Receivable—Delinquent | | | | | | 75 | 75 | 30,000 |
| Estimated Uncollectible Delinquent Taxes | | | | | | 5 | 5 | 4,000 |
| Accounts Receivable | | | | | | | | 10,000 |
| Estimated Uncollectible Accounts Receivable | | | | | | | | 1,000 |
| Inventory | 4,000 | | 6,000 | | | | | |
| Vouchers Payable | 3,500 | 27,000 | 7,000 | 7,500 | 28,000 | 65 | 65 | 22,000 |
| Due to Intragovernmental Service Fund | | | | | | | | 3,000 |
| Reserve for Encumbrances | 11,000 | 15,000 | 15,000 | 11,000 | 15,000 | 35 | 35 | 12,000 |
| Reserve for Encumbrances of Prior Years | 5,000 | 12,000 | 8,000 | 8,750 | | 40 | | 5,000 |
| Reserve for Inventory | 4,000 | | 6,000 | | | | | |
| Fund Balance | 22,500 | 17,400 | ? | 19,350 | ? | 105 | 105 | ? |
| Estimated Revenues | 200,000 | 360,000 | 300,000 | 405,000 | 300,000 | 500 | 500 | 400,000 |
| Revenues | 184,500 | 366,000 | 280,000 | 407,450 | 310,000 | 450 | 450 | 385,000 |
| Appropriations | 190,000 | 375,000 | 290,000 | 408,000 | 333,000 | 525 | 525 | 420,000 |
| Expenditures | 175,000 | 354,000 | 270,000 | 387,350 | 305,000 | 475 | 475 | 402,000 |
| Encumbrances | 11,000 | 15,000 | 15,000 | 11,000 | 15,000 | 35 | 35 | 12,000 |
| Expenditures Chargeable to Reserve for Encumbrances of Prior Years | 4,500 | 11,400 | 7,000 | 8,700 | | 30 | | 4,900 |

| | | |
|---|---:|---:|
| Cash ................................... | $ 1,100 | |
| Taxes Receivable—Current* ................ | 8,200 | |
| Estimated Uncollectible Taxes—Current ...... | | 150 |
| Taxes Receivable—Delinquent .............. | 2,500 | |
| Estimated Uncollectible Taxes—Delinquent ... | | 1,650 |
| Miscellaneous Accounts Receivable........... | 4,000 | |
| Estimated Uncollectible Accounts ........... | | 400 |
| Due from Intragovernmental Service Fund .... | 5,000 | |
| Expenditures† ........................... | 75,500 | |
| Encumbrances ........................... | 3,700 | |
| Revenues** ............................. | | 6,000 |
| Due to Utility Fund ...................... | | 1,000 |
| Vouchers Payable ........................ | | 2,000 |
| Reserve for Encumbrances—Prior Year ....... | | 4,400 |
| Reserve for Encumbrances ................. | | 3,700 |
| Direct Credit to Fund Balance†† ............ | | 700 |
| Appropriations ........................... | | 72,000 |
| Fund Balance ............................ | | 8,000 |
| | $100,000 | $100,000 |

\* The current tax roll and miscellaneous accounts receivable, recorded on the accrual basis as sources of revenue, amounted to $50,000 and $20,000, respectively. These items have been recorded on the books subject to a 2% provision for uncollectible accounts.

† Includes $4,250 paid during the fiscal year in settlement of all purchase orders outstanding at the beginning of the fiscal year.

\*\* Represents the difference between the budgeted (estimated) revenue of $70,000 and the actual revenue realized during the fiscal year.

†† Represents the proceeds from sale of equipment damaged by fire.

Required:

(1) Prepare an Analysis of Changes in Fund Balance for the year ending June 30, 19X2.

(2) Prepare a formal Balance Sheet at June 30, 19X2. (AICPA adapted.)

**Problem 5-8.** The following balances of the accounts of the General Fund of the City of Pineville were those in the accounts just before the closing entries were made on December 31, 19X0.

| | | |
|---|---:|---:|
| Actual Revenues ........................ | | $407,450 |
| Appropriations ........................... | | 408,000 |
| Cash .................................... | $ 57,480 | |
| Due from Other Funds .................... | 14,500 | |
| Encumbrances ........................... | 18,640 | |
| Estimated Revenues....................... | 405,000 | |
| Expenditures ........................... | 387,350 | |

| | | |
|---|---:|---:|
| Expenditures Chargeable to Reserve for Encumbrances, Prior Years .............. | 8,700 | |
| Reserve for Encumbrances, Current Year ..... | | 18,640 |
| Reserve for Encumbrances, Prior Years ....... | | 8,750 |
| Reserve for Stores ......................... | | 2,500 |
| Reserve for Uncollected Taxes .............. | | 46,420 |
| Stores Inventory ........................... | 2,250 | |
| Tax Anticipation Notes Payable ............. | | 20,000 |
| Taxes Receivable........................... | 46,420 | |
| Fund Balance .............................. | | 17,450 |
| Vouchers Payable .......................... | | 11,130 |

Additional information which is available is summarized as follows:
1.  A special reserve for contingencies in the amount of $2,000 as of December 31, 19W9, was closed out during the year when it was proved to have been unnecessary.
2.  A reserve for stores was created out of fund balance at December 31, 19X0, by order of the Council in the amount of $2,500.
3.  Taxes of $1,000, levied and collected in prior years, were refunded during the year.
Prepare a formal analysis of changes in fund balance for the City of Pineville on the basis of the information given above.

**Problem 5-9.**  The following closing entries were made for Arizona City at December 31, 19X0:

| | | | |
|---|---|---:|---:|
| (a) | Revenues ........................... | $328,000 | |
| | Fund Balance ...................... | 5,000 | |
| | Estimated Revenues ................ | | $333,000 |
| (b) | Appropriations ...................... | 350,000 | |
| | Reserve for Encumbrances ............ | 15,000 | |
| | Expenditures ...................... | | 320,000 |
| | Encumbrances ..................... | | 15,000 |
| | Fund Balance ..................... | | 30,000 |
| (c) | Fund Balance ...................... | 1,500 | |
| | Reserve for Inventory .............. | | 1,500 |

The following additional data were known:
1.  Prior to the posting of the above closing entries, the balance of the Fund Balance account was $20,000.
2.  At December 31, 19W9, the balance in the Encumbrances account was $20,000. The orders included in that total were received and paid for in 19X0.
3.  Arizona City has not changed its method of closing since it was incorporated on January 1, 19W9.
4.  On September 30, 19X0, the City Council approved a change of the amount of the petty cash fund and its related reserve from $2,500 to $2,000.
Prepare a statement analyzing the changes in Fund Balance for the year ended December 31, 19X0.

# 6

# Revenue Accounting

In a fund accounting context, revenues are " additions to assets which: (a) do not increase any liability; (b) do not represent the recovery of an expenditure; (c) do not represent the cancellation of certain liabilities without a corresponding increase in other liabilities or a decrease in assets; and (d) do not represent contributions of fund capital in Enterprise and Intragovernmental Service Funds."[1] More generally, revenues are increases in assets or decreases in liabilities that increase the residual equity of a fund.

## CLASSIFICATION OF REVENUE ACCOUNTS

The objective in creating a chart of accounts is to provide a vehicle for summarizing information in a useful form. Revenues are classified in accounts in order to produce information that management may use to (1) prepare and control the budget, (2) control the collection of revenues, (3) prepare financial statements for reporting to the public, and (4) prepare financial statistics. A classification of revenue accounts by source (together with appropriate reports) provides the basic data for all these purposes.

GENERAL FUND REVENUES. Revenues must be related in the accounts to the

[1] *GAAFR,* p. 168.

funds to which the revenues are applicable. The following are the main revenue classes for the General Fund:

Taxes (including penalties and interest on delinquent taxes)
Licenses and permits
Intergovernmental revenues (including grants, shared revenues, and payments in lieu of taxes)
Charges for services (excluding revenues of public enterprises)
Fines and forfeits
Miscellaneous revenues (including interest earnings, rents and royalties, sales of and compensation for loss of fixed assets, contributions from public enterprises, escheats, contributions and donations from private sources, and balances from discontinued funds)

The classes given above are not account titles. They are broad group headings, just as Current Assets and Fixed Assets are category groupings on the balance sheet of a private enterprise, which are useful for reporting purposes. For example, no account would be set up for fines and forfeits. Instead, individual accounts would be provided for each type of revenue falling in that class, including Court Fines, Library Fines, and Forfeits. To arrive at the total revenue accrued or received from fines and forfeits it would be necessary to combine the balances of these accounts.

REVENUES OF OTHER FUNDS. The revenue classes described for the General Fund are suitable for the funds of a governmental unit other than Enterprise, Intragovernmental Service, and Trust and Agency Funds. For example, taxes may be a revenue source of Special Revenue Funds and Debt Service Funds, while a special assessments category may be added to either the taxes or miscellaneous revenue classification, as appropriate, for the Special Assessment Fund. Similarly, accounts entitled Sales of Bonds and Premiums on Bonds Sold may be added to the Miscellaneous Revenue category for Capital Projects Funds. Clearly, no other fund is likely to have the variety of revenue sources that the General Fund has.

Enterprise and Intragovernmental Service Funds use account titles similar to those that would be used for the revenue accounts of business enterprises. Too, capital and revenue transactions will be carefully distinguished in the accounts of these nonexpendable funds; both are generally considered revenues in expendable fund accounting.

DISTINCTION BETWEEN REVENUES OF A FUND AND REVENUES OF A GOVERNMENTAL UNIT. A distinction must be made between the revenues of a fund and the revenues of the governmental unit as a whole. Some receipts or accruals constitute fund revenues but are not revenues of the governmental unit, i.e., they increase the ownership equity of the fund but not that of the unit. To illustrate, proceeds from the sale of bonds are revenues of the Capital Projects Fund because they increase its ownership equity and do not create any liability in that Fund. They are not, however, revenues of the governmental unit, since the bonds are a liability of the unit. Similarly, charges for services rendered to departments financed out of the General Fund are revenues of the Intragovernmental Service Fund but not of the governmental unit as a whole, since these charges must be paid by the departments. Other examples are balances from discontinued funds and contributions from public enterprises.

In classifying revenues for the purpose of state-wide or national financial statistics, only those of the governmental unit as a whole should be included. These usually consist of the revenues of the General Fund, revenues of Special Revenue Funds, special assessments collected from property owners, and the revenues of enterprises operated by the governmental unit. Further, some accountants prefer to supplement the fund statements with consolidated or consolidating statements for these funds, the unit as a whole, or its major subdivisions, where interfund revenues are significant in amount. Others prefer to refer to interfund revenues as "transfers" rather than as "revenues."

This chapter is concerned with the accounting for the principal sources of revenues of the General Fund and Special Revenue Funds. Those types of revenue that are peculiar to another fund, such as special assessments and proceeds from the sale of bonds, are discussed with the related fund.

## TAXES

A tax is a forced contribution made to a government to meet public needs. Typically, the amount of the tax bears no direct relationship to any benefit received by the taxpayer.

The amount of any tax is computed by the application of a rate or rates set by the governmental unit to a defined base, such as value of property, amount of income, or number of units. From the standpoint of administration, taxes may be divided into two groups—those that are self-assessing and those that are not. The latter group, of which the general property tax on realty (real property) and personalty (personal property) is the chief representative, requires that the governmental unit take action to establish the amount of the tax base to which the rate or rates will be applied. Taxes on income, inheritance, severance of natural resources, gasoline, general sales, tobacco, alcoholic beverages, and chain stores are self-assessing; that is, the taxpayer is expected to determine the amount of the tax base, apply the proper rate or rates thereto, and submit the payment with the return that shows the computation.

When the taxpayer has thus assessed his own tax, verification of the amount of tax requires (1) a determination that the tax base has been properly reported by the taxpayer and (2) a determination that the proper rates have been applied accurately to the tax base to arrive at the total amount of the tax. The most difficult problem is the first, of course; for example, in the case of the income tax it is necessary to ascertain that all income that should have been reported has been disclosed. Furthermore, investigation should not be limited to those taxpayers who file returns. The governmental unit must also make certain that all taxpayers who should pay taxes have filed returns.

Self-assessing taxes are usually accounted for on a cash basis because the return and the remittance are ordinarily made at the same time. Further, there may be no objectively measurable basis upon which to set up accruals because the amount of the tax is not known before the return is filed. In some jurisdictions income tax returns are filed at a specified time and the tax is paid in installments. In such a case, since the amount of the tax is known, the revenues are accrued as soon as the return is filed. Some taxes require the attachment of stamps to an article to indicate that the tax has been paid. For example, liquor taxes and tobacco taxes are frequently paid through the purchase of stamps to be affixed to bottles or packages. In such cases the taxes are considered to be revenue as soon as the stamps are sold to the manufacturer, dealer, or other businessman, even though the articles to which the stamps are affixed may not be sold for an indefinite period following the purchase of the tax stamps.

## General Property Taxes

General property taxes are ad valorem taxes in proportion to the assessed valuation of real or personal property. The procedure in the administration of general property taxes is as follows: (1) The assessed valuation of each piece of real property and of the taxable personal property of each taxpayer is determined by the local tax assessor; (2) a local board of review hears complaints regarding assessments; (3) county and state boards of equalization assign equalized values to taxing districts; (4) the legislative body levies the total amount of taxes which it needs, but not in excess of the amount permitted by law; (5) the tax levy is distributed among taxpayers on the basis of the assessed value of property owned by them; (6) taxpayers are billed; (7) tax collections are credited to taxpayers' accounts; (8) tax collections are enforced by the imposition of penalties and the sale of property for taxes. Each of these steps in general property tax administration is discussed below.

ASSESSMENT OF PROPERTY. The valuing of property for purposes of taxation is called assessment. The assessment of property for local taxes is usually performed by an elected or appointed official known as an assessor. The assessed value of each piece of real property or of the personal property of every taxpayer is recorded on a sheet known as an assessment roll, which contains columns entitled as follows for the tax roll of real property:

Taxpayer's Name and General Description of Property
Block and Lot Number
Value of Land
Value of Improvements
Total Assessed Valuation

Each such sheet contains the assessed value of several pieces of property or the assessed values of the personal property of several owners. In the case of real property, for each piece of property there will be a separate continuing record on which the assessed valuation for that piece alone, together with its full description, is recorded.

The total assessed value of real estate in the governmental unit is the sum of the assessed values of the individual pieces of property within its jurisdiction; the total assessed value of personal property is the sum of the assessed values of the personal property of the individual owners residing within the limits of the governmental unit. Thus several governmental units, such as a state, county, city, and school district, may tax each piece of property. Ordinarily only one of these jurisdictions will have the assessment responsibility, and separate assessment rolls are prepared for each of the governmental units for the property within its jurisdiction.

REVIEW OF ASSESSMENT. After each property owner is notified of the assessment of his property, he is permitted to protest his assessment to a local reviewing board, which may be composed of officials of the government or of non-official residents of the governmental unit. The board hears objections to assessments, weighs the evidence, and changes the assessment if it considers a change to be proper. A taxpayer who is not satisfied with board action may appeal his assessment to the courts.

EQUALIZATION OF ASSESSMENTS. In most states the assessment of property is made by a local government. The taxes of the state and perhaps even the county are, therefore, levied on the basis of assessments made by a number of different assessors, each of whom may have different ideas as to the valuations that should be assigned to property. The law usually requires that the assessment be made at a figure which is the equivalent of "fair market value" in the accountant's terminology, but in practice the actual valuations in a state or even a county will cover a wide range of percentages of market value. Let us assume that the following information is available:

| Taxing District | Market Values, All Property | Assessed Value, All Property | City Levies | Tax Rate 4 ÷ 3 |
|---|---|---|---|---|
| 1 | 2 | 3 | 4 | 5 |
| City A | 10,000,000 | 10,000,000 | 100,000 | 1% |
| City B | 10,000,000 | 5,000,000 | 100,000 | 2% |

If taxpayer Able of City A and taxpayer Baker of City B have properties that have a market value of $10,000, each will pay city taxes of $100. But suppose that City A and City B are in the same county and that the county tax rate is set at 1 percent of assessed values. Able's county tax will be $100, while Baker's will be one-half that amount for property having the same market value.

The inequity described in the preceding paragraph can be avoided if the county will equalize assessments. Equalization requires that the county (1) supervise the assessors in its jurisdiction so that they make their assessments at a uniform percentage of fair market value or (2) assign taxes to be collected from the assessing districts on the basis of market values rather than assessed values. In the latter case the county would assign the amount of tax to be collected from each city; in the foregoing illustration City A and City B, both having market values of all property of $10,000,000, should be assigned the same amount, let us say $50,000. County tax rates in the two cities then would be computed as follows:

| Taxing District | Assessed Value, All Property | County Levy | County Tax Rate |
|---|---|---|---|
| 1 | 2 | 3 | 4 |
| City A | 10,000,000 | 50,000 | .5% |
| City B | 5,000,000 | 50,000 | 1.0% |

Lack of equalization or poor equalization leads to "competitive underassessment" in the several assessing districts and to widespread dissatisfaction with the property tax as a revenue source.

LEVYING THE TAX. Taxes are levied through the passage of a tax levy act or ordinance, usually passed at the time the appropriation act or ordinance is passed. The levy is ordinarily applicable to only one year.

Tax levies are made in one or two lump sums in some governmental units, whereas in others the levies are very detailed. A statute or even a charter may require that certain taxes are to be levied for specified purposes. In that event the legislative body must indicate specifically the amount levied for each purpose. Another effect of detailed tax levies is to require the creation of Special Revenue Funds. For example, if a special levy is made for parks, it is necessary to create a Special Revenue Fund for parks to insure that the taxes collected are not used for any other purposes.

*Determining the tax rate.* As indicated above, the tax rate is determined by dividing the amount of taxes levied by the assessed valuation. Thus, if a government has an assessed valuation of $10,000,000 and its total tax levy is $250,000, the tax rate is 2.5 percent of or 25 mills per dollar of assessed value ($250,000 ÷ $10,000,000). The total tax rate consists of the tax rate for general purposes and special tax rates, if any, for particular purposes. For example, if we assume that the total levy of $250,000 consisted of $150,000 for general purposes, $10,000 for park purposes, $50,000 for schools, and $40,000 for debt service, the tax rates would be as follows:

| Purpose | Rate (in mills per dollar of assessed value) |
|---|---|
| General | 15 |
| Parks | 1 |
| Schools | 5 |
| Debt Service | 4 |
| | 25 |

Maximum tax rates are frequently prescribed for governmental units by constitution, statutes, or charters. The legislative body must recognize such limitations as it plans the total levy. If the amount the legislative body would like to produce from the tax will produce a rate higher than the maximum permitted by law, the amount of the levy must be reduced. When a government finds itself thus limited in the amount of taxes it can levy, it would ordinarily review the assessment process in the hope that the total assessed valuation, the tax base, could be increased.

*Determining the amount due from each taxpayer.* The amount of tax due from each taxpayer is arrived at by multiplying the assessed value of his property by the tax rate. For example, if a taxpayer owns real estate with an assessed value of $10,000 and the city tax rate is 25 mills per dollar of assessed value, his city tax will be $250 ($10,000 × .025).

SETTING UP TAXES RECEIVABLE AND BILLING TAXPAYERS. As soon as the amount due from each taxpayer is determined, it is entered on the tax roll.

*The tax roll.* A tax roll is a record showing the amount of taxes levied against each piece of real property and against each owner of personal property.

The assessment roll previously described may be used for this purpose by the addition of several columns, or tax rolls may be prepared separately. If the assessment and tax rolls are combined, the column headings may be as follows:

Taxpayer's Name and General Description of Property
Block and Lot Number
Value of Land
Value of Improvements
Total Assessed Valuation
Composite Tax Rate
Total Tax
Bill Number
Payment
    Date Paid
    Amount of Tax
    Penalties
Liens

The foregoing list of column headings indicates that the tax roll is to be used not only for the recording of the amount of taxes levied but also for tax collections. In addition, it will serve as a subsidiary ledger supporting the Taxes Receivable controlling accounts in the general ledger. If interest and penalties on delinquent taxes are accrued at the end of each year, provision is made for showing the accruals.

A more convenient subsidiary ledger may be maintained on individual property tax cards that contain a description of each piece of property, the owner's name, assessment information, tax levy information, and payment information. They provide a continuous tax history of each piece of property for, unlike the tax roll, a new card is not made out for each tax levy. These cards are similar to the accounts receivable subsidiary ledger accounts of a commercial enterprise, except that they are organized by items of property rather than by taxpayer. An example of such a card is shown in Figure 6-1.

Notice that the focus of the real estate tax ledger is on the property. This facilitates grouping of the property by districts, both on the assessment roll and on the tax roll, and facilitates calculation of total assessed valuations and tax levies by jurisdictions. Personal property levies are ordinarily handled separately from the property tax levy; that is, a taxpayer's real property and personal property taxes are shown on separate bills and recorded in separate subsidiary records.

*Recording taxes on the books.* Some of the entries to record taxes on the books have already been introduced in the General Fund chapter. For example, when taxes are levied, the accrual basis entry in each fund is a debit to Taxes Receivable—Current and credits to Estimated Uncollectible Current Taxes and

Figure 6-1

## A GOVERNMENTAL UNIT
### Real Estate Tax Ledger

Ward _____ Lot _____  Property No. _____

Subdivision _____ County Lot _____ Block _____ Acres _____

House No. _____ Street _____ Description _____

Address _____

| Assessed to | Year | Ref. | Assessed Valuation | Composite Tax Rate | Amount of Tax | Paid or Canceled | | | Balance of Tax |
|---|---|---|---|---|---|---|---|---|---|
| | | | | | | Date | Taxes | Int. & P'lty | |
| | | | | | | | | | |

184

to Revenues. Later, when the taxes become delinquent, an entry is made debiting Taxes Receivable—Delinquent and Estimated Uncollectible Current Taxes and crediting Taxes Receivable—Current and Estimated Uncollectible Delinquent Taxes.

It should be emphasized at this point that separate Taxes Receivable accounts should be set up for each kind of taxes, such as real property taxes, personal property taxes, and income taxes that may have been accrued. Further, all of these taxes should be recorded in such a way that the amount applicable to each individual year can be readily determined. One way to accomplish this objective is to set up control accounts for each kind of taxes receivable by years.

Because the proportion of the total tax levy made for each purpose may vary from year to year, it is important to be able to identify each year's levy so that the proper Taxes Receivable accounts may be credited and the proceeds of tax collections may be allocated to the proper fund. For example, suppose that the tax levy is $100,000 both for this year and for last year but that the levies are divided as follows:

| | This Year | | Last Year | |
| Purpose | Amount Levied | Percentage of Total | Amount Levied | Percentage of Total |
| --- | --- | --- | --- | --- |
| General | $ 46,700 | 46.7 | $ 40,000 | 40.0 |
| Parks | 13,300 | 13.3 | 13,300 | 13.3 |
| Schools | 26,700 | 26.7 | 33,400 | 33.4 |
| Sinking Fund | 13,300 | 13.3 | 13,300 | 13.3 |
| | $100,000 | 100.0 | $100,000 | 100.0 |

The part of the proceeds of this year's tax levy that is to be placed in the General Fund is found by multiplying the amount collected from the levy by 46.7 percent. Thus, if $90,000 is collected, $42,030 is placed to the credit of the General Fund ($90,000 × 46.7 percent). On the other hand the amount of collections from last year's levy that is to be placed to the credit of the General Fund is obtained by multiplying the collections from that levy by 40 percent. For example, if collections amount to $10,000, the sum of $4,000 ($10,000 × 40 percent) is placed to the credit of the General Fund. Collections from the other levies are allocated to the proper funds in the same manner. It is evident, therefore, that tax collections cannot be applied to the proper funds unless the amount collected from each levy is known.

RECORDING TAX COLLECTIONS.   Let us assume that if full details regarding delinquent taxes were to be shown on the balance sheet, the Taxes Receivable account for a governmental unit would appear as follows:

Real Property Taxes Receivable—Delinquent:

| | | | |
|---|---:|---:|---:|
| Levy of 19X9 | $30,000 | | |
| 19X8 | 20,000 | | |
| 19X7 | 10,000 | | |
| 19X6 | 5,000 | | |
| 19X5 and prior | 3,000 | $68,000 | |
| Less: Estimated Uncollectible | | | |
| Delinquent Taxes | | 10,000 | $58,000 |

Personal Property Taxes Receivable—Delinquent:

| | | | |
|---|---:|---:|---:|
| Levy of 19X9 | $20,000 | | |
| 19X8 | 15,000 | | |
| 19X7 | 10,000 | | |
| 19X6 | 4,000 | | |
| 19X5 and prior | 5,000 | $54,000 | |
| Less: Estimated Uncollectible | | | |
| Delinquent Taxes | | 15,000 | 39,000 |
| Total Taxes Receivable—Delinquent .... | | | $97,000 |

As taxes are collected, the entry in the recipient fund is as follows:

| | | |
|---|---:|---:|
| Cash | 100,000 | |
| Taxes Receivable—Current | | 80,000 |
| Taxes Receivable—Delinquent | | 20,000 |

To record collection of current and delinquent taxes, as follows:

| Year of Levy | Amount |
|---|---:|
| 19Y0 (Current) | $ 80,000 |
| 19X9 | 10,000 |
| 19X8 | 5,000 |
| 19X7 | 3,000 |
| 19X6 | 1,000 |
| 19X5 | 500 |
| 19X4 | 500 |
| | $100,000 |

*Collection of a government's taxes by another unit.* Frequently one governmental unit acts as collecting agent for other units. In that case, each governmental unit certifies its tax levy to the collecting unit, which in turn bills the taxpayers. These taxes are handled by the collecting unit in an Agency Fund, for which the accounting procedures are discussed in Chapter 12.

The accounting procedure thus far outlined is for governmental units that collect their own taxes, but it is also applicable to those that do not collect their own taxes. In the latter case the collecting unit transmits a report indicating the amount collected from each year's levy of real property taxes and of personal property taxes. The receiving unit, on the basis of this report, distributes the proceeds among the various funds and credits the proper general ledger accounts. Thus the only difference between the accounting procedure for a governmental unit that collects its own taxes and one that does not is that the latter does not prepare a tax roll and probably does not keep a record of the amounts paid or owed by the individual taxpayers. The latter records are kept for it by the collecting governmental unit.

*Discounts on taxes.* A few governmental units allow discounts on taxes paid before a certain date. These discounts should be considered as revenue deductions; that is, the tax revenues should be credited only for the net amount of the tax, and an Estimated Discounts on Taxes account should be provided. For example, if the tax levy was $300,000, on which it is estimated that discounts of $2,000 will be taken, the entry to record the levy of the tax and the estimate of discounts is as follows:

| | | |
|---|---:|---:|
| Taxes Receivable—Current .................... | 300,000 | |
|     Estimated Uncollectible Current Taxes ...... | | 9,000 |
|     Estimated Discounts on Taxes ............. | | 2,000 |
|     Revenues ............................... | | 289,000 |
|     To record levy of taxes and estimated losses as | | |
|     well as estimated discounts to be taken. | | |

As taxes are collected and discounts are taken, the discounts are charged against the estimate. For example, if tax collections amounted to $150,000 and discounts to the amount of $1,500 had been taken, the entry to record the transaction would be as follows:

| | | |
|---|---:|---:|
| Cash......................................... | 150,000 | |
| Estimated Discounts on Taxes ................. | 1,500 | |
|     Taxes Receivable—Current ................ | | 151,500 |
|     To record collection of taxes and net discounts | | |
|     thereon. | | |

As the discount period is passed, the following entry is made:

| | | |
|---|---:|---:|
| Estimated Discounts on Taxes ................. | 500 | |
|     Revenues ............................... | | 500 |
|     To record increase in revenues by amount of esti- | | |
|     mated discounts which were not taken. | | |

In a few governmental units the law requires that discounts be authorized by appropriations. In such cases the levy of taxes is recorded by the standard entry and the collection of taxes would signal the following entry:

```
Cash.......................................   XX
Expenditures...............................    X
    Taxes Receivable—Current ................            XXX
    To record collection of taxes and the allowance of
    discounts.
```

This method of accounting for discounts has the effect of overstating both revenues and expenditures and is therefore not desirable. It should be used only in cases where the law makes it impossible to use the first method.

*Taxes collected in advance.*   Sometimes a taxpayer will pay his subsequent years taxes before they are due, possibly before the tax has been levied or billed. Such tax collections are subsequent period revenue, not revenue of the period in which they are collected. They may be recorded either in the General Fund or in a Trust Fund, the entry in either case being as follows:

```
Cash.......................................   2,500
    Taxes Collected in Advance ..................           2,500
    To record collection of taxes on next year's roll.
```

These tax collections represent a deferred credit to revenues, and the Taxes Collected in Advance account is therefore shown as a deferred credit—a liability— on the balance sheet. The entries made subsequently, when the taxes are levied and the Taxes Receivable accounts are set up, depend on where the transaction is originally recorded. If the cash from the advance tax collections was recorded in a Trust Fund, an entry must be made transferring the money out of that fund to the proper funds. This Trust Fund entry is as follows:

```
Taxes Collected in Advance (or Trust Fund Balance) ..   2,500
    Cash.......................................           2,500
    To record paying to each fund of proper amount of
    taxes belonging to it.
```

The corresponding entry in each of the funds receiving the cash is

```
Cash.......................................   1,000
    Taxes Receivable—Current ..................           1,000
    To record receipt of cash from Trust Fund representing
    share of taxes collected in advance applicable to this
    fund.
```

If, on the other hand, the taxes collected in advance are recorded in the General Fund, and the taxes are also applicable to other funds, the entry after the Taxes Receivable accounts are set up is as follows:

Taxes Collected in Advance ...................... 2,500
    Taxes Receivable—Current ...................              1,000
    Cash.......................................              1,500
    To record application of taxes collected in advance to
    reduce taxes receivable of General Fund and to record
    transfer of cash to other funds on account of advanced
    tax collections applicable to them.

In each of the other funds affected, an entry is made debiting Cash and crediting Taxes Receivable—Current.

If the amount of taxes collected in advance exceeds the amount levied, the excess is either refunded or continues as a deferred credit until the next levy is made. If, on the other hand, the amount collected is less than the amount levied, the taxpayer is billed for the difference.

ENFORCING THE COLLECTION OF TAXES.  The laws applicable to most jurisdictions prescribe a date after which unpaid taxes become delinquent, whereupon they are subject to specified penalties and to the accrual of interest. Taxes, interest, and penalties in most states become a lien against property without any action on the part of the governmental unit. At the expiration of a specified period of time the governmental unit has the right to sell the property in order to satisfy its lien. Any excess of the amount received from the sale of the property over the amount of taxes, interest, penalties, and the cost of holding the sale is turned over to the property owner. If the proceeds from the sale of the property are insufficient to cover the amount due, the law may or may not make the property owner liable for the difference.

The property owner is given the privilege of redeeming the property within a certain period of time. If the property was purchased by an individual, it can be redeemed by payment to the buyer of the purchase price plus interest. If it was bid in by the governmental unit, the property can be redeemed by payment of the taxes, interest, penalties, and other charges. If the property is not redeemed by the specified date, the acquirer secures title.

In the usual case more than one governmental unit is involved in the process of selling property for delinquent taxes and in the related redemption of the property. If each government were left to enforce its own lien and sell the property for taxes, not only would the cost of sale be greatly increased but such a procedure would also result in considerable confusion. Accordingly, the statutes ordinarily make provision for the transfer of delinquent tax rolls to a single governmental unit. This unit attempts to collect the delinquent taxes and goes through all the steps necessary to enforce the lien. In the absence of statutory provisions, each unit receives from the collecting unit its proportionate share of tax collections.

*Recording interest and penalties on taxes.*  Some governmental units accrue interest and penalties on delinquent taxes, while others do not record them as revenues until they are collected. If they are accrued, they are added to the tax roll or other subsidiary record. The entry to record the accrual of interest and penalties is as follows:

```
Interest and Penalties Receivable ................     15,000
     Estimated Uncollectible Interest and
          Penalties ...............................                1,000
     Revenues ..................................               14,000
     To record revenues from interest and penalties on
     delinquent taxes and to allow for the amount of
     such revenues that it is estimated will never be col-
     lected.
```

If interest and penalties are not accrued, but are recorded as revenues only at the time the cash is received, the entry to record revenues from this source is as follows:

```
Cash.......................................     10,000
     Revenues ..................................               10,000
     To record receipt of interest and penalties on delin-
     quent taxes.
```

In both of the foregoing cases, it is essential to identify the revenues from interest and penalties with the particular tax levy to which they apply. The reasons for this distinction are the same as those given for recording taxes receivable by year of levy.

*Accounting for tax sales.*   When the period specified by law is passed without payment of taxes, penalties, and interest, the assets are converted into tax liens:

```
Tax Liens Receivable .........................     28,000
     Taxes Receivable—Delinquent ..............               25,000
     Interest and Penalties Receivable on Taxes ....                3,000
     To record conversion of delinquent taxes and of
     interest and penalties thereon to tax liens, as follows:
```

| Levy of | Taxes | Interest and Penalties | Total |
|---------|-------|-----------|-------|
| 19X8 | $10,000 | $1,000 | $11,000 |
| 19X7 | 15,000 | 2,000 | 17,000 |
| | $25,000 | $3,000 | $28,000 |

Subsidiary taxes and interest receivable records for each of the pieces of property are, of course, credited at this time; and subsidiary records of the individual tax liens would be established.

Court and other costs are ordinarily incurred in the process of converting property into tax liens and in the subsequent effort to sell the properties. In some jurisdictions the costs of holding a tax sale are charged to expenditures because the law provides that such costs are covered by interest and penalties levied against the property. In most cases, however, the cost should be added to the amount of the tax lien:

| | | |
|---|---|---|
| Tax Liens Receivable ............................ | 1,000 | |
| Cash........................................ | | 1,000 |

To record court costs and other costs required in the conversion of delinquent taxes and interest and penalties thereon into tax liens.

At the time the assets are converted into tax liens, the related estimated uncollectible accounts are converted into Estimated Uncollectible Tax Liens accounts. The amount to be transferred is necessarily an estimate of the results of the tax sale, together with an estimate of the proper allowances for uncollectible delinquent taxes and interest and penalties.

| | | |
|---|---|---|
| Estimated Uncollectible Delinquent Taxes ........... | 2,000 | |
| Estimated Uncollectible Interest and Penalties ........ | 100 | |
| Estimated Uncollectible Tax Liens ............. | | 2,100 |

To transfer estimated uncollectible taxes, interest, and penalties to estimated uncollectible tax liens.

The proceeds from the sale of the property may be more than, less than, or exactly the same as the amount of the tax liens. If they are the same there is simply a debit to Cash and a credit to Tax Liens Receivable. If the property is sold for more than the amount of the liens, the entry would be as follows:

| | | |
|---|---|---|
| Cash........................................ | 30,000 | |
| Tax Liens Receivable ....................... | | 29,000 |
| Due to Property Owners Trust Fund .......... | | 1,000 |

To record sale of tax liens for an amount in excess of their carrying value.

The amount due to the Property Owners Trust Fund would be transferred to that fund and would be held there in trust for subsequent payment to the property owner.

On the other hand, if the cash received from the sale of the property is not sufficient to cover the tax liens, and if taxes are a lien only against the property, the difference is charged to Estimated Uncollectible Tax Liens:

| | | |
|---|---|---|
| Cash........................................ | 27,000 | |
| Estimated Uncollectible Tax Liens ................ | 2,000 | |
| Tax Liens Receivable ....................... | | 29,000 |

To record the sale of property for taxes and to charge the difference between cash received and the amount of the tax liens to estimated uncollectible tax liens.

If the governmental unit bids in properties at the time of the sale, it becomes, as would any other purchaser, subject to the redemption privilege by the property owners. As properties are redeemed, an entry is made debiting Cash and crediting Tax Liens Receivable.

If properties are not redeemed and the governmental unit decides to use them for its own purposes—for example, for playgrounds—the Tax Liens Receivable accounts are removed from the funds in which they are carried through the following entry:

| | | |
|---|---|---|
| Expenditures................................... | 1,000 | |
| Estimated Uncollectible Tax Liens................. | 700 | |
| Tax Liens Receivable ........................ | | 1,700 |
| To record the removal of tax sale property from the asset category. | | |

The debit to Expenditures represents the estimated salable value of the tax liens, while the debit to Estimated Uncollectible Tax Liens represents the difference between the salable value of the liens and the value at which they are carried on the books.

Since the property will be part of the governmental unit's general fixed assets, it is necessary to record it in the General Fixed Assets group of accounts. The entry to record this transaction there is as follows:

| | | |
|---|---|---|
| Land ......................................... | 300 | |
| Buildings ...................................... | 700 | |
| Investment in General Fixed Assets— General Fund Revenues...................... | | 1,000 |
| To record property acquired at tax sale and not redeemed. | | |

It should be noted that these fixed assets are capitalized at the market value of the tax liens outstanding against them (in this case, $1,000). The joint cost incurred should be allocated between the land and building in proportion to their relative fair values. The apportionment between land and buildings must sometimes be made arbitrarily, although an appraisal or the assessed values usually provide a reasonable allocation basis.

As noted earlier, several governmental units may have liens on the same piece of property. The accounting procedure for the sale of the property is the same as that for property sold to satisfy the lien of only one governmental unit. The proceeds from the sale of the property are distributed among the various units to satisfy their liens, and any remaining cash is turned over to the property owner. If the proceeds are not sufficient to cover all the liens, each governmental unit receives a proportionate share of the money realized, unless statues specify another basis of distribution.

### General Property Tax Statements

Property tax statements are prepared to provide adequate disclosure of the details of property taxes. These statements may be divided into two classes: (1)

those that are directly integrated with the financial statements of the current period, and (2) those that show data for this period as well as for a number of other periods.

The annual financial report (see Chapter 17) is divided into two segments: a financial section and a statistical section. The general property tax statements that are directly related to the financial statements of the current period, called subsidiary financial statements, belong in the financial section of the annual report, while those that show data for a number of periods are known as statistical statements and appear in the statistical section. The first four statements illustrated here are subsidiary financial statements and the last four are statistical statements. Each is discussed in detail below.

STATEMENT OF CHANGES IN TAXES RECEIVABLE (FIGURE 6-2). This statement contains complete analyses of the Current Taxes and Delinquent Taxes Receivable accounts for the current fiscal year. It shows the transfers from current to

Figure 6-2

A GOVERNMENTAL UNIT
Statement of Changes in Taxes Receivable
For Fiscal Year Ended December 31, 19X5

|  | Total | Current Taxes | Delinquent Taxes |
|---|---|---|---|
| Taxes receivable, January 1, 19x5 ..... | $ 160,000 |  | $160,000 |
| Add: |  |  |  |
| Taxes levied .................... | $8,000,000 | $8,000,000 |  |
| Transfers from current taxes ....... | 100,000 |  | $100,000 |
| Total additions ................ | 8,100,000 | 8,000,000 | 100,000 |
| Total ..................... | $8,260,000 | $8,000,000 | $260,000 |
| Deduct: |  |  |  |
| Collections ..................... | $7,950,000 | $7,900,000 | $ 50,000 |
| Transfers to delinquent taxes ....... | 100,000 | 100,000 |  |
| Cancellations and abatements ...... | 30,000 |  | 30,000 |
| Total deductions .............. | $8,080,000 | $8,000,000 | $ 80,000 |
| Taxes receivable December 31, 19x5 .. | $ 180,000 |  | $180,000 |

delinquent status and provides an analysis of the Total Taxes Receivable at the end of the year.

STATEMENT OF TAXES RECEIVABLE BY FUNDS (FIGURE 6-3). This is an analysis of the Taxes Receivable account or accounts that appear in the yearend balance

Figure 6-3

A GOVERNMENTAL UNIT

Detailed Statement of Taxes Receivable by Funds

December 31, 19X8

|  | Total | General Fund | Debt Service Fund |
|---|---|---|---|
| Real estate taxes: |  |  |  |
| 19X8..................... | $ 70,000 | $55,000 | $15,000 |
| 19X7..................... | 15,000 | 12,000 | 3,000 |
| 19X6 and prior........... | 1,500 | 1,000 | 500 |
|  | $ 86,500 | $68,000 | $18,500 |
| Personal property taxes: |  |  |  |
| 19X8..................... | $ 7,000 | $ 5,500 | $ 1,500 |
| 19X7:.................... | 2,000 | 1,500 | 500 |
| 19X6 and prior........... | 5,000 | 4,000 | 1,000 |
|  | $ 14,000 | $11,000 | $ 3,000 |
|  | $100,500 | $79,000 | $21,500 |

Figure 6-4

A GOVERNMENTAL UNIT

Statement of Changes in Tax Liens Receivable

For Fiscal Year Ended December 31, 19X9

| | | |
|---|---|---|
| Tax liens receivable—beginning of year ........... | | $ 78,000 |
| Add: | | |
| Tax liens acquired— | | |
| Transfers from taxes receivable ............... | $20,000 | |
| Interest, penalties, and costs on | | |
| taxes transferred ........................ | 3,000 | 23,000 |
| Total ................................. | | $101,000 |
| Deduct: | | |
| Payments received ........................... | $22,000 | |
| Tax liens canceled or abated .................. | 3,000 | |
| Property transferred to General Fixed Assets ..... | 5,000 | $ 30,000 |
| Tax liens receivable—end of year ................ | | $ 71,000 |

Figure 6-5

## A GOVERNMENTAL UNIT
Detailed Statement of Tax Liens December 31, 19X9

| | Amount of Tax | Interest & Penalties Accrued to Date of Sale | Costs of Sale | Total Amount of Liens | Less Estimated Uncollectibles | Net Amount of Liens |
|---|---|---|---|---|---|---|
| Taxes of: | | | | | | |
| 19X8 | $18,700 | $2,800 | $ 500 | $22,000 | $ 3,500 | $18,500 |
| 19X7 | 12,800 | 1,800 | 400 | 15,000 | 2,500 | 12,500 |
| 19X6 | 8,500 | 1,300 | 200 | 10,000 | 1,500 | 8,500 |
| 19X5 | 6,800 | 1,000 | 200 | 8,000 | 1,000 | 7,000 |
| 19X4 and prior years | 13,600 | 2,000 | 400 | 16,000 | 1,500 | 14,500 |
| Total | $60,400 | $8,900 | $1,700 | $71,000 | $10,000 | $61,000 |
| Made up as follows: | | | | | | |
| General Fund | $42,280 | $6,230 | $1,190 | $49,700 | $ 7,000 | $42,700 |
| A Special Revenue Fund | 12,080 | 1,780 | 340 | 14,200 | 2,000 | 12,200 |
| Debt Service Funds | 6,040 | 890 | 170 | 7,100 | 1,000 | 6,100 |
| Total (as above) | $60,400 | $8,900 | $1,700 | $71,000 | $10,000 | $61,000 |

sheets of the several funds. Taxes Receivable are subdivided by years, and real estate and personal property taxes are shown separately.

STATEMENT OF CHANGES IN TAX LIENS RECEIVABLE (FIGURE 6-4). Like the Statement of Changes in Taxes Receivable, this statement shows a complete analysis of the Tax Liens Receivable account for the year.

DETAILED STATEMENT OF TAX LIENS (FIGURE 6-5). This statement shows a complete analysis of the tax liens receivable at the end of the year. The details making up the total amount of liens, the estimated uncollectible amounts by years, and an analysis of liens according to fund complete the statement.

STATEMENT OF ASSESSED VALUE AND ESTIMATED FAIR VALUE OF ALL TAXABLE PROPERTY (FIGURE 6-6). This statement presents information over a period of time regarding the assessed and estimated values of both real and personal property and culminates in an annual ratio of total assessed value to total fair value. The assessed value of property is an important determinant of the amount of taxes that can be raised, and it is therefore important to know the relationship between assessed value and fair value. If additional taxes are needed, they may be provided by an increase in the ratio of total assessed value to total fair value or by an increase in the tax rate, as well as by an increase in the total fair value of property. Therefore a rise or a fall in the tax rate must be judged in the light of the assessed valuation, for a fall in the tax rate may have been compensated for by a rise in the ratio of assessed value to fair value. Further, unless

**Figure 6-6**

A GOVERNMENTAL UNIT

Statement of Assessed Value and Estimated Fair Value of
All Taxable Property For Fiscal Years Ended December 31, 19X3–19Y2

| Assessment Period | Real Property (in thousands of dollars) | | Personal Property (in thousands of dollars) | | Ratio of Total Assessed Value to Total Fair Value |
| | Assessed Value | Estimated Fair Value | Assessed Value | Estimated Fair Value | |
| --- | --- | --- | --- | --- | --- |
| 19X3 | $ 25,000 | $ 50,000 | $ 9,000 | $ 18,000 | 50% |
| 19X4 | 50,000 | 100,000 | 15,000 | 31,000 | 50 |
| 19X5 | 55,000 | 110,000 | 25,000 | 50,000 | 50 |
| 19X6 | 57,000 | 114,000 | 27,000 | 56,000 | 50 |
| 19X7 | 63,000 | 126,000 | 31,000 | 60,000 | 50 |
| 19X8 | 92,000 | 150,000 | 40,000 | 75,000 | 59 |
| 19X9 | 120,000 | 190,000 | 53,000 | 81,000 | 64 |
| 19Y0 | 126,000 | 201,000 | 49,000 | 82,000 | 60 |
| 19Y1 | 150,000 | 240,000 | 57,000 | 95,000 | 62 |
| 19Y2 | 175,000 | 275,000 | 63,000 | 110,000 | 62 |

the ratio of assessed value to fair value is known, comparable tax rates for different governmental units cannot be compiled.

STATEMENT OF TAX RATES AND TAX LEVIES (FIGURE 6-7). This statement shows the tax rates and tax levies on property within the jurisdiction of a governmental unit for all the governmental units that levy taxes on property therein. It therefore provides an indication of the tax burden on property in A Governmental Unit.

STATEMENTS OF TAX LEVIES AND TAX COLLECTIONS (FIGURES 6-8 AND 6-9). One of the most important facts contributing to an evaluation of the financial

**Figure 6-7**

### A GOVERNMENTAL UNIT
Statements of Tax Rates and Tax Levies
For Fiscal Years Ended December 31, 19X7–19Y6

#### Tax Rates

| Assessment Period | City | County | School | Total |
|---|---|---|---|---|
| 19X7 | 15 mills | 8 mills | 10 mills | 33 mills |
| 19X8 | 15 | 9 | 11 | 35 |
| 19X9 | 15 | 9 | 11 | 35 |
| 19Y0 | 16 | 9 | 14 | 39 |
| 19Y1 | 16 | 10 | 14 | 40 |
| 19Y2 | 16 | 10 | 14 | 40 |
| 19Y3 | 16 | 10 | 14 | 40 |
| 19Y4 | 16 | 10 | 14 | 40 |
| 19Y5 | 16 | 10 | 19 | 45 |
| 19Y6 | 18 | 10 | 17 | 45 |

#### Tax Levies

| Assessment Period | City | County | School | Total |
|---|---|---|---|---|
| 19X7 | $ 375,000 | $ 200,000 | $ 250,000 | $ 825,000 |
| 19X8 | 750,000 | 450,000 | 550,000 | 1,750,000 |
| 19X9 | 825,000 | 495,000 | 605,000 | 1,925,000 |
| 19Y0 | 912,000 | 513,000 | 798,000 | 2,223,000 |
| 19Y1 | 1,008,000 | 630,000 | 882,000 | 2,520,000 |
| 19Y2 | 1,472,000 | 920,000 | 1,288,000 | 3,680,000 |
| 19Y3 | 1,926,000 | 1,200,000 | 1,680,000 | 4,800,000 |
| 19Y4 | 2,016,000 | 1,266,000 | 1,764,000 | 5,040,000 |
| 19Y5 | 2,400,000 | 1,500,000 | 2,850,000 | 6,750,000 |
| 19Y6 | 3,150,000 | 1,750,000 | 2,975,000 | 7,875,000 |

**Figure 6-8**

## A GOVERNMENTAL UNIT
### Statement of Tax Levies and Tax Collections
### January 1 to May 30, 19Y0

| | Total Tax Levy for Year | Uncollected at Beginning of This Year | Amount Collected This Month | Amount Collected from Beginning of This Year to Date | Amount Uncollected at This Date | Ratio of | | |
| | | | | | | Column 3 to Column 2 | Column 5 to Column 3 | Column 6 to Column 2 |
| | 2 | 3 | 4 | 5 | 6 | 7 | 8 | 9 |
|---|---|---|---|---|---|---|---|---|
| 19X1 | $500,000 | $ 30,500 | $ 1,567 | $ 5,093 | $25,407 | 6.1% | 16.7% | 5.1% |
| 19X2 | 450,000 | 35,750 | 1,789 | 6,613 | 29,137 | 7.9 | 18.5 | 6.5 |
| 19X3 | 425,000 | 45,475 | 2,140 | 9,868 | 35,607 | 10.7 | 21.7 | 8.4 |
| 19X4 | 400,000 | 53,600 | 2,560 | 13,024 | 40,576 | 13.4 | 24.3 | 10.1 |
| 19X5 | 430,000 | 68,370 | 3,429 | 19,553 | 48,817 | 15.9 | 28.6 | 11.4 |
| 19X6 | 460,000 | 87,860 | 5,223 | 29,257 | 58,603 | 19.1 | 33.3 | 12.7 |
| 19X7 | 500,000 | 108,500 | 9,342 | 45,244 | 63,256 | 21.7 | 41.7 | 12.7 |
| 19X8 | 505,000 | 123,725 | 10,355 | 53,820 | 69,905 | 24.5 | 43.5 | 13.8 |
| 19X9 | 504,000 | 140,350 | 11,960 | 66,385 | 73,965 | 27.8 | 47.3 | 14.7 |
| 19Y0 | 505,000 | 150,420 | 13,197 | 75,360 | 75,060 | 29.8 | 50.1 | 14.9 |

# A GOVERNMENTAL UNIT
## Statement of Tax Levies and Tax Collections
### Fiscal Years Ended December 31, 19X5–19Y4

| Tax Year | Total Tax Levy | Collections of Current Year's Taxes During Fiscal Period | Proportion of Levy Collected During Fiscal Period | Collections of Prior Years' Taxes During Fiscal Period | Total Collections | Ratio of Total Collections to Tax Levy | Accumulated Delinquent Taxes | Ratio of Accumulated Delinquent Taxes to Current Year's Tax Levy |
|---|---|---|---|---|---|---|---|---|
| 19X5 | $ 500 | $375 | 75% | $150 | $ 525 | 105% | $125 | 25% |
| 19X6 | 600 | 425 | 71 | 120 | 545 | 91 | 180 | 30 |
| 19X7 | 750 | 550 | 73 | 150 | 700 | 93 | 230 | 31 |
| 19X8 | 850 | 600 | 71 | 225 | 825 | 97 | 255 | 30 |
| 19X9 | 900 | 650 | 72 | 265 | 915 | 102 | 240 | 27 |
| 19Y0 | 1,000 | 750 | 75 | 270 | 1,020 | 102 | 220 | 22 |
| 19Y1 | 1,050 | 800 | 76 | 200 | 1,000 | 95 | 270 | 26 |
| 19Y2 | 1,100 | 825 | 75 | 250 | 1,075 | 98 | 270 | 27 |
| 19Y3 | 1,200 | 900 | 75 | 325 | 1,225 | 102 | 295 | 23 |
| 19Y4 | 1,300 | 950 | 73 | 170 | 1,120 | 86 | 450 | 35 |

**Figure 6-9**

strength of a government is the success with which taxes are being collected. No matter what its taxing power, a government will suffer financial embarrassment if it is unable to collect the taxes that it levies. These statements provide information regarding both tax levies and tax collections. The main difference between them is that the first is prepared during the year and shows collections from the beginning of the year to the date of the statement and for the current month, whereas the second is prepared at the end of the fiscal year and shows information regarding the success with which each year's levy has been collected, collections of delinquent taxes during each fiscal period, and accumulated delinquent taxes. These data are important in evaluating the financial health of the government and the trend of that health.

## LICENSES AND PERMITS

Governments have the right to permit, control or forbid many activities of individuals or corporations. The privilege of performing an act that would otherwise be illegal is granted by means of licenses or permits. Revenues from them may be divided into business and nonbusiness categories. In the business category are alcoholic beverages, health, corporations, public utilities, professional and occupational, and amusements licenses, among others. In the nonbusiness category may be found building, motor vehicles, motor vehicle operators, hunting and fishing, marriage, burial, and parking meters.

The rates for licenses and permits are established through legislative action, that is, by the passage of an ordinance or statute. In contrast to property taxes, however, there is no need for completely new rates to be established each year. Instead, the legislative body usually makes adjustments in the rates of particular licenses from time to time as the need arises.

Revenue from licenses and permits is not considered as such until it is received in cash, since the amount is not known until the licenses and permits are issued. Proper control over these revenues must insure not only that the revenues actually collected are properly handled but also that all the revenues which should be collected are collected. In other words, the governmental unit must see that all those who should secure licenses or permits do so. For example, if a license is required for the operation of a motor vehicle, the governmental unit must see that no vehicle is operated without one. Of course, the governmental unit must also see to it that the revenues actually collected are accounted for. This feature of control is accomplished in part through the use of controlled financial stationery. That is, licenses and permits are assigned series of numbers, and, when these documents are given to the employees who are to handle them, a record is made of the numbers on them. Thereafter, employees are required to account for the documents either by cash or by unused and spoiled documents.

# INTERGOVERNMENTAL REVENUE

Intergovernmental revenues consist of grants (grants in aid), shared revenues, and payments received from other governmental units in lieu of taxes. Grants are made on the basis of need, are not related to the several revenue sources of the granting government, and are ordinarily made for specific purposes. Shared revenues are collected by one governmental unit but are distributed among other units or classes of governments, usually on the basis of the amount collected. Payments in lieu of taxes are amounts paid to one government by another to reimburse the payee for revenues lost because the payor government does not pay taxes. The maximum amount usually would be computed by determining the amount that the receiving government would have collected had the property of the paying government been subject to taxation.

REVENUE ACCOUNTS. A total of nine classifications of intergovernmental revenues may be prepared for a municipality by listing the three kinds of intergovernmental revenue under Federal, state, and local unit categories. For example, there would be grants from local units, shared revenues from local units, and payments from local units in lieu of taxes (in each case the local units should be identified). Similar categories would be applied to Federal and state revenues sources.

As already indicated, grants are ordinarily made for a specified purpose. Accordingly, all grants—whether from Federal, state or local government sources —should be recorded in the appropriate fund and classified according to the function for which the grants are to be spent. Grants may be classified in such functions as general government, public safety, highways and streets, sanitation, and health. Shared revenues, on the other hand, should be classified into accounts according to the source of the revenue. Payments in lieu of taxes are classified only by governmental source—Federal, state, or local unit.

ACCOUNTING FOR INTERGOVERNMENTAL REVENUE. Intergovernmental revenues should be accrued as they become due from the paying government. First attention must be given to selecting the fund in which the revenue is to be recorded. Because grants are restricted to special purposes, they must be accounted for in Special Revenue or Trust Funds. Presumably the receiving government would record payments in lieu of taxes in the same fund and manner as it records its receipts of taxes. State collected, locally shared taxes should be identified in the subsidiary Revenue Ledger as to the kind of tax being received.

The paying government would have to make appropriations for its expenditures for grants and payments in lieu of taxes. On the other hand, if the state is collecting taxes for its local governments, the collections and payments are not revenues and expenditures but are simply receipts and disbursements made for the local units. Accordingly, they should be accounted for in an Agency Fund as described in Chapter 12.

## CHARGES FOR SERVICES

These revenues consist of charges made by various departments for services rendered by them. Although the revenues of Enterprise Funds are also derived from the sale of services to the public, because of their importance, the funds are treated separately. Similarly, special assessments for improvements can in a sense be considered revenues of the department that constructs the improvements financed from them; but they are not so treated, because of their special nature.

It is important to distinguish between revenues derived from departmental earnings and those from licenses and permits. Only those charges that result directly from the activity of the department and that are made for the purpose of recovering part of the expense of the department are considered charges for current services. Some of these charges may involve the issuance of permits, but the revenues should not be classed as coming from permits but rather as charges for services.

Some of these revenues are not recorded until they are collected in cash. If collection does not occur at the time the services are rendered or immediately thereafter, revenue should be recorded as the persons or governments served are billed. The following entries illustrate some transactions that result in revenues being recorded as soon as they are earned:

| | | |
|---|---|---|
| Due from Other Governmental Units.............. | 25,000 | |
| Revenues ............................... | | 25,000 |

To record earnings resulting from charges to other governmental units for patients quartered in hospitals and for board of prisoners. Entries in subsidiary accounts: *Debit* each governmental unit. *Credit* Hospital Fees, $10,000; Prison Fees, $15,000.

| | | |
|---|---|---|
| Accounts Receivable .......................... | 25,000 | |
| Revenues ............................... | | 25,000 |

To record street lighting, street sprinkling, and garbage collection charges made to property owners. Entries in subsidiary accounts: *Debit* each person for whom service was rendered. *Credit* Street Lighting Charges, $5,000; Sewerage Charges, $10,000; Refuse Collection Fees, $10,000.

The following entry, on the other hand, illustrates some of the transactions in which revenues are not accrued:

| | | |
|---|---|---|
| Cash......................................... | 88,200 | |
| Revenues ............................... | | 88,200 |

To record receipt of cash representing charges for services. Entries in subsidiary accounts:

*Credit*

| | |
|---|---|
| Sale of Maps and Publications .................... | $ 1,200 |
| Special Police Services .......................... | 3,000 |
| Special Fire Protection Services ................. | 54,000 |
| Building Inspection Fees ........................ | 5,000 |
| Plumbing Inspection Fees ...................... | 5,000 |
| Swimming Pool Inspection Fees ................. | 2,000 |
| Golf Fees..................................... | 7,000 |
| Fees for Recording Legal Instruments ............. | 6,000 |
| Animal Control and Shelter Fees ................. | 5,000 |
| | $88,200 |

As implied by the foregoing materials, the chart of accounts for charges for services should be based on the activity for which the charge is made. These activities can be classified according to the function of the government in which the activity is carried on. For example, under the general government function we would expect to find accounts for the following:

1. Court costs, fees, and charges
2. Recording of legal instruments
3. Zoning and subdivision fees
4. Plan checking fees
5. Sale of maps and publications

## FINES AND FORFEITS

Revenues from fines and forfeits do not usually form an important part of a governmental unit's income and are usually accounted for on a cash basis. Fines are penalties imposed for the commission of statutory criminal offenses or for violation of lawful administrative rules. Penalties for the delinquent payment of taxes are not included in this category of revenue, since they are considered part of tax revenues. Similarly, penalties for late payment of utility bills are considered utility operating revenues. Fines and other penalties included in this section are primarily those imposed by the courts.

The money from forfeits is usually first accounted for in a Trust Fund. For example, assume that a person has been released on bail and that he has forfeited his bail. When bail is received, an entry is made in a Trust Fund debiting Cash or another asset account and crediting the proper Trust Fund Balance account. Unless the law provides otherwise, when bail is forfeited, the money is transferred to the General Fund. The entries to record the transfer in the Trust Fund and General Fund, respectively, are as follows:

*Trust Fund:*

| | | |
|---|---|---|
| Bail Fund Balance .............................. | 5,000 | |
| Cash........................................ | | 5,000 |

To record reduction of Trust Fund Balance through
transfer of forfeited bail to the General Fund.

*General Fund:*

| | | |
|---|---|---|
| Cash......................................... | 5,000 | |
| Revenues ................................. | | 5,000 |

To record receipt of money representing forfeited bail.

## MISCELLANEOUS REVENUE

Included in the miscellaneous category are such sources of revenue as interest earnings, rents and royalties, sales and compensation for loss of fixed assets, contribution from public enterprises, escheats, contributions and donations from private sources, and balances from discontinued funds. It may be noted that all the revenues discussed in this chapter may be found in General and Special Revenue Funds; some of them may also appear in other funds, as we shall see. In addition, other funds may have their own sources of revenue which have not been described here but will be treated in subsequent chapters. For example, the account "Sales of Bonds" will be found in the Capital Projects Fund, where it is used to record the receipt of proceeds from the sale of bonds, exclusive of premiums and accumulated interest. As already noted, this account would represent revenue to the Capital Projects Fund, but proceeds from the sale of bonds would not represent revenue for the governmental unit as a whole. Most of the revenues in the miscellaneous category are self-explanatory, but a discussion of some of them may prove useful.

INTEREST EARNINGS.   During the last decade the short-term investment of cash available in excess of current needs has been authorized by legislative bodies throughout the country. Thus, in addition to interest on long-term investments of Debt Service and Trust Funds, for example, interest earned on short-term investments of idle cash has become a substantial general revenue source in many municipalities. Interest should be accrued as it is earned by the governmental unit.

SALES AND COMPENSATION FOR LOSS OF FIXED ASSETS.   Although fixed assets financed from General and Special Revenue Funds are not carried as part of the assets of such funds, the net proceeds from the sale and compensation for loss of these assets form a part of the revenue of these funds. As a general rule, such revenue should be recorded in the fund that financed the acquisition of the asset that has been sold or destroyed. Since identification of the source from which assets were financed may be difficult, and since in many instances the funds that financed the purchase of assets have gone out of existence before the assets are disposed of, the net proceeds from the sale and compensation for loss of general fixed assets usually flow into the General Fund and are considered revenues of that Fund. As we shall see, proceeds from the sale and compensation for loss of assets carried in Intragovernmental Service Funds, Enterprise Funds, and Trust Funds would ordinarily be accounted for in those funds rather than in the General Fund.

## REVENUE LEDGER

The subsidiary Revenue Ledger contains accounts for each source of revenue; its general ledger control accounts are Estimated Revenues and Revenues. To minimize the number of accounts in the ledger and, more importantly, to facilitate comparisons of actual and estimated revenues, one account is used for each revenue source. For example, Figure 6-10 is the account for motor vehicle license revenues. When the Estimated Revenues general ledger account is debited at the beginning of the year to record revenue plans, the subsidiary Revenue Ledger accounts for the specific sources of that revenue also are debited. As the Revenues account is credited, the corresponding revenue source accounts are credited in the subsidiary Revenue Ledger. Thus the account balances present at all times a series of comparisons of plans and achievements. The general ledger control accounts compare planned and actual revenue totals, while the

**Figure 6-10**

| A GOVERNMENTAL UNIT Revenue Ledger | | | | | |
|---|---|---|---|---|---|
| Account No.: 322.2 Class: Licenses and Permits Account Name: Motor Vehicle Licenses | | | | | |
| Date | Reference | Folio | Estimated Revenue Dr. | Actual Revenue Cr. | Balance Dr. or (Cr.) |
| 19X6 Jan. 3 June 30 | Budget Estimate Licenses Issued | G. J. 1 C. R. 41 | $34,000 — | — $34,500 | $34,000 (500) |

subsidiary accounts present such comparisons with respect to each revenue source.

At the end of the fiscal period, the function of the Revenue Ledger has been fulfilled. If the Ledger is to be filed away—if new (physically) accounts are to be used in the next period—no subsidiary revenue ledger closing entries are required. The Revenue Ledger can be filed away with its year-end balances unchanged. But if the same ledger accounts, sheets or cards, are to be used in the next period, the accounts must be closed.

The entry closing out revenues in both the General Ledger and Revenue Ledger is as follows:

| | | |
|---|---:|---:|
| Revenues .................................. | 428,700 | |
| Fund Balance ............................. | 2,300 | |
|    Estimated Revenues ...................... | | 431,000 |

To record closing out of actual revenues and estimated revenues. Entries in subsidiary accounts:

| | Debit To Close Out Excess of Actual Revenues Over Estimated Revenues | Credit To Close Out Deficiency of Actual Revenues Under Estimated Revenues |
|---|---:|---:|
| Penalties and Interest on Delinquent Taxes ....... | | $ 300 |
| Motor Vehicle Licenses........................ | $ 500 | |
| Street and Curb Permits ...................... | 1,000 | |
| Alcoholic Beverage Licenses ................... | 1,000 | |
| Amusement Licenses .......................... | 500 | |
| Professional and Occupational Licenses ........... | 150 | |
| Municipal Court Fines ........................ | 100 | |
| Interest Earnings ............................. | 200 | |
| Rents and Royalties .......................... | 300 | |
| Share of Income Taxes ........................ | | 3,800 |
| Share of Gasoline Taxes ....................... | | 2,700 |
| Marriage Licenses ............................ | 350 | |
| Special Police Services ........................ | 300 | |
| Health Inspection Fees ........................ | 100 | |
| Sales of Fixed Assets ......................... | 100 | |
| Balances from Discontinued Funds .............. | | 100 |
| | $4,600 | $6,900 |

**Figure 6-11**

A GOVERNMENTAL UNIT

General Fund

Statement of Revenues—Estimated and Actual

for Fiscal Year

| | Estimated Revenues | Actual Revenues | Actual Over (Under) Estimated |
|---|---|---|---|
| Taxes: | | | |
| General property taxes | $288,000 | $288,000 | — |
| Penalties and interest on delinquent general property taxes | 1,000 | 700 | $ (300) |
| Total taxes | $289,000 | $288,700 | $ (300) |
| Licenses and Permits: | | | |
| Business | $ 20,300 | $ 21,950 | $ 1,650 |
| Nonbusiness | 26,600 | 28,100 | 1,500 |
| Total licenses and permits | $ 46,900 | $ 50,050 | $ 3,150 |
| Intergovernmental Revenue: | | | |
| Share of state income taxes | $ 37,000 | $ 33,200 | $(3,800) |
| Share of state gasoline taxes | 25,000 | 22,300 | (2,700) |
| Total intergovernmental revenue | $ 62,000 | $ 55,500 | $(6,500) |
| Charges for Services: | | | |
| General government | $ 1,000 | $ 1,000 | $ — |
| Public safety | 4,000 | 4,300 | 300 |
| Health | 1,800 | 2,250 | 450 |
| Total charges for services | $ 6,800 | $ 7,550 | $ 750 |
| Fines and Forfeits: | | | |
| Fines | $ 9,000 | $ 9,100 | $ 100 |
| Forfeits | 500 | 500 | — |
| Total fines and forfeits | $ 9,500 | $ 9,600 | $ 100 |
| Miscellaneous Revenues: | | | |
| Interest earnings | $ 2,200 | $ 2,400 | $ 200 |
| Rents | 5,000 | 5,300 | 300 |
| Sales of fixed assets | 5,100 | 5,200 | 100 |
| Conscience money | 200 | 200 | — |
| Balances from discontinued funds | 4,300 | 4,200 | (100) |
| Total miscellaneous revenues | $ 16,800 | $ 17,300 | $ 500 |
| Total revenues | $431,000 | $428,700 | $(2,300) |

Figure 6-12

## A GOVERNMENTAL UNIT
### General Fund
#### Statement of Actual and Estimated Revenue
For Month Ending March 31, 19X2, and Three Months Ending March 31, 19X2

| Revenue Source | Total Estimated 19X2 | March | | | Year to Date | | | |
|---|---|---|---|---|---|---|---|---|
| | | Estimated | Actual | Over or Under* Estimate | Estimated | Actual | Over or Under* Estimate | Balance To Be Collected |
| **Taxes:** | | | | | | | | |
| General property taxes | $290,600 | $48,500 | $46,990 | $1,510* | $106,500 | $103,435 | $3,065* | $187,165 |
| Penalties and interest on delinquent taxes | 1,150 | 100 | 90 | 10* | 300 | 250 | 50* | 900 |
| Total taxes | $291,750 | $48,600 | $47,080 | $1,520* | $106,800 | $103,685 | $3,115* | $188,065 |
| Licenses and permits | $ 56,300 | $ 4,800 | $ 7,000 | $2,200 | $ 15,000 | $ 18,000 | $3,000 | $ 38,300 |
| **Fines and Forfeits:** | | | | | | | | |
| Fines | $ 6,500 | $ 500 | $ 550 | $ 50 | $ 1,600 | $ 1,675 | $ 75 | $ 4,825 |
| Forfeits | 3,000 | 250 | 250 | — | 800 | 825 | 25 | 2,175 |
| Total fines and forfeits | $ 9,500 | $ 750 | $ 800 | $ 50 | $ 2,400 | $ 2,500 | $ 100 | $ 7,000 |

Figure 6-12 (cont.)

| | | | | | | | | |
|---|---|---|---|---|---|---|---|---|
| Intergovernmental Revenue: | | | | | | | | |
| Federal grants | $ 15,000 | $ — | $ — | $ — | $ — | $ — | $ — | $ 15,000 |
| State grants | 47,200 | 5,200 | 5,300 | 100 | 17,000 | 18,000 | 1,000 | 29,200 |
| Total intergovernmental revenue | $ 62,200 | $ 5,200 | $ 5,300 | $ 100 | $ 17,000 | $ 18,000 | $1,000 | $ 44,200 |
| Charges for Services: | | | | | | | | |
| Public safety | $ 6,800 | $ 575 | $ 550 | $ 25* | $ 1,600 | $ 1,550 | $ 50* | $ 5,250 |
| Highways and streets | 5,200 | 440 | 450 | 10 | 1,300 | 1,375 | 75 | 3,825 |
| Total charges for services | $ 12,000 | $ 1,015 | $ 1,000 | $ 15* | $ 2,900 | $ 2,925 | $ 25 | $ 9,075 |
| Miscellaneous Revenue: | | | | | | | | |
| Interest | $ 7,200 | $ 610 | $ 580 | $ 30* | $ 1,800 | $ 1,775 | $ 25* | $ 5,425 |
| Rents | 5,100 | 1,000 | 1,010 | 10 | 2,000 | 2,015 | 15 | 3,085 |
| Sale of fixed assets | 4,300 | 500 | 500 | — | 1,500 | 1,550 | 50 | 2,750 |
| Total miscellaneous revenue | $ 16,600 | $ 2,110 | $ 2,090 | $ 20* | $ 5,300 | $ 5,340 | $ 40 | $ 11,260 |
| Total revenues | $448,350 | $62,475 | $63,270 | $ 795 | $149,400 | $150,450 | $1,050 | $297,900 |

The difference between the debits and credits to the Revenue Ledger account balances is, of course, the amount of the General Ledger debit to Fund Balance, $2,300. If actual revenues had exceeded estimates, there would have been a credit to Fund Balance.

## REVENUE STATEMENTS

The detailed data regarding estimated and actual revenues that are maintained in the accounts of the Revenue Ledger are the source of information presented to administrators and the public in formal revenue statements. The significance of comparing estimated and actual revenues can hardly be overemphasized.

STATEMENT OF REVENUES—ESTIMATED AND ACTUAL (FIGURE 6-11). This statement is prepared only at year end, since it contains no basis for comparisons of estimates and administration until the year has been completed. (1) The comparison of estimated and actual revenues at year end is valuable in the preparation of future estimates. Usually the finance officer will be called upon to explain why his estimates fell short of or exceeded actual revenues, and, if his errors are due to failure to take certain factors into account, he will take steps to remedy the situation in making future estimates. (2) The statement is likely to prevent the finance officer from purposely overestimating or underestimating revenues over a period of years, for a series of such statements will make evident these shortcomings. Overestimates lead to the making of appropriations in excess of revenues, so that the governmental unit ends its operations with a deficit. Underestimates are most likely to occur in a government in which the estimating officer is administratively independent of the chief executive. In such cases the estimates may be continually understated, without any danger of administrative action, because of the estimator's political bias or because of a sincere belief that underestimation is the proper means of maintaining a balanced budget. (3) The comparison of estimated and actual revenues may reveal that actual collections have not been as great as they should have been. Investigation may reveal laxness or fraud in assessment or collection procedures.

STATEMENT OF ACTUAL AND ESTIMATED REVENUE (FIGURE 6-12). It is important that the administration recognize during the year whether revenues are being collected at the proper rate. A comparison of monthly revenues with estimates will provide prompt notice that parking meter or court fines revenues, for example, are falling behind schedule. When the Statement of Actual and

Estimated Revenues provides such notice, the administration can take steps to satisfy itself as to the reasons for the deficiencies and, if necessary, adjust the rate and amount of expenditures.

**Question 6-1.** The term *competitive* underassessment is used in the "Equalization of Assessments" section of Chapter 6. What does the term mean? How does the process of equalization discourage underassessment?

**Question 6-2.** In a certain governmental unit, homesteads are exempt from taxation up to $2,500 of their assessed value except taxes levied for the payment of bonds issued prior to enactment of the homestead exemption law and for the payment of the interest on such bonds. The assessed valuation of the municipality in 19X9 was $100,000,000, out of which properties with an assessed value of $20,000,000 were entitled to the exemption privilege. The tax levy for 19X9 was as follows: (*a*) for all expenses excepting interest and bond retirements, $700,000; (*b*) for interest and bond retirements, $100,000, out of which $70,000 is applicable to bonds issued prior to the enactment of the homestead exemption act and $30,000 to bonds issued after passage of the act. Calculate the tax rate or tax rates of the governmental unit in question.

**Question 6-3.** Referring to Question 6-2, assume that taxpayer *A* resides in a homestead with an assessed valuation of $10,000. What is his 19X9 tax bill?

**Question 6-4.** Is it better to consider discounts on taxes as direct deductions from revenue or as expenditures?

**Question 6-5.** Is it better to consider estimated losses on taxes receivable as direct deductions from revenue or as expenditures?

**Question 6-6.** A municipality removes from the General Fund all taxes delinquent more than one year. As these taxes are collected, the proceeds are transferred to the General Fund. (*a*) What effect will the removal of the delinquent taxes have on the financial condition of the General Fund? (*b*) How will the revenues of the General Fund be affected by the collections of delinquent taxes?

**Question 6-7.** In some cases no provision for loss is made when uncollected taxes, interest, and penalties are transferred to tax liens. If there is a loss on such a lien, what accounts would you charge? How would you apportion the loss between those accounts?

**Question 6-8.** The taxes of City *A* are collected by County *C*, while City *B* collects its own taxes. In what respects will the tax accounting procedures for the two cities differ?

**Question 6-9.** For which of the following would you set up accounts in the Revenue Ledger?

**Case I.** Taxes
      General Property Taxes
        Real Property
        Personal Property
          Tangible Personal
          Intangible Personal

**Case II.**  Intergovernmental Revenue
   State Shared Revenues
   Property Taxes
   Individual Income Taxes
   Corporate Income Taxes

**Question 6-10.**  (*a*) What is the difference between state-collected, locally shared taxes, and grants-in-aid? (*b*) A statute provides that 50 per cent of state motor vehicle license collections are to be distributed annually among the municipalities and counties (that is, county territory outside of municipalities) on the basis of the number of licenses issued to residents thereof during the year. Are such payments a distribution of state-collected, locally shared taxes, or grants-in-aid? (*c*) Would your answer be different if the statute had provided, in addition, that the money received by the municipalities and counties was to be employed only for road purposes?

**Question 6-11.**  (*a*) What is the difference between revenues from charges for current services and license revenues? (*b*) A department charges $10, the approximate cost of inspection, for issuing a building permit. Would you classify this as revenues from permits or as charges for current services?

**Question 6-12.**  Both tax rates and license rates are established by legislative action. Which rates (license or tax) are likely to remain in effect over a longer period of time?

**Question 6-13.**  The controller of the City of *F*, who is independent of the chief executive, purposely underestimates revenues and publishes revenue statements which show actual revenues only.

   a.  How can one discover the controller's practice?

   b.  The controller, when discovered in the practice, "points with pride" to the City's solvency and states that his underestimates have kept the City from overspending. Comment.

**Question 6-14.**  What purposes do revenue statements serve in the administration of the General Fund?

**Problem 6-1.**  The 19X5, 19X6, and 19X7 tax rates for the City of *K* are:

|  | *Rate per $100 of Assessed Value* | | |
| --- | --- | --- | --- |
|  | *19X5* | *19X6* | *19X7* |
| General Fund | $1.00 | $1.10 | $1.20 |
| Library Fund | .09 | .09 | .09 |
| Municipal Bonds—Redemptions | .20 | .18 | .16 |
|  | $1.29 | $1.37 | $1.45 |

The total assessed value for 19X7 was $88,400,000.
Required:
   Compute the amount of taxes levied for each fund for 19X7.

**Problem 6-2.**  In the City of *K* (Problem 6-1), collections were made in 19X7 as follows:

|            |              |
|------------|--------------|
| 19X5 levy  | $1,000,000   |
| 19X6 levy  | 100,000      |
| 19X7 levy  | 50,000       |
|            | $1,150,000   |

Required:

Compute the amount of collections applicable to each fund for each year.

**Problem 6-3.** On the basis of the following facts, determine the assessed value of the County of Z:

| Kind of Property | True Value |
|------------------|------------|
| Real Estate: | |
| Homesteads on platted property up to $4,000 ....... | $ 18,000,000 |
| Homesteads on unplatted property up to $4,000...... | 3,200,000 |
| Homesteads on platted property in excess of $4,000 .. | 3,500,000 |
| Homesteads on unplatted property in excess of $4,000. | 100,000 |
| Other real estate................................. | 192,300,000 |
| Personal Property: | |
| Household goods and furniture ................... | 32,510,000 |
| Livestock, agricultural products, stocks of merchandise, and so on ................................... | 72,490,000 |
| Other personal property ........................ | 17,500,000 |
| Money and Credits .............................. | 175,000,000 |

*Basis of Assessment*

Real estate is assessed at 55 per cent of true value. Homesteads on platted property up to $4,000 true value are assessed at 30 per cent of true value, and homesteads on unplatted property up to $4,000 true value are assessed at 25 per cent of true value. Homesteads on platted property in excess of $4,000 true value are assessed 52 per cent of true value, and homesteads on unplatted property in excess of $4,000 true value are assessed at 40 per cent of true value.

Household goods and furniture, including musical instruments, sewing machines, wearing apparel of members of family, and all personal property actually used by the owner for personal and domestic purposes or for the furnishing or equipment of the family residence are assessed at 30 per cent of true value.

Livestock, poultry, all agricultural products, stocks of merchandise, together with the furniture and fixtures used therewith, manufacturer's materials and manufactured articles, and all tools, implements, and machinery which are not permanently attached to and a part of the real estate where located are assessed at 40 per cent of true value. Other personal property is assessed at 55 per cent of its true value.

Money and credits are assessed at 98 per cent of their true value.

**Problem 6-4.** On the basis of the following data, prepare a statement similar to the one in Figure 6-8.

CITY OF *T*
Statement of Tax Levies and Tax Collections
January 1–January 31, 19X0

| Year | Total Tax Levy for Year | Uncollected Beginning of This Year | Amount Collected This Month |
|------|------|------|------|
| 19W1 | $1,000,000 | $    60,000 | $    3,000 |
| 19W2 | 950,000 | 70,000 | 4,000 |
| 19W3 | 925,000 | 80,000 | 6,000 |
| 19W4 | 900,000 | 70,000 | 5,000 |
| 19W5 | 930,000 | 90,000 | 8,000 |
| 19W6 | 960,000 | 90,000 | 9,000 |
| 19W7 | 1,000,000 | 100,000 | 10,000 |
| 19W8 | 1,000,000 | 110,000 | 20,000 |
| 19W9 | 1,100,000 | 120,000 | 20,000 |
| 19X0 | 1,100,000 | 1,100,000 | 400,000 |

**Problem 6-5.** On the basis of the following data, prepare a statement similar to that illustrated in Figure 6-9:

CITY OF *B*
Statement of Tax Levies and Tax Collections
for Fiscal Periods 19W1–19X0

| Fiscal Period | Total Tax Levy | Collection of Current Taxes During Fiscal Period | Collection of Delinquent Taxes During Fiscal Period | Accumulated Delinquent Taxes |
|------|------|------|------|------|
| 19W1 | $1,427,315.71 | $1,389,195.28 | $26,716.03 | $ 87,070.23 |
| 19W2 | 1,436,788.34 | 1,393,933.07 | 34,292.51 | 95,632.99 |
| 19W3 | 1,418,678.05 | 1,371,841.33 | 42,809.66 | 99,660.05 |
| 19W4 | 1,441,288.72 | 1,372,060.94 | 52,716.33 | 116,171.50 |
| 19W5 | 1,267,183.83 | 1,174,818.47 | 55,140.92 | 153,395.94 |
| 19W6 | 1,095,953.92 | 1,034,642.38 | 73,807.71 | 140,899.77 |
| 19W7 | 1,081,375.23 | 1,028,771.11 | 56,725.53 | 136,764.82 |
| 19W8 | 1,153,631.75 | 1,121,232.23 | 56,965.77 | 112,198.57 |
| 19W9 | 1,162,104.72 | 1,138.005.55 | 38,949.86 | 97,457.88 |
| 19X0 | 1,215,650.32 | 1,193,508.49 | 32,885.76 | 86,713.95 |

**Problem 6-6.** On the basis of the following data, prepare a statement for the Village of *J* analyzing the changes in the Tax Sale Certificates account during 19X0:

| Tax sale certificates canceled | $20,000 |
| Transfers from taxes receivable | 90,000 |
| Property transferred to general fixed assets | 42,000 |
| Payments received | 55,000 |
| Interest, penalties, and costs on taxes transferred | 5,000 |
| Balance, January 1 | 43,000 |

**Problem 6-7.** From the following data, prepare a statement analyzing the changes in the Taxes Receivable account during 19X5:

Tax collections on current taxes were $900,000 and on delinquent taxes $225,000. Taxes levied amounted to $1,725,000.

Taxes to the amount of $200,000 became delinquent.

On January 1, the balance of current taxes receivable was $215,000 and of delinquent taxes receivable, $855,000.

Taxes canceled on the current year's levy amounted to $8,000 and on delinquent taxes to $12,000.

**Problem 6-8.** City AAA had the following transactions, among others, in 19X7:

1. The Council estimated that revenue of $150,000 would be generated for the General Fund in 19X7. The sources and amounts of expected revenue are as follows:

| Property tax | $ 90,000 |
| Parking meters | 5,000 |
| Business licenses | 30,000 |
| Amusement licenses | 10,000 |
| Beer licenses | 15,000 |
| | $150,000 |

2. Property taxes of $91,000 were levied by the Council; $1,000 of these taxes are expected to be uncollectible.

3. The following collections were made by the City:

| Property taxes | $ 80,000 |
| Parking meters | 5,500 |
| Business licenses | 28,000 |
| Amusement licenses | 9,500 |
| Beer licenses | 18,000 |
| | $141,000 |

Required:
(1)  Record the transactions:
 (a)  In the General Journal.
 (b)  In the Revenue Subsidiary Ledger.
 (c)  In the revenue control accounts.
(2)  Prepare a trial balance of the balances in the Revenue Subsidiary Ledger after the postings. Show agreement with the control accounts.
(3)  Make the closing entry for the revenue accounts in the General Journal.

**Problem 6-9.** The following is a list of the revenue accounts in the General Fund Revenue Ledger of the City of *P* at December 31, 19X0:

| Revenue Source | Estimated | Actual |
|---|---|---|
| Amusement Licenses | $     500 | $     500 |
| Sale of "No Parking" Signs | 300 | 300 |
| Interest on Bank Deposits | 500 | 500 |
| Real Estate Taxes (Net) | 100,000 | 95,000 |
| Personal Property Taxes (Net) | 58,000 | 50,000 |
| Penalties and Interest on Delinquent Taxes | 5,000 | 5,500 |
| Sales Taxes | 42,000 | 42,000 |
| Plumbing Installation Permits | 5,000 | 4,800 |
| Motor Vehicle Registration Fees Received From State | 17,000 | 15,500 |
| Golf Fees | 2,000 | 2,100 |
| Street Lighting Charges | 1,000 | 1,200 |
| Marriage Licenses | 600 | 400 |
| Burial Permits | 1,000 | 1,200 |
| Subscriptions to City Publications | 500 | 450 |
| Alcoholic Beverage Licenses | 19,000 | 18,000 |
| Sales of Sewerage Sludge | 800 | 600 |
| Library Fines | 1,000 | 1,100 |
| Donations From Private Sources | 5,000 | 5,000 |
| Building Permits | 3,000 | 3,100 |
| Special Police Services | 2,000 | 1,800 |
| Sale of Fixed Assets | 1,000 | 500 |
| Gasoline Tax Received From State | 28,000 | 28,000 |
| Special Fire Protection Services | 200 | 300 |
| Court Fines | 5,000 | 4,200 |
| Cigarette Tax Received From State | 12,000 | 12,500 |
| Interest on Investments | 300 | 300 |
| Hospital Fees | 5,000 | 5,500 |
| Rent From Public Buildings | 2,000 | 2,000 |
| Bus Company Franchise Fees | 3,000 | 3,000 |
| Taxi Licenses | 500 | 600 |
| | $321,200 | $305,950 |

Required:

(1) Set up "T" accounts for the General Ledger accounts and enter in them the total amounts of estimated revenues and actual revenues, respectively; also set up a "T" account for Fund Balance.

(2)   Set up the following (subsidiary) Revenue Ledger accounts (see Figure 6-10) and post the amounts of estimated aṇd actual revenue thereto:
   Real Estate Taxes
   Court Fines
   Building Permits
(3)   Prepare a journal entry to close out the estimated and actual revenues, showing both the General Ledger and Revenue Ledger (that is, subsidiary) accounts.
(4)   Post the amounts shown in the closing entry to the General Ledger accounts and to those subsidary revenue accounts for which you have set up accounts.
(5)   Prepare a statement, properly arranged, comparing the estimated and actual revenues of the General Fund of the City of *P* for the year ended December 31, 19X0.

**Problem 6-10.**   The following are the estimated revenues for the City of *A* at January 1, 19X0:

| | |
|---|---:|
| Taxes | $175,000 |
| Interest and Penalties | 2,000 |
| Fines and Fees | 700 |
| Permits | 300 |
| Animal Licenses | 900 |
| Rents | 500 |
| Other Licenses | 3,500 |
| Interest | 1,000 |

The city reports its transactions on a cash basis.
At the end of January, the following collections had been made:

| | |
|---|---:|
| Taxes | $90,000 |
| Interest and Penalties | 1,000 |
| Fines and Fees | 50 |
| Permits | 140 |
| Animal Licenses | 800 |
| Rents | 45 |
| Other Licenses | 2,000 |

An unanticipated grant-in-aid of $5,000 was received from the state.
Collections for the remaining eleven months were as follows:

| | |
|---|---:|
| Taxes | $70,000 |
| Interest and Penalties | 800 |
| Fines and Fees | 400 |
| Permits | 30 |
| Animal Licenses | 70 |
| Rents | 455 |
| Other Licenses | 300 |
| Interest | 900 |

Required:
(1)  Prepare the entries necessary to record on the books the estimated revenues as well as revenue collections.
(2)  Post to "T" accounts and to subsidiary revenue accounts (see Figure 6-10).
(3)  Prepare closing entries.
(4)  Post to the "T" accounts and to the subsidiary revenue accounts.
(5)  Prepare a statement of estimated revenues compared with actual revenues for 19X0.

**Problem 6-11.**  From the following accounts taken from a municipality's report for the fiscal year ended June 30, 19X9, prepare a statement of estimated revenue compared with actual.

|  | Estimated | Actual |
|---|---|---|
| Property Taxes | $1,126,000 | $1,127,000 |
| Permits | 5,200 | 5,850 |
| Sales of Maps and Publications | 29,000 | 11,275 |
| Motor Fuel Tax | 106,000 | 161,725 |
| Rents and Royalties | 3,500 | 3,200 |
| Licenses | 35,000 | 65,900 |
| Severance Tax | 200 | 190 |
| Contributions | 36,000 | 27,450 |
| Interest Earnings | 22,000 | 54,800 |
| Gross Receipts Taxes | 1,200 | 1,300 |
| Fines and Forfeits | 25,000 | 35,600 |
| Refuse Collection Charges | 2,000 | 2,875 |
| Special Police Services | 25 | 350 |
| Special Fire Protection Services | — | 75 |
| Court Costs, Fees, and Charges | 10,000 | 14,800 |
|  | $1,401,125 | $1,512,390 |

**Problem 6-12.**  The following is a list of the estimated and actual General Fund revenues for the fiscal year ended June 30, 19X0, for the State of $Y$:

|  | Estimated | Actual |
|---|---|---|
| Sales Tax | $11,826,000 | $11,701,526 |
| Gasoline Inspection | 750,000 | 806,408 |
| Amusement Taxes | 400,000 | 623,815 |
| Oil Inspection | 100,000 | 106,028 |
| Capital Issues | 5,000 | 12,671 |
| Miscellaneous Taxes | — | 6,019 |
| Tobacco Products Taxes | 210,000 | 210,000 |
| Interest Earnings | 50,000 | 11,671 |

| | | |
|---|---:|---:|
| Motor Fuel Tax | 2,750,000 | 2,360,000 |
| Escheats | 14,500 | 918 |
| Contributions from Public Enterprises | — | 3,823 |
| Refund of Imprest Cash—Revenue Department | — | 25,000 |
| Property Tax | 175,000 | 153,744 |
| Utilities Commission Fees | — | 10 |
| State Board of Elections | — | 6,208 |
| Inheritance Taxes | 750,000 | 530,617 |
| Licenses | 3,500,000 | 3,496,866 |
| Franchise Taxes | 7,267,800 | 7,245,754 |
| Insurance Department Fees | 14,700 | 15,692 |
| Income Taxes | 7,690,000 | 8,088,119 |
| Secretary of State Fees | 60,000 | 71,682 |
| Governor's Office Fees | 15,000 | 18,551 |
| | $35,578,000 | $35,495,122 |

Required:
Prepare a statement of estimated and actual revenues for the fiscal year ended June 30, 19X0.

# 7

# Expenditure Accounting

The budget prepared by the executive branch contains the plans the chief executive wants to carry out during a fiscal year. The legislative branch reviews the plans, and by providing appropriations it enters into a contract with the executive branch for putting into effect those plans—or as much of the plans as it endorses. The executive branch is then charged with the responsibility of carrying out the contract in both a legal and an efficient manner.

## ACCOUNTING CONTROLS

The accounting system is a powerful tool for control of both legality and efficiency. Though its most obvious role is financial, it may also be used to record and report quantitative data of all kinds. The statistical data that must be estimated and accumulated to plan and control virtually all the operations of a government are best used in conjunction with financial data, and frequently it is feasible to accumulate the two kinds of data simultaneously. The accounting system will be discussed in relation to the following problems:

1. Misapplication of assets
2. Illegal expenditures
   2.1 Overspending of appropriations
   2.2 Spending for illegal purposes

3. Use of improper methods and procedures
4. Unwise or inappropriate expenditures
5. Allocation and allotments of appropriations.

Discussion of these problems and potential methods of control serves as an excellent introduction to expenditure accounting principles and procedures. In general the principles are those of internal control, and there is no intention of presenting an exhaustive discussion of that topic here.[1]

MISAPPLICATION OF ASSETS. Not-for-profit organizations own many assets, starting with but not restricted to cash, that are desirable to those who do not own them. The accounting system is a principal means of preventing the misuse or theft of assets. Control to prevent misapplication of assets is provided by a combination of operational procedures, including the entire set of preaudit procedures, and by the postaudit. Sound operational procedures are founded on the separation of responsibility for operation, for custody, and for control. For example, a large storeroom for office supplies should be under the care of the storekeeper who is given adequate personnel and appropriate physical facilities for maintaining control over the supplies entrusted to him. The operating personnel who need office supplies should be able to obtain office supplies only by means of requisitions that become the basis for reducing the storekeeper's responsibility. The accounting department, exercising the control function, should maintain a record of supplies for which the storekeeper is responsible, and periodic physical inventory counts and analyses should be performed to establish the agreement between the goods on hand and the goods listed in the control records.

The preaudit is usually performed by or under the direction of the chief accounting officer of the governmental unit and is designed to determine whether prescribed procedures have been followed in the acquisition of goods and services. Discussion of preaudit procedures appears later in this chapter.

Finally, the examination of the financial statements and their supporting records by an independent postauditor is a powerful deterrent to misapplication of assets. Chapter 18 is devoted to auditing.

ILLEGAL EXPENDITURES. Expenditures may be illegal because the appropriations that allegedly authorize them have been exceeded or because the expenditures are made for purposes not contemplated by the appropriation. Control of overspending of appropriations is, of course, basically the responsibility of the individual department head; but ultimate control is ordinarily exercised by the chief accounting officer.

The accounting system provides records that permit the comparison of expenditures with appropriations or allotments and also provides current infor-

---

[1] See Committee on Auditing Procedure, Statements on Auditing Procedure Number 33, *Auditing Standards and Procedures,* Chapter V (New York: American Institute of Certified Public Accountants, 1963), and the Committee's 1949 work, *Internal Control.*

mation regarding the encumbrances that are outstanding. The department head can exercise effective control only if he is provided with current information as to the unexpended and unencumbered balances of his allotments or appropriations. Expenditures that are made on purchase orders are ordinarily subject to approval by the chief accounting officer at the time the order is placed. Other expenditures are ordinarily controlled by the preaudit work of the accounting department; though in some cases it may be desirable to encumber the appropriations for amounts that are obviously committed, such as certain contractual services and even payroll. Certainly payroll expenditures should be controlled in part at the time of hiring and again in the preaudit procedure.

Expenditures may legally be made only for purposes that are contemplated by the legislators when they make appropriations. For example, the purchase of liquor for the entertainment of highway contractors could not legally be made out of governmental funds unless the legislative body had appropriated funds to be used for the purpose. In other cases the legislature may specifically prohibit purchases of certain items, such as passenger cars. Again the primary responsibility for prevention of illegal expenditures rests with the operating agency, but the final control as to legality is usually exercised by the chief accounting officer in the central administration. Such control typically is imposed at the purchase order point as orders are presented for encumbrance; expenditures that are not encumbered should be controlled at the preaudit point.

USE OF IMPROPER METHODS AND PROCEDURES. Assuring the use of proper methods and procedures is an integral part of the process of internal control. The central financial administrative agencies, including those of the chief accounting officer, the treasurer, the purchasing agent, and the budget officer, should work together in specifying the forms, methods, and procedures to be used within the framework of applicable law. Examples of specific procedures will be discussed in a succeeding section of this chapter.

Responsibility for operational control necessarily belongs to the operating units of the government, and the heads of such agencies are primarily responsible for compliance with specified methods and procedures. The ultimate responsibility rests with the central agencies; the chief accountant's control is exercised through his preaudit procedures, which provide him with an overview of methods and procedures in use.

UNWISE OR INAPPROPRIATE EXPENDITURES. A situation encountered frequently in governments is that in which the operating agencies have an appropriation against which a proposed expenditure may legally be charged but the central financial administrative agencies question the wisdom or appropriateness of the expenditure. Lump sum appropriations provide substantial flexibility to the operating agency and for that reason are highly desirable. A sound accounting and reporting system generates reliable comparisons of plans and accomplishments that provide an after-the-fact control on the agency in such cases, and the head of the agency should have ultimate responsibility for his decisions. This responsibility is removed from him if he is subject to veto by a central purchasing agent, a central budget officer or the chief accountant. *The central financial administrative agencies should not have authority to prevent such expenditures,* though they should certainly be free to suggest the possibility of a mistake if an operating agency is ordering what is known to be a three-year supply of an item or is ordering Cadillacs to be used as highway patrol cars.

The foregoing discussion of the placement of expenditure controls should be tempered by acknowledging that the size of the government has a substantial effect on the ways in which these controls are exercised. In a very small governmental unit control may be highly centralized because of the ease with which central financial administrative officers, or even the chief executive, can review operations. As the size of the government expands, responsibility tends to be concentrated in the departments. As the departments increase in size, as the quality of their supervisory personnel improves, and as the ability of a central officer to be conversant with all operations decreases, power tends to shift to the departments. This is particularly true in unintegrated, loosely knit governments such as those of many states.

ALLOCATION AND ALLOTMENT OF APPROPRIATIONS. A discussion of accounting controls would be incomplete without recognizing the importance of executive control of rates of expenditure and purposes of expenditure. After the appropriation ordinance or act is passed, the executive branch of the government is expected to control the budget properly. As noted in Chapter 3, the appropriation ordinance or act does not specify the rate at which expenditures are to be made throughout the year nor, in the case of lump-sum appropriations, does it specify the details of expenditure. Thus, allotments and allocations—executive assignments of appropriations to specific periods of time or to specific classifications of expenditures—may be established to control the departments' use of the appropriations. When assignments are made, only the assigned portion of the annual appropriation constitutes valid expenditure authority at the operating agency level.

The following schedule of events is typical of the process of control by allotments (and, by inference, of allocations):

1. The chief executive calls for departmental allocation and allotment schedules. Each department head at this time knows the maximum amount that his department may spend; he must determine how much of the appropriations he believes should be spent during each period and he must determine, if a lump sum of appropriation has been made, how the sum is to be spread among his activities. The latter distribution will be made in essentially the same way as his original budget estimates were made. Work programs set up to show both the allocation to activities and the allotment by periods may be utilized to support the schedules he will submit to the chief executive.

2. The chief executive receives from the director of finance or the budget officer statements showing estimated receipts by months, quarters, or other planning periods.

3. The departmental allocation and allotment schedules are submitted to the chief executive with their support.

4. The departmental schedules are tabulated to show total allocations and allotments requested for each period of the year.

5. Adjustments are then made, as far as possible, to bring the amount of expenditures to be authorized within the actual resources available each period. The periodic work programs are helpful in this connection, and the chief executive will work with department heads to determine what adjustments are necessary and desirable.

6. The allocations and allotments are approved by the chief executive and certified to the finance officer who sets up the proper accounts for each unit so as to show both the amounts allocated and the allotments into which the appropriation allocation is divided. If the budget is to be effectively controlled, organization units must stay within both their appropriations allocations and the amounts alloted to them for a particular period.

None of the foregoing should be taken to mean that all governmental units use allotments or that very many use both time and expenditure classification assignments. In the case of line-item appropriations, there is no necessity for allocation by expenditure classification, and many governmental units may have no need to allot expenditures by periods.

## EXPENDITURE ACCOUNTING PROCEDURES

Expenditures are classified and coded during the preaudit step of the budget process. Preaudit consists of approving transactions before they have taken place, as in the case of purchase orders, or before they have been recorded, as in the case of expenditures. Responsibility for the function is usually assigned to the chief accounting officer, although large departments, especially at the state and national levels, have accountants who perform some or all of the preaudit functions. The preaudit is, in the case of expenditures, directed to the control of methods and procedures involved in the expenditure process as well as the prevention of illegal expenditures and the stealing and misuse of assets.

Most governmental units use some form of the voucher system which requires that all disbursements must be authorized by an approved voucher. The voucher itself constitutes an outline of the work that must be performed in making sure that appropriate procedures have been followed in the process of requisitioning, purchasing, receiving, and approving invoices for payment. Figure 7-3 provides an example of an accounts payable voucher.

Since accounting procedures for each of the main objects of expenditure are different, the procedures to be briefly discussed will be those for personal services, supplies, and other services and charges.

## Personal Services

The steps in accounting for personal services are (1) determining rates of pay, (2) ascertaining the amounts earned by employees, (3) recording payments made to employees, and (4) charging the resultant expenditure to the proper accounts.

DETERMINING RATES OF PAY. At the time an employee is hired his rate of pay is set by reference to the authority in use in his governmental unit. The legislative body has the ultimate authority and may determine rates of pay directly, or the power to do so may be delegated to the chief executive or to a civil service commission. Rates that are set legislatively may be expressed in an appropriation ordinance, an annual wage and salary ordinance, or in a continuing ordinance.

DETERMINING AMOUNTS DUE EMPLOYEES. Since an employee's pay depends cn his rate of pay and the amount of time he works, time or attendance records must be kept for employees. These records are the responsibility of each department head, but of course he can delegate the time-keeping duty. Mechanical time-recording devices may be used, but the typical record is a time sheet, which may or may not be a part of the same form used for the payroll.

In most cities the time records are submitted to a central payroll or accounting department. There is a substantial trend towards centralization of payroll preparation in state governments, but many state departments are large enough to support an efficient payroll department.

Since there are many procedures and bookkeeping devices available for payroll, a description of payroll procedures can at best give examples from the broad range available.

A payroll register form is illustrated in Figure 7-1. In this case it is assumed that the same form is used both for time-keeping and payroll preparation. The names of employees, classes of position, and rates of pay are filled in by the accounting department by appropriate means. Master records are kept under the control of the chief accounting officer or the head of the payroll division. Changes in the master records for dismissals, position changes, pay changes, and the like will be submitted to the accounting department so that the records are kept up to date both as to proper pay rates and the proper expenditure accounts to be charged.

The payroll sheets are run off at the beginning of the payroll period and sent to the respective departments. Between the start and end of the payroll period, new employees may have been hired. The time-keeper is notified of these by the accounting department and adds their names to the payroll sheet. At the

Figure 7-1

**A GOVERNMENTAL UNIT**

Payroll Register for Payroll Period

Department: Public Welfare

| Name, Class No., and Title | Salary Rate | Days | | | | | | | Worked | | | | | | | Total Days | Gross Amount of Pay | Deductions For | | | | Net Amount |
|---|---|---|---|---|---|---|---|---|---|---|---|---|---|---|---|---|---|---|---|---|---|---|
| | | 1 | 2 | 3 | | | | 14 | 15 | | | 31 | | | | | | Pensions | Withholding | FICA Taxes | Bonds | |
| | | 16 | 17 | 18 | | | | 29 | 30 | | | | | | | | | | | | | |
| McNulty, George T70 Chief Probation Officer | $325.00 | W | W | H | | | | SL | W | | | W | | | | 16 | $162.50 | $7.50 | $9.20 | $4.47 | $5.00 | $136.33 |

Signed _____ In Charge of Time Rolls

Approved _____ Appointing Officer

Symbols: W = Worked
V = Vacation
H = Nonworking day
SL = Sick leave, no deduction
O = Absence without leave, full deduction

Approved by Civil Service Commission

Signed _____ Secretary

Approved _____ Comptroller

226

Figure 7-2

## A GOVERNMENTAL UNIT
### Payroll Register
### For Payroll Period

Department: Public Welfare

| Hours or Days | Earnings | | | | Deductions | | | | | | Net Pay | Period Ending | Date | Name of Employee | Fund | Check Number | Net Amount |
| | Rate | Regular | Over-time | Gross Pay | W. Tax | FICA | Retire-ment | Bonds | Other | | | | | | | | |
| | | | | | | | | | Amount | Code | | | | | | | |
| 1 | 2 | 3 | 4 | 5 | 6 | 7 | 8 | 9 | 10 | 11 | 12 | 13 | 14 | 15 | 16 | 17 | 18 |
| 16 | $325.00 | $162.50 | | $162.50 | $9.20 | $4.47 | $7.50 | $5.00 | | | $136.33 | May 31, 19— | May 31, 19— | George McNulty | General | 13,463 | $136.33 |

end of the payroll period, the payroll sheets are transmitted to the accounting department. Here the amount of pay due each employee and the deductions therefrom, such as for pensions and Federal income taxes, are calculated and recorded on the payroll sheets.

A second type of payroll register is illustrated in Figure 7-2. It is intended for use (1) with a separate time record and (2) in computers and bookkeeping machines that reduce the payroll operation to a minimum number of operations. Present Federal payroll laws require that employees receive a record of the amounts earned, deducted, and paid them and that the employer maintain a detailed record of payroll information for each employee, and governments are not excepted from the requirement. Using bookkeeping machines, a governmental unit can produce in one operation the payroll register, the statement of the employee's earnings and deductions (columns 1–13 may be posted simultaneously to a check stub having the same headings as columns 1–13), the employee payroll ledger (columns 1–13 may be posted simultaneously to the ledger card having the same headings as columns 1–13), and the check (columns 14–18 may be printed simultaneously on prenumbered checks having the same headings as columns 14–18).

The payroll is not considered completed until it has been audited. Auditing of payrolls consists of verifying (1) that employees have been placed on the payroll by the appropriate authority, (2) that persons listed actually worked the time for which they are being paid, (3) that calculations are correct, (4) that classes of positions and rates of pay correspond with the provisions of the salary and wage ordinance or other documents designating rates of pay for employees, and (5) that, in the case of salaries and wages subject to appropriation, a sufficient amount is available to the credit of the appropriation to absorb the salary and wage expenses chargeable to it. This work may be performed by various departments. For example, the civil service commission may verify the classes of positions and rates of pay for civil service employees on the payroll. The budget officer may be required to ascertain that appropriations for particular departments have sufficient balances against which to charge the salary and wage expenses. On the other hand, all these functions may be entrusted to the governmental unit's finance officer.

The above discussion relates primarily to permanent employees hired on either an hourly or salary basis. The payroll procedure for temporary employees is not materially different except that master records may not be used. In this case, too, it is necessary to ensure that employees have been placed on the payroll by the appropriate authority, that employees worked the time they are being paid for, that the payroll has been properly calculated, that rates of pay are as authorized, that the expenditures, if subject to appropriation, have been appropriated for, and that a sufficient amount is available to the credit of the appropriation against which the expenditures are to be charged.

RECORDING PAYMENTS MADE TO EMPLOYEES. After the payroll has been completed and approved (Figure 7-1) or in the process of payroll preparation (Figure 7-2), checks are made out for the employees and, at the designated time, are distributed. Under a proper system of internal control, employees having anything to do with the preparation of time reports, payrolls, or checks are not permitted to distribute the checks to employees. At frequent intervals, endorsements on checks are verified by comparison with the signature cards on file in the accounting department.

CHARGING PERSONAL SERVICE EXPENSES TO PROPER ACCOUNTS. The costs of services of personnel that are chargeable directly to departments or other organizational units are accumulated in the payroll process by the account to be charged. Costs of maintenance and construction personnel may be assignable to a number of expenditure accounts, as may the cost of personnel whose duties cause them to move from one department or activity to another. In these latter cases supervisors or the individual employees may be required to keep and submit records indicating time spent in the several assignments so that proper allocations of payroll costs to expenditure accounts may be made. As soon as the payroll has been approved, an entry is made to record the authorization of the liability and to charge the proper accounts, as follows:

| | | |
|---|---|---|
| Expenditures.................................. | 10,000 | |
| Vouchers Payable .......................... | | 10,000 |
| To record payroll for period May 1–15, 19X0, chargeable as follows: | | |

| | |
|---|---|
| Council.......................... | 1,000 |
| Executive Department .............. | 2,000 |
| Courts........................... | 2,000 |
| Board of Elections................. | 200 |
| Etc. ............................. | 4,800 |
| | 10,000 |

The amounts shown in the explanation to the above entry would be posted to the "Expenditures" columns of the individual appropriation accounts in the expenditures ledger.

As employees are paid, an entry is made debiting Vouchers Payable and crediting Cash. Frequently, a special payroll bank account is provided, in which case one check is prepared for the amount of the entire payroll and is deposited to the credit of the account. The entry is made when the check for the total payroll is drawn, and the payroll checks are charged against this bank account.

### Supplies

The accounting procedure for supplies may be divided into two parts: (1) accounting for *purchases,* and (2) accounting for the *use of supplies.*

PURCHASES.   The details of purchasing procedure vary according to whether
(1) the supplies are purchased directly by individual departments or through a
central purchasing agency and (2) the supplies are purchased for a central
storeroom or directly for departments. Nearly all cities and state governments,
as well as the national government, use varying degrees of central purchasing.
Throughout this chapter it is assumed that purchases are made through a central agency. If a central storeroom is not used, all supplies are delivered directly
to the departments; and even if a storeroom is used, many deliveries will be
made directly to departments.

The purchasing procedure and the related accounting procedure consist of
the following steps: (1) preparing purchase requisitions and placing them with
the purchasing agent, (2) securing prices or bids, (3) placing orders, (4) receiving the supplies, (5) receiving the invoice and approving the liability, and
(6) paying the liability. All of these steps, except that relating to the payment
of the liability, are discussed below.

The first step in the purchasing procedure is the filing of a requisition with
the purchasing agent, asking him to secure the desired supplies. If the governmental unit has a central storeroom, many purchase requisitions are likely to be
initiated by storekeepers as soon as the amount on hand has reached a predetermined minimum. Where no central storeroom exists, requisitions are filed by the
organization units needing supplies. Even if a central storeroom is maintained,
there are many occasions for departments to file requisitions for supplies that
cannot be economically carried in stock.

Although the work of the purchasing agent is extremely technical, an
understanding of the expenditure process requires an understanding of the
function he performs and something of his methods. The purchasing agent is a
specialist in the acquisition of personal property. He is trained to discover and
evaluate the goods that are available for various needs and to determine how
best to acquire the goods to fill those needs. These activities may readily be
identified as staff services; that is, they are intended to assist operating officials
and employees to discharge their assigned responsibilities effectively. The purchasing function consists primarily of service to the other units of the government and of certain controls to be exercised over the purchasing process.

Responsibility for control of methods of purchasing is usually assigned to
the purchasing agent. A twofold duty is thus imposed: first, the government
should obtain the proper goods at the proper price; and second, there should be
maintained safeguards that will prevent misappropriation of public moneys.
The following discussion outlines some of the methods which the purchasing
agent should (and should not) use to discharge his responsibilities.

Upon receipt of a requisition from a storeroom or department the purchasing agent first determines whether the item or items are properly described. The
law usually requires that all purchases over a minimum amount, ranging typically from $250 to $1,000, be made by formal competitive bids; smaller purchases must in many jurisdictions be made by an informal competitive process

such as obtaining bids by telephone. If bids are to be truly competitive, the bidders must understand precisely what is desired. Descriptions of articles, called specifications, must state explicitly what is to be provided. Bidders then understand what they are expected to provide and can be held responsible for failure of their merchandise to conform to specifications.

The purchasing agent should not be assigned, and usually is not assigned, responsibility for the following: (1) control of overspending of appropriations, (2) control of unwise expenditures, and (3) control to insure that an appropriation exists for an expenditure of the nature contemplated. Basic responsibility for all of these rests with the department originating the requisition; the chief accounting officer usually must approve the purchase order with respect to responsibilities (1) and (3) above. In some governmental units the finance officer is asked to review requisitions for adequacy of appropriation and for legality of the nature of the expenditure, but usually these controls are exercised just prior to the placement of the purchase order.

After the specifications for the items to be bought have been properly selected or prepared, the purchasing agent sends out requests for bids. At the time specified in the request the bids are opened and the award is made to the lowest and best bidder. Normally the purchasing agent makes the award, but for purchases over a certain amount the approval of the chief executive and, in the case of local governments, sometimes also the legislative body may be required.

The next step is to place a purchase order, prepared by the purchasing agent, with the vendor selected. As already indicated, to insure proper budgetary control, provision is ordinarily made that no purchase order is valid unless approved by the finance officer. Accordingly, the finance officer is required to certify that a sufficient amount is available to the credit of the appropriation to which the purchase is chargeable. The finance officer will reduce the balance available to the credit of the appropriation before certifying the purchase order. The certified purchase order is then transmitted to the vendor. Even when supplies are ordered for a central storeroom financed through an Intragovernmental Service Fund, and even though no appropriation is necessary for the expenditures made out of that fund, it is advisable to have a certification by the finance officer that funds are legally available for this expenditure.

The supplies are received by the requisitioning departments or by the central storeroom. In either case a receiving report is filled out indicating the kinds and quantities of supplies received. In an effective purchasing system the purchasing agent and the receiving agency would work together to verify that the goods received conform to specifications. The receiving report is used later to compare the quantities received with the quantities ordered and the quantities filled. If the supplies apply to a contract for delivery over a period of time, the receiving report is used also as the basis for making an entry on the bidding form, the order form, or some special form reducing the quantities of supplies remaining to be received on the contract.

Since most vendors allow a cash discount for the prompt payment of bills, governmental units find it desirable to audit invoices promptly to insure payment within the discount period. To facilitate the work of auditing invoices, some governmental units furnish the vendor with invoice blanks. The auditing of invoices consists of determining that (1) the purchase has been made as required by law, (2) each invoice is for materials or services actually received, (3) the quantities agree with the receiving report, (4) the unit prices are those indicated on the purchase order, (5) extensions and footings are correct, (6) the invoice price does not exceed the encumbrance or, if it does, that the unencumbered balance of the appropriation is sufficient to cover the excess, (7) prescribed purchasing procedures were used, and (8) an appropriation is available to which the purchase may legally be charged.

After an invoice has been audited and the expenditures have been found to comply with all of these requirements, a voucher is prepared signifying the approval of the liability and designating the accounts to be charged (see Figure 7-3). The law, particularly of small governmental units, sometimes requires that vouchers be approved by the legislative body. Approval of vouchers is a function of the executive department but, in cases in which internal control is weak, legislative approval may make a contribution to the control of expenditures.

ACCOUNTING FOR SUPPLIES USED.   As in all governmental activities, the law to some degree determines the practices by which a government provides and accounts for supplies used by its departments, but within the legal framework there may be substantial latitude. Two legal assumptions are dealt with in the following paragraphs: (1) The Expenditures account is to be charged with the amount of supplies purchased (purchases basis). (2) The Expenditures account is to be charged with the amount of supplies consumed (consumption basis).

On the *purchases* basis the appropriation is provided on the basis of estimated purchases and the Expenditures account is charged with all actual purchases during the year. Inventory may or may not be recorded; in the typical situation, it is not. When the government is on the purchases basis and no inventory is recorded, stores accounting is quite simple. Assuming that the usual entry has been made encumbering the purchase order, the approval of the invoice gives rise to the following entry:

| | | |
|---|---|---|
| Reserve for Encumbrances | 10,000 | |
| Expenditures | 9,500 | |
| Vouchers Payable | | 9,500 |
| Encumbrances | | 10,000 |

To record approval of invoice, cancellation of encumbrance, and reduction of appropriation by amount of actual expenditure. Subsidiary accounts:

| Organization Unit | Encumbrances Canceled | Expenditure Charged |
|---|---|---|
| Department of Public Works | 10,000 | 9,500 |

Figure 7-3

(a) Front.

A GOVERNMENTAL UNIT
Accounts Payable Voucher

No. _____
Date _____

Payee

Requisition No. _____
Purchase Order No. _____
_____
_____        Terms _____
_____        Date Due _____

| Invoice Date | Invoice Number | Description | Amount |
|---|---|---|---|
| | | | |
| | | | |
| | | | |
| | | | |
| | | | |
| | | | |
| | | | |
| | | | |
| | | | |
| | | Cash Discount | |
| | | Net | |

Audited and Found O.K. _____

Entry Authorized _____

Payment Authorized _____

Figure 7-3 (cont.)

(b) Reverse.

| Accounts Payable Voucher | | | | |
|---|---|---|---|---|
| Charge These Accounts | | | | Summary |
| Code | Description | G. L. | S. L. | Voucher No. _____ |

Voucher No. _____
Voucher Date _____
Due Date _____
Date Paid _____
Check No. _____

Amount      $ _____
Discount      _____
Net      $ _____

PAYEE

_____
_____
_____

Journalized _____
Posted _____
_____

The amounts shown in the explanation to the entry are posted to the "Encumbrances" and "Expenditures" columns of the individual appropriation accounts carried in the Expenditure Ledger (see Figure 7-5). The foregoing entry would also serve to record in a General or Special Revenue Fund the supplies received from a central storeroom operated through an Intragovernmental Service Fund.

Failure to record inventory leads to a management problem (perhaps unrecognized) because inventories are not likely to be subject either to custodial control or budgetary consideration. On the other hand, recording the inventory tends to point out to management the need for controlling the inventory in terms of both physical custody and total investment. Too, the budget authorities of the executive and legislative branches need data concerning both the inventory and estimated consumption if they are to give intelligent consideration to budget requests.

Each department should take a physical inventory of supplies at the end of the fiscal year. Let us assume that departments do not keep perpetual inventory records, that this is the first time that departments have taken a physical inventory, and that the cost of supplies on hand is ascertained to be $20,000. In that case, if the departments are all financed either from the General Fund or from some Special Revenue Fund, the following entry is made as soon as the value of materials on hand is determined:

| | | |
|---|---|---|
| Inventory of Supplies | 20,000 | |
| Reserve for Inventory of Supplies | | 20,000 |
| To record inventories of supplies on hand in following organization units: | | |
| | | |
| Department of Public Works | 10,000 | |
| Police Department | 1,000 | |
| Fire Department | 1,000 | |
| Etc. | 8,000 | |
| | 20,000 | |

The foregoing entry may be thought of as a combination of two entries: (1) debit Inventory of Supplies and credit Fund Balance and (2) debit Fund Balance and credit Reserve for Inventories. Inventories of future years will differ in amount; what change should be made in the two accounts in the preceding entry? Most authorities agree that both accounts should show the cost of the inventory on hand at the end of the year when the purchases basis is used.

When the accounting for stores is on the *consumption* basis, the appropriation is provided on the basis of estimated consumption, the Expenditures account is charged with actual consumption, and inventory will always be recorded. The inventory may be kept on either the periodic or the perpetual basis. The entry to record the inventory for the first time is the same as that previously given for the purchases basis; that is, debit Inventory of Supplies and credit Reserve for Inventories.

When a periodic inventory is used with the consumption basis, typical operating entries (encumbrance and subsidiary ledger entries omitted) are as follows:

| | | |
|---|---|---|
| Expenditures.............................. | 150,000 | |
| Vouchers Payable ....................... | | 150,000 |
| To record the purchase of stores for the year. | | |

| | | |
|---|---|---|
| Inventory of Supplies ....................... | 2,500 | |
| Expenditures........................... | | 2,500 |
| To record the increase in inventory during the fiscal period, or to record the inventory at the end of the first year of the fund's existence. | | |

These entries are usually accompanied by an entry to adjust the reserve account, even though the supplies are available to finance subsequent period expenditures. The entry to adjust the Reserve for Inventory of Supplies in this case would be:

| | | |
|---|---|---|
| Fund Balance............................. | 2,500 | |
| Reserve for Inventory of Supplies .......... | | 2,500 |
| To adjust the reserve to equal the valuation of the supplies on hand. | | |

The debits and credits in the last two entries are reversed if the inventory has decreased.

When a perpetual inventory is used with the consumption basis, typical entries to be made after the inventory has been first recorded are as follows (encumbrances and subsidiary ledger entries again omitted) :

| | | |
|---|---|---|
| Inventory of Supplies ....................... | 150,000 | |
| Vouchers Payable ....................... | | 150,000 |
| To record the purchases of supplies. | | |

| | | |
|---|---|---|
| Expenditures.............................. | 147,000 | |
| Inventory of Supplies .................... | | 147,000 |
| To charge Expenditures with the amount of stores issued. | | |

| | | |
|---|---|---|
| Expenditures.............................. | 500 | |
| Inventory of Supplies .................... | | 500 |
| To record inventory shortage, per physical inventory. (If there is an overage, the accounts debited and credited in this entry are reversed.) | | |

| Fund Balance .............................. | 2,500 | |
| Reserve for Inventory of Supplies .......... | | 2,500 |

To adjust the reserve for the increase in inventory
during the period. (If there has been a decrease in
inventory during the period, the entry is reversed.)

The last entry is made on the assumption that the Reserve for Inventory of Supplies is to be maintained at an amount equal to the inventory. If the inventory varies substantially from normal levels, it may be desirable to maintain the Reserve for Inventory of Supplies account at the normal figure in order accurately to indicate the Fund Balance available for appropriation in the succeeding year.

SUPPLIES ACQUIRED FOR A STOREROOM FINANCED FROM AN INTRAGOVERNMENTAL SERVICE FUND. The accounting for these supplies is described in Chapter 13, which deals with Intragovernmental Service Funds.

## Other Services and Charges

When services are acquired under contract, an entry is made encumbering appropriations for the amount of the estimated contractual liability at the time the contract is awarded. As services and the related invoices are received, the entries setting up encumbrances are reversed and the actual expenditures are recorded. When contractual services are of small amount or of a regularly recurring and relatively constant amount, the appropriations for them are not ordinarily encumbered.

Depreciation and interest expenses present accounting problems that are discussed in subsequent chapters.

FIXED ASSETS AND RETIREMENT OF DEBT. The foregoing discussion applies to the acquisition of relatively small fixed assets, such as furniture and minor equipment. It does not apply to fixed assets of major dimension or to the retirement of bonds or other long-term debts. These subjects are discussed in subsequent chapters.

CLASSIFYING AND RECORDING EXPENDITURES. As we have seen, expenditures must be approved before they may be recorded as liabilities. Approval is evidenced by a voucher, which is illustrated in Figure 7-3. The approved voucher is entered in a voucher register, illustrated in Figure 7-4. The information necessary for recording each transaction in the voucher register is obtained from the vouchers. At the time he audits invoices or payrolls the audit clerk determines to which accounts and funds expenditures are chargeable. By using a prearranged code he can designate the proper account easily.

In many cases postings to the detailed expenditures accounts are made directly from the vouchers, especially if it is desirable to show more information in the account than can be obtained from the voucher register. This would be

Figure 7-4

A GOVERNMENTAL UNIT

Voucher Register

Sheet No. _____

Month of _____ 19 ___

| Day | Details | Voucher No. | Payment | | Amount | Code | Funds | | | |
|-----|---------|-------------|---------|---------|--------|------|---------|-----------------|------------------|---------------------------|
| | | | Date | Check No. | | | General | Special Revenue | Capital Projects | Intra-governmental Service |
| | | | | | | | | | | |

238

true, for example, of the voucher register here illustrated, which shows only the total charge against each fund.

## CLASSIFICATION OF EXPENDITURES

Expenditures of a governmental unit are classified in order to serve several purposes. First, the money that belongs to a governmental unit is in the treasury in various funds; the appropriations for the expenditures must necessarily be classified according to the funds that are in the treasury, and, as we have seen, the expenditures must be related to the appropriations. Second, appropriate classification provides information that will be helpful in the preparation of the budgets for succeeding years. Third, appropriate classification provides information to control the expenditure of funds in an economical fashion. Fourth, the properly classified expenditures provide information for the financial statements and for financial statistics that may be used for comparative purposes.

Since appropriations are expressed in terms of specified funds, the basic classification of expenditures is in accord with the sources of the appropriations, the several funds. To produce all the required information, the expenditures of a fund are also classified by function, activity, organization unit, character and object. In preparing statements that describe in a broad fashion the operation of a governmental unit the fund classification may be ignored, but it cannot be ignored in the accounting process.

The National Committee on Governmental Accounting has prepared a standard classification of accounts, including expenditure accounts.[2] The classification is intended to be complete, so that the appropriate accounts for the several funds of any governmental unit may be selected from the classification. The budgeting, accounting, and reporting systems of A Governmental Unit should utilize the same structure of accounts; and if the same standard classification is used by all governmental units, the comparison of and summation of expenditures for various purposes on a local, state, and national basis is facilitated.

CLASSIFICATION BY FUNCTION. A Governmental Unit's functions are the broad purposes that the government exists to fulfill. A typical governmental unit provides a wide spectrum of services; many provide services that are the same in objective as those of other governmental units. For example, the typical city, county, and state governments are all involved in the provision of public safety. If they all select from a standard classification the accounts necessary to record their expenditures for public safety it becomes possible to accumulate a total figure for a state or for the nation as a whole. Further, it becomes possible to compare expenditures of one city or county with another city or county having comparable size and problems. The functional classification provides the basic structure for the classification of expenditures.

The following is a standard classification of expenditures by function:

2 *GAAFR,* "Appendix B: Use of Account Classifications," pp. 175–201.

| | *Broad Functions, Functional Classifications* | | *Functions* |
| *Code\** | *Title* | *Code* | *Title* |
| --- | --- | --- | --- |
| 1000– 1999 | General Government | 1000 | Legislative Branch |
| | | 1100 | Executive Branch |
| | | 1200 | Judicial Branch |
| 2000– 2999 | Public Safety | 2000 | Police Protection |
| | | 2100 | Fire Protection |
| | | 2200 | Correction |
| | | 2300 | Protective Inspection |
| 3000– 4999 | Public Works | 3000 | Highways and Streets |
| | | 4000 | Sanitation |
| 5000– 6999 | Health and Welfare | 5000 | Health |
| | | 6000 | Welfare |
| 7000– 7999 | Education (Schools) | | |
| 8000– 9999 | Culture-Recreation | 8000 | Libraries |
| | | 9000 | Parks |
| 10000–14999 | Conservation of Natural Resources | 10000 | Water Resources |
| | | 11000 | Agricultural Resources |
| | | 12000 | Mineral Resources |
| | | 13000 | Fish and Game Resources |
| | | 14000 | Other Natural Resources |
| 15000–15999 | Urban Redevelopment and Housing | | |
| 16000–16999 | Economic Development and Assistance | | |
| 17000–17999 | Economic Opportunity | | |
| 18000–19999 | Debt Service | 18000 | Interest |
| | | 19000 | Principal |
| 20000–20999 | Paying Agent's Fees | | |
| 21000–21999 | Intergovernmental Expenditures | | |

* For explanation of code numbers, see section headed "Coding Expenditure Accounts," which follows.

CLASSIFICATION BY ACTIVITY. An activity is a specific line of work carried on by a governmental unit in order to perform one of its functions. Ordinarily it is necessary to carry on several activities in order to fulfill a function. The typical activities for the police protection and sanitation functions are given below:[3]

[3] For explanation of code numbers, see section headed "Coding Expenditure Accounts," which follows.

```
2000  Police Protection Function
      2010  Police Administration
      2020  Crime Control and Investigation
            2021  Criminal Investigation
            2022  Vice Control
            2023  Patrol
            2024  Records and Identification
            2025  Youth Investigation and Control
            2026  Custody of Prisoners
            2027  Custody of Property
            2028  Crime Laboratory
      2030  Traffic Control
            2031  Motor Vehicle Inspection and Regulation
      2040  Police Training
      2050  Support Services
            2051  Communications Services
            2052  Automotive Services
            2053  Ambulance Services
            2054  Medical Services
            2055  Special Detail Services
            2056  Police Stations and Buildings

4000  Sanitation Function
      4010  Sanitary Administration
      4020  Street Cleaning
      4030  Waste Collection
      4040  Waste Disposal
      4050  Sewage Collection and Disposal
            4051  Sanitary Sewer Construction
            4052  Sanitary Sewer Maintenance
            4053  Sanitary Sewer Cleaning
            4054  New Sewer Services
            4055  Sewer Lift Stations
            4056  Sewage Treatment Plants
      4060  Weed Control
```

The activity classification is essential to secure cost data for budget preparation and managerial control. Unit cost accounting is possible only if: (1) expenditures are classified by activities and (2) statistics concerning units of output are accumulated. Even if unit costs are not to be computed, it is desirable to compare the costs of an activity with the benefits expected from it in order to make an intelligent decision as to whether the scope of the activity should be increased, decreased, or left unchanged. Accumulation of cost data by activities also permits comparison of such costs between governmental units and, by addition, accumulation of expenditures by function.

CLASSIFICATION BY ORGANIZATION UNIT. Sound budgetary control requires that authority and responsibility for carrying on the activities of the government be assigned in a definite fashion to its officials. The assignment of appropriations and their related expenditures to organization units is essential if department heads are to be held responsible for planning their activities and for controlling those activities that are authorized by the legislative body through the appropriations process. The classification of expenditures by organization unit is therefore important because it provides the means whereby expenditure can be controlled and responsibility can be definitely allocated.

If the planning and execution of functions and activities is to be properly controlled, there must be proper allocation of activities to departments. Ideally a major department would be assigned responsibility for a function and its subunits would be assigned responsibility for the several activities necessary to carry out the function. However, in an actual situation it may not be feasible to attain the ideal. For example, it may be appropriate to assign activities of a governmental unit in such a way that those requiring engineering skill will all be in the same department, perhaps called the Department of Public Works. The Department head might be assigned responsibility for sanitation and streets, both of which are major functions, and also for building inspection, plumbing inspection, electrical inspection, gas inspection, air conditioning inspection, boiler inspection, elevator inspection, and weights and measures, all in the public safety function. Within that Department of Public Works each of the many activities involved in the two major functions, together with each of the other miscellaneous activities, should be assigned to individual organizational subunits. Again speaking ideally, each organizational unit (or subunit) in the Department of Public Works should have responsibility for a single activity. *A minimum requirement is that responsibility for an activity should be assigned to only one organization unit.* Those units that cover more than one activity should have their budgeting, accounting, reporting and administration arranged so that assignments or allocations of costs may be made by activity. Organization by activity is highly desirable because of the possibility of precise assignment of authority and responsibility and because of the simplicity of accounting and control of activities that results.

From the foregoing description it is clear that no major difficulty is caused when a department is responsible for activities in more than one function. This arrangement may be highly desirable in order for a governmental unit to take advantage of the training and experience of officers or employees whose skills are in short supply. This arrangement also emphasizes that the functional classification's chief importance is in broad scale reporting rather than in operations.

CLASSIFICATION BY CHARACTER. The classification by character is a classification by period benefited by the expenditure. The three groupings are current expenses, capital outlays, and debt service. Current expenses are those expenditures that are expected to be consumed within the current period, that is, those that benefit the current period. Capital outlays are those that are expected to benefit not only this period but also several or many periods in the future. Desks, trucks, and buildings are examples of capital outlays. Inasmuch as the distinction between capital outlays and current expenses is sometimes difficult to make, it is necessary to establish policies that can be used in making these classification decisions. For example, the decision as to whether to charge test tubes for a laboratory as a current expense or a capital outlay should be based on experience with test tubes. If most of them, say 95 percent, will be broken in the course of the current year, they probably should be classified as current expenses even though the other 5 percent may last for several years. The decision may also be made on the basis of cost; no major violence will be done to the fairness of financial reporting if capital outlay items costing less than some arbitrary and relatively small sum are treated as current expenses.

Payments of maturing long-term debt principal, interest on debt, and related service charges, together with payments made to Debt Service Funds for the foregoing purposes, are debt service expenditures. Though these are sometimes said to be expenditures that are made for past benefits, it is clear that in those cases in which debt proceeds were used to acquire capital outlay items the expenditures may "benefit" past, present, and future periods.

CLASSIFICATION BY OBJECT OF EXPENDITURE. The object-of-expenditure classification groups expenditures according to the article purchased or the service obtained. The following is a standard classification of objects of expenditure related to the character classification as indicated:

| Character | Object of Expenditure |
|---|---|
| 01–03* Current Expenses | 01 Personal Services |
| | 02 Supplies |
| | 03 Other Services and Charges |
| 04–07 Capital Outlays | 04 Land |
| | 05 Buildings |
| | 06 Improvements Other Than Buildings |
| | 07 Machinery and Equipment |
| 08–10 Debt Service | 08 Debt Principal |
| | 09 Interest |
| | 10 Debt Service Charges |

* For explanation of code numbers, see section headed "Coding Expenditure Accounts," which follows.

The object-of-expenditure classifications under capital outlays are obviously directly applicable to purchased assets rather than to those constructed by the governmental unit. In the latter case it may be useful to use the object-of-expenditure classifications under current expenses for the accumulation of costs. These classifications should be understood to be subordinate to the classifications listed above under capital outlays; for example, the personal service costs, materials and supplies, and other services and charges incurred in the construction of the city hall by the city's own work force would culminate in a classification under capital outlay called "Buildings."

The objects of expenditure listed above under Current Expenses are major classifications. A small municipality, or a small organizational unit in a larger municipality, might find that "personal services," "supplies," and "other services and charges" provide enough detail for administrative and reporting purposes. In most cases, however, each of those classifications would be broken down into greater detail. Personal services could be subdivided into salaries, wages, employer contributions to the retirement system, insurance, sick leave, terminal pay, and the like. The supplies category may be detailed in whatever ways are found to be useful. A minimum breakdown would include office supplies, operating supplies, and repair and maintenance supplies. Other services and charges include such costs as professional services, communication, transportation, advertising, printing and binding, and the like. It is obvious that in certain circumstances it might be very useful to the administration to break down some or all of the foregoing into greater detail. For example, it might be useful to divide communication into such categories as telephone, telegraph, and postage.

The main objects of expenditure ordinarily provide sufficient detail for reports to the public. Decisions as to greater amounts of detail by object of expenditure in the accounts should be based on the administrative need for such information for planning and controlling the operations of the governmental unit.

### Coding Expenditure Accounts

To facilitate the accounting work and the preparation of financial statistics, accounts are coded—that is, are assigned numbers or symbols that can be used in the place of the account titles. The codes form a convenient shorthand for verbal, written, and machine reference. All accounts would be coded; but since the coding of expenditure accounts is more difficult than the coding of other accounts, only their coding will be illustrated. The coding system shown here is only one of several that may be used.

In the preceding tables, numbers have been placed beside the several function, activity, character, and object-of-expenditure classifications. These numbers represent an assumed assignment of codes for A Governmental Unit. The following transactions and their coding illustrate the use of the code numbers on the assumption that the several activities or subactivities listed in the foregoing materials have been assigned to organizational units such as departments, bureaus, or sections:

1. Salaries were paid to the policemen in the Patrol division.
   Code No. 2023–01
       Function: Public Safety (2000–2999)
                 Police Protection (2000)
       Activity: Crime Control and Investigation (2020)
              Patrol (2023)
       Organization Unit: Patrol Division (2023)
       Character: Current Expenses (01–03)
       Object: Personal Services (01)
2. Travel expenses of the head of the Sanitation Division were paid:
   Code No. 4010–03
       Function: Public Works (3000–4999)
                 Sanitation (4000)
       Activity: Sanitary Administration (4010)
       Organization Unit: Sanitation Division Administration (4010)
       Character: Current Expenses (01–03)
       Object: Other Services and Charges (03)
3. New benches were purchased for the City Court.
   Code No. 1000–07
       Function: General Government (1000–1999)
       Activity: Legislative Branch (1000)
       Organization Unit: City Court (1000)
       Character: Capital Outlay (04–07)
       Object: Machinery and Equipment (07)

The examples provide several instances in which additional information, and therefore additional coding, might be desirable. In the second example it might be desirable to have information regarding the specific object of expenditure for "Other Services and Charges." If so, an additional digit, let us say "5," could be added to the "03" to designate travel expenses, and Travel Expenses in the "Other Services and Charges" category would be coded "035." Such additional coding would be applicable throughout all the departments of the governmental unit. Similarly, in example 3 it might be desirable to divide machinery and equipment into various categories, of which "Furniture" might be one and might be assigned the number "3." The code to designate the purchase of the benches then would have been "073."

The foregoing code has provided no designation of fund. Two possible ways of providing this information might be used. First, a code of one or more digits might be developed to identify the funds, and this code might be placed ahead of the function and activity coding illustrated above. Another possibility is to assign all accounts bearing numbers between, let us say, 1000 and 22000 to the General Fund and develop additional code numbers for the other funds.

The existence of a code similar to the one described above emphasizes that the chart of accounts for expenditures is based upon two classifications: organizational unit and object of expenditure. Given the assignment of programs or activities to organization units, the organizational unit and object of expenditure become the basis of managerial planning and control. Data that have been classified by organization unit and by object may subsequently be used in various combinations to produce summaries for the other types of classifications because the accounts have been coded to show fund, function, activity, and character. The following is a part of the heading of a subsidiary appropriation-expenditure ledger sheet:

---

Code No.  2023–01

Function:  Public Safety-Police Protection

Activity:  Crime Control and Investigation—Patrol

Organization Unit:  Police Department—Patrol Division

Character:  Current Expenses

Object:  Personal Services

---

The code provides full information regarding function, activity, organization unit, character, and object. If the total cost of police protection is desired, all the accounts that bear numbers from 2000–2099 may be summarized. If the total cost of personal services for the Police Department is desired, all the personal services accounts (01) bearing numbers from 2000–2099 may be summarized. Total costs of public safety may be derived by summarizing the balances of all the accounts bearing numbers from 2000–2999; that is to say, after the costs of the Police, Fire, Corrections, and Protective Inspection Departments have been determined, those costs may be added to obtain the total costs for the public safety function.

## SUBSIDIARY ACCOUNTS FOR EXPENDITURES

In order to illustrate the use of expenditure subsidiary accounts, let us assume for the moment that allotments of appropriations are not made, that is, that the entire amount of an operating agency's appropriations are available to it from the start of the period. In this situation the Appropriations account in the General Ledger is used to record the appropriation; the related Expenditures and Encumbrances accounts in the General Ledger contain the information for reductions of the appropriations as orders are placed and expenditures made, whether or not allotments are made. These three are control accounts for the subsidiary appropriation-expenditure ledger. Each account in this ledger shows not only the amount appropriated but also the expenditures and encumbrances charged against the appropriation. Thus, all the information about an appropriation is recorded in one subsidiary account (see Figure 7-5) in order (1)

Figure 7-5

Code No.: 2120–02
Function: Public Safety
Organization Unit: Fire Department
Bureau of Fire Fighting
Activity: Fire Fighting
Character: Current Expenses
Object: Supplies
Year: 19X1

**Cumulative Allotments**

| Original | | | Revisions | | |
|---|---|---|---|---|---|
| Jan. | $ 350 | July ——— | Jan. | $2,300 | July ——— |
| Feb. | 700 | Aug. ——— | Feb. | 2,600 | Aug. ——— |
| Mar. | 1,000 | Sept. ——— | Mar. | 2,900 | Sept. ——— |
| Apr. | 1,400 | Oct. ——— | Apr. | 3,250 | Oct. ——— |
| May | 1,700 | Nov. ——— | May | 3,550 | Nov. ——— |
| June | 2,000 | Dec. ——— | June | 3,800 | Dec. ——— |

## A GOVERNMENTAL UNIT
### Appropriation-Expenditure Ledger

| | | Encumbrances | | | | Expenditures | | | | |
|---|---|---|---|---|---|---|---|---|---|---|
| | | Order | | | | | | | | |
| Date | Description | No. | Issued Dr. | Filled or Canceled Cr. | Balance Dr. | Voucher No. | Amount Dr. | Total Expenditures Dr. | Appropriations Cr. | Unencumbered Balance Cr. |
| 1 | 2 | 3 | 4 | 5 | 6 | 7 | 8 | 9 | 10 | 11 |
| 1/3 | Appropriation | — | — | — | — | — | — | — | 3,800 | 3,800 |
| 1/3 | Clothing | 2 | 200 | — | 200 | — | — | — | — | 3,600 |
| 1/7 | Lubricants | 4 | 45 | — | 245 | — | — | — | — | 3,555 |
| 1/23 | Clothing | 2 | — | 200 | 45 | 39 | 205 | 205 | — | 3,550 |
| 12/10 | Clothing | 20 | 300 | — | 300 | — | — | 3,000 | — | 500 |
| 12/31 | Closing Entry | — | — | — | — | — | — | — | (500) | — |

to minimize the number of accounts needed to record expenditure information and, (2), more importantly, to provide better budgetary control. Such an account makes it possible to tell at a glance the status of each appropriation.

The account illustrated in Figure 7-5 is for supplies for the Bureau of Fire Fighting in the Fire Department. There are other appropriations, not illustrated, for the Bureau's personal services, other services and charges, and, perhaps, capital outlay. At the beginning of the year, when the appropriations entry is made, the appropriation is entered in the "Appropriations" column[4] and added to the "Unencumbered Balance" column. The unencumbered balance is reduced by expenditures and by purchase orders placed. This form of account provides valuable information to the finance officer as he controls the expenditures of the departmental units. Regulations are set up providing that no purchase order or contract is valid unless it is approved by the finance officer. Upon approval the purchase order becomes the basis for an entry debiting Encumbrances and crediting Reserve for Encumbrances. The entry debiting Encumbrances in the general ledger is supported by an entry recording the purchase order in the "Encumbrances–Order Issued" column of the subsidiary ledger account. At the same time the unencumbered balance is reduced by the amount of the encumbrance. When an expenditure is made for an item not encumbered previously (1) the Expenditures account in the General Ledger is debited, (2) the "Expenditures—Amount" column in the subsidiary Appropriation—Expenditure Ledger account is debited and (3) the "Unencumbered Balance" is reduced by the amount of the expenditure. Thus at any time the finance officer can determine whether there is an unencumbered balance sufficient to authorize a purchase order or an expenditure.

When an encumbered expenditure is made, it is necessary in the General Ledger to reverse the encumbering entry as well as to record the expenditure. The credit to Encumbrances in the General Ledger is supported by an entry in the "Encumbrances—Order Filled or Canceled" column in the Appropriation-Expenditure Ledger account. If the amount of the expenditure is not the same as the amount of the purchase order, it is also necessary to adjust the unencumbered balance. (This adjustment is made automatically in most mechanized accounting systems.) If the amount of the purchase order exceeds the expenditure, the difference is added to the unencumbered balance; if the expenditure exceeds the purchase order, the unencumbered balance is reduced.

### Entries in Subsidiary Ledger

We have observed that as soon as the appropriation ordinance is passed, an entry is made to record it. If estimated revenues are not included in the budgetary entry, it is as follows:

4 If allotments are made only the allotted appropriations are credited to the "Appropriations" column of the appropriation-expenditure ledger accounts and added to the "Unencumbered Balance" column.

| | | |
|---|---:|---:|
| Fund Balance ........................... | 426,000 | |
| Appropriations ....................... | | 426,000 |

To record appropriations. Entries in subsidiary accounts are as follows (amounts to be posted to the subsidiary Appropriation-Expenditure Ledger accounts are indicated by an asterisk):

Credit Appropriations:
General Government:
Council:
Current Expenses:

| | | | |
|---|---:|---:|---:|
| Personal Services .......... | 8,400* | | |
| Supplies ................. | 600* | | |
| Other Services and Charges.. | 800* | 9,800 | |

Capital Outlays:

| | | | |
|---|---:|---:|---:|
| Equipment ............... | | 1,500* | 5,500 |

Executive Department:
Current Expenses:

| | | | |
|---|---:|---:|---:|
| Personal Services ........... | 10,000* | | |
| Supplies ................. | 1,200* | | |
| Other Services and Charges.. | 1,100* | 12,300 | |

Capital Outlays:

| | | | |
|---|---:|---:|---:|
| Equipment ............... | | 1,500* | 7,000 |

Research and Investigation:
Current Expenses:

| | | | |
|---|---:|---:|---:|
| Personal Services .......... | 1,900* | | |
| Materials and Supplies ..... | 75* | | |
| Other Charges ............. | 25* | 2,000 | |

Capital Outlays:

| | | | |
|---|---:|---:|---:|
| Equipment ............... | | 300* | 2,300 |
| Total General Government | | | 57,030 |

| | |
|---|---:|
| Interest ......................... | 14,400* |
| Retirement of Bonds ............. | 34,000* |
| Total Appropriations .......... | 426,000 |

Even though expenditures are carefully planned, additions to certain appropriations may be necessary. Some governmental units are prohibited by law from making such changes, and other methods are available for taking care of contingencies that may arise. Sometimes a lump-sum contingent appropriation is made and assigned to the mayor or city manager. Either he or the legislative body may have legislative authorization to make transfers from the contingency appropriation to the several departments. Such an entry, assuming a transfer of $8,000 has been authorized, is as follows:

Appropriations.................................... 8,000
    Appropriations...............................         8,000
    To record transfer of appropriations. Entries in sub-
    sidiary accounts: *Debit* Contingencies, $8,000. *Credit*
    Executive Department, $8,000.

Note that the Appropriations account carried in the general ledger is not affected; the only change is in the subsidiary accounts. If no contingent appropriation has been provided, an additional appropriation may be desired and legal. Unless additional revenue is provided at the same time, the appropriation is debited to the Fund Balance account (it decreases the planned year-end balance), as follows:

Fund Balance.................................... 8,000
    Appropriations...............................         8,000
    To record additional appropriations. Entries in sub-
    sidiary accounts: *Credit* Executive Department, $8,000.

To the extent that additional revenues are expected to cover the appropriation, the Estimated Revenues account is debited instead of the Fund Balance account.

Obviously the necessity for changes in specific appropriations is reduced if a lump-sum appropriation is made. Suppose that during the year it is found advantageous to have work done by the department's employees that was originally intended to be performed by contract. If it is necessary to hire additional employees to do the work, and if there have been separate departmental appropriations for personal services and other services and charges, there will have to be a change in the appropriation if the correct decision is to be carried out. On the other hand, if the department has received a lump-sum appropriation, no change in the appropriation is necessary and the departmental decision can be carried out without complication. Some have objected that such freedom of action is not desirable because it implies lack of legislative control over the executive branch. It is true that the executive branch in such circumstances has substantial freedom of action. On the other hand, if the accounting and reporting systems are properly designed to compare the budgeted and actual expenditures, the legislative body will have an opportunity to observe the change in plan through the reports and, if appropriate, to call the executive branch to account for the change. Since the executive branch obtains its funds from the legislative branch, the knowledge that it will be called to account for its decisions provides a powerful deterrent to inappropriate action.

Throughout the year the general ledger entries to the three controlling accounts—Appropriations, Expenditures, and Encumbrances—will be supported by entries in the subsidiary expenditures ledger. At any point in time it should be possible to post all of the journals and prepare a list of account balances in the subsidiary ledger that would equal the net difference in the three control accounts, computed as follows:

Appropriations .............................                                        $X
Less:   Expenditures and Encumbrances:
        Expenditures........................    $Y
        Encumbrances .....................     Z                  Y + Z
        Control figure ...................              $X − (Y + Z)

This balancing process should be carried out at least monthly.

### Closing Entries

At the end of the year the expenditure accounts contain the information necessary for preparation of the financial statements relating to expenditures. The accumulation of that information concludes the functions of the subsidiary accounts and they are ready to be closed out or, if new ledger sheets or cards are to be used for succeeding years, to be stored away. The closing entry for the controlling accounts for Appropriations, Expenditures and Encumbrances was given in Chapter 4. It is repeated below, but subsidiary accounts have been added to show how they are affected by this entry if they are to be closed.

In the closing entry given below, the total of unencumbered balances is $6,100, which is both the sum of the subsidiary ledger account balances and the amount that is credited to the Fund Balance account by the general journal entry. Note that the effect of the closing process in the general ledger is to close the unencumbered appropriations [Appropriations − (Expenditures + Encumbrances)] to the Fund Balance account, thereby adjusting the Fund Balance account for the difference between planned and actual expenditures and for the fact that the Reserve for Encumbrances account has now become a Fund Balance reservation, i.e., it is no longer a memorandum offset account but a Fund Balance Reserve. The amount to be posted to each of the individual Appropriation − Expenditure Ledger accounts is exactly equal to the amount of the unencumbered balance of that Expenditure account. The journal entry, including instructions for closing the subsidiary expenditures ledger, is given below. Note that the total debits and credits in the Appropriation-Expenditure Ledger closing entry do *not* balance, but that the difference equals the $6,100 closed to Fund Balance in the General Ledger.

Appropriations ............................ 426,000
Expenditures........................... 399,900
Encumbrances ......................... 20,000
Fund Balance .......................... 6,100

To record closing out of appropriations, expenditures, encumbrances. Entries (debits) in subsidiary accounts:

|  | Personal Services | Supplies | Other Services and Charges | Capital Outlays |
|---|---|---|---|---|
| General Government: |  |  |  |  |
| Council ......................... |  | 200 |  | 100 |
| Executive Department ............. |  | 150 | 150 |  |
| Courts ......................... |  |  | 100 | 100 |
| Department of Finance: |  |  |  |  |
| General Supervision ............. |  | 100 |  |  |
| Bureau of Accounts .............. | 75 |  |  |  |
| Bureau of Treasury .............. |  | 20 |  |  |
| Bureau of Purchases ............. |  |  | 75 |  |
| Department of Law ............... | 100 |  |  |  |
| City Clerk ...................... |  | 100 | 55 |  |
| Planning and Zoning ............. | 50 |  | 75 |  |
| Civil Service Commission .......... |  |  |  | 100 |
| Public Safety: |  |  |  |  |
| Department of Police |  |  |  |  |
| Administration .................. |  | 40 |  |  |
| Bureau of Records .............. |  | 100 | 60 |  |

~~~~~~~~~~~~~~~~~~~~~~~~~~~~~~~~~~~~~~~~~~~~~~~~~~~~~~~~~~~~~~~~~~~~~~~~~~~~~~~~~~~~~~~~~~~~~~~~~~~~~~~~~~~~~~~~~~~~~~~~~

| Bureau of Fire Fighting .......... |  | 500 |  |  |
| Department of Traffic Engineering ... |  |  | 75 |  |
| Department of Licensed Occupations.. |  | 25 |  |  |
| Highways and Streets ............... | 500 | 100 | 100 |  |
| Health and Welfare ................. | 1,000 | 350 | 100 | 500 |
| Culture-Recreation.................. | 125 | 100 | 75 |  |
| Education ......................... | 200 |  |  |  |
|  | 2,650 | 1,785 | 865 | 800 |
|  |  |  |  | 865 |
|  |  |  |  | 1,785 |
|  |  |  |  | 2,650 |
| Total ...................... |  |  |  | 6,100 |

An example of the posting of one of the above subsidiary ledger entries is provided by Figure 7-5 for the Bureau of Fire Fighting. On December 10, 19X1, the account shows encumbrances outstanding amounting to $300 and an unencumbered balance of $500. The latter amount is transferred to Fund Balance by the above journal entry, posted in the "Appropriations" column as a debit.

### Reserve for Encumbrances of Prior Years

When encumbered appropriations may legally be carried forward into the following year as authority for expenditure, the expenditure accounts of the prior year, properly dated, may be carried forward to the following year as the basis for accounting for expenditures chargeable to the Reserve for Encumbrances (Prior Year). In this case the encumbered balances of the expenditure accounts are not closed out in the closing entries described above; rather, an amount equal to the Reserve for Encumbrances usually is left in the "Appropriations" and "Unencumbered Balance" columns. Though technically there is no unencumbered balance, these subsidiary accounts are now controlled by the Reserve for Encumbrances (Prior Year) and Expenditures (Prior Year) Accounts—and only the former has a balance at the start of the new year. Another possibility is to create a new set of accounts such as the one in Figure 7-6, to which the encumbered balance of the Supplies account of the Bureau of Fire Fighting has been carried forward. Regardless of whether encumbered balances are transferred to the Reserve for Encumbrance (Prior Year) subsidiary accounts or retained in the old expenditure accounts, the accounts containing these balances constitute a separate ledger in support of the Reserve for Encumbrances of prior years and therefore must not be grouped with the new year's exependiture accounts.

## EXPENDITURE STATEMENTS

The data contained in the individual appropriation-expenditure subsidiary accounts are the basis for the several different kinds of expenditure statements necessary to assist in the management and control of the operation of the governmental unit and to report upon that operation at the end of each fiscal period. The following discussions pertain to both the General Fund and any Special Revenue Funds that the governmental unit may have.

*Year-end statements.* The Statement of Expenditures and Encumbrances Compared with Appropriations, Figure 7-7, or a variant of that statement, is the only year-end expenditure statement recommended by the National Committee on Governmental Accounting. Its principal purpose is to report on executive accountability for not spending more than the amount of appropriations. It also may have some value because of the historical record of the appropriations, expenditures, unexpended balances, and unencumbered balances that it contains.

Figure 7-6

Code No.: 2105-C
Function: Public Safety
Organization Unit: Department of Fire
Bureau of Fire Fighting

## A GOVERNMENTAL UNIT

Reserve for Encumbrances of Prior Years Account

Activity: Fire Fighting
Object: Supplies
Year: 19X2

| Date | Explanation | Debit | Credit |
|------|-------------|-------|--------|
| Jan. 3<br>15 | Transferred from Appropriation Account, 19X1<br>Expenditures | $280.00 | $300.00 |

Figure 7-7

## A GOVERNMENTAL UNIT
### General Fund
Statement of Expenditures and Encumbrances Compared with Appropriations
For the Fiscal Year Ended December 31, 19X5

| Function, Activity, and Object* | Appropriations (after revisions) | Expenditures | Unexpended Balance | Encumbrances | Unencumbered Balance |
|---|---|---|---|---|---|
| General Government: | | | | | |
| Legislative: | | | | | |
| Personal Services | $ 20,000 | $ 19,000 | $ 1,000 | $ 400 | $ 600 |
| Supplies | 3,000 | 2,750 | 250 | — | 250 |
| Other Services and Charges | 4,000 | 3,900 | 100 | 100 | — |
| Capital Outlays | 500 | 500 | — | — | — |
| Total Legislative | $ 27,500 | $ 26,150 | $ 1,350 | $ 500 | $ 850 |
| Judicial | 25,000 | 23,000 | 2,000 | 1,750 | 250 |
| Executive | 75,000 | 73,000 | 2,000 | 1,250 | 750 |
| Total General Government | $ 127,500 | $ 122,150 | $ 5,350 | $ 3,500 | $ 1,850 |
| Public Safety† | 200,000 | 198,500 | 1,500 | 1,000 | 500 |
| Highways and Streets† | 100,000 | 99,400 | 600 | 500 | 100 |
| Sanitation† | 60,000 | 57,500 | 2,500 | 2,000 | 500 |
| Health† | 50,000 | 49,225 | 775 | 575 | 200 |
| Welfare† | 40,000 | 38,750 | 1,250 | 1,000 | 250 |
| Culture—Recreation† | 55,000 | 54,000 | 1,000 | 1,000 | — |
| Education† | 500,000 | 495,000 | 5,000 | 3,000 | 2,000 |
| Total | $1,132,500 | $1,114,525 | $17,975 | $12,575 | $5,400 |

* The amount and nature of detail to be included in this statement depend upon the amount and nature of the detail in which appropriations are made. For example, appropriations may be made in lump sum or in detail, for activities or for departmental units.
† Itemize by activity or organization unit and by object, if possible.

Since the first column of the statement is for revised appropriations, the amount of detail presented in the statement is determined by the detail in which appropriations are made. For example, in Figure 7-9 the detailed information regarding activity and object of expenditure is assumed to be available and is the basis for the amount of detail. If the legislative body had provided appropriations on a lump-sum basis for each of the major departments in the city, the functional and departmental classifications would have been used. If the activities of the governmental unit had been assigned to the departments for which appropriations were made, the activity information would, essentially, have been available through the departmental classifications.

The appropriations information in Figure 7-7 is *after* revisions have been made. Detailed appropriations information may be provided in three columns entitled "Appropriations," "Revisions," and "Final Appropriations." When substantial changes have been made in appropriations, the supplemental information regarding changes may be useful and should be provided in the statement (Figure 7-7) or in notes thereto.

When encumbrances are negligible at the end of the year, the expenditure and encumbrance information may be included in a single column. The statement in this case should clearly indicate that the combination has been made, and it would not contain an "Unexpended Balance" column.

The use of the heading "Statement of Expenditures and Encumbrances Compared with Appropriations" implies that a similar statement would be provided for encumbrances of prior years and their related expenditures. The column headings might be as follows: "Reserve for Encumbrances (Year)," "Expenditures (Year)," and "Credit (Charge) to Fund Balance." The National Committee on Governmental Accounting recommends a "Statement of Expenditures and Encumbrances Compared with Authorizations" with column headings similar to those in Figure 7-8. Such a statement takes the place of the Statement of Expenditures and Encumbrances Compared with Appropriations and a statement pertaining to Reserve for Encumbrances of prior years and expenditures chargeable thereto.

If the governmental unit uses lump-sum appropriations, the lack of detail in the Statement of Expenditures and Encumbrances Compared with Appropriations may make it desirable to present a statement in which a considerably greater amount of detail can be presented—the Statement of Expenditures, Classified by Function, Organization Unit, Character, and Object, Figure 7-9. The first column has been headed "Function and Activity (or Organization Unit)." The assumption has been made that each activity has been assigned to a specific organization unit; if this is so, the statement contains the fully classified historical detail of expenditures for a fiscal year. These kinds of data may be useful for planning, for comparison of expenditures with expected expenditures, and for the needs of those in such professions as economics and political science for information regarding the nature of expenditures.

Figure 7-8

# A GOVERNMENTAL UNIT

General Fund

Statement of Expenditures and Encumbrances Compared with Authorizations

For the Fiscal Year Ended December 31, 19X5

| Function, Activity, and Object | 19X4 | | | 19X5 | | | |
|---|---|---|---|---|---|---|---|
| | Reserve for Encumbrances | Expenditures | Credit (Charge) To Fund Balance | Appropriations (Revised) | Expenditures | Encumbrances | Unencumbered Balance |

Figure 7-9

A GOVERNMENTAL UNIT

General Fund

Statement of Expenditures, Classified by Function, Organization Unit, Character, and Object

For the Fiscal Year Ended December 31, 19X1

| Function and Activity (or Organization Unit) | Grand Total | Current Expenses | | | | Capital Outlays | | | | |
|---|---|---|---|---|---|---|---|---|---|---|
| | | Total Current Expenses | Personal Services | Supplies | Other Services and Charges | Total Capital Outlays | Land | Buildings | Improvements Other Than Buildings | Machinery and Equipment |
| General Government: | | | | | | | | | | |
| Council.............. | $ 5,100 | $ 3,800 | $ 3,500 | $ 150 | $ 150 | $ 1,300 | — | — | — | $ 1,300 |
| Executive Department... | 46,730 | 40,200 | 37,350 | 1,300 | 1,550 | 6,530 | — | — | — | 6,530 |
| Judiciary ............. | 2,200 | 2,000 | 1,900 | 75 | 25 | 200 | — | — | — | 200 |
| Total General Government...... | $ 54,030 | $ 46,000 | $ 42,750 | $ 1,525 | $ 1,725 | $ 8,030 | — | — | — | $ 8,030 |

258

Figure 7-9 (cont.)

| Function and Activity (or Organization Unit) | Grand Total | Current Expenses | | | | Capital Outlays | | | | |
|---|---|---|---|---|---|---|---|---|---|---|
| | | Total Current Expenses | Personal Services | Supplies | Other Services and Charges | Total Capital Outlays | Land | Buildings | Improvements Other Than Buildings | Machinery and Equipment |
| Public Safety.......... | 85,370 | 64,100 | 58,050 | 2,850 | 3,200 | 21,270 | — | — | $ 6,000 | 15,270 |
| Highways and Streets...... | 28,300 | 18,000 | 15,000 | 1,800 | 1,200 | 10,300 | — | — | 9,000 | 1,300 |
| Sanitation ......... | 26,700 | 16,000 | 13,500 | 1,500 | 1,000 | 10,700 | — | — | 8,700 | 2,000 |
| Health ........... | 41,400 | 13,800 | 12,000 | 1,300 | 500 | 27,600 | $5,000 | — | 12,000 | 10,600 |
| Welfare........... | 17,000 | 12,000 | 4,000 | 200 | 7,800 | 5,000 | — | — | — | 5,000 |
| Culture—Recreation ...... | 17,400 | 8,500 | 7,500 | 200 | 800 | 8,900 | 2,000 | — | 1,500 | 5,400 |
| Education ......... | 81,300 | 69,800 | 63,000 | 3,800 | 3,000 | 11,500 | — | — | — | 11,500 |
| Interest ......... | 14,400 | 14,400 | — | — | 14,400 | — | — | — | — | — |
| Total Current Expenses and Capital Outlays... | $365,000 | $262,600 | $215,800 | $13,175 | $33,625 | $103,300 | $7,000 | — | $37,200 | $59,100 |
| Retirement of Bonds....... | 34,000 | | | | | | | | | |
| Total.............. | $399,900 | | | | | | | | | |

Figure 7-10

# A GOVERNMENTAL UNIT
## General Fund
### Statement of Actual and Estimated Expenditures
For the Month of March 31, 19X5 and Three Months Ending March 31, 19X5

| Function, Activity or Organization, and Object | Appropriations (Revised) | March Estimated | March Actual | March Actual (Over) Under Estimated | January-March Estimated | January-March Actual | January-March Actual (Over) Under Estimated | Unexpended Balance | Encumbrances | Unencumbered Balance |
|---|---|---|---|---|---|---|---|---|---|---|
| **General Government:** | | | | | | | | | | |
| Legislative: | | | | | | | | | | |
| Personal Services | $ 20,000 | $ 1,667 | $ 1,667 | $ — | $ 5,000 | $ 5,000 | $ — | $ 15,000 | $ — | $ 15,000 |
| Supplies | 3,000 | 300 | 275 | 25 | 800 | 770 | 30 | 2,230 | 400 | 1,830 |
| Other Services and Charges | 4,000 | 333 | 350 | (17) | 1,000 | 990 | 10 | 3,010 | 75 | 2,935 |
| Capital Outlays | 500 | — | — | — | 500 | 500 | — | — | — | — |
| Total Legislative | $ 27,500 | $ 2,300 | $ 2,292 | $ 8 | $ 7,300 | $ 7,260 | $ 40 | $ 20,240 | $ 475 | $ 19,765 |
| Judicial* | 25,000 | 2,500 | 2,400 | 100 | 6,000 | 5,900 | 100 | 19,100 | 1,100 | 18,000 |
| Executive* | 75,000 | 7,500 | 7,550 | (50) | 18,000 | 17,500 | 500 | 57,500 | 2,500 | 5,500 |
| Total General Government | $ 127,500 | $ 12,300 | $ 12,242 | $ 58 | $ 31,300 | $ 30,660 | $ 640 | $ 96,840 | $ 4,075 | $ 92,765 |

**Figure 7-10 (cont.)**

| Function, Activity or Organization, and Object | Appropriations (Revised) | March | | | January-March | | | Unexpended Balance | Encumbrances | Unencumbered Balance |
|---|---|---|---|---|---|---|---|---|---|---|
| | | Estimated | Actual | Actual (Over) Under Estimated | Estimated | Actual | Actual (Over) Under Estimated | | | |
| Public Safety* | 200,000 | 21,000 | 20,500 | 500 | 50,000 | 49,000 | 1,000 | 151,000 | 10,800 | 140,200 |
| Highways and Streets* | 100,000 | 8,500 | 8,400 | 100 | 24,000 | 23,850 | 150 | 76,150 | 4,100 | 72,050 |
| Sanitation* | 60,000 | 7,500 | 7,200 | 300 | 15,000 | 15,100 | (100) | 44,900 | 3,800 | 41,100 |
| Health* | 50,000 | 5,000 | 4,950 | 50 | 12,000 | 11,750 | 250 | 38,250 | 2,250 | 36,000 |
| Welfare* | 40,000 | 3,500 | 3,600 | (100) | 10,000 | 9,500 | 500 | 30,500 | 4,500 | 26,000 |
| Culture—Recreation* | 55,000 | 4,500 | 4,250 | 250 | 14,000 | 13,425 | 575 | 41,575 | 4,125 | 37,450 |
| Education* | 500,000 | 40,000 | 39,150 | 850 | 120,500 | 119,750 | 750 | 380,250 | 15,900 | 364,350 |
| Total | $1,132,500 | $102,300 | $100,292 | $2,008 | $276,800 | $273,035 | $3,765 | $859,465 | $49,550 | $809,915 |

* Information by activity or organization unit and by object if possible (see text for comment regarding the degrees of detail desirable when the statement is used for various purposes).

261

ALLOTMENTS, ALLOCATIONS, AND INTERIM STATEMENTS. The principal interim statement is the Statement of Actual and Estimated Expenditures, which provides both monthly and year-to-date figures for expenditures, presented in Figure 7-10. If this statement is to be prepared for publication, summary data by functions and activities or organization units should be appropriate. If it is to be prepared as a management report, more detailed information regarding, for example, objects of expenditure would presumably be required.

The preparation of this statement requires either that appropriations be made in the amount of detail desired for the statement or that the executive branch of the government provide allocations of lump-sum appropriations for the degree of detail desired for the statement. For example, referring to Figure 7-10, if the legislative branch received a lump-sum appropriation for 19X5 in the amount of $27,500, the amounts in the appropriations column for Personal Services, Supplies, Other Services and Charges, and Capital Outlays might not have been provided by the City Council. However, if the mayor or city manager approved allocations for those objects of expenditure, the allocation data can be used in lieu of appropriations. Under such circumstances, the first column should be retitled, perhaps as "Appropriations (Revised) and Allocations," with an asterisk being used to separate the two kinds of figures in the column.

Allotments are also assumed by the Statement of Actual and Estimated Expenditures. The two columns headed "Estimated" are the result of allotments of appropriations. The existence of time allotments permits the statement to be used as a basis of managerial control; that is, the chief executive and the city council can tell from the Statement whether the allotments are being heeded by the supervisors.

In many governmental units the supervisors are provided with copies of their appropriation-expenditure subsidiary ledger accounts or with summaries of those accounts on a monthly basis. These accounts or summaries keep the supervisor up-to-date as to his expenditure position. Many supervisors go even further and require personnel within their organizational unit to maintain a record that parallels the appropriation-expenditure accounts for the unit. By this means the supervisor has available to him information on a basis even more timely than can be provided by the central accounting office. The duplication of records is undesirable, but it may be necessary unless the supervisor can be given day-to-day information regarding his appropriations, expenditures, and encumbrances.

Question 7-1.   Designate the functions to which the following activities apply:
Granting aid to libraries
Operating a museum
Retirement of debt
Enacting laws
Judicial activities

Detecting crime
Preventing fires
Supervising banks
Maintaining a sewer system
Operating hospitals
Payment of old age assistance
Operating a jail
Operating a park
Payments for pupils attending schools of another governmental unit
Rendering aid to dependent children
Activities of parole boards
Personnel administration
Providing Pasteur treatments
Operating a hospital for the blind
Operating a school
Operating an old soldiers' home
Constructing and maintaining highways
Fighting fires
Prosecuting offenders
Administering elections
Rendering legal advice to the legislative body
Payment of interest
Inspecting buildings
Keeping accounts

**Question 7-2.** The following is a part of an expenditure statement. Set up account headings to designate the function, organization unit, and so forth, with which the accounts are identified. You may disregard code numbers for the accounts.

Public Safety:

Police Department:

Current Expenses:

| | | |
|---|---|---|
| Personal Services | $40,000 | |
| Materials and Supplies | 2,000 | |
| Other Services and Charges | 2,000 | $44,000 |

Capital Outlays:

| | | |
|---|---|---|
| Equipment | | 6,000 |

Total Police Department ............................................. $50,000

Fire Department:

Current Expenses:

| | | |
|---|---|---|
| Personal Services | $30,000 | |
| Supplies | 1,500 | |
| Other Services and Charges | 2,000 | $33,500 |

Capital Outlays:

| | | |
|---|---|---|
| Equipment | | 6,500 |

Total Fire Department ............................................. 40,000

Total Public Safety ............................................. $90,000

**Question 7-3.** Distinguish between an expenditure in the governmental accounting sense and an expense in the commercial accounting sense.

**Question 7-4.** Explain how an accounting system can be designed to produce information for all of the bases of expenditure classification and still produce information useful for managerial purposes.

**Question 7-5.** Name the controlling accounts which one might expect to find in use in the General Fund.

**Question 7-6.** In a certain municipality the purchase of materials is charged against an appropriation set up for that purpose. Subsequently, as materials are withdrawn, their cost is charged to the appropriations of the departments by which they are withdrawn. What is wrong with this procedure, and what remedy would you propose?

**Question 7-7.** (a) Should the inventory of materials and supplies carried in the General Fund of a governmental unit be recorded at cost, at cost or market, whichever is lower, or on some other basis? (b) Would your answer be different if the inventory was owned by a municipal water utility?

**Question 7-8.** On January 2, 19X1, materials costing $100 were transferred from perpetual inventory to the Police Department. Give the journal entry or entries to be made.

**Question 7-9.** A governmental unit takes advantage of purchase discounts by paying its bills promptly. Should the full purchase price be recorded on the records with the discounts treated as revenue, or should the purchases be recorded at their net cost (that is, after deduction of discounts)?

**Question 7-10.** It has been suggested that the amounts paid by the General Fund to a pension fund for the city's share of pension fund contributions be charged to the departments in which the covered employees work. Do you agree? Explain.

**Question 7-11.** In one municipality vouchers must be approved not only by the finance officer but also by the four members of the finance committee of the city council. In your opinion is the approval of the finance committee desirable? Give reasons.

**Question 7-12.** Do you think that information concerning expenditures chargeable to the reserve for encumbrances of prior years should be reported on the same statement as are appropriation expenditures? Why?

**Question 7-13.** Explain how you would decide whether or not a planned expenditure should be encumbered.

**Problem 7-1.** The following information is for the City of A for the year ended December 31, 19X5:

| | |
|---|---|
| Rent of equipment—constructing bridges | $ 3,500 |
| Wages—snow and ice removal | 3,000 |
| Salaries—Board of Elections | 15,000 |
| Compensation insurance—firemen | 1,000 |
| Postage—City Council | 350 |
| Wages—street repair | 10,000 |
| Rent of equipment—repair of bridges | 1,000 |
| Purchase of land—Police Department | 15,000 |
| Salaries—policemen | 40,000 |

| | |
|---|---:|
| Salaries—City Court Judges | 10,000 |
| Salary—Mayor | 18,000 |
| Purchase of comptometers—Bureau of Accounts | 1,000 |
| Heat, light and power—Police Department | 1,000 |
| Salaries—Councilmen | 15,000 |
| Telephone and telegraph—City Council | 300 |
| Purchase of desks—Council | 175 |
| Compensation insurance—policemen | 1,000 |
| Wages—resurfacing streets | 15,000 |
| Postage—Bureau of Purchases | 500 |
| Wages—constructing bridges | 17,500 |
| Salaries and wages—construction of new fire station | 7,500 |
| Purchase of police cars | 10,000 |
| Printing of ballots | 1,000 |
| Telephone and telegraph—Fire Department | 850 |
| Interest on bonds | 40,000 |
| Salaries—Department of Highways (all chargeable to maintenance) | 8,000 |
| Purchase of land—Fire Department | 15,000 |
| Wages—constructing streets | 30,000 |
| Salaries—firemen | 60,000 |
| Rent of equipment—Fire Department | 750 |
| Traveling expenses—Mayor | 650 |
| Salaries—Bureau of Accounts | 7,500 |
| Telephone and telegraph—Police | 2,000 |
| Contributions to pension funds | 10,000 |
| Repairs to Fire Department buildings—by contract | 3,500 |
| Retirement of serial bonds | 50,000 |
| Purchase of materials—construction of police station | 5,000 |
| Telephone and telegraph—Bureau of Purchases | 100 |
| Purchase of bookcases for City Court | 500 |
| Repair of streets— contract | 5,000 |
| Construction of bridge—by contract | 2,000 |
| Grants to other governmental units | 5,000 |
| Heat, light, and power—Bureau of Purchases | 500 |
| Purchase of law books for City Court | 1,000 |
| Salaries—Civil Service Commissioners | 12,000 |
| Purchase of materials—construction of fire station | 10,000 |
| Wages—repair of bridges | 3,500 |
| Heat, light, and power—Fire Department | 2,500 |
| Salaries—Bureau of Purchases | 7,000 |

Required:
   (1)   Prepare a statement for the City of *A* for the year ended December 31, 19X5, classifying expenditures by character, function, and object. Divide the statement

into three sections—a current expenses section, a capital outlays section, and a debt service section. Within each section arrange the expenses by function, showing under each function the objects going to make up the function.

(2)   Prepare a statement classifying expenditures by organization units.

**Problem 7-2.**  The following data were taken from the accounts of the Town of Ridgedale after the books had been closed for the fiscal year ending June 30, 19X3:

| | Balance 6/30/X2 | 19X3 Changes Debits | 19X3 Changes Credits | Balances 6/30/X3 |
|---|---|---|---|---|
| Cash ........................ | $180,000 | $ 955,000 | $ 880,000 | $255,000 |
| Taxes Receivable .............. | 20,000 | 809,000 | 781,000 | 48,000 |
| | $200,000 | | | $303,000 |
| Estimated Uncollectible Taxes .... | $ 4,000 | 6,000 | 9,000 | $ 7,000 |
| Vouchers Payable .............. | 44,000 | 880,000 | 889,000 | 53,000 |
| Due to Intragovernmental Service Fund ....................... | 2,000 | 7,000 | 10,000 | 5,000 |
| Due to Debt Service Fund ....... | 10,000 | 60,000 | 100,000 | 50,000 |
| Reserve for Encumbrances ....... | 40,000 | 40,000 | 47,000 | 47,000 |
| Fund Balance ................. | 100,000 | 20,000 | 61,000 | 141,000 |
| | $200,000 | $2,777,000 | $2,777,000 | $303,000 |

The following additional data are available:

1.  The budget for the year provided for estimated revenues of $1,000,000 and appropriations of $965,000.

2.  Expenditures totaling $895,000, in addition to those chargeable against Reserve for Encumbrances, were made.

3.  The actual expenditure chargeable against Reserve for Encumbrances was $37,000.

Required:

Prepare a worksheet to compare estimated revenues with actual revenues and encumbrances and expenditures with appropriations and other authorizations. The worksheet should have the following column headings:

| Heading |
|---|
| Balance Sheet, 6/30/X2 |
| 19X3 Transactions (Debit & Credit) |
| Estimated Revenues |
| Actual Revenues |
| Encumbrances and Expenditures |
| Appropriations and Other Authorizations |
| Balance Sheet, 6/30/X3 |

(AICPA)

**Problem 7-3.** The following information pertains to the operations of the General Fund of the X County. Functions of this county government include operating the county jail and caring for the county courts.

Funds to finance the operations are provided from a levy of county tax against the various towns of the county, from the state distribution of unincorporated business taxes, from board of jail prisoners assessed against the towns and against the state and from interest on savings accounts.

The balances in the accounts of the Fund on January 1, 19X0, were as follows:

| | |
|---|---:|
| Cash in savings accounts | $ 60,650 |
| Cash in checking accounts | 41,380 |
| Cash on hand (undeposited prisoners' board receipts) | 320 |
| Inventory of jail supplies | 3,070 |
| Due from towns and state for board of prisoners | 3,550 |
| General Fund balance | 108,970 |

The budget for the year 19X0 as adopted by the county commissioners provided for the following items of revenue and expenditure:

| | | |
|---|---|---:|
| (1) | Town and county taxes | $ 20,000 |
| (2) | Jail operating costs | 55,500 |
| (3) | Court operating costs | 7,500 |
| (4) | Unincorporated business tax | 18,000 |
| (5) | Board of prisoners (revenue) | 5,000 |
| (6) | Commissioners' salaries and expenses | 8,000 |
| (7) | Interest on savings | 1,000 |
| (8) | Miscellaneous expenses | 1,000 |

General Fund balance was appropriated in sufficient amount to balance the budget. At December 31, 19X0, the jail supply inventory amounted to $5,120, cash of $380 was on hand, and $1,325 of prisoners' board bills were unpaid. The following items represent all of the transactions which occurred during the year, with all current bills vouchered and paid by December 31, 19X0:

| | |
|---|---:|
| Item (1) was transacted exactly as budgeted. | |
| Item (2) cash expenditures amounted to | $ 55,230 |
| Item (3) amounted to | 7,110 |
| Item (4) amounted to | 18,070 |
| Item (5) billings amounted to | 4,550 |
| Item (6) amounted to | 6,670 |
| Item (7) amounted to | 1,050 |
| Item (8) amounted to | 2,310 |

During the year, $25,000 was transferred from the savings accounts to the checking accounts.

Required:
From the above information, prepare a worksheet providing columns to show:
(1) The transactions for the year. (Journal entries not required.)
(2) Variances between budgeted and actual revenues and expenditures for the year.
(3) Balance sheet of the General Fund, December 31, 19X0.
(AICPA.)

**Problem 7-4.** The following is a list of the accounts in the General Fund Expenditure Ledger of the City of *B* at December 31, 19X0:

| Organization Unit | Appropriations Current Expenses | Appropriations Capital Outlays | Expenditures Current Expenses | Expenditures Capital Outlays | Encumbrances Outstanding Current Expenses | Encumbrances Outstanding Capital Outlays |
|---|---|---|---|---|---|---|
| Public Works Department (Sanitation Function) ......... | $22,000 | $ 7,500 | $21,000 | $ 6,700 | — | $ 750 |
| Public Works Department (Highways and Streets Function) ... | 20,000 | 30,000 | 19,000 | 28,000 | $1,000 | 1,000 |
| Civil Service Commission .............. | 7,500 | — | 6,700 | — | 750 | — |
| Welfare Department... | 30,000 | 1,500 | 26,000 | 800 | 2,250 | 100 |
| Court .............. | 7,500 | — | 6,700 | — | — | — |
| Council............. | 15,000 | 3,000 | 13,500 | 3,000 | — | — |
| City Clerk's Office .... | 15,000 | 3,000 | 15,000 | 1,500 | — | 500 |
| Department of Police .. | 40,000 | 7,500 | 38,500 | 6,000 | 1,000 | 1,000 |
| Mayor ............. | 20,000 | 1,500 | 18,000 | 500 | 1,500 | 750 |
| Department of Finance .......... | 15,000 | 1,500 | 13,500 | 1,500 | 1,500 | — |
| Department of Law ... | 15,000 | — | 9,000 | — | — | — |
| Department of Fire.... | 30,000 | 7,500 | 19,000 | 4,000 | 750 | 750 |
| Department of Health . | 20,000 | 6,000 | 19,000 | 5,000 | 500 | 500 |
| Retirement of Bonds... | 15,000* | — | 15,000* | — | — | — |
| Interest ............. | 7,500 | — | 7,500 | — | — | — |

* Not part of current expenses; shown in "Current Expenses" column to save space.

Required:
(1) Set up "T" accounts for the General Ledger accounts and enter in them the proper totals of appropriations, expenditures, encumbrances, and reserve for encumbrances, respectively; set up a "T" account for Fund Balance. *Hint*—Set up "T" accounts for Appropriations (to include both current expenses and capital outlays), for Expenditures, and so forth. You need not distinguish between current expenses, capital outlays, and retirement of debt in your *General Ledger* accounts.

(2)  Set up the following (subsidiary) expenditure accounts (see Figure 7-5) and post appropriations, expenditures, and encumbrances to them:

City Clerk's Office—Current Expenses
Department of Fire—Capital Outlays
Department of Law—Current Expenses
Mayor—Capital Outlays
Public Works Department—Highways—Current Expenses
Welfare Department—Public Welfare—Current Expenses

(3)  Prepare a journal entry to close out appropriations, expenditures, and encumbrances, showing both the General Ledger and Expenditure Ledger (subsidiary) accounts.

(4)  Post the amounts shown in the closing entry to the General Ledger accounts and to those subsidary accounts for which you have set up accounts.

(5)  Prepare a statement, properly arranged, comparing appropriations with expenditures and encumbrances of the General Fund for 19X0.

**Problem 7-5.**  An appropriation was made by the Council for Council Supplies for $9,000. During the year these transactions occurred:

1.  Council ordered $4,000 (estimated cost) of supplies on January 10, 19X5, with order number 72.

2.  Council ordered $2,000 (estimated cost) of supplies on January 29, 19X5, with order number 73.

3.  On February 12, 19X5, order number 72 arrived. Its actual cost was $4,300.

4.  On March 2, 19X5, order number 73 arrived. Its actual cost was $1,900.

5.  On October 5, 19X5, Council bought some supplies for cash. Cost was $2,600.

6.  The City received a $100 quantity discount for the supplies bought for the Council.

Required:

Prepare an Expenditures Subsidiary Ledger account for the Council's Supplies. As a minimum you should have dollar columns for Encumbrances Dr. and Cr., Expenditures, Appropriations, and Balance. (See Figure 7-5.)

**Problem 7-6.**  The account on page 270 appears in the Expenditures Ledger of the City of X. You are to restate the account to show the correct recording of the transactions and to show correct balances.

**Problem 7-7.**  The account on page 271 is found in the Expenditure Subsidiary Ledger of the City Hospital. It contains the appropriation for the supplies for the Outpatient Clinic, together with certain entries which the staff has made. You are to reconstruct the account as it would appear if it had been properly kept.

**Problem 7-8.**  The following information summarizes the operation of the Library Fund of the City of Hillsdale:

1.  The account balances at December 31, 19X0, were as follows:

| | |
|---|---|
| Cash | $2,350 |
| Reserve for Encumbrances | 1,000 |
| Fund Balance | 1,350 |

2.  Effective January 1, 19X1, the City Council dedicated a portion of the property taxes of the City, together with all receipts from parking meters, to the Library Fund. The Council's estimate of revenues from these sources follows:

## CITY OF X
### Expenditure Ledger

Acc. No. 1110-02
Office of the Mayor
Supplies

| 19X2 Date | Description | Encumbrances Dr. | Encumbrances Cr. | Expenditures | Appropriations | Balance |
|---|---|---|---|---|---|---|
| Jan. 1 | Budget | | | | $3,800 | $3,800 |
| 5 | Purchase Order 8—Stationery | $ 500 | | | | 3,300 |
| 10 | Invoice 498—telephone bill | | | $ 20 | | 3,280 |
| 25 | Invoice for P.O. 8 | | $ 495 | 495 | | 3,280 |
| Feb. 1 | Bill from Stores Fund | 200 | | | | 3,080 |
| 8 | Returned Stationery | | | | 50 | 3,130 |
| 9 | Purchase Order 250—Supplies | 100 | | | | 3,230 |
| Mar. 5 | Invoice for P.O. 250 | | 100 | 105 | | 3,230 |
| 15 | Allowance on Supplies | | | | 5 | 3,225 |
| June 10 | Transferred Supplies to Fire Department | | | | 50 | 3,175 |
| 15 | P.O. 2561—Printing and Supplies | 2,000 | | | | 1,175 |
| Aug. 15 | Invoice for P.O. 2561 | | 2,000 | 2,100 | | 1,075 |
| Nov. 15 | Transfer of Appropriation to City Manager's Office | | | 500 | | 575 |

| Date | Description | Reference | | Encumbrances | | Expenditures | Appropriation | Balance |
|---|---|---|---|---|---|---|---|---|
| | | No. Vr. | No. Order | Created | Liquidated | | | |
| Jan. 1 | Budget | | | | | | $3,800 | $3,800 |
| 3 | Examination table | | 45 | $ 45 | | | | 3,755 |
| 4 | Adhesive tape | 101 | | | | $ 10 | | 3,765 |
| 5 | Medical Supplies | | 50 | 125 | | | | 3,640 |
| 6 | Bandages | | 52 | 60 | | | | 3,580 |
| 7 | Supplementary Appropriation | | | | | | 200 | 3,780 |
| 8 | Examination table | 120 | 45 | (45) | | 45 | | 3,735 |
| 9 | Medical supplies | 121 | 50 | | $125 | 125 | | 3,735 |
| 10 | Bandages | 125 | 52 | | 55 | 55 | | 3,735 |
| 11 | Quantity discount on Vr. 121 | | | | 10 | | | 3,725 |
| 12 | Transfer of appropriation to Operating Room | | | | | 300 | | 3,425 |

| | |
|---|---:|
| Property Taxes | $ 50,000 |
| Parking Meters | 135,000 |
| | $185,000 |

3. Planned expenditures for 19X1 were as follows:

| | |
|---|---:|
| General Administration | $ 50,000 |
| Library-on-Wheels | 40,000 |
| Books | 90,000 |
| | $180,000 |

The Council's approval of expenditures included $1,000 for books ordered in 19X0.

4. Taxes in the amount of $52,500 were levied. It was expected that of this amount $2,000 would prove uncollectible.

5. Receipts during the year consisted of the following items:

| | |
|---|---:|
| Property Taxes | $ 51,500 |
| Parking Meter Collections | 136,000 |
| Refund on Books Bought This Year | 300 |
| | $187,800 |

6. The following purchase orders were placed:

| | |
|---|---:|
| General Administration | $ 30,000 |
| Library-on-Wheels | 10,000 |
| Books | 80,000 |
| | $120,000 |

7. Certain of the orders placed in 19X0 and 19X1 were received. The vouchers, together with amount of the related purchase orders, are summarized below:

| | Ordered | Vouchered |
|---|---:|---:|
| General Administration | $ 20,000 | $ 21,500 |
| Library-on-Wheels | 10,000 | 10,000 |
| Books | 80,000 | 85,000 |
| | $110,000 | $116,500 |

8. Additional vouchers were prepared for the following purposes:

| | |
|---|---|
| General Administration | $27,000 |
| Library-on-Wheels | 30,000 |
| Books | 6,000 |
| Refund of Overpayment of Taxes | 400 |
| | $63,400 |

9. Vouchers were paid in the total amount of $178,000.

10. A physical inventory of $2,000 was taken on December 31, 19X1, and the City Council directed that it be properly recorded.

11. The Council passed an ordinance that expenditures must be charged against appropriations of the year in which the expenditures are made.

Required:

(1) Prepare a worksheet or sheets that will show closing entries and balance sheet information at December 31, 19X1, and will summarize the information needed for the usual revenue and expenditure statements.

(2) Prepare the statements mentioned above, together with an analysis of changes in Fund Balance.

**Problem 7-9.** K City had the following trial balance on January 1, 19X1:

| | | |
|---|---|---|
| Cash | $ 7,000 | |
| Taxes Receivable, Delinquent | 48,000 | |
| Estimated Uncollectible Taxes, Delinquent | | $ 4,000 |
| Due from Water Fund | 500 | |
| Vouchers Payable | | 11,000 |
| Due to Taxpayers | | 1,000 |
| Reserve for Encumbrances, 19X0 | | 3,000 |
| Fund Balance | | 36,500 |
| | $55,500 | $55,500 |

The following information summarizes the transactions of the City during 19X1:

1. The City Council approved the following budget for 19X1:

**Expenditures:**

| | |
|---|---|
| City Manager | $20,000 |
| Police Department | 10,000 |
| Fire Department | 10,000 |
| Streets and Roads | 20,000 |
| | $60,000 |

**Revenues:**

| | |
|---|---|
| Property Taxes | $40,000 |
| Fines and Fees | 5,000 |
| Miscellaneous | 5,000 |
| | $50,000 |

2.   The Council approved the levy of taxes in the amount of $40,000. It was estimated that $2,000 of the amount would never be collected.

3.   Cash collected during the year may be summarized as follows:

| | |
|---|---:|
| Prior year's levies | $45,000 |
| 19X1 levy | 11,000 |
| Fines and fees | 4,000 |
| Taxes written off in prior years | 500 |
| Interest | 500 |
| Service charges | 2,000 |
| | $63,000 |

4.   Orders placed during the year were as follows:

| | |
|---|---:|
| City Manager | $ 4,000 |
| Police Department | 3,000 |
| Fire Department | 3,000 |
| Streets and Roads | 5,000 |
| | $15,000 |

5.   Payrolls vouchered during the year were as follows:

| | |
|---|---:|
| City Manager | $15,000 |
| Police Department | 7,000 |
| Fire Department | 6,500 |
| Streets and Roads | 14,000 |
| | $42,500 |

6.   Invoices vouchered during the year are listed as follows:

| | |
|---|---:|
| City Manager | $ 4,500 |
| Police Department | 3,000 |
| Fire Department | 3,000 |
| Streets and Roads | 4,000 |
| Invoices for 19X0 Orders | 3,100 |
| | $17,600 |

The above invoices completed all orders except one dated June 1, 19X1, for an attachment for the road grader for $950.

7. Analysis of collections revealed that Taxpayer *A*, to whom the City owed $1,000 on January 1, 19X1, for overpayment of taxes, had paid his tax for 19X1 less $1,000.

8. The General Fund rendered services in the amount of $250 to the Water Fund.

9. The City Council made an additional appropriation in the amount of $5,000 for a bond maturity which was overlooked in the preparation of the budget.

10. The bond matured and was vouchered.

11. Cash paid on account of vouchers payable totalled $65,000.

12. Delinquent Taxes in the amount of $500 were written off on the authority of the Council.

Required:

(1) A worksheet or worksheets summarizing the year's operations in such a way that the required statements may be easily prepared.

(2) A statement which summarizes the results of the year's operations with respect to revenues.

(3) A statement which summarizes the results of the year's operations with respect to expenditures.

(4) A statement which summarizes the changes in Fund Balance.

**Problem 7-10.** From the following information, prepare a statement for the year 19X6 showing operating budget appropriations, expenditures, and other commitments against the appropriations, as well as unencumbered balances, for the Town of *E:*
The following appropriations were included in the operating budget adopted:

Administrative expenses:

| | |
|---|---:|
| Salaries | $ 3,600 |
| Other services and charges | 600 |
| Supplies | 1,800 |

Assessment and collection of taxes:

| | |
|---|---:|
| Salaries | 5,000 |
| Other services and charges | 100 |
| Supplies | 800 |

Police department:

| | |
|---|---:|
| Salaries | 25,000 |
| Supplies | 1,500 |
| Other services and changes | 4,250 |

Fire department:

| | |
|---|---:|
| Salaries | 15,000 |
| Supplies | 500 |
| Other services and charges | 1,300 |

Street repairs and maintenance:

| | |
|---|---:|
| Salaries and wages | 5,550 |
| Materials and supplies | 7,400 |
| Interest on bonds | 21,000 |
| Payment of bonds | 45,000 |
| | $138,400 |

(AICPA, adapted.)

No provision was made in this budget for purchase of new equipment or for capital improvements.

Cash disbursements for all divisions of the accounts were recorded in the same cash disbursement book. A summary of the amounts so recorded for the year follows:

| Name and Description | | Total Payments | |
|---|---|---|---|
| Telephone Co.: | | | |
| Telephone service: | | | |
| Collector's Office .......................... | $    84 | | |
| Police Department ...................... | 167 | | |
| Fire Department ........................ | 85 | | |
| Treasurer's Office........................ | 540 | $    876 | |
| Payrolls: | | | |
| Salaries of policemen ..................... | $24,500 | | |
| Salaries of firemen ........................ | 14,800 | | |
| Salary of Treasurer ....................... | 2,500 | | |
| Salary of Assistant to Treasurer ............ | 1,100 | | |
| Salary of Tax Collector ................... | 3,000 | | |
| Salary of Assessor ........................ | 2,000 | | |
| Salary of Superintendent of Streets .......... | 2,000 | | |
| Wages of street employees.................. | 3,450 | 53,350 | |
| A.B.C. Stationery Co.: | | | |
| Tax duplicates, tax cash books, etc. .......... | $    300 | | |
| Treasurer's books, ledger sheets, etc. ........ | 450 | 750 | |
| W & B Garage Co.: | | | |
| Repairs to police cars ..................... | $    550 | | |
| Tires for police cars ...................... | 300 | | |
| Repairs to fire trucks ..................... | 450 | 1,300 | |
| Gulf Oil Corporation: | | | |
| 11,000 gallons of gasoline delivered to disbursing pump at police station at 20¢ per gallon. (All gasoline purchased is charged to police department. Periodical adjustments are made for gasoline used by other departments. During the year the fire department used 3,000 gallons.) | | 2,200 | |
| Penrod Printing Company: | | | |
| Purchase order, vouchers, checks, etc. ....... | $    600 | | |
| Tax bills ................................ | 425 | 1,025 | |

Colonial Outfitters:

| | | |
|---|---|---|
| Police uniforms and sundry supplies ......... | $ 900 | |
| Firemen's uniforms and sundry supplies ..... | 300 | 1,200 |

Barrett Company:

15,000 gallons of tarvia at 20¢ per gallon ....   3,000

(Of the above, 10,000 gallons were used in
the repair of existing roads and the balance
was used in the construction of new streets.)

State Trust Co.:

For interest on coupon bonds .............   21,000

Consolidated Stone and Sand Co.:

300 tons crushed stone at $20 per ton........   6,000

(Of the above, 250 tons were used in the repair of existing roads and the balance was
used in the construction of new streets.)

American Fabric & Rubber Co.:

Repairs to fire line hose ...................   150

Johnson Radio Company:

Incidental repairs to police radio system .....   450

State Trust Company:

For payment of bonds .....................   45,000

Johnson's Food Store:

Food for prisoners .......................   300

DeCozen Motor Co.:

Cars for Police Department ...............   3,750

RCA Mfg. Co.:

Short-wave receivers and transmitters, including installation, per contract .............   1,250

$141,601

The following commitments and accrued expenses remained unpaid at December 31, 19X6:

| Name and Description | Total Payments |
|---|---|
| Payroll: | |
| Wages accrued—street department ......... | $ 95 |
| Penrod Printing Company: | |
| Stationery and vouchers for treasurer's office | 250 |
| (Not received until January 15, 19X7) | |

Johnson Radio Company:
Repairs to police radio ................... 85
Telephone Company:
Telephone bill for December:

| | | |
|---|---:|---:|
| Treasurer's Office ...................... | $50 | |
| Collector's Office ...................... | 14 | |
| Police Department ..................... | 23 | |
| Fire Department....................... | 12 | 99 |
| | | $529 |

# 8

# Capital Projects Funds

Capital Projects Funds are employed to account for resources received from bond or other long-term general obligation debt issues, grants or shared revenues from other governments, transfers from other funds or other sources, and used, except as indicated below, to acquire major, long-lived capital facilities. A Capital Projects Fund is, in substance, a special type of Special Revenue Fund, differing from the latter primarily in that (1) resources are used to acquire capital facilities rather than to finance current operations, and (2) the accountability focus is upon compliance with provisions of bond indentures, grant stipulations, or similar constraints and upon the project, the duration of which may span several operating periods.

Capital Projects Funds constitute both a replacement for and an expansion of Bond Funds, formerly recommended by the NCGA. Under prior recommendations, Bond Funds were used to account for the proceeds of all general obligation bond issues except those of Special Assessment and Enterprise Funds.[1] Capital projects are now frequently financed, fully or partially, through intergovernmental grants, shared revenues, and long-term debt instruments other than bonds, as well as through bond issues. Thus, under former recommendations, several different types of funds (Special Revenue, Bond, etc.) might be required to account for a single project. Another purpose of the changed recom-

[1] Bond Funds are discussed briefly at the end of this chapter.

mendations is to assure that capital projects are accounted for uniformly and in a manner that articulates with the capital program or capital budget.

The intent of present NCGA recommendations is that proceeds of all general obligation long-term debt issuances should be accounted for through Capital Projects Funds *except* (1) refunding issues, which are expended and accounted for through Debt Service Funds, and (2) Special Assessment and Enterprise Fund issues that are primary obligations of and will be serviced by these types of funds. The NCGA recommendations are somewhat vague, however, with respect to proceeds of long-term general obligation debt incurred for purposes other than capital outlay or refunding (e.g., to finance operating deficits, provide disaster relief, etc.). It would appear that such transactions might be acceptably accounted for through Capital Projects, Special Revenue, or even Bond Funds.

Not all fixed asset acquisitions are financed through Capital Projects Funds. Fixed assets of limited cost may be acquired with resources of almost any fund; and major fixed assets may be acquired through the General or Special Revenue Funds when long-term debt or special purpose grants are not involved, as well as through Special Assessment and Enterprise Funds.

### Number of Funds Required

Separate Capital Projects Funds are usually established for each project or debt issue because (1) the nature of such projects varies widely, they typically involve significant amounts of resources, and they are usually budgeted on an individual project or debt issue basis and (2) legal and contractual requirements differ significantly among such projects. Where debt issues are involved, a major purpose of the Capital Projects Fund is to show that the proceeds were used only for authorized purposes and that unexpended balances or deficits have been handled in accordance with applicable contractual agreements or legal provisions. A single Capital Projects Fund will suffice, however, where a single debt issue is used to finance several projects or a series of closely related projects is financed through a single grant or by internal transfers from the General or Special Revenue Funds. Combined statements are generally used to present financial operation or position data where a government has more than one Capital Projects Fund in operation during a given year.

### Capital Projects Fund Life Cycle

A Capital Projects Fund is established upon project or debt issue authorization. The accrual and inflows, expenditures and encumbrances, and balances of project-related resources are then recorded within the Fund accounting records. The Fund is abolished at the conclusion of the project (or expenditure of debt issue proceeds for other purposes) and the accounting records retained to evidence the fiscal stewardship of the government.

## Costs Charged to Projects

All expenditures necessary to bring the facility in question to a state of readiness for its intended purpose are properly chargeable as Capital Project Fund costs. In addition to the direct cost of items such as land, buildings, materials, and labor, total project cost would therefore include such related items as engineering and architect fees, transportation costs, damages occasioned by the project, and other costs associated with the endeavor.

Although it may be contended that interest costs during the construction period and a share of general government overhead are proper project costs, such costs are rarely charged to the project unless they are reimbursable, such as under terms of the grant through which the project is financed. Too, where costs such as overhead are reimbursable, the reimbursable amount is frequently calculated in accordance with a predetermined formula rather than by being derived directly from cost accounting or similar records.

This is not to say that no overhead costs are charged to the project unless reimbursable. Overhead is charged to the project, for example, to the extent that such costs are included in charges for goods or services provided for the project through Intragovernmental Service Funds. Because of past manipulative abuses, however, and since intergovernmental grants are often intended only to supplement existing resources, charges for overhead may be specifically excluded from "project cost" as defined by statute, contractual agreement, or administrative determination.

## Alternative Accounting Approaches and Entries

Several approaches to Capital Projects Fund accounting are acceptable. One must look to the substance of procedures employed in a particular situation, rather than their form or terminology, in assessing their appropriateness.

A major reason underlying differences in acceptable accounting approaches is that Capital Projects Fund budgetary practices vary widely in accordance with variations in the nature of such projects and the overall budgetary approach used by a particular government. Accounting is a service function, of course, and as such must be adapted to differences in information needs in each situation.

Where the capital budget is officially enacted, often by incorporation within the general budget, the type and level of the appropriations made determines the minimum budgetary control and account detail required. Obviously, management information needs may necessitate additional degrees of budgetary control or account detail.

Where appropriations are made in rather explicit line item or category detail, as is often the case where a city or county is to construct a capital facility largely with its own work crews and equipment, appropriate Capital Projects Fund accounting procedures would correspond closely with those for the General Fund. Expenditure subsidiary ledger accounts should be controlled by Appropriations, Expenditures, and Encumbrances accounts in such circumstances.

On the other hand, the procedures illustrated by the NCGA presume that (1) expenditure authorizations are made either in total for the project as a whole or in broad categorical terms and (2) the requisite degree of budgetary control exercised over Capital Projects Funds does not necessitate the use of an Appropriations account. In such situations, often found in practice, the expenditure ledger would be controlled only by the Expenditures and Encumbrances accounts. In other words, a lesser degree of continuous budgetary control would be exercised than in General and Special Revenue Fund accounting.

Finally, some accountants (the authors included) consider use of the term "revenues" to be at best questionable, perhaps misleading, in describing Capital Project Fund inflows from bond issue proceeds and interfund transfers. Such items are "revenues" only in the literal or technical fund entity accounting usage of that term, of course, not from the standpoint of the organization as a whole. Since Capital Projects Funds typically have few "revenue" sources and transactions, and since statements analyzing changes in Fund Balance and/or Appropriations comprise the major operating statements prepared for this type fund, these "Revenues" may acceptably be credited (1) directly to either Fund Balance or Appropriations rather than to Revenues, or (2) to Fund Balance or Appropriations temporary (nominal) accounts, such as Proceeds from Sale of Bonds or Transfers from General Fund, in which the term "revenue" does not appear.

The approach demonstrated below was chosen because (1) it corresponds closely to that illustrated by the NCGA, and (2) the reader is assumed to be competent in General Fund accounting and readily able to adapt that approach to Capital Projects Fund accounting where he should—or must—do so. The accounts affected under the alternative approaches referred to above are also indicated (within parentheses) in the illustrative examples which follow.

### Establishment of Fund

A Capital Projects Fund ledger is established upon project authorization. Details related to the authorization are entered therein either by narrative memorandum entry or by a formal entry such as:

| | | |
|---|---|---|
| Projects Authorized ......................... | 400,000 | |
| Fund Balance (or Appropriations) .......... | | 400,000 |
| To record project authorization. | | |

As assets are accrued or received, the entries are as follows:

IF A MEMORANDUM AUTHORIZATION ENTRY WAS MADE:

| | | |
|---|---:|---:|
| Due from General Fund | 50,000 | |
| Due from County | 50,000 | |
| Due from Federal Government | 200,000 | |
|    Revenues (or Fund Balance or | | |
|       Appropriations) | | 300,000 |
| To record accrual of project resources other than | | |
| from borrowing. | | |

| | | |
|---|---:|---:|
| Cash | 101,000 | |
|    Revenues (or Fund Balance or | | |
|       Appropriations) | | 100,000 |
|    Premium on Bonds | | 1,000 |
| To record sale of bonds at a premium. | | |

IF A FORMAL AUTHORIZATION ENTRY WAS MADE:

| | | |
|---|---:|---:|
| Due from General Fund | 50,000 | |
| Due from County | 50,000 | |
| Due from Federal Government | 200,000 | |
|    Projects Authorized | | 300,000 |
| To record accrual of project resources other than | | |
| from borrowing. | | |

| | | |
|---|---:|---:|
| Cash | 101,000 | |
|    Projects Authorized | | 100,000 |
|    Premium on Bonds | | 1,000 |
| To record sale of bonds at a premium. | | |

In this illustration a $400,000 project has been authorized, to be financed from four sources: a General Fund transfer, a county contribution, a Federal grant, and a bond issue. Note that (1) if a formal project authorization entry was made, the Projects Authorized "resource" account is removed when assets are received or accrued, (2) a premium on bonds does not serve to increase the project authorization, and (3) Appropriations and Estimated Revenue accounts are not employed. Estimated Revenue accounts would serve little purpose in the usual situation, since resources for capital projects are generally obtained from only a few sources and estimation presents little problem. An Appropriations account may, as noted, be used in the same manner as in the General Fund.

### Disposition of Premiums, Discounts, Accrued Interest

Premiums and discounts on debt issuances are interest rate adjustments. Therefore, premiums should be transferred to the appropriate Debt Service Fund and, theoretically, an amount equal to any discount should be transferred from the Debt Service Fund to the Capital Projects Fund. Where a series of debt issuances is involved, only the net premium or discount is of concern; and disposition of the net premium or discount is deferred until all debt instruments have been issued. Because of legal difficulties—and since at the origination of the project there probably will be no resources in the appropriate Debt Service Fund—a discount must usually be written off, and the project authorization (Fund Balance or Appropriations) reduced accordingly. Alternatively, the discount may be written off to Expenditures (1) as a matter of expediency, (2) to avoid revising a formal appropriation made previously, or (3) because the discount is considered a necessary cost of acquiring the item in question.

Interest on bonds is usually paid annually or semiannually. In order to simplify the debt service process, the holder of a bond is paid the full amount of interest due for the annual or semiannual period, regardless of how long he has owned the bond. Where bonds are sold between interest dates, therefore, the purchaser must also pay for the interest accrued on the bond, since he will receive interest for the full period at the next interest payment date. Accrued interest thus received should be transferred to the Debt Service Fund from which the bond interest will be paid.

To illustrate, assume the bonds in our example were sold between interest dates, when $200 interest was accrued, at a $1,000 discount. The appropriate entries would be:

IF A MEMORANDUM AUTHORIZATION ENTRY WAS MADE:

| | | |
|---|---:|---:|
| Cash................................................. | 99,200 | |
| Discount on Bonds ............................ | 1,000 | |
|     Revenues (or Fund Balance or | | |
|         Appropriations) ......................... | | 100,000 |
|     Accrued Interest Payable .................. | | 200 |
|     To record sale of bonds at a discount between interest payment dates. | | |
| | | |
| Revenues (or Fund Balance or | | |
|     Appropriations) ............................ | 1,000 | |
|     Discount on Bonds ....................... | | 1,000 |
|     To reduce the project authorization and write off bond discount. | | |

(Alternatively, the sale of bonds may be recorded net—that is, only $99,000 credited to Revenues (or to Fund Balance or Appropriations) and no discount account established—if it is known at the time of the bond sale that any discount will serve to reduce the project authorization.)

| | | |
|---|---:|---:|
| Accrued Interest Payable ..................... | 200 | |
|     Cash..................................... | | 200 |
|     To record transfer of bond interest received to Debt Service Fund. | | |

IF A FORMAL AUTHORIZATION ENTRY WAS MADE:

| | | |
|---|---|---|
| Cash........................................... | 99,200 | |
| Discount on Bonds ............................ | 1,000 | |
| Projects Authorized......................... | | 100,000 |
| Accrued Interest Payable ................... | | 200 |
| To record sale of bonds at a discount. | | |

| | | |
|---|---|---|
| Fund Balance (or Appropriations) ............... | 1,000 | |
| Discount on Bonds ........................ | | 1,000 |
| To reduce the project authorization and write off bond discount. | | |

| | | |
|---|---|---|
| Accrued Interest Payable...................... | 200 | |
| Cash...................................... | | 200 |
| To record transfer of bond interest received to Debt Service Fund. | | |

Should resources subsequently be transferred to the Capital Projects Fund from another fund to compensate for the discount after it had been written off, the entries would be:

IF A MEMORANDUM AUTHORIZATION ENTRY WAS MADE:

| | | |
|---|---|---|
| Cash........................................... | 1,000 | |
| Revenues (or Fund Balance or Appropriations) ............................ | | 1,000 |
| To record transfer to make up for bond discount previously written off. | | |

IF A FORMAL AUTHORIZATION ENTRY WAS MADE:

| | | |
|---|---|---|
| Cash........................................... | 1,000 | |
| Fund Balance (or Appropriations) .............. | | 1,000 |
| To record transfer to make up for bond discount previously written off. | | |

A net premium would be disposed of by recording its transfer to the appropriate Debt Service Fund:

| | | |
|---|---|---|
| Premium on Bonds ............................. | 1,000 | |
| Cash...................................... | | 1,000 |
| To record transfer of bond premium to Debt Service Fund. | | |

Premiums and interest received upon bond issuance are sometimes recorded directly in a Debt Service Fund. This practice is not objectionable so long as an adequate audit trail is maintained.

### Operation of Fund

As noted earlier, a Capital Projects Fund continues in existence until the project(s) is(are) completed and the related resources have been expended or transferred to other funds. The Fund is abolished when its purpose is served.

In extremely simple situations, such as where the project consists of purchasing existing facilities for a single payment or transferring resources to another fund (e.g., to finance a deficit or establish an Enterprise Fund), the life of the Capital Projects Fund may be brief and its transaction entries uncomplicated. Assuming in the first example above (bonds sold at a premium, which has been transferred to the Debt Service Fund) that receivables were collected and the assets expended or transferred *immediately,* the following entries would be made:

| | | |
|---|---|---|
| Cash.................................... | 300,000 | |
| Due from General Fund................... | | 50,000 |
| Due from County........................ | | 50,000 |
| Due from Federal Government ........... | | 200,000 |
| To record collection of receivables. | | |
| | | |
| Expenditures (or Fund Balance or Appropriations) .......................... | 400,000 | |
| Cash.................................... | | 400,000 |
| To record immediate expenditure or transfer of all assets of the fund. | | |

Any necessary closing entries would then be made and the Fund abolished. Had Revenues and Expenditures accounts been used the closing entry is simply:

| | | |
|---|---|---|
| Revenues ................................ | 400,000 | |
| Expenditures............................ | | 400,000 |
| To close fund accounts. | | |

Had the Fund Balance or Appropriations account been credited for asset accruals and debited upon their expenditure, no closing entry would be required.

In the usual case, however, a Capital Projects Fund is used to finance construction projects where the government acts as a general contractor, possibly using its own employees and equipment for part or all of the work. In this situation accounting procedures are more complicated and closely resemble those of the General Fund.

## CAPITAL PROJECTS FUND CASE ILLUSTRATION

Typical Capital Projects Fund transactions and entries will now be illustrated through use of an extended case example. The case example is summarized in worksheets presented as Figures 8-13 and 8-14. Only the numbered journal entries that follow are posted to the worksheets in Figures 8-13 and 8-14; those that are not numbered illustrate alternative approaches or varied situations that may be encountered in Capital Projects Fund accounting.

Only general ledger accounts are used in the illustration, though one or more subsidiary ledgers may be employed if warranted by a need for more detailed data. It is assumed in the case illustration that (1) the bonds sold at a discount, which has been written off, leaving a $399,000 project authorization, (2) the Revenues account has been credited for assets received or accrued, (3) the project is begun in one year and completed in the next, and (4) an Appropriations account is not used, since the entire Fund Balance is appropriated in "lump-sum" fashion for the project as a whole. As noted earlier, under this approach the expenditure subsidiary ledger (if used) would be controlled only by the Encumbrances and Expenditures accounts.

The trial balance of the Capital Projects Fund as we begin the case illustration is as follows:

| | | |
|---|---|---|
| Cash................................... | 399,000 | |
| Revenues................................ | | 399,000 |
| | 399,000 | 399,000 |

### Transactions and Entries—First Fiscal Year

Let us assume that this project involves a bridge to be constructed partly by a contractor and partly by city labor. A contract is entered into with Jones & Company for construction of certain parts of the bridge, at an estimated cost of $300,000.

| | | | |
|---|---|---|---|
| (1) | Encumbrances ......................... | 300,000 | |
| | Reserve for Encumbrances ........... | | 300,000 |
| | To record encumbrance for contract let. | | |

Orders were placed for materials estimated to cost $5,000.

| | | | |
|---|---|---|---|
| (2) | Encumbrances ......................... | 5,000 | |
| | Reserve for Encumbrances ........... | | 5,000 |
| | To record encumbrances for orders placed. | | |

Payroll, $16,000, was paid.

| | | | |
|---|---|---|---|
| (3) | Expenditures .......................... | 16,000 | |
| | Cash ............................. | | 16,000 |
| | To record payroll. | | |

A bill for $120,000 was received from Jones & Company for part of the work.

| | | | |
|---|---|---|---|
| (4) | Reserve for Encumbrances ............... | 120,000 | |
| | Encumbrances ..................... | | 120,000 |
| | To reverse, in part, entry setting up encumbrances. | | |

(5)  Expenditures ............................ 120,000
      Contracts Payable...................         120,000
      To record expenditures.

The materials previously ordered were received; the bill was for $4,800.

(6)  Reserve for Encumbrances ............... 5,000
      Encumbrances .....................         5,000
      To reverse entry setting up encumbrances.

(7)  Expenditures ........................... 4,800
      Vouchers Payable ...................         4,800
      To record expenditures.

Payment of $120,000 was made to Jones & Company.

(8)  Contracts Payable....................... 120,000
      Cash ..............................         120,000

An order estimated to cost $12,000 was placed.

(9)  Encumbrances ......................... 12,000
      Reserve for Encumbrances ............         12,000
      To record encumbrances on order placed.

Had several related projects been financed through the Fund, several Appropriations accounts would be established or separate Expenditures accounts employed in the general ledger. In addition, separate subsidiary records would be established to support each project control account. Again, note that nothing precludes use of a complete budgetary accounting approach, including Estimated Revenues and/or Appropriations accounts, in a manner similar to General Fund accounting.

PRECLOSING TRIAL BALANCE.   Upon posting the numbered entries above to the Capital Projects Fund accounts, the following unadjusted, preclosing trial balance (Figure 8-13) could be drawn at the close of the first year's activities:

| | | |
|---|---:|---:|
| Cash.................................. | 263,000 | |
| Vouchers Payable ...................... | | 4,800 |
| Revenues ............................. | | 399,000 |
| Expenditures.......................... | 140,800 | |
| Encumbrances ......................... | 192,000 | |
| Reserve for Encumbrances ............... | | 192,000 |
| | 595,800 | 595,800 |

ADJUSTING ENTRIES—PROJECT INCOMPLETE.   The accounts should be adjusted, as appropriate, prior to preparation of year-end statements. Most of the usual types of adjusting entries have already been presented and need not be discussed again here. One type of adjustment warrants special attention, however, as it is unique to project- and purpose-oriented funds such as Capital Projects and Special Assessment Funds.

An adjusting entry will be necessary to properly state the Fund's resources and the Fund Balance (or Appropriations) account where (1) a memorandum project authorization entry was made (rather than a formal entry) at the inception of the project and (2) all resources to be made available to the Fund have not been received or accrued by year-end. The adjustment required involves the same accounts as does the formal project authorization entry discussed earlier, but the amounts will equal the difference between the amount expected to be available for the project and the resources received or accrued to date. For example, if only $150,000 of the bonds (par value) in the example above had been issued by year end, the following adjustment would be required prior to statement preparation:

| | | |
|---|---|---|
| Bonds Authorized—Unissued .................. | 250,000 | |
| Fund Balance (or Appropriations) .......... | | 250,000 |
| To record bond issue and expenditure authority not recorded previously. | | |

Had the $150,000 been an amount estimated to be available from a Federal grant in process (rather than from unissued bonds), an account such as Estimated Federal Grant Proceeds would have been debited. Adjustments of this type are reversed at the beginning of the subsequent period.

Failure to make such adjustments will result in understatement of the assets (or resources) and the Fund Balance (or Appropriations) account. Moreover, it will result in a Fund Balance deficit being reported in all cases where the sum of the expenditures to date and encumbrances at year-end exceeds the assets received or accrued to date, even when total project expenditures and encumbrances to date are well within the project authorization.

CLOSING ENTRY—PROJECT INCOMPLETE. Unlike General Fund appropriations, authorizations to make Capital Projects Fund expenditures are not usually limited as to time; that is, the authorization normally continues until the project is completed. Although it may be argued that closing entries need not be prepared for uncompleted projects, the preferred approach is to close the Revenues, Expenditures, and Encumbrances accounts to Fund Balance in order to summarize operating results to date and Fund financial status at year end. Closing the Expenditures account annually also facilitates capitalization of the cost of construction in progress in the General Fixed Asset accounts. Closing entries are made as follows:

| | | | |
|---|---|---|---|
| (C1) | Revenues ........................... | 399,000 | |
| | Fund Balance ..................... | | 399,000 |
| | To close Revenues account at year end. | | |

(C2)  Fund Balance ........................     332,800
         Expenditures.....................                       140,800
         Encumbrances  ...................                       192,000
         To close Expenditures to date and Encum-
         brances at year end.

If an Appropriations account is used, the total balance is not closed at this time. Rather, only an amount equal to the sum of the Expenditures and Encumbrances is closed; the remaining Appropriations continue as expenditure authority in the subsequent period.

Appropriations .............................     332,800
         Expenditures............................                       140,800
         Encumbrances ..........................                       192,000
         To close Expenditures and Encumbrances to Ap-
         propriations.

Note that the Fund Balance account is unaffected by closing entries relating to an uncompleted project where Appropriations accounts are used. Fund Balance equal to the total authorization has been appropriated; the Fund Balance account will be affected only if Appropriations are revised or if total Expenditures for the project differ from total Appropriations.

Some accountants prefer not to close the Encumbrances account at year end, that is, they prefer to leave the Encumbrances account in its usual offset relationship with the Reserve for Encumbrances account. The advantages of this approach are that it avoids (1) the possibility that Encumbrances will be inadvertently capitalized in the General Fixed Asset account group along with the Expenditures, and (2) the need to re-establish the Encumbrances account at the start of the subsequent period. Under this acceptable alternative, the Encumbrances account is deducted from the Fund Balance (or Appropriations) account in the balance sheet, and affects neither the Fund Balance (or Appropriations) account balance nor analyses thereof; the Reserve for Encumbrances is added to the unencumbered fund balance (Fund Balance less Encumbrances) to derive total fund balance. This method is illustrated in the discussion of Bond Funds at the close of this chapter.

Similarly, as noted above, there are those who prefer not to make year-end closing entries at all, but to close the accounts only after the project is complete. Under this approach (1) the balance of the Expenditures account includes total project expenditures, from project inception to date, and (2) both Expenditures and Encumbrances are deducted from Fund Balance (or Appropriations) in balance sheets prepared prior to project completion—that is, neither affects the Fund Balance (or Appropriations) account directly nor appears in analyses thereof—and the Reserve for Encumbrances is added to the unexpended and unencumbered Fund Balance amount to derive total fund balance.

## Major Statements at Close of the Fiscal Year—Project Incomplete

Assuming that the journal entries illustrated thus far for the Capital Projects Fund had been posted to the accounts (see Figure 8-13), the statements in Figures 8-1 (A) and 8-1 (B) and 8-2 (A) and 8-2 (B) could be prepared.

Figure 8-1 (A)

A GOVERNMENTAL UNIT
Capital Projects Fund
Balance Sheet at Close of Fiscal Year (Date)
(Project Incomplete)

*Assets*

| | |
|---|---|
| Cash ...................................... | $263,000 |

*Liabilities, Reserves, and Fund Balance*

| | |
|---|---|
| Vouchers payable ........................... | $ 4,800 |
| Reserve for encumbrances .................... | 192,000 |
| Fund balance (Figure 8-2(A)) ................. | 66,200 |
| | $263,000 |

Figure 8-1 (B)

A GOVERNMENTAL UNIT
Capital Projects Fund
Balance Sheet at Close of Fiscal Year (Date)
(Project Incomplete)

*Assets*

| | |
|---|---|
| Cash ...................................... | $263,000 |

*Liabilities and Fund Balance*

Liabilities:

| | |
|---|---|
| Vouchers payable ........................ | $ 4,800 |

Fund Balance:

| | | |
|---|---|---|
| Reserved for encumbrances.........$192,000 | | |
| Unreserved (or Unencumbered) ..... 66,200 | 258,200 |
| | $263,000 |

Figure 8-2 (A)

A GOVERNMENTAL UNIT
Capital Projects Fund
Analysis of Changes in Fund Balance (Account)
For the Fiscal Year Ended (Date)
(Project Incomplete)

| | | |
|---|---|---:|
| Initial project authorization .................... | | $400,000 |
| Less: Discount on bonds ..................... | | 1,000 |
| Net project authorization ...................... | | $399,000 |
| | | |
| Fund balance, beginning of year ................ | | $ –0– |
| | | |
| Add: Revenues............................. | | 399,000 |
| | | $399,000 |
| | | |
| Less: Expenditures .............. | $140,800 | |
| Encumbrances ............ | 192,000 | 332,800 |
| | | |
| Fund balance, end of year .................... | | $ 66,200 |

The distinctions between Figures 8-1 (A) and 8-2 (A) and Figures 8-1 (B) and 8-2 (B) warrant careful study.

Figures 8-1 (A) and 8-2 (A) are based on illustrations contained within *Governmental Accounting, Auditing, and Financial Reporting*. The "Fund Balance" presented in the Balance Sheet (Figure 8-1 (A)) and for which changes are analyzed in Figure 8-2 (A) agrees with the Fund Balance *account* in the general ledger and is thus in fact the *unreserved* Fund Balance. The Reserve for Encumbrances is actually *reserved* Fund Balance, since Encumbrances have been closed to the Fund Balance account, but it is shown in a separate "Reserves" classification on the Balance Sheet and is excluded from the ending balance in the Analysis of Changes in Fund Balance (account). Though subject to criticism conceptually, the approach illustrated in Figures 8-1 (A) and 8-2 (A) has certain practical advantages in that (1) it is simple and unconfusing, as the figures shown for Fund Balance and Reserve for Encumbrances agree with the balances of these accounts in the general ledger, and (2) it highlights the amount of resources available for future commitment ($66,200). Highlighting the total Fund Balance ($258,200) is often thought to be less desirable since the Reserve for Encumbrances ($197,000) represents assets already committed.

Figures 8-1 (B) and 8-2 (B) are more correct conceptually than their counterparts in that the ambiguous "Reserve" category is eliminated from the Balance Sheet (Figure 8-1 (B)) and in that the Analysis of Changes in Fund

Figure 8-2 (B)

A GOVERNMENTAL UNIT
Capital Projects Fund
Analysis of Changes in Fund Balance (Total)
For the Fiscal Year Ended (Date)
(Project Incomplete)

| | | |
|---|---|---:|
| Initial project authorization ................... | | $400,000 |
| Less: Discount on bonds .................... | | 1,000 |
| | | $399,000 |
| Fund balance, beginning of year ............... | | $ –0– |
| Add: Revenues............................. | | $399,000 |
| | | $399,000 |
| Less: Expenditures ................ | $140,800 | |
| Encumbrances .............. | 192,000 | 332,800 |
| Unreserved fund balance, end of year .......... | | $ 66,200 |
| Fund balance reserved for encumbrances, end of year ................................... | | 192,000 |
| Total fund balance, end of year ............... | | $258,200 |

Balance (Figure 8-2 (B)) includes both its reserved and unreserved portions. Alternatively, the Analysis of Changes in Fund Balance (Total) shown in Figure 8-2 (B) could better be presented in columnar form:

| | *Unreserved* | *Reserved* | *Total* |
|---|---:|---:|---:|
| Fund Balance, beginning of year ......... | $ –0– | $ –0– | $ –0– |
| Changes during the year: | | | |
| Revenues ......................... | 399,000 | –0– | 399,000 |
| Expenditures ...................... | (140,800) | –0– | (140,800) |
| Encumbrances ..................... | (192,000) | 192,000 | –0– |
| Fund Balance, end of year.............. | $ 66,200 | $192,000 | $ 258,200 |

Both approaches have found wide usage and general acceptance in practice. Obviously, it is important for both the accountant and the user of the statements to be aware of the method on which they are based.

Expenditures and encumbrances should be itemized in appropriate detail either within the statement analyzing changes in fund balance or in schedules cross-referenced to that statement. Budgetary comparisons should also be presented, particularly where significant variations have occurred. Presentation of a separate Statement of Estimated and Actual Revenues (Figure 8-3) is authoritatively recommended, though revenues may be itemized within the Analysis of Changes in Fund Balance or in supplementary schedules thereto if there are neither a large number of sources nor significant variations between estimated and actual amounts.

Note particularly that neither the long-term debt incurred to finance the project nor the fixed assets acquired thereby appear in statements of the Capital Projects Fund. The long-term debt is established in the General Long-Term Debt account group upon incurrence; fixed assets are capitalized at year-end in the General Fixed Assets account group. The only exception to this rule occurs in situations where (1) bond anticipation (or similar) notes are issued for periods of over one year in the expectation of lower bond interest rates in the future, (2) such notes are established as liabilities of the Capital Projects Fund, as they are to be liquidated from ultimate bond sale proceeds, and (3) the receipt and expenditure of the bond sale proceeds are accounted for through the Capital Projects Fund. Alternatively, (1) the bond anticipation note liability may be established in the General Long-Term Debt group of accounts, and (2) proceeds of the bond sale, considered a refunding issue, expended to retire the notes through a Debt Service Fund (see Chapter 10).

**Figure 8-3**

A GOVERNMENTAL UNIT
Capital Projects Fund
Statement of Revenue—Estimated and Actual
For the Fiscal Year Ended (Date)

|  | Estimated Revenue | Actual Revenue | Actual over (under) Estimated |
|---|---|---|---|
| Transfer from General Fund ............. | $ 50,000 | $ 50,000 | $   – |
| Contribution by county ................. | 50,000 | 50,000 | – |
| Federal grant-in-aid .................... | 200,000 | 200,000 | – |
| Sale of bonds .......................... | 100,000 | 99,000 | (1,000) |
|  | $400,000 | $399,000 | $(1,000) |

## Transactions and Entries—Second Fiscal Year

To conclude the illustration, let us assume that the project was completed in the next fiscal year and that the transactions or events and the corresponding entries (see Figure 8-14) were as follows:

The Encumbrances account is re-established in its usual off-set relationship with the Reserve for Encumbrances account by reversing the portion of the previous closing entry related to Encumbrances.

| | | | |
|---|---|---|---|
| (10) | Encumbrances ......................... | 192,000 | |
| | Fund Balance (or Appropriations) .... | | 192,000 |
| | To re-establish encumbrances closed at end of previous year. | | |

The materials ordered were received together with an invoice for $12,400.

| | | | |
|---|---|---|---|
| (11) | Reserve for Encumbrances .............. | 12,000 | |
| | Encumbrances .................... | | 12,000 |
| | To reverse entry setting up encumbrances. | | |
| (12) | Expenditures ......................... | 12,400 | |
| | Vouchers Payable ................. | | 12,400 |
| | To record expenditures. | | |

Jones & Company completed its part of the work; its bill was for $180,000, the balance of its contract.

| | | | |
|---|---|---|---|
| (13) | Reserve for Encumbrances .............. | 180,000 | |
| | Encumbrances .................... | | 180,000 |
| | To reverse remaining encumbrances. | | |
| (14) | Expenditures ......................... | 180,000 | |
| | Contracts Payable.................. | | 180,000 |
| | To record expenditures. | | |

Total additional payments for labor amounted to $60,000.

| | | | |
|---|---|---|---|
| (15) | Expenditures ......................... | 60,000 | |
| | Cash ............................. | | 60,000 |
| | To record expenditures. | | |

Jones & Company's bill was paid, except for 5 per cent of the total contract, which was retained pending inspection and final approval of the completed project.

| | | | |
|---|---|---|---|
| (16) | Contracts Payable...................... | 180,000 | |
| | Contracts Payable-Retained Percentage. | | 15,000 |
| | Cash ............................. | | 165,000 |
| | To record payment of contract balance, less retained percentage. | | |

All other outstanding bills were paid.

| (17) | Vouchers Payable ..................... | 17,200 | |
| | Cash ............................. | | 17,200 |
| | To record payment of vouchers. | | |

CLOSING ENTRY—PROJECT COMPLETED. When the project is completed, an entry is made closing Expenditures into the Fund Balance account. The entry is as follows:

| (C3) | Fund Balance ........................ | 252,400 | |
| | Expenditures...................... | | 252,400 |
| | To record closing out of expenditures. | | |

Had an Appropriations account been used, any balance therein would be eliminated upon project completion and the unneeded Appropriations returned to Fund Balance:

| Appropriations .............................. | 258,200 | |
| Expenditures............................ | | 252,400 |
| Fund Balance ............................ | | 5,800 |
| To record closing of expenditures and return of unneeded appropriations to fund balance. | | |

BALANCE SHEET—PROJECT COMPLETED. After the above entries have been posted (see Figure 8-14), the balance sheet in Figure 8-4 can be prepared.

**Figure 8-4**

A GOVERNMENTAL UNIT
Capital Projects Fund
Balance Sheet During, or at Close of, Fiscal Year (Date)
(Project Completed)

*Assets*

| Cash ........................................ | $20,800 |

*Liabilities and Fund Balance*

| Contracts payable—retained percentage .......... | $15,000 |
| Fund balance .............................. | 5,800 |
| | $20,800 |

Note again that the resulting fixed assets are not set up in the Capital Projects Fund even when the project is completed. Instead, as already indicated, they are shown as part of the General Fixed Assets group of accounts. Again, bonds payable are not shown in the Capital Projects Fund balance sheet, but are carried as part of the General Long-Term Debt accounts.

Since the project is completed, the Fund has largely accomplished its purpose. From the above Balance Sheet (Figure 8-4) it is evident that, were it not for the Fund Balance, the Fund could be abolished as soon as the completed project was approved and the retained percentage on the contract paid.

DISPOSING OF FUND BALANCE OR DEFICIT.  From the foregoing example it is apparent that any existing Fund Balance must be disposed of before the Fund is dissolved. Frequently, the legislative body specifies what shall be done with such a balance. In the absence of legislative restrictions, however, the balance is usually transferred to the Debt Service Fund from which the bonds or other related debt will be retired. The rationale for such action is that the balance arose because project expenditure requirements were overestimated, with the result that a larger amount than necessary was borrowed. Where resources were provided by intergovernmental grants or intragovernmental transfers, it may be either necessary or appropriate to refund a portion of these resources in disposing of the fund balance.

Government managers are well advised to provide in project authorizations, bond indentures, or otherwise for the possibility that costs have been overestimated and a Fund Balance might need to be disposed of at the conclusion of the project. In the absence of written authorization to rebate unneeded monies or transfer them to the related Debt Service Fund, officials may be precluded from doing so and forced to hold them, possibly indefinitely, until they are needed for the express purpose for which they were secured. Such situations have arisen occasionally, for example, in cases in which money was borrowed "for the sole and exclusive purpose of extending existing waterlines and no other purposes." Should the waterlines now extend well beyond the urban area and a fund balance remain, it is obviously preferable to transfer or rebate the unneeded balance rather than be forced to retain the money—possibly without even being able to invest it if the terms cited above are literally interpreted—until such time as population growth might justify further waterline expansion.

A Capital Projects Fund deficit would ordinarily be disposed of in one of two ways. If small, it would probably be eliminated by transferring money from the General Fund; if large, it would probably be disposed of by additional borrowing.

ANALYSIS OF CHANGES IN FUND BALANCE—PROJECT COMPLETED.  The Analysis of Changes in Fund Balance is the major Capital Projects Fund statement. A statement similar to the one in Figure 8-5 would be prepared at the end of the year in which the project was completed and the fund balance disposed of.

Figure 8-5

A GOVERNMENTAL UNIT
Capital Projects Fund
Analysis of Changes in Fund Balance
For the Fiscal Year Ended (Date)

| | | |
|---|---:|---:|
| Net Project Authorization .......................... | | $399,000 |
| Fund balance, beginning of year ................ | | 66,200 |
| Add:  Revenues.....................$   –0– | | |
| Prior year encumbrances | | |
| re-established .............. 192,000 | | 192,000 |
| | | $258,200 |
| Less:  Expenditures ................. 252,400 | | |
| Transfers to Debt | | |
| Service Fund ................  5,800 | | 258,200 |
| Fund balance, end of year ..................... | | $   –0– |

## INVESTMENT OF IDLE CASH

Significant sums of cash are commonly involved in capital project fiscal management. Cash receipt, investment, and disbursement therefore warrant careful planning, timing, and control.

Prudent financial management requires that loan transactions not be closed (and interest charges begun) in the usual situation until the cash is needed. There may be exceptions to this rule, of course, as in cases where investments yield the government more than enough to cover the related interest costs. Similarly, significant sums should not be permitted to remain on demand deposit, but should be invested in high grade government securities, certificates of deposit, or savings accounts until such time as they are to be disbursed.

Both the authority to invest idle cash and the disposition of investment earnings should be agreed upon and documented in the project authorization ordinance and in other contractual agreements. Investment earnings might be used, for example, to reduce the government's share of the project cost or to increase the project expenditure authorization. Where monies have been borrowed and interest expense is being incurred, however, investment earnings should normally be transferred to the appropriate Debt Service Fund.

Governments generally manage idle Capital Projects Fund cash far better today than in earlier years. There continue to be isolated instances of intentional or careless mismanagement, however, such as leaving significant sums of cash on demand deposit with favored banks for months or years at a time or using investment earnings for general government purposes in an unauthorized manner. The latter practice has the effect of financing current expenditures through long-term debt. Such practices at least border on fraud and should not be condoned.

## FINANCING SEVERAL PROJECTS THROUGH ONE FUND

Earlier in this chapter it was noted that a single Capital Projects Fund may be used to finance several projects where only one debt issue or grant is involved or the projects are financed through internal transfers from other funds. For example, the capital project may consist of several "general improvements," possibly financed through a general obligation bond issue. Each project undertaken may be separately budgeted in such cases and, in any event, each must be separately controlled and accounted for within the fund accounts.

Separate project control and accounting within a single fund is best done by establishing a series of appropriately designated Appropriations or Fund Balance, Expenditures, and Encumbrances and Reserve for Encumbrances accounts in the general ledger. These general ledger accounts jointly control a similar series of separate project expenditure subsidiary accounts or ledgers. This approach is illustrated in Figure 8-6.

Accounting for these funds corresponds with procedures discussed above. Closing entries differ only in that several Appropriations, Expenditures, and Encumbrances accounts are employed. After all projects to be financed from the fund have been completed and all liabilities liquidated, any remaining fund balance or deficit is disposed of as indicated earlier and the fund is terminated.

Financial statements prepared for multiproject Capital Projects Funds should present information related to each project as well as for the Fund as a whole. This may be accomplished either by columnar or "pancake" presentation. The columnar approach is illustrated by the following statement headings:

A GOVERNMENTAL UNIT
Capital Projects Fund
Balance Sheet (Date)

|  | *Total* | *Completed Projects Project "A"* | *Incomplete Projects Project "B"* | *Projects Not Yet Determined* |
|---|---|---|---|---|

The "pancake" method of presentation is illustrated by the statement headings and partial statement shown in Figure 8-7.

Figure 8-6

APPROACH TO ACCOUNTING CONTROL
SEVERAL PROJECTS FINANCED THROUGH ONE
CAPITAL PROJECTS FUND

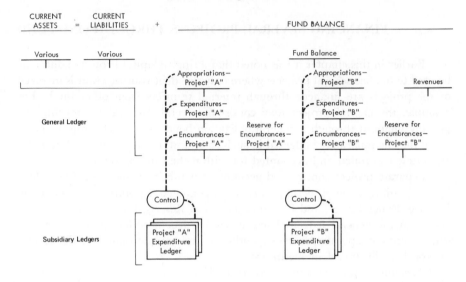

Figure 8-7

A GOVERNMENT UNIT
Capital Projects Fund
Statement of Appropriations, Expenditures, and Encumbrances
For Fiscal Year Ended (Date)

| | Appropriations | Expenditures | Encumbrances | Unencumbered Balance |
|---|---|---|---|---|
| Project "A" | | | | |
| Total Project "A" | $ 500,000 | $200,000 | $ 10,000 | $290,000 |
| Project "B" | | | | |
| Total Project "B" | $ 700,000 | $600,000 | $ 90,000 | $ 10,000 |
| Total—All Projects | $1,200,000 | $800,000 | $100,000 | $300,000 |

## COMBINED CAPITAL PROJECTS FUNDS STATEMENTS

Three financial statements are required to present the results of operation and financial position of a Capital Projects Fund: (1) Balance Sheet, (2) Analysis of Changes in Fund Balance, and (3) Statement of Revenue—Estimated and Actual. In many cases a Statement of Expenditures and Encumbrances Compared with Appropriations will also be necessary. Alternatively, as indicated earlier, revenue and expenditure and encumbrance data may be detailed within the statement analyzing changes in fund balances when only a few revenue sources or expenditure and encumbrance categories are involved.

In order both to focus attention on capital projects activities as a whole and to reduce the number of separate statements required, statements of the several Capital Projects Funds of a government are usually presented in combined form. With adequate disclosure in either columnar or "pancake" format, such combined statements also fulfill the requirement for separate statements for each fund. In no case, however, should combined totals be shown without the details applicable to each fund either being presented within the statement itself or being incorporated by reference therein to a statement or schedule containing the separate fund details. Presentation of consolidated statements in which interfund transactions, receivables, or payables have been eliminated is expressly prohibited by the NCGA.

A Combined Balance Sheet for several Capital Projects Funds is shown in Figure 8-8. The "Bridge Fund" is that illustrated in this chapter; the other data are assumed for illustrative purposes. As indicated in this statement, a distinction is frequently made between completed and incomplete projects in combined balance sheets and in combined analyses of changes in fund balances. For incomplete projects it is important to disclose the unexpended and unencumbered fund balances in the balance sheet and/or statement analyzing changes in fund balance, either parenthetically, by footnote, or through use of an Appropriations account(s).

A Combined Analysis of Changes in Fund Balances is illustrated in Figure 8-9. This statement is identical to that which would be prepared for a single fund, except that it contains a "total" column and a separate column for each fund.

If a government has numerous Capital Projects Funds (that is, more than six or seven), it may be desirable to prepare combined schedules for groups of funds and use such combined data, appropriately described and referenced to the schedules, in preparation of the combined balance sheet for all Capital Projects Funds. A similar technique often proves useful in connection with statements of multiproject funds. The partial statement and schedule shown in Figure 8-10 illustrate this approach.

Figure 8-8

## A GOVERNMENTAL UNIT
### Capital Projects Funds
### Combined Balance Sheet (Date)

| | | Completed Projects | | Incomplete Projects | |
| --- | --- | --- | --- | --- | --- |
| Assets | Total All Funds | Bridge Fund | Sewer System Fund | Civic Center Fund | General Improvements Fund |
| Cash | $ 44,800 | $ 20,800 | $ 10,000 | $ 5,000 | $ 9,000 |
| Investments | 550,000 | | | 450,000 | 100,000 |
| Due from other funds (itemize) | 50,000 | | | 30,000 | 20,000 |
| Due from county | 25,000 | | | 15,000 | 10,000 |
| Total assets | $669,800 | $ 20,800 | $ 10,000 | $500,000 | $139,000 |
| *Liabilities, Reserves,\* and Fund Balances* | | | | | |
| Liabilities: | | | | | |
| Vouchers payable | $ 60,000 | | | $ | $ 60,000 |
| Contracts payable | 50,000 | | | | 50,000 |
| Contracts payable—retained percentage | 25,000 | $ 15,000 | $ 10,000 | | |
| Due to other funds (itemize) | 10,000 | | | | 10,000 |
| Total liabilities | $145,000 | $ 15,000 | $ 10,000 | $ | $120,000 |

Reserves* and Fund Balances:

| | | | | | |
|---|---|---|---|---|---|
| Reserve for encumbrances | $500,000 | $ | | $490,000 | $ 10,000 |
| Fund balance** (Figure 8-9) | 24,800 | $ 5,800 | 10,000 | 10,000 | 9,000 |
| Total reserves and fund balances | $524,800 | $ 5,800 | | $500,000 | 19,000 |
| Total liabilities, reserves, and fund balances | $669,800 | $ 20,800 | $ 10,000 | $500,000 | $139,000 |

* As noted in the text, "Reserves" are "Reserved Fund Balance"; hence (1) the major caption "Liabilities and Fund Balances" is more correct conceptually than "Liabilities, Reserves, and Fund Balances," and (2) the "Reserves" may appear within a "Fund Balances" section rather than as a separate element of the "Reserves and Fund Balances" section illustrated here.

** Appropriations are "Appropriated Fund Balance." Hence, where Appropriations are made the Fund Balance would appear:

Fund Balance:
  Appropriated (or Appropriations)
  Unappropriated (or Available)

Figure 8-9

## A GOVERNMENTAL UNIT
### Capital Projects Funds
### Combined Analysis of Changes in Fund Balances (Period)

| | Total All Funds | Completed Projects | | Incomplete Projects | |
| --- | --- | --- | --- | --- | --- |
| | | Bridge Fund | Sewer System Fund | Civic Center Fund | General Improvements Fund |
| Initial project authorization .......... | $2,175,000 | $400,000 | $575,000 | $500,000 | $700,000 |
| Less: Discount on bonds .......... | 3,000 | 1,000 | – | – | 2,000 |
| Net project authorization .......... | $2,172,000 | $399,000 | $575,000 | $500,000 | $698,000 |
| Fund balance,* 1/1/B .......... | $ 901,200 | $ 66,200 | $200,000 | $500,000 | $135,000 |
| Add: | | | | | |
| Revenues (itemize or reference statement of) .......... | $ 500,000 | $ – | $200,000 | $ – | $300,000 |
| 19A Encumbrances re-established .......... | 457,000 | 192,000 | 150,000 | – | 115,000 |
| Total additions .......... | $ 957,000 | $192,000 | $350,000 | $ – | $415,000 |
| Total 1/1/B balance and additions .......... | $1,858,200 | $258,200 | $550,000 | $500,000 | $550,000 |

Deduct:

| | | | | | |
|---|---|---|---|---|---|
| Expenditures (itemize or reference statement of) | $1,333,400 | $252,400 | $550,000 | $ – | $531,000 |
| Transfer to Debt Service Fund | 5,800 | 5,800 | – | – | – |
| Reserve for encumbrances-19B | 500,000 | – | – | 490,000 | 10,000 |
| Total deductions | $1,839,200 | $258,200 | $550,000 | $490,000 | $541,000 |
| Fund Balance, *12/31/B (Figure 8-8) | $ 19,000 | $ – | $ – | $ 10,000 | $ 9,000 |

* Alternatively, separate analyses of Appropriated (Appropriations) and Unappropriated Fund Balances may be prepared or Fund Balances above may be classified as between Appropriated and Unappropriated.

Figure 8-10

A GOVERNMENTAL UNIT
Capital Projects Funds
Combined Balance Sheet (Date)

| | Completed Projects | | Incomplete Projects | |
| --- | --- | --- | --- | --- |
| Total All Funds | Bridge Fund | Sewer System Fund | Civic Center Fund | General Improvements Fund (Schedule A) |

Schedule A

A GOVERNMENTAL UNIT
General Improvements Capital Project Fund
Balance Sheet (Date)

| Total | Project "A" | Project "B" | Projects Not Yet Determined |
| --- | --- | --- | --- |

## BOND FUNDS

Earlier in this chapter we observed that Capital Projects Funds are an expansion and replacement of Bond Funds formerly recommended by the NCGA. Bond Fund accounting is discussed briefly in concluding this chapter inasmuch as (1) Bond Funds were a longstanding feature of previous NCGA recommendations and widely used in practice, and (2) they may continue to be found in practice.

As noted earlier, Bond Funds are used to establish accountability for the acquisition and use of the proceeds of general obligation bond issues. As in the case of Capital Projects Funds, a separate Bond Fund is normally established for each bond issue.

Bond Fund accounting procedures are virtually identical to those for Capital Projects Funds in which Appropriations accounts are established and procedures similar to those of General Fund accounting are employed. The authorization of the bond issue begins the Bond Fund life cycle and is recorded formally:

Bonds Authorized—Unissued . . . . . . . . . . . . . . . . . . 100,000
     Appropriations . . . . . . . . . . . . . . . . . . . . . . . . . . . 100,000
To record authorization of bonds.

Note that (1) the Bonds Authorized—Unissued account is considered a resource account similar to the Projects Authorized account illustrated earlier for the

Capital Projects Fund, and (2) the Appropriations account is credited for the expenditure authority. An unappropriated fund balance results only if appropriations are for less than the maximum expenditure authority or final project costs differ from the amount authorized.

The Bonds Authorized—Unissued account is removed upon receipt of the bond proceeds in the same manner as the Projects Authorized account was removed in the Capital Projects Fund example. Should all bonds not be sold as of a balance sheet date, the Bonds Authorized—Unissued account is listed under "Assets and Other Resources" on the balance sheet.

Premiums, discounts, and accrued interest received upon the sale of bonds are disposed of in the manner discussed for Capital Projects Funds. Again, accounting during a fiscal period parallels that for the General Fund.

Assume that $75,000 of the bonds authorized were issued during the first year of a Bond Fund's existence and that Expenditures and Encumbrances amounted to $40,000 and $15,000, respectively. The closing entry for the uncompleted project, if prepared, would be:

| | | |
|---|---|---|
| Appropriations............................... | 40,000 | |
| Expenditures.............................. | | 40,000 |
| To close expenditures against appropriations. | | |

Alternatively, encumbrances may be closed at year end and re-established at the beginning of the subsequent year.

A simplified Bond Fund Balance Sheet prepared at the end of its first fiscal year might appear as in Figures 8-11 (A) or 8-11 (B). Note the treatment of

**Figure 8-11 (A)**

A GOVERNMENTAL UNIT
Bond Fund Balance Sheet (Date)
(Project Incomplete)

*Assets and Other Resources*

| | | |
|---|---|---|
| Cash....................................... | | $39,800 |
| Bonds authorized—unissued .................. | | 25,000 |
| | | $64,800 |

*Liabilities, Reserves, and Appropriations*

| | | |
|---|---|---|
| Vouchers payable ........................... | | 4,800 |
| Reserve for encumbrances ..................... | | 15,000 |
| Appropriations (unexpended balance) .. | $60,000 | |
| Less: Encumbrances ............... | 15,000 | 45,000 |
| | | $64,800 |

Figure 8-11 (B)

A GOVERNMENTAL UNIT
Bond Fund Balance Sheet (Date)
(Project Incomplete)

*Assets and Other Resources*

| | |
|---|---|
| Cash ........................................ | $39,800 |
| Bonds authorized—unissued .................... | 25,000 |
| | $64,800 |

*Liabilities and Fund Balance*

| | | |
|---|---|---|
| Liabilities: | | |
| Vouchers payable ......................... | | $ 4,800 |
| Fund Balance: | | |
| Reserved for encumbrances.......... | $15,000 | |
| Unencumbered appropriations ...... | 45,000 | 60,000 |
| | | $64,800 |

the Encumbrances and Reserve for Encumbrances accounts, which are carried forward to the subsequent period in their usual offset relationship in Figure 8-11 (A); Encumbrances has been deducted from Appropriations to derive the "Unencumbered Appropriations" amount in Figure 8-11 (B). Note also that Figure 8-11 (B) does not contain a separate "Reserves" section, but that reserves are shown in the "Fund Balance" section.

A statement comparing expenditures with appropriations would also be prepared at year end. For the sake of brevity, this statement is illustrated only following completion of the project.

Figure 8-12

A GOVERNMENTAL UNIT
Bond Fund
Statement of Expenditures Compared with Appropriations
For Fiscal Years (Dates)

| | | |
|---|---|---|
| Appropriations (entire project)................ | | $100,000 |
| Less: Expenditures: | | |
| Of this year .................... | $56,500 | |
| Of prior years .................. | 40,000 | |
| Total expenditures ........................ | | 96,500 |
| Unexpended fund balance .................... | | $ 3,500 |
| Less: Transfers to Debt Service Fund ......... | | 3,500 |
| Fund balance, (date) ........................ | | $ — |

Figure 8-13

## A GOVERNMENTAL UNIT
### Capital Projects Fund
### Worksheet for First Fiscal Year (Date)

| | Trial Balance (Beginning of Illustration) Dr. | Cr. | Transactions (First Year) Dr. | Cr. | Preclosing Trial Balance (Project Incomplete) Dr. | Cr. | Closing Entries (Project Incomplete) Dr. | Cr. | Balance Sheet (Project Incomplete) Dr. | Cr. |
|---|---|---|---|---|---|---|---|---|---|---|
| Cash | 399,000 | | | (3) 16,000 (8) 120,000 | 263,000 | | | | 263,000 | |
| Revenues | | 399,000 | | | | 399,000 | (C1) 399,000 | | | |
| Encumbrances | | | (1) 300,000 (2) 5,000 (9) 12,000 | (4) 120,000 (6) 5,000 | 192,000 | | | (C2) 192,000 | | |
| Reserve for Encumbrances | | | (4) 120,000 (6) 5,000 | (1) 300,000 (2) 5,000 (9) 12,000 | | 192,000 | | | | 192,000 |
| Expenditures | | | (3) 16,000 (5) 120,000 (7) 4,800 | | 140,800 | | | (C2) 140,800 | | |
| Contracts Payable | | | (8) 120,000 | (5) 120,000 | | | | | | |
| Vouchers Payable | | | | (7) 4,800 | | 4,800 | | | | 4,800 |
| Fund Balance | | | | | | | (C2) 332,800 | (C1) 399,000 | | 66,200 |
| | 399,000 | 399,000 | 702,800 | 702,800 | 595,800 | 595,800 | 399,000 | 399,000 | 263,000 | 263,000 |

Figure 8-14

## A GOVERNMENTAL UNIT
### Capital Projects Fund
### Worksheet for Second Fiscal Year (Date)

| | Trial Balance (Beginning of Second Year) Dr. | Cr. | Transactions (Second Year) Dr. | Cr. | Preclosing Trial Balance (Project Completed) Dr. | Cr. | Closing Entries (Project Completed) Dr. | Cr. | Balance Sheet (Project Completed) Dr. | Cr. |
|---|---|---|---|---|---|---|---|---|---|---|
| Cash .......... | 263,000 | | | (15) 60,000  (16) 165,000  (17) 17,200 | 20,800 | | | | 20,800 | |
| Revenues ....... | | | (10) 192,000 | | | | | | | |
| Encumbrances .. | | | (11) 12,000  (13) 180,000 | | | | | | | |
| Reserve for Encumbrances | | 192,000 | | (11) 12,000  (13) 180,000 | | | | | | |
| Expenditures .... | | | (12) 12,400  (14) 180,000  (15) 60,000 | | 252,400 | | | (C3) 252,400 | | |
| Contracts Payable ...... | | | (16) 180,000 | (14) 180,000 | | | | | | |
| Vouchers Payable ... | | 4,800 | (17) 17,200 | (12) 12,400 | | | | | | |
| Fund Balance ... | | 66,200 | | (10) 192,000 | | 258,200 | (C3) 252,400 | | | 5,800 |
| Contracts Payable— Retained Percentage .... | | | | (16) 15,000 | | 15,000 | | | | 15,000 |
| | 263,000 | 263,000 | 833,600 | 833,600 | 273,200 | 273,200 | 252,400 | 252,400 | 20,800 | 20,800 |

Assuming that the project was completed during the second fiscal year at a total cost of $96,500, the closing entry would be:

| | | |
|---|---|---|
| Appropriations .............................. | 60,000 | |
| Expenditures............................. | | 56,500 |
| Fund Balance ............................. | | 3,500 |

To close current period expenditures and the balance of the appropriations account to fund balance upon completion of the project.

Statements of Bond Fund expenditures compared with appropriations (Figure 8-12) are usually prepared in cumulative form. Note again that the Fund Balance account is affected only when total costs differ from authorized expenditures unless an amount less than the full project authorization has been appropriated. Fund balances or deficits are disposed of in the manner discussed for Capital Projects Funds.

**Question 8-1.** A Capital Projects Fund is, in essence, a special type of Special Revenue Fund. Explain.

**Question 8-2.** Must all municipal capital outlays be financed and accounted for through Capital Projects Funds? Explain.

**Question 8-3.** What is the "life cycle" of a Capital Projects Fund?

**Question 8-4.** Why is each identifiable capital project of material porportions usually financed and accounted for through a separate Capital Projects Fund? In what situations might several capital projects properly be financed and accounted for through a single Capital Projects Fund?

**Question 8-5.** What is the difference between a Capital Projects Fund and a Bond Fund? Why did the NCGA recommend changing from the latter to the former?

**Question 8-6.** The governing board of a city recently levied a gasoline tax "for the express purpose of financing the construction of a civic center, servicing debt issued to do so, or both" and instructed the Comptroller to establish a Gasoline Tax Fund to account for the receipt, expenditure, and balances of the tax proceeds. What type fund should be established?

**Question 8-7.** Why might the term "revenues" be objected to when used to describe inflows of Capital Projects Fund resources from debt issues or interfund transfers?

**Question 8-8.** A municipality sold bonds and then, finding that it would not need the money for several months, invested it. (1) Assuming that interest in the amount of $500 was received, give the entry to record this transaction. (2) Now assume that the bonds had originally been sold at a discount of $300 and give the entry to record the receipt of such interest. (3) Finally, assume that the appropriations amounted to $100,000, that the bonds were sold at par, but that it now appears that the project will cost $100,500. Can the $500 be used to finance the additional expenditure without authorization from the legislative body?

**Question 8-9.** Why are statements for several Capital Projects Funds often presented in combined form?

**Question 8-10.** What type statement presentation is appropriate to present the details of Capital Projects Fund revenues, expenditures and/or encumbrances of a particular period?

**Question 8-11.** Why might a grantor not permit general municipal overhead to be charged to a capital project financed by its grant, or insist that allowable (reimburseable) overhead be calculated by means of a predetermined formula related to direct project costs?

**Question 8-12.** Is it permissible to record bond premiums and accrued bond interest received upon the issuance of bonds directly in the accounts of a Debt Service Fund rather than recording them initially in the Capital Projects Fund and subsequently transferring them to the Debt Service Fund?

**Question 8-13.** At the beginning of the year $100,000 of an issue of serial bonds to be used to finance a capital project was sold at a discount of $1,000. Subsequently there was a rise in the price of the bonds so that the remaining $200,000 of the same issue was sold several months later at a premium of $2,000. How should these premiums and discounts be recorded? Give entries.

**Question 8-14.** Assume the same facts as in Question 8-13, except that the bonds were sold at a discount of $2,000 and at a premium of $1,000, respectively. Give the necessary entries.

**Question 8-15.** Assume the same facts as in Question 8-13, except that the first sale was in one year and the second sale was during the following year. Would the premiums and discounts be handled in the same way as those described in Question 8-13? If not, in what way should they be handled? Give entries.

**Question 8-16.** Why should a competent governmental accountant or auditor review proposed bond indentures, ordinances establishing Capital Projects (or Bond) Funds, and similar instruments or agreements before they are agreed to or enacted?

**Question 8-17.** In certain Capital Projects Fund accounting situations it might be appropriate to: (1) employ Estimated Revenue, Revenue, Appropriations, Expenditures, Encumbrances, and Reserve for Encumbrances accounts in a manner paralleling that of General Fund accounting; (2) debit and credit the Fund Balance account for expenditures incurred and revenues received or accrued, respectively; or (3) utilize only the Fund Balance, Expenditures, Encumbrances, and Reserve for Encumbrances equity accounts. Briefly describe a situation in which each of these approaches would be appropriate.

**Question 8-18.** What similarities exist between and among the Fund Balance, Appropriations, and Revenues accounts?

**Question 8-19.** What problems might one encounter in attempting to determine the proper disposition of a Capital Projects Fund balance remaining after the project has been completed and all Capital Projects Fund liabilities have been paid?

**Question 8-20.** What disposition should be made of a Capital Projects Fund *deficit* remaining at the conclusion of the project?

**Question 8-21.** Neither the fixed assets acquired through a Capital Projects Fund nor the long-term debt issued to finance capital projects are normally accounted for therein. Why? Where are such fixed assets and long-term debt accounted for, and are there exceptions to this general rule?

**Question 8-22.** Proceeds of certain general obligation long-term debt issues are not accounted for through Capital Projects Funds. When is this the case? Through which funds or fund types are such debt proceeds accounted for?

**Question 8-23.** The Balance Sheet presented in Figure 8-1 (A) contains the caption "Liabilities, Reserves, and Fund Balance." Why is this caption considered objectionable by many accountants?

**Question 8-24.** Upon authorization of a capital project and establishment of a Capital Projects Fund, the project authorization may be recorded either by memorandum (narrative only) entry or by formal journal entry. (1) Under what circumstances might a narrative memorandum entry be more appropriate than a formal journal entry, and vice versa? (2) What is the nature of the Projects Authorized account and what disposition is made of its balance?

**Question 8-25.** Should expenditures and/or encumbrances relating to construction in progress being financed through a Capital Projects Fund be capitalized in the General Fixed Assets group of accounts?

**Question 8-26.** How does the Bonds Authorized—Unissued account differ from the Projects Authorized account?

**Question 8-27.** Why must one look to the substance and effect of Capital Projects Fund accounting procedures, rather than only to the form (terminology, accounts employed, etc.), in order to determine their propriety?

**Question 8-28.** Some accountants prefer to close Capital Projects Fund Revenues, Expenditures and Encumbrances accounts at year end, even if the project is incomplete, while others prefer that their balances not be closed until the project is completed. Is either approach acceptable? Discuss the effect and the advantages and disadvantages of each approach.

**Problem 8-1.** The following transactions and events occurred in Lanesburg Township during 19X4:

1. The township assembly agreed that a new police and fire department building would be constructed, at a cost not to exceed $150,000, on land owned by the township. (Memorandum authorization entry.)

2. Cash with which to finance the project was received from the following sources:

| | |
|---|---:|
| Transfer from General Fund | $ 10,000 |
| State-Federal grant | 50,000 |
| Bank of Lanesburg (long-term note) | 90,000 |
| | $150,000 |

3. Cash was disbursed from the Capital Projects Fund as follows:

| | |
|---|---:|
| Construction contract | $140,000 |
| Architect fees | 5,000 |
| Engineering charges | 1,000 |
| Transfer to General Fund | 4,000 |
| | $150,000 |

Required:

Prepare general journal entries to record the above facts in at least three distinctly different, but acceptable, manners in the Capital Projects Fund accounts.

**Problem 8-2.** The following transactions and events relating to a capital project undertaken by Williams County occurred during 19X4.

1. The Board of Commissioners approved a street improvement program expected to cost $500,000 and authorized a $300,000 bond issue to partially finance the improvements; the remaining resources needed are to be provided by a Federal grant and an interfund transfer. Capital Project Fund accounting records were established and the plans and authorizations recorded therein by memorandum entry.

2.  Proceeds of the bond sale, $303,000, were recorded in the Capital Projects Fund.
3.  A purchase order was issued for materials estimated to cost $120,000.
4.  Engineering costs were paid, $15,000.
5.  Right-of-way acquisition costs, $30,000, were paid.
6.  The Board of Commissioners was notified that a $125,000 Federal street improvement grant had been approved and would be received in two equal installments. The first installment will be received in 19X4, the second in 19X5.
7.  The bond premium (2) was transferred to the appropriate Debt Service Fund.
8.  The materials ordered above (3) arrived, except for items expected to cost $10,000, which were delayed temporarily, together with an invoice for $112,000.
9.  Freight charges paid on the materials received, $700.
10.  Materials expected to cost $40,000 were ordered.
11.  The first installment of the Federal grant was received.
12.  The interfund transfer due from the General Fund was established as a receivable in the Capital Projects Fund accounts.
13.  Equipment rental costs paid during 19X4 were $20,000; in addition, $3,000 of such costs are accrued at year end.
14.  Wages paid workers on the project during 19X4 totaled $90,000; an additional $6,000 is accrued at year end.
15.  The Revenues, Expenditures, and Encumbrances accounts were closed at year end.

Required:

Prepare a columnar worksheet to reflect the foregoing transactions and events and from which a pre-closing trial balance, Statement of Changes in Fund Balance, and Balance Sheet may be prepared. Separate Revenue accounts should be employed for each major source, though only one Expenditure account and one Encumbrance account need be used. Your worksheet entries should be keyed to the numbered items in the problem.

**Problem 8-3. Part I.** The following transactions took place in the village of Alffton during 19A:

1.  A bond issue of $120,000 was authorized for the construction of a library. A Capital Projects Fund journal and ledger were established and a narrative entry made to record the project authorization..
2.  The bonds were sold at a premium of $900.
3.  The cost of issuing the bonds, $800, was paid.
4.  An order was placed for materials estimated to cost $65,000.
5.  Salaries and wages amounting to $5,000 were paid.
6.  The premium was transferred to the Debt Service Fund.

Required:

(a)  Prepare all entries, including closing entries, to record the transactions for 19A.
(b)  Post to "T" accounts.
(c)  Prepare a balance sheet as of December 31, 19A.
(d)  Prepare a statement analyzing the changes in the Fund Balance account for the year ended December 31, 19A.

**Problem 8-3. Part II.** The following transactions took place during 19B:

7.  The materials were received; the actual cost was found to be $65,000.
8.  Salaries and wages amounting to $40,100 were paid.
9.  All bills outstanding were paid.
10.  The project was completed. The accounts were closed and the remaining balance was to be transferred to the Debt Service Fund.

Required:
(a)   Prepare all journal entries, including closing entries, to record the transactions for 19B.
(b)   Post to "T" accounts.
(c)   Prepare a statement analyzing the changes in the Fund Balance account for the year ended December 31, 19B.
(d)   Prepare a statement analyzing the changes in the Fund Balance account for the two years ended December 31, 19B.

**Problem 8-4.**   From the data in Problem 8-3, Parts I and II:
a.   Prepare a columnar worksheet for the two year period ending December 31, 19B, using the following columnar headings:
(1)   19A Transactions
(2)   Closing Entries, 12/31/19A
(3)   Post-Closing Trial Balances, 12/31/19A
(4)   19B Transactions
(5)   Closing Entries, 12/31/19B
(6)   Post-Closing Trial Balance, 12/31/19B
b.   Prepare a statement analyzing the changes in the Fund Balance account for the two year period ended December 31, 19B. (Note: Part (b) should be omitted if Problem 8-3, Parts I and II, is also assigned.)

**Problem 8-5. Part I.**   The following transactions took place in Mills County during 19X4.
1.   A bond issue of $500,000 was authorized for the construction of a bridge; in as much as all the bonds were not to be sold immediately, the bond authorization was recorded in the accounts. (Credit-Appropriations)
2.   One half of the bonds were sold; the sale was at par.
3.   The cost of handling the bonds, $700, was paid from and charged as an expenditure of, the Capital Projects Fund.
4.   A contract was entered into with White & Company for the construction of the bridge at a cost of $420,000.
5.   A bill for $175,000 was received from White & Company for work done on the bridge to date.
6.   Salaries of state engineers amounting to $5,350 were paid to the state.
Required:
(a)   Prepare journal entries. (Do not prepare closing entries.)
(b)   Post to "T" accounts.
(c)   Prepare a balance sheet as of December 31, 19X4.

**Problem 8-5. Part II.**   The following transactions took place during 19X5:
7.   The bill due White & Company was paid.
8.   A bond issue of $400,000 was authorized for the purpose of constructing a garage; another Capital Projects Fund was established. The authorization was recorded in the accounts.
9.   Bonds (garage) to the amount of $200,000 were sold at a $4,000 premium.
10.   The cost of handling the bonds amounted to $2,500, which was paid.
11.   Orders were placed for materials (garage project) estimated to cost $52,000.
12.   A bill for $125,000 was received from White & Company for further work performed on the bridge contract.
13.   Salaries and wages paid amounted to $51,000; of this total $4,000 applies to the bridge project and the remainder to the garage project.
14.   The materials ordered (11) were received; the actual cost, $53,000, was vouchered for later payment.

15. An order was placed for materials (garage project) estimated to cost $100,000.
16. The net bond premium was transferred to the appropriate Debt Service Fund.

Required:

(a)   Prepare journal entries. (Do not prepare closing entries.)
(b)   Post to "T" accounts.
(c)   Prepare a combined balance sheet for the Capital Projects Funds as of December 31, 19X5.
(d)   Prepare a combined statement analyzing the changes in the Appropriations accounts for the two years ended December 31, 19X5.

**Problem 8-6. Part I.**  From the data in Problem 8-5, Parts I and II, prepare columnar worksheets for the two year period ended December 31, 19X5. The worksheet for the Bridge (Capital Projects) Fund should have columnar headings as follows:

| 19X4 Transactions | | Trial Balance, 12/31/19X4 | | 19X5 Transactions | | Trial Balance, 12/31/19X5 | |
|---|---|---|---|---|---|---|---|
| Debit | Credit | Debit | Credit | Debit | Credit | Debit | Credit |

The worksheet for the Garage (Capital Projects) Fund should contain similar headings relating to 19X5 transactions and balances. Entries should be keyed to the numbered items in Problem 8-5.

**Problem 8-6. Part II.**  In Part I of this problem, as in Problem 8-5, the accounts were not closed at year end. Prepare the journal entries that would have been necessary during 19X4 and 19X5 if these Bridge (Capital Projects) Fund temporary accounts had been closed annually: (a) both the Expenditures and Encumbrances accounts, and (b) only the Expenditures account.

**Problem 8-6. Part III.**  (Omit if Problem 8-5 is assigned.) From the worksheet prepared in Part I and supplemental calculations, prepare:

a.   A Combined Balance Sheet for the Capital Projects Funds as of December 31, 19X5.

b.   A combined statement analyzing the changes in the Appropriations accounts for the two years ended December 31, 19X5.

**Problem 8-7. Part I.**  From the data in Problem 8-5, Parts I and II, prepare a columnar worksheet for the two years ended December 31, 19X5, under the following changed conditions: (1) both projects are to be accounted for within a single Capital Projects Fund; (2) project authorization entries are prepared in memorandum form and bond issue proceeds are to be credited directly to Fund Balance accounts; (3) two sets of Expenditures, Encumbrances, and Reserve for Encumbrances accounts are to be employed; and (4) the Expenditures and Encumbrances accounts are to be closed at the end of each year. The worksheet should have columnar headings as follows:

| Columns | Heading |
|---|---|
| 1–2 | 19X4 Transactions |
| 3–4 | Closing Entries, 12/31/19X4 |
| 5–6 | Post-closing Trial Balance, 12/31/19X4 |
| 7–8 | 19X5 Transactions |
| 9–10 | Closing Entries, 12/31/19X5 |
| 11–12 | Post-closing Trial Balance, 12/31/19X5 |

Asset and liability accounts need not be separately identified by project within the accounts. Worksheet entries should be keyed to the numbered items in Problem 8-5.

**Problem 8-7. Part II.** Based on your observations in solving Part I of this problem, why is the use of "resource" accounts such as Projects Authorized and Bonds Authorized-Unissued considered by many governmental accountants to be essential in certain Capital Projects Fund situations?

**Problem 8-8.** A bond issue utilized to finance a capital project of Smithson Township sold at a $3,000 discount. Although for several months the council was uncertain as to whether any or all of the deficiency would be financed from other sources, it subsequently ordered that $2,000 be transferred to the Capital Projects Fund from the General Fund and reduced the project authorization by the remaining $1,000. The clerk carried out the council's mandate immediately.

Required:
(a) Assuming the Bond Discount account was closed previously, what entries should the clerk make to record the transfer and project authorization reduction?
(b) What entries should he make if the Bond Discount account has a $3,000 debit balance?

**Problem 8-9.** Upon receiving approval of a $4,000,000 water pollution abatement grant in 19A, a county controller established appropriate Capital Projects Fund accounting records and made a journal entry therein to reflect the project authorization. In 19B he was notified that the grant was being reduced to only $3,000,000 because of Federal fund shortages and budgetary revisions. (1) How should the grant reduction be reflected in the Capital Projects Fund accounting records? (2) How would your answer differ if the $4,000,000 grant proceeds had been received in 19A and a $1,000,000 check was drawn in 19B payable to the Federal grantor agency? (Assume in both cases that 19B closing entries have not yet been prepared.)

**Problem 8-10.** The trial balances of the General Fund and the Capital Projects Fund of the City of Wadeton as of January 1, 19X4, are as follows:

### General Fund

| | | |
|---|---:|---:|
| Cash ....................................... | $ 27,000 | |
| Taxes Receivable—Current ..................... | 57,000 | |
| Allowance for Uncollectible Current Taxes ........ | | $ 3,500 |
| Taxes Receivable—Delinquent .................. | 41,000 | |
| Allowance for Uncollectible Delinquent Taxes ..... | | 11,000 |
| Interest and Penalties Receivable on Taxes ....... | 4,200 | |
| Allowance for Uncollectible Interest and Penalties.. | | 1,000 |
| Accounts Receivable ......................... | 35,000 | |
| Allowance for Uncollectible Accounts............ | | 3,000 |
| Vouchers Payable ............................ | | 82,000 |
| Contracts Payable ............................ | | 48,000 |
| Reserve for Encumbrances—19X3 ............... | | 10,000 |
| Fund Balance ................................ | | 6,200 |
| | $164,700 | $164,700 |

### Capital Projects Fund

| | | |
|---|---|---|
| Projects Authorized .......................... | $150,000 | |
| Appropriations ............................... | | $150,000 |
| | $150,000 | $150,000 |

The following transactions took place in the two funds during the year:

1. The city council passed a General Fund appropriation ordinance. Revenues were estimated at $310,000 and appropriations amounted to $300,000, as follows:

| | |
|---|---|
| City Court | $ 14,000 |
| Board of Directors | 3,000 |
| Department of Finance | 25,000 |
| General Government | 218,000 |
| Transfer to Debt Service Fund | 40,000 |
| | $310,000 |

2. Taxes totaling $250,000 were accrued; and a 2 percent allowance for uncollectible current taxes was set up.

3. Bonds with a par value of $150,000 were sold at a premium of $2,000, the proceeds to be used for the construction of a municipal library.

4. The cost of printing the bonds and miscellaneous handling charges connected with their sale amounted to $300, and were paid. (Hint—debit Premium on Bonds)

5. The net premium was transferred to the General Fund.

6. The actual cost of the materials ordered in 19X3 for the public works department, the only order set up as an encumbrance of that year, was $10,000—and a voucher was prepared accordingly.

7. A contract was let for partial construction of the library. The Abner Contracting Company was awarded the contract on a bid of $95,000.

8. On February 1, orders were placed for materials for the following:

| | |
|---|---|
| City Court | $ 2,400 |
| Board of Elections | 1,800 |
| Department of Finance | 1,300 |
| Library Construction | 10,200 |
| | $ 15,700 |

9. The materials ordered on February 1 were received. Invoices for these materials follow:

| | |
|---|---|
| City Court | $ 2,300 |
| Board of Elections | 1,900 |
| Department of Finance | 1,400 |
| Library Construction | 10,000 |
| | $ 15,600 |

10. Current taxes of $49,000 became delinquent, and $2,000 of the allowance for uncollectible current taxes was transferred to the allowance for uncollectible delinquent taxes.

11. Payroll vouchers were approved for the following:

| | |
|---|---|
| City Court | $ 12,000 |
| Department of Finance | 19,000 |
| General Government | 41,000 |
| Library Construction | 11,000 |

12. A bill was received from the Abner Contracting Company for $15,000.

13. Collections were made as follows:

| | |
|---|---|
| Current Taxes | $230,000 |
| Delinquent Taxes | 5,500 |
| Interest and Penalties Receivable on Taxes | 520 |
| Accounts Receivable | 29,000 |
| Miscellaneous Revenues Not Previously Accrued | 72,000 |

14. The approved payroll vouchers (11) were paid.

15. Judgments incurred in connection with the construction of the library totaled $7,500.

16. Materials were ordered by the city for library construction at an estimated cost of $12,500.

17. The Abner Contracting Company was paid.

18. Interest and penalties accrued on delinquent taxes amounted to $4,000; a provision of 10 percent was made for estimated uncollectible interest and penalties on delinquent taxes.

19. Vouchers for bills for materials ordered on February 1 (9) were paid.

20. Delinquent taxes of 19X2 in the amount of $300, written off as uncollectible in 19X4, were collected.

21. A bill was received from the Abner Contracting Company for $40,000.

22. The judgments (15) were paid.

23. The city council certified $2,200 of delinquent taxes to be uncollectible, and they were written off.

24. The Abner Contracting Company was paid.

25. Current taxes collected amounted to $15,000.

26. Vouchers payable of $82,000 carried in the General Fund were paid.

27. Serial bonds to the amount of $40,000 matured, and that amount was transferred from the General Fund to the Debt Service Fund.

28. The payroll for library construction work to the amount of $7,000 was approved and paid.

29. The matured serial bonds (27) were retired, together with $8,000 interest thereon, from Debt Service Fund.

30. The materials ordered for the library at an estimated cost of $12,500 were received; the invoice was for $13,000.

31. The Abner Contracting Company submitted a bill covering the remaining cost of the contract.

32. Orders were placed for materials for general government departments at an estimated cost of $100,000.

33. A cash payroll for general government departments amounting to $57,000 was paid.

34. The materials ordered for the general government departments were received, together with a bill for $105,000. (Purchase method.)

35. Taxes were collected in advance, $500, from a taxpayer planning an extended trip.

36. Materials were ordered for the fire department at an estimated cost of $3,000.

37. Contracts payable in the General Fund to the amount of $48,000 were paid.

38. The Abner Contracting Company was paid, except for 5 per cent of the contract that was held pending final approval of the project.

39. The balance in the Capital Projects Fund was calculated and transferred to the General Fund.

40. Closing entries were prepared.

Required:

(a) Prepare columnar worksheets in good form for the General and Capital Projects Funds setting forth the trial balance at January 1, 19X4, the transactions and events occurring during 19X4, the pre-closing trial balance at year end, the changes in Fund Balance(s), and balance sheet (after-closing trial balance) data at December 31, 19X4. Prepare your worksheets for the general ledger accounts of each fund on the assumption that subsidiary ledgers are used, as appropriate, in accounting for each fund. Key your worksheets to the problem data.

(b) Prepare a statement anlyzing the changes in the Fund Balance account of the General Fund during 19X4. Your solution should include both planned (budgeted) and actual data.

(c) Prepare a statement analyzing the changes in the Appropriations account of the Capital Projects Fund during 19X4.

**Problem 8-11.** This problem incorporates the information within Problem 8-10, but is to be solved in a manner that meets the following requirements:

Required:

(a) Prepare columnar worksheets as indicated in Requirement (a) of Problem 8-10, but assume that subsidiary ledgers are *not* maintained and budgetary control is exercised in the general ledgers as follows:

*General Fund:*

Estimated Revenues and Revenues—in total

Appropriations, Expenditures, and Encumbrances—Categorized as indicated in item (1) of Problem 8-10.

*Library (Capital Projects) Fund*

Appropriations—in total

Expenditures and Encumbrances—classified according to (1) Materials, (2) Payroll, and (3) Contracted and Other.

(b) Prepare an Analysis of Changes in the Fund Balance Account of the General Fund during 19X4. Your solution should be itemized as indicated above, and should include both planned (budgeted) and actual data.

(c) Prepare a detailed Analysis of Changes in the Appropriations Account for the Capital Projects Fund during 19X4.

# 9

# Special Assessment Funds

The typical services rendered by a government are beneficial to the general public, but some improvements or services are so evidently of primary benefit to a citizen or group of citizens that all or a part of their cost is charged to the properties or persons benefited. Special Assessment Funds are established to account for the financing of such improvements or services through special charges levied against the properties or persons benefited. Typical improvements are sewers, street paving and widening, curbs, and sidewalks; typical services are street cleaning and street lighting.

The accounting procedure for Special Assessment Funds established to finance *service* activities parallels that for the General Fund. Such funds are, in effect, a type of Special Revenue Fund. All that is required is that proper records be kept of the amount assessed against and collected from each property or person and that the money be applied to the purposes of the Fund. This chapter will deal with *improvements* financed through special assessments for three reasons: (1) Special Assessment Funds are used to finance construction projects more often than services; (2) most services provided on a continuing basis are best financed and accounted for through Enterprise Funds, discussed in Chapter 14, and (3) accounting procedures for improvement projects are more complicated than for services.

## OVERVIEW

The typical construction-related Special Assessment Fund is actually a Capital Projects—Debt Service Fund combination. Accounting for construction activities financed through Special Assessment Funds is virtually identical to that discussed for Capital Projects Funds; therefore, that discussion (Chapter 8) is quite relevant here. Debt service aspects of Special Assessment Funds are generally rather uncomplicated.

Special Assessment Fund projects normally must originate with a petition (requesting the project) signed by over 50 per cent of the property owners within the geographic area in which the improvement is requested. In some jurisdictions the government may undertake improvement projects and assess the property owners even if fewer than half of them desire the project, but usually it may do so only if the general public health and welfare will be endangered if the improvement is not made.

In the usual case the government acts as a general contractor-trustee on behalf of the property owners within the special district, though in some cases the assessments levied may be deemed a special tax on certain property or property owners. Special assessment activities may be governed by a host of state or local legislative requirements and customs. These must be given due regard in the determination of appropriate accounting and reporting procedures in a particular situation.

Financing construction through special assessments presents various problems. (1) Detailed construction records must be kept in order to determine the actual cost[1] of the project. (2) Because the individual assessments in such cases are usually large, the owners of the property assessed are frequently extended the privilege of paying assessments in installments over a number of years. In addition, special assessments often are not levied until the project has been completed and all costs are known. Hence construction expenditures are usually financed from other sources, such as bonds, notes, or a combination of the two, and assessment principal and interest collected are used to service the debt. (3) All the cash receipts of the Special Assessment Fund are to be used for specified purposes, and the accounts preferably should provide for a segregation of cash by purpose. Accounts such as Cash for Construction, Cash for Payment of Notes and Interest, Cash for Bond Payments, and Cash for Interest Payments may be used for this purpose. Similarly, since the usual Special Assessment Fund is, in substance, a Capital Projects—Debt Service Fund hybrid, it is useful to segregate the fund balance according to the use to which the net assets it represents may be put.

Though specific approaches to special assessment projects vary, the more complex ones generally go through seven distinct phases:

[1] The discussion of capital project "cost" in Chapter 8 is equally applicable here.

1. Authorization of the project
2. Financing the construction
3. Construction of the improvement
4. Assessment determination and levy
5. Collection of assessments and interest thereon
6. Servicing debt principal and interest
7. Disposing of balances or deficits and terminating the fund

Some special assessment projects follow this order exactly, but not all projects involve all phases, nor are the phases always sequenced as in the above listing. In simpler situations where (1) construction is to be done under a fixed price

**Figure 9-1**

### ILLUSTRATIVE SPECIAL ASSESSMENT
### FUND PHASES AND ACTIVITIES

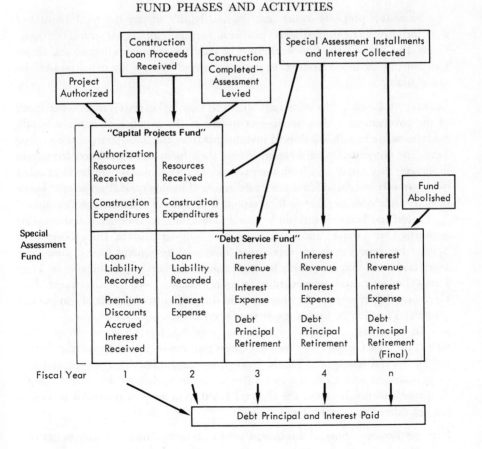

contract and (2) costs are assessed and collected prior to payment being made to the contractor, the Special Assessment Fund functions only as a Capital Projects Fund and phases 2 and 6 are eliminated. In other cases (1) assessments are levied before all project costs are known, (2) some assessments may be designated for construction use and others for debt service, and (3) construction, assessment and collection, and debt service activities may be carried on simultaneously. (See Figure 9-1.) In the third situation just noted—where construction, assessment and collection, and debt service activities overlap—particular care must be taken to assure that assets designated for one purpose are not used for another. Separate Cash and Fund Balance accounts prove especially useful in such cases. This is the most complex type of situation usually encountered in Special Assessment Fund accounting, and is the basis for the illustrative example within this chapter.

### Interim Financing of the Special Assessment Project

Since few property owners are financially able to pay the total amount of a major assessment immediately, provision is usually made for installment payments. But the construction work must be paid for upon completion, and therefore must be financed from other sources. Several interim financing possibilities are available.

INTERFUND LOANS.    In some instances cash may be borrowed from other funds of the government, either pending or in lieu of the issuance of notes or bonds. Such loans are usually considered investments from the standpoint of the lending fund, and interest is paid thereon. Where such loans are considered temporary in nature, they are repaid from the proceeds of special assessment bond or other debt issues. If interfund loans are made in lieu of issuing special assessment bonds or other indebtedness, they will be repaid from special assessment collections.

Interfund loans should not be made unless they are both legal and properly authorized, of course, and intermediate or long-term loans from General or Special Revenue Funds are rarely used in special assessment project financing. Interfund loans may frequently be made from Debt Service, Enterprise, or Trust Funds, however, and are generally an extremely safe form of investment. Furthermore, they may provide a higher yield than other investments of comparable safety and involve no brokerage or similar costs.

In other instances, governments may establish an Intragovernmental Service Fund (see Chapter 13) for the express purpose of providing interim financing for Special Assessment Funds. Intragovernmental Service Fund capital may be provided in such cases through a special tax levy, through issuance of bonds, or through a transfer from the General Fund. As money is repaid, it is used to finance other special assessment projects.

SALE OF BONDS.    Special assessment project interim financing may be secured through bond issues. Either general-special assessment bonds or special-special assessment bonds may be issued. A general-special assessment bond is secured by the full faith and credit of the governmental unit; that is, maturing interest or principal payments must be met from other resources of the unit if assessment collections are inadequate to do so. A special-special assessment bond is one that may not become a charge against the governmental unit as a whole but is secured only by the assessments collected or the properties benefited. Technically, the government's responsibility in the case of special-special assessment bonds is merely to enforce collections and to handle proceeds properly. In practice, a government normally will be equally vigilant in enforcing collection of assessments relating to either type of bond issue and will see that neither type is permitted to be in default. Default of any bond issue with which it is even casually associated may severely affect a government's credit rating and, hence, both its ability to borrow for other purposes and the interest rate it must pay.

Usually serial bonds are issued with maturity dates arranged so that part of the issue may be retired as soon as a special assessment installment is collected. Specific bonds may be payable from particular installment collections. In that case, bonds may be payable only from the collections of the installment to which they apply and no other. Bonds are sometimes made liens against specific pieces of property. In that case, each bond is payable only from the assessments levied against the particular pieces of property with which it is identified.

ISSUANCE OF NOTES.   An interval of time may elapse between the authorization of the bond issue and the sale of the bonds. Certain formalities may delay the sale of the bonds or their issuance may be intentionally delayed because of unfavorable bond market conditions. But contractors often must be paid as the work progresses, and the government must meet its payrolls. If the sale of the bonds must (or should) be delayed, short-term notes may be issued in the interim. In such cases the government may borrow on open note from a local bank or may issue more formal "bond anticipation notes."

Sometimes intermediate- or long-term notes are issued in lieu of bonds, even though bonds could be sold immediately. This should be done, of course, if notes can be issued at a lower effective interest rate (including issue costs) than bonds. Too, the issuance of short- or intermediate-term notes may make it possible to delay the authorization and sale of bonds (or long-term notes) until after the project is completed and the exact cost of construction is determined. The advantage of this procedure is that the exact amount of bonds or other long-term debt instruments that must be issued is known at the later date.

## Levying and Collecting Assessments

Assessments are levied in some cases when the project is completed and in others as soon as construction is authorized. A brief description of assessment procedures will be of help in understanding special assessment accounting.

ASSESSMENT PROCEDURES.   Assessments are levied on the basis of benefit. The benefited area is designated as the *benefit district*. Usually such districts are numbered and are referred to by number. The area of a benefit district varies with the size and nature of the project and the methods of assessing. For example, the widening of a long street will involve a greater benefit area than the widening of a short street. The benefit district and the properties assessed consist of all the parcels that are deemed to be benefited by the improvement, regardless of how far they may be from it.

The governmental unit as a whole may receive some benefit from an improvement and may therefore bear part of the cost. The governmental unit's share will vary, since property owners are not expected to pay more than the amount of benefit accruing to their properties; nor may they legally be required to do so under terms of usual state or local statutes. If the total of the estimated assessments (based on presumed benefits) is less than the cost of the improvement, the government will make up the difference; but, if the total of these estimated assessments equals or exceeds the estimated cost of the improvement, the government may assume no part of the cost. *The methods of determining total benefits as well as the distribution of cost between the benefited properties and the government at large are governed by many arbitrary rules.*

The governmental unit may also share in the cost of special assessment improvements in the capacity of a property owner. For example, a police station, a fire station, or other government property may be located within the benefit district. Obviously it would be unfair to exempt this property from assessments and spread the cost over the privately owned property. The governmental unit, in the same manner as any property owner, must pay its share of the costs involved. However, assessments ordinarily cannot be levied on properties owned by governments independent of the governmental unit constructing the project (for example, state or county property within a city) unless statutes authorize such assessments. In some cases the governmental unit levying the assessment bears all or a portion of such nonassessable costs, as well as those that might prove to be uncollectible for other reasons.

ASSESSMENT ROLES AND RECORDS.   Special assessments and interest receivable may be recorded either on a special assessment roll or on individual special assessment records. A special assessment roll, much like a property tax roll, is a record showing the assessments levied against each piece of property, payments received thereon, and related information. A form for a special assessment roll is illustrated in Figure 9-2. Some governments find it more practicable to use individual special assessment records similar to the one illustrated in Figure 9-3. Still others use both types of records, that is, the individual records are established from the assessment roll and payments are posted to both records in order to achieve improved accounting and/or internal control. Sometimes the same record is used to show both ad valorem taxes and special assessments receivable from each particular piece of property.

Figure 9-2

**A GOVERNMENTAL UNIT**
Special Assessment Roll

| Name of Property Owner | Legal Description of Property | Total Assessment | Payments | | | | | |
|---|---|---|---|---|---|---|---|---|
| | | | Date | Principal | Interest | Date | Principal | Interest |
| | | | | | | | | |

Figure 9-3

**A GOVERNMENTAL UNIT**
Individual Special Assessment Record

Name of Owner _____  Date Assessed _____

Legal Description _____

Total Assessment _____  Interest Rate _____  No. of Installments _____

| Installment No. | Principal | Interest | Additional Interest | | Payments | | | | | | Remarks |
|---|---|---|---|---|---|---|---|---|---|---|---|
| | | | Date | Amount | Date | Principal | Interest | Date | Principal | Interest | |
| | | | | | | | | | | | |

327

ALLOWANCE FOR UNCOLLECTIBLE ASSESSMENTS.  In spite of the fact that some of the assessments may prove to be uncollectible, usually no allowance for uncollectible assessments is set up. This is because the government is acting in a trustee capacity; as such, its duty is to see that the assessments are collected and properly disbursed. If delinquent assessments are not paid, the government may secure a lien against the property, and it may have the property sold to satisfy the lien. The accounting procedure involved in such cases is described later in this chapter.

The trust character of Special Assessment Funds is especially evident in those instances where bonds are a lien against specific properties. Here the government may use the proceeds from the assessments levied against these properties only for the payment of such bonds. Further, certain bonds may be payable from specified installments of assessments levied against particular pieces of property. Even if general-special assessment bonds are issued, an allowance for uncollectible assessments is often considered impractical in such situations. If an allowance for uncollectible assessments is established, all assessments must be increased proportionately. Not only might this be considered inequitable, it might also be illegal—since properties may not be assessed for more than the amount of the benefit accruing to them as a result of the project.

For these reasons, deficiencies resulting from uncollectible assessments usually must be made up by the governmental unit. A practical and workable approach to this problem is for an Allowance for Uncollectible Special Assessments to be established in an amount equal to the additional contributions (over the government's normal share) expected to be made by the governmental unit as a result of special assessment levies apt to be assumed by the government because (1) they prove to be illegal, as when they exceed property value increments occasioned by the improvements or (2) the property owner is unable to pay the levy and, as a matter of policy or charity, it is forgiven rather than being collected through public sale of the property. A "resource account" such as Estimated Additional Governmental Unit Contributions should be established in the same amount as the allowance and both accounts should be adjusted periodically, as appropriate.

FINANCING THE GOVERNMENT'S CONTRIBUTION.  The governmental unit may finance its contributions to project cost in various ways. If the amount is large, it may issue general bonds for this purpose. The bond proceeds would be handled first through a Capital Projects Fund and then transferred to the Special Assessment Fund.

If the government's share of the assessment cost is small, it may be financed from a special tax levy or through an appropriation from the General Fund. Even if the government's part of the cost is large, it may be met through an appropriation or special tax levy. But in that case the government will likely pay its share in installments. Whether the government will finance its share through a bond issue or a tax levy will depend on existing circumstances. For example, if the government is subject to a tax limit and is close to that limit, it is more likely to issue bonds. On the other hand, if it has limited borrowing power, it may resort to taxation.

## Interest Income and Expense

Interest costs on bonds arise because property owners are permitted to pay by installments, so the property owners are expected to bear the interest cost. The interest rate charged on deferred assessments may be higher than that which government pays for several reasons. For example, some property owners may choose to pay the full amount of the assessment immediately in order to save interest costs. Statutes may provide for the abatement of interest to property owners making full payment. If the government has issued callable bonds, it may reduce interest expenses by calling them in and redeeming them. However, if the bonds are not callable, are callable only at a significant call penalty, or cannot be purchased in the open market, the government will continue to pay the full amount of interest, even though its interest income will be reduced. Theoretically, the government should refuse to accept immediate payment of the full amount assessed, if not required by law to do so, unless the sum collected can be invested at a net yield rate equal to that charged on assessments receivable. But in actual practice the governmental unit sometimes finds it desirable to receive full payment if the interest losses will be small; in many cases it can invest such collections at a higher yield rate than is charged on the assessment receivables. Finally, the government normally cannot begin charging interest until assessments are levied, usually after the project is completed. Interest expenses up to the time of the first interest collections should be considered a cost of the project to be assessed to property owners. If interest charges are not included as part of the cost to be recovered from assessments, the interest rate charged on deferred assessments must be sufficient to recoup all interest expenses occasioned by the special assessment project.

## Cash Accounts

All Special Assessment Fund cash is to be used for specified purposes. The accounts should, in the opinion of the authors, provide for a segregation of cash by purpose, though such segregation is not mandatory. As indicated earlier, accounts entitled Cash for Construction, Cash for Payment of Notes and Interest, Cash for Bond Payments, and Cash for Interest Payments may be used. Alternatively, a single Cash Control account may be established in the general ledger and separate subsidiary ledger Cash accounts employed. A schematic arrangement indicating possible sources of the several categories of cash is presented in Figure 9-4. The student will find this figure a useful reference guide to the analysis and recording of cash collections. Use of a single Cash account is considered acceptable by the authors only in those situations in which only one category of cash is contained in a Special Assessment Fund at any given time. Thus a single account would suffice where (1) no interim financing is

**Figure 9-4**

### SPECIAL ASSESSMENT FUND
#### Typical Sources of Cash

Case A: The project is financed by contribution from the government and by assessment. The governmental unit pays its share of the costs promptly. Bonds are issued to permit deferral of assessment payments.

Case B: The project is financed by contribution from the government and by assessment. The governmental unit defers one-half of its payments to future years. Notes are issued to finance construction and to permit the issuance of bonds for the exact amount necessary to finance the deferred assessments. Assessments are levied upon completion of the project.

| Cash Account Debited | Source of Cash | |
| --- | --- | --- |
| | Case A | Case B |
| Cash for Construction | Governmental unit's share of cost<br>First assessment installment(s)<br>Bond proceeds (excluding premiums) | One-half of governmental unit's share of cost<br>Note proceeds |
| Cash for Payment of Notes and Interest | | Installment(s) of governmental unit's share of cost<br>Bond proceeds (excluding premiums)<br>Installment(s) of assessments receivable |
| Cash for Payment of Bonds | Assessment Collections | Assessment Collections |
| Cash for Payment of Interest | Bond premium<br>Interest on assessment installments | Bond premium<br>Interest on assessment installments |

required, that is, construction costs are paid directly from assessment receipts, or (2) interim financing is obtained without a premium or accrued interest being received and the amount borrowed exactly equals construction costs, payment of interest expense is deferred until interest on assessments is collected, and construction costs are paid prior to the collection of assessments or interest thereon. Such cases are relatively rare.

## Fund Balance(s)

As in the case of separate Cash accounts, separate Fund Balance accounts are not required by the NCGA. The Committee states that:

> The *Fund Balance* account...indicates, prior to completion of construction, the balance authorized to be expended for completion of the project. Upon completion, it indicates the surplus or deficit resulting from actual construction costs, and, subsequent to construction, it summarizes the relationship between interest expenses on outstanding special assessment bonds and interest earnings on special assessments receivable.[2]

The authors agree that information of the type referred to above is indispensable to proper Special Assessment Fund management and accountability. The use of a single Fund Balance account would disclose the required information, however, only in those cases in which (1) every asset and liability account is distinctively labelled as relating to construction, debt principal, or interest, or (2) as discussed above in connection with accounting for cash, each phase of the Special Assessment Fund life cycle is neatly divided and all fund assets, liabilities, or balances at any specific point in time relate to a single use category. Such situations are rare.

Where multiple Fund Balance and Cash accounts are not utilized, *all* resources available to the fund prior to the completion of construction might be expended, either intentionally or unintentionally, for construction purposes. In such instances (1) resources intended for debt service may be illegally used for construction, (2) legally authorized construction cost ceilings may be exceeded, (3) the security of fund creditors may be endangered, (4) bond indenture provisions or other contractual agreements may be violated, (5) supplemental assessments may have to be levied against the persons or properties benefited by the project, if possible, or (6) the public at large may be forced to bear more than its fair share of the project cost when General Fund resources must be used to "bail out" the Special Assessment Fund. Though not everyday occurrences, situations such as these arise all too often. Thus, the authors strongly advocate the use of separate Fund Balance accounts and illustrate their use in the examples within this chapter.

2 *GAAFR,* p. 91.

### Recording the Project Authorization

Authorization of the project begins the Special Assessment Fund life cycle. Authorization usually originates with the legislative body or special district commissioners, after due notice has been given and hearings held, and should be documented as a matter of public record.

As in the case of Capital Projects Funds, authorization may be recorded in the Special Assessment Fund accounts either narratively or by formal entry. In either case the entry should be referenced to the authorization ordinance or other documentation. If a formal authorization entry is made, it will appear as follows:

| | | |
|---|---|---|
| Improvements Authorized ..................... | 750,000 | |
|     Fund Balance—Construction (or | | |
|        Appropriations) ....................... | | 750,000 |
|     To record authorization of special assessment project. See minutes of council: Book 4, page 17. | | |

When assets are accrued the Improvements Authorized account is removed from the books:

| | | |
|---|---|---|
| Assets (various) ............................. | 750,000 | |
|     Improvements Authorized ................. | | 750,000 |
|     To record accrual of assets and removal of general resource account. | | |

Appropriate authority must also be secured and documented if bonds are to be issued or other debt is to be incurred in the course of the project. A narrative memorandum entry will suffice, though some accountants prefer preparation of a formal entry, to record the authority to incur debt. Formal recording is of less consequence here than in those cases illustrated previously with respect to Capital Projects Funds (Chapter 8), since only the authority to incur indebtedness is involved, not that for the project itself. Furthermore, were it not for the authority to levy special assessments, authorization to issue bonds would be meaningless; were there no provision for paying the bonds and interest thereon, no one would buy them. On the other hand, formal bond authorization entries are used frequently in order to establish accounting system control over unissued bonds. In this case the unissued bonds, or records thereof, constitute a subsidiary ledger under general ledger control.

Several approaches to entering debt issuance authority in the accounts may be encountered in practice, most of which are not uncommon to commercial accounting. Probably the simplest method is to make an entry such as the one immediately following at the time the authority is granted and reverse it upon incurring the debt.

AUTHORITY TO ISSUE BONDS GRANTED:
Unissued Bonds .............................    350,000
    Bonds Eligible to be Sold .................                  350,000
    To record authorization of special-special bond
    issue.

A PORTION OF THE BONDS IS SOLD:
(a)  Bonds Eligible to be Sold .................    100,000
      Unissued Bonds.....................                  100,000
    To reverse bond issue authorization entry to
    the extent bonds have been sold.
(b)  Cash—Interest Payments .................       500
    Cash—Construction .....................       xxx
    Discount on Bonds Payable...............       xxx
      Bonds Payable......................                  100,000
      Accrued Interest on Bonds Payable.....                   500
    To record the sale of bonds at a discount
    between interest dates.

Should a balance sheet be prepared prior to issuance of all bonds authorized, the Unissued Bonds and Bonds Eligible to be Sold accounts would be shown short in the liability section.

Another approach is to make the following entries upon bond authorization and sale, respectively:

AUTHORITY TO ISSUE BONDS GRANTED:
Bonds Authorized—Unissued .................    350,000
    Bonds Payable ..........................                  350,000
    To record authorization of special-special bond
    issue.

A PORTION OF THE BONDS IS SOLD:
Cash for Interest Payments ...................       500
Cash for Construction .......................       xxx
Discount on Bonds Payable ...................       xxx
    Bonds Authorized—Unissued .............                  100,000
    Accrued Interest on Bonds Payable .........                   500
    To record the sale of bonds at a discount between
    interest dates.

Under this method, the par or face value of bonds outstanding at any time is the difference between the balances of the Bonds Payable and Bonds Authorized —Unissued accounts, less any treasury bonds held. The Bonds Authorized—Unissued account would serve as the general ledger control account over unissued bonds.

Again, the authors consider the preparation of formal debt authorization entries (as opposed to narrative memorandum entries) to be strictly optional, that is, a matter of personal preference. The only exception is when (1) a narrative, rather than formal, project authorization entry was made, and (2) statements are to be prepared prior to receipt or accrual of all resources (other than interest) to be available to the Fund. Here, as in the Capital Projects Fund, it is necessary to prepare an adjusting entry prior to statement preparation to properly reflect the Fund's resources and Fund Balance. An adjustment of the type shown below is essential when expenditures to date plus encumbrances outstanding at the statement date exceed the amount of resources received or accrued to date, since in its absence a deficit may be reported erroneously. Assuming that only $100,000 of the $350,000 bond issue above had been issued, the adjustment required would be:

| | | |
|---|---|---|
| Bonds Authorized—Unissued .................. | 250,000 | |
| Fund Balance—Construction (or | | |
| Appropriations) ...................... | | 250,000 |
| To record bond issue authorization not previously | | |
| recorded. | | |

Where the assessments have not been levied by statement date, an account such as Assessments Authorized or Unassessed Project Costs should be debited. Adjusting entries of this type would be reversed after the accounts are closed and statements have been prepared.

### Bond Premium or Discount

As indicated previously, premiums and discounts on long-term investments or arising from the sale of bonds represent interest-rate adjustments. The NCGA has consistently recommended that premiums and discounts on special assessment bonds be amortized in a systematic and rational manner over the life of the bond issue in order to properly report interest expense. Assumably it would likewise favor amortization of premiums or discounts on long-term Special Assessment Fund investments in order to properly compute interest income and, hence, Fund Balance—Interest.

Others contend that proper matching of interest revenue and expense is of minor importance in Special Assessment Fund accounting. The crucial matter, they contend, is whether or not sufficient Cash—Interest is available to cover interest disbursements. Thus, in practice, premiums and discounts are frequently closed directly to an appropriate Fund Balance account in the period in which they arise.

As in Capital Projects Funds, only the net proceeds of a bond issue are considered available for construction purposes and discounts are commonly closed to the Fund Balance—Construction (or Appropriations) account. If the discount subsequently is made up by transfer from another fund, the Fund Balance—Construction account is increased back to the original authorization amount.

A major difference between Capital Projects and Special Assessment Funds, however, is that the latter also serves as a Debt Service Fund for special assessment liabilities. If interest charged on assessments receivable approximates the *nominal* rate of interest paid, the direct write-off treatment may be appropriate. It is inappropriate and misleading, however, if the interest rate charged on assessments equals or exceeds the *yield* rate at which the bonds were sold, as sufficient Cash—Interest received over that to be disbursed for interest payments may be received well after the end of the construction period, and after the construction costs must be paid. Nevertheless, it represents a resource which may be borrowed against in order to pay the full amount of authorized construction costs on schedule. Fund Balance—Construction need be reduced, therefore, only if total interest disbursements over the life of the fund are expected to exceed total interest receipts.

Premiums are credited to Fund Balance—Interest if written off directly. Although periodic interest income—interest expense matching is affected and the amount at which the Fund Balance—Interest account is reported differs during the life of the fund from that when premiums are amortized, (1) the Fund Balance—Construction account is not affected, and (2) the Fund Balance —Interest account will be the same at the end of the Fund's life under either method, because the periodic differences would off-set each other by that time. Direct write-off of bond premiums is less objectionable than direct write-off of discounts, therefore, and may frequently be justified on the basis of expediency, particularly where reported periodic net interest income or expense is not materially affected.

The same logic, in reverse, may be applied in deciding whether or not premiums or discounts on long-term investments of Special Assessment Funds should be amortized. Inasmuch as Special Assessment Fund cash is rarely invested on a long-term basis, alternative entries are not illustrated here.

For the reasons cited above, the authors prefer to amortize special assessment bond premiums or discounts. Thus the illustrations and examples within this chapter assume that bond premiums or discounts are amortized in some rational and systematic manner rather than written off directly to a Fund Balance account.

## Variations in Budgeting and Accounting Technique

Although contributions from the General Fund or other funds to the Special Assessment Fund would be incorporated in the operating budget of the contributing fund, Special Assessment Fund budgeting and budgetary accounting practices vary among governments. As in Capital Projects Funds, Special Assessment Fund expenditures may be appropriated for in varying degrees of specificity. Where Special Assessment Fund expenditures are incorporated within the current operating budget other than in total, it will generally be necessary to employ several appropriations accounts or to have a general ledger Appropriations control account and several expenditure subsidiary ledger accounts. Accounting procedures would then closely parallel those of the General Fund. As in the Capital Projects Funds chapter (Chapter 8), the reader is assumed to be competent in General Fund accounting procedures and able to adapt Special Assessment Fund accounting to that approach where appropriate.

In the usual case the government considers itself to be acting in a trustee capacity in special assessment situations and does not enact that fund's budget into law. Special assessment project costs are fixed by contract in some cases; in others, only the approximate total cost may be reasonably estimable. In any event, the project authorization is commonly considered appropriated on a total project basis, that is, the total Fund Balance—Construction (and Bonds and Interest) is deemed to be appropriated on a lump-sum basis. In such situations the use of an Appropriations account would serve no useful purpose where only one project is financed through the Fund, and Expenditures and Encumbrances would be accounted for in the manner illustrated for Capital Projects Funds. This latter approach is illustrated in the examples within this chapter; Appropriations appears in parentheses in the entries illustrated where that account would be affected under the alternative approach.

## TRANSACTIONS AND ENTRIES—FIRST FISCAL YEAR

The following transactions and entries are typical of the first year of operation of a Special Assessment Fund. (These transaction entries are summarized in worksheet form in Figure 9-12.) Discussions of some of the transactions will be found later in the chapter.

*Transactions*

1. A special assessment project was authorized in the amount of $500,000.
2. Bonds totaling $350,000 (par) were sold at a premium of $1,000.
3. Assessments were made against property owners and the general government. Current assessments were $50,000; deferred assessments, $350,000; and the governmental unit's share of the cost was $100,000.
4. A construction contract was let for $440,000.
5. Current assessment installments were collected in the amount of $45,000.
6. The governmental unit paid $50,000 of its share of the cost.
7. An additional installment of $40,000 of assessments came due.
8. The unpaid portion of the first assessment installment became delinquent.
9. Interest in the amount of $17,500 became due on assessments.
10. Interest in the amount of $15,750 became due on bonds; premium of $200 was amortized.
11. Interest in the amount of $17,000 was collected.

12. Bond interest of $15,750 was paid.
13. A contractor's bill of $100,000 was approved for payment.
14. Property was condemned and the judgments totaled $40,000.
15. The judgments were paid.

*Entries*

(1) Narrative memorandum entry
or
Improvements Authorized ............... 500,000
    Fund Balance—Construction (or
    Appropriations)..................... 500,000
    To record authorization of special assessment
    project.

(2) Cash—Construction ................... 350,000
    Cash—Interest Payments............... 1,000
    Unamortized Premiums on Bonds ..... 1,000
    Bonds Payable...................... 350,000
    To record sale of bonds at a premium.

(3) IF A MEMORANDUM AUTHORIZATION ENTRY WAS MADE:
    Assessments Receivable—Current ........ 50,000
    Assessments Receivable—Deferred ........ 350,000
    Governmental Unit's Share of Cost........ 100,000
    Fund Balance—Construction (or
    Appropriations) .................. 500,000
    To record levy of assessments and govern-
    mental unit's share of cost.

    IF A FORMAL AUTHORIZATION ENTRY WAS MADE:
    Assessments Receivable—Current ........ 50,000
    Assessments Receivable—Deferred ........ 350,000
    Governmental Unit's Share of Cost........ 100,000
    Improvements Authorized .......... 500,000
    To record levy of assessments and govern-
    ment's share of cost.

(4) Encumbrances ....................... 440,000
    Reserve for Encumbrances .......... 440,000
    To record awarding of contract.

(5) Cash—Construction ................... 45,000
    Assessments Receivable—Current .... 45,000
    To record collection of current assessments.

(Note: In this example it is assumed that assessments due in the first year are to be used for construction; proceeds of deferred assessments are to be used for bond retirement.)

(6)   Cash—Construction ....................        50,000
         Governmental Unit's Share of Cost. ...                    50,000
         To record transfer of money to cover gov-
         ernmental unit's share of cost.

(7)   Assessments Receivable—Current ........        40,000
         Assessments Receivable—Deferred ....                      40,000
         To record assessments becoming currently
         receivable.

(8)   Assessments Receivable—Delinquent ......         5,000
         Assessments Receivable—Current .....                       5,000
         To record delinquent assessments represen-
         tating first installments.

(9)   Interest Receivable ....................        17,500
         Interest Revenues .................                       17,500
         To record interest receivable on all of the
         unpaid installments.

(10)  Unamortized Premiums on Bonds ........           200
         Interest Expenses ....................        15,550
         Interest Payable ...................                      15,750
         To record interest due on bonds and pre-
         mium amortization.

(Note: Premiums or discounts may be amortized either on interest payment
dates or at year end.)

(11)  Cash—Interest Payments ...............        17,000
         Interest Receivable ................                      17,000
         To record receipt of interest.

(12)  Interest Payable .......................        15,750
         Cash—Interest Payments ...........                        15,750
         To record payment of interest.

(13)  (a)   Reserve for Encumbrances ..........       100,000
              Encumbrances ................                       100,000
              To record cancellation of encum-
              brances by amount of actual liability.

       (b)   Expenditures .....................       100,000
              Contracts Payable .............                     100,000
              To record liability on account of con-
              tract.

(14)  Expenditures ...........................        40,000
         Judgments Payable .................                       40,000
         To record condemnation awards made.

(15)  Judgments Payable ....................        40,000
         Cash—Construction .................                       40,000
         To record payment of judgments.

## Trial Balance before Closing Entries

On the basis of these fifteen journal entries (see Figure 9-12) the preclosing trial balance of the Special Assessment Fund would appear as follows:

| | | |
|---|---:|---:|
| Cash—Construction................ | $ 405,000 | |
| Cash—Interest Payments ............ | 2,250 | |
| Assessments Receivable—Current ..... | 40,000 | |
| Assessments Receivable—Delinquent .. | 5,000 | |
| Assessments Receivable—Deferred .... | 310,000 | |
| Governmental Unit's Share of Cost ... | 50,000 | |
| Interest Receivable ................ | 500 | |
| Interest Expenses .................. | 15,550 | |
| Expenditures...................... | 140,000 | |
| Encumbrances .................... | 340,000 | |
| Contracts Payable ................. | | $ 100,000 |
| Bonds Payable ................... | | 350,000 |
| Unamortized Premiums on Bonds .... | | 800 |
| Interest Revenues ................. | | 17,500 |
| Reserve for Encumbrances .......... | | 340,000 |
| Fund Balance—Construction (or Appropriations) ................. | | 500,000 |
| | $1,308,300 | $1,308,300 |

## Closing Entries at End of Fiscal Year

At the end of each year an entry is made closing out the Interest Revenues and the Interest Expenses accounts. The entry, if revenues exceed expenses, is as follows:

| | | | |
|---|---|---:|---:|
| (C1) | Interest Revenues ....................... | 17,500 | |
| | Interest Expenses .................... | | 15,500 |
| | Fund Balance—Interest .............. | | 1,950 |
| | To record closing out of interest accounts. | | |

The appropriation of special assessment moneys is for a project rather than a time period; the time period is relatively insignificant in the life of the fund. Just as in Capital Projects Funds, therefore, the Expenditures account may be closed out at the end of each fiscal year, or it may be closed out only at the time construction is completed. Similarly, the Encumbrances account may be closed at year end and re-established at the beginning of the subsequent year, or it may be carried forward in the usual off-set relationship with the Reserve for Encumbrances account. If both Expenditures and Encumbrances are closed at the end of the fiscal year, the approach assumed in this example, the entry is as follows:

| (C2) | Fund Balance—Construction (or Appropriations) .................... | 480,000 | |
|---|---|---|---|
| | Expenditures...................... | | 140,000 |
| | Encumbrances ..................... | | 340,000 |
| | To record closing out of expenditures for construction at the end of the fiscal year. | | |

If, alternatively, Encumbrances were not closed, the entry would be:

Fund Balance—Construction (or Appropriations).. 140,000
Expenditures............................ 140,000
To record closing out of expenditures; encumbrances not closed.

Expenditures for construction should be capitalized as work in progress in the General Fixed Assets group of accounts at the end of the fiscal year (See Chapter 11). Encumbrances should *not* be capitalized as part of the cost of general fixed assets.

### Balance Sheet for Uncompleted Project

After the above closing entries were posted (see Figure 9-12), the Special Assessment Fund balance sheet would appear as illustrated in Figure 9-5.

Figure 9-5

A GOVERNMENTAL UNIT
Special Assessment Fund
Balance Sheet
At Close of Fiscal Year

*Assets*

| | | |
|---|---|---|
| Cash: | | |
| For construction ............................. | $405,000 | |
| For interest payments .......................... | 2,250 | $407,250 |
| Assessments receivable: | | |
| Current ....................................... | $ 40,000 | |
| Delinquent (Note: To be used to finance construction) | 5,000 | |
| Deferred ..................................... | 310,000 | 355,000 |
| Governmental unit's share of cost .................... | | 50,000 |
| Interest receivable ............................... | | 500 |
| Total assets ................................. | | $812,750 |

*Liabilities, Reserves, and Fund Balances*

Liabilities:

| | | | |
|---|---|---|---|
| Contracts payable .............................. | | $100,000 | |
| Bonds payable ...................... | $350,000 | | |
| Unamortized premiums on bonds ...... | 800 | 350,800 | $450,800 |
| Reserve for encumbrances ......................... | | | 340,000 |
| Fund balance—construction ....................... | | | 20,000 |
| Fund balance—interest ........................... | | | 1,950 |
| Total liabilities, reserves, and fund balance ........ | | | $812,750 |

The Fund Balance—Construction account in this balance sheet (Figure 9-5) represents the *unencumbered* project authorization, that is, it is the difference between construction-related assets, liabilities, and reserves. Note that the *unexpended* fund balance available for construction purposes is $360,000, which may be presented in the balance sheet as follows:

| | | |
|---|---|---|
| Fund balance—construction: | | |
| Reserved for encumbrances ....... | $340,000 | |
| Unencumbered ................. | 20,000 | |
| Total ....................... | | $360,000 |

Presentation of Fund Balance—Construction in this manner is preferable to the more usual method illustrated in Figure 9-5, because it leaves no doubt in the reader's mind as to whether the Reserve for Encumbrances is a liability or a fund balance account.

The Fund Balance—Interest account in Figure 9-4 represents the cumulative difference between interest revenues and interest expenses reported to date. The figure may be readily proved:

| | |
|---|---|
| Cash—Interest Payments ........................ | $2,250 |
| Interest Receivable ............................ | 500 |
| | $2,750 |
| Less: Unamortized Premiums on Bonds .......... | 800 |
| Fund Balance—Interest ........................ | $1,950 |

By way of comparison, had (1) an Appropriations account been used, (2) the Unamortized Premiums on Bonds been closed directly to Fund Balance—Interest rather than amortized, and (3) the Encumbrances account not been closed at year end, the liabilities and fund balances section of the balance sheet illustrated in Figure 9-5 would appear as follows:

*Liabilities, Reserves, Appropriations, and Fund Balance*

Liabilities:

| | | |
|---|---:|---:|
| Contracts payable ............................. | $100,000 | |
| Bonds payable ................................ | 350,000 | $450,000 |

Reserves, Appropriations and Fund Balance:

| | | |
|---|---:|---:|
| Reserve for encumbrances ...................... | $340,000 | |
| Appropriations (unexpended balance)... $360,000 | | |
| Less—encumbrances................. 340,000 | 20,000 | 360,000 |
| Fund balance—interest .......................... | | 2,750 |

Total liabilities, reserves, appropriations, and
fund balance .................................. $812,750

Under this approach there usually will be no balance in the Fund Balance—Construction account until the project has been completed and all costs are known. At that time the difference between the remaining Appropriations and the Expenditures in the year of project completion would be closed to Fund Balance—Construction.

The Fund Balance—Interest account would equal the net current assets available for interest payments under this method, since the bond premium was closed directly to that account. This figure may also be readily proved:

| | |
|---|---:|
| Cash—Interest Payments........................ | $2,250 |
| Interest Receivable ............................ | 500 |
| Fund Balance—Interest ........................ | $2,750 |

Finally, note the presentation of the Reserve for Encumbrances, Appropriations, and Encumbrances accounts in the partial balance sheet above. Again, in this case a preferable presentation would be:

*Liabilities and Fund Balances*

Liabilities:

| | | |
|---|---:|---:|
| Contracts payable ............................. | $100,000 | |
| Bonds payable ................................ | 350,000 | |
| Total ...................................... | | $450,000 |

Fund balance:

Construction:

| | | |
|---|---:|---:|
| Reserved for encumbrances ......... | $340,000 | |
| Appropriated .......... $360,000 | | |
| Less: Encumbered .... 340,000 | 20,000 | |
| Unexpended balance ....................... | $360,000 | |
| Interest ...................................... | 2,750 | |
| Total ...................................... | | 362,750 |

Total liabilities and fund balances.................... $812,750

## Analysis of Changes in Fund Balances

A statement analyzing the changes in Special Assessment Fund balances should be prepared at the end of each fiscal year. Where an Appropriations account is in use, the appropriate statement would be an analysis of changes in Appropriations, though both are required where both have changed during the period.

Several formats for such statements are in general use, most of which are

**Figure 9-6**

A GOVERNMENTAL UNIT
Special Assessment Fund
Analysis of Changes in Fund Balances
For the Year Ended (Date)
(Project Incomplete)

|  | Total | Construction | Interest |
|---|---|---|---|
| Project authorization .................. | $500,000 | $500,000 | |
| Fund balance, beginning of year (date) ... | $ — | $ — | $ — |
| Additions: | | | |
| Special assessments levied ............ | $400,000 | $400,000 | — |
| Governmental unit's share of cost ...... | 100,000 | 100,000 | — |
| Interest revenues ................... | 17,500 | — | $ 17,500 |
| Total additions ................... | $517,500 | $500,000 | $ 17,500 |
| Total balances and additions ........... | $517,500 | $500,000 | $ 17,500 |
| | | | |
| Deductions: | | | |
| Expenditures ...................... | $140,000 | $140,000 | — |
| Encumbrances* .................... | 340,000 | 340,000 | — |
| Interest expenses† .................. | 15,550 | — | $ 15,550 |
| Total deductions ................. | $495,550 | $480,000 | $ 15,550 |
| Fund balance, end of year (date) ........ | $ 21,950 | $ 20,000 | $ 1,950 |

* Alternatively, Encumbrances may be deducted from Fund Balance—Construction in the Balance Sheet rather than being closed at year end and re-established in the accounts at the beginning of the following year.

† The bond premium is being amortized in this example; thus the Interest Expenses account reports the difference between the cash interest paid or accrued ($15,750) and the portion of the premium amortized during the period ($200). Were this not the case, the entire premium ($1,000) would be added to Fund Balance—Interest, and Interest Expenses would reflect the cash interest paid or accrued ($15,750). The difference in reported Fund Balance—Interest under these methods is reduced each period by the amount of premium amortization; the reported Fund Balance—Interest is the same under both methods only after amortization is completed.

illustrated at some point within this chapter. The authors prefer a columnar presentation of statements analyzing changes in these accounts, such as that illustrated in Figure 9-6, though the NCGA requires only that the amounts shown in the "Total" column of that statement be presented. In most situations presentation of total data only will not, in our opinion, constitute adequate disclosure unless supplemented by parenthetical or footnote explanation of the detail shown in the other columns of the statement illustrated in Figure 9-6.

## TRANSACTIONS AND ENTRIES—SECOND YEAR

Let us assume that construction of the project was completed during the second year. The following list of transactions and entries (see Figure 9-13) illustrates the operation of the Fund during this year:

*Transactions*

1. Encumbrances were re-established in the accounts (if closed at end of first fiscal year).
2. Deferred assessments in the amount of $40,000 became due.
3. Interest amounting to $17,500 became receivable.
4. Delinquent assessments of $4,000 were collected.
5. The remaining part of the governmental unit's share of the cost of the improvement was transferred.
6. Contracts payable of $100,000 were paid.
7. Current assessments of $75,000 were collected.
8. Interest of $16,500 was collected.
9. Interest of $15,750 was paid; premium on bonds was amortized.
10. Supervisory expenses of engineers, amounting to $5,000, were paid.
11. The project was completed and a bill was received from the contractor for the remaining part of the cost of the contract ($340,000).
12. Bonds to the amount of $70,000 were retired.
13. Current assessments receivable of $5,000 became delinquent.
14. The amount due on the contract was paid except for $44,000, which was retained pending final approval of the project.

*Entries*

1. Encumbrances ..........................     340,000
   Fund Balance—Construction (or
       Appropriations)....................                340,000
   To re-establish encumbrances closed out at
   the end of the previous year.

(Note: This entry is not required if the Encumbrances account was not closed at the end of the previous year.)

2. Assessments Receivable—Current ..........   40,000
   Assessments Receivable—Deferred .....               40,000
   To record the setting up of deferred install-
   ments that have become due.

3. Interest Receivable .....................   17,500
   Interest Revenues ...................                17,500
   To record interest receivable.

4. Cash—Construction .....................   4,000
   Assessments Receivable—Delinquent ...                4,000
   To record collection of delinquent assess-
   ments representing first installments.

(Recall that assessments due in the first year, and now delinquent, were designated for construction purposes.)

5. Cash—Construction .....................   50,000
   Governmental Unit's Share of Cost .....               50,000
   To record transfer of remaining part of
   amount due from governmental unit.

6. Contracts Payable......................   100,000
   Cash—Construction .................                  100,000
   To record payment of part of contract.

7. Cash—Bond Payments ..................   75,000
   Assessments Receivable—Current ......                75,000
   To record collection of current assessments
   receivable.

8. Cash—Interest Payments.................   16,500
   Interest Receivable ..................                16,500
   To record interest collections.

9. Unamortized Premiums on Bonds ..........   200
   Interest Expenses ......................   15,550
   Cash—Interest Payments.............                  15,750
   To record payment of interest and amortiza-
   tion of premium on bonds.

10. Expenditures ...........................   5,000
   Cash—Construction .................                  5,000
   To record payment of supervisory expenses.

11. (a) Reserve for Encumbrances ...........   340,000
      Encumbrances .................                340,000
      To record cancellation of encum-
      brances.

   (b) Expenditures ......................   340,000
      Contracts Payable ..............                340,000
      To record construction expenditures
      and corresponding liability to con-
      tractors.

12.   Bonds Payable .........................     70,000
      Cash—Bond Payments ..............                70,000
      To record retirement of bonds.

13.   Assessments Receivable—Delinquent .......     5,000
      Assessments Receivable—Current ......                5,000
      To record setting up delinquent assessments
      separately.

14.   Contracts Payable......................     340,000
      Contracts Payable—Retained
         Percentage......................                44,000
         Cash—Construction .................                296,000
      To record retention of part of amount due on
      contract and payment of remaining part.

## Closing Entries—Project Completed

As before, entries are made at the end of the fiscal year closing out the Interest Revenues, Interest Expenses and Expenditures accounts. Encumbrances are not of concern at this point since none are outstanding. The closing entries required are as follows:

(C1)   Interest Revenues .......................     17,500
      Interest Expenses....................                15,550
      Fund Balance—Interest ..............                1,950
      To record closing of interest revenues and
      expenses to fund balance—interest.

(Recall that the premium on bonds is being amortized in this example. Had the premium been closed directly as an addition to Fund Balance—Interest in the first year, reported interest expense for the second year would have been $15,750, the amount of cash interest paid or accrued for the period, and Fund Balance—Interest increased by only $1,750 in the entry above.)

(C2)   Fund Balance—Construction (or
      Appropriations) .......................     345,000
      Expenditures........................                345,000
      To record closing out of expenditures.

Had an Appropriations account(s) been in use, (1) its balance would now stand at $15,000, and (2) there would be no balance as yet in the Fund Balance —Construction account. The following additional entry would be required if this approach had been used rather than that used in our example:

Appropriations................................     15,000
      Fund Balance—Construction .................                15,000
      To close unneeded appropriations to fund balance—
      construction upon completion of construction.

Note that the alternative approaches have now converged insofar as they relate to the Fund Balance—Construction account. The balance sheet at this point would be identical in this regard, regardless of the approach employed.

### Balance Sheet—Project Completed

After the above closing entries are posted, the balance sheet of the Special Assessment Fund will appear as indicated in Figure 9-7.

**Figure 9-7**

A GOVERNMENTAL UNIT
Special Assessment Fund
Balance Sheet
At Close of Fiscal Year

*Assets*

| | | |
|---|---|---|
| Cash: | | |
| For construction.............................. | $ 58,000 | |
| For bonds payments ........................... | 5,000 | |
| For interest payments ......................... | 3,000 | $ 66,000 |
| Assessments receivable: | | |
| Delinquent (Note: $1,000 is to be used to finance construction) ......................... | $ 6,000 | |
| Deferred ..................................... | 270,000 | 276,000 |
| Interest receivable .............................. | | 1,500 |
| Total assests ............................... | | $343,500 |

*Liabilities and Fund Balance*

| | | | |
|---|---|---|---|
| Liabilities: | | | |
| Contracts payable—retained percentage ............ | | $ 44,000 | |
| Bonds payable ...................... | $280,000 | | |
| Unamortized premiums on bonds ...... | 600 | 280,600 | $324,600 |
| Fund balance: | | | |
| Construction.................................. | | $ 15,000 | |
| Interest ......................................... | | 3,900 | 18,900 |
| Total liabilities and fund balance ............... | | | $343,500 |

Had the premium on bonds been written off to Fund Balance—Interest in the first year, the Liabilities and Fund Balance section of the balance sheet illustrated in Figure 9-7 would appear as:

*Liabilities and Fund Balance*

Liabilities:

| | | |
|---|---|---|
| Contracts payable—retained percentage ............ | $ 44,000 | |
| Bonds payable .............................. | 280,000 | $324,000 |

Fund Balance:

| | | |
|---|---|---|
| Construction ................................. | $ 15,000 | |
| Interest ..................................... | 4,500 | $ 19,500 |
| | | $343,500 |

Note again that the difference results from the balance of the unamortized bond premium being carried in the accounts in one case but having been closed to Fund Balance—Interest in the other. Where the premium is amortized, it causes

**Figure 9-8**

A GOVERNMENTAL UNIT
Special Assessment Fund
Balance Sheet (Alternative Form)
At Close of Fiscal Year

| | *Fund for* | | |
|---|---|---|---|
| | *Construction* | *Payment of Bonds* | *Payment of Interest* |
| *Assets* | | | |
| Cash .......................... | $58,000 | $ 5,000 | $3,000 |
| Assessments receivable: | | | |
| Delinquent ................... | 1,000 | 5,000 | |
| Deferred ..................... | | 270,000 | |
| Interest receivable .............. | | | 1,500 |
| | $59,000 | $280,000 | $4,500 |

*Liabilities and Fund Balance*

| | | | |
|---|---|---|---|
| Liabilities: | | | |
| Contracts payable—retained percentage ..................... | $44,000 | | |
| Bonds payable ............... | | $280,000 | |
| Unamortized premiums on bonds . | | | $ 600 |
| Fund balance .................. | 15,000 | | 3,900 |
| | $59,000 | $280,000 | $4,500 |

Fund Balance—Interest to be increased by periodic increments—since reported interest expense is reduced each period via premium amortization—whereas Fund Balance—Interest is increased immediately where the direct write-off method is used. These alternative methods will converge—that is, the Fund Balance—Interest account will report the same amount in both cases—when the premium amortization is completed at the end of the life of the bond issue.

COLUMNAR FORM OF BALANCE SHEET. If special assessment projects are financed from the sale of special assessment bonds, the Special Assessment Fund really consists of three funds: (1) a Capital Projects Fund that accounts for the proceeds from the sale of the bonds used to finance construction, (2) a Special Revenue Fund that accounts for the special assessments used to retire the bonds, and (3) a Special Revenue Fund that accounts for interest collected on deferred special assessments and used to pay interest on the bonds. This fact is evident from the foregoing entries and from the balance sheets illustrated in Figures 9-5 and 9-7. It can be demonstrated further by rearranging the balance sheet in Figure 9-7 in the manner illustrated in Figure 9-8.

Had the bond premium been written off directly to Fund Balance—Interest, the Liabilities and Fund Balance section of the balance sheet illustrated in Figure 9-8 would appear:

|  | *Fund for* | | |
|---|---|---|---|
|  | *Construction* | *Payment of Bonds* | *Payment of Interest* |

*Liabilities and Fund Balance*

| | | | |
|---|---|---|---|
| Liabilities: | | | |
| Contracts payable—retained | | | |
| percentage .................. | $44,000 | | |
| Bonds payable ................ | | $280,000 | |
| Fund balance .................. | 15,000 | | $4,500 |
| | $59,000 | $280,000 | $4,500 |

Advocates of writing-off bond premiums directly to Fund Balance—Interest stress the ease and clarity with which this latter presentation may be communicated to the layman, that is, that writing-off premiums or discounts avoids potential problems inherent in attempting to explain their nature and theoretically correct accounting treatment to the layman.

SUBSIDIARY SCHEDULE OF INSTALLMENTS RECEIVABLE AND BONDS PAYABLE. If bonds are identified with and are made payable from particular installments, a subsidiary schedule similar to the one illustrated in Figure 9-9 must be prepared. This schedule shows for each installment the amount of cash and other assets that will ultimately be used in paying bonds and interest, the amount of bonds and interest payable, and the related balance or deficit. The schedule sup-

**Figure 9-9**

A GOVERNMENTAL UNIT
Special Assessment Fund
Schedule of Installments to be Applied
To Payment of Bonds and Interest

*Date*

*Years*

| | | 19— | 19— | 19— | 19— |
|---|---|---|---|---|---|

*Installment No.*

| | Total | 2 | 3 | 4 | 5 |
|---|---|---|---|---|---|
| Cash for bond payments ......... | $ 5,000 | $ 5,000 | | | |
| Cash for interest payments ....... | 3,000 | 3,000 | | | |
| Assessments receivable: | | | | | |
| Delinquent ................. | 5,000 | 5,000 | | | |
| Deferred ................... | 270,000 | | $90,000 | $90,000 | $90,000 |
| Interest receivable ............. | 1,500 | 1,500 | | | |
| | $284,500 | $14,500 | $90,000 | $90,000 | $90,000 |

*Liabilities and Fund Balance*

| | | | | | |
|---|---|---|---|---|---|
| Bonds payable ................ | $280,000 | $10,000 | $90,000 | $90,000 | $90,000 |
| Fund balance—interest ......... | 4,500 | 4,500 | | | |
| | $284,500 | $14,500 | $90,000 | $90,000 | $90,000 |

ports the accounts illustrated in the last two columns of the above balance sheet, assuming that the premium was written off.

Note that the delinquent assessments of $1,000 are not shown here since it was assumed in the example that the first installment was to be used to finance construction. When the $1,000 is collected, it will not be used for the retirement of bonds but for meeting construction expenditures, and therefore it is not shown in this schedule.

### Analysis of Changes in Fund Balance—Project Complete

The preferred format of the Analysis of Changes in Fund Balances statement that would be prepared at the end of the second fiscal year is shown in Figure 9-10. Note that there is no Fund Balance—Bonds; the assets dedicated to their retirement equal the liability for bond principal (see Figure 9-8). A

**Figure 9-10**

A GOVERNMENTAL UNIT

Special Assessment Fund

Analysis of Changes in Fund Balances

For the Fiscal Year Ended (Date)

(Second Fiscal Year—Project Completed)

|  | Total | Construction | Interest |
|---|---|---|---|
| Project authorization ................. | $500,000 | $500,000 | |
| Expenditures of prior years ......... | ( 140,000) | ( 140,000) | |
| Encumbrances at beginning of year.. | ( 340,000) | ( 340,000) | |
| Fund balance, beginning of year (date).. | $ 21,950 | $ 20,000 | $ 1,950 |
| Additions: | | | |
| Encumbrances re-established* ...... | $340,000 | $340,000 | |
| Interest revenues ................. | 17,500 | | $17,500 |
| Total additions ................. | $357,500 | $340,000 | $17,500 |
| Total balance and additions .......... | $379,450 | $360,000 | $19,450 |
| Deductions: | | | |
| Expenditures .................... | $345,000 | $345,000 | |
| Interest expenses† .............. | 15,550 | | $15,550 |
| Total deductions .............. | $360,550 | $345,000 | $15,550 |
| Fund balance, end of year (date) ..... | $ 18,900 | $ 15,000 | $ 3,900 |

* Alternatively, the Encumbrances account may have been brought forward from the previous year in its usual off-set relation with the Reserve for Encumbrances account rather than being closed to Fund Balance—Construction at the end of the prior year and re-established at the beginning of the current year. For clarification of this point refer to the textual material and the notes to Figure 9-6.

† The amount reported as interest expenses each period and the balance of the Fund Balance—Interest account will differ from that shown here if bond premiums or discounts are closed directly to Fund Balance—Interest rather than being amortized. For clarification of this point refer to the textual material and the notes to Figure 9-6.

Fund Balance—Bonds account would appear therefore only where bond-related assets differ from the bond principal owed.

Had an Appropriations account been employed in our example, the Fund Balance—Construction account would have had a zero balance prior to preparation and posting of closing entries at the end of the second fiscal year. A statement of changes in the Appropriations account would be required where that account is used, and the Fund Balance—Construction account would require analysis only after project construction was completed.

Figure 9-11

A GOVERNMENTAL UNIT

Special Assessment Fund

Statement of Expenditures Compared with Appropriations

For Fiscal Years (Date)

(Project Completed) ·

| | | | |
|---|---|---|---|
| Appropriations | | $500,000 | |
| Less: Expenditures | | | |
| Of this year | $345,000 | | |
| Of prior years | 140,000 | 485,000 | |
| Unexpended balance | | | $15,000 |
| Less—Transferred to fund balance—construction ... | | | 15,000 |
| | | | $  – |

A typical Statement of Expenditures Compared with Appropriations is illustrated in Figure 9-11. The analysis of the Fund Balance—Construction account in this situation would be as follows:

| | |
|---|---|
| Balance, beginning of year | $ –0– |
| Add: Unneeded appropriations canceled | 15,000 |
| Balance, end of year | $15,000 |

### Capitalizing Expenditures

The fixed assets acquired through Special Assessment Fund expenditures are general assets of the government and should be recorded in the General Fixed Assets group of accounts (see Chapter 11). Since special assessment projects are, to a great extent, financed by private property owners, the question arises as to whether the government should capitalize the entire cost of the project or only that portion of the cost which it financed.

Since the government financed only part of the project, it might seem that it should not capitalize the complete cost. But the improvement cannot be considered the property of assessment payers; they are not at liberty to do as they please with it. Too, the government is responsible for the maintenance and repair of the improvement. Moreover, especially where levies are assessed against property owners who are not in favor of the project, assessments may be viewed as a form of taxation. Property owners have, in substance, contributed assessment payments and the resulting improvements to the community at large. For all practical purposes, therefore, the improvement can be considered as belonging to the governmental unit. Accordingly, the entire cost should be capitalized by the governmental unit, but the capitalization should be so recorded that it will be possible to distinguish the portion of the project costs financed by the governmental unit from that financed by the private owners.

## ACTIVITIES SUBSEQUENT TO PROJECT COMPLETION

The Capital Projects Fund aspects of the Special Assessment Fund life cycle have been concluded upon completion of construction and payment of construction costs. Any balance within the Fund Balance—Construction account may now be disposed of in the manner discussed below.

The Special Assessment Fund will continue to function in a Debt Service Fund capacity until all assessments receivable have been collected and all Special Assessment Fund debt has been liquidated. At that time, any Fund Balance —Interest and Fund Balance—Bonds (or other debt type) will be appropriately disposed of and the fund terminated.

### Disposing of Fund Balances

At any time prior to abolition of the fund there may be three distinct types of fund balances. First, a fund balance may result from an excess of authorized expenditures over actual expenditures. Second, an excess of interest revenues over interest expenses gives rise to fund balance during or at the end of the fund's life cycle, or both. Third, though less common than the preceding, a fund balance may result from an excess of assets earmarked for debt principal retirement over debt principal owed. These are referred to as construction balance, interest balance, and debt principal balance, respectively, in the discussions which follow.

The disposal of a construction balance varies according to the interim financing method and with the assessment procedure employed. Where interim financing is involved the construction balance would normally be reclassified as debt service balance. Where interim borrowing is not involved and the levy is made *after* the project is completed, there can be no balance, since the assessment will be made large enough to recover only the actual cost of construction. If assessments are levied *before* the project is completed, rebates may be granted in the form of cash or a reduction of the unpaid assessments. However, either statutes or sound management may prohibit the payment of rebates or the reduction of assessments until all outstanding debt has been paid, so that, in the event some assessments prove uncollectible, the balance may be applied to the retirement of the debt.

In cases where (1) the timing of assessment and interest collections coincides with debt service requirements, and (2) an excess of interest revenues over interest expenses is expected to recur each year, it may be appropriate to reduce the interest rate charged on assessments receivable so that the interest balance is eliminated or minimal by the time the fund is to be terminated. The relevant balance is that *anticipated* immediately prior to fund termination, however, not the amount of the Fund Balance—Interest account at an earlier date. Since the Fund Balance—Interest account is not actuarially based, it may have a credit balance, particularly in the early years of the Special Assessment Fund life cycle, in situations in which an ultimate interest deficit is virtually assured. This would result, for example, if 9 percent bonds were sold to yield 8 percent, assessments yield 6 percent, and the premium is closed to Fund Balance—Interest rather than being amortized. (This is an excellent example of why both the NCGA and the authors recommend amortization of premiums and discounts.)

Such situations may also be encountered where bonds are sold at par or premiums or discounts are amortized. To illustrate, assume that (1) a series of five bonds issues of equal denomination were sold at par with nominal rates of 2 percent, 4 percent, 6 percent, 8 percent, and 10 percent respectively, (2) one fifth of the bonds mature annually in the order indicated by the nominal interest rate listing, and (3) assessments yield 7 percent and are collected equally over the five year period. A sizeable, but illusionary, Fund Balance—Interest might be reported in earlier years, though a deficit would arise later.

Recall, too, that some property owners may pay their assessments early. Investment of these monies may yield more or less than the rate charged on assessments. They often yield less because such collections tend to occur sporadically, in amounts too small to be invested individually at reasonable yield rates; that is, collections may have to be accumulated until their total warrants investment. In the meantime they generate little or no interest income. For these and other reasons, reduction of interest charges or disposal of an interest balance is usually deferred until all debt principal and interest have been paid. Interest balance remaining after all debt is liquidated should generally be rebated or used to make up a deficit in another aspect of the Fund's activities. Alternatively, it may be transferred to another Special Assessment Fund or to the General Fund, particularly if the interest balance is small or is deemed to be attributable to the government's contribution to the special assessment project.

Bondholders may insist that assessments receivable in an amount greater than bond principal owed be earmarked for bond retirement. A Fund Balance—Bonds would be reported in such cases and, assuming that collection of assessments so designated exceed the bond principal owed, would require disposition after the bonds are paid. One would expect in such a case that a Fund Balance—Construction deficit resulted from this excessive earmarking of assessments receivable and that the debt principal balance would be used to offset that deficit. In any event, a debt principal balance would normally be disposed of in the same manner as a construction balance.

DISPOSING OF DEFICITS.    Instead of having positive balances, a Special Assessment Fund may have three deficits—a *construction deficit,* an *interest deficit,* or a *debt principal deficit.*

Most construction deficits arise where assessments are levied *before* the completion of the project. If assessments are levied *after* the project is completed, the total construction cost is known—and the assessments plus the governmental unit's share of the cost are made large enough to cover the actual construction costs. More specifically, a construction deficit remaining upon termination of a Special Assessment Fund might indicate one of these:

1. If assessments were levied *before* completion of the project—that (a) actual costs exceeded the amount authorized and assessed or (b) some assessments proved uncollectible; or,
2. If assessments were levied *after* completion of the project—that actual construction costs exceeded (a) the estimated and authorized amount that had been borrowed and/or (b) the assessable amount, or (c) that the project authorization was not properly scaled down following the sale of bonds at a discount.

The deficit may be made up through the levy of supplemental assessments. If the assessments are payable in installments, the latter may be adjusted to reflect the supplemental levy or a separate supplementary roll may be made. Frequently a supplemental levy will not be deemed politically feasible, however, particularly where elected officials forced (or encouraged) the project to be undertaken. The project may have become an emotional issue of concern to some or all of the property owners in the district, for example, many of whom may be quite vocal, influential, or both. In such cases the government may make up the deficit through an additional contribution or from interest or debt principal balances.

Interest deficits for any one year are disposed of by charging them against accumulated Fund Balance—Interest. If it appears that an interest deficit will exist at the conclusion of the Fund's debt service function, it may be necessary to raise interest rates. On the other hand, interest deficits may be made up by a transfer from the General Fund. Or, if legal, they may be eliminated by applying construction or debt principal balances against the interest deficit. Although the last method penalizes those who have paid their assessments in full, it has the advantage of eliminating the ill feeling or litigation that may accompany a rise in the interest rate. As noted earlier, in many instances those assessment owners who have paid in full are responsible for the decline in interest earnings. That is, if bonds cannot be retired as soon as collections are made from those paying in full—or the money cannot be invested promptly at a yield commensurate with the interest paid on the bonds—the government will continue to pay the same amount of interest on the outstanding bonds, but its interest earnings will be reduced.

A debt principal deficit would be disposed of as appropriate in the circumstances. If the debt is of the special-special assessment type and is secured only by the delinquent assessments levied against certain properties, the government would have no legal obligation to see that creditors receive full payment. As discussed earlier, however, default on any obligation with which a government is even casually associated may have a significant detrimental effect on that government's credit standing. Thus, if possible, the government might make up the deficit in some manner, even though it was not legally obligated to do so. Accounting and other procedures related to delinquent assessments are discussed in more detail in the concluding section of this chapter.

TRANSACTIONS AND ENTRIES ILLUSTRATING DISPOSAL OF FUND BALANCES AND DEFICITS. The following transactions and entries illustrate the accounting procedure involved in disposing of construction, interest, and debt principal balances and deficits.

*Transactions*

a.  Construction balance amounted to $62,000. Rebates were made in cash as follows: to property owners, $10,000; to the governmental unit, $2,000. A reduction of $50,000 was made in assessments.
b.  Cash representing construction balance of $50,000 was used to retire bonds.
c.  Construction balance was $10,000 and was applied toward eliminating an interest deficit of a corresponding amount.
d.  A construction deficit of $100,000 was eliminated through supplemental assessments of $90,000, together with a supplemental contribution by the governmental unit of $10,000.
e.  Interest and debt principal balances of $1,000 and $9,000, respectively, were transferred to the General Fund.

*Entries*

a.  Fund Balance—Construction ................ 62,000
       Cash—Construction.. ...................                 12,000
       Assessments Receivable—Deferred .......                 50,000
       To record making of cash rebates and the re-
       duction in assessments.

b.  Fund Balance—Construction ................ 50,000
    Bonds Payable............................ 50,000
       Cash—Construction .....................                 50,000
       Fund Balance—Bonds ...................                  50,000
       To record use of cash representing construc-
       tion balance for the retirement of bonds.

c.  Fund Balance—Construction ................ 10,000
    Cash—Interest Payments ................... 10,000
       Fund Balance—Interest ................                  10 000
       Cash—Construction .....................                 10,000
       To record application of construction balance
       to elimination of interest deficit.

d.  Assessments Receivable—Supplemental ....... 90,000
    Governmental Unit's Share of Cost—
    Supplemental .......................... 10,000
      Fund Balance—Construction ............        100,000
      To record levy of supplemental special assess-
      ments to eliminate deficit.

e.  Fund Balance—Interest ................... 1,000
    Fund Balance—Bonds .................... 9,000
      Cash—Interest ......................        1,000
      Cash—Bond Payments.................        9,000
      To record transfer of cash representing in-
      terest and debt principal fund balances to the
      General Fund.

## COMBINED STATEMENTS

A governmental unit may have many special assessment projects. In that case, it must establish a separate fund for each project. In presenting balance sheets or other statements of these funds, it is important to retain the identity of each fund. It is desirable also, as in the case of Capital Projects Funds, to group special assessment projects in accordance with whether they represent completed projects or uncompleted projects. The following is an illustration of the heading for a combined Special Assessment Fund balance sheet:

A GOVERNMENTAL UNIT
Special Assessment Funds
Balance Sheet (Date)

|  | Completed Projects | | Uncompleted Projects | |
|---|---|---|---|---|
| Total | No. 59 | No. 60 | No. 61 | No. 62 |

If the governmental unit has many special assessment projects, it may wish to prepare a combined balance sheet in which (1) all assets, liabilities, reserves, and balances are combined, or (2) combined data for groups of Special Assessment Funds make up the main combined statement totals. In such case, a subsidiary schedule(s) showing the amount of assets, liabilities, reserves, and balances applicable to each Fund must be prepared. The schedule(s) heading would be similar to the one illustrated above for a combined columnar balance sheet. In other words, as in the case of Capital Projects Funds, the combined balance sheet(s) becomes a subsidiary schedule(s), and figures in the "Total" column of the schedule(s) must correspond with the amounts shown in the main balance sheet.

The Analysis of Changes in Fund Balances statement may also be prepared in combined form following these format modification guidelines. Too, these guidelines are equally applicable to combined statements of cash receipts and disbursements or other Special Assessment Fund combined statements or analyses.

## ACCOUNTING FOR DELINQUENT SPECIAL ASSESSMENTS

We have already discussed the accounting procedure for assessments receivable up to the time they become delinquent. In this section, we discuss the procedure relating to the collection of delinquent special assessments.

Special assessments are usually made, by statute, a lien against the property against which they are levied; and, at the expiration of a certain period of time, the property may be sold at a public sale and the proceeds used to satisfy the lien. Let us assume that the governmental unit incurred certain costs, such as advertising and auctioneer's fees, in holding the sale. The entry to record these costs would be as follows:

| | | |
|---|---|---|
| Cost of Holding Sale .............................. | 200 | |
| Accounts Payable ............................. | | 200 |
| To record the costs of holding a sale of special assessment property. | | |

The entry to record the sale of property for unpaid special assessments is as follows:

| | | |
|---|---|---|
| Cash—Bond Payments ......................... | 10,000 | |
| Cash—Interest Payments ........................ | 150 | |
| Cash—Other Payments......................... | 200 | |
| Assessments Receivable—Delinquent ........... | | 2,000 |
| Assessments Receivable—Deferred ............. | | 8,000 |
| Interest Receivable ......................... | | 150 |
| Cost of Holding Sale ........................ | | 200 |
| To record sale of property for nonpayment of special assessments. | | |

The entry to record payment of the cost of holding the sale is as follows:

| | | |
|---|---|---|
| Accounts Payable .................................. | 200 | |
| Cash—Other Payments ........................ | | 200 |
| To record payment of costs of holding a sale of special assessment property. | | |

Note that the proceeds may be applied to satisfy not only the assessments receivable, but also the interest receivable up to the date of sale and the cost of holding the sale. Of course, specific authorization by ordinance or statute is required for the use of the proceeds to cover interest and the cost of holding the sale.

The excess of the amount realized from the sale of the property over the amount of special assessments, interest, and the cost of holding the sale is held in a Trust Fund for the benefit of the property owner until claimed by him. The transaction is recorded in that fund by debiting Cash and crediting the Property Owner's Trust Fund Balance account. If, on the other hand, the proceeds are not sufficient to cover special assessments, interest, and the cost of the sale, the property owner would ordinarily not be called upon to make up the difference.

The proceeds realized by the governmental unit from the sale of property for delinquent assessments may be used for various purposes. If general-special assessment bonds have been issued, the governmental unit may have paid the bond and interest as they fell due with money borrowed from other funds. The proceeds would then be used to pay off the loans. If special-special assessment bonds are used, neither bonds due nor the interest on bonds may have been paid, and the proceeds will in such cases be used to retire the bonds and pay the interest. If unmatured bonds are not callable, are callable only at a significant premium, or are not available at a reasonable price on the open market, the governmental unit may not be able or willing to retire them prior to maturity. Instead, bonds and interest will have to be paid as they fall due, and the governmental unit will be faced with the problem of investing the money in the interim.

If the amount realized from the sale of the property is insufficient to cover the principal of the bonds and the interest, and the property owner cannot be called upon to make up the difference, the procedure followed depends on whether special-special assessment or general-special assessment bonds were issued. If special-special assessment bonds were issued, the bondholder will bear the loss unless the government chooses to do so, often after first bidding in the property itself. On the other hand, if general-special assessment bonds were issued, the deficiency must be made up by the governmental unit. Frequently, if the property cannot be sold for a sufficient amount to meet bonds and interest, the governmental unit bids it in. The entry to record this transaction is as follows:

| | | |
|---|---:|---:|
| Assessment Sale Certificates | 10,350 | |
|     Assessments Receivable—Delinquent | | 2,000 |
|     Assessments Receivable—Deferred | | 8,000 |
|     Interest Receivable | | 150 |
|     Cost of Holding Sale | | 200 |
|     To record bidding in of property for assessment | | |

If the governmental unit bids in the property, payments on bonds and interest falling due often must be met, pending the disposition of the property, through interfund or bank loans.

The property owner usually has the right to redeem his property within a certain period of time by paying the purchaser the price paid at the public sale plus interest and costs. If the sales price was not sufficient to pay the assessments, the property owner often must also pay the remaining assessments in order to redeem the property.

If the property was purchased by a private buyer, the redemption is handled through a Trust Fund. On the other hand, if the property is bid in by the governmental unit, the transaction is handled in the Special Assessment Fund. For example, if the property was bid in by a municipality and a loan was made to finance maturing bonds and interest and to meet the cost of holding the sale, the entry to record the redemption of the property is as follows:

| | | |
|---|---|---|
| Cash—Payment of Loans | 5,350 | |
| Cash—Bond Payments | 5,000 | |
| Cash—Interest Payments | 50 | |
| Assessment Sale Certificates | | 10,350 |
| Interest Revenues | | 50 |
| To record redemption of property bid in by governmental unit. | | |

It should be noted that the Interest Revenues account consists of accrued interest from the time the property was bid in until the time of redemption. Interest prior to the date of bidding in the property is included in the Assessment Sale Certificates account.

If the property is not redeemed within the required period of time, the purchaser acquires title to it. If the property was bid in by the governmental unit, it gets title. No entries are necessary to record this fact, the next entry being made when the property is sold by the governmental unit and the proceeds are used to pay the bonds and interest. Since the entry would be similar to the one described immediately above, it will not be illustrated here.

If the governmental unit intends to keep the property, an entry must be made in the Special Assessment Fund to close out the Assessment Sale Certificates account. This will result in a deficit in the Fund unless an amount of money equal to the balance in the Assessment Sale Certificates account for the property is transferred from the General Fund (or another fund) to the Special Assessment Fund. The entry to record the receipt of the cash by the Special Assessment Fund is as follows:

| | | |
|---|---|---|
| Cash—Bond Payments | 10,000 | |
| Cash—Interest Payments | 150 | |
| Cash—Other Payments | 200 | |
| Assessment Sale Certificates | | 10,350 |
| To record transfer of cash from the General Fund equal to the balance in the Assessment Sale Certificates account as a result of the bidding in of the delinquent property by this municipality. | | |

If money has already been advanced as a loan from the General Fund to the Special Assessment Fund, the loan will be canceled and only the difference between the loan and the amount of the assessment sale certificate will be transferred from the General Fund. If we assume that $5,350 had been borrowed from the General Fund, the entry to record the cancellation of the loan and the receipt of money to cover bond payments yet to be made is as follows:

| | | |
|---|---|---|
| Cash—Bonds Payments......................... | 5,000 | |
| Due to General Fund ........................... | 5,350 | |
|     Assessment Sale Certificates .................. | | 10,350 |
|     To record cancellation of liability to General Fund | | |
|     and receipt of money from that fund for payment | | |
|     of bonds. | | |

It is assumed immediately above that the entire amount of special assessment bonds outstanding is to be paid at one time. If bonds are to be retired in installments, two procedures might be followed. One procedure is to transfer at one time cash equivalent to the full amount of the assessment sale certificate, as was assumed in the above entry. In that case, Special Assessment Fund cash is invested, and the earnings on investments are used to pay interest on bonds. The other procedure is to transfer each year an amount sufficient only to retire that part of the bonds and interest falling due during that year which the Special Assessment Fund is unable to pay because of the transfer of the property. In this case Due from General Fund, rather than Cash — Bond Payments, would be debited in the preceding entry.

Two additional facts should be noted about special assessments. First, the law may provide for penalties on delinquent special assessments. These are accounted for in the same manner as interest on delinquent special assessments. In fact, an examination of the interest rates that governmental units are sometimes permitted to charge will reveal that these interest charges also include penalties, although they are referred to as *interest*. Sometimes the term *interest and penalties* is used.

Second, the same property will no doubt be subject to ad valorem real estate taxes as well as the special assessments, and unpaid taxes are also a lien against the property. Sometimes a single lien is secured against the property to cover both ad valorem taxes and special assessments. The proceeds from the sale of the property are in that event used to satisfy both liens. For example, the Illinois Supreme Court[3] has held that liens of general taxes and local improvement special assessments are on a parity, with no priority of one over the other.

[3] *People* v. *The Taylorville Sanitary District, et al., 371 Ill. 280 (1939), 20 N. E. (2d) 576.*

**Figure 9-12**

## A GOVERNMENTAL UNIT
### Special Assessment Fund Worksheet for First Fiscal Year
#### (Project Uncompleted)

| | Transactions—First Fiscal Year (Project Begun) Dr. | Cr. | Pre-Closing Trial Balance (End of First Fiscal Year) Dr. | Cr. | Closing Entries (End of First Fiscal Year) Dr. | Cr. | Post-Closing Trial Balance (End of First Fiscal Year) Dr. | Cr. |
|---|---|---|---|---|---|---|---|---|
| Cash—Construction ........ | (2) 350,000 (5) 45,000 (6) 50,000 | (15) 40,000 | 405,000 | | | | 405,000 | |
| Cash—Interest Payments ... | (2) 1,000 (11) 17,000 | (12) 15,750 | 2,250 | | | | 2,250 | |
| Unamortized Premiums on Bonds ............. | (10) 200 | (2) 1,000 | | 800 | | | | 800 |
| Bonds Payable ............. | | (2) 350,000 | | 350,000 | | | | 350,000 |
| Assessments Receivable—Current........... | (3) 50,000 (7) 40,000 | (5) 45,000 (8) 5,000 | 40,000 | | | | 40,000 | |

| Account | Transactions Dr | Transactions Cr | Trial Balance Dr | Trial Balance Cr | Closing Dr | Closing Cr | Balance Sheet Dr | Balance Sheet Cr |
|---|---|---|---|---|---|---|---|---|
| Assessments Receivable—Deferred | (3) 350,000 | (7) 40,000 | 310,000 |  |  |  | 310,000 |  |
| Governmental Unit's Share of Cost | (3) 100,000 | (6) 50,000 | 50,000 |  |  |  | 50,000 |  |
| Fund Balance—Construction |  | (3) 500,000 |  | 500,000 | (C2) 480,000 |  |  | 20,000 |
| Encumbrances | (4) 440,000 | (13a) 100,000 | 340,000 |  |  | (C2) 340,000 |  |  |
| Reserve for Encumbrances | (13a) 100,000 | (4) 440,000 |  | 340,000 |  |  |  | 340,000 |
| Assessments Receivable—Delinquent | (8) 5,000 |  | 5,000 |  |  |  | 5,000 |  |
| Interest Receivable | (9) 17,500 | (11) 17,000 | 500 |  |  |  | 500 |  |
| Interest Revenues |  | (9) 17,500 |  | 17,500 | (C1) 17,500 |  |  |  |
| Interest Expenses | (10) 15,550 |  | 15,550 |  |  | (C1) 15,550 |  |  |
| Interest Payable | (12) 15,750 | (10) 15,550 |  | 15,750 |  |  |  |  |
| Expenditures | (13b) 100,000<br>(14) 40,000 |  | 140,000 |  |  | (C2) 140,000 |  |  |
| Contracts Payable |  | (13b) 100,000 |  | 100,000 |  |  |  | 100,000 |
| Judgments Payable | (15) 40,000 | (14) 40,000 |  | 40,000 |  |  |  |  |
| Fund Balance—Interest |  | (15) 1,950 |  | 1,950 |  | (C1) 1,950 |  | 1,950 |
|  | 1,777,000 | 1,777,000 | 1,308,300 | 1,308,300 | 497,500 | 497,500 | 812,750 | 812,750 |

Figure 9-13

## A GOVERNMENTAL UNIT
### Special Assessment Fund
### Worksheet for Second Fiscal Year
#### (Project Completed)

| | Beginning Trial Balance | | Transactions—Second Fiscal Year | | Pre-Closing Trial Balance (End of Second Fiscal Year) | | Closing Entries (End of Second Fiscal Year) | | Post-Closing Trial Balance (End of Second Fiscal Year) | |
|---|---|---|---|---|---|---|---|---|---|---|
| | Dr. | Cr. | Dr. | Cr. | Dr. | Cr. | Dr. | Cr. | Dr. | Cr. |
| Cash—Construction | 405,000 | | (4) 4,000 (5) 50,000 | (6) 100,000 (10) 5,000 (14) 296,000 | 58,000 | | | | 58,000 | |
| Cash—Interest Payments | 2,250 | | (8) 16,500 | (9) 15,750 | 3,000 | | | | 3,000 | |
| Unamortized Premiums on Bonds | | 800 | (9) 200 | | | 600 | | | | 600 |
| Bonds Payable | | 350,000 | (12) 70,000 | | | 280,000 | | | | 280,000 |
| Assessments Receivable—Current | 40,000 | | (2) 40,000 | (7) 75,000 (13) 5,000 | | | | | | |
| Assessments Receivable—Deferred | 310,000 | | | (2) 10,000 | 270,000 | | | | 270,000 | |
| Governmental Unit's Share of Cost | 50,000 | | | (5) 50,000 | | | | | | |
| Fund Balance—Construction | | 20,000 | | | | 360,000 | (C2) 345,000 | | | 15,000 |
| Encumbrances | | | (1) 340,000 | (11a) 340,000 | | | | | | |
| Reserve for Encumbrances | | 340,000 | (11a) 340,000 | (1) 340,000 | | | | | | |

| | | | | | | | |
|---|---|---|---|---|---|---|---|
| Assessments Receivable— | | | | | | | |
| Delinquent | 5,000 | (13) 5,000 | (4) 4,000 | 6,000 | | | |
| Interest Receivable | 500 | (3) 17,500 | (8) 16,500 | 1,500 | | | |
| Interest Revenues | | (3) 17,500 | 17,500 | (C1) 17,500 | | | |
| Interest Expenses | | (9) 15,550 | 15,550 | | (C1) 15,550 | | |
| Expenditures | | (10) 5,000 | 345,000 | | (C2) 345,000 | | |
| | | (11b) 340,000 | | | | | |
| Contracts Payable | 100,000 | (6) 100,000 | (11b) 340,000 | | | | |
| | | (14) 340,000 | | | | | |
| Fund Balance—Interest | | 1,950 | 1,950 | | (C1) 1,950 | | |
| Cash—Bond Payments | | (7) 75,000 | (12) 70,000 | 5,000 | | 5,000 | |
| Contracts Payable— | | | | | | | 3,900 |
| Retained Percentage | | (14) 44,000 | 44,000 | 44,000 | | | |
| | 812,750 | 812,750 | 1,758,750 | 704,050 | 362,500 | 343,500 | |

**Question 9-1.** Inasmuch as special assessments may be levied to finance either routine services or special improvement projects, why does this chapter deal almost exclusively with the latter?

**Question 9-2.** Making a formal "Improvements Authorized" journal entry is considered essential in certain Special Assessment Fund situations, but serves little or no useful purpose in others. Explain.

**Question 9-3.** A Special Assessment Fund may be, in essence, either a Capital Projects Fund or a combination Capital Projects-Debt Service Fund. Explain.

**Question 9-4.** Why might the use of a series of distinctively titled Cash accounts be appropriate in certain Special Assessment Fund situations but of little value in others?

**Question 9-5.** List the various means by which Special Assessment Fund interim financing may be secured and discuss the different manners in which notes may be employed for this purpose.

**Question 9-6.** Distinguish between general-special and special-special bonds.

**Question 9-7.** Why does a governmental unit frequently bear part of the cost of a special assessment improvement project?

**Question 9-8.** Despite the fact that some special assessments are expected to be uncollectible, an Allowance for Uncollectible Special Assessments is rarely established. Why is this so? Could such an allowance properly be established? Explain.

**Question 9-9.** Would it be advisable to prepare a statement comparing revenues and expenditures of a Special Assessment Fund each year? Explain.

**Question 9-10.** How does the use of multiple Fund Balance accounts in Special Assessment Fund accounting differ from that in Capital Projects Fund accounting?

**Question 9-11.** The extended illustration of Special Assessment Fund accounting and reporting within this chapter contained three "funds-within-a-fund", the separate identities of which were maintained through use of distinctively titled Fund Balance accounts. Under what circumstances would four "funds-within-a-fund" be employed in Special Assessment Fund accounting?

**Question 9-12.** How does use of the Improvements Authorized account in Special Assessment Fund accounting differ from that of the Projects Authorized account in the Capital Projects Fund?

**Question 9-13.** Why do many governmental accountants insist that special assessment bond issue discounts be amortized, while they are less concerned about whether or not premiums are amortized?

**Question 9-14.** Though several capital projects might be financed and accounted for through a single Capital Projects Fund, a separate Special Assessment Fund is virtually always required for each special assessment project. Why is this so?

**Question 9-15.** Why will the Fund Balance accounts of a Special Assessment Fund have different balances during the Fund's life cycle if Appropriations accounts are used than if they are not used, but not immediately prior to its termination?

**Question 9-16.** Should the total cost of a special assessment project be capitalized in the General Fixed Assets accounts? Only the governmental unit's share of the cost? Why?

**Question 9-17.** Is the Fund Balance-Construction account likely to have a balance upon completion of an improvement project constructed on open account or under contract and paid for by assessments levied at the conclusion of the project and collected immediately? Why?

**Question 9-18.** Why would a Fund Balance-Construction account balance remaining at the conclusion of the construction phase of a Special Assessment Fund normally be closed to the Fund Balance-Debt Principal account?

**Question 9-19.** When a government "bids in" property at a public sale held to satisfy liens against properties upon which assessments are delinquent, it receives an "assessment sale certificate." Explain the meaning of the term within quotation marks. How much cost (or disbursements) would be involved if a government bid in property for $5,000 and costs of holding the sale were $100?

**Question 9-20.** Compare the usage of the Unissued Bonds and Bonds Authorized-Unissued accounts in Special Assessment Fund accounting with that in Capital Projects Fund accounting.

**Question 9-21.** A municipality plans to widen an existing two lane residential street into a four lane thoroughfare and assess the cost of the improvement to residents of the neighborhood in which the street is located. Might the residents raise valid objections to the plan from the standpoints of legality or equity? Explain.

**Quesion 9-22.** Why might the interest rate charged on deferred special assessments properly be set at a rate higher than that paid by the governmental unit on debt it incurs to finance the projects?

**Question 9-23.** Why should great care be exercised in determining special assessment benefit district boundaries? Why should assumption by the governmental unit of special assessments originally levied against privately owned properties be subject to action by its governing board and to special audit scrutiny?

**Question 9-24.** Suppose that it is decided to use interest on assessments to make up a discount on bonds in the amount of $1,000. Give the entries to record (a) the receipt of the interest and (b) its use in eliminating the discount.

**Problem 9-1.** The following transactions took place during 19X4 in the City of Flowersville:

1. The construction of neighborhood street pavements estimated to cost $150,000 and to be financed from special assessments was authorized. (Formal authorization entry)
2. Pending the collection of assessments, construction was financed through the issue of notes for $90,000.
3. A contract was entered into with Acher & Wallace for the construction of the pavements at a cost of $140,000.
4. Assessments to the amount of $120,000 were levied; the municipality agreed to contribute $30,000 as its share of the cost of financing the project.
5. A bill was received from Acher & Wallace for $50,000.
6. Supervisory engineering expenses amounting to $5,000 were paid.
7. Acher & Wallace was paid.
8. All assessments and the city's contribution were collected.
9. A bill was received from Acher & Wallace for the remaining amount due on the contract.
10. Notes payable outstanding and interest of $3,000 were paid.
11. The project was completed.
12. Acher & Wallace was paid in full, except for $10,000 which was retained pending the final inspection and approval of the project.

Required:
(a) Prepare journal entries, including closing entries.
(b) Post to "T" accounts.
(c) Prepare a Balance Sheet as of December 31, 19X4.

(d)   Prepare a statement analyzing the changes in the Fund Balance account(s).
(e)   What disposition should be made of the Fund Balance?

**Problem 9-2. Part I.**   From the information given in Problem 9-1, prepare a columnar worksheet to reflect the transactions of the Special Assessment Fund of the City of Flowersville. Your worksheet headings should be as follows:

| 19X4 Transactions | | Closing Entry(ies) | | Post-closing Trial Balance December 31, 19X4 | |
|---|---|---|---|---|---|
| Debit | Credit | Debit | Credit | Debit | Credit |

**Problem 9-2. Part II.**   Prepare journal entries to reflect items 1, 2, and 4 of problem 9-1 under the assumption that a formal project authorization entry is *not* made.

**Problem 9-3. Part I.**   The following is a list of transactions which took place in the City of N during 19X4:

1.   The city commission authorized the paving of certain streets at an estimated cost of $200,000, the work to be performed by the city's own labor forces. The project is to be financed in the following manner:

| | |
|---|---|
| City's share | $ 50,000 |
| 19X4 assessment installment | 15,000 |
| Deferred assessments (nine installments) | 135,000 |
| | $200,000 |

(Memorandum entry)

2.   Special-special assessment bonds were sold at par in the amount of $135,000. These bonds will be paid from the deferred assessments.

3.   Assessments were levied and the city's share of project costs was accrued.

4.   The city paid over its share of the estimated cost.

5.   Assessments of $13,000 were collected.

6.   Materials estimated to cost $92,000 were ordered.

7.   The Tact Company was paid $3,000 in surveying fees.

8.   The materials ordered (6) were received. The actual cost was $92,500, and the invoice was approved for payment.

9.   A bill for $4,500 was received from the Petri Construction Company covering rental charges for equipment and was approved for payment.

10.   Payrolls paid during the year amounted to $67,000.

11.   Judgments for $10,000 on account of condemnation of property were awarded and paid.

12.   Interest on bonds to the amount of $3,000 became due.

13.   Vouchers payable amounting to $94,000 were paid.

14.   Uncollected current assessments became delinquent.

15.   Interest accrued on deferred assessments amounted to $3,500.

Required:
(a)   Prepare all journal entries, exclusive of closing entries.
(b)   Post to "T" accounts.
(c)   Prepare a balance sheet as of December 31, 19X4.

(d)   Prepare the entries that would have been made to reflect items 1-3 above if a formal authorization entry was made.

**Problem 9-3. Part II.**   Transactions taking place in 19X5 were as follows:

16.   Another special assessment installment became due.
17.   Collections were made as follows:

| | |
|---|---:|
| 19X4 installments | $ 1,200 |
| Current installments | 10,500 |
| Interest collected | 3,300 |

18.   Interest due on bonds was paid.
19.   Uncollected current assessments became delinquent.
20.   Payrolls amounted to $5,000 and were paid.
21.   Interest on bonds to the amount of $4,000 became due.
22.   Interest on assessments to the amount of $4,500 accrued.
23.   The cost of selling properties for unpaid special assessments was $65, which was paid out of construction cash.
24.   Property A, on which no assessments had been paid, was sold. Total unpaid special assessments on this parcel of property amounted to $1,200, accumulated interest was $70, and the cost of selling the property was $20. The property was sold for $1,290.
25.   Properties E and L, on which no assessments had been paid, were offered for sale. The price offered was not satisfactory, and the governmental unit bid them in. Unpaid assessments, interest, and cost of holding the sale of these properties were as follows:

| Property | Unpaid Assessments | Interest | Cost of Holding Sale |
|:---:|:---:|:---:|:---:|
| E | $2,000 | $180 | $25 |
| L | 2,200 | 135 | 20 |

26.   Property E was redeemed by the owner, who paid, in addition to all other interest and charges due, interest of $40.
27.   Bonds to the amount of $15,000 were called in and retired, and interest of $500 due thereon was paid.
28.   Property L was taken over by the city and is to be used for recreation purposes. The city paid the full amount of the assessment certificate out of the General Fund.

Required:
(a)   Prepare all journal entries, including closing entries.
(b)   Post to "T" accounts.
(c)   Prepare a Balance Sheet as of December 31, 19X5.
(d)   Prepare a statement analyzing the changes in the Fund Balance account(s) for the two years ended December 31, 19X5.

**Problem 9-4.**   From the information given in Problem 9-3, Parts I and II:
(a)   Prepare a columnar worksheet to reflect the transactions of the Special Assessment Fund for the two years ended December 31, 19X5. Your worksheet headings should be those shown on p. 370.

| Columns | Heading |
|---------|---------|
| 1-2 | 19X4 Transactions |
| 3-4 | Trial Balance, 12/31/19X4 |
| 5-6 | 19X5 Transactions |
| 7-8 | Pre-closing Trial Balance, 12/31/19X5 |
| 9-10 | Closing Entries, 12/31/19X5 |
| 11-12 | Post-closing Trial Balance, 12/31/19X5 |

(b)   Prepare a Balance Sheet as of December 31, 19X5. (Omit if Problem 9-3, Parts I and II, is also assigned.)

(c)   Prepare a statement analyzing the changes in the Fund Balance account(s) for the two years ended December 31, 19X5. (Omit if Problem 9-3, Parts I and II, is also assigned.)

**Problem 9-5.**   You were engaged as auditor of the City of Druid as of July 1, 19X4. You found the following accounts, among others, in the General Fund for the fiscal year ending June 30, 19X4:

*Special Cash*

| Date | Reference | Dr. | Cr. | Balance |
|------|-----------|-----|-----|---------|
| 8/1/X3...................... | CR 58 | 301,000 | | 301,000 |
| 9/1/X3...................... | CR 60 | 80,000 | | 381,000 |
| 12/1/X3..................... | CD 41 | | 185,000 | 196,000 |
| 2/1/X4...................... | CD 45 | | 9,000 | 187,000 |
| 6/1/X4...................... | CR 64 | 50,500 | | 237,500 |
| 6/30/X4.................... | CD 65 | | 1.67,000 | 70,500 |

*Bonds Payable*

| Date | Reference | Dr. | Cr. | Balance |
|------|-----------|-----|-----|---------|
| 8/1/X3...................... | CR 58 | | 300,000 | 300,000 |
| 6/1/X4...................... | CR 64 | | 50,000 | 350,000 |

*Construction in Progress—Main Street Improvement Project*

| Date | Reference | Dr. | Cr. | Balance |
|------|-----------|-----|-----|---------|
| 12/1/X3..................... | CD 41 | 185,000 | | 185,000 |
| 6/30/X4.................... | CD 65 | 167,000 | | 352,000 |

*Interest Expense*

| Date | Reference | Dr. | Cr. | Balance |
|------|-----------|-----|-----|---------|
| 2/1/X4...................... | CD 45 | 9,000 | | 9,000 |
| 6/1/X4...................... | CR 64 | | 500 | 8,500 |

*Assessment Income*

| Date | Reference | Dr. | Cr. | Balance |
|------|-----------|-----|-----|---------|
| 9/1/X3..................... | CR 60 | | 80,000 | 80,000 |

*Premium on Bonds*

| Date | Reference | Dr. | Cr. | Balance |
|------|-----------|-----|-----|---------|
| 8/1/X4.................... | CR 58 | | 1,000 | 1,000 |

The accounts resulted from the project described below:

The City Council authorized the Main Street Improvement Project and a bond issue of $350,000 to permit deferral of assessment payments. According to the terms of the authorization the property owners were to be assessed 80 percent of the estimated cost of construction and the balance was made available by the City during October 19X3. On September 1, 1973 the first of five equal annual assessment installments was collected in full from the property owners. The deferred assessments were to bear interest at 8 percent from September 1, 19X3.

The project was expected to be completed by October 31, 19X4.

Required:

(a)   Prepare a Special Assessment Fund worksheet in which you record the transactions of the Main Street Improvement Project as they should have been made by the City. A formal authorization entry should not be made; and the bond premium should be written off to Fund Balance—Interest. Show the closing entries at June 30, 19X4, and show the account balances at that date. (Formal journal entries are not required.)

(b)   Prepare the formal journal entries that should be made to correct the General Fund accounts and to record properly therein the results of transactions of the Main Street Improvement Project.

(c)   Prepare a columnar Balance Sheet at June 30, 19X4, showing the balances of the various "funds" within the Special Assessment Fund.

(d)   Prepare a columnar Analysis of Changes in Fund Balance(s) for the year ended June 30, 19X4.

(AICPA, adapted)

**Problem 9-6. Part I.**   The following is a trial balance of the Special Assessment Fund of the City of Victorville as of January 1, 19X5.

| | | |
|---|---|---|
| Assessments Receivable-Deferred | $450,000 | |
| City's Share of Cost | 80,000 | |
| Bonds Payable | | $530,000 |
| | $530,000 | $530,000 |

Special assessments were levied after all construction had been completed. The special assessments and the city's share of cost are payable in ten equal installments beginning in 19X5. Collections from these sources are to be used to retire the serial bonds outstanding, which mature at a rate of $53,000 annually. Interest charged on deferred special assessments is to be used to pay bond interest.

The following transactions took place during 19X5:
1. The first installment became current.
2. Interest accrued on assessments amounted to $13,500.
3. Collections of current assessments amounted to $44,000.
4. The city's 19X5 installment was paid from the General Fund.
5. Collections of interest amounted to $13,400.
6. Bonds in the amount of $53,000 were retired.
7. Interest paid on bonds amounted to $13,000.
8. Uncollected current assessments became delinquent.

The following transactions took place during the years 19X6 to 19Y2, inclusive:
9. The installments for 19X6–19Y2 became current.
10. Interest becoming receivable on assessments during this period amounted to $108,850.
11. Collections during this period were as follows:

| | |
|---|---:|
| Current assessments | $296,000 |
| Interest on assessments | 103,000 |
| City's installments | 56,000 |
| Delinquent assessments | 2,000 |

12. Payments were made as follows during these seven years:

| | |
|---|---:|
| Bonds | 352,000 |
| Interest | 99,000 |

13. The uncollected current assessments became delinquent.
14. Cash for interest payments to the amount of $75 was used to pay the county for the cost of holding the sale of delinquent properties.
15. At the end of 19Y2, the properties listed below, on which the last two (19Y1 and 19Y2) installments had not been paid, were put up for sale. Property L was sold to an individual for $2,745, and properties M and N were bid in for this fund.

| | Unpaid Assessments | Accrued Interest | Cost of Sale | Total |
|---|---:|---:|---:|---:|
| L .............. | $2,500 | $220 | $25 | $2,745 |
| M.............. | 3,000 | 260 | 25 | 3,285 |
| N .............. | 2,300 | 210 | 25 | 2,535 |

The following transactions took place during 19Y3:
16. The installment for this year became current.
17. Interest accrued on assessments amounted to $3,000.

18.  Collections for this fund during the year were as follows:

| | |
|---|---|
| 19Y3 installment | $42,000 |
| Delinquent assessments | 10,000 |
| Interest on assessments | 5,200 |
| City's installment | 8,000 |

19.  Bonds retired this year amounted to $59,000.
20.  Interest expenses on bonds paid amounted to $6,200.
21.  Property M was redeemed by the owner, who was charged additional interest of $15.
22.  The uncollected portion of the 19Y3 installment became delinquent.
The following transactions took place during 19Y4:
23.  The final installment became current.
24.  Interest receivable on assessments amounted to $2,400.
25.  Property N was transferred to the General Fixed Assets of the city, and this fund was reimbursed from the General Fund for the amount of the special assessment sale certificate.
26.  Collections from assessments were as follows:

| | |
|---|---|
| 19Y4 installment | $42,050 |
| City's installment | 8,000 |

27.  Cash for interest payments of $40 was used to pay the county for holding a delinquent assessment sale.
28.  Property P, with a total unpaid assessment of $1,300, plus $200 interest (previously accrued) and $40 for cost of sale, was sold for $1,540.
29.  All delinquent installments were collected.
30.  All interest receivable was collected.
31.  The remaining bonds were retired.
32.  Interest paid on bonds amounted to $1,600.
33.  The excess cash remaining was rebated and the fund was terminated.
Required:
Prepare a columnar worksheet to reflect the transactions affecting the Special Assessment Fund of the City of Victorville. Use a "debits over credits" worksheet with the following headings:

| Columns | Heading |
|---|---|
| 1 | Trial Balance, 1/1/19X5 |
| 2–3 | 19X5 Transaction and Closing Entries |
| 4 | Trial Balance, 12/31/19X5 |
| 5–6 | 19X6–Y2 Summary Transactions and Closing Entries |
| 7 | Trial Balance, 12/31/19Y2 |
| 8–9 | 19Y3 Transactions and Closing Entries |
| 10 | Trial Balance, 12/31/19Y3 |
| 11–12 | 19Y4 Transactions and Closing Entries |
| Optional 13 | Trial Balance, 12/31/19Y4 |

**Problem 9-6. Part II.** Prepare the following financial statements for the Special Assessment Fund of the City of Victorville in columnar form:
(a) A Comparative Balance Sheet, setting forth the balances as of December 31, 19X4, 19X5, 19Y2, 19Y3 and 19Y4.
(b) A Comparative Analysis of Changes in Fund Balance-Interest, with column headings as follows:

| Year Ended December 31, 19X5 | Seven (7) Years Ended December 31, 19Y2 | Year Ended December 31, 19Y3 | Year Ended December 31, 19Y4 |
| --- | --- | --- | --- |

**Problem 9-7.** The following transactions took place in the City of Dixonville during 19A:
1. The legislative body authorized the widening of a street at an estimated cost of $450,000.
2. Bonds to the amount of $300,000 were authorized and were sold at a discount of $1,300.
3. The city agreed to contribute $120,000 as its share of the estimated cost; the remainder was assessed against property owners. The assessments were made payable in installments, and certain series of bonds were to be paid from certain installments and no others. Assessment installments and bonds to be retired therefrom were as follows:

| Nos. | Due Date | Amount of Installment | Amount of Bonds to Be Retired |
| --- | --- | --- | --- |
| 1 | 19A | $30,000 | – |
| 2–9 | 19B-I | 33,000 | $33,000 |
| 10 | 19J | 36,000 | 36,000 |

4. A contract was entered into with the Fane Construction Company for the construction of the project at a cost of $360,000.
5. Supervisory engineering expenses amounting to $10,000 were paid.
6. The city's contribution was received in full; and assessments of $27,000 were received.
7. The remainder of the first installment became delinquent.
8. Judgments to the amount of $120,000 were awarded for property condemned.
9. A bill for $100,000 was received from the Fane Construction Company.
10. Payments were made as follows:

| | |
| --- | --- |
| Judgments payable | $120,000 |
| Fane Construction Company | 100,000 |

11. and 12. Interest of $8,200 became receivable; of this amount $7,500 was collected.
13. and 14. Interest of $6,100 became payable; of this amount $4,000 was paid.

The transactions taking place in 19B were as follows:

15. Delinquent assessments of $1,500 were collected.
16. A bill was received from the Fane Construction Company for the remaining amount due on the contract.
17. Interest payable at the close of the last fiscal year was paid.
18. and 19. Interest of $9,000 became receivable during this year; interest receivable collected amounted to $8,900.
20. Assessments receivable coming due during 19B were reclassified accordingly.
21 and 22. Interest of $7,100 became payable; of this amount $3,550 was paid.
23. and 24. Current assessments amounting to $32,000 were collected; the remaining part of the second installment became delinquent.
25. The Fane Construction Company was paid the full amount of the contract, except for $50,000 which was retained pending final approval of the project.
26. Collections (transaction 23) were applied to the payment of bonds.

The transactions taking place in 19C were as follows:

27. Interest payable at the close of 19B was paid.
28. The city agreed to contribute $10,000 for the purpose of eliminating the deficit.
29. The remaining part of the deficit was to be eliminated through the levy of supplemental assessments. Supplemental assessments were subsequently levied and were made payable in three equal annual installments, the first becoming due promptly.
30. Notes were issued to cover the last two annual installments of the supplemental assessments.
31. Assessments receivable coming due in 19C were reclassified as current.
32. Assessments (not supplemental) were collected as follows:

| | |
|---|---:|
| From 1st installment | $   750 |
| From 2nd installment | 750 |
| From 3rd installment | 32,250 |

33. The proceeds, in so far as applicable, were used to retire bonds.
34. The uncollected portion of the third installment was set up as delinquent.
35. and 36. Interest on assessments to the amount of $7,900 became receivable during this year; interest receivable collected amounted to $7,750.
37. and 38. Interest on bonds to the amount of $6,240 became payable; of this amount $3,120 was paid.
39. The first installment of the supplemental assessment was collected in full, except for $800 which is now delinquent.
40. The city paid its contribution.
41. Interest on supplemental assessments collected was $464; an additional $16 was receivable at December 31, 19C.
42. The project was found to be satisfactory and the Fane Construction Company was paid the amount due it. The additional cash necessary for this purpose was borrowed from the General Fund.
43. Interest on notes to the amount of $360 was paid.

Required:

(a) Prepare a columnar worksheet to reflect the transactions of the Dixonville Special Assessment Fund for the three years ending December 31, 19C. The columnar heading of the worksheet should be as shown on p. 376.

| Columns | Heading |
|---------|---------|
| 1–2 | 19A Transaction and Closing Entries |
| 3–4 | Trial Balance, 12/31/19A |
| 5–6 | 19B Transaction and Closing Entries |
| 7–8 | Trial Balance, 12/31/19B |
| 9–10 | 19C Transaction and Closing Entries |
| 11–12 | Trial Balance, 12/31/19C |

(b)   Prepare an Analysis of Changes in Fund Balance(s) for the three years ended December 31, 19C. The statement should be prepared in such manner that the changes occurring each year are readily observable, as is the Fund Balance available at the end of 19A, 19B, and 19C, and should include both reserved and unreserved amounts.

**Problem 9-8. Part I.**   The City of Poseyton voted a bond issue for the purpose of constructing a modern sewer system in a section of the city. The cost is to be borne by general revenues of the city and by assessments levied against properties in the area of the improvement.

The following transactions and events related to this project occurred during 19X4:

1.   February 1-The city engineer submitted to the city council an estimate of the construction cost of the project, showing a total of $445,000. Preliminary planning costs were expected to amount to $15,000. The council approved the estimate and project, subject to voter approval of the necessary bond issue.

2.   April 1-A Ten year 6 percent special-general bond issue of $460,000 was approved by the voters of the city.

3.   April 10-A contract covering preliminary planning (estimated to cost $15,000) was entered into by the project trustees.

4.   April 15-The assessment roll was certified on the basis of $415,000, due in ten equal annual installments starting May 1, 19X5. Interest at 6 percent per annum from May 1, 19X4 is to be paid on each installment due date, based on the total assessment outstanding. Interest is charged at 10 percent per annum on delinquent assessments and interest receivable.

5.   April 30-The preliminary plans were completed and an invoice of $13,700 was received from the planning contractor (in full). The trustees borrowed $25,000 from the General Fund of the city to pay this and other costs. The invoice was paid on May 5.

6.   May 20-A contract for construction was entered into at a price of $420,000, subject to certain possible future adjustments.

7.   June 1-$200,000 of the authorized bonds were sold at 101. The entire issue was dated June 1, 19X4, with interest payable December 1 and June 1 each year. The bonds mature at the rate of $46,000 per year, starting June 1, 19X5.

8.   July 31-A partial payment of $26,100 was made to the contractor, which amount was 90 percent of the amount due based on percentage-of-completion. The balance is being held pending project completion, state inspection, and acceptance by the trustees. The loan from the General Fund was repaid.

9.   November 1-The remaining bonds were sold at 98 and accrued interest.

10.   August 1 to December 31-Payments to the contractor amounted to $284,400, 10 percent of the amount due having been withheld pending completion. Costs of $4,210 incurred in connection with administering the construction project were paid

during the period. The bond interest was paid at due date. The city paid $2,300 on its part of the cost of the project.

Required:

Prepare the following:

(a) A columnar worksheet reflecting the transactions of the Special Revenue Fund of the City of Poseyton during the year ended December 31, 19X4. The worksheet should be headed as follows:

| 19X4 Transactions | | Closing Entries 12/31/19X4 | | Post-closing Trial Balance 12/31/19X4 | |
|---|---|---|---|---|---|
| Dr. | Cr. | Dr. | Cr. | Dr. | Cr. |

Assume that (1) a formal project authorization entry is made in which the Appropriations account is credited. Worksheet entries should be keyed to the numbered items in the problem; a net bond premium is to be closed at year end to Fund Balance-Interest, but a net discount should be closed to Fund Balance-Construction.

(b) A columnar Balance Sheet at December 31, 19X4, presenting the assets, liabilities, and balances attributable to each "fund" within the Special Assessment Fund.

(c) A columnar Analysis of Changes in Fund Balance(s) for the year ended December 31, 19X4.

(AICPA, adapted)

**Problem 9-8. Part II.** The following transactions and events affected the Special Assessment Fund of the City of Poseyton during 19X5:

11. January 2-The assessment installment maturing in 19X5 was reclassified as current.

12. March 31-The project was completed and the contractor submitted a final invoice for $90,000, including the cost of modifications requested and agreed to by the trustees.

13. April 12-The contractor was paid $81,000 on the above invoice, the balance being withheld pending state inspection of the construction work and acceptance of the project by the trustees.

14. April 14-Landscaping and other costs not included within the construction contract were paid, $15,000.

15. April 18-A construction deficiency was discovered during the inspection. At the request of the contractor, who was now involved in an out-of-state project, the deficiency was repaired by Public Works Department employees at a cost of $4,000. The Public Works Department is financed through the General Fund.

16. April 28-The amount necessary to cover the excess construction costs to be borne by the city was appropriated from the General Fund. This amount, less the $4,000 due to the General Fund from the Special Assessment Fund, was paid to the Special Assessment Fund.

17. April 29-The amount due the contractor was paid.

18. May 1-December 30-Collections were made as follows: assessments, $47,000, including $8,000 from one person who paid the entire assessment levied against his property; interest was collected only from those property owners also paying their assessments. No additional interest was charged those paying by December 30.

19.  June 1-The bond principal and interest due was paid.

20.  December 1-The bond interest due was paid.

21.  December 31-Unpaid current assessments and interest due as of May 1 were declared delinquent and interest at 10 percent per annum from May 1 was accrued thereon.

Required:

Prepare the following:

(a)  A columnar worksheet reflecting the transactions of the Special Revenue Fund of the City of Poseyton for the year ended December 31, 19X5. The worksheet should be headed as follows:

| *Trial Balance 12/31/19X4* | | *19X5 Transactions* | | *Closing Entries 12/31/19X5* | | *Post-closing Trial Balance 12/31/19X5* | |
|---|---|---|---|---|---|---|---|
| *Dr.* | *Cr.* | *Dr.* | *Cr.* | *Dr.* | *Cr.* | *Dr.* | *Cr.* |

Alternatively, you may continue using the worksheet prepared for Part I of this problem, adding the columns and headings required.

(b)  A Balance Sheet at December 31, 19X5, with comparative 19X4 year end balances.

(c)  An Analysis of Changes in Fund Balance(s) for the two years ended December 31, 19X5. The beginning balance, changes, and ending balance of each year should be clearly presented within the statement.

# 10

# Debt Service Funds

The purpose of Debt Service Funds is "to account for the payment of interest and principal on long-term debt other than special assessment and revenue bonds."[1] The responsibility of providing for the retirement of long-term, general obligation debt is ordinarily indicated by the terms of the indenture or other contract by which the debt is created. (The term "general obligation" indicates that the "full faith and credit" of the governmental unit has been pledged to the repayment of the debt.) Even when the governmental unit so obligates itself, the primary responsibility for repayment may be assigned to resources other than taxes. For example, when improvements are to be paid for by owners of benefited property, bonds issued to finance the improvements are expected to be repaid by the assessments made against the property benefited and the accounting for the debt and its repayment is done through the Special Assessment Fund (Chapter 9). Similarly, when general obligation bonds are issued for the benefit of a public enterprise, the public enterprise frequently has full or partial responsibility for repayment out of revenues. If the enterprise has full or primary responsibility for payment of the obligation, the accounting therefor should be done in the Enterprise Fund (Chapter 14) and a Debt Service Fund is not necessary.

[1] *GAAFR, op. cit.,* p. 7.

### Types of Long-Term Debt

Classified on the basis of the formality of the document representing the liability, there are three kinds of long-term debt: bonds, notes, and time warrants.

A *bond* is a written promise, ordinarily signed by two officials of the governmental unit and bearing its seal, to pay a specified principal sum at a specified future date, usually with interest at a specified rate. *Term bonds* are those for which all of the principal is payable at the specified maturity date. *Serial bonds*, which are by far the most widely used type, provide for periodic maturities ranging up to the maximum period permitted by law in the respective states. Specific arrangements of maturities may vary widely. Regular serial bonds are repayable in equal annual installments over the life of the issue. In some cases the beginning of the repayment series is deferred a specified number of years in the future, after which equal annual installments are to be paid. In some cases the indenture provides for increasing amounts of annual payments computed so that the total annual payment of interest and principal is a constant sum over the life of the issue. Other arrangements may be set up by the bond indenture.

*Notes* are less formal documents indicating an obligation to repay borrowed funds. *General obligation notes* that are to be repaid within one year of the date of issue are normally carried as liabilities of the General Fund, while those that are to be repaid over a longer period of time justify the creation of related Debt Service Funds.

*Warrants* are orders by authorized legislative or executive officials upon the treasurer of the governmental unit directing the treasurer to pay a specified sum to order or bearer. If these warrants are to be paid more than one year after the date of issue, they also justify the Debt Service Fund treatment. Arrangements of maturity dates of notes and warrants may have substantial diversity; Debt Service Funds for notes or warrants are not discussed separately below because the accounting for them is similar to that for bonds.

### Timing of Debt Service Payments

The pattern of payment of debt service for long-term debt is based on a major objective of state and local government finance: So that the drain on each year's resources will be relatively constant, annual debt service requirements should not fluctuate materially. This objective has implications for the payment of interest and debt retirement. Interest expense is an annual cost and is directly proportional to the principal amount of debt outstanding. Interest costs and regular serial bonds therefore meet the objective quite well. On the other hand, a term maturity twenty years in the future requires the governmental unit to accumulate the amount of principal due twenty years hence by means of annual contributions that, together with earnings on the invested contributions, will equal the principal amount. The operation of a Debt Service Fund for a term issue of bonds will therefore be substantially different from the operation of a Fund used to meet the debt service requirements of a serial issue.

## Sources of Financing

The money for repayment of long-term debt may come from a number of sources with varying legal restrictions. The typical source is property taxes. A special tax rate may be assessed for a single bond issue, or a total annual rate may be used with a proration of the proceeds to several debt issues. There is a growing tendency for legislative bodies to earmark a tax for a specified purpose, with a proviso that the proceeds may be used either for current operating expenses or to repay debt that has been created to finance a specified purpose. The total proceeds of the tax would in such a case go into a Special Revenue Fund; the portion of the proceeds allocated to debt repayment would be transferred to a Debt Service Fund (and a portion might be transferred to a Capital Projects Fund). Even in cases where the law does not require a Debt Service Fund,

> The latter [Debt Service] fund is necessary to maintain the separate identity and character of general debt operations by governmental units and to permit the proper disclosure thereof in financial statements and reports.[2]

Still another method of payment of debt is required by a bond indenture or other contract that specifies that the debt shall be repaid out of "the first revenues accruing to the treasury." The effect of such an agreement is to cause the government to contribute the necessary amounts to the Debt Service Fund from the General Fund; the obligation has first call on the revenues of the General Fund.

When a term issue is to be repaid by a fund accumulating to the par or face amount of the issue at date of maturity, the assets of the fund during its lifetime will be invested in income-producing securities. The income from these securities constitutes still another form of revenue for the Debt Service Fund. In such cases the contract with the bond holders ordinarily requires equal annual revenues for the Fund from contributions or from special tax levies of the same annual amount. Since the assets of the Fund will increase annually from the contributions or special tax levy and from the earnings on the invested assets, it is necessary to estimate the rate at which Fund assets will earn and to use the estimated rate in calculating the amount of the annual contribution necessary to accumulate the required maturity value of the liability.

Finally, maturing bonds may be refunded, that is, they may be retired by either (1) exchanging new bonds for old ones or (2) selling a new bond issue

---

[2] *GAAFR, op. cit.*, p. 37.

and using the proceeds to retire an old issue. The new bond issue constitutes the financing source in refunding transactions.

### Debt Service Fund for a Refunding Issue

A Debt Service Fund is not needed where new bonds are simply exchanged for old ones and no cash changes hands. The only accounting requirement in this case is that the General Long-Term Debt group of accounts (Chapter 11) be adjusted to reflect the retirement of the old bonds and issuance of the new ones.

A Debt Service Fund is needed, however, if the new bonds are sold and the proceeds are used to retire the maturing issue. The Debt Serivce Fund may be in existence only for a few moments in this situation, as its function is merely to record the receipt of the new issue proceeds and their use to retire the old issue. Assuming that a $1,000,000 bond issue was sold at par to refund an old bond issue in that amount, the Debt Service Fund entries would be:

| | | |
|---|---|---|
| Cash .................................. | 1,000,000 | |
|     Revenues........................... | | 1,000,000 |
|     To record receipt of the proceeds from sale of the new issue. | | |
| Expenditures ........................... | 1,000,000 | |
|     Cash ............................. | | 1,000,000 |
|     To record expenditure of the proceeds to retire the old issue. | | |
| Revenues............................... | 1,000,000 | |
|     Expenditures ...................... | | 1,000,000 |
|     To close the accounts of the Debt Service Fund for the bonds retired and to abolish the fund. | | |

Alternatively, since the Debt Service Fund serves merely as a refunding conduit, some accountants prefer to make the following "self-closing" entries in refunding situations:

| | | |
|---|---|---|
| Cash ................................. | 1,000,000 | |
|     Fund Balance (or Appropriations) ....... | | 1,000,000 |
|     To record receipt of the proceeds from sale of the new (refunding) bond issue. | | |
| Fund Balance (or Appropriations) .......... | 1,000,000 | |
|     Cash ............................. | | 1,000,000 |
|     To record the expenditure of the proceeds to retire the old issue. | | |

Again, the General Long-Term Debt group of accounts (Chapter 11) must be adjusted to reflect the new issue outstanding and the retirement of the old one.

## Debt Service Fund for a Serial Issue

To illustrate the operation of a Debt Service Fund for a serial issue we shall assume that a governmental unit issued 5 percent Flores Park Serial Bonds on January 1, 19X1, in the amount of one million dollars to finance the purchase and development of a park. The bond indenture calls for annual payments of $100,000 to retire the principal. The debt service requirements (principal and interest) are to be provided by a property tax levied for that specific purpose. The following journal entries record the transactions for the first year of operation of the Flores Park Debt Service Fund. They are summarized in the worksheet presented as Figure 10-1.

| | | | |
|---|---|---:|---:|
| (1) | Estimated Revenues | 155,000 | |
| | Appropriations | | 150,000 |
| | Fund Balance | | 5,000 |
| | To record the budget for the fund for the fiscal year. | | |
| (2) | Taxes Receivable—Current | 156,000 | |
| | Estimated Uncollectible Current Taxes | | 1,000 |
| | Revenues | | 155,000 |
| | To record the taxes levied for the year. | | |
| (3) | Cash | 151,000 | |
| | Taxes Receivable—Current | | 151,000 |
| | To record collection of taxes for the year. | | |
| (4) | Expenditures | 100,000 | |
| | Matured Bonds Payable | | 100,000 |
| | To record the fund's liability for payment of the first annual serial maturity. | | |
| (5) | Expenditures | 50,000 | |
| | Matured Interest Payable | | 50,000 |
| | To record the accrual of interest payable at the end of the year. | | |
| (6) | Matured Bonds Payable | 100,000 | |
| | Matured Interest Payable | 50,000 | |
| | Cash | | 150,000 |
| | To record payment of liabilities. | | |
| (7) | Taxes Receivable—Delinquent | 5,000 | |
| | Estimated Uncollectible Current Taxes | 1,000 | |
| | Taxes Receivable—Current | | 5,000 |
| | Estimated Uncollectible Delinquent Taxes | | 1,000 |
| | To record the transfer of taxes receivable and the related estimated uncollectible taxes from current to delinquent status. | | |

## Figure 10-1

### A GOVERNMENTAL UNIT
#### Debt Service Fund—Flores Park Serial Bonds
#### Summary of Accounting Operations
#### For the Year Ended December 31, 19X1

| | 19X1 Transactions | | Closing Entries | | Post-closing Trial Balance December 31, 19X1 | |
|---|---|---|---|---|---|---|
| | Dr. | Cr. | Dr. | Cr. | Dr. | Cr. |
| Estimated Revenues | 155,000(1) | | | 155,000(C1) | | |
| Appropriations | | 150,000(1) | 150,000(C2) | | | |
| Fund Balance | | 5,000(1) | | | | 5,000 |
| Taxes Receivable—Current | 156,000(2) | 151,000(3) | | | | |
| | | 5,000(7) | | | | |
| Estimated Uncollectible Current Taxes | 1,000(7) | 1,000(2) | | | | |
| Revenues | | 155,000(2) | 155,000(C1) | | | |
| Cash | 151,000(3) | 150,000(6) | | | 1,000 | |
| | 100,000(4) | | | | | |
| | 50,000(5) | | | | | |
| Expenditures | 150,000(6) | | | 150,000(C2) | | |

384

| | | |
|---|---|---|
| Matured Bonds Payable | 100,000(6) | 100,000(4) |
| Matured Interest Payable | 50,000(6) | 50,000(5) |
| Taxes Receivable —Delinquent | 5,000(7) | |
| Estimated Uncollectible Delinquent Taxes | 1,000(7) | |

5,000

6,000   6,000

1,000

6,000

*Closing Entries*

(C1)   Revenues ............................   155,000
          Estimated Revenues ...............               155,000
          To close the revenue accounts.


(C2)   Appropriations........................   150,000
          Expenditures......................               150,000
          To close the expenditure accounts.


It should be emphasized that the operations of the Debt Service Fund—Flores Park Serial Bonds—could have been financed by any one or a combination of the revenue sources described earlier in this chapter.


### Sinking Fund Requirements

Term bonds ordinarily are repaid from a fund accumulated over the life of the bonds by means of annual additions to the fund and by earnings of the fund assets. Figure 10-2, "Schedule of Sinking Fund Requirements," has been prepared for the City Hall bonds of A Governmental Unit. These are 5 1/2 percent, 20-year term bonds issued January 1, 19X0. They are to be repaid out of "the first revenues accruing to the Treasury." The latter terminology indicates that the source of revenues for the Debt Service Fund for these bonds will be the General Fund of A Governmental Unit.

The first payment to the sinking fund is scheduled for the end of year 1. A similar payment will be made at the end of each succeeding year until, when the twentieth payment has been made, the fund is supposed to equal one million dollars. An assumed earnings rate of 6 percent has been used in the development of Figure 10-2. The amount of the required annual additions was determined by selecting from a table the amount of an ordinary annuity of one dollar per period at 6 percent for twenty periods. This amount, $36.7855912, is the amount to which an annual annuity of one dollar would accumulate in twenty years at six percent. Since the desired amount to be accumulated is one million dollars, it was necessary to divide the one million dollars by $36.7855912 to obtain the $27,185 that is the amount of the required annual additions. As indicated in the schedule, the last addition is somewhat less than the preceding ones because of rounding errors. In any event, the final payment in 19Y9 will be in the amount that brings the sinking fund resources to $1,000,000, the amount required to retire the term bonds.

The schedule of sinking fund requirements provides the amounts of the budgetary requirements for the Debt Service Fund for the duration of the Fund, provided the accumulation process proceeds as planned or departs from the plan by immaterial amounts. The required fund balance at the end of each year provides a standard against which the actual accumulation may be compared. If the actual accumulation falls short or exceeds the required fund

Figure 10-2

SCHEDULE OF SINKING FUND REQUIREMENTS
(Assuming an Annual Earnings Rate of 6 Percent)

| Year | Required Annual Additions | Required Fund Earnings | Required Fund Increases | Required Fund Balances |
|------|---------------------------|------------------------|-------------------------|------------------------|
| 1 (19X0) | $ 27,185 | | $ 27,185 | $ 27,185 |
| 2 (19X1) | 27,185 | $ 1,631 | 28,816 | 56,001 |
| 3 (19X2) | 27,185 | 3,360 | 30,545 | 86,546 |
| 4 (19X3) | 27,185 | 5,193 | 32,378 | 118,924 |
| 5 (19X4) | 27,185 | 7,135 | 34,320 | 153,244 |
| 6 (19X5) | 27,185 | 9,195 | 36,380 | 189,624 |
| 7 (19X6) | 27,185 | 11,377 | 38,562 | 228,186 |
| 8 (19X7) | 27,185 | 13,691 | 40,876 | 269,062 |
| 9 (19X8) | 27,185 | 16,144 | 43,329 | 312,391 |
| 10 (19X9) | 27,185 | 18,743 | 45,928 | 358,319 |
| 11 (19Y0) | 27,185 | 21,499 | 48,684 | 407,003 |
| 12 (19Y1) | 27,185 | 24,420 | 51,605 | 458,608 |
| 13 (19Y2) | 27,185 | 27,516 | 54,701 | 513,309 |
| 14 (19Y3) | 27,185 | 30,799 | 57,984 | 571,293 |
| 15 (19Y4) | 27,185 | 34,278 | 61,463 | 632,756 |
| 16 (19Y5) | 27,185 | 37,965 | 65,150 | 697,906 |
| 17 (19Y6) | 27,185 | 41,874 | 69,059 | 766,965 |
| 18 (19Y7) | 27,185 | 46,018 | 73,203 | 840,168 |
| 19 (19Y8) | 27,185 | 50,410 | 77,595 | 917,763 |
| 20 (19Y9) | 27,171* | 55,066 | 82,237 | 1,000,000 |
| | $543,686 | $456,314 | $1,000,000 | $1,000,000 |

*The last year's addition needs to be only $27,171 because of rounding errors.

balances by substantial amounts, a new schedule of sinking fund requirements should be computed by starting from the actual accumulation and computing the annual additions and fund earnings required to produce one million dollars by the end of the twentieth year. The calculation of the new schedule may be based on an altered expected annual earnings rate.

Reasons for differences between the actual and planned accumulation of a sinking fund are many. Contributions or other revenues may fall short or exceed the planned, as may earnings on investments. Capital gains or losses on the disposition of investments are not contemplated in the accumulation schedule (except as they may be included in the expected earnings rate). Finally, a Debt Service Fund's resources may be used to purchase some of the bonds it is set up to service. If the bonds are kept alive in the Fund, with interest being paid to itself, the planned accumulation is not affected by the purchase. But both the National Committee on Governmental Accounting and the AICPA Committee on Governmental Accounting and Auditing have recommended that such bonds be retired unless legal or contractual provisions prohibit retirement.[3] Retirement takes out of use assets originally intended to be held to maturity of the debt issue and hence removes some of the Fund's earning capacity. This in turn requires recalculation of the accumulation schedule and, in many cases, an increase in the annual revenues other than earnings on investments that build the Fund Balance. The decision to retire or not to retire treasury bonds should be made by balancing the costs of continuing the bonds alive in the Fund with the cost of recalculating the accumulation schedule and changing the annual revenues required by the Fund.

### Debt Service Fund for a Term Issue

To illustrate the operation of a Debt Service Fund for a term issue we shall use the City Hall bonds described above and the schedule of sinking fund requirements presented in Figure 10-2. At the end of the first year of the Fund's operation, 19X0, there would have been a balance of $27,185 in both the Fund Balance and Cash accounts of the Debt Service Fund. These would have resulted from the first payment to the sinking fund of the required annual additions. The following journal entries (summarized in Figure 10-3) record the transactions of the City Hall Bonds Debt Service Fund for the second year of operation, 19X1:

| | | | |
|---|---|---|---|
| (1) | Required Additions ........................ | 82,585 | |
| | Required Earnings ........................ | 1,631 | |
| | Appropriations ........................ | | 55,400 |
| | Fund Balance ........................ | | 28,816 |
| | To record the budget for 19X1. | | |

The budget for 19X1 is as follows:

| | | |
|---|---|---|
| Required additions (to be provided by the General Fund) .................. | 82,585 | |
| Required earnings .................... | 1,631 | 84,216 |
| Appropriations: | | |
| Annual interest charges .............. | 55,000 | |
| Fiscal agent's fee .................... | 400 | 55,400 |
| Required Fund increase ................ | | 28,816 |

---

[3] *GAAFR, op. cit.*, p. 36.

The required additions figure is computed as follows:

| | |
|---|---:|
| Required addition to sinking fund ............... | 27,185 |
| Annual interest charges........................ | 55,000 |
| Fiscal agent's fee ............................ | 400 |
| | 82,585 |

The term "Required Additions" is the account title used by the National Committee on Governmental Accounting; in this set of circumstances perhaps a better term would be "Required Contributions." Note that the credit to Fund Balance is the amount of "Required Fund Increases" for Year 2 (19X1) in Figure 10-2.

| | | | |
|---|---|---:|---:|
| (2) | Investments............................. | 26,000 | |
| | Unamortized Premiums on Investments...... | 270 | |
| | Interest Receivable on Investments......... | 520 | |
| |     Unamortized Discounts on Investments .. | | 80 |
| |     Cash.............................. | | 26,710 |
| | To record the purchase of investments, together with the related premiums, accrued interest, and discounts. | | |

(Alternatively, (1) the interest receivable on investments at the time of purchase may be debited to Interest Earnings rather than Interest Receivable on Investments, (2) entry 5 omitted except in the year end adjustment process, after which it would be reversed; and (3) interest collections credited to Interest Earnings.)

| | | | |
|---|---|---:|---:|
| (3) | Due from General Fund .................. | 82,585 | |
| |     Revenues (or Additions or Contributions) ................... | | 82,585 |
| | To accrue the contribution from the General Fund. | | |
| (4) | Cash................................... | 82,585 | |
| |     Due From General Fund ............. | | 82,585 |
| | To record the receipt of the contribution from the General Fund. | | |
| (5) | Interest Receivable on Investments......... | 1,650 | |
| |     Interest Earnings (or Earnings) ........ | | 1,650 |
| | To record accrual of interest revenue on investments. | | |
| (6) | Cash................................... | 1,750 | |
| |     Interest Receivable on Investments...... | | 1,750 |
| | To record collection of interest receivable. | | |

Figure 10-3

## A GOVERNMENTAL UNIT
### Debt Service Fund—City Hall Term Bonds
### Summary of Accounting Operations
### for the Year Ended December 31, 19X1

| | Post-closing Trial Balance December 31, 19X0 | | 19X1 Transactions | | Closing Entries | | Post-closing Trial Balance December 31, 19X1 | |
|---|---|---|---|---|---|---|---|---|
| | Dr. | Cr. | Dr. | Cr. | Dr. | Cr. | Dr. | Cr. |
| Cash | 27,185 | | 82,585(4) 1,750(6) | 26,710(2) 55,000(9) 400(12) | | | 29,410 | |
| Fund Balance | | 27,185 | | 28,816(1) | | 9(C2) | | 56,010 |
| | 27,185 | 27,185 | | | | | | |
| Required Additions | | | 82,585(1) | | | 82,585(C1) | | |
| Required Earnings | | | 1,631(1) | | | 1,631(C2) | | |
| Appropriations | | | | 55,400(1) | 55,400(C3) | | | |
| Investments | | | 26,000(2) | | | | 26,000 | |
| Unamortized Premiums on Investments | | | 270(2) | 30(7) | | | 240 | |
| Interest Receivable on Investments | | | 520(2) 1,650(5) | 1,750(6) | | | 420 | |

| Account | | | |
|---|---|---|---|
| Unamortized Discounts on Investments | 20(7) | | 60 |
| Due from General Fund | 80(2) | | |
| Revenues (or Additions or Contributions) | 82,585(3) | 82,585(4) | 82,585(C1) |
| Interest Earnings (or Earnings) | 10(7) | 82,585(3) | 1,640(C2) |
| | | 1,650(5) | |
| Expenditures | 55,400(8) | | 55,400(C3) |
| Matured Interest Payable | 55,000(10) | 55,000(8) | |
| Vouchers Payable | 55,000(11) | 400(8) | |
| | 400(12) | 55,000(10) | |
| Cash with Fiscal Agent | 55,000(9) | 55,000(11) | |
| | | 56,070 | 56,070 |

(7)  Unamortized Discounts on Investments . . . . . .     20
     Interest Earnings . . . . . . . . . . . . . . . . . . . . . . . .     10
         Unamortized Premiums on Investments . .               30
     To record amortization of premiums and
     discounts on investments and the resultant
     correction of interest earnings.

(8)  Expenditures . . . . . . . . . . . . . . . . . . . . . . . . . . .  55,400
         Matured Interest Payable . . . . . . . . . . . . .            55,000
         Vouchers Payable . . . . . . . . . . . . . . . . . . .           400
     To record accrual of interest payments on the
     bonds and the payment of agent's fees.

(9)  Cash with Fiscal Agent . . . . . . . . . . . . . . . . . .  55,000
         Cash . . . . . . . . . . . . . . . . . . . . . . . . . . . . . .          55,000
     To record transfer of cash for payment of
     interest on the bonds to the fiscal agent.

(10) Matured Interest Payable . . . . . . . . . . . . . . . .  55,000
         Vouchers Payable . . . . . . . . . . . . . . . . . . .          55,000
     To record the vouchering of the interest lia-
     bility.

(11) Vouchers Payable . . . . . . . . . . . . . . . . . . . . . . .  55,000
         Cash with Fiscal Agent . . . . . . . . . . . . . . .          55,000
     To record payment of the interest by the
     fiscal agent.

(12) Vouchers Payable . . . . . . . . . . . . . . . . . . . . . . .     400
         Cash . . . . . . . . . . . . . . . . . . . . . . . . . . . . . .             400
     To record payment of the fiscal agent's fee.

(C1) Revenues (or Additions or Contributions) . . . .  82,585
         Required Additions . . . . . . . . . . . . . . . . . .          82,585
     To record the closing of the Revenues and
     Required Additions accounts.

(C2) Interest Earnings (or Earnings) . . . . . . . . . . . .   1,640
         Required Earnings . . . . . . . . . . . . . . . . . . .           1,631
         Fund Balance . . . . . . . . . . . . . . . . . . . . . . .               9
     To close the earnings and estimated earnings
     accounts and to transfer the difference to
     Fund Balance.

When the budget was recorded in journal entry number 1, the credit to Fund Balance was $28,816, the amount of the required fund increase for the second year according to Figure 10-2, "Schedule of Sinking Fund Requirements." The $9 difference between estimated and actual earnings for year 2 will produce a higher figure for Fund Balance at the end of year 2 than that required by the schedule of sinking fund requirements.

(C3)   Appropriations . . . . . . . . . . . . . . . . . . . . . . . . . .      55,400
        Expenditures. . . . . . . . . . . . . . . . . . . . . . . .                          55,400
        To close the estimated and actual expendi-
        tures accounts.

## Accrual of Interest Payable

The National Committee on Governmental Accounting does not recommend accrual of the year end balances of interest payable on term or serial
bonds unless the revenues to pay the interest have been accrued or received. If
a fund on a calendar-year basis paid the interest on its bonds as it fell due on,
let us say, October 31, 19X1, there is no question but that the Debt Service
Fund would be obligated, as of December 31, 19X1, for the interest for the
additional two months of 19X1. On the other hand, the 19X1 budget has provided for the payment of the interest expense falling due in the current year,
and the following year's budget will provide for payment of interest falling due
in 19X2. Since there is no way to show as assets, as of December 31, 19X1, the
revenues that will be used to pay the interest for the months of November and
December, 19X1, the accrual of those two months' interest would result in an
unwarranted deficit in a Debt Service Fund servicing serial bonds and an unwarranted shortage of the required fund balance in a fund accounting for the
service of term bonds. Thus, interest payable at year end is not normally recorded in the Debt Service Fund accounts, though it may be shown parenthetically or by footnote.

## Balance Sheet Prior to Maturity

Separate balance sheets for each of the Debt Service Funds of A Governmental Unit could be prepared, of course; but where a number of funds
exists it is customary to combine them as shown in Figure 10-4. The balance
sheet might include such additional assets as Cash with Fiscal Agents, Taxes
Receivable—Current, Tax Liens Receivable, and Interest and Penalties Receivable on Taxes. In addition, the unamortized premiums and discounts on
investments may be presented in the balance sheet rather than showing the
investment figure at net cost. Similarly, there may be such liability accounts as
Matured Bonds Payable and Matured Interest Payable. In the case of term
bonds it is essential that the actuarial requirement for the fund should be
footnoted in order that readers of the statement may compare the actual
achievement of the fund with the actuarial requirement.

If the number of Debt Service Funds exceeds five or six, the format of
Figure 10-4 becomes unwieldy and perhaps impossible to use. One option in
such cases is to present a summary Debt Service Funds balance sheet in which
the totals of each kind of account for all funds is presented. Then supporting

Figure 10-4

A GOVERNMENTAL UNIT
Debt Service Funds
Balance Sheet
December 31, 19X1

| | | *19Z0* | *19Y9* |
| | | *Flores* | *City* |
| *Assets* | *Total* | *Park* | *Hall* |
| --- | --- | --- | --- |
| Cash .............................. | $30,410 | $1,000 | $29,410 |
| Taxes receivable—delinquent (net of | | | |
|   estimated uncollectible taxes) ....... | 4,000 | 4,000* | |
| Investments ....................... | 26,180 | | 26,180† |
| Interest receivable on investments ..... | 420 | | 420 |
|    Total assets ..................... | $61,010 | $5,000 | $56,010 |

| *Liabilities and Fund Balances* | | | |
| --- | --- | --- | --- |
| Fund balances .................... | $61,010 | $5,000 | $56,010** |

* A "Combined Schedule of Delinquent Taxes by Funds" will be included in the annual report to provide an overview of the success of the collection of taxes on a government-wide basis. The net delinquent tax figure for cash fund should be referenced to and supported by it.

† A "Combined Schedule of Investments—All Funds" will be included in the annual report to provide complete information regarding individual investments (interest rates, maturity dates, par value and unamortized premiums and discounts) of each fund. The net investment figure should be referenced to and supported by it.

** The actuarial requirement is $56,001.

schedules may be prepared presenting each fund's share of each item presented in the summary balance sheet.

**Balance Sheet at Maturity**

The Balance Sheet of A Governmental Unit's City Hall Term Bonds Debt Service Fund at the date of maturity of the bonds, December 31, 19Y9, is presented in Figure 10-5. It presents two problems. In the first place, though most of the investments have been converted into cash, $26,000 of investments remain to be liquidated. If these securities are marketable at or above cost, their liquidation represents a minor problem. The Interest Receivable on Investments will also be liquidated with the sale of the investments. A more difficult problem is presented when the source of revenues for the Debt Service Fund is property taxes. Delinquent taxes that may remain on the balance sheet of the

Debt Service Fund at maturity may ultimately be collected, but cash is required immediately for the payment of the bonds. If the government has other Debt Service Funds, and if the law permits, part of the cash available in other Debt Service Funds may be used. When delinquent taxes are collected, the lendor Debt Service Fund is replenished. Money may be loaned to the Debt Service Fund from the General Fund for this purpose, or the delinquent tax receivables may be transferred to the General Fund when the necessary money is transferred from the General Fund to the Debt Service Fund. If the law prohibits such interfund loans, or interfund "sales" of delinquent receivables, short-term borrowing from nongovernment sources may be necessary.

The second problem is the disposition of the Fund Balance. If the law permits, the balance will be transferred to another Debt Service Fund, especially if the latter's contributions or earnings are short of requirements. Similarly, if the Fund had a deficit, it might be made up by transfers from the General Fund, by an additional tax levy, or by transfers of balances of other Debt Service Funds. Normally the fund balance or deficit of a Debt Service Fund will be small because adjustments will have been made from time to time throughout the life of the Fund. Deficits are sometimes particularly large, however, because of failure to make contributions at proper intervals, failure to compute actuarial requirements properly, or losses on investments. A special tax may have to be levied in such instances; or, if the deficit is large, the bonds may have to be refunded; and there may even be a default.

**Figure 10-5**

A GOVERNMENTAL UNIT
City Hall Bonds Debt Service Fund
Balance Sheet
December 31, 19Y9

*Assets*

| | |
|---|---:|
| Cash | $ 975,000 |
| Investments | 26,000 |
| Interest receivable on investments | 1,500 |
| Total assets | $1,002,500 |

*Liabilities and Fund Balance*

| | |
|---|---:|
| Matured bonds payable | $1,000,000 |
| Fund balance | 2,500 |
| Total liabilities and fund balance | $1,002,500 |

## Statements of Operation

Both those managing Debt Service Funds and the investing and taxpaying public will be interested in the results of operation of Debt Service Funds. Two statements are prepared for this purpose: A statement of Cash Receipts and Disbursements and a Statement of Revenues, Expenditures, and Fund Balances. The former will not be illustrated because the authors believe that it is in general not as useful as the latter and because of its largely self-explanatory nature. A Statement of Revenues, Expenditures, and Fund Balances for the Debt Service Funds of A Governmental Unit is presented in Figure 10-6. Additional revenue accounts that might appear in the statement include Interest and Penalties on Property Taxes; Revenue From Other Agencies, such as shared taxes from higher governments; and Gains or Losses on Disposition of Investments. All readers of the statement will be interested in comparing the actuarial requirement for the increases in fund balances with the actual ac-

**Figure 10-6**

### A GOVERNMENTAL UNIT
Debt Service Funds
Statement of Revenues, Expenditures, and Fund Balances
For the Year Ended December 31, 19X1

|  | Total | 19Z0 Flores Park | 19Y9 City Hall |
|---|---|---|---|
| Revenues: |  |  |  |
| Property taxes | $155,000 | $155,000 |  |
| Contribution from General Fund | 82,585 |  | $82,585 |
| Interest on investments | 1,640 |  | 1,640 |
| Total revenues | $239,225 | $155,000 | $84,225 |
| Expenditures: |  |  |  |
| Redemption of serial bonds | $100,000 | $100,000 |  |
| Interest on bonds | 105,000 | 50,000 | $55,000 |
| Fiscal agent's fees | 400 |  | 400 |
| Total expenditures | $205,400 | $150,000 | $55,400 |
| Excess (deficit) to fund balance | $ 33,825 | $ 5,000* | $28,825† |
| Fund balances, January 1, 19X1 | 27,185 | –0– | 27,185 |
| Fund balances, December 31, 19X1 | $ 61,010 | $ 5,000 | $56,010 |

\* The actuarial requirement for 19X1 was $0.
† The actuarial requirement for 19X1 was $28,816.

complishment of the Funds; for this reason the actuarial requirements are footnoted.

Interim financial statements may be prepared for the benefit of management. However, the few expenditures of a Debt Service Fund are more precisely budgetable than those of, for example, the General Fund and hence are more easily controlled by the finance officer in charge of them. Accordingly, the National Committee on Governmental Accounting recommends that summary interim Statements of Expenditures and Encumbrances Compared with Appropriations be prepared for all funds rather than individual statements for each fund.[4]

## Single Debt Service Fund for Several Bond Issues

As a general rule, the number of Debt Service Funds should be held to a minimum. The law or contractual requirements in some cases may make it necessary to have a Debt Service Fund for each bond issue, but in other cases the law may permit a single Debt Service Fund to provide for a number of issues. The latter arrangement is particularly desirable for all the issues to be financed from the general property tax. In such cases the budget for the single Debt Service Fund would be prepared by analyzing the debt service requirements for each bond issue. That is, the Required Additions, Required Earnings, and Appropriations accounts would be set up in sum as they would have been set up for individual Debt Service Funds for each issue. No attempt is made to allocate revenues to specific issues in such cases, nor is there any segregation of assets and liabilities.

When a balance sheet is prepared for a single Debt Service Fund that is servicing several issues, two portions of the balance sheet may require specific identification of debt issues. (1) If a matured debt issue is shown as a liability of the Fund, then it should be identified by name. (2) In addition, the Fund Balance figure should be supported by a schedule of actuarial requirements for each of the debt issues.

### Pooling of Assets

Even though the law may require that the accounts of each Debt Service Fund be kept separate, it may be legally feasible to pool the assets of some or all of the Debt Service Funds in order to achieve maximum efficiency and safety in the investment program. For example, a single investment counsel may be able to serve as easily for a major investment as for several minor ones. More importantly, the investments may be diversified when a substantial sum is involved, economies of purchase may result from the investment of large sums

[4] *GAAFR, op. cit.,* p. 40.

rather than small ones, and a smaller proportion of the total assets may need to be kept in cash (nonearning) form if the assets are pooled. In such cases well defined rules for determination of the equity of each Debt Service Fund in the assets and in the profits and losses from investments must be established and detailed records must be maintained.

**Question 10-1.** What is the nature of the Fund Balance account in the Debt Service Fund at year end?

**Question 10-2.** A sinking fund was established for the purpose of retiring Dorchester Street Bridge bonds, which had a 20-year maturity. In the fifth year $40,000 of Dorchester Street Bridge bonds were acquired by the Debt Service Fund. Should these bonds be canceled, or should they be held alive until maturity? Why?

**Question 10-3.** Give the entries to record the following: (a) the sale of sinking fund investments bought at a par value of $100,000 at a profit of $2,000; (b) the sale of general sinking fund investments bought at a par value of $95,000 at a loss of $1,500.

**Question 10-4.** City Z's Debt Service Fund pays interest on the City Hall Bonds on February 1 and August 1. Should interest payable be accrued at December 31, the end of the Fund's fiscal year? Why?

**Question 10-5.** (a) General sinking fund securities have risen in value. Should the appreciation in value be recorded on the books? (b) Would your answer be different if the securities had declined in value?

**Question 10-6.** A fund was established for the retirement of bonds of $100,000 maturing at the end of ten years. Annual contributions of $10,000 are to be made, but all earnings on the contributions are to be transferred to the General Fund. Is this fund a sinking fund in the sense in which the term is used in the present chapter? Give reasons for your answer.

**Question 10-7.** A certain municipality provides that its sinking fund is to be built up from various licenses and fines. The revenues from these sources have been as follows: 19X7, $5,000; 19X8, $3,000; 19X9, $8,000. Can you see what is wrong with such a provision?

**Question 10-8.** What disposition should be made of the balance remaining in a Debt Service Fund after the bonds mature and are paid?

**Question 10-9.** Why is there no discussion of comparative periodic statements in the Debt Service Fund chapter?

**Question 10-10.** What are the advantages of pooling the investments of a city's Debt Service Funds?

**Question 10-11.** What are the main sources of assets for a Debt Service Fund?

**Problem 10-1.** Set up a schedule showing the required sinking fund contributions and required earnings if it is assumed that a $100,000 bond issue is to be retired in ten years and contributions are to earn 3 percent interest compounded annually. The required annual addition is $8,723.

**Problem 10-2.** On January 1, 19X1, Central City issued bonds amounting to $100,000 and maturing in 5 years.

At the same time an appropriation was made for the General Fund to pay the first year's contribution to a sinking fund on December 31, 19X1. The General Fund was to make a similar contribution each year thereafter to maturity.

Each year the contribution and earnings were received on December 31 and the cash in the fund on January 1 was invested.
The investments all had the same maturity date as did the sinking fund bonds.
At maturity sinking fund bonds were set up in the sinking fund, and cash for their retirement was transmitted to fiscal agents. Surplus was transferred to the General Fund.
A comparison of sinking fund earnings with requirements showed the following:

| Year | Excess of Earnings Over Requirements | Deficiency of Earnings Over Requirements |
|------|--------------------------------------|------------------------------------------|
| 19X2 | $300 | |
| 19X3 | | $500 |
| 19X4 | 400 | |
| 19X5 | 200 | |

Required:
(a)  Prepare a schedule showing required contributions and earnings. (Assume that sinking fund investments will earn 3 percent per year, compounded annually. According to sinking fund tables, the required annual contribution on the basis of this rate of interest is $18,835.94.)
(b)  Prepare journal entries, including closing entries, to be made each year.
(c)  Prepare a balance sheet as of Decembebr 31 of each year.

**Problem 10-3.**  N City has the following trial balance in the Debt Service Fund on January 1, 19X0:

| | | |
|---|---|---|
| Cash.................................... | $10,623.00 | |
| Investments (Net of discount of $312.50) ...... | 45,687.50 | |
| Interest Receivable ........................ | 498.66 | |
| Fund Balance ............................. | | $56,809.16 |
| | $56,809.16 | $56,809.16 |

The following information is available for the calendar year 19X0:
1.  The accumulation schedule for the fund shows $8,723 as the required annual addition and $1,692.72 as the required fund earnings.
2.  The General Fund budget contains an appropriation for the annual addition.
3.  The Fund buys on January 15 a $10,000, 4 percent bond, interest dates January and July, for 101 plus accrued interest.
4.  The General Fund contribution is received.
5.  Interest is received on July 2 on the bonds bought in transaction 3.
6.  Other interest collected during the year totals $1,400.
7.  On December 31 the accrued interest on investments other than those bought this year totals $475.80.
8.  Straight-line amortization of the discount on investment is $73.50.

Required:
(a)  Prepare a worksheet summarizing the activities of the Debt Service Fund for the year. Include closing entries.
(b)  Prepare a balance sheet after closing entries.

**Problem 10-4.** The City of *B*, pursuant to state law, consolidated all of its Debt Service Funds into one Fund, the balance sheet for which was as follows:

CITY OF *B*
Debt Service Fund
Balance Sheet
December 31, 19X9

*Assets*

| | | |
|---|---:|---:|
| Cash ................................... | | $150,000 |
| Taxes receivable—delinquent................ | $ 90,000 | |
| Less: Estimated uncollectible delinquent | | |
| taxes ................................. | 10,000 | 80,000 |
| Investments ............................ | $276,000 | |
| Less—Discounts on investments ............. | 1,000 | 275,000 |
| | | $505,000 |

*Fund Balance*

| | |
|---|---:|
| Fund Balance | |
| School bonds............................ | 252,500 |
| Library bonds ......................... | 176,750 |
| Recreation bonds....................... | 75,750 |
| | $505,000 |

The state Supreme Court subsequently held the law authorizing consolidated Debt Service Funds unconstitutional.
Required:
Recast the above balance sheet so as to comply with the court decision (that is, show the financial condition of *each* fund).

**Problem 10-5.** From the following data prepare a statement comparing sinking fund additions and earnings for 19X0 with requirements of that year.
Required additions for current year, $20,000
Required earnings, $30,000
Actual additions $20,000
Interest earned, $29,000
Amortization of discounts, $550
Amortization of premiums, $2,300

# 11

# General Fixed Assets;
# General Long-Term Debt;
# Introduction to Interfund
# Transactions and Relationships

The funds for which accounting principles have been presented thus far have been separate, self-balancing entities which may have seemed unrelated to one another. Fixed assets purchased through the funds have mysteriously disappeared from the accounts, as has the liability for general obligation long-term indebtedness. These mysteries are explained in this chapter. The first part deals with the accounting procedure for General Fixed Assets and explains the relationship between them and the funds from which they are financed. The second part is concerned with the accounting procedure for a government's general obligation long-term debt and points out the relationship of the indebtedness to the General Fund, the Capital Projects Funds, and the Debt Service Funds. The third part provides a formal introduction to the subject of interfund transactions and relationships.

## GENERAL FIXED ASSETS

Fixed assets are those assets (1) of significant value, (2) having a useful life extending beyond the year of acquisition, and (3) used, or to be used, in the conduct of the government's activities. Although by definition fixed assets are material and significant, fixed asset records and control are often found to be deficient in practice. The importance of properly recording fixed assets in the accounts should not be overlooked or minimized, for only through proper recording can they be controlled and their use evaluated.

### "General" Fixed Assets Defined

Though accounting for a government's fixed assets parallels that for those of commercial enterprises in most regards, there are certain marked differences. One major distinguishing characteristic of governmental accounting for fixed assets is the clear-cut distinction maintained between (1) General Fixed Assets, and (2) fixed assets accounted for within specific fund entities.

The funds discussed thus far have been termed *expendable* funds, for they are vehicles through which the sources and uses of appropriable resources are accounted for. Acquisition of fixed assets is a *use* of expendable fund resources since the assets thereby acquired are not appropriable and belong to the organization as a whole, not to a particular fund. Therefore, none of the funds discussed thus far has had acquisitions of capital assets recorded therein *as fixed assets*; in every case the acquisition of such assets has been accounted for as a fund *expenditure,* since the assets are considered *general* fixed assets and are capitalized in the General Fixed Assets *nonfund group of accounts.*

> GENERAL FIXED ASSETS. Those fixed assets of a governmental unit which are not accounted for in an Enterprise, Trust, or Intragovernmental Service Fund.[1]

In funds discussed in succeeding chapters (Trust, Intragovernmental Service, and Enterprise Funds), acquisitions of fixed assets are accounted for, for the most part at least, in the same manner as in the accounts of for-profit enterprises. Fixed assets acquired through resources of these funds are *not* general fixed assets, but are capitalized within the accounts of the acquiring fund. The discussion here relates primarily to *general* fixed assets. However, the general definitions, asset account classifications, illustrative record formats, and most of the other topics are applicable to *all* governmental fixed assets. Differences between accounting for *general* fixed assets and for fixed assets capitalized within specific fund entities will be observed in succeeding chapters.

### Acquisition and Initial Valuation

As in commercial accounting, a government's fixed assets are initially recorded at cost, generally defined as "consideration given or consideration received, whichever is more clearly determinable." Importantly, "cost" includes all normal and necessary costs incurred to bring the asset into a state of readiness for the use for which it is intended.

[1] *GAAFR, op. cit.,* p. 161.

Common ways by which governments acquire fixed assets include outright purchase, construction contract, construction by government personnel, gift, and foreclosure. Frequently, two or more methods are used in the acquisition of a single asset. For example, the governmental unit may have part of a bridge constructed by contract and part by its own labor force.

ACQUISITION BY PURCHASE. Where assets are purchased, it is important to record as part of their cost not only the stated purchase price but also all expenses incidental to their acquisition. Among these are legal expenses, brokers' fees, the cost of engineering or other tests to determine the condition of structures, and the cost of repairing secondhand equipment preparatory to use.

CONSTRUCTION BY CONTRACT. The major elements of the cost of assets acquired by contract can readily be determined usually, particularly if a "turnkey" contract is involved, since that cost consists primarily of the amount charged by the contractor. However, cognizance must be taken of all other costs incidental to the project, such as the cost of preliminary engineering surveys, supervision expenses, and other overhead.

CONSTRUCTION BY GOVERNMENTAL UNIT. The procedure in recording the cost of assets constructed by the governmental unit's own labor force is discussed in Chapter 15.

ACQUISITION BY GIFT. Assets acquired by gift are capitalized at their estimated fair market value at time of receipt. Where the government must incur expenses to secure or assure title, repair the property prior to use, or for similar reasons, these costs should be considered as part of the total cost of the asset.

ACQUISITION BY FORECLOSURE. The valuation should normally be the lower of (1) the amount of taxes or special assessments due, penalties and interest thereon, and foreclosure costs applicable thereto, or (2) the appraised value of the property. Both amounts should be included within the fixed asset records.

OTHER ACQUISITION METHODS. Two other methods by which governments may acquire property are by eminent domain and escheat. *Eminent domain* is the power of government to seize private property for public use, compensation to the owner normally being determined through the courts. Property thus acquired is accounted for in the same manner as that acquired in a negotiated purchase.

Acquisition by *escheat* occurs when title to property is vested in or reverts to the government because the rightful owner does not come forward to claim it or because he dies without known heirs. Fixed assets obtained in this manner are accounted for in the same manner as gifts, that is, they are capitalized in the General Fixed Assets accounts at estimated fair market value at acquisition.

**Classification**

The NCGA recommends that governmental fixed assets be classified as (1) Land, (2) Buildings, (3) Improvements Other Than Buildings, (4) Equipment, or (5) Construction in Progress.

1.  *Land.* The cost of land includes the amount paid for the land itself, costs incidental to the acquisition of land, and expenses incurred in preparing the land for use. Costs incidental to the acquisition of land are legal expenses for perfection of title, fees to brokers, and so forth. The expenses of preparing land for use include, among others, the cost of demolishing buildings (less salvage value), the cost of relocating structures, and expenses connected with clearing land. As stated previously, governmental units may pay special assessments on their properties located in special assessment districts. Since special assessment improvements are presumed to benefit the properties assessed, the special assessments paid by the governmental unit as an owner of property should be added to the cost of the land.

2.  *Buildings.* The "buildings" classification includes (1) relatively permanent structures used to house persons or property, and (2) fixtures which are permanently attached to and made a part of buildings and which cannot be removed without cutting into the walls, ceilings, or floors or without in some way damaging the building. Where land and buildings are acquired in the same transaction, the total cost should be allocated between them, either according to terms of the acquisition agreement or in accordance with the best available estimate of their relative fair values.

3.  *Improvements Other Than Buildings.* Examples of items in this category are bridges, sidewalks, streets, dams, tunnels, and fences.

4.  *Equipment.* Examples are trucks, automobiles, pumps, desks, typewriters, and bookcases. Since equipment is movable, it must be accounted for with particular care.

5.  *Construction Work in Progress.* The cost of construction work undertaken but incomplete at a balance sheet date. These costs are appropriately reclassified upon project completion.

Where several fixed assets are acquired simultaneously for a single sum and objective valuations for each asset are not established in the course of negotiations, the total cost incurred should be allocated among the assets in proportion to their estimated relative fair market values. Approximations of relative fair values may be obtained through appraisal, by inquiry of those consumating the transaction, from approximations made by the governing board or a responsible official of the unit, or from other sources such as property tax assessment records.

In order to record and report the manner in which fixed assets were acquired, both currently and cumulatively, the NCGA recommends that the credit side of the General Fixed Assets account group be classified according to the *source* of the resources used for fixed asset acquisition. In previous chapters we have observed that General Fixed Asset acquisition may be financed through three major fund types:

1. *Capital Projects Funds*—major facilities acquired through long-term borrowing, intergovernmental grants-in-aid, interfund transfers, or some combination of sources.
2. *Special Assessment Funds*—facilities or improvements partially or fully financed by property owners benefiting directly from them.
3. *General or Special Revenue Funds*—various general fixed assets, particularly equipment, from general or special revenues.

Inasmuch as general or special revenues may be transferred to Capital Projects and Special Assessment Funds, and since other governments often assist in fixed asset acquisition, it is not sufficient merely to classify fixed asset sources by fund or fund type. Rather, they should be classified by the original funding source, for example (1) general obligation bonds, (2) Federal grants, (3) state grants, (4) General Fund revenues, (5) Special Revenue Fund revenues, (6) special assessments, or (7) gifts. Therefore, a single acquisition may require credits to several Investment in General Fixed Assets (source) accounts. Figure 11-1 presents an overview of the accounting equation applicable to General Fixed Assets accounting.

## Recording Fixed Asset Acquisitions

Practice varies considerably as to (1) the timing of the updating of the General Fixed Assets account group, and (2) the extent of subsidiary account use. Computerized systems may be programmed to generate General Fixed Asset entries continually, periodically, or at year end. In less than fully automated systems, (1) some accountants prefer to update the GFA ledger whenever a relevant transaction occurs; (2) others maintain a GFA journal which is posted to the GFA ledger periodically during the year or at year end; and (3) still others update the GFA ledger only at year end, perhaps based on worksheet analyses of fund capital outlay expenditures. Regardless of individual preference, there should be an established, workable system by which General Fixed Assets subsidiary records are prepared and the account group is updated prior to statement preparation, at least annually. Likewise, the extent to which subsidiary ledgers are employed is a matter of individual preference and the detailed information desired or required. Normally the Land, Buildings, Improvements Other Than Buildings, Construction Work in Progress, and Investment in General Fixed Assets accounts are *controlling* accounts and details of assets owned and the means by which they were financed are maintained in subsidiary ledgers.

Figure 11-1

GENERAL FIXED ASSETS ACCOUNTING OVERVIEW

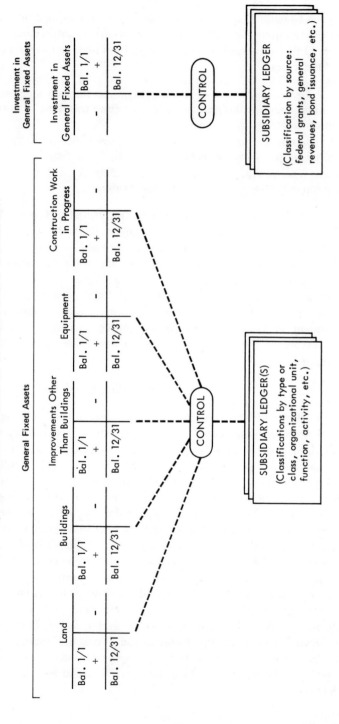

The following trial balance illustrates the account relationship:

| | | |
|---|---:|---:|
| Land .............................. | 700,000 | |
| Buildings ........................... | 2,500,000 | |
| Improvements Other Than Buildings .... | 1,100,000 | |
| Equipment ......................... | 619,200 | |
| Construction Work in Progress.......... | 480,800 | |
| Investment in General Fixed Assets from: | | |
| General Obligation Bonds........... | | 2,500,000 |
| Federal Grants .................... | | 1,500,000 |
| General Fund Revenues ............. | | 1,150,000 |
| Special Assessments ................ | | 250,000 |
| | 5,400,000 | 5,400,000 |

The entries to record the capital expenditures in each fund have already been given. However, in order to illustrate more clearly the relationship between these funds and the General Fixed Assets accounts, some of the fund entries will be repeated, and the corresponding entry in the General Fixed Assets group of accounts will be indicated.

ASSETS FINANCED FROM THE GENERAL OR SPECIAL REVENUE FUNDS. Let us assume that of the expenditures of $399,900 shown on page 138, $103,300 represented expenditures for fixed assets. The entry in the General Fund at the time the expenditure is made is as follows:

| | | |
|---|---:|---:|
| Expenditures.............................. | 103,300 | |
| Vouchers Payable ...................... | | 103,300 |
| To record purchase of land, buildings and equipment. | | |

A companion entry would be made in the General Fixed Assets group of accounts as follows:

| | | |
|---|---:|---:|
| Land ....................................... | 7,000 | |
| Buildings................................... | 37,200 | |
| Equipment ................................. | 59,100 | |
| Investment in General Fixed Assets ......... | | 103,300 |
| To record cost of fixed assets financed from current revenues. | | |

| Investment in GFA subsidiary accounts: | *Cr.* |
|---|---:|
| General Fund Revenues ................... | 103,300 |

To repeat, if the General Fund purchases had been made at several different times, each might have been recorded in the General Fixed Assets group of accounts immediately upon acquisition; or they might have been accumulated into a summary entry recorded prior to the preparation of statements.

ASSETS FINANCED THROUGH CAPITAL PROJECTS FUNDS. As indicated earlier, construction expenditures may be closed out at the end of each year or, less preferably, they may not be closed out until construction is completed. Assuming that expenditures are closed annually, the entry in the Capital Projects Fund at the end of the first year is:

| | | |
|---|---|---|
| Fund Balance (or Appropriations) .............. | 140,800 | |
| Expenditures............................. | | 140,800 |
| To close expenditures to date. | | |

Whether or not the foregoing entry is made, and whether or not encumbrances are closed, the following entry is required in the General Fixed Assets group of accounts:

| | | |
|---|---|---|
| Construction Work in Progress ................ | 140,800 | |
| Investment in General Fixed Assets ......... | | 140,800 |
| To record construction work in progress financed through Capital Projects Fund. | | |

| | |
|---|---|
| Investment in GFA subsidiary accounts: | *Cr.* |
| General Fund Revenues .................... | 17,600 |
| County Grants ........................... | 17,600 |
| Federal Grants............................ | 70,400 |
| General Obligation Bonds ................. | 35,200 |
| | 140,800 |

The distribution of sources as among General Fund revenues, county grants, Federal grants, and issuance of general obligation bonds would be made in proportion to the expected total contribution of each to the project. Note also that *encumbered* amounts, whether or not closed out at year end, are *not* capitalized; only *expended* amounts are capitalized.

When the project is completed, during the second year in our example, the entry in the Capital Projects Fund (page 296) is:

| | | |
|---|---|---|
| Fund Balance (or Appropriations) .............. | 252,400 | |
| Expenditures............................. | | 252,400 |
| To record closing out of final expenditures for completed project. | | |

In the General Fixed Assets account group, the entry is:

| | | |
|---|---|---|
| Improvements Other Than Buildings ........... | 393,200 | |
| Construction Work in Progress ............ | | 140,800 |
| Investment in General Fixed Assets ........ | | 252,400 |
| To record the cost of completed project financed through Capital Projects fund and to close the Construction Work in Progress account: | | |

(Entry continued)

Investment in GFA subsidiary:

|  | Cr. |
|---|---|
| General Fund Revenues .................... | 32,400 |
| County Grants ........................... | 32,400 |
| Federal Grants........................... | 129,600 |
| General Obligation Bonds ................. | 58,000 |
|  | 252,400 |

The subsidiary entry pertaining to sources was determined by the following calculation:

|  | Total | General Fund | County Grant | Federal Grant | Bond Issue |
|---|---|---|---|---|---|
| Final project revenues ......... | $399,000 | $50,000 | $50,000 | $200,000 | $99,000 |
| Less:  Fund balance transferred to Debt Service Fund........ |  |  |  |  | (5,800) |
| Final project cost/sources....... | $393,200 | $50,000 | $50,000 | $200,000 | $93,200 |
| Less:  Amounts credited to sources in previous Construction Work in Process entry(ies) | (140,800) | (17,600) | (17,600) | (70,400) | (35,200) |
| Balance to be credited to Investment in General Fixed Asset subsidiary ledger source accounts ................. | $252,400 | $32,400 | $32,400 | $129,600 | $58,000 |

ASSETS FINANCED THROUGH SPECIAL ASSESSMENT FUNDS. The procedure for recording fixed assets acquired through Special Assessment Funds closely parallels that for Capital Projects Funds. Expenditures, but *not* encumbrances, incurred for uncompleted projects are capitalized currently; upon completion of the project, all costs are appropriately classified.

Assuming that expenditures were closed at year end, the following entry was made in the Special Assessment Fund (see page 340).

| Fund Balance—Construction (or Appropriations).. | 140,000 |  |
|---|---|---|
| Expenditures ........................... |  | 140,000 |

To close out construction work in process expenditures.

The following entry should be made in the General Fixed Assets account group:

| Construction Work in Progress ................. | 140,000 |  |
|---|---|---|
| Investment in General Fixed Assets ......... |  | 140,000 |

To record construction work in progress financed through Special Assessment Fund.

(Entry continued)

Investment in GFA subsidiary accounts:      *Cr.*

| | |
|---|---|
| Special Assessments .............. | 112,000 |
| General Fund Revenues .......... | 28,000 |
| | 140,000 |

Again, the source subsidiary ledger account entries were based on total expected revenue sources, that is, the government's share of this project was to be $100,000 of the $500,000 total cost, or 20 percent.

Upon completion of the project, the following closing entry was made in the Special Assessment Fund:

| | | |
|---|---|---|
| Fund Balance—Construction (or Appropriations) | 345,000 | |
| Expenditures........................... | | 345,000 |
| To record closing out of expenditures. | | |

The following entry, supported by the schedule below, should be made in the General Fixed Assets group of accounts:

| | | |
|---|---|---|
| Improvements Other Than Buildings ........... | 485,000 | |
| Construction Work in Progress ............. | | 140,000 |
| Investment in General Fixed Assets ......... | | 345,000 |
| To record completion of special assessment project. | | |

Investment in GFA subsidiary accounts:      *Cr.*

| | |
|---|---|
| Special Assessments .............. | 288,000 |
| General Fund Revenues .......... | 57,000 |
| | 345,000 |

Calculation:

| | Total | Special Assessments | General Fund Transfer |
|---|---|---|---|
| Final project resources for construction ................... | $500,000 | $400,000 | $100,000 |
| Less: Unneeded fund balance returned to General Fund ........ | (15,000) | | (15,000) |
| Final project cost/sources .......... | $485,000 | $400,000 | $ 85,000 |
| Less: Amounts credited to sources in previous Construction Work in Process entry(ies)............... | (140,000) | (112,000) | (28,000) |
| Balance to be credited to Investment in GFA subsidiary source accounts | $345,000 | $288,000 | $ 57,000 |

ASSETS ACQUIRED THROUGH FORECLOSURE. We noted earlier that fixed assets acquired through foreclosure should be recorded at the lower of (1) fair market value, and (2) the amount of taxes or assessments, penalties and interest due on the property, and costs of foreclosure and sale. To illustrate, assume that a building with an estimated value of $2,000 was acquired through foreclosure. At the time of foreclosure, the following were due a Special Revenue Fund:

| | |
|---|---:|
| Taxes.............................. | $ 900 |
| Penalties ........................... | 100 |
| Interest ........................... | 75 |
| Costs of foreclosure and sale .......... | 25 |
| | $1,100 |

Further assuming that these receivables had been reclassified as Tax Liens Receivable prior to the decision to retain the property for the government's use, the following entry should be made in the Special Revenue Fund:

| | | |
|---|---:|---:|
| Expenditures..................................... | 1,100 | |
| Tax Liens Receivable ......................... | | 1,100 |
| To record acquisition of land through foreclosure; estimated fair market value, $2,000. | | |

The accompanying entry in the General Fixed Assets account group would be:

| | | |
|---|---:|---:|
| Land .......................................... | 1,100 | |
| Investment in General Fixed Assets ............ | | 1,100 |
| To record acquisition of land through foreclosure of tax liens. | | |

| | |
|---|---:|
| Investment in GFA subsidiary accounts: | *Cr.* |
| Special Revenue Fund Revenues................ | 1,100 |

Note that the Investment in General Fixed Asset subsidiary credit is to "Special Revenue Fund Revenues," rather than to Foreclosures (or some similar account). Note also that had the fair market value of the property been less than charges against it, say $800, the Special Revenue Fund expenditure would be recorded at $800 and $300 would be charged against the allowance for uncollectible accounts.

In all of the examples cited thus far, there has been a clear-cut indication within a fund ledger that a fixed asset has been acquired and should be capitalized, that is, there has been a charge to the Expenditures account of some fund. Laws or custom in some jurisdictions do not permit charging fixed asset acquisitions through foreclosure to the Expenditures account, however. Rather, the uncollectible amount must be charged as a bad debt, and the following entry would appear in the fund ledger:

```
Allowance for Uncollectible Tax Liens..............  1,100
    Tax Liens Receivable ........................          1,100
    To record acquisition of property through foreclosure;
    estimated fair market value, $2,000. (State laws do not
    permit charging the Expenditures account.)
```

Thus, "bad debt" entries such as the above must be examined, as they may call for a General Fixed Assets entry. (Again, the Investment in Fixed Assets subsidiary credit would be to Special Revenue Fund Revenues, since these were forgone to acquire the property.)

Finally, some have suggested that fixed assets be capitalized at the *higher* of collections forgone and appraisal, contending that the "true value" is thereby reflected in the accounts. We feel that the *lower* of the two figures is preferable since:

1. *Where receipts forgone is the lower:*
   a. The amount forgone is the "cost" of the property.
   b. It is objectively measurable.
   c. It is verifiable.
   d. The Fund and General Fixed Asset ledgers articulate.
2. *Where fair market value is lower:*
   a. A loss has, in substance, been realized.
   b. The estimated value of the consideration received would represent a more realistic and conservative figure at which to capitalize the asset.

ASSETS ACQUIRED THROUGH GIFTS. Inasmuch as no fund assets were relinquished in acquiring property donated to the government, transactions of this type are recorded *only* in the General Fixed Assets account group. Donated property should be recorded in the GFA group at estimated fair market value to the unit at the time of the donation:

```
Land .........................................  1,500
    Investment in General Fixed Assets  ............        1,500
    To record land received by gift at estimated fair mar-
    ket value.
Investment in GFA subsidiary accounts:            Cr.
    Private Gifts  .............................      1,500
```

### Establishing Property Records

After the cost of other value of a fixed assets has been determined, it is recorded on an individual property record. The National Committee on Governmental Accounting recommends recording the following information relative to each unit of property:

1. Class code
2. Sequence or payment voucher number

3. Date of acquisition
4. Name and address of vendor
5. Abbreviated description
6. Department, division, or unit charged with custody
7. Location
8. Cost
9. Fund and account from which purchased
10. Method of acquisition
11. Estimated life
12. Date, method, and authorization of disposition[2]

A separate record is established for each "unit" of property. (A unit of property is any item which can be readily identified and accounted for separately.) These records of individual properties constitute the subsidiary accounts which support the General Fixed Assets accounts in the general ledger. The forms illustrated below are typical of those used in manual systems. Similar data may be maintained in computer files, of course, with records or analyses available on demand.

LAND RECORDS. A property record form for Land is illustrated in Figure 11-2. Note that provision is made on this record for showing the legal description of the land, its location, its use, the authority for acquiring it, the method of financing its acquisition, and similar information. Note also the references to the general ledger control account and to the accounting documents approving and supporting the expenditure.

RECORDS FOR BUILDING AND OTHER IMPROVEMENTS. A property record form for Buildings or Improvements Other Than Buildings is illustrated in Figure 11-3. This form is similar to that illustrated in Figure 11-2, except that it does not show the legal description of the property and that provision is made for recording deductions resulting from retirements. Note also that reference is made to construction work orders. With the aid of this reference, it is possible to substantiate the original cost of each structure and improvement and the cost of additions or replacements made after the property was acquired.

EQUIPMENT RECORDS. An individual property record form for equipment— in this case, office furniture—is illustrated in Figure 11-4. Different kinds of property records may be needed for different types of equipment. For example, the form illustrated in Figure 11-4 would not be suitable for automotive equipment. Records for this type of equipment should show, in addition to the information carried on the card here illustrated, data as to depreciation, number

2 *GAAFR, op. cit.,* p. 95.

Figure 11-2

## A GOVERNMENTAL UNIT
### Land Ledger

| Department _____ | General Ledger Control |
|---|---|
| _____ | Date _____ Amount _____ |
| Legal Description _____ | Date _____ Revised Amount _____ |
| _____ | **Plat Book** |
| _____ | Plat Book Page No._____ |
| _____ | Property No. _____ |
| _____ | **Legal Authorization** |
| _____ | Date _____ Ordinance No. _____ |
| _____ | Date _____ Ordinance No. _____ |
| _____ | **Deed** |
| Location _____ | Reversion Clause? Yes_____ No_____ |
| | If yes, give deed conditions _____ |
| Size _____ | _____ |
| Purpose for Which Obtained _____ | _____ |
| | Grantor _____ |
| Present Use _____ | Type of Deed _____ Date _____ |
| _____ | Recorded _____ Vol._____ Page_____ |
| _____ | No._____ |
| _____ | Copy on File with_____ |

**For Land Purchased**

| | | |
|---|---|---|
| Date_____ | Amount_____ | Voucher No._____ |
| Date_____ | Amount_____ | Voucher No._____ |
| Date_____ | Amount_____ | Voucher No._____ |
| Date_____ | Amount_____ | Gen.Jour.Page _____ |

**For Land Otherwise Acquired**

Date_____ Amount _____ Reference _____
Explanation_____

| **Method of Financing** | | **Disposition Made** |
|---|---|---|
| Method | Amount | Date |
| Bonds_____ | | How Disposed of _____ |
| Current Revenues_____ | | Price _____ |
| Gifts, Bequests_____ | | Receipt Document _____ |
| _____ | | Other References _____ |

of miles driven annually, total annual cost of operation, and annual rentals earned. Postings to such a record would be made at the end of each year from the individual equipment property records illustrated in Figure 15-7.

**Figure 11-3**

A GOVERNMENTAL UNIT

Buildings or Improvements Other Than Buildings Ledger

| | |
|---|---|
| Number _____ | Authorization |
| Department _____ | Date _____ Ordinance No. _____ |
| Location _____ | Date _____ Ordinance No. _____ |
| | General Ledger Control |
| Purpose for Which Obtained _____ | Date _____ Amount _____ |
| | Date _____ Revised Amount _____ |
| Present Use _____ | Date _____ Revised Amount _____ |
| Estimated Life _____ | For Assets Constructed |
| | Date Completed _____ |
| | Cost _____ |
| | Work Order No. _____ |

| Methods of Financing | For Assets Purchased |
|---|---|
| | Date _____ Cost _____ |
| Original Amount / Additions or Deductions* | Voucher No. _____ |
| | For Donated Assets |
| Current Revenues ____ ____ | Date _____ |
| Gifts ____ ____ | Amount _____ |
| Special Assessments: | Reference _____ |
| Govt. Share ____ ____ | Explanation _____ |
| Property Owners' Share ____ ____ | _____ |
| Bonds ____ ____ | _____ |

| | Additions |
|---|---|
| | Date _____ Cost _____ |
| Disposition Made _____ | Work Order No. _____ |
| | Date _____ Cost _____ |
| | Work Order No. _____ |
| Date _____ | |
| Salvage Proceeds ____ G.J. or C.R.* Page ____ | Deductions |
| | Date _____ Amount _____ |
| Cost of Dismantling _____ | References _____ |
| Retirement Order No. _____ | |

**Figure 11-4**

A GOVERNMENTAL UNIT

Equipment Ledger

```
                                              Item No. _____
 Description _____

 Department _____ Division _____
 Serial No. _____ Make _____ Model _____
 Date Received _____ Purchase Order No. _____ Estimated Life _____

 Cost _____ Vo.No. _____          Additions
 Freight _____ Vo.No. _____   Date _____ Amount _____
                 Vo.No. _____   Reference _____
 Total Original Cost _____
 Date _____ Revised Cost _____   Date _____ Amount _____
 Date _____ Revised Cost _____   Reference _____

         Method of Financing
              Original   Additions or        Deductions
              Amount     Deductions*   Date _____ Amount _____
 Current Revenues _____  _____   Reference _____
 Gifts            _____  _____
                                      Disposition _____

 Remarks _____     Date _____ Amount _____
 _____     Reference _____
```

## Classifying Individual Property Records

As we have seen, *General* Fixed Assets are set up in a separate group of accounts. In the general ledger, they are divided into five main classes—Land, Buildings, Improvements Other Than Buildings, Equipment, and Construction Work in Progress. The totals of the balances carried on the individual property records must agree, of course, with the totals shown in the General Fixed Assets general ledger.

The individual property records may be classified in a variety of ways: asset class, department, activity, source, etc. In computerized systems it is common to file records centrally, by classes, and generate reports on other bases as needed.

In manual systems, the cards need not be arranged in five main groups with one group covering Land, another Buildings, and so forth. Where only one set is maintained, cards are commonly grouped by departments, and under each department the cards are arranged in the five subgroups. Improvements Other Than Buldings are still further subdivided by classes of property—for example, sidewalks, streets, and bridges. Equipment, too, is subdivided into a number of classes: automotive equipment, office machinery, office equipment and so forth. Each of these types of equipment may be subdivided still further. For example, office equipment might be subdivided as follows: bookcases, books, carpets, chairs, coat trees, desk lamps, desks, drafting tables, filing equipment, lockers, map cases, mimeograph equipment, safes, telephone switchboards, time clocks, visible index equipment, water coolers, and so forth. All the cards falling within a particular subclass are grouped together. For example, all cards for office equipment used by a particular organization unit would be placed in one group. In that manner, it is possible to arrive readily at the total cost of office equipment used by the department, as well as to establish accounting control of the office equipment. Similarly, all cards for other classes of equipment are grouped together. Subcontrol accounts may or may not be established for various subclasses of equipment, depending on the number of items included under each subclass. For example, if a department has many items of office equipment it may establish a subcontrol account entitled "Office Equipment," which would be supported by the cards set up for the individual items of office equipment.

If a department is composed of several subdivisions, or if its property is located in various places, separate control accounts are established for each subdivision or location. For example, if a municipality has several fire stations, each of which is located in a different part of the city, separate control accounts would be established for the fixed assets at each fire station. Thus, the cards for the property in Station A would be arranged as follows:

Land
Improvements Other Than Buildings
Fire-Fighting Equipment
 Aerial-Ladder Trucks[3]
 Chemical Engines
 Combination Fire Trucks
 Fire Extinguishers
 Fire Hose
 Ladders
 Pumpers
 Squad Wagons

[3] A separate card is prepared for each piece of equipment listed under each of the groups. For example, if station A had more than one aerial-ladder truck, a separate card would be provided for each.

Household Equipment
   Beds
   Chairs
   Stoves
   etc.

To arrive at the total cost of the fixed assets used by the fire department, it is necessary to add the amounts shown for land, structures and improvements, and equipment for each fire station and for the fire department headquarters, as illustrated below:

| Station | Total | Land | Buildings | Equipment |
|---|---|---|---|---|
| Headquarters | $ 30,000 | – | – | $ 30,000 |
| Station A | 60,000 | $10,000 | $ 20,000 | 30,000 |
| Station B | 100,000 | 20,000 | 40,000 | 40,000 |
| Station C | 145,000 | 30,000 | 55,000 | 60,000 |
| Station D | 25,000 | 5,000 | 10,000 | 10,000 |
| Total Fire Department | $360,000 | $65,000 | $125,000 | $170,000 |

Obviously, computerization of General Fixed Assets records can often save a great deal of clerical effort, as well as make available data which cannot economically be routinely maintained using manual methods.

### Additions, Betterments, and Renewals

Before the cost of additions to fixed assets is recorded, it should be determined that the expenditure has actually bettered the asset. In general, expenditures for work performed on fixed assets should be analyzed to determine what part of the expenditure has resulted in bettering the asset and what part has merely restored the asset to its former condition (a renewal or overhaul). The part that has bettered the asset should be capitalized and added to the original cost or other value of the asset, whereas the other part (renewal) should be treated as a current expense. No hard or fast rules can be laid down as to what constitues a repair or a betterment. In general, if the useful life of the asset is significantly prolonged or the asset is made more useful, the expenditure may be said to have resulted in a betterment.

Additions to fixed assets are not classified according to whether they are buildings, other improvements, or equipment until they are completed. As noted earlier, costs incurred are accumulated in the Construction Work in Progress account during the construction period and are reclassified by asset type following completion of the project.

## Depreciation Not Recorded

Another major distinction between governmental and commercial accounting results from the ninth principle set forth by the National Committee on Governmental Accounting:

*Depreciation*
9. Depreciation on general fixed assets should *not* be recorded in the general accounting records. Depreciation charges on such assets may be computed for *unit cost* purposes, provided such charges are recorded *only* in memorandum form and do *not* appear in the fund accounts.[4]

The Committee did not deny the existence of depreciation as "an economic fact of life." However, it saw no constructive purpose in recording depreciation expense related to General Fixed Assets, primarily because governments do not determine periodic net income. (Depreciation *is* usually recorded on assets capitalized in specific funds, as will be discussed subsequently.) In prohibiting the recording of depreciation "in the fund accounts," the committee inferred that *expense* accounting is incompatible with *expenditure* accounting typically associated with governmental expendable funds. Inasmuch as the General Fixed Assets account group is not a fund, the statement quoted above would not bar recording depreciation therein, though it is seldom done in practice.

This long-standing and well-accepted NCGA recommendation has been debated for many years and is probably its most controversial pronouncement. Many individuals and groups have argued that depreciation of General Fixed Assets should be recognized. One of the more recent and more vigorous arguments for recognition of depreciation (and expenses generally) *in addition to expenditures* was that put forth by the American Accounting Association's Committee on Accounting Practices of Not-for-Profit Organizations. This committee recommended that:

1. The accounting records and related reports of a not-for-profit organization should disclose the cost of use or consumption of the assets allocated to services and/or time periods as appropriate by an acceptable depreciation technique;

2. Depreciation accounting should be recognized as an integral part of accounting for resources. (Because statutory and regulatory requirements for property accounting cannot be ignored, not-for-profit organizations may find it necessary to make multiple recordings and disclosures of individual transactions. Where there are specific legal prohibitions against formally recording and reporting depreciation, not-for-profit organizations should use supplementary records and statements to the extent necessary to furnish interested parties with relevant fixed asset depreciation data.)[5]

[4] *GAAFR*, p. 10. (Emphasis added.)
[5] "Report of the Committee on Accounting Practices of Not-for-Profit Organizations," *The Accounting Review,* Supplement to Vol. 46, 1971, p. 119.

A summary of the major issues of the depreciation controversy, as seen by the AAA committee, is contained in Table 11-1.

Table 11-1

THE DEPRECIATION CONTROVERSY:
SUMMARY OF MAJOR ISSUES

| *Against Recognition* | *For Recognition* |
| --- | --- |
| *Serves no useful purpose.* Depreciation accounting is necessary only to measure profit—NFP organizations are not organized for profit and *profit or loss determination is irrelevant.* | Accrual accounting is essential to an understanding of the financial status (and change in status) of all organizations—should be cognizant of total NFP resource availability, utilization, and capital implementation or diminution. |
| Taxes, not fixed assets, provide revenue—recognition would *violate the matching concept.* | Expenses need not physically "produce" revenue directly. In reality we *match* revenues and expenses *to periods,* often separately. |
| NFP organizations exist on a year-to-year basis—*are not going-concerns.* | Where power of self-perpetuation exists via taxes, NFP entities *are extremely "going"*— it is more necessary to give full accounting than in private enterprise because of this power and their broad social impact and responsibility. |
| Recognition would result in *double-charging* current generation. | Cost determination separate from "price determination." *Are now unaware of costs or who bears them*—may be triple charging or half charging. Cost determination and "price-setting" are separate problems—accrual cost data are often useful in setting pricing policies. |
| Recognition *might result in a deficit*—this would upset the public. | We should *report clearly* and *truthfully*—many organizations acquire excess resources in some periods and deplete these subsequently. Such should be reported. |

Source: "Report of the Committee on Accounting Practices of Not-for-Profit Organizations," *The Accounting Review,* Supplement to Vol. 46, 1971, pp. 117–118.

**Table 11-1 (cont.)**

| *Against Recognition* | *For Recognition* |
| --- | --- |
| Recognition would be *confusing*—fund and budgetary considerations dominate NFP accounting. *Expenditures* are *budgeted* and must be accounted for—*depreciation* expense is NOT *budgeted*. | Funds and budgets are control devices and adherence must be reported. A single report will suffice only where budget is expense-based. Otherwise, we must *separate* current *fund budgetary accounting from financial accounting* as is done in profit-oriented organizations. Alternatively, we can adjust budgetary statements for capital outlay and depreciation. |
| Recognition is *technically unmanageable* in fund accounting structure—a good place for a debit but no place for the credit as fixed assets are not in fund accounts. | Several *expedient alternatives* are *available*—for example, hospitals account for depreciation through expense-equity adjustment of fund structure and/or account classification. |
| Recognition of depreciation would be *misleading* as: | Failure to recognize depreciation is *more misleading*. The contra arguments are *irrelevant* because: |
| a. *"Reserve"* for depreciation *implies cash* availability. | a. This argument was settled years ago—it is a *nomenclature problem*. |
| b. *"Value"* of fixed assets *is academic question*—"Cost" is all that is of importance. | b. There is *no attempt to measure "value"* but rather costs consumed and the cost of service potentials remaining within the organization. |
| c. *Asset was donated*—NFP has no depreciation expense. | c. The *donation was a contribution of capital*—the source of capital does not determine the measurement of its consumption. |
| d. We *may not replace* fixed assets or will replace through public subscription or individual donation. | d. See c above—also, expense measurement and asset replacement are *separate problems*. |
| *Fixed assets are a heritage* of past administrations—is unfair to charge current administration with past mistakes. | *Currently not accountable for use of them at all*—should use or dispose of, clearly indicating reasons and effects. |
| Fixed assets *do not depreciate if properly maintained*. | *Depreciation and maintenance are* largely *separate problems*. Even so, who is to determine adequacy or propriety of current maintenance? Maintenance expenditures frequently are *deferable* to the next administration, or at least until after the next election. |

Table 11-1 (cont.)

| *Against Recognition* | *For Recognition* |
| --- | --- |
| *Depreciation* is an estimate—*it cannot be accurately computed.* | Informed *estimates* are certainly *preferable to nonaccounting.* |
| What purpose is served in reporting depreciation on the *White House?* the *Statue of Liberty?* | Probably none—infinite useful life and/or small initial cost may result in *immateriality,* and hence not require depreciation accounting. |
| *No one* (citizens, legislators, creditors, etc.) *is interested* in depreciation. | They *have not been "exposed"* to true accrual accounting for NFP organizations. Presented via readable, meaningful financial reports, information concerning total resource stewardship (as opposed to current line item dollar accountability) might awaken a generally apathetic citizenry. Many *managements now receive* unpublished data relating to depreciation. |
| The *expense* of depreciation accounting *would exceed* the *benefits.* | *Inexpensive* if there are reasonably accurate records essential to physical control of assets. |
| *Can determine depreciation costs via memorandum records,* special studies, etc. | *Current "non-accounting" practices based on this premise are disappointing.* In addition, control is established when integrated into system. |

### Sale, Retirement, or Replacement

Inasmuch as depreciation of General Fixed Assets is not usually recorded, an asset's carrying value in the accounts normally remains at original cost throughout the period of its use. Removal of the asset's carrying value upon its disposal is in most cases simply a matter of reversal of the acquisition entry. The accounting procedure upon disposal is, in sum:

1. *General Fixed Assets.* Remove the asset carrying value by debiting the Investment in General Fixed Assets account(s) and crediting the asset account(s) in the general and subsidiary ledgers.
2. *Fund receiving proceeds of sale.* Record any salvage value, insurance proceeds, or other receipts as Revenue in the accounts of the recipient fund.

Thus, if a fire truck with a book value of $10,000 is sold for $2,000, the following entries are made:

ENTRY IN GENERAL FUND:

| Cash........................................ | 2,000 | |
| Revenues—Sales of Equipment ............. | | 2,000 |
| To record sale of fire truck. | | |

ENTRY IN GENERAL FIXED ASSETS GROUP OF ACCOUNTS:

| Investment in Fixed Assets—General | | |
| Fund Revenues .......................... | 10,000 | |
| Equipment ............................. | | 10,000 |
| To record sale of fire truck with book value of $10,000. | | |

Note that although only $2,000 was realized from the sale of the truck, the full book value, $10,000, must be written off in the General Fixed Asset account group. Of course, the individual property record for the particular truck would be canceled.

If the above truck is traded in on a new truck costing $12,000, and an allowance of $3,000 is made on the old truck, the transaction is recorded as follows:

ENTRY IN GENERAL FUND:

| Expenditures................................. | 9,000 | |
| Cash....................................... | | 9,000 |
| To record purchase of fire truck costing $12,000, net of trade-in allowance of $3,000. | | |

ENTRIES IN GENERAL FIXED ASSETS GROUP OF ACCOUNTS:

| Investment in Fixed Assets—General | | |
| Fund Revenues .......................... | 10,000 | |
| Equipment ............................. | | 10,000 |
| To record disposal (trade-in) of old fire truck with book value of $10,000. | | |

| Equipment ............................... | 12,000 | |
| Investment in Fixed Assets—General | | |
| Fund Revenues ...................... | | 12,000 |
| To record purchase of fire truck at a cost of $9,000 plus trade-in allowance on old fire truck of $3,000. | | |

Thus far we have assumed that the assets were sold to private persons. Sometimes property accounted for in a nonexpendable fund is sold to a department financed through an expendable fund. Let us assume, for example, that an enterprise sells equipment at book value to the public works department, which is financed from the General Fund. The following entries would be made:

ENTRY IN ENTERPRISE FUND:

| Due from General Fund ...................... | 15,000 | |
| Allowance for Depreciation-Equipment .......... | 1,000 | |
| Equipment ............................. | | 16,000 |
| To record sale of equipment to department of public works at net book value. | | |

ENTRY IN GENERAL FUND:

| | | |
|---|---|---|
| Expenditures................................... | 15,000 | |
| Due to Enterprise Fund ................... | | 15,000 |

To record purchase of equipment from Enterprise
Fund for department of public works and liability
owing to that fund.

ENTRY IN GENERAL FIXED ASSETS GROUP OF ACCOUNTS:

| | | |
|---|---|---|
| Equipment ................................... | 15,000 | |
| Investment in Fixed Assets—General | | |
| Fund Revenues ......................... | | 15,000 |

To record purchase of equipment for public works
department.

The entries to record retirements are more complicated because it is important to take into account the cost of retirement as well as the proceeds received from the sale of salvage. For example, assume that a fire station was torn down, that the book value of the building was $60,000, that the cost of tearing it down was $1,000, and that $5,000 was realized from the sale of salvage. The entries to record these transactions are as shown below.

ENTRY IN GENERAL FIXED ASSETS GROUP OF ACCOUNTS:

| | | |
|---|---|---|
| Investment in Fixed Assets—Bond Issues ......... | 60,000 | |
| Buildings .............................. | | 60,000 |

To record retirement of fire station.

ENTRIES IN GENERAL FUND:

| | | |
|---|---|---|
| Expenditures................................ | 1,000 | |
| Cash.................................. | | 1,000 |

To record cost of dismantling building, such cost
to be reimbursed from sale of salvage.

| | | |
|---|---|---|
| Cash....................................... | 5,000 | |
| Expenditures........................... | | 1,000 |
| Revenues ............................. | | 4,000 |

To record sale of salvage and reimbursement for
cost of dismantling fire station.

On the other hand, if the cost of dismantling was $2,000, and if only $1,000 had been realized from the sale of salvage, the General Fund entries would be as follows:

| | | |
|---|---|---|
| Expenditures.................................... | 2,000 | |
| Cash....................................... | | 2,000 |

To record cost of dismantling building, such cost to be
reimbursed from sale of salvage.

| | | |
|---|---|---|
| Cash......................................... | 1,000 | |
| Expenditures............................... | | 1,000 |

To record sale of salvage and to reduce the dismantling
cost by the amount of cash realized from the sale of
salvage.

Asset retirements should be properly authorized and documented. A typical Asset Retirement Order form appears as Figure 11-5.

### Transfer of Fixed Assets

Fixed assets should not be transferred from one location to another, or from one use to another, without formal written authorization by the proper authority. Unless transfers are formally authorized, fixed assets cannot be properly controlled. An order authorizing the transfer of fixed assets is illustrated in Figure 11-6.

The nonreciprocal transfer of fixed assets between departments financed from the same fund does not affect the general ledger accounts of the fund. However, a new property card must be prepared or the old one modified to indicate the new location and use of the asset. Nonreciprocal transfers between departments financed from different funds may affect both the general ledger accounts and the individual property records. For example, if equipment was transferred from the Water Department to the Fire, Police, and Public Works Departments, the entries to record this transaction (assuming the three departments receiving the equipment are financed from the General Fund) are as follows:

ENTRY IN ENTERPRISE FUND:

| | | |
|---|---|---|
| Retained Earnings (or Governmental Unit's Contribution) | 10,000 | |
| Allowance for Depreciation—Equipment | 20,000 | |
| Equipment | | 30,000 |

To record transfer of equipment to other departments as follows:

| Department | Cost of Equipment | Accumulated Depreciation | Net Book Value |
|---|---|---|---|
| Police | $ 5,000 | $ 3,000 | $ 2,000 |
| Fire | 10,000 | 6,500 | 3,500 |
| Public Works | 15,000 | 10,500 | 4,500 |
| | $30,000 | $20,000 | $10,000 |

ENTRY IN GENERAL FIXED ASSETS GROUP OF ACCOUNTS:

| | | |
|---|---|---|
| Equipment | 10,000 | |
| Investment in Fixed Assets—Enterprise Fund Transfers | | 10,000 |

To record transfer of equipment by water utility to following departments:

| | |
|---|---|
| Police Department | $ 2,000 |
| Fire Department | 3,500 |
| Public Works Department | 4,500 |
| | $10,000 |

Figure 11-5

## A GOVERNMENTAL UNIT
### Asset Retirement Order

Number _____   Date _____

Retired from _____   Department _____

| Identification | | Date of Purchase | Description | Cost (Including Additions) | Accumulated Depreciation | Salvage Value | Cost of Dismantling | Date | Voucher No. or Receipt No. | Account | | |
|---|---|---|---|---|---|---|---|---|---|---|---|---|
| Property No. | Mfg's. No. | | | | | | | | | Name | No. | Amount Debit or Credit* |
| | | | | | | | | | | | | |

Remarks _____

Requested by _____

Approved _____

Approved _____

Noted on Property Record _____

Figure 11-6

## A GOVERNMENTAL UNIT
### Asset Transfer Order

Number _____

Transferred from _____ Department

Requested by _____ Department

Date _____

| Identification | | Date of Purchase | Description | Cost | Accumulated Depreciation | Net Value | Account | | | |
|---|---|---|---|---|---|---|---|---|---|---|
| Inventory or Property No. | Mfg's. No. | | | | | | Name | No. | Amount | |
| | | | | | | | | | Debit or Credit* | |

Received by _____ Date _____ Remarks _____

Charge Accepted _____

Approved _____ Dept. Head

Noted on Property Record _____

Approved _____ Property Clerk

427

A separate property record is established for this equipment in each department, of course. No entry is made in the General Fund accounts, however, since no appropriable General Fund assets were either provided or used as a result of the transfer.

### Property Damaged or Destroyed

Expenditures for repairs necessary to restore damaged property to its former condition are charged to the Expenditures account in the fund from which the cost of repairs is financed and are classified as current expenses. If the expenditures not only restore the asset to its former condition but also result in bettering it, the excess of the total amount expended over the amount required to restore the asset to its former condition is capitalized in the General Fixed Assets group of accounts.

As an illustration, let us assume that an asset is damaged and that $40,000 is spent for its repair and $10,000 for its betterment. If the expenditures are financed out of the General Fund, the entries are as follows:

ENTRY IN GENERAL FUND:
Expenditures............................... 50,000
    Cash ................................. 50,000
    To record expenditures for repairs to damaged police station, of which $10,000 are due to betterments. Subsidiary accounts:

|  | Current | Capital |
|---|---|---|
| *Organization Unit* | *Expenses* | *Outlays* |
| Department of Police............... | 40,000 | 10,000 |

ENTRY IN GENERAL FIXED GROUP OF ACCOUNTS:
Buildings................................... 10,000
    Investment in Fixed Assets—General
    Fund Revenues ......................... 10,000
    To record improvement of police station.

An entry also is made in the individual property record for the particular police station to indicate the $10,000 increase in the book value of the station building.

Let us assume further that the total book value of the police station is $100,000, that the station is destroyed by fire, and that the governmental unit collects insurance of $90,000. The following entries would be made in the General Fixed Assets group of accounts and in the General Fund, respectively, to record these transactions:

ENTRY IN GENERAL FIXED ASSETS GROUP OF ACCOUNTS:
Investment in Fixed Assets—Bond Issue ....... 100,000
    Buildings............................. 100,000
    To record destruction of police station by fire.

ENTRIES IN GENERAL FUND:

| | | |
|---|---|---|
| Cash...................................... | 90,000 | |
| Revenues ............................. | | 90,000 |

To record collection of insurance on police station destroyed by fire.

| | | |
|---|---|---|
| Fund Balance............................. | 90,000 | |
| Reserve for Restoring Police Station ...... | | 90,000 |

To create a reserve equal to the portion of the insurance proceeds to be used in restoring the police station.

The reserve is created to make certain that the cash received from the insurance company is not appropriated for other than replacement purposes. Of course, if the governmental unit does not intend to restore the property, no reservation is necessary. Similarly, if the total cost of reconstruction is less than the amount of insurance proceeds received, the amount of the reservation would be correspondingly smaller.

Although the NCGA does not mention write-downs of General Fixed Assets because of damage, obsolescence, or abandonment, it would seem reasonable to do so where circumstances dictate. Thus, it would not seem reasonable to continue carrying a 1926 model fire engine, now confined to the kiddie park, at its original cost of $26,000. Similarly, wrecked vehicles or damaged items of equipment that are not to be repaired probably should be written down to their salvage value. Write-downs are accomplished in the same manner as removals, discussed above.

### Inventory of Fixed Assets

A physical inventory of equipment should be taken either as a continuous process or at the end of each year. If assets are properly recorded when they are acquired, and if retirements and transfers are accurately recorded, the inventory as disclosed by physical inspection should equal the amounts shown by the records. All variations between the two should be investigated.

If it is discovered that certain fixed assets are missing, an investigation should be made. If they cannot be located the General Fixed Assets accounts must be reduced by the book value of the missing fixed assets, and the fixed asset subsidiary accounts and departmental records must be adjusted accordingly. Significant shortages should be disclosed in the statements explaining the changes in fixed assets (Figures 11-8 and 11-10); further, they are indicative of weaknesses in the internal control and accounting systems.

An interesting problem arises with respect to taking an inventory of property for the first time. For example, assume that a governmental unit has not kept records of its fixed assets and that the officials decide to begin keeping such a record. Obviously, the first step would be to take an inventory. As a result of the inventory, information should be available as to (1) the name or description of each asset, (2) any identification marks, such as the manufacturer's number, (3) the location of the asset, (4) its estimated life, and (5) other data necessary to set up an individual property record for each asset. One of the difficult tasks in this connection is to arrive at the value at which to record the assets. If invoices or other documents indicating the cost of an asset are available, these can be used. If such documents are not available, it is necessary to estimate the original cost of the equipment, or appraise it as of the date of the inventory, and to record it at the appraised value.

### Statements of General Fixed Assets

The NCGA suggests that three major statements and one major schedule pertaining to the General Fixed Assets account group be prepared. These include (1) a Statement of General Fixed Assets (Figure 11-7), supplemented by a Schedule of General Fixed Assets—By Functions and Activities (Figure 11-9), (2) a Statement of Changes in General Fixed Assets—By Functions and Activities (Figure 11-10), and (3) a Statement of Changes in General Fixed Assets—By Sources (Figure 11-8).

The Statement of General Fixed Assets (Figure 11-7) presents a summary of the assets, by major category, and their sources. The supplementary Schedule

**Figure 11-7**

A GOVERNMENTAL UNIT
Statement of General Fixed Assets (Date)

General fixed assets:

| | |
|---|---:|
| Land | $   709,600 |
| Buildings | 2,487,200 |
| Improvements other than buildings | 1,978,200 |
| Equipment | 643,100 |
| Construction work in progress | 300,000 |
| Total general fixed assets | $6,118,100 |

Investment in general fixed assets from:

| | |
|---|---:|
| General obligation bonds | $2,558,000 |
| Federal grants | 1,629,600 |
| County grants | 50,000 |
| Special assessments | 650,000 |
| General revenues | 1,227,900 |
| Private gifts | 1,500 |
| Special revenues | 1,100 |
| Total investment in general fixed assets | $6,118,100 |

# A GOVERNMENTAL UNIT

Statement of Changes in General Fixed Assets—by Sources

For the Fiscal Year Ended (Date)

| | Total | Land | Buildings | Improvements Other than Buildings | Equipment | Construction Work in Process |
|---|---|---|---|---|---|---|
| General fixed assets (beginning of year) .... | $5,400,000 | $700,000 | $2,500,000 | $1,100,000 | $619,200 | $480,800 |
| Additions from: | | | | | | |
| General obligation bonds ........... | $ 168,200 | | | $ 93,200 | | $ 75,000 |
| Federal grants ................. | 225,000 | | | 200,000 | | 25,000 |
| County grants ................. | 50,000 | | | 50,000 | | |
| Special assessments ............. | 400,000 | | | 400,000 | | |
| General revenues* ............... | 238,300 | $ 7,000 | $ 37,200 | 135,000 | $ 59,100 | |
| Special revenues* ............... | 1,100 | 1,100 | | | | |
| Private gifts ................. | 1,500 | 1,500 | | | | |
| | $1,084,100 | $ 9,600 | $ 37,200 | $ 878,200 | $ 59,100 | $100,000 |
| Total balance and additions ......... | $6,484,100 | $709,600 | $2,537,200 | $1,978,200 | $678,300 | $580,800 |
| Deductions: | | | | | | |
| Cost of assets sold or traded ......... | $ 32,800 | | | | $ 32,800 | |
| Cost of assets lost by fire ........... | 50,000 | | $ 50,000 | | | |
| Cost of assets worn out and written off .. | 2,400 | | | | 2,400 | |
| Cost of construction work in process of prior year completed† ............... | 280,800 | | | | | $280,800 |
| | $ 366,000 | | $ 50,000 | | $ 35,200 | $280,800 |
| General fixed assets (end of year) ........ | $6,118,100 | $709,600 | $2,487,200 | $1,978,200 | $643,100 | $200,000 |

* Includes amounts transferred to and expended through Capital Projects and Special Assessment Funds.
† Included in costs capitalized to Land, Buildings, Improvements Other than Buildings, and Equipment.

431

Figure 11-9

A GOVERNMENTAL UNIT

Schedule of General Fixed Assets—By Functions and Activities (Date)

| Function and Activity | Total | Land | Buildings | Improvements Other than Buildings | Equipment |
|---|---|---|---|---|---|
| General government: | | | | | |
| Council .................. | $ 20,000 | | | | $ 20,000 |
| Executive department ...... | 13,080 | | | | 13,080 |
| Courts .................. | 100,148 | $ 22,437 | $ 72,700 | | 5,011 |
| Research and investigation ...... | 63,000 | | | | 63,300 |
| General government buildings ...... | 580,000 | 100,000 | 400,000 | 50,000 | 30,000 |
| Total general government ...... | $ 986,100 | $141,600 | $ 573,500 | $ 90,000 | $181,000 |
| Public safety: | | | | | |
| Police protection ...... | $ 233,000 | $ 79,000 | $ 130,000 | $ 1,500 | $ 22,500 |
| Fire protection............ | 316,600 | 27,000 | 120,000 | 6,200 | 163,400 |
| Protective inspection........ | 6,000 | | | | 6,000 |
| Other inspection.......... | 2,000 | | | | 2,000 |
| Correction .............. | 8,600 | 18,000 | 55,000 | 4,000 | 9,000 |
| Total public safety ...... | $ 643,600 | $124,000 | $ 305,000 | $ 11,700 | $202,900 |

| | | | | | |
|---|---:|---:|---:|---:|---:|
| Highways | $2,310,000 | $200,500 | $ 270,000 | $1,819,400 | $ 20,100 |
| Sanitation and waste removal | 306,000 | 71,000 | 53,000 | 22,600 | 159,400 |
| Public welfare | 101,400 | 68,000 | 24,000 | 2,000 | 7,400 |
| Schools | 1,138,800 | 35,000 | 1,047,400 | 17,000 | 39,400 |
| Libraries | 202,000 | 47,000 | 122,600 | 3,500 | 28,900 |
| Recreation | 130,200 | 22,500 | 91,700 | 12,000 | 4,000 |
| Total allocated to functions | $5,818,100 | $709,600 | $2,487,200 | $1,978,200 | $643,100 |
| Construction work in progress | 300,000 | | | | |
| Total general fixed assets | $6,118,100 | | | | |

of General Fixed Assets—By Functions and Activities (Figure 11-9) indicates
the areas in which they are utilized. In practice, this schedule is often prepared
on an organizational unit basis—rather than along the broader functional

**Figure 11-10**

A GOVERNMENTAL UNIT

Statement of Changes in General Fixed Assets—By Functions and Activities

For the Fiscal Year Ended (Date)

| Function and Activity | General Fixed Assets (Beginning of Year) | Additions | Deductions | General Fixed Assets (End of Year) |
|---|---|---|---|---|
| General government: | | | | |
| Council . . . . . . . . . . . . . . . . . | $  18,400 | $  2,100 | $  500 | $  20,000 |
| Executive department . . . . . . | 11,580 | 1,500 | | 13,080 |
| Courts . . . . . . . . . . . . . . . . . | 98,548 | 2,200 | 600 | 100,148 |
| | | | | |
| Research and investigation. . | 61,800 | 1,200 | | 63,000 |
| General government building | 516,000 | 84,000 | 20,000 | 580,000 |
| Total general government | $ 923,500 | $ 101,400 | $ 38,800 | $ 986,100 |
| Public safety: | | | | |
| Police protection . . . . . . . . . . | 222,500 | 21,600 | 11,100 | 233,000 |
| Fire protection . . . . . . . . . . . . | 311,500 | 18,400 | 13,300 | 316,600 |
| Protective inspection . . . . . . . | 6,100 | | 100 | 6,000 |
| Other inspection. . . . . . . . . . | 2,000 | | | 2,000 |
| Correction. . . . . . . . . . . . . . | 81,800 | 4,600 | 400 | 86,000 |
| Total public safety. . . . . . . | $ 623,900 | $ 44,600 | $ 24,900 | $ 643,600 |
| Highways . . . . . . . . . . . . . . . . . | $1,591,900 | $ 718,100 | | $2,310,000 |
| Sanitation and waste removal | 298,000 | 10,000 | 2,000 | 306,000 |
| Public welfare. . . . . . . . . . . . . | 101,400 | | | 101,400 |
| Schools. . . . . . . . . . . . . . . . . . | 1,070,000 | 84,000 | 15,200 | 1,138,800 |
| Libraries . . . . . . . . . . . . . . . . . | 197,400 | 7,000 | 2,400 | 202,000 |
| Recreation. . . . . . . . . . . . . . . . | 113,100 | 19,000 | 1,900 | 130,200 |
| Construction work in progress. . | 480,800 | 100,000 | 280,800 | 300,000 |
| | $5,400,000 | $1,084,100 | $366,000 | $6,118,100 |

categories illustrated—in order to present departmental utilization of, and responsibilities for, General Fixed Assets.

The Statement of Changes in General Fixed Assets—By Functions and Activities (Figure 11-10)—or by organizational unit—compliments the Schedule of General Fixed Assets—By Functions and Activities (Figure 11-9). Similarly, the Statement of Changes in General Fixed Assets—By Sources connects the present Statement of General Fixed Assets (Figure 11-8) with the former one by summarizing current period acquisitions and disposals.

## GENERAL LONG-TERM DEBT

The same type of clear-cut distinction maintained between fixed assets of specific funds and General Fixed Assets is maintained as between (1) long-term debt attributed to a specific fund, and (2) General Long-Term Debt. Thus, the liability for *unmatured general obligation* long-term debt is not established in the accounts of the Capital Projects or other fund through which debt proceeds are expended, nor in a Debt Service Fund, but in the General Long-Term Debt group of accounts.

### "General" Long-Term Debt Defined

General Long-Term Debt may be defined as (1) the unmatured or defaulted principal, (2) of bonds, warrants, notes, and other forms of long-term indebtedness, that (3) is secured by the full faith and credit of the government and (4) is not deemed a primary obligation of any specific fund of the organization. Simply stated, it is the unmatured general obligation indebtedness of the government as a whole, assuming none is in default. Excluded from the definition of General Long-Term Debt are (1) obligations of Special Assessment Funds, discussed previously, and of Enterprise and Trust Funds and (2) matured general obligation debt that has been set up as a liability of a Debt Service Fund. Such obligations are not *general* debt, but are specific obligations of particular funds, though the government as a whole may be contingently liable for them.

The General Long-Term Debt group of accounts replaces the General Bonded Debt and Interest account group of pre-1968 NCGA recommendations. The 1968 committee recommendations are both more realistic and on sounder theoretical grounds, as they (1) broaden the scope of the account group to include all unmatured general obligation debts not accounted for in a fund, not just that which is bonded, and (2) eliminate the previous requirement that unmatured interest—the total cash interest to be paid if the debt remains outstanding for its entire original issue period—be recorded as a liability. Information on future interest payments occasioned by an organization's existing debt structure is presented within the statistical section of financial reports.

## Overview of General Long-Term Debt Accounting

The same type of balanced listing of dollar and item accountability maintained for General Fixed Assets is maintained also for General Long-Term Debt. Though a distinction is made in the accounts as between term and serial indebtedness, the accounting process for General Long-Term Debt may be visualized as in Figure 11-11.

Simply stated, accounting for General Long-Term Debt may be divided into three phases:

1. *When Debt Is Incurred.* The principal of the debt owed is credited to an appropriate liability account; the corresponding debit is to an "Amount To Be Provided for Payment of Debt Principal" or similar account, indicating the extent to which future revenues are committed to the retirement of debt principal.

2. *While Unmatured Debt Is Outstanding.* As resources for the retirement of General Long-Term Debt are accumulated, usually in Debt Service Funds, the "Amount to be provided..." account is reduced and an "Amount Available..." account established or increased to reflect their availability.

3. *When Debt Matures.* The matured debt is established as a liability of the fund through which it is to be paid—usually a Debt Service Fund—and the liability and related "Amount Available..." and/or "Amount to be Provided..." accounts are reversed from the General Long-Term Debt group of accounts.

Practice varies somewhat as to the timing of the entries up-dating the General Long-Term Debt account group. As a general rule (1) entries to record incurrence of debt are made immediately upon its incurrence, (2) entries to record accumulation of debt retirement resources are made in the course of the year end adjustment process; and (3) entries to record debt maturity are prepared at such time as the liability is established in the accounts of the payer fund, usually a Debt Service Fund.

### Relation to Term Debt

In order to illustrate the relationship among the Capital Projects and Debt Service Funds and the General Long-Term Debt group of accounts, recall to mind the 19Y9 City Hall Bonds example of the previous chapter. Upon issuance of the debt instruments at par, entries would be required as follows:

Entry in capital projects fund:

| | | |
|---|---|---|
| Cash ................................ | 1,000,000 | |
| Revenues (or Fund Balance or Appropriations) ................. | | 1,000,000 |
| To record receipt of term bond proceeds sold at par. | | |

Figure 11-11

GENERAL LONG-TERM DEBT GROUP OF ACCOUNTS

RESOURCES TO BE PROVIDED + RESOURCES AVAILABLE = GENERAL LONG-TERM DEBT PAYABLE

**Amount to be Provided**

| (1) Debt Incurred | (2) Resources Accumulated in Debt Service Funds for Debt Retirement | (3) Related to Matured Debt |
|---|---|---|
| | Balance | |
| Balance | | |

**Amount Available**

| (2) Resources Accumulated in Debt Service Funds for Debt Retirement | (3) Related to Matured Debt |
|---|---|
| Balance | |

**Debt Payable**

| (3) Matured Debt — Set Up as Debt Service Fund Liability | (1) Debt Incurred |
|---|---|
| | Balance |

CONTROL

Debt Z

Debt B

Debt A

Description, terms, etc. ....

| REF | (dr.) MATURED | (cr.) INCURRED | BALANCE |
|---|---|---|---|

437

ENTRY IN GENERAL LONG-TERM DEBT ACCOUNTS:
Amount to be Provided for Payment
of Term Bonds . . . . . . . . . . . . . . . . . . . . . . .    1,000,000
    Term Bonds Payable . . . . . . . . . . . . . . .             1,000,000
To record issuance of term bonds.

The liability is recorded at par or maturity value in the GLTD accounts, even if the debt is issued at a premium or discount. The proceeds are expended through the Capital Projects Funds and assets are capitalized in the General Fixed Assets group of accounts following procedures previously discussed.

Recall, however, that a 19Y9 City Hall Bonds Debt Service Fund was established to service this debt. At the end of its first year there was a balance of $27,185 in that Fund, requiring the following adjustment to be made at year end in the GLTD accounts:

Amount Available in Debt Service Funds—
Term Bonds . . . . . . . . . . . . . . . . . . . . . . . . . . . . .    27,185
    Amount to be Provided for Payment of
    Term Bonds . . . . . . . . . . . . . . . . . . . . . . . . . . .            27,185
To record amount available for retirement of term bonds.

Similarly, at the end of the second year the 19Y9 City Hall Debt Service Fund had net assets (Fund Balance) of $56,010, occasioning the following GLTD adjustment:

Amount Available in Debt Service Funds—Term
Bonds . . . . . . . . . . . . . . . . . . . . . . . . . . . . . . . . .    28,825
    Amount to be Provided for Payment of Term
    Bonds . . . . . . . . . . . . . . . . . . . . . . . . . . . . . . . .            28,825
To record increase in the amount available for retirement of term bonds from $27,185 to $56,010.

Similar entries would be made at least annually throughout the life of the Debt Service Fund and the debt issue.

In the 19Y9 City Hall Bonds example, over $1 million had been accumulated in the Debt Service Fund—and reflected in the General Long-term Debt accounts—prior to bond maturity. When the bonds mature, the following related entries are needed:

ENTRY IN DEBT SERVICE FUND:
Expenditures . . . . . . . . . . . . . . . . . . . . . . . . . .    1,000,000
    Matured Bonds Payable . . . . . . . . . . . . .            1,000,000
To record maturity of bonds.

ENTRY IN GENERAL LONG-TERM DEBT ACCOUNTS:
Term Bonds Payable . . . . . . . . . . . . . . . . . . .    1,000,000
    Amount Available in Debt Service
    Funds—Term Bonds . . . . . . . . . . . . . .            1,000,000
To record term bonds maturing and established as a liability of a Debt Service Fund.

Had an amount less than the principal of the maturing bonds been accumulated in the Debt Service Fund (and reflected in the GLTD accounts), the difference would be credited to the "Amount to be Provided. . ." account upon the liability being transferred. Thus, had only $800,000 been available in the 19Y9 City Hall Bond Debt Service Fund upon debt maturity, the GLTD entry would have been:

```
Term Bonds Payable ......................  1,000,000
    Amount Available in Debt Service Funds—
    Term Bonds ........................             800,000
    Amount to be Provided for Payment of
    Term Bonds ........................             200,000
        To record term bonds maturing and established
        as a liability of a Debt Service Fund.
```

In this case, assuming no defaut occurred, additional resources would have been transferred to the Debt Service Fund or part of the debt would have been refunded or extended.

### Relation to Serial Debt

Most serial Debt Service Funds are essentially "flow-through" vehicles through which current period principal and interest requirements and payments are accounted for. Such funds are apt to have minimal (if any) balances at year-end, and do not normally necessitate entries in the General Long-Term Debt group of accounts. The appropriate GLTD entry upon maturity of debt principal in such situations is simply the reverse of the entry made to reflect debt incurrence.

Where debt principal maturities are staggered over a period of years, the government may equalize its annual debt service provisions, thereby accumulating resources in "low requirement" years for use during "high requirement" years. Where a significant excess of serial Debt Service Fund assets over current year principal and interest requirements exists, the serial bond Debt Service Fund becomes similar to a term bond Debt Service Fund and should be accounted for similarly. The required annual adjustment to the GLTD accounts in such cases is again simply a matter of reclassifying from the "Amount to be Provided. . ." account to the "Amount Available. . ." account an amount sufficient to bring the latter into agreement with the Fund Balance account in the serial bond Debt Service Fund.

### Relation to Non-GLTD Issuances

We have observed that long-term indebtedness of Special Assessment, Enterprise, and Trust Funds are usually specific fund liabilities rather than General Long-Term Debt. In many instances, however, governments have guaranteed the timely servicing of such indebtedness in order to make the is-suances more saleable and/or to obtain a lower interest rate on such debt than would otherwise be possible. Though such arrangements usually do not call for formal GLTD entries—as the liability is shown in the balance sheet of the principal debtor fund—the organization's contingent liability on the debt should be disclosed in the Statement of General Long-Term Debt (Figure 11-15). Should the servicing of such debt be in arrears, the contingent liability may become an actual liability, of course, and would then be established in the GLTD accounts.

As a general rule, then, a liability is accounted for in the fund primarily liable therefor, with disclosure required within the statements of the fund secondarily liable—or in GLTD statements if the government as a whole is secondarily liable. Application of this general rule proves difficult at times, and sound judgment and adequate disclosure often prove essential. For example, it may be difficult on occasion to determine (1) where the primary liability for a debt falls; (2) particularly where industrial revenue bonds or obligations of special boards or commissions are involved, which obligations the government should be—or might be—deemed contingently liable for under existing statutes or agreements; (3) where "moral" obligations to guarantee debt have been implied or acknowledged, which will prove enforceable and/or will be enforced against the government; or (4) at what stage a contingent liability becomes an actual liability.

An example of the National Committee's rationale in regard to matters such as these may be found in the accounting procedure it recommends where (1) a general obligation debt is incurred for the benefit of a municipal enter-prise, and (2) the debt is to be serviced through the Enterprise Fund "as a matter of discretionary financial policy" rather than as a party to the debt instrument. Here the Committee recommends that:

1. The original bond authorization be recorded in a Capital Projects Fund in the same manner as any other general obligation bond issue.
2. The sale of the bonds be recorded in the General Long-Term Debt Group of Accounts and the Capital Projects Fund.
3. The bond proceeds be transferred from the Capital Projects Fund to the Enterprise Fund.
4. The assets acquired from the bond proceeds be retained and accounted for in the Enterprise Fund.
5. The amount of bonds outstanding be shown as a liability of the Enterprise Fund (also) with the account title "Advance from Municipality—General Obligation Bonds."[6]

Though such a procedure results in (1) a single liability being shown twice—

6 *GAAFR*, pp. 56–57.

both in the Enterprise Fund and within the General Long-Term Debt account group, and (2) a payable being established within the Enterprise Fund accounts for which there is no corresponding receivable account, the NCGA defends its position by citing the necessity of accounting to reflect legal compliance and

> ...the overriding importance of determining the correct financial position of each fund and balanced account group as individual entities rather than a single over-all financial position for the governmental unit as a consolidated single entity.[7]

The complexities, inconsistencies, and financial statement distortion implicit in the NCGA recommendations cited above are unacceptable to the authors. A better approach would seem to be:

1. *If Enterprise Fund servicing of debt is truly discretionary*—the liability should be established within the General Long-Term Debt group of accounts, the proceeds transferred to the Enterprise Fund should be deemed a capital contribution, and the discretionary arrangement should be disclosed both in the GLTD and the Enterprise Fund statements.

2. *If Enterprise Fund servicing of debt is expected or mandatory*—
   a. in addition to the entries illustrated above a receivable from the Enterprise Fund should be established in the Debt Service Fund, and/or the appropriate amount should be reflected in the GLTD accounts as an amount *expected* to be provided by the Enterprise Fund; or,
   b. If the liability is, in substance, that of the Enterprise Fund, both the proceeds and the liability should be accounted for within the Enterprise Fund accounts—perhaps after first being passed through a Capital Projects Fund—and the government's contingent (in substance) liability should be disclosed in the GLTD statements.

### Premiums and Discounts

Notice again that premiums and discounts on General Long-Term Debt issues are not reflected within the GLTD group of accounts, nor are they reflected or amortized within the accounts of a fund entity. We observed earlier that (1) premiums are usually transferred to a Debt Service Fund, and therefore affect the Amount Available account within the GLTD group, and (2) discounts are written off and either other resources must be secured to compensate for the discount or the project must be scaled down. In effect, then, premiums and discounts on General Long-Term Debt issues "disappear" in this multiple fund and account group environment. This is of minimal consequence, of course, to the increasing number of government managers who realize the

7 *GAAFR,* p. 57.

problems and dangers of printing stated rates on debt issues and issue bonds at par on a bid basis.

### Establishing GLTD Records

A file should be established for each debt issue at an early date, preferably while it is in the planning stage. Here should be maintained copies of, or references to, all pertinent correspondence, ordinances or resolutions, advertisements for the authorization referendum, advertisements or calls for bids, bond indentures or other agreements, debt service schedules, and the like.

The debt instruments themselves should be prenumbered and carefully controlled at all stages of their life cycle. Most government bonds are "bearer" instruments with interest coupons attached, which makes strict control essential.

Subsidiary records such as that illustrated in Figure 11-12 should be established for each serial debt issue. Note that this form also serves as, or supports, an interest payable subsidiary ledger. Although the form illustrated is entitled "Bond and Interest Record," the general format is easily adapted to other forms of long-term debt. An appropriate form for registered debt is shown in Figure 11-13.

As debt principal and interest are paid, whether by the government itself or through a fiscal agent, periodic reports such as that shown in Figure 11-14 should be prepared. Paid coupons and bonds should be marked "Paid" or "Canceled," reconciled with reports of this type, and retained at least until the records have been audited. Paid bonds and coupons are typically destroyed periodically, usually by cremation, in order to conserve storage space and avoid even the slightest possibility of re-issue or double payment. The number of each bond or coupon destroyed should be recorded, attested to by two or more responsible officials who have verified the accuracy of the list and witnessed the bond and coupon destruction, and filed for reference. Bonds and interest coupons may be destroyed by the fiscal agent. In this case, the certified statement of items destroyed (provided by the fiscal agent) should be recorded and filed for reference. As an extra safeguard, some governments require that canceled bonds and interest coupons be microfilmed prior to being destroyed.

### GLTD Statements, Schedules, and Statistical Tables

Although the National Committee on Governmental Accounting sets forth only one financial statement dealing exclusively with general obligation long-term debt, many of the statistical tables (and one combined statement) recommended relate to General Long-Term Debt. The major debt-related presentations suggested are discussed briefly below.

The major statement recommended by the Committee is the Statement of General Long-Term Debt (Figure 11-15). This summary statement of general

# A GOVERNMENTAL UNIT
## Bond and Interest Record

Title _____

Kind of Bonds and Maturities _____

Purpose _____

Amount of Issue _____

Date of Bonds _____

Interest Dates _____

Authorized by _____ Date of Sale _____

Interest Rates _____

Legality Approved by _____ Effective Interest Rate _____

Purchaser _____

Denomination of Bonds _____

Discount _____

Date of Delivery _____ Sale Price _____ Premium _____

Accrued Interest _____

Are Any Bonds of This Issue Registered? _____ Where Payable _____

| Date of Maturity | Interest Due | | | Principal Due | | | Principal and Interest Due Each Date |
|---|---|---|---|---|---|---|---|
| | Coupon No. | Bonds Numbered | Amount | Bonds Numbered | Amount | | |
| | | | | | | | |
| | | | | | | | |

Figure 11-13

## A GOVERNMENTAL UNIT
### Registered Bond Record

Purpose and Title of Issue_____Date of Issue_____
Interest Rate_____Payable on_____
Principal Payable at_____

| Item No. | Date | Bond No. | Name Registered in or Transferred to | Address | Amount | Maturity Date | Amount of Interest Each Period |
|---|---|---|---|---|---|---|---|
| | | | | | | | |

Figure 11-14

## A GOVERNMENTAL UNIT
### Report from Fiscal Agent

Date_____

| Title of Issue | Bonds Paid | | Coupons Paid | | Total Paid |
|---|---|---|---|---|---|
| | Quantity | Amount | Quantity | Amount | |
| | | | | | |

obligation long-term debt and the amounts available and to be provided for its retirement should be supported by a combined schedule of Bonds (and other long-term debt) Payable (Figure 11-16). Many governmental reports also

**Figure 11-15**

CITY OF JACKSONVILLE, FLORIDA
Statement of General Long-Term Debt
September 30, 19X0 and 19W9

*Amount Available and to be Provided for*
*the Payment of General Long-Term Debt*

|  | 19X0 | 19W9 |
|---|---|---|
| Serial bonds: |  |  |
| Amount available for retirement of serial bonds | $ 4,559,393 | $ 4,975,860 |
| Amount to be provided for retirement of serial bonds | 81,550,607 | 83,940,140 |
|  | $86,110,000 | $88,916,000 |
|  |  |  |
| General notes: |  |  |
| Amount to be provided for retirement of general notes | – | 59,737 |
|  | $86,110,000 | $88,975,737 |

*General Long-Term Debt Payable*

|  | 19X0 | 19W9 |
|---|---|---|
| Serial bonds payable: |  |  |
| General obligation bonds payable | $58,735,000 | $60,811,000 |
| General bonds payable from specific revenue sources other than ad valorem taxes | 27,375,000 | 28,105,000 |
|  | $86,110,000 | $88,916,000 |
|  |  |  |
| General notes payable | – | 59,737 |
|  | $86,110,000 | $88,975,737 |

| Note: | General obligation bonds payable include amounts due to independent agencies as follows: | 19X0 | 19W9 |
|---|---|---|---|
|  | Duval County Hospital Authority | $19,620,000 | $19,750,000 |
|  | Jacksonville Port Authority | 30,630,000 | 31,340,000 |
|  |  | $50,250,000 | $51,090,000 |

Source: Adapted from a recent edition of *Financial Statements and Supplementary Information, with Report of Certified Public Accountants,* City of Jacksonville, Florida.

Figure 11-16

## CITY OF JACKSONVILLE, FLORIDA
### Combined Schedule of Bonds Payable
### September 30, 19X0

| Purpose | Interest Rates | Interest Dates | Source of Payment | Principal Issued | Principal Outstanding Sept. 30, 19X0 | Year of Final Principal Maturity |
|---|---|---|---|---|---|---|
| **General obligation bonds:** | | | | | | |
| **General government issues:** | | | | | | |
| Duval County Certificates of 19W3 — Construction of juvenile shelter and parking facility | 2.5–3.1 | 7–1/1–1 | Ad valorem taxes | $ 4,500,000 | $ 3,260,000 | 19Y3 |
| 19W2 general improvement bonds — $3,900,000 allocated for construction of Haydon Burns and Myrtle Avenue Branch Libraries; $2,000,000 allocated for City Hall Annex parking lot and Northside waterfront development; $1,750,000 allocated for park and marina and Southside waterfront development | 2.5–3.2 | 9–1/3–1 | Ad valorem taxes | 7,650,000 | 5,225,000 | 19Y1 |
| **Due to independent agencies:** | | | | | | |
| Duval County Hospital Authority — Constructing and equipping new hospital | 3.2–6.0 | 2–1/8–1 | Ad valorem taxes | 20,000,000 | 19,620,000 | 19Z5 |
| Jacksonville Port Authority — $9,000,000 allocated for construction of Jacksonville International Airport; $25,000,000 allocated for rebuilding and expanding port facilities | 3.1–6.0 / 3.0–5.5 | 8–1/2–1 / 7–1/1–1 | Ad valorem taxes | 34,000,000 | 30,630,000 | 19Z7 |
| | | | | 66,150,000 | 58,735,000 | |

General bonds:

| | | | | | | | |
|---|---|---|---|---|---|---|---|
| Auditorium certificates of indebtedness | Construction of auditorium | 3.5–3.7 | 10-1/4-1 | General revenues other than ad valorem and cigarette taxes | 2,500,000 | 1,000,000 | 19X4 |
| Utilities tax revenue refunding bonds | Refund utilities tax revenue bonds | 3.0–6.0 | 1-1/7-1 | Utilities tax and net revenues of Coliseum-Auditorium facilities | 29,500,000 | 26,375,000 | 19Z2 |
| | | | | | 32,000,000 | 27,375,000 | |
| | | | | | 98,150,000 | 86,110,000 | |

Bonds payable by Enterprise Funds:

| | | | | | | | |
|---|---|---|---|---|---|---|---|
| Sewer District II revenue bonds | Construction of waste treatment facility on Imeson Airport property | 4.5 | 10-1/4-1 | Utilities tax and Sewer District II net revenues | 2,840,000 | 2,115,000 | 19Z8 |
| Municipal Parking revenue bonds | Construction of off-street parking facilities | 3.75 | 12-1/6-1 | Municipal parking system revenues | 4,000,000 | 1,772,000 | 19Y5 |
| Gator Bowl revenue bonds | Construction of Gator Bowl improvements | 3.0–3.875 | 5-1/11-1 | Gator Bowl revenues | 700,000 | 590,000 | 19Z0 |
| Recreation revenue bonds | Construction of Sam Wolfson Baseball Park | 3.75 | 3-1/9-1 | Baseball parks and parking facilities at Sports Complex revenues | 400,000 | 98,000 | 19X4 |
| Motor Vehicle Inspection revenue bonds | Construction of Motor Vehicle Inspection facilities | 4.2–5.0 | 1-1/6-1 | Motor Vehicle Inspection revenues | 1,250,000 | 1,250,000 | 19Y6 |
| | | | | | 9,190,000 | 5,825,000 | |
| Totals | | | | | $107,340,000 | $91,935,000 | |

See notes accompanying individual fund statements.

Source: Adapted from a recent edition of *Financial Statements and Supplementary Information, With Report of Certified Public Accountants*, City of Jacksonville, Florida.

CITY OF JACKSONVILLE, FLORIDA
Summary of Debt Service Requirements to Maturity
September 30, 19X0

*General Obligation Bonds Payable from Ad Valorem Taxes*

| Year | General Government Issues | | Due to Independent Agencies | | Total | |
|---|---|---|---|---|---|---|
| Ending | Principal | Interest | Principal | Interest | Principal | Interest |
| 19X1 | $ 585,000 | $ 247,715 | $ 915,000 | $ 2,059,044 | $ 1,500,000 | $ 2,306,759 |
| 19X2 | 605,000 | 231,740 | 985,000 | 2,009,766 | 1,590,000 | 2,241,506 |
| 19X3 | 630,000 | 214,942 | 1,055,000 | 1,958.339 | 1,685,000 | 2,173,281 |
| 19Z4 | — | — | 2,910,000 | 268,356 | 2,910,000 | 268,356 |
| 19Z5 | — | — | 3,310,000 | 151,313 | 3,310,000 | 151,313 |
| 19Z6 | — | — | 1,720,000 | 59,030 | 1,720,000 | 59,030 |
| 19Z7 | — | — | 480,000 | 480 | 480,000 | 480 |
| 19Z8 | — | — | — | — | — | — |
| Totals | $8,485,000 | $1,689,822 | $50,250,000 | $30,965,663 | $58,735,000 | $32,655,485 |

Source: Adapted from a recent edition of *Financial Statements and Supplementary Information, With Report of Certified Public Accountants,* City of Jacksonville, Florida.

include a statement of changes either in General Long-Term Debt or in total long-term debt.

In order to present the resource requirement of the existing debt structure, for each future year and in total, a Summary of Debt Service Requirements to Maturity—accompanied by a detailed schedule(s) of the requirements of each issue of general obligation long-term debt—is recommended for inclusion within the statistical tables. Figure 11-17 contains a typical summary statement; had long-term notes or warrants been outstanding, additional columns for these would have been added.

A number of other debt-related statistical tables are included in the annual report of a municipality in order to assist bond holders, bond rating firms, and others in assessing the organization's debt structure and debt service ability and to demonstrate legal compliance. Both legal compliance and the amount of additional general obligation debt which may be issued in the future are indicated in the Computation of Legal Debt Margin (Figure 11-18). The calculation varies somewhat according to the laws governing a particular organization, but is typically made along the following lines:

**Figure 11-17**

| General Bonds Payable from Specific Revenue Sources Other than Ad Valorem Taxes | | Revenue Bonds Payable from Enterprise Funds | | | | Total Debt Service |
|---|---|---|---|---|---|---|
| Principal | Interest | Principal | Interest | Total Principal | Total Interest | Requirements |
| $ 760,000 | $ 957,514 | $ 586,000 | $ 233,458 | $ 2,846,000 | $ 3,497,731 | $ 6,343,731 |
| 970,000 | 910,365 | 608,000 | 208,430 | 3,168,000 | 3,360,301 | 6,528,301 |
| 1,025,000 | 860,408 | 634,000 | 181,789 | 3,344,000 | 3,215,478 | 6,559,478 |
| — | — | 50,000 | 9,450 | 2,960,000 | 277,806 | 3,237,806 |
| — | — | 55,000 | 7,087 | 3,365,000 | 158,400 | 3,523,400 |
| — | — | 55,000 | 4,612 | 1,775,000 | 63,642 | 1,838,642 |
| — | — | 60,000 | 2,025 | 540,000 | 2,505 | 542,505 |
| — | — | 15,000 | 337 | 15,000 | 337 | 15,337 |
| $27,375,000 | $12,016,823 | $5,825,000 | $2,145,243 | $91,935,000 | $46,817,551 | $138,752,551 |

1. *Calculation of Legal Debt Limit.* The general obligation debt issue ceiling is first calculated. In most jurisdictions, this is set forth by law as a percentage of the assessed value of taxable properties.

2. *Indication of Net Debt Outstanding Applicable to Debt Limit.* In the usual case the gross long-term debt is indicated, from which is subtracted (1) amounts available for debt retirement, and (2) debts which are not general obligations or that for other reasons are not covered by the debt limit statutes.

3. *Calculation of Legal Debt Margin.* This is the difference between the debt ceiling (1) and the debt outstanding in respect to the ceiling (2).

The Computation of Direct and Overlapping Debt (Figure 11-19), indicates the total long-term debt burden or "debt saturation" of the populace within the unit's jurisdiction. Finally, the magnitude, relationship, and trends of the bonded debt burden and debt servicing ability are indicated in a ten-year historical presentation of the Ratio of General Bonded Debt to Assessed Value and Net Bonded Debt per Capita (Figure 11-20) and the Ratio of Annual Debt Service Expenditures for General Bonded Debt to Total General Expenditures (Figure 11-21).

**Figure 11-18**

### CITY OF GROSSE POINTE, MICHIGAN
Legal Debt Margin, June 30, 19Y0

| | | | |
|---|---|---:|---:|
| 19X9 State Equalized Valuation ................................ | | | $43,013,252 |
| Debt Limit—10% of State equalized valuation ..................... | | | $ 4,301,325 |
| Amount of Debt Applicable to Debt Limit: | | | |
| General obligation bonds: | | | |
| 19W4 Park Improvement.............. | $ 45,000 | | |
| 19X1 Park Improvement.............. | 55,000 | | |
| 19X5 Sewer System Improvement ...... | 1,120,000 | | |
| 19W6 Street Improvement*........... | 22,000 | $1,242,000 | |
| Revenue bonds: | | | |
| 19W5 Water Supply and Sewage | | | |
| Disposal System† ................. | 60,000 | | |
| 19W5 Automobile Parking System** .... | 210,000 | 270,000 | |
| Contracts: | | | |
| Voting machines .................... | 2,218 | | |
| Parking lot properties: | | | |
| James S. Holden Co.** ............. | 85,000 | | |
| Cadieux Properties, Inc.**.......... | 6,000 | 93,218 | |
| Total ..................................... | | 1,605,218 | |
| Less debt which is not general obligation: | | | |
| Revenue bonds ..................... | 270,000 | | |
| Contracts for parking lot properties ..... | 91,000 | 361,000 | |
| Total amount applicable to debt limit ................... | | | 1,244,218 |
| Legal Debt Margin ............................................ | | | $ 3,057,107 |

* Motor vehicle highway bonds payable from gas and weight taxes received from the State of Michigan.
† Bonds payable from the revenues of the Water Supply and Sewage Disposal System.
** Contracts payable from the revenues of the Automobile Parking System.

Source: Adapted from a recent edition of *Financial Statements and Supplementary Information, and Accountants' Opinion*, City of Grosse Pointe, Michigan.

Figure 11-19

CITY OF BIRMINGHAM, ALABAMA
Statement of Direct and Overlapping Debt
August 31, 19X0

| | Gross Debt Less Sinking Fund | Percentage of Debt Applicable to this Municipality | Municipality Share of Debt |
|---|---|---|---|
| This Municipality: | | | |
| Gross Bonded Debt (Table VI) | $50,845,000 | | |
| Less: Sinking Fund Assets (Table VI) | 10,232,867 | | |
| Direct Net Debt (Table VI) | $40,612,133 | 100% | $40,612,133 |
| Jefferson County, Alabama (Fiscal Year ended September 30, 19X0): | | | |
| Total Bonds and Warrants Outstanding | 16,959,000* | 49 | 8,309,991 |
| Jefferson County Board of Education (Fiscal Year ended September 30, 19X0): | | | |
| Total Bonds and Warrants Outstanding | 3,060,000† | 49 | 1,499,000 |
| Total Direct and Overlapping Debt | | | $50,421,124 |

Note: The debt for schools of the City Board of Education of the City of Birmingham, Alabama, is included in the City's general obligation debt shown above.

* All of the Gross Debt of Jefferson County is payable from one of several specially pledged revenues. Each of the specially pledged revenues produces a substantial margin of revenue above the necessary debt service requirements.

† The entire debt of the Jefferson County Board of Education is paid by appropriation of the General Fund of Jefferson County. No portion of this Debt Service is paid from the school funds of the City of Birmingham.

Source: Adapted from a recent edition of *Financial Report,* City of Birmingham, Alabama.

## INTERFUND RELATIONSHIPS

Thus far in this chapter we have indicated how the transactions in the various expendable funds affect the General Fixed Assets and General Long-Term Debt account groups. The entries starting on p. 453 illustrate how certain transactions in one fund affect another fund or funds:

**Figure 11-20**

CITY OF ATLANTA, GEORGIA

Ratio of Net General Bonded Debt to Assessed Value

and Net Bonded Debt Per Capita, Last Ten Years (in Thousands)

| Year | Population | Assessed Value for Bond Purposes | Gross Bonded Debt | Less: Funds Available for Debt Retirement | Net Bonded Debt | Ratio of Net Bonded Debt To Assessed Value | Net Bonded Debt Per Capita |
|---|---|---|---|---|---|---|---|
| 19X0 | 487,455 | $1,075,573 | $ 76,811 | $1,444 | $ 75,367 | 7.01 | $154.61 |
| 19X1 | 489,400 | 1,116,698 | 74,173 | 841 | 73,332 | 6.57 | 149.84 |
| 19X2 | 491,300 | 1,148,770 | 71,502 | 1,272 | 70,230 | 6.11 | 142.95 |
| 19X3 | 493,200 | 1,203,521 | 83,565 | 2,424 | 81,141 | 6.74 | 164.52 |
| 19X4 | 495,200 | 1,280,457 | 80,691 | 3,893 | 76,798 | 6.00 | 155.08 |
| 19X5 | 497,100 | 1,335,204 | 102,040 | 4,677 | 97,363 | 7.29 | 195.86 |
| 19X6 | 499,000 | 1,411,544 | 109,085 | 5,528 | 103,559 | 7.34 | 207.53 |
| 19X7 | 513,200 | 1,473,696 | 117,100 | 5,227 | 111,873 | 7.59 | 217.99 |
| 19X8 | 507,800 | 1,676,098 | 113,157 | 4,414 | 108,743 | 6.49 | 214.15 |
| 19X9 | 502,500 | 1,800,797 | 129,160 | 4,224 | 124,936 | 6.98 | 248.63 |

Source: Adapted from a recent *Annual Report of the Director of Finance,* Atlanta, Georgia.

**Figure 11-21**

CITY OF ROCHESTER, MINNESOTA

Ratio of Annual Debt Service Expenditures for General Bonded Debt

to Total General Expenditures Last Ten Years

| Fiscal Year | Principal | Interest | Total Debt Service | Total General Expenditures | Ratio of Debt Service to General Expenditures (percent) |
|---|---|---|---|---|---|
| 19X1 | 135,000 | $60,390 | $195,390 | $3,459,162 | 5.648% |
| 19X2 | 140,000 | 87,522 | 227,522 | 3,464,419 | 6.567 |
| 19X3 | 140,000 | 93,375 | 233,375 | 3,625,675 | 6.437 |
| 19X4 | 155,000 | 84,275 | 239,275 | 3,613,823 | 6.621 |
| 19X5 | 160,000 | 80,400 | 240,400 | 3,878,341 | 6.199 |
| 19X6 | 160,000 | 76,400 | 236,400 | 4,134,202 | 5.718 |
| 19X7 | 180,000 | 57,785 | 237,785 | 3,956,148 | 6.010 |
| 19X8 | 150,000 | 55,143 | 205,143 | 4,934,845 | 4.150 |
| 19X9 | 165,000 | 50,840 | 215,840 | 5,354,174 | 4.031 |
| 19Y0 | 170,000 | 46,165 | 216,165 | 5,280,998 | 4.093 |

Source: Adapted from a recent edition of *Annual Financial Report,* City of Rochester, Minnesota.

*Transactions Originating in the General Fund*

1. A loan was made from the General Fund to the Debt Service Fund.

ENTRY IN GENERAL FUND:
Due from Debt Service Fund ................. 40,000
   Cash.................................... 40,000
   To record loan made to Debt Service Fund.

ENTRY IN DEBT SERVICE FUND:
Cash...................................... 40,000
   Due to General Fund .................... 40,000
   To record loan from General Fund.

2. A sinking fund contribution was made from the General Fund to the Debt Service Fund.

ENTRY IN GENERAL FUND:
Expenditures.............................. 50,000
   Cash.................................... 50,000
   To record payment of contribution to Debt Service Fund.

ENTRY IN DEBT SERVICE FUND:
Cash...................................... 50,000
   Revenues (or Additions or Contributions) .... 50,000
   To record receipt of contribution from General Fund.

ENTRY IN GENERAL LONG-TERM DEBT GROUP OF ACCOUNTS:
Amount Available for Retirement of Term Bonds   50,000
   Amount to Be Provided for Retirement
   of Term Bonds ........................ 50,000
   To decrease amount to be provided and to increase the amount available for the retirement of term bonds.

3. The governmental unit is required to pay part of the cost of special assessment improvements.

ENTRY IN GENERAL FUND:
Expenditures.............................. 100,000
   Due to Special Assessment Fund .......... 100,000
   To record governmental unit's liability for contribution toward construction of special assessment improvements.

ENTRY IN SPECIAL ASSESSMENT FUND:
Due from General Fund ................... 100,000
   Fund Balance (or Appropriations) ........ 100,000
   To record amount due from General Fund for governmental unit's share of cost of project.

4. Services were performed by a department financed through the General Fund for a special assessment project.

ENTRY IN GENERAL FUND:
Due from Special Assessment Fund.............    10,000
    Expenditures............................             10,000
    To record reduction of expenditures by cost of
    services rendered on special assessment projects.

ENTRY IN SPECIAL ASSESSMENT FUND:
Expenditures...............................    10,000
    Due to General Fund ....................             10,000
    To record cost of services performed by a depart-
    ment financed through the General Fund.

*Transactions Originating in Capital Projects Fund*

1. Premiums on bonds were transferred to the General Fund.

ENTRY IN CAPITAL PROJECTS FUND:
Unamortized Premiums on Bonds .............    1,000
    Cash..................................             1,000
    To record transfer of premiums to the General
    Fund.

ENTRY IN GENERAL FUND:
Cash...................................    1,000
    Revenues .............................             1,000
    To record receipt of cash representing premiums
    on bonds.

2. Proceeds from the sale of bonds issued were transferred (immediately upon receipt) from the Capital Projects Fund to finance:
   (a) the governmental unit's share of special assessment improvement costs
   (b) a deficit in the General Fund.

ENTRY IN CAPITAL PROJECTS FUND:
Fund Balance (or Appropriations or
   Expenditures) .........................    100,000
    Cash..................................             100,000
    To record immediate transfer of proceeds out of
    Capital Projects Fund.

(a) ENTRY IN SPECIAL ASSESSMENT FUND:
Cash—Construction .....................    100,000
    Governmental Unit's Share of Cost .....             100,000
    To record receipt of cash representing gov-
    ernmental unit's share of cost.

(b) ENTRY IN GENERAL FUND:
Cash ..................................    100,000
    Revenues (or Fund Balance)..........             100,000
    To record receipt of proceeds from the sale
    of bonds issued to fund a deficit.

3. Services were rendered by workers paid from a Capital Projects Fund for a department financed through the General Fund.

ENTRY IN CAPITAL PROJECTS FUND:
Due from General Fund ........................ 5,000
    Expenditures............................... 5,000
    To record reduction of construction expenditures by cost of services rendered Department X.

ENTRY IN GENERAL FUND:
Expenditures................................. 5,000
    Due to Capital Projects Fund ............... 5,000
    To record amount due to Capital Projects Fund on account of services rendered Department X.

4. Capital Projects Fund balance was transferred to the General Fund (or to a Debt Service Fund).

ENTRY IN CAPITAL PROJECTS FUND:
Fund Balance ................................ 4,000
    Cash........................................ 4,000
    To record transfer of balance out of Capital Projects Fund to General Fund (or Debt Service Fund).

ENTRY IN GENERAL FUND (OR DEBT SERVICE FUND):
Cash......................................... 4,000
    Revenues (or Fund Balance) ................ 4,000
    To record receipt of Capital Projects Fund balance.

ENTRY IN GENERAL LONG-TERM DEBT GROUP OF ACCOUNTS (if previous entry is in Debt Service Fund):
Amount Available for Retirement of (Type of)
    Bonds ..................................... 4,000
    Amount to Be Provided for Retirement of (Type of) Bonds....................... 4,000
    To record receipt of Capital Projects Fund balance by Debt Service Fund and corresponding increase in amount available for retirement of bonds.

Since, at this point in the book, not all of the funds in governmental accounting have been presented, the foregoing entries are not illustrative of all funds. Additional funds are presented in the next three chapters, and in each case typical relationships of the fund with other funds are illustrated. Finally, a comprehensive "Summary of Interfund Accounting" is presented in Chapter 14.

**Question 11-1.** Distinguish between *interfund transactions* and *interfund relationships*.
**Question 11-2.** Distinguish between a *fund* and an *account group* such as General Fixed Assets.

**Question 11-3.** What criteria must be met for an asset to be classified as a *fixed* asset? A *general* fixed asset?

**Question 11-4.** Generally speaking, what is meant by the term *cost* when determining what costs should be assigned to a fixed asset?

**Question 11-5.** A governmental unit acquired land, buildings, other improvements, and certain equipment for a single lump-sum purchase price. How should the portion of the total cost attributable to the various assets acquired be determined?

**Question 11-6.** Fixed assets may be acquired through exercise of a government's power of *eminent domain* and by *escheat*. Distinguish between these terms.

**Question 11-7.** A municipality was granted certain land for use as a playground. The property was appraised at $10,000 at the time of the grant. Subsequently, all land in the neighborhood rose in value by 20 percent. Should the increase be reflected in the records?

**Question 11-8.** A municipality owns a fire station and is required to pay assessments of $10,000 as an owner of property in the benefited area. As a result of the improvements, the property has risen in value by $15,000. Should the asset be written up, and, if so, by how much?

**Question 11-9.** The NCGA recommended in 1968 that the General Bonded Debt And Interest account group formerly recommended be replaced by a General Long-Term Debt Group of Accounts. Why?

**Question 11-10.** What liabilities are accounted for through the General Long-Term Debt group of accounts? Which items of long-term debt are excluded?

**Question 11-11.** Why are General Fixed Assets and General Long-Term Debt not shown in the same group of accounts?

**Question 11-12.** What entries or disclosures should be made in the General Long-Term Debt group of accounts, or statements pertaining thereto, with regard to general-special debt of Special Assessment Funds?

**Question 11-13.** A municipality's share of special assessment costs was $250,000. To finance these costs, the municipality issued bonds for a corresponding amount. Should these bonds be shown as part of the General Long-Term Debt group of accounts or in the Special Assessment Fund? Explain.

**Question 11-14.** On June 1, 19W3, $300,000 par value of 20-year term general obligation sinking fund bonds were issued by a governmental unit. Only $50,000 had been accumulated in the Debt Service (Sinking) Fund by May 30, 19Y4, the end of the unit's fiscal year, and there was no possibility of retiring the bonds from resources of other funds that year. Should the matured bonds be shown in the General Fund or in the Debt Service Fund, or should they continue to be carried in the General Long-Term Debt group of accounts? Why?

**Question 11-15.** An asset was financed out of a Special Revenue Fund and was carried in the General Fixed Assets group of accounts. Subsequently the asset was sold. To which fund would you credit the proceeds? Why?

**Question 11-16.** Assume that the asset referred to in the preceding question was financed from a Special Assessment Fund or a Capital Projects Fund. To which fund should the proceeds from the sale of this asset be credited? Explain.

**Question 11-17.** Records of fixed assets owned by Lucas County have never been maintained in a systematic manner, and the auditor has recommended that an inventory be taken and that a General Fixed Assets group of accounts be established and maintained. The governing board agrees that it needs better fixed asset control, but has tentatively concluded that no action will be taken in this regard because the appraisal fee estimates provided by reputable appraisal firms far exceed the amount of resources available for such an undertaking. What suggestions or comments, if any, would you offer upon your advice being sought by members of the board?

**Question 11-18.** Near the end of 19X5, a city purchased a luxury automobile for use by the mayor at a cost of $6,000. The vehicle was wrecked during 19X6 and sold for salvage for $600. Assuming that the automobile was purchased from General Fund resources and the salvage proceeds were also recorded there, what entries would be made in 19X5 and 19X6 to reflect these facts? Might misleading inferences be drawn from the General Fund statements for 19X6?

**Question 11-19.** An accountant who is accustomed to commercial accounting and reporting procedures, but unfamiliar with those of governments, was surprised and concerned to find that neither depreciation of general fixed assets nor gains or losses upon their disposal is recognized in government accounts and reports. Upon learning further that bond discount or premium related to general long-term debt is not amortized, and that interest expense is reported essentially on a cash basis by governments, he expressed further concern—concluding that these asset- and liability-related accounting and reporting procedures are inappropriate, misleading, and not in accordance with generally accepted accounting principles. Do you agree? Why?

**Question 11-20.** A neighborhood improvement program expected to cost $100,000 and to be financed entirely by special assessments was undertaken in the City of Xavier. Assessments of $8,000 levied against a large parcel of property within the special assessment district remained unpaid by its absentee owner as the final phase of the program was begun, and the clerk ordered the property to be sold at a sheriff's sale. The city bid in the property at $63,000 and, upon deciding to keep it for a public playground, the aldermen instructed the clerk to write off the delinquent assessment, scale down the improvement program accordingly, and record the property in the General Fixed Assets group of accounts at $1. What objection might be raised with regard to the actions and instructions of the aldermen?

**Problem 11-1.** A street improvement project expected to cost $200,000 and to be financed 70:20:10 by special assessments, a Federal grant, and General Fund contributions, respectively, was undertaken in 19X2. Assessments and contributions were levied and accrued based upon these estimates. Total expenditures incurred and encumbrances at year end were as follows:

|  | Expenditures (Cumulative) | Encumbrances (At Year End) |
|---|---|---|
| December 31, 19X2 | $ 70,000 | $35,000 |
| December 31, 19X3 | 170,000 | 30,000 |
| December 31, 19X4 | 195,000 | –0– |

A $10,000 state grant-in-aid was received for the project during 19X4, the year in which the project was completed. The resources remaining upon completion of the project were refunded pro rata to the Federal government and the General Fund.

Required:
  Prepare the entries that would be made in the General Fixed Assets group of accounts at the end of each year.

**Problem 11-2.** The following is a balance sheet of the Capital Fund of the City of Newton as presented in its annual report:

CITY OF NEWTON
Capital Fund
Balance Sheet
November 30, 19XX

| | | | |
|---|---|---|---|
| Cash in Banks: | | Bonded Debt: | |
| Unexpended bond | | Maturing within One | |
| proceeds .......... | $ 17,364.39 | Year: | |
| Bond Sinking Funds .. | 318,471.48 | Public Improvement | |
| | $ 335,835.87 | Serial Bonds ..... | $ 128,000.00 |
| | | Public Improvement | |
| | | Sinking Fund | |
| | | Bonds .......... | 20,000.00 |
| Amount Necessary to Be | | Maturing After One | |
| Raised by Taxation to | | Year: | |
| Retire Future Bond | | Public Improvement | |
| Maturities .......... | 2,118,528.52 | Serial Bonds ..... | 1,901,000.00 |
| | | Public Improvement | |
| | | Sinking Fund | |
| | | Bonds .......... | 388,000.00 |
| | | | $2,437,000.00 |
| Amount Necessary to | | | |
| Be Raised by | | | |
| Taxation to Pay | | Interest Payable in | |
| Interest in Future | | Future Years ......... | 950,000.00 |
| Years .............. | 950,000.00 | | |
| Land, Structures, and | | Fixed Property Balancing | |
| Equipment.......... | 2,710,316.77 | Account ............ | 2,727,681.16 |
| | $6,114,681.16 | | $6,114,681.16 |

The unexpended bond proceeds represent part of the money received from the sale of serial bonds. The project has been completed, and the money is not needed to finance construction, the cost of the project having been overestimated.

Required:
Prepare statements of (1) General Fixed Assets and (2) General Long-Term Debt, respectively.

**Problem 11-3.** The City of Bergen entered into the following transactions during 19X4:
1. A bond issue was authorized to provide funds for the construction of a new municipal building estimated to cost $500,000. (Formal authorization entry; credit Appropriations.) The bonds were to be paid in 10 equal installments, due March 1 of each year, beginning in 19X5.
2. An advance of $40,000 was received from the General Fund to underwrite a deposit on the land contract of $60,000. The deposit was made.

3. Bonds of $450,000 were sold for cash at 102 and the premium was transferred to a Debt Service Fund. It was decided not to sell all of the bonds because the cost of the land was less than was expected.

4. Contracts amounting to $390,000 were let to Michela and Company, the lowest bidder, for the construction of the municipal building..

5. The temporary advance from the General Fund was repaid and the balance on the land contract was paid.

6. Based on the architect's certificate, warrants were issued for $320,000 for the work completed to date.

7. Warrants paid in cash by the treasurer amounted to $310,000.

8. Because of changes in the plans, the contract with Michela and Company was revised to $440,000; the remaining bonds were sold at 101, and the premium was transferred to a Debt Service Fund.

9. The building was completed and additional warrants amounting to $115,000 were issued to the contractor in final payment for the work. All warrants were paid by the treasurer.

10. The Capital Projects Fund was closed, the balance being transferred to the Debt Service Fund.

Required:

(a) Record the above and closing entries in Capital Projects Fund "T" accounts or on a worksheet. Designate the entries by the numbers which identify the items above.

(b) Prepare applicable balance sheets of other funds and account groups of the City of Bergen as of December 31, 19X4, considering only the bond issue proceeds and expenditures from the Capital Projects Fund.

(AICPA, adapted)

**Problem 11-4.** The City Hall Bond Fund was established on July 1, 19X2 to account for the construction of a new City Hall financed by the sale of bonds. The building was to be constructed on a site owned by the City.

The building construction was to be financed by the issuance of 10-year $2,000,000 general obligation bonds bearing interest at 4 percent. Through prior arrangements $1,000,000 of these bonds were sold on July 1, 19X2. The remaining bonds are to be sold on July 1, 19X3.

The only funds in which transactions pertaining to the new City Hall were recorded were the City Hall Bond Fund and the General Fund. The Bond Fund's trial balance follows:

CITY OF LARNACA

City Hall Bond Fund

June 30, 19X3

|  | Debit | Credit |
|---|---|---|
| Cash.......................... | $ 893,000 | |
| Appropriation expenditures .......... | 140,500 | |
| Encumbrances .................... | 715,500 | |
| Accounts payable ................. | | $ 11,000 |
| Reserve for encumbrances ........... | | 723,000 |
| Appropriations.................... | | 1,015,000 |
|  | $1,749,000 | $1,749,000 |

An analysis of the Appropriation Expenditures account follows:

|  |  | Debit |
|---|---|---|
| 1. | A progress billing invoice from General Construction Company (with which the City contracted for the construction of the new City Hall for $750,000—other contracts will be let for heating, air conditioning, etc.) showing 10 percent of the work completed ........ | $ 75,000 |
| 2. | A charge from the General Fund for work done by Public Works Department employees in clearing the building site ................................ | 11,000 |
| 3. | Payments to suppliers for building materials and supplies purchases ............................. | 14,500 |
| 4. | Payment of interest on bonds outstanding ........ | 40,000 |
|  |  | $140,500 |

An analysis of the Reserve for Encumbrances account follows:

|  |  | Debit (Credit) |
|---|---|---|
| 1. | To record contract with General Construction Company ...................................... | $(750,000) |
| 2. | Purchase orders placed for materials and supplies.. | (55,000) |
| 3. | Receipt of materials and supplies and payment therefore.................................. | 14,500 |
| 4. | Payment of General Construction Company invoice less 10 percent retention .................... | 67,500 |
|  |  | $(723,000) |

An analysis of the Appropriations account follows:

|  |  | Debit (Credit) |
|---|---|---|
| 1. | Face value of bonds sold ................... | $(1,000,000) |
| 2. | Premium realized on sale of bonds ........... | (15,000) |
|  |  | $(1,015,000) |

Required:

(a) Prepare a worksheet for the City Hall Bond (Capital Projects) Fund at June 30, 19X3, showing.

1. Preliminary trial balance.
2. Adjustments. (Formal journal entries are not required.)
3. Adjusted trial balance, before closing. (Closing entries are not required.)

(b) Prepare the formal adjusting journal entries for the following funds and groups of accounts. (Closing entries are not required.)
1. General Fixed Assets.
2. Debt Service Fund.
3. General Long-Term Debt.

(AICPA, adapted)

**Problem 11-5.** The accounts of the City of Daltonville were kept by an inexperienced bookkeeper during the year ended December 31, 19X5. The following trial balance of the General Fund was available when you began your examination:

CITY OF DALTONVILLE
General Fund
Trial Balance
December 31, 19X5

| | | |
|---|---:|---:|
| Cash ......................................... | $ 75,600 | |
| Taxes receivable—current year .................. | 29,000 | |
| Estimated losses—current year taxes receivable..... | | $ 9,000 |
| Taxes receivable—prior year .................... | 4,000 | |
| Estimated losses—prior year taxes receivable....... | | 5,100 |
| Appropriations ............................... | | 174,000 |
| Estimated revenues ........................... | 180,000 | |
| Building addition constructed .................. | 25,000 | |
| Serial bonds paid............................. | 8,000 | |
| Expenditures ................................ | 140,000 | |
| Special assessment bonds payable ............... | | 50,000 |
| Revenues .................................... | | 177,000 |
| Accounts payable ............................ | | 13,000 |
| Fund Balance................................ | | 33,500 |
| | $461,600 | $461,600 |

Your examination disclosed the following:
1. The estimate of losses of $9,000 for current year taxes receivable was found to be a reasonable estimate.
2. The Building Addition Constructed account balance is the cost of an addition to the municipal building. The addition was constructed during 19X5 and payment was made from the General Fund as authorized.
3. The Serial Bonds Paid account reports the annual retirement of general obligation bonds issued to finance the construction of the municipal building. Interest payments of $3,800 for this bond issue are included in Expenditures.
4. A physical count of the current operating supplies at December 31, 19X5, revealed an inventory of $6,500. The decision was made to record the inventory in the accounts; expenditures are to be recorded on the basis of usage rather than purchases.
5. Operating supplies ordered in 19X4 and chargeable to 19X4 appropriations were received, recorded and consumed in January 19X5. The outstanding purchase

orders for these supplies, which were not recorded in the accounts at year end, amounted to $4,400. The vendors' invoices for these supplies totaled $4,700. Appropriations lapse one year after the end of the fiscal year for which they are made.

6. Outstanding purchase orders at December 31, 19X5, for operating supplies totaled $5,300. These purchase orders were not recorded on the books.

7. The special assessment bonds were sold at par in December 19X5 to finance a street paving project. No contracts have been signed for this project and no expenditures have been made.

8. The balance in the Revenues account includes credits for $10,000 for a note issued to a bank to obtain cash in anticipation of tax collections to pay current expenses and for $900 for the sale of scrap iron from the City's water plant. The note was still outstanding at year end. The operations of the water plant are accounted for by a separate fund.

Required:
(a) Prepare the formal adjusting and closing journal entries for the General Fund.
(b) The foregoing information disclosed by your examination was recorded only in the General Fund even though other funds or groups of accounts were involved. Prepare the formal adjusting journal entries for any other funds or groups of accounts involved.

(AICPA, adapted)

**Problem 11-6. Part I.** From the information given in Problem 11-5, prepare a columnar worksheet to reflect the adjustments and corrections needed in order to establish appropriate funds and account groups for the City of Daltonville. Your worksheet headings should be as follows:

| Column(s) | | Worksheet Heading |
|---|---|---|
| 1 | | General Fund Trial Balance (Uncorrected), 12/31/19X5 |
| 2–3 | | Adjusting and Correcting Entries, 12/31/19X5 |
| 4–5 | | Closing Entries, 12/31/19X5 |
| 6–9 | | Corrected Post-Closing Trial Balances, 12/31/19X5 |
| | 6–7 | General Fund |
| | 8–9 | Special Assessment Fund |
| 10–12 | | Journal Entries Required, 12/31/19X5 |
| | 10 | General Long-Term Debt |
| | 11 | General Fixed Assets |
| | 12 | Enterprise (Water) Fund |

**Problem 11-6. Part II.** Assuming the worksheet prepared in Part I will suffice for year end statement preparation and as a basis for establishing ledgers for funds and account groups other than the General Fund, and that no adjusting or correcting entries have been made in the General Fund accounts, prepare a *compound* entry to correct the balance sheet accounts of the General Fund at December 31, 19X5.

**Problem 11-7.** Your examination of the financial statements of the Town of Ecalpon for the year ended June 30, 19X6, disclosed that the Town's inexperienced bookkeeper was uninformed regarding governmental accounting and recorded all transactions in the General Fund. (Proper records had been established and maintained in prior years.) The following General Fund trial balance was prepared by the bookkeeper:

TOWN OF ECALPON
General Fund
Trial Balance
June 30, 19X6

| | | |
|---|---:|---:|
| Cash .............................. | $ 12,900 | |
| Accounts Receivable ....,.............. | 1,200 | |
| Taxes Receivable, Current Year ......... | 8,000 | |
| Tax Anticipation Notes Payable ......... | | $ 15,000 |
| Appropriations ....................... | | 350,000 |
| Expenditures ........................ | 344,000 | |
| Estimated Revenues................... | 290,000 | |
| Revenues ........................... | | 320,000 |
| Town Property ...................... | 16,100 | |
| Bonds Payable ...................,.... | 36,000 | |
| Fund Balance ....................... | | 23,200 |
| | $708,200 | $708,200 |

Your audit disclosed the following:

1. The accounts receivable balance was due from the Town's water utility for the sale of scrap iron. Accounts for the municipal water utility operated by the Town are maintained in a separate fund, by an experienced bookkeeper.

2. The total tax levy for the year was $280,000, of which $10,000 was abated during the year. The Town's tax collection experience in recent years indicates an average loss of 5 percent of the net tax levy for uncollectible taxes. Current year taxes receivable become delinquent August 1, 19X7.

3. On June 30, 19X6, the Town retired at face value 4 percent General Obligation Serial Bonds totaling $30,000. The bonds were issued on July 1, 19X4, in the total amount of $150,000. The principal and interest paid during the year were recorded in the Bonds Payable account. No other long-term debt is outstanding.

4. At the beginning of the year, to service various departments the Town Council authorized a supply room with an inventory not to exceed $10,000. During the year supplies totaling $12,300 were purchased and charged to Expenditures. The physical inventory taken at June 30 disclosed that supplies totaling $8,400 were used.

5. Expenditures for 19X6 included $2,600 applicable to purchase orders issued in the prior year. Outstanding purchase orders at June 30, 19X6, not recorded in the accounts amounted to $4,100.

6. The amount of $8,200, due from the state for the Town's share of state gasoline taxes, was not recorded in the accounts.

7. Equipment costing $7,500 was removed from service and sold for $900 during the year and new equipment costing $17,000 purchased. These transactions were recorded in the Town Property account.

Required:

(a) Prepare the formal adjusting and closing journal entries for the General Fund.

(b) Prepare the formal adjusting journal entries required for any other funds or groups of accounts. (The bookkeeper had recorded all transactions in the General Fund.)

(AICPA, adapted)

**Problem 11-8.** From the information in Problem 11-7, prepare the following for the Town of Ecalpon:

a. A worksheet to adjust, correct, and close the General Fund accounts at June 6, 19X6, with columnar headings as follows:

| Columns | Heading |
| --- | --- |
| 1–2 | Uncorrected Trial Balance, 6/30/19X6 |
| 3–4 | Adjustments and Corrections |
| 5–6 | Corrected Pre-closing Trial Balance, 6/30/19X6 |
| 7–8 | Closing Entries |
| 9–10 | Corrected Post-closing Trial Balance, 6/30/19X6 |

b. A Statement of Changes in Fund Balance of the General Fund for the year ended June 30, 19X6, with the following columnar headings:

| Unappropriated | Reserved for Encumbrances, 19X5 | Reserved for Encumbrances, 19X6 | Reserved for Authorized Supplies Inventory | Total |
| --- | --- | --- | --- | --- |

**Problem 11-9.** The following transactions of the Village of Lakeside are not related unless the transactions are given under the same Roman numeral or unless the connection is specifically stated; not all of the Village's transactions are given. You are to make all of the journal entries to which each transaction gives rise. Use general journal paper and form; no explanation is required. Use the date columns to indicate the fund or account group in which each entry is made, using these abbreviations:

| Fund or Account Group | Abbreviation |
| --- | --- |
| General | GF |
| Special Revenue | SR |
| Capital Projects | CP |
| Special Assessment | SA |
| Debt Service | DS |
| General Fixed Assets | GFA |
| General Long-Term Debt | GLTD |

Separate the journal entries from each other by putting the transaction number and letter on the line above each entry.

    I.    Interest of $3,000 was paid on an issue of general sinking fund bonds.

   II.    A serial issue of general bonds matured in the amount of $50,000 and was paid.

  III.    a.    General obligation sinking fund, 6 percent, 20-year bonds were authorized (formal entry) in the amount of $500,000 (see VII).

           b.    The bonds were issued at a discount of $5,000 and the project authorization was reduced accordingly.

c. The sole purpose of the bond issue was to acquire for $490,000 a piece of property consisting of a parcel of land occupied by a building. The land was worth $50,000. The property was purchased and the fund closed, the balance being transferred to the sinking fund.

IV. Ben E. Factor gave the Village eighty acres of land to be used as a park. The parcel had cost Mr. Factor $20,000 in 1945; its present market value is $80,000.

V. A fire truck, bought in 1948 at a cost of $4,000, was sold for $500; the proceeds were placed in the General Fund.

VI. a. A special assessment project was approved in the amount of $75,000. (Formal authorization entry.)

b. The Village borrowed $50,000 at 6 percent interest for 3 months to finance special assessment construction.

c. The Village's share of the cost was paid in the amount of $15,000.

d. A contract for $74,000 was let to the ABC Company.

e. The Village Engineer certified that the project was one-half completed. The contractor was paid one-half of the contract price, subject to a retained percentage of 5 percent.

f. The contract was completed.

g. The property owners were assessed for all costs.

h. All assessments were collected in full.

i. The fund's business was completed and it was terminated.

VII. a. The schedule of accumulation for the Debt Service (sinking) Fund (see III) showed an annual contribution requirement of $14,355 and estimated earnings of $985 for the current year.

b. The contribution was received.

c. The contribution was invested.

d. Actual earnings totaled $960.

e. The Debt Service (sinking) Fund books were closed.

**Problem 11-10.** Each of the following transactions is independent of the others. (1) Following each transaction a fund or account group is named. Prepare, without explanation, the entry or entries required to record the transaction in the designated fund or account group. (2) You are also to designate any other fund or account group in which the transaction gives rise to an entry or entries, either immediately or by year end, using the following symbols:

| | |
|---|---|
| General Fund | GF |
| Special Revenue Fund | SR |
| Capital Projects Fund | CP |
| Special Assessment Fund | SA |
| Debt Service Fund | DS |
| General Fixed Assets | GFA |
| General Long-Term Debt | GLTD |

1. A truck which was used for garbage disposal was sold for $400. The original cost of the truck was $8,500; it had an expected useful life of five years and was four years old at date of sale. General Fixed Assets.

2. An issue of $100,000 of 20-year, 5 percent sinking fund bonds was authorized for the construction of a bridge over the Yahara River. General Long-Term Debt.

3. An anonymous donor gave the city 500 acres of land on the outskirts of the city. The City Council dedicated the land to park use. The original cost of the property to the donor was $500,000; he had paid taxes of $10,000 a year on it for 10 years; the market value at date of donation was $750,000. General Fixed Assets.

4. The City Council ordered an inventory to be taken and an appropriate reserve to be placed on the books. It voted to consider appropriation expenditures to be based on purchases. The inventory was taken and found to total $10,000. General Fund.

5. Invoices totaling $15,700 were received and vouchered for goods which were ordered last year. Encumbered appropriations do not lapse. The invoices covered all of the orders outstanding at the end of the prior year; the orders had totaled $16,000. General Fund.

6. The post-closing trial balance of the General Fund at December 31, 19X4, contained a Reserve for Encumbrances of $20,000. The appropriations for 19X5 were $270,000, which included the orders which were placed in the preceding year. Special Revenue Fund.

7. General obligation bonds of $100,000 par were sold at 101. Capital Projects Fund.

8. A bond issue was authorized in the amount of $50,000 for the payment of the total cost of a special assessment paving project. Special Assessment Fund.

9. The Expenditures account in the Capital Projects Fund has a balance of $129,000; Appropriations, a balance of $130,000. Construction has been completed. Closing entries are to be made for the Capital Projects Fund. The bonds are serial bonds. Capital Projects Fund.

10. General obligation bonds of $100,000 were sold at 99. Capital Projects Fund.

11. A special assessment project of $100,000 was authorized. Special Assessment Fund.

12. A contract for a paving project was signed for $75,000. Special Assessment Fund.

13. The budget for the Debt Service Fund (contributions $20,000, interest $2,500) becomes available at the beginning of the year. Prepare the journal entry to record the budget. Debt Service Fund.

14. The sinking fund annual contribution of $20,000 became receivable. Debt Service Fund.

15. Bought a desk for the city attorney's office, $500, with General Fund cash. General Fund.

16. Prepare the closing entries, without dollar amounts, for a Debt Service (sinking) Fund which is completing a year which is neither its first nor its last. Debt Service (Sinking) Fund.

17. Last year a city building project was incomplete, but expenditures of $100,000 were closed. Now the project is complete and closing entries are made. This year's expenditures total $50,000. General Fixed Assets.

**Problem 11-11.** Insurance proceeds of $40,000, received after a fire damaged a municipal building, were recorded in a Capital Projects Fund while renovation was in process. A total of $70,000 was spent on the building, of which $50,000 was attributable to restoring it to its pre-fire condition, and the additional amount needed was transferred to the Capital Projects Fund from the General Fund. A billing error was discovered after the contractor was paid, and he refunded $1,500 to the Capital Projects Fund; this amount was later transferred to a Debt Service Fund, by order of the Council, to ultimately be used to repay the indebtedness incurred when the building was constructed five years earlier.

Required:
(a)  What entries would be made in the city's accounts to reflect these transactions and events assuming all occurred in 19X1?
(b)  What entries would be made if (a) the fire damage occurred and the insurance proceeds were received in 19X1; (b) the General Fund transfer, completion of the project, and payment of the contractor's original bill occurred during 19X2; and (c) the billing error was discovered in 19X3 and the refund and transfer to the Debt Service Fund took place in that year?

**Problem 11-12.**  You were engaged to examine the financial statements of the City of Homer for the year ended June 30, 19X9, and found that the bookkeeper had recorded all transactions in the General Fund. You were furnished the General Fund Trial Balance, which appears below:

CITY OF HOMER
General Fund
Trial Balance
June 30, 19X9

*Debits*

| | |
|---|---:|
| Cash | $ 125,180 |
| Cash for Construction | 174,000 |
| Taxes Receivable—Current | 8,000 |
| Assessments Receivable—Deferred | 300,000 |
| Inventory of Materials and Supplies | 38,000 |
| Improvements Authorized | 15,000 |
| Estimated Revenues | 4,135,000 |
| Interest Expense | 18,000 |
| Encumbrances | 360,000 |
| Expenditures | 4,310,000 |
| Total Debits | $9,483,180 |

*Credits*

| | |
|---|---:|
| Estimated Uncollectible Current Taxes | $ 7,000 |
| Vouchers Payable | 62,090 |
| Interest Payble | 18,000 |
| Liability Under Street Improvement Project | 10,000 |
| Bonds Payable | 300,000 |
| Premium on Bonds | 3,000 |
| Reserve for Inventory | 36,000 |
| Reserve for Encumbrances | 360,000 |
| Appropriations | 4,450,000 |
| Interest Revenue | 21,000 |
| Fund Balance | 106,090 |
| Revenues | 4,110,000 |
| Total Credits | $9,483,180 |

Your audit disclosed the following:

1. Years ago the City Council authorized the recording of inventories, and a physical inventory taken on June 30, 19X9, showed that materials and supplies with a cost of $37,750 were on hand at that date. The inventory is recorded on a perpetual basis.

2. Current taxes are now considered delinquent and it is estimated that $5,500 of such taxes will be uncollectible.

3. Discounts of $32,000 were taken on property taxes. An appropriation is not required for discounts, but an allowance for them was not made at the time the tax levy was recorded. Discounts taken were charged to Expenditures.

4. On June 25, 19X9, the State Revenue Department informed the city that its share of a state-collected, locally-shared tax would be $75,000.

5. New equipment for the Police Department was acquired at a cost of $90,000 and was properly recorded in the General Fund.

6. During the year 100 acres of land was donated to the city for use as an industrial park. The land had a value of $250,000. No recording has been made.

7. The City Council authorized the paving and widening of certain streets at an estimated cost of $365,000, which included an estimated $5,000 cost for planning and engineering to be paid from the General Fund. The remaining $360,000 was to be financed by a $10,000 contribution from the city and $350,000 by assessments against property owners payable in seven equal annual installments. A $15,000 appropriation was made for the city's share at the time the annual budget was recorded, and the total $365,000 was also recorded as an appropriation. The following information is also relevant to the street improvement project:

(a) Property owners paid their annual installment plus a $21,000 interest charge in full.

(b) Special assessment bonds of $300,000 were authorized and sold at a premium of $3,000. An $18,000 liability for interest was properly recorded. The city does not amortize bond premium or discount.

(c) The city's $15,000 share was recorded as an expenditure during the year. The $5,000 for planning and engineering fees were paid. Construction began July 5, 19X8, and the contractor has been paid $200,000 under the contract for construction which calls for performance of the work at a total cost of $360,000. This $360,000 makes up the balance in the Reserve for Encumbrances.

(d) The Cash for Construction account was used for all receipts and disbursements relative to the project. It is made up of the proceeds of the bond issue and collection of assessment installments and interest minus payments to the contractor.

Required:

Prepare a worksheet to adjust (but not close) the account balances at June 30, 19X9, and to distribute them to the appropriate funds or groups of accounts. It is recommended that the worksheet be in the order of the General Fund Trial Balance and have the following column headings:

(a) Balance per books.
(b) Adjustments—debit.
(c) Adjustments—credit.
(d) General Fund.
(e) Special Assessment Fund.
(f) General Fixed Assets.

(Number all adjusting entries. Formal journal entries or financial statements are not required. Supporting computations should be in good form.)

(AICPA, adapted)

**Problem 11-13.** The City of Patonton trial balances on January 1, 19X4 were as follows:

### General Fund

| | | |
|---|---:|---:|
| Cash ........................................ | $ 7,000 | |
| Taxes Receivable, Delinquent .................... | 48,000 | |
| Allowance for Uncollectible Taxes Receivable, | | |
| Delinquent ................................. | | $ 4,000 |
| Due from Water Fund ......................... | 500 | |
| Vouchers Payable ............................. | | 11,000 |
| Due to Taxpayers ............................. | | 1,000 |
| Reserve for Encumbrances, 19X3 ................. | | 3,000 |
| Fund Balance ................................. | | 36,500 |
| | $55,500 | $55,500 |

### General Long-Term Debt

| | | |
|---|---:|---:|
| Amount to Be Provided for Payment of Bonds ....... | 75,000 | |
| Bonds Payable ................................ | | 75,000 |
| | $75,000 | $75,000 |

The following information summarizes the transactions of the City during 19X4:
1. The City Council approved the following General Fund budget for 19X4:

| | |
|---|---|
| Expenditures | $60,000 |
| Revenues | 50,000 |

2. The Council approved the levy of general property taxes of $40,000. It was estimated that $2,000 of the amount would never be collected.
3. Upon petition of the property owners in Foggy Bottom Subdivision, a paving project expected to cost $50,000 was authorized by the Council. (Prepare a formal authorization entry.) The City had been having such high maintenance costs for Foggy Bottom streets that the Council agreed that the City should pay one-half of the cost of the project.
4. A contract for $40,000 was signed for the principal paving work.
5. The City Engineer and the Street Department performed part of the work on the paving project at a cost of $10,000.
6. Property owners and the City were assessed on June 30, 19X4. Property owners are to pay one-fifth of their assessments each year starting January 1, 19X5, with interest at 6 percent from June 30, 19X4.
7. The paving project was financed by borrowing $50,000 from a local bank on short-term notes.
8. Bonds were authorized to pay the City's share of the cost of the paving project. (Prepare a formal authorization entry.) The bonds carry an interest rate of 6 per-

cent, and one-fifth of the face value matures annually starting one year from date of issue.

9. Some of the cash collections during the year are summarized as follows:

| | |
|---|---:|
| Prior year's levies | $45,000 |
| 19X4 levy | 11,000 |
| Fines and fees | 4,000 |
| Taxes written off in prior years | 500 |
| Interest | 500 |
| Service charges | 2,000 |
| | $63,000 |

10. Orders placed during the year totaled $15,000.

11. Payrolls vouchered during the year totaled $52,500.

12. The bonds referred to in transaction 8 were sold at 101. The proceeds were properly distributed and accounted for, the premiums being transferred to a Debt Service Fund, and the Capital Projects Fund for the issue was closed.

13. The paving contractor was paid $40,000 on the basis of the City Engineer's statement of completion.

14. Bonds were sold at par to finance the property owners' share of the cost of the project. The bonds were dated July 1, 19X4, and bear interest at 5 percent.

15. The paving notes were paid without interest.

16. Invoices vouchered during the year in the General Fund were as follows:

| | |
|---|---:|
| Invoices for 19X4 orders | $14,500 |
| Invoices for 19X3 orders | 3,100 |
| | $17,600 |

The above invoices completed all orders except one dated June 1, 19X4, for $950.

17. Analysis of collections revealed that Taxpayer A, to whom the City owed $1,000 on January 1, 19X4 for overpayment of taxes, had settled his obligation to the City by paying his tax for 19X4, less $1,000.

18. A department financed through the General Fund rendered services in the amount of $250 to the Water Fund.

19. The City Council made an additional appropriation in the amount of $5,000 for a bond maturity which was overlooked in the preparation of the budget.

20. The bonds mentioned in transaction 12 matured and were vouchered.

21. Cash paid on vouchers payable totaled $65,000.

22. Delinquent taxes in the amount of $500 were written off on the authority of the Council.

23. The General Fund was reimbursed from the Special Assessment Fund for the services rendered in transaction 5.

24. Included in General Fund expenditures is an amount of $1,500 for interest on bonded debt issued in 19X3.

Required:

For each fund (except the Water Fund) and account group needed to record properly the above transactions, prepare a worksheet to facilitate the preparation of statements describing the fund's operations and position at December 31, 19X4.

**Problem 11-14.** From the following information, prepare balance sheet working papers of each of the following funds or account groups of the. City of *M* as of February 28, 19X6: (1) General Fund, (2) Special Assessment Fund, (3) Capital Projects Fund and (4) General Fixed Assets.

The City of *M* has established the above funds and account group in its accounting system and, in addition, has a Debt Service (Sinking) Fund and a General Long-Term Debt group of accounts. Detail for the latter fund and account group is omitted in this problem and working papers of these are not required.

The City of *M* keeps its accounts on the accrual basis, except with respect to interest receivable and payable not yet due. It makes provision in its tax roll for state road taxes, state school taxes, and county taxes which are collected by it as agent for the state and the county.

Ledger account balances as of February 28, 19X6, are presented as follows:

|  | *Balance* |
|---|---:|
| **General Fund:** | |
| Cash in Depositories ............................. | $ 125,000 |
| Petty Cash ...................................... | 500 |
| Taxes Receivable—Current ........................ | 215,000 |
| Taxes Receivable—Delinquent ..................... | 20,000 |
| Taxes Receivable for Other Units—Current .......... | 18,000 |
| Interest and Penalties Receivable on Delinquent Taxes.. | 1,400 |
| Vouchers Payable ............................... | 130,000 |
| Notes Payable ................................... | 116,200 |
| Due to Special Assessment Fund .................... | 8,400 |
| Due to Other Governmental Units—State ............ | 21,600 |
| Due to Other Governmental Units—County .......... | 5,400 |
| Fund Balance .................................... | 44,900 |
| Appropriations .................................. | 921,800 |
| Expenditures ................................... | 900,000 |
| Estimated Revenues ............................. | 950,000 |
| Revenues........................................ | 953,600 |
| Revenues Not Anticipated ......................... | 8,200 |
| Taxes Collected in Advance ....................... | 14,800 |
| Emergency Note ................................. | 5,000 |
| **Special Assessments Fund:** | |
| Cash in Depositories ............................. | 316,600 |
| Special Assessments Receivable .................... | 320,000 |
| Due from General Fund—Municipality's Share of Assessment Improvement Costs ....................... | 8,400 |
| Special Assessment Liens ......................... | 20,000 |
| Improvements Other Than Buildings—Completed* .... | 75,000 |
| Improvements Other Than Buildings—In Progress* .... | 28,000 |
| Vouchers Payable................................. | 15,000 |

| | *Balance* |
|---|---|
| Notes Payable | 90,000 |
| Contracts Payable—Uncompleted Contracts | 130,000 |
| Bonds Payable | 350,000 |
| Reserve for Authorized Expenditures** | 183,000 |
| Fund Balance-Construction | — |
| Fund Balance-Interest | — |
| Capital Projects Fund: | |
| Cash in Depositories | 120,000 |
| Accounts Receivable | 15,000 |
| Buildings—Completed* | 120,000 |
| Buildings—Uncompleted* | 50,000 |
| Bonds Authorized—Unissued | 100,000 |
| Vouchers Payable | 25,000 |
| Contracts Payable—Uncompleted Contracts | 68,700 |
| Contracts Payable—Completed Contracts | 60,000 |
| Expenditures | 309,000 |
| Reserve for Authorized Expenditures** | 560,300 |
| General Fixed Assets (Balances as at March 1, 19X6): | |
| Land | 1,200,000 |
| Buildings | 3,400,000 |
| Improvements Other Than Buildings | 640,000 |
| Machinery and Equipment | 325,000 |
| Construction Work in Progress | — |
| Investment in General Fixed Assets | 5,565,000 |

\* Accounts such as these are frequently employed in Capital Projects and Special Assessment Fund accounting in lieu of Expenditures accounts or to reestablish construction work in process in the accounts after closing entries have been made.
\*\* Synonymous with "Appropriations" described in Chapters 8 and 10.

Your audit discloses the following:
1. Provisions for estimated losses against receivables (after abatements) in the General Fund are to be provided as follows:

| | |
|---|---|
| Taxes receivable—current | 10% |
| Taxes receivable—delinquent, and interest and penalties thereon | 20 |
| Taxes receivable for other units—current | 10 |

2. Abatements of City taxes not reflected are $4,900 for 19X5, $710 for 19X4, and $340 for 19X3. Interest and penalties applicable to abated taxes were $80 for 19X4 and $20 for 19X3. Taxes become delinquent at the end of the year following the year in which they are levied.
3. The state and county taxes, amounting to $36,000 and $9,000 respectively, were credited to Fund Balance as part of the entry setting up the tax roll. The current balances in the Due to Other Governmental Units accounts represent cash collected

to date for these units. Such cash, which has not as yet been remitted to the units, has been credited to the Taxes Receivable for Other Units—Current account.

4. The taxes collected in advance ($14,800) were subject to a discount of $800, currently charged to the Expenditures account.

5. The emergency note was issued on February 1, 19X6, to meet an emergency appropriation. This note is to be retired through taxation during the fiscal year beginning March 1, 19X6. Fund Balance was charged for the amount of the appropriation, which equaled the amount of the note.

6. Unrecorded interest due on special assessment liens amounts to $540.

7. No provision has been made for retained percentages of $5,000 on uncompleted special assessment contracts.

8. The Reserve for Authorized Expenditures account in the Special Assessment Fund shows that on work completed to February 28, 19X6, authorizations have exceeded expenditures by $1,400, an amount considered too small to be rebated.

9. Unrecorded commitments on unfilled orders for the General, Special Assessment, and Capital Projects Funds amounted to $30,000, $45,000, and $18,000, respectively.

10. Current year Capital Projects Fund expenditures relate to the building under construction.

(AICPA, adapted)

**Problem 11-15.** At the start of your examination of the accounts of the City of Waterford, you discovered that the bookkeeper failed to keep the accounts by funds. The following trial balance of the General Fund for the year ended December 31, 19X9, was available.

CITY OF WATERFORD

General Fund

Trial Balance

December 31, 19X9

|  | Debit | Credit |
|---|---|---|
| Cash | $ 207,500 | |
| Taxes Receivable—Current | 148,500 | |
| Estimated Uncollectible Taxes—Current | | $ 6,000 |
| Expenditures | 760,000 | |
| Revenues | | 992,500 |
| Donated Land | 190,000 | |
| River Bridge Bonds Authorized—Unissued | 100,000 | |
| Construction Work in Progress—River Bridge | 130,000 | |
| River Bridge Bonds Payable | | 200,000 |
| Contracts Payable—River Bridge | | 25,000 |
| Contracts Payable—River Bridge (Retained Percentage) | | 5,000 |
| Vouchers Payable | | 7,500 |
| Fund Balance | | 300,000 |
| Total | $1,536,000 | $1,536,000 |

Your examination disclosed the following:
1. The budget for the year 19X9, not recorded on the books, estimated revenues and expenditures as follows: revenues $815,000; expenditures $775,000.
2. Outstanding purchase orders at December 31, 19X9 for operating expenses not recorded on the books totaled $2,500.
3. Included in the Revenues account is a credit of $190,000 representing the value of land donated by the state as a grant-in-aid for construction of the River Bridge.
4. Interest payable in future years totals $60,000 on River Bridge bonds sold at par for $200,000.
5. Examination of the subledger containing the details of the Expenditures account revealed the following items included therein:

| | |
|---|---:|
| Current operating expenses | $472,000 |
| Additions to structures and improvements (other than bridges)... | 210,000 |
| Equipment purchases for police department | 10,000 |
| General obligation street improvement bonds paid | 50,000 |
| Interest paid on general obligation bonds | 18,000 |

Required:
Prepare a worksheet showing the General Fund trial balance given, adjusting entries, and distributions to the proper funds or groups of accounts at December 31, 19X9. (Do not prepare closing entries). The following column headings are recommended:

| Columns | Headings |
|---|---|
| 1–2 | General Fund Trial Balance (Uncorrected)—Debit |
| | Credit |
| 3–4 | Adjustments—Debit |
| | Credit |
| 5–6 | Corrected General Fund Trial Balance (Pre-Closing)—Debit |
| | Credit |
| 7 | Capital Projects Fund Trial Balance (Pre-Closing) |
| 8 | General Fixed Assets Group |
| 9 | General Long-Term Debt Group |

Number all adjusting and transaction entries. Formal journal entries are not required.

(AICPA, adapted)

# 12

# Trust and Agency Funds

A *Trust* Fund is established to account for assets received and held by a government acting in the capacity of trustee or custodian. An *Agency* Fund is established to account for assets received by a government in its capacity as an agent for individuals, businesses, or other governments.

The difference between Trust Funds and Agency Funds is often one of degree. Trust Funds, for example, may be subject to complex administrative and financial provisions set forth in trust agreements, may be in existence for long periods of time, and may involve investment or other management of trust assets. Thus, Trust Fund management and accounting may be more complex than that required for Agency Funds. Agency Funds, on the other hand, are primarily clearance devices for cash collected for others, held briefly, and then disbursed to authorized recipients. The government acts in a fiduciary capacity, however, in all of its trust and agency relationships. Too, accounting for Agency Funds and for the simpler types of expendable Trust Funds is virtually identical. Trust and Agency Funds may therefore be considered together as one class of funds.

It is important to note that enterprise trust and agency relationships (such as utility customer deposits) are accounted for within Enterprise Funds (Chapter 14) following the "funds within a fund" approach. Separate Trust or Agency Funds need not be established in such cases; all that is required is that the restricted asset and related liability accounts be distinctively titled as trust- or agency-related.

## Budgetary Considerations

In the usual trust or agency relationship, the government merely manages or transmits fund resources in accordance with specific instructions or customary trust or agency practices. It may hold legal title to assets of these Funds, but rarely has beneficial title to them and may not normally expend them for usual operating purposes. For these reasons, Trust and Agency Fund revenues and expenditures are rarely incorporated in a government's operating budget or subjected to formal budgetary control through the accounting process.

There are exceptions, of course. The most usual of these is when a Trust Fund is in substance a Special Revenue Fund, that is, its resources are available for certain operating purposes. In such cases—e.g., Revenue Sharing Trust Funds of state or local governments—logic would dictate that the Trust Fund be accounted for as if it were a Special Revenue Fund.

## The Accountability Focus

The accountability focus in General and Special Revenue Fund accounting is primarily upon operating budget compliance within a specified time period. In Capital Projects and Special Assessment Fund accounting, attention is generally focused mainly upon the project, rather than a specific period, and upon the capital program or capital budget. The accountability focus in Trust and Agency Fund accounting, on the other hand, is upon the manner in which the government fulfilled its fiduciary responsibilities during a specified period of time and upon those unfilled responsibilities remaining at the end of the period.

The aim in Trust Fund accounting is therefore to insure that the money or other resources are handled in accordance with the terms of the trust agreement and/or applicable trust laws. The accounting procedure for Agency Funds must insure that collections are properly handled and are turned over promptly to the party for whom they are collected. The net amount of resources in a Trust or Agency Fund is usually indicated in a Fund Balance account, though in some cases (see retirement and pension fund discussions following) different account titles may be used. The accounts of this type measure the *accountability* of the governmental unit as trustee or agent for the use and disposition of the resources in its care. In the case of the Agency Fund the accountability concept very closely approaches the liability concept, and even in the Trust Fund there is an obligation for the government to use Fund resources to discharge the assigned function. Failure to comply with trust terms would ordinarily be grounds for the forfeiture of Fund resources.

## Financial Statements Required

A Balance Sheet, Statement of Changes in Fund Balance, and Statement of Cash Receipts and Disbursements should be prepared at least annually for all Trust and Agency Funds. Examples of each of these are included in the section of this chapter dealing with public employee retirement funds. Additional statements or schedules are often needed to fully disclose operating or position data for certain types of Trust or Agency Funds. Several of these, such as statements analyzing pension fund reserves and schedules of investments or taxes receivable, are illustrated in this chapter. Combined statements are usually prepared where a governmental unit is responsible for several Trust and Agency Funds (see Figure 12-15).

## TRUST FUNDS

A variety of trust relationships, varying from elemental to extremely complex, may be encountered in the governmental environment. Some of these would not necessitate the creation of a Trust Fund. For example, where earnings of an independently trusteed fund are remitted to the government to supplement library operations—and finance a relatively minor percentage of total library operating expenditures—they may be considered revenues of the fund through which library activities are financed. On the other hand, if trust earnings provide a substantial portion of total library operating resources, the entire library operation may be financed through a Trust Fund.

Trust Funds may be classified in several ways. Some are established *internally* for administrative expediency, for example, while others are set up pursuant to formal agreements with *external* persons or groups, such as by trust indenture.

Trust Funds may also be classified as *public* and *private*. A public Trust Fund is one whose principal, earnings, or both must be used for a public purpose. An example is a fund established to account for resources received by bequest which are to be used to provide health care for the indigent. A private Trust Fund is one that will ordinarily revert to private individuals or will be used for private purposes. A guaranty deposits fund is an example of a private Trust Fund. The accounting procedure will not be determined by whether the Fund is public or private, however, but by whether it is expendable or nonexpendable.

By far the most important classification of Trust Funds from an accounting standpoint is between those that are *expendable* and those that are *nonexpendable*. As the name implies, expendable Trust Funds are those whose entire resources may be expended. Pension funds and special deposits funds are examples of expendable Trust Funds. Pension fund expenditures take the form of pension payments to beneficiaries; expenditures of deposit funds are in the form of refunds to the depositors.

Nonexpendable Trust Funds are those in which the principal (corpus), and perhaps the earnings, must be held intact. A loan fund whose principal and earnings must be kept intact represents a good example of a nonexpendable

Trust Fund. Such a fund is usually established upon the gift or bequest of a sum of money or other property to be used in making loans for specified purposes. Since loans are expected to be repaid, the Fund is not expended when the loans are made. In the absence of uncollectible loans, the Fund becomes more or less permanent, cash being replaced by accounts or notes receivable when loans are made. The Fund's balance will increase if interest charges exceed bad debt losses and administrative costs, if any, charged to the Fund.

Finally, some Trust Funds are expendable as to earnings but nonexpendable as to principal (corpus). In this case two funds are usually established (1) a nonexpendable principal Trust Fund, and (2) an expendable earnings Trust Fund.

An exhaustive treatment of trust law and accounting is beyond the scope of this text. Rather, the more usual types of Trust Funds found in state and local governments are briefly considered here and the fundamental accounting and reporting procedures applicable in typical situations are illustrated. The reader desiring a more comprehensive general knowledge of the subject should find the relevant chapter in any standard advanced accounting text helpful. Determination of appropriate systems and procedures in specific cases, however, may require a search of the more technical accounting, legal, and insurance literature or the assistance of specialists within one or more of these fields.

### Expendable Trust Funds

Two examples of expendable Trust Funds are illustrated below, namely, a guaranty deposits fund and a retirement or pension fund.

Accounting for the former is relatively uncomplicated; for the latter, rather complex. In view of their complexities and growing significance in government finance, two approaches to retirement or pension fund accounting are illustrated.

GUARANTY DEPOSITS FUND. Most governments require deposits for some purpose. For example, contractors may be required to post deposits with the government to guarantee satisfactory performance of their contracts. These deposits must be accounted for so that they may be returned to the depositors if contract performance is satisfactory or, if performance is not satisfactory, used to defray the costs of having the defective performance corrected.

The accounting procedure for a guaranty deposits fund is simple. As deposits are received, Cash is debited and a Deposits Fund Balance account is credited. Subsequently, as deposits are refunded, these entries are reversed. The Balance Sheet of such a fund would, therefore, contain only a few accounts, as indicated by the statement presented in Figure 12-1.

PENSION AND RETIREMENT FUNDS. Public employee retirement plans provide examples of more complex expendable Trust Funds common to governments.

Figure 12-1

A GOVERNMENTAL UNIT
Guaranty Deposits Fund
Balance Sheet
At Close of Fiscal Year (Date)

*Assets*

| | |
|---|---|
| Cash ...................... | $ 3,370 |
| Investments .............. | 15,000 |
| | $18,370 |

*Fund Balance*

| | |
|---|---|
| Deposits fund balance ........ | $18,370 |

Pension or retirement plans of governments, like those of businesses, should be managed and accounted for on an actuarial basis, and the provisions of Accounting Principles Board (APB) Opinion Number 8 are generally applicable to them.

Many types of retirement plans are in existence in governments. Local governments often have retirement systems, though in some states employees of all governmental units of a certain type (e.g., municipalities) or all employees within certain functional fields (e.g., teachers, policemen, firemen) are included in a statewide retirement system. In some cases these plans are integrated with Federal social security benefits; in others, employees are not covered under that program. The administrative mechanisms established also differ widely. In some instances the retirement system is managed and accounted for by the finance department or some other executive agency of the government. In other cases an independent board, or even a separate corporation, is charged with retirement system management and accountability.

Of far more consequence to accounting and reporting, to sound public finance policy, and to the public interest generally, is the disparate array of financial management practices relating to retirement systems. The NCGA noted that:

Judged by virtually any yardstick—monetary value, growth, impact on governmental budgets and personnel management, or economic significance to individual government employees, public employee retirement systems are among the most significant of those governmental operations which must be accounted for in trust funds.

Some retirement systems, unfortunately, are not properly funded on an actuarial basis and rely on uncertain and often inadequate legislative appropriations to finance benefit payments during any fiscal period. At the opposite end of the scale are an increasing number of systems which are set up on the actuarial reserve basis with all liabilities, present and prospective, adequately funded and properly managed. In between these two extremes are numerous retirement systems and funds which are designed to be actuarily [sic] sound ...but which have comparatively minor and manageable...deficits resulting from such circumstances as inadequate legislative provision for prior service costs, investment restrictions, or...liberal increases in benefits without commensurate and timely increases in employer and/or employee contributions.[1]

Differences in actuarial soundness often are attributable to differences in laws regarding retirement systems or in the political environments in which they function, or both. In some cases, for example, the government's legal liability to retirees is limited to the amount in the retirement fund; proration is required if available resources are inadequate to meet current demands. Too, increased retiree payments may be promised in the heat of a political campaign without consideration being given to the financial position of the retirement fund or the means of paying for liberalized benefits. There is little doubt, however, but that retirement fund accounting generally is adversely affected by the short run, current operating focus of governmental budgeting and accounting for nonenterprise activities. In too many instances such funds have been operated on a cash receipts and disbursements basis, and accounted for as Special Revenue Funds, when the nature of the plan required a long-run management and accountability focus. Where the government's legal obligation or intent is to manage and account for the retirement fund over a period of many years, "pay-as-you-go" or "terminal funding" procedures are usually inappropriate. They result at best in significant understatement of the government's liabilities; at worst, they lead to drastic increases in employee or employer contributions to the fund or to reduced payments being made to retirees.

RETIREMENT FUND EXAMPLE (NO BUDGETARY ACCOUNTS). In order to illustrate the proper accounting approach for a soundly managed public employee retirement fund of medium complexity, let us assume that such a fund is already in operation and its beginning trial balance appears as in Figure 12-2. For purposes of this example, assume also that: (1) the plan is financed by employer contributions, employee contributions, and investment earnings, (2) the equities of employees resigning or dying prior to retirement are returned to them or to their estates, but employer contributions on their behalf remain in the fund; (3) employer contributions and earnings thereon vest[2] to the benefit of the employee only upon retirement, (4) earnings of the fund are

---

[1] *GAAFR*, pp. 76–77.

[2] Employer contributions or pension benefits "vest" when they are irrevocably owed to the employee or his estate. The trend today is toward employer contributions being vested immediately or within a relatively short period (five to ten years), rather than only upon retirement.

**Figure 12-2**

### A GOVERNMENTAL UNIT
Retirement Fund
Trial Balance
At Beginning of Fiscal Year (Date)

|                                              | Dr.       | Cr.       |
| -------------------------------------------- | --------- | --------- |
| Cash                                         | 56,000    |           |
| Due from General Fund                        | 8,000     |           |
| Interest Receivable                          | 3,000     |           |
| Investments                                  | 980,000   |           |
| Unamortized Premiums on Investments          | 5,000     |           |
| Due to Resigned Employees                    |           | 3,000     |
| Annuities Payable                            |           | 2,800     |
| Reserve for Employee Contributions           |           | 470,200   |
| Reserve for Employer Contributions           |           | 260,100   |
| Actuarial Deficiency—Reserve for             |           |           |
| Employer Contributions                       |           | 300,000   |
| Reserve for Retiree Annuities                |           | 315,900   |
| Fund Balance (deficit)                       |           | (300,000) |
|                                              | 1,052,000 | 1,052,000 |

apportioned according to a predetermined formula among employee equity, employer equity, and retiree equity in the fund, and (5) actuarial requirements are recorded by year-end adjusting entries.

The following transactions or events occurred during the year, and would be recorded as indicated. (See summary worksheet, Figure 12-7.)

EMPLOYER AND EMPLOYEE CONTRIBUTIONS WERE ACCRUED IN THE GENERAL FUND:

| (1) Due from General Fund                    | 175,000   |         |
| -------------------------------------------- | --------- | ------- |
| Contributions—Employees                      |           | 125,000 |
| Contributions—Employer                       |           | 50,000  |

To record employee and employer contributions due from General Fund.

(Though the employer contribution would be budgeted in the General or other Funds through which employee payrolls are paid, the retirement fund in this example is not under formal continuous budgetary control during the period.)

A CHECK WAS RECEIVED FROM THE GENERAL FUND:

(2)  Cash ................................  170,000
    Due from General Fund ............      170,000
    To record receipt of contributions from the
    General Fund.

ACCRUED INTEREST AND PREMIUM AMORTIZATION ON INVESTMENTS WAS RE-
CORDED:

(3)  Interest Receivable .....................  45,000
    Unamortized Premiums on Investments .      200
    Interest Earnings ...................      44,800
    To record accrued interest receivable and
    amortization of premiums on investments.

(Investment premiums and discounts are amortized as a part of the accrual basis calculation of investment earnings.)

A PORTION OF THE INTEREST RECEIVABLE WAS COLLECTED:

(4)  Cash ................................  40,000
    Interest Receivable ..................      40,000
    To record receipt of interest receivable.

AN EMPLOYEE RETIRED; EMPLOYER CONTRIBUTIONS IN HIS BEHALF VESTED AND HIS RETIREMENT BENEFIT FORMULA WAS DETERMINED:

(5)  Reserve for Employee Contributions ........  10,000
    Reserve for Employer Contributions ........  5,000
    Reserve for Retiree Annuities ..........      15,000
    To record reclassification of equities upon
    an employee's retirement and vesting of the
    government's contributions in his behalf.

(Note: The employer's contribution has now vested to the benefit of the retiree.)

THREE EMPLOYEES RESIGNED AND ONE DIED PRIOR TO RETIREMENT:

(6)  Reserve for Employee Contributions ........  25,000
    Due to Deceased Employee's Estate.....      10,000
    Due to Resigned Employees ...........      15,000
    To record amounts due upon employee re-
    signations and the death of one employee
    prior to retirement.

(Note: Employer contributions do not vest in this example unless the employee remains in the government's employ until retirement.)

Cᴏᴏᴋ Cʜᴇᴄᴋs ᴡᴇʀᴇ ᴍᴀɪʟᴇᴅ ᴛᴏ ᴛᴡᴏ ᴏꜰ ᴛʜᴇ ʀᴇsɪɢɴᴇᴅ ᴇᴍᴘʟᴏʏᴇᴇs ᴀɴᴅ ᴛᴏ ᴛʜᴇ ᴇsᴛᴀᴛᴇ ᴏꜰ ᴛʜᴇ ᴅᴇᴄᴇᴀsᴇᴅ ᴇᴍᴘʟᴏʏᴇᴇ:

| | | | |
|---|---|---|---|
| (7) | Due to Deceased Employee's Estate........ | 10,000 | |
| | Due to Resigned Employees .............. | 12,000 | |
| | Cash............................... | | 22,000 |
| | To record payments to former employees and to the estate of a deceased employee. | | |

Aɴɴᴜɪᴛɪᴇs ᴘᴀʏᴀʙʟᴇ ᴡᴇʀᴇ ᴀᴄᴄʀᴜᴇᴅ:

| | | | |
|---|---|---|---|
| (8) | Expenditures........................... | 24,000 | |
| | Annuities Payable .................. | | 24,000 |
| | To record accrual of liability for annuities payable. | | |

Aɴɴᴜɪᴛɪᴇs ᴘᴀʏᴀʙʟᴇ ᴡᴇʀᴇ ᴘᴀɪᴅ, ᴇxᴄᴇᴘᴛ ꜰᴏʀ ᴛʜᴀᴛ ᴛᴏ ᴏɴᴇ ᴇᴍᴘʟᴏʏᴇᴇ ᴡʜᴏ ɪs ᴏᴜᴛ ᴏꜰ ᴛʜᴇ ᴄᴏᴜɴᴛʀʏ:

| | | | |
|---|---|---|---|
| (9) | Annuities Payable ...................... | 23,000 | |
| | Cash.............................. | | 23,000 |
| | To record payment of annuities. | | |

Aᴅᴅɪᴛɪᴏɴᴀʟ ɪɴᴠᴇsᴛᴍᴇɴᴛs ᴡᴇʀᴇ ᴍᴀᴅᴇ:

| | | | |
|---|---|---|---|
| (10) | Investments........................... | 150,000 | |
| | Unamortized Discounts on Investments | | 7,000 |
| | Cash............................ | | 143,000 |
| | To record investments made. | | |

Aᴛ ʏᴇᴀʀ ᴇɴᴅ ᴛʜᴇ ꜰᴏʟʟᴏᴡɪɴɢ ᴀᴅᴊᴜsᴛɪɴɢ ᴀɴᴅ ᴄʟᴏsɪɴɢ ᴇɴᴛʀɪᴇs ᴡᴇʀᴇ ᴍᴀᴅᴇ. Tʜᴇ ᴀᴄᴛᴜᴀʀʏ ɪɴᴅɪᴄᴀᴛᴇᴅ ᴛʜᴀᴛ ᴀᴅᴅɪᴛɪᴏɴᴀʟ ᴄᴏɴᴛʀɪʙᴜᴛɪᴏɴs ᴡᴏᴜʟᴅ ɴᴇᴇᴅ ᴛᴏ ʙᴇ ᴍᴀᴅᴇ ɪꜰ ᴛʜᴇ ꜰᴜɴᴅ ᴡᴇʀᴇ ᴛᴏ ʙᴇ ᴀᴄᴛᴜᴀʀɪᴀʟʟʏ sᴏᴜɴᴅ:

| | | | |
|---|---|---|---|
| (11) | Fund Balance ....................... | 20,000 | |
| | Actuarial Deficiency—Reserve for Employer Contributions ............. | | 20,000 |
| | To record the change in the actuarial deficiency of the fund. | | |

(The order of the latter account title is often reversed, that is, it may be "Reserve for Employer Contributions—Actuarial Deficiency.")

Cᴏɴᴛʀɪʙᴜᴛɪᴏɴs ᴀᴄᴄᴏᴜɴᴛs ᴡᴇʀᴇ ᴄʟᴏsᴇᴅ ᴛᴏ ᴛʜᴇ ʀᴇsᴘᴇᴄᴛɪᴠᴇ ʀᴇsᴇʀᴠᴇ ᴀᴄᴄᴏᴜɴᴛs:

| | | | |
|---|---|---|---|
| (12) | Contributions—Employees ............. | 125,000 | |
| | Contributions—Employer ............... | 50,000 | |
| | Reserve for Employee Contributions ... | | 125,000 |
| | Reserve for Employer Contributions ... | | 50,000 |
| | To close Contributions Accounts. | | |

(Note: Alternatively these contributions might have been credited to the reserve accounts originally.)

INTEREST EARNINGS WERE APPORTIONED AMONG EMPLOYER, EMPLOYEE, AND RETIREE EQUITIES:

| | | | |
|---|---|---|---|
| (13) | Interest Earnings ..................... | 44,800 | |
| | Reserve for Employee Contributions ... | | 18,300 |
| | Reserve for Employer Contributions ... | | 15,700 |
| | Reserve for Retiree Annuities ........ | | 10,800 |
| | To record apportionment of interest earnings. | | |

THE EXPENDITURES ACCOUNT WAS CLOSED:

| | | | |
|---|---|---|---|
| (14) | Reserve for Retiree Annuities ............ | 24,000 | |
| | Expenditures ..................... | | 24,000 |
| | To close the Expenditures account. | | |

As noted earlier, the following statements should be prepared annually for all Trust and Agency Funds: (1) a Balance Sheet; (2) an Analysis of Changes in Fund Balance(s); and (3) a Cash Receipts and Disbursements Statement. In addition, a statement analyzing changes in reserve accounts should be prepared for pension or retirement funds (and for other Trust or Agency Funds if changes are significant). Actuarial assumptions and actuarial position should be clearly disclosed in the statements or by footnote. The required statements are illustrated, using the retirement fund data given, in Figures 12-3, 12-4, 12-5, and 12-6.

Most of the "reserves" shown on the Retirement Fund Balance Sheet (Figure 12-3) are actually liabilities rather than equity accounts. Thus, it may be more appropriate to present the "Liabilities, Reserves, and Fund Balances" section of the Balance Sheet in Figure 12-3 (using the terminology in this example, rather than that which might be more appropriate) as follows:

| | | |
|---|---|---|
| Liabilities: | | |
| Due to resigned employees .............. | $ 6,000 | |
| Annuities currently payable ............ | 3,800 | |
| Reserve for retiree annuities ............ | 317,700 | |
| Reserve for employee contributions ...... | 578,500 | |
| Reserve for actuarial deficiency-employer contributions ...................... | 320,000 | $1,226,000 |
| | | |
| Fund Balance: | | |
| Reserve for employer contributions ....... | $320,800 | |
| Unreserved (deficit) .................. | (320,000) | 800 |
| | | $1,226,800 |

Obviously, a much different impression is communicated by the above presentation than by that of Figure 12-3.

Figure 12-3

A GOVERNMENTAL UNIT
Retirement Fund
Balance Sheet
At Close of Fiscal Year (Date)

*Assets*

| | | |
|---|---:|---:|
| Cash ...................................... | | $ 78,000 |
| Due from General Fund ....................... | | 13,000 |
| Interest receivable .......................... | | 8,000 |
| Investments (at par; fair market value, $xx) ...... | $1,130,000 | |
| Unamortized premiums on investments ........ | 4,800 | |
| Unamortized discounts on investments .......... | (7,000) | 1,127,800 |
| Total Assets ............................. | | $1,226,800 |

*Liabilities, Reserves, and Fund Balances*

| | |
|---|---:|
| Due to resigned employees ..................... | $ 6,000 |
| Annuities currently payable .................... | 3,800 |
| Reserve for employee contributions ............. | 578,500 |
| Reserve for employer contributions .............. | 320,800 |
| Actuarial deficiency—Reserve for employer contributions ............................. | 320,000 |
| Reserve for retiree annuities .................... | 317,700 |
| Fund balance (deficit) ......................... | (320,000) |
| Total Liabilities, Reserves, and Fund Balances ... | $1,226,800 |

Note: This statement is prepared in conformity with illustrations in *Governmental Accounting, Auditing, and Financial Reporting.* An alternate presentation is discussed within the textual material in this Chapter.

Figure 12-4

A GOVERNMENTAL UNIT
Retirement Fund
Analysis of Changes in Fund Balance
For the Fiscal Year Ended (Date)

| | |
|---|---:|
| Fund balance, beginning of year ............ | $(300,000) |
| Increase in actuarial deficiency—reserve for employer contributions ................. | (20,000) |
| Fund balance, end of year ................ | $(320,000) |

Figure 12-5

## A GOVERNMENTAL UNIT
### Retirement Fund
### Analysis of Changes in Retirement Reserves
### For the Fiscal Year Ended (Date)

| | Total | Reserve for Employee Contributions | Reserve for Employer Contributions | Actuarial Deficiency-Reserve for Employer Contributions | Reserve for Retiree Annuities |
|---|---|---|---|---|---|
| Balances, beginning of year | $1,346,200 | $470,200 | $260,100 | $300,000 | $315,900 |
| Additions: | | | | | |
|   Employee contributions | $ 125,000 | $125,000 | — | — | — |
|   Employer contributions | 50,000 | — | $ 50,000 | — | — |
|   Interest earnings | 44,800 | 18,300 | 15,700 | — | $ 10,800 |
|     Total additions | $ 219,800 | $143,300 | $ 65,700 | — | $ 10,800 |
| Total balance and additions | $1,566,000 | $613,500 | $325,800 | $300,000 | $326,700 |
| Transfers: Annuities awarded | — | (10,000) | (5,000) | — | 15,000 |
| Actuarial adjustments | 20,000 | — | — | 20,000 | — |
| Total revised balances | $1,586,000 | $603,500 | $320,800 | $320,000 | $341,700 |
| Deductions: | | | | | |
|   Expenditures—annuities | $ 24,000 | — | — | — | $ 24,000 |
|   Rebates—deaths | 10,000 | $ 10,000 | — | — | — |
|   Rebates—resignations | 15,000 | 15,000 | — | — | — |
|     Total deductions | $ 49,000 | $ 25,000 | — | — | $ 24,000 |
| Balances, end of year | $1,537,000 | $578,500 | $320,800 | $320,000 | $317,700 |

**Figure 12-6**

A GOVERNMENTAL UNIT
Retirement Fund
Statement of Cash Receipts and Disbursements
For the Fiscal Year Ended (Date)

| | | |
|---|---:|---:|
| Cash balance, beginning of year ............ | | $ 56,000 |
| Receipts: | | |
| Employee contributions ................. | $125,000 | |
| Employer contributions ................. | 45,000 | |
| Interest.............................. | 40,000 | |
| Total receipts ....:................... | | 210,000 |
| Total cash available ..................... | | $266,000 |
| Disbursements: | | |
| Investments purchased.................. | $143,000 | |
| Rebates—resignations ................. | 12,000 | |
| Rebates—deaths ...................... | 10,000 | |
| Annuity payments .................... | 23,000 | |
| Total disbursements ................. | | 188,000 |
| Cash balance, end of year ................ | | $ 78,000 |

Because various usages of the term "reserve" persist in the insurance industry, and because some are proper reserves while others may represent liabilities, separate liability, reserve, and fund balance subheadings are not usually employed within the balance sheet or in combined statements including pension or retirement fund data.

PENSION FUND EXAMPLE (WITH BUDGETARY ACCOUNTS). The above example is consistent with NCGA recommendations and those of Opinion Number 8 of the Accounting Principles Board. In that example it was assumed that it was necessary to maintain records of individual employee contributions, actuarial requirements were reflected through adjusting entries at year-end, and the retirement fund was not subjected to continuous budgetary control. Further, only one Fund Balance account was employed, that is, neither the cause of a deficiency nor the source of a balance was disclosed. By way of contrast, we now consider briefly the procedures that might be used in accounting for a pension fund in which (1) budgetary accounting for revenues is employed, (2) an actuarially based Pension Fund Reserve account—which is adjusted to the actuarially determined amount by the budgetary entry at the beginning of each

Figure 12-7

## A GOVERNMENTAL UNIT
### Retirement Fund
### Worksheet for the Year Ended (Date)

| | Trial Balance (Beginning of Year) | | Transactions and Adjustments (During Year) | | Closing Entries (End of Year) | | Balance Sheet (End of Year) | |
|---|---|---|---|---|---|---|---|---|
| | Dr. | Cr. | Dr. | Cr. | Dr. | Cr. | Dr. | Cr. |
| Cash.............. | 56,000 | | (2) 170,000 (4) 40,000 | (7) 22,000 (9) 23,000 (10) 143,000 | | | 78,000 | |
| Due from General Fund ......... | 8,000 | | (1) 175,000 | (2) 170,000 | | | 13,000 | |
| Interest Receivable ........... | 3,000 | | (3) 45,000 | (4) 40,000 | | | 8,000 | |
| Investments .............. | 980,000 | | (10) 150,000 | | | | 1,130,000 | |
| Unamortized Premiums on Investments ........... | 5,000 | | | (3) 200 | | | 4,800 | |
| Due to Resigned Employees ...... | | 3,000 | (7) 12,000 | (6) 15,000 | | | | 6,000 |
| Annuities Payable ........... | | 2,800 | (9) 23,000 | (8) 24,000 | | | | 3,800 |
| Reserve for Employee Contributions............ | | 470,200 | (5) 10,000 (6) 25,000 | | | (12) 125,000 (13) 18,300 | | 578,500 |

| Account | Debit | | Credit | | |
|---|---|---|---|---|---|
| Reserve for Employee Contributions | 260,100 | (5) 5,000 | (12) 50,000 | (13) 15,700 | 320,800 |
| Actuarial Deficiency—Reserve for Employer Contributions | 300,000 | (11) 20,000 | | | 320,000 |
| Reserve for Retiree Annuities | 315,900 | (5) 15,000 | (14) 24,000 | (13) 10,800 | 317,700 |
| Fund Balance | 300,000 | (11) 20,000 | | | 320,000 |
| | 1,352,000 | 1,352,000 | | 1,553,800 | 1,553,800 |
| Contributions—Employees | (1) 125,000 | (12) 125,000 | | | |
| Contributions—Employer | (1) 50,000 | (12) 50,000 | | | |
| Interest Earnings | (3) 44,800 | (13) 44,800 | | | |
| Due to Deceased Employee's Estate | (7) 10,000 | (6) 10,000 | | | |
| Expenditures | (8) 24,000 | (14) 24,000 | | | |
| Unamortized Discounts on Investments | (10) 7,000 | 7,000 | | | |
| | 709,000 | 709,000 | 243,800 | 243,800 | 1,553,800 1,553,800 |

year—is used in lieu of the several reserve accounts in the previous example, and (3) the source or cause of a fund balance or deficit is reported by closing the difference between estimated and actual revenues and expenditures to appropriately titled Fund Balance accounts at year end, rather than to the Pension Fund Reserve account. This second example illustrates the approach formerly recommended by the NCGA. Were an Appropriations account used it would affect the Pension Fund Reserve account in the manner in which the Fund Balance account is affected by budgetary and closing entries in General Fund Accounting. This example is summarized in worksheet form in Figure 12-9.

### Transactions

1. Required employees' contributions, $15,000; required contributions from governmental unit, $15,000; required earnings, $600.
2. The required contributions, divided equally between deductions from employees' salaries and the governmental unit's contribution, were calculated as follows: General Fund, $27,000 and Special Assessment Fund, $3,000. However, only $13,000 was appropriated for the pension fund in the General Fund budget and no revision was possible.
3. The amounts due from the General Fund and the Special Assessment Fund were paid.
4. Securities with a par value of $20,000 were acquired for $20,350, including $50 for accrued interest purchased.
5. Securities with a par value of $8,000 were acquired at a discount of $100. They were acquired at an interest payment date and no accrued interest was purchased.
6. Semi-annual interest payments on investments were received, $400, of which $50 represents accrued interest purchased.
7. Premiums on investments in the amount of $30 and discounts on investments in the amount of $10 were amortized.
8. At the end of the year, interest in the amount of $375 became receivable.
9. Premiums on investments in the amount of $25 and discounts on investments in the amount of $15 were amortized.
10. Pensions in the amount of $120 became payable.
11. Pensions payable in the amount of $90 were paid.
12. Closing entries were prepared.

### Entries

| | | | |
|---|---|---|---|
| 1. | Required Contributions—Employees | 15,000 | |
| | Required Contributions—Governmental Unit | 15,000 | |
| | Required Earnings | 600 | |
| | Pension Fund Reserve | | 30,600 |
| | To record required contributions and required earnings. | | |

(Note: The "Required" accounts are equivalent to Estimated Revenue accounts; an Appropriations account might also be used in a fund of this type and procedures similar to General Fund accounting employed.)

| | | | |
|---|---|---|---|
| 2. | Due from General Fund ................. | 25,000 | |
| | Due from Special Assessment Fund ......... | 3,000 | |
| | Contributions—Governmental Unit..... | | 13,000 |
| | Contributions—Employees .......... | | 15,000 |
| | To record amounts due from General Fund and Special Assessment Fund for contributions representing deductions from employees' salaries and the governmental unit's share. | | |

(Recall that the government was unable to pay the full amount actuarially required to the pension fund and appropriated a lesser amount.)

| | | | |
|---|---|---|---|
| 3. | Cash................................... | 28,000 | |
| | Due from General Fund ............. | | 25,000 |
| | Due from Special Assessment Fund ..... | | 3,000 |
| | To record collection of amounts due from General Fund and Special Assessment Fund. | | |
| 4. | Investments............................ | 20,000 | |
| | Unamortized Premiums on Investments ..... | 300 | |
| | Accrued Interest on Investments Purchased . | 50 | |
| | Cash.............................. | | 20,350 |
| | To record purchase of investments at a premium and the accrued interest on investments purchased. | | |

(Alternatively, the accrued interest purchased could be debited to the Earnings account and the full amount collected credited to Earnings in entry 6.)

| | | | |
|---|---|---|---|
| 5. | Investments........................... | 8,000 | |
| | Unamortized Discounts on Investments . | | 100 |
| | Cash.............................. | | 7,900 |
| | To record purchase of investments at a discount. | | |
| 6. | Cash ................................. | 400 | |
| | Accrued Interest on Investments Purchased | | 50 |
| | Earnings .................... | | 350 |
| | To record receipt of semiannual interest on investments. | | |
| 7. | Unamortized Discounts on Investments .... | 10 | |
| | Earnings ............................. | 20 | |
| | Unamortized Premiums on Investments . | | 30 |
| | To record amortization of premiums and discounts on investments. | | |

8. Interest Receivable on Investments . . . . . . . .　375
　　Earnings . . . . . . . . . . . . . . . . . . . . . . . . . . . . 　　　375
　　To record interest receivable on investments.

9. Unamortized Discounts on Investments . . . .　15
　　Earnings . . . . . . . . . . . . . . . . . . . . . . . . . . . .　10
　　　Unamortized Premiums on Investments .　　　25
　　To record amortization of premiums and
　　discounts on investments.

10. Pension Expenditures . . . . . . . . . . . . . . . . . . . .　120
　　　Pensions Payable. . . . . . . . . . . . . . . . . . . . .　　　120
　　To record pensions payable.

11. Pensions Payable. . . . . . . . . . . . . . . . . . . . . . . .　90
　　　Cash . . . . . . . . . . . . . . . . . . . . . . . . . . . . . . .　　　90
　　To record payment of pensions payable.

12. (a)　Pension Fund Reserve. . . . . . . . . . . . . . .　120
　　　　Pension Expenditures . . . . . . . . . . . .　　　120
　　　To close out pension expenditures.

(Had an Appropriations account been in use it would be closed in the above entry and the Pension Fund Reserve affected only by the difference between Appropriations and Pension Expenditures.)

　(b)　Contributions-Employees . . . . . . . . . . . .　15,000
　　　Contributions-Governmental Unit . . . .　13,000
　　　Fund Balance-Government Contribu-
　　　　tions . . . . . . . . . . . . . . . . . . . . . . . . . . . .　2,000
　　　　Required Contributions-Employees.　　　15,000
　　　　Required　Contributions-Govern-
　　　　　mental Unit . . . . . . . . .　. . . . . . . .　　　15,000
　　　　To close out actual and requi..d con-
　　　　tributions.

　(c)　Earnings . . . . . . . . . . . . . . . . . . . . . . . . . . .　695
　　　　Required Earnings . . . . . . . . . . . . . .　　　600
　　　　Fund Balance-Earnings. . . . . . . . . . .　　　95
　　　To close out actual and required earn-
　　　ings.

A Balance Sheet for the Pension Fund in this second example is shown in Figure 12-8. (Compare this statement with that in Figure 12-3.) The accounting cycle illustrated would be repeated in the subsequent year.

### Nonexpendable Trust Funds

There are two types of nonexpendable Trust Funds: those in which neither the principal nor the earnings of the fund may be expended, and those in which earnings may be expended but principal must be kept intact. A loan fund is an example of the former type; examples of the latter type are some

**Figure 12-8**

A GOVERNMENTAL UNIT
Pension Fund
Balance Sheet
At Close of Fiscal Year

*Assets*

| | | | |
|---|---|---|---|
| Cash ............................... | | | $    60 |
| Investments .......................... | | $28,000 | |
| Unamortized premiums on investments ... | $245 | | |
| Less: Unamortized discounts on investments ........................ | 75 | 170 | 28,170 |
| Interest receivable on investments ........ | | | 375 |
| | | | $28,605 |

*Liabilities, Reserves, and Fund Balances*

| | |
|---|---|
| Pensions payable....................... | $    30 |
| Pension fund reserve (actuarially based) ... | 30,480 |
| Fund balance-government contributions ... | (2,000) |
| Fund balance-earnings.................. | 95 |
| | $28,605 |

common forms of endowment funds. The accounting procedure for simpler nonexpendable funds does not differ materially from that for expendable Trust Funds. Where both expendable and nonexpendable aspects are involved, however, (1) a careful distinction between trust principal (corpus) and income must be maintained, and (2) income determination procedures may be uniquely defined by the trust instrument or applicable laws. The same principles and distinctions apply as in trust accounting generally, that is, the creator or donor has the right to specify which items of revenue, expense, gain, or loss are to affect trust principal and which are deemed to relate to trust earnings. Where both expendable and nonexpendable trust aspects are involved, separate expendable and nonexpendable Trust Funds usually are established.

LOAN FUNDS. The following transactions and entries are illustrative of the operation of a loan fund.

*Transactions*

1. A cash donation of $100,000 was received for the purpose of establishing a loan fund.

Figure 12-9

## A GOVERNMENTAL UNIT
### Pension Fund
### Worksheet for the Year Ended (Date)

| | Transactions and Adjustments (During Year) | | Closing Entries (At Year End) | | Balance Sheet (At Year End) | |
|---|---|---|---|---|---|---|
| | Dr. | Cr. | Dr. | Cr. | Dr. | Cr. |
| Required Contributions—Employees .......... | (1) 15,000 | | | | | |
| Required Contributions—Governmental Unit ...... | (1) 15,000 | | | | | |
| Required Earnings .................... | (1) 600 | | | | | |
| Pension Fund Reserve ................. | | (1) 30,600 | (12a) 120 | (12b) 15,000<br>(12b) 15,000<br>(12c) 600 | | 30,480 |
| Due from General Fund ............... | (2) 25,000 | (3) 25,000 | | | | |
| Due from Special Assessment Fund ....... | (2) 3,000 | (3) 3,000 | | | | |
| Contributions—Governmental Unit ........ | | (2) 13,000 | (12b) 13,000 | | | |
| Contributions—Employees ............. | | (2) 15,000 | (12b) 15,000 | | | |
| Cash ............................ | (3) 28,000<br>(6) 400 | (4) 20,350<br>(5) 7,900<br>(11) 90 | | | 60 | |
| Investments ...................... | (4) 20,000<br>(5) 8,000 | | | | 28,000 | |
| Unamortized Premiums on Investments ...... | (4) 300 | (7) 30 | | | 245 | |
| Accrued Interest on Investments Purchased ...... | (4) 50 | (6) 50 | | | | |
| Unamortized Discounts on Investments Purchased .... | (7) 10<br>(9) 15 | (5) 100 | | | | 75 |

| | | | | | | | | |
|---|---|---|---|---|---|---|---|---|
| Earnings .................. | (7) | 20 | (6) | 350 | (12c) | 695 | | 375 |
| | | | | | | | | |
| Interest Receivable on Investments ...... | (9) | 10 | (8) | 375 | | | (12a) | 120 |
| Pension Expenditures ...... | (8) | 375 | | | | | | 30 |
| Pensions Payable ...... | (10) | 120 | (10) | 120 | | | | |
| | (11) | 90 | (12b) | 2,000 | | | | 2,000 |
| Fund Balance—Government Contributions ...... | | | | | | | | |
| Fund Balance—Earnings ...... | | | | | (12c) | 95 | | 95 |
| | | 115,990 | | 115,990 | | 30,815 | | 30,680 |
| | | | | | | 30,815 | | 30,680 |

2.   Loans amounting to $60,000 were made.
3.   A loan of $1,000 was repaid with interest of $20.
4.   Earnings were closed out.

*Entries*

1.  Cash ...................................   100,000
      Loan Fund Balance ..................                 100,000
      To record receipt of cash and establishment
      of loan fund.

2.  Loans Receivable  .......................   60,000
      Cash ...............................                  60,000
      To record loans made.

3.  Cash ...................................   1,020
      Loans Receivable ....................                 1,000
      Earnings  ...........................                    20
      To record repayment of loan with interest.

4.  Earnings  ..............................   20
      Loan Fund Balance ..................                    20
      To record closing out of earnings and increase
      in loan fund balance.

A loan fund Balance Sheet prepared after posting the above entries is shown in Figure 12-10.

**Figure 12-10**

A GOVERNMENTAL UNIT
Loan Fund
Balance Sheet at Close of Fiscal Year

*Assets*

Cash  .........................................   $ 41,020
Loans receivable  .............................     59,000
                                                  _____
                                                  $100,020

*Fund Balance*

Loan fund balance  ............................   $100,020

Note that there is only one Loan Fund Balance account in the above statement, that is, no distinction is made between the original capital and the $20 increase during the period. Such a distinction is not required, though separate "contributed" and "earned" capital accounts may be maintained, since earnings increase the amount of the Fund capital available for loans.

A question arises as to what would happen if the cost of administration were payable out of the Fund. In that case it would technically cease to be a nonexpendable fund, since administration expenses would reduce its balance. Provision is sometimes made, however, for meeting administration expenses out of earnings; and in that case, administrative expenses might be deemed deductible in determining *net* earnings. Strictly speaking, however, we have another type of Trust Fund, one whose principal must be kept intact but whose earnings may be expended. (This type of fund is discussed below.) Note also that though theoretically the loan fund illustrated above is nonexpendable, in actual practice the fund balance may be reduced through bad loans.

ENDOWMENT FUNDS. Some trusts are most easily accounted for by establishing both an expendable Trust Fund and a nonexpendable Trust Fund. For example, an individual may donate money or other property with a view to having the income therefrom used to finance certain activities. Since the donor intended the principal to be held intact and the income alone expended, two funds may be established: (1) a nonexpendable Trust Fund to account for the principal, and (2) an expendable Trust Fund to account for the earnings.[3]

A trust agreement of the type just described imposes problems that are the same as, and require the use of the same principles as, those of accounting for a trust that provides for payment of trust income to a life beneficiary with the principal payable to a remainderman at death of the beneficiary. As noted earlier, a discussion of the principles of trust accounting is found in standard advanced accounting texts and is beyond the scope of this book. Selected principles are illustrated in the following transactions and entries for an endowment fund:

*Transactions*

1. Cash in the amount of $210,000 was received for the establishment of a fund whose income is to be used in granting scholarships.

2. Investments with a par value of $200,000 were purchased at a premium of $3,000 plus accrued interest of $400.

3. A check in the amount of $3,000 was received in payment of interest on the investments.

4. Premiums in the amount of $125 were amortized.

5. Securities with a par value of $1,000, to which unamortized premiums in the amount of $14 were applicable, were sold for $1,005 plus accrued interest of $10.

6. Securities with a par value of $2,000, to which $28 in unamortized premiums were applicable, were sold for $2,050 plus accrued interest of $25.

---

[3] Alternatively, a single Trust Fund having separate Fund Balance–Principal and Fund Balance—Earnings accounts may be established. In this case, the gains, losses, revenues and expenses attributed to principal (corpus) are closed to the Fund Balance–Principal account; those entering into the determination of trust income, and expenditures of earnings for their designated uses, are closed to Fund Balance—Earnings.

7.  Interest receivable in the amount of $2,600 was recorded.
8.  Premiums in the amount of $120 were amortized.
9.  The total earnings to date were recorded as a liability of the Endowment Principal Fund to the Endowment Earnings Fund.
10. A $2,500 payment was made from the Endowment Principal Fund to the Endowment Earnings Fund.
11. A $2,000 scholarship grant was made out of the Endowment Earnings Fund. (Note: This is an outright grant, not a loan.)

*Entries*

1.  ENTRY IN ENDOWMENT PRINCIPAL FUND:

| | | |
|---|---:|---:|
| Cash .............................. | 210,000 | |
|     Endowment Principal Fund Balance .. | | 210,000 |
|     To record receipt of cash for establishment of endowment fund. | | |

2.  ENTRY IN ENDOWMENT PRINCIPAL FUND:

| | | |
|---|---:|---:|
| Investments ......................... | 200,000 | |
| Unamortized Premiums on Investments ... | 3,000 | |
| Accrued Interest on Investments Purchased | 400 | |
|     Cash ........................... | | 203,400 |
|     To record purchase of investments at a premium and accrued interest on investments purchased. | | |

3.  ENTRY IN ENDOWMENT PRINCIPAL FUND:

| | | |
|---|---:|---:|
| Cash .............................. | 3,000 | |
|     Accrued Interest on Investments Purchased | | 400 |
|     Earnings ....................... | | 2,600 |
|     To record collection of interest. | | |

(Alternatively, the accrued interest purchased could have been debited to Earnings in entry 2 and the total interest collection credited to Earnings in entry 3.)

4.  ENTRY IN ENDOWMENT PRINCIPAL FUND:

| | | |
|---|---:|---:|
| Earnings .......................... | 125 | |
|     Unamortized Premiums on Investments | | 125 |
|     To record amortization of premiums on investments. | | |

5.  ENTRY IN ENDOWMENT PRINCIPAL FUND:

| | | |
|---|---:|---:|
| Cash .............................. | 1,015 | |
| Endowment Principal Fund Balance ..... | 9 | |
|     Investments ..................... | | 1,000 |
|     Unamortized Premiums on Investments | | 14 |
|     Earnings ....................... | | 10 |
|     To record sale of investments at a loss of $9; to record also interest income of $10. | | |

6. ENTRY IN ENDOWMENT PRINCIPAL FUND:

| | | |
|---|---|---|
| Cash ............................... | 2,075 | |
| Investments ....................... | | 2,000 |
| Unamortized Premiums on Investments | | 28 |
| Endowment Principal Fund Balance .. | | 22 |
| Earnings ......................... | | 25 |

To record sale of investments at a profit of $22 and to record also interest income of $25.

7. ENTRY IN ENDOWMENT PRINCIPAL FUND:

| | | |
|---|---|---|
| Interest Receivable on Investments ....... | 2,600 | |
| Earnings ......................... | | 2,600 |

To record interest accrued on investments.

8. ENTRY IN ENDOWMENT PRINCIPAL FUND:

| | | |
|---|---|---|
| Earnings ........................... | 120 | |
| Unamortized Premiums on Investments | | 120 |

To record amortization of premiums on investments.

9. (a) ENTRY IN ENDOWMENT PRINCIPAL FUND:

| | | |
|---|---|---|
| Earnings ......................... | 4,990 | |
| Due to Endowment Earnings Fund | | 4,990 |

To record liability of endowment principal fund to endowment earnings fund for earnings to date.

(b) ENTRY IN ENDOWMENT EARNINGS FUND:

| | | |
|---|---|---|
| Due from Endowment Principal Fund.. | 4,990 | |
| Endowment Earnings Fund Balance ................... | | 4,990 |

To record amount due from endowment principal fund for earnings to date.

10. (a) ENTRY IN ENDOWMENT PRINCIPAL FUND:

| | | |
|---|---|---|
| Due to Endowment Earnings Fund... | 2,500 | |
| Cash ...................... | | 2,500 |

To record payment of part of total amount due to endowment earnings fund.

(b) ENTRY IN ENDOWMENT EARNINGS FUND:

| | | |
|---|---|---|
| Cash .......................... | 2,500 | |
| Due from Endowment Principal Fund ...................... | | 2,500 |

To record receipt of part of total amount due from endowment principal fund.

11. ENTRY IN ENDOWMENT EARNINGS FUND:

| | | |
|---|---|---|
| Endowment Earnings Fund Balance ...... | 2,000 | |
| Cash ........................... | | 2,000 |

To record payment of scholarship.

After the preceding entries are posted to the accounts, the Endowment Fund Balance Sheets illustrated in Figures 12-11 and 12-12 may be prepared.

If endowments are in the form of fixed properties, these constitute the principal fund and the net income therefrom is transferred to an expendable fund. Both the revenues and the expenses connected with administering the property—for example, rents, repairs, decorating expenses, and janitor's wages —would be accounted for in the principal fund. The net earnings would be transferred to the earnings fund and expended for the purpose designated—for example, granting scholarships.

Figure 12-11

### A GOVERNMENTAL UNIT
Endowment Principal Fund
Balance Sheet at Close of Fiscal Year

*Assets*

| | | |
|---|---|---|
| Cash .............................. | | $ 10,190 |
| Investments ......................... | $197,000 | |
| Unamortized premiums on investments ... | 2,713 | 199,713 |
| Interest receivable on investments ........ | | 2,600 |
| | | $212,503 |

*Liabilities and Fund Balance*

| | |
|---|---|
| Due to Endowment Earnings Fund ....... | $  2,490 |
| Endowment principal fund balance ....... | 210,013 |
| | $212,503 |

Figure 12-12

### A GOVERNMENTAL UNIT
Endowment Earnings Fund
Balance Sheet at Close of Fiscal Year

*Assets*

| | |
|---|---|
| Cash ...................................... | $ 500 |
| Due from Endowment Principal Fund .......... | 2,490 |
| | $2,990 |

*Fund Balance*

| | |
|---|---|
| Endowment Earnings Fund balance ............ | $2,990 |

It is important, in such cases, to account carefully for the income and expenses of the principal fund so that the net income may be properly computed. Whether depreciation is charged as an expense will depend on the provisions of the trust document or the implied intent of the donor. If the grant contemplates the replacement of worn-out property, depreciation must be charged in an amount sufficient to preserve the principal intact. On the other hand, if the property is not to be replaced, depreciation might not be charged as an expense in determining trust income. If the trust instrument is silent as to depreciation of fixed assets held in trust, and the donor's intent in this regard is unclear, state statutes control. If there are no relevant state statutes, the general rule is that depreciation or amortization of those assets comprising the original trust principal either is not recorded or is charged against trust *principal*, not earnings, as are gains and losses on sales of investments present when the trust was established. If depreciation and amortization are recorded, that related to assets acquired by the trustee with other trust assets is charged to *earnings*. Some authorities feel that this question has not been conclusively settled, however, and that the trend now appears to be toward charging depreciation in determining trust earnings. Obviously, accounting for such items as depreciation and investment gains and losses should be covered in the trust instrument. Competent legal advice should be sought whenever such questions are not explicitly treated in that document.

POOLED INVESTMENT FUNDS. Pooled investment Trust Funds are "in-house mutual funds" through which the investment of resources of various governmental fund entities may be centrally administered. A government might set up a single pooled investment fund or it might employ a series of such funds to serve certain types of funds, such as a Special Assessment Fund pooled investment fund, a Trust Fund pooled investment fund, and so forth. The fund may be managed by an employee(s) of the government or by an individual or organization independent of the government.

Not every government would benefit from establishing a fund or funds of this type, of course, though numerous advantages accompany their use where warranted by the potential magnitude of investments for the government as a whole. Among the benefits that may accrue through use of pooled investment funds are these:

1. *Improved investment management*—through giving high-level recognition to the need for investing idle cash, centralizing investment management authority and responsibility, and, to some extent, overcoming management problems occasioned by the necessity to manage resources of many separate fund accounting entities.

2. *Higher investment yield*—because (a) the time cash remains idle is minimized, that is, monies need not be accumulated in individual funds until

they warrant investment, but may be invested collectively whenever total investable cash of the several funds warrants investment, (b) brokerage costs per dollar invested may be substantially reduced by investing larger sums and reducing the number of investment and disinvestment transactions, (c) some high yield, high grade securities are available only in rather large denominations, and (d) the "average" investable cash of the government as a whole may be kept invested rather than only minimum amounts within various funds, that is, various funds may "buy in" and "sell out" as their cash requirements dictate.

3. *Diversification of investments*—which (a) permits the establishment of a reasoned investment policy and (b) spreads the benefits of unexpected gains and the risks of unexpected losses among many funds rather than attributing them to a single fund.

All pertinent legal or contractual provisions must be observed in establishing and operating pooled investment funds, of course. Beyond such compliance, it is essential that policies relating to issues and procedures such as those enumerated below be established, committed to writing, and followed consistently:

1. *Valuation of a participating fund's share in the pool*—upon investment, disinvestment, at year end.
2. *Distribution of earnings*—whether based upon average (simple or weighted) investment or upon some other method; the frequency with which the method is to be applied (annually, quarterly, daily); the effect of "buying in" and "selling out."
3. *Distribution of gains or losses*—valuation dates; whether gains or losses are to be distributed currently or averaged, possibly over a period of several years.

Practices vary widely in regard to questions such as these. A discussion of the ramifications and possible effects of alternative policies, though inviting, is beyond the scope of this text.

In order to illustrate the basic accounting procedures for pooled investment funds, let us assume that (1) a Special Assessment Funds pooled investment fund is established, and (2) Public Improvement Fund 726 (PI 726) participates in this investment pool. Some typical transactions are described below; to highlight the interfund aspects of this situation, entries are indicated both for the pooled investment Trust Fund and for PI 726, one of the member funds.

*Transactions*

1. The Pooled Investment Fund was established by transfers as follows: PI 726; $50,000; PI 741, $70,000; PI 750, securities (cost $75,000 to PI 750; fair market value upon pooling, $80,000).

2. Investments were made as follows: bonds, $105,000 (including $5,000 premium); certificates of deposit, $15,000.

3. Additional cash, $5,000, was received from PI 741.

4. Interest on bonds was received, $6,000; premium amortization for the period was recorded.

5. One fourth of the bonds were sold at the interest due date for $28,000 in order to meet cash needs of PI 750 (see below).

6. Cash, $25,000, was returned to PI 750 to meet its debt service requirements.

7. Accrued interest receivable on certificates of deposit at year-end, $700.

8. Accounts were closed at year-end; earnings and the investment gain were distributed (not disbursed) to member fund equity accounts in accordance with the agreed formula.

*Entries*

1. (a) ENTRY IN POOLED INVESTMENT FUND:

| | | |
|---|---:|---:|
| Cash | 120,000 | |
| Investments | 80,000 | |
| Fund Balance | | 200,000 |

To record original investments upon establishment of fund.

(Both the Investments and Fund Balance accounts are control accounts in this example. The Investments account subsidiary ledger would contain details of each investment made; the individual member fund equities in the investment pool would be recorded in the Fund Balance subsidiary ledger. The transfer of securities from PI 750 must be recorded in the Pooled Investment Fund at fair market value upon transfer. Either the cost or equity method might be followed in recording the transaction in the accounts of PI 750.)

(b) ENTRY IN PI 726:

| | | |
|---|---:|---:|
| Pooled Investments (or Equity in Investment Pool) | 50,000 | |
| Cash | | 50,000 |

To record transfer of cash to the investment pool.

2. ENTRY IN POOLED INVESTMENT FUND:

| | | |
|---|---:|---:|
| Investments | 115,000 | |
| Unamortized Premiums on Investments | 5,000 | |
| Cash | | 120,000 |

To record investments made.

(Note: Investments could be debited for $120,000 and no separate premium account used; the premium account is illustrated here solely to emphasize the need for amortization of investment premiums and discounts.)

3. ENTRY IN POOLED INVESTMENT FUND:

| | | |
|---|---|---|
| Cash | 5,000 | |
| Fund Balance | | 5,000 |
| To record receipt of cash from PI 741. | | |

4. ENTRY IN POOLED INVESTMENT FUND:

| | | |
|---|---|---|
| Cash | 6,000 | |
| Unamortized Premiums on Investments | | 1,000 |
| Earnings | | 5,000 |
| To record receipt of bond interest and premium amortization. | | |

5. ENTRY IN POOLED INVESTMENT FUND:

| | | |
|---|---|---|
| Cash | 28,000 | |
| Investments | | 25,000 |
| Unamortized Premiums on Investments | | 1,000 |
| Gain on Sale of Investments | | 2,000 |
| To record sale of one fourth of the bonds at interest date. | | |

6. ENTRY IN POOLED INVESTMENT FUND:

| | | |
|---|---|---|
| Fund Balance | 25,000 | |
| Cash | | 25,000 |
| To record disinvestment by PI 750. | | |

7. ENTRY IN POOLED INVESTMENT FUND:

| | | |
|---|---|---|
| Accrued Interest Receivable | 700 | |
| Earnings | | 700 |
| To record interest accrued on certificates of deposit at year end. | | |

8. (a) ENTRY IN POOLED INVESTMENT FUND:

| | | |
|---|---|---|
| Earnings | 5,700 | |
| Gain on Sale of Investments | 2,000 | |
| Fund Balance | | 7,700 |
| To distribute earnings and gain to member fund equity accounts per agreed formula: | | |

| | |
|---|---|
| PI 726 | $2,156 |
| PI 741 | 2,695 |
| PI 750 | 2,849 |
| | $7,700 |

(b) ENTRY IN PI 726:

| | | |
|---|---|---|
| Pooled Investments (or Equity in Investment Pool) | 2,156 | |
| Earnings | | 1,596 |
| Gain on Sale of Investments | | 560 |
| To record share of pooled investment earnings and gains. | | |

(Alternatively the gain on sale of investments might have been credited in the Pooled Investment Fund to an account such as Reserve for Investment Gains and Losses—which would be changed or credited for subsequent gains or losses—rather than being distributed currently. Such an approach has the effect of smoothing reported income of the constituent funds where gains and losses tend to balance out over a period of years.)

A Balance Sheet for the Pooled Investment Fund prepared on a cost basis appears in Figure 12-13. (Note that the equity of each member fund is separately stated.) An Income Statement, a Statement Analyzing Changes in Fund Balances, and a Statement of Cash Receipts and Disbursements would also be prepared for this fund. In addition, the composition of its investment portfolio should be disclosed in a separate statement or schedule, or by footnote, if not indicated within the Balance Sheet.

**Figure 12-13**

A GOVERNMENTAL UNIT
Pooled Investment Trust Fund
Balance Sheet at Close of Fiscal Year

*Assets*

| | | |
|---|---:|---:|
| Cash ..................................... | | $ 14,000 |
| Investments ............................. | $170,000 | |
| Unamortized premiums on investments ........ | 3,000 | 173,000 |
| Interest receivable on investments ............. | | 700 |
| | | $187,700 |

*Fund Balance*

| | |
|---|---:|
| Fund Balance—PI 726 ....................... | $ 52,156 |
| Fund Balance—PI 741 ....................... | 77,695 |
| Fund Balance—PI 750 ....................... | 57,849 |
| | $187,700 |

Finally, recall that the above transactions and entries are intended to be illustrative only and that more complex accounting aspects and procedural variations may be encountered in practice. For example, where member funds "buy in" and "sell out" frequently, in whole or in part, there is strong support for regularly revaluing the pooled investment fund assets at fair market value as is common in accounting for mutual funds (regulated investment trusts). Even if the accounts continue to be carried at cost, fair market value data must generally be used in arriving at equitable policies and procedures relative to income distribution and of member fund equity upon withdrawal.

## AGENCY FUNDS

Agency Funds are conduit or clearinghouse funds established to account for assets (usually cash) received for and paid to other funds, individuals, or organizations. The assets thus received are usually held only briefly; investment or other fiscal management complexities are rarely involved, except in situations such as that of the Tax Agency Fund illustrated later in this chapter.

Not all agency relationships arising in the conduct of a government's business require that an Agency Fund be established. For example, payroll deductions for such items as insurance premiums and income tax withholdings create agency responsibilities which may often be accounted for (as liabilities) in the fund through which the payroll is paid. On the other hand, where payrolls are paid from several funds it may be more convenient to transfer withheld amounts to an Agency Fund in order that a single check and remittance report may be forwarded to the recipient. As a general rule, Agency Funds should be used whenever (1) the volume of agency transactions, the magnitude of the sums involved, and/or the management and accounting capabilities of government personnel make it either unwieldy or unwise to account for agency responsibilities through other funds, or (2) financial management or accounting for interfund transactions or relationships is expedited through their use.

### Simpler Agency Funds

Though agency relationships are commonly viewed as arising between the government and individuals or organizations external to it, recall that each fund of the government is a distinct legal entity. Interfund or intragovernmental Agency Funds may prove useful in (1) alleviating some of the awkwardness occasioned by the use of numerous fund accounting entities in governments, and (2) establishing clear-cut audit trails where a single transaction affects several funds. Thus, though a special imprest[4] bank account will often suffice, some governments establish an Agency Fund where (1) receipts must be allocated among several funds or (2) a single expenditure is financed through several funds. In the former case, a single check may be deposited in an Agency Fund and separate checks payable to the various funds drawn against it; in the latter, checks drawn against several funds are placed in an Agency Fund and a single check drawn against it in payment for the total expenditure. Likewise,

---

[4] An imprest bank account is one to which deposits are made periodically in an amount equal to the sum of the checks written thereon; when all checks written have cleared, the bank's account balance will equal a predetermined amount, often zero. Imprest bank accounts are often used to enhance cash control and/or to facilitate bank-book reconciliations.

some governments account for all receipts and disbursements through an Agency Fund, with interfund settlement being made periodically. Such a procedure is particularly useful in manual accounting systems as it (1) avoids the necessity of preparing separate deposit slips daily for each fund, as well as daily use of numerous different check forms, and (2) assists in centralization of the financial management function, such as through means of a single voucher system. Again, judgment should be exercised in deciding whether an Agency Fund is useful in such cases; a special imprest checking account may serve the government's needs adequately without necessitating the additional record-keeping occasioned by the establishment of an Agency Fund.

Whether the agency relationship is external or internal, the accounting in situations discussed thus far is not complicated. All that is required is that entries such as the following be prepared upon receipt and disbursement of monies:

UPON RECEIPT:
Cash (or other assets) ........................ 100,000
    Fund Balance (or Due to......) ...........       100,000

UPON DISBURSEMENT:
Fund Balance (or Due to......) ............. 100,000
    Cash (or other assets) ....................       100,000

Note that although a Fund Balance account is commonly used in Agency Fund accounting, all Agency Fund assets are owed to some fund, person, or organization. The government has no equity in the Fund's assets, and a liability account may appropriately be substituted for the Fund Balance account. Too, where there is more than one claimant to Agency Fund assets, separate liability or Fund Balance accounts (or separate subsidiary accounts) are required.

### More Complex Agency Funds

In the examples above, the Agency Fund required little management action or expertise. Other Agency Funds, such as the Tax Agency Fund illustrated below, may involve significant management responsibilities and more complex accounting procedures.

In order to avoid duplication of assessment and collection effort and to enforce tax laws as equitably and economically as possible, all taxes levied upon properties within a state, county, or other geographic area may be billed and collected by one of the governments. That unit therefore becomes an agent for the other taxing units and establishes an Agency Fund such as the Tax Agency Fund described below. In the usual case, the several taxing bodies (e.g., the state, county, school districts) certify the amounts or rates at which taxes are to be levied for them by the designated government. The latter then levies the total tax, including its own, against specific properties and proceeds to collect the tax. In addition, it normally makes pro rata payments of collections to the various taxing bodies during the year, often quarterly, and charges a collection or service fee to the other units.

The following example illustrates the general approach to tax Agency Fund accounting. Though not illustrated here, detailed records of levies and collections relative to each property taxed, by year of levy, are required.[5] Collections pertaining to each year's levy are distributed among the taxing bodies in the ratio of each unit's levy to the total levy of that year.

### Case of City A

City A serves as the collecting agent for several governmental units. City A's levies and those certified by the other units for 19X2 and 19X3 are as follows:

|  | 19X3 | | 19X2 | |
| --- | --- | --- | --- | --- |
|  | Amount Levied | Percentage of Total | Amount Levied | Percentage of Total |
| City A* | $100,000 | 25.0 | $ 91,200 | 24.0 |
| School District B | 200,000 | 50.0 | 188,100 | 49.5 |
| Park District X | 50,000 | 12.5 | 49,400 | 13.0 |
| Sanitary District Y | 50,000 | 12.5 | 51,300 | 13.5 |
|  | $400,000 | 100.0 | $380,000 | 100.0 |

\* Although these taxes are the taxes of the collecting governmental unit, they are treated in the same manner as if they were being collected for it by another unit.

The Tax Agency Fund trial balance at December 31, 19X2 consists of $75,000 of Taxes Receivable for Other Units and a Taxes Fund Balance of $75,000. These amounts arose entirely from the 19X2 levy. Transactions and entries illustrated for the General Fund of City A are similar to those that would be made by the other recipient governmental units.

### Transactions

1. The 19X3 levies are placed on the tax roll and recorded on the books.
2. Collections of interest and penalties (not previously accrued in the Agency Fund) of $15,000 and taxes of $300,000 are received. Collections are identified by type, year, and governmental unit (see the explanation for the journal entry) so that distributions may be made in accordance with the original levies.

[5] These records are discussed and illustrated in Chapter 8, "Revenue Accounting."

3. The collections (transaction 2) are paid from the Tax Agency Fund to the respective governmental units, except for a 2 per cent collection charge levied upon the *other* governments.

*Entries*

1. ENTRY IN GENERAL FUND:

| | | |
|---|---:|---:|
| Taxes Receivable—Current .............. | 100,000 | |
| Estimated Uncollectible Current Taxes.. | | 1,000 |
| Revenues ......................... | | 99,000 |
| To record the 19X3 tax levy. | | |

ENTRY IN TAX AGENCY FUND:

| | | |
|---|---:|---:|
| Taxes Receivable for Other Units* ........ | 400,000 | |
| Taxes Fund Balance................ | | 400,000 |

To record 19X3 taxes placed on the tax roll. *Credit* Taxes Fund Balance subsidiary accounts:

| | |
|---|---:|
| City of *A*-Uncollected................ | 100,000 |
| School District B-Uncollected ......... | 200,000 |
| Park District X-Uncollected .......... | 50,000 |
| Sanitary District Y-Uncollected ....... | 50,000 |
| | 400,000 |

\* Taxes Receivable for Other Units may be classified into two accounts, Current and Delinquent, if desired. The distinction would be apparent in the subsidiary records, however, since (1) taxes are levied by year, and (2) a separate ledger account or column would be provided for each year's levy against each property.

(Appropriate subsidiary records for Taxes Receivable for Other Units by taxpayer would be maintained.)

2. ENTRY IN TAX AGENCY FUND:

| | | |
|---|---:|---:|
| Cash ................................ | 315,000 | |
| Taxes Receivable for Other Units ..... | | 300,000 |
| Taxes Fund Balance ............... | | 15,000 |

To record collections of taxes and interest and penalties classified as follows:
Subsidiary taxpayer records would be credited for appropriate amounts.
*Debit* Taxes Fund Balance subsidiary accounts:

| | |
|---|---:|
| City of *A*-Uncollected................ | 74,250 |
| School District B-Uncollected ......... | 149,625 |
| Park District X-Uncollected .......... | 37,875 |
| Sanitary District Y-Uncollected ....... | 38,250 |
| | 300,000 |

*Credit* Taxes Fund Balance subsidiary accounts:

| | |
|---|---:|
| City of *A*-Collected | 77,850 |
| School District B-Collected | 157,050 |
| Park District X-Collected | 39,825 |
| Sanitary District Y-Collected | 40,275 |
| | 315,000 |

3. ENTRY IN TAX AGENCY FUND:

| | | |
|---|---:|---:|
| Taxes Fund Balance | 315,000 | |
| Cash | | 310,257 |
| Due to General Fund | | 4,743 |

To record payment of amounts collected, with the retention of a 2 per cent collection charge for taxes collected for *other* governmental units.

*Debit* Taxes Fund Balance subsidiary accounts:

| | |
|---|---:|
| City of *A*-Collected | 77,850 |
| School District B-Collected | 157,050 |
| Park District X-Collected | 39,825 |
| Sanitary District B-Collected | 40,275 |
| | 315,000 |

ENTRIES IN GENERAL FUND:

| | | |
|---|---:|---:|
| Cash | 77,850 | |
| Taxes Receivable-Current | | 56,250 |
| Taxes Receivable-Delinquent | | 18,000 |
| Interest and Penalties Receivable on Taxes | | 3,600 |

To record receipt of collections of taxes and interest and penalties from Tax Agency Fund.

| | | |
|---|---:|---:|
| Due from Tax Agency Fund | 4,743 | |
| Revenues | | 4,743 |

To record revenues charged for tax services rendered to other governmental units.

*Credit* subsidiary revenue account:

| | |
|---|---:|
| Tax Collection Fees | 4,743 |

The preparation of the tax roll, the accounting for taxes and handling the collections involves considerable expense, and the collecting unit usually charges for these services. The charges are legitimate financial expenses, and provision is made for them in the budget. The usual practice, illustrated in the foregoing transactions, is for the collecting unit to retain a portion of the taxes and interest and penalties collected rather than to go through the process of billing the charges to the several governmental units. To further illustrate the procedure, the journal entry which School District B would make to record receipt of cash from the Tax Agency Fund (Transaction 3 above) follows.

| | | |
|---|---|---|
| Cash...................................... | 153,909 | |
| Expenditures............................... | 3,141 | |
| Taxes Receivable-Current ............... | | 112,500 |
| Taxes Receivable-Delinquent.............. | | 37,125 |
| Interest and Penalties Receivable on Taxes. .. | | 7,425 |
| To record receipts of amounts collected by City | | |
| A less collection charge of 2 per cent. | | |

The Balance Sheet of the Tax Agency Fund of City $A$ after the foregoing transactions have been recorded is presented in Figure 12-14.

**Figure 12-14**

CITY $A$

Tax Agency Fund

Balance Sheet at Close of Fiscal Year

*Assets*

| | |
|---|---|
| Cash ................................... | $ 4,743 |
| Taxes receivable for other units ............ | 175,000 |
| | $179,743 |

*Liabilities and Fund Balance*

| | |
|---|---|
| Due to General Fund..................... | $ 4,743 |
| Taxes fund balance ..................... | 175,000 |
| | $179,743 |

**Question 12-1.** Trust Funds and Agency Funds, though separate fund types, are treated in the same chapter in this text and are often spoken of collectively as "Trust and Agency" Funds. In what ways are they similar and how do they differ?

**Question 12-2.** Compare the primary forms of accountability as among (1) the General and Special Revenue Funds, (2) Capital Projects and Special Revenue Funds, and (3) Trust and Agency Funds.

**Question 12-3.** A single trust agreement often gives rise to two separate Trust Funds. When is this so, and may a single trust agreement result in the establishment of three, four, or more separate funds?

**Question 12-4.** In certain situations an expendable Trust Fund may be virtually identical to a Special Revenue Fund and should be budgeted and accounted for as though it were a Special Revenue Fund. Explain.

**Question 12-5.** What is the difference between a nonexpendable Trust Fund and an Agency Fund?

**Question 12-6.** Accounting for separate Trust and Agency Funds on a "funds within a fund" approach was not illustrated in this chapter. Is it possible and/or permissible

Figure 12-15

A GOVERNMENTAL UNIT
Trust and Agency Funds
Balance Sheet at Close of Fiscal Year

| Assets | Total All Funds | Expendable Trust Funds | | | | | Nonexpendable Trust Funds | | Agency Fund |
|---|---|---|---|---|---|---|---|---|---|
| | | Deposits Fund | Retirement Fund | Pension Fund | Pooled Investment Fund | Endowment Earnings Fund | Endowment Principal Fund | Loan Fund | Tax Agency Fund |
| Cash | $ 151,883 | $ 3,370 | $ 78,000 | $ 60 | $ 14,000 | $ 500 | $ 10,190 | $ 41,020 | $ 4,743 |
| Loans receivable | 59,000 | | | | | | | 59,000 | |
| Investments | 1,540,000 | 15,000 | 1,130,000 | 28,000 | 170,000 | | 197,000 | | |
| Unamortized premiums on investments | 10,758 | | 4,800 | 245 | 3,000 | | 2,713 | | |
| Unamortized discounts on investments | (7,075) | | (7,000) | (75) | | | | | |
| Interest receivable on investments | 11,675 | | 8,000 | 375 | 700 | | 2,600 | | |
| Due from Endowment Principal Fund | 2,490 | | | | | 2,490 | | | |
| Due from General Fund | 13,000 | | 13,000 | | | | | | |
| Taxes receivable for other units | 175,000 | | | | | | | | 175,000 |
| | $1,956,731 | $18,370 | $1,226,800 | $28,605 | $187,700 | $2,990 | $212,503 | $100,020 | $179,743 |

*Liabilities, Reserves, and Fund Balances*

| | Total | | | | | | | | | |
|---|--:|--:|--:|--:|--:|--:|--:|--:|--:|--:|
| Due to resigned employees | $ 6,000 | | | $ 6,000 | | | | | | |
| Annuities currently payable | 3,800 | | | 3,800 | | | | | | |
| Pensions payable | 30 | | | | $ 30 | | | | | |
| Due to Endowment Earnings Fund | 2,490 | | | | | | | $ 2,490 | | |
| Due to General Fund | 4,743 | | | | | | | | | $ 4,743 |
| Reserve for employee contributions | 578,500 | | | 578,500 | | | | | | |
| Reserve for employer contributions | 320,800 | | | 320,800 | | | | | | |
| Actuarial deficiency—Reserve for employee contributions | 320,000 | | | 320,000 | | | | | | |
| Reserve for retiree annuities | 317,700 | | | 317,700 | | | | | | |
| Pension fund reserve | 30,480 | | | | 30,480 | | | | | |
| Fund balance (Deficit) | 372,188 | $18,370 | $18,370 | (320,000) | (1,905) | $187,700 | $2,990 | 210,013 | $100,020 | 175,000 |
| | $1,956,731 | $18,370 | $18,370 | $1,226,800 | $28,605 | $187,700 | $2,990 | $212,503 | $100,020 | $179,743 |

to account for more than one type of trust or agency relationship within a single Trust or Agency Fund?

**Question 12-7.** Classify the following as to whether they are expendable Trust Funds, nonexpendable Trust Funds, or Agency Funds:

a. A fund established to handle tax collections by a governmental unit for other governments.

b. A pension fund.

c. A loan fund.

d. A fund whose principal is to be held intact but whose income must be expended for bravery awards.

e. A fund established to handle deposits.

f. A fund established to handle that part of the proceeds from the sale of property for taxes which is to be refunded to the property owner.

g. A fund whose principal and income are both to be used in granting scholarships.

**Question 12-8.** How do the Trust and Agency Funds discussed in this chapter differ from those of business enterprises?

**Question 12-9.** A county's fee officers (sheriff, county clerk, etc.) deposit their collections with the county treasurer. Once a month, the county auditor determines the accounts to which such collections apply and makes the proper entries. Most of these collections apply to the General Fund, but some of them apply also to other funds. (a) Should these collections, pending their allocation, be handled through the General Fund or a Trust and Agency Fund? (b) Assuming they are handled through the General Fund, what entry should be made in that fund (1) when the money is collected and (2) when the allocation is made? Assume $14,000 applies to the General Fund and $1,000 to other funds.

**Question 12-10.** Although Fund Balance and Reserve accounts are commonly used in Trust and Agency Funds, they may actually be *liability* accounts within these funds. Explain.

**Question 12-11.** Taxes for Sanitary District R are collected by the County of C. The county clerk maintains the records of the individual taxpayers and enters in them the amount due from each taxpayer. For rendering this service, the clerk is permitted to add to each taxpayer's bill 2 cents for each governmental unit. For example, if a taxpayer is charged with taxes for the county, city, and sanitary district, 6 cents is added to his bill. Taxes are collected by the county treasurer, who is allowed a fee of 2 percent of the amount collected. Before transmitting the proceeds of any collections to a governmental unit, the treasurer deducts the county clerk's fee and his own fee. (a) Should the county clerk's fee be included as part of the sanitary district's tax levy? If not, should such fee be recorded at all on the sanitary district's books? (b) Should the treasurer's fees be included as part of the tax levy of the sanitary district? How would you treat such fees on the sanitary district's books?

**Question 12-12.** Why might the Balance Sheet prepared for a Pension Fund report a Fund Balance *deficit* when it also reports assets far in excess of the amount shown as Pensions Payable?

**Question 12-13.** What is the difference between a Special Assessment Fund and a private Trust Fund?

**Question 12-14.** Why might a governmental unit establish a Pooled Investments Fund? What types of policies and procedures should be set forth clearly and adhered to consistently with regard to a fund of this sort?

**Question 12-15.** In what respects are a Pension Fund and a Debt Service Sinking Fund similar and in what respects do they differ? (Assume that both are actuarially based and that budgetary entries are made in the accounts of both at the beginning of each year.)

**Question 12-16.** How might *internal* (interfund or intragovernmental) Agency Funds be used to facilitate a governmental unit's financial management and accounting processes?

**Question 12-17.** In accounting for a Tax Agency Fund, why is it necessary to maintain records of taxes levied and collected for each taxing authority involved by year of levy?

**Question 12-18.** According to the terms of A's will, the city is to become the owner of an apartment building. The net income from the building is to be added to the Policemen's Pension Fund. (a) Is this an expendable or nonexpendable Trust Fund? (b) Suppose that, in computing net income, the city does not take depreciation into account. Is the fund expendable or nonexpendable?

**Question 12-19.** The earnings of a nonexpendable (as to corpus) Trust Fund are used to support the operation of a municipal museum, art gallery, and park complex. Should these activities be accounted for through the General Fund, a Special Revenue Fund, or a Trust Fund?

**Question 12-20.** What is meant by "pay-as-you-go" and "terminal funding" as these terms are used with regard to pension plans or funds?

**Question 12-21.** A trust indenture states that the principal (corpus) of the trust is to be maintained intact in perpetuity. Yet, although the governmental trustee did not violate the terms of the trust agreement—and it was not subsequently revised—the principal (corpus) had decreased to less than half its original amount five years after the trust was created. Why or how might this have happened?

**Question 12-22.** What are the major differences in the accounting for pension funds (1) that are not actuarially based, (2) that are adjusted to an actuarial basis at year end, and (3) that are both actuarially based and for which budgetary accounts are established within the account structure?

**Question 12-23.** Discuss the merits of writing down long-term bond investments to the lower of cost or market (1) in a retirement or pension fund, and (2) in a pooled investments fund.

**Question 12-24.** What accounting differences would you find with respect to a pooled investments fund and the member funds where all use the cost method of accounting for pooled investments as opposed to where the equity (based on market value) method is used by all?

**Problem 12-1.** Prepare the general journal entries required to record the following transactions in the general ledgers of the State, the County General Fund and the County Tax Agency Fund. You may omit formal entry explanations, but should key the entries to the numbered items in this problem.

1. The County Tax Agency Fund has been established to account for the County's duties of collecting the State property taxes. The levies for the year 19X0 were $600,000 for the County General Fund and $480,000 for the State. It is expected that uncollectible taxes will be $10,000 for the State and $15,000 for the County.
2. Collections were $300,000 for the County and $240,000 for the State.
3. The County is entitled to a fee of 1 percent of taxes collected for other governments. The County sends the State the amount due.
4. The fee is transmitted from the Tax Agency Fund to the County General Fund.
5. Uncollectible taxes in the amount of $5,000 for the State and $6,000 for the County are written off.

**Problem 12-2.** The following is a trial balance of the Tax Agency Fund of the City of *F* as of June 30, 19X0:

| | | |
|---|---:|---:|
| Cash ............................... | $ 90,000 | |
| Taxes Receivable for County X ............ | 22,500 | |
| Taxes Receivable for City Y .............. | 48,000 | |
| Taxes Receivable for School District Z ....... | 69,000 | |
| Taxes Fund Balance—County X ........... | | $ 37,500 |
| Taxes Fund Balance—City Y .............. | | 78,000 |
| Taxes Fund Balance—School District Z. ..... | | 114,000 |
| | $229,500 | $229,500 |

The following transactions took place:
1. Cash to the amount of $89,400 was paid over as follows:

| Unit | Amount Due | Collection Fee | Amount Paid Over |
|:---:|---:|---:|---:|
| X | $15,000 | $100 | $14,900 |
| Y | 30,000 | 200 | 29,800 |
| Z | 45,000 | 300 | 44,700 |

2. The collection fees were paid over to the General Fund.
3. Taxes were levied as follows:

| Unit | Amount Levied |
|:---:|---:|
| X | $ 50,000 |
| Y | 100,000 |
| Z | 150,000 |

Required:
(a) Prepare journal entries.
(b) Post to "T" accounts.
(c) Prepare a Balance Sheet as of November 30, 19X0.
or
(d) In lieu of requirements a, b, and c, prepare a worksheet from which these requirements might readily be fulfilled.

**Problem 12-3.** The City of Robinsburg collects, in addition to its own taxes, those of other units. The following are the tax levies for 19X1 and 19X2:

| | 19X1 | 19X2 |
|---|---:|---:|
| City | $220,800 | $240,000 |
| School District | 144,000 | 160,000 |
| Park District | 115,200 | 100,000 |
| | $480,000 | $500,000 |

Collections during 19X2 were as follows:

| | |
|---|---|
| 19X1 levy | $ 67,000 |
| 19X2 levy | 464,000 |

The city tax levies are in turn distributed among the following funds:

| | Mills per Dollar of Assessed Value | |
|---|---|---|
| Fund | 19X1 | 19X2 |
| General | 8.76 | 8.51 |
| Library | 1.44 | 1.61 |
| Debt Retirement | 1.80 | 1.38 |
| Total | 12.00 | 11.50 |

Required:
(a) Compute the amount of the collection of each levy applicable to each governmental unit.
(b) Compute the amount of the collection from each city levy applicable to each city fund. (Assume no collection fee is charged against City tax collections.)
(c) Prepare the journal entry to be made on the city's books to record the collection of taxes in 19X2 (that is, the collection of 19X1 and 19X2 taxes in 19X2).
(d) Assuming that the municipality charges a fee of 2 percent for collecting other units' taxes, prepare the entry to record on the city's books the collection of the fee and its transfer to the General Fund. Prepare also an entry to record the transmittal of the money to the other units (districts) for which it is collected by the city.
(e) Prepare the entries to be made transferring the city's collections to the proper city funds, and the entries in each fund.

**Problem 12-4.** Prepare journal entries to record the following transactions:
1. Property A was sold for unpaid taxes covering 19X4 and 19X5 levies and interest and penalties, as follows:

| Levy of | Taxes | Interest and Penalties |
|---|---|---|
| 19X5 | $7,500 | $750 |
| 19X4 | 6,200 | 940 |

The cost of holding the sale was $65, and the property was sold for $17,500.
2. The taxpayer redeemed the property promptly; no additional penalties or interest were assessed.
3. Assume the same facts as in the first transaction except that the property was sold for $12,000.
4. Assume the same facts as in the first transaction except that the governmental unit bid in the property. (Note: Set up an allowance for estimated losses on tax

sale certificates through debiting Allowance for Uncollectible Delinquent Taxes, $750, and Allowance for Uncollectible Interest and Penalties, $65.)

5. The governmental unit decided to use the property for recreational purposes. The taxes all belonged to the General Fund. (Assume the salable value of the property is 85 percent of the amount of the tax sale certificate.)

**Problem 12-5.** The following is a trial balance of the Policemen's Retirement Fund of the City of Cherrydale:

CITY OF CHERRYDALE

Policemen's Retirement Fund

Trial Balance

January 1, 19X0

| | | |
|---|---:|---:|
| Cash .............................. | $ 6,000 | |
| Investments ........................ | 52,000 | |
| Interest Receivable on Investments ...... | 450 | |
| Pensions Payable ..................... | | $ 150 |
| Pension Fund Reserve ................. | | 58,010 |
| Fund Balance-Earnings ................ | | 290 |
| | $58,450 | $58,450 |

The following transactions took place during the year:

1. Required contributions from employees amounted to $22,000 and from the governmental unit, $22,000; required earnings, $2,000.

2. The required contributions became due from the General Fund ($38,000) and a Special Revenue Fund ($6,000). One half of these amounts represents the employees share of contributions.

3. Payments were received from the General Fund, $30,000, and the Special Revenue Fund, $4,000.

4. Securities were acquired for cash as follows:

    (a) First Purchase:

| | |
|---|---:|
|         Par Value........................... | $20,000 |
|         Premiums ........................... | 300 |
|         Interest accrued at date of purchase...... | 200 |

    (b) Second Purchase:

| | |
|---|---:|
|         Par Value........................... | $15,000 |
|         Discounts .......................... | 150 |

5. Interest received on investments amounted to $3,000, including interest receivable on January 1, 19X0, and accrued interest purchased.

6. Premiums and discounts in the amounts of $50 and $30, respectively, were amortized.

7. Pensions paid, including pensions accrued at January 1, 19X0, amounted to $1,800.

8. Pensions accrued at December 31, 19X0, amounted to $190.

Required:
  (a)  Prepare journal entries, including closing entries.
  (b)  Post to "T" accounts.
  (c)  Prepare a balance sheet as of December 31, 19X0.

**Problem 12-6.**

a.  Prepare a solution to Problem 12-5 by designing and completing an appropriate worksheet rather than making journal entries and posting to "T" accounts.

b.  In addition to preparing a Balance Sheet at December 31, 19X0, prepare an Analysis of Changes in Fund Balance for the year then ended, using the following columnar headings:

| Pension Fund Reserve | | Fund Balance—Earnings | |
|---|---|---|---|
| *Actual* | *Planned* | *Actual* | *Planned* |

Assume that planned pension expenditures were $1,700.

**Problem 12-7.**  The following is a trial balance of the Child Welfare Principal Trust Fund of the City of Sweeney Bluff as of January 1, 19X3:

| | | |
|---|---|---|
| Cash .................................... | $ 98,000 | |
| Land.................................... | 70,000 | |
| Buildings ............................... | 162,000 | |
| Accumulated Depreciation ................. | | $ 65,000 |
| Accrued Wages Payable .................. | | 150 |
| Accrued Taxes Payable ................... | | 1,800 |
| Due to Child Welfare Earnings Trust Fund ... | | 15,000 |
| Fund Balance—Trust Principal ............. | | 248,050 |
| | $330,000 | $330,000 |

The endowment was in the form of an apartment building. Endowment principal is to be kept intact, and the net earnings are to be used in financing child welfare activities.

The following transactions took place during the year:
  1.  Expenses and accrued liabilities paid in cash were as follows:

| | |
|---|---|
| Heat, light, and power ............................. | $ 5,200 |
| Janitor's wages (including $150 previously accrued)...... | 3,000 |
| Painting and decorating ........................... | 3,750 |
| Repairs........................................... | 1,500 |
| Taxes (including $1,800 previously accrued) .......... | 3,750 |
| Management fees .................................. | 4,500 |
| Miscellaneous expenses ........................... | 1,500 |
| | $23,200 |

2.   A special assessment of $2,000 levied by the municipality against the property was paid.

3.   Rents for 19X3 (all collected) amounted to $45,000.

4.   The amount due to the Child Welfare Earnings Trust Fund at January 1, 19X3 was paid.

5.   Expenditures of $15,000 were paid from the Child Welfare Earnings Trust Fund to finance 19X3 summer camp activities.

6.   The following adjustments were made at the close of the year:

| | |
|---|---|
| Depreciation .................... | $6,000 |
| Accrued Taxes ................. | 1,900 |
| Accrued Wages................. | 170 |

Required:

(a)   Prepare a Balance Sheet as of December 31, 19X3, and a Combined Statement of Net Income and Change in Fund Balance for the fiscal year ended December 31, 19X3, for the Child Welfare Principal Trust Fund. (Support these statements with a worksheet, "T" account, or other analysis.)

(b)   Prepare a Balance Sheet as of December 31, 19X3, for the Child Welfare Earnings Trust Fund. An analysis of changes in Fund Balance for the year then ended should be included within the Balance Sheet. (Assume that the Child Welfare Earnings Trust Fund had no activities or balances other than those indicated in the problem.)

(c)   Should an analysis of changes in Fund Balance normally be presented for a fund, either in a separate statement or within the Balance Sheet, even if no change has occurred during a period? Explain.

**Problem 12-8.**   The city of New Arnheim has engaged you to examine the following Balance Sheet which was prepared by the city's bookkeeper:

### CITY OF NEW ARNHEIM
#### Balance Sheet
#### June 30, 19X9

*Assets*

| | |
|---|---|
| Cash ...................................... | $   159,000 |
| Taxes receivable—current ..................... | 32,000 |
| Supplies on hand ............................ | 9,000 |
| Marketable securities ........................ | 250,000 |
| Land........................................ | 1,000,000 |
| Fixed assets ................................ | 7,000,000 |
| Total ..................................... | $8,450,000 |

*Liabilities*

| | |
|---|---|
| Vouchers payable ........................... | $    42,000 |
| Reserve for supplies inventory ............... | 8,000 |
| Bonds payable ............................. | 3,000,000 |
| Fund balance ............................. | 5,400,000 |
| Total ................................... | $8,450,000 |

Your audit disclosed the following information:
1.  An analysis of the Fund Balance account:

| | | |
|---|---|---|
| Balance, June 30, 19X8 ...................... | | $2,100,000 |
| Add: | | |
| Donated land ........................... | $  800,000 | |
| Federal grant-in-aid ..................... | 2,200,000 | |
| Creation of endowment fund .............. | 250,000 | |
| Excess of actual tax revenue over estimated revenue ............................. | 24,000 | |
| Excess of appropriations closed out over expenditures and encumbrances ............... | 20,000 | |
| Net income from endowment funds .......... | 10,000 | 3,304,000 |
| | | 5,404,000 |
| Deduct: | | |
| Excess of Cultural Center operating expenses over income .......................... | | 4,000 |
| Balance, June 30, 19X9 ...................... | | $5,400,000 |

2.  In July, 19X8, land appraised at a fair market value of $800,000 was donated to the city for a Cultural Center which was opened on April 15, 19X9. Building construction expenditures for the project were financed from a federal grant-in-aid of $2,200,000 and from an authorized 10-year $3,000,000 issue of 6 percent general obligation bonds sold at par on July 1, 19X8. Interest is payable on December 31 and June 30. The fair market value of the land and the cost of the building are included respectively in the Land and Fixed Assets accounts.
3.  The Cultural Center receives no direct state or city subsidy for current operating expenses. A Cultural Center Endowment Fund was established by a gift of marketable securities having a fair market value of $250,000 at date of receipt. The endowment principal is to be kept intact. Income is to be applied to any operating deficit of the center.

4. Other data:

(a)   It is anticipated that $7,000 of the 19X8–X9 tax levy is uncollectible.

(b)   The physical inventory of supplies on hand at June 30, 19X9, amounted to $12,500.

(c)   Unfilled purchase orders for the General Fund at June 30, 19X9, totaled $5,000.

(d)   On July 1, 19X8, an all-purpose building was purchased for $2,000,000. Of the purchase price, $200,000 was allotted to the land. The purchase had been authorized under the budget for the year ended June 30, 19X9.

Required:

(a)   Prepare a worksheet showing adjustments and distributions to the proper funds or groups of accounts. The worksheet should be in the form of the city of New Arnheim's balance sheet and have the following column headings:

| Column(s) | Headings |
| --- | --- |
| 1 | Balance per Books |
| 2–3 | Adjustments—Debit |
| | —Credit |
| 4 | General Fund |
| 5–6 | City Cultural Center Endowment Fund: |
| | Principal |
| | Revenues |
| 7 | General Fixed Assets |
| 8 | General Long-Term Debt |

Number all adjusting entries. (Formal journal entries are not required.) Supporting computations should be in good form.

(b)   Assuming the amounts reflected in the above Balance Sheet were all in the General Fund, prepare the formal entry required, in compound form, to correct the accounts of the General Fund at June 30, 19X9.

(AICPA, adapted)

**Problem 12-9. Part I.**   Cultura Township had not been operating a public library prior to October 1, 19X1. On October 1, 19X1, James Jones died, having made a valid will that provided for the gift of his residence and various securities to the town for the establishment and operations of a free public library. The gift was accepted, and the library funds and operation were placed under the control of trustees. The terms of the gift provided that not in excess of $5,000 of the principal of the fund could be used for the purchase of equipment, building rearrangement, and purchase of such "standard" library reference books as, in the opinion of the trustees, were needed for starting the library. Except for this $5,000, the principal of the fund is to be invested and the income therefrom used to operate the library in accordance with appropriations made by the trustees. The property received from the estate by the trustees was as follows:

| Description | Face or Par | Appraised Value |
|---|---|---|
| Residence of James Jones: | | |
| Land .............................. | | $ 2,500 |
| Building (25-year estimated life) ........ | | 20,000 |
| Bonds: | | |
| AB Company......................... | $34,000 | 32,000 |
| C & D Company .................... | 10,000 | 11,200 |
| D & G Company .................... | 20,000 | 20,000 |
| Stocks: | | |
| M Company, 6% preferred............. | 12,000 | 12,600 |
| S Company, 5% preferred ............. | 10,000 | 9,600 |
| K Company, common (300 shares) ...... | No par | 12,900 |
| GF Company (200 shares) ............. | 4,000 | 14,500 |

The following events occurred in connection with the library operations up to June 30, 19X2:

1. 100 shares of GF Company stock were sold on November 17, for $6,875.
2. Cash payments were made for: (a) Alteration of the house—$1,310, (b) General reference books—$725, (c) Equipment having an estimated life of ten years—$2,180. The trustees state that these amounts are to be charged to principal under the applicable provision of the gift.
3. The library started operation on January 1, 19X2. The trustees adopted the following budget for the year ended December 31, 19X2:

| | |
|---|---|
| Estimated income from Trust Principal Fund earnings transfer ...... | $5,000 |
| Estimated income from fines, etc. ............................. | 200 |
| Appropriation for salaries ...................................... | 3,600 |
| Appropriation for subscriptions ................................ | 300 |
| Appropriation for purchase of books ........................... | 800 |
| Appropriation for utilities, supplies, etc. ........................ | 400 |

4. The following cash receipts were reported during the six months to June 30, 19X2:

| | |
|---|---|
| a. Sale of C and D Company bonds, including accrued interest of $80 ................................................. | $11,550 |
| b. Interest and dividends .................................... | 3,100 |
| c. Fines ..................................................... | 20 |
| d. Gift for purchase of books .............................. | 200 |
| Total ................................................ | $14,870 |

5.  The following cash payments were made during the six months to June 30, 19X2:

| | | |
|---|---|---:|
| a. | Purchase of 100 shares of no-par common stock of L and M Company, including commission and tax cost of $50............. | $ 9,655 |
| b. | Payment of salaries....................................... | 1,500 |
| c. | Payment of property taxes applicable to the year ended December 31, 19X1 based on an assessment as of June 30, 19X1.......... | 200 |
| d. | Purchase of books........................................ | 900 |
| e. | Magazine subscriptions.................................... | 230 |
| f. | Supplies and other expense ............................... | 260 |
| | Total ............................................... | $12,745 |

6.  On June 30, 19X2, there were miscellaneous library expenses unpaid, but accrued, amounting to $90. Also there were outstanding purchase orders for books in the amount of $70.

Required:

Assuming the township records budgetary accounts with respect to library operations, prepare in detail the worksheet(s) necessary to show the results of operations to June 30, 19X2, and the financial position of the Trust Fund(s) related to the library as of June 30, 19X2. Where alternate treatment of an item is acceptable, explain the alternate treatment and state the justification for your treatment. In designing your worksheet(s), you should observe the requirements of Part II of this problem in order that those requirements may be fulfilled readily from the worksheet(s) prepared here.

**Problem 12-9. Part II.**  From the worksheet(s) prepared in Part I, construct the following formal statements relative to Cultura Township's library endowment and library operations:

1.  A Balance Sheet(s) for the Trust Fund(s) at June 30, 19X2.
2.  A detailed Statement of Actual and Estimated Revenues for the library operation for the six months ended June 30, 19X2.
3.  A detailed Statement of Appropriations, Expenditures and Encumbrances for the library operation for the six months ended June 30, 19X2.
4.  A summary Analysis of Changes in the Fund Balance Account with respect to the trust earnings for the six months ended June 30, 19X2, supported by the statements prepared to fulfill requirements 2 and 3.
5.  A detailed Analysis of Changes in Fund Balance with respect to the trust principal for the nine month period ended June 30, 19X2.

(Statements should be in good form and cross-referenced appropriately.)

**Problem 12-10.**  The City of Linde, organized on January 1, 19X1, has never kept accounts on a double-entry system. During 19X8 the city council employed you to install a system of accounts. You made a study and determined the values of assets and liabilities in order to inaugurate the proper system as of January 1, 19X9, the beginning of the city's fiscal year, as follows:

| | |
|---|---:|
| 1.  City taxes receivable—19X8 and prior years (including 10 percent considered uncollectible) ........................... | $ 21,900 |

2. Investment in securities:
   a. Earmarked to bond retirement......................... 136,680
   b. Donated by J. Stark on July 1, 19X8, the net income from
      which is to supplement library operations. The cost of all the
      stock to Stark was $50,000. Appraised value on July 1 .... 65,400

3. Cash:
   a. For general operations, including $3,000 in petty cash .... 18,000
   b. Earmarked to investments for bond retirement (represents
      interest earned over the actuarial estimate) .............. 840
   c. Balance of cash donated by J. Stark, the net income from
      which is to supplement library operations .............. 12,000
   d. Undistributed balance of cash received from J. Stark invest-
      ments and apartment rents .......................... 3,000

4. Buildings:
   a. For general operations ............................... 235,000
   b. Apartment building donated by J. Stark on July 1, 19X8.
      Net rental income before depreciation is to be used in the
      operation of the library. Cost to Stark, July 1, 19X0, $96,000
      (exclusive of cost of land); estimated life of 50 years, with no
      salvage value. Appraised value on July 1, 19X8 .......... 90,000

5. Equipment:
   a. For general use ..................................... 280,000
   b. Apartment furniture purchased with donated cash, October
      1, 19X8; estimated life 10 years, with no salvage value.
      Cost ............................................... 36,000

6. Streets and curbs financed by special assessments levied in prior
   years (all collected). The city contributed one-third of the cost.. 300,000

7. Land:
   a. General use ....................................... 60,000
   b. Apartment building site ............................. 10,000

8. Supplies:
   a. For general operation ............................. 1,800
   b. For apartment house operation, purchased by income cash.. 300
   c. Originally purchased for general operation, transferred to
      and used in library operations; no settlement has been made 2,400

9. Vouchers payable—for general operations ................. 16,000

10. Five percent (5%) 30-year bonds payable, issued at par on Janu-
    ary 1, 19X6 (for purchase of land, buildings, and equipment) .. 400,000

Required:
List the funds or account group titles that would be required for the City of Linde
on the basis of the above information, leaving at least 15 lines between each title.
Under each title make one summary journal entry to record all of the required

accounts and amounts as of December 31, 19X8. You may omit formal entry explanations, but you should state any assumptions made and show calculations, as appropriate.

(AICPA, adapted)

**Problem 12-11.**   Prepare a columnar analytical worksheet to serve as a basis upon which an appropriate double-entry accounting system may be established for the City of Linde (Problem 12-10.) Use these headings.

| Worksheet Column(s) | Heading |
| --- | --- |
| Date/Reference | Key |
| Account/Explanation | Account Titles |
| 1–2 | Combined Totals |
| 3–4 | General Fund |
| 5–6 | Nonexpendable (Principal) Trust Fund |
| 7–8 | Expendable (Earnings) Trust Fund |
| 9–10 | Debt Service Fund |
| 11 | General Fixed Assets Group |
| 12 | General Long-Term Debt Group |

You are to cross-reference (Key) your worksheet to the numbered and lettered items in Problem 12-10; other entries needed should be keyed A, B, C, etc.

**Problem 12-12. Part I.**   Joseph Colvin, a prominent citizen and former mayor of the City of Farleyton, gave a downtown commercial office building to the City in trust, with the stipulation that the net rental and interest income be used to provide scholarships and loans to city employees. The trust was established on July 1, 19X1, and the trust instrument specifies that:

1.   The property and Trust Fund are to be managed by a board of trustees appointed by the aldermen of the City of Farleyton.

2.   Twenty percent of the net rental income is to be used for scholarships, the balance for loans. Estimates of current year earnings may be used in determining the amounts of scholarships and loans that may be awarded and approved in order that resources of the Trust Fund may be made available to qualified applicants as soon as possible. Financial statements are to be prepared semi-annually to assist the trustees in managing the fund and in assessing the stewardship of the trustees.

3.   Scholarships may be awarded only to city employees or specified members of their immediate families pursuing (or desiring to pursue) college or university coursework and who (a) earn above average scores on standardized entrance exams and/or (b) maintain a stipulated grade average or class standing.

4.   Loans may be made to city employees to assist them (a) in meeting college or university expenses for themselves or specified members of their immediate families, or (b) when they are in financial difficulty because of accident or illness. Interest is charged at 5 percent per annum, compounded semi-annually, on the unpaid balance of loans, and increases the balance available for loans; bad debt losses reduce the amount of the fund available for loans. Repayment terms are within the discretion of the trustees.

5.   Income is to be determined on the accrual basis of accounting. The building, furniture, and fixtures constituting the trust assets were to be recorded in the accounts

at fair market value at July 1, 19X1. Depreciation of the building is to be charged in determining net income, but that on the furniture and fixtures is chargeable to corpus. Depreciation on building is to be calculated at three percent (3%) per year on the original cost; that on furniture and fixtures at 10 percent. A full period's depreciation is to be charged in the semi-annual period in which an asset is acquired; none is to be charged to the semi-annual period in which assets are sold or otherwise disposed of. The trustees may acquire additional or replacement furniture and fixtures as needed, but such acquisitions will reduce its scholarship and loan authority in the proportion that net income is distributed. Gains and losses on assets comprising the original trust corpus shall be charged to corpus; those on assets acquired by the trustees shall be charged to current earnings.

6. To facilitate accounting and auditing, appropriate accounts are to be maintained in a single Colvin Scholarship and Loan Fund. Net assets need not be segregated by purpose, but the balance of each fund should be readily determinable from the accounts and the semi-annual financial statements.

The trust was established on July 1, 19X1. The trial balance of the Trust Fund at January 1, 19X4, is as follows:

### COLVIN SCHOLARSHIP AND LOAN FUND
Trial Balance

January 1, 19X4

| | | |
|---|---:|---:|
| Cash-Checking Account | 6,750 | |
| Cash-Savings and Loan Association | 8,000 | |
| Loans Receivable | 130,000 | |
| Accrued Interest Receivable-Loans | 10,000 | |
| Investments | 45,000 | |
| Accrued Interest Receivable-Investments | 500 | |
| Building | 650,000 | |
| Accumulated Depreciation-Building | | 48,750 |
| Furniture and Fixtures | 100,000 | |
| Accumulated Depreciation-Furniture and Fixtures | | 25,000 |
| Scholarships Payable | | 3,000 |
| Accounts Payable | | 1,500 |
| Reserve for Loans Outstanding | | 130,000 |
| Reserve for Loan Interest Receivable | | 10,000 |
| Fund Balance-Principal | | 725,000 |
| Fund Balance-Loans | | 6,000 |
| Fund Balance-Scholarships | | 1,000 |
| | 950,250 | 950,250 |

No furniture and fixtures were purchased by the trustees between July 1, 19X1, and December 31, 19X3, and no loans or interest have been written off as uncollectible.

The following transactions and events occurred during the first six months of 19X4:

1. Based on the available balance and anticipated 19X4 earnings, the board of

trustees awarded scholarships amounting to $8,500 and approved loans of $50,000. A reserve was established to reflect the loans authorized.

2.   Scholarship payments and loan disbursements amounted to $9,000 and $30,000, respectively. An approved loan application in the amount of $2,000 was withdrawn by the applicant; the balance will probably be disbursed in the Fall.

3.   Rentals received, $50,000; $1,500 was receivable at June 30.

4.   Maintenance and other expenses paid, including the accounts payable at January 1, $6,000; $800 of such expenses were payable at June 30.

6.   Loan and related interest collections amounted to $21,000 and $2,300, respectively.

7.   A loan receivable from a former employee of $4,000, together with interest receivable thereon of $400, was determined to be uncollectible and was written off by order of the board of trustees.

8.   Interest on investments received, $2,100; $800 was accrued at June 30. The trustees were notified that dividends of $200 had been credited to the savings and loan association account for the six months ended June 30.

9.   Furniture and fixtures valued at $20,000 upon formation of the trust were replaced at a cost of $30,000. The invoice for these items is unpaid at June 30; the furniture and fixtures replaced were sold for $7,000 cash.

10.   Accrued interest receivable on loans outstanding at June 30 totaled $11,000.

Required:

Prepare a worksheet to reflect the activities of the Colvin Scholarship and Loan Fund during the six months ended June 30, 19X4 and the balances at that date. The worksheet should be headed as follows:

| Columns | Heading |
| --- | --- |
| 1–2 | Trial Balance, 1/1/19X4 |
| 3–4 | Transactions and Adjustments |
| 5–6 | Adjusted Trial Balance, 6/30/19X4 |
| 7–8 | Pro Forma Closing Entries, 6/30/19X4 |
| 9–10 | Balance Sheet, 6/30/19X4 |

With the exception of changes in reserves, transactions and events are reflected in temporary accounts rather than being recorded directly in Fund Balance accounts. Adjustments are journalized and posted semi-annually, but the accounts are closed only at year end.

**Problem 12-12. Part II.**   From the worksheet prepared in Part I:

a.   Prepare a Balance Sheet for the Colvin Scholarship and Loan Fund at June 30, 19X4, with these columnar headings:

| Total | Principal | Scholarships | Loans |
| --- | --- | --- | --- |

b.   Prepare an Analysis of Changes in Fund Balances of the Colvin Scholarship and Loan Fund for the six months ended June 30, 19X4. The columnar headings should be as follows

| Column(s) | Heading |
|---|---|
| 1 | Total |
| 2 | Principal |
| 3 | Scholarships |
| 4–8 | Loans |

The heading and sub-headings of the Loans columns (4-8) should be:

| | | Loans | | |
|---|---|---|---|---|
| Total | Unreserved | | Reserved for: | |
| | | Loans Outstanding | Loan Interest Receivable | Loans Approved |

c. Prepare a Statement of Net Income for the Colvin Scholarship and Loan Fund for the six months ended June 30, 19X4. (Cross-reference the statements prepared as appropriate.)

d. Upon reviewing the financial statements prepared above, Letha Farley Colvin is concerned that the trustees may have acted improperly and seeks your opinion on the matter. Why is she concerned, and what opinion or explanation would you offer?

# 13

# Intragovernmental Service Funds

Intragovernmental Service (IGS) Funds, sometimes referred to as "working capital" or "revolving" funds, are established in order to finance, administer, and account for the provision of goods and services by one department of a government to its other departments. This type of fund serves internal users only (or primarily) and should be distinguished from Enterprise Funds, through which provision of goods or services for compensation to the general public is financed and accounted for.

IGS Funds are internal *intermediary* fiscal and accounting entities through which some of the expenditures of other departments are made. They are used in order (1) to attain greater economy, efficiency, and effectiveness in the acquisition and distribution of common goods or services utilized by several or all departments within the organization, and (2) to facilitate an equitable sharing of costs among the various departments served and, hence, among the funds of the organization. As noted earlier, they may also be used to provide interim financing for Special Assessment and Capital Projects Funds.

Activities handled through IGS Funds in practice vary widely both as to type and complexity of operation. Among the simpler types are those used (1) to distribute common or joint costs, such as the cost of telephone, two-way radio or other communication facilities, among departments, (2) to acquire, distribute, and allocate costs of a few selected items of inventory, such as office supplies or gasoline, or (3) to provide temporary loans to other funds in deficit situations or prior to the receipt of debt issue or grant proceeds. Activities of a more complex nature commonly accounted for through IGS Funds include motor pools; duplicating and printing facilities; repair shops and garages; cement and asphalt plants; and purchasing, warehousing, and distribution services and facilities.

## Overview of Accounting Principles

Intragovernmental Service Funds are established to provide continuing services, usually on a break-even basis. As contrasted with expendable funds discussed in earlier chapters, IGS Funds are *nonexpendable* or *self-sustaining* funds and are accounted for on essentially the same basis as a private business of a similar type.

The use of generally accepted principles of business accounting indicates that fixed assets will be recorded in the Funds, as will long-term debt for which the IGS Fund is responsible. Depreciation is recognized and recorded in order that Fund capital will not be impaired.

The above statement that depreciation is accounted for "in order that Fund capital will not be impaired" is significant. Where all fixed assets utilized by the IGS Fund activity are accounted for therein and are expected (properly or improperly) to be replaced through its resources, depreciation accounting results in the determination of full cost (historical) for reimbursement and other decision-making purposes. On the other hand, where only part of the fixed assets are capitalized in or to be replaced through the IGS Fund—the balance usually being recorded in General Fixed Assets—depreciation is formally recorded *only* on these fixed assets in the IGS Fund. The resultant "cost" in this latter case may be appropriate for purposes of reimbursement and maintenance of Fund capital, but it must be supplemented by depreciation expense data relative to non-IGS Fund fixed assets if meaningful cost analyses and "make or buy" and similar decisions are to be made.

Many goods and services usually financed by IGS Funds are available on a commercial basis. Therefore, one of the benefits of applying generally accepted principles of business accounting to IGS Funds is the ability to compare the cost of services provided through IGS Funds with the cost of the same services if procured commercially.

Another benefit from the production of accurate cost information is its effect on administrators in making decisions. For example, consider the case of a machine shop in which special projects are undertaken for other departments. A department head, having seen a device advertised for $1,500, comes to the machine shop manager and asks for an estimate of the cost to manufacture the device. If the machine shop computes costs on the same basis as a private business, the department head receives a reply which permits an accurate direct comparison of total cost-to-produce with total cost-to-buy. But suppose the machine shop has an appropriation which pays all labor costs and provides fixed assets for the shop and the manager computes the cost to the department head on the basis of direct materials cost plus a small percentage to cover minor overhead items. The department head will accept the lower price because it represents the lower charge to his own appropriation, but the total cost to the government may far exceed $1,500.

Finally, production of accurate cost data means that the departments that utilize the services of the IGS Fund may be charged on an equitable basis for the cost of the services utilized. Recall again, however, that "reimbursable cost" and "full cost" may differ, e.g., where depreciation is not recorded on all fixed assets utilized by the IGS Fund activity.

### Cost Accounting in the IGS Fund

The variety of activities that may be financed through an IGS Fund indicates the variety of cost accounting systems that may be required for managerial control. Job order, process, or standard cost systems may be appropriate; the system used should produce accurate cost data and provide managerial control. Some of the simpler fundamental aspects of cost accounting systems are illustrated in Chapter 15; a more complete exposition is beyond the scope of this book.

### Creation of the IGS Fund

Ordinarily an IGS Fund will be created by constitutional, charter, or legislative action, though the chief executive may be permitted by legislation to do so. Capital to finance IGS Fund activities may come from appropriations from the General Fund, the issue of general bonds or other debt instruments, transfers from other funds, or advances from another government. Capital may also be augmented by confiscation of all, or excessive, inventories of materials and supplies that a fund's future "clients" (a governmental unit's departments) may have on hand at a specified time. Finally, IGS Fund capital may be increased by setting prices which will produce a profit that is retained in the Fund.

If the General Fund provides capital for the IGS Fund, the following entries will be made:

ENTRY IN GENERAL FUND:

| | | |
|---|---|---|
| Expenditures .......................... | 50,000 | |
|     Cash ............................... | | 50,000 |
|     To record capital provided to IGS Fund. | | |

ENTRY IN IGS FUND:

| | | |
|---|---|---|
| Cash ................................. | 50,000 | |
|     Contribution from General Fund | | |
|         (or Capital) ........................ | | 50,000 |
|     To record receipt of capital from General Fund. | | |

If the General Fund is to ultimately be repaid from IGS Fund resources, the following entries would be made rather than those above:

ENTRIES IN GENERAL FUND:
| | | |
|---|---|---|
| Advance to IGS Fund ..................... | 50,000 | |
| Cash .............................. | | 50,000 |
| To record capital advance to IGS Fund. | | |

| | | |
|---|---|---|
| Fund Balance ........................... | 50,000 | |
| Reserve for Advance to IGS Fund ....... | | 50,000 |
| To record reservation of fund balance because of advance to IGS Fund. | | |

ENTRY IN IGS FUND:
| | | |
|---|---|---|
| Cash .................................... | 50,000 | |
| Advance from General Fund ............. | | 50,000 |
| To record advance from General Fund. | | |

Note that the terms "advance to" and "advance from" are used in the above case rather than "due to" and "due from." The term "advance" is customarily used in connection with intermediate- and long-term receivables and payables, whereas "due to" and "due from" connote short-term relationships. Note also that a reserve was established in the General Fund in order to indicate that the asset "Advance to IGS Fund" does not represent currently appropriable resources.

If proceeds from the sale of bonds are transferred from the Capital Projects Fund to finance an IGS Fund, the following entries will be made:

ENTRY IN CAPITAL PROJECTS FUND:
| | | |
|---|---|---|
| Appropriations (or Fund Balance or Expenditures) | 100,000 | |
| Cash ............................... | | 100,000 |
| To record transfer of proceeds to provide IGS Fund capital. | | |

ENTRY IN IGS FUND:
| | | |
|---|---|---|
| Cash .................................. | 100,000 | |
| Contribution from General Obligation Bonds (or Capital)....................... | | 100,000 |
| To record receipt of capital from sale of bonds. | | |

## Pricing Policies

The preceding discussions relative to pricing were based on the assumption that the prices charged by the IGS Fund would be based on (historical) cost, and most authorities assume that cost is the proper pricing basis. Where IGS Fund activities are very modest in scope and do not use full-time personnel or incur significant other costs, charges to user funds may be based on direct costs. This might be the case, for example, where (1) very limited group purchasing and warehousing is done only occasionally or as a small part of the overall purchasing operation, or (2) where the IGS Fund is essentially a "flowthrough" or clearance device for common costs, such as two-way radio facility rentals. In the more usual case, however, the activity involves substantial amounts of personnel, space, materials, and other overhead costs that are recovered through billing user departments for more than the direct cost of the goods or services provided.

The Intragovernmental Service Fund usually has a captive clientele, since in most governments the departments may not use another source of supply if a service or material is available through the IGS Fund. This makes it possible for IGS Fund prices to be set at levels that will produce a substantial profit or loss.

In some cases IGS Fund capital has been built up by means of substantial annual profits. The increase in capital was paid for, of course, by the funds that financed the appropriations used to buy IGS Fund services or supplies. There have even been instances in which the retained earnings of an IGS Fund provided the basis for a cash "dividend" that was transferred as "revenue" to the General Fund. To the extent that IGS Fund revenues were derived from departments financed by the General Fund, the profit thus transferred merely had the effect of offsetting excessive charges to it previously; but if departments or activities financed through other funds patronized the IGS Fund, the effect of overcharging was (subtly) to transfer resources from these other funds to the General Fund.

Use of IGS Fund charges to divert restricted resources to other purposes cannot be condoned. Such practice erodes confidence in the organization's administrators and in the accounting system, constitutes indirect fraud at best, and at worst results in illegal usage of intergovernmental grant, trust, or other restricted resources.

### Pricing Methods

The pricing method used by an IGS Fund is usually based on estimates of total costs and total consumption of goods or services. From these two estimates a rate is developed which is applied to each purchase. If the cost of materials to be issued by a Stores Fund during the coming year was expected to be $300,000 and other costs of fund operation were estimated at $12,000, goods would be priced to departments at $1.04 for every $1.00 of direct cost of materials issued. Similarly, rental rates of automotive equipment may be based on time or mileage, or both. If a truck was expected to be driven 12,000 miles during the year at a total cost of $1,200, the departments probably would be charged $.10 per mile.

Where IGS Fund charges to departments are based on predetermined price schedules, (1) IGS Fund expenses are charged to appropriately titled expense accounts, and (2) IGS Fund "sales" are credited to an account such as Billings to Departments and debited to a Due From (name) Fund account. Where goods or services provided are charged to user departments on the basis of direct cost plus estimated overhead, IGS Fund overhead expenses incurred are debited to an Overhead account and amounts charged to user departments for overhead reimbursement are credited to Overhead or to an Overhead Applied account. The difference between overhead incurred and that billed to user departments during a period is referred to as "under-applied or -absorbed" or "over-applied or -absorbed" overhead.

The alternative to using predetermined rates such as those described in the preceding paragraphs is to charge the departments on the basis of actual costs determined at the end of each month, quarter, or year. Though this method is often used for uncomplicated IGS Funds, a predetermined rental rate is generally used for more complex operations for the following reasons: (1) Some IGS Fund expenses may not be determinable until the end of the month (or later), whereas it may be desirable to bill departments promptly so that they know how much expense or expenditure is charged to their jobs and activities at any time. (2) Charges based on actual monthly costs are likely to spread the burden unequally among departments. For example, assume that the costs of extensive equipment repairs made in June are included in the charges to the departments using the equipment during that month. In this situation, those departments that used the equipment in June would be billed for costs more properly allocated to several months or years, while the departments that used the equipment in previous or succeeding months would not bear their "fair share" of these costs. Furthermore, even if one department used the equipment throughout the year, charges based on actual monthly costs often would result in an unequitable distribution of costs among jobs and activities carried on by the department (as between June and other months in this example).

### Relation to the Budget

The level of activity of an Intragovernmental Service Fund will be determined by the demand of the government's departments for its services. Separate IGS Fund appropriations are rarely made, and formal budgetary control is seldom introduced into IGS Fund accounts, because (1) the IGS activity must be able to respond to service demands, not constrained by inflexible appropriation levels, and (2) the appropriations to the various user departments constitute an indirect budgetary ceiling on the IGS activities.

Sound management requires that *flexible* budgetary techniques be employed in the planning and conduct of major IGS Fund activities. Furthermore, the NCGA has suggested that IGS Fund finances be included in the operating budget in the following manner:

> The total amount of proposed *expenditures* for a Service Fund activity in the budget should be offset by the amount of billings to departments, leaving no net appropriations from general revenues of the government.[1]

[1] *GAAFR,* p. 71. (Emphasis added.)

Although IGS Fund accounting is focused upon accrual accounting for revenues and expenses (not expenditures), the NCGA felt that IGS revenue and expenditure data should be included as an integral part of the annual budget document:

> ...in order to have a comprehensive financial plan for all of the governmental unit's operations during the fiscal year, to provide proper legislative and managerial control over the fund's operations, and to insure uniformity of financial policy and administration among all of the unit's operating departments.[2]

Laws or custom in some cases prohibit the incurrence of obligations against or disbursement of cash from IGS Funds without appropriation authority. Where this is the case, it is necessary to record not only those transactions that affect the actual position and operations of the fund (that is, those transactions that affect the actual revenues, expenses, assets, liabilities, and capital) but also those relating to appropriations, expenditures, and encumbrances. Since this is the unusual case, rather than the usual one, the major examples that follow illustrate the accounting for proprietary accounts only; supplementary entries at the conclusion of the chapter illustrate the modifications necessary for budgetary accounting in IGS Funds.

## IGS FUND ACCOUNTING ILLUSTRATED

Two illustrations of Intragovernmental Service Fund activities, accounting, and reporting comprise the next section of this chapter. The IGS Fund activities illustrated are a central automotive equipment operation and a Stores Fund.

### A Central Automotive Equipment Unit

Assume that a Central Automotive Equipment Fund has been created and that some of the assets needed have been acquired. The IGS Fund balance sheet prior to beginning operations is presented in Figure 13-1. The balance sheet data also provide the starting point for the worksheet summarizing this example, Figure 13-5; the "Proprietary Accounts" section of that worksheet summarizes this phase of our example.

Fund resources will be used to buy automobiles, trucks, tractors, and the like. The usage of each machine and the cost of operation on a per mile or per hour basis will be estimated and records of actual cost will be kept so that they may be compared with estimates and may be used in making estimates for coming years. Such records also are useful in making decisions concerning efficiency of management and economy of operation of various types and brands of equipment.

[2] *GAAFR,* p. 70.

The following transactions and entries (see Figure 13-5) illustrate more specifically how a central equipment bureau usually operates.

Figure 13-1

A GOVERNMENTAL UNIT
Central Automotive Equipment (IGS) Fund
Balance Sheet (Date)

*Assets*

| | | |
|---|---:|---:|
| Current assets: | | |
| Cash ........................... | | $ 75,000 |
| Fixed assets: | | |
| Land .......................... | $10,000 | |
| Buildings ..................... | 40,000 | |
| Machinery and equipment ........ | 10,000 | 60,000 |
| | | $135,000 |

*Contributed Capital*

| | |
|---|---:|
| Contributed capital from General Fund | $135,000 |

*Transactions*

1. Purchased equipment on credit for $40,000.
2. Materials and supplies purchased on credit, $10,000.
3. Salaries and wages paid, $19,000, distributed as follows:

| | |
|---|---:|
| Mechanics' Wages ............ | $9,000 |
| Indirect Labor ................ | 3,000 |
| Superintendent's Salary ........ | 3,500 |
| Office Salaries ............... | 3,500 |

4. Heat, light, and power paid, $2,000.
5. Depreciation:

| | |
|---|---:|
| Buildings..................... | $2,400 |
| Machinery and Equipment ...... | 9,200 |

6. Total billings to departments for services rendered, $42,800, of which $30,000 is chargeable to the General Fund and $12,800 is chargeable to the Enterprise Fund.

7. Vouchers payable in the amount of $42,500 were paid, of which $35,000 relates to the equipment puchased.
8. Office expenses paid, $200.
9. Materials and supplies issued during period, $7,000.
10. Accrued salaries and wages, $1,000, distributed as follows:

| | |
|---|---|
| Mechanics' Wages .............. | $500 |
| Indirect Labor................. | 150 |
| Superintendent's Salary .......... | 175 |
| Office Salaries ................. | 175 |

*Entries*

1. Machinery and Equipment ..............    40,000
   Vouchers Payable ..................        40,000
   To record purchase of equipment.

2. Inventory of Materials and Supplies ........    10,000
   Vouchers Payable ..................        10,000
   To record purchase of materials and supplies.

3. Mechanics' Wages ......................    9,000
   Indirect Labor.......................    3,000
   Superintendent's Salary .................    3,500
   Office Salaries .........................    3,500
   Cash ............................        19,000
   To record expenses for salaries and wages.

4. Heat, Light and Power .................    2,000
   Cash ............................        2,000
   To record heat, light, and power expense.

5. Depreciation—Buildings .................    2,400
   Depreciation—Machinery and Equipment ..    9,200
   Allowance for Depreciation—Buildings ..        2,400
   Allowance for Depreciation—Machinery
     and Equipment ..................        9,200
   To record depreciation expenses.

6. Due from General Fund .................    30,000
   Due from Enterprise Fund ...............    12,800
   Billings to Departments ..............        42,800
   To record billings to departments.*

7. Vouchers Payable ......................    42,500
   Cash ............................        42,500
   To record payment of vouchers payable.

\* In the General Fund, Expenditures will be charged, while in the Enterprise Fund an expense or asset account will be charged. In both cases, the credit will be to Due to Central Automotive Equipment (Intragovernmental Service) Fund.

*Entries*

8. Office Expenses ......................... 200
   Cash ............................... 200
   To record miscellaneous office expenses.

9. Cost of Materials and Supplies Used ....... 7,000
   Inventory of Materials and Supplies .... 7,000
   To record cost of materials and supplies used.

10. Mechanics' Wages ...................... 500
    Indirect Labor......................... 150
    Superintendent's Salary ................. 175
    Office Salaries and Wages ............... 175
    Accrued Salaries and Wages Payable ... 1,000
    To record accrued salaries and wages.

After these entries have been posted (see Figure 13-5) the trial balance of the accounts of the IGS Fund will appear as follows:

| | | |
|---|---:|---:|
| Cash ...................................... | $ 11,300 | |
| Due from General Fund .................... | 30,000 | |
| Due from Enterprise Fund ................. | 12,800 | |
| Inventory of Materials and Supplies ........... | 3,000 | |
| Land ..................................... | 10,000 | |
| Buildings ................................ | 40,000 | |
| Allowance for Depreciation—Buildings ........ | | $ 2,400 |
| Machinery and Equipment .................. | 50,000 | |
| Allowance for Depreciation—Machinery and | | |
| Equipment ............................ | | 9,200 |
| Vouchers Payable ......................... | | 7,500 |
| Accrued Salaries and Wages Payable .......... | | 1,000 |
| Contributed Capital from General Fund........ | | 135,000 |
| Billings to Departments ..................... | | 42,800 |
| Cost of Materials and Supplies Used .......... | 7,000 | |
| Mechanics' Wages ........................ | 9,500 | |
| Indirect Labor ........................... | 3,150 | |
| Superintendent's Salary .................... | 3,675 | |
| Depreciation—Buildings ................... | 2,400 | |
| Depreciation—Machinery and Equipment ...... | 9,200 | |
| Heat, Light, and Power .................... | 2,000 | |
| Office Salaries ........................... | 3,675 | |
| Office Expenses .......................... | 200 | |
| | $197,900 | $197,900 |

Closing entries may be made in a variety of methods. Some accountants prefer to make one compound entry closing all revenue and expense accounts directly to Retained Earnings. Others prefer a multiple-step approach through which (1) the various direct cost accounts are summarized in a single Direct Cost account, (2) the Direct Cost account and all other accounts are closed to a Cost of Services Rendered account, (3) the Cost of Services Rendered and Billings to Departments (and other revenue) accounts are closed to an Excess of Billings to Departments over Costs (or vice versa) account, and (4) the latter account is closed to Retained Earnings. Any reasonable closing entry or combination of entries will suffice that (1) updates the Retained Earnings account to its period end balance and (2) brings the temporary proprietary accounts to a zero balance so that they are ready for use during the succeeding period. The following two-step approach is patterned after that illustrated by the NCGA:

| | | | |
|---|---|---|---|
| 11. | Billings to Departments | 42,800 | |
| | Cost of Materials and Supplies Used ... | | 7,000 |
| | Mechanics' Wages | | 9,500 |
| | Indirect Labor | | 3,150 |
| | Superintendent's Salary | | 3,675 |
| | Depreciation—Buildings | | 2,400 |
| | Depreciation—Machinery and Equipment | | 9,200 |
| | Heat, Light, and Power | | 2,000 |
| | Office Salaries | | 3,675 |
| | Office Expenses | | 200 |
| | Excess of Net Billings to Departments Over Costs | | 2,000 |
| | To close revenue and expense accounts and determine the excess of net charges over costs of services for the period. | | |
| | | | |
| 12. | Excess of Net Billings to Departments Over Costs | 2,000 | |
| | Retained Earnings | | 2,000 |
| | To close net income for the period to Retained Earnings. | | |

In Figures 13-2, 13-3, and 13-4 are presented the Balance Sheet, Analysis of Change in Retained Earnings, and Operating Statement, respectively, for the Central Automotive Equipment Fund based on the foregoing transactions. These statements may be derived readily from the "Proprietary Accounts" portion of the worksheet in Figure 13-5. As indicated before, the fixed assets of the Fund appear on the balance sheet with their related allowances for depreciation.

Since departments are billed for overhead charges, including depreciation, part of the money received from departments represents depreciation charges. The money representing depreciation charges may be debited to a restricted cash account or set up in a separate fund to insure its availability to replace assets; or it may be made part of the Fund's general cash and used for various purposes, pending the replacement of the assets. In the present case, it is assumed that no segregation is made, nor is a retained earnings reserve established.

Figure 13-2

A GOVERNMENTAL UNIT
Central Automotive Equipment (IGS) Fund
Balance Sheet at Close of Fiscal Year (Date)

*Assets*

Current Assets:

| | | |
|---|---:|---:|
| Cash | $11,300 | |
| Due from General Fund | 30,000 | |
| Due from Enterprise Fund | 12,800 | |
| Inventory of materials and supplies | 3,000 | $ 57,100 |

Fixed Assets:

| | | | |
|---|---:|---:|---:|
| Land | | $10,000 | |
| Buildings | $40,000 | | |
| Less: Allowance for depreciation ... | 2,400 | 37,600 | |
| Machinery and equipment | $50,000 | | |
| Less: Allowance for depreciation ... | 9,200 | 40,800 | 88,400 |
| Total assets | | | $145,500 |

*Liabilities, Contributed Capital, and Retained Earnings*

Liabilities:

| | | |
|---|---:|---:|
| Vouchers payable | $ 7,500 | |
| Accrued salaries and wages payable | 1,000 | $ 8,500 |
| Contributed capital from General Fund | | 135,000 |
| Retained earnings (Figure 13-3) | | 2,000 |
| Total liabilities, contributed capital, and retained earnings | | $145,500 |

Long-term debt incurred for IGS Fund purposes is not shown in the Fund balance sheet unless the resources of the Fund are to be used to retire the debt. Usually the debt will be paid out of general taxation or other sources, such as enterprise earnings in the case of IGS Funds furnishing services to a utility department. However, if an IGS Fund is dissolved, some of its assets may be used to retire outstanding debt.

The operating statement of an Intragovernmental Service Fund is similar to an industrial or commercial income and expense (net income) statement. This similarity is evident from the statement in Figure 13-4, which is based on the entries previously illustrated.

The above procedure applies to those cases where a central equipment bureau owns the equipment. However, the procedure would not be materially

**Figure 13-3**

A GOVERNMENTAL UNIT

Central Automotive Equipment (IGS) Fund

Analysis of Charges in Retained Earnings for (Period)

| | | |
|---|---|---|
| Balance, beginning of period.................. | $ | — |
| Add: Excess of net billings to | | |
| departments over costs (Figure 13-4) ......... | | 2,000.00 |
| Balance, end of period ...................... | | $2,000.00 |

**Figure 13-4**

A GOVERNMENTAL UNIT

Central Automotive Equipment (IGS) Fund

Statement of Operations for (Period)

| | | | |
|---|---|---|---|
| Billings to departments ...................... | | | $42,800 |
| Less: Costs of materials and supplies used ..... | | $ 7,000 | |
| Other operating costs: | | | |
| Mechanics' Wages.................. | $9,500 | | |
| Indirect labor .................... | 3,150 | | |
| Superintendent's salary ............. | 3,675 | | |
| Depreciation—building ............. | 2,400 | | |
| Depreciation— | | | |
| machinery and equipment ......... | 9,200 | | |
| Heat, light and power .............. | 2,000 | | |
| Office salaries..................... | 3,675 | | |
| Office expenses ................... | 200 | | |
| Total other operating costs ...... | | 33,800 | |
| Total cost of services rendered ......... | | | 40,800 |
| Excess of billings to departments over costs .... | | | $ 2,000 |

different if the equipment was owned by the individual departments or was classified in the General Fixed Assets category. In fact, the only difference is that billings to departments probably would be reduced by the amount of the depreciation charges. Depreciation should be computed in such an event; but the computation usually would be made primarily for statistical purposes, to determine the total cost (including depreciation) of operating each piece of equipment, and for determining total activity cost. Depreciation expense would not be formally recorded as part of the expenses of operating the central equipment bureau, nor would depreciation charges be included in the operating statement. No allowance for depreciation need be provided in such situations, but a record should be kept for each fixed asset indicating the cumulative amount of depreciation, based on the depreciation charges calculated for statistical purposes.

## A Central Stores Fund

Another example of accounting for Intragovernmental Service Fund transactions is to be found in a Central Stores Fund. Such a fund is established for the purpose of purchasing and storing materials for eventual distribution to departments; and, as in this example, departmental billings are usually based on direct inventory cost plus an overhead factor. To simplify the discussion, it is again assumed that appropriations are not required for the Fund's expenditures.

The first step in the accounting process occurs here when an invoice for supplies of inventory items is approved for payment. At that time, an entry is made to record the purchase and to set up the liability. The entry is as follows:

| | | |
|---|---|---|
| Inventory of Materials and Supplies .............. | 20,000 | |
| Vouchers Payable ......................... | | 20,000 |
| To record the purchase of materials and supplies. | | |

Note that the debit is not made to a Purchases account but directly to an Inventory of Materials and Supplies account. The reason is that perpetual inventory records should be kept where a central storeroom is in operation.

Materials or supplies purchased for central storerooms are not charged against departmental appropriations until the materials or supplies are withdrawn from the storeroom. One procedure in withdrawing materials and charging appropriations is as follows: When a department needs materials, a stores requisition is prepared. This requisition is made out in duplicate (at least) and is presented to the storekeeper. The storekeeper issues the items called for on the requisition and has the employee receiving them sign one copy of the requisition. This copy is retained by the storekeeper as evidence that the materials have been withdrawn; it is also the basis for posting the individual stock record cards to reduce the amount shown to be on hand. Subsequently, individual items on the requisition are priced and the total cost of materials withdrawn on the particular requisition is computed. Sometimes requisitions are priced before they are filled, in order to see that the cost of materials requisitioned does not exceed a department's unencumbered appropriation, but this procedure is not always practicable.

In the perpetual inventory record, the unit cost should include the purchase price plus transportation expenses. If the IGS Fund capital is to be kept intact, it is necessary also to recover overhead costs, such as the salary of the purchasing agent, wages of storekeepers, and amounts expended for heat, light, and power.

| | Balance Sheet (Beginning of Period) | | Transactions and Adjustments | |
|---|---|---|---|---|
| | Dr. | Cr. | Dr. | Cr. |
| **Proprietary Accounts** | | | | |
| Cash ...................... | 75,000 | | | (3) 19,000 |
| | | | | (4) 2,000 |
| | | | | (7) 42,500 |
| | | | | (8) 200 |
| Land ....................... | 10,000 | | | |
| Buildings ................... | 40,000 | | | |
| Machinery and Equipment ..... | 10,000 | | (1) 40,000 | |
| Contributed Capital from | | | | |
| General Fund.............. | | 135,000 | | |
| | 135,000 | 135,000 | | |
| Vouchers Payable ............ | | | (7) 42,500 | (1) 40,000 |
| | | | | (2) 10,000 |
| Inventory of Materials and | | | | |
| Supplies .................. | | | (2) 10,000 | (9) 7,000 |
| Mechanics' Wages ........... | | | (3) 9,000 | |
| | | | (10) 500 | |
| Indirect Labor .............. | | | (3) 3,000 | |
| | | | (10) 150 | |
| Superintendent's Salary ........ | | | (3) 3,500 | |
| | | | (10) 175 | |
| Office Salaries ............... | | | (3) 3,500 | |
| | | | (10) 175 | |
| Heat, Light and Power......... | | | (4) 2,000 | |
| Depreciation—Building ....... | | | (5) 2,400 | |
| Depreciation—Machinery and | | | | |
| Equipment ................. | | | (5) 9,200 | |
| Accumulated Depreciation— | | | | |
| Building .................. | | | | (5) 2,400 |
| Accumulated Depreciation— | | | | |
| Machinery and Equipment ... | | | | (5) 9,200 |
| Due from General Fund ....... | | | (6) 30,000 | |
| Due from Enterprise Fund ..... | | | (6) 12,800 | |

Figure 13-5

| Pre-closing Trial Balance (End of Period) | | Closing Entries (End of Period) | | Balance Sheet (End of Period) | |
|---|---|---|---|---|---|
| Dr. | Cr. | Dr. | Cr. | Dr. | Cr. |
| 11,300 | | | | 11,300 | |
| 10,000 | | | | 10,000 | |
| 40,000 | | | | 40,000 | |
| 50,000 | | | | 50,000 | |
| | 135,000 | | | | 135,000 |
| | 7,500 | | | | 7,500 |
| 3,000 | | | | 3,000 | |
| 9,500 | | | (11) 9,500 | | |
| 3,150 | | | (11) 3,150 | | |
| 3,675 | | | (11) 3,675 | | |
| 3,675 | | | (11) 3,675 | | |
| 2,000 | | | (11) 2,000 | | |
| 2,400 | | | (11) 2,400 | | |
| 9,200 | | | (11) 9,200 | | |
| | 2,400 | | | | 2,400 |
| | 9,200 | | | | 9,200 |
| 30,000 | | | | 30,000 | |
| 12,800 | | | | 12,800 | |

|  | Balance Sheet (Beginning of Period) | | Transactions and Adjustments | |
|---|---|---|---|---|
|  | Dr. | Cr. | Dr. | Cr. |
| Billings to Departments ....... |  |  |  | (6) 42,800 |
| Office Expenses .............. |  |  | (8) 200 |  |
| Cost of Materials and Supplies Used .................... |  |  | (9) 7,000 |  |
| Accrued Salaries and Wages Payable .................. |  |  |  | (10) 1,000 |
| Excess of Net Billings to Departments Over Costs (Summary) ............... |  |  |  |  |
| Retained Earnings............ |  |  |  |  |
|  |  |  | 176,100 | 176,100 |
| **Budgetary Accounts*** |  |  |  |  |
| Budget Requirements ......... |  |  | (A) 80,000 | (1b) 40,000 |
|  |  |  |  | (2b) 10,000 |
|  |  |  |  | (3) 19,000 |
|  |  |  |  | (4) 2,000 |
|  |  |  |  | (8) 200 |
|  |  |  |  | (10) 1,000 |
| Appropriations .............. |  |  |  | (A) 80,000 |
| Encumbrances ............... |  |  | (B) 40,500 | (1a) 40,500 |
|  |  |  | (C) 9,700 | (2a) 9,700 |
|  |  |  | (D) 5,000 |  |
| Reserve for Encumbrances ..... |  |  | (1a) 40,500 | (B) 40,500 |
|  |  |  | (2a) 9,700 | (C) 9,700 |
|  |  |  |  | (D) 5,000 |
| Expenditures ............... |  |  | (1b) 40,000 |  |
|  |  |  | (2b) 10,000 |  |
|  |  |  | (3) 19,000 |  |
|  |  |  | (4) 2,000 |  |
|  |  |  | (8) 200 |  |
|  |  |  | (10) 1,000 |  |
|  |  |  | 257,600 | 257,600 |

* Used only where it is desirable or necessary to control Appropriations, Expenditures, and Encumbrances within the IGS Fund account structure.

**Figure 13-5 (cont.)**

| Pre-closing Trial Balance (End of Period) | | Closing Entries (End of Period) | | Balance Sheet (End of Period) | |
|---|---|---|---|---|---|
| Dr. | Cr. | Dr. | Cr. | Dr. | Cr. |
| | 42,800 | (11) 42,800 | | | |
| 200 | | | (11) 200 | | |
| 7,000 | | | (11) 7,000 | | |
| | 1,000 | | | | 1,000 |
| | | (12) 2,000 | (11) 2,000 | | |
| | | | (12) 2,000 | | 2,000 |
| 197,900 | 197,900 | 44,800 | 44,800 | 157,100 | 157,100 |
| 7,800 | | | (13) 2,800 | 5,000 | |
| | 80,000 | (13) 80,000 | | | |
| 5,000 | | | (13) 5,000 | | |
| | 5,000 | | | | 5,000 |
| 72,200 | | | (13) 72,200 | | |
| 85,000 | 85,000 | 80,000 | 80,000 | 5,000 | 5,000 |

As noted earlier, these expenses usually are allocated to each requisition based on a predetermined percentage of the cost of the materials withdrawn. The percentage is determined by dividing the estimated total stores expenses by the total estimated cost of materials to be issued. Assuming that total stores expenses for the forthcoming year are estimated to be $20,000 and that the cost of the materials to be withdrawn during the period is estimated at $500,000, the overhead rate applicable to materials issued is 4 percent ($20,000 ÷ $500,000). The amount of overhead to be charged upon the issue of materials that cost the Stores Fund $2,585 is $103.40 (4 percent of $2,585).

As soon as the requisition is priced, information is available for the purpose of billing the department withdrawing the materials. The entry to record the issue and billing is as follows:

| | | |
|---|---|---|
| Due from General Fund .................... | 2,688.40 | |
|     Inventory of Materials and Supplies ....... | | 2,585.00 |
|     Overhead Applied (or Overhead) ......... | | 103.40 |
|     To record issuance of materials and supplies to | | |
|     Department of Public Works on Requisition 1405. | | |

Note that the General Fund is billed for both the cost of the materials and a portion of the estimated overhead expenses ($2,585.00 + $103.40). Alternatively, the gross Billings to Departments might be recorded and a Cost of Materials and Supplies Issued account used to record the direct cost of stores issued. The entry in this case would be:

| | | |
|---|---|---|
| Due from General Fund .................... | 2,688.40 | |
| Cost of Materials and Supplies Issued ........ | 2,585.00 | |
|     Billings to Departments.................. | | 2,688.40 |
|     Inventory of Materials and Supplies........ | | 2,585.00 |
|     To record the billing and cost of materials issued | | |
|     to Department of Public Works on Requisition | | |
|     1405. | | |

Entries to record actual overhead expenses in the IGS Fund are made at the time the expenses are incurred, not at the time materials are issued. For example, at the time that storekeepers' salaries are approved for payment the following entry is made:

| | | |
|---|---|---|
| Overhead (or Operating Expenses) ............... | 1,000 | |
|     Vouchers Payable ........................ | | 1,000 |
|     To record storekeepers' salaries. Subsidiary ledger: | | |
|     *Debit* Salaries and Wages, $1,000. | | |

At the end of the year, if overhead rates have been correctly estimated, the exact amount of overhead will have been recovered. Otherwise, the IGS Fund will have either underabsorbed or overabsorbed overhead.

Under the system of accounting for materials described here, the inventory of materials and supplies on hand can be ascertained from the records at any time. To insure that the materials and supplies shown by the records are actually on hand, a physical inventory should be taken at least annually. Usually the actual amount on hand will be smaller than the amount shown by the records. The variation may be due to such factors as shrinkage, breakage, theft, or improper recording. In any event, the records must be adjusted to correspond with the actual physical count by making entries on each perpetual inventory card affected. The Inventory of Materials and Supplies account in the general ledger must also be adjusted, of course. If the amounts according to physical count are less than the amounts shown on the records, the entry is as follows:

| | | |
|---|---|---|
| Overhead (or Operating Expenses) | 2,000 | |
| Inventory of Materials and Supplies | | 2,000 |
| To record inventory losses as revealed by actual physical count. Subsidiary ledger: *Debit* Inventory Losses, $2,000. | | |

Inventory losses must be recovered if the capital of the IGS Fund is to be kept intact and should be taken into account in estimating the overhead expenses of the central storeroom for the purpose of establishing the overhead rate to be applied to requisitions.

Closing entries for the Stores Fund would parallel those illustrated earlier for the Central Automotive Equipment Fund. Similarly, a Balance Sheet, Analysis of Changes in Retained Earnings, and Operating Statement like those illustrated in Figures 13-2, 13-3, and 13-4 should be prepared at least annually.

Thus far we have discussed the entries to be made in the IGS Fund. Corresponding entries are, of course, made for the departments receiving the particular materials. In the case of a public works department, whose activities are financed from the General Fund, the entry is as follows:

| | | |
|---|---|---|
| Expenditures | 2,688.40 | |
| Due to IGS Fund | | 2,688.40 |
| To record receipt of materials by the Department of Public Works and its liability to IGS Fund. Subsidiary ledger: *Debit* Department of Public Works, $2,688.40. | | |

Materials withdrawn by departments from a central storeroom and on hand in the departments at the close of the year should be treated the same as those acquired directly from vendors. Sometimes a storeroom system for a single department is financed through an IGS Fund. Materials and supplies are accounted for in that case in the same manner as those handled through a central storeroom established for all departments.

### Disposition of Under- or Over-Applied Overhead

In the usual case, under- or over-applied overhead is closed at year-end and thus affects both income determination for the period and the ending balance of the Retained Earnings account. Alternatively, it may be the basis for supplemental billings or refunds or credits to the user departments; or, if it is caused by cyclical or similar factors the under- or over-applied overhead may be carried forward to the succeeding period on the assumption that overhead incurred and applied will equal over a span of two or more years.

### Disposition of Retained Earnings

The necessity of basing charges to departments on estimates means that in the usual case an IGS Fund, even one that is intended to break even, has a profit or loss at the end of a year. The profit or loss may be disposed of in one of the following ways:

1. It may be charged or credited to the billed departments in accordance with their usage. If the intent is for the fund to break even, this procedure is theoretically the correct one.
2. The amount may be closed to Retained Earnings with the intent of adjusting the following year's billings to eliminate the balance. This procedure is a practical substitute for the first.
3. The amount may be closed to and left in Retained Earnings, or even transferred to Fund Capital—without subsequent adjustment of billing rates—on the theory that the Fund is to be increased or decreased in size. Transfers to Fund Capital should not be permitted without proper legislative or administrative authorization and supervision.
4. As indicated earlier, an amount of money equal to the profit may be transferred to the General Fund; occasionally this is required by law.

In the absence of specific instructions, the profit or loss should be closed to Retained Earnings. No refunds, supplemental billings or transfers should be made in the absence of specific authorization or instructions in this regard.

### Dissolution of an IGS Fund

When the services provided by an Intragovernmental Service Fund are no longer needed, or when some more preferable method of providing them is found, the Fund is dissolved. The net current assets of a dissolved fund are usually transferred to the funds from which the capital was originally secured. However, as stated before, if capital was secured by incurring general obligation long-term debt, the net current assets are not transferred to the Capital Projects Fund but to the Debt Service Fund that will retire the debt.

Fixed assets are usually transferred to departments financed from the funds that contributed the capital or to the departments that can best use them. Unless they are transferred to one of the governmental unit's enterprises, the assets are recorded in the General Fixed Assets accounts of the government. If transferred to an enterprise, they are set up as part of the Enterprise Fund.

### Accounting for Budgetary Operations

Thus far we have assumed that no appropriations were made by the legislative body of the governmental unit for IGS Funds. The accounting procedure outlined is also applicable in its entirety to IGS Funds subject to appropriations and budgetary control, but these require additional accounting. In this section, we point out the modifications in accounting procedure necessary to record appropriations, expenditures, and encumbrances.

We have selected for illustration purposes *one* way in which budgetary requirements may be accounted for satisfactorily within the usual IGS Fund accounting framework. There are other equally satisfactory approaches, such as through adaptation of the Federal government accounting approach to state and local government IGS Fund accounting.

The approach illustrated is a dual expense/expenditure accounting system, a combination of the accounting equations for expendable and nonexpendable funds. It is shown graphically in Figure 13-6. Note that the left two-thirds of Figure 13-6 contains the usual commercial accounting equation, summarized here for ease of illustration; the right one-third contains the self-balancing budgetary account structure.

ACCOUNTING FOR APPROPRIATIONS.    If an activity financed from an IGS Fund is to be operated as a self-supporting entity, appropriation accounts and the expenditures and encumbrances chargeable to them must be kept separate and distinct from the proprietary accounts, for many of the transactions affecting appropriations do not affect the profit or loss of the Fund and vice versa. For example, expenditures for fixed assets are capitalized and do not affect profits or losses, but they are charges against appropriations. On the other hand, depreciation expenses reduce profits, but usually no appropriation is made for them as they do not affect net appropriable assets.

It should also be evident from the discussion above that there is not necessarily any relationship between the estimated revenues of an IGS Fund and the appropriations made for it. Thus, as we have seen, appropriations are frequently made for some expenditures that are not chargeable against revenues (for example, the acquisition of fixed assets), and no appropriations are made for some expenses chargeable to revenues (for example, depreciation expenses). Accordingly, appropriations are not offset by estimated revenues but by an account indicating budgetary requirements. For example, if we assume the figures illustrated, the entry setting up appropriations for an IGS Fund is as follows:

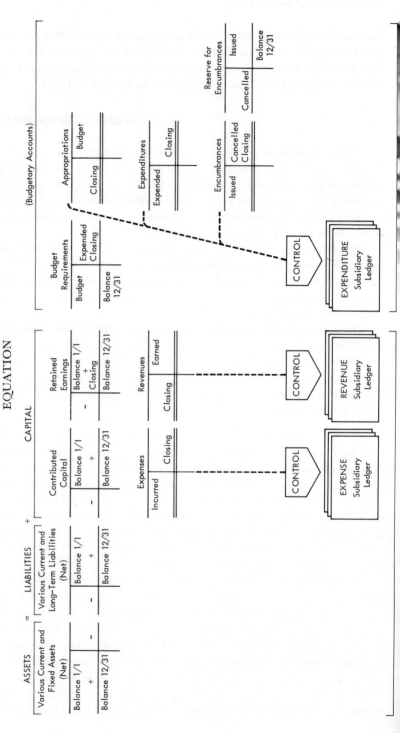

Figure 13-6

BUDGETARY ACCOUNTING WITHIN THE
INTRAGOVERNMENTAL SERVICE FUND ACCOUNTING
EQUATION

| A. | Budget Requirements | 80,000 | |
| | Appropriations | | 80,000 |
| | To record appropriations. | | |

As will be observed momentarily, the Budget Requirements account is essentially a "plug" utilized in order to fit the budgetary accounts neatly within the IGS Fund accounting equation. Since revenue estimates are not ordinarily subject to legal limitation or control, they need not be formally recorded. A memorandum account showing such estimates should be kept, however.

CHARGING EXPENDITURES AND ENCUMBRANCES TO APPROPRIATIONS. The following transactions and entries illustrate how appropriations are recorded and controlled. These transactions are similar to those given on pp. 537–39. It is thus possible to note readily what *additional* entries are necessary to record and to control appropriations. (To conserve space, the proprietary entries are *not* repeated here.) The transactions below are numbered to correspond with those of the Central Automotive Equipment Fund presented earlier in this Chapter. The letters A (above), B, C and D identify budgetary transactions that have no proprietary accounting effect; transactions 5, 6, 7 and 9 in the example do not appear here because they have no budgetary accounting effect. Both phases of this example are summarized in the two-part worksheet presented as Figure 13-5.

*Transactions*

B. Equipment estimated to cost $40,500 was ordered.
1. The equipment was received; the actual cost was $40,000.
C. Materials and supplies estimated to cost $9,700 were ordered.
2. The materials and supplies were received; the actual cost was $10,000.
3. Salaries and wages paid, $19,000.
4. Heat, light, and power paid, $2,000.
8. Office expenses paid, $200.
D. A purchase order was placed for materials estimated to cost $5,000.
10. Accrued salaries and wages, $1,000.

*Entries*

| B. | Encumbrances | 40,500 | |
| | Reserve for Encumbrances | | 40,500 |
| | To record placing order for equipment. | | |
| 1. | (a) Reserve for Encumbrances | 40,500 | |
| | Encumbrances | | 40,500 |
| | To reverse entries setting up encumbrances. | | |
| | (b) Expenditures | 40,000 | |
| | Budget Requirements | | 40,000 |
| | To record reduction of budget requirements and appropriations on account of equipment purchased. | | |

| C. | Encumbrances | 9,700 | |
| | Reserve for Encumbrances | | 9,700 |
| | To record order placed for materials and supplies. | | |

| 2. | (a) | Reserve for Encumbrances | 9,700 | |
| | | Encumbrances | | 9,700 |
| | | To reverse entry setting up encumbrances. | | |
| | (b) | Expenditures | 10,000 | |
| | | Budget Requirements | | 10,000 |
| | | To record reduction of budget requirements and appropriations on account of purchase of materials and supplies. | | |

| 3. | Expenditures | 19,000 | |
| | Budget Requirements | | 19,000 |
| | To record reduction of budget requirements and appropriations on account of salaries and wages paid. | | |

| 4. | Expenditures | 2,000 | |
| | Budget Requirements | | 2,000 |
| | To record reduction of budget requirements and appropriations on account of heat, light, and power expenses paid. | | |

5–7. (No budgetary effect)

| 8. | Expenditures | 200 | |
| | Budget Requirements | | 200 |
| | To record reduction of budget requirements and appropriations by amount of office expenses paid. | | |

9. (No budgetary effect)

| D. | Encumbrances | 5,000 | |
| | Reserve for Encumbrances | | 5,000 |
| | To record purchase order placed for materials and supplies. | | |

| 10. | Expenditures | 1,000 | |
| | Budget Requirements | | 1,000 |
| | To record reduction of budget requirements and appropriations by amount of accrued salaries and wages. | | |

The foregoing entries are based on the assumption that appropriations are charged as soon as expenditures are incurred, regardless of when they are paid, but that no adjustments are made for expenditures applicable to more than one year. For example, it is assumed that no adjustment is made in the budgetary accounts for materials purchased during the year that remain on hand at the close of the year (purchases basis). It is assumed also that depreciation is not charged to appropriations. These assumptions are in accordance with conditions existing in many governmental units.

TRIAL BALANCE BEFORE CLOSING ENTRIES. Assuming the foregoing entries had been posted (see Figure 13-5), the trial balance of the *budgetary account group* would be as follows:

| | | |
|---|---:|---:|
| Budget Requirements | 7,800 | |
| Expenditures | 72,200 | |
| Encumbrances | 5,000 | |
| Reserve for Encumbrances | | 5,000 |
| Appropriations | | 80,000 |
| | 85,000 | 85,000 |

CLOSING ENTRIES FOR THE BUDGETARY GROUP. The closing entries are made for the purpose of determining to what extent expenditures exceed or are under appropriations and to close out the budgetary accounts. However, if encumbered appropriations do not lapse and encumbrances are outstanding at the close of the fiscal year, a balance sufficient to cover these encumbrances must be retained in the Budget Requirements account. The closing entries here are as follows:

| | | | |
|---|---|---:|---:|
| 13. | Appropriations | 80,000 | |
| | Expenditures | | 72,200 |
| | Encumbrances | | 5,000 |
| | Budget Requirements | | 2,800 |
| | To close out appropriations, expenditures, and encumbrances. | | |

BALANCE SHEET—BUDGETARY ACCOUNTS. A post-closing trial balance or a balance sheet of the budgetary group of accounts after closing entries are posted (see Figure 13-5) contains only accounts to show budget requirements for encumbrances outstanding at the close of the fiscal year. If we assume the closing entries illustrated, the statement would appear as shown in Figure 13-7.

When the actual amount of the expenditure is determined during the following year, an entry is made debiting the Reserve for Encumbrances account and crediting the Budget Requirements account by the amount of the encumbrances (in this case, $5,000).

**Figure 13-7**

A GOVERNMENTAL UNIT
Intragovernmental Service Fund
Balance Sheet—Budgetary Group
at Close of Fiscal Year

| | |
|---|---:|
| Budget requirements | $5,000 |
| Reserve for encumbrances | $5,000 |

## IGS FUND STATEMENTS

The National Committee on Governmental Accounting recommends that a Balance Sheet (Figure 13-2), an Analysis of Changes in Retained Earnings (Figure 13-3), and a Statement of Operations (Figure 13-4) be prepared for Intragovernmental Service Funds. Statements of several IGS Funds may be presented in combined form, with separate columns for each Fund. Preparation of Combined Operating Statements of IGS Funds financing dissimilar activities is often not feasible, however, and may result in a complex and confusing presentation.

A Statement of Changes in Financial Position, usually on a cash or working capital basis, should also be prepared for IGS Funds. A Statement of Changes in Financial Position prepared on a cash basis ("cash flow" statement) is presented in Figure 13-8. The worksheet from which it was derived is shown in

**Figure 13-8**

A GOVERNMENTAL UNIT
Central Automotive Equipment (IGS) Fund
Statement of Changes in (Cash) Financial Position
For the Year Ended (Date)

| | | | |
|---|---|---|---|
| Cash, beginning of period (Figure 13-1) ...... | | | $75,000 |
| Cash was applied to: | | | |
| Operations— | | | |
| Excess of billings to departments over costs (Figure 13-4) ................... | | $ 2,000 | |
| Adjustments to derive cash applied— | | | |
| Add: Depreciation expense......... | $11,600 | | |
| Increase in vouchers payable (operations) .............. | 2,500 | | |
| Increase in accrued salaries and wages payable......... | 1,000 | | |
| | $15,100 | | |
| Less: Increase in billings receivable . | $42,800 | | |
| Increase in inventories ....... | 3,000 | | |
| | $45,800 | | |
| Net adjustments—deduct.............. | | 30,700 | |
| Cash applied to operations .............. | | | $28,700 |
| Other applications— | | | |
| Purchase of equipment................. | | | 35,000 |
| Total cash applied (decrease in cash) ....... | | | $63,700 |
| Cash, end of period (Figure 13-2) ........... | | | $11,300 |

Figure 13-9. A Statement of Changes in Financial Position prepared on a working capital basis ("funds flow" statement) is presented in Figure 13-10. It is accompanied by a Schedule of Changes in Net Working Capital (Figure 13-11) and a supporting worksheet (Figure 13-12).

Several acceptable alternative approaches to the preparation and presentation of the Statement of Changes in Financial Position are in popular usage. The main point to observe is that (1) whereas in expendable fund accounting the primary focus of accountability is upon changes in financial position ("funds flow" or "cash flow," in essence), and revenue and expense data comparable to that of business accounting must be derived analytically if it is desired, (2) in

**Figure 13-9**

## A GOVERNMENTAL UNIT
### Central Automotive Equipment (IGS) Fund
Worksheet for Statement of Changes in Financial Position (Cash Basis)
For the Year Ended (Date)

| Debits | Trial Balance (At Beginning of Period) | Changes Dr. | Changes Cr. | After-closing Trial Balance (At End of Period) |
|---|---|---|---|---|
| Cash | 75,000 | | (g) 63,700 | 11,300 |
| Due from General Fund | — | (b) 30,000 | | 30,000 |
| Due from Enterprise Fund | — | (b) 12,800 | | 12,800 |
| Inventory of Materials and Supplies | — | (c) 3,000 | | 3,000 |
| Land | 10,000 | | | 10,000 |
| Buildings | 40,000 | | | 40,000 |
| Machinery and Equipment | 10,000 | (b) 40,000 | | 50,000 |
| | 135,000 | | | 157,100 |

| Credits | | | | |
|---|---|---|---|---|
| Allowance for Depreciation—Building | — | | (d) 2,400 | 2,400 |
| Allowance for Depreciation— Machinery and Equipment | — | | (d) 9,200 | 9,200 |
| Vouchers Payable | — | | (c) 2,500 (f) 5,000 | 7,500 |
| Accrued Salaries and Wages Payable | — | | (e) 1,000 | 1,000 |
| Contributed Capital from General Fund | 135,000 | | | 135,000 |
| Retained Earnings | — | | (a) 2,000 | 2,000 |
| | 135,000 | | | 157,100 |

**Figure 13-9 (cont.)**

|                                                              | *Provided*  | *Applied* |
|--------------------------------------------------------------|-------------|-----------|
| Cash was applied to:                                         |             |           |
| Operations—                                                  |             |           |
| Excess of net billings to departments over costs .......................... | (a) 2,000 | |
| Adjustments to derive cash effect:                           |             |           |
| Increase in billings receivable ............               |             | (b) 42,800 |
| Increase in inventories .................                   |             | (c) 3,000 |
| Increase in vouchers payable (inventories) .               | (c) 2,500   |           |
| Depreciation expense ..................                     | (d) 11,600  |           |
| Increase in accrued salaries and wages payable ........................... | (e) 1,000 | |
|                                                              | 17,100      | 45,800    |
| Net cash applied to operations .............               |             | 28,700    |
| Other Applications—                                          |             |           |
| Purchase of equipment ...................                   |             | (f) 35,000 |
| Decrease in cash ...........................                | (g) 63,700  | 63,700    |

(a) The excess of net billings to departments over costs (net income) is a convenient starting point in logically deriving the net cash provided or required by operations (cash effect). The derivation—a reconciliation of cash flow from operations and net income—is accomplished through entries (b)-(e).

(b) Cash inflow from billings was less than total billings shown in the Statement of Operations because some billings have not yet been collected.

(c) Although Costs of Materials and Supplies Used, $7,000, was deducted on the Statement of Operations, the inventory on hand has increased by $3,000. However, only $500 more cash was required than has been deducted in the Statement of Operations, since $2,500 of Vouchers Payable is owed at year-end on inventory purchases.

(d) Depreciation expense is a proper expense deduction but did not require cash this period, so it is added back in deriving current period cash flow from operations. (Acquisitions take cash; see item (f) below.)

(e) The accrued salaries and wages payable have not yet taken cash, but have been properly included in expense. Thus this amount is added back in the derivation of the net current period cash effect of operations.

(f) Although $40,000 of equipment was acquired, $5,000 remains owed on it and the net "use" or "application" of cash therefore was only $35,000.

(g) The net change in cash is the connecting link and numerical accuracy proof figure tying together the two parts of this worksheet.

nonexpendable fund accounting, the primary accountability and accounting focus is upon revenue and expense measurement similar to that of business enterprise accounting, and data on changes in financial position ("funds flow" or "cash flow") must usually be derived analytically. Note also that the alternative measurements commonly employed in governmental accounting—changes in financial position, as defined (revenues and expenditures), and net income

Figure 13-10

A GOVERNMENTAL UNIT
Central Automotive Equipment (IGS) Fund
Statement of Changes in (Working Capital) Financial Position
For the Year Ended (Date)

| | | |
|---|---|---:|
| Net working capital, beginning of period (Figure 13-11) ... | | $75,000 |
| Working capital provided by: | | |
| Operations— | | |
| Excess of billings to departments over costs | | |
| (Figure 13-4) .............................. | $ 2,000 | |
| Adjustment to derive working capital provided— | | |
| Add: Depreciation expense.................... | 11,600 | |
| | $13,600 | |
| Working capital applied to: | | |
| Purchase of equipment........................... | 40,000 | |
| Decrease in working capital during the period........... | | 26,400 |
| Net working capital, end of period (Figure 13-11) ....... | | $48,600 |

Figure 13-11

A GOVERNMENTAL UNIT
Central Automotive Equipment (IGS) Fund
Schedule of Changes in Net Working Capital
For the Year Ended (Date)

| | Working Capital | | |
|---|---|---|---|
| | Beginning of | End of | |
| Current Assets | Period | Period | Change |
| Cash ................................. | $75,000 | $11,300 | $(63,700) |
| Due from General Fund .............. | — | 30,000 | 30,000 |
| Due from Enterprise Fund ............ | — | 12,800 | 12,800 |
| Inventory ........................... | — | 3,000 | 3,000 |
| | $75,000 | $57,100 | $(17,900) |
| Current Liabilities | | | |
| Vouchers payable .................... | $ — | $ 7,500 | $ 7,500 |
| Accrued salaries and wages payable. ..... | — | 1,000 | 1,000 |
| | — | $ 8,500 | $ 8,500 |
| Working capital .................... | $75,000 | $48,600 | $ 26,400 |

Figure 13-12

A GOVERNMENTAL UNIT
Central Automotive Equipment (IGS) Fund
Worksheet for Statement of Changes in Financial Position
(Working Capital Basis) For the Year Ended (Date)

| Debits | Beginning of Period | Changes Dr. | Changes Cr. | End of Period |
|---|---|---|---|---|
| Net Working Capital .................. | 75,000 | | (4) 26,400 | 48,600 |
| Land ............................. | 10,000 | | | 10,000 |
| Buildings ......................... | 40,000 | | | 40,000 |
| Machinery and Equipment ........... | 10,000 | (3) 40,000 | | 50,000 |
| | 135,000 | | | 148,600 |

| Credits | | | | |
|---|---|---|---|---|
| Allowance for Depreciation—Building .. | — | | (2) 2,400 | 2,400 |
| Allowance for Depreciation— Machinery and Equipment ......... | — | | (2) 9,200 | 9,200 |
| Contributed Capital from General Fund. | 135,000 | | | 135,000 |
| Retained Earnings ................... | — | | (1) 2,000 | 2,000 |
| | 135,000 | | | 148,600 |

| | Provided | Applied |
|---|---|---|
| Working capital provided by: | | |
| Operations— | | |
| Excess of net billings to departments over costs ........................... | (1) 2,000 | |
| Adjustments to derive working capital effect: | | |
| Add: Depreciation expense ............. | (2) 11,600 | |
| Net working capital provided by operations... | 13,600 | |
| Working capital applied to: | | |
| Purchase of equipment .................... | | (3) 40,000 |
| Decrease in net working capital ............... | (4) 26,400 | |
| | 40,000 | 40,000 |

(revenues and expenses)—are readily reconcilable. The one selected for measurement in the accounts (the primary accounting focus) is that which is considered the more useful and relevant on a day-to-day basis in achieving or demonstrating the type of accountability customarily sought.

The Statement of Changes in Financial Position is discussed briefly and illustrated again in the next chapter (Chapter 14). One interested in a more thorough discussion of its preparation and presentation will find the topic covered adequately in most contemporary intermediate accounting textbooks. The Statement of Changes in Financial Position is also the topic of Opinions 3 and 19 of the Accounting Principles Board.

**Question 13-1.** Why are Intragovernmental Service Funds often referred to as "revolving" or "working capital" funds?

**Question 13-2.** Intragovernmental Service Funds are *nonexpendable* funds. How does this cause IGS Fund accounting to differ from that for *expendable* funds?

**Question 13-3.** The bookkeeper of a municipality asks your advice with respect to whether Due from IGS Fund, Advance to IGS Fund, or an Expenditure account should be debited upon General Fund resources being transferred to establish an Intragovernmental Service Fund. What do you recommend?

**Question 13-4.** Resources were transferred from the General Fund to establish an Intragovernmental Service Fund, an Advance to IGS account being debited in the former. What additional General Fund entry(ies) might be required at or before year end?

**Question 13-5.** In what manner should IGS Fund temporary proprietorship accounts be closed at period end?

**Question 13-6.** Why are terms such as "Billings to Departments" and "Excess of Net Billings to Departments Over Costs" generally used in Intragovernmental Service Fund accounting and reporting rather than more familiar terms such as "Sales" and "Net Income"?

**Question 13-7.** Why is an IGS Fund not normally subjected to fixed budgetary control?

**Question 13-8.** Accounting for an Intragovernmental Service Fund that is controlled by a fixed budget is often called "double accounting." Why?

**Question 13-9.** In what ways might the original capital required to establish an Intragovernmental Service Fund be acquired?

**Question 13-10.** What advantages might accrue to a governmental unit establishing an Intragovernmental Service Fund to account for the acquisition, storage, and provision of supplies for the various departments?

**Question 13-11.** What major benefits should accrue from accurate cost data being maintained for activities accounted for through an Intragovernmental Service Fund?

**Question 13-12.** In what type situation would the *direct* cost of the goods or services provided (with no provision for items such as depreciation or overhead) be the appropriate basis for IGS Fund reimbursement? Explain.

**Question 13-13.** Why are predetermined price schedules or overhead rates commonly employed in Intragovernmental Service Fund billings to user departments?

**Question 13-14.** An Intragovernmental Service Fund established by a county is intended to operate on a break-even basis. How might profits or losses and/or a Retained Earnings balance remaining at year end be disposed of?

**Question 13-15.** A City operates a motor pool as an Intragovernmental Service Fund. List and evaluate the ways that over- or underabsorbed overhead may be treated.

**Question 13-16.** Why might all of the fixed assets owned by a government and used in conducting activities financed through an Intragovernmental Service Fund not be accounted for therein? Give examples and indicate where such assets would be accounted for.

**Question 13-17.** Under what circumstances would it be improper for an Intragovernmental Service Fund to include depreciation in charges to other funds for services rendered or materials supplied?

**Question 13-18.** An Intragovernmental Service Fund was established through the sale of bonds. What disposition should be made of the assets of the Fund if it is dissolved?

**Question 13-19.** Referring to Question 13-18, suppose that the bonds are being retired from a Debt Service Fund. Should the charges to departments for services include depreciation on buildings and equipment financed from these bonds, assuming (a) these departments are all financed from the General Fund and (b) these departments are all financed from funds other than the General Fund?

**Question 13-20.** In a certain state a question has arisen as to whether the maintenance of one of the state office buildings should be financed by a single appropriation for maintenance or whether maintenance expenses should be financed through an Intergovernmental Service Fund. If an Intergovernmental Service Fund were established, the departments would be charged rent based on the amount of space occupied and an appropriation would be made to each department for this purpose. Which of these two methods would you recommend? Why?

**Question 13-21.** The mayor wants to increase the size of an Intragovernmental Service Fund by setting a higher-than-cost rate of reimbursement. What response would you make to his suggestion?

**Question 13-22.** How should overtime premiums incurred in the conduct of IGS Fund activities be charged to user departments where IGS Fund charges are based on direct costs plus overhead? (AICPA, adapted)

**Question 13-23.** How does the Budget Requirements account sometimes used in Intragovernmental Service Fund accounting differ from the Estimated Revenues account of the General or a Special Revenue Fund, the Required Contributions or Required Earnings account(s) of a Debt Service Fund, and the Required Contributions or Required Earnings account(s) of a Pension Trust Fund?

**Problem 13-1.** The following is a trial balance prepared for the Central Stores Department Fund of a state agency at December 31, 19X6.

| | | |
|---|---:|---:|
| Sales to Departments .............................. | | $150,000 |
| Sales Returns and Allowances ..................... | $   2,000 | |
| Purchases ....................................... | 100,600 | |
| Freight In ...................................... | 1,000 | |
| Wages ........................................... | 25,000 | |
| Office Salaries ................................. | 6,000 | |
| Office Expenses ................................. | 1,000 | |
| Miscellaneous General Expenses.................... | 2,000 | |
| Land ............................................ | 40,000 | |
| Buildings ....................................... | 90,000 | |
| Allowance for Depreciation—Buildings ............. | | 12,000 |
| Equipment ....................................... | 65,000 | |
| Allowance for Depreciation—Equipment ............ | | 10,000 |

| | | |
|---|---:|---:|
| Cash .......................................... | 15,000 | |
| Due from General Fund ....................... | 48,000 | |
| Notes Receivable ............................. | 2,000 | |
| Inventory .................................... | 70,000 | |
| Prepaid Insurance ............................ | 700 | |
| Accounts Payable ............................. | | 13,300 |
| Bonds Payable ................................ | | 95,000 |
| Contributed Capital .......................... | | 165,000 |
| Retained Earnings ............................ | | 23,000 |
| | $468,300 | $468,300 |

Adjustments:

Insurance expired, $400.

Accrued wages, $1,000; accrued salaries, $300.

Accrued interest payable, $3,000.

Closing inventory, $80,000.

Depreciation:

Buildings, 4 percent.

Equipment, 8 percent.

Required:

Prepare a Balance Sheet (including an analysis of change in the Retained Earnings account therein) at December 31, 19X6 and a Statement of Operations for the Central Stores Department Fund for the period ended December 31, 19X6.

**Problem 13-2.** The following is a trial balance of an Intragovernmental Service Fund of the City of Bevton at July 1, 19X0:

| | | |
|---|---:|---:|
| Cash .......................................... | $ 50,000 | |
| Land ......................................... | 55,000 | |
| Buildings .................................... | 32,000 | |
| Allowance for Depreciation—Buildings ............. | | $ 8,000 |
| Machinery .................................... | 26,000 | |
| Allowance for Depreciation—Machinery ........... | | 5,000 |
| Equipment ................................... | 36,000 | |
| Allowance for Depreciation—Equipment ........... | | 9,200 |
| Due from General Fund ....................... | 77,600 | |
| Inventory of Materials ........................ | 25,000 | |
| Vouchers Payable ............................. | | 55,000 |
| Capital Contributed from General Fund ........... | | 200,000 |
| Retained Earnings ............................ | | 31,400 |
| Work in Process Inventory ..................... | 7,000 | |
| | $308,600 | $308,600 |

The following transactions took place during the year:

1. Materials were received, together with an invoice in the amount of $63,000.
2. Payrolls were approved and paid as follows:

| Direct labor | $12,000 |
|---|---|
| Indirect labor | 3,000 |
| Plant office | 6,000 |

3. Electric bills of $4,000 were paid.

4. The city treasurer transferred cash from the General Fund to the Intragovernmental Service Fund for the amount due to the IGS Fund for past services.

5. Vouchers payable as of July 1, 19X0, were paid in full.

6. Telephone and telegraph charges of $500 were paid.

7. Plant office supplies were purchased on account for $200.

8. The General Fund was billed $95,000 for materials manufactured for and used by departments financed through the General Fund.

9. Materials used by the Intragovernmental Service Fund activity, during this period, all direct, $60,000.

10. Insurance premiums paid amounted to $500, of which $400 is applicable to succeeding years.

11. A small secondhand machine was purchased for $700 cash.

12. Repair bills incurred and paid during this period amounted to $1,200.

13. Depreciation charges:

| Buildings | $1,600 |
|---|---|
| Machinery | 2,600 |
| Equipment | 3,600 |

14. Work in process on June 30, 19X1, amounted to $7,000.

Required:

Prepare a Balance Sheet for the Intragovernmental Service Fund as of June 30, 19X1, and a detailed Statement of Operations for the fiscal year ended June 30, 19X1. The change in the Retained Earnings account should be reflected in the Balance Sheet. Support the statements by a worksheet, "T" account analysis, or computation schedules; and cross-reference the statements appropriately.

**Problem 13-3.** The City of Morristown operates a printing shop through an Intragovernmental Service Fund to provide printing services for all departments. The Central Printing Fund was established by a contribution of $30,000 from the General Fund on January 1, 19X5, at which time the equipment was purchased. The after-closing trial balance on June 30, 19X8, was as follows:

|  | Debits | Credits |
|---|---|---|
| Cash | $35,000 | |
| Due from General Fund | 2,000 | |
| Accounts Receivable | 1,500 | |
| Supplies Inventory | 3,000 | |
| Equipment | 25,000 | |
| Accumulated Depreciation—Equipment | | $ 8,750 |
| Accounts Payable | | 4,750 |
| Advance from General Fund | | 20,000 |
| Retained Earnings | | 33,000 |
|  | $66,500 | $66,500 |

The following transactions occurred during fiscal year 19X9:
1. The Publicity Bureau, financed by the General Fund, ordered 30,000 multicolor travel brochures printed at a cost of $1.20 each. The brochures were delivered.
2. Supplies were purchased on account for $13,000.
3. Employee salaries were $30,000. One-sixth of this amount was withheld for taxes and is to be paid to the City's Tax Fund; the employees were paid.
4. Taxes withheld were remitted to the Tax Fund.
5. Utility charges for the year billed by the Enterprise Fund, $2,200.
6. Supplies used, $10,050.
7. Other billings during the period were: Special Assessment Fund, $300; Special Revenue Fund, $4,750.
8. Inventory of supplies at year end, $5,900.
9. Unpaid receivable balances at June 30, 19X9, were: General Fund, $3,000; Special Revenue Fund, $750.
10. Printing Press #3 was repaired by the central repair shop, operated from the Maintenance Fund. A statement for $75 was received, but has not been paid.
11. The Accounts Receivable at June 30, 19X8, were paid in full.
12. Accounts Payable as of June 30, 19X9, $2,800.
13. Depreciation expense was recorded.

Required:
(a) Journalize all transactions and adjustments required in the Central Printing Fund accounts.
(b) Prepare closing entries for the Central Printing Fund accounts at June 30, 19X9.
(c) Prepare an after-closing trial balance of the Central Printing Fund accounts as of June 30, 19X9.

**Problem 13-4.** From the information in Problem 13-3, prepare a columnar work-sheet to reflect the beginning balances, transactions and adjustments, closing entries (results of operations), and ending balances of the Central Printing Fund of the City of Morristown for the year ended June 30, 19X9.

**Problem 13-5.** The following transactions took place during the fiscal year beginning July 1, 19X0, and relate to an Intragovernmental Service Fund of the City of Marcille.
1. Budget requirements for the year were estimated at $70,000 and an appropriation was made for this amount.
2. Materials were ordered as follows:

| | |
|---|---:|
| Sand .................... | $ 6,200 |
| Filler .................. | 7,200 |
| Asphalt ................. | 16,400 |
| Crushed rock ............ | 8,200 |

3. Telephone and telegraph charges of $300 were paid.
4. Plant office supplies were purchased for $100 cash.
5. The materials ordered were received, together with an invoice. The actual cost of the materials ordered was as follows:

| | |
|---|---:|
| Sand .................... | $ 6,000 |
| Filler .................. | 7,200 |
| Asphalt ................. | 16,500 |
| Crushed rock ............ | 8,000 |

6. Payrolls were approved as follows:

| | |
|---|---|
| Direct labor .............. | $ 6,000 |
| Indirect labor ............ | 2,000 |
| Plant office.............. | 3,000 |

7. Electric bills for $2,000 were paid.
8. An order was placed for a small machine estimated to cost $280.
9. The equipment (machine) was received, together with an invoice for $300.
10. Repair bills paid this period amounted to $700.
11. Additional materials order amounted to $15,000.

Required:

(a) Prepare journal entries, including closing entries, for the budgetary transactions (only). You need not include subsidiary entries.

(b) Post to general ledger (control) "T" accounts.

(c) Prepare a Balance Sheet for the budgetary group of accounts as of June 30, 19X1.

**Problem 13-6.** The following transactions and events occurred in Beatty County during its fiscal year ended September 30, 19X3:

1. An Intragovernmental Service Fund was established on October 1, 19X2, to account for the acquisition and issuance of materials and supplies. In addition to a General Fund contribution of $40,000, the following items on hand were transferred at cost to comprise IGS Fund capital:

| Department | Cost |
|---|---|
| Assessor ................. | $ 3,300 |
| Health ................ | 1,400 |
| Highway* .............. | 48,600 |
| Administrative............ | 1,700 |
| Sheriff.................. | 800 |
| | $55,800 |

* Financed through the Gasoline Tax Fund; the remaining departments are financed from the General Fund.

2. Storage bins and other furniture and equipment needed for the central storeroom were purchased on October 3, 19X2, for $6,000 and vouchered for payment. The storeroom is located in a small building adjacent to the courthouse. The small building was constructed several years ago at a cost of $18,000, and its useful life remaining at October 1, 19X2, was estimated at 10 years; the bins and other furniture and equipment should last 15 years. It is expected that within 10-15 years the central storeroom will be moved to the basement of the courthouse and the building in which it is presently housed will be demolished to provide additional parking space.

3. The general budget for Beatty County for the 19X3 fiscal year was adopted on October 15, 19X2. Departmental appropriations for materials and supplies included therein were as follows:

| Department | Cost |
|---|---|
| Assessor ................ | $ 5,000 |
| Health ................ | 2,000 |
| Highway ................ | 250,000 |
| Administrative........... | 3,000 |
| Sheriff.................. | 1,500 |
| | $261,500 |

The General Fund cash contribution to the IGS Fund was included within the General Fund appropriations, but the inventories transferred were charged to the Fund Balance account(s) of funds from which they were contributed. The inventories transferred had been recorded properly and were fully reserved for in the accounts prior to their transfer to the IGS Fund. No additional appropriation was made for the IGS Fund, but the estimated departmental expenditures for materials and supplies from the IGS Fund were shown as estimated revenues of that Fund in the budget, offset by estimated IGS Fund expenditures.

4. Materials and supplies were issued during the first six months' operations of the central storeroom as follows:

| Department | Inventory Cost to IGS Fund | Billing to Department |
|---|---|---|
| Assessor ............. | $ 1,800 | $ 1,908 |
| Health ............. | 400 | 424 |
| Highway ............ | 80,000 | 84,800 |
| Administration ...... | 1,300 | 1,378 |
| Sheriff.............. | 300 | 318 |
| | $83,800 | $88,828 |

5. Materials and supplies estimated to cost $190,000 were ordered by central storeroom personnel during the year.

6. Costs of operating the storeroom during the year were vouchered as follows:

| | |
|---|---|
| Salaries and wages ........ | $ 9,000 |
| Insurance .............. | 550 |
| Heat, light and power ..... | 700 |
| Janitorial ............... | 300 |
| Miscellaneous .......... | 450 |
| | $11,000 |

7. Materials and supplies received and vouchered for payment during the year cost $187,000; goods on order at year end, included in item 5 above, were expected to cost $10,000.

8. Materials and supplies were issued from the central storeroom during the last six months of the 19X3 fiscal year as follows:

| Department | Inventory Cost to IGS Fund | Billing to Department |
|---|---|---|
| Assessor ............. | $ 2,900 | $ 3,074 |
| Health ............. | 1,700 | 1,802 |
| Highway ........... | 109,050 | 115,593 |
| Administration ...... | 1,450 | 1,537 |
| Sheriff.............. | 1,100 | 1,166 |
| | $116,200 | $123,172 |

9. At year end, $3,000 remained payable from the General Fund to the IGS Fund.

10. Vouchers payable from the IGS Fund at year end totaled $11,400.

11. Adjustment data:
   a. Salaries and wages accrued at year end, $150;
   b. It was determined that $300 of the insurance premiums paid during 19X3 were applicable to subsequent years;
   c. Inventory at hand (cost) per physical inventory taken at September 30, 19X3, $42,700.

Required:

(a) Prepare a worksheet to reflect the transactions and adjustments, pre-closing trial balance, closing entries, and ending balances of the Intragovernmental Service Fund of Beatty County for the year ended September 30, 19X3. Use detailed revenue and expense accounts such as those illustrated in the Central Automotive Equipment Fund example in this chapter (see Figure 13-4) and incorporate such budgetary accounts as you deem necessary in the circumstances. Assume that a perpetual inventory system is in use, and that any excess of billings over cost (or vice versa) is to be retained in the IGS Fund rather than being disposed of through supplemental billings or credit memorandums.

(b) Prepare the adjusting entry that would be made at year end in the IGS Fund if any excess of costs over billings (or vice versa) must be reflected in supplemental billings or credit memorandums prior to closing the accounts. (Round to nearest one-half percent and to the nearest whole dollar.)

**Problem 13-7.** From the information contained within Problem 13-6:

a. Prepare a worksheet to reflect the transactions and adjustments, pre-closing trial balance, closing entries, and ending balances of Beatty County's Intragovernmental Service Fund for the year ended September 30, 19X3, under the assumption that Overhead and Overhead Applied control accounts similar to those illustrated in the Central Stores Fund example in this chapter are employed.

b. Prepare the adjusting entry that would be made at year end in the IGS Fund if any excess of billings over costs (or vice versa) must be disposed of by supplemental billings or credit memorandums prior to the accounts being closed. (Round to the nearest one-half percent and to the nearest whole dollar.)

**Problem 13-8.** The following is a trial balance of an Intragovernmental Service Fund (established to finance the operations of a central garage) of the City of Zeffler at January 1, 19X5:

| | | |
|---|---:|---:|
| Land | $ 35,000 | |
| Buildings | 70,000 | |
| Allowance for Depreciation—Buildings | | $ 10,000 |
| Equipment | 180,000 | |
| Allowance for Depreciation—Equipment | | 60,000 |
| Cash | 45,000 | |
| Inventory: | | |
| Gasoline | 4,000 | |
| Oil and Grease | 2,000 | |
| Tires | 6,500 | |
| Parts | 13,500 | |
| Due from General Fund | 20,000 | |
| Vouchers Payable | | 75,000 |
| Contributed Capital | | 228,000 |
| Retained Earnings | | 3,000 |
| | $376,000 | $376,000 |

1. Wages and salaries (all chargeable to 19X5) were as follows:

| | |
|---|---:|
| Salary of superintendent | $10,000 |
| Mechanics' wages | 39,000 |
| Garage office salaries | 6,500 |

2. Purchases (on account) were as follows:

| | |
|---|---:|
| Gasoline | $20,000 |
| Oil and grease | 2,000 |
| Tires | 16,000 |
| Parts | 30,000 |

3. Departments are charged at a predetermined rate based on mileage. During the year 19X5, billings to departments amounted to $140,000, all of which was payable from the General Fund. At December 31, 19X4, $25,000 was owed the Intragovernmental Service Fund from the General Fund.

4. Other expenses were as follows:

Heat, light and power, $10,000, which is due to the Enterprise Fund.

Depreciation:

Buildings, 5 percent of original cost.

Equipment, 10 percent of original cost.

5. Vouchers payable paid amounted to $35,000.

6. Closing inventories were as follows:

| | |
|---|---|
| Gasoline ......................... | $ 7,000 |
| Oil and grease ................... | 1,500 |
| Tires .......................... | 11,500 |
| Parts .......................... | 15,000 |

7. Accrued salaries and wages were as follows:

| | |
|---|---|
| Salary of superintendent ........... | $   250 |
| Mechanics' wages ............... | 830 |
| Garage office salaries ............. | 180 |

Required:

(a)  Prepare a worksheet reflecting the beginning balances, transactions and adjustments, operations, and ending balances of the Intragovernmental Service Fund of the City of Zeffler for 19X5.

(b)  Prepare a Balance Sheet as of December 31, 19X5, and a combined Statement of Operations and Changes in Retained Earnings for the year ended December 31, 19X5, for the IGS Fund.

**Problem 13-9.** Cole County maintains an Intragovernmental Service Fund for financial control of a garage operated to serve several departments. It is the county's policy to maintain the Fund accounts so that the departments served will be charged their several shares of the operating cost for a fiscal year. Current billings are made to the departments for services based on charges for actual materials and supplies and actual direct labor plus estimated overhead. Differences between total overhead actually incurred and the estimated amounts billed to departments are adjusted through supplemental billing at the end of each fiscal year. Adjustments to physical inventories are handled through overhead.

1.  Garage overhead for the fiscal year ended December 31, 19X9, was comprised of the physical inventory adjustments referred to and the following expenses: superintendence, $8,000; office salaries, $4,300; office supplies, $200; garage depreciation, $2,000; heat and light, $620; miscellaneous, $80.

2.  Accounts payable at December 31, 19X9, amounted to $1,100. All payrolls had been paid.

3.  The garage originally cost $50,000, financed by a capital advance from the General Fund; at January 1, 19X9, the accumulated depreciation thereagainst was $4,000. On that date, records of the Fund showed cash, $11,000; inventories of gas, oil and grease, $1,050; inventories of repair and maintenance materials, $2,250; a balance of $900 on account of services previously rendered the General Fund; accounts payable of $700; capital advances from the General Fund of $50,000; and a cumulative "surplus" account.

4.  Physical inventories at December 31, 19X9, were as follows:

| | |
|---|---|
| Gas, oil, and grease ............... | $  890 |
| Repair and maintenance materials ... | 2,000 |

5. Summaries of certain transactions for the fiscal year ended December 31, 19X9, appear in journal entry form as follows:

(a)  Due from General Fund ................. $11,300
     Due from Highway Fund ................ 8,305
     Due from Police Fund .................. 9,960
     Due from Fire Fund .................... 5,585
     Billings for Services Rendered to
       Departments .................... $35,150
     To record charges to departments for services billed, as follows:

|  |  |  | | Repairs and Maintenance | |
|  |  |  | Actual Cost | | Estimated |
| | | Gas, Oil, | | | Overhead |
| | | Grease | | Direct | (135% of |
| Department | Total | (at cost) | Materials | Labor | Direct Labor) |
|---|---|---|---|---|---|
| General .... | $11,300 | $ 3,950 | $1,240 | $2,600 | $ 3,510 |
| Highway ... | 8,305 | 2,460 | 910 | 2,100 | 2,835 |
| Police ...... | 9,960 | 2,280 | 1,100 | 2,800 | 3,780 |
| Fire ....... | 5,585 | 1,540 | 520 | 1,500 | 2,025 |
|  | $35,150 | $10,230 | $3,770 | $9,000 | $12,150 |

(b)  Cash ................................. $29,900
     Due from General Fund ............ $10,400
     Due from Highway Fund ........... 7,000
     Due from Police Fund .............. 8,000
     Due from Fire Fund ............... 4,500
     To record cash received for services billed.

(c)  Purchases—Gas, oil, and grease .......... $10,100
     Purchases—Repair and maintenance
       materials .......................... 3,589
     Accounts Payable ................... $13,680
     To record purchases for the period.

Required:

Prepare a worksheet to reflect the beginning balances, transactions and adjustments, operations, and ending balances of the Intragovernmental Service Fund of Cole County for 19X9. The worksheet columnar headings should appear as follows:

| | | Transactions & Adjustments During | | Results of Operations, | | Balance Sheet | |
| Trial Balance January 1, 19X9 | | the Fiscal Year Ended December 31, 19X9 | | Fiscal Year Ended December 31, 19X9 | | December 31, 19X9 | |
|---|---|---|---|---|---|---|---|
| Debits | Credits | Debits | Credits | Debits | Credits | Debits | Credits |

(AICPA, adapted)

**Problem 13-10.** The following account balances are taken from the books of the City of *M* on June 30, 19X9, the close of the fiscal year.
Required:
(a) Segregate the data into the applicable fund or account-group trial balances, supplying the needed account titles.
(b) Prepare closing entries.

| | |
|---|---:|
| Accounts payable—general | $ 6,000 |
| Appropriations—general | 106,000 |
| Bonds payable—general—term | 300,000 |
| Bonds payable—special assessment—District No. 1 | 25,000 |
| Bonds payable—premium—special assessment—District No. 1 | 1,000 |
| Building—garage | 20,000 |
| Building—garage—accumulated depreciation | 5,000 |
| Buildings—other | 300,000 |
| Capital outlays for construction—bridge | 70,000 |
| Capital outlays for construction—special assessment—District No. 1 | 26,000 |
| Cash | 47,600 |
| Contracts payable—bridge | 5,000 |
| Depreciation—garage | 2,500 |
| Encumbrances—bridge | 25,000 |
| Encumbrances—general | 7,000 |
| Equipment—garage | 50,000 |
| Equipment—accumulated depreciation | 10,000 |
| Equipment—other | 75,000 |
| Estimated revenues | 100,000 |
| Expenditures—general | 104,000 |
| Garage—original appropriation | 60,000 |
| Inventory of materials and supplies—garage | 1,500 |
| Inventory of materials and supplies—general | 4,000 |
| Labor—garage | 5,000 |
| Land—garage | 4,000 |
| Land—Other | 20,000 |
| Materials and supplies used—garage | 2,000 |
| Overhead—garage | 2,500 |
| Public improvements | 1,250,000 |
| Reserve for authorized expenditures—bridge* | 100,000 |
| Reserve for authorized expenditures—special assessments** | 25,000 |
| Reserve for encumbrances—bridge | 25,000 |
| Reserve for encumbrances—general | 7,000 |
| Revenues—garage | 12,500 |
| Revenues—general | 102,000 |
| Revenues—interest on special assessments—District No. 1 | 1,000 |

| | |
|---|---:|
| Special assessments receivable—District No. 1, deferred .......... | 18,000 |
| Special assessments receivable—District No. 1, delinquent......... | 400 |
| Fund balance ............................................... | 1,419,000 |
| Taxes receivable—delinquent .............................. | 75,000 |

   * Synonymous with "Appropriations-bridge" described in Chapter 8.
  ** Synonymous with "Appropriations-special assessments" described in Chapter 9.

### Explanatory data:

1. The city has deposited all cash in a single bank account. The fund segregation will require a separate account for each fund. The cash is attributable as follows: garage, $2,000; bridge, $35,000; construction of pavement, $2,000; special assessment bond payments, $1,600; interest on special assessment bonds, $2,000; balance, general city.
2. $3,000 of the special assessment construction expenditures were paid from general city (General Fund) cash.
3. The city's share of special assessment construction, unpaid, is $5,000.
4. The municipal garage has supplied services in the amount of $1,000 for the General Fund for which no settlement has been made.
5. The municipal garage was built and equipped out of general taxes. The "surplus" earned by the garage to July 1, 19X8, is $3,000.

(AICPA, adapted)

**Problem 13-11.** From the following information, prepare a worksheet for the City of Previtson for the year ended June 30, 19X8, showing opening balances, entries in the various accounts to reflect transactions for the year, closing entries and fund balance sheets at the end of the year.
The balance sheet of the City of Previtson at July 1, 19X7, is submitted as follows:

### CITY OF PREVITSON
Combined Balance Sheet—All Funds: July 1, 19X7
General Fund

#### Assets

| | |
|---|---:|
| Cash ............................................... | $50,000 |
| Taxes receivable—delinquent ........................ | 25,000 |
| Long-term advance to Revolving Fund.................. | 15,000 |
| | $90,000 |

#### Liabilities

| | |
|---|---:|
| Accounts payable .................................... | $30,000 |
| Due to Revolving Fund .............................. | 5,500 |
| Reserve for encumbrances ........................... | 4,500 |
| Reserve for advance to Revolving Fund ............... | 15,000 |
| Fund balance ....................................... | 35,000 |
| | $90,000 |

## Transportation Revolving Fund

| | | | |
|---|---|---|---|
| Cash ................... | $ 9,500 | Long-term advance from | |
| Due from General Fund .. | 5,500 | General Fund.......... | $15,000 |
| | $15,000 | | $15,000 |

Transactions for fiscal year ended June 30, 19X8:

1. Estimated total General Fund revenues were $200,000, including $75,000 of miscellaneous revenues.
2. Appropriations made totaled $175,000.
3. The council levied property taxes of $125,000. Based on experience, the losses will be 5 percent.
4. Receipts from current tax revenues amounted to $85,000; receipts from miscellaneous sources were $80,000.
5. Delinquent taxes received, $23,500; the balance is considered uncollectible.
6. General Fund materials and supplies received and vouchered for payment amounted to $95,000, including $4,000 in complete fulfillment of all orders outstanding at July 1, 19X7; budgeted orders placed amounted to $100,000, and orders outstanding at the end of the year amounted to $4,000.
7. Salary and wage payments amounted to $72,000, as budgeted; vouchered bills paid were $90,000.
8. Collections on taxes written off in prior years were $1,650.
9. Taxes collected in advance were $1,000 (in addition to those collected earlier).
10. In order to finance the construction of certain local roadways, the council voted to set up a Special Assessment Fund and levied a special assessment of $75,000 on 1/1/19X8, collectible in equal proportions over a period of three years, with interest from date of assessment at the rate of 6 percent per year.
11. Pending collection of special assessments, 5 percent bonds in the amount of $25,000 were sold at a premium of $200 on January 1, 19X8. The premium is considered too small to be amortized over the life of the bonds.
12. Construction contracts were let in the amount of $50,000.
13. Contractors were paid $20,000, less 10 percent retained percentage.
14. Special assessments collected amounted to $23,000, representing $22,500 principal on current assessments due for the payment of bonds and $500 interest on deferred assessments to pay interest on outstanding bonds. Interest on special assessments is accounted for on the cash basis.
15. Outstanding bonds of $12,000 were paid, plus interest of $625; no interest payable was accrued at June 30, 19X8.
16. The Transportation Revolving Fund purchased trucks for $9,000, of which $5,000 remains unpaid on open account.
17. The Transportation Revolving Fund charged the General Fund for transportation services applicable to General Fund activities in the amount of $3,000, at cost, including depreciation on trucks of $1,200; other operating expenses, all paid, totaled $1,600.
18. The Transportation Revolving Fund was paid $6,000 from the General Fund; accounts payable outstanding in the Revolving Fund at June 30, 19X8 were $2,000.

(AICPA, adapted)

**Problem 13-12.** The Village of Z was incorporated January 1, 19X6. The following events occurred in that year:

1. The Council approved the following general budget:

| | |
|---|---:|
| Revenues .......................................... | $200,000 |
| Expenditures: | |
| Current purposes ................................ | $160,000 |
| Establishment of Stores Fund ...................... | 10,000 |
| Debt service requirements ........................ | 3,600 |
| Equipment ..................................... | 24,000 |
| | $197,600 |

2. The Council borrowed $40,000 from the Village State Bank on tax anticipation notes.

3. The General Fund contributed $10,000 to the Stores Fund (an Intragovernmental Service Fund) as a permanent investment in inventory.

4. The Council decided (prior to preparing the budget) that a Village Hall was needed, and an issue of sinking fund bonds ($80,000 par value) was approved by the voters on January 2, 19X6. The bonds are dated January 1, 19X6, bear interest at 4 percent, and mature in 20 years.

5. The Village decided to pave Main Street, and a special assessment project was authorized to pave the street at a cost of $40,000.

6. The Village Hall bonds were sold at 101 and accrued interest of $600.

7. The assessments were levied at the authorized total amount, less the Village's share of $3,000. All assessments were collected during the year, together with the Village's contribution, which was considered for "current purposes."

8. Contracts were made for the paving, $40,000, and for the Village Hall, $76,000. The paving contract was completed, but had not been inspected and approved, at December 31. The contractor was paid all but 5 percent of the contract amount; the balance was retained to insure compliance with the terms of the paving contract.

9. Property taxes were levied in the amount of $160,000; it was expected that 1 percent of this amount would prove uncollectible.

10. Cash collections during the year were as follows:

| | |
|---|---:|
| Property taxes ........................... | $154,000 |
| Miscellaneous revenues .................... | 36,000 |
| | $190,000 |

11. The following purchase orders were issued during the year:

| | |
|---|---:|
| Operating expenditures ...................... | $60,000 |
| Equipment ................................ | 30,000 |
| Stores (for the Stores Fund) .................. | 8,000 |
| | $98,000 |

12. The following schedule summarizes certain of the orders received and vouchers prepared during the year:

|  | Ordered | Vouchered |
|---|---|---|
| Operating expenditures .................... | $57,000 | $152,000 |
| Equipment ............................. | 20,000 | 19,600 |
| Debt service requirements ................. |  | 3,600 |
| Tax anticipation notes .................... |  | 20,000 |
| Stores (for the Stores Fund) ............... |  | 8,400 |
|  | $85,000 | $203,600 |

The vendor was paid the full amount due from the Stores Fund; General Fund vouchers totaling $180,000 were paid, including the debt service requirements budgeted.

13. A retiree was paid $1,000 from the Stores Fund to operate the warehouse. He issued materials that cost $7,200 to departments financed through the General Fund at a billed figure of $8,800. This bill was paid from the General Fund during the year.

14. The actuarial table prepared for the sinking fund aspect of the Debt Service Fund showed a $2,000 contribution and earnings of $25 required for 19X6. The only contribution made was the budgeted amount paid from the General Fund. The Debt Service Fund trustee bought securities for $1,800 during the year and received $80 of revenue therefrom. Interest on the bonds was paid from the Debt Service Fund.

15. The Village Hall was three-fourths completed at year end according to the supervising architect. A payment of $57,000 on the contract was approved and made. An additional $2,000 was paid to the General Fund to reimburse it for landscaping work done by employees of a department financed through the General Fund.

16. The operating expenditures (see item 12) included withholding and FICA taxes that were transferred to an Agency Fund on each payroll date. The amount of these taxes was $3,000. At December 31, the other governmental units had been paid $2,000 from the Agency Fund.

17. At the end of the year an inventory of supplies held by the several departments financed from the General Fund was found to be $7,500. The Council decided that the inventory should be recorded, but that the inventory could not legally affect Expenditures.

Required:

Prepare a worksheet designed to provide data for appropriate statements of all funds and account groups needed by the Village of Z. Include the closing entries necessary to produce correct year end balances.

# 14

# Enterprise Funds; Summary of Interfund Accounting

Enterprise Funds are established to account for the financing of self-supporting enterprises that render goods or services to the public at large on a consumer charge basis. These funds should be distinguished from Intragovernmental Service Funds, established to account for activities involved in rendering goods or services to other departments of the governmental unit, and from those departments (such as libraries and highway departments) that provide incidental services to the public for compensation. Among the many types of self-supporting activities of governments financed through Enterprise Funds are electric generation and/or distribution systems, water systems, natural gas distribution systems, sewer systems, public docks and wharves, hospitals, nursing homes, off-street parking lots and garages, toll highways and bridges, public housing, airports, garbage collection and disposal services, public transportation systems, liquor wholesaling and retailing operations, swimming pools, and golf courses.

The National Committee on Governmental Accounting suggests a "principal revenues" test for determining whether an activity should be accounted for through an Enterprise Fund. Specifically, it suggests that:

> ...if a substantial amount of the revenues used to finance an activity or series of related activities in a single fund is derived from user charges, the fund can be appropriately classified and accounted for as an Enterprise Fund.[1]

[1] *GAAFR*, p. 50.

577

Issuance of revenue bonds to finance an activity is also seen by the Committee as indicative of the self-supporting nature of an activity that should be accounted for through an Enterprise Fund. Application of these criteria in practice is important, since it is not uncommon to find enterprise activities improperly accounted for through the General Fund or in Special Revenue or Special Assessment Funds.

A discussion of Enterprise Fund accounting principles and procedures comprises the principal topic of this chapter. The chapter is concluded by a summary review of interfund (or multifund) accounting concepts that is designed to assist the reader in (1) reviewing the material covered thus far, (2) integrating his knowledge of appropriate accounting principles and procedures for the various types of funds and account groups commonly employed by state and local governments, and (3) gaining conceptual dexterity in the application of appropriate accounting principles and procedures in the multiple entity accounting environment of governments.

## ENTERPRISE FUND ACCOUNTING

Enterprise activities may be administered through a department of a general purpose government, a separate board or commission under the jurisdiction of the government, or an independent special district not under the general purpose government's jurisdiction. Regardless of organizational location or the type of activity involved, certain characteristics, principles, and procedures are common to all Enterprise Fund accounting.

### Characteristics of Enterprise Fund Accounting

For purposes of discussion, the major distinguishing characteristics of Enterprise Fund accounting may be categorized conveniently under the following headings: (1) accounting principles, (2) restricted asset accounts, and (3) budgeting and appropriations. Other features of certain enterprise situations (payments in lieu of taxes, Utility Acquisition Adjustment accounts, etc.) will be discussed later in the chapter.

ACCOUNTING PRINCIPLES. Enterprise Funds, like Intragovernmental Service Funds, are nonexpendable or self-sustaining funds. Thus it is essential that a distinction be maintained between capital contributions and revenues and that revenues and expenses be accounted for on an accrual basis so that periodic net income or loss can be determined. Fixed assets and long-term debt related to enterprise activities are accounted for in the Enterprise Fund, as are depreciation and amortization.

More specifically, the accounting principles or standards utilized should be those used in accounting for privately owned enterprises of similar types and sizes. Many municipally owned utilities are required by supervisory commissions to follow the same accounting as that prescribed for privately owned utilities of the same class. Likewise, pronouncements of the Accounting Principles Board of the American Institute of Certified Public Accountants and its predecessor and successor organizations are applicable to many governmental enterprises.

Transactions between the enterprise and other government departments should be accounted for in the same manner as "outsider" transactions. Therefore, goods or services provided by an Enterprise Fund to departments of the government financed from other funds should be billed at regular, predetermined rates; and all goods or services provided the enterprise by other governmental departments should be billed to it on the same basis that other users are charged. If this is not done, operating and position statements of all funds may be distorted.

Finally the National Committee on Governmental Accounting recommends that a separate fund be established for each governmental enterprise and that all transactions or events relating to a specific enterprise be recorded within the appropriate Enterprise Fund records. The major exception to this general rule occurs in the case of related activities, such as water and sewer utilities, which may be merged because of their complementary nature or because joint revenue bonds are used in financing such operations.

RESTRICTED ASSET ACCOUNTS. Enterprise activities may involve transactions or relationships which, if encountered in a general government situation, would require the use of several separate and distinct fund entities. Thus, utilities may require customers to post deposits (Trust), may acquire or construct major capital facilities (Capital Projects), or may have sinking fund or other debt-related resources (Debt Service). In some cases, certain enterprise-related intrafund "funds" are required to be established under terms of bond indentures or similar agreements.

In keeping with its recommendation that governmental enterprises follow appropriate commercial accounting principles, the NCGA recommends that the term "funds" be interpreted in this instance in the usual commercial accounting connotation of restricted assets. Thus, Enterprise Funds may contain several "funds within a fund," since the use of distinctively titled intrafund restricted asset accounts (offset by liability or equity reserve accounts) is deemed preferable to the use of a series of separate fund entities in Enterprise Fund accounting. Application of the "funds within a fund" approach is demonstrated in the illustrative example within this chapter.

BUDGETING AND APPROPRIATIONS. As in the case of Intragovernmental Service Funds, careful planning and realistic *flexible* budgeting should be considered prerequisites to sound Enterprise Fund management. It is not desirable, however, to control the expenditures of enterprises by means of rigid appropriations. Their levels of activities are controlled by the demands for their goods or services, and the demand affects both revenues and expenditures. An increase in expenditures above a planned level may be highly desirable if it is due to an increase in the number of customers or in the volume of goods or services provided to existing customers. (Presumably revenues would be correspondingly or appropriately increased in such cases.) If expenditures are controlled by inflexible (fixed dollar) appropriations, the necessary expansion of activities may be delayed. Thus the NCGA states that:

> In the interests of managerial flexibility and practicality...it is recommended that no formal system of budgetary accounting and control be employed for enterprise funds, but that, instead, the budgetary estimates upon which the legally adopted budget is based be retained in memorandum form and utilized in the preparation of comprehensive operating statements.[2]

Despite the undesirability of the practice and NCGA recommendations to the contrary, many governmental units continue to make appropriations for enterprises in the same manner as for other departments. It is necessary in such cases, as in Intragovernmental Service Funds in similar situations, to record not only those transactions that affect the actual operations of the enterprise (transactions that affect the revenues, expenses, assets, liabilities, reserves and equity) but also those that affect appropriations, expenditures, and encumbrances. Budgetary accounting procedures for self-supporting enterprises discussed at the end of Chapter 13 are equally applicable to Enterprise Funds. Thus, in order to simplify the following discussion we assume that appropriations are not made for the Enterprise Fund.

### Enterprise Fund Accounting Illustrated

Services of the type generally referred to as "public utilities" are among the most common enterprise activities undertaken by local governments. Such activities invariably involve significant amounts of assets, liabilities, revenues, and expenses and are seldom considered within contemporary undergraduate accounting courses. For these reasons, we have chosen an electric utility example to illustrate Enterprise Fund accounting procedures. The illustrative example is presented in several topical phases and is summarized in the worksheet presented in Figure 14-6. The numbers appearing in parentheses to the left of the journal entries both give continuity to the illustrative example and serve to cross-reference the journal entries and the worksheet (Figure 14-6).

ESTABLISHMENT OF FUND AND ACQUISITION OF PLANT.   The acquisition of a utility may be financed wholly or partially by the sale of bonds to be retired from utility earnings, by contributions or grants from a governmental unit, and by contributions from prospective customers. If we assume that the acquisition of a utility plant is financed through a contribution from the governmental unit,

2 *GAAFR*, p. 51.

the entry to record the receipt of the contribution and the establishment of the Fund is as follows:

(1)  Cash ................................. 400,000
     Contribution from Municipality .......             400,000
     To record governmental unit's contribution
     for acquisition of utility.

The next step is the acquisition of the plant. To simplify the discussion, let us assume further that a private electricity generation and distribution plant already in operation is acquired at book value. The entries to record the acquisition are as follows:

(2)  Land ................................. 50,000
     Buildings ............................. 100,000
     Improvements Other than Buildings ........ 550,000
     Machinery and Equipment .............. 150,000
     Accounts Receivable..................... 62,000
     Inventory of Materials and Supplies ........ 10,000
          Allowance for Depreciation—Buildings ..     10,000
          Allowance for Depreciation—
          Improvements Other than Buildings ..     70,000
          Allowance for Depreciation—Machinery
          and Equipment ..................     40,000
          Allowance for Uncollectible Accounts ...     12,000
          Bonds Payable .....................     500,000
          Vouchers Payable ..................     10,000
          ABC Electric Company ..............     280,000
     To record the acquisition of the assets and
     liabilities of the ABC Electric Company.

(3)  ABC Electric Company .................. 280,000
     Cash ...............................     280,000
     To record payment to ABC Electric
     Company.

Note that the accounts for both original cost and accumulated depreciation of assets were brought forward from the books of ABC Electric Company. This practice is in keeping with recommendations of the National Association of Railroad and Utilities Commissioners (NARUC) that assets be accounted for at "original cost" to the utility *first* placing them in public service. This is the prevailing practice in regulated utility accounting. Alternatively, it is also acceptable to record the assets at their net cost to the Enterprise Fund and not to establish depreciation allowance accounts initially.

The practice of recording assets and accumulated depreciation on the books of the purchaser at book value to the seller (defined in regulatory accounting as "original cost") rather than at fair market value is somewhat akin to the depreciation recapture provisions of the Internal Revenue Code in that both arose to curb abuses of depreciation accounting. In the absence of an "original cost" policy, for example, Utility A might (1) acquire new assets with an estimated useful life of 20 years; (2) depreciate them over a relatively short period, say 5 years, thus charging their full cost against revenues and—since a given level of earnings would be permitted by the regulatory body—to the consumer public; and (3) sell the fully depreciated (on the books) assets at fair market value to Utility B, which would charge its cost of the assets (fair market value) to depreciation expense and, ultimately, to the same consumer public. This sequence of events would constitute, in the view of many, a "double-charge" against the public. Thus, regulatory policies pertaining to fixed assets typically are based on the assumption that the public should be charged with depreciation of the original cost of specific assets only once; and many regulatory bodies require the rate of return permitted to be calculated on an "original cost" basis and/or allow only depreciation based on "original cost" to be deducted from revenues in determining net income for regulatory purposes. Such policies obviously are justified pragmatically rather than theoretically.

Had ABC Electric been purchased for $350,000, instead of at its $280,000 book value, the acquisition would have been recorded in the books of a *regulated* utility as follows:

| | | |
|---|---:|---:|
| Land | 50,000 | |
| Buildings | 100,000 | |
| Improvements Other than Buildings | 550,000 | |
| Machinery and Equipment | 150,000 | |
| Accounts Receivable | 62,000 | |
| Inventory of Materials and Supplies | 10,000 | |
| Utility Plant Acquisition Adjustments | 70,000 | |
| 　　Allowance for Depreciation—Buildings | | 10,000 |
| 　　Allowance for Depreciation—Improvements | | |
| 　　　　Other than Buildings | | 70,000 |
| 　　Allowance for Depreciation—Equipment | | |
| 　　　　and Machinery | | 12,000 |
| 　　Allowance for Uncollectible Accounts | | 40,000 |
| 　　Bonds Payable | | 500,000 |
| 　　Vouchers Payable | | 10,000 |
| 　　ABC Electric Company | | 350,000 |
| 　　To record acquisition of the assets and liabilities | | |
| 　　of the ABC Electric Company. | | |

The Utility Plant Acquisition Adjustments account is often improperly considered to represent goodwill. It does not represent a payment for anticipated excess earnings, however, as does purchased goodwill. The Acquisitions Adjustment account merely shows the difference between the book value of the assets on the seller's books and their fair market value at the date of sale; it is necessary only because of the "original cost" accounting policy of regulatory bodies. The

Acquisition Adjustments account is amortized in a rational and systematic manner over the lives of the assets that caused its establishment, that is, over the lives of those assets whose fair market value exceeded their book value at the date of the sale. For regulatory reporting purposes, the amortization is shown as a nonoperating expense; for general purpose reporting, depreciation of the specific assets with which it is identified is adjusted upwards to show properly the depreciation expense of the enterprise on a "purchase cost" basis.

It is important to re-emphasize the fact that the Utility Plant Acquisition Adjustments account is a product of usual regulatory policies. Although its use may be justified from a regulatory standpoint, it is contrary to accounting's cost concept and emphasis upon the firm.

Furthermore, recording assets purchased at the seller's book value is also contrary to generally accepted principles of accounting for business enterprise. Possibly hoping indirectly to discourage use of the Acquisitions Adjustment account, the NCGA does not mention it within *GAAFR*. Thus, unless its use is required by a regulatory body of appropriate jurisdiction, it should *not* be used and assets acquired should be recorded at their cost to the purchaser (or at fair market value if donated).

ACCOUNTING FOR ROUTINE OPERATING TRANSACTIONS. The following transactions and entries illustrate the operation of an Enterprise Fund for a utility. The accounting procedures for (1) the receipt and expenditure of bond proceeds, (2) utility debt service and related "funds," and (3) customers' deposits require use of intrafund restricted asset accounts and are discussed in a subsequent phase of the example. To simplify the discussion, all revenues, with the exception of interest revenues, are assumed to be credited to an Operating Revenues control account; and all expenses, with the exception of depreciation, taxes, and interest, are assumed to be charged to an Operating Expenses control account. Detailed operating revenue and expense accounts are illustrated in Figures 14-4 and 14-5.

*Transactions*

1. Total salaries and wages paid, $127,200.
2. Materials costing $59,000 were received.
3. Revenues billed during the year, $300,000.
4. Equipment costing $50,500 was purchased.
5. Telephone and telegraph bills paid, $500.
6. Rental due on equipment rented to the State Public Works Department, $7,000.
7. Fire insurance premiums paid, $1,000 (2-year policy).
8. Collection on accounts receivable, $290,000.
9. Bill received from Intragovernmental Service Fund for services rendered, $12,800.
10. Bonds paid, $50,000.

11. Interest paid, $20,000.
12. Interest received, $1,000.
13. Taxes paid, $10,500.
14. Vouchers payable in the amount of $70,000 were paid.
15. A subdivision electricity system, valued at $30,000, was donated to the utility by the subdivision developer.
16. Necessary adjusting entries were based on the following data:

|   |   |   |
|---|---|--:|
| a. | Accrued salaries and wages payable | $ 6,000 |
| b. | Accrued interest payable | 2,000 |
| c. | Accrued interest receivable | 200 |
| d. | Accrued taxes payable | 7,500 |
| e. | Prepaid insurance | 600 |
| f. | Ending inventory of materials and supplies | 30,000 |
| g. | Estimated losses on accounts receivable | 1,500 |
| h. | Depreciation: | |
|   | Buildings | 5,000 |
|   | Improvements other than buildings | 15,000 |
|   | Machinery and equipment | 16,000 |
| i. | Unbilled receivables | 21,000 |

*Entries*

(4)  1. Operating Expenses ................. 127,200
       Cash......................... 127,200
       To record payment of salaries and
       wages.

(5)  2. Inventory of Materials and Supplies ... 59,000
       Vouchers Payable .............. 59,000
       To record purchase of materials.

(6)  3. Accounts Receivable ................. 300,000
       Operating Revenues ............ 300,000
       To record operating revenues.

(7)  4. Machinery and Equipment .......... 50,500
       Vouchers Payable .............. 50,500
       To record purchase of equipment.

(8)  5. Operating Expenses ................. 500
       Cash......................... 500
       To record telephone and telegraph ex-
       penses.

(9)  6. Due from State Public Works Depart-
       ment .......................... 7,000
       Nonoperating Revenues-Equipment
       Rental ....................... 7,000
       To record rental of equipment to State
       Public Works Department.

(10)    7. Operating Expenses ................     1,000
            Cash..........................                      1,000
            To record insurance premium pay-
            ments.

(11)    8. Cash.............................   290,000
            Accounts Receivable ............                290,000
            To record collection of accounts receiv-
            able.

(12)    9. Operating Expenses ................    12,800
            Due to Intragovernmental Service
            Fund ......................                         12,800
            To record cost of services rendered by
            Intragovernmental Service Fund.

(13)   10. Bonds Payable .....................    50,000
            Cash..........................                     50,000
            To record retirement of part of issue
            of serial bonds.

(14)   11. Interest Expense....................    20,000
            Cash..........................                     20,000
            To record payment of interest.

(15)   12. Cash.............................     1,000
            Interest Revenues ..............                   1,000
            To record receipt of interest revenues.

(16)   13. Taxes ...........................    10,500
            Cash..........................                    10,500
            To record payment of taxes.

(17)   14. Vouchers Payable .................    70,000
            Cash..........................                     70,000
            To record payment of vouchers.

(18)   15. Improvements Other than Buildings....    30,000
            Contribution from Subdividers.....                30,000
            To record dedication of subdivision
            distribution lines to the utility.

(Tapping fees or similar charges paid by customers should also be credited to
contributions from customers to the extent they exceed recovery of hook-up
costs.)

(19)   16. (a) Operating Expenses .............     6,000
                Accrued Salaries and Wages
                Payable ..................                      6,000
                To record salaries and wages ac-
                crued.

           (b) Interest Expense ...............     2,000
                Accrued Interest Payable......                  2,000
                To record accrued interest payable.

(c) Accrued Interest Receivable ......     200  
     Interest Revenue ............             200  
     To record accrued interest receivable.

(d) Taxes ........................     7,500  
     Accrued Taxes Payable ......             7,500  
     To record accrued taxes.

(e) Prepaid Insurance .............     600  
     Operating Expenses ..........             600  
     To record unexpired insurance.

(f) Operating Expenses .............     39,000  
     Inventory of Materials and Supplies ...................             39,000  
     To record operating expenses in connection with materials used during year.

(g) Operating Expenses .............     1,500  
     Allowance for Uncollectible Accounts ................             1,500  
     To record estimated losses on accounts receivable.

(h) Depreciation Expense ............     36,000  
     Allowance for Depreciation—Buildings ................             5,000  
     Allowance for Depreciation—Improvements Other than Buildings ................             15,000  
     Allowance for Depreciation—Machinery and Equipment ..             16,000  
     To record depreciation for fiscal year.

(i) Unbilled Accounts Receivable .....     21,000  
     Operating Revenues .........             21,000  
     To record unbilled receivables and revenues at year end.

ACCOUNTING FOR RESTRICTED ASSET ACCOUNTS. As indicated earlier, an enterprise's restricted assets are accounted for within the Enterprise Fund accounts rather than through separate fund entities. This is accomplished through use of distinctively titled restricted asset accounts, offset by liability or equity reserve accounts—by establishing "funds" within the fund—so that a single fund serves the purpose of several separate fund entities. Before studying the procedures that follow, note how the Trial Balance (Figure 14-1) and the Balance Sheet (Figure 14-2) presented at the conclusion of this example are designed to separate these intrafund "funds" from the unrestricted assets and other liabilities and equities.

The types of restricted asset situations that may be encountered in practice vary widely, from simple customer deposits "funds" to complex series of "funds" required under terms of bond indentures, through legislative decree, or for administrative purposes. Several of the more common restricted asset situations are presented here to illustrate the use of intrafund restricted asset accounts, sometimes referred to as "secondary account groups," in Enterprise Fund accounting. In the following illustrations we use distinctively titled asset and liability accounts for each "fund" and adjust the appropriate reserve accounts by inspection at period-end. "Fund" revenues and expenses are recorded in the Electricity (Enterprise) Fund revenue and expense control accounts under the assumption that any "fund" detail needed is provided in subsidiary records. Alternatively, we might have used detailed "fund" revenue and expense accounts and closed them at period-end either (1) directly to the appropriate reserve account, or (2) to the Retained Earnings account, followed by an entry adjusting the appropriate reserve account.

*Customer deposits.* A utility frequently requires its customers to post deposits, on which it normally pays interest, as a partial protection against bad debt losses. The following transactions and entries illustrate the procedure in recording the deposits, earnings thereon, interest paid to depositors, forfeited deposits, and the return of deposits upon termination of service:

*Transactions*

1. Deposits of $11,000 were received.
2. Deposits in the amount of $10,000 were invested (assume that no premiums, discounts, or accrued interest purchases were involved).
3. Interest accrued on investments but not received, $200.
4. Interest accrued on deposits but not paid, $150.
5. A customer's deposit was declared forfeited for nonpayment of his account.
6. A customer moving to another town requested that his service be disconnected. His final bill was offset against his deposit and the balance remitted to him.
7. The appropriate reserve account was adjusted at period end to equal the net assets of the "fund."

*Entries*

(20) 1. Customers' Deposits—Cash ........... 11,000
      Customers' Deposits Payable .......        11,000
      To record receipt of customers' deposits.

(21) 2. Customers' Deposits—Investments ..... 10,000
      Customers' Deposits—Cash .......        10,000
      To record investment of customers' deposits.

(22) 3. Customers' Deposits—Accrued Interest
      Receivable ..................... 200
      Interest Revenue ................        200
      To record interest revenues.

(23)  4. Interest Expense...................... 150
      Customers' Deposits—Accrued Inter-
        est Payable ....................          150
      To record interest expenses.

(24)  5. (a) Customers' Deposits Payable ....... 12
      Customers' Deposits—Accrued
        Interest Payable ...............   2
      Allowance for Uncollectible
        Accounts ....................   8
          Accounts Receivable .........          22
      To record forfeiture of customer's
      deposit, offset against overdue receiv-
      able, and write-off of the uncollecti-
      ble balance.

     (b) Cash ........................... 14
          Customers' Deposits—Cash ....          14
      To reclassify forfeited customer de-
      posits cash to unrestricted cash.

(25)  6. Customers' Deposits Payable .......... 15
      Customers' Deposits—Accrued Interest
        Payable.........................   3
          Accounts Receivable .............          10
          Customers' Deposits—Cash .......          8
      To record offsetting of customers' final
      bill against his deposit account and remit-
      tance of the balance due him.

(26)  7. Retained Earnings ................... 60
      Reserve for Earnings on Customers'
        Deposits ......................          60
      To reserve Retained Earnings to indicate
      that net assets of the Customers' Deposits
      Fund are available only for customer
      deposit interest requirements.

*Construction financed by bond issue.*   Accounting for Enterprise Fund construction financed through the sale of bonds is not unlike that for private construction. Both the authorization of the bond issue and appropriations, if any,
are normally recorded in memorandum form rather than formally within the accounts. The following transactions and entries illustrate appropriate procedures
in the typical case.

### Transactions

1.  Bonds in the amount of $200,000 (par) were sold at a premium of $2,000.
2.  The premium cash was reclassified as being restricted for debt service.
3.  A contract was entered into with Smith & Company for the construction
    of part of the project at a cost of $100,000.

4.  Materials costing $41,000 were purchased by the utility and delivered to the construction site.

5.  The bill for materials was paid.

6.  A bill for $30,000 was received from Smith & Company.

7.  Smith & Company was paid.

8.  The utility paid $56,000, representing the cost of construction labor and supervisory expenses.

9.  Smith & Company completed its part of the construction project and submitted its bill for $70,000.

10. Smith & Company was paid in full except for $10,000, which was retained pending final inspection and approval of the project.

11. The completed project was found to be satisfactory and was set up on the records as a fixed asset.

12. Smith & Company was paid the final amount due.

13. The remaining bond cash was transferred to the Enterprise debt service "fund."

*Entries*

| | | | | |
|---|---|---|---|---|
| (27) | 1. Construction—Cash................. | 200,000 | | |
| | Cash............................. | 2,000 | | |
| | Unamortized Premiums on Bonds.. | | 2,000 | |
| | Bonds Payable ................. | | 200,000 | |
| | To record sale of bonds at a premium. | | | |

| | | | |
|---|---|---|---|
| (28) | 2. Debt Service—Cash................. | 2,000 | |
| | Cash......................... | | 2,000 |
| | To record restriction of premium cash for debt service purposes. | | |

    3.  No entry is necessary to record entering into a contract; a narrative memorandum entry may be made.

| | | | |
|---|---|---|---|
| (29) | 4. Construction Work in Progress ....... | 41,000 | |
| | Construction Vouchers Payable ... | | 41,000 |
| | To record cost of construction materials. | | |

| | | | |
|---|---|---|---|
| (30) | 5. Construction Vouchers Payable ....... | 41,000 | |
| | Construction—Cash............. | | 41,000 |
| | To record payment of bill for materials. | | |

| | | | |
|---|---|---|---|
| (31) | 6. Construction Work in Progress ....... | 30,000 | |
| | Construction Contracts Payable ... | | 30,000 |
| | To record receipt of bill from Smith & Company for part of cost of contract. | | |

| | | | |
|---|---|---|---|
| (32) | 7. Construction Contracts Payable. ...... | 30,000 | |
| | Construction—Cash............. | | 30,000 |
| | To record payment of amount now due on contract. | | |

(33) 8. Construction Work in Progress .......    56,000
      Construction—Cash..............          56,000
      To record cost of labor and supervisory
      expenses.

(34) 9. Construction Work in Progress .......    70,000
      Construction Contracts Payable ...         70,000
      To record receipt of bill from Smith
      & Company to cover remaining cost
      of contract.

(35) 10. Construction Contracts Payable .......    70,000
      Construction—Cash..............         60,000
      Construction Contracts Payable—
        Retained Percentage ..........         10,000
      To record payment of amount due on
      contract and retention of part of
      amount due pending final approval of
      project.

(36) 11. Improvements Other than Buildings....    197,000
      Construction Work in Progress.....      197,000
      To close out Construction Work in
      Progress account and to set up cost of
      completed improvements.

(37) 12. Construction Contracts Payable—
      Retained Percentage ............    10,000
      Construction—Cash.............        10,000
      To record final payment to contractor.

(38) 13. Debt Service—Cash.................    3,000
      Construction—Cash.............        3,000
      To record transfer of unused bond
      proceeds to sinking fund.

Interest expenses during the construction period on money borrowed to finance the construction are usually capitalized in accounting for a privately owned regulated utility. And, even if the utility does not borrow money for construction, it may capitalize the interest (imputed) it would have paid if it had borrowed money for this purpose. The reason is that the utility is deprived of the use of the money for revenue-producing purposes until the project is completed and is in a position to earn revenue. Adding this "cost" to other project costs, and thus allowing it to enter the rate basis, will permit the utility to recover a like amount through additional depreciation charges against revenues or, where the allowable return is stated as a percentage of the book value of assets, to derive a higher dollar return during the asset's useful life.

The propriety of capitalizing interest expense incurred or imputed during construction as a cost of the project is highly debatable. Furthermore, it is a question on which the NCGA is silent.

Most accountants (1) oppose the capitalization of any interest expense, incurred or imputed, on the basis that interest is a financing cost, not a construction cost, and (2) argue against capitalization of imputed interest, in particular, on the grounds that it is not an actual cost incurred. Those favoring capitalization contend that (1) the magnitude of public utility construction projects or acquisitions is usually so great that one could not be expected to pay the costs without borrowing, i.e., that interest should be considered an ordinary and necessary cost of major construction or acquisition projects; and (2) a major reason for accounting for publicly owned utilities along the lines of privately owned utilities is to be able to effect valid comparisons between and among them; failure to capitalize construction period interest in Enterprise Funds in the same manner as in privately owned utilities would distort such comparisions.

Either practice, capitalization or noncapitalization of interest during the construction or acquisition period, appears to have substantial authoritative support. The authors prefer that if interest is capitalized it be limited to the amount actually incurred, in other words, that imputed interest not be capitalized.

If interest incurred is capitalized, it is necessary to take account of unamortized premiums and discounts so that the actual interest expense (rather than the cash or nominal interest) is capitalized. For example, let us assume that interest accrued in the amount of $4,500 is attributable to a construction project that extended over the full year, and that the amount of premium to be amortized during the construction period is $100. The entry to record interest expense and the amortization of premiums is as follows:

| | | |
|---|---|---|
| Interest Expense | 4,400 | |
| Unamortized Premiums on Bonds | 100 | |
| Accrued Interest Payable | | 4,500 |
| To record interest expense and reduction of same by amount of premium amortized. | | |

Subsequently an entry would be made capitalizing the net interest expense as follows:

| | | |
|---|---|---|
| Improvements Other than Buildings | 4,400 | |
| Interest Expense | | 4,400 |
| To record charging interest expense to construction. | | |

Should imputed interest be capitalized, a credit to a rather unorthodox account such as Imputed Interest Expense Capitalized to Construction would be required. Such an account might conceivably be closed either to current period income, contributed capital, or Retained Earnings, depending upon one's interpretation of its nature.

*Debt service and related accounts.* A variety of intrafund "funds" related to bond issues may be required (in addition to a construction or Capital Projects "fund") under terms commonly found in contemporary bond indentures. Among the most usual of these are:

1. *Term Bond Principal Sinking Fund.* Often referred to merely as a "Sinking" fund, its purpose is to segregate stipulated amounts of assets, and earnings thereon, for the eventual retirement of term bond principal.

2. *Revenue Bond Debt Service Fund.* This type of intrafund "fund," commonly referred to as an "Interest and Redemption," "Interest and Sinking," or "Bond and Interest" fund, is often required to assure timely payment of serial revenue bond interest and principal. A common indenture provision is that one-sixth of the next semi-annual interest payment, plus one-twelfth of the next annual principal payment, be deposited monthly in a "fund" of this type.

3. *Principal and Interest Reserve Fund.* Often referred to simply as a "Reserve" fund, intrafund "funds" of this type are often required to provide bondholders an additional "cushion" or safety margin. "Funds" of this sort are usually required to be accumulated to a specific sum within the first 60 months after bonds are issued and are to be used (1) to pay matured bonds and interest if the resources in the Debt Service "fund" prove inadequate, or (2) if not required earlier to cover deficiences, to retire the final bond principal and interest maturities.

4. *Contingencies Fund.* This intrafund "fund," sometimes referred to as the "Emergency Repair" or "Operating Reserve" fund, is intended to afford bondholders even more security by providing in advance for emergency expenditures or for operating asset renewal or replacement. Thus, the bondholder receives additional assurance that the operating facilities will not be permitted to deteriorate in order that bond principal and interest requirements be met—or the utility be forced into receivership—because of such unforeseen expenditure requirements. Like the Principal and Interest Reserve "fund," the Contingencies "fund" is usually required to be accumulated in a specific amount early in the life of the bond issue.

The principles and procedures of accounting for both term and serial bond Debt Service Funds were covered in detail in Chapter 10 and are fully applicable to the first two types of intrafund "funds" listed above. The only difference is that such "funds" are accounted for on a "funds within a fund" basis within the Enterprise Fund—through use of a series of self-balancing restricted asset, liability, and equity reserve intrafund account groups—rather than through separate accounting entities.

In order to illustrate the operation and accounting for debt service-related "funds" within an Enterprise Fund, let us assume that Debt Service, Principal and Interest Reserve, and Contingencies "funds," as described in items 2, 3, and 4 above, are required under terms of an enterprise bond indenture. A total of $5,000 has already been classified as Debt Service-Cash (Construction "fund" transactions 2 and 13) as a result of a bond issue premium ($2,000) and unused bond issue proceeds ($3,000). The following transactions illustrate typical activities related to these restricted asset accounts:

Transactions

1. The Debt Service "fund" was increased by $25,000; $10,000 each was added to the Principal and Interest Reserve "fund" and to the Contingencies "fund."

2. Interest on bonds, $15,000, was paid.

3. A $7,000 unforeseen emergency repair was incurred and is to be paid from the Contingencies "fund."

4. Principal and Interest Reserve "fund" cash, $9,000, was invested.

5. Interest was earned on the above investment, $450, of which $300 was received in cash.

6. Bond interest payable had accrued at year end, $6,000; premium of $300 was amortized.

7. The appropriate reserve accounts were adjusted at year end to equal the net assets of the "funds."

Entries

| | | | | |
|---|---|---|---|---|
| (39) | 1. | Debt Service—Cash...................... | 25,000 | |
| | | Principal and Interest Reserve—Cash .... | 10,000 | |
| | | Contingencies—Cash .................. | 10,000 | |
| | | Cash............................... | | 45,000 |
| | | To record amounts restricted and set aside for these funds. | | |
| (40) | 2. | Interest Expense........................ | 15,000 | |
| | | Debt Service—Cash................. | | 15,000 |
| | | To record payment of bond interest. | | |
| (41) | 3. | Operating Expenses ................... | 7,000 | |
| | | Contingencies—Vouchers Payable .... | | 7,000 |
| | | To record liability for emergency repair expense. | | |
| (42) | 4. | Principal and Interest Reserve— | | |
| | | Investments........................ | 9,000 | |
| | | Principal and Interest Reserve—Cash.. | | 9,000 |
| | | To record investment of fund cash. | | |
| (43) | 5. | Principal and Interest Reserve—Cash .... | 300 | |
| | | Principal and Interest Reserve— | | |
| | | Accrued Interest Receivable ........... | 150 | |
| | | Interest Revenue ................... | | 450 |
| | | To record interest earned and received. | | |

| (44) | 6. Interest Expense...................... | 5,700 | |
|---|---|---|---|
| | Unamortized Premiums on Bonds ........ | 300 | |
| | Debt Service—Accrued Bond Interest | | |
| | Payable ....................... | | 6,000 |
| | To record bond interest accrued and | | |
| | amortization of bond premium. | | |
| (45) | 7. Retained Earnings .................... | 22,450 | |
| | Reserve for Bond Debt Service ...... | | 9,000 |
| | Reserve for Bond Principal and Interest | | |
| | Payments Guarantee ............. | | 10,450 |
| | Reserve for Contingencies........... | | 3,000 |

Retained Earnings reserves need to be adjusted to equal "fund" net assets only prior to statement preparation. Continuous adjustment merely constitutes "busy work," though such practice is technically correct and may occasionally be found. The purpose of these reserves is to indicate that restricted intrafund "fund" net assets are not available for "dividends" to the General Fund or for other purposes. The reserves also constitute the balancing accounts of the self-balancing "funds within a fund."

Adjusting Entries.    For ease of illustration, we have included most of the required adjusting entries within the various phases of our example in this chapter. Most of the adjusting entries required were similar to those common in commercial accounting; and, as in commercial accounting, those of an accrual nature would be reversed at the beginning of the subsequent period. The adjusting entries that may be less familiar to the reader, and therefore deserve special attention at this point, are those relating to unbilled receivables and amortization of the Utility Plant Acquisition Adjustments account.

Accurate determination of the revenue earned during a year requires that significant amounts of unbilled receivables be accrued at year-end, particularly if the amount of such receivables varies materially from year to year. This is not to say that a cut-off point in the billing cycle cannot be used, or that other expediency methods that do not distort reported net income or financial position cannot be employed. Such methods should be used only after careful consideration of possible distortions or biases thereby introduced, however, and should be applied consistently each year.

As indicated previously, the Utility Plant Acquisition Adjustments account, when employed, is set up either as a fixed asset or as a deferred charge and is amortized (prorated over time) in a systematic and rational manner. The amortization entry is as follows:

| Amortization of Utility Plant Acquisition Adjust- | | |
|---|---|---|
| ments ...................................... | `XX,XXX | |
| Allowance for Amortization of Utility Plant | | |
| Acquisition Adjustments .................. | | XX,XXX |
| To record amortization of utility plant acquisition | | |
| adjustments. | | |

The Allowance for Amortization of Utility Plant Acquisition Adjustments is a valuation account and is deducted from the Utility Plant Acquisition Adjustments account in the balance sheet. The Utility Plant Acquisition Adjustments account and the related allowance would be shown in the balance sheet as follows:

```
Utility plant acquisition adjustments .............  XX, XXX
Less: Allowance for amortization of utility plant
    acquisition adjustments ....................  XX, XXX
Unamortized utility plant acquisition adjustments  ..           XX, XXX
```

When assets are disposed of, any related balances in the Utility Plant Acquisition Adjustments and Allowance for Amortization of Utility Plant Acquisition Adjustments accounts should be removed in the same entry in which the "original cost" asset and depreciation allowance accounts are reduced. Otherwise, the acquisition adjustments accounts will be overstated and the gain or loss reported on the disposal transaction will be misstated.

When the amortization process is completed, an entry may be made debiting the Allowance for Amortization of Utility Plant Acquisition Adjustments account and crediting the Utility Plant Acquisition Adjustments account for corresponding amounts to clear their balances. These amounts would then be added to the appropriate asset and depreciation allowance accounts.

Recall again, however, that the Utility Plant Acquisition Adjustments account is peculiar to the *regulated* industry environment and is *not* a standard feature of Enterprise Fund accounting. Remember also that, although the Adjustments account and the related Amortization and Amortization Allowance accounts must appear in statements prepared for regulatory purposes, it may be necessary to allocate these to the asset and expense accounts relating to the properties being carried at "original cost" (that required the Acquisition Adjustments account to be established) and to prepare modified financial statements in order that general purpose reports present fairly the financial position and operating results of the Enterprise Fund.

PRECLOSING TRIAL BALANCE. An adjusted, preclosing trial balance for the Electric (Enterprise) Fund, based on the journal entries in this chapter having numbers in parentheses by them, appears as Figure 14-1. In order to illustrate the "funds within a fund" approach common to Enterprise Fund accounting, this trial balance has been modified from the usual trial balance format in that (1) it is divided into two major sections, entitled "General Accounts" and "Restricted Accounts," respectively, and (2) subtotals have been included to indicate the self-balancing nature of many Enterprise Fund intrafund "funds."

This is not to say that all intrafund restricted account groups are self-balancing, for they need not be. Thus, had we not assumed in our example that the net assets of the Customers' Deposits "fund" were restricted to guarantee future interest liabilities to customers (1) there would have been no need to

Figure 14-1

A GOVERNMENTAL UNIT

Electric (Enterprise) Fund

Preclosing (Adjusted) Trial Balance (Date)

General Accounts:

| | | |
|---|---:|---:|
| Cash ............................... | $ 86,814 | |
| Accounts Receivable ................ | 71,968 | |
| Allowance for Uncollectible Accounts ... | | $ 13,492 |
| Unbilled Accounts Receivable .......... | 21,000 | |
| Accrued Interest Receivable .......... | 200 | |
| Due from State Public Works Department | 7,000 | |
| Inventory of Materials and Supplies...... | 30,000 | |
| Prepaid Insurance ................... | 600 | |
| Land .............................. | 50,000 | |
| Buildings .......................... | 100,000 | |
| Allowance for Depreciation—Buildings ... | | 15,000 |
| Improvements Other Than Buildings .... | 777,000 | |
| Allowance for Depreciation— | | |
|   Improvements Other Than Buildings .. | | 85,000 |
| Machinery and Equipment ............ | 200,500 | |
| Allowance for Depreciation—Machinery | | |
|   and Equipment .................... | | 56,000 |
| Vouchers Payable .................... | | 49,500 |
| Due to Intragovernmental Service Fund .. | | 12,800 |
| Accrued Salaries and Wages Payable .... | | 6,000 |
| Accrued Interest Payable ............. | | 2,000 |
| Accrued Taxes Payable ............... | | 7,500 |
| Bonds Payable ...................... | | 650,000 |
| Unamortized Premiums on Bonds........ | | 1,700 |
| Contribution from Municipality ........ | | 400,000 |
| Contribution from Subdividers ......... | | 30,000 |
| Retained Earnings ................... | 22,510 | |
| Operating Revenues .................. | | 321,000 |
| Operating Expenses................... | 194,400 | |
| Depreciation Expense ................. | 36,000 | |
| Taxes ............................. | 18,000 | |
| Nonoperating Revenue—Equipment | | |
|   Rental .......................... | | 7,000 |
| Interest Revenue .................... | | 1,850 |
| Interest Expense .................... | 42,850 | |
| Subtotal ....................... | $1,658,842 | $1,658,842 |

**Figure 14-1 (cont.)**

| | | | |
|---|---|---|---|
| | Restricted or Secondary Accounts: | | |
| Customers' Deposits "Fund" | Customers' Deposits—Cash | $ 978 | |
| | Customers' Deposits—Investments | 10,000 | |
| | Customers' Deposits—Accrued Interest Receivable | 200 | |
| | Customers' Deposits Payable | | $ 10,973 |
| | Customers' Deposits—Interest Payable | | 145 |
| | Reserve for Earnings on Customers' Deposits | | 60 |
| | Subtotal | $ 11,178 | $ 11,178 |
| Debt Service "Fund" | Debt Service—Cash | $ 15,000 | |
| | Debt Service—Accrued Interest Payable | | $ 6,000 |
| | Reserve for Bond Debt Service | | 9,000 |
| | Subtotal | $ 15,000 | $ 15,000 |
| Principal and Interest Reserve "Fund" | Principal and Interest Reserve—Cash | $ 1,300 | |
| | Principal and Interest Reserve—Investments | 9,000 | |
| | Principal and Interest Reserve—Accrued Interest Receivable | 150 | |
| | Reserve for Bond Principal and Interest Payments Guarantee | | $ 10,450 |
| | Subtotal | $ 10,450 | $ 10,450 |
| Contingencies "Fund" | Contingencies—Cash | $ 10,000 | |
| | Contingencies—Voucher Payable | | $ 7,000 |
| | Reserve for Contingencies | | 3,000 |
| | Subtotal | $ 10,000 | $ 10,000 |
| | Total | $1,705,470 | $1,705,470 |

establish a Reserve for Earnings on Customers' Deposits and (2) this "fund" would not be self-balancing.

Closing Entries. As observed earlier, any reasonable closing entry(ies) that brings the temporary proprietorship accounts to a zero balance and updates the Retained Earnings account is acceptable. Inasmuch as a multiple-step closing approach was illustrated in Chapter 13, the compound entry approach is demonstrated here:

| (46) | Operating Revenues .................... | 321,000 | |
|---|---|---|---|
| | Nonoperating Revenue—Equipment Rental | 7,000 | |
| | Interest Revenue ...................... | 1,850 | |
| | Operating Expenses .................. | | 194,400 |
| | Depreciation Expense ................ | | 36,000 |
| | Taxes ............................... | | 18,000 |
| | Interest Expense .................... | | 42,850 |
| | Retained Earnings .................. | | 38,600 |
| | To close the temporary proprietorship accounts and update Retained Earnings. | | |

Subsidiary accounts would also be closed at this time, of course.

FINANCIAL STATEMENTS.   The four major Enterprise Fund financial statements recommended by the National Committee on Governmental Accounting are (1) a balance sheet, (2) an analysis of changes in retained earnings, (3) a revenue and expense statement, and (4) a statement of sources and application of "cash funds" (statement of changes in financial position). Each of these statements is illustrated and commented upon in subsequent sections of this chapter.

The Committee also recommends annual preparation of (1) a schedule of operating expenses, budgeted and actual, and (2) a schedule of fixed assets and depreciation, including changes therein. Other statements may also be desirable or required, of course, depending upon the type of enterprise and the needs of managers, regulatory authorities, creditors, and the public. The NCGA suggests, for example, that it might be useful to prepare statements detailing changes in the Cash and Investment accounts of intrafund restricted asset account groups.

*Balance sheet.*   A Balance Sheet for the Electric (Enterprise) Fund is illustrated in Figure 14-2. Note that the balance sheet exhibited is similar to that of a profit-seeking public utility. Like the balance sheet of a business enterprise, or that of many nonexpendable Trust and Intragovernmental Service Funds, this statement contains both fixed assets and long-term liabilities of the governmental enterprise.

The balance sheet presented in Figure 14-2 follows the arrangement recommended by the National Association of Railroad and Utilities Commissioners, in which fixed assets precede current assets and long-term debt precedes current liabilities. This arrangement of utility balance sheets is consistent with the usual relative importance of fixed assets and long-term liabilities in this "capital-intensive" industry—current assets and liabilities are often relatively insignificant by comparison. The familiar "order of liquidity" arrangement is also acceptable for utility balance sheets, however, and will normally be preferable for nonutility types of Enterprise Fund balance sheets. Illustrative formats of the Statement of Changes in Assets Restricted for Revenue Bond Debt Service and the Schedule of Fixed Assets and Depreciation—which usually are presented to complete the Enterprise Fund disclosure—are shown in Figures 14-10 and 14-11, respectively.

Figure 14-2

# A GOVERNMENTAL UNIT
## Electric (Enterprise) Fund
### Balance Sheet (Date)

*Assets*

| | | | |
|---|---|---|---|
| Plant and Equipment: | | | |
| Land | | $ 50,000 | |
| Buildings | $100,000 | | |
| Less: Allowance for depreciation | 15,000 | 85,000 | |
| Improvements other than buildings | $777,000 | | |
| Less: Allowance for depreciation | 85,000 | 692,000 | |
| Machinery and equipment | $200,500 | | |
| Less: Allowance for depreciation | 56,000 | 144,500 | |
| Total Plant and Equipment | | | $971,500 |
| Current Assets: | | | |
| Cash | | $ 86,814 | |
| Accounts receivable | $ 71,968 | | |
| Less: Allowance for uncollectible accounts.. | 13,492 | 58,476 | |
| Unbilled accounts receivable | | 21,000 | |
| Accrued interest receivable | | 200 | |
| Due from State Public Works Department | | 7,000 | |
| Inventory of materials and supplies | | 30,000 | |
| Prepaid insurance | | 600 | |
| Total Current Assets | | | 204,090 |
| Restricted Assets: | | | |
| Customers Deposits: | | | |
| Cash | $ 978 | | |
| Investments | 10,000 | | |
| Accrued interest receivable | 200 | $ 11,178 | |
| Debt Service: | | | |
| Cash | | 15,000 | |
| Principal and Interest Reserve: | | | |
| Cash | $ 1,300 | | |
| Investments | 9,000 | | |
| Accrued interest receivable | 150 | 10,450 | |
| Contingencies: | | | |
| Cash | | 10,000 | |
| Total Restricted Assets | | | 46,628 |
| Total Assets | | | $1,222,218 |

**Figure 14-2 (cont.)**

*Liabilities, Reserves, Contributions, and Retained Earnings*

Long-Term Liabilities:

| | | |
|---|---:|---:|
| Bonds payable .......................... | $650,000 | |
| Unamortized premiums on bonds ........... | 1,700 | |
| Total Long-Term Liabilities ............ | | $651,700 |

Current Liabilities (Payable from Current Assets):

| | | |
|---|---:|---:|
| Vouchers payable ....................... | $ 49,500 | |
| Due to Intragovernmental Service Fund....... | 12,800 | |
| Accrued salaries and wages payable .......... | 6,000 | |
| Accrued interest payable .................. | 2,000 | |
| Accrued taxes payable .................... | 7,500 | |
| Total Current Liabilities (Payable from Current Assets) ..................... | | 77,800 |

Liabilities Payable From Restricted Assets:

| | | |
|---|---:|---:|
| Customers' deposits payable ................ | $ 10,973 | |
| Interest payable on customers' deposits ....... | 145 | |
| Debt Service—Accrued bond interest payable .. | 6,000 | |
| Contingencies—Vouchers payable ............ | 7,000 | |
| Total Liabilities Payable From Restricted Assets ............................ | | 24,118 |
| Total Liabilities ...................... | | $753,618 |

Reserves:

| | | |
|---|---:|---:|
| Reserve for earnings on customers' deposits .... | $ 60 | |
| Reserve for bond debt service ............... | 9,000 | |
| Reserve for bond principal and interest guarantee ........................... | 10,450 | |
| Reserve for contingencies................... | 3,000 | |
| Total Reserves ....................... | | 22,510 |

Contributions:

| | | |
|---|---:|---:|
| Contributions from municipality ........... | $400,000 | |
| Contributions from subdividers.............. | 30,000 | |
| Total Contributions ................... | | 430,000 |
| Retained earnings (Figure 14-3)............... | | 16,090 |
| Total Liabilities, Reserves, Contributions, and Retained Earnings........................... | | $1,222,218 |

Notice the asset categorization as among plant and equipment, current assets, and restricted assets in the Balance Sheet in Figure 14-2 and the parallel division of liabilities into long-term liabilities, current liabilities payable from current assets, and liabilities payable from restricted assets. Such intrastatement categorization permits ready "across the balance sheet" comparisons and analyses.

The Contributions from Municipality account shows the amount of capital invested in the utility by the governmental unit. As indicated earlier, this account is credited for the amount expended by the governmental unit in acquiring the utility. Similarly, the account is credited for subsequent capital contributions made by the governmental unit to the utility, such as those to make up a deficit or to increase its capital. The NCGA position is that the Contributions from Municipality account should not be reduced by amounts transferred each year from the Enterprise Fund to the General Fund. (For example, the governmental unit may transfer all or a portion of utility profits to the General Fund each year.) Such transfers are deemed by the NCGA to first reduce Retained Earnings, since they usually are distributions of earnings rather than disinvestments of capital. Only when Retained Earnings has been reduced to zero are such transfers deemed to reduce the governmental unit's capital contribution. (A temporary advance to an Enterprise Fund should be recorded in "Advance To/

**Figure 14-3**

### A GOVERNMENTAL UNIT
Electric (Enterprise) Fund
Analysis of Changes In Retained Earnings
For Period Ended (Date)

| | | |
|---|---:|---:|
| Retained Earnings, beginning of period* .......... | | $ — |
| Additions:  Net income (Figure 14-4) .......... | | 38,600 |
| Total beginning balance and additions ........... | | $38,600 |
| Deductions: | | |
| Increase in reserve for customers' deposits ....... | $ 60 | |
| Increase in reserve for bond debt service ........ | 9,000 | |
| Increase in reserve for bond principal and | | |
| interest guarantee ........................ | 10,450 | |
| Increase in reserve for contingencies ............ | 3,000 | |
| Total deductions ......................... | | 22,510 |
| Retained Earnings, end of period (Figure 14-2) ..... | | $16,090 |

* There is no beginning balance since this statement was prepared at the end of the first operating period.

From" accounts and the nature of the transaction should be documented in the minutes of the governing body.)

*Analysis of changes in retained earnings.* An analysis of changes in the Retained Earnings account during the period is contained in Figure 14-3. Since our example consisted of the initial year's transactions, the beginning balance is zero; the ending balance of the Retained Earnings account is the beginning balance for the subsequent period, of course.

As in commercial enterprise accounting, the main causes of change in the Retained Earnings account of an Enterprise Fund are (1) net income or loss, (2) "dividends" paid the governmental unit, and (3) increases or decreases in

**Figure 14-4**

A GOVERNMENTAL UNIT
Electric (Enterprise) Fund
Statement of Revenue and Expense
For the Period Ended (Date)

| | | |
|---|---:|---:|
| Operating revenues: | | |
| Residential sales ............................ | $185,200 | |
| Commercial sales .......................... | 91,300 | |
| Industrial sales ........................... | 62,500 | |
| Public street lighting ..................... | 12,000 | |
| Total operating revenues .................. | | $321,000 |
| Less: Operating revenue deductions: | | |
| Operating expenses (Figure 14-5) .............. | $194,400 | |
| Depreciation* ............................. | 36,000 | |
| Taxes .................................... | 18,000 | |
| Total operating revenue deductions ........... | | 248,400 |
| Operating income* ......................... | | $ 72,600 |
| Add: Nonoperating income: | | |
| Equipment rental .......................... | $ 7,000 | |
| Interest revenue .......................... | 1,850 | |
| Total nonoperating income ................. | | 8,850 |
| Total operating and nonoperating income ........ | | $ 81,450 |
| Less: Nonoperating expenses: | | |
| Interest expense .......................... | | 42,850 |
| Net Income .................................. | | $ 38,600 |

\* Where net revenue is calculated on a cash basis for purposes of computing debt service coverage, an "Operating Revenue before Depreciation" figure is frequently presented, from which depreciation is deducted in determining "Operating Income."

Figure 14-5

A GOVERNMENTAL UNIT

Electric (Enterprise) Fund

Detailed Statement* of Operating Expenses

for Fiscal Year Ended (Date)

Production Expenses:

Electric generating—

| | | |
|---|---|---|
| Supervision | $ 8,000 | |
| Station labor | 15,000 | |
| Fuel | 54,000 | |
| Water | 4,000 | |
| Supplies and expenses | 8,400 | $89,400 |

Maintenance of plant and equipment—

| | | |
|---|---|---|
| Supervision | $ 4,000 | |
| Maintenance of structures and improvements .. | 8,000 | |
| Maintenance of boiler plant equipment ....... | 10,000 | |
| Maintenance of generating and electric plant equipment | 10,000 | 32,000 |
| Power purchased | | 2,000 |
| Total production expense | | $123,400 |

Distribution Expenses:

| | | |
|---|---|---|
| Supervision | $ 2,500 | |
| Services on consumers' premises | 4,500 | |
| Street lighting and signal system | 4,000 | |
| Overhead system | 18,200 | |
| Maintenance and servicing of mobile equipment... | 3,000 | |
| Utility storeroom expenses | 4,000 | |
| Total distribution expenses | | 36,200 |

Accounting and Collection Expenses:

| | | |
|---|---|---|
| Customers' contracts and orders | $ 2,500 | |
| Meter reading | 3,500 | |
| Collecting offices | 1,000 | |
| Delinquent accounts—collection expense | 2,000 | |
| Customers' billing and accounting | 4,000 | |
| Provision for doubtful accounts | 1,800 | |
| Total accounting and collection expense ..... | | 14,800 |

| | |
|---|---|
| Sales Promotion Expenses | 1,000 |

* The detailed amounts in this statement cannot be derived from the example in the chapter. They have been hypothesized for illustrative purposes only.

**Figure 14-5 (cont.)**

Administrative and General Expenses:

| | | |
|---|---:|---:|
| Salaries of executives .......................... | $ 8,000 | |
| Other general office salaries ................... | 3,500 | |
| General office supplies and expenses ............ | 400 | |
| Insurance ..................................... | 2,000 | |
| Employees' welfare expenses ................... | 1,500 | |
| Pension fund contributions .................... | 2,800 | |
| Miscellaneous general expenses................. | 800 | |
| Total administrative and general expense .... | | 19,000 |
| Total operating expenses ....................... | | $194,400 |

reserved or appropriated Retained Earnings accounts. Statements analyzing changes in reserves also should be prepared if significant changes therein occurred during the period.

*Statement of revenue and expense.* A Statement of Revenue and Expense (Income Statement) should be prepared on both an interim and annual basis for each Enterprise Fund. *The NCGA recommends that budgetary or period-to-period comparative data be included in revenue and expense statements, or that both types of statements be prepared.* Comparative data is omitted here only in the interest of clarity of illustration.

The Statement of Revenue and Expense shown in Figure 14-4 illustrates the usual utility format in which (1) a distinction is maintained between operating revenues and expenses and nonoperating revenues and expenses, and (2) operating expenses are summarized, being supported by a detailed Schedule of Operating Expenses (Figure 14-5). Had there been many significant types of operating revenues, these too might have been shown in summary and supported by a detailed schedule. The format for an interim Statement of Revenue and Expense is shown in Figure 14-12.

*Statement of changes in financial position.* The fourth primary statement recommended for Enterprise Funds by the NCGA is the Statement of Sources and Application of Cash Funds. The Accounting Principles Board of the AICPA subsequently recommended in Opinion 19 that (1) a statement of this nature should be titled "Statement of Changes in Financial Position," (2) the statement should be based on a broad concept of cash or working capital that embraces all changes in financial position, and (3) the concept or basis of preparation should be clearly disclosed.

As noted in Chapter 13, considerable flexibility of both concept and format are permissible insofar as statements summarizing changes in financial position are concerned. It is imperative, however, that all important financing and in-

Figure 14-6

## A GOVERNMENTAL UNIT
### Electric (Enterprise) Fund
### Worksheet for the Period Ended (Date)

| | Transactions and Adjustments Dr. | Transactions and Adjustments Cr. | Pre-closing Trial Balance (End of Period) Dr. | Pre-closing Trial Balance (End of Period) Cr. | Closing Entries (Revenues and Expenses) Dr. | Closing Entries (Revenues and Expenses) Cr. | Balance Sheet (End of Period) Dr. | Balance Sheet (End of Period) Cr. |
|---|---|---|---|---|---|---|---|---|
| Cash ............... | (1) 400,000 (11) 290,000 (15) 1,000 (24b) 14 (27) 2,000 | (3) 280,000 (4) 127,200 (8) 500 (10) 1,000 (13) 50,000 (14) 20,000 (16) 10,500 (17) 70,000 (28) 2,000 (39) 45,000 | 86,814 | | | | 86,814 | |
| Contribution from Municipality ...... | | (1) 400,000 | | 400,000 | | | | 400,000 |
| Land ....................... | (2) 50,000 | | 50,000 | | | | 50,000 | |
| Buildings.................... | (2) 100,000 | | 100,000 | | | | 100,000 | |
| Allowance for Depreciation—Buildings ......... | | (2) 10,000 (19h) 5,000 | | 15,000 | | | | 15,000 |
| Improvements Other Than Buildings ...... | (2) 550,000 (18) 30,000 (36) 197,000 | | 777,000 | | | | 777,000 | |
| Allowance for Depreciation—Improvements Other Than Buildings ...... | | (2) 70,000 (19h) 15,000 | | 85,000 | | | | 85,000 |
| Machinery and Equipment ...... | (2) 150,000 (7) 50,500 | | 200,500 | | | | 200,500 | |

Figure 14-6 (cont.)

| | Transactions and Adjustments | | Pre-closing Trial Balance (End of Period) | | Closing Entries (Revenues and Expenses) | | Balance Sheet (End of Period) | |
|---|---|---|---|---|---|---|---|---|
| | Dr. | Cr. | Dr. | Cr. | Dr. | Cr. | Dr. | Cr. |
| Allowance for Depreciation—Machinery and Equipment ........ | | (2) 40,000<br>(19h) 16,000 | | 56,000 | | | | 56,000 |
| Accounts Receivable ........ | (2) 62,000<br>(6) 300,000 | (11) 290,000<br>(24a) 22<br>(25) 10 | 71,968 | | | | 71,968 | |
| Allowance for Uncollectible Accounts ........ | (24a) 8 | (2) 12,000<br>(19g) 1,500 | | 13,492 | | | | 13,492 |
| Inventory of Materials and Supplies ........ | (2) 10,000<br>(5) 59,000 | (19f) 39,000 | 30,000 | | | | 30,000 | |
| Bonds Payable ........ | (13) 50,000 | (2) 500,000<br>(27) 200,000 | | 650,000 | | | | |
| Vouchers Payable ........ | (17) 70,000 | (2) 10,000<br>(5) 59,000<br>(7) 50,500 | | 49,500 | | | | 49,500 |
| ABC Electric Company ........ | (3) 280,000 | (2) 280,000 | | | | | | |
| Operating Expenses ........ | (4) 127,200<br>(8) 500<br>(10) 1,000<br>(12) 12,800<br>(19a) 6,000<br>(19f) 39,000<br>(19g) 1,500<br>(41) 7,000 | (19e) 600 | 194,400 | | (46) 194,400 | | | |
| Operating Revenues ........ | | (6) 300,000<br>(19i) 21,000 | | 321,000 | (46) 321,000 | | | |
| Due from State Public Works Department ...... | (9) 7,000 | | 7,000 | | | | 7,000 | |
| Nonoperating Revenues—Equipment Rental ... | | (9) 7,000 | | 7,000 | (46) 7,000 | | | |
| Due to Intragovernmental Service Fund ........ | | (12) 12,800 | | 12,800 | | | | 12,800 |

606

| Account | Debit (Ref / Amount) | | |
|---|---|---|---|
| Interest Expense | (14) 20,000<br>(19b) 2,000<br>(23) 150<br>(40) 15,000<br>(44) 5,700 | 42,850 | (46) 42,850 |
| Interest Revenue | (15) 1,000<br>(19c) 200<br>(22) 200<br>(43) 450 | 18,000 | 1,850   (46) 1,850   (46) 18,000 |
| Taxes | (16) 10,500<br>(19d) 7,500 | | |
| Contribution from Subdividers | (18) 30,000 | 30,000 | 30,000 |
| Accrued Salaries and Wages Payable | (19a) 6,000 | 6,000 | 6,000 |
| Accrued Interest Payable | (19b) 2,000 | 2,000 | 2,000 |
| Accrued Interest Receivable | (19c) 200 | 200 | 200 |
| Accrued Taxes Payable | (19d) 7,500 | 7,500 | 7,500 |
| Prepaid Insurance | (19e) 600 | 600 | 600 |
| Depreciation Expense | (19h) 36,000 | 36,000 | (46) 36,000 |
| Unbilled Accounts Receivable | (19i) 21,000 | 21,000 | 21,000 |
| Customers' Deposits—Cash | (20) 11,000<br>(21) 10,000<br>(24b) 14<br>(25) 8 | 978 | 978 |
| Customers' Deposits Payable | (20) 11,000 | 10,973 | 10,973 |
| Customers' Deposits—Investments | (21) 10,000 | 10,000 | 10,000 |
| Customers' Deposits—Accrued Interest Receivable | (22) 200 | 200 | 200 |
| Customers' Deposits—Accrued Interest Payable | (23) 150<br>(24a) 2<br>(25) 3 | 145 | 145 |
| Retained Earnings | (26) 60<br>(45) 22,450 | 22,510 | 16,090<br>(46) 38,600 |
| Reserve for Earnings on Customers' Deposits | (26) 60 | 60 | 60 |
| Construction—Cash | (27) 200,000<br>(30) 41,000<br>(32) 30,000<br>(33) 56,000<br>(35) 60,000<br>(37) 10,000<br>(38) 3,000 | | |

### Figure 14-6 (cont.)

| Account | Transactions and Adjustments Dr. | Transactions and Adjustments Cr. | Pre-closing Trial Balance (End of Period) Dr. | Pre-closing Trial Balance (End of Period) Cr. | Closing Entries (Revenues and Expenses) Dr. | Closing Entries (Revenues and Expenses) Cr. | Balance Sheet (End of Period) Dr. | Balance Sheet (End of Period) Cr. |
|---|---|---|---|---|---|---|---|---|
| Unamortized Premiums on Bonds | (44) 300 | (27) 2,000 | | 1,700 | | | | 1,700 |
| Debt Service—Cash | (28) 2,000 (38) 3,000 (39) 25,000 | (40) 15,000 | 15,000 | | | | 15,000 | |
| Construction Work in Progress | (29) 41,000 (31) 30,000 (33) 56,000 (34) 70,000 | (36) 197,000 | | | | | | |
| Construction Vouchers Payable | (30) 41,000 | (29) 41,000 | | | | | | |
| Construction Contracts Payable | (32) 30,000 | (31) 30,000 | | | | | | |
| Construction Contracts Payable—Retained Percentage | (35) 70,000 | (34) 70,000 | | | | | | |
| Principal and Interest Reserve—Cash | (37) 10,000 (39) 10,000 (43) 300 | (35) 10,000 (42) 9,000 | 1,300 | | | | 1,300 | |
| Contingencies—Cash | (39) 10,000 | | 10,000 | | | | 10,000 | |
| Contingencies—Vouchers Payable | | (41) 7,000 | | 7,000 | | | | 7,000 |
| Principal and Interest Reserve—Investments | (42) 9,000 | | 9,000 | | | | 9,000 | |
| Principal and Interest Reserve—Accrued Interest Receivable | (43) 150 | | 150 | | | | 150 | |
| Debt Service—Accrued Bond Interest Payable | | (44) 6,000 | | 6,000 | | | | 6,000 |
| Reserve for Bond Debt Service | | (45) 9,000 | | 9,000 | | | | 9,000 |
| Reserve for Bond Principal and Interest | | | | | | | | |
| Payments Guarantee | | (45) 10,450 | | 10,450 | | | | 10,450 |
| Reserve for Contingencies | | (45) 3,000 | | 3,000 | | | | 3,000 |
| | 3,623,664 | 3,623,664 | 1,705,470 | 1,705,470 | 329,850 | 329,850 | 1,391,710 | 1,391,710 |

**Figure 14-7**

## A GOVERNMENTAL UNIT
Electric (Enterprise) Fund
Statement of Changes in (Unrestricted Cash) Financial Position
For Period Ended (Date)

Sources of unrestricted cash:
Operations:

| | | | |
|---|---|---|---|
| Net Income (Figure 14-4) ................. | | $ 38,600 | |
| Add:  Expenses not currently requiring unrestricted cash outlays— | | | |
| Depreciation of facilities and equipment .................... | $ 36,000 | | |
| Increase in current liabilities ......... | 67,800 | 103,800 | |
| Deduct:  Deductions from expenses not affecting cash requirements: | | | |
| Amortization of bond premium ........... | $    300 | | |
| Increase in current receivables (net of allowance for uncollectible accounts)..... | 36,676 | | |
| Increase in inventory of materials and supplies........................... | 20,000 | | |
| Increase in prepaid insurance ........... | 600 | ⟨57,576⟩ | |
| Total provided by operations .............. | | | $ 84,824 |

Other sources:

| | | |
|---|---|---|
| Contribution from municipality ............. | 400,000 | |
| Assumption of ABC bonds payable .......... | 500,000 | |
| Assumption of ABC vouchers payable ....... | 10,000 | |
| Issuance of bonds ........................ | 202,000 | |
| Contribution from subdividers ............. | 30,000 | |
| Total provided by other sources ........ | | 1,142,000 |
| Total provided  ........................... | | $1,226,824 |

Uses of unrestricted cash:

| | |
|---|---|
| Acquisition of land ........................ | 50,000 |
| Acquisition of buildings .................... | 90,000 |
| Acquisition of improvements other than buildings ............................. | 707,000 |
| Acquisition of machinery and equipment ....... | 160,500 |
| Acquisition of initial accounts receivable ....... | 50,000 |
| Acquisition of initial inventory of materials and supplies................................ | 10,000 |
| Retirement of bonds ....................... | 50,000 |

**Figure 14-7 (cont.)**

| | | | |
|---|---|---|---|
| Increases in net assets restricted for: | | | |
| Customers' deposits ...................... | $ 60 | | |
| Debt service ........................... | 9,000 | | |
| Principal and interest reserve .............. | 10,450 | | |
| Contingencies ......................... | 3,000 | 22,510 | |
| Total uses................................ | | | 1,140,010 |
| Increase in unrestricted cash .................. | | | $ 86,814 |

vesting activities be disclosed, even those that do not directly affect cash or other working capital elements.[3] A Statement of Changes in Financial Position prepared on the cash concept preferred by the NCGA is illustrated in Figure 14-7; the worksheet by which it was derived is presented as Figure 14-8. A Statement of Changes in Financial Position prepared on the working capital concept is contained in Figure 14-9.

*Other statements and schedules.* As noted earlier, other statements and schedules may be needed to complete the annual financial presentation for an Enterprise Fund or on an interim basis. Formats for two of the more common of those prepared annually, the Statement of Changes in Assets Restricted for Revenue Bond Service and the Schedule of Fixed Assets and Depreciation, are presented for A Governmental Unit's Water and Sewer (Enterprise) Fund in Figures 14-10 and 14-11, respectively. The format for the Comparative Statement of Revenue and Expense that should be prepared monthly or quarterly for the Water and Sewer (Enterprise) Fund is shown in Figure 14-12.

## SUMMARY OF INTERFUND ACCOUNTING

At this point in the text all the funds and nonfund account groups commonly employed in state and local government accounting have been presented and discussed. It should be evident by now that the use of separate funds and account groups is the dominating characteristic of contemporary governmental accounting.

It should also be evident that mastery of fund accounting concepts and procedures, both as to individual funds and nonfund account groups and collectively as they relate to one another, is essential to obtaining an in-depth understanding of governmental accounting. Although the procedural details have been described in this and preceding chapters, it is appropriate at this

---

[3] A detailed discussion of the underlying concepts and preparation techniques for the statement of changes in financial position is beyond the scope of this text. The reader desiring a detailed treatment of this topic is referred to Accounting Principles Board (APB) Opinions 3 and 19 and to any standard intermediate accounting textbook.

point to summarize and review some of the principal concepts that evolve from these discussions of accounting procedures for each fund and account group.

INDEPENDENT FISCAL AND ACCOUNTING ENTITIES.    Each fund and nonfund account group is an independent fiscal entity and must be accounted for as such. The accounting system must be so devised that the assets, liabilities, capital or balances (reserves, unreserved fund balance, contributed capital, retained earnings), revenues, and expenditures or expenses are identified with the particular fund or nonfund account group entity to which they apply. It follows that each entity must have a self-balancing group of accounts. It does *not* follow that a separate ledger must be established for each fund and nonfund account group. The accounts required may be maintained either (1) in separate ledgers or (2) in a single ledger or computer file in which the fund and nonfund entities are distinguished through an appropriate account classification code.

A fund does not necessarily consist only of cash. It may also contain other assets—such as receivables, inventories, and even fixed assets—as well as the liabilities (either in total or those that have matured) that are to be discharged from its resources. Cash segregated for certain purposes does not necessarily constitute a fund, though it may constitute either a fund or a "fund" in the Enterprise Fund and commercial accounting sense.

TYPES OF INDEPENDENT FISCAL ENTITIES.    We have classified the various funds and nonfund account groups into three categories for purposes of discussion and analysis:

Expendable funds:
  General
  Special Revenue
  Capital Projects
  Special Assessment
  Debt Service
  Trust (expendable)
  Agency

Nonexpendable funds:
  Intragovernmental Service
  Enterprise
  Trust (nonexpendable)

Nonfund account groups:
  General Fixed Assets
  General Long-Term Debt

The expendable fund, nonexpendable fund, nonfund account group classification is a useful one since (1) many conceptual and procedural similarities are shared by the funds or nonfund account groups within each category, and (2) major conceptual and procedural characteristics distinguish each of the three

**Figure 14-8**

A GOVERNMENTAL UNIT

Electric (Enterprise) Fund

Worksheet for Statement of Changes in (Unrestricted Cash)

Financial Position For the Year Ended (Date)

(First Year of Operation by Governmental Unit)

| Debits | Beginning of Period | Changes Dr. | | Changes Cr. | End of Period |
|---|---|---|---|---|---|
| Cash ........................... | — | (21) | 86,814 | | 86,814 |
| Land ........................... | — | (2) | 50,000 | | 50,000 |
| Buildings ....................... | — | (2) | 100,000 | | 100,000 |
| Improvements Other Than Buildings | — | (2) | 550,000 | | 777,000 |
| | | (5) | 30,000 | | |
| | | (9) | 197,000 | | |
| Machinery and Equipment ........ | — | (2) | 150,000 | | 200,500 |
| | | (3) | 50,500 | | |
| Accounts Receivable .............. | — | (2) | 62,000 | | 71,968 |
| | | (13) | 9,968 | | |
| Inventory of Materials and Supplies.. | — | (2) | 10,000 | | 30,000 |
| | | (14) | 20,000 | | |
| Due from State Public Works Dept .. | — | (13) | 7,000 | | 7,000 |
| Accrued Interest Receivable ....... | — | (13) | 200 | | 200 |
| Prepaid Insurance ................ | — | (15) | 600 | | 600 |
| Unbilled Accounts Receivable ...... | — | (13) | 21,000 | | 21,000 |
| Customers' Deposits—Cash ........ | — | (16) | 978 | | 978 |
| Customers' Deposits—Investments .. | — | (16) | 10,000 | | 10,000 |
| Customers' Deposits—Accrued Interest Receivable ............. | — | (16) | 200 | | 200 |
| Debt Service—Cash ............... | — | (17) | 15,000 | | 15,000 |
| Principal and Interest Revenue— Cash .......................... | — | (18) | 1,300 | | 1,300 |
| Contingencies—Cash .............. | — | (19) | 10,000 | | 10,000 |
| Principal and Interest Reserve— Investments .................... | — | (18) | 9,000 | | 9,000 |
| Principal and Interest Reserve— Accrued Interest Receivable ..... | — | (18) | 150 | | 150 |
| | — | | | | 1,391,710 |

**Figure 14-8 (cont.)**

| Credits | Beginning of Period | Changes Dr. | Changes Cr. | End of Period |
|---|---|---|---|---|
| Contribution from Municipality .... | — | | (1) 400,000 | 400,000 |
| Allowance for Depreciation— | | | | |
| Buildings ..................... | — | | (2) 10,000 | 15,000 |
| | | | (6) 5,000 | |
| Allowance for Depreciation— | | | | |
| Improvements Other Than | | | | |
| Buildings ..................... | — | | (2) 70,000 | 85,000 |
| | | | (6) 15,000 | |
| Allowance for Depreciation— | | | | |
| Machinery and Equipment ...... | — | | (2) 40,000 | 56,000 |
| | | | (6) 16,000 | |
| Allowance for Uncollectible Accounts | — | | (2) 12,000 | 13,492 |
| | | | (13) 1,492 | |
| Bonds Payable .................. | — | (4) 50,000 | (2) 500,000 | 650,000 |
| | | | (8) 200,000 | |
| Vouchers Payable ............... | — | | (2) 10,000 | 49,500 |
| | | | (20) 39,500 | |
| Due to Intragovernmental Service | | | | |
| Fund ........................ | — | | (20) 12,800 | 12,800 |
| Contribution from Subdividers ..... | — | | (5) 30,000 | 30,000 |
| Accrued Salaries and Wages Payable | — | | (20) 6,000 | 6,000 |
| Accrued Interest Payable .......... | — | | (20) 2,000 | 2,000 |
| Accrued Taxes Payable ........... | — | | (20) 7,500 | 7,500 |
| Customers' Deposits Payable........ | — | | (16) 10,973 | 10,973 |
| Customers' Deposits—Accrued | | | | |
| Interest Payable ............... | — | | (16) 145 | 145 |
| Retained Earnings ............... | — | (7) 60 | (12) 38,600 | 16,090 |
| | | (11) 22,450 | | |
| Reserve for Earnings on Customers' | | | | |
| Deposits ..................... | — | | (7) 60 | 60 |
| Unamortized Premiums on Bonds ... | — | (10) 300 | (8) 2,000 | 1,700 |
| Contingencies—Vouchers Payable .. | — | | (19) 7,000 | 7,000 |
| Debt Service—Accrued Bond | | | | |
| Interest Payable ............... | — | | (17) 6,000 | 6,000 |
| Reserve for Bond Debt Service ..... | — | | (11) 9,000 | 9,000 |
| Reserve for Bond Principal and | | | | |
| Interest Payments Guarantee ..... | — | | (11) 10,450 | 10,450 |
| Reserve for Contingencies .......... | — | | (11) 3,000 | 3,000 |
| | — | | | 1,391,710 |

**Figure 14-8** (cont.)

|  | Sources | Uses |
|---|---|---|
| *Unrestricted cash was provided by:* | | |
| Operations— | | |
| Net Income (Figure 14-4) | (12) 38,600 | |
| Adjustments to derive cash effect: | | |
| Depreciation expense | (6) 36,000 | |
| Increase in current liabilities | (20) 67,800 | |
| Amortization of bond premium | | (10) 300 |
| Increase in current receivables (net) | | (13) 36,676 |
| Increase in materials and supplies inventory | | (14) 20,000 |
| Increase in prepaid insurance | | (15) 600 |
| | 142,400 | 57,576 |
| | | (√) 84,824 |
| | 142,400 | 142,400 |
| Net Provided by Operations | (√) 84,824 | |
| Other Sources— | | |
| Contributions from Municipality | (1) 400,000 | |
| Assumption of ABC bond liability | (2) 500,000 | |
| Assumption of ABC vouchers payable | (2) 10,000 | |
| Contributions from subdividers | (5) 30,000 | |
| Issuance of bonds | (8) 202,000 | |
| | 1,142,000 | |
| *Unrestricted cash used for:* | | |
| Acquisition of ABC Electric Company properties: | | |
| Land | | (2) 50,000 |
| Buildings | | (2) 90,000 |
| Improvements other than buildings | | (2) 480,000 |
| Machinery and equipment | | (2) 110,000 |
| Accounts receivable | | (2) 50,000 |
| Inventory | | (2) 10,000 |
| Other acquisitions: | | |
| Machinery and equipment | | (3) 50,500 |
| Improvements other than buildings | | (9) 197,000 |
| | | (5) 30,000 |
| Retirement of bonds payable | | (4) 50,000 |
| Increase in Customers' Deposits fund equity | | (16) 60 |
| Increase in Debt Service fund equity | | (17) 9,000 |
| Increase in Principal and Interest Payments | | |
| Guarantee fund equity | | (18) 10,450 |
| Increase in Contingencies fund equity | | (19) 3,000 |
| | | 1,140,010 |
| Increase in cash | | (21) 86,814 |
| | 1,226,824 | 1,226,824 |

**Figure 14-8 (cont.)**

| Changes in Unrestricted Cash Worksheet Key | Problem Transaction and Worksheet Key | Explanation |
|:---:|:---:|:---|
| (1) | (1) | Establishment of Electricity (Enterprise) Fund. |
| (2) | (2) (3) | Acquisition of ABC Electric Company. |
| (3) | (7) | Acquisition of machinery and equipment (assumes voucher related thereto was paid). |
| (4) | (13) | Retirement of bond principal. |
| (5) | (18) | Subdivider donation of electricity distribution system. |
| (6) | (19h) | Depreciation recorded. |
| (7) | (26) | Established Reserve for Earnings on Customers' Deposits. |
| (8) | (27) | Issued bonds for construction. |
| (9) | (36) | Construction of improvements. |
| (10) | (44) | Amortization of bond premium. |
| (11) | (45) | Established reserves. |
| (12) | (46) | Net income determined and closed to Retained Earnings. |
| (13–21) | | Derived logically. |

categories from the others. Thus, we have seen that (1) the primary focus of expendable fund accounting is upon flows (revenues and expenditures) and balances of appropriable resources, usually in relation to budgetary estimates or limitations, and that expendable funds are comprised primarily of current assets and related current liabilities, (2) the nonfund account groups provide accountability for nonappropriable (fixed) assets and for long-term liabilities that are not to be discharged from assets of a particular fund during the current accounting period, and (3) the nonexpendable funds are accounted for in generally the same manner as are private commercial enterprises, that is, the accounting focus is upon revenues and expenses (not expenditures) and both current and fixed assets and liabilities are included within the nonexpendable fund accounts.

DIFFERENCES IN BUDGETARY CONTROL EMPHASIS. The revenue and expenditure transactions of most expendable funds are customarily planned and controlled through the use of rather rigid fixed dollar budgets and appropriations. This is particularly true of the General, Special Revenue, Capital Projects, and Debt Service Funds. In order to facilitate budgetary control and comparision in these funds, both budgetary and proprietary accounts are maintained within their account structures.

On the other hand, nonexpendable fund activities are more commonly planned through flexible budgeting techniques because their transactions are determined by the level of demand for their goods or services or by other factors.

Figure 14-9

A GOVERNMENTAL UNIT
Electric (Enterprise) Fund
Statement of Changes in (Working Capital) Financial Position
For Period Ended (Date)

*Sources of Working Capital*

| | | |
|---|---:|---:|
| Operations: | | |
| Net Income (Figure 14-4) ................... | $ 38,600 | |
| Add:   Expenses not currently requiring working capital— | | |
|      Depreciation of facilities and equipment | 36,000 | |
| Deduct:   Deductions from expense not currently providing working capital— | | |
|      Amortization of bond premium ...... | ⟨300⟩ | |
| Total provided by operations ................ | | $ 74,300 |
| Other Sources: | | |
| Contribution from municipality .............. | $400,000 | |
| Contributions from subdividers............... | 30,000 | |
| Assumption of ABC bonds................... | 500,000 | |
| Issuance of bonds .......................... | 202;000 | |
|      Total provided from other sources .......... | | 1,132,000 |
| Total provided ........................... | | $1,206,300 |

*Uses of Working Capital*

| | | | |
|---|---:|---:|---:|
| Acquisition of land .......................... | | 50,000 | |
| Acquisition of buildings ...................... | | 90,000 | |
| Acquisition of improvements other than buildings.. | | 707,000 | |
| Acquisition of machinery and equipment ......... | | 160,500 | |
| Retirement of bonds ......................... | | 50,000 | |
| Increase in net assets restricted for: ............. | | | |
|      Customers' deposits ........................ | $    60 | | |
|      Debt service ............................. | 9,000 | | |
|      Principal and interest reserve ................ | 10,450 | | |
|      Contingencies ........................... | 3,000 | 22,510 | |
| Total uses................................. | | | 1,080,010 |
| Increase in working capital ................... | | | $   126,290 |

Figure 14-10

A GOVERNMENTAL UNIT
Water and Sewer (Enterprise) Fund
Format for Statement of Changes in Assets Restricted for Revenue Bond
Debt Service for the Fiscal Year Ended December 31, 19X2

| | Cash With Fiscal Agents | Debt Service | Reserve | Contin-gency | Total |
|---|---|---|---|---|---|
| Cash balance, January 1, 19X2 . . . . . . . . . . . | | | | | |
| Cash receipts: | | | | | |
| Transfers from operating cash . . . . . . . . . . | | | | | |
| Interest earnings on investments . . . . . . . . | | | | | |
| Transfer from Revenue Bond Debt Service cash . . . . . . . . . . . . . . . . . . . . | | | | | |
| Total cash available . . . . . . . . . . . . . . . . . | | | | | |
| Cash disbursements: | | | | | |
| Principal payments . . . . . . . . . . . . . . . . . . | | | | | |
| Interest payments . . . . . . . . . . . . . . . . . . | | | | | |
| Fiscal agents' fees . . . . . . . . . . . . . . . . . . | | | | | |
| Purchase of investments . . . . . . . . . . . . . . | | | | | |
| Transfer to fiscal agent . . . . . . . . . . . . . . | | | | | |
| Total disbursements . . . . . . . . . . . . . . . . | | | | | |
| Cash balance, December 31, 19X2 . . . . . . . | | | | | |
| Investment balance, January 1, 19X2 . . . . . | | | | | |
| Additions . . . . . . . . . . . . . . . . . . . . . . . . . . | | | | | |
| Deductions . . . . . . . . . . . . . . . . . . . . . . . | | | | | |
| Investment balance, December 31, 19X2 . . . | | | | | |
| Total cash and investments, December 31, 19X2 . . . . . . . . . . . . . . . . . . . . . . . . . . . . | | | | | |

Thus, budgetary accounts are not usually included in their account structures. In those cases where nonexpendable funds are subject to budget and appropriation controls, budgetary accounts may be made a part of their accounting system but are not ordinarily combined with the proprietary accounts. Furthermore, usually only those budgetary constraints embodied in legal provisions are included as part of the nonexpendable fund accounting system; all other budgetary operations are recorded in budget memoranda accounts. For example,

Figure 14-11

A GOVERNMENTAL UNIT

Water and Sewer (Enterprise) Fund

Format for Schedule of Fixed Assets and Depreciation

For the Fiscal Year Ended December 31, 19X2

| | Assets | | | | Allowance for Depreciation | | | |
|---|---|---|---|---|---|---|---|---|
| | *Balances (Beginning of Year)* | *Additions* | *Deductions* | *Balances (End of Year)* | *Balances (Beginning of Year)* | *Depre- ciation Taken* | *Balances (End of Year)* | *Net Book Value* |
| Land | | | | | | | | |
| Buildings: | | | | | | | | |
| Water system | | | | | | | | |
| Sewer system | | | | | | | | |
| Total—buildings | | | | | | | | |
| Improvements Other Than Buildings: | | | | | | | | |
| Water mains | | | | | | | | |
| Water towers and reservoirs | | | | | | | | |
| Water service connections | | | | | | | | |
| Sewer gathering lines | | | | | | | | |
| Sewage disposal plant | | | | | | | | |
| Total—Improvements other than buildings | | | | | | | | |

Machinery and equipment:
Water meters
Fire hydrants
Water purification plant and
    equipment
Pumping equipment
Laboratory equipment
Tools and working equipment
Automobiles and trucks
Office furniture and equipment
Other equipment
    Total machinery and equipment
Construction Work in Progress
Grand Totals

**Figure 14-12**

A GOVERNMENTAL UNIT
Water and Sewer (Enterprise) Fund
Format for Comparative Statement of Revenue and Expense
For the Months of September, 19X1 and 19X2 and
Nine Months Ending September 30, 19X1 and 19X2

|  | | *Nine Months Ending* | |
|---|---|---|---|
| *September 19X2* | *September 19X1* | *Sept. 30, 19X2* | *Sept. 30, 19X1* |

Operating Revenues:
  Metered water sales
  Bulk water sales
  Sewer service charges
  Sales of stores
  Customers' forfeited discount
    Total operating revenues
Less: Operating revenue deductions before
  depreciation:
  Operating expenses
  Cost of stores sold
  Taxes
    Total operating revenue deductions before
    depreciation
Net Operating Income Before Depreciation
Less: Depreciation
Net Operating Income

Add: Non-operating Income:
  Rent—Non-operating property
  Interest earnings
  Income Before Non-operating Expenses

Less: Non-operating expenses:
  Interest expense—Revenue bonds
  Interest expense—General obligation bonds
  Fiscal agents' fees
    Total Non-operating Expenses
Net Income

Note: Alternatively the statement may compare actual results to date with the flexible budget for the period.

estimated revenues of nonexpendable funds rarely need to be recorded formally in the accounts.

SEPARATION OF RELATED ASSETS AND LIABILITIES. The use of special purpose fund and nonfund account group entities often results in related assets and liabilities being accounted for through different accounting entities. For example, special assessment improvements are included in the General Fixed Assets accounts, whereas special assessment debt is shown as a liability of a Special Assessment Fund. Likewise, though bond issue proceeds are accounted for through a Capital Projects Fund, the related liability is included in the General Long-Term Debt group of accounts.

DIFFERENCES IN RECORDING ASSETS AND LIABILITIES. Because of the differing natures of the funds and account groups, identical types of assets and liabilities may be included in some funds and excluded from others. For example, fixed assets and bonds payable are included within an Enterprise Fund but not in the General Fund. Again, special assessment bonds payable are shown as a liability of the appropriate Special Assessment Fund, but the special assessment improvements are not capitalized therein.

DIFFERENCES IN THE BASIS OF ACCOUNTING. Differences in the nature and accounting focus of the various funds also cause differences in the bases of accounting employed. The modified accrual basis is used for some, whereas the full accrual basis is employed for others.

The basis upon which appropriations are made *dictates* the basis of accounting in those funds subject to rigid budgetary control. The modified accrual basis is recommended for those funds most commonly subject to formalized budgetary control—the General, Special Revenue, and Debt Service funds—because it parallels the usual manner in which budgets are prepared and appropriations are made. The modified accrual basis results in revenues being recorded only when appropriable resources become available; and expenditures for interest on long-term debt are reflected in the period in which they are to be paid, the period for which an appropriation will be made, rather than on the basis of time remaining prior to maturity.

Where the modified accrual basis of accounting is used, it may be necessary to adjust the asset and liability accounts at year end, and to increase or decrease the Fund Balance (either reserved or unreserved) accounts correspondingly, in order that the financial position of the fund may be reported properly. For example, inventory adjustments are handled in this manner when appropriations are based on inventory purchases rather than on usage. Furthermore, it may be necessary to issue supplementary revenue and expenditure statements where, because of local legal requirements or custom, those prepared routinely are not in accordance with generally accepted principles of accounting.

The full accrual basis is followed in accounting for nonexpendable funds because it is essential here to determine periodic net income or loss. Under this basis, revenues are recorded as soon as they are earned, regardless of when they will be collected; and expenses are recorded when incurred, regardless of when they will be paid. Furthermore, depreciation and amortization are recorded within the accounts of nonexpendable funds in order that all expenses may be reported and capital increments or decrements may be fairly presented.

ACCOUNTS OF FUNDS V. ACCOUNTS OF THE GOVERNMENTAL UNIT. Much of the foregoing summary points up a final observation: In governmental accounting the sum of the parts may not equal the whole. Rather, the revenues of the governmental unit as a whole are likely to be smaller than the sum of the revenues of its various funds, and the same may be said for expenditures. For example, consider the contributed revenues of the Debt Service Fund or the billings for services of an Intragovernmental Service Fund. These items represent revenues to the individual funds, but not to the governmental unit. In the same manner, certain fund expenditures may not be expenditures from the standpoint of the government as a whole.

Though some practicing accountants and academicians believe that interfund revenues, expenditures, receivables, and payables should be eliminated in the preparation of state and local government financial statements, such eliminations are vigorously opposed by the NCGA. Its opposition is predicated on the fact that most funds are created by law. Where this is the case, neither the accountant nor the management ordinarily has the authority to cancel or offset interfund receivables or payables; authority equivalent to that which established the funds would be required for such cancellation. Therefore, financial statement presentations of state and local governments usually follow the law, and (1) interfund receivables and payables appear in both individual fund and combined fund balance sheets, and (2) individual fund revenue and expenditure data do not add to meaningful totals to the extent that they include amounts that are not revenues or expenditures of the governmental unit as a whole.

**Question 14-1.** How should one determine whether a particular activity should be accounted for through an Enterprise Fund?

**Question 14-2.** The garbage collection and disposal services of a local government might be accounted for through the General Fund, a Special Revenue Fund, a Special Assessment Fund, or an Enterprise Fund. Indicate the circumstances in which each of these fund types might be the appropriate accounting vehicle for such an activity.

**Question 14-3.** How does one distinguish between an Intragovernmental Service and an Enterprise Fund?

**Question 14-4.** Contrast and explain the accounting distinction made between revenues and capital investments or disinvestments in a nonexpendable fund such as the Enterprise Fund with that made in an expendable fund.

**Question 14-5.** What is the purpose of net worth reserves in Enterprise Fund accounting?

**Question 14-6.** An asset costing $10,000 was transferred from the General Fixed

Assets group of accounts of a governmental unit to the governmental unit's enterprise. What effect would this transfer have on the General Fund and the Enterprise Fund, respectively?

**Question 14-7.** Township City is located adjacent to a freeway leading to a nearby metropolitan area and has grown rapidly from a small village to a city of 75,000. Its population is expected to continue to double every ten years in the foreseeable future. The city has owned and operated the local electricity generation and distribution system since its inception many years ago and has never charged itself for electricity consumption. The newly employed comptroller of Township City seeks your advice in this regard. What is your response?

**Question 14-8.** (a) A utility bills its customers separately for services and for sales taxes. Should billings for sales taxes be included in Enterprise Fund revenues? (b) Suppose that the utility is not allowed to bill customers for the sales tax. However, rates have been raised by approximately the amount of the tax. Should the revenues be reduced by the amount of the sales tax? (c) Give the entries to show how the payment of the taxes by the governmental utility (enterprise) would be recorded in each of the above cases.

**Question 14-9.** A certain city, wishing to acquire a privately owned utility, had an appraisal made of the property. The appraisers valued the assets on the basis of original cost less accrued depreciation and arrived at a value of $400,000. The owners refused to sell the plant for less than $425,000, however, and the municipality paid the full amount asked. Give the entry necessary to record the cash purchase of the utility by the municipality.

**Question 14-10. Part I.** A utility's engineer claims that no depreciation charges should be made during 19X1 on certain machines because these machines are operating with 95 percent efficiency, the same level as during the previous year. Are the engineer's claims correct?

**Question 14-10. Part II.** The engineers of a municipal utility claim that depreciation should not be charged since the city is spending money for maintaining the plant. Is their claim correct?

**Question 14-11.** It is sometimes claimed that to include depreciation among the expenses and to provide money out of earnings to retire bonds which were used to finance the acquisition of the assets being depreciated is to overcharge the current generation of customers. Through retiring the debt, the customers are paying for the old plant, and through depreciation charges they are paying for a new plant. Is this claim correct? Explain.

**Question 14-12.** Why is it not necessary to reserve Enterprise Fund Retained Earnings to the extent that assets are set aside in an equipment replacement intrafund "fund"? (Note particularly that this procedure is contrary to the practice followed in the case of a sinking "fund," where an amount corresponding to the addition made to the sinking fund is added to the appropriate reserve account.)

**Question 14-13.** Having been told repeatedly during his many years of service that depreciation was charged "in order to provide for the replacement of fixed assets," a member of a government's election utility (Enterprise Fund) board of directors was visibly upset upon being advised by the controller that it would be necessary for the utility to go deeply in debt "in order to replace some of our fixed assets." "How can it be true," he asks, "that we have operated profitably each year, have an $850,000 Retained Earnings balance and total Accumulated Depreciation account balances of $6,000,000, have never made transfers to the General Fund, and yet have Cash and Investments totaling only $100,000?"

**Question 14-14. Part I.** A pension fund is maintained through contributions from both a municipal utility and its employees and is administered by an independent pension board. (a) Should such a fund be shown as part of the Enterprise Fund? (b) Would your answer be different if contributions were made only by the utility?

**Question 14-14. Part II.** A utility carries a pension fund as part of the Enterprise Fund. Should earnings on pension fund investments be included in Enterprise Fund revenues?

**Question 14-15.** A local government council has jurisdiction over the electricity generation and distribution franchise rights in its area. Having exhausted its taxing and general obligation debt issue authority, it is considering the possibility of terminating the franchise held by a privately owned regulated utility now serving the area. Certain members of the council have proposed that this be done, noting that a municipally owned utility is not subject to state or Federal regulation, state or local property taxes, and Federal or state income taxes. They suggest that the present owners of the utility be offered municipal utility revenue bonds in the amount of the unamortized original cost values of the fixed assets on the utility books; in addition, the present owners would be permitted to keep the cash and investments now held by the utility to the extent that they exceed its current liabilities, and the municipality would assume the outstanding bonds of the utility. The proponents of the plan further suggest that the excess of the receipts of the municipally owned utility over current expenses and debt service requirements be transferred to the General Fund and used to finance current operations of the municipality. Assuming you are a newly elected member of the council, what questions would you raise with regard to the proposal?

**Question 14-16.** It is sometimes suggested that the amount contributed to a municipally-owned enterprise by the municipality or donated to it by others should be amortized to Retained Earnings as the property thereby acquired is depreciated in the accounts. Proponents of this amortization procedure believe that, in its absence, the Retained Earnings account is understated. Do you agree with the procedure proposed? Why?

**Question 14-17.** Does the term "accrual" refer to *what* is measured or to *when* measurement occurs? Explain.

**Question 14-18.** Why does the NCGA recommend the modified accrual basis of accounting for some funds and the accrual basis for others? Is this not inconsistent?

**Question 14-19.** A city controller has expressed his desire to convert the city's fund and nonfund account group records, now maintained in separate ledgers, to a system in which all accounts would be maintained within a single general ledger. Is this permissible? Explain.

**Question 14-20.** Which of the funds and nonfund account groups have what might be described as a budget? Explain.

**Question 14-21.** In governmental accounting, some funds are accounted for primarily on a period basis while the project is a more significant basis for reporting for others. State which basis is appropriate for each of the funds and nonfund account groups we have studied.

**Question 14-22. Part I.** In what funds may "Buildings" properly appear as an account title?

**Question 14-22. Part II.** For which types of funds are profit and loss (income determination) accounting procedures employed?

**Question 14-23.** If two companies which compose an economic unit have intercompany receivables and payables, these are eliminated in the preparation of a consolidated balance sheet. Should interfund receivables and payables be eliminated from the balance sheet of a governmental unit? Explain.

**Question 14-24.** Contrast and explain the differences in the accounting for bond premiums or discounts as among those arising upon the issue of general obligation construction bonds, special assessment bonds, and enterprise revenue bonds.

**Question 14-25.** What is the nature of the residual equity account(s) in each of the following funds?
a. General Fund
b. Special Revenue Fund
c. Capital Projects Fund
d. Debt Service Fund
e. Special Assessment Fund

(Note: Reserved or appropriated balance accounts need not be discussed.)

**Problem 14-1.** The City of Lenn operates its own municipal airport. The trial balance of the Airport Fund as of January 1, 19X0, was as follows:

| | | |
|---|---:|---:|
| Cash | $ 37,000 | |
| Accounts Receivable | 50,000 | |
| Allowance for Uncollectible Accounts | | $ 2,000 |
| Land | 200,000 | |
| Structures and Improvements | 700,000 | |
| Allowance for Depreciation—Structures and Improvements | | 50,000 |
| Equipment | 250,000 | |
| Allowance for Depreciation—Equipment | | 90,000 |
| Vouchers Payable | | 48,000 |
| Bonds Payable | | 800,000 |
| Governmental Unit's Contribution | | 200,000 |
| Retained Earnings | | 47,000 |
| | $1,237,000 | $1,237,000 |

The following transactions took place during the year:
1. Revenues collected in cash: aviation revenues, $340,500; concession revenues, $90,0000; revenues from airport management, $30,000; revenues from sales of petroleum products, etc. (net revenue, after deducting all costs relating to the sales), $10,500.
2. Expenses, all paid in cash with the exception of $24,000, which remained unpaid at December 31, were: operating, $222,000; maintenance, $75,000; general and administrative, $73,000.
3. Bad debts written off during the year, $1,900.
4. The vouchers payable outstanding on January 1, 19X0 were paid.
5. Bonds paid during the year, $50,000, together with interest of $40,000.
6. The remaining accounts receivable outstanding on January 1, 19X0, were collected.
7. Accounts receivable on December 31, 19X0 amounted to $30,000, all applicable to aviation revenues, of which $1,400 is estimated to be uncollectible.
8. Accrued interest payable at the end of the year amounted to $3,000.
9. Depreciation charges:

| | |
|---|---:|
| Structures and improvements | $14,000 |
| Equipment | 21,000 |

Required:

(a)   Prepare a worksheet to reflect the beginning trial balance, the transactions and adjustments during 19X0, the revenues and expenses of the year (or closing entries), and the ending balance sheet data.

(b)   Prepare a Balance Sheet for the Airport Fund as of December 31, 19X0.

(c)   Prepare a Revenue and Expense Statement for the Airport Fund for the fiscal year ended December 31, 19X0.

**Problem 14-2.**   The following is a list of the accounts of the Electric Utility Fund of the City of Ditten as of June 1, 19X7:

| | | |
|---|---:|---:|
| Cash ......................................... | $100,000 | |
| Construction Fund—Cash ....................... | 30,000 | |
| Deposits Fund—Cash ........................... | 2,000 | |
| Construction Fund—Expenditures ................ | 100,000 | |
| Construction Fund—Vouchers Payable............. | | $ 40,000 |
| Bonds Authorized—Unissued .................... | 50,000 | |
| Accounts Receivable .......................... | 77,000 | |
| Deposits Fund—Interest Payable ................ | | 350 |
| Deposits Fund—Interest Receivable ............. | 400 | |
| Deposits Fund—Investments .................... | 10,000 | |
| Deposits Funds—Surplus ....................... | | 2,050 |
| Deposits Payable ............................. | | 9,000 |
| Sinking Fund—Cash ........................... | 20,000 | |
| Sinking Fund—Investments .................... | 50,000 | |
| Sinking Fund—Unappropriated Surplus............ | | 5,000 |
| Unappropriated Surplus ....................... | | 139,000 |
| Vouchers Payable ............................. | | 5,000 |
| Inventory of Materials ........................ | 10,000 | |
| Allowance for Uncollectible Accounts ............. | | 4,600 |
| Appropriations ............................... | | 180,000 |
| Reserve for Retirement of Sinking Fund Bonds (Actuarial Requirement) ...................... | | 65,000 |

You are given the following additional information:

The electric utility was formerly accounted for in the same manner as any other department. Beginning with June 1, 19X7, the utility is to be accounted for as a self-supporting enterprise, no formal records are to be kept of appropriations or other authorizations, and proper account terminology is to be employed.

Fixed assets of the utility consist of the following:

| Assets | Cost | Allowance for Depreciation |
|---|---:|---:|
| Land .................... | $150,000 | — |
| Structures and Improvements | 320,000 | $60,000 |
| Equipment .............. | 105,000 | 30,000 |
| | $575,000 | $90,000 |

The utility began operations many years ago upon receiving a $360,000 cash contribution from the General Fund; the contribution was credited to Unappropriated Surplus.

Construction Fund expenditures were for construction work in progress.

Bonds outstanding amount to $300,000 at June 1, 19X7.

Required:

(a)  Prepare a worksheet from which to prepare a corrected Balance Sheet for the Electric Utility Fund of the City of Ditten at June 1, 19X7. Your worksheet columns should be headed as follows:

| Column(s) | Headings |
| --- | --- |
| 1–2 | Ledger Balances, June 1, 19X7—Dr. |
|  | Cr. |
| 3–4 | Adjustments and Corrections—Dr. |
|  | Cr. |
| 5–6 | Balance Sheet, June 1, 19X7—Dr. |
|  | Cr. |
| 7–10 | Balance Sheet Detail—Dr. (Cr.) |
| | Operations Construction Fund Sinking Fund Deposits Fund |

(b)  Prepare a Balance Sheet for the Electric Utility Fund of the City of Ditten as of June 1, 19X7, in proper and customary form.

**Problem 14-3.**  The City of Larkspur provides electric energy for its citizens through an operating department. All transactions of the Electric Department are recorded in a self-sustaining fund supported by revenue from the sales of energy. Plant expansion is financed by the issuance of bonds which are repaid out of revenues.

All cash of the Electric Department is held by the City Treasurer. Receipts from customers and others are deposited in the Treasurer's account. Disbursements are made by drawing warrants on the Treasurer.

The following is the postclosing trial balance of the Department as at June 30, 19X7:

| | | |
| --- | --- | --- |
| Cash on Deposit with City Treasurer .......... | $ 2,250,000 | |
| Due from Customers ........................ | 2,120,000 | |
| Other Current Assets ........................ | 130,000 | |
| Construction in Progress .................... | 500,000 | |
| Land ...................................... | 5,000,000 | |
| Electric Plant ............................. | 50,000,000* | |
| Accumulated Depreciation—Electric Plant ...... | | $10,000,000 |
| Accounts Payable and Accrued Liabilities ....... | | 3,270,000 |
| 5% Electric Revenue Bonds Payable .......... | | 20,000,000 |
| Accumulated Earnings ...................... | | 26,730,000 |
| | $60,000,000 | $60,000,000 |

* The plant is being depreciated on the basis of a 50-year composite life.

During the year ended June 30, 19X8, the Department had the following transactions:

1. Sales of electric energy, $10,700,000.
2. Purchases of fuel and operating supplies, $2,950,000.
3. Construction expenditures relating to miscellaneous system improvements (financed from operations), $750,000.
4. Fuel consumed, $2,790,000.
5. Miscellaneous plant additions and improvements constructed and placed in service at mid-year, $1,000,000.
6. Wages and salaries paid, $4,280,000.
7. Sale at par on December 31, 19X7 of 20-year 5 percent Electric Revenue bonds, dated January 1, 19X8, with interest payable semi-annually, $5,000,000.
8. Expenditures out of bond proceeds for construction of Larkspur Steam Plant Unit No. 1 and control house, $2,800,000.
9. Operating materials and supplies consumed, $150,000.
10. Payments received from customers, $10,500,000.
11. Expenditures out of bond proceeds for construction of Larkspur Steam Plant Unit No. 2, $2,200,000.
12. Warrants drawn on City Treasurer in settlement of accounts payable, $3,045,000.
13. The Larkspur Steam Plant was placed in service June 30, 19X8.
14. Interest on bonds paid during the year, $500,000.

Required:

(a) A worksheet for the Electric Department Fund showing:
    1. The balance sheet amounts at June 30, 19X7.
    2. The transactions for the year and closing entries. (Note: Formal journal entries are not required.)
    3. The balance sheet amounts at June 30, 19X8.

(b) A Statement of Changes in Financial Position (working capital basis) of the Electric Department Fund during the year ended June 30, 19X8, accompanied by a schedule of Changes in Working Capital.

**Problem 14-4.** From the following formation about the Water Department Fund of the City of Northwood: (1) prepare a worksheet showing the original trial balance, corrections and adjustments, corrected revenue and expense data, and balance sheet accounts; and (2) prepare in proper form a Balance Sheet, Statement of Revenue and Expense, and Analysis of Changes in the Retained Earnings for the year ended December 31, 19X4, for the Water Department Fund.

## LEDGER BALANCES, DECEMBER 31, 19X4

| | |
|---|---:|
| Cash—Operating Fund | $ 178,000 |
| Cash—Consumers' Deposits | 3,000 |
| Postage on Meter | 1,000 |
| Accounts Receivable: | |
|     Consumer billing | 65,000 |
|     Service | 17,000 |
|     Sundry | 700 |
| Due from Other Funds | — |
| Supplies Inventory | 40,000 |
| Goods on Order (Note 2) | 145,000 |

| | |
|---|---:|
| Investments—Consumers' Deposits | 74,000 |
| Property, Plant and Equipment | 6,000,000 |
| Accumulated Depreciation | 1,350,000 |
| Unfilled Orders (Note 2) | 145,000 |
| Warrants Payable | 50,100 |
| Due to Other Funds | — |
| Consumers' Advance Service Payments | — |
| Accounts Payable—Trade | 47,000 |
| Accounts Payable—County | 56,000 |
| Water Consumers' Deposits | 77,000 |
| Revenue Bonds Payable | 300,000 |
| Contributed Capital | 4,000,000 |
| Retained Earnings | 648,000 |
| Revenue Billings | 1,000,000 |
| Expense: | |
|     Production | 440,000 |
|     Distribution | 251,000 |
|     Office | 190,000 |
|     Administrative and General | 105,000 |
| Cost of Installations, Repairs, and Parts | 140,000 |
| Interest on Consumers' Deposits | 1,600 |
| Interest on Bonds | 16,000 |
| Billing Allowances and Adjustments | 5,000 |

Notes: (1) Revenue bonds mature serially at $30,000 each year.
      (2) Contra accounts are employed to establish accounting control over unfilled purchase orders outstanding. The Goods on Order account normally has a debit balance.

Examination of the records soon after December 31, 19X4 discloses the following data:

1. Included in error in Accounts Payable-Trade:
   a. For reimbursement of metered postage due to General Fund (Postage on meter at December 31, 19X4, $200.) ......... $ 500
   b. Due to other City funds ............................. 18,500
2. Items included in book inventory that were not received until 19X5 ............................................... $ 2,000
3. Computation of inventory items chargeable to distribution expense understated by................................... 1,200
4. Classified as Accounts Payable—Trade, should be Accounts Payable—County........................................ 10,000
5. Unfilled orders not of record ............................. 3,000
6. 19X5 expense purchases recorded as 19X4 liabilities and charged to expense as follows:
   a. Production expense ...................... $700

    b.   Distribution expense ...................... 500

    c.   Office expense .......................... 900

    d.   Administrative and general expense ........ 400

7.  Included in Accounts Receivable—Service, but actually due from other funds ...................................... 600

8.  Credit balances included in Accounts Receivable—Service .... 1,400

9.  Included in Accounts Receivable—Sundry but due from other City funds .......................................... 150

10.  Required adjustment to reduce Unfilled Orders Account to proper estimates of the cost of purchase orders outstanding .... 2,600

11.  Cancelled purchase order included in Unfilled Orders. This order was a duplication of a previously recorded expenditure.. 40,000

12.  Unrecorded receivable from City departments for water consumed ................................................ 5,000

13.  Unrecorded warrant payable for production expense ......... 2,300

14.  Overcharges in November consumer billings discovered ....... 1,150

15.  Unbilled receivables at December 31, 19X4 (unbilled receivables of $198,000 had been properly adjusted for at December 31, 19X3) .............................................. 230,000

16.  Minutes of the Council meeting of October 7, 19X4 contain a motion (passed) that a reserve for equipment replacement be established .......................................... 600,000

(AICPA, adapted)

**Problem 14-5.** The following information pertains to the operation of the Water Fund of the City of Marion. Included in the operations of this Fund are those of a Special Replacement Fund for the Water Department, the accounts of which are a part of the accounts of the Water Fund.

The balances in the accounts of this fund on January 1, 19X5 were as follows:

| | |
|---|---|
| Cash .................................................... | $ 6,126 |
| Accounts Receivable (net of $1,200 estimated to be uncollectible) .. | 7,645 |
| Stores .................................................. | 13,826 |
| Investments—Replacement Fund............................. | 21,700 |
| Property, Plant and Equipment ............................. | 212,604 |
| Accumulated Depreciation ................................. | 50,400 |
| Vouchers Payable ........................................ | 4,324 |
| Customers' Deposits* ..................................... | 1,500 |
| Replacement Fund Reserve ................................ | 21,700 |
| Retained Earnings ........................................ | 21,977 |
| Bonds Payable ........................................... | 60,000 |
| Contributed Capital ...................................... | 102,000 |

    * No restrictions are placed on deposits received or investment income thereon; interest is not paid on deposits.

The following items represent all transactions of the fund for the year ended December 31, 19X5:

| | | |
|---|---|---:|
| 1. | Services billed ........................................ | $146,867 |
| 2. | Accounts collected ................................... | 147,842 |
| 3. | Uncollectible accounts of prior years written off; current provision made, $750 ...................................... | 1,097 |
| 4. | Invoices and payrolls approved and vouchered for current expense ............................................... | 69,826 |
| 5. | Invoices approved and vouchered for Water Department stores purchased .......................................... | 31,424 |
| 6. | Stores issued for use in operation ........................ | 32,615 |
| 7. | Supplies secured from General Fund stores and used in operation (cash transferred to General Fund)...................... | 7,197 |
| 8. | Vouchers approved for payment of annual serial maturity bonds, including interest of $3,000 ............................. | 23,000 |
| 9. | Depreciation (replacement reserve and assets adjusted also, "to fully reserve and fund" the accumulated depreciation) ........ | 10,600 |
| 10. | Deposits received ...................................... | 400 |
| | Deposits refunded ..................................... | 240 |
| 11. | Invoices approved and vouchered for replacement of fully depreciated equipment which had cost $6,200 .................. | 7,800 |
| 12. | Invoices approved and vouchered for additions to plant ...... | 12,460 |
| 13. | Interest received on investments; none is accrued at year end.. | 1,102 |
| 14. | Purchased securities as necessary to fully invest the Replacement Fund to the nearest whole $100 ........................ | compute |
| 15. | Approved vouchers paid (general) ........................ | 133,316 |
| 16. | Stores inventory per physical count at December 31, 19X5 (any shortages or overages are assumed to be related to operating expenses) ............................................. | 11,820 |

Required:

(a)  A worksheet analysis of the beginning trial balance, transactions and adjustments during 19X5, revenues and expenses, and balance sheet at December 31, 19X5, of the Water Fund of the City of Marion.

(b)  A Balance Sheet of the Water Fund as of December 31, 19X5.

(c)  An Operating Statement of the Water Department for 19X5.

(d)  An Analysis of Changes in Retained Earnings of the Water Fund during 19X5.

(AICPA, adapted)

**Problem 14-6.**  The following transactions or events are concerned with regulated utilities and with restricted asset intrafund "funds" within Enterprise Funds. Each is independent of the others unless stated otherwise.

a. Amortization of the Utility Plant Acquisition Account has been completed on an item of equipment still in service in Utility T. The equipment was acquired by Utility T from Utility X for $125,000; its cost new to Utility X was $175,000, and it had a book value of $90,000 when it was sold to Utility T. Both the original cost account and the accumulated depreciation account were recorded on Utility T's books at the time it acquired the equipment.

b. A machine bought by Utility B from Utility A for $300,000 (now 80 percent depreciated) was traded in on a replacement machine (list price $500,000); $450,000 difference was paid, $350,000 of this amount being paid from the Equipment Replacement Fund. Utility A had acquired the machine new at a cost of $400,000; the related accumulated depreciation account had a balance of $150,000 when the machine was acquired by Utility B, which recorded it at net book value in the Machinery and Equipment account at that time. The machine had a fair market value of $25,000 when it was traded in by Utility B. The Equipment Replacement Fund is fully reserved; the reserve is adjusted at the time a transaction affects it.

c. Same situation as (b), but the replacement machine was bought on open account; no cash was disbursed at that time.

d. Depreciation and amortization adjustments for the year ended September 30, 19X8, were recorded by Utility F. Among its assets is a building acquired 10 years ago from Utility N for $210,000, exclusive of land cost. At that time the building had a remaining useful life expectancy of 30 years and a net book value of $150,000 to Utility N, which had constructed it at a cost of $175,000.

e. Assume that the building referred to in (d) above was destroyed by fire on March 31, 19X9 and that insurance proceeds of $300,000 were accrued immediately.

f. Bond interest in the amount of $10,000 was paid at December 31, 19X9, the end of a utility's fiscal year, from the Bond Interest Payments Fund. An additional $2,000 was accrued, also to be paid from the Bond Interest Payments Fund, and bond discount of $350 was amortized.

g. A utility recorded accrued additional interest payable on customer's deposits of $9,600 (accrued during the year) at the end of 19X3 and accrued interest receivable on invested customers' deposits of $3,200. Interest earned on customers' deposits can be used only to pay interest thereon, and distinctively titled customers' deposits revenue and expense accounts are maintained in the utility's general ledger.

h. The customers' deposits accounts were closed. In addition to the information in part (g) above, assume that interest received on invested deposits of $10,000 had been recorded earlier, as had interest expense of $30 on the accounts of a consumer leaving the service area who was paid a total of $180 accumulated interest on his deposit. Further, assume that interest receivable on customers' deposits invested and additional interest payable on customers' deposits of $2,900 and $6,200 (additional), respectively, had been accrued at the close of the preceding year, at which time the total cumulative interest owned on customers' deposits was reported at $109,300.

Required:
Prepare general journal entries in compound form to record the transactions or events described. You may omit formal entry explanations, but should show all significant computations.

**Problem 14-7.** The following is a trial balance of the *budgetary* accounts of the Enterprise Fund of the Enterprise Fund of the City of Youngston as of January 1, 19X8:

| | | |
|---|---|---|
| Budget Requirements ............. | $21,000 | |
| Reserve for Encumbrances ........ | | $21,000 |
| | $21,000 | $21,000 |

The following transactions took place during the year:
1. Appropriations of $320,000 were made. (All expenditures, with the exception of depreciation and losses on uncollectible accounts, have been appropriated for.)
2. The materials ordered at the close of the previous year were received, together with a bill for $22,000.
3. Total salaries and wages paid amounted to $90,000.
4. An order was placed for equipment estimated to cost $60,000.
5. An order was placed for materials estimated to cost $40,000.
6. The equipment was received; the actual cost was $62,000.
7. The materials were received; the actual cost was $39,000.
8. Telephone and telegraph charges of $500 were paid.
9. Interest paid amounted to $15,000.
10. Taxes paid amounted to $2,000.
11. An order was placed for materials estimated to cost $24,000.
12. Bonds of $30,000 (principal amount) were retired.
13. A transfer of $10,000 was made to the City's General Fund. (Note: This transfer was appropriated for.)
14. Adjustments at year end were made as follows:
   a. Accrued salaries and wages payable, $5,400.
   b. Accrued interest payable, $4,000.
   c. Accrued taxes, $5,300.

Required:
(a) Prepare journal entries, including closing entries, to reflect the budgetary transactions.
(b) Post to "T" accounts.
(c) Prepare a Balance Sheet for the budgetary group of accounts as of December 31, 19X8.

**Problem 14-8.** The Township of Hamlet finances its operation from revenues provided by property taxes, water distribution, fines levied by the Municipal Court, and interest on savings accounts.

Hamlet maintains only a General Fund. You were engaged to conduct the audit for the year ended December 31, 19X6, and determined the following:
1. General Fund account balances on January 1, 19X6 were:

| | |
|---|---|
| Cash in savings accounts ..................... | $ 62,030 |
| Cash in checking accounts.................... | 38,450 |
| Cash on hand (undeposited water receipts) ...... | 160 |
| Water works supplies ........................ | 2,640 |
| Due from water customers.................... | 1,670 |
| Fund balance .............................. | 104,950 |

2. The budget for 19X6 adopted by the city commission and the transactions relat-

ing to the budget (with all current bills vouchered and paid on December 31, 19X6) for the year were:

|  | Budget | Transactions |
|---|---|---|
| Property taxes | $26,750 | $26,750 |
| Water works costs | 66,500 | 64,360* |
| City constable and court fees | 10,000 | 9,550 |
| Water revenues | 10,000 | 12,060** |
| Court fines | 12,500 | 11,025 |
| Commissioners' salaries and expenses | 6,000 | 5,470 |
| Interest on savings accounts | 2,000 | 2,240 |
| Miscellaneous expenses | 1,200 | 2,610 |

  \* Cash expenditures.
\*\* Billings.

3. The commissioners appropriated sufficient General Fund balance to equalize budgeted revenues and appropriations. The difference was caused by anticipated repairs to water mains. It was also necessary to transfer $15,000 from a savings account to a checking account to pay for these repairs during 19X6.

4. Your count of cash on December 31, 19X6, determined that there was $250 on hand that was not deposited until January 2, 19X7.

5. All billings for water during 19X6 were paid with the exception of statements totaling $1,230 which were mailed to customers the last week of December.

6. All water works supplies were consumed during the year on the repair of water mains. Hamlet's charter specifies that appropriation expenditures are to be based on purchases.

Required:

(a) Prepare a worksheet for the Township of Hamlet for the year ended December 31, 19X6. Column headings should provide for: (1) a trial balance, (2) transactions for the year, (3) variances from budget and (4) a balance sheet at December 31, 19X6. Formal statements and journal entries are not required. (Assume that the water distribution system may properly be accounted for in the General Fund.)

(b) Should a separate Enterprise Fund be established to account for the water distribution activity? Why?

(AICPA, adapted)

**Problem 14-9.** The following transactions were among those affecting the City of Sterlington during 19X2. Required: (1) Set up an answer sheet like that illustrated on p. 635. (2) Indicate for each transaction (by means of the appropriate numerals) the accounts debited and credited in the General Fund. If two entries in the General Fund are required, place such entries one above the other. (3) If a transaction requires an entry(ies) in a fund(s) or nonfund account group(s) other than the General Fund, indicate those affected by printing the appropriate letter symbol(s) in the column headed "Other Funds or Account Groups Affected." If no entry is required for a transaction, state "None." (Example: Payment by the General Fund of a bill owed by the Special Revenue Fund.

## ANSWER SHEET FORMAT

| Transaction Number | General Fund | | Other Funds or Account Groups Affected | "13" Account Explanation |
| | Dr. | Cr. | | |
|---|---|---|---|---|
| Example | 3 | 2 | SR | |
| 1. | | | | |
| 20. | | | | |

| Symbol | Fund or Account Group | Number | Account Titles |
|---|---|---|---|
| CP | Capital Projects | 1 | Appropriations |
| GLD | General Long-Term Debt | 2 | Cash |
| G | General | 3 | Due from other funds |
| GFA | General Fixed Assets | 4 | Due to other funds |
| DS | Debt Service | 5 | Encumbrances |
| SA | Special Assessment | 6 | Estimated Revenue |
| SR | Special Revenue | 7 | Expenditures |
| TA | Trust or Agency | 8 | Fund Balance |
| E | Enterprise | 9 | Reserve for Encumbrances |
| IGS | Intragovernmental Service | 10 | Revenues |
| | | 11 | Taxes Receivable-Current |
| | | 12 | Vouchers Payable |
| | | 13 | Other (explain) |

### Description of transactions:

The following transactions were among those affecting the City of Sterlington during 19X2:

1. The 19X2 budget was approved. It provided for $520,000 of General Fund revenues and $205,000 of School Fund revenues.

2. Appropriations were made for the General Fund, $516,000.

3. General taxes were levied, $490,000; approximately $10,000 of this amount will prove uncollectible or will be abated.

4. Contractors were paid $200,000 for construction of an office building. The payment was from proceeds of a general bond issue of 19X0.

5. Bonds of a general issue authorized previously were sold at par for $60,000.

6. Orders were placed for uniforms for the Police Department at an estimated cost of $7,500.

7. Payment of salaries of town officers was made in the amount of $11,200 (disregard withholding considerations.)

8. The uniforms ordered above (item 6) were received and vouchers approved for the invoice price of $7,480.

9.   Fire equipment was purchased for $12,500 and a voucher approved in that (the encumbered) amount.

10.   A payment of $5,000 was made by the General Fund to a fund for the redemption of general obligation bonds.

11.   Of the taxes levied (item 3), $210,000 was collected during 19X2; the balance are now delinquent.

12.   Supplies for general administrative use were requisitioned from the Stores Fund. A charge of $1,220 was made for the supplies; they cost the Stores Fund $1,150. (Supplies are accounted for on a perpetual basis in the Stores Fund; on a purchases basis in other funds.)

13.   The General Fund advanced $30,000 cash to provide working capital for a fund out of which payment will be made for a new sewage installation. Eventual financing will be by means of charges to property owners on the basis of benefit received; thus, the advance should be repaid within two or three years.

14.   Equipment used by the Public Works Department was sold for $7,000 cash. This sale was not included in the budget. The equipment had been acquired 10 years earlier, at which time its useful life was estimated at 20 years.

15.   Receipts from licenses and fees amounted to $16,000.

16.   An advance of $10,000 was made from the General Fund to a fund for the operation of a central printing service used by all departments of the municipal government. (This had not been budgeted and is not expected to be repaid.)

17.   Taxes amounting to $1,240 written off as uncollectible in 19X0 were collected. No amount was budgeted for such collections.

18.   A total of $1,000 of the advance made in item 16 was returned because it was not needed.

19.   The city received a cash bequest of $75,000 for the establishment of a scholarship fund.

20.   Previously approved and recorded vouchers for Police Department salaries of $6,200 and for the transfer of $500 to the Police Pension Fund were paid.

**Problem 14-10.** The transactions and events described below occurred in Joiner Junction Township during 19X5. Prepare all general journal entries necessary to reflect the transactions or events described, clearly indicating the fund or nonfund account group in which each entry is made. Omit subsidiary ledger entries and formal entry explanations; state any assumptions made concisely.

1.   A $50,000, 10 year, 6 percent special-special bond issue of the Shady Lane Subdivision Improvement Fund was sold at 95 plus $250 accrued interest to finance the property owner's share of costs of construction. Neither the township nor the property owners will make up the deficiency; interest charged on deferred assessments should just cover the cash interest requirements of the bond issue.

2.   Property owners involved in the Shady Lane Subdivision project were assessed $50,000, the amounts coming due equally over a 10-year period beginning in 19X5. The municipality's share of the cost, $10,000, was included in the General Fund budget and was set up as a liability for that Fund when property owners were assessed.

3.   A $100,000 general obligation bond issue (5 percent, 20 year term) sold at 102 plus $1,000 accrued interest. In accordance with terms of the bond issue authorization, the premium and accrued interest were deposited directly to the Bond Principal and Interest Payments Fund.

4.   A Central Equipment Repair Fund was established by transfer of $40,000 of the bond issue proceeds. This transfer is viewed as invested equity (rather than debt equity) in the new fund.

5. The township's share of the Shady Lane project cost was paid from the bond issue (3) proceeds rather than from the General Fund.

6. Sinking fund accounts were closed based on the following information:

| | Budgeted (Actuarial) Requirements | Actual |
|---|---|---|
| General Fund transfers ........ | $3,500 | $1,800 |
| Transfer of bond premium .... | — | 2,000 |
| Sinking fund earnings ......... | 200 | 150 |
| Transfer of accrued interest..... | — | 1,000 |
| Interest payments ............ | 2,000 | 1,500 |

7. The Central Equipment Repair Fund billed the General Fund departments $1,000, and the Shady Lane Subdivision Improvement Fund $500, for services rendered.

8. The Joiner Junction Power Company was acquired by the municipality for $2,000,000. The cash remaining from the general obligation bond issue was transferred to the Electric Transmission Fund (not to be repaid) and revenue bonds were given power company shareholders for the balance of the purchase price.

Power Company Books

| Asset | Cost | Accumulated Depreciation | Appraised Fair Market Value |
|---|---|---|---|
| Land and Rights-of-Way | $    90,000 | $   — | $   480,000 |
| Buildings and Improvements | 60,000 | 30,000 | 360,000 |
| Equipment | 240,000 | 180,000 | 300,000 |
| Transmission Lines | 1,500,000 | 600,000 | 1,260,000 |
| | $1,890,000 | $810,000 | $2,400,000 |

The utility will continue to be regulated by the Public Service Commission and must adhere to its "original cost" policies in regulatory reports and in rate determination cases.

9. The Shady Lane Subdivision Improvement Fund year-end closing entry was made based upon the following information (assume that adjustments required have been posted):

a. Construction activity to date (all projects are still in progress):

| | | |
|---|---|---|
| 1. | Expenditures ..................... | $25,000 |
| 2. | Encumbrances outstanding .......... | 15,000 |

b. Interest expense and revenue:

| | | |
|---|---|---|
| 1. | Amounts paid/received ............. | — |
| 2. | Accrued interest payable ............ | 1,000 |
| 3. | Accrued interest receivable .......... | 600 |

10. Closing entries were made for the Shady School Memorial Trust Fund. This fund is nonexpendable as to principal. Sixty percent of the earnings inure to the "Shady School Student Assistance Fund" to provide low interest loans to needy graduates of that school who wish to pursue higher education; the balance accrues to the "Shady School Maintenance Fund." Revenues of the Memorial Fund were: Rentals, $15,000; Interest, $10,000; Gain on Sale of Land, $6,000. Expenses were: Operating Expenses, $12,000; Depreciation (corpus), $4,000.

**Problem 14-11.** Valle City had the following transactions in 19X7. Record transactions in all funds and account groups affected in general journal form, designating the fund or account group. The transactions are separate except where several appear under one Arabic numeral. Make all entries to which the transactions give rise.

1. General Fund current taxes of $85,000, subject to an estimated loss of $6,500, became delinquent.

2. A long-term advance of $500,000 was made from the General Fund to establish a fund to buy and hold stores and issue them to the City's various departments.

3. The annual General Fund contribution of $10,000 to the sinking fund for City Hall bonds became due and payable.

4. a. A trust that is expendable as to income and nonexpendable as to principal received $75,000 of rental payments from tenants of trust properties.

b. Trust expenses of $60,000 were paid and depreciation of $5,000 was recorded.

c. Land carried on the trust books at $16,000 was sold for $20,000.

d. Trust books were closed at year end.

5. A 6 percent serial bond issue of $250,000 was sold at par to fund a General Fund deficit.

6. The General Fund liability of $7,500 for contributions to the employees' pension fund was accrued.

7. A lot appraised at $50,000 was received as a gift from an individual for the purpose of establishing a playground.

8. a. Furniture for the mayor's office estimated to cost $500 was ordered.

b. The furniture and a bill therefore were received; the actual cost was $525.

9. Term (sinking fund) bonds amounting to $100,000 matured, together with $2,000 interest thereon.

10. Term (sinking fund) bonds to the amount of $200,000 were sold at a premium of $1,000. They are 5 percent bonds and will mature in 20 years; the par amount is to be used to finance a construction project.

11. The office building construction project financed from the bonds referred to in the preceding transaction was completed. Construction expenditures to the amount of $197,000 were closed; proper disposition was made of the balance. (Prepare closing and disposition of balance entry.)

12. a. Special assessment improvements of $750,000 were authorized.

b. Special assessment notes of $550,000 were sold at par.

c. Assessments of $550,000, maturing in 10 equal installments (the first installments coming due in six months), were levied on private property; the remainder of the cost is to be paid by the municipality.

d. The municipality authorized the issuance of bonds for the purpose of financing part of its share of the cost ($200,000).

e. The bonds were sold at a premium of $2,500.

f. The proceeds from the sale of the bonds, as well as the premium, were transferred to the proper fund or funds.

g. The municipality authorized the issuance of special assessment bonds of $550,000 to retire the special assessment notes.

h. The bonds were sold at par.

i. Construction expenditures during the first year amounted to $100,000; encumbrances at year end were $500,000.

j. Interest accrued at year end: on the bonds (e), $2,200; on the notes (b), $3,000; and on the bonds (g), $5,000. No interest payments were made during the year.

k. Interest accrued on deferred assessments at year end, $12,000; no interest collections were made during the year.

l. The books were closed at year end.

**Problem 14-12.** You have been engaged by the Town of Nihill to examine its June, 30, 19X4, balance sheet. You are the first CPA to be engaged by the Town and find that acceptable methods of municipal accounting have not been employed. The Town clerk stated that the books had been closed and presented the following balance sheet:

TOWN OF NIHILL

Balance Sheet

June 30, 19X4

*Assets*

| | |
|---|---:|
| Cash | $ 36,200 |
| Taxes receivable | 21,900 |
| Accounts receivable | 9,000 |
| Investments | 84,200 |
| Prepaid expenses | 21,000 |
| Fixed assets | 245,400 |
| Total | $417,700 |

*Liabilities*

| | |
|---|---:|
| Accounts payable | $  6,500 |
| Bonds payable | 200,000 |
| Fund balance | 211,200 |
| Total | $417,700 |

The Town of Nihill was formed as a separate political unit on July 1, 19X2. The Town was formerly a real estate development within the Township of Hamton. Your audit disclosed the following information:

1. On July 1, 19X3, the Town received a bequest of $50,000 in cash and a house with a fair market value of $40,000. The house was recorded on the books as an investment at its fair market value at July 1, 19X3. The bequest arose under the terms of a will which provided that the house would be used as a public library and the $50,000 would be established as a nonexpendable trust fund whose income would be used to buy library books. Securities costing $49,200 were purchased in July, 19X3, by the Town for the trust fund and in June 19X4, securities with a cost of $5,000 were sold for $6,800. The trust fund had dividend and interest income of $2,100 during the year of which $1,900 was expended. In addition the Town expended from general funds $9,000 for conversion of the house to library purposes

and $19,000 for books; these last amounts were charged to expenditures. The Town has no other investments. The decision was made to account for the library trust earnings in a separate fund.

2. Taxes levied for the year amounted to $84,300, of which $62,400 was collected and $800 has been identified as being illegal and requiring abatement. In addition, it is anticipated that $1,400 of the remaining 19X3-X4 levy will prove uncollectible.

3. The water company that had been formed by the developer to service the real estate development was purchased by the Town on July 1, 19X3. The seller accepted 5 percent general obligation bonds in settlement. Details of the sales contract follow:

| | | |
|---|---:|---:|
| Plant and equipment .......................... | | $108,000 |
| Assets and liabilities assumed: | | |
| Prepaid expenses (inventories) ................ | $19,000 | |
| Accounts receivable ........................ | 8,000 | |
| Total.................................. | $27,000 | |
| Accounts payable .......................... | 5,000 | 22,000 |
| Sales price .............................. | | $130,000 |

Cash arising from the operation of the water plant, except for a $1,000 working fund, is used for the general purposes of the Town. At June 30, 19X4, the following accounts pertain solely to the operation of the water plant: Accounts Receivable, Prepaid Expenses, and Accounts Payable.

4. A $300,000 issue of 5 percent general obligation bonds was authorized on July 1, 19X3. In addition to the settlement for the purchase of the water company, bonds in the amount of $70,000 were sold at 100 on that date, and $65,400 of the proceeds had been used up to June 30, 19X4, to obtain other equipment for the Town. Interest is payable on June 30 and December 31; no interest payments are in arrears. Commencing June 30, 19X5, bonds in the amount of $10,000 are to be retired each June 30.

5. A shipment of supplies for the water plant was received in June 19X4 and included in Prepaid Expenses, but the invoice for $700 was recorded in July. An order was placed in June with a printer for stationery to be used by the Town's governing body. The stationery was delivered in July and cost $500. The remaining composite life of the water company plant and equipment at July 1, 19X3, was estimated at 30 years.

Required:

Prepare a balance sheet worksheet to adjust the Town clerk's account accumulations as of June 30, 19X4, and distribute them to the appropriate funds or nonfund groups of accounts. The worksheet should be in the format of the Town clerk's balance sheet and have the following column headings:

1. Balance per Books.
2. Adjustments-Debits.
3. Adjustments-Credits.
4. General Fund.
5. Library Endowment Principal Fund.
6. Library Fund.

7. General Fixed Assets.
8. Enterprise Fund.
9. Capital Projects Fund.
10. General Long-Term Debt.

(Formal journal entries are not required. Supporting computations should be in good form.)

(AICPA, adapted)

**Problem 14-13.** The Village of Huttig was incorporated January 1, 19X0. You are to prepare worksheets for its several funds. Include the closing entries necessary to produce the correct year-end balances. The following transactions occurred during the year 19X0:

1. The Council approved the following budget:

| | |
|---|---|
| Revenues ................................... | $60,000 |
| Expenditures: | |
| Current expenditures ....................... | $50,000 |
| Sinking fund contribution ................... | 1,000 |
| Equipment .............................. | 8,500 |
| | $59,500 |

2. The First Huttig State Bank loaned the Village $10,000 on tax anticipation notes.

3. A General Fund transfer of $2,500 was made to establish an Intragovernmental Service (Working Capital) Fund to provide a permanent investment in inventory.

4. The Village decided to build a village hall and an issue of sinking fund bonds, $30,000 par value, was authorized. The bonds bear interest at 6 percent and mature in 20 years. A fund ledger was established and the authorization was recorded in the accounts.

5. The Village decided to pave Main Street; a special assessment project was authorized to pave the street at a cost of $20,000.

6. The bond issue was sold at a price of 101 and accrued interest of $100.

7. The assessments were levied at the authorized total amount, less the Village's share of $1,000. All assessments were collected during the year, together with the Village's contribution.

8. Contracts were made for the paving, $20,000, and for the Village Hall, $28,000. The paving contract was completed but not approved at December 31; the contractor was paid all but 5 percent, which was retained to insure compliance with the terms of the contract.

9. Property taxes were levied in the amount of $50,000; it was expected that 1 percent of this amount would prove uncollectible.

10. Cash collections during the year were as follows:

| | |
|---|---|
| Property taxes ............................. | $48,500 |
| Miscellaneous revenues ..................... | 9,000 |
| | $57,500 |

11. The following purchase orders were issued during the year:

| | |
|---|---:|
| Various operating expenditures ................ | $25,000 |
| Various items of equipment ................... | 7,500 |
| Stores for the IGS (Working Capital) Fund ...... | 2,000 |
| | $34,500 |

12. The following schedule summarizes certain expenditures made during the year:

| | Ordered | Vouchered |
|---|---:|---:|
| Various operating expenditures ............... | $24,250 | $48,000 |
| Various items of equipment ................... | 7,500 | 7,400 |
| Tax anticipation notes ....................... | | 5,000 |
| Stores for the IGS (Working Capital) Fund ...... | 2,000 | 2,100 |
| | $33,750 | $62,500 |

13. The IGS (Working Capital) Fund purchases were paid for in full; General Fund payments of $50,000 were made on the above vouchers.

14. A local man was paid $250 from the IGS (Working Capital) Fund to operate the warehouse in his spare time. He issued materials which cost $1,800 to General Fund departments at a billed figure of $2,200. This bill was paid during the year from the General Fund.

15. The actuarial table prepared for the sinking fund showed a $1,000 contribution and earnings of $50 for 19X0. (Actuarial requirements are entered in the accounts.) The contribution was paid. Securities were acquired for the sinking fund for $950 during the year and $40 of revenue was received therefrom.

16. The Village Hall was three-fourths completed according to the supervising architect. Payment of $20,500 was approved and paid. An additional $1,500 was paid to the General Fund to reimburse it for preliminary landscaping work done by employees paid from the General Fund.

17. The operating expenditures (see item 12) included withholding and FICA taxes which had been transferred to the Agency Fund on each payroll date (included in vouchers paid). The amount of these taxes was $750. At December 31, $500 had been paid out of the Agency Fund.

**Problem 14-14.** The Balance Sheet of the City of Antagon as of June 30, 19X5, shows a surplus of $258,216. The statement has been criticized as not giving a satisfactory reflection of the financial position of the city. You are asked (a) to revise the statement in accordance with acceptable methods of governmental accounting, and (b) to provide a detailed analysis of the changes in the General Fund balance for the year ended June 30, 19X5. You may prepare your revised balance sheet in columnar form if you prefer, or you may submit an appropriate worksheet in lieu of a formal balance sheet.

The balance sheet, as prepared, is as follows:

### Assets

|  | Balance 6/30/X4 | Balance 6/30/X5 |
|---|---|---|
| Cash | $ 20,485 | $ 2,873 |
| Taxes receivable | 54,200 | 36,690 |
| Accounts receivable | 12,362 | 13,584 |
| Investments | 42,000 | 42,000 |
| Prepaid expenses | 6,487 | 5,374 |
| Fixed assets | 696,565 | 710,465 |
| Total | $832,099 | $810,986 |

### Liabilities

|  | Balance 6/30/X4 | Balance 6/30/X5 |
|---|---|---|
| Warrants payable | $ 30,900 | $ 46,970 |
| Bonds payable | 490,000 | 480,000 |
| Reserve for depreciation | 22,300 | 25,800 |
| Surplus | 288,899 | 258,216 |
|  | $832,099 | $810,986 |

Additional information is available as follows: (1) Taxes levied for the year ended June 30, 19X5 amounted to $64,300, of which $37,600 was collected and $650 was abated. Abatement of prior years' taxes was $3,108. It is anticipated that an additional $1,350 of the 19X4-X5 levy will finally be uncollectible and that an additional $3,500 of 19X3 and prior taxes will prove uncollectible, but these additional uncollectible amounts were not included in preparation of the above balance sheet. (2) Revenue other than from taxes was reported as $20,210, but $4,300 of this amount was collected for other governments and has not been paid nor set up as a liability and $1,200 was from interest on investments. The investments are held in trust; the income is to be used for library upkeep. The $3,050 cost of library upkeep for the year is included in expenditures. The trust was established on June 29, 19X4. (3) Expenditures amounted to $153,400 during the year. Included herein is interest on bonds of $15,000, purchase of general fixed assets of $18,900, retirement of general obligation bonds of $10,000, and the abatement of this and prior years' taxes. The $10,000 of bonds retired and the $18,900 of assets purchased were also credited to surplus and debited to bonds payable and fixed assets, respectively. (4) Included in fixed assets is $174,964 as of June 30, 19X4, and $169,964 as of June 30, 19X5, of property of the municipal water plant. The revenue of the plant and the expenses, including depreciation of $8,500 and bond interest on $90,000 of 3 percent bonds outstanding against the plant, have been netted, and the profit of $9,307 has been transferred to surplus. The reserve for depreciation, the accounts receivable and the prepaid expenses at both balance sheet dates are applicable to the water plant operations. Also, $5,025 in 19X4 and $8,750 in 19X5 of the warrants payable are applicable to this department. The cash arising from the department's operations, except for a $500 working fund, is used for general purposes of the city. No water plant fixed assets were purchased during the period, nor were any sold. The municipality has never contributed capital to the water plant; its only financing through the years, other than from consumer charges, has been secured through issue of revenue bonds.

# 15

# Cost Accounting, Finding, and Analysis

Every organization, whether privately owned or governmental, has only a limited amount of scarce resources at its disposal. Thus, every decision affecting future resource allocation—and each evaluation of past resource utilization—necessarily involves either implicit or explicit comparison of the costs incurred, or to be incurred, with the benefits received or expected. It is extremely important, therefore, that planners, decision-makers, managers, and evaluators at all levels (including the citizenry) be provided reliable, relevant, and timely information as to both past and prospective costs of governmental services, products, and activities in order that each may better perform his function.

Any listing of the specific uses of cost information is necessarily incomplete —as its present and potential uses are both pervasive and dynamic. Among the more important specific uses of governmental cost information are:

1.  *Budgeting.* Budgetary planning, preparation and support, that is, making decisions concerning the allocation of scarce resources among relatively unlimited demands. Appropriate cost records and forecasts are prerequisites to effective program or performance budgeting.

2.  *Cost and Efficiency Analyses.* Interperiod, intraunit and interunit analyses of costs and cost trends to determine their direction and to indicate relative efficiency.

3.  *"Make or Buy" Decisions.* Where goods or services are available from non-

governmental sources, whether the unit is effecting savings by performing the function in question or should contract for it.

4. *Fee Determination.* Determination of service or product fee schedules, amounts to be assessed to property owners in special assessment projects, and costs reimbursable under terms of contracts or grants.

5. *Capitalization and Analysis of Construction Projects.* Calculation of the total cost of assets constructed by the unit, for comparison with project cost estimates and as a basis for capitalizing the asset in the appropriate accounting records.

6. *Reporting.* Supplementing fund expenditure reports with data on total and/or unit costs of programs, projects, or other activities.

Cost accounting, the principal concern of this chapter, is often broadly defined as the art of determining the cost of a product, service or activity. The authors prefer a narrower definition and use the term "cost accounting" to refer to a continuous process of analyzing, classifying, recording, and summarizing costs within the discipline and controls of the formal accounting system and reporting them to users on a regular basis. The determination or estimation of costs by more informal procedures and/or on an irregular basis is referred to as "cost finding."

Following a brief introduction to cost concepts, terminology and behavior, the remainder of this chapter is devoted primarily to cost accounting and cost finding. These topics normally comprise the subject of one or more separate courses in the contemporary collegiate accounting curriculum, of course, and this chapter should be viewed as introductory in nature. A detailed, complete presentation of the subject is beyond the scope of this book.[1]

## COST CONCEPTS, TERMINOLOGY, AND BEHAVIOR

That differing concepts and measures of "cost" are relevant in differing analyses and decision situations is axiomatic to financial management. Varying usages of the term "cost" cause no little confusion and frustration to the novice accountant and to the layman, however, and the term is best used only with an appropriate modifier.

### Cost Concepts

One of the more common errors made, both by the novice and in contemporary practice, is that of considering *expenditures* to be synonymous with *cost*— and thus erroneously considering total or per unit expenditures to be equivalent to total or per unit cost of a product or service. The systems of appropriation-

[1] For a more complete treatment of cost accounting and cost finding, see Charles T. Horngren, *Cost Accounting: A Managerial Emphasis* (Englewood Cliffs, N.J.: Prentice-Hall, Inc., 1972.)

expenditure accounting for expendable funds described in the earlier chapters of this book provide necessary records of the "things" (services, materials or supplies, debt service, fixed assets) for which a government incurs expenditures. The result is essentially a record of *input*—of funds (working capital) applied— and the systems described typically do not incorporate information as to the goods or services actually rendered to the public or the total resources consumed in doing so. Rather, the emphasis of expendable fund accounting and reporting, especially that for the General Fund and Special Revenue Funds, is upon controlling the expenditure of appropriable resources. These records of input are not intended to be accurate in terms of total costs: (1) in many governments, the records are maintained on the cash basis; (2) depreciation is not taken into consideration; (3) purchases of General Fixed Assets and retirement of General Long-Term Debt are treated as current period expenditures; and (4) overhead costs are not likely to be assigned to operating units or activities.

In contrast to the working capital utilization or input approach of appropriation-expenditure accounting, cost accounting and cost finding are usually concerned with measurement of the *total* costs or expenses incurred by an organization or activity in producing goods or rendering services and, where possible, relating these costs to *output* in terms of volume and cost per unit of goods produced or services rendered. Both are akin to Enterprise and other nonexpendable fund cost measurement rather than to expendable fund appropriable resource flow measurement. The process of assigning *all* costs, direct and indirect, to measurable services or products distinguishes both cost accounting and cost finding from expenditure accounting. Calculation of the total and unit cost of the work done is the usual end-product of both approaches to the problem of costing. Figure 15-1, discussed later, illustrates the relationship of current expenditures and total activity expenses or product costs.

When used without modifiers, both "cost accounting" and "cost finding" refer to the measurement or determination of total and/or per unit *long-run historical* costs incurred in producing an asset (a building, for example) or costs expired (expenses) in providing a service (e.g., garbage collection and disposal). Thus, long-run historical costing—often referred to as "full" or "absorption" costing—may be considered "general purpose" costing, and is the usual basis of cost accounting systems or cost finding calculations. Nonroutine or special situation decisions may require derivation of "special purpose" cost data, however, and the use of long-run cost data may be inappropriate and misleading in some circumstances.

Special purpose data of the types described in this and the remaining paragraphs of this section are not normally maintained in the accounts, but are derived on an "as needed" basis from a variety of sources. *Current replacement costs* are more relevant than historical costs in some situations, such as where one is planning to replace specific assets, for example. Too, *opportunity costs*— the benefits foregone by using resources for one purpose rather than another—

Figure 15-1

RECONCILIATION OF EXPENDITURES
AND COSTS OR EXPENSES
(Activity Financed Through Expendable Fund)

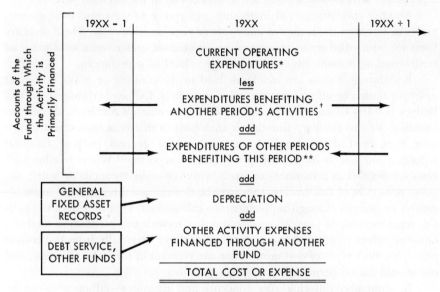

* Excludes debt principal retirement and capital outlay expenditures.

† For example, prepaid insurance and inventory adjustments where
expenditures are recorded on a "purchases" basis and other accrual
and deferral adjustments for items reflected in the Expenditures account
for the period that are applicable to previous or future periods.

** Adjustments for items such as those in note 2 that are reflected in
the Expenditures account in a previous or future period but are
applicable to 19XX.

are often relevant in making choices among alternative courses of action, as
when one must decide whether to use a structure for governmental purposes or
to sell it and build another elsewhere (or use the sale proceeds for other purposes). In addition, differential or marginal costs often are more relevant to
short-run decisions than are long-run cost data. *Differential* costs are the total
"out-of-pocket" costs involved in changing the level or type of an activity.
(*Incremental* costs refer to additional differential costs; *decremental* costs are
decreases in differential costs.) *Marginal cost,* on the other hand, is the short-run
cost change *per unit* of increasing or decreasing the level of an existing service
or production activity.

Short-run data should be evaluated carefully and used cautiously in governmental decision making, because decisions based on short-run costs and con-

siderations often become built into the long-run scheme of things and have significant long-run cost effects. Thus, though the cost of paving an additional mile of street is a relevant figure, the estimated increased maintenance costs this will require in future years is equally relevant to the decision of whether to pave a particular street—and should not be overlooked in the decision process.

Another cost measure, of increasing importance to state and local governments in recent years, is that of *allowable* or *reimbursable costs*. These costs are those for which the organization will be reimbursed under terms of a grant or contractual agreement, usually with a higher level of government.

Reimbursable costs are usually defined in the contract or grant document or by regulation or administrative directive, such as Office of Management and Budget (OMB) Circulars A-21 and A-87. A government's reimbursable cost accounting (or cost finding) situation is analogous to that of a commercial enterprise that must determine both net income for general purpose financial reporting and taxable income for special purpose reporting.[2] Where reimbursable costs are defined in a manner consistent with (or easily reconcilable with) on-going principles of full costing, they may be determined directly from available records or derived through supplementary calculations. It is necessary to establish separate, special purpose cost accounting records or cost finding analyses, however, where reimbursable cost stipulations differ materially from full costing principles. Both types of cost information are relevant in the latter situation, and one should not be permitted to supplant the other.

In summary, differing cost concepts and measures—either long-run or short-run, and on either a total or per unit basis—may be appropriate in different situations. The distinctions among the various cost concepts and measures, as well as their uses and limitations, should be borne in mind—and great care must be exercised in order to assure that reliable cost data appropriate to the decision or evaluation at hand are made available on a timely basis. To summarize briefly, the four major cost concept categories discussed thus far are:

1. *Budgetary "Costs,"* expendable fund expenditure and encumbrance data available from fund-based financial statements, do not constitute full costs, though they are often a convenient starting point in cost finding analyses.

2. *Special Purpose or Short-run "Costs,"* such as replacement, differential, marginal, or opportunity costs, are not normally the basis of on-going cost accounting systems but are determined on an "as needed" basis.

3. *Reimbursable Costs* are stipulated or expressly defined costs that must be determined through cost accounting or finding; these should not supplant full cost determinations where the two differ in concept.

4. *Full Cost,* also referred to as "total cost" or "absorption cost," is the cost

---

2 It is also analogous to that of a hospital or nursing home that must substantiate medicare reimbursement requests as well as prepare general purpose financial statements, a regulated industry that must prepare both general purpose and prescribed financial reports, or a company whose securities are subject to SEC reporting requirements.

concept or basis underlying most general purpose, on-going cost accounting systems or cost-finding determinations.

Again, the term "cost," when used without a modifier, should refer to full costing, the fourth cost concept enumerated above. This is the sense in which that term is used in the remainder of this chapter.

### Cost Elements

The components of the total cost of producing a specific product or performing a specific service activity are commonly classified as follows:

1. *Direct Labor.* Labor costs incurred directly in the production of the good or service that are conveniently traceable thereto.
2. *Direct Materials.* Costs of materials used directly in the production of goods or services that are conveniently traceable thereto.
3. *Overhead.* Indirect labor costs, indirect material costs, and all other costs (such as supervision, minor supplies, rent, utilities, small tools) reasonably associated with provision of the goods or services.

The total of direct labor and direct material costs are commonly referred to as "prime" costs; the total of direct labor costs and overhead costs, as "conversion" costs. These elements are illustrated in Figure 15-2.

### Figure 15-2

### COST ELEMENTS

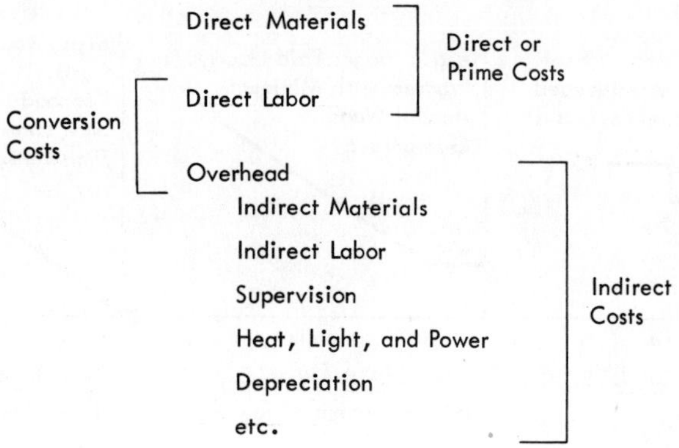

### Cost Behavior

Costs may also be categorized according to their behavior patterns at various levels of activity for purposes of analysis, evaluation, and projection. (Such categories are not normally the basis for cost account classification or reporting.) The major classifications of cost by behavior, that is, changes in total cost occasioned by a change in activity level, are variable, fixed, semivariable, or semifixed. These cost patterns are illustrated graphically in Figure 15-3.

A *fixed* cost factor is one that remains constant over a wide range of activity, that is, the total cost is fixed but the cost per unit of product produced or service provided decreases as the number of units increases. Rental expense of $500 per month is a fixed cost. *Semifixed* or "step" costs are fixed at certain activity levels or ranges but increase to succeedingly higher plateaus as activity increases. Supervision costs, in a situation in which one foreman is required for every ten laborers or for each shift, is an example of a semifixed or step cost. As more laborers are required or additional work shifts are necessitated by higher

**Figure 15-3**

COST BEHAVIOR PATTERNS

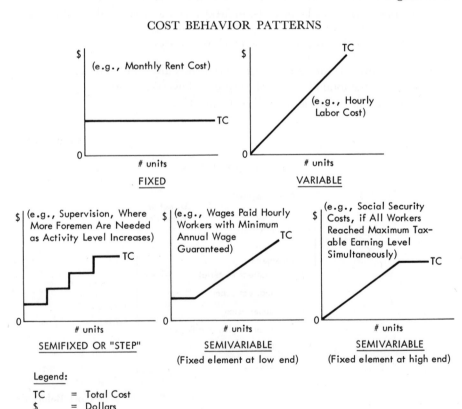

Legend:

TC = Total Cost
$ = Dollars
# units = Number of units of goods
          produced or services provided

levels of activity, total supervision costs increase in steps—but are fixed within specified activity ranges.

*Variable* costs are fixed per unit within a wide range of activity and thus increase in direct proportion to the change in activity level. Material that costs $4 per unit or labor that costs $3 per hour are examples of variable costs. *Semi-variable* costs are those that are primarily variable but contain some elements of fixed costs at either the low or high end of the range of activity. Labor costs, where hourly workers are guaranteed a minimum annual wage, is an example of the former; social security or unemployment taxes, where most or all workers exceed the maximum earnings base upon which such taxes are computed, serve to illustrate the latter. A costing system in which only variable costs are capitalized, and in which all fixed costs are considered "period costs" (current expenses) is referred to as "variable costing" or "direct costing." Though the latter term is not very descriptive of the features of the method, it is a widely used term. Variable or direct costing is *not* generally accepted for external reporting purposes, but often provides valuable insight for short-run decision-making purposes.

Where costs may be categorized realiably as between fixed and variable costs, one may readily determine the "break-even" point in situations where revenues are received in direct proportion to goods or services produced or provided. The break-even calculation is based on the assumption that production and sales are in equal quantities and that if one unit is sold another must be acquired to replace it in inventory. Thus if fixed costs are to be recouped, or a profit realized, this must come from the gross margin, or "contribution margin," the difference between the revenue received per unit and the variable cost of acquiring an additional unit. For example, if goods or services have a variable cost of $3 per unit and are sold (or reimbursed for) at $5 per unit, the contribution margin is $2 per unit. If the activity through which they are produced incurs fixed overhead and other costs of $8,000 per year, then 4,000 units ($8,000 fixed costs ÷ $2 unit contribution margin) must be produced and/or sold during the year in order for the activity to break-even—for its revenues to exactly equal its total fixed and variable costs. Stated differently, it must have sales or other revenues of $20,000 (4,000 units × $5 unit sales price) in order to cover all costs. Should a profit of $1,000 be desired, one may simply view this as if it were added fixed costs to be recouped, that is, $8,000 fixed costs plus the $1,000 profit must be recouped through the contribution margin, and sales of 4,500 units ($9,000 ÷ $2 unit contribution margin) or $22,500 (4,500 units × $5 unit sales price) must be achieved. Similarly, if the activity receives a subsidy or for other reasons it is desired or necessary to cover only part of its fixed costs, the amount that must be covered may be divided by the unit contribution margin and the number of units that must be provided and/or sold, and the total dollars of sales or other revenues required, may be determined in this manner.

Two additional points concerning cost behavior warrant mention. First, most costs are either fixed or variable within narrow ranges. Thus, the semi-variable costs (fixed element at low end) illustrated in Figure 15-3 could be considered fixed if the activity level was near the vertical axis and variable if it was toward or beyond the middle of the horizontal axis. The more narrow the range of expected activity, therefore, the more likely are the costs to behave in a predictable manner. The expected activity level span over which fixed and variable cost classifications and computations are deemed to be reliable is known as the "relevant range." Second, cost behavior patterns are subject to change through time, either because of factor supply and demand shifts or because of a variety of internal or external factors. Both the classifications and dollar amounts of cost factors should be based on thorough analysis and reevaluated frequently to assure their accuracy and reliability.

The remainder of this chapter is devoted to a general discussion of cost accounting and cost finding. Again, a thorough and detailed presentation of these topics is beyond the scope of this book; the reader desiring a more complete understanding of these subjects is directed to one of the several excellent cost accounting texts available.

## COST ACCOUNTING—OVERVIEW

The NCGA defines cost accounting as:

> That method of accounting which provides for assembling and recording all the elements of cost incurred to accomplish a purpose, to carry on an activity or operation, or to complete a unit of work or a specific job.[3]

Recall that we earlier indicated a preference for the narrower interpretation of the term, that is, cost accounting is used here to refer to a continuous process of analyzing, classifying, recording, and summarizing cost data within the discipline and controls of the formal accounting system and reporting them to users on a regular basis. Cost finding, the determination or estimation of costs by less formal procedures and/or on an irregular basis, is discussed in a later section of this chapter.

The usefulness and importance of cost accounting to governmental financial planning, management, and evaluation was noted in the introduction to this chapter. The observations of the American Accounting Association's Committee on Accounting Practices of Not-for-Profit Organizations regarding society's interest in adequate governmental cost accounting appear equally relevant:

> Cost accounting has long been recognized by those in the profit-oriented environment as a useful tool for promoting efficiency. Yet cost accounting may be even more important in many NFP organizations than in the private sector because (1) all or a broader sector of society's interest may be involved than is the case for a single commercial enterprise, (2) the profit motive is lacking as a regulating device or a measure of operating efficiency in the NFP

[3] *GAAFR*, p. 157.

environment, (3) of the frequent lack of a powerful interest group (such as stockholders) to constantly review and evaluate management's effectiveness, and (4) some NFP organizations, particularly governments, have the power to enforce the exacting of revenues and thus ensure self-perpetuation even when they are inefficient.[4]

Despite widespread recognition of the usefulness of cost data, there is ample opportunity for further implementation of cost accounting systems within governments. The same American Accounting Association Committee observed that:

> The potentials of cost accounting techniques have scarcely begun to be realized in the NFP field. . . . NFP accounting has been tailored to fulfill legalistic fund and budgetary requirements and little attention has been given (outside the hospital field and in some NFP-owned utilities and other self-sustaining activities) to developing accrual-based cost accounting.[5]

The most interesting and beneficial type of information that can be given to citizens is the answer to the question, "What did we receive for our taxes?" The answer should be in terms of project or program costs incurred and service rendered, not merely objects of expenditure.

### Cost Centers

The identification of cost centers and of operations or products to be costed is an essential step in the development of any cost accounting system. All governments are divided into organizational units. Each unit is typically responsible for a number of activities, and these activities are assigned to organizational subunits. Ideally each subunit would be assigned one activity or operation, and no more than one subunit would be engaged in a given activity, but the ideal is seldom attained. In the usual case the subunit is responsible for several operations or activities within an organizational unit, and two or more subunits are involved in some of the activities. Each cost center has both input and output relative to the activity or activities in which it engages, though the output, in particular, may not be objectively measurable in some cases. Many of the operations that are not now thought to be objectively measurable may later prove to be objectively measurable and be brought under the control provided by unit cost accounting systems and analyses. Examples of operations and their units of measurement are given at several points later in this chapter.

### Basic Cost Accounting Approaches

The appropriate approach to cost data accumulation for a cost center depends on the nature of the activity(ies) involved. One of two widely used ap-

---

4 "Report of the Committee on Accounting Practices of Not-for-Profit Organizations," *The Accounting Review*, Vol. 46 (Supplement), p. 92.

5 *Ibid.*

proaches, referred to as "job order" and "process" costing, respectively, will fit most cost center activity patterns. In a few situations it may be necessary to use both approaches, or a combination of them, in accounting for a single cost center, but the basic nature of the approaches remains unchanged and universal.

The *job order* approach is appropriate where the goods or services produced or provided are of a heterogeneous nature, that is, where they are of a "tailor made" or "special order" nature and are separable, discrete activities (jobs). The job order approach in governments is typlified by cost accounting systems for construction projects, vehicle repair, and intergovernmental grant activities. It also has application in personal service activities such as building inspection and social welfare casework. Job order costing is illustrated graphically in Figure 15-4.

The *process costing* approach, on the other hand, is used where many units of a homogeneous good or service are produced in or provided by a cost center characterized by a pattern of routine, repetitive activities, perhaps in mechanized work situations. Water purification and distribution systems, sewerage collection and disposal, and garbage removal and disposal activities commonly fit this activity costing pattern, as do cashiering, accounting and data processing, and similar activities. The process costing approach is illustrated graphically in Figure 15-5.

### Reconciliation of Cost and General Accounts

Where activities financed through a self-sustaining or nonexpendable fund are to be costed, the cost accounts are readily made a part of and controlled by the usual accounting system. Thus, cost accounting is both more readily implemented and its reliability more easily controlled in enterprise and similar situations. (See Figure 15-6.)

Where activities subject to costing are financed through an expendable fund, such as the General or a Special Revenue Fund, cost finding is often more appropriate than cost accounting inasmuch as expenditure data provide only a starting point for cost determination in many cases. It is axiomatic, however, that cost data that are not controlled by the general records are likely to be inaccurate unless great care is exercised.

Cost accounting systems under expendable fund general ledger control may be designed and implemented readily where (1) all fixed assets are rented, either from sources external to the government or an Intragovernmental Service Fund, and there are no other significant differences between fund expenditures and encumbrances and activity expenses, and (2) for *reimbursable* costing purposes, where the expendable fund is accounted for on a basis consistent with grant- or contract-stipulated cost principles. Even where the costing and expenditure accounting bases do not totally conform, it may be practicable to gain effective general ledger control over the cost accounts by a reconciliation process. Assume,

Figure 15-4

JOB ORDER COSTING APPROACH ILLUSTRATED

(General and Subsidiary Ledgers)

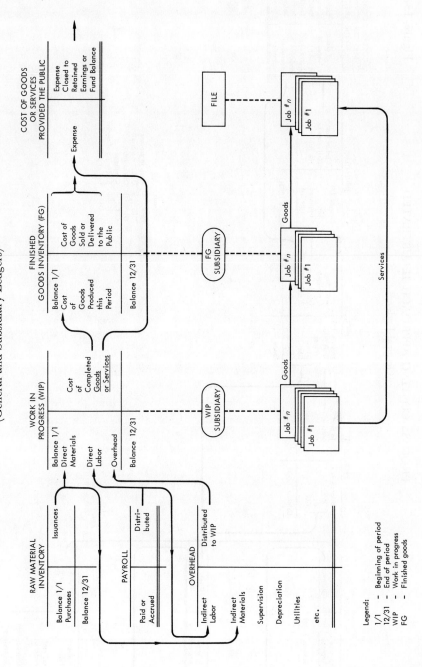

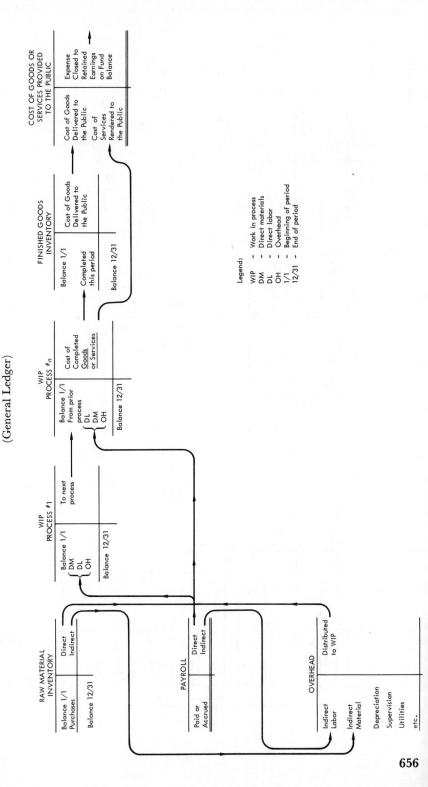

**Figure 15-5**

PROCESS COSTING APPROACH ILLUSTRATED
(General Ledger)

Legend:

WIP — Work in process
DM — Direct materials
DL — Direct labor
OH — Overhead
1/1 — Beginning of period
12/31 — End of period

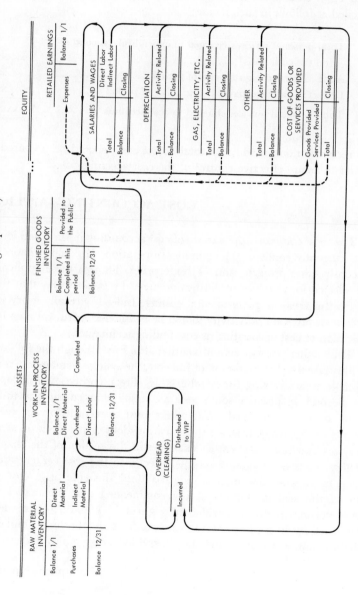

Figure 15-6

PROCESS COSTING APPROACH
(Related to the Accounting Equation)

for example, that the only difference between proper costing and expenditure accounting in a given situation is that personal services expenditures are recorded on a cash basis. Personal services expenditures and expenses may be reconciled as follows in such a case:

| | |
|---|---:|
| Total personal services charged to expenditure accounts (on the cash basis) .............................. | $ xxxxxx |
| Add: Accrued payroll, end of period .............. | xx |
| Deduct: Accrued payroll, beginning of period ........ | xxx |
| Total personal services charged to cost accounts ........ | $ xxxxxx |

Such reconciliations, made on a total object basis, should be prepared regularly in order to assure effective control of the cost accounts.

## COST ACCOUNTING—APPLICATIONS

The most common applications of cost accounting in state and local governments currently concern (1) equipment operation, (2) maintenance activities, (3) construction projects, and (4) enterprises. Though these applications have been selected for purposes of illustration here, this is *not* to say that they are the only fruitful areas of governmental costing. Indeed, virtually every identifiable government program or activity should be considered a fruitful area for possible application of cost accounting or cost finding techniques.

Three other points warrant mention also. First, though the following examples illustrate the determination of full cost, the systems demonstrated are readily adaptable to accounting for reimbursable, direct (prime), variable, and other costs. Second, in practice some costs are easily charged directly to the job or process cost center involved, while others must be recorded initially in "clearing accounts" and later distributed to the various jobs or processes on some rational and systematic basis. The earlier examples in this section of the chapter assume that most costs are readily traceable directly to the cost centers; detailed discussion of clearing accounts is deferred until the enterprise cost accounting phase of this section. Finally, it is recommended that the reader review the general costing models illustrated in Figures 15-4 and 15-5 frequently as he studies each application in this section in order to relate the examples presented to the accounting equation and the general ledger accounts of these models.

### Equipment Operation Costs

The operating departments may rent or lease equipment, either from a central equipment bureau financed through an Intragovernmental Service Fund or from external sources, or they may use equipment classified as General Fixed Assets. If the equipment is handled through a central equipment bureau, it is important to know the cost of operating each piece in order that (1) the central equipment bureau may recover the cost from the departments using the equipment, (2) each user department or activity may be charged a proper share of the cost, (3) managers may determine which pieces of equipment are operating efficiently enough to warrant their continued use and which should be scrapped or sold, and (4) managers may determine which of several brands is the most economical to operate. Thus, it is important to know the cost of operating each piece of equipment whether it is recorded in General Fixed Assets or is operated through a central equipment bureau.

It is assumed here that the equipment is operated by a central equipment bureau that is financed and accounted for through an Intragovernmental Service (IGS) Fund. However, to repeat, cost determination is equally necessary where departments operate equipment classified as General Fixed Assets.

SECURING DIRECT COSTS. The expenses involved in operating a piece of equipment include the cost of gasoline, oil, tires, and other operating supplies consumed, repair and maintenance costs, depreciation of the equipment, and general overhead.

The basic data for arriving at the cost of operating each piece of equipment are gathered in an individual equipment record like that illustrated in Figure 15-7. This record should be prepared at least annually, though monthly posting is common; monthly or quarterly cost reports are obviously preferable to annual reports from a managerial usefulness perspective.

OVERHEAD COSTS. Overhead includes all expenses connected with operating the central equipment bureau that cannot be assigned directly to any one piece of equipment. These include, among others, the salaries of the superintendent and foremen; the cost of such supplies as grease, paint, and rags; depreciation of the bureau's facilities and equipment; and the cost of operating the garage office. These expenses may be first compiled in separate expense accounts and subsequently distributed to all pieces of equipment on some systematic and rational basis. One of the bases frequently used to allocate repair superintendence costs, for example, is the number of labor hours spent on each piece of equipment during the month. A labor hour is one hour of work by one employee. Thus, if one mechanic works for four hours on an automobile, the job is said to have required four labor hours, as is the case if four employees each work one hour on the automobile.

DISTRIBUTING OVERHEAD COSTS. A common method of distributing overhead expenses among the items of equipment is to allocate them in proportion to the number of direct labor hours spent in repairing and maintaining each piece of equipment. This may be done as follows: (1) The expenses shown in the individual overhead expense accounts are added to arrive at the total equipment overhead expenses for the month. (2) Provision is made for accumulating the total direct labor hours for the month and the number spent in maintaining and repairing each vehicle. (3) The total overhead cost per direct labor hour is then

**Figure 15-7**

A GOVERNMENTAL UNIT
Individual Equipment Record
for Year Ending _____ 19__

1. Equipment No. _____ Serial No. _____
2. Motor No. _____
3. Make _____
4. Type _____
5. Capacity _____
6. Date Purchased _____
7. Original Cost _____ $_____
8. Value Start of This Year _____ $_____

9. Estimated Salvage Value _____ $_____
10. Remaining Depreciation _____ $_____
11. Estimated Depreciation This Year _____ $_____
12. Estimated Hours or Miles This Year _____
13. Depreciation Rate per Hour _____ $_____
   per Mile _____ $_____
14. Rental Rates { Date _____ Rate _____ per Mi. or Hr.
              { Date _____ Rate _____ per Mi. or Hr.

| Month | Gasoline | | Oil | | Tires and Supplies | Mainte-nance and Repairs | Overhead | Deprecia-tion | Total Cost | Miles Run | Hours Run | Cost per Mile or Hour | Miles per Gallon | Rentals Earned (Credits) |
|---|---|---|---|---|---|---|---|---|---|---|---|---|---|---|
| 1 | 2 | | 3 | | 4 | 5 | 6 | 7 | 8 | 9 | 10 | 11 | 12 | 13 |
| | Gals. | Amt. | Qts. | Amt. | Amt. | Amt. | Amt. | Amt. | Amt. | | | Amt. | | Amt. |
| | | | | | | | | | | | | | | |

660

computed by dividing the total overhead expenses for the month by the total number of direct labor hours. (4) The amount of overhead chargeable to each piece of equipment is determined (by multiplying the number of direct labor hours spent on it by the rate per direct labor hour) and is posted to column 6 of the equipment record.

To illustrate, if the total overhead expenses during a period amounted to $2,000 and a total of 2,000 direct labor hours was spent repairing and maintaining equipment, the overhead expense rate would be $1.00 per direct labor hour. If 30 labor hours were spent on a particular piece of equipment, $30 of overhead expense would be posted to its individual equipment record. (In the general ledger, the $30 would be debited to Repairs and Maintenance and credited to Overhead or Overhead Applied.)

DEPRECIATION. Depreciation must be taken into account in order to determine the total cost of operating a piece of equipment. One commonly used method for calculating depreciation of equipment is the work (or use) unit method. Under this method, the expected net cost (original cost less expected salvage value at disposal) of using each piece of equipment during its useful life is first determined. The expected net cost is then divided by the total number of work (or use) units expected during the useful life of the asset, and the charge to each activity is determined by multiplying the number of equipment work (or use) units applicable to the activity by the rate per work (or use) unit. For example, assume that a truck was acquired at a cost of $2,400, that it is expected to be driven 40,000 miles during its useful life to the government, and that the salvage value of the truck upon its disposal is expected to be approximately $400. The depreciation rate would be $.05 per mile ($2,000 ÷ 40,000). If the truck was driven 1,500 miles during the month of July, $75 (1,500 × $.05) of depreciation expense would to be posted to its individual equipment record.

The last column in the individual equipment record refers to rentals earned. Rentals were discussed in Chapter 13 and need not be considered again here.

STATEMENT OF EQUIPMENT COSTS. As indicated before, one of the purposes of securing equipment costs is to measure the efficiency of each piece of equipment. Accordingly, a statement showing the total cost of operating the piece of equipment, the number of miles or hours operated, and the cost per mile or hour is normally prepared both at the end of each month or quarter and annually. These unit costs serve as an index of the efficiency of equipment operation. This statement contains the same columns as the individual equipment record form illustrated in Figure 15-7, except that an "Equipment Number" column is substituted for the first column in the record.

### Maintenance Activity Costs

Many of the maintenance activities of a government are suitable for accumulation of data on work accomplished and for calculation of unit costs. The following are examples of the operations susceptible of unit cost measurement and the units of measurement employed.

### BUREAU OF SANITATION

| *Operation or Account Title* | *Work Unit* |
| --- | --- |
| Waste Collection: | |
| Loading and Hauling Nonburnables .............. | Tons or Cubic Yards |
| Maintenance of Dumps ......................... | Tons or Cubic Yards |
| Loading and Hauling Burnables .................. | Tons or Pounds |
| Dead Animals and Other Special Collection ........ | Number and Kind |
| Incinerator Operation and Maintenance: | |
| Charging ...................................... | Tons |
| Firing ........................................ | Tons |
| Removing Ashes ............................... | Tons or Pounds |
| Street Cleaning: | |
| Machine Sweeping (including removal of sweepings) .. | Cleaning Mile |
| Beat Patrol (cleaning sections) .................... | Cleaning Mile |

COMPILING COSTS AND UNITS OF WORK. If accurate unit costs are to be secured, both the total cost of an activity and the number of units of work must be compiled. One method of compiling such information is through the use of work orders like the one illustrated in Figure 15-8. These work orders taken together constitute a work and cost ledger.

Note that provision is made for filling in the cost of labor, the cost of materials, the cost of equipment use, overhead costs, total cost of the job, number of units of work involved, and the cost per unit. The scope of this book does not permit a detailed outline of the procedure for compiling the various elements of cost, but the procedure will be discussed briefly.

A daily record is kept by the foreman or timekeeper of the amount of work put in by each employee on each job. This form also provides space for filling in the number of units of work completed. The form is transmitted, probably daily, to the accounting department, where the hours are multiplied by the rate per hour to arrive at the cost of labor put in on the particular activity. This total is then posted to the work order. The amount of time worked is also entered on the payroll register and forms the basis for calculating the amount of pay due hourly employees.

A daily report is prepared showing the amount of materials and supplies used in connection with each activity. The number of the requisition on which the materials were withdrawn is shown on this report. On the basis of the requisitions, the cost of materials used is determined by the accounting department and is entered on the work order in the work and cost ledger. It should be noted

Figure 15-8

## A GOVERNMENTAL UNIT
### Work Order

Control Account _____  No. _____ Job or Operation _____  Page No. _____

Unit Cost Standard _____  Per _____ For Fiscal Year _____  No. _____ 19 ___

| Date | Field Labor | | Materials | | | | | | Equipment Expense | | Engineering and Overhead | Total Cost | Work Units | Unit Costs |
|------|------|------|------|------|------|------|------|------|------|------|------|------|------|------|
| | Hours | Amount | Req. No. | Quan. | Description | Price | Amount | | Hours | Amount | | | | |
| | | | | | | | | | | | | | | |
| | | | | | | | | | | | | | | |
| | | | | | | | | | | | | | | |

that reference here is to materials that can be definitely allocated to a particular job or activity, as, for example, materials used in repairing streets. If the materials are such that they cannot be allocated to a particular job or activity, they are considered part of overhead expenses.

We have indicated before how costs for equipment use are determined and that these costs are recovered by charging a rental fee per mile or hour of use. The foreman records the number of hours or the number of miles worked on each activity by each piece of equipment. When the report is turned in to the accounting department, total equipment use costs for the activity are determined by multiplying the number of miles or hours used by the proper rental rates. The amount is then posted to the work order. The procedure is not materially different if equipment is rented from a private trucking company. Usually the company charges a rental rate per hour or mile, and the cost of equipment use is determined by multiplying the number of miles or hours used for the particular activity by the rate per mile or hour.

As already stated, certain expenses cannot be charged directly to individual activities and must therefore be allocated on some systematic and rational basis. Among these are supervisory salaries; heat, light, and power; and watchmen's wages. From a theoretical standpoint even a part of the cost of operating the general accounting office should be charged to each activity. But, since this is seldom practical, only the overhead of the department carrying on the activity is usually allocated.

One of two procedures may be followed. The first, illustrated briefly earlier, is to accumulate such costs in "suspense" or "clearing" accounts until the end of the accounting period, by which time the total amount of overhead will have been determined. The actual overhead costs incurred during the period are then distributed among jobs and operations on the basis of some factor common to all, such as direct labor cost or the number of direct labor hours, that is thought to be reasonably well correlated with overhead costs incurred. For example, if total overhead expenses of $50,000 are to be distributed among all the activities on the basis of direct labor costs and the total direct labor cost for all such activities is $500,000, the rate to be applied to each activity is 10 percent. Therefore, if the total direct labor cost on activity $A$ is $20,000, the amount of overhead to be applied to that activity is $2,000 ($20,000 $\times$ 10 percent).

The second procedure is to use a factor such as that just illustrated as a basis of apportioning overhead costs continually throughout the period (on an estimated basis) rather than awaiting actual cost determination at period end. Thus, at the beginning of the year the total amount of overhead chargeable to all activities and the total direct labor cost for all activities are estimated. The predetermined overhead application rate is arrived at by dividing the estimated total overhead cost by the estimated total direct labor cost. The amount of overhead applicable to each activity is in turn secured by multiplying the cost of the direct labor put in on the activity by the predetermined overhead application (allocation) rate.

For example, if estimated overhead costs of $100,000 are to be distributed among activities for which the total direct labor cost is estimated to be $500,000, the overhead rate will be 20 percent ($100,000 ÷ $500,000). The amount to be charged to an activity at any time would be arrived at by multiplying the total direct labor cost for the activity by the predetermined rate. Of course, if the actual overhead cost or total direct labor cost incurred is either greater or smaller than the amount originally estimated, adjustments must be made at the end of the year by pro-rating the unapplied or overapplied overhead among the activities or by increasing or decreasing the rate for the following year.

After these overhead costs are determined, they, too, are posted to the work orders and the cost ledger. The total cost is then arrived at by adding the costs of labor, materials and supplies, equipment use, and overhead. As we have indicated before, provision is made for posting the total number of work (or use) units to the work order. The cost per unit can be established by dividing the total cost by the number of work (or use) units.

UNIT COST STANDARDS.    Provision is made on the work order for filling in the unit cost standard. Though standard costs are discussed briefly at a later point in the chapter, it is appropriate to note at this point that a unit cost standard is defined as the minimum cost necessary to perform a unit of work of acceptable quality. Unit cost standards are developed scientifically by studying the necessary operations and the trend of unit costs over a period of time, eliminating from consideration those that are the result of abnormal operating conditions. By comparing actual unit costs with unit cost standards, it is possible to tell to what extent the actual unit costs depart from possible minimum costs. Furthermore, by analyzing the causes of the variance between standard and actual cost, one may obtain hints as to the causes of inefficiency and insight relative to factor use and cost trends and probable future costs.

COST STATEMENTS.    Cost statements are prepared on the basis of the data collected on the individual work orders. These statements show the various operations connected with a particular activity, standard work units, the total cost of carrying on the activity, units of work done, unit cost, number of man hours, units per man hour, number of equipment hours, and units per equipment hour. Figure 15-9 illustrates the appropriate form for a cost statement.

### Construction Costs

Cost accounting is used in construction work for two reasons: (1) to determine whether the operations involved in constructing the project are being, or were, performed efficiently, and (2) to arrive at the total cost of the project.

Figure 15-9

Department _____
Bureau _____

## A GOVERNMENTAL UNIT
### Work and Cost Statement
for Month

| Operation | Standard Work Units | Total Cost | Units of Work Done | Unit Cost | No. of Man Hours | Units per Man Hour | No. of Equipment Hours | Units per Equipment Hour |
|---|---|---|---|---|---|---|---|---|
| **Street Cleaning** | | | | | | | | |
| 1 White Wing | Cleaning Mi. | | | | | | | |
| 2 Broom Gang | " | | | | | | | |
| 3 Machine Sweeping | " | | | | | | | |
| 4 Machine Flushing | " | | | | | | | |
| 5 Hose Flushing | " | | | | | | | |
| 6 Street Sprinkling | " | | | | | | | |
| 7 Sweepings Removed | Cu. Yds. | | | | | | | |
| 8 Snow and Ice Removed | " " | | | | | | | |
| **Street Repairs** | | | | | | | | |
| 11 Concrete Street Repairs | Sq. Yds. | | | | | | | |
| 12 Brick Street Repairs | " | | | | | | | |
| 13 Asphalt Street Repairs | " | | | | | | | |
| 14 Macadam Surface Treatment | " | | | | | | | |
| 15 Plumbers' and Utility Cuts | " " | | | | | | | |
| 16 Cold Patch Repairs | Tons | | | | | | | |
| 17 Curb and Gutter | Lin. Feet | | | | | | | |
| 22 Sidewalk Repairs | Sq. Ft. | | | | | | | |
| 23 Sidewalk Construction | " " | | | | | | | |

The following are some of the operations involved in the construction of sewers, for example, and the units of measure used to determine unit costs:

| Operation | Unit of Measure |
| --- | --- |
| Earth Excavation—Hand | cubic yards |
| Earth Excavation—Machine | cubic yards |
| Rock Works | cubic yards |
| Sheeting and Bracing | lineal feet of trench |
| Underdrain | lineal feet |
| Laying Pipe | lineal feet |
| Form Work | lineal feet |
| Placing Concrete | lineal feet or cubic yards |
| Backfilling | cubic yards |
| Surface Restoration | square yards |

By comparing the unit cost of performing these operations with unit cost standards, it is possible to determine whether or not work is being carried on at the lowest possible cost.

COMPILING COSTS AND UNITS OF WORK. The data necessary for computing both total and unit construction costs are accumulated on a construction work order, a form for which is illustrated in Figure 15-10. Note that provision is made for recording both estimated and actual costs. The estimated cost of a project is determined before the project is approved, of course. To increase their reliability, the estimates are detailed by objects, separate estimates being made for materials, labor, equipment, use, and overhead costs. Where construction activities cannot be expressed in terms of unit costs, the number of units and unit cost columns are left blank or "N.A." (not applicable) is inserted there.

Estimated cost data are based on engineering forecasts. The kinds and quantities of materials to be used, the amount of labor, and the amount of equipment use are estimated by the governmental unit's engineering department. The quantities are priced on the basis of current quotations for materials, payroll and other labor reports, and reports of equipment use. Of course, in pricing materials, labor, and equipment use, cognizance is also taken of probable price trends during the construction period. Estimated overhead is applied either on the basis of labor hours or on the basis of the total cost of materials, labor, and equipment use.

Thus far we have discussed the procedure for accumulating the data on which estimated costs are based. The actual cost of materials, labor, and so forth must be recorded as the work progresses. Under a cost accounting system the procedure for recording construction costs is generally the same as that for recording maintenance costs. To make the discussion clearer, each element of cost will be considered separately.

**Figure 15-10**

(*a*) Front

## A GOVERNMENTAL UNIT
### Construction Work Order

No. _____

Date _____

To _____

You are directed to initiate and complete the work described below.

_____

_____

_____

*Estimates*

| Kind of Work | Mate-rials | Labor | Equip-ment | Over-head | Total | No. of Units | Unit Cost |
|---|---|---|---|---|---|---|---|
| | | | | | | | |
| Totals | | | | | | | |

Approved _____

**Figure 15-10**

(b) Reverse

## Construction Work Order

Work Order No. _____  Work Completed _____ 19___

ACCUMULATION OF COSTS

| Kind of Work | Materials | Labor | Equipment | Overhead | Total Cost | Units | Actual Unit Cost | Total Estimated Cost | Excess or Deficiency* of Total Actual over Estimated Cost | Estimated Unit Cost | Excess or Deficiency* of Actual Unit Cost over Estimated Unit Cost |
|---|---|---|---|---|---|---|---|---|---|---|---|
| | | | | | | | | | | | |
| Totals | | | | | | | | | | | |
| Over or Under* Estimate | | | | | | | | | | | |

Data for the cost of materials issued from inventories are secured from requisitions. Where materials are ordered directly for a particular job, as is frequently the case in construction projects, the cost of materials used is based on the purchase invoices and on invoices and interdepartmental bills for transportation and handling charges.

Data for the cost of labor on each project are obtained from daily labor reports. In the usual case, a daily record is kept by the foremen or by a timekeeper of the amount of work put in by each employee on each job. This form also provides space for filling in the number of work units completed where appropriate. The daily labor report forms are transmitted to the accounting department at regular intervals, preferably daily, where the hours worked are multiplied by the workers' hourly pay rates to arrive at the cost of labor put in on each activity. The total is then posted to the work order, either individually or based on summaries prepared at regular intervals. The hours worked or the total labor cost, or both, are also entered on the payroll register and form the basis for calculating the amount of pay due employees.

Construction projects are charged with the cost of equipment use in the same manner as are maintenance jobs. A record is kept of the number of hours that each piece of equipment is used on the job, and the cost chargeable to the project is arrived at by multiplying the number of hours worked by the rate per hour. The cost of the use of hired private equipment is usually arrived at by multiplying the number of units by the agreed rate per unit—for example, the number of hours worked by the rate per hour or cubic yards of earth excavated by the rate per cubic yard.

As noted earlier, overhead expenses consist of all expenses other than the cost of direct materials, direct labor, and equipment use. They include such costs as workmen's compensation insurance and a portion of general and administrative expenses. If the actual amount of the overhead cost applicable to a particular project is determinable, it is allocated directly to the project. All other overhead is applied on some predetermined basis, such as the cost of labor or the total cost of materials, labor, and equipment use. Sometimes an estimated overhead rate is applied in the manner discussed earlier.

ENTRIES. The entries necessary to record the cost of construction work in progress and the cost of the completed project were illustrated in Chapter 11. It should be remembered that the individual property records for assets constructed by the governmental unit are set up on the basis of the data contained in the construction work order.

COST STATEMENTS. Two types of cost statements are prepared monthly or at less frequent intervals on the basis of the data contained in the individual construction work orders. The first is a statement summarizing, for completed projects or project phases, the information contained in the construction work orders (Figure 15-10). The second is a statement showing the unit costs of construction operations carried on during the month or other period. A form for this statement is illustrated in Figure 15-11.

### Cost Accounting as Applied to Enterprises

The principles and procedures discussed in connection with cost accounting for a governmental unit's general activities are equally applicable to the activities carried on by an enterprise. However, some phases of cost accounting are peculiar to, or especially significant in, enterprise cost accounting. These include the use of clearing accounts and the allocation of joint expenses, both discussed earlier to some extent, and the use of cost units and cost statements that are different from those illustrated previously in this chapter. Each of these is discussed separately below.

CLEARING ACCOUNTS. Certain expenditures are incurred under circumstances that prevent their being charged to the proper accounts at the time they are incurred. Even if the expenses can be charged directly to specific activities, they are sometimes recorded in a clearing account in order that the *total* expenses may be computed before they are distributed among the various accounts. (See Figure 15-6.) For example, it may be desirable not only to allocate shop expenses among the various activities for whose benefit the shop is operated but also to know the *total* shop expenses for a particular period of time. The charges are therefore first recorded in clearing accounts, and then transferred from these accounts to the expense accounts. Clearing accounts are often established for stores inventories and usage, transportation, and shop costs.

In discussing the accounting procedure for materials issued from a central storeroom (Chapter 11), we indicated that charges to departments consist of two elements—the direct cost of the materials and overhead charges. Overhead charges may be accumulated in the Stores Expenses—Clearing (or Overhead) account and then redistributed to the proper accounts either at year end or, by use of predetermined application rates, throughout the year. Since the subject is treated in Chapter 11, that discussion will not be repeated here.

A Transportation Expenses—Clearing account may be charged with the cost of operating the enterprise's vehicles. The procedure in charging expenses to individual pieces of equipment and to the Transportation Expenses—Clearing account should be evident from the discussion earlier in this chapter. The Transportation Expenses—Clearing account is reduced as charges are made to the various jobs and activities on which the equipment was used (see the second entry below).

The Shop Expenses—Clearing account is used to accumulate the cost of operating enterprise shops. At certain intervals, the account is cleared by charging the proper job or activity accounts and crediting the clearing account. Charges to jobs and activities may be made on the basis of the actual cost of materials, labor, and overhead chargeable to each job or activity, on the basis

Figure 15-11

## A GOVERNMENTAL UNIT
### Report of Construction Operation Costs
### for Period

| Operation | Standard Work Units | Units of Work Done | | | Unit Cost | | | Total Cost | | | Production Ratios | |
|---|---|---|---|---|---|---|---|---|---|---|---|---|
| | | Last Month | This Month | This Year to Date | Last Month | This Month | Last Year to Date | This Year to Date | This Month | Last Year to Date | This Year to Date | Units per Labor Hour | Units per Equipment Hour |
| Underdrain | Lin Ft. | | | | | | | | | | | | |
| Form Work | " " | | | | | | | | | | | | |
| Backfilling | Cu. Yds. | | | | | | | | | | | | |

of some predetermined rates, or on a combination of both approaches. Thus, the principles involved in allocating shop and transportation expenses are essentially the same as those involved in charging inventory and general overhead expenses, discussed in this chapter and in Chapter 11.

The following is an example of how the Shop Expenses—Clearing account may be used. The same procedure would, of course, be followed for the other clearing accounts. At the time the expenditure chargeable to the clearing account is first incurred, an entry is made debiting the Shop Expenses—Clearing account and crediting Cash or a liability account. For example, if the payroll for mechanics is $5,000, the transaction is recorded thus:

| | | |
|---|---|---|
| Shop Expenses—Clearing ........................ | 5,000 | |
| Vouchers Payable ........................... | | 5,000 |
| To record expenses for garage labor. | | |

As the particular jobs and activities are charged, the following entry is made:

| | | | |
|---|---|---|---|
| Operating Expenses........................... | | 7,000 | |
| Construction Work in Progress ................. | | 3,000 | |
| Shop Expenses—Clearing .................... | | | 10,000 |
| To record distribution of clearing expenses among jobs and activities, as follows: | | | |
| Operating expenses: | | | |
| Transmission Expenses: | | | |
| Repairs to Transmission System ............ | | | 2,000 |
| Maintenance of Poles, Towers, Fixtures, and Conduits: | | | |
| Repairs to Poles, Towers, and Fixtures ...... | | 2,000 | |
| Repairs to Underground Conduits ........... | | 1,000 | 3,000 |
| Distribution Expenses: | | | |
| Repairs to Distribution Structures and Equipment ............................... | | 1,000 | |
| Repairs to Overhead Distribution Conductors . | | 500 | |
| Repairs to Underground Distribution Conductors................................. | | 500 | 2,000 |
| Total Operating Expenses ............... | | | 7,000 |

CONSTRUCTION WORK IN PROGRESS:

| *Work Order No.* | *Amount* | |
|---|---|---|
| 11 ..................................... | 1,000 | |
| 12 ..................................... | 500 | |
| 13 ..................................... | 1,000 | |
| 14 ..................................... | 300 | |
| 15 ..................................... | 200 | |
| Total Construction Work in Progress ...... | | 3,000 |
| Grand Total ........................ | | 10,000 |

Entries would also be made in the "Rentals Earned" column of each individual equipment record (Figure 15-7) showing the total amount of charges applied to jobs and activities for work done by or with the equipment.

Activities and jobs are not charged until clearing accounts are cleared out. Accordingly, it is important to distribute the expenses carried in the account among the various jobs and activities to which they apply and to reduce the clearing account correspondingly. It is especially important to distribute the expenses carried in the clearing accounts before the close of the year, so that all the expenses applicable to the particular year may be included as part of the cost of operations of that year. A clearing account should have no balance at the end of the fiscal year, except where the expenses charged to the account are applicable in part to the succeeding year. Such balances are shown among the deferred debits on the asset side of the balance sheet.

ALLOCATION OF JOINT EXPENSES. Some governmental units operate electric and water utilities under joint management. In some cases both utilities are financed from one fund, whereas in other cases separate funds are set up for each. To insure proper accounting for each utility, it is preferable that each be accounted for in a separate fund. It will be assumed throughout the following discussion that separate Enterprise Funds are used, although the same governmental unit operates both utilities.

The accounting procedure for each utility is the same as that for utilities operated separately rather than jointly. The only point to note about jointly operated utilities is the importance of allocating joint costs (expenses) equitably to each enterprise. An example of such joint costs is the salary of the superintendent where the same man is in charge of both the water and the electric plant. It is usually impracticable to keep a record of the time devoted by the superintendent to each utility, and therefore his salary, and other expenses that cannot be definitely allocated to either utility, must be apportioned on a somewhat arbitrary basis. For example, administrative expenses incurred jointly by both utilities might be allocated equally, based on estimates of time spent, or on the basis of the amount of gross revenue earned by each, if no better allocation basis can be determined.

Another accounting problem that arises when the two utilities are jointly operated is occasioned by the use by one utility of the services of the other. For example, assume that the water plant furnishes water to the electric plant, and the electric plant furnishes electricity to the water plant. As noted in Chapter 14, each utility should bill the other at standard established rates and should record as an expense the charges for services rendered by the other. On the other hand, the plant furnishing the service should record as a revenue the amount charged to the plant using the service.

To illustrate and review, assume that the water utility supplies the electric utility with water at a cost of $10,000. The entries in the accounts of each fund are:

ENTRY IN WATER (ENTERPRISE) FUND:
Due from Electric Fund ...................... 10,000
    Operating Revenues ......................             10,000
To record sale of water to electric utility.

ENTRY IN ELECTRIC (ENTERPRISE) FUND:
Operating Expenses ........................ 10,000
    Due to Water Fund ......................             10,000
To record purchase of water from water utility.

Postings would be made to the proper subsidiary operating revenue accounts and operating expense accounts.

COST UNITS AND STATEMENTS.    An example of cost units used by water utilities for both maintenance and construction purposes appears on pp. 678–79. On the basis of the data compiled on the work orders, statements are prepared monthly or quarterly to show unit costs for various maintenance and construction activities carried on by the utility. These statements are similar to the ones illustrated in Figures 15-9 and 15-11.

In addition to the monthly or quarterly cost statements, statistical statements based on the cost data are prepared at the close of the fiscal year. Examples of some of the statements prepared by water utilities and included in their annual financial reports are given in Figures 15-12 through 15-16. These state-

**Figure 15-12**

A GOVERNMENTAL UNIT
Water Works
Cost of Pumping per Million Gallons
for Fiscal Years Ending
December 31, 19X6–19Y5

| Year | Millions of Gallons Pumped | Total Cost | Cost per Million Gallons |
|------|---------------------------|-------------|--------------------------|
| 19X6 | 5,972.42 | $ 87,867.10 | $14.71 |
| 19X7 | 6,342.16 | 92,006.19 | 14.51 |
| 19X8 | 6,095.93 | 79,154.90 | 12.98 |
| 19X9 | 7,730.86 | 107,024.78 | 13.84 |
| 19Y0 | 8,756.26 | 107,897.18 | 12.32 |
| 19Y1 | 7,805.63 | 97,013.62 | 12.43 |
| 19Y2 | 7,365.49 | 90,220.88 | 12.25 |
| 19Y3 | 7,872.23 | 93,220.88 | 11.86 |
| 19Y4 | 7,308.91 | 90,301.12 | 12.35 |
| 19Y5 | 7,206.26 | 90,072.32 | 12.50 |

**Figure 15-13**

A GOVERNMENTAL UNIT
Water Works
Cost of Purification per Million Gallons
for Fiscal Years Ending
December 31, 19X6–19Y5

| Year | Millions of Gallons Purified | Total Cost | Cost per Million Gallons |
|------|------|------|------|
| 19X6 | 4,364.74 | $ 33,306.06 | $ 7.63 |
| 19X7 | 5,123.26 | 43,083.82 | 8.41 |
| 19Y5 | 6,088.30 | 53,340.34 | 8.76 |

**Figure 15-14**

A GOVERNMENTAL UNIT
Water Works
Cost of Transmission and Distribution per Million Gallons Pumped
for Fiscal Years Ending
December 31, 19X6–19Y5

| Year | Millions of Gallons Pumped | Total Cost | Cost per Million Gallons |
|------|------|------|------|
| 19X6 | 5,972.42 | $ 26,517.54 | $ 4.44 |
| 19X7 | 6,342.16 | 27,271.29 | 4.30 |
| 19Y5 | 7,206.26 | 30,266.29 | 4.20 |

ments show the following: (1) cost of pumping per million gallons, (2) cost of purification per million gallons, (3) cost of transmission and distribution per million gallons pumped, (4) operating revenues, operating revenue deductions, net operating revenues, and net income, and (5) cost per foot of main laid, classified by size.

Figure 15-15

A GOVERNMENTAL UNIT
Water Works
Operating Revenues, Operating Revenue Deductions,
Net Operating Revenues, and Net Income
for Fiscal Years Ending
December 31, 19X6–19Y5

| Year | Operating Revenues | Operating Revenue Deductions | Net Operating Revenues | Net Income |
|---|---|---|---|---|
| 19X6 | $444,520 | $369,220 | $75,300 | $65,000 |
| 19X7 | 486,000 | 405,900 | 80,100 | 70,000 |
| 19Y5 | 503,000 | 426,700 | 76,300 | 65,000 |

Figure 15-16

A GOVERNMENTAL UNIT
Water Works
Cost per Foot of Main Laid, Classified by Size
for Fiscal Years Ending
December 31, 19X6–19Y5

| | 2″ | | 4″ | | | 24″ | |
|---|---|---|---|---|---|---|---|
| Year | No. of Feet Laid | Unit Cost | No. of Feet Laid | Unit Cost | | No. of Feet Laid | Unit Cost |
| 19X6 | 700 | $1.0136 | 16,150 | $1.3484 | | — | — |
| 19X7 | 3,405 | .593 | 19,711 | 1.2061 | | — | — |
| 19X8 | — | — | 54,720 | 1.1623 | | 2,147 | $9.1633 |
| 19X9 | 2,920 | .7351 | 22,529 | 1.1204 | | — | — |
| 19Y0 | 2,380 | .653 | 22,548 | 1.1733 | | — | — |
| 19Y1 | 1,510 | .6056 | 13,330 | 1.0669 | | 7,434 | 9.7357 |
| 19Y2 | — | — | 12,910 | 1.0321 | | — | — |
| 19Y3 | — | — | 5,812 | .8940 | | — | — |
| 19Y4 | 480 | .7533 | — | — | | — | — |
| 19Y5 | 502 | .7044 | 1,461 | 1.0921 | | — | — |

| *Type of Work* | *Units of Measurement* |
|---|---|
| **Maintenance of Mains:** | |
| Opening Blowoffs and Flushing Mains ................ | No. of |
| Thawing Main Pipes ............................. | No. of |
| Locating Main Pipe Leaks ........................ | No. Located |
| Inspecting, Cleaning, and Oiling Main Gates .......... | No. of |
| Emergency Main Shut-Offs and Turn-Ons ........... | No. of |
| Repairing Main Pipes ............................ | No. of Jobs |
| Lowering Mains ................................. | Lineal Feet |
| Repairing Main Gates ............................ | No. of Jobs |
| Resetting and Grading Main Gate Boxes ............. | No. of Boxes |
| **Maintenance of Hydrants:** | |
| Inspecting Hydrants ............................. | No. of |
| Flushing Hydrants ............................... | No. of |
| Oiling and Packing Hydrants ...................... | No. of |
| Thawing, Pickling, and Pumping Hydrants ........... | No. of |
| Painting Hydrants .............................. | No. of |
| Inspecting, Cleaning, and Oiling Hydrant Gates ....... | No. of |
| Repairing Hydrants .............................. | No. of Jobs |
| Grading and Resetting Hydrant Gate Boxes .......... | No. of |
| **Maintenance of Services:** | |
| Repacking and Tightening Service Meter Connections . | No. of |
| Cleaning Services (Cellar work) ..................... | No. of |
| Thawing Services ................................ | No. Thawed |
| Shut-Offs and Turn-Ons ......................... | No. of |
| Cleaning Service for Stop Boxes .................... | No. of |
| Repairing Services ............................... | No. of Jobs |
| Lowering Service Pipes ........................... | Lineal Feet |
| Resetting and Grading Service Boxes ............... | No. of |
| Repairing and Lighting Trenches .................. | No. of |
| **Maintenance of Meters:** | |
| Flushing or Inspecting Meters on Premises............ | No. of |
| Packing or Cleaning Ground Meter Boxes ............ | No. of |
| Removing or Resetting Meters or Meter Interiors ...... | No. of |
| Testing Meters ................................. | No. of |
| Repairing Meters ................................ | No. of |
| Fixing Meter Parts .............................. | No. of |
| **Construction of Mains:** | |
| Excavation ..................................... | Lineal Feet |
| Laying Pipe .................................... | Lineal Feet |
| Backfilling ..................................... | Lineal Feet |

| Type of Work | Units of Measurement |
|---|---|
| Hydrants ........................................ | No. of |
| Connections ..................................... | Lineal Feet |
| Hydrants: | |
| Establishing New Hydrants on Existing Mains ........ | No. of |
| Inserting Hydrant Gates .......................... | No. of |
| Replacing Hydrants ............................. | No. of |
| Pumping ........................................ | Millions of Gallons |
| Filtering ........................................ | Millions of Gallons |
| Transmission and Distribution ...................... | Millions of Gallons |

## Cost Standards and Variance Analyses

Total and unit cost and cost trend data provided by job order or process cost accounting systems constitute valuable financial management information. The ideal cost accounting system, however, also employs cost standards and variance analyses.

A "standard" is a predetermined criteria by which subsequent performance may be evaluated. A "cost standard" or "standard cost," you will recall, is the minimum total or per unit cost necessary to complete a project, a phase of a project, or a given program, activity, or unit of work of the quality desired.

Inasmuch as the use of poor or inappropriate standards may result in misleading analyses and erroneous evaluations of performance, standard costs should be determined carefully and reviewed frequently. It is essential, for example, that cost standards established be both representative of efficient (or acceptable) levels of performance and realistically attainable in the work environment or situation subject to standard costing and variance analysis. It is of less importance whether the standards are integrated within the account structure or are maintained in memorandum form, though the former is usually preferable.

Though the self-study and evaluation necessary to establish viable cost standards is often of significant benefit to management, an even more significant financial management payoff can result from the added post-event evaluation capabilities afforded by variance analysis procedures. *Variance analysis* is the process of determining the nature, magnitudes, and causes of differences between planned and actual performance and/or costs of performance. Whereas only total and/or unit costs are available under cost systems not employing standards, standard cost systems provide information as to "what should have been" as well as "what was." In other words, both the planned or expected and actual total and/or unit costs are known—and deviations between standard and actual cost may be analyzed for clues concerning inefficiency levels and causes, probable cost trends, and methods by which performance may be improved.

Although a detailed discussion of standard costing and variance analysis is beyond the scope of this book, a brief example of its application and usefulness is offered to illustrate its potential in governmental financial management.

VARIANCE ANALYSIS EXAMPLE. Assume that a particular activity is deemed satisfactory if 10,000 units of output can be achieved at a cost of $2.00 per unit, or $20,000. This standard is based on the assumption that 1/4 hour of labor ($2.00/hr.) and 3 units of material (@ 50¢) are needed to complete one unit. During 19XX 9,600 units were produced at a cost of $2.25 per unit, or $21,000. (Assume also that overhead costs are immaterial.)

The usual steps involved in variance analysis are explained, illustrated, and commented upon briefly below:

*First step.*

| | |
|---|---|
| *Planned Total Cost* (9,600 units @ $2.00) = | $19,200 |
| *Actual Total Cost* (9,600 units @ $2.25) = | 21,600 |
| *Total Variance (Unfavorable)* | $ 2,400 |

(Note: without a standard, the only data available would be the actual cost of $21,600. Had costs in the preceding year been $24,700, for example, it might appear that this year's performance was "good.")

*Second step.* The *Total Variance,* $2,400, can be further analyzed by cause through analysis of information on the actual time and material used and determination of unit costs and variances:

*Planned cost per unit:*

| Materials | 3 @ 50c | = $1.50 |
|---|---|---|
| Labor | 1/4 hr. @ $2.00 = | .50 |
| | | $2.00 |

*Actual cost per unit:*

| Materials | 3 @ 60c | = $1.80 | $.25 per unit |
|---|---|---|---|
| | | | Unfavorable (UF) |
| Labor | 1/5 @ $2.25 | = .45 | Variance |
| | | $2.25 | |

The *Unit Cost Variance* may now be separated:

| Materials: | $1.80 − $1.50 = | $.30 UF |
|---|---|---|
| Labor: | $ .50 − $ .45 = | .05 Favorable (F) |
| | | $.25 UF |

*Third step.* An analysis such as the following provides even more insight as to the underlying causes of these variances:

| Materials | Standard at Standard | | | |
|---|---|---|---|---|
| | 3 | .50 | = $1.50 | Use Variance = $0 |
| | Actual at Standard | | | |
| | 3 | .50 | = 1.50 | Price Variance |
| | Actual at Actual | | | = $.30 UF |
| | 3 | .60 | = 1.80 | |

TOTAL Materials Variance $.30 UF per unit

| Labor | Standard at Standard | | | |
|---|---|---|---|---|
| | 1/4 | $2.00 | = $.50 | Time Variance = $.10 F |
| | Actual at Standard | | | |
| | 1/5 | $2.00 | = .40 | Pay rate |
| | Actual at Actual | | | Variance = .05 UF |
| | 1/5 | $2.25 | = .45 | |

TOTAL Labor Variance   $.05 F per unit

A WORD OF CAUTION. While we emphasize the potential benefits of standard costing and variance analysis to governmental financial management, they do not constitute a panacea. Standard costing and variance analysis techniques can be no better than the standards themselves. Moreover, variance analyses do not provide "pat" answers, but offer clues or "leads" to areas warranting management attention.

An unfavorable variance is not always "bad," nor is a favorable variance always "good." One often must be intimately familiar with a specific project or activity in order to analyze the variances in sufficient depth to be able to evaluate underlying causes of variation, their near-term significance, and their probable long-range implications. Thus, the unfavorable materials price variance in the example above could be the result either of inefficient purchasing or of excellent purchasing performance, such as by the purchasing department having provided the required quality of material at 60¢ per unit during a period in which the general market price of the item in question spurted to 70¢ per unit from the 50¢ per unit expected (standard) cost. Likewise, the favorable pay rate variance might reflect (1) increased efficiency resulting from use of more skilled workers where greater productivity more than offsets the increased rate of pay they command, or (2) a temporary increase in productivity of the usual work force resulting from an overall wage boost—with the work force expected to return to lower, more normal productivity levels in the near future—which carries unfavorable long-range cost connotations.

## COST FINDING

Many of the advantages of cost accounting may be obtained without a complete "full" cost accounting information system. Further, as noted earlier, "full" cost is not relevant to every decision or information need. For the preparation of the budget, for example, information and estimates based on the expenditure accounts may be more useful than costs containing elements (for example, depreciation) that are not budgeted. Similarly, control of costs by top administrators may be just as easy, or perhaps easier, if the costs for which a supervisor is held responsible consist only of those elements over which he has control ("controllable costs"). A supervisor can control such direct costs as personnel and materials; but depreciation expenses may have been determined by his superior or his predecessor, and overhead costs assigned to his operations usually are not subject to his control. Thus, control over costs at the point where they are incurred ordinarily does not require knowledge of total cost, though a "controllable cost" accounting system may be needed.

Attaining most of the other advantages of cost accounting noted at the beginning of this chapter requires knowledge of total costs, but having this information made available routinely through a formal cost accounting system may not be essential to effective day-to-day administration. Among the activities for which information need be available only periodically or occasionally are: decisions as to whether the city's work force should do a job or whether it should be contracted, the setting of rates and negotiating contracts for services rendered by the city, reporting to officials and the public, and determination of the cost of fixed assets constructed.

### Cost Finding Approaches

Cost finding, as contrasted with cost accounting, has been described as the determination or estimation of costs, however defined, by less formal procedures and/or on an irregular basis. In the usual case it involves taking available fund expenditure or other data and recasting, supplementing, and manipulating it in order to derive the cost data or estimate sought.

The illustration in Figure 15-1 might well have been titled "The Usual Cost Finding Approach," inasmuch as it serves as a general cost-finding model as well as to illustrate the reconciliation of expenditures and costs or expenses. To illustrate utilization of the cost finding approach, assume that the street maintenance function is financed through the General Fund, that it is desired to derive the *expense* of operating that department's vehicle fleet, and that the following information has been gathered from a variety of sources:

1. Total expenditures for vehicle acquisition, operation, and maintenance during the period were $72,000.
2. Of this total, $20,000 was for new vehicle acquisition and $8,000 was for major overhauls, that should be capitalized; the balance was for routine maintenance.
3. Depreciation of the vehicles has been calculated at $84,000.
4. Maintenance expenditures of $1,000 were made for supplies not used this

period; supplies acquired through prior period expenditures, but used for maintenance this period, cost $4,000.
5. Insurance premiums for policies on all vehicles are paid through a Special Revenue Fund; the portion expired this period and applicable to the street maintenance vehicle fleet is determined to be $2,000.

*Cost Calculation:*

| | | |
|---|---:|---:|
| Total *Expenditures*, this period .......................... | | $72,000 |
| Less: Expenditures benefiting other periods: | | |
| Acquisition of new vehicles ................ | $20,000 | |
| Major Overhauls ........................ | 8,000 | |
| Purchase of supplies not used this period ...... | 1,000 | 29,000 |
| Current Period Expenditures ...................... | | $43,000 |
| Plus: Expenditures of other periods benefiting this period: | | |
| Depreciation of vehicles ................... | $84,000 | |
| Supplies purchased previously but used this period .............................. | 4,000 | |
| Insurance expense ....................... | 2,000 | 90,000 |
| Total *Expense*, this period............................. | | $133,000 |

This general approach is useful in all situations where the basic records available are expenditure-based and expense or cost data is desired. It is equally useful in determining reimbursable, controllable, direct (prime), variable, or other costs from expenditure-based data. Note also in the above example that total expenditures and total expenses were far different, indicating the severity of the potential error of anyone confusing these two very different concepts in either total or per unit calculations.

Another cost finding approach is that common in reimbursable cost finding situations. Inasmuch as this approach is best developed and most widely used in the health care industry, it is illustrated through a hospital example.

## A Hospital Cost Finding Example

The American Hospital Association recommends that hospitals use a "controllable cost" accounting system to control day-to-day activities and that full and reimbursable costs be determined by use of cost finding techniques.[6] Data for budgeting and current control over costs are produced by use of cost accounting centers, for which are accumulated the direct costs that are controllable by the department head or lower-level supervisor. These cost centers tradition-

---

[6] *Cost Finding and Rate Setting for Hospitals* (Chicago: The Association, 1968), p. 1. This AHA book contains extensive discussions on, and a comprehensive illustration of, hospital cost finding. The illustration in this chapter is necessarily brief and general.

ally are referred to as *special service* or *patient service* departments or activities if their services are rendered directly to patients; they are referred to as *general service* departments or activities if they provide services to the hospital as a whole. In recent years they have increasingly been categorized simply as "revenue producing" or "nonrevenue producing." A system of worksheet (or computerized) procedures is then utilized to provide for the allocation and accumulation of cost data so that information equivalent to that produced by a full cost accounting system is produced.

METHODS OF COST ALLOCATION. Three methods, known by various terms or simply by number, are currently accepted and widely used for making the cost allocations. The results produced by the methods differ enough to require that a single method should be adopted and used consistently if period-by-period comparisons are to be made.

Under Method 1, often referred to as the "direct" or "single step" method, the costs of nonrevenue producing (general service) cost centers are distributed only to the revenue producing (special service and patient service) cost centers. Revenue producing patient service cost centers—classified here as Inpatients, Nursery, Outpatients, Emergency, and Private Ambulatory—are not the cost centers to which most costs are charged directly. However, all costs are ultimately charged to them by the worksheet procedure.

Under Method 2, often termed the "step down" method, a nonrevenue producing (general service) department's costs may be distributed to other nonrevenue producing (general service) departments as well as to revenue producing (special service and patient service) cost centers. After a department's costs have been distributed, it does not receive distributions from other departments, however, even though it may benefit from their services. Therefore an attempt is made to allocate departmental costs in such an order that the inaccuracies will be minimized; that is, the departments that receive the least service from the others will be closed out first.

Under Method 3, sometimes known as the "double step" or "double distribution" method, the costs of each nonrevenue producing (general service) department are distributed to every other department it serves. Again, an attempt is made to distribute first the costs of the departments that receive the least service from others. Even though a department's costs have been allocated, it may receive distributions from other departments during the "first round" allocation process. The amounts are then reallocated as in Method 2.[7]

Method 3 is the most accurate of those described above; Method 1, the

---

[7] A fourth method, which may be called the "mathematical" or "scientific" method, is more accurate than any of the three common methods discussed but appears to be used rather infrequently, possibly due to its use of complex simultaneous equations to apportion costs among all departments and ultimately allocate all general service costs to special service and patient cost centers. Mathematical solution of a distribution involving as many unknowns as are present in a hospital usually is not feasible in the absence of computer capability; hence this method is not discussed in detail here.

least accurate. Method 2 is a widely used compromise and is used in a further description of cost allocation worksheet technique.

The usual worksheet procedures involve three basic steps: (1) rearrangement of direct costs, (2) allocation of nonrevenue producing (general service) department costs, and (3) allocation of revenue producing (special service) department costs. Each of these steps is discussed in the following paragraphs.

REARRANGEMENT OF DIRECT COSTS.   In some cases direct cost centers established because of supervisory assignments contain costs allocable to two or more identifiable activities. For example, budgeting and day-to-day cost control may dictate the use of a dietary cost center. All raw food and food preparation costs are assigned to this center and are the responsibility of the dietitian. But for allocation purposes it must be recognized that a hospital cafeteria usually serves individuals or groups in addition to inpatients. Hence, before the allocation of dietary costs to other departments is begun, they must be separated into those costs applicable to the cafeteria, those applicable to the nursery, and those applicable to inpatients. The separation should be based on priced requisitions of food and analysis of payroll costs incurred for cafeteria and other dietary functions. The cost center data that are the basis of succeeding steps in this example may be assumed to already reflect rearrangements of direct costs such as that just described.

ALLOCATION OF NONREVENUE PRODUCING (GENERAL SERVICE) DEPARTMENT COSTS.   The following is a list of typical nonrevenue producing (general service) departments and their usual bases of allocation to other nonrevenue pro-

**Figure 15-17**

### A HOSPITAL
#### Cost Apportionment

Schedule No.: <u>B–11</u>
Cost Center: <u>Nursing Service</u>
For Fiscal Year: _____
Basis of Apportionment: <u>Nursing Staff Hours</u>

| Cost Center | Statistical Data | Cost Apportionment |
|---|---|---|
| Inpatients | 175,000 | $306,250 |
| Nursery | 25,000 | 43,750 |
| Total | 200,000 | $350,000 |

| Cost Center | Total | Provision for Depreciation | Employee Health and Welfare | Nursing Service | Social Service |
|---|---|---|---|---|---|
| 1 | 2 | 3 | 4 | 13 | 17 |
| **General Service Cost Centers** | | | | | |
| Provision for Depreciation.... | $ 45,000 | $45,000 | | | |
| Employee Health and Welfare | 40,000 | $ 50 | $40,500 | | |
| Operation of Plant ......... | 65,000 | 600 | $ 200 | | |
| Maintenance of Plant ....... | 35,000 | 400 | 1,300 | | |
| Laundry and Linen Service . | 30,000 | 800 | 1,350 | | |
| Housekeeping .............. | 60,000 | 300 | 2,300 | | |
| Dietary—Raw Food ........ | 46,000 | | | | |
| —Other............. | 61,000 | 800 | 2,500 | | |
| Cafeteria ................. | 52,000 | 1,200 | 800 | | |
| Maintenance of Personnel ... | 5,000 | 7,050 | 200 | | |
| Nursing Service............. | 310,000 | 400 | 11,300 | $350,000 | |
| Medical Supplies and Expense | 85,000 | 800 | 1,200 | | |
| Pharmacy ................. | 50,000 | 450 | 400 | | |
| Medical Records........... | 20,000 | 600 | 900 | | |
| Social Service ............. | 10,000 | 300 | 300 | | $12,500 |
| Nursing School ............. | 27,000 | 2,550 | 1,050 | | |
| Intern-Resident Service ..... | 48,000 | 150 | 1,850 | | |
| Administration and General . | 160,000 | 2,500 | 4,300 | | |
| Cost of Meals Sold ......... | | | | | |
| Cost of Rooms Rented ...... | | | | | |
| **Special Service Cost Centers** | | | | | |
| Operating Service.......... | 76,000 | 4,500 | 2,550 | | |
| Delivery Room ............. | 20,000 | 850 | 850 | | |
| Anesthesia ................. | 12,000 | 350 | | | |
| Radiology ................. | 56,000 | 2,200 | 1,850 | | |
| Laboratory ................ | 81,000 | 1,200 | 2,850 | | |
| Blood Bank ................ | 34,000 | 300 | 400 | | |
| BMR—EKG .............. | 8,000 | 200 | 100 | | |
| Oxygen Therapy ........... | 6,000 | 400 | 50 | | |
| Physical Therapy ........... | 25,000 | 800 | 600 | | |
| Cost of Medical Supplies Sold | | | | | |
| Cost of Drugs Sold ........ | | | | | |
| **Inpatient Cost Centers** | | | | | |
| Inpatients ................. | | 12,150 | | $306,250 | $ 6,500 |
| Nursery .................. | 2,000 | 850 | | 43,750 | |
| **Outpatient Cost Centers** | | | | | |
| Outpatients ................ | 15,000 | 1,500 | 500 | | 5,500 |
| Emergency................. | 20,000 | 750 | 800 | | 500 |
| Total ................ | $1,504,000 | $45,000 | $40,500 | $350,000 | $12,500 |

Figure 15-18

| Subtotal | Deduct Recovery of Expenses | Nursing School | Intern-Resident Service | Subtotal After Deductions | Administrative and General | Total |
|---|---|---|---|---|---|---|
| 18 | 19 | 20 | 21 | 22 | 23 | 24 |
| $  85,000 | $ 8,500 | $76,500 | | | | |
| 75,000 | | | $75,000 | | | |
| 202,000 | | | | $  202,000 | | |
| 23,500 | 23,000 | | | 500 | | |
| 6,500 | 6,700 | | | (200) | $202,300 | |
| 108,000 | | $ 7,500 | $10,000 | 125,500 | $ 20,742 | $  146,242 |
| 36,000 | | 6,500 | 7,500 | 50,000 | 8,264 | 58,264 |
| 14,000 | | | 8,000 | 22,000 | 3,636 | 25,636 |
| 66,000 | | | | 66,000 | 10,908 | 76,908 |
| 86,000 | | | | 86,000 | 14,214 | 100,214 |
| 34,000 | | | | 34,000 | 5,619 | 39,619 |
| 9,000 | | | | 9,000 | 1,487 | 10,487 |
| 7,000 | | | | 7,000 | 1,157 | 8,157 |
| 31,000 | | | | 31,000 | 5,124 | 36,124 |
| 4,500 | | | | 4,500 | | 4,500 |
| 35,000 | | | | 35,000 | | 35,000 |
| 570,500 | | 52,000 | 36,000 | 658,500 | 108,835 | 767,335 |
| 51,000 | | 4,500 | | 55,500 | 9,173 | 64,673 |
| 29,500 | | 3,600 | 7,000 | 40,100 | 6,628 | 46,728 |
| 30,500 | | 2,400 | 6,500 | 39,400 | 6,513 | 45,913 |
| $1,504,000 | $38,200 | $76,500 | $75,000 | $1,465,800 | $202,300 | $1,465,800 |

ducing (general service) departments and to revenue producing (special service and patient service) cost centers:

| *Nonrevenue Producing*<br>*(General Service) Cost Center* | *Basis of Allocation* |
|---|---|
| Provision for Depreciation .......... | For Buildings:   Floor Space |
| | For Equipment:   Equipment in Use |
| Employee Health and Welfare ....... | Dollars of Payroll |
| Operation of Plant ................ | Floor Space |
| Maintenance of Plant.............. | Floor Space |
| Laundry and Linen Service ........ | Pounds of Laundry Used |
| Housekeeping .................... | Hours of Service |
| Dietary—Raw Food .............. | To Cafeteria:   Priced Requisitions |
| | To Inpatients:   Meals Served |
| Dietary—Other .................. | To Cafeteria: Per Cent of Raw Food Costs |
| | To Inpatients: Meals Served |
| Cafeteria ....................... | Sales Value of Meals Served |
| Maintenance of Personnel ......... | Number of Employees Housed |
| Nursing Service .................. | Hours of Service |
| Medical Supplies and Expense ...... | Priced Requisitions |
| Pharmacy....................... | Priced Requisitions |
| Medical Records ................. | Hours of Service |
| Social Service ................... | Hours of Service |
| Nursing School .................. | Hours of Service |
| Intern-Resident School ........... | Hours of Service |
| Administration and General ........ | Accumulated Costs of Other Centers |

A worksheet illustrating the allocation of Nursing Service costs to other centers is given in Figure 15-17. Nursing staff hours for the period were 200,000; total cost was $350,000. By dividing $350,000 by 200,000 an hourly rate of $1.75 is produced; this rate times the nursing hours spent in a cost center produces the nursing service allocation to that center. A similar worksheet allocation is prepared for each general service cost center.

Data provided by the worksheet allocations described in the preceding paragraph are summarized on the "Cost Apportionment—General Services" worksheet, Figure 15-18. Note that the provision for depreciation is distributed first (in column 3) and that depreciation becomes a part of the total cost of the employee health and welfare center which is distributed. As a further example note that the direct cost of nursing service is $310,000 (column 1) but that the amount ditributed in column 13, $350,000, includes cost distributions made in preceding columns.

The result of the distributions made in Figure 15-18 is the accumulation of total costs for special service centers and partial costs for patient service centers. A comparison of the statistics on output of the special service centers with their accumulated total costs will produce total unit costs. These data may be reported for the purposes previously cited in a statement such as "Special Services Costs," Figure 15-19.

ALLOCATION OF SPECIAL SERVICE DEPARTMENT COSTS.    After total costs have been computed for special service departments they are distributed to the patient cost centers. A worksheet such as that illustrated in Figure 15-17 for the apportionment of nursing service costs is prepared for each of the special service centers. The apportionments are made on the bases indicated in Figure 15-19, the report of "Special Services Costs," except that if some of the units are not uniform, a weighting process may be used. That is to say, if certain kinds of physical therapy treatments are more expensive than others, the more expensive ones may be appropriately weighted to allocate the total cost of treatments more accurately.

A worksheet for accumulation of total patient center costs is illustrated in Figure 15-20. The data from the allocation worksheets for each special service cost center are entered in it to accumulate total costs.

After total costs have been computed they may be compared with statistical data concerning output of the patient centers to arrive at total unit costs. Reporting of these data is illustrated in Figure 15-21, "Inpatient and Outpatient Costs."

**Figure 15-19**

### A HOSPITAL
Special Services Costs
For Fiscal Year

| Special Service Cost Center | Total Costs | Units of Service Rendered | | Average Cost Per Unit |
|---|---|---|---|---|
| Operating Service | $146,242 | 5,879 | hours | $24.88 |
| Delivery Room | 58,264 | 1,167 | deliveries | 49.92 |
| Anesthesia | 25,636 | 6,555 | hours | 3.91 |
| Radiology | 76,908 | 29,015 | films | 2.65 |
| Laboratory | 100,214 | 70,780 | examinations | 1.42 |
| Blood Bank | 39,619 | 1,752 | transfusions | 22.61 |
| BMR—EKG | 10,487 | 1,772 | examinations | 5.92 |
| Oxygen Therapy | 8,157 | 8,526 | hours | .96 |
| Physical Therapy | 36,124 | 1,111 | treatments | 3.25 |
| Cost of Medical Supplies Sold | 4,500 | | | |
| Cost of Drugs Sold | 35,000 | | | |

Figure 15-20

# A HOSPITAL
## Cost Apportionment—Special Services
### For Fiscal Year

| Cost Center | Accumulated Costs* | Inpatients | Nursery | Outpatients | Emergency | Private Ambulatory |
|---|---|---|---|---|---|---|
| 1 | 2 | 3 | 4 | 5 | 6 | 7 |
| **Special Service Cost Centers:** | | | | | | |
| Operating Service | $ 146,242 | $ 137,442 | $ 8,800 | | | |
| Delivery Room | 58,264 | 58,264 | | | | |
| Anesthesia | 25,636 | 24,600 | 1,036 | | | |
| Radiology | 76,908 | 34,200 | 1,708 | $ 2,200 | $ 5,300 | $33,500 |
| Laboratory | 100,214 | 80,500 | 1,500 | 7,914 | 700 | 9,600 |
| Blood Bank | 39,619 | 37,400 | 500 | | 1,719 | |
| BMR—EKG | 10,487 | 7,800 | 100 | 500 | 100 | 1,987 |
| Oxygen Therapy | 8,157 | 6,100 | 1,500 | | 557 | |
| Physical Therapy | 36,124 | 11,200 | | 9,924 | | 15,000 |
| Cost of Medical Supplies Sold | 4,500 | 4,100 | 400 | | | |
| Cost of Drugs Sold | 35,000 | 26,600 | 200 | 2,800 | 1,100 | 4,300 |
| **Inpatient Cost Centers:** | | | | | | |
| Inpatients | 767,335 | 767,335 | | | | |
| Nursery | 64,673 | | 64,673 | | | |
| **Outpatient Cost Centers:** | | | | | | |
| Outpatients | 46,728 | | | 46,728 | | |
| Emergency | 45,913 | | | | 45,913 | |
| Private Ambulatory | | | | | | |
| Total | $1,465,800 | $1,195,541 | $80,417 | $70,066 | $55,289 | $64,287 |

**Figure 15-21**

## A HOSPITAL
### Inpatient and Outpatient Costs
### for Fiscal Year

| Cost Center | Total Costs* | Units of Service Rendered | Average Cost Per Unit |
|---|---|---|---|
| **Inpatient Cost Centers:** | | | |
| Inpatients | $1,195,541 | 53,161 patient days | $22.49 |
| Nursery | 80,417 | 7,393 new born days | 10.88 |
| **Outpatient Costs Centers:** | | | |
| Outpatients | 70,066 | 9,886 visits | 7.09 |
| Emergency | 55,389 | 5,518 visits | 10.04 |
| Private Ambulatory | 64,387 | 13,025 visits | 4.94 |

\* From "Total" line, Figure 15-20.

Hospitals are not, of course, the first organizations to use cost finding. Broadly speaking, any special study of costs is "cost finding," as is a system of cost accounting. However, the formal acceptance of cost finding as a preferred solution to the problem of obtaining total cost is unusual; the usefulness of the approach for hospital administration indicates that it may be useful in other areas of fund accounting.

**Question 15-1.** Explain the meaning of the statement made in the chapter that "every decision affecting future resource allocation—and each evaluation of past resource utilization—necessarily involves either implicit or explicit comparison of the costs incurred, or to be incurred, with the benefits received or expected."

**Question 15-2.** What is the principal difference between financial accounting generally and cost accounting? Between cost accounting and cost finding?

**Question 15-3.** How do *budgetary* costs differ from *full* costs?

**Question 15-4.** Fixed costs are variable per unit and variable costs are fixed per unit. Explain.

**Question 15-5.** Distinguish between the following terms:
a.  Replacement cost and opportunity cost
b.  Marginal cost and differential cost
c.  Incremental cost and decremental cost
d.  Process costs and controllable costs
e.  Reimbursable costs and job order costs
f.  Fixed costs and variable costs
g.  Semifixed costs and semivariable costs
h.  Direct costs and indirect costs
i.  Prime cost and conversion cost

    j.   Short-run costs and long-run costs
    k.   Absorption costing and variable (or "direct") costing
    l.   Relevant cost center and relevant range.

**Question 15-6.** Discuss the desirability of a cost accounting system as compared with a cost finding system.

**Question 15-7.** Do you think that a cost finding system should be used in a municipality? For all activities? Characterize the types of activities for which you think cost finding is suitable.

**Question 15-8.** Mention at least three factors that are likely to make the unit cost of collecting and hauling garbage in two cities differ.

**Question 15-9.** What are cost *standards* and of what value are they in municipal cost accounting?

**Question 15-10.** What are the major benefits and limitations of standard costing?

**Question 15-11.** "The existence of an effective costing system is a prerequisite to an effective performance budgeting system." Discuss.

**Question 15-12.** Why is it important that reimbursable costing, though necessary, not be permitted to supplant cost determination on another basis?

**Question 15-13.** Discuss the advisability of comparing the unit costs of one hospital with those of another hospital.

**Question 15-14.** The XYZ Hospital has an appropriation for *Clerical Help* which includes the salaries of clerks in the administrator's office, admissions office, accounting office, and out-patient clinic. Discuss the implications of this arrangement for cost accounting and cost finding purposes.

**Question 15-15.** A city operates both an electric utility and a water utility. The electric utility uses water to generate steam, and the water utility uses electricity for pumping purposes. If both utilities make a sufficient profit each year from sales of services to customers to provide the money necessary for the retirement of bonds, should the charges made by the electric utility to the water utility (or vice versa) for services be sufficiently high to yield a profit or should they be limited to the cost of rendering the service (exclusive of profits)?

**Question 15-16.** Indicate some of the dangers inherent in relying upon short-run cost data in decision-making.

**Question 15-17.**
    a.   Define direct labor and indirect labor.
    b.   Discuss three reasons for distinguishing between direct and indirect labor.
    c.   Give three costing methods of accounting for the premium costs of overtime direct labor. Under what circumstances would each method be appropriate? (AICPA, adapted)

**Question 15-18.**
    a.   Define standard costs.
    b.   What are the advantages of a standard cost system?
    c.   Present arguments in support of each of the following three methods of treating standard cost variances for purposes of financial reporting:
        1.   They may be carried as deferred charges or credits on the balance sheet.
        2.   They may appear as charges or credits on the income statement.
        3.   They may be allocated between inventories and cost of goods sold. (AICPA, adapted)

**Question 15-19. Part I.** After reading an article you recommended on cost behavior, your client asks you to explain the following excerpts from it:

1. "*Fixed costs* are variable per unit of output and *variable costs* are fixed per unit of output (though in the long run all costs are variable)."

2. "*Depreciation* may be either a fixed cost or a variable cost, depending on the method used to compute it."

Required:

For each excerpt:

(a)  Define the *underscored* terms. Give examples where appropriate.

(b)  Explain the meaning of the excerpt to your client.

**Question 15-19. Part II.**  A breakeven chart, as illustrated below, is a useful technique for showing relationships between costs, volume, and profits or contribution to overhead.

Required:

(a)  Identify the numbered components of the breakeven chart.

(b)  Discuss the significance of the concept of the "relevant range" to breakeven analyses.

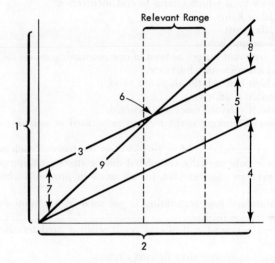

(AICPA, adapted)

**Question 15-20.**  The following statements pertain to cost accounting, budgeting, and the control of operations through the use of cost data. Complete each statement by selecting the best answer choice for each item. Write the appropriate letter on a separate answer sheet. Select only one answer for each item.

1.  Job order cost accounting is a method for determining the cost of units of goods or services

a.  Where production or provision is a continuous process.

b.  Which are indistinguishable from any others produced or provided.

c.  Where each is unique in specialized production or provision.

d.  When an estimated cost system is employed.

2.  One employing very tight (high) standards in a standard cost system should expect that

a.  Costs will be controlled better than if lower standards were used.

    b.   Employees will be strongly motivated to attain the standards.

    c.   No incentive bonus will be paid.

    d.   Most variances will be unfavorable.

3.   Standard costing will produce the same results as actual or conventional costing when standard cost variances are distributed to

    a.   Cost of goods sold or services provided.

    b.   A revenue or expense account.

    c.   Cost of goods sold or services provided and inventories or deferred charges.

    d.   A balance sheet account.

4.   Flexible budgeting is a reporting system wherein the

    a.   Budget standards may be adjusted at will.

    b.   Reporting dates vary according to the levels of activity reported upon.

    c.   Statements included in the budget report vary from period to period.

    d.   Planned level of activity is adjusted to the actual level of activity before the budget comparison report is prepared.

5.   Manufacturing overhead should be allocated on the basis of

    a.   An activity basis which relates to cost incurrence.

    b.   Direct labor hours.

    c.   Direct labor cost.

    d.   Direct machine hours.

6.   The term "relevant range" as used in cost accounting means the range

    a.   Over which costs may fluctuate.

    b.   Over which cost relationships are valid.

    c.   Of probable production.

    d.   Over which relevant costs are incurred.

7.   Process cost accounting is the method to be used in assigning costs to products or services

    a.   Which are manufactured or provided on the basis of each order received.

    b.   Which are only partially completed during the accounting period.

    c.   As an average cost per unit for all units in process during the accounting period.

    d.   When standard cost accounting is not used in a continuous process manufacturing or service facility.

8.   Overapplied overhead will always result when a predetermined overhead rate is employed and

    a.   Production is greater than defined capacity.

    b.   Actual overhead costs are less than expected.

    c.   Defined capacity is less than normal capacity.

    d.   Overhead incurred is less than overhead applied.

9.   The difference over a period of time between actual overhead and applied overhead will usually be minimal when the predetermined overhead rate is based on

    a.   Normal (or practical) capacity.

    b.   Designed capacity.

    c.   Direct labor hours.

    d.   Direct machine hours.

10.   If a predetermined overhead rate is not employed and the volume of production or service provision is reduced from the level planned, the cost per unit would be expected to

    a.   Remain unchanged for fixed costs and increase for variable costs.

    b.   Increase for fixed costs and remain unchanged for variable costs.

    c.   Increase for fixed costs and decrease for variable costs.

    d.  Decrease for fixed costs and decrease for variable costs.
11.  Management by exception refers to management's
    a.  Having no predetermined plan.
    b.  Considering only rare events.
    c.  Taking action on items selected at random.
    d.  Considering only items which vary materially from plans.
12.  As applied to cost accounting, a cost center is a
    a.  Unit of activity for which costs are accumulated.
    b.  Cost accounting department.
    c.  Plant accounting department.
    d.  Production department.
13.  Absorption costing differs from direct costing in the
    a.  Amount of costs assigned to individual units of product.
    b.  Amount of net income that will be reported when there is no change in inventory.
    c.  Amount of fixed costs that will be incurred.
    d.  Kinds of activities for which they may be used to report.
14.  An understatement of work in process inventory at the end of a period will
    a.  Understate cost of goods manufactured in that period.
    b.  Overstate current assets.
    c.  Overstate gross profit from sales in that period.
    d.  Understate net income for that period.
15.  Cost-profit-volume analysis is most important for the determination of the
    a.  Volume of operation necessary to break even.
    b.  Relationship between revenues and costs at various levels of operations.
    c.  Variable revenues necessary to equal fixed costs.
    d.  Sales revenue necessary to equal variable costs.
16.  Reporting under the direct costing concept is accomplished by
    a.  Including only direct costs in the income statement.
    b.  Matching variable costs against revenues and treating fixed costs as period costs.
    c.  Treating all costs as period costs.
    d.  Eliminating the work in process inventory account. (AICPA, adapted)

## Question 15-21.

a.  Explain the meanings of the terms (1) cost, (2) expense, and (3) loss as used for financial reporting in conformity with generally accepted accounting principles. In your explanation discuss the distinguishing characteristics of the terms and their similarities and interrelationships.

b.  Classify each of the following items as a cost, expense, loss or other category and explain how the classification of each item may change:

    1.  Cost of goods sold or services provided.
    2.  Bad debts expense.
    3.  Depreciation expense for plant machinery.
    4.  Spoiled goods.

c.  The terms "period cost" and "product cost" are sometimes used to describe certain items in financial statements. Define these terms and distinguish between them. To what types of items do each apply? (AICPA, adapted)

## Question 15-22.

(Reference to a standard intermediate or cost accounting text may be required in answering this question.) Inventories usually are an important asset in manufacturing, merchandising, or service activities. A proper balance of inventory quantities is desirable from several standpoints. Maintaining such a balance is dependent upon a number of factors including ordering at the proper time and in the correct lot size. Serious penalites may attend both overstocking and stockout situations.

Required:

a. Define "cost" as applied to the valuation of inventories.

b. In connection with inventory ordering and control, certain terms are basic. Explain the meaning of each of the following:

1. Economic order quantity.
2. Reorder point.
3. Lead time.
4. Safety stock.

c.

1. What are the costs of carrying inventories? Explain.
2. How does overstocking add to the cost of carrying inventories?

d.

1. What are the consequences of maintaining minimal or inadequate inventory levels?
2. What are the difficulties of measuring precisely the costs associated with understocking?

e. What factors should be considered in computing:

1. Optimum investment in inventory. Identify both those costs which do and those which normally do not explicitly appear on formal accounting records.
2. Economic order quantity.
3. Minimum stock reorder point.

f. Discuss the propriety of including carrying costs (of normal inventory, overstocking, and understocking) in the inventory cost:

1. For external reporting.
2. For internal decision making.

(AICPA, adapted)

**Problem 15-1.** (Expenditure apportionment) Counties $X$ and $Y$ operate a sanitarium jointly. Operating and maintenance costs, after revenues applicable to them have been deducted, are apportioned on the basis of the number of patient-days (the care of one patient for one day) attributable to each county. Expenditures for fixed assets, after rental income has been deducted, are distributed on the basis of the assessed value of the taxable property of each county. Settlements are made every six months.

You are given these facts for the first six months of 19X3:

| | | |
|---|---:|---:|
| Operating and maintenance expenditures . . . . . . . . . | | $73,000 |
| Revenues earned in connection with operations . . . . . | | 1,000 |
| Number of patient-days: | | |
| County $X$ . . . . . . . . . . . . . . . . . . . . . . . . . . . . . . . . . . . | 17,500 | |
| County $Y$. . . . . . . . . . . . . . . . . . . . . . . . . . . . . . . . . . . . | 11,300 | |
| Capital outlays . . . . . . . . . . . . . . . . . . . . . . . . . . . . . . . . | | 2,400 |
| Rental income . . . . . . . . . . . . . . . . . . . . . . . . . . . . . . . | | 560 |
| Assessed valuation of taxable property: | | |
| County $X$ . . . . . . . . . . . . . . . . . . . . . . . . . . . . . . . . . . | $129,000,000 | |
| County $Y$. . . . . . . . . . . . . . . . . . . . . . . . . . . . . . . . . . . . | 86,000,000 | |

Required:

Prepare a statement showing the apportionment of sanitarium expenditures for the first six months of 19X3 between the counties.

**Problem 15-2.**   (Cost finding) The County of Milton operates a quarry financed from an Intragovernmental Service Fund for the purpose of obtaining rock needed for highway construction purposes. A small amount of rock is also sold to a municipality located near by. The operations of the quarry are financed through charges made to the county highway department and the nearby municipality.

The following is a summary of transactions taking place in 19X7:

|  | Tons | Pounds | Per Ton |
|---|---|---|---|
| Sales to highway department: |  |  |  |
| Crushed rock—from bins | 3,173 | 1,100 | $3.00 |
| Crushed rock—from quarry | 892 | 1,180 | 2.50 |
| Rubble—from quarry | 347 | 100 | 1.00 |
| Rock dust—from quarry | 71 | 1,500 | .50 |
| Sales to City of A: |  |  |  |
| Crushed rock—from quarry | 207 | 1,200 | 2.55 |
| Rock dust—from quarry | 145 | 100 | .50 |

Expenditures were incurred as follows:

|  | Extracting | Crushing | Other |
|---|---|---|---|
| Labor | $5,351 | $ 397 |  |
| Dynamite | 82 |  |  |
| Repairs to machinery and equipment | 147 | 1,328 |  |
| Building repairs | 84 |  |  |
| Oil and supplies | 124 |  |  |
| Tools | 286 |  |  |
| Purchase of machinery and equipment | 500 | 1,500 |  |
| Taxes, insurance, and royalty |  |  | $989 |
| Freight on crushed rock |  |  | 937 |
| Labor unloading rock |  |  | 229 |
| Repairs and sundry expense |  |  | 162 |
| Power |  | 225 |  |

Use the short ton (2,000 pounds) in making your computations. Machinery and equipment used in the extracting operation originally cost $30,300 and has a composite useful life of 15 years; that used in the crushing facility, an original cost of $21,830 and a composite useful life of 10 years.

Required:

Prepare a revenue and expense statement for the Quarry Fund of the County of Milton for the year ending December 31, 19X7.

**Problem 15-3.**   (Cost determination; cost statements) The City of Y operates a central equipment bureau, renting out the equipment to various departments as needed. The following is a condensed statement of the expenses and miles or hours of use of each piece of equipment for the year ending December 31, 19X0:

| Equipment No. | Operating Expenses | Mainte- nance Expenses | Other Expenses | Miles or Hours* Used | Rental Rate per Mile or Hour* |
|---|---|---|---|---|---|
| 1 | $ 93 | $ 71 | $284 | 4,210 | $ .1215 |
| 2 | 135 | 142 | 187 | 7,812 | .0903 |
| 3 | 127 | 99 | 260 | 2,712* | .4464* |
| 4 | 436 | 347 | 149 | 5,140* | .3600* |
| 5 | 288 | 124 | 178 | 3,260* | .3402* |
| 6 | 161 | 70 | 209 | 11,140 | .0560 |
| 7 | 355 | 650 | 693 | 541* | 2.0028* |

The equipment was used during the year by the following departments, among others, which were charged at the rental rates indicated above:

| Equipment No. | Department Using the Equipment | Miles or Hours* Used |
|---|---|---|
| 1 | Mayor .......................................... | 4,210 |
| 2 | Department of Public Safety: | |
| | Division of Weights and Measures ................. | 3,712 |
| | Department of Health: | |
| | Food and Sanitary Division ...................... | 4,100 |
| 3 | Department of Public Works: | |
| | Division of Construction and Repairs: | |
| | Job B ...................................... | 600* |
| | Job C ...................................... | 300* |
| | Job D ...................................... | 1,500* |
| 4 | Department of Public Works: | |
| | Bureau of Streets and Alleys ..................... | 5,112* |
| 5 | Department of Public Works: | |
| | Bureau of Streets and Alleys ..................... | 1,210* |
| | Bureau of Sewers ............................. | 1,712* |
| 6 | Department of Health: | |
| | Nursing Division .............................. | 5,200 |
| | Board of Elections ............................ | 2,315 |
| | Department of Law............................. | 3,625 |
| 7 | Department of Public Works: | |
| | Bureau of Street Cleaning: | |
| | Street A .................................... | 150* |
| | Street B .................................... | 175* |
| | Street C .................................... | 200* |

Required:

(a) Prepare a statement showing the cost of operating each piece of equipment, the earnings for each piece, and the net profit or loss, for the year ending December 31, 19X0.

(b) Prepare a statement showing for each organization unit the number of miles or hours worked for it by each piece of equipment, the amount charged to it on account of the use of each piece, and the total charges to it on account of equipment use.

(c) Prepare a statement showing the amounts charged to the various construction and repair jobs and to the streets cleaned.

**Problem 15-4.** (Cost determination—reciprocal services provided). The Public Works Department of the City of K has an agreement with the municipally-owned electric utility whereby street lighting is charged to the Department at the cost of generation, transmission, and distribution.

The total cost of generating, transmitting, and distributing electricity, exclusive of charges for use of equipment was $317,077 in 19X6. The Public Works Department charges the utility for the use of municipal equipment, such charges being based on actual cost of operation to the department. During 19X6, equipment units number of hours operated and costs of operation are as follows:

| Equipment No. | Cost of Operation | Total Miles or Hours* Operated | Miles or Hours* Operated for Utility |
|---|---|---|---|
| 3 | $840 | 15,000 | 10,000 |
| 11 | 966 | 4,600* | 3,100* |
| 12 | 600 | 2,500* | 2,300* |

The utility generated a total of 66,382,000 K.W.H. (kilowatt hours) which were disposed as follows:

Used by utility itself:

| | |
|---|---|
| Station auxiliaries ..................... | 3,925,000 K.W.H. |
| Other use by utility ................... | 565,000 |
| Sales to Public Works Department ......... | 1,567,000 |
| Sales to other consumers ................. | 54,525,000 |
| Lost and unaccounted for ................ | 5,800,000 |
| Total............................... | 66,382,000 K.W.H. |

Required:

Prepare a statement for the Enterprise (Electric Utility) Fund of the City of K showing the cost of electricity furnished to the Public Works Department for street lighting during the year ending December 31, 19X6.

**Problem 15-5.** (Cost finding and unit cost determination) On the basis of the following data, prepare a statement for the City of R for the year ending June 30, 19X1, showing the total cost of refuse collection and the cost per ton or cubic yard, as the case may be (carry unit costs to three decimal places).

| | Garbage | Rubbish | Dead Animals |
|---|---|---|---|
| By City Forces: | | | |
| Salaries and wages ............ | $512,000 | $215,000 | $4,100 |
| Materials and supplies ........ | 32,000 | 28,800 | — |
| Equipment use* ............. | 116,050 | 70,500 | 2,200 |
| Tons collected .............. | 193,000 | — | — |
| Cubic yards collected ........ | — | 312,000 | — |

* Includes depreciation and rentals, but excludes capital outlays of $231,586. The equipment has a composite useful life of 7 years.

|  | Garbage | Rubbish | Dead Animals |
|---|---|---|---|
| By Contract: | | | |
| Cost ..................... | 81,600 | 16,400 | 3,300 |
| Tons collected .............. | 27,000 | — | — |
| Cubic yards collected ........ | — | 26,000 | — |

Overhead is calculated at an additional 12 percent of total direct costs in the case of city force collection and 5 percent in the case of collection by contract.

**Problem 15-6.** (Cost finding and unit cost determination) On the basis of the following data, prepare a statement of the City of $K$ for the year ending June 30, 19X9, showing the total expenses of the street cleaning division and unit costs for each activity (carry unit costs to three decimal places).

| Activity | Unit | No. of Units | Total Cost |
|---|---|---|---|
| Ashes and trash collection .... | Cubic yards ............ | 450,000 | $230,000 |
| Garbage collection ........... | Tons ................. | 7,000 | 57,000 |
| Garbage disposal............. | Tons ................. | 9,000 | 6,200 |
| Streets cleaned by hand broom | M square yards ......... | 69,000 | |
| | or | | 42,500 |
| | Cubic yards sweepings ... | 15,000 | |
| Streets cleaned by hand and truck patrol ............... | M square yards ......... | 97,000 | |
| | or | | 21,000 |
| | Cubic yards sweepings ... | 5,000 | |
| Flushing ................... | M square yards ......... | 43,000 | 4,500 |
| Gutter cleaning ............. | M square yards ......... | 3,500 | |
| | or | | 10,000 |
| | Cubic yards sweepings ... | 6,000 | |
| Alley cleaning ............... | M square yards ......... | 700 | |
| | or | | 3,500 |
| | Cubic yards sweepings ... | 1,400 | |
| Sweeping and collection of leaves | M square yards ......... | 18,000 | |
| | or | | 18,000 |
| | Cubic yards sweepings ... | 14,000 | |

Add overhead of 12 percent of total direct cost in each case.

**Problem 15-7.** (Cost behavior) One of the following graphs describes the behavior of the cost, expense, income or valuation amount that would appear on *a series of annual financial statements* for each of the following independent situations. All policy decisions and events that caused changes in the behavior patterns of the charted amounts took place in the middle of the time span portrayed in the graphs.

The vertical axes of the graphs represent the annual dollar amount of cost, expense income or valuation, as the case may be, and the horizontal axes represent the passage of time. The axes intersect at zero.

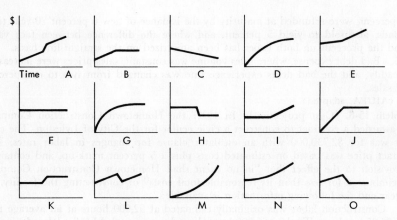

Required:

For each of the following items, select the graph which *best* describes the behavior of the cost, expense, income or valuation amount, as the case may be. A graph may be selected for more than one answer.

1. Interest income on sinking fund investments, where annual payments to the fund were constant.

2. Inventory valuation, where sales volume was constant, prices were constant, and the inventory turnover ratio was steadily increasing.

3. Inventory valuation, where inventory quantities were constant, prices were rising steadily, and the valuation basis was changed from FIFO to LIFO.

4. Cost of goods sold, where physical inventory and sales quantities were constant, prices were rising steadily, and the inventory valuation basis was changed from FIFO to LIFO.

5. Bond interest expense, where the original 5 percent bonds, issued at a discount and amortized on the straight-line basis, were refunded at maturity by the issuance of new 5 percent bonds at face value.

6. Finished goods inventory valuation, where inventory quantities were constant, costs were constant, and the valuation basis was changed from absorption costing to direct costing.

7. Cost depletion charges to income, where quantities mined and sold were decreasing.

8. Bonds payable, where 5% bonds were sold to yield 6 percent and the bond liability was carried at its effective amount.

9. Cost of goods sold, where prices were constant and quantities sold were declining steadily.

10. Gross margin, where sales volume was constant, prices were constant, and the basis for valuing finished goods was changed from absorption costing to direct costing.

11. Accumulated depreciation, where there were no additions or retirements, accelerated depreciation was used, and the assets became fully depreciated.

12. Bond interest expense, where the original 5% bonds, issued at face value, were refunded at maturity by the issuance of new 6% bonds to yield 6½ percent, with the difference between face value and the proceeds being amortized on the straight-line basis.

13. Bond interest expense, where the original 5% bonds, sold to yield 6 percent to maturity and amortized on the effective rate basis, were refunded at maturity by the issuance of new 6% bonds at face value.

14. Bond interest expense, where the original 6%, 20-year term bonds, sold to yield

5 percent, were refunded at maturity by the issuance of new 6 percent 20-year term bonds, also sold to yield 5 percent, and where the difference between face value and the proceeds on both issues has been amortized on the straight-line basis.

15. Bad debt expense, where sales volume was constant, sales prices were increasing steadily, and the bad debts experience rate was changed from two to one percent of sales.

(AICPA, adapted)

**Problem 15-8.** (Cost projection) In 19X1 the Hometown Construction Company was awarded a contract to construct a civic center for the City of Lyleston. The contract was for $2,730,000 with an escalator clause for changes in labor rates. The contract price was based on estimated costs plus a 5 percent mark-up, and contained a provision to the effect that "in no event shall Hometown Construction Company be reimbursed for less than its reasonable total costs" of constructing the facility.

At year end the following information is available:

1. Construction labor was originally estimated at 92,000 hours at an average rate of $3.25 per hour. To date 65,800 hours have been expended by the labor force and it is estimated that an additional 65,000 will be needed to complete the job.

2. Effective January 1, 19X2 the construction force union contract provides for a 4 percent increase in the basic hourly rate.

3. Material costs were originally estimated at $1,375,000. Purchase orders totaling $1,250,000 for 90 percent of the material have been placed. The remaining materials will cost 7 percent more than originally estimated because of general price increases.

4. The electrical work estimated at $130,000 was subcontracted for $127,500.

5. In a supplemental contract it was agreed that the air conditioning equipment installed would be modified at a contract price of $42,000. The subcontractor set a price of $40,000 for this extra work.

6. Total costs incurred to date aggregate $1,605,000.

Required:

Prepare an estimate at December 31, 19X1, of the probable final cost of the civic center to the City of Lyleston.

(AICPA, adapted)

**Problem 15-9.** (Revenue and expense estimates; pro forma operating statement)  The Metropolitan Area Transit Authority, Inc. has been established to inaugurate express bus service between the City of Thorne and a nearby suburb (one-way fare $.25) and is considering the purchase of either 32- or 52-passenger buses, on which pertinent estimates are as follows:

|  | 32-Passenger Bus | 52-Passenger Bus |
|---|---|---|
| Number of each to be purchased | 6 | 4 |
| Useful life | 8 years | 8 years |
| Purchase price of each bus | $80,000 | $110,000 |
| Mileage per gallon of fuel | 5 | 3 |
| Salvage value per bus | $ 6,000 | $ 7,000 |
| Drivers' hourly wage | $ 3.50 | $ 4.20 |
| Price per gallon of fuel | $ .30 | $ .30 |
| General and Administrative expenses | $24,000 | $ 24,000 |
| Other annual cash expenses | $ 5,000 | $ 3,000 |
| Maintenance cost per mile | .04 | .05 |

The buses would be in operation five days per week generally, but the routes would not be run during weekends or on major holidays. During the four daily rush hours all buses would be in service and are expected to operate at full capacity (state law prohibits standees) in both directions of the route, each bus covering the route 12 times (6 round trips) during that period. During the remainder of the 16-hour day, it is estimated that 500 passengers would be carried and Thorne would operate only 4 buses on the route. Part-time drivers would be employed to drive the extra hours during the rush hours. A bus traveling the route all day would go 480 miles and one traveling only during rush hours would go 120 miles a day during the 260-day year.

Required:

Prepare a pro forma (estimated) statement of annual operations (revenue and expense) for the Thorne Metropolitan Area Transit Authority, Inc., accompanied by schedules of estimated annual revenue, estimated annual drivers' wages, and estimated annual cost of fuel.

(AICPA, adapted)

**Problem 15-10.** (Cost and revenue projection; marginal income; break-even)  Ruidoso County Park and Recreation Authority operates a ski shop, restaurant and lodge during the 120-day ski season from November 15 to March 15. The administrator is considering changing the manner of operations and keeping the Lodge open all year. Results of the operations for the year ended March 15, 19X7, were as follows:

| | Ski Shop | | Restaurant | | Lodge | |
|---|---|---|---|---|---|---|
| | Amount | Per cent | Amount | Per cent | Amount | Per cent |
| Revenue ......... | $27,000 | 100% | $40,000 | 100% | $108,000 | 100% |
| Costs: | | | | | | |
| Costs of goods sold ......... | 14,850 | 55 | 24,000 | 60 | | |
| Supplies ........ | 1,350 | 5 | 4,000 | 10 | 7,560 | 7 |
| Utilities ........ | 270 | 1 | 1,200 | 3 | 2,160 | 2 |
| Salaries ........ | 1,620 | 6 | 12,000 | 30 | 32,400 | 30 |
| Insurance ...... | 810 | 3 | 800 | 2 | 9,720 | 9 |
| Property taxes on building .. | 540 | 2 | 1,600 | 4 | 6,480 | 6 |
| Depreciation .... | 1,080 | 4 | 2,000 | 5 | 28,080 | 26 |
| Total costs .... | 20,520 | 76 | 45,600 | 114 | 86,400 | 80 |
| Net income or (loss) ......... | $ 6,480 | 24% | $(5,600) | (14)% | $21,600 | 20% |

1.  The lodge has 100 rooms and the rate from November 15 to March 15 is $10 per day for one or two persons. The occupancy rate from November 15 to March 15 is 90 percent.

2.  Ski shop and restaurant sales vary in direct proportion to room occupancy.

3.  For the ski shop and restaurant, cost of goods sold, supplies, and utilities vary in direct proportion to sales. For the lodge, supplies and utilities vary in direct proportion to room occupancy.

4. The ski shop, restaurant and lodge are located in the same building. Depreciation on the building is charged to the lodge. The ski shop and restaurant are charged with depreciation only on equipment. The full cost of the restaurant equipment became fully depreciated on March 15, 19X7, but the equipment has a remaining useful life of 3 years. The equipment can be sold for $1,200 but will be worthless in 3 years. All depreciation is computed by the straight-line method.

5. Insurance premiums are for annual coverage for public liability and fire insurance on the building and equipment. All building insurance is charged to the lodge.

6. Salaries are the minimum necessary to keep each facility open and are for the ski season only except for the lodge security guard who is paid $5,400 per year.

Two alternatives are being considered for the future operation of Ruidoso Ski Lodge:

1. The administrator believes that during the ski season the restaurant should be closed because "it does not have enough revenue to cover its out-of-pocket costs." It is estimated that lodge occupancy would drop to 80 percent of capacity if the restaurant were closed during the ski season. The space utilized by the restaurant would be used as a lounge for lodge guests.

2. The administrator is considering keeping the lodge open from March 15 to November 15. The ski shop would be converted into a gift shop if the lodge should be operated during this period with conversion costs of $1,000 in March and $1,000 in November each year. It is estimated that revenues from the gift shop would be the same per room occupied as revenues from the ski shop, that variable costs would be in the same ratio to revenues and that all other costs would be the same for the gift shop as for the ski shop. The occupancy rate of the lodge at a room rate of $7 per day is estimated at 50 percent during the period from March 15 to November 15 whether or not the restaurant is operated.

Required:

(Ignore possible income taxes and use 30 days per month for computational purposes.)

(a) Prepare a projected income statement for the ski shop and lodge from November 15, 19X7, to March 15, 19X8, assuming the restaurant is closed during this period and all facilities are closed during the remainder of the year.

(b) Assume that all facilities will continue to be operated during the 4-month period of November 15 to March 15 of each year.

   1. Assume that the lodge is operated during the 8 months from March 15 to November 15. Prepare an analysis which indicates the projected marginal income or loss of operating the gift shop and lodge during this 8-month period.

   2. Compute the minimum room rate which should be charged to allow the lodge to break even during the 8 months from March 15 to November 15 assuming the gift shop and restaurant are not operated during this period.

   (AICPA, adapted)

**Problem 15-11.** (Cost determination from cash and balance sheet data; statistical calculations) You have been requested by the Hillcrest Blood Bank, a not-for-profit organization, to assist in developing certain information from the Bank's operations. You determine the following:

1. Blood is furnished to the blood bank by volunteers and, when necessary, by professional donors. During the year 2,568 pints of blood were taken from volunteers and professional blood donors.

2. Volunteer donors who give blood to the bank can draw against their account when needed. An individual who requires a blood transfusion has the option of paying for the blood used at $25 per pint or replacing it at the blood bank. Hospitals purchase blood at $8 per pint.

3. The Hillcrest Blood Bank has a reciprocal arrangement with a number of other banks that permits a member who requires a transfusion in a different locality to

draw blood from the local bank against his account in Hillcrest. The issuing blood bank charges a set fee of $14 per pint to the home blood bank.

4. If blood is issued to hospitals but is not used and is returned to the blood bank, there is a handling charge of $1 per pint. Only hospitals are permitted to return blood. During the year 402 pints were returned. The blood being returned must be in usable condition.

5. Blood can be stored for only 21 days and then must be discarded. During the year 343 pints were outdated. This is a normal rate of loss.

6. The blood bank sells serum and supplies at cost to doctors and laboratories. These items are used in processing blood and are sold at the same price that they are billed to the blood bank. No blood bank operating expenses are allocated to the cost of sales of these items.

7. Inventories of blood are valued at the sales price to hospitals. The sales price to hospitals was increased on July 1, 19X1. The inventories are as follows:

|  | Pints | Sales Price | Total |
|---|---|---|---|
| June 30, 19X1 | 80 | $6 | $480 |
| June 30, 19X2 | 80 | 8 | 640 |

8. The following financial statements are available:

### HILLCREST BLOOD BANK
#### Balance Sheet

|  | June 30, 19X1 | June 30, 19X2 |
|---|---|---|
| *Assets* | | |
| Cash ..................................... | $ 2,712 | $ 2,093 |
| U.S. Treasury bonds ...................... | 15,000 | 16,000 |
| Accounts receivable—sales of blood: | | |
| Hospitals ............................. | 1,302 | 1,448 |
| Individuals............................. | 425 | 550 |
| Inventories: | | |
| Blood ................................. | 480 | 640 |
| Supplies and serum ...................... | 250 | 315 |
| Furniture and equipment, less depreciation ..... | 4,400 | 4,050 |
| Total assets ......................... | $24,569 | $25,096 |
| *Liabilities and Balance* | | |
| Accounts payable—supplies ................. | $   325 | $   275 |
| Balance—excess of assets over liabilities ........ | 24,244 | 24,821 |
| Total liabilities and balance ............. | $24,569 | $25,096 |

### HILLCREST BLOOD BANK
Statement of Cash Receipts and Disbursements
For the Year Ended June 30, 19X2

| | | | |
|---|---:|---:|---:|
| Balance, July 1, 19X1: | | | |
|   Cash in bank .......................... | | | $ 2,712 |
|   U. S. Treasury bonds ..................... | | | 15,000 |
|     Total.................................. | | | 17,712 |
| Receipts: | | | |
|   From hospitals: | | | |
|     Hillcrest Hospital ....................... | $7,702 | | |
|     Good Samaritan Hospital ................. | 3,818 | $11,520 | |
|   Individuals............................... | | 6,675 | |
|   From other blood banks .................... | | 602 | |
|   From sales of serum and supplies ........... | | 2,260 | |
|   Interest on bonds ......................... | | 525 | |
|   Gifts and bequests......................... | | 4,928 | |
|     Total receipts ........................... | | | 26,510 |
|     Total to be accounted for .................. | | | 44,222 |
| Disbursements: | | | |
|   Laboratory expense: | | | |
|     Serum ............................... | $3,098 | | |
|     Salaries .............................. | 3,392 | | |
|     Supplies .............................. | 3,533 | | |
|     Laundry and miscellaneous .............. | 277 | 10,300 | |
|   Other expenses and disbursements: | | | |
|     Salaries .................................. | 5,774 | | |
|     Dues and subscriptions...................... | 204 | | |
|     Rent and utilities ......................... | 1,404 | | |
|     Blood testing ............................. | 2,378 | | |
|     Payments to other blood banks for blood given to | | | |
|       members away from home ................ | 854 | | |
|     Payments to professional blood donors ....... | 2,410 | | |
|     Other expenses .......................... | 1,805 | | |
|     Purchase of U. S. Treasury bond ............ | 1,000 | 15,829 | |
|     Total disbursements ..................... | | | 26,129 |
| Balance, June 30, 19X2 ...................... | | | $18,093 |
| Composed of: | | | |
|   Cash in bank ............................. | | | $ 2,093 |
|   U. S. Treasury bonds ...................... | | | 16,000 |
|     Total.................................. | | | $18,093 |

Required:
(a) Prepare a statement on the accrual basis of the total expense of taking and processing blood.
(b) Prepare a schedule computing (1) the number of pints of blood sold and (2) the number of pints withdrawn by members.
(c) Prepare a schedule computing the expense per pint of taking and processing the blood that was used.
(AICPA, adapted)

**Problem 15-12.** (Variance analysis) You are preparing your long form report in connection with the examination of State Gas Company at December 31, 19X7. The report will include an explanation of the 19X7 increase in operating revenues.
The following information is available from the company records:

| | 19X6 | 19X7 | Increase (Decrease) |
|---|---|---|---|
| Average number of customers .... | 27,000 | 26,000 | (1,000) |
| MCF sales .................... | 486,000 | 520,000 | 34,000 |
| Revenue .................... | $1,215,000 | $1,274,000 | $59,000 |

Required:
Prepare an explanation of the 19X7 increase in operating revenues, accompanied by an analysis accounting for the effect of changes in:
1. Average number of customers.
2. Average gas consumption per customer.
3. Average rate per MCF sold (MCF = thousand cubic feet).

**Problem 15-13.** (Standard costs and variance analysis) A state furniture shop that builds modular office furniture units for the various state agencies uses a standard cost system in accounting for its production costs.
The standard cost of a unit of furniture follows:

| | | |
|---|---|---|
| Lumber, 100 feet @ $150 per 1,000 feet ............ | | $15.00 |
| Direct labor, 4 hours @ $2.50 per hour ............ | | 10.00 |
| Manufacturing overhead: | | |
| Fixed (30% of direct labor at normal capacity) .... | $3.00 | |
| Variable (60% of direct labor at standard wage rate) | 6.00 | 9.00 |
| | | $34.00 |

The following flexible monthly overhead budget is in effect:

| Direct Labor Hours | Estimated Overhead |
|---|---|
| 5,200 ........................................ | $10,800 |
| 4,800 ........................................ | 10,200 |
| 4,400 ........................................ | 9,600 |
| 4,000 (normal capacity)........................ | 9,000 |
| 3,600 ........................................ | 8,400 |

The actual unit costs for the month of December, 19X8 were as follows:

| | |
|---|---|
| Lumber used (110 feet @ $120 per 1,000 feet) . . . . . . | $13.20 |
| Direct labor (4¼ hours @ $2.60 per hour) . . . . . . . . . | 11.05 |
| Manufacturing overhead ($10,560 ÷ 1,200 units) . . . . | 8.80 |
| | $33.05 |

Required:

Prepare a schedule which shows (1) the total variance, (2) an analysis of the total and per unit materials and labor variances, and (3) the total and per unit overhead budget variance, from standard cost for the month of December, 19X8.

**Problem 15-14.** (Cost finding—hospital) The General Fund of the General Hospital of *D* Village has the expense accounts and balances in its trial balance at December 31, 19X4, shown on pp. 709–10, additional information is given relating to the allocation of expenses.

Required:

Prepare the following for the year ended December 31, 19X4:

a. A worksheet showing the apportionment of the cost of the Provision for Depreciation to other centers (see Figure 15-17).

b. A worksheet showing the apportionment of Nursing Service costs to other centers. NOTE: Student must proceed with requirement "d" until total Nursing Service costs are obtained before he can fulfill requirement "b." Total Administrative and General costs must be similarly obtained in order to fulfill requirement "c".

c. A worksheet showing the apportionment of Administrative and General costs to other centers.

d. A worksheet showing "Cost Apportionment—General Services" (see Figure 15-18).

e. A statement of "Special Services Costs" (see Figure 15-19).

f. A worksheet showing the "Cost Apportionment—Special Services" (see Figure 15-20).

g. A statement of "Inpatient and Outpatient Costs" (see Figure 15-21).

(Round to the nearest whole dollar; and round the final figure in a column where necessary.)

**Problem 15-15.** (Water supply construction and operations; worksheet; balance sheet) Four municipalities—Rose City, Copperville, Pineboro, and Coletown—formed the Spring Valley Water Commission for the construction and operation of a joint water supply. The project was estimated to cost $10,000,000 and to have a capacity of 100 million gallons daily (MGD).

It was agreed that the capital costs were to be apportioned among the participating municipalities according to the daily water allotments, but no municipality should be charged for the cost of any part of the project unless it were to receive benefit therefrom.

Capital assessment:

The four municipalities allotted the entire estimated supply of 100 MGD among themselves and agreed to an initial assessment (subject to subsequent adjustment) of the estimated cost of $10,000,000 in proportion to these allotments, as follows:

| | Trial Balance Amounts | Floor Space Occupied | Cost of Equipment in Use | Pounds of Laundry Used | Hours of Nursing Service | Priced Requisitions Medical Supply | Pharmacy |
|---|---|---|---|---|---|---|---|
| Provision for Depreciation: | | | | | | | |
| Building | $ 10,000 | | | | | | |
| Equipment | 10,000 | | | | | | |
| Operation and Maintenance of Plant | 40,000 | 2,000 | $ 3,000 | | | | |
| Laundry Service | 15,000 | 500 | 1,000 | 1,000 | | | |
| Housekeeping | 72,000 | 500 | 1,000 | 3,000 | | | |
| Dietary (Service to inpatients only) | 55,000 | 3,000 | 5,000 | — | | | |
| Nursing Service | 160,000 | 500 | 1,000 | | | | |
| Medical Supply | 46,000 | 1,500 | 4,000 | 5,000 | 8,000 | | |
| Pharmacy | 25,000 | 1,500 | 2,000 | 1,000 | | | |
| Medical Records | 5,000 | 500 | 1,000 | | | | |
| Administration and General | 48,000 | 2,000 | 5,000 | | | | |
| Operating and Delivery Service | 42,000 | 15,000 | 20,000 | 20,000 | 20,000 | $10,000 | $ 4,000 |
| Radiology | 22,000 | 5,000 | 25,000 | 3,000 | 10,000 | 1,000 | 1,000 |
| Laboratory Services | 65,000 | 10,000 | 10,000 | 2,000 | | | 1,000 |
| Cost of Drugs Sold | | | | | | | 30,000 |
| Inpatients | | 45,000 | 25,000 | 100,000 | 200,000 | 34,000 | 6,000 |
| Nursery | 1,000 | 5,000 | 5,000 | 6,000 | 34,000 | 2,000 | 1,000 |
| Outpatients | 8,000 | 5,000 | 4,000 | 4,000 | 20,000 | 1,000 | 1,000 |
| Emergency Room | 10,000 | 3,000 | 8,000 | 5,000 | 8,000 | 3,000 | 1,000 |
| Private Ambulatory | | | | | | | |
| | $634,000 | 100,000 | $120,000 | 150,000 | 300,000 | $50,000 | $45,000 |
| Patient days | 42,079 | | | | | | |
| Newborn days | 8,305 | | | | | | |
| Outpatient visits | 12,046 | | | | | | |
| Emergency visits | 5,156 | | | | | | |
| Private ambulatory visits | 5,491 | | | | | | |
| Prescriptions filled | 8,328 | | | | | | |

| | Hours of Operating and Delivery Room Use | Number of X-Ray Films (Radiology) | Number of Laboratory Examinations | Retail Price of Drugs Sold | Hours of Housekeeping Service | Hours of Service on Medical Records |
|---|---|---|---|---|---|---|
| Medical Supply | | | | | 500 | |
| Pharmacy | | | | | 500 | |
| Medical Records | | | | | 2,000 | |
| Administration and General | | | | | 8,000 | |
| Operating and Delivery Service | | | | | 2,000 | |
| Radiology | | | | | 2,000 | |
| Laboratory Services | | | | | 3,500 | |
| Cost of Drugs Sold | | | | | | |
| Inpatients | 19,000 | 23,000 | 107,000 | $40,000 | 49,000 | 5,000 |
| Nursery | 1,000 | 1,000 | 2,000 | 1,000 | 1,000 | |
| Outpatients | | 2,000 | 5,000 | 5,000 | 5,000 | 1,500 |
| Emergency Room | | 5,000 | 1,000 | 2,000 | 1,500 | 500 |
| Private Ambulatory | | 19,000 | 10,000 | 2,000 | | |
| | 20,000 | 50,000 | 125,000 | $50,000 | 75,000 | 7,000 |

|  | MGD | Assessment |
|---|---|---|
| Rose City | 30 | $ 3,000,000 |
| Copperville | 20 | 2,000,000 |
| Pineboro | 10 | 1,000,000 |
| Coletown | 40 | 4,000,000 |
|  | 100 | $10,000,000 |

All capital assessments were collected in full except that of Copperville, which paid only 90 percent of its assessment.

*Expenditure to December 31, 19X7*

At the close of 19X7, Spider Dam and Crabtree Reservoir were completed, and pipe lines had been laid—namely, twin pipe lines from Spider Dam to the point where Rose City takes off the water and a single pipe line below that point. The cost per mile of the twin pipe lines was twice the cost per mile of the single line, and it was assumed that the twin lines were constructed for the benefit of all the municipalities. For convenience, the capital costs are identified by classes as follows:

Class A. Cost of Spider Dam and other costs at the headworks.

Class B. Twin pipe lines from Spider Dam and the headworks to the Rose City take-off—a distance of five miles. (In accordance with the agreement, the expenditures under Classes A and B are to be distributed to all of the four participating municipalities on the basis of the contract allotments.)

Class C. Single pipe line from Rose City take-off to Copperville take-off—a distance of three miles. (This capital cost is accordingly apportionable to Copperville, Pineboro, and Coletown.)

Class D. Single pipe line from Copperville take-off to Pineboro take-off—a distance of two miles. (This capital cost is apportionable to Pineboro and Coletown.)

Class E. Single pipe line from Pineboro take-off to Coletown take-off—a distance of ten miles. (This entire capital cost is chargeable to Coletown.)

The capital costs up to January 1, 19X8, when operation began, were as follows:

Construction costs:

Headworks:

| Spider Dam | $2,000,000 |
|---|---|
| Pumping station | 300,000 |
| Power house | 200,000 |
| Total | $2,500,000 |

Aqueduct:

$100,000 per mile of single pipe line.

Land, rights of way, etc.:

| Class A | $1,993,100 |
|---|---|
| Class B | 447,800 |
| Class C | 198,900 |
| Class D | 104,200 |
| Class E | 256,000 |
| Total | $3,000,000 |

Engineering costs:

Direct charges to classes:

| | |
|---|---|
| Class A .............................. | $ 440,000 |
| Class B .............................. | 120,000 |
| Class C .............................. | 80,000 |
| Class D .............................. | 60,000 |
| Class E .............................. | 100,000 |
| Total.............................. | $ 800,000 |

Indirect charges—$200,000 (to be apportioned to classes in proportion to direct engineering costs).

Administrative expenses—$500,000 (to be apportioned to classes in proportion to all construction costs up to January 1, 19X8, exclusive of land and engineering costs).

*Operating assessment 19X8.* It was further agreed that the operating costs were to be apportioned according to actual water consumption, but in no event was the basis for any municipality's portion to be less than the contract allotment. The surplus or deficit resulting from each year's operations was to be credited or charged to the succeeding year's operating assessments. In 19X8 the average daily consumption was as follows:

| | MGD |
|---|---|
| Rose City | 40 |
| Copperville | 10 |
| Pineboro | 5 |
| Coletown | 25 |
| | 80 |

The 19X8 operating expenses, estimated at $100,000, had been assessed as follows:

| | |
|---|---|
| Rose City | $ 30,000 |
| Copperville | 20,000 |
| Pineboro | 10,000 |
| Coletown | 40,000 |
| | $100,000 |

Rose City was the only municipality that paid its operating assessment in 19X8.

*Expenditures 19X8.* The actual expenditures for 19X8 were as follows:

Capital:

It was necessary to build a surge tank to prevent water surges from breaking the aqueduct. The tank cost $100,000 and was constructed halfway between the Rose City and Copperville take-off points. It was agreed that this surge tank was of benefit to all the participating municipalities.

Operating:

$71,000

The following were paid from capital division cash in addition to the capital and operating expenses listed above: 19X8 engineering expenses of $16,000, 50 percent of which was to be apportioned to the capital division and 50 percent to the operating division; and 19X8 administrative expenses of $25,000, 80 percent of which was to be apportioned to the operating division and 20 percent to the capital division. The portions of the engineering and administrative expenses chargeable to the capital division are to be applied to the several classes of property on the basis of the engineering and the construction costs, respectively, to January 1, 19X8.

*Water sales 19X8.* The Spring Valley Water Commission, in anticipation of the under-consumption of water on the part of some of the participating municipalities, entered into a contract with Glendale for 19X8, whereby this municipality agreed to pay $30 a million gallons for water. The contract provided that Glendale would take a minimum of ten million gallons a day. Glendale paid the commission $7,500 a month on account; its consumption for the year was 3,300 million gallons. There were no expenses chargeable to the water sales division except $30,000, representing the cost of connecting the pipe lines (which is not included in the above $71,000 operating expenses and is to be considered a water sales expense during 19X8), also paid from capital division cash.

Profits from the sale of water to municipalities not participating in the project were to be apportioned annually to the participating municipalities on the basis of operating expenses charged to them.

*General data and requirement.* The accounts of the commission are kept in three self-balancing divisions, namely: "capital," "operating," and "water sales." At the end of 19X8, all inter-divisional balances are settled in cash to the extent that funds are available in the divisions.

Required:

Prepare a balance sheet (with supporting schedules and work papers) showing assets and liabilities of each division separately as of December 31, 19X8, including the balances due from and due to the respective municipalities, and the equities of the participating municipalities.

(AICPA, adapted)

# 16

# Cash

Cash is probably the single most important asset of fund-oriented organizations. A substantial portion of the assets of many funds is held in cash; cash is the asset that is most likely to be misappropriated. It poses further problems of management because of the lack of synchronization between the inflows and outflows of cash in the typical situation. The organization must decide upon the minimum amount of cash necessary to conduct its operations, it must compute the costs of cash insufficiencies and determine how to overcome them, it must weigh the cost of holding excessive amounts of idle cash against the cost of investing, and it must determine when and how to invest excess cash.

### The Treasurer

In the typical governmental organization the treasurer has responsibility for and control over the collection, custody, and disbursement of cash. The treasurer usually reports to the director of finance, and there is substantial agreement that he should be a civil service or merit system employee rather than an elected official. There are, of course, elected treasurers and tax collectors in many cities and in some states. While organizational arrangements do not insure either good or bad administration, basing the selection of the treasurer on the election process is certainly unwise. It is likely to produce officials without appropriate training, there may be cases in which desirable continuity is broken

714

by the election process, and, most important, the necessities of getting elected and the strict administration of the collection process do not seem to mix.

The treasurer should be paid by means of a salary. The fee system of compensation is likely to produce uneven administration because large tax bills may be assiduously pursued for the large fees that are involved, while small tax bills are ignored.

In some cases an official may legally collect taxes and hold the money temporarily as a debtor of the governmental unit instead of depositing it to the credit of the government. For example, a tax collector is sometimes not required to turn the cash over immediately upon collection but does so only at stated intervals. In the meantime he deposits the money to the credit of his own personal account; and when the time for settlement comes, he draws a check on this account for the amount to be turned over. This practice is to be condemned. All money collected by an official should be deposited at once to the credit of the governmental unit.

### Accounting for Cash Receipts

The principal procedures for safeguarding the handling of cash include the following: (1) assign duties so that employees who handle cash do not have access to the accounting records, (2) use prenumbered financial stationery, and (3) require the prompt deposit of all cash receipts, intact, to the credit of the governmental unit.

These provisions for safeguarding cash apply both to the receipts of the treasury office and to departmental collections. It is not feasible for all receipts to come to the treasury directly; some originate in departments. Departmental collections should either be transmitted to the treasury office or be deposited promptly in the bank to the credit of the governmental unit. In the latter case the depository should issue two deposit tickets, one to be kept by the depositing department and the other to be transmitted to the treasurer's office. Appropriate documents should be submitted in support of the amount deposited or transmitted to the treasury office.

Receipts flow into the treasury from a great many sources, and they must be classified properly so that the correct accounts may be credited. The primary classification is by fund, of course. Within each of the funds the receipts must be classified as to source; this classification determines whether nonrevenue sources, such as those that decrease assets and increase liabilities, or revenues will be credited. Many of these accounts are control accounts supported by subsidiary ledgers, and it is essential that the appropriate account in the related subsidiary ledger be identified.

Collections are typically evidenced by documents, and the information necessary for the foregoing classification is obtained from the documents. For example, tax receipts are evidenced by tax bills; ideally every time a tax is paid the collecting unit would retain one part of the tax bill. It would then have the data necessary to determine the fund classification, the taxes receivable control account, and the individual taxpayer's accounts. Similarly, license collections are evidenced by carbon copies of the licenses issued. Ordinarily licenses are not set up as receivables, and the carbon copies of the licenses are used as a basis for fund classification, the credit to the revenues control account in the proper fund, and credits to the individual licenses accounts in the revenue subsidiary ledger of the appropriate fund.

In the simplest situation documents are physically grouped for the purpose of securing control totals. They are first grouped by fund and then by main sources within each fund. As a result of these groupings the amounts necessary for the purpose of crediting the proper control accounts for each fund in the general ledger (that is, the Taxes Receivable account for each fund, the Accounts Receivable account, the Revenues account, etc.) are secured. A still further grouping of documents is required to arrive at the amounts to be posted to the subsidiary accounts. The foregoing procedure is necessary no matter what the distribution of duties may be. For example, if the accounting department and the treasurer's office are under the control of two independent officials, the treasurer is concerned only with classifying the documents so that he can arrive at the amount of cash applicable to each fund. As soon as he obtains these data, he turns the documents over to the accounting department. On the other hand, if the treasury and the accounting department are under the supervision of the same official, such as a director of finance, the grouping of the receipt documents by main sources and by funds is frequently made by the treasurer. On the basis of these groupings the treasurer prepares a daily cash report, a copy of which is turned over to the accounting department with the grouped documents on which the report is based. The accounting department compares the report with the grouped documents and uses the report as a basis for making entries in the Revenues and Receipts Register (Figure 16-1). On the other hand, a detailed cash report must be prepared by the accounting department if the treasurer reports collections only by funds. The detailed cash report is used for making entries in the revenues and receipts register.

When the money is collected by the departments instead of by the treasurer, the departments are frequently required to classify their collections by fund and source. In many governmental units departments are not permitted to deposit their collections with the treasurer until they secure a pay-in warrant from the accounting officer. The accounting officer reviews the departmental groupings of documents to satisfy himself that they have been properly classified by fund and source. The report may be prepared in triplicate; all copies, together with the grouped documents, are presented for approval to the accounting officer, who signs the three copies and retains one copy and the accompanying documents. The other two copies are turned over to the department, which then deposits the money with the treasurer. The treasurer in turn signs the two re-

## Figure 16-1

### A GOVERNMENTAL UNIT
### Revenue and Receipts Register
### Month of _____

| | | General Fund | | | | | | | | Special Revenue | |
| | | Taxes | | | | Interest & Penalties on Taxes | Motor Vehicle Licenses | Rents | Other Receipts | | Taxes | |
| | | Real Estate | | Personal Property | | | | | | | Real Estate | |
| Day | Total for Day | Year | Amount | Year | Amount | | | | Name of Account | Amount | Year | Amount |
| | | | | | | | | | | | | |
| | | | | | | | | | | | | |

maining copies and returns one copy to the department as evidence that he has received the money. The pay-in warrants are used as a basis for an entry in the Revenues and Receipts Register. In the treasurer's office the warrants are used as a basis for preparing the treasurer's daily report of collections.

Certain departments may maintain their own detailed accounts. For example, the water department may keep the individual accounts of the water customers. In that case the cashier's stubs are not turned over to the treasurer or to the accounting department but are retained by the department and used in posting to the individual Accounts Receivable. The department submits a summary of the revenues collected, and this summary is used as a basis for crediting the Accounts Receivable controlling account and any other controlling accounts of the proper funds. As indicated earlier, the foregoing discussion presumes a very elementary accounting system. Various types of mechanical, electric, and electronic equipment require appropriate modifications. For example, physical groupings of documents may be unnecessary where summaries produced by tabulating or computing equipment provide the necessary totals.

### Recording Collections

A very simple Revenue and Receipts Register is illustrated in Figure 16-1. It is based on the assumption that the government has only a few sources of receipts and a hand-kept or machine-kept system. If a governmental unit has many sources it obviously would be impracticable to use a column for each source. In such a case subregisters would be established for certain of the accounts. For example, one subregister might be established for licenses and permits, another for revenues from the use of money and property, and so forth.

In some systems receipts are not entered in any register but are posted to the accounts directly from the daily reports of cash collections. The daily cash collection reports may be summarized at the end of each month into a journal entry that is posted to the accounts. In any event the detailed accounts, such as each taxpayer's account, usually are credited from the documents themselves and not from any of the registers.

### Accounting for Cash Disbursements

The process of preparation of vouchers signifying the approval of liabilities has already been described (Chapter 7). The voucher and the check may be prepared at the same time. Vouchers are prepared in duplicate (at least), and they are designed so that the original can be used as a check and the duplicate can be used as the basis for an entry in the voucher register and as evidence of the approval of the claim. In some systems additional voucher copies are filed by vendor, date due, voucher number, fund, etc. The original of the voucher document becomes a check when it is signed by the treasurer.

An alternative disbursement procedure is to use a voucher, a warrant, and a check. The voucher designates the approval of the claim and serves as a basis for charging the proper expenditure and other accounts, whereas the warrant is an order by the accounting officer on the treasurer to pay the amount specified. The treasurer then may issue a check to cover the warrant. Sometimes the warrant is designed so that it becomes a check when the bank account is designated thereon and it is signed by the treasurer.

Disbursements are recorded in a Check Register, a simple form for which is illustrated in Figure 16-2. If a special payroll bank account has been established, the payroll sheets themselves may be converted into a check register by adding a column for the payroll check numbers opposite the employee names on these sheets. If no special payroll account is set up, the same procedure may be followed; but it is necessary also to record in the check register the total amount of checks issued. The check register is usually produced as a by-product of the check-writing process in mechanized systems.

### Cash Statements

Cash statements can be classified into those prepared during the year primarily for the purpose of administration and those prepared for external reporting purposes. The first group includes statements comparing actual with estimated receipts, statements dealing with cash planning, and statements of tax collections. Other cash statements are those showing receipts, disbursements, and balances of the several funds.

The Comparative Statement of Monthly Receipts (Figure 16-3) is prepared at the end of each month for those funds for which it will be useful—usually for the General Fund and for Special Revenue Funds, the funds for which appropriations are required.

The Cash Budget (Figure 16-4) is prepared, at least monthly, in order that the cash position of the governmental unit may be carefully controlled. The minimum balance of cash required for operating purposes must be carefully computed. Schedules of estimated receipts from both revenue sources and from maturities of investments, together with estimated disbursements for expenditures and for maturities of notes payable, provide the information regarding prospective cash available for investment and cash insufficiencies that must be made good by disinvestment or borrowing. In recent years governments have become acutely aware of the cost of leaving excess cash idle, even for a few hours or days, and active investment programs have resulted.

The Statement of Tax Levies and Tax Collections was discussed earlier and is illustrated in Figure 6-8. It shows tax collections both for the current month and from the beginning of the year to date and supplements in part the Comparative Statement of Monthly Receipts (Figure 16-3). Whereas the latter shows merely the total amount of taxes collected—it is supposed to show pri-

Figure 16-2

**A GOVERNMENTAL UNIT**

Check Register

Month of _____

| Day | Name | Check No. | General | | | Funds Special Revenue | Capital Projects |
|---|---|---|---|---|---|---|---|
| | | | Bank A | Bank B | Bank C | Bank A | Bank B |
| | | | | | | | |
| | | | | | | | |

Figure 16-3

## A GOVERNMENTAL UNIT
### General Fund
Comparative Statement of Monthly Receipts for Month Ending March 31, 19X1
and Three Months Ending March 31, 19X1

| Sources of Receipts | Total Estimated 19X1 | March | | | Total to Date | | | |
|---|---|---|---|---|---|---|---|---|
| | | Esti-mated | Actual | Over or Under* Estimate | Esti-mated | Actual | Over or Under* Estimate | Balance |
| General Property Taxes: | | | | | | | | |
| Current and Delinquent | $290,600 | $48,500 | $46,990 | $1,510* | $106,500 | $103,435 | $3,065* | $187,165 |
| Interest and Penalties on Taxes | 1,150 | 100 | 90 | 10* | 300 | 250 | 50* | 900 |
| Licenses and Permits | 56,300 | 4,800 | 7,000 | 2,200 | 15,000 | 18,000 | 3,000 | 38,300 |
| Fines and Forfeits | 9,500 | 750 | 800 | 50 | 2,400 | 2,500 | 100 | 7,000 |
| Interest | 7,200 | 610 | 580 | 30* | 1,800 | 1,775 | 25* | 5,425 |
| Intergovernmental Revenues | 62,200 | 5,200 | 5,300 | 100 | 17,000 | 18,000 | 1,000 | 44,200 |
| Charges for Current Services | 6,800 | 575 | 550 | 25* | 1,600 | 1,550 | 50* | 5,250 |
| Collections of Accounts Receivable | 5,200 | 440 | 450 | 10 | 1,300 | 1,375 | 75 | 3,825 |
| Sale of Fixed Assets | 5,100 | 1,000 | 1,010 | 10 | 2,000 | 2,015 | 15 | 3,085 |
| Transfers from Other Funds | 4,300 | 500 | 500 | — | 1,500 | 1,550 | 50 | 2,750 |
| Total Receipts | $448,350 | $62,475 | $63,270 | $ 795 | $149,400 | $150,450 | $1,050 | $297,900 |

**Figure 16-4**

## A GOVERNMENTAL UNIT
### General Fund
### Cash Budget
### For the Six Months Ending June 30, 19X5

| | Period | | |
|---|---|---|---|
| | *1* | *2* | *3* |
| Balance, first of period | $100 | $100 | $100 |
| Add: | | | |
|   Estimated receipts, revenue sources | $435 | $200 | $205 |
|   Maturities of investments | 40 | 50 | 70 |
|     Total additions | $475 | $250 | $275 |
| Available for the period | $575 | $350 | $375 |
| Deduct: | | | |
|   Estimated disbursements for expenditures | $450 | $310 | $240 |
|   Maturities of notes payable | – 0 – | – 0 – | – 0 – |
|     Total deductions | $450 | $310 | $240 |
| Balance, end of period | $125 | $ 40 | $135 |
| Deduct, minimum balance | 100 | 100 | 100 |
| Cash excess—available for investment | $ 25 | | $ 35 |
| Cash insufficiency—requires disinvestment or borrowing | | $ 60 | |

marily the trend of collections of the entire tax roll—the former shows the amount collected from each year's levy, by fund.

The Statement of Cash Receipts and Disbursements for the Special Assessment Funds (Figure 16-5) is important because of the cash operations of those funds. In addition, in cases requiring segregation of cash for construction, cash for bond principal payments, and cash for interest payments the statement should be prepared to give evidence that the distinction between the various kinds of cash is being recognized by officials.

The Statement of Cash Receipts and Disbursements for Trust and Agency Funds (Figure 16-6) should be prepared because cash transactions are the primary types of transactions that take place in most Trust and Agency Funds.

The Combined Statement of Cash Receipts and Disbursements—All Funds (Figure 16-7) is a summary statement showing cash receipts and disbursements for each fund and indicating in summary form the changes that have taken place in the cash account(s) of each fund or group of related funds. Note that the cash receipts and cash disbursements data shown include interfund transactions, the assumption being that interfund balances are settled by check or journal entries, but that interfund transactions are highlighted so that the *net* cash receipts, disbursements, and balances of the government as a whole are also evident. In some jurisdictions it is traditional to show the banks in which the cash of each fund is being held; in others only the total ending balances are detailed by name of bank, and the average balances held by each bank during the period may be noted.

The foregoing are not the only cash receipts and disbursements statements that may be needed, for circumstances may require that the cash accounts of other funds be similarly analyzed. Clearly these statements may be prepared not only at the end of a month or a year but also at other times as necessity demands.

**Figure 16-5**

A GOVERNMENTAL UNIT
Special Assessment Funds
Statement of Cash Receipts and Disbursements for Fiscal Year

|  | | *District No.* | |
|  | *Total* | *1* | *2* | *3* |
|---|---|---|---|---|
| Cash balance—beginning of year | $188,000 | $17,000 | $33,000 | $ 44,000 |
| Receipts: | | | | |
| Current special assessments | $122,000 | $10,000 | $18,000 | $ 33,000 |
| Delinquent special assessments | 16,000 | 2,000 | 2,000 | 4,000 |
| Governmental unit's share of cost | 34,000 | 3,000 | 4,000 | 10,000 |
| Interest on assessments | 36,000 | 3,000 | 5,000 | 10,000 |
| Proceeds from sale of bonds | 100,000 | — | — | 50,000 |
| Total receipts | $308,000 | $18,000 | $29,000 | $107,000 |
| Total | $496,000 | $35,000 | $62,000 | $151,000 |
| Disbursements: | | | | |
| Capital outlays—construction | $180,000 | $15,000 | $30,000 | $ 45,000 |
| Bonds redeemed | 60,000 | 5,000 | 10,000 | 15,000 |
| Interest | 18,000 | 2,000 | 3,000 | 4,000 |
| Total disbursements | $258,000 | $22,000 | $43,000 | $ 64,000 |
| Cash balance—end of year | $238,000 | $13,000 | $19,000 | $ 87,000 |

Figure 16-6

A GOVERNMENTAL UNIT
Trust and Agency Funds
Statement of Cash Receipts and Disbursements for Fiscal Year

| | Total All Funds | Expendable Trust Funds | | | Nonexpendable Trust Funds | | Agency Fund |
| --- | --- | --- | --- | --- | --- | --- | --- |
| | | Performance Deposits Fund | Employees Pension Fund | Endowment Earnings Fund | Endowment Principal Fund | Loan Fund | |
| Cash balance beginning of year | $ 76,000 | $20,000 | $ 5,000 | $ 1,000 | $ 10,000 | $15,000 | $25,000 |
| Add, Receipts: | | | | | | | |
| Deposits | $ 25,000 | $25,000 | | | | | |
| Taxes for other units (itemize) | 50,000 | | | | | | $50,000 |
| Contributions | 13,000 | | $13,000 | | | | |
| Gifts | 60,000 | | | | $ 60,000 | | |
| Sale of investments | 14,500 | 14,500 | | | | | |
| Loans repaid | 20,000 | | | | | $20,000 | |
| Revenue from earnings of Endowment Principal Fund | 50,000 | | | $50,000 | | | |
| Interest | 57,500 | 500 | 2,000 | | 55,000 | | |
| Total receipts | $290,000 | $40,000 | $15,000 | $50,000 | $115,000 | $20,000 | $50,000 |
| Total receipts and balances | $366,000 | $60,000 | $20,000 | $51,000 | $125,000 | $35,000 | $75,000 |

| Less, Disbursements: | | | | | | | |
|---|---|---|---|---|---|---|---|
| Taxes paid to other units (itemize) | $ 70,000 | | | | | | $70,000 |
| Deposits refunded | 50,000 | $50,000 | | | | | |
| Pensions paid | 5,000 | | $ 5,000 | | | | |
| Band concerts | 41,000 | | | $41,000 | | | |
| Loans made | 30,000 | | | | | $30,000 | |
| Transfers to Endowment Earnings Fund | 50,000 | | | | $ 50,000 | | |
| Investments purchases | 83,000 | | 13,000 | | 70,000 | | |
| Total disbursements | $329,000 | $50,000 | $18,000 | $41,000 | $120,000 | $30,000 | $70,000 |
| Cash balance, end of year | $ 37,000 | $10,000 | $ 2,000 | $10,000 | $ 5,000 | $ 5,000 | $ 5,000 |

Figure 16-7

A GOVERNMENTAL UNIT

Combined Statement of Cash Receipts and Disbursements

All Funds for Fiscal Year

| | Cash Balance, Beginning of Year | Receipts | | Disbursements | | Cash Balance, End of Year |
|---|---|---|---|---|---|---|
| Fund | | Regular | Inter-Fund | Regular | Inter-Fund | |
| General | $180,000 | $300,000 | $ 15,000 | 390,000 | $ 90,000 | $ 15,000 |
| Special Revenue | 40,000 | 50,000 | — | 70,000 | 5,000 | 15,000 |
| Capital Projects | 60,000 | 40,000 | 10,000 | 50,000 | 10,000 | 50,000 |
| Debt Service | 100,000 | 150,000 | — | 200,000 | — | 50,000 |
| Intragovernmental Service | 45,000 | 5,000 | 100,000 | 130,000 | — | 20,000 |
| Special Assessment | 55,000 | 150,000 | 10,000 | 180,000 | 20,000 | 15,000 |
| Trust and Agency | 25,000 | 50,000 | — | 55,000 | — | 20,000 |
| Enterprise | 50,000 | 200,000 | 10,000 | 200,000 | 20,000 | 40,000 |
| Total | $555,000 | $945,000 | $145,000 | $1,275,000 | $145,000 | $225,000 |

### Funds and Bank Accounts

From the viewpoint of accounting there is no need for a separate bank account for each fund since the segregation of cash by funds on the books is sufficient. An independent fund may be said to exist even if no separate bank account is provided for it. Legal requirements may force the use of separate bank accounts for each fund, however, and a policy decision may be made requiring such separate accounts. Further, use of separate bank accounts may be appropriate because of weaknesses in the accounting or internal control systems or to facilitate the bank reconciliation process.

The use of one bank account for all funds may lead to hidden interfund borrowing; that is, cash applicable to one fund may be used to meet the expenditures of another fund. Such hidden borrowing is most likely to be resorted to in cases in which statutes prohibit interfund loans. Regular preparation of statements indicating balances, both positive and negative, will reveal the practice, but some administrators or legislators may feel that a policy of separate bank accounts is desirable.

If the governmental unit has many funds, the establishment of separate bank accounts for each is likely to hinder the effective administration of cash. For example, some governmental units have hundreds of Trust Funds, and others have separate tax levy funds for each department. Use of separate bank accounts for each of these funds would complicate the accounting procedure considerably with respect both to normal operating transactions and to cash borrowing and investment.

While no policy can be dogmatically advocated, it would seem that the proper procedure would be somewhat as follows: Given the existence of an accounting system that dependably indicates the amount of cash in each fund and, as appropriate, its intended or designated use, a separate bank account need not be established for each fund. Separate bank accounts should probably be established for each type of fund; that is, a separate bank account might be established for the General Fund, for Debt Service Funds, for all Capital Projects Funds, and so forth.

## Interfund Settlements

Either as a result of interfund borrowing or as a result of the performance by a department financed from one fund of services for a department financed from another fund, a fund may have money coming from another fund and may in turn owe money to the same fund or to other funds. Many governmental units settle interfund transactions at the end of each month. Others make settlements at more or less frequent intervals. The procedure in making interfund settlements depends on whether or not a separate bank account is provided for each of the funds. If separate bank accounts are provided, interfund settlements are made by check; otherwise they are made through a journal entry. In either case the settlement should be authorized in the same manner as other cash transactions.

## Reconciliations

As in private businesses, bank statements must be reconciled periodically (preferably monthly) with the cash balances carried on the books of the treasurer and on the books of the controller. This can be a considerable chore in manual systems, though modern computer systems are programmed to perform the reconciliation process.

The extent of the reconciliation required between the cash account as shown on the treasurer's records and on the bank statement will depend on the method of recording disbursements on the treasurer's books. If the treasurer records checks as disbursements as soon as they are issued, checks outstanding must be taken into account. If, contrary to sound financial administration, the treasurer does not record checks as disbursements until they have cleared through the bank, then the only item to be taken into account in making the reconciliation is cash on hand for deposit.

The extent of reconciliation between the balance of the Cash account(s) shown on the controller's books and that shown on the bank statements will vary. If the Cash account(s) on the controller's books is reduced as soon as warrants are issued, it is necessary to take into account, in addition to outstanding checks, the warrants issued by the controller for which the treasurer has not yet issued checks. Otherwise only outstanding checks and deposits in transit need to be taken into account.

### Concluding Comment

Generally speaking, public sector cash management has made tremendous strides in recent years and is far more effective today than it was even five or ten years ago. Among the several factors contributing to this progress are increases in (1) the number of full-time, professionally trained municipal financial managers; (2) the computer capabilities of many governments, permitting them to overcome the inherent limitations of fund accounting systems and improve their cash planning and investment programs; (3) the competitiveness in the money market, which has made it possible to invest large sums profitably even when they are available only overnight or over a weekend; (4) computer capabilities of banks and other financial institutions, permitting them to invest and disinvest the governmental depositor's cash rapidly and efficiently; and (5) the literature and professional development courses designed to assist state and local governments do a better job of cash management. The era in which even medium-size local governments often maintained 50 to 250 separate checking accounts, each with a different check form, and in which large sums were left in bank demand deposits at no interest for long periods is largely past. Progress has not been universal, of course, but many municipal finance officers today can point with pride to the fact that shrewd cash management yields to the government interest returns far in excess of their own salary, perhaps even far more than that of the entire financial management and accounting staff.

**Question 16-1.** In a certain state, warrants are issued to payees by the state controller, who requests the state treasurer to make payment to the payees named in the warrants. Although these warrants have no bank designated on them, they are accepted by banks and eventually find their way to the state treasurer for payment. The treasurer then writes a check for the amount of warrants presented by each of the banks. Should unpaid warrants be considered as a cash disbursement or should they be shown as a liability on the balance sheet? Give a reason or reasons for your answer.

**Question 16-2.** Suppose that the state controller in Question 16-1 issues the warrant to the payee and that the warrant indicates the bank by which it is to be paid, but that the warrant is not valid until countersigned by the state treasurer. How should warrants issued by the controller but not yet signed by the treasurer be shown on the balance sheet?

**Question 16-3.** The treasurer of the City of F does not consider a disbursement as such until the checks have cleared through the bank, whereas the treasurer of the School District of F considers disbursements as such as soon as the checks are issued, regardless of when they clear. Which treasurer in your opinion is following the more proper procedure?

**Question 16-4.** Why is it improper for an official to deposit government money to the credit of his own personal account?

**Question 16-5.** (a) Is it necessary to have a separate bank account for each fund? (b) What are the advantages and disadvantages of providing a separate bank account for each fund? (c) Under what circumstances would you recommend the establishment of a separate bank account for each fund?

**Question 16-6.** In a certain city checks must be signed by the mayor, the comptroller, and the treasurer. Do you think three signatures are necessary? If not, indicate how many signatures should be required and which of these three officers should sign.

**Question 16-7.** The legislative body of a municipality has established a relief fund through a special levy authorized for this purpose by the state legislature. The city also has a mayor's contingency fund set up by order of the mayor out of an appropriation made for his department. Can the mayor's contingency fund lend money to the relief fund? Can the relief fund lend money to the mayor's contingency fund?

**Question 16-8.** Discuss the propriety of netting cash overdrafts against cash balances in the combined balance sheet of a governmental unit.

**Problem 16-1.** The following are the opening cash balances and receipts and disbursements for special assessment districts 8, 11, 13, and 16 of the City of F for the year ending December 31, 19X0:

|  | District | | | |
| --- | --- | --- | --- | --- |
|  | 8 | 11 | 13 | 16 |
| Cash Balances: | | | | |
| For Construction ................. | $30,000 | $45,000 | $60,000 | $ 15,000 |
| For Bond Payments............... | 15,000 | 22,500 | 30,000 | 7,500 |
| For Interest Payments ............ | 3,000 | 4,500 | 6,000 | 750 |
| Receipts: | | | | |
| Interest ........................ | 2,500 | 3,000 | 3,500 | 500 |
| Sale of Bonds ................... | 70,000 | — | — | 80,000 |
| Current Assessments—For | | | | |
| Construction.................. | — | — | 15,000 | 10,000 |
| Delinquent Assessments—For Bonds.. | 15,000 | 7,500 | 1,500 | 1,500 |
| Delinquent Assessments—For | | | | |
| Construction.................. | 2,000 | 2,500 | 2,000 | 3,000 |
| Sale of Notes ................... | 20,000 | — | — | 5,000 |
| Municipality's Share of Cost ........ | 15,000 | 20,000 | 10,000 | 15,000 |
| Payments: | | | | |
| Capital Outlays ................. | 75,000 | 56,000 | 80,000 | 110,000 |
| Interest ........................ | 2,000 | 3,000 | 4,000 | 500 |
| Bond Retirement ............... | 17,000 | 20,000 | 20,000 | 7,500 |

Required:
Prepare a statement showing opening cash balances, receipts, disbursements, and closing cash balances for each district and for all the districts combined.

**Problem 16-2.**  The City of *F* maintains three bank accounts. On June 30, 19X0, the balances according to the bank statements were as follows:

| | |
|---|---|
| Loop National Bank | $48,199 |
| U. S. National Bank | 96,516 |
| Best National Bank | 76,325 |

The balances according to the treasurer's books on that day were as follows:

| Fund | Loop National Bank | U.S. National Bank | Best National Bank |
|---|---|---|---|
| General | | | $62,000 |
| Special Revenue | $51,950 | | |
| Debt Service | | $40,800 | |
| Water Utility | | 44,200 | |

The treasurer considers disbursements as such as soon as he issues checks. The balances of cash according to the comptroller's books were as follows:

| Fund | Amount |
|---|---|
| General | $72,500 |
| Special Revenue | 42,750 |
| Debt Service | 40,650 |
| Water Utility | 33,500 |

The comptroller considers cash disbursements as such as soon as warrants are issued. The following checks are still outstanding:

| General Fund | | Debt Service Fund | |
|---|---|---|---|
| #3614 | $   450 | #6112 | $   130 |
| 4812 | 110 | 6997 | 250 |
| 4813 | 270 | 6998 | 875 |
| 4816 | 4,850 | 6999 | 13,000 |
| 4822 | 2,000 | 7000 | 2,000 |
| 4823 | 412 | | |
| 4824 | 68 | | |

| Special Revenue Fund | | Water Utility Fund | |
|---|---|---|---|
| #2190 | $   140 | #1409 | $   75 |
| 2191 | 275 | 1416 | 42 |
| 2305 | 412 | 1512 | 97 |
| 2306 | 1,500 | 1513 | 1,500 |
| 2307 | 3,200 | 1514 | 110 |
| 2308 | 840 | 1515 | 67 |
| | | 1516 | 143 |

Warrants issued for which checks have not yet been written are as follows:

| Fund | Amount |
|------|--------|
| General | $3,200 |
| Special Revenue | 750 |
| Debt Service | 6,200 |
| Water Utility | 850 |

Interest credited by the bank but not taken up by the city is as follows:

| Fund | Amount |
|------|--------|
| General | $1,000 |
| Special Revenue | 350 |
| Debt Service | 6,200 |
| Water Utility | 700 |

The following deposits were in transit on June 30:

| Fund | Amount |
|------|--------|
| General | $8,500 |
| Special Revenue | 2,000 |
| Debt Service | 615 |
| Water Utility | 4,200 |

Exchange charged by the bank and not yet recorded on the city's books is as follows:

| Fund | Amount |
|------|--------|
| General | $ 35 |
| Special Revenue | 35 |
| Debt Service | 16 |
| Water Utility | 42 |

Required:

Prepare a statement reconciling the cash accounts as shown by the bank statements with the balances shown on the treasurer's records and on the comptroller's records, respectively.

**Problem 16-3.** From the following information for the City of *R*, prepare a summary statement of cash receipts, disbursements, and balances properly classified by funds as of December 31, 19X0:

Cash Balances, January 1, 19X0:

    Electric Fund .......................... $ 42,520

    General Fund .......................... 22,915

    Pension Fund ......................... 14,630

    Public School Fund .................... 14,650

    Special Assessment Fund ................ 26,885

Receipts of 19X0:

    Electric Fund:

        Sales ............................... 462,350

        Accounts Receivable Collections ......... 22,620

        Public Street Lighting ................. 19,840 (a)

        Rents .............................. 3,575

    General Fund:

        Current Taxes ....................... 405,500

        Taxes Paid by Electric Fund ............ 12,360 (b)

        Parking Meters ...................... 5,702

        Dog Licenses ........................ 3,508

        Police Fines ......................... 10,650

        Interest Earnings ..................... 1,200

        Concessions ......................... 3,700

        State Gas Tax ....................... 18,300

        Weights and Measures ................. 4,650

        Clinic Fees ......................... 3,420

        Golf Fees ........................... 7,810

    Pension Fund:

        Taxes .............................. 32,720 (c)

        Employees' Contribution .............. 37,000

        Interest on Investments ................ 5,436

    Public School Fund:

        Taxes .............................. 151,000 (d)

        State Appropriation ................... 75,500

    Special Assessment Fund:

        Installment Collections ................. 24,680

        City's Share ........................ 8,000 (e)

        Interest Collections ................... 6,270

Disbursements during 19X0:

    Electric Fund .......................... 489,139*

    General Fund .......................... 472,210†

    Pension Fund ......................... 55,800

    Public School Fund .................... 190,287

    Special Assessment Fund ................ 51,630

\* Includes item (b).

† Includes items (a), (c), (d), and (e).

**Problem 16-4.** The following data were taken from the treasurer's report of the City of *Y* for the fiscal year ended December 31, 19X0.

CITY OF *Y*

Statement of Cash Receipts, Disbursements, and Balances

for Fiscal Year Ended December, 31, 19X0

| Fund | Opening Balance | Receipts | Disbursements | Closing Balance |
|------|----------------|----------|---------------|-----------------|
| General | $1,271,432 | $4,305,206 | $4,271,431 | $1,305,207 |
| Capital Projects I | 31,009 | 75,743 | 54,692 | 52,060 |
| Special Assessment | 103,597 | 298,385 | 386,072 | 15,910 |
| School | 325,196 | 2,194,825 | 2,505,247 | 14,774 |
| Pension Trust | 2,128 | 17,144 | 15,724 | 3,548 |
| Capital Projects II | 69,155 | 172,873 | 179,370 | 62,658 |
| Sewage Disposal | 1,237,825 | 615,412 | 1,104,383 | 748,854 |
| Central Fire Alarm | — | 50,000 | 21 | 49,979 |
| | $3,040,342 | $7,729,588 | $8,516,940 | $2,252,990 |

The following transfers were made during the year and shown in the comptroller's records but not in the treasurer's books:

| Transferred from | Transferred to | Amount |
|------------------|----------------|--------|
| Special Assessment | Capital Projects | $ 8,125 |
| General | Sewage Disposal | 62,350 |
| General | School | 844,068 |
| Sewage Disposal | General | 13,500 |
| General | Central Fire Alarm | 1,275 |

Required:
(a)  Prepare a statement showing receipts, disbursements, and balances according to the comptroller's records.
(b)  Prepare a statement reconciling the cash balances according to the comptroller's records with the cash balances according to the treasurer's books.

**Problem 16-5.** On the basis of the following data, prepare a statement reconciling the receipts and disbursements as recorded by the county clerk of the County of *F* and as shown on the books of the country sanitorium.

According to the records of the sanitorium, it received $110,000 during 19X3, whereas on the county clerk's books the sanitorium was charged with receipts of $110,233. The sanitorium received money from the sale of farm products in December to the amount of $967, which was not recorded on the county clerk's books until January, 19X4. On the other hand, the county clerk recorded the receipt of $1,200 from the state for the benefit of the sanitorium, but the sanitorium did not receive the money until 19X4 and therefore did not record it as a receipt of 19X3.

According to the county records, the sanitorium disbursed $121,375 during 19X3, whereas according to the sanitorium records, it disbursed $122,300 during that period. However, disbursements of $925 were charged as such on the sanitorium's books in December, 19X3, whereas they were not recorded on the county clerk's records until January, 19X4.

**Problem 16-6.** The following transfers were made between a state's funds during the fiscal year ended May 31, 19X5:

The General Fund transferred money to other funds as follows:

| | |
|---|---:|
| Administration | $    20,000 |
| Debt Service Fund I | 50,000,000 |
| Debt Service Fund II | 45,000,000 |
| Debt Service Fund III | 4,103,125 |
| Debt Service Fund IV | 4,962,349 |
| Liquid Fuels Tax Fund | 5,000,000 |
| School Employees Retirement Fund | 312,200 |
| Motor License Fund | 4,200,000 |
| State Stores Fund | 7,500,000 |
| Flood Control Fund | 275,000 |
| State Employees' Retirement Fund | 415,000 |
| Liquor License Fund | 1,200,000 |

The state stores fund transferred $2,250,000 to the Liquid Fuels Tax Fund.
In addition to the transfer from the General Fund, the State Employees' Retirement Fund received money from the following:

| | |
|---|---:|
| Fish Fund | $     5,350 |
| Banking Department Fund | 19,575 |
| State Stores Fund | 172,500 |
| Game Fund | 12,400 |
| Manufacturing Fund | 7,425 |
| State Workmen's Insurance Fund | 11,600 |

The General Fund received money from the following funds:

| | |
|---|---:|
| Administration Fund | $    20,000 |
| Motor License Fund | 18,752,000 |
| State Insurance Fund | 1,000,000 |
| Liquid Fuels Tax Fund | 5,510,000 |
| Federal Rehabilitation Fund | 259,000 |
| Federal Vocational Eduction Fund | 697,880 |
| Liquor License Fund | 1,000,000 |

Required:
Prepare a statement analyzing the interfund transactions.

**Problem 16-7.** The Village of *P* operates on an accrual basis with respect to both revenues and expenditures. It maintains two bank accounts at the Grovers State Bank, one for the General Fund and one for the Capital Projects Fund. You are asked to prepare from the following data (a) a statement reconciling the balances per bank with the balances of each for each fund per comptroller's books on December 31, 19X5, before any correcting entries are made, and (b) journal entries necessary to correct the comptroller's records.

1. Balance per bank statement: (a) General Fund, $76,500; (b) Capital Projects Fund, $32,700.
2. On December 30, 19X5, the treasurer wrote check G112 for $95 in payment of a voucher chargeable against the Capital Projects Fund. The comptroller caught this error but the check had already been cashed. To date no action has been taken on this matter.
3. Capital Projects accounts receivable to the amount of $300 were collected on December 31, 19X5, and shown on the records, but were not deposited until January 2, 19X6.
4. Due to an oversight General Fund money received on December 31, 19X5, ($250 from taxes receivable, $50 from fines, and check B904 described below) was not recorded until its deposit on January 5, 19X6. The total deposit on that day, which included also January 19X6, receipts, was $2,000 and the entire amount was recorded as a January, 19X6, receipt on the comptroller's books.
5. The bank made service charges of $75. Of this amount $35 was chargeable to the General Fund and the remainder to the Capital Projects Fund. These charges have not been recorded by the city.
6. Check G108 was for $250 but was recorded in error on the comptroller's books as $230 because the voucher payable was for that amount.
7. Check B904 is a payment in lieu of taxes made to the General Fund and turned over to that Fund on December 31, 19X5, but not put through for collection by the General Fund until January 5, 19X6. (See 4 above.)
8. The following checks were outstanding:

| General Fund | | Capital Projects | |
|---|---|---|---|
| G114 | $210 | B901 | $ 75 |
| G115 | 350 | B902 | 15 |
| G116 | 400 | B903 | 92 |
| G117 | 150 | B904 | 1,000 |

9. Checks G116 and G117 were written on December 31, 19X5. Check G116 was mailed on that day while check G117 was not mailed until January 5, 19X6. Both were recorded by the comptroller as December disbursements.

**Problem 16-8.** The Z City Council on January 3, 19X6, created a Library Fund by levying a special tax in the amount of $145,000 and appropriating $120,000 for library purposes. The amounts received by the city from this levy for each month during the year were as follows:

| | | | |
|---|---|---|---|
| January ........... | $10,145 | July .............. | $10,220 |
| February .......... | 13,440 | August ............ | 11,361 |
| March ............. | 15,670 | September ......... | 12,446 |
| April ............. | 10,492 | October ........... | 11,756 |
| May ............... | 11,170 | November .......... | 10,660 |
| June .............. | 14,240 | December .......... | 12,008 |

The following vouchers were certified, and the following warrants were issued each month:

|          | Vouchers | Warrants |           | Vouchers | Warrants |
|----------|----------|----------|-----------|----------|----------|
| January..... | $ 7,147 | $ 7,147 | July ......... | $14,875 | $14,272 |
| February.... | 9,610 | 9,810 | August ...... | 12,950 | 13,124 |
| March ..... | 10,340 | 10,460 | September.... | 9,236 | 9,140 |
| April ....... | 10,620 | 10,787 | October ..... | 10,520 | 10,620 |
| May ....... | 11,750 | 11,490 | November ... | 8,560 | 7,475 |
| June ....... | 13,680 | 13,684 | December .... | 7,250 | 3,926 |

The city treasurer during the year paid warrants amounting to $109,376.
Required:

(a)  Set up "T" accounts as they should appear on the books of (1) the comptroller, and (2) the treasurer.

(b)  Prepare a statement reconciling the comptroller's cash with that of the treasurer.

(c)  Prepare closing entries and post to "T" accounts.

(d)  Prepare a balance sheet as of December 31, 19X6.

**Problem 16-9.**  The Cobleskill City Council passed a resolution requiring a yearly cash budget by fund for the City beginning with its fiscal year ending September 30, 19X3. The City's financial director has prepared a list of expected cash receipts and disbursements, but he is having difficulty subdividing them by fund. The list follows:

Cash receipts

    Taxes:

| | |
|---|---:|
| General property | $ 685,000 |
| School | 421,000 |
| Franchise | 223,000 |
| | 1,329,000 |

    Licenses and permits:

| | |
|---|---:|
| Business licenses | 41,000 |
| Automobile inspection permits | 24,000 |
| Building permits | 18,000 |
| | 83,000 |

    Intergovernmental revenue:

| | |
|---|---:|
| Sales tax | 1,012,000 |
| Federal grants | 128,000 |
| State motor vehicle tax | 83,500 |
| State gasoline tax | 52,000 |
| State alcoholic beverage licenses | 16,000 |
| | 1,291,500 |

    Charges for services:

| | |
|---|---:|
| Sanitation fees | $ 121,000 |
| Sewer connection fees | 71,000 |
| Library revenues | 13,000 |
| Park revenues | 2,500 |
| | 207,500 |

Bond issues:

| | |
|---|---:|
| Civic center | 347,000 |
| General obligation | 200,000 |
| Sewer | 153,000 |
| Library | 120,000 |
| | 820,000 |

Other

| | |
|---|---:|
| Proceeds from the sale of investments | 312,000 |
| Sewer assessments | 50,000 |
| Rental revenue | 48,000 |
| Interest revenue | 15,000 |
| | 425,000 |
| | $4,156,000 |

*Cash disbursements*

| | |
|---|---:|
| General government | $  671,000 |
| Public safety | 516,000 |
| Schools | 458,000 |
| Sanitation | 131,000 |
| Library | 28,000 |
| Rental property | 17,500 |
| Parks | 17,000 |
| | 1,838,500 |

Debt service:

| | |
|---|---:|
| General obligation bonds | 618,000 |
| Street construction bonds | 327,000 |
| School bonds | 119,000 |
| Sewage disposal plant bonds | 37,200 |
| | 1,101,200 |

| | |
|---|---:|
| Investments | 358,000 |
| State portion of sales tax | 860,200 |

Capital expenditures:

| | |
|---|---:|
| Sewer construction (assessed area) | 114,100 |
| Civic center construction | 73,000 |
| Library construction | 36,000 |
| | 223,100 |
| | $4,381,000 |

The financial director provides you with the following additional information:
1. A bond issue was authorized in 19X2 for the construction of a civic center. The debt is to be paid from future civic center revenues and general property taxes.

2.  A bond issue was authorized in 19X2 for additions to the library. The debt is to be paid from general property taxes.

3.  General obligation bonds are paid from general property taxes collected by the general fund.

4.  Ten percent (10%) of the total annual school taxes represents an individually voted tax for payment of bonds the proceeds of which were used for school construction.

5.  In 19X0, a wealthy citizen donated rental property to the City. Net income from the property is to be used to assist in operating the library. The net cash increase attributable to the property is transferred to the library on September 30 of each year.

6.  All sales taxes are collected by the City; the state receives 85 percent of these taxes. The state's portion is remitted at the end of each month.

7.  Payment of the street construction bonds is to be made from assessments previously collected from the respective property owners. The proceeds from the assessments were invested and the principal of $312,000 will earn $15,000 interest during the coming year.

8.  In 19X2, a special assessment in the amount of $203,000 was made on certain property owners for sewer construction. During fiscal 19X3, $50,000 of this assessment is expected to be collected. The remainder of the sewer cost is to be paid from a $153,000 bond issue to be sold in fiscal 19X3. Future special assessment collections will be used to pay principal and interest on the bonds.

9.  All sewer and sanitation services are provided by a separate Enterprise Fund.

10.  The federal grant is for fiscal 19X3 school operations.

11.  The proceeds remaining at the end of the year from the sale of civic center and library bonds are to be invested.

Required:

Prepare a budget of cash receipts and disbursements by fund for the year ending September 30, 19X3. All interfund transfers of cash are to be included. (AICPA)

# 17

## Reporting

Reporting is the last phase of the budget cycle for which the executive branch of the government is responsible. In the annual financial report the executive branch demonstrates its compliance with the legal and contractual requirements, including fund and appropriational requirements, under which the government is operated by making a presentation that is in conformity with generally accepted accounting principles. The annual financial report is designed to provide the legislative body, creditors, investors, students of public finance, political scientists, and the general public with the information that each group needs.

Interim statements are primarily designed to meet the needs of administrative personnel such as the chief executive, supervisors at the several levels of government, and budget examiners, though legislators may be interested in them as indications of whether budget plans are being followed. The interim statements help management to determine how well the executive branch is complying with legal requirements and that it will be able to make appropriate financial disclosures at the end of the period. In addition, these statements provide important means of control over current operations, including the revelation of variations from plan that may require alterations in the plan or corrections of operations.

The annual financial report and interim (usually monthly) reports are the subjects of the principal subdivisions of this chapter.

## THE ANNUAL FINANCIAL REPORT

The annual financial report is prepared by the finance officer of a governmental unit. His most obvious objective is to show the city's financial condition and the financial results of its operations, but he may also use it to transmit information to the public that is not specifically related to finances.

### The Principle of Full Disclosure

Generally accepted accounting principles applicable to municipalities have been discussed earlier, but the principle of disclosure is particularly applicable to the financial statements themselves and merits discussion here. Generally accepted accounting principles applicable to business enterprises include the principle of adequate disclosure. The principle of adequate disclosure in effect states that the financial statements *should communicate* all information necessary for fair presentation in conformity with generally accepted accounting principles and *should not* be misleading. The criteria for determining whether an item requires disclosure are as follows: (1) an item of information should be disclosed if there is a reasonable probability that it might affect the judgments made or conclusions reached by a "reasonably informed" reader of the financial statements; (2) a mass of detailed information, overly condensed presentations, and highly technical or vague language that might be a barrier to effective communication should be avoided. In short, the object is to present the financial information in such a manner that its significance is apparent to a reasonably informed reader without burying him in trivia. If the item titles and amounts in the financial statements are not sufficiently informative, for example, the preparer of the statements is expected to add in the statements or in footnotes thereto all information that will be significant to a decision by statement users; likewise, if there has been a change in accounting principles, both the change and the effect of the change warrant disclosure. In the past a company has not been required to analyze its sales or profits by customer classes, by industry or type of product, or on a geographical basis. The trend of the requirements of the accounting profession and governmental agencies is in the direction of requiring additional disclosures, and in the present environment of emphasis upon consumer and investor protection this is an accelerating trend.

Because of the sensitivity of public expenditures ("that's my tax money you are spending"), "full disclosure" is a more accurate term for the disclosure principle in government than is "adequate disclosure." The public has an inherent right to know the significant details of governmental operations. Every tendency of demands upon government is to provide additional information; to conduct all government business in open meetings; and to tell the public the details of contracts, expenditures on campaigns, expenditures by lobbyists, and the like. In this atmosphere there is a continuing pressure to disclose fully the details of the public's financial business, both in summary and in detail.

The National Committee on Governmental Accounting emphasized the need for full disclosure at several points in *GAAFR*. You will recall, for example, that the second NCGA principle is:

2. If there is a conflict between legal provisions and generally accepted accounting principles applicable to governmental units, legal provisions must take precedence. Insofar as possible, however, the governmental accounting system should make possible the full disclosure and fair presentation of financial position and operating results in accordance with generally accepted principles of accounting applicable to governmental units.[1]

The Committee elaborated on this principle as follows:

In the administration of governmental financial programs, it sometimes happens that specific legal provisions run counter to recognized principles and practices of governmental accounting. These differences often result from the fact that certain laws governing fiscal operations are antiquated and difficult to change.

...in a society which operates under the rule of law, accounting, like all other management tools and procedures of public administration, must at all times comply with all laws governing it.

However, in cases where such compliance is not fully in agreement with recognized accounting principles, it is recommended that the governmental unit also prepare such additional or supplementary financial statements as may be necessary to present fairly the financial position and results of operations of its constituent funds and balanced account groups for the fiscal period in conformity with generally accepted accounting principles applicable to governmental units and consistently applied.[2]

The following NCGA observations and recommendations are equally to the point:

Accounting principles and procedures detailed in this volume [*GAAFR*] are so designed that when adhered to [they] will enhance the fiscal control, will denote compliance with legal requirements, and will result in a financial report disclosing fiscal responsibility. However, *preparation of a report which reflects fiscal stewardship responsibilities only is insufficient in many respects* for use by management, for making policy decisions, and for statistical purposes, *and may be considered as falling short of a prime requisite of financial reporting —full disclosure* of financial activities.

...the finance officer should *not* assume that by preparing a report which demonstrates conformance with legal requirements that this prevents addi-

[1] *GAAFR,* p. 4.
[2] *Ibid.,* pp. 4–5.

tional reporting of fiscal data in total and/or other than on a fund basis. He should also assume responsibility for preparing *supplemental* fiscal data basic in reaching essential administrative and management decisions, formulating fiscal policy, informing the general and investing public, and submitting financial data to central compiling agencies, such as national bureaus of statistics. *Adherence to legal requirements is paramount but this should not be construed as establishing maximum reporting requirements. Supplementary information may be equally valuable in meeting another basic requirement —full disclosure—*since this will provide readers with some understanding of the finances of the reporting governmental unit.[3]

## Content of the Annual Financial Report

The typical annual financial report consists of an introductory section, including a letter of transmittal; financial statements; and statistical tables. Each of these is discussed below.

INTRODUCTORY SECTION. After a title page and a table of contents, the chief finance officer's letter of transmittal will appear. It is ordinarily addressed to the chief executive and the legislative body of the governmental unit, but in a larger sense it is directed to all those who are interested in the financial position and results of operation of the unit. For example, the finance officer of a city may want to describe the legal constraints and the policy requirements under which the city operates and under which the statements are prepared. These would include the basis of accounting used by the city in the preparation of its budget and in operations. Certainly he would want to include the financial and related highlights of the year being reported upon; his comments about the trend of city finances for the future would be appropriate. For example, he might describe population projections and their expected effect upon requirements for city services and city resources.

The introductory section usually contains the report of the independent certified public accountant or other postauditor upon his examination of the financial statements.

The foregoing by no means exhaust the possible useful elements of the introductory section. For example, in some circumstances it may be appropriate to move some of the statistical materials from the statistical section of the annual report to the introductory section, where they and remarks upon them will receive more attention. It may also be considered desirable to list principal officials of the city, display an organization chart, or reproduce the Certificate of Conformance received from the Municipal Finance Officers' Association of the United States and Canada for the prior year's financial report and indicate whether this year's financial report is, in the finance officer's opinion, also in compliance with generally accepted accounting principles for municipal governments.

[3] *Ibid.*, p. 233. (Emphasis added.)

Financial Statements. The National Committee on Governmental Accounting recommends that the annual report contain, as a minimum, the following four combined statements and three combined schedules in the indicated order[4]:

1. Combined Balance Sheet—All Funds (Figure 17-1).
2. Combined Statement of Revenue—Estimated and Actual, General and Special Revenue Funds (Figure 17-2).
3. Combined Statement of General Governmental Expenditures and Encumbrances Compared with Authorizations—General and Special Revenue Funds (Figure 17-3).
4. Combined Statement of Cash Receipts and Disbursements—All Funds (Figure 17-4).
5. Combined Schedule of Delinquent Taxes Receivable by Funds (Figure 17-5).
6. Combined Schedule of Bonds Payable (Figure 17-6).
7. Combined Schedule of Investments—All Funds (Figure 17-7).

Presentation of these statements and schedules at the beginning of the financial section and ahead of the individual fund statements provides the reader with "an overview and broad perspective" of the government's financial position and the results of its financial operations. The combined statements present a summary set of information that may satisfy the user's needs without the necessity for examining the statements of each fund. These combined statements may then be supplemented, as the user desires, by examination of the statements of the individual funds and account groups that are presented thereafter.

As noted earlier, the National Committee on Governmental Accounting strongly opposes the preparation of *consolidated* financial statements.[5] It is their belief that *combined* statements properly recognize the legal facts of the independence of the several funds and account groups. Unlike the corporate holding company that has control of the destiny of its subsidiaries, the city government may not, at will, cancel the funds' interfund receivables and payables or use the excess cash in one fund to meet the financial crisis in another. Even the use of a total column in a columnar form of combined balance sheet is held to be inappropriate, since it implies that the account balances are additive, whereas as a matter of fact (law, contract) they may not be additive.

---

[4] *GAAFR*, p. 110. The figures in this chapter are adapted from *GAAFR*.

[5] We also noted earlier that some accountants prefer to supplement the individual fund and nonfund account group statements with consolidated or consolidating statements (in which interfund balances and the effects of interfund transactions are eliminated) rather than with combined statements. Combined statements are by far the more widely used, though the use of consolidated and consolidating statements to fulfill the "overview" function appears to be increasing.

Figure 17-1

A GOVERNMENTAL UNIT
Combined Balance Sheet—All Funds
December 31, 19X4

| | General Fund | Special Revenue Funds | Debt Service Funds | Capital Projects Funds | Enterprise Fund | Intra-governmental Service Fund | Trust and Agency Funds | Special Assessment Funds | General Fixed Assets | General Long-Term Debt |
|---|---|---|---|---|---|---|---|---|---|---|
| Assets and Other Debits | | | | | | | | | | |
| Asset 1 | | | | | | | | | | |
| Asset 2 | | | | | | | | | | |
| — | | | | | | | | | | |
| — | | | | | | | | | | |
| — | | | | | | | | | | |
| Asset n | | | | | | | | | | |
| Total Assets and Other Debits | | | | | | | | | | |
| Liabilities | | | | | | | | | | |
| Liability 1 | | | | | | | | | | |
| Liability 2 | | | | | | | | | | |
| — | | | | | | | | | | |
| — | | | | | | | | | | |
| Liability n | | | | | | | | | | |
| Total Liabilities | | | | | | | | | | |

Reserves, Fund Balances, and
Retained Earnings

Reserve 1
Reserve 2
Fund Balance
Retained Earnings

Total Reserves, Fund Balances
and Retained Earnings

Observations on Figure 17-1:

1. The amounts of the individual fund and account group assets, other debits, liabilities, reserves, fund balances and retained earnings are entered in the respective fund and account group columns.

2. There is no total column for the sums of the funds and account groups. As has been observed in this chapter, the balances of various accounts, such as Cash, may not properly be added because of the independent natures of the several funds.

745

**Figure 17-2**

## A GOVERMENTAL UNIT
Combined Statement of Revenues—
Estimated and Actual—General and Special Revenue Funds
For the Fiscal Year Ended December 31, 19X4

| Source and Fund | Estimated Revenues | Actual Revenues | Actual Over (Under) Estimated |
|---|---|---|---|
| Taxes: | | | |
| General | | | |
| Special Revenue | | | |
| Total Taxes | | | |
| Licenses and Permits: | | | |
| General | | | |
| Intergovernmental Revenue: | | | |
| General | | | |
| Special Revenue | | | |
| Total Intergovernmental Revenue | | | |
| Charges for Services: | | | |
| General | | | |
| Special Revenue | | | |
| Total Charges for Services | | | |
| Fines and Forfeits: | | | |
| General | | | |
| Miscellaneous Revenue: | | | |
| General | | | |
| Special Revenue | | | |
| Total Miscellaneous Revenue | | | |
| Total Revenue | | | |

Combined statements relating to operation are desirable only for the funds that are concerned with the discharge of the government's general responsibilities: the General and Special Revenue Funds. Hence only those two types of funds are included in the "Combined Statement of Revenue—Estimated and Actual" (Figure 17-2), and in the "Combined Statement of General Governmental Expenditures and Encumbrances Compared with Authorizations" (Figure 17-3). The "Combined Statement of Cash Receipts and Disbursements" (Figure 17-4), on the other hand, can properly cover all funds since it carries no analytical implications other than those applicable to cash flow.

The individual balance sheets of the several funds and account groups may not be the appropriate places to list the delinquent taxes, bond liabilities, and

Figure 17-3

A GOVERNMENTAL UNIT

Combined Statement of General Governmental Expenditures and

Encumbrances Compared with Authorizations—General and Special Revenue Funds

For the Fiscal Year Ended December 31, 19X4

| Function and Fund | Reserve for Encumbrances 19X3 | Expenditures 19X3 | Credit (Charge) to Fund Balance | 19X4 Appropriations (Revised) | 19X4 Expenditures | Encumbrances December 31, 19X4 | 19X4 Unencumbered Balance |
|---|---|---|---|---|---|---|---|
| General Government: | | | | | | | |
| General Fund | | | | | | | |
| Special Revenue Fund 1 | | | | | | | |
| Total General Government | | | | | | | |
| Public Safety | | | | | | | |
| General Fund | | | | | | | |
| Special Revenue Fund 2 | | | | | | | |
| Special Revenue Fund 3 | | | | | | | |
| Total Public Safety | | | | | | | |
| Other | | | | | | | |
| Total of General and Special Revenue Funds | | | | | | | |

**Figure 17-4**

A GOVERNMENTAL UNIT
Combined Statement of Cash Receipts and
Disbursements—All Funds
For the Fiscal Year Ended December 31, 19X4

| Fund, Classified by Type | Balance 1–1–X4 | Receipts | Disburse- ments | Balance 12–31–X4 |
|---|---|---|---|---|
| General Fund | | | | |
| Special Revenue Funds: | | | | |
|   Special Revenue Fund 1 | | | | |
|   Special Revenue Fund 2 | | | | |
|   Special Revenue Fund n | | | | |
| Debt Service Funds | | | | |
| Other | | | | |
|   Total All Funds | | | | $ XXXXX |
| Classified by Depository: | | | | |
|   Change and petty cash funds | | | | $ XXXX |
|   Bank 1 | | | | XXXXX |
|   Bank 2 | | | | XXX |
|   Bank n | | | | XXX |
|   Totals, 12–31-X4 | | | | $ XXXXX |

**Figure 17-5**

A GOVERNMENTAL UNIT
Combined Schedule of Delinquent Taxes Receivable by Funds
December 31, 19X4

| Delinquent Taxes by Year | Total | General | Funds Special Revenue | Debt Service |
|---|---|---|---|---|
| Delinquent Taxes: | | | | |
|   19X3 | | | | |
|   19X2 | | | | |
|   19X1 | | | | |
| Total delinquent taxes | | | | |
| Less: Estimated uncollectible delinquent taxes | | | | |
| Net delinquent taxes receivable | * | * | * | * |

* Totals for the several types of funds would be keyed to balance sheets for those types of funds.

# A GOVERNMENTAL UNIT
## Combined Schedule of Bonds Payable
### December 31, 19X4

| | Interest Rates and Dates | Issue Date | Final Maturity Date | Annual Serial Payments | Bonds | | | | Debt Service Fund Balance—Term Bonds | | |
|---|---|---|---|---|---|---|---|---|---|---|---|
| | | | | | Authorized | Issued | Retired | Outstanding | Requirement | Actual | Actual (Under) Over Requirement |
| General Obligation Bonds | | | | | | | | | | | |
| Issue 1 | | | | | | | | | | | |
| Issue 2 | | | | | | | | | | | |
| Issue — | | | | | | | | | | | |
| Issue n | | | | | | | | | | | |
| Total general obligation bonds* | | | | | | | | | | | |
| Revenue Bonds | | | | | | | | | | | |
| Issue 1 | | | | | | | | | | | |
| Issue 2 | | | | | | | | | | | |
| Issue — | | | | | | | | | | | |
| Issue n | | | | | | | | | | | |
| Total revenue bonds† | | | | | | | | | | | |
| Special Assessment Bonds | | | | | | | | | | | |
| Improvement District 1 | | | | | | | | | | | |
| Improvement District 2 | | | | | | | | | | | |
| Improvement District — | | | | | | | | | | | |
| Improvement District n | | | | | | | | | | | |
| Total special assessment bonds** | | | | | | | | | | | |

\* Referenced to "Statement of Long-Term Debt."

† Referenced to balance sheet(s) of Enterprise Fund(s).

\*\* Referenced to balance sheet(s) of Special Assessment Fund(s).

Figure 17-7

## A GOVERNMENTAL UNIT
Combined Schedule of Investments—All Funds
December 31, 19X4

| Description | Bond Certificate Numbers | Interest Rates (%) | Maturity Dates | Par Value | Unamortized Premiums | Unamortized Discount | Total Book Value |
|---|---|---|---|---|---|---|---|
| General Fund: | | | | | | | |
| Issue 1 | | | | | | | |
| Issue 2 | | | | | | | |
| Total General Fund | | | | ⎸⎸ | ⎸⎸ | ⎸⎸ | ⎸⎸ |
| Debt Service Funds: | | | | | | | |
| Issue 1 | | | | | | | |
| Issue 2 | | | | | | | |
| Issue — | | | | | | | |
| Issue n | | | | | | | |
| Total Debt Service Funds | | | | ⎸⎸ | ⎸⎸ | ⎸⎸ | ⎸⎸ |
| Trust and Agency Funds: | | | | | | | |
| Issue 1 | | | | | | | |
| Issue 2 | | | | | | | |
| Issue — | | | | | | | |
| Issue n | | | | | | | |
| Total Trust and Agency Funds | | | | ⎸⎸ | ⎸⎸ | ⎸⎸ | ⎸⎸ |
| Enterprise Funds: | | | | | | | |
| Issue 1 | | | | | | | |
| Issue 2 | | | | | | | |
| Total Enterprise Funds | | | | ⎸⎸ | ⎸⎸ | ⎸⎸ | ⎸⎸ |

Note: The totals of each type of fund would be referenced to the related balance sheet.

investments in detail. In such statements as a combined balance sheet the full disclosure requirements discussed above often cannot be met because of space limitations. Further, summations of these aspects of a city's finances may facilitate analysis of its financial position by statement users. Accordingly, it is desirable to include among the combined statements the "Combined Schedule of Delinquent Taxes Receivable by Funds" (Figure 17-5); "Combined Schedule of Bonds Payable," (Figure 17-6); and "Combined Schedule of Investments— All Funds" (Figure 17-7). In these schedules the details of the accounts can be itemized by fund or account group.

In addition to the seven combined statements, the financial statements section of the annual report will contain statements pertaining to each fund and account group. The following is a list of the additional statements that might appear. The statements have been presented in the several chapters of this book. The list is illustrative; an annual report may have a greater or smaller number of statements than is found in the list. The statements the finance officer will want to include depend upon the number of funds, the magnitude of transactions in the funds, and his evaluation of the importance of analyzing the changes that have taken place in certain funds and accounts during the year.

*Figure*

### General Fund*

| | Figure |
|---|---|
| Balance Sheet | 5-2 |
| Analysis of Changes in Fund Balance | 5-3, 5-4, 5-5, 5-6, or 5-7 |
| Statement of Revenues—Estimated and Actual | 6-11 |
| Statement of Expenditures and Encumbrances Compared with Authorizations | 7-8 |
| Statement of Expenditures Classified by Function, Organization Unit, Character, and Object | 7-9 |

### Capital Projects Fund(s)

| | |
|---|---|
| Balance Sheet | 8-1 |
| Analysis of Changes in Fund Balance | 8-2 or 8-10 |
| Statement of Revenues—Estimated and Actual | 8-3 |

### Special Assessment Fund(s)

| | |
|---|---|
| Balance Sheet | 9-5, 9-7, or 9-8 |
| Analysis of Changes in Fund Balance | 9-6 or 9-10 |
| Schedule of Installments to be Applied to Payment of Bonds and Interest | 9-9 |
| Statement of Expenditures Compared with Appropriations | 9-11 |

* Statements similar to those of the General Fund would be appropriate for Special Revenue Funds.

*Figure*

### Debt Service Fund(s)

| | |
|---|---|
| Balance Sheet | 10-4, 10-5 |
| Statement of Revenues, Expenditures, and Fund Balances | 10-6 |

### Trust and Agency Fund(s)

| | |
|---|---|
| Balance Sheet | 12-1, 12-3, 12-8, 12-10, or 12-11, 12-12, 12-13, or 12-14 |
| Analysis of Changes in Fund Balance | 12-4 |

### Intragovernmental Service Fund(s)

| | |
|---|---|
| Balance Sheet | 13-1 or 13-2 |
| Analysis of Changes in Retained Earnings | 13-3 |
| Statement of Operations | 13-4 |
| Statement of Changes in Financial Position† | 13-8 or 13-18 |

### Enterprise Fund(s)

| | |
|---|---|
| Balance Sheet | 14-2 |
| Analysis of Changes in Retained Earnings | 14-3 |
| Statement of Revenue and Expense | 14-4 |
| Statement of Changes in Financial Position | 14-7 or 14-9 |

### General Fixed Assets

| | |
|---|---|
| Statement of General Fixed Assets | 11-7 |
| Statement of Changes in General Fixed Assets— | |
| By Sources | 11-8 |
| By Functions and Activities | 11-10 |
| Schedule of General Fixed Assets—By Functions and Activities | 11-9 |

### General Long-Term Debt

| | |
|---|---|
| Statement of General Long-Term Debt | 11-15 |

† Though not required by the NCGA in *GAAFR,* it is often appropriate to prepare a Statement of Changes in Financial Position for an Intragovernmental Service Fund.

STATISTICAL TABLES. The statistical section of the annual financial report should contain all the data necessary for a full understanding of the position and prospects of the governmental unit. The financial statements are limited to presentations of information from the accounts describing the transactions of the last year or, at most, the last two years. Many of the statistical tables provide supplemenary financial information, sometimes covering periods as long as ten or more years; but the tables are by no means limited to fiscal data. Social, economic, physical or geographic, environmental, cultural, and political information that may contribute to an understanding of the governmental unit's finances are appropriate.

The National Committee on Governmental Accounting has stated that the following tables, which are largely self-explanatory, are "essential to adequate and full understanding of financial affairs."[6] The list may properly be described as comprehensive.

General Governmental Expenditures by Function—Last Ten Fiscal Years (Figure 17-8).

General Revenues by Source—Last Ten Fiscal Years (Figure 17-9).

Tax Revenues by Source—Last Ten Fiscal Years (Figure 17-10).

Property Tax Levies and Collections—Last Ten Years (Figure 17-11).

Assessed and [Estimated] Actual Value of Taxable Property—Last Ten Fiscal Years (Figure 17-12).

Property Tax Rates and Tax Levies—All Overlapping Governments—Last Ten Fiscal Years (Figure 17-13).

Special Assessment Collections—Last Ten Fiscal Years (Figure 17-14).

Ratio of Net General Debt to Assessed Value and Net Bonded Debt Per Capita —Last Ten Fiscal Years (Figure 11-20).

Computation of Direct and Overlapping Debt (Figure 11-19).

Computation of Legal Debt Margin (Figure 11-18).

Ratio of Annual Debt Service Expenditures for General Bonded Debt to Total General Expenditures, Last Ten Years (Figure 11-21).

Schedule of Revenue Bond Coverage—Last Ten Fiscal Years (Figure 17-15).

Debt Service Requirements to Maturity—General Obligation Bonds (Figure 17-16).

Summary of Debt Service Charges to Maturity (Figure 11-17).

Schedule of Insurance in Force (Figure 17-17).

Salaries and Surety Bonds of Principal Officials (Figure 17-18).

Miscellaneous Statistical Data (Figure 17-19).

**Figure 17-8**

A GOVERNMENTAL UNIT
General Governmental Expenditures by Function
Last Ten Fiscal Years

| Fiscal Year | General Government | Public Safety | Highways and Streets | Sanitation | Health | Welfare | Other |
|---|---|---|---|---|---|---|---|

6 *GAAFR*, pp. 114–15.

Figure 17-9

## A GOVERNMENTAL UNIT
### General Revenues by Source Last Ten Fiscal Years

| Fiscal Year | Taxes | Licenses and Permits | Intergovernmental Revenue | Charges for Services | Fines and Forfeits | Miscellaneous Revenue |
| --- | --- | --- | --- | --- | --- | --- |

Figure 17-10

## A GOVERNMENTAL UNIT
### Tax Revenues by Source Last Ten Fiscal Years

| Fiscal Year | Total Taxes | General Property Taxes | General Sales Taxes | Income Taxes | Business Gross Receipts Taxes | Other Taxes |
| --- | --- | --- | --- | --- | --- | --- |

Figure 17-11

### A GOVERNMENTAL UNIT
Property Tax Levies and Collections Last Ten Fiscal Years

| Fiscal Year | Total Tax Levy | Current Tax Collections | Percent of Levy Collected | Delinquent Tax Collections | Total Tax Collections | Total Collections as Percent or Current Levy | Outstanding Delinquent Taxes | Outstanding Delinquent Taxes as Percent of Current Levy |
|---|---|---|---|---|---|---|---|---|

Figure 17-12

### A GOVERNMENTAL UNIT
Assessed and (Estimated) Actual Value of Taxable Property Last Ten Fiscal Years

| Fiscal Year | Real Property | | Personal Property | | Total | | Ratio of Total Assessed to Total Estimated Actual Value |
|---|---|---|---|---|---|---|---|
| | Assessed Value | Estimated Actual Value | Assessed Value | Estimated Actual Value | Assessed Value | Estimated Actual Value | |

Figure 17-13

A GOVERNMENTAL UNIT

Property Tax Rates and Tax Levies—All Overlapping Governments

Last Ten Fiscal Years

| *Fiscal Year* | *City* | *School District* | *County* | *State* | *Other* | *Total* |
|---|---|---|---|---|---|---|
| | | | *Tax Rates* | | | |
| 19X1 | | | | | | |
| 19X2 | | | | | | |
| 19X3 | | | | | | |
| 19X4 | | | | | | |
| 19X5 | | | | | | |
| 19X6 | | | | | | |
| 19X7 | | | | | | |
| 19X8 | | | | | | |
| 19X9 | | | | | | |
| 19Y0 | | | | | | |
| | | | *Tax Levies* | | | |
| 19X1 | | | | | | |
| 19X2 | | | | | | |
| 19X3 | | | | | | |
| 19X4 | | | | | | |
| 19X5 | | | | | | |
| 19X6 | | | | | | |
| 19X7 | | | | | | |
| 19X8 | | | | | | |
| 19X9 | | | | | | |
| 19Y0 | | | | | | |

Note: The following items, if not explained elsewhere in the report, should be indicated and explained as supplementary notes to this table:

Amount and source (constitution, statute, or charter) of any tax rate limits.

Scope of tax rate limits—operations, debt service, or both.

Due date for current taxes.

Date taxes become delinquent.

Penalties for delinquency.

Discounts, if any, allowed and dates on which computed.

Procedure for enforcing collection of delinquent taxes.

If taxes of reporting unit are collected by another governmental unit, give name of collecting unit and state basis on which current collections are distributed to reporting unit; e.g., 100 percent of levy, or only in the proportion of its levy to all levies. Indicate basis of compensating collecting unit—flat dollar amount, percentage of collections, etc.

**Figure 17-14**

## A GOVERNMENTAL UNIT
### Special Assessment Collections Last Ten Fiscal Years

| Fiscal Year | Current Assessments Due | Current Assessments Collected | Ratio of Collections to Amount Due | Total Outstanding Current and Delinquent Assessments |
|---|---|---|---|---|

**Figure 17-15**

## A GOVERNMENTAL UNIT
### Schedule of Revenue Bond Coverage Last Ten Fiscal Years

| (1) Fiscal Year | (2) Gross Revenue* | (3) Expenses† | (4) Net Revenue Available for Debt Service** | Debt Service Requirements | | | (8) Coverage†† |
|---|---|---|---|---|---|---|---|
| | | | | (5) Principal | (6) Interest | (7) Total | |

\* As defined in applicable bond indentures or governing laws. In many instances, revenue for debt coverage is on a cash basis.

† Total expenses exclusive of depreciation and bond interest.

\*\* Gross revenue in column (2) minus expenses in column (3).

†† Column (4) divided by column (7).

Figure 17-16

## A GOVERNMENTAL UNIT
### Debt Service Requirements to Maturity—General Obligation Bonds*

| Fiscal Year | Principal | Interest | Total Requirements |
|---|---|---|---|

\* Identical separate tables should also be prepared for any revenue bonds and special assessment bonds which are outstanding, as well as for any other long-term debt outstanding.

Figure 17-17

## A GOVERNMENTAL UNIT
### Schedule of Insurance in Force—End of Fiscal Year

| Type of Coverage and Name of Company | Policy Number | Policy Period | | Details of Coverage | Coinsurance | Liability Limits | Annual Premium |
|---|---|---|---|---|---|---|---|
| | | From | To | | | | |

**Figure 17-18**

A GOVERNMENTAL UNIT
Salaries and Surety Bonds
of Principal Officials
For Fiscal Year Ended (Date)

| *Name and Title of Official* | *Annual Salary* | *Amount of Surety Bond* |
| --- | --- | --- |

## INTERIM STATEMENTS

The statements that are prepared on an interim basis, usually monthly or quarterly, are primarily for the use of administrators and, in the case of municipalities in which legislators are intimately concerned with current operations, for legislators. Balance sheets and statements that summarize operations to date may have only limited circulation among those members of the public who are interested in the governmental unit's financial operations or they may be published and distributed widely.

The administrators need information on a current basis if they are to control the activities under their command. Once plans have been made, control is a process of comparing plans and accomplishments. The following statements, prepared monthly, provide for such comparison:

Statement of Actual and Estimated Revenue—Prepared for General, Special Revenue, and Debt Service Funds (Figure 6-12)

Statement of Actual and Estimated Expenditures—Prepared for General and Special Revenue Funds (Figure 7-10)

Comparative Statement of Revenue and Expense—Prepared for Enterprise and Intragovernmental Service Funds (Figure 14-12)

These statements have been illustrated and their uses discussed in the respective chapters (see Figure numbers above) in which they appear.

Cash management, discussed in Chapter 16, is a part of the overall management problem and requires appropriate interim information, which is provided by the following statements:

Combined Statement of Cash Receipts and Disbursements—All Funds (Figure 16-7)

Combined Forecast of Cash Position—All Funds (Figure 16-4)

These two statements were discussed in Chapter 16.

Figure 17-19

A GOVERNMENTAL UNIT
Miscellaneous Statistical Data*

Date of Incorporation
Date First Charter Adopted
Date Present Charter Adopted
Form of Government
Area—Square Miles—By ten-year periods for last forty years
Miles of Streets and Alleys
    Streets—Paved
    Streets—Unpaved
    Alleys
    Sidewalks
Miles of Sewers:
    Storm
    Sanitary
Building Permits:
    Permits Issued (each year for last ten years)
    Value of Buildings (each year for last ten years)
Fire Protection:
    Number of Stations
    Number of Employees
Police Protection:
    Number of Employees
    Number of Law Violations
    Jail (Facilities and Populations)
    Vehicular Patrol Units

Recreation:
    Parks—Number of Acres and Facilities
    Number of Golf Courses
    Number of Playgrounds
    Number of Swimming Pools
    Number of Other Recreation Facilities
Education:
    Number of Schools (by type)
    Number of Administrative Personnel
    Number of Teachers
    Number of Students
    Average Daily Attendance (by school)
Each Enterprise:
    Number of users or consumers
    Data on use or consumption
    Plant Capacity
    Data on Distribution System
Number of Street Lights
Employees (as of date)
    Merit System
    Exempt
    Total

760

Elections:

Number of Registered Voters

Number of Votes Cast in:

    Last General Election

    Last Municipal Election

Percentage of Registered Voters Voting in:

    Last General Election

    Last Municipal Election

Population:

    Census Population Count for Last Four Censuses

    Age Distribution of Population Last Four Censuses

    Income Level of Population Last Four Censuses

    Current Population Estimate (state source)

    Retail Sales—By Year for Last Ten Years

    Per Capita Income—For Years Available

    Principal Taxpayers

    List Name and Type of Business of Ten Largest Taxpayers

* The data suggested here are applicable to a municipal government. They would necessarily have to be modified for other units of government.

The statements above are those recommended by the NCGA. A variety of other interim statements and schedules may be found in practice.

## POPULAR REPORTS

In addition to the more formal interim and annual financial presentations, many local governments distribute summary "highlight" or other reports prepared specifically for the nonaccountant lay citizenry. A variety of popular report approaches may be found in practice, but most are typified by the use of highly condensed financial data presentations, graphic illustrations (bar charts, line graphs, photograms, etc.), and explanatory materials written in nontechnical language for the express purpose of communicating the major aspects of the government's financial position, operating results, and/or future financial plans to the general public. Most popular reports are kept short—the usual range is 2 to 10 pages—in order to hold the attention of the layman while communicating as much information as possible within the fewest pages possible. Sometimes these "reports to the general citizenry" are published in a local newspaper, either to attain the highest possible readership or because this is required by law.

Reports of this type cannot replace the formal annual and interim reports, of course, and are intended to supplement rather than supplant them. In fact, many popular reports include a note to the effect that the complete financial reports are available to, or for inspection by, any interested person. (In the opinion of the authors, a notation of this type should appear conspicuously in all popular reports.) Properly done, the popular report can serve a major role in (1) general public relations, (2) interesting lethargic citizens in the government's activities and programs and making them aware of major aspects of its financial activities, position, and plans, and (3) reducing the number of complete annual report copies needed, and thereby the associated publication costs, since popular reports may serve the needs of many users who might otherwise receive the larger, complete reports.

**Question 17-1.** Recast the following balance sheet so that it will show properly the financial condition of the City of $K$:

CITY OF $K$
General Fund Balance Sheet, March 31, 19X6

*Assets*

| | |
|---|---|
| Current assets | $ 300,000 |
| Fixed assets | 8,196,000 |
| | $8,496,000 |

*Liabilities and Fund Balance*

Liabilities:

| | | |
|---|---|---|
| Current liabilities | $ 350,000 | |
| Bonded indebtedness | 3,400,000 | $3,750,000 |
| Balance | | 4,746,000 |
| | | $8,496,000 |

**Question 17-2.** Explain what is wrong with the following statement:

### CITY OF X
### General Fund Balance Sheet, December 31, 19X5

*Assets*

| | | |
|---|---|---|
| Cash | | $82,000 |
| Taxes receivable | $100,000 | |
| Less: Allowance for uncollected taxes | 100,000 | — |
| | | $82,000 |

*Liabilities and Fund Balance*

| | |
|---|---|
| Tax anticipation notes | $80,000 |
| Fund balance | 2,000 |
| | $82,000 |

**Question 17-3.** What differences in classification of expenditures would you expect to find between an expenditure statement prepared primarily for the use of the city manager and one prepared for consumption by political scientists?

**Problem 17-1.** In connection with the audit of the City of Z, you are handed the following analysis of the changes in the Fund Balance account of the General Fund. The municipality is required to keep its accounts for both revenues and expenditures on an accrual basis.

### CITY OF Z
### General Fund
### Statement of Changes in Fund Balance
### For Fiscal Year Ending June 30, 19X7

| | | |
|---|---|---|
| Fund Balance, June 1, 19X6 .............. | | $ 75,000 |
| Add: Excess of revenues over expenditures: | | |
| Revenues ........................... | $350,000 | |
| Less: Expenditures ..................... | 305,000 | 45,000 |
| Fund Balance, June 30, 19X7 ............. | | $120,000 |

Among the revenues are included $15,000 estimated revenues not realized and $335,000 actual revenues, consisting among other items of cash receipts from the following sources: (1) collections applicable to the 19X8 tax levy, $3,000; (2) sale of fixed assets carried in the Enterprise Fund, $2,500; (3) special tax levy made for the purpose of establishing an Intragovernmental Service Fund, $75,000; (4) sale of general fixed assets which were financed by a general sinking fund bond issue still outstanding, $3,000; (5) sale of fixed assets originally financed 75 percent from special assessments and 25 percent from General Fund revenues, $1,500; (6) a transfer from the Debt Service Fund to the General Fund, the money transferred to be used to retire sinking fund bonds, $150,000; (7) tax levy for the retirement of serial bonds, $15,000; (8) borrowed from the Enterprise Fund, $750.

The expenditures consist, among others, of the following items: (1) payments on account of the retirement of sinking fund bonds, $127,000; (2) payments for the retirement of serial bonds, $14,550; (3) repayment of a loan made from the Trust Fund, $450; (4) city's share of cost of special assessment project, $3,000; (5) purchase of general fixed assets, $10,000.

Included also among the expenditures are unliquidated encumbrances of $22,000 outstanding on June 30, 19X7, as well as expenditures of $5,000 for which encum-brances amounting to $5,500 were outstanding on July 1, 19X6.

Required:

Prepare a corrected statement analyzing the changes in fund balance and showing separately each item and amount by which revenues or expenditures should be increased or decreased. Show also any other adjustments needed to show the correct fund balance on June 30, 19X7.

**Problem 17-2.** The following statement is taken from a state's financial report. (References are to schedules carried in the report but not reproduced here.)

### Capital Balance Sheet
#### Assets, Investment, and Liabilities, June 30, 19X9

*Capital Assets*

| | | |
|---|---|---:|
| Debt Service Fund Assets...................... | | $ 23,528,921.16 |
| Consisting of: | | |
| (a) Cash in State Treasury (Schedule A1) .... | $ 774,144.82 | |
| (b) Investments and Bonds (Schedule B1) .... | 12,707,000.00 | |
| (c) County Notes Receivable (Schedule B2) .. | 10,047,776.34 | |

Investments in Railroad Stocks (Schedule B3) (*Assume they apply to a trust fund.*) ................................ 5,233,584.00

| | Par Value | Market Value | |
|---|---|---|---:|
| (a) X Railroad Stocks .......... | $3,000,200 | $ 4,410,294.00 | |
| (b) Atlantic and X Railroad Stocks ................... | 1,266,600 | 823,290.00 | |
| (c) Miscellaneous Stocks ........ | 775,080 | — | |

Fixed Assets:

Consisting of:

State Highways, State Institutions, Departmental Buildings,

Real Estate, Equipment, and other fixed assets ............ $290,171,055.22

$318,933,560.38

## Capital Liabilities

| | | |
|---|---|---|
| State Debt (Schedule B4) .................... | | $167,360,000.00 |
| Consisting of: | | |
| (a) State Highway Bonds ................. | $97,171,000.00 | |
| (b) General Fund Bonds .................. | 54,979,000.00 | |
| (c) Special School Building Bonds .......... | 12,710,000.00 | |
| (d) Veterans' Loan Bonds ................ | 2,500,000.00 | |
| Total Capital Liabilities ............ | | $167,360,000.00 |
| Capital Surplus .............................. | | 151,573,560.38 |
| (Value of Fixed Assets in excess of Funded Debt of State) | | |
| | | $318,933,560.38 |

Required:

Recast this statement so as to show properly the financial condition of the state. You may split up this statement into as many statements as you think desirable. Assume actuarial sinking fund requirements of $23,520,800.

**Problem 17-3.** In connection with the audit of the accounts of the City of $X$, you are handed the following balance sheet which has been prepared by the city comptroller:

### CITY OF $X$
### Balance Sheet
### December 31, 19X8

#### Assets

| | General Fund | Debt Service (Sinking) Fund |
|---|---|---|
| Cash ................................. | $ 58,000 | $ 82,000 |
| Taxes Receivable ....................... | 155,000 | 17,500 |
| Amount to Be Provided for Retirement of Bonds | | 168,000 |
| Total ............................... | $213,000 | $267,500 |

#### Liabilities, Reserves, and Surplus

| | General Fund | Debt Service (Sinking) Fund |
|---|---|---|
| Bonds Payable ........................... | | $250,000 |
| Vouchers Payable ....................... | $ 81,000 | |
| Reserve for Uncollected Taxes ............. | 155,000 | 17,500 |
| Operating Deficit ....................... | 23,000* | |
| Total ............................... | $213,000 | $267,500 |

* Red.

Upon investigation you discover the following additional facts:

1. Estimated losses on taxes receivable are $10,000 in the General Fund and $1,000 in the Debt Service Fund.

2. Actuarial requirements of the Debt Service Fund at December 31, 19X8, $110,000.

3. Of the total bonds payable $100,000 represents serial bonds payable (not matured); $15,000 represents matured serial bonds; and the remainder is represented by sinking fund bonds payable which have not yet matured.

4. Matured interest payable on sinking fund bonds, $2,700, and on serial bonds, $2,100.

5. Interest payable in future years on sinking fund bonds, $10,000, and on serial bonds, $30,000.

Required:

Prepare a columnar balance sheet on an *accrual basis* containing separate columns for the funds or groups of accounts that you think it desirable to list separately. Your balance sheet should conform to sound municipal accounting principles.

**Problem 17-4.** A governmental authority was constituted about July 1, 19X6, to carry out certain recreational activities for which the authority was to buy or construct equipment.

It was decided that the accounts of the authority will be kept and the statements presented in conformity with the principles of accounting endorsed by the National Committee on Governmental Accounting. From the following information, prepare columnar work sheets recording the transactions of the authority so as to facilitate the preparation of appropriate statements for the year ended June 30, 19X7:

1. An advance of $50,000 was made by the government creating the authority to finance the initial construction and activities, to be repaid out of operating revenues.

2. From the Intragovernmental Service Fund thus created, $10,000 was transferred to the General Fund for current operating expenses until revenues could be realized.

3. A budget of recreational activities for the year was adopted as follows:

*Revenues*

| | | |
|---|---:|---:|
| Licenses | $ 50,000 | |
| Fees | 100,000 | |
| Sales | 30,000 | |
| Miscellaneous | 10,000 | $190,000 |

*Expenditures*

| | | |
|---|---:|---:|
| Administration | $ 10,000 | |
| Bathing pavilion | 65,000 | |
| Boating | 25,000 | |
| Park maintenance | 54,000 | |
| Interest on bonds | 6,000 | |
| Sinking fund requirements | 20,000 | 180,000 |

4. Purchases of supplies were made for central stores to the amount of $36,000 and paid in full.

5. A 7-year bond issue of $200,000 for improvements was authorized as of July 1, 19X6, bearing interest at 6½ percent per annum, payable semiannually. It was disposed of on August 1st at par and accrued interest of $1,000.

6. Contracts amounting to $165,000 were let for improvements. Work was com-

pleted and contracts paid to the extent of $156,000, which included $1,000 extras, leaving $10,000 in progress on June 30, 19X7.

7. Additional construction work was supplied through the Intragovernmental Service Fund to the extent of $34,000, which included $18,000 labor paid in cash, $14,000 material from stores at cost, and $2,000 overhead. The Intragovernmental Service Fund was reimbursed in full for this service.

8. Other services (labor only) supplied to authority activities and paid for by the Intragovernmental Service Fund were as follows, including 10 percent or $920 for overhead:

| | | |
|---|---:|---:|
| Bathing pavilion | $3,300 | |
| Boating | 1,100 | |
| Park maintenance | 5,720 | $10,120 |

Of the above, $2,200 for park maintenance was incomplete and not billed as of June 30, 19X7. Otherwise, reimbursement to the Intragovernmental Service Fund was completed.

9. Revenues collected during the year were as follows:

| | | |
|---|---:|---:|
| Licenses | $ 48,500 | |
| Fees | 101,400 | |
| Sales | 29,200 | |
| Miscellaneous | 9,400 | $188,500 |

In addition there were $1,600 of licenses billed but not collected, on which possible losses should not exceed 20 percent.

Of the fees collected, it was necessary to refund $210.

Of the licenses collected, $500 represented advance payments on account of the following year.

10. Supplies were issued to authority departments by the central stores as follows, the figures in each case including 10 percent or a total of $1,050 for working-capital-fund overhead:

| | | |
|---|---:|---:|
| Administration | $ 330 | |
| Bathing pavilion | 2,640 | |
| Boating | 1,650 | |
| Park maintenance | 6,930 | $11,550 |

Transfers were made to the Intragovernmental Service Fund to the amount of $10,600 on account of these items.

11. Contracts and orders issued during the year for operating expenses totaled $83,000. These were liquidated to the extent of $81,160, leaving $1,200 for the bathing pavilion, and $640 for boating, or a total of $1,840 outstanding at June 30th.

12. Vouchers approved during the year for payrolls, invoices, and miscellaneous, including those covering contracts and orders liquidated, as well as other items, were as follows:

| | | |
|---|---:|---:|
| Administration .............................. | $ 9,450 | |
| Bathing pavilion .......................... | 59,160 | |
| Boating .................................... | 21,600 | |
| Park maintenance ......................... | 41,000 | |
| Interest ................................... | 6,000 | $137,210 |

Treasury warrants were issued and paid in settlement of these items to the amount of $135,610.

13.　Transfer was made to the Debt Service Fund for $18,000 of the amount due it from the General Fund, leaving the remainder as still owing. Securities costing $18,000 were purchased for this Fund, and income thereon was realized to the amount of $300. Among the securities purchased were $5,000 bonds of the authority, which were immediately retired. No revenues were planned for the year ended June 30, 19X7.

14.　The sum of $5,000 was repaid to the Intragovernmental Service Fund on the advance made to the General Fund.

15.　Purchases of office and general equipment to the amount of $20,000 were made from the Intragovernmental Service Fund. This equipment is to be written off by charges to overhead at the rate of 5 percent per year, beginning with the current year.

16.　Overhead expense of the Intragovernmental Service Fund paid for the year was $2,600. The physical inventory of stores at the end of the year was $12,300. Stores adjustments are considered to be part of overhead. Operating accounts were closed to the retained earnings account of the fund. The sum of $1,000 was repaid to the central government to apply on the advance made to the authority.

17.　Among the invoices paid during the year from the General Fund were items totaling $16,540 for park maintenance equipment. (AICPA)

**Problem 17-5.**　From the following municipal trial balance at the close of a fiscal year but before closing the books, prepare a balance sheet, properly subdivided into funds, after giving effect to necessary entries of the General Fund and the Debt Service (Sinking) Fund as of the close of the year and to settlements of all interfund balances other than permanent advances:

| | Debit | Credit |
|---|---:|---:|
| Accounts Receivable, General Fund ......... | $　3,321.74 | |
| Appropriation Balances (unencumbered), | | |
| 　General Fund ......................... | | $　1,117.09 |
| Assessments Receivable .................... | 72,621.70 | |
| Capital Projects Fund Cash ................ | 2,005.60 | |
| Capital Projects Fund Balance (unencumbered) | | 678.00 |
| Bonds Payable, General .................... | | 250,000.00 |
| Bonds Authorized and Unissued ............. | 8,000.00 | |
| Contracts Payable, Capital Projects Fund ..... | | 4,700.00 |
| Due Stores Fund from Capital Projects Fund .. | | 1,227.60 |
| Due Stores Fund from General Fund ........ | | 1,593.96 |
| Due Stores Fund from other Funds ......... | 2,821.56 | |

| | | |
|---|---:|---:|
| Estimated Revenues .......................... | 1,500.00 | |
| Fixed Property ............................ | 897,640.00 | |
| Fixed Property (Income-Producing, Trust | | |
| Fund) ................................. | 62,000.00 | |
| General Fund Cash ........................ | 1,842.10 | |
| Income Account, Debt Service Fund ......... | | 1,960.00 |
| Interest Account, Special Assessments ........ | 620.00 | |
| Loan from General to Stores Fund .......... | 25,000.00 | |
| Public Benefit Receivable (Assessment Fund) .. | 6,400.00 | |
| Reserve for Encumbrances, General Fund..... | | 2,827.10 |
| Reserve for Loan to Stores Fund............. | | 25,000.00 |
| Reserve for Retirement of Bonds ............ | | 160,000.00 |
| Estimated Uncollectible Taxes .............. | | 2,875.00 |
| Debt Service (Sinking) Fund Cash ........... | 1,450.00 | |
| Debt Service (Sinking) Fund Investments ..... | 160,000.00 | |
| Debt Service (Sinking) Fund Requirements ... | 1,000.00 | |
| Debt Service (Sinking) Fund Balance ........ | | 490.00 |
| Special Assessment Bonds .................. | | 80,000.00 |
| Special Assessment Fund Cash .............. | 1,872.65 | |
| Stores Fund Working Capital (Loan from | | |
| General Fund) ......................... | | 25,000.00 |
| Stores Fund Cash ......................... | 1,408.22 | |
| Stores Inventory ......................... | 15,942.80 | |
| Fund Balance Receipts, General Fund ....... | | 896.00 |
| Special Assessment Fund Balance ............ | | 1,514.35 |
| Investment in Fixed Assets ................. | | 647,640.00 |
| Taxes Receivable, General Fund ............ | 6,972.61 | |
| Temporary Loans, General Fund ............ | | 3,000.00 |
| Trust Funds Balance ...................... | | 96,320.00 |
| Trust Fund Cash ......................... | 6,820.00 | |
| Trust Fund Investments .................... | 27,500.00 | |
| Vouchers Payable, Capital Projects Fund ..... | | 3,400.00 |
| Vouchers Payable, General Fund ............ | | 1,327.30 |
| Work in Process, Stores Fund .............. | 4,827.42 | |
| | $1,311,566.40 | $1,311,566.40 |

(AICPA)

# 18

# Auditing

Auditing is the process of collecting and evaluating evidence in order to formulate an independent, professional opinion about assertions made by management. The typical readers of a financial or operational report issued by management have no opportunity to review the operations in question or to assess the credibility of management's representations, and few could do a good job given the opportunity. The auditor's review provides an expert's independent, professional judgment on the matters that he covers in his report. The purpose of the opinion is to add credibility to those representations properly made by management and to reduce the credibility of those that the auditor does not consider to be appropriate. These representations may take the form of financial statements, reports on the activities of organizations in carrying out programs assigned by legislative action, or implied representations regarding the carrying out of basic managerial responsibilities. For example, management is responsible for compliance with legal requirements and for carrying out programs economically and efficiently. The auditor may be asked to give his opinions on the foregoing matters even when management's representation is an implied one.

CLASSIFICATIONS OF AUDITS. The term *preaudit* has been used in connection with revenues and expenditures to characterize the work that is done to control the accuracy of the collection and recording of revenues and the incurring and recording of expenditures and disbursements. Preaudit work is a part of the constructive accounting and control processes and is not, therefore, included in the definition of auditing as given above.

Audits may be classified as *internal* or *external* on the basis of the relationship of the auditor to the agency being examined. It is customary for management to use internal auditors to review the operation of the agency, including employees' compliance with managerial policies, and to report to management upon these matters. Though the internal auditor's responsibility is ordinarily of the *postaudit* type (i.e., he is not directly involved in the constructive accounting processes), he reports to top management of the agency. External auditors are independent of the auditee agency and owe their responsibility to the legislative body, the public, and other governmental units.

The National Committee on Governmental Accounting has further divided postaudits into general or special categories:

> General audits are those which embrace all financial operations and records of a governmental unit and are made after the close of an accounting period. Special audits are those which are restricted to some segment of the unit's financial transactions or which cover all financial transactions for a period of time shorter or longer than the normal operating period (usually a fiscal year).

Another useful classification of audits is the *financial* audit as opposed to the *operational* or *managerial* or *performance* audit. Perhaps they may best be described by analyzing the purposes of audits.

PURPOSES OF THE AUDIT.   A governmental audit performed by an independent external auditor will have one or more of the following four major purposes: (1) To ascertain whether, in the auditor's opinion, the statements *present fairly* the financial position and results of operations of the organization in conformity with generally accepted accounting principles applied on a basis consistent with that of the preceding year. The typical examination of financial statements has this objective, together with the following one. (2) To determine *compliance* with legal provisions relating to finances—the *regularity* of fiscal operations. These two purposes include a determination of the adequacy of accounting records and procedures and a verification of the financial stewardship of the organization's management. An audit having these two objectives would be characterized a "financial and compliance" audit or a "fiscal" audit. Though the contract for a financial audit engagement does not ordinarily provide for recommendations for improvement, the professional auditor will feel an obligation to make suggestions to management regarding the possibilities for improvement that have come to his attention during the audit. Many believe that such audits also serve as control devices to prevent the loss of public funds through fraud or inefficiency. (3) To evaluate the *effectiveness* with which the operations of an agency attain the objectives of the agency's programs (*program results*). This may include an evaluation of whether the activities contemplated in the statutes are properly designed to attain legislative intent. (4) To evaluate the *economy and efficiency* with which the agency management carries out its programs. Technically economy deals with a minimization of expenditure, whereas efficiency implies a maximization of benefits for costs consumed. An audit having either or both of the last two objectives would be called an "operational" or "performance" audit.

All of the foregoing purposes have to do with an evaluation of the responsibility and accountability of public officials. The first two deal with compliance with fiscal requirements. The last two emphasize managerial effectiveness. An audit that is intended to fulfill all these purposes or objectives may be referred to as a "full" or "comprehensive" audit. The scope of a comprehensive audit, and the components to which a given audit may be limited, are summarized in Figure 18-1.

Few audits of governments today are intended to include all aspects of the comprehensive audit in depth. Rather, audits are increasingly being designed to meet the specific needs of agency managers, other governments, investors, and the public in a given situation. Thus, while some attention may be given to all areas of the comprehensive audit, one aspect may receive the principal thrust of the audit effort while the others receive secondary attention. The primary thrust of most contemporary general audits of governments is upon the financial and compliance aspects, though special audits are often directed toward the efficiency and economy or effectiveness (program results) aspects. These various audit aspects (or thrusts) are not mutually exclusive, but overlap significantly. The overlapping nature of these alternate audit thrusts, the minimum coverage deemed to be acceptable by most authorities today, and the evolutionary trend of governmental auditing are illustrated graphically in Figure 18-2.

MANAGEMENT'S REPRESENTATIONS. In giving an opinion on the fairness of financial statements the auditor is dealing with representations specifically made by management. Assuming the representations made are proper, the purpose of an opinion on these statements is clearly to add credibility to these representations. However, the same thing may be said of the other three objectives. If it does not publicly address itself to the other matters, management implicitly asserts that it has complied with the law, that it has achieved agency and program objectives or made reasonable progress toward them, and that it has operated economically and efficiently. Though these representations may not be in as specific form as those having to do with finances, they may still be evaluated and the auditor's opinion may be as useful as if specific representations had been made.

CLASSIFICATION OF EXTERNAL AUDITORS. External audits are performed by persons who are independent of the administrative organization of the unit audited. There are three groups of independent auditors: (1) those who are officials of the governmental unit being examined, (2) those who are officials of

Figure 18-1

THE POTENTIAL SCOPE OF A GOVERNMENTAL AUDIT

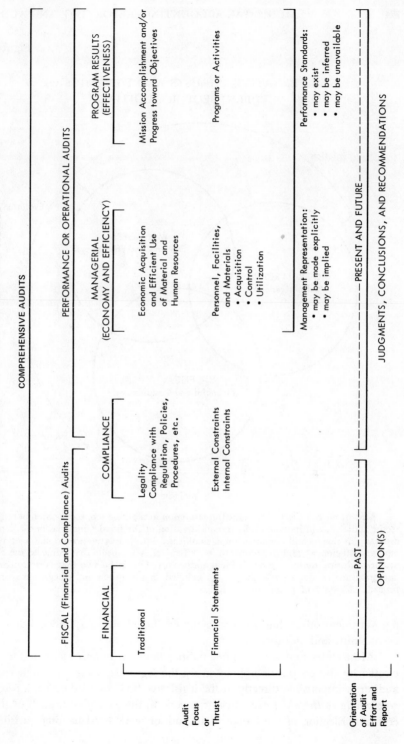

Figure 18-2

ALTERNATIVE THRUSTS AND DYNAMICS OF
PUBLIC SECTOR AUDITING

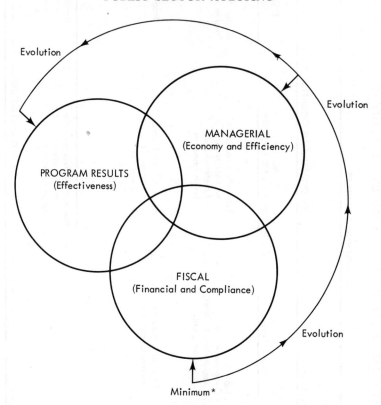

\* Most authorities believe that the *minimum* acceptable scope of contemporary public sector audits should include in-depth consideration of the fiscal (financial and compliance) aspects plus review and comment upon significant aspects relative to the managerial (economy and efficiency) and program results (effectiveness) aspects that come to the auditor's attention during the course of his fiscal audit work. Others believe that certain managerial and program results aspects should be included in the *minimum* acceptable scope (and procedural steps) of public sector audits.

a government other than the one being examined, and (3) independent public accountants and auditors.

Most states and a few municipalities have an independent auditor either elected by the people or appointed by the legislative body. In such cases the auditor is responsible directly to the legislative body or to the people; *he is not responsible to the chief executive* or anyone in the executive branch of the government. Election of the independent auditor works well in some jurisdictions;

but in others only minimal qualifications are needed to seek the office and the auditor may be elected "on the coattails of" the governor. The elected auditor's independence and effectiveness are impaired significantly in the latter situation.

The term "auditor" is sometimes applied to the principal accounting officer of a state. In such cases he is not, of course, an independent external auditor. In other cases the external auditor is vested with some of the pre-audit responsibilities; for example, he may be required by law to rule upon the legality of proposed expenditures upon request by the operating agencies. Such a provision is unsound. The constructive accounting processes are a part of the executive function; assigning a portion of them to an auditor who is not responsible to the chief executive represents a division of the chief executive's authority and, hence, his responsibility. In addition, the provision results in the auditor's reviewing his own work as he performs the audit function.

State audit agencies in some states have the responsibility of auditing local governmental units, either at or without the request of the units. Such audit agencies do not necessarily audit any of the state agencies. Most local governmental audits are made by independent certified public accountants or registered accountants, however, and state agencies increasingly are concerning themselves with (1) setting standards for the scope and minimum procedures of local government audits in their jurisdiction, (2) reviewing reports prepared by independent auditors to assure that they are in compliance with these standards, (3) performing "spot check" or test audit procedures where audit coverage appears to be insufficient, and (4) accumulating reliable and useful statewide statistics on local government finance for use by both the executive and legislative branches of the state government.

SELECTION OF THE AUDITOR. The auditor should be selected by the legislative body on the basis of the quality of work that he may be expected to do. Many governments attempt to select an auditor by competitive bidding, but most accountants feel that this device imposes unprofessional pressures upon the auditors and is not conducive to selection of the best-qualified. Commodities for which precise specifications may be prepared may be profitably acquired by competitive bids, but professional qualities cannot be so defined.

The inappropriateness and adverse effects of securing professional audit services on the basis of competetive bidding were set forth clearly in a *Joint Statement on Competetive Bidding for Audit Services in Governmental Agencies* by the American Institute of Certified Public Accountants and the Municipal Finance Officers Association of the United States and Canada. Issued in 1955 and revised in 1961, this statement reads, in part, as follows:

> Competitive bidding...is not an effective procedure in arranging for an independent audit.
> It is not effective for the simple reason that an audit is not something which can be covered by rigid specifications. *An audit is a professional service requir-*

*ing professional independence, skill, and judgment. An independent auditor should have as much latitude as he may find necessary* to be assured that the records are in order and that the system of accounts is functioning properly.

It may be that public officials continue to use competitive bidding in the belief that it is legally required with respect to professonal services. If this impression exists, legal opinion should be sought in order to settle the question.

If selected by a process of competitive bidding, the independent auditor will approach his work with an awareness that he has somewhat demeaned his profession in accepting an engagement on a bid basis. Moreover, he will generally be hampered by either overly detailed or inadequate specifications which he had no part in framing and therefore may be required to perform work which, in his professional judgment, need not be done, or precluded from doing work which he knows ought to be done.

Independent auditors should not be subject to arbitrary dictation in matters pertaining to their work, and *auditing should not be placed on the lowest possible standard of performance* which can be made acceptable.

This statement is not intended to challenge the right of government officials to obtain some estimate of their auditing expenses. Once a governmental agency has decided to engage an independent auditor, it ought to discuss the engagement with the auditor it believes to be the best qualified to render the most satisfactory service. After the independent auditor has surveyed the fiscal records and identified the principal problems, it should be possible to develop an understanding on the scope of his audit and on the length of time which will be required for its completion. The independent auditor should then be in a position, if required, to give an estimate of the cost of the service which is not likely to be exceeded unless he encounters unforeseen problems.

This approach to the selection of an auditor, reflecting a legitimate concern for costs, is perfectly reasonable and acceptable. But *no one gains—indeed, everyone is likely to lose—when auditors are selected by competitive bidding on the basis of the lowest possible price.*

It would be in the best interest of all concerned for political subdivisions employing a certified public accountant or a firm of certified public accountants to do so in the same way in which they would select an attorney, doctor, or other professional advisor—choose the one in whom they have the most confidence, discuss the work to be done, and agree on the basis for the fee.[1]

The position of the National Committee on Governmental Accounting is consistent with the logic of the *Joint Statement* cited above. Specifically, the NCGA stated that independent auditors:

> ...should be selected only on the basis of professional competence and experience. This will not only mean that the auditor should be a certified public accountant authorized to practice in the jurisdiction being audited, but that he should have appropriate experience in the audit of governmental units and a demonstrated high level of attainment in such a professional practice. There must be a clear recognition on the part of both public officials concerned and independent accountants that auditing services are truly professional in nature. This being the case, the audit services should be compensated on the basis of

---

[1] *GAAFR,* p. 129. (Emphasis added.)

professional fees agreed upon in advance of the engagement and not on the basis of competitive bids. . . .[2]

Selection of independent public auditors by means of competitive bids appears to have decreased significantly in local governments following issuance of the *Joint Statement* and the NCGA position statement. However, several federal agencies, in particular, have insisted upon securing audit services on the basis of competetive bids in recent years, and it appears that refusal of accountants to bid when requests for bids are issued might be construed as a violation of anti-trust laws. Thus, resolution of this problem lies in the future.

THE AUDIT CONTRACT.    In order to assure that there is no misunderstanding as to the nature, scope, or other aspects of the independent auditor's engagement, the contract should be in written form. Frequently it takes the form of an exchange of correspondence, though formal contracts are generally considered preferable. Among the matters to be covered in the contract are the following items: (1) the type and purpose of the audit—including a clear specification of the audit scope, any limitation of the scope, and the parties at interest, (2) the exact departments, funds, agencies, and the like to be audited, (3) the period the audit is to cover, (4) approximate beginning and completion dates and the date of delivery of the report, (5) the number of copies of the report, (6) the information and assistance that the auditee will provide for the auditor, (7) the means of handling unexpected problems, such as the discovery of a fraud which requires a more extensive audit than was agreed upon, and the manner by which—and to whom—the auditor is to report upon fraud, malfeasance, etc., coming to his attention, (8) the terms of compensation and reimbursement of the auditor's expenses, and (9) the place at which the audit work will be done.

Preliminary steps in the audit of an organization that uses fund accounting include familiarization with the nature of the organization, investigation of its system of internal control, and familiarization with the principles of accounting in use. The auditor must also acquaint himself with the legal and contractual provisions that govern the agency's fiscal and reporting activities. These include the restrictions governing the provision and disbursement of revenues and those controlling the funds and budget practices to be used. Some of these steps, or portions of them, often must be taken before the auditor can determine whether he should accept the engagement or before the terms of the engagement may be intelligently agreed upon.

## AUDITING STANDARDS

AICPA AUDITING STANDARDS.    The American Institute of Certified Public Accountants has approved a set of standards of quality for the performance of an audit.

2 *Ibid.,* p. 128.

*General standards*

1. The examination is to be performed by a person or persons having adequate technical training and proficiency as an auditor.
2. In all matters relating to the assignment an independence in mental attitude is to be maintained by the auditor or auditors.
3. Due professional care is to be exercised in the performance of the examination and the preparation of the report.

*Standards of field work*

1. The work is to be adequately planned and assistants, if any, are to be properly supervised.
2. There is to be a proper study and evaluation of the existing internal control as a basis for reliance thereon and for the determination of the resultant extent of the tests to which auditing procedures are to be restricted.
3. Sufficient competent evidential matter is to be obtained through inspection, observation, inquiries and confirmations to afford a reasonable basis for an opinion regarding the financial statements under examination.

*Standards of reporting*

1. The report shall state whether the financial statements are presented in accordance with generally accepted principles of accounting.
2. The report shall state whether such principles have been consistently observed in the current period in relation to the preceding period.
3. Informative disclosures in the financial statements are to be regarded as reasonably adequate unless otherwise stated in the report.
4. The report shall either contain an expression of opinion regarding the financial statements, taken as a whole, or an assertion to the effect that an opinion cannot be expressed. When an overall opinion cannot be expressed, the reasons therefore should be stated. In all cases where an auditor's name is associated with financial statements the report should contain a clear-cut indication of the character of the auditor's examination, if any, and the degree of responsibility he is taking.[3]

Audit procedures must be distinguished from audit standards. Standards deal with quality, while procedures are the actual work that is performed. Standards govern the auditor's judgment in deciding which procedures will be used, the way they will be used, when they will be used, and the extent to which they will be used. No listing of audit procedures will be attempted here. Many of the procedures for a governmental unit are essentially the same as those for the

[3] Committee on Auditing Procedure, American Institute of Certified Public Accountants, *Statement On Auditing Standards,* Codification of Auditing Standards and Procedures No. 1 (New York: AICPA, 1973) par, 150.02, p. 5.

examination of a profit-seeking organization; however, the procedures used must be tailored to the characteristics of the organization, which include legal requirements and restrictions, generally accepted accounting principles, and the objectives of the audit. The AICPA standards cited above were designed to control the quality of examinations of financial statements of profit-seeking enterprises. In general they are applicable to the examinations of financial statements of organizations that use fund accounting, but some interpretation seems desirable. For example, an auditor may have adequate technical training and proficiency to audit a profit-seeking enterprise but lack the knowledge of governmental accounting or of the laws of a specific government that is necessary for an adequate audit of a government. In such a case he should refuse the engagement or take steps to acquire the necessary knowledge. (Special applications of the "Standards of Reporting" are discussed later in the chapter.) Additional guidance and interpretation are provided by the governmental auditing standards set forth by the Comptroller General of the United States.

GOVERNMENTAL AUDITING STANDARDS. Though there are many similarities between auditing profit-seeking and governmental organizations, there are also many differences. Though the NCGA offered some guidance relative to auditing, there was no comprehensive statement of governmental auditing standards prior to issuance of *Standards for Audit of Governmental Organizations, Programs, Activities & Functions*[4] by the Comptroller General of the United States in 1972.

The Comptroller General noted in the foreward of the *Standards* document that:

> Public officials, legislators, and the general public want to know whether governmental funds are handled properly and in compliance with existing laws and whether governmental programs are being conducted efficiently, effectively, and economically. They also want to have this information provided, or at least concurred in, by someone who is not an advocate of the program but is independent and objective.
>
> This demand for information has widened the scope of governmental auditing so that such auditing no longer is a function concerned primarily with financial operations. Instead, governmental auditing now is also concerned with whether governmental organizations are achieving the purposes for which programs are authorized and funds are made available, are doing so economically and efficiently, and are complying with applicable laws and regulations. The standards contained in this statement were developed to apply to audits of this wider scope.[5]

These standards are intended for application in audits of all governmental organizations, programs, activities and functions—whether they are performed

---

4 Comptroller General of the United States, *Standards for Audit of Governmental Organizations, Programs, Activities & Functions* (Washington, D.C.: United States General Accounting Office, 1972).

5 Ibid., p. i.

by auditors employed by federal, state, or local governments; independent public accountants; or others qualified to perform parts of the audit work contemplated under the standards. Likewise, they are intended to apply to both internal audits and audits of contractors, grantees, and other external organizations performed by or for a governmental entity.

The standards set forth by the Comptroller General recognize and incorporate the standards of the AICPA. The AICPA standards are recognized as being necessary and appropriate to financial statement audits, but insufficient for the broader scope of governmental auditing. The governmental auditing standards are built around the three elements of a comprehensive audit discussed earlier:

1. *Financial and compliance*—determines (a) whether financial operations are properly conducted, (b) whether the financial reports of an audited entity are presented fairly, and (c) whether the entity has complied with applicable laws and regulations.

2. *Economy and efficiency*—determines whether the entity is managing or utilizing its resources (personnel, property, space, and so forth) in an economical and efficient manner and the causes of any inefficiencies or uneconomical practices, including inadequacies in management information systems, administrative procedures, or organizational structure.

3. *Program results*—determines whether the desired results or benefits are being achieved, whether the objectives established by the legislature or other authorizing body are being met, and whether the agency has considered alternatives which might yield desired results at a lower cost.[6]

Provision for such a broad audit scope is not intended to imply that all audits are now being conducted in this manner or that all audits should be of such an extensive scope. Further, it is recognized in the *Standards* document that the standards set forth there are "purposely forward-looking" and that they include some concepts and areas of audit coverage that are still evolving in practice. For these reasons the standards are structured so that any one of the three elements can be performed separately if this is deemed desirable. Thus it is *essential* (1) that audit contracts or letters of engagement specifically identify which of the three elements are to be covered and (2) that the auditor's report indicate which were included in the audit. Obviously, in the governmental environment "an audit" is not necessarily synonymous with "an audit"—as the scope and depth of audit engagements vary considerably.

The standards of governmental auditing set forth by the U. S. Comptroller General are as follows:

[6] *Ibid.,* p. 2.

*General standards*

1.  The full scope of an audit of a governmental program, function, activity, or organization should encompass:
    a.  An examination of financial transactions, accounts, and reports, including an evaluation of compliance with applicable laws and regulations.
    b.  A review of efficiency and economy in the use of resources.
    c.  A review to determine whether desired results are effectively achieved.
    In determining the scope for a particular audit, responsible officials should give consideration to the needs of the potential users of the results of that audit.
2.  The auditors assigned to perform the audit must collectively possess adequate professional proficiency for the tasks required.
3.  In all matters relating to the audit work, the audit organization and the individual auditors shall maintain an independent attitude.
4.  Due professional care is to be used in conducting the audit and in preparing related reports.

*Examination and evaluation standards*

1.  Work is to be adequately planned.
2.  Assistants are to be properly supervised.
3.  A review is to be made of compliance with legal and regulatory requirements.
4.  An evaluation is to be made of the system of internal control to assess the extent it can be relied upon to ensure accurate information, to ensure compliance with laws and regulations, and to provide for efficient and effective operations.
5.  Sufficient, competent, and relevant evidence is to be obtained to afford a reasonable basis for the auditor's opinions, judgments, conclusions, and recommendations.

*Reporting standards*

1.  Written audit reports are to be submitted to the appropriate officials of the organizations requiring or arranging for the audits. Copies of the reports should be sent to other officials who may be responsible for taking action on audit findings and recommendations and to others responsible or authorized to receive such reports. Copies should also be made available for public inspection.
2.  Reports are to be issued on or before the dates specified by law, regulation, or other arrangement and, in any event, as promptly as possible so as to make the information available for timely use by management and by legislative officials.
3.  Each report shall:
    a.  Be as concise as possible but, at the same time, clear and complete enough to be understood by the users.

b. Present factual matter accurately, completely, and fairly.

c. Present findings and conclusions objectively and in language as clear and simple as the subject matter permits.

d. Include only factual information, findings, and conclusions that are adequately supported by enough evidence in the auditor's working papers to demonstrate or prove, when called upon, the bases for the matters reported and their correctness and reasonableness. Detailed supporting information should be included in the report to the extent necessary to make a convincing presentation.

e. Include, when possible, the auditor's recommendations for actions to effect improvements in problem areas noted in his audit and to otherwise make improvements in operations. Information on underlying causes of problems reported should be included to assist in implementing or devising corrective actions.

f. Place primary emphasis on improvement rather than on criticism of the past; critical comments should be presented in balanced perspective, recognizing any unusual difficulties or circumstances faced by the operating officials concerned.

g. Identify and explain issues and questions needing further study and consideration by the auditor or others.

h. Include recognition of noteworthy accomplishments, particularly when management improvements in one program or activity may be applicable elsewhere.

i. Include recognition of the views of responsible officials of the organization, program, function, or activity audited on the auditor's findings, conclusions, and recommendations. Except where the possibility of fraud or other compelling reason may require different treatment, the auditor's tentative findings and conclusions should be reviewed with such officials. When possible, without undue delay, their views should be obtained in writing and objectively considered and presented in preparing the final report.

j. Clearly explain the scope and objectives of the audit.

k. State whether any significant pertinent information has been omitted because it is deemed privileged or confidential. The nature of such information should be described, and the law or other basis under which it is withheld should be stated.

4. Each audit report containing financial reports shall:

a. Contain an expression of the auditor's opinion on whether the information contained in the financial reports is presented fairly. If the auditor cannot express an opinion, the reasons therefore should be stated in the audit report.

b. State whether the financial reports have been prepared in accordance with generally accepted or prescribed accounting principles applicable to the organization, program, function, or activity audited and on a consistent basis from one period to the next. Material changes in accounting policies and procedures and their effect on the financial reports are to be explained in the audit report.

c. Contain appropriate supplementary explanatory information about the contents of the financial reports as may be necessary for full and informative disclosure about the financial operations of the organization, program, function, or activity audited. Violations of legal or other regulatory requirements, including instances of noncompliance, shall be explained in the audit report.[7]

## AUDITING PROCEDURES

A comprehensive, authoritative coverage of municipal auditing procedures is contained in *Audits of State and Local Governmental Units*,[8] an AICPA industry audit guide. The municipal auditor will find a wealth of useful information in this publication and should be thoroughly familiar with its contents. Further guidance is contained in the "Auditing of Governmental Units" chapter of *GAAFR*[9]; in addition, several states and state CPA societies prescribe or recommend minimum audit programs or procedures. Finally, audit guides are available for many Federal programs; these should be studied carefully by the auditor in formulating his audit program. The *Audit Guide and Standards for Revenue Sharing Recipients*[10] has almost universal significance in governmental auditing. The auditor should inquire as to the existence and availability of audit guides pertinent to other Federal programs in which the auditee organization participates—audit guides are available for most of the larger ones—as they not only provide useful guidance but may impose specific accounting, auditing and/or reporting requirements.

## THE FISCAL (FINANCIAL AND COMPLIANCE) AUDIT ELEMENT

Legal compliance is considered an integral part both of managerial responsibility and accountability and of the fiscal audit of governments. The legal constraints under which governments operate and the control orientation of governmental accounting systems have been commented upon at numerous points throughout this book. Obviously the accountability process is incomplete if the audit of the financial statements does not include the legal compliance aspects within its scope or these are not included in the auditor's report.

### Auditing Standards

The AICPA standards are designed for the financial aspects of the fiscal audit element and have been incorporated within the Comptroller General's

7 *Ibid.,* pp. 6–9.

8 Committee on Governmental Accounting and Auditing, American Institute of Certified Public Accountants, *Audits of State and Local Governmental Units,* Exposure draft, April 1973 (New York: The Institute, 1973). Publication of this guide was imminent as this text went to press.

9 *GAAFR,* pp. 127–47.

10 Department of the Treasury, Office of Revenue Sharing, *Audit Guide and Standards for Revenue Sharing Recipients* (USGPO, October, 1973).

standards. The laws, regulations, or other legal constraints under which the government operates establish the standards against which legal compliance is measured.

## Audit Procedures

The procedures commonly employed in financial auditing are covered adequately in the several standard auditing textbooks available. The procedures involved in auditing legal compliance will vary with the circumstances. Either the government's attorney or the auditor must determine the legal provisions of laws, ordinances, bond indentures, grants, etc., that are applicable in the situation. The auditor then determines the extent to which they have been complied with and the adequacy of the disclosure in the financial statements in this regard, The auditor must also assure himself that the auditee has not incurred significant unrecorded liability through failure to comply with, or through violation of, pertinent laws and regulations.

## The Audit Report

The auditor's report on his fiscal examination is discussed under four headings: (1) scope, (2) statements, (3) opinion, and (4) comments. Operational (performance) audit element reporting follows a similar pattern, though it typically is longer and includes additional topics.

SCOPE. In the first paragraph of the "Auditor's Short Form Report" (Figure 18-3) the auditor describes the scope of his examination. The wording used in Figure 18-3 states that a satisfactory examination has been performed for the specified statements. If the scope of his examination was unsatisfactory in any respect, the auditor must decide whether the alternative procedures (if any) that he employed were satisfactory and what the effect on his opinion has been.

It is essential that the auditor list the statements about which he is rendering an opinion. The typical annual report contains both financial and satistical statements. Ordinarily the auditor does not give an opinion on the statistical statements, and his scope paragraph should state whether they are covered by his opinion. Some auditors insert a disclaimer in front of those statements to which the opinion does not apply to further assure that the reader is not confused in this regard.

STATEMENTS. As has already been emphasized, the statements about which the auditor gives an opinion are the responsibility of the administration of the unit he is auditing. As a matter of fact, the statements may be and often are prepared by the auditor, but both he and the officials involved should recognize that the latter have the primary responsibility for their fairness. The auditor should secure for his work papers an affirmation from the officials indicating that the statements present fairly the organization's financial condition and results of operations.

If the auditor's contract requires that he prepare (as well as audit) the financial reports, the auditor will prepare and present the statements in the same form as would the officials. In this case, his report will also constitute his letter of transmittal.

OPINION. The second paragraph of the "Auditor's Short Form Report" (Figure 18-3) contains the model language suggested by the American Institute of Certified Public Accountants for an "unqualified" opinion—that is, an opinion based on an examination of financial statements conducted in conformity with generally accepted auditing standards applied to statements that acceptably meet the terms set out in the second paragraph. If the audit or the statements are less than satisfactory in some material respect, the auditor must give a qualified opinion or an adverse opinion or, if he is unable to form an opinion, he must disclaim an opinion. In giving a "qualified" opinion the auditor states that, in spite of the audit's scope or procedures or the statements' content being less than satisfactory in some specified respect, he has arrived at an overall opinion on the statements. If the statements are not fairly presented in conformity with generally accepted accounting principles and standards, the auditor must specify the flaw or flaws and give an "adverse" opinion—state that the statements are *not* fairly presented. Because of major omissions of auditing procedures or because of major uncertainties regarding one or more statement items, the auditor may not know whether the statements are fairly presented. He will therefore disclaim an opinion (issue a "disclaimer") on the fairness of the statements taken as a whole. After expressing an adverse opinion or issuing a disclaimer of opinion he may give an opinion on the statement items that he believes *are* fairly stated (a "piecemeal" opinion).

A number of reasons for alteration in the language of the opinion are cited following; the list is not intended to be exhaustive.

1. The scope of the audit may have been unsatisfactory in some respect.
2. The auditor may feel that the statements do not present "financial position" or "results of operation."
3. He may believe that there are no "generally accepted principles of accounting" for the type of organization that he has audited.
4. He may feel that the auditee's statements as prepared are not in conformity with principles of accounting that he believes to be "generally accepted."
5. He may believe that the principles used in preparing the statements have not been applied on a basis consistent with that of the preceding year.
6. He may consider the disclosures to be insufficient in the circumstances.

Each of these problems requires the auditor to reach a decision concerning the

Figure 18-3

AUDITOR'S SHORT FORM REPORT

---

OFFICIAL LETTERHEAD
OF
AUDITING FIRM OR AGENCY

Date

The Honorable (name), Mayor
Members of the City Council
City of Sample
Sample, State

Gentlemen:

We have examined the balance sheets of the various funds of the City of Sample, State, as of December 31, 19X2, and the related statements of operations for the year then ended. Our examination was made in accordance with generally accepted auditing standards, and accordingly included such tests of the accounting records and such other auditing procedures as we considered necessary in the circumstances.

In our opinion, the accompanying balance sheets and related statements of operations present fairly the financial position of the various funds and balanced account groups for the City of Sample, State, at December 31, 19X2, and the results of their operations for the year then ended, in conformity with generally accepted accounting principles applicable to governmental entities, applied on a basis consistent with that of the preceding fiscal year. It is our further opinion that the accounting requirements of the bond ordinance under which the city's water and sewer bonds, Series 19W4, were issued have been met.

Very truly yours,

(signed)
NAME OF FIRM
Certified Public Accountants

---

type of opinion that he can and should render. Generally speaking, if the problem is not so great that referring to it and taking exception to it would negate an expression of opinion on the statements taken as a whole, he will render a qualified opinion. If the problem that he cites is so grave that a qualified opinion is not appropriate, he must express an adverse opinion if the problem is one of fairness or he must disclaim an opinion if the problem is one of uncertainty. *If the auditor's name is connected with a set of statements, the responsibility that he assumes must be clearly stated.*

COMMENTS.  While the independent auditor is engaged primarily and in most cases exclusively to give an opinion on the financial statements and, perhaps, the extent of legal compliance, one of his most valuable services can be to provide analyses and recommendations on matters that he has discovered in the process of his examination. For this reason many accountants will go beyond the short form report that has been discussed above. The additional materials may be presented in either a long form report, which is comparable in formality to the short form report, or in the form of letters to responsible officials.

The long form report includes the scope and opinion materials that have already been discussed, but in addition the auditor will provide discussions, analyses, and recommendations regarding operational matters that came to his attention during his examination of financial statements. Illustrative of the subject matter of these comments are such topics as accounting systems and procedures; protection, utilization, and disposition of assets; number of funds; organizational arrangements; and insurance and bonding practices. The auditor may need also to comment upon compliance or lack of compliance of officials with legal and contractual requirements. An official should not be criticized for using a procedure that is in compliance with the law; if the auditor believes that the procedure is subject to criticism, he should criticize in his report the legal requirements. Similarly, he may have to criticize officials for efficient procedures if they are not in strict compliance with the law. Again he may want to recommend changes in the law.

The auditor must tentatively evaluate internal control in order properly to plan his audit, and he continues his evaluation as he performs the audit. In many cases he has recommendations for improvements. Usually such recommendations are provided in a letter that is separate from his audit report, but there are some auditors who include this important topic in their comments in the long form report.

Source: *GAAFR,* p. 209. This is an adaptation by the NCGA of the standard short form opinion prescribed by the AICPA Committee on Auditing Procedure (now the Auditing Standards Executive Committee). The AICPA committees have consistently preferred that the phrase "applicable to governmental entities" be omitted, that is, that reference be made simply to "generally accepted accounting principles." The apparent logic of this preference is that no reference to the specific source of the principles is necessary when they have been authoritatively and clearly set forth, as in *GAAFR,* and have become generally accepted in practice.

If the auditor does not provide a long form report, the comments that have just been discussed may be included in a letter or letters to responsible government officials. However, it can be argued convincingly that the public at large is the governmental auditor's client, and that issuance of a long-form report is far preferable to issuance of a short-form report, even if the latter is accompanied by a management advisory letter.

## THE OPERATIONAL (PERFORMANCE) AUDIT ELEMENTS

Audit work of professional quality requires the preexistence of a number of factors. There must be a body of competent auditors who are willing to express an opinion. These individuals must be equipped with techniques of evidence gathering that are satisfactory for the requirements of the audit. The existence of a professional organization implies self-imposed standards of performance that control the quality of audit work. There must be persons who are interested in receiving and using the opinions that the auditors render, whatever the subject of the audit may have been. Finally, there must be standards of performance by which the organization can be judged, and there must be explicit or implicit representations of compliance with these standards made by the management of the audited entity.

The outstanding example of a governmental organization engaged in operational auditing is the United States General Accounting Office. Its work exemplifies the requirements for operational audit work of professional quality. In the past the GAO's audits were generally performed by employees who were certified public accountants. They brought with them the generally accepted auditing standards of the accounting profession. The accountants were assisted in their audit work by lawyers whose duties included the review of the legality of proposed and actual executive department expenditures. Increasing emphasis upon audits of managerial performance has led to the recruiting of engineers and others whose technical backgrounds are useful in evaluating operations. The GAO reports to the Congress of the United States, and Congress has increasingly assigned the evaluation of executive branch performance to the GAO.

### Standards of Managerial Performance

Standards of operational performance are not nearly so well defined as are those of financial auditing, nor are managerial representations as to operational performance likely to be so definite. Performance auditing is concerned with administrative activities that are designed to achieve the objectives of the functions, programs, and activities that have been assigned to the client agencies by legislative action. Accordingly, the standards of performance must deal with how well the organization is managed and, concomitantly, whether the agency has achieved the objectives set out for it by legislative action.

In financial auditing the standards of agency performance are reasonably explicit—compliance with generally accepted accounting principles and compliance with laws, policies, and procedures that govern fiscal operations. In the field of operational auditing there may be occasional explicit representations by management as to accomplishment, but more often there is no explicit representation but only the implicit managerial responsibility for economical, efficient, and effective performance.

Operational auditing standards of performance are derived from and implied by many different sources. One of the most important sources is legislative statement of policy. When legislation creates programs and activities and provides financing for them, the appointed agency has the responsibility of carrying out legislative direction; it may properly be held accountable through the audit process for compliance and accomplishment. It is important to note that legislative prescription is not always best designed to achieve legislative intent. A proper function of an auditor who reports to the legislative body is to comment upon achievement of legislative intent as well as compliance of the agency with programs and activities the legislature designed to achieve its objectives. For example, the GAO was requested by the Congress to evaluate the efficacy of the Head Start program. In such circumstances the auditor has a responsibility to evaluate both administrative compliance with legally prescribed programs and the efficacy of well-administered programs in achieving legislative objectives.

Many professional organizations formally state desirable policies and levels of performance in their fields of proficiency. The auditor may properly look to such statements for standards to be used in evaluating the performance of agencies operating in such professional fields.

The auditor may also use comparisons as standards of quality and achievement for the operation to be examined. Accomplishments of the audited agency in the past and of other organizations, trends, statistics of accomplishment at the national or local levels, and the like may form the basis for such comparisons. Statistical data measuring the output of the agency are particularly useful.

Generally accepted principles of management may be used as criteria for managerial performance. Management should explicitly plan its objectives, programs, policies, standards, and organizational arrangements. It must assign responsibility and delegate authority. It must set up procedures that will provide for proper use and control of its resources. It must set up record keeping and reporting systems and provide for internal audit of its activities. It must select personnel of appropriate quality.

Management's own statements of standards, goals, objectives, and other criteria of success, together with reports thereon, are useful standards and sources of evaluation, respectively.

Finally, there are certain commonsense standards of performance that the agency must expect to be used in judging it. Duplication of effort, backlogs of work, failures to enforce agreements, failure to use good management techniques, obsolete or excessive inventories, use of government property for private benefit, failure to coordinate activities with agencies doing related work—all of these are indications of operational misfeasance or malfeasance that should be used by the auditor who is evaluating performance.

## Auditing Standards

The generally accepted auditing standards developed by the American Institute of Certified Public Accountants for the guidance of members in conducting and reporting upon examinations of financial statements have in general been used by its members in both management services and auditing engagements, including those involving operational auditing. The "General Standards" and "Standards of Field Work" have been accepted as directly pertinent, while the standards of reporting clearly must be evaluated with respect to specific engagements. For example, the first AICPA standard of reporting says that "the report shall state whether the financial statements are presented in accordance with generally accepted principles of accounting." This standard would be clearly inapplicable to the report that an auditor might give following an operational auditing examination. On the other hand, AICPA standard of reporting number four concludes with this sentence: "In all cases where an auditor's name is associated with financial statements the report should contain a clearcut indication of the character of the auditor's examination, if any, and the degree of responsibility he is taking." With appropriate modifications to recognize that financial statements are not the matters being examined, this statement is clearly applicable to operational auditing.

Though at this writing the extent of the impact of *Standards for Audit of Governmental Organizations, Programs, Activities and Functions* on governmental auditing could not be assessed, certainly it will be significant. Not only are these standards designed specifically for governmental audits, but the federal government has the authority to require their implementation wherever federal funds are involved—which encompasses most state and local governmental units and many nongovernment and quasi-governmental organizations. As noted earlier, these standards are normative rather than descriptive, that is, they portray what should be or might be, not necessarily the level of current practice. As such they provide guidelines for the upgrading of governmental audit practice, at least, and probably point the direction of the evolution of governmental auditing in the future.

## Audit Procedures

The techniques of operational auditing are in many ways similar to those of financial audits. The auditor's objective is to find sufficient evidence to support his opinion. He must review the legal background of agency operations, the administrative requirements of laws or contracts, the policies of the agency, and the management controls and systems, including financial and operating reports. He must examine organizational arrangements, flows of financial and operational data, and documentary evidence. He must analyze, inspect, observe, count, trace, compare, question, and obtain confirmations. The collection of evidence by these methods, and others, must be directed to the specific objectives of the audit, whether they be those of a financial audit, an operational audit, or a comprehensive audit covering all aspects of agency operation and representations of management.

The auditor's findings of fact, cause, and effect will ordinarily be divisible into categories: a group of findings that is favorable to the management of the auditee agency and a group that is not. When the auditor identifies a problem that is not favorable to the management, he will want to determine how widespread it is in the agency. He will want to evaluate the materiality of the problem and its effects on costs both directly and indirectly. He must attempt to determine the causes of inefficiency and consider and evaluate the options for eliminating them. The problem must be related to the personnel responsible for it, and the auditor will want to discuss his findings and his proposed options with the management personnel who are responsible. Their review is exceedingly important because of their intimate relationship with and knowledge of the agency. Only after the auditor has gone through this process is he in a position to select the option that he wants to recommend and to formulate his report.

## Reporting

The audit report should clearly state the scope of the examination, including its objectives. For example, the auditor might be expected to ascertain the extent to which the objectives set out in legislation have been achieved or whether the administration of the act has been carried out economically and efficiently. Certainly the organization or organizations subject to examination must be identified. In some cases programs that have common or similar goals or similar patterns of activities may and probably should be examined by audits that cross organizational lines.

Another section of an operational audit report will include the findings of fact and, to the extent they can be identified, the causes and effects of the situations or events described in the findings. This is an appropriate spot for commendations of especially good management and results. It is essential here that the auditor assess the efficacy of managers within the environment in which they work, not some hypothetical ideal environment, and that he evaluate their actions in terms of the information available at the time decisions had to be made. This is crucial to a fair, undistorted evaluation, since "hindsight is always 20/20."

A third section of the report should contain the auditor's recommendations for improvement. These should flow out of the statements of fact, cause, and effect that will already have appeared in the report. Frequently the auditor will have worked with agency personnel to solve problems; full credit should be given to the agency for its suggested solutions and for taking prompt action on those recommendations that have already been put into effect. Recommendations that have not been implemented may well be divided into those that are capable of implementation without additional legislation and those that are not. Special attention is justified for (1) recommendations of prior audits that the auditee agency has not put into effect, and (2) recommendations with which the auditee agency management disagrees.

The work of the auditor may well be justifiable by means of specific accomplishments. The auditor should summarize dollars collected and dollars saved because of his recommendations where such summarization is possible. Mention of financial or other benefits that are not measurable in quantitative terms may be appropriate.

## CONCLUDING COMMENT

Both the theory and the practice of governmental auditing are evolving rapidly. A major factor underlying this rapid evolution, or "quiet revolution," has been the widespread realization that the traditional financial audit has limited utility in governments—that the accountability process remains incomplete in the absence of an independent audit of at least certain aspects of legal compliance, economy and efficiency, and effectiveness. What is taking place, in effect, may be described as an effort to meld the traditional financial audit with legal compliance evaluation and with selected techniques of systems analysis, operations research, value engineering, and other tools of the modern internal auditor, mathematician, engineer, and management consultant—and to bring these to bear in the management and evaluation of governments through the audit process. The ultimate results of this significant change in scope and emphasis remain to be seen, but great strides already have been made in several federal, state, and local audit agencies.

**Question 18-1.** Compare the responsibilities of a municipality's officers and its independent auditor for the financial report.

**Question 18-2.** In the course of an audit of the books of a municipality, you find that the financial statements, when prepared on the basis required by law, do not reflect the true financial condition or financial operations of the municipality. What would be your procedure?

**Question 18-3.** In making an audit, how would you ascertain that expenditures were properly appropriated for?

**Question 18-4.** You are called in to audit the books of a municipality for which taxes are collected by a county. How would you verify that taxes receivable controlling accounts are correct?

**Question 18-5.** In your audit of the taxes receivable of a county which collects both its own taxes and taxes for other units, how would you verify that the taxpayers' individual account balances, as shown in the records, are correct?

**Question 18-6.** A municipal golf course charges $4.00 for eighteen holes played during regular hours but only $2.50 for nine holes played in the two and one-half hours prior to dusk. It has been found that the clerk has been charging players at the daytime rate but recording the receipts as twilight hour receipts and pocketing the difference. What steps would you recommend to insure that all receipts will be properly accounted for hereafter?

**Question 18-7.** Describe briefly the contents of the audit report of a governmental unit.

**Question 18-8.** A municipality requires auditors to submit bids as to how much they would charge for the annual audit. The audit contract is awarded to the lowest bidder. What is wrong with this method of hiring auditors?

**Question 18-9.** Upon completion of your audit and presentation of the report to a city council one of the councilmen takes exception to the phrase "in our opinion" which appears in your audit. He states that you were engaged to make a sufficiently complete and detailed examination to determine all pertinent facts about the city; that if you have not completed all the work necessary to that end, you should continue your investigation as long as necessary, but that he wants a certificate consisting of positive statements of fact, without any qualification or questions of "opinion." Discuss the logic of the councilman's remarks and the position which you would take. (AICPA)

**Question 18-10.** A councilman requests that you, an independent public accountant, render an opinion on the budget presented to the council by the city manager. Discuss the position which you would take with respect to his request. (AICPA)

**Question 18-11.** The comptroller of D City is responsible for approval of all receipts of city funds and all disbursements thereof. The city council takes the position that, since he is auditing both receipts and disbursements for accuracy and legality, no additional audit by independent accountants is necessary. What position would you, a new councilman, take?

**Question 18-12.** The state auditor has for years been responsible for examinations of the financial operations of all state agencies. A bill is under consideration to add to his duties those of the chief accounting officer of the state. You are testifying before a legislative committee which is considering the bill. What is the tenor of your testimony?

**Question 18-13.** Auditing has been defined as the process of collecting and evaluating evidence in order to formulate an opinion about assertions made by management. About what assertions is the external auditor giving his opinion as the result of a financial audit? About what assertions is the external auditor giving his opinion as the result of an operational audit?

**Question 18-14.** What are the factors required if there are to be audits of professional quality, whether they be financial audits or operational audits?

**Question 18-15.** By what standards of performance may the auditor evaluate the efficacy and efficiency of management in government?

**Question 18-16.** The auditor's report on a financial audit has scope and opinion sections. What sections would you expect to find in the audit report of an operational audit?

*The purpose of the auditing chapter is to impress students of governmental accounting with the proper functions of the independent auditor and with the principles which guide the auditor. In view of this limited objective, no problems have been provided.*

# II

# FEDERAL AND INSTITUTIONAL
# ACCOUNTING AND REPORTING

# 19

# Federal Government Accounting

The Federal Government of the United States is engaged in an unparalleled myriad of functions, programs and activities both here and abroad. It is simultaneously the country's largest single employer and consumer. Some 2.5 million full-time civilian personnel are employed within its various departments and agencies to carry out its many functions. Federal disbursements were estimated to approach $250 billion during 1973, up almost six-fold from the 1950 level, and Federal Government purchases of goods and services now comprise almost 20 percent of our gross national product.

The accounting system of the Federal Government is actually a series of systems, subsystems, sub-subsystems, etc., which track its financial activities around the world. Federal accounting is similar to that of state and local governments in that it has been heavily influenced by legislation and regulation. Likewise, it serves as a major tool of fund and appropriation control, both over and within the various departments and agencies. It is noticeably different in that (1) accounting is concerned with budgetary and financial operations and position both of the individual agencies and of the Federal Government as a whole, (2) "dual-track" agency systems provide for both "expenditure" (in the governmental sense) and "expense" (in the financial accounting sense) accounting and reporting, and (3) the agency or department is generally considered the primary accounting entity; fund and appropriation accounting is incorporated within each agency accounting system. Financial reports for the Government as a whole are compiled by the Treasury Department's Bureau of Accounts from the central cash accounts it maintains and from monthly reports submitted to it by the agencies.

## OVERVIEW OF THE FEDERAL FINANCIAL MANAGEMENT ENVIRONMENT

The importance of budgeting, accounting and reporting to governmental financial management and accountability was recognized by those drafting the Constitution of the United States. Thus, they included a mandate (Article I, Section 9) that:

> No money shall be drawn from the treasury, but in consequence of appropriations made by law; and a regular statement and account of the receipts and expenditures of all public money shall be published from time to time.

From the outset, therefore, financial management was seen as a shared function of the legislative and executive branches of the Federal Government. Then as now, the "power of the purse string" was vested in Congress, while the executive branch was charged with administering the activities of the Government and reporting on its stewardship both to the Congress and to the public.

### Landmark Legislation

Federal budgeting, accounting, reporting and auditing were mostly within the purview of the Secretary of the Treasury for over a century and evolved slowly, little affected by legislation. The pace of legislation and change has quickened during the past 50 years or so, however, beginning with the landmark Budget and Accounting Act of 1921. Included in the 1921 act are provisions that (1) require the President to submit an executive (proposed) budget at the beginning of each regular session of Congress, (2) established the Office of Management and Budget (OMB)—then the Bureau of the Budget (BOB)—within the Executive Office of the President, and (3) established the General Accounting Office, headed by the Comptroller General, to assist the Congress in its oversight of the executive branch and to serve as the independent legislative auditor of the Federal Government.

Numerous laws pertaining to Federal financial management and accountability have been enacted since 1921, the most significant being the Budget and Accounting Procedures Act of 1950. Based largely on the recommendations of the First Hoover Commission, the 1950 Act, as amended, provides that:

A unified system of central accounting and reporting be established in the Treasury Department to provide data on the financial operations and position of the Government as a whole.

Each executive agency furnish the Treasury Department with such reports or other information as the Secretary of the Treasury may require to operate a central accounting and reporting system for the Government as a whole.

An adequate and effective agency accounting system be established and maintained by the head of each agency.

Agency accounting and reporting systems be integrated with the central accounting system of the Treasury Department.

Both individual agency accounting systems and the central accounting systems within the Treasury Department conform with the principles, standards, and related requirements prescribed by the Comptroller General, and that such compliance be examined in the course of audits by the General Accounting Office.

The Comptroller General, the Secretary of the Treasury, and the Director of the Office of Management and Budget conduct a continuous joint program (Joint Financial Management Improvement Program) for the improvement of accounting and financial reporting in the Government.

### Financial Management Roles and Responsibilities

The general outlines of the individual and shared financial management roles and responsibilities within the Federal Government, apparent in the legislation cited above, are summarized in Figure 19-1. The major financial management roles and responsibilities of the legislative and executive branches are discussed below briefly in the following order:

*Legislative Branch*
  Congress
  General Accounting Office (Comptroller General)
*Executive Branch*
  President
  Office of Management and Budget
  General Services Administration
  Secretary of the Treasury
  Federal Agencies
*Joint*
  Joint Financial Management Improvement Program

CONGRESS. Authority for all programs of the executive branch rests with the Congress, which also provides for their financing through the enactment of appropriations. Although the President *proposes* programs and appropriations through the executive budget, the Congress enacts the *actual* budget—which invariably differs somewhat from the executive budget—through a series of individual appropriation bills. Thus the actual budget is enacted piecemeal, not in total, at the will of the Congress.

Congress also exercises general oversight over the executive branch by means of committee investigations, budgetary and other hearings, and audits and other studies by the General Accounting Office.

Figure 19-1

FEDERAL FINANCIAL MANAGEMENT ROLES AND
RESPONSIBILITIES—A SUMMARY

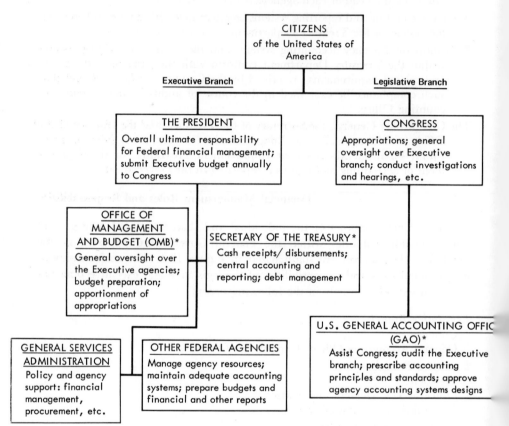

* Members, with the Director of the U.S. Civil Service Commission, of the Joint
Financial Management Improvement Program Steering Committee.

GENERAL ACCOUNTING OFFICE.    A multitude of roles and responsibilities have
been assigned to the GAO since its inception in 1921. Among these roles and
responsibilities are:

1.  *Assisting the Congress in the general oversight of the executive branch.*
    Though all GAO activities are related to this purpose, specific activities
    related hereto include (a) assigning staff members to assist Congressional
    Committees, and (b) conducting special studies and investigations at the
    request of Congress.

2. *Serving as the independent legislative auditor of the Federal Government.* The GAO audit staff conducts audits of all branches of the Government, both here and abroad.

3. *Prescribing principles and standards for Federal agency accounting systems.* This is done through the *General Accounting Office Policy and Procedures Manual For Guidance of Federal Agencies,* published in loose-leaf form and updated periodically.

4. *Assisting agencies in accounting systems design.* To this end the GAO (a) provides technical assistance upon request to Federal agencies designing or modifying accounting systems, (b) approves those agency statements of principles and agency system designs which comply with requirements set forth in the GAO *Manual,* (c) includes recommendations for systems improvement in its audit reports, (d) conducts an on-going program of agency system review, and (e) circulates illustrative examples of suggested and notable accounting and reporting practices among the agencies.

5. *Reporting to Congress on the status of agency accounting systems.* This is done through providing members of Congress copies of all audit reports and through an annual summary report to Congress on this subject.

PRESIDENT. The President of the United States has ultimate responsibility for financial management and accountability of the executive branch of the Government. In fulfilling his responsibilities he relies heavily upon the heads of the executive agencies, particularly the Treasury and OMB, to which a great deal of authority is delegated.

Though the President can only suggest to Congress the appropriations he desires, he has the power to veto appropriation bills passed by the Congress. He cannot modify a bill, however, but must approve or disapprove it in its entirety. A Presidential veto can be overridden only by a two-thirds vote of Congress. Further, since appropriations are viewed by the executive branch as authorizations to obligate the Government, not orders to do so, the President may instruct the Office of Management and Budget not to release appropriations for purposes he does not favor. The propriety of "reserving" or "impounding" appropriations for this reason has been questioned by Congress from time to time, including recent years, and has evoked much debate in both governmental and academic circles.

OFFICE OF MANAGEMENT AND BUDGET. An agency within the Executive Office of the President, the OMB has broad financial management powers as well as the responsibility of preparing the executive budget. Among the other duties assigned OMB are:

To study and recommend to the President changes relative to (a) the existing organizational structure of the agencies, their activities and methods of business, etc., (b) appropriations, (c) the assignment of particular activities or tasks within the executive branch, and (d) any need for reorganization of the executive branch.

To apportion appropriations (enacted) among the agencies and establish "reserves" in anticipation of cost savings, contingencies, etc.

To develop programs and regulations for improved gathering, compiling, and disseminating of statistical data pertaining to the Government and its agencies.

Upon request, to furnish statistical data and other assistance to Congress.

Numerous bulletins, circulars and other directives relating to Federal budgeting, accounting and reporting have been issued by OMB.

GENERAL SERVICES ADMINISTRATION. Several government-wide financial management policy and support functions formerly assigned to the OMB were reassigned to the General Services Administration (GSA) by executive order in 1973. GSA now has principal executive branch policy and agency-support responsibility for financial management, procurement, contracting and property management, and automated data processing systems management. Its Office of Federal Financial Management Policy, established to carry out these new responsibilities, is expected to play an increasingly significant role in all areas of Federal financial management, including budgeting, accounting, reporting, and auditing.

SECRETARY OF THE TREASURY. The Secretary of the Treasury is both the chief accountant and the banker of the Federal Government. His functions include:

Central accounting and reporting for the Government as a whole.

Cash receipt and disbursement management—including supervision of the Federal depository system and disbursing cash for virtually all civilian agencies.

Management of the public debt—including the scheduling of borrowing to meet current needs, repayment of principal, and meeting interest requirements.

Investment of Trust Funds.

Supervision of agency borrowing from the treasury.

Numerous directives issued by the Secretary of the Treasury affect Federal accounting and reporting, the most comprehensive being the *Treasury Department Fiscal Manual for Guidance of Departments and Agencies.*

FEDERAL AGENCIES. The efficacy of Federal financial management is determined by the economy, efficiency and effectiveness achieved at the agency or department level. Likewise, Federal budgeting, accounting, and reporting can be no better than that of the related departmental or agency systems and subsystems upon which the central systems are dependent. Among the many accounting-related functions and activities of the agencies arc these:

To prepare agency budget requests for submission to the President through OMB.

To establish and maintain effective systems of accounting and internal control in conformity with the principles and standards prescribed by GAO.

To furnish reports and other information requested by the Treasury, OMB, and GAO.

With OMB assistance, to achieve insofar as possible (a) consistency in accounting and budgetary classifications, (b) synchronization between accounting and budgetary classifications and the agency's organizational structure, and (c) adequate support of budget requests by data on performance and program costs, by organizational units.

To report to Congress on actions taken pursuant to recommendations for improvement contained within GAO reports.

Though they are to comply with the broad principles and standards set forth in the GAO *Manual,* agency accounting systems are "tailor made" to the needs of the agency and vary widely in design and procedure. Most agencies have developed accounting policies and procedures manuals that serve both as a guide to agency personnel and as valuable reference material to others interested in the systems and procedures of a particular agency. In addition, most have internal audit staffs that continually study and evaluate the agency's activities.

JOINT FINANCIAL MANAGEMENT IMPROVEMENT PROGRAM. The Joint Financial Management Improvement Program (JFMIP) is a Government-wide cooperative effort to coordinate and improve financial management within the Federal complex. Begun informally in 1947, and officially authorized by the Budget and Accounting Act of 1950, the JFMIP operates under the joint leadership of the Comptroller General, the Secretary of the Treasury, the Director of OMB, and the Chairman of the U.S. Civil Service Commission.

A steering committee comprised of representatives of each central agency coordinates the JFMIP activities. It meets regularly to consider problem areas, initiate research projects and evaluate financial management progress throughout the Government. The JFMIP has played a major coordinative role and provides an essential vehicle for carrying out joint endeavors such as those contained in the Legislative Reorganization Act of 1970 to the effect that the Secretary of the Treasury and the Director of OMB, in cooperation with the Comptroller General, are to develop, establish, and maintain:

Insofar as practicable, a standardized information and data processing system for budgetary and fiscal data.

A standard classification of programs, activities, receipts, and expenditures of Federal agencies.

### Fund Structure

Fund structures employed in Federal Government accounting may be broadly classified as between (1) funds derived from general taxing and revenue powers and from business operations, also known as "Federal" or "Government-owned" funds, and (2) funds held by the Government in the capacity of custodian or trustee, sometimes referred to as "Not Government-owned" or "Trust and Agency" funds. Six types of funds are employed within these two broad categories:

| *Government-owned or "Federal" Funds* | *Trust or Custodian Funds* |
|---|---|
| General Fund | Trust Funds |
| Special Funds | Deposit Funds |
| Revolving Funds | |
| Management Funds | |

GENERAL FUND. The General Fund of the Federal Government is similar in many respects to that of a state or local government. There is only one General Fund; it is used to account for collections that are not dedicated to specific purposes; and the bulk of Congressional appropriations or other authorizations to the various agencies are financed through it.

SPECIAL FUNDS. Special Funds are much like Special Revenue Funds of municipalities. They are established to account for the receipt and expenditure of appropriable resources (1) earmarked by law or contractual agreement for some specified purpose, but (2) not generated by operations for which continuing authority to reuse such receipts has been granted. There are many Special Funds in the Federal Government, though most involve relatively small amounts of money.

REVOLVING FUNDS. Revolving Funds are employed to account for the continuous cycles of commercial-type operations of the Federal Government in which revenues generated are, for the most part at least, automatically available for agency use without need for further action by Congress. There are two types of funds within this category:

1. Public Enterprise Funds—the revenues of which are derived primarily from user charges levied outside the Federal Government. These are similar to Enterprise Funds of municipalities.
2. Intragovernmental Industrial or Working Capital Funds—also known as "Stock" Funds—financed by charges to user agencies within the Government. These are similar to Intragovernmental Service Funds of municipalities.

MANAGEMENT FUNDS. Management Funds are established to facilitate the financing of and accounting for—on a "suspense" or "clearing account" basis—agency operations that ultimately will be charged to two or more appropriations. Management Funds are used, for example, to account for central payment of transportation vouchers and for research projects conducted jointly by several agencies.

TRUST FUNDS. Trust Funds are established to account for the receipt and expenditure of resources by the Federal Government in the capacity of trustee for the benefit of specific individuals or classes of individuals. The Federal Old-Age and Survivors Insurance Trust Fund, the National Service Life Insurance Fund, and the Highway Trust Fund are examples of Federal Trust Funds. The principles of Trust Fund accounting discussed in Chapter 12 are generally applicable to Federal Trust Fund accounting.

DEPOSIT FUNDS. These Funds, similar to municipal Agency Funds, are employed to facilitate the accounting for collections either (1) held in suspense temporarily and later refunded or paid into some other Federal fund, or (2) held by the Government as a banker, or in some other agency capacity, and to be paid out at the direction of the owner.

## OVERVIEW OF THE BUDGETARY PROCESS

Federal agencies may incur obligations requiring either current or future disbursements from one or more of the Government's funds only if Congress has granted budgetary authority to do so. Budgetary authority is usually granted in the form of appropriations, though it may also be granted in the form of "contract authorizations"—which permit obligations to be incurred in either a definite or indefinite amount, but require a subsequent appropriation to liquidate the obligations—or in a variety of other forms.

Most appropriations for current operations provide obligational authority only within the year for which they are granted (one-year or annual appropriations), though disbursements to liquidate them may occur in the two following years. In some cases—such as where major facility construction or research are involved—the appropriation continues as valid obligational authority for several years (multiple-year appropriations) or until expended (no-year appropriations). Occasionally appropriations are made on a permanent basis (permanent appropriations), particularly for activities financed from Revolving and Trust Funds, and agency receipts are available to the agency without additional authorization from Congress. Similarly, Congress may authorize an agency to spend debt receipts, a form of authority sometimes referred to as "back-door financing." Should the new fiscal year begin before an agency's appropriations are enacted—which has occurred with increasing frequency in recent years—Congress passes a "continuing resolution" authorizing the agency to incur obligations under the assumption that the current year appropriations will be identical to those of the prior year.[1]

1 One reason why Congressional appropriations often are not finalized by the July 1 start of the new fiscal year is that an appropriation may not be enacted prior to enactment of legislation authorizing the agency to conduct the program(s) for which budget authority is sought. Thus, not only must new programs be authorized, but many prior year program authorizations expire each year and must be considered for renewal before the budget requests may be considered and appropriations made. For these and other reasons, the use of continuing resolutions has increased in recent years. (Some agencies have operated for the full fiscal year on this basis.)

A Federal agency therefore may have several types of obligational authority available during a given year—e.g., from different appropriations, some definite and some indefinite in amount, some one-year and others multiple-year or no-year, and so on. Thus, budgetary accounting in a Federal agency may be far more complex than in a municipality.

## The Budget Cycle

The Federal budget cycle[2] may be divided into four stages: (1) formulation by the executive branch, (2) congressional action on appropriations, (3) execution of the enacted budget, and (4) budgetary reporting and auditing. These stages are summarized in Figure 19-2; the approximate time frame of the budgetary process for a given fiscal year is shown in Figure 19-3.

FORMULATION OF THE EXECUTIVE BUDGET.   As may be observed from Figure 19-3, the budget submitted to the Congress by the President in January of each year represents many months of planning, analysis and compilation efforts spanning the entire executive branch of the Federal Government. The approximate timing, steps and interagency relationships of this formulation process are summarized in Figure 19-4.

In studying Figure 19-4, note the continuous exchange of information, proposals, evaluations and policy determination among the President, OMB and the other executive agencies. The process of executive budget formulation may be described concisely as follows: (1) During the spring, each agency evaluates its programs, identifies policy issues and prepares budgetary estimates and projections for the fiscal year to begin in 1–1½ years—taking into account both anticipated program changes and alternative means of achieving its objectives. (2) After review in the agency and by OMB, and OMB-agency conferences on major issues or questions involved, preliminary budget plans are transmitted to the President. (3) The President reviews the preliminary agency budget plans—together with preliminary projections of the economic outlook and revenue estimates provided him by the Treasury Department, the Council of Economic Advisors and OMB—and issues general budgetary and fiscal policy guidelines for the fiscal year in question. The agencies then receive tentative policy decisions and planning parameters to serve as guidelines for preparing formal agency budget requests. (4 )Agency budgets compiled in accordance with these guidelines are reviewed by OMB. After OMB hearings and additional OMB-agency conferences to resolve questions or differences remaining, revised agency budgets are submitted to the President. (5) After the President again reviews the overall

---

2 For a more extended discussion of the Federal budget process see David J. Ott and Attiat F. Ott, "The Budget Process," in *Federal Budget Policy*, rev. ed., (Washington, D. C.: The Brookings Institution, 1969), pp. 22–47, or Committee on Government Operations, House of Representatives, 91st Congress, 1st Session, *The Budget Process in the Federal Government* (USGPO: 1969).

Figure 19-2

## THE FEDERAL BUDGET PROCESS

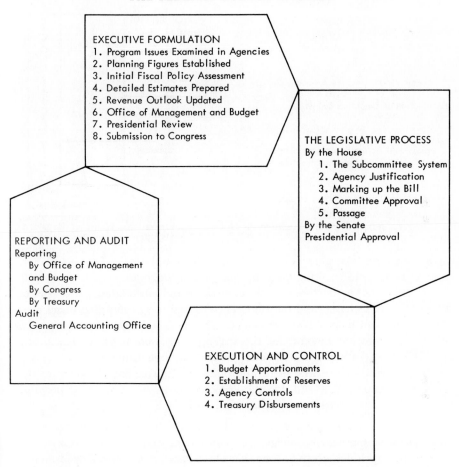

EXECUTIVE FORMULATION
1. Program Issues Examined in Agencies
2. Planning Figures Established
3. Initial Fiscal Policy Assessment
4. Detailed Estimates Prepared
5. Revenue Outlook Updated
6. Office of Management and Budget
7. Presidential Review
8. Submission to Congress

THE LEGISLATIVE PROCESS
By the House
1. The Subcommittee System
2. Agency Justification
3. Marking up the Bill
4. Committee Approval
5. Passage
By the Senate
Presidential Approval

REPORTING AND AUDIT
Reporting
By Office of Management
and Budget
By Congress
By Treasury
Audit
General Accounting Office

EXECUTION AND CONTROL
1. Budget Apportionments
2. Establishment of Reserves
3. Agency Controls
4. Treasury Disbursements

Source: Michael E. Levy, et al., *The Federal Budget: Its Impact on the Economy,* Fiscal 1973 Edition (New York: The Conference Board, 1972) p. 16.

economic outlook, revised revenue estimates, and individual agency requests, he orders the executive budget to be finalized for presentation to the Congress.

CONGRESSIONAL ACTION.   The manner in which the Congress reviews the executive budget and arrives at agency appropriations (or other authorizations) is illustrated in Figure 19-5. Congressional appropriations are not based directly on expenditures, but on authority to obligate the Government to ultimately make disbursements for expenditures or loans. Thus, an agency's total "budget authority" (BA) is comprised of "new obligational authority" (NOA)—authority to

**Figure 19-3**

MAJOR STEPS IN THE FEDERAL BUDGET PROCESS

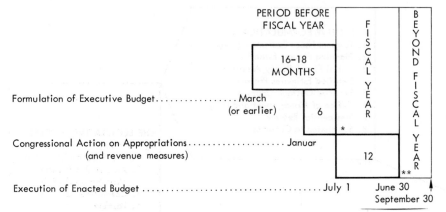

Source: Adapted from Committee on Government Operations, House of Representatives, *The Budget Process in the Federal Government* (USGPO: April, 1969), p. 4.

incur obligations for agency programs—and "loan authority" (LA)—authority to incur obligations covering the principal of loan programs.

In studying Figure 19-5, note the committee and subcommittee processes of both houses of Congress and the conference committees (comprised of selected members of both houses) through which differences in bills passed by the two houses are resolved in determining the final appropriations bill to be sent to the President. Recall also that a series of appropriations bills (usually about 12) are passed each year—there is no single appropriation bill enacting a budget for the government as a whole—and that the President may not modify an appropriation bill, but must accept or reject each in its entirety.

EXECUTION OF THE ENACTED BUDGET. The major steps involved in execution and control of the enacted budget (appropriations and other authorizations) are summarized in Figure 19-6. Note that OMB "apportions" the appropriations or other budget authority to the agencies on a time period (usually quarterly) or activity basis. This is done to assure orderly use of agency authority and to prevent overspending (over-obligation) early in the period that might cause the agencies to request supplemental authority later in the year. Note again that OMB may "reserve" amounts as it sees fit—sometimes called "impounding" by those who do not favor this process—to further protect against over-obligation at the agency level, to assist in cash planning, and/or to restrict expenditures in program areas in which the President believes that the appropriations enacted are excessive.[3]

[3] Use of the term "reserve" by OMB to designate amounts that are *not* to be expended should be distinguished from the more usual use of that term in agency accounting (as in accounting generally) to indicate the purposes for which expenditures *are* to be incurred.

Each agency "allots" its apportioned obligation authority among its various programs and/or organizational subunits. Thus, an agency has only a portion of its annual obligational authority available to it at any time—the apportioned part—and only the alloted apportionments comprise valid obligational authority at the agency field office level.

Figure 19-4

## FORMULATION OF THE EXECUTIVE BUDGET

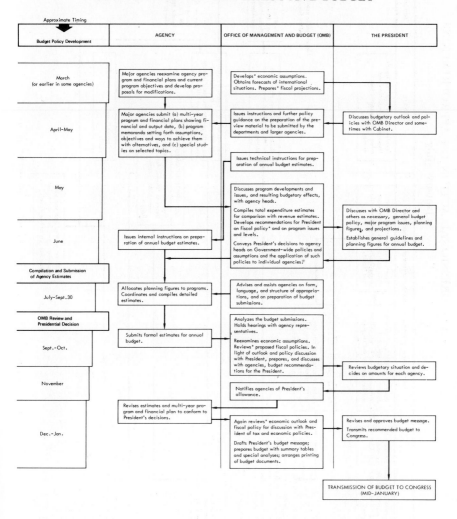

| Approximate Timing | AGENCY | OFFICE OF MANAGEMENT AND BUDGET (OMB) | THE PRESIDENT |
|---|---|---|---|
| **Budget Policy Development** | | | |
| March (or earlier in some agencies) | Major agencies reexamine agency program and financial plans and current program objectives and develop proposals for modifications. | Develops* economic assumptions. Obtains forecasts of international situations. Prepares* fiscal projections. | |
| April-May | Major agencies submit (a) multi-year program and financial plans showing financial and output data, (b) program memoranda setting forth assumptions, objectives and ways to achieve them with alternatives, and (c) special studies on selected topics. | Issues instructions and further policy guidance on the preparation of the preview material to be submitted by the departments and larger agencies. | Discusses budgetary outlook and policies with OMB Director and sometimes with Cabinet. |
| | | Issues technical instructions for preparation of annual budget estimates. | |
| May | | Discusses program developments and issues, and resulting budgetary effects, with agency heads. | Discusses with OMB Director and others as necessary, general budget policy, major program issues, planning figures, and projections. |
| June | Issues internal instructions on preparation of annual budget estimates. | Compiles total expenditure estimates for comparison with revenue estimates. Develops recommendations for President on fiscal policy* and on program issues and levels. Conveys President's decisions to agency heads on Government-wide policies and assumptions and the application of such policies to individual agencies. | Establishes general guidelines and planning figures for annual budget. |
| **Compilation and Submission of Agency Estimates** | | | |
| July-Sept.30 | Allocates planning figures to programs. Coordinates and compiles detailed estimates. | Advises and assists agencies on form, language, and structure of appropriations, and on preparation of budget submissions. | |
| **OMB Review and Presidential Decision** | | | |
| Sept.-Oct. | Submits formal estimates for annual budget. | Analyzes the budget submissions. Holds hearings with agency representatives. Reexamines economic assumptions. Reviews* proposed fiscal policies. In light of outlook and policy discussion with President, prepares, and discusses with agencies, budget recommendations for the President. | Reviews budgetary situation and decides on amounts for each agency. |
| November | | Notifies agencies of President's allowance. | |
| Dec.-Jan. | Revises estimates and multi-year program and financial plan to conform to President's decisions. | Again reviews* economic outlook and fiscal policy for discussion with President of tax and economic policies. Drafts President's budget message; prepares budget with summary tables and special analyses; arranges printing of budget documents. | Revises and approves budget message. Transmits recommended budget to Congress. |
| | | | TRANSMISSION OF BUDGET TO CONGRESS (MID-JANUARY) |

Source: Adapted from *The Budget Process in the Federal Government*, p. 5.

## Figure 19-5

## CONGRESSIONAL ACTION ON APPROPRIATIONS
(January—July*)

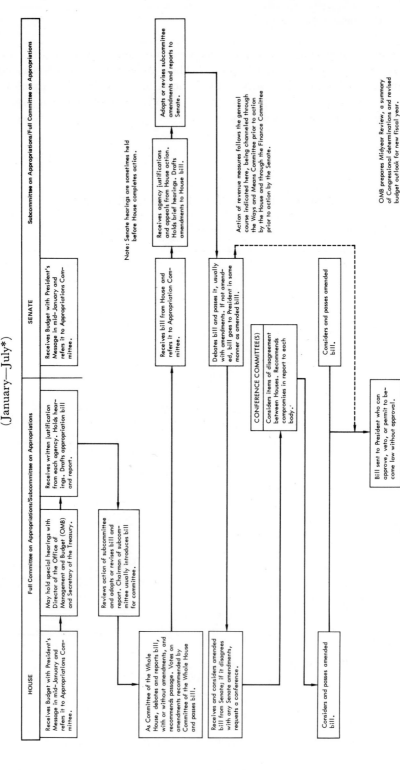

Source: Adapted from *The Budget Process in the Federal Government*, p. 6.

REPORTING AND AUDIT.    Agency accounting and reporting is a responsibility of agency management. In addition to preparing financial and managerial reports for internal use and for others interested in its activities and status, the agency also prepares such reports as may be required by the Treasury, the Congress, or OMB. Again, the central reporting function (for the government as an entity) is carried out by the Treasury Department, based on its central accounting records and the monthly reports filed with it by the agencies.

Independent legislative audit of the agencies is performed by the GAO. Note that the GAO audit is also viewed as an integral part of the agency management process (See Figure 19-6). Accordingly, GAO audits increasingly have been management-assistance oriented in recent years. GAO findings and recommendations for corrective action are reported to the President, the Congress, and the agencies—and the agencies must respond to the GAO reports and inform Congress as to their progress and plans relative to the implementation of GAO suggestions.

## An Evolutionary Process

The Federal budgetary process is dynamic, not static, and evolves continually. Though the pace of change usually may be categorized as "evolutionary," it has been accelerated on two particular occasions recently.

The first far-reaching change was occasioned by President Johnson's executive order of August 1965 calling for introduction of a Planning-Programming-Budgeting System (PPB or PPBS) in the Federal Government. This order was followed by a series of OMB (then BOB) and Treasury Department directives, as well as revision of the GAO *Manual.* Extensive PPB staffs were assembled in many agencies and much effort was invested in program structure design, preparing cost-benefit and alternative course of action analyses, and the like. As might be expected, numerous problems developed in attempting to implement PPB rapidly throughout the Federal establishment, there were occasional abuses of the approach, and those who looked upon it as a panacea were inevitably disillusioned. Though the PPB approach has been only partially implemented— and despite recurring nomenclature changes and claims that PPB is "dead" in the Federal Government—its basic concepts and approaches have had a significant impact on the Federal budgetary process.

A second major factor impacting on the Federal budgetary process recently has been the *Report of the President's Commission on Budget Concepts*[4] issued in October 1967. The bipartisan Commission offered 13 major recommendations for improving the budgetary process and presentations and expressed its views on a total of 117 different points related thereto.

----

[4] *Report of the President's Commission on Budget Concepts,* USGPO, 1967, 109 pages. See also *Staff Papers and Other Materials Reviewed by the President's Commission,* USGPO, 1967, 512 pages.

**Figure 19-6**

## EXECUTION OF ENACTED BUDGET

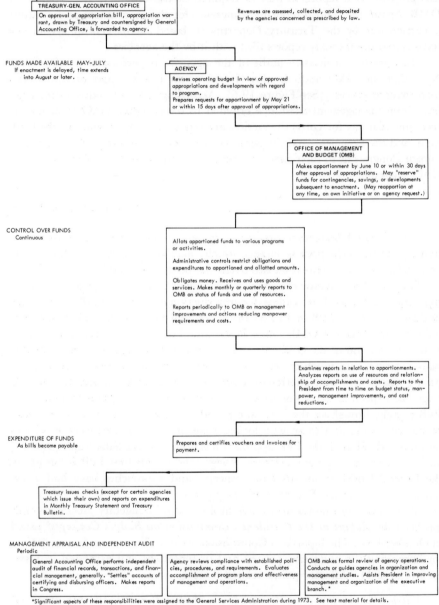

Source: Adapted from *The Budget Process in the Federal Government,* p. 7.

No doubt the most important Commission recommendation was that a single, unified budget should replace the three then-existing budget concepts.[5] This suggestion was implemented in the FY 1969 budget, as were many other Commission recommendations.

Probably the most significant Commission recommendation *not* implemented to date is that calling for budget expenditures and receipts (including revenues) to be reported on the accrual basis instead of the checks-issued and collections-received bases now used. The Bureau of the Budget (now OMB) and the Treasury Department issued instructions to the executive agencies for implementing this recommendation, the GAO *Manual* was revised accordingly, and agencies began submitting "trial run" statements to the Treasury Department on the accrual basis in July 1968. Significant problems were encountered with several aspects of accrual measurement, particularly the measurement of contract construction and intergovernmental grant expenditures on a "constructive receipt" basis and the accrual of personal taxes.

Implementation of the accrual basis was postponed on several occasions as the OMB, the Treasury Department and the Comptroller General studied the problems encountered in the tests underway and the reliability of the data being gathered. In July 1971 they requested the Central Agency Steering Committee on Implementation of the Recommendations of the President's Commission on Budget Concepts to study the direction and timing of the implementation of accrual budgeting and budgetary reporting in the Federal Government.[6] Following the September 1971 report of the Steering Committee, the OMB Director advised the Comptroller General (in May 1972) that conversion of the budget to the accrual basis was being deferred indefinitely. Several other recommendations of the President's Commission on Budget Concepts also continue under study, including those to the effect that budget information available to Congress and the public should be (1) more detailed, that is, aggregate figures should be broken into quarterly or semi-annual data, and (2) more comprehensive, by including estimates extending further into the future.

## ACCOUNTING PRINCIPLES AND STANDARDS
## FOR FEDERAL AGENCIES

The accounting principles and standards for Federal agencies prescribed by the Comptroller General are contained in Chapter 2, "Accounting Principles And Standards," of Title 2—"Accounting," of the *GAO Manual For*

[5] These were (1) the "administrative budget," which excluded the Trust funds; (2) the "consolidated cash statement (budget)," which included all funds but was on a checks-paid basis; and (3) the Federal sector of the national income and product accounts, which constituted a third "budget" concept.

[6] Federal agencies have for many years been required by law to adopt accrual accounting. The extent to which they do so varies significantly, however, and some agencies have made little progress toward achieving reliable accrual accounting data.

*Guidance of Federal Agencies.* A portion of Title 2 is published separately as *Accounting Principles And Standards For Federal Agencies* (revised 1972). Selected major aspects of these principles and standards are discussed below.

### Purposes and Objectives

The fundamental purposes underlying Federal agency accounting are:

To provide information necessary for effective and economical management of its operations and the resources entrusted to it. (Managerial Control)

To enable the management to report on the discharge of its responsibilities for the resources and operations for which it is accountable. (Accountability)

This dual purpose necessitates a system of accounting and related records providing reliable and auditable information on the agency's resources, liabilities and obligations, expenditures, revenues, and costs (expired) for information and control uses by internal agency managers, other agencies and authorities having control responsibilities, the Congress, and the public.

The objectives of Federal agency accounting set forth in the Budget and Accounting Procedures Act of 1950 are:

Full disclosure of the financial results of agency activities.

Production of adequate financial information needed for agency management purposes.

Effective control over and accountability for all funds, property, and other assets for which each agency is responsible.

Reliable accounting reports to serve as the basis for preparation and support of agency budget requests, for controlling the execution of budgets, and for providing financial information required by OMB.

Suitable integration of agency accounting with the central accounting and reporting operations of the Treasury Department.

Proper accounting is an inherent responsibility of agency management. Though the agency head may delegate the authority for accounting systems design and operation, he must bear the ultimate responsibility for the systems. Thus, he should assure himself that:

A proper accounting system is established based on the accounting principles and standards prescribed by the Comptroller General.

The information provided by the accounting system lends itself to effective use.

The information is used by responsible agency officials in programming the agency's activities, in preparing budget data, and in achieving and maintaining an acceptable level of operational economy and efficiency.

## Standards for Internal Management Control

Among the more important objectives of an agency's internal management control system are:

To promote efficiency and economy of operations.

To restrict obligations and costs to a minimum, consistent with efficiently and effectively carrying out the agency's purposes, within the limits of congressional appropriations and other authorizations and restrictions.

To safeguard assets against waste, loss and improper or unwarranted use.

To assure that all agency revenues are properly accounted for and collected.

To assure the accuracy and reliability of financial, statistical, and other reports.

Twelve standards for internal management control are prescribed by the Comptroller General:

1. *Policies.* Agency management policies adopted should be clearly stated, systematically communicated throughout the organization, consistent with applicable laws or other external regulations and policies, and designed to promote effective, efficient and economical operations.

2. *Organization.* The organizational structure should be carefully planned and lines of authority and responsibility for agency activity performance should be clearly identified.

3. *Segregation of Duties and Functions.* Internal checks on performance and to minimize the possibility of irregular acts should be provided by segregating duties as among authorization, performance, recordkeeping, custody of resources, and review.

4. *Planning.* An effective agency-wide planning system should be established in order to determine and justify resource needs and to facilitate effective, efficient and economical operation.

5. *Procedures.* Procedures adopted to carry out agency operations should be as simple, efficient, and practicable as circumstances permit.

6. *Authorization and Record Procedures.* An adequate system of authorization and record procedures must be implemented to promote compliance with prescribed requirements and restrictions of applicable laws, regulations, and internal management policies; to prevent illegal or unauthorized transactions or acts; and to provide proper accounting records of the assets, liabilities and obligations, receipts and revenues, expenditures, costs (expired), and appropriations for which the agency is responsible.

7. *Information System.* Essential operating and financial data should be provided through an adequate, reliable and efficiently operated agency information system.

8. *Supervision and Review.* The performance of all duties and functions should be properly supervised and subject to review through an effective internal audit activity.

9. *Qualifications of Personnel.* Education, training, experience, competence, integrity, and other qualifications of personnel must be appropriate for the responsibilities assigned.

10. *Personal Accountability.* Each official and employee must be fully aware of his assigned responsibilities and understand the nature and consequences of his performance. Each must be held fully accountable for the faithful, honest, and efficient discharge of his duties and functions.

11. *Expenditure Control.* Expenditure control procedures must be devised to assure that needed goods and services are acquired at the lowest possible cost, that those paid for are actually received and are in consonance with the agreements under which they are acquired, that acquisitions are consistent with legal and other authorizations or policies, and that resources are used effectively.

12. *Safeguarding of Resources.* All resources for which the agency is responsible must be appropriately safeguarded to prevent misuse, waste, deterioration, destruction or misappropriation.

### Standards for Accounting Systems

Agency accounting systems must not only assist in demonstrating compliance with statutory requirements, including the principles and standards set forth by the Comptroller General, but must fulfill the needs of Congress, of higher level executive agencies such as the OMB and the Treasury Department, and of agency managers. Thus, an agency's accounting system must meet all recurring internal and external needs for cost and other financial data for planning, programming, budgeting, control and reporting. Stated differently, the accounting system must provide not only the basis for control over funds, property, and other assets, but must provide an accurate and reliable basis for developing and reporting costs of performance in accordance with (a) major organizational segments, (b) budget activities, and (c) the PPB program structure adopted by the agency.

Several other broad accounting system principles or standards also are prescribed:

1. *Usefulness.* The financial data produced by the system should be useful. It must be promptly presented and clearly reported so that its significance is understood by both internal and external users.

2. *Accounting for Responsibilities.* The system should be designed so that major assignments of responsibility can be reported on readily.

3. *Consistency of Account Classifications.* Planning, programming, budgeting, and accounting classifications should be consistent with each other and synchronized with the agency's organization structure to the extent practicable.

4. *Technical Requirements.* The system should provide complete and reliable records of the resources and operations of the agency entity. The records

should embrace all agency assets, as well as its liabilities and obligations, receipts and revenues, expenditures, and costs (expenses). Financial transactions should be adequately supported by pertinent documents available for audit. Furthermore, interfund and interagency transactions and balances should be separately identified in agency records and statements to facilitate the preparation of consolidated financial reports for the Government.

5. *Qualified Personnel.* Agency officials are entitled to and should demand a high degree of technical competence in selecting and retaining top accounting personnel.

6. *Truthfulness and Honesty.* The highest standards of truthfulness and honesty should be applied in agency accounting. Accordingly, financial transactions should not be recorded in a manner that will produce materially inaccurate, false or misleading information.

7. *Simplicity.* Accounting procedures should be as simple and understandable as practicable. Excessive details and unnecessary refinements in the accounting records should be avoided.

8. *Accuracy, Reliability, and Materiality.* In determining the degree of precision to be sought in making allocations of cost (expense) or revenues, or in computing other items where judgements and estimates are employed, the materiality and relative significance of the items involved should be considered carefully. Meticulous procedures which do not produce materially more accurate results or provide other offsetting benefits should be avoided.

9. *Updating Needed.* Agency accounting systems should be (a) reviewed from time to time to assure that they continue to meet the test of usefulness to users and (b) modified as appropriate in light of changing circumstances.

## The Accrual Basis of Accounting

Federal agencies are required by law to maintain accounts on the accrual basis. Appropriate records on obligations incurred and liquidated must be kept to provide information to assist in expenditure control and disbursement planning and for reporting on the status of appropriations and funds. Agency accounting systems that provide information primarily in terms of obligations (encumbrances) and disbursements are incomplete if they cannot also produce the data needed to properly disclose information on financial and property resources, liabilities, revenues and expenditures, and costs (expenses) of operations by major areas of responsibility and activity.[7]

A Federal agency's accounting system therefore must include data on "obligations" (encumbrances), "accrued expenditures" (expenditures), "applied costs" (expenses) and cash disbursements—not one or the other. This is sum-

[7] The accrual basis may be followed in day-to-day accounting procedures or the system may be maintained on a cash or obligation basis and converted to the accrual basis periodically (at least monthly) prior to statement preparation.

marized succinctly in Figure 19-7, in which the purchase of materials serves as an example.

Figure 19-7

### TIMING OF THE RECORDING OF PURCHASE OF MATERIALS UNDER ACCRUAL METHOD OF ACCOUNTING

| | *Recorded in Accounting Records in Month in Which* | | | |
|---|---|---|---|---|
| *Transaction* | *Order Is Placed* | *Materials Are Delivered* | *Materials Are Used* | *Bill Is Paid* |
| Placing an order for materials | As an *obligation* | | | |
| Materials delivered | | As an *accrued expenditure* | | |
| Materials used or consumed | | | As an *applied cost* | |
| Payment made for materials | | | | As a *disbursement* of cash |

Source: U. S. General Accounting Office, *Frequently Asked Questions about Accrual Accounting in the Federal Government,* 1970, p. 5.

### Fund Control

"Fund control" refers to management control over the use of fund authorizations to assure that (1) funds are used only for authorized purposes, (2) they are used economically and effectively, and (3) obligations and disbursements do not exceed the amounts authorized. The last of these is important not only because of constitutional requirements related to disbursements and the fact that Congressional appropriations are in terms of obligational authority, but also to assure compliance with the Antideficiency Act—which forbids incurring obligations or making disbursements which would create deficiencies in appropriations and funds. Thus, each agency accounting system must record its appropriations and other authorizations, apportionments, and allotments—as well as its related obligations, expenditures, and disbursements.

## Accounting Entity and Account Structure

Federal agency accounting entities may be the entire agency, subdivisions thereof, or one or more legally established funds. The preferred entity and account structure is one in which accounts relating to all sources of funds used to finance agency activities are incorporated into a single, integrated accounting system. Thus, while fund entities are of paramount importance at the central accounting level, the agency or subunit is normally the primary accounting entity at the agency level—and fund detail is maintained within that accounting entity. The basic structure of a Federal agency's accounts usually is:

| Balance Sheet Accounts | Assets Liabilities Investment of the U. S. Government |
| Temporary Accounts | Revenues Costs (expenses) Budgetary accounts |

The accounting equation and the basic accounting procedures of a typical agency are illustrated both graphically and by a case example later in this chapter.

ASSETS.  For the most part, the principles and standards of asset accounting set forth by the Comptroller General relate to standard intermediate accounting topics such as cash, receivables, and property—including determination of the cost of property upon acquisition, treatment of purchase discounts as deductions from cost rather than as revenue, accounting for materials on a consumption basis rather than on a purchase basis, and the need for taking inventory periodically. Two points deserve special mention, however.

The first relates to the Cash accounts. Since the Treasury Department disburses cash for most Federal agencies, agency Cash accounts (Fund Balances with U. S. Treasury) are segregated by fund and appropriation. As will be explained later, this is a principal manner in which fund control is exercised in the accounts; and the Cash accounts (other than Petty Cash and Cash on Hand) offset the budgetary accounts in the agency ledger.

Second, though the Comptroller General stops short of requiring depreciation accounting in all agencies and in all situations, depreciation accounting is clearly encouraged. Specifically, the *Principles and Standards* document states:

A basic responsibility of agency management is to fully and fairly account for all resources entrusted to or acquired by the agency. This responsibility extends to the consumption of those resources through use in carrying out operations and is just as applicable to long-lived physical facilities as it is to expendable materials.

Although depreciation is not represented by current expeditures of funds, and although there is no precise way to arrive at an accurate measure of depreciation as a current cost, it is nonetheless a real cost.[8]

At the same time, it is stated that:

...the activities carried on in the Federal Government are so varied in nature that a uniform requirement to account for depreciation of capital assets cannot be justified.

Procedures shall be adopted by each agency to account for depreciation... whenever a need arises for periodic determination of the cost of all resources consumed in performing services. This information is needed when:

1. The financial results of operations in terms of costs of performance in relation to revenue earned, if any, are to be fully disclosed in financial reports.

2. Amounts to be collected in reimbursement for services performed are to be determined on the basis of the full cost of performance pursuant to legal requirements or administrative policy.

3. Investment in fixed assets used is substantial and there is a need to assemble total costs to assist management and other officials in making comparisons, evaluating performance, and devising future plans.

4. Total cost of property constructed by an agency is needed to determine the amount to be capitalized.[9]

The Comptroller General's emphasis on the need for cost information (discussed below) would seem to require depreciation accounting in most situations.

LIABILITIES.   Principles and standards relating to agency liability accounting include requirements that (1) liabilities incurred be accounted for and reported irrespective of whether funds are available or authorized for their payment, and (2) the accounting system provide for separate identification of funded and unfunded liabilities. Other topics covered in the GAO *Manual* include the need to disclose all contingent liabilities; the necessity in accounting for Federal insurance, pension and similar programs requiring actuarial basis measurement to disclose the current costs of such programs as they accrue and the estimated liabilities accrued at the reporting date, irrespective of the degree to which funds have been appropriated or otherwise obtained for such payments; the requirement that real property acquired under lease-purchase contracts be recorded as an asset (and a correponding liability be established) upon acceptance of the property; the need to account for liabilities under construction or other contracts on a "constructive receipt" basis rather than only upon project comple-

---

[8] The Comptroller General of the United States, *Accounting Principles and Standards for Federal Agencies, 1972 (Revision),* (USGPO, 1972), p. 37.

[9] *Ibid.,* pp. 37–38.

tion or cash disbursement; and accounting for Working Fund advances and employee leave costs.

INVESTMENT OF THE U. S. GOVERNMENT.  The Investment of the U. S. Government represents the residual equity of the Federal Government in the agency. The major causes of change in this account are:

Additions:
  Congressional appropriations
  Property and services obtained from other Federal agencies without reimbursement
  Certain borrowings from the U. S. Treasury
  Net income from operations

Reductions:
  Funds returned to the U. S. Treasury
  Property transferred to other Federal agencies without reimbursement
  Net loss from operations

Broadly speaking, the Investment of the U. S. Government includes all unobligated appropriations, obligations, expenditures, revenues and reimbursements —that is, the budgetary and operating accounts may be viewed as subsets or subsidiary to this account. Alternatively, the temporary budgetary accounts may be viewed as a separate subgroup, since only the net income and appropriation expenditures are closed to the Invested Capital account, and the Federal agency accounting equation may be visualized as shown in Figure 19-8.

REVENUES.  The discussion of the nature, control, use of the accrual basis of accounting, and reporting of revenues in the *Manual* is similar to that commonly found in intermediate accounting texts. It is important to note that appropriations are *not* considered revenues (but are considered to be capital contributions when expended). Rather, the term refers to agency operating revenues such as from billings for services and to gains upon property disposal.

COSTS (EXPENSES).  The term "cost" is defined as the financial measure of *resources consumed* in accomplishing a specified purpose, carrying out an activity, or completing a unit of work or a specific project. This topic is covered extensively in the *Principles and Standards* document and would seem especially relevant in view of the audit standards issued by the Comptroller General (Chapter 18). Further, Public Law 84-863 requires Federal agencies to install accounting systems that produce appropriate data on the cost of operations.

The importance attributed to cost accounting and cost finding by the Comptroller General is indicated by the following excerpts from the *Principles and Standards* document:

Cost information provides a common financial denominator for the measurement and evaluation of efficiency and economy in terms of resources used in performance.

The production and reporting of significant cost information are essential ingredients of effective financial management. Such information must be available to agency management officials, the Office of Management and Budget, and the Congress for devising and approving realistic future financial plans (budgeting). It is needed in making meaningful comparisons and in keeping costs within limits established by law, regulation, or agency management policies.

Every expenditure should be conceived as a cost of some essential, planned activity. Because costs furnish important measures of performance, they deserve the unremitting attention of management officials.

Efficient use of resources is a management responsibility. The use of cost information to achieve this objective places positive emphasis on the receipt of value for resources used. In turn, this emphasis results in giving greater prominence to cost aspects in the planning of operations as opposed to placing exclusive emphasis on not exceeding budgetary authorizations with a resulting lack of emphasis on value received.[10]

Cost accounting or cost finding systems of Federal agencies should provide for accumulation of cost information by: (1) major organizational segments, (2) budget activities, and (3) the PPB structure of the agency. In order to facilitate cost (expense) determination, expenditures should be categorized according to whether they pertain to current expenses or the acquisition of assets and by object, e.g., labor, materials, and contractor services.

### Financial Reporting

Although agency managers determine the internal reports needed, four basic financial reports are required of all Federal agencies: (1) Statement of Assets and Liabilities (Balance Sheet), (2) Statement of Operations, (3) Statement of Sources and Application of Funds, and (4) Statement of Changes in the Investment of the United States. These and other statements are illustrated in the final section of this chapter. Furthermore, agencies must report on the status of all appropriations or other authorizations, separate statements should be prepared for each fund, and the agencies must prepare any other financial reports required by the Congress, its committees, or the central agencies. Combined or consolidated statements should be prepared where they will throw further light on the financial condition or financial operations of the agency.

Reporting standards prescribed relate to (1) Fairness of Presentation, (2) Compliance with Prescribed Requirements, (3) Timeliness, and (4) Usefulness.

---

10 *Accounting Principles and Standards for Federal Agencies,* pp. 46–47.

The standards relating to *fairness* of presentation may be summarized as follows:

1. *Completeness and Clarity.* All essential facts are to be included and disclosed adequately.
2. *Accuracy, Reliability and Truthfulness.* Not only should reports be accurate, reliable and truthful, but all appropriate steps should be taken to avoid bias, obscurement of significant facts, and presentation of misleading information.
3. *Accounting Support.* The financial reports are assumed to be supported in the accounts unless other data sources are disclosed and explained.
4. *Excluded Costs.* The exclusion of any significant costs should be explained in the notes to the statement.
5. *Form, Content, and Arrangement.* This shall be as simple as possible and emphasize communication of significant information to report users.
6. *Extent of Detail.* While detail should be sufficient to provide a clear and complete report, unnecessary detail should be avoided—especially where its inclusion obscures significant financial data.
7. *Performance Under Limitations.* Financial performance should be reported in relation to statutory or other limitations prescribed by higher authorities, particularly where these affect operational economy, efficiency, or effectiveness.
8. *Consistency.* Data reported is assumed to be based on accounting records maintained on a consistent basis unless material changes in accounting policies and methods are disclosed and their effects are explained.
9. *Terminology.* This should be consistent and nontechnical.

The *compliance* standard states that reports must comply with (1) applicable laws and regulations relative to the nature, accounting basis, content, frequency, and distribution of reports, and (2) applicable restrictions pertaining to information that is classified for national security purposes. The *timeliness* standard requires that reports be produced promptly in order to be of maximum usefulness, while the *usefulness* standard calls for reports to be carefully designed with an eye to their usefulness and suggests that unnecessary reports be abolished.

## FEDERAL AGENCY ACCOUNTING AND REPORTING ILLUSTRATED

This concluding section of the chapter is comprised of: (1) an overview of the Federal agency accounting equation and the usual account and ledger relationships, (2) a case illustration of Federal agency accounting, and (3) illustrative agency financial statements. Although specific methods of accounting vary among agencies, as do their functions and financing methods, the approach illustrated is fairly typical and serves to highlight the major aspects of Federal agency accounting and reporting.

### Overview of the Federal Agency Accounting Equation

Figure 19-8 contains a graphic illustration of the accounting equation and the usual account and ledger relationships of a Federal agency financed through General Fund appropriations and billings for services rendered. Observe that (1) The accounting equation may be expressed as "Assets = Liabilities + Investment of the United States Government", (2) The equity section, the Investment of the United States Government, is subdivided into Invested Capital and Unexpended Appropriations subsections. The former is proprietary in nature, whereas the latter is budgetary, (3) The budgetary account credit balances are offset by the Fund Balance with U. S. Treasury and Estimated Appropriation Reimbursements (estimated operating revenues) accounts initially. Subsequently they are offset by these accounts and the Reimbursements to Appropriations (actual operating revenues) account; (4) Revenues and Expenses (Applied Costs) are accounted for, as well as Expended Appropriations (Accrued Expenditures)—which is viewed as both an expenditure and a capital increment account. Other capital increments and decrements also are accounted for separately from Revenues and Expenses. Thus, the typical Federal agency accounting system is a dual system in which (1) budgetary and proprietary accounting are accomplished simultaneously, and (2) the distinction between capital transactions, including appropriation expenditures, and current revenues and expenses is maintained.

The illustration in Figure 19-8 is rather comprehensive. It warrants careful study and should be reviewed from time to time in conjunction with the case example and the illustrative financial statements that follow.

### A Case Illustration[11]

In order to illustrate the principal aspects of Federal agency accounting, let us assume that (1) a newly created agency began its first year of operations on July 1, 19X0, concluding it on June 30, 19X1, and (2) its activities are financed through a single General Fund appropriation and reimbursements for services rendered. To simplify the illustration, we also (1) assume that general ledger control accounts similar to those in Figure 19-8 are employed, (2) limit our presentation to general ledger entries, and (3) in order to demonstrate the entire cycle, make summary entries where similar transactions typically recur throughout the year.

DESCRIPTION OF THE AGENCY.    The agency's primary function is rendering ser-

11 This case illustration is adapted from that presented in Chapter 8000, Title 2, of the *GAO Manual for the Guidance of Federal Agencies*.

vices to other agencies. Reimbursements received or accrued are available to the agency without further appropriation and are thus credited to its appropriation accounts. The agency renders personal services for the most part, but also acquires and uses materials and equipment; it has no field offices. Reimbursable expenses are billed to user agencies monthly on the basis of direct labor and materials costs incurred and estimated overhead (based on a predetermined percentage of direct cost).

The agency maintains both a general accounting system and a job-order (work order) cost accounting system. A perpetual inventory system is employed, as is the accrual basis of accounting. The Allotment-Expenditure subsidiary ledger format typically used is shown in Figure 19-9.

ILLUSTRATIVE TRANSACTIONS AND ENTRIES. Most of the remainder of this chapter is devoted to the presentation of a series of selected illustrative transactions or events and the entries made to record their effects. A columnar worksheet summarizing the case illustration entries is presented in Figure 19-10. This worksheet, together with the illustrative entries and Figures 19-8 and 19-9, presents a concise summary of the major aspects of accounting for a typical Federal service agency.

*Summary of Transactions and Events*

1. Congress appropriated $175,000 from the General Fund to finance the agency during the fiscal year; in addition, appropriation reimbursements from charges for services to be rendered during the year are estimated at $40,000.
2. The OMB apportioned $170,000 of the Congressional appropriation, reserving $5,000 for possible cost savings and contingencies.
3. Administrative allotments were made by agency management as follows:

| | |
|---|---:|
| 1st quarter | $ 55,000 |
| 2nd quarter | 58,000 |
| 3rd quarter | 44,000 |
| 4th quarter | 50,000 |
| | $207,000 |

4. Purchase orders were placed for materials estimated to cost $37,000.
5. Materials estimated to cost $30,000 were received; the invoice was for $30,500.
6. Materials costing $25,000 were used by the agency.
7. A one year insurance policy was purchased at mid-year at a cost of $200.
8. Travel advances made to agency employees totaled $1,000.
9. An employee submitted an expense report for $300, of which $200 was covered by travel advances; he is to be reimbursed for the remaining $100.

# Figure 19-8

## AN OVERVIEW OF THE FEDERAL AGENCY ACCOUNTING EQUATION AND ACCOUNT/LEDGER RELATIONSHIPS

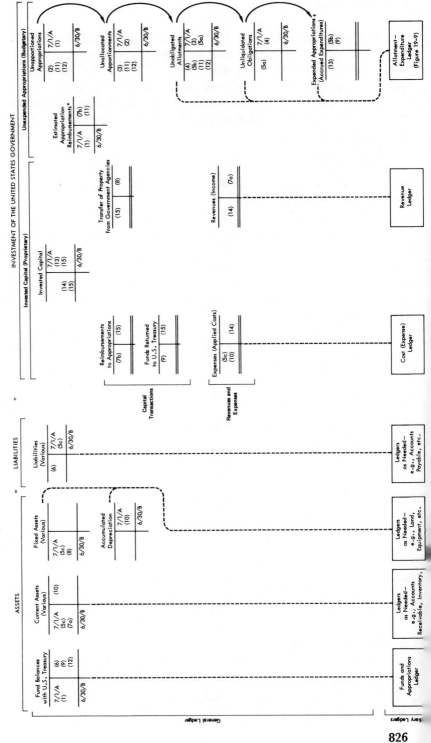

**Figure 19-8 Note**

&ast; This account may be considered an asset (or "assets and other debits") account rather than a budgetary account.

† This account is more properly classified under "capital transactions"; it is shown in the "Unexpended Appropriations" section here to better illustrate Federal agency budgetary accounting.

*Legend:*

7/1/A—Beginning-of-period balances

*Budgetary and Operating*

1. Unapportioned Appropriations enacted by Congress and Estimated Appropriation Reimbursements (estimated agency operating revenues) are established in the accounts.

2. Appropriations are apportioned to Agency by OMB.

3. Apportioned appropriations are allotted (usually by months or quarters) to Agency programs, field offices, etc. by Agency top management.

4. Allotted appropriations are obligated (encumbered) for goods or services ordered or other commitments made.

5. Goods or services are received or other expenditures are made: (a) Obligation entry is reversed; (b) the Expended Appropriations (Accrued Expenditures) are recorded and Unobligated Allotments is reduced accordingly; and (c) the related assets or expenses and liabilities are established in the accounts.

6. Liabilities are paid through Treasury disbursement officer.

7. Revenues usable by the Agency without the need for further Congressional action are received or accrued: (a) Asset (Cash or receivable) and revenue are recorded, and (b) The Reimbursements to Appropriations and reductions in Estimated Appropriation Reimbursements yet to be received or accrued are reflected. [Note: The debit in Reimbursements to Appropriations will be closed to Invested Capital to offset the credit to that account upon the Expended Appropriations account being credited thereto in closing—in order that only the expended Congressional appropriations serve to increase the Invested Capital Account. See entry 15 below.]

*Capital Transactions*

8. Fixed assets are transferred to the Agency from another Agency at no cost to the recipient Agency. [This would be reflected as Transfers of Property To Government Agencies on the books of the transferor Agency.]

9. Cash in excess of the Agency's needs was released to the Treasury for other uses. (This constitutes a U. S. Government *disinvestment* in this Agency.)

*Adjusting Entries*

10. Depreciation and other asset consumption charges are recorded as Expenses (Applied Costs).

11. Estimated Appropriation Reimbursements is adjusted to the balance properly carried forward to the succeeding year and corresponding adjustments are made to the Unapportioned Appropriations, Unallocated Apportionments and Unobligated Allotments accounts.

12. Unobligated appropriations that lapse at year end are recorded as reductions of the Fund Balances with U. S. Treasury, Unapportioned Appropriations, Unallocated Apportionments and Unobligated Allotments.

*Closing Entries*

13. Expended Appropriations (Accrued Expenditures) for the period are closed to Invested Capital to reflect the additional investment by the U. S. Government in the Agency financed through appropriations.

14. Agency Expenses, net of Revenues (Income) from Agency operations, are closed to Invested Capital at year end.

15. Other Invested Capital increment and decrement accounts are closed at period end.

6/30/B—Balances at period end, after closing.

## Figure 19-9

FEDERAL AGENCY ALLOTMENT—EXPENDITURE LEDGER FORMAT

ALLOTMENT—EXPENDITURE LEDGER

Allotment Class/Code _____
Division or Activity _____
Apportioned Appropriation _____

Allotments: 1st Quarter _____
2nd Quarter _____
3rd Quarter _____
4th Quarter _____

| Date | Explanation | Document Reference | Object Code | Accrued Expenditures | Obligations | | Allotments | Unobligated Allotments |
| | | | | | Liquidated | Incurred | | |
|------|-------------|--------------------|-------------|----------------------|-------------|----------|------------|------------------------|
| | | | | | | | | |

10. Overhead expenses of $26,450 were incurred, of which $1,330 is payable to other Federal Government agencies.

11. Equipment estimated to cost $10,200 was ordered.

12. The equipment arrived, together with an invoice for $10,000.

13. Equipment was transferred from another Federal Government agency at no cost to this (recipient) agency. The equipment had originally cost $5,750 and accumulated depreciation of $750 had been recorded on the transferor agency's books.

14. Equipment that originally cost $1,000, on which accumulated depreciation of $100 had been recorded, was sold for $950 cash.

15. The proceeds of the equipment sale were transferred to the U. S. Treasury.

16. The agency's liability for employees annual leave accrued during the year amounted to $9,600.

17. Direct labor costs incurred during the year totaled $108,000. Withholdings that must be matched by the agency amounted to $10,150; income taxes withheld were $19,000; and employee leave taken amounted to $8,100.

18. Agency billings for services rendered to other Federal agencies were $39,000.

19. Accounts receivable collected during the period totaled $36,500.

20. Collections of receivables were deposited intact with the U. S. Treasury.

21. Vouchers scheduled for payment by the depository during the year were as follows: To Government agencies, $37,780; To others, $152,220.

22. Depreciation of agency equipment during the year was estimated at $1,500.

23. Direct salary costs of $4,000 were accrued at year end; the physical inventory was in agreement with the perpetual records.

24. Deposits with the U. S. Treasury in the amount of $1,500 had not been confirmed by the depository to the agency at period end, nor had payments of $800 of vouchers scheduled for payment.

25. Unobligated appropriations lapse at year end; all reimbursable costs have been billed and no further appropriation reimbursements are expected to result from this year's activities.

26. Closing entries were prepared at period end.

*Entries*

| 1. | Fund Balances with U. S. Treasury | 175,000 | |
|---|---|---|---|
| | Estimated Appropriation Reimbursements | 40,000 | |
| | Unapportioned Appropriations | | 175,000 |
| | Unallocated Apportionments | | 40,000 |
| | To record appropriation and estimated appropriation reimbursements. | | |

(Were the $40,000 Estimated Appropriation Reimbursements subject to OMB apportionment, the entire $215,000 would be credited to Unapportioned Appropriations.)

Figure 19-10

# ILLUSTRATIVE FEDERAL AGENCY
## Worksheet for the Fiscal Year Ended June 30, 19X1

| | Transactions | | Adjustments | | Closing Entries (Changes in Invested Capital of U.S. Government)* | | Balance Sheet | |
|---|---|---|---|---|---|---|---|---|
| | Dr. | Cr. | Dr. | Cr. | Dr. | Cr. | Dr. | Cr. |
| Fund Balances with U.S. Treasury | 175,000(1)<br>36,500(20) | 1,000(8)<br>190,000(21) | | 700(24)<br>9,300(25) | | | 10,500 | |
| Estimated Appropriation Reimbursements | 40,000(1) | 39,000(18b) | 5,000(25) | 1,000(25) | | | | |
| Unapportioned Appropriations | 170,000(2) | 175,000(1) | | | | | | |
| Unallocated Apportionments | 207,000(3) | 40,000(1)<br>170,000(2) | 3,000(25) | | | | | |
| Unobligated Allotments | 37,000(4)<br>30,500(5c)<br>200(7b)<br>300(9b)<br>26,450(10b)<br>10,200(11)<br>10,000(12c)<br>126,250(17b) | 207,000(3)<br>30,000(5b)<br>10,200(12b) | 4,000(23b)<br>2,300(25) | | | | | |
| Unliquidated Obligations* | 30,000(5b)<br>10,200(12b) | 37,000(4)<br>10,200(11) | | | | | | 7,000 |
| Expended Appropriations (Accrued Expenditures) | | 30,500(5c)<br>200(7b)<br>300(9b)<br>26,450(10b)<br>10,000(12c)<br>126,250(17b) | | 4,000(23b) | 197,700(26b) | | | |
| Inventories | 30,500(5a) | 25,000(b) | | | | | 5,500 | |

| Account | Dr | Cr | Dr | Cr | Dr | Cr | Dr | Cr |
|---|---|---|---|---|---|---|---|---|
| Direct Costs | 25,000(6); 108,000(17a); 100(7a); 300(9a); 26,450(10a); 9,600(16); 10,150(17a) | 200(7a); 100(9a); 25,120(10a); 10,000(12a); 86,950(17a) | 4,000(23a) | | 137,000(26a) | | | 100 |
| Prepaid Expenses | 100(7a) | | | | 48,100(26a) | | | |
| Overhead Expenses | 300(9a) | | 1,500(22) | | | | | 2,850 |
| Travel Advances | 1,000(8) | | | | | | | 2,150 |
| Accounts Payable—Federal | 37,780(21) | 200(9a); 1,330(10a); 39,300(17a) | | | | | 800 | |
| Equipment | 10,000(12a); 5,750(13) | 1,000(14) | | | 14,750 | | | 2,150 |
| Accumulated Depreciation—Equipment | 100(14) | 750(13) | | 1,500(22) | | | | |
| Transfer of Property from Government Agencies | 5,000(13) | | | | 5,000(26c) | | | |
| Undeposited Collections | 950(15); 36,500(20) | | | | 520(6a) | 950(26c) | | 1,500 |
| Other Income | 50(13) | | | | | | | |
| Funds Returned to U.S. Treasury | 950(15) | | | | | | | |
| Liability for Accrued Leave | 8,100(17a) | 9,600(16) | | | | 39,000(26b) | | 1,500 |
| Accounts Receivable—Federal | 39,000(18a) | 36,500(19) | | | 39,000(26a) | | 2,500 | |
| Billings for Services (Sales) | 39,000(18a) | | | | | 39,000(26b) | | |
| Reimbursements to Appropriations | 39,000(18b) | | 4,000(23a) | | | | | 4,000 |
| Accrued Liabilities | | | | 800(24) | | | | 800 |
| Deposits in Transit | | 1,500(24) | | | 146,050(26a) | 158,700(26b) | 1,500 | |
| Disbursements in Transit | | | | | | 4,050(26c) | | 16,700 |
| Invested Capital | | | | | | | | |
| | 1,451,150 | 1,451,150 | 21,300 | 21,300 | 387,800 | 387,800 | 35,650 | 35,650 |

* These columns may be titled "Investment of the U.S. Government" and the Unliquidated Obligations account (and any continuing appropriation accounts) closed thereto and reestablished in the accounts at the beginning of the succeeding period. The authors prefer to clearly separate the Invested Capital (proprietory) and Appropriation (budgetary) components of the "Investment of the U.S. Government" data category.

2.  Unapportioned Appropriations ............  170,000
        Unallocated Apportionments .........             170,000
    To record OMB apportionments of appro-
    priation.

3.  Unallocated Apportionments .............  207,000
        Unobligated Allotments .............             207,000
    To record allotment of apportioned appro-
    priations.

(This is a summary entry. In practice an entry would be made each quarter; the $207,000 is the total of the allotments made during the year.)

4.  Unobligated Allotments .................   37,000
        Unliquidated Obligations ............              37,000
    To record obligations outstanding for mate-
    rials on order.

(The Unliquidated Obligations account—sometimes called Unfilled Orders—is similar to the Encumbrances account used in municipal accounting.)

5.  (a)  Inventories ........................   30,500
            Accounts Payable—Nonfederal ....              30,500
         To record cost of materials purchased
         and the liability therefor.
    (b)  Unliquidated Obligations ............   30,000
            Unobligated Allotments .........              30,000
         To reverse estimated obligations pre-
         viously recorded.
    (c)  Unobligated Allotments .............   30,500
            Expended Appropriations (or
                Accrued Expenditures) ........              30,500
         To charge allotment with cost of mate-
         rials purchased.

(Entries b and c may be combined as follows:

Unliquidated Obligations ............   30,000
Unobligated Allotments .............      500
    Expended Appropriations (or
        Accrued Expenditures) ........              30,500
    To record the expenditure for mate-
    rials, remove the obligation previously
    recorded, and reduce the allotment by
    the excess of actual materials cost over
    that estimated.

Similarly, had the order cost less than estimated, the Unobligated Allotments account would be credited for the difference between estimated and actual cost.)

6.  Direct Costs ............................. 25,000
       Inventories ......................... 25,000
       To record direct materials used.

7.  (a)  Prepaid Expenses ................... 100
         Overhead Expenses ................. 100
            Accounts Payable—Nonfederal .... 200
            To record liability for insurance policy
            acquired.

(Alternatively, the entire $200 might be set up as Prepaid Expense and an adjusting entry made at period end for the portion consumed.)

    (b)  Unobligated Allotments .............. 200
            Expended Appropriations (or
            Accrued Expenditures) .......... 200
            To charge allotment with the cost of insurance acquired.

8.  Travel Advances ........................ 1,000
       Fund Balances with U. S. Treasury .... 1,000
       To record travel advances to employees.

9.  (a)  Overhead Expenses .................. 300
            Travel Advances ................ 200
            Accounts Payable—Nonfederal .... 100
            To record travel expenses, reduction of
            travel advances and liability for expenses not advanced previously.
    (b)  Unobligated Allotments .............. 300
            Expended Appropriations (or
            Accrued Expenditures) ......... 300
            To charge the allotment with travel expenses incurred.

10. (a)  Overhead Expenses .................. 26,450
            Accounts Payable—Federal ....... 1,330
            Accounts Payable—Nonfederal .... 25,120
            To record overhead expenses incurred.

(Federal agencies separate Federal and nonfederal payables and receivables to assist in the preparation of consolidated reports.)

    (b)  Unobligated Allotments .............. 26,450
            Expended Appropriations (or
            Accrued Expenditures) ......... 26,450
            To charge allotment with overhead expenses incurred.

11. Unobligated Allotments .................. 10,200
       Unliquidated Obligations ............ 10,200
       To record obligation incurred for equipment ordered.

12. (a) Equipment .......................... 10,000
        Accounts Payable-Nonfederal .....           10,000
        To record acquisition of equipment.
    (b) Unliquidated obligations ............. 10,200
        Unobligated Allotments ..........           10,200
        To reverse estimated obligation record-
        ed when equipment was ordered.
    (c) Unobligated Allotments .............. 10,000
        Expended Appropriations (or
        Accrued Expenditures) .........           10,000
        To charge allotment for cost of equip-
        ment purchased.

(Alternatively, entries b and c may be combined, with the $200 excess of esti-
mated over actual costs being credited to Unobligated Allotments. See entry 5.)

13. Equipment ............................ 5,750
        Accumulated Depreciation—Equipment           750
        Transfers of Property from Government
        Agencies ........................         5,000
        To record transfer of equipment from an-
        other agency at book value.

14. Undeposited Collections................. 950
    Accumulated Depreciation—Equipment .... 100
        Equipment .......................         1,000
        Other Income ......................           50
        To record sale of equipment for more than
        book value.

15. Funds Returned to U. S. Treasury ......... 950
        Undeposited Collections..............           950
        To record transfer of equipment sale pro-
        ceeds to the prescribed miscellaneous re-
        ceipts account of the Treasury.

(Had the proceeds been needed to finance equipment replacement in the current
or succeeding year, they might have been retained by the agency. If this were
the case, the proceeds would be placed in a Deposit Fund of the Treasury and
the appropriate budgetary account credited. Here it is assumed that the proceeds were transferred to the Treasury for general Government use.)

16. Overhead Expenses...................... 9,600
        Liability for Accrued Leave ...........         9,600
        To charge accrued employee leave cost as an
        expense.

(Accrued employee leave costs are established as expenses and liabilities as
earned. During the payroll period in which the leave is taken, the liability is re-

duced by the amount of leave taken and the leave cost, together with other payroll costs, are charged against the allotment. See entry 17.)

17.  (a)  Direct Costs ........................        108,000
          Overhead Costs .....................         10,150
          Liability for Accrued Leave ..........          8,100
              Accounts Payable—Federal .......                        39,300
              Accounts Payable—Nonfederal ....                        86,950
              To record payroll and related costs and
              reduce the liability for employee leave
              by the amount taken during the pay-
              roll period.
      (b)  Unobligated Allotments ..............        126,250
              Expended Appropriations (or
                  Accrued Expenditures) ........                       126,250
              To charge the allotment with payroll
              and related expenditures.

18.  (a)  Accounts Receivable—Federal ........         39,000
              Billings for Services (or Sales) .....                    39,000
              To record billings for services ren-
              dered.
      (b)  Reimbursements to Appropriations.....         39,000
              Estimated Appropriation
                  Reimbursements .............                          39,000
              To record reimbursements to appro-
              priations resulting from billings for ser-
              vices and reduce the Estimated Appro-
              priations Reimbursements account by
              the amount of the actual reimburse-
              ments.

(The Estimated Appropriation Reimbursements account balance should reflect the amount estimated *yet* to be received. Had reimbursements arising from billings for services exceeded the estimate recorded at the beginning of the year— for example, had they amounted to $42,000—the entry would appear as follows:

      (a)  Accounts Receivable—Federal ........         42,000
              Billings for Services (or Sales) .....                    42,000
              To record billings for services.
      (b)  Reimbursements to Appropriations.....         42,000
              Estimated Appropriation
                  Reimbursements .............                          40,000
              Unallocated Apportionments .....                          2,500
              To record appropriation reimburse-
              ments, reduce the Estimated Appro-
              priation Reimbursements account to
              zero, and record the additional autho-
              rization arising upon actual reimburse-
              ments exceeding those estimated.

Note the additional appropriation recorded in this situation.)

19. Undeposited Collections.................     36,500
       Accounts Receivable—Federal .........                36,500
    To record collection of receivables.

20. Fund Balances with U. S. Treasury ........     36,500
       Undeposited Collections..............                36,500
    To record deposits with Treasury.

21. Accounts Payable—Federal ..............     37,780
    Accounts Payable—Nonfederal ...........    152,220
       Fund Balances with U. S. Treasury ....               190,000
    To record scheduling of vouchers for pay-
    ment by disbursing officer.

22. Overhead Expenses......................      1,500
       Accumulated Depreciation—Equipment                    1,500
    To record depreciation of equipment.

23. (a)  Direct Costs .......................      4,000
            Accrued Liabilities .............                 4,000
         To record accrued salaries.
    (b)  Unobligated Allotments .............      4,000
            Expended Appropriations (or
               Accrued Expenditures) .........               4,000
         To charge the allotment for accrued
         salaries.

24. Deposits in Transit......................      1,500
       Disbursements in Transit .............                   800
       Fund Balances with U. S. Treasury ....                  700
    To record deposits for which no depository
    confirmation has been received at period end
    and vouchers scheduled for payment for
    which payment notification has not been
    received at period end.

(Deposits in Transit and Disbursements in Transit, the latter being equivalent
to checks outstanding, are set up formally—rather than only in reconciliations—
at period end. This is done both for control purposes and to assist in the preparation of government-wide financial reports.)

25. Unapportioned Appropriations ...........      5,000
    Unallocated Apportionments .............      3,000
    Unobligated Allotments .................      6,300
       Estimated Appropriation
          Reimbursements ..................                   1,000
       Fund Balances with U. S. Treasury ....               13,300
    To record lapsed appropriations and reduce
    appropriations by the excess of estimated
    over actual reimbursements.

(It is assumed here that the appropriation is of the annual or one-year type.
Had any unobligated appropriations not lapsed, only the lapsed portions would
be canceled. Likewise, were further reimbursements expected from this period's

activity a portion or all of the Estimated Appropriation Reimbursements account would be carried forward to the succeeding period. Note that the Unliquidated Obligations account is carried forward as it serves as expenditure and disbursement authority during the two years following the year in which the obligations are incurred.)

26. (a) Invested Capital .................... 146,050
        Billings for Services (or Sales) ......... 39,000
        Other Income ..................... 50
            Direct Costs .................... 137,000
            Overhead Expenses ............. 48,100
        To close revenue and expense accounts
        and reduce Invested Capital by the
        excess of expenses over revenues.
    (b) Expended Appropriations (or Accrued
        Expenditures) .................... 197,700
        Reimbursements to
            Appropriations .............. 39,000
        Invested Capital ............... 158,700
        To close the expenditures and reim-
        bursements accounts and increase the
        Invested Capital account by the net
        additional investment of the U. S. Gov-
        ernment during the period that was
        financed through current appropria-
        tions.

(Observe that closing the Billings for Services account in entry 26 (a) increased the Invested Capital account by $39,000; the identical $39,000 balance in the Reimbursements to Appropriations account serves to avoid double counting this amount by causing the Invested Capital to be increased in entry 26 (b) only by those expenditures financed through current appropriations, exclusive of reimbursements.)

    (c) Transfers of Property from Government
        Agencies ....................... 5,000
        Funds Returned to U. S.
            Treasury .................... 950
        Invested Capital ............... 4,050
        To close other capital investment and
        disinvestment accounts and increase
        the Invested Capital account accord-
        ingly.

## Reporting

The principal financial statements prepared for Federal agencies, both on an interim basis and at year end, include the following:

1. Statement of Assets and Liabilities (Figure 19-11);
2. Statement of Changes in the Investment of the United States Government (Figure 19-12);

**Figure 19-11**

ILLUSTRATIVE FEDERAL AGENCY
Statement of Assets and Liabilities
June 30, 19X1

*Assets*

Current Assets:

| | | |
|---|---:|---:|
| Fund balances with U. S. Treasury | $10,500 | |
| Deposits in transit | 1,500 | |
| Accounts receivable—federal | 2,500 | |
| Travel advances | 800 | |
| Inventories | 5,500 | |
| Prepaid expenses | 100 | $20,900 |
| Fixed Assets: | | |
| Equipment | $14,750 | |
| Less: Accumulated depreciation | 2,150 | 12,600 |
| Total Assets | | $33,500 |

*Liabilities and Investment of
the United States Government*

Current Liabilities:

| | | |
|---|---:|---:|
| Disbursements in transit | $ 800 | |
| Accrued liabilities | 4,000 | |
| Accounts payable—nonfederal | 650 | |
| Accounts payable—federal | 2,850 | $ 8,300 |
| Other Liabilities: | | |
| Liability for accrued leave | | 1,500 |
| Total Liabilities | | $ 9,800 |
| Investment of the United States Government (Figure 19-12): | | |
| Invested capital | $16,700 | |
| Unexpended appropriations | 7,000 | 23,700 |
| Total Liabilities and Investment of the United States Government | | $33,500 |

3. Statement of Expenses (Figure 19-13);
4. Statement of Sources and Applications of Funds (Figure 19-14);
5. Statement of Status of Appropriations (Figure 19-15); and
6. Reconciliation of Program Costs with Obligations (Figure 19-16).

**Figure 19-12**

### ILLUSTRATIVE FEDERAL AGENCY
Statement of Changes in the Investment of
the United States Government
For the Fiscal Year Ended June 30, 19X1

| | | |
|---|---:|---:|
| Balance of Investment of the United States Government, July 1, 19X0...................... | | $ — |
| Add: | | |
| Appropriations*................................ | $175,000 | |
| Revenues (Figure 19-13).......................... | 39,050 | |
| Transfer of property from Government Agencies ...... | 5,000 | $219,050 |
| Less: | | |
| Expenses (Figure 19-13).......................... | $185,100 | |
| Funds returned to U. S. Treasury.................. | 950 | |
| Unobligated appropriations lapsing during the year ... | 9,300 | 195,350 |
| Balance of Investment of the United States Government, June 30, 19X1 ..................... | | $ 23,700 |
| Composed of: | | |
| Invested Capital............................... | $ 16,700 | |
| Unexpended appropriations: | | |
| Unapportioned appropriations† ........ $ — | | |
| Unallotted apportionments† ........... — | | |
| Unobligated allotments† .............. — | | |
| Unliquidated obligations ............. 7,000 | 7,000 | $ 23,700 |

\* Alternatively, the Expended Appropriations and Unliquidated Obligations balances may be added in lieu of adding total appropriations and deducting unobligated appropriations lapsing during the year.

† Accounts having zero balances normally are excluded from the financial statements. These accounts are shown here to illustrate how they would appear on interim statements and, if all unobligated appropriations do not lapse, at year end.

As noted earlier, the first four statements listed above are required of all agencies. The latter two are primarily for internal and intragovernmental use.

Except where a report or statement format is prescribed, agency managers have considerable latitude both as to the financial statements to be prepared for the agency and statement format. Thus, both the statements issued and the statement formats may vary somewhat from those illustrated here, and additional statements may be prepared to fulfill agency management purposes or requests of OMB, Treasury or Congress.

Figure 19-13

## ILLUSTRATIVE FEDERAL AGENCY
Statement of Expenses (Net)
For the Fiscal Year Ended June 30, 19X1

Expenses:

Direct Costs:

| | | |
|---|---:|---:|
| Direct labor | $112,000 | |
| Direct material | 25,000 | $137,000 |

Overhead expenses:

| | | |
|---|---:|---:|
| Salaries and wages | $ xx | |
| Heat, light and power | xx | |
| Rent | xx | |
| Printing | xx | |
| Travel | 300 | |
| Depreciation | 1,500 | |
| Annual leave | 9,600 | |
| etc. | xx | 48,100 |
| Total expenses | | $185,100 |

Revenues:

| | | |
|---|---:|---:|
| Billings for services | $ 39,000 | |
| Other income | 50 | |
| Total revenues | | 39,050 |
| Net expenses (or Excess of expenses over revenues) | | $146,050 |

**Question 19-1.** Governmental accounting is said to involve two fundamental objectives: managerial control and accountability. Explain.

**Question 19-2.** List the major types of data that a Federal agency accounting system should provide on a routine, recurring basis.

**Question 19-3.** Explain the meaning of the following terms in Federal accounting:
  a. Apportionment
  b. Reserves (by OMB)
  c. Allotment
  d. Obligation
  e. Accrued Expenditure
  f. Obligation Incurred
  g. Cost (or Applied cost)
  h. Reimbursements to Appropriations
  i. Fund Balance with U.S. Treasury

**Question 19-4.** Distinguish among and between the following: obligations, accrued expenditures, disbursements, and applied costs.

**Question 19-5.**
  a. List the Federal fund types.
  b. In a parallel column, list the types of municipal funds in a manner that "matches" the municipal funds to the Federal funds to the extent practicable.

Figure 19-14

ILLUSTRATIVE FEDERAL AGENCY

Statement of Sources and Applications of Funds

(Statement of Change in Financial Position—Working Capital Basis)

For the Fiscal Year Ended June 30, 19X1

Funds provided by:

| | | |
|---|---:|---:|
| Appropriation from Congress ............ | $175,000 | |
| Less: Appropriations lapsing during the year | 9,300 | $165,700 |
| Revenues—Billings for services ........... | | 39,000 |
| Sale of equipment ..................... | | 950 |
| Total funds provided ................. | | $205,650 |

Funds applied to:

Cost of current year's operations:

| | | | |
|---|---:|---:|---:|
| Expenses (Figure 19-13) .............. | | $185,100 | |
| Adjustments to derive working capital effect— | | | |
| Deduct: Depreciation ............. | $ 1,500 | | |
| Leave earned but not taken | 1,500 | 3,000 | |
| | | $182,100 | |
| Purchase of equipment ................. | | 10,000 | |
| Funds returned to U.S. Treasury......... | | 950 | |
| Total funds applied ................ | | | 193,050 |
| Increase in working capital ............... | | | $ 12,600 |

The Increase in Working Capital is Accounted

For As Follows:

| Current Assets: | 7/1/19X0 | 6/30/19X1 | Increase (Decrease) |
|---|---:|---:|---:|
| Fund balances with U.S. Treasury ... | $ — | $ 10,500 | $ 10,500 |
| Deposits in transit ................ | — | 1,500 | 1,500 |
| Accounts receivable—federal ........ | — | 2,500 | 2,500 |
| Travel advances .................. | — | 800 | 800 |
| Inventories ...................... | — | 5,500 | 5,500 |
| Prepaid expenses.................. | — | 100 | 100 |
| | $ — | $ 20,900 | $ 20,900 |
| Current Liabilities: | | | |
| Disbursements in transit ............ | — | 800 | 800 |
| Accrued liabilities ................ | — | 4,000 | 4,000 |
| Accounts payable—nonfederal ....... | — | 650 | 650 |
| Accounts payable—federal ......... | — | 2,850 | 2,850 |
| | $ — | $ 8,300 | $ 8,300 |
| Working capital ................... | $ — | $ 12,600 | $ 12,600 |

## ILLUSTRATIVE FEDERAL AGENCY    Figure 19-15
### Statement of Status of Appropriations
### June 30, 19X1

*Current Fiscal Year Appropriation*

| | | |
|---|---:|---:|
| Appropriation(s) .................................... | $175,000 | |
| Reimbursements .................................... | 39,000 | |
| Total appropriation and reimbursements ............. | | $214,000 |
| Less: Appropriations lapsing during the year .......... | | 9,300 |
| | | $204,700 |
| Less: Unexpended appropriation at June 30, 19X1: | | |
|     Unapportioned appropriations ................. | $ | |
|     Unallotted apportionments .................... | — | |
|     Unobligated allotments ...................... | — | |
|       Unobligated balance of appropriation ......... | $ — | |
|     Unliquidated obligations....................... | 7,000 | |
|       Unexpended balance of appropriation ......... | | 7,000 |
| Current Appropriation Expended (Accrued Expenditures) in the current fiscal year .......................... | | $197,700 |

*Prior Fiscal Years' Appropriations*

| | | |
|---|---:|---:|
| Unliquidated obligations, July 1, 19X0 .............. | $ — | |
| Less: Unliquidated obligations, June 30, 19X1 ....... | — | |
| Prior year appropriations expended in current fiscal year .. | | — |
| Total appropriation expended (accrued expenditures) .... | | $197,700 |

## ILLUSTRATIVE FEDERAL AGENCY    Figure 19-16
### Reconciliation of Program Costs with Obligations
### For the Fiscal Year Ended June 30, 19X1

| | | |
|---|---:|---:|
| Total expenses (Figure 19-13).......................... | | $185,100 |
| Equipment purchases ................................ | | 10,000 |
| **Total program costs (including capital outlays)** .... | | $195,100 |
| Less: Expenses not chargeable to current appropriation: | | |
|     Depreciation ................................ | $1,500 | |
|     Leave earned but not taken .................... | 1,500 | 3,000 |
| **Total adjusted program costs**...................... | | 192,100 |
| Add: Increase in inventories........................... | $5,500 | |
|     Increase in prepaid expenses .................... | 100 | 5,600 |
| **Accrued expenditures** (Figure 19-15) ................ | | 197,700 |
| Add: Increase in unliquidated obligations .............. | | 7,000 |
| **Obligations incurred** .............................. | | $204,700 |

Note: Key terms are set in boldface for illustrative purposes.

**Question 19-6.** Why are intragovernmental transactions and balances (receivables and payables) of a Federal agency distinguished in the accounts from those not involving other Federal agencies?

**Question 19-7.** Briefly state the Comptroller General's position with respect to depreciation accounting by Federal agencies.

**Question 19-8.** List the types of financial statements issued by Federal agencies.

**Question 19-9.** How is fund accounting accomplished in a Federal agency where the agency is the accounting entity?

**Question 19-10.** Explain the following types of appropriations or other types of obligational authority:
  a.  Contract authorization
  b.  Multiple year appropriations
  c.  No year appropriations
  d.  Permanent appropriations
  e.  Continuing resolutions

**Question 19-11.** Audits performed by the U.S. General Accounting Office are considered both part of the reporting and audit phase of Federal financial management and an integral part of agency management. Explain.

**Question 19-12.** Compare the Investment of the United States Government accounts with (a) the Fund Balance account of a municipal fund (expendable), and (b) the Contributions and Retained Earnings accounts of a municipal Enterprise Fund.

**Question 19-13.** What types of problems might you expect to encounter in accounting for (a) accrued expenditures on the basis of constructive receipt, and (b) personal income tax accruals?

**Question 19-14.** Compare the manner in which budgetary accounting is accomplished in a Federal agency with that of a municipality.

**Problem 19-1.** The trial balance of Able Agency at July 1, 19X6, the start of its 19X7 fiscal year, was as follows:

| | | |
|---|---:|---:|
| Fund Balances with U.S. Treasury | 40,000 | |
| Inventories | 10,000 | |
| Equipment | 25,000 | |
| Accumulated Depreciation | | 5,000 |
| Unliquidated Obligations—19X6 | | 30,000 |
| Invested Capital of the U.S. Government | | 40,000 |
| | 75,000 | 75,000 |

The following transactions and events occurred during the month of July 19X6:
  1.  Able Agency was notified that its fiscal 19X7 appropriation was $2,500,000.
  2.  The Office of Management and Budget apportioned $600,000 to Able Agency for the first quarter of the 19X7 fiscal year.
  3.  Able Agency's chief executive allotted $500,000 of the first quarter appropriation apportionment.
  4.  Obligations incurred during the month for equipment, materials, and program costs amounted to $128,000.
  5.  Goods and services ordered during the prior year were received:

|  | Obligated for | Actual Cost |
|---|---|---|
| Materials ........................ | $ 20,000 | $ 21,000 |
| Program A costs ................... | 7,000 | 7,000 |
| Program B costs .................. | 3,000 | 3,000 |
|  | $ 30,000 | $ 31,000 |

6.  Goods and services ordered during July 19X6 were received:

|  | Obligated for | Actual Cost |
|---|---|---|
| Materials ........................ | $ 6,000 | $ 5,000 |
| Equipment ....................... | 10,000 | 10,000 |
| Program A costs ................... | 30,000 | 32,000 |
| Program B costs .................. | 80,000 | 81,000 |
|  | $126,000 | $128,000 |

7.  Depreciation for the month of July was estimated at $200, chargeable to Overhead.

8.  Materials issued from inventory during July were for: Program A, $18,000; Program B, $7,000; and general (Overhead), $3,000.

9.  Liabilities placed in line for payment by the U.S. Treasurer totaled $145,000.

10.  Other accrued expenditures at July 31, 19X6, not previously recorded, were: Program A, $1,000; Program B, $6,000; and general (Overhead), $1,500.

Required:

a.  Prepare the general journal entries necessary to record the transactions and events affecting Able Agency during the month of July 19X6. (Key entries to problem data; omit entry explanations.)

b.  Prepare a trial balance for Able Agency at July 31, 19X6. (Assume that closing entries are made annually.)

c.  What is the invested capital of the U. S. Government in Able Agency at July 31, 19X6? The total investment of the U. S. Government?

**Problem 19-2.**  From the information in Problem 19-1:

1.  Prepare a worksheet summarizing the activities of Able Agency during the month of July 19X6. Your worksheet should be cross-referenced to the numbered items in that problem and should be headed as follows:

| Columns | Heading |
|---|---|
| 1–2 | Trial Balance, July 1, 19X6 |
| 3–4 | Entries during July, 19X6 |
| 5–6 | Trial Balance, July 31, 19X6 |

2.  Prepare a Statement of Status of Appropriations for Able Agency at July 31, 19X6.

**Problem 19-3.** The trial balance accounts of $X$ Agency at June 30, 19X1, the end of its first year of operations, appears below. The data is adjusted for all items except the lapsing of appropriations.

| | | | |
|---|---|---|---|
| Accounts Payable—Federal .... | 8,000 | Inventories ................... | 700 |
| Accounts Receivable— | | Liability for Accrued Leave .... | 1,200 |
| Nonfederal ............... | 12,000 | Overhead ................... | 30,000 |
| Accrued Liabilities .......... | 500 | Prepaid Expenses ........... | 200 |
| Accumulated Depreciation .... | 1,000 | Reimbursements to | |
| Deposits in Transit .......... | 3,000 | Appropriations.............. | 18,000 |
| Depreciation ............... | 1,000 | Revenues ................... | 18,000 |
| Direct Costs ............... | 79,300 | Transfer of Property from | |
| Disbursements in Transit ...... | 4,000 | Government Agencies ...... | 15,000 |
| Equipment ................. | 20,000 | Travel Advances ............. | 400 |
| Estimated Appropriation | | Unallocated Apportionments .. | 10,000 |
| Reimbursements .......... | 1,500 | Unapportioned Appropriations.. | 12,000 |
| Expended Appropriations ...... | 114,000 | Undeposited Collections ...... | 2,500 |
| Fund Balances with U.S. | | Unliquidated Obligations ...... | 7,000 |
| Treasury ................. | 25,100 | Unobligated Allotments........ | 3,000 |

Other information: (1) All appropriations are one-year appropriations. (2) No further reimbursements on account of this year's activities are expected. (3) The transfer of property from government agencies consisted of equipment.

Required:

a. Entries to adjust the appropriations (budgetary) accounts and to close the books at June 30, 19X1.

b. A Statement of Assets and Liabilities of $X$ Agency at June 30, 19X1.

c. A Statement of Changes in the Investment of the United States Government in $X$ Agency for the year ended June 30, 19X1.

d. A Reconciliation of Program Costs with Obligations for $X$ Agency for the year ended June 30, 19X1.

**Problem 19-4.** Innovation Agency, established during 19X2, is financed by no-year appropriations and from billings for certain of its services. Its trial balance at the beginning of 19X3 was as follows:

| | Dr. | Cr. |
|---|---|---|
| Fund Balances with the U.S. Treasury ............ | 15,000 | |
| Accounts Receivable—Federal ................. | 9,000 | |
| Materials and Supplies ....................... | 41,000 | |
| Plant and Equipment ........................ | 60,000 | |
| Accumulated Depreciation ..................... | | 2,000 |
| Accounts Payable—Federal ................... | | 8,000 |
| Invested Capital ............................ | | 100,000 |
| Unobligated Allotments ...................... | | 10,000 |
| Unliquidated Obligations ..................... | | 5,000 |
| | 125,000 | 125,000 |

A summary of the transactions and events affecting Innovation Agency during 19X3 follows:

1. Additional appropriations of $500,000 were made for the agency. Billings for services, available to the agency without further appropriation, were estimated at $200,000.

2. All but 5 percent of the current year's appropriation was apportioned to the agency by the OMB.

3. Agency management allocated all but $50,000 of the increased obligational authority available to the agency.

4. Billings for services totaled $215,000, all to Federal agencies; collections amounted to $210,000, all deposited with the U.S. Treasury to the credit of Innovation Agency by payor agencies.

5. Purchase orders were placed for materials, supplies, and equipment estimated to cost $183,000.

6. Equipment was transferred to the agency at no cost from another agency. The equipment had originally cost $70,000; accumulated depreciation of $40,000 had been recorded thereon by the transferor agency.

7. The equipment received by transfer (item 6) proved unsatisfactory and was sold for cash at book value.

8. The equipment sale proceeds were returned to the U. S. Treasury for general government use.

9. Orders were received from industrial suppliers as follows:

|  | Estimated Cost | Actual Cost |
| --- | --- | --- |
| Materials and supplies ............ | 66,000 | 68,000 |
| Equipment ..................... | 120,000 | 120,000 |

10. Employee annual leave earned amounted to $25,000.

11. Employee salaries amounted to $400,000, including $12,000 annual leave taken. Withholdings that must be matched totaled $24,000; income taxes withheld were $40,000; and withholdings on private insurance plans totaled $14,000.

12. Materials and supplies used during the year cost $90,000.

13. A two-year insurance policy costing $1,000 was purchased at mid-year.

14. Depreciation of agency plant and equipment during the period was recorded, $16,000.

15. Vouchers were scheduled for payment by the U. S. Treasurer as follows: Federal, $88,000; Nonfederal, $530,000.

16. All deposits were confirmed by the U. S. Treasury, but $14,000 of disbursements were in transit at year end.

Required:

From the above information prepare for Innovative Agency:

a. A worksheet summarizing the financial activities during 19X3. Your worksheet should be keyed to the problem data items and should be headed as follows:

| Columns | Heading |
| --- | --- |
| 1–2 | Trial Balance, Beginning of 19X3 |
| 3–4 | Transactions and Adjustments—19X3 |
| 5–6 | Preclosing Trial Balance, End of 19X3 (Optional) |
| 7–8 | Closing Entries, End of 19X3 |
| 9–10 | Postclosing Trial Balance, End of 19X3 |

b.   A Statement of Assets and Liabilities (Balance Sheet) at the end of 19X3.

c.   A Statement of Changes in the Investment of the United States Government during the 19X3 fiscal year.

d.   A Reconciliation of Program Costs with Obligations for the 19X3 fiscal year.

# 20

# Accounting for Hospitals

The scope and complexity of the hospital environment have undergone swift and dramatic changes in recent years. Correspondingly, hospital financial management and accounting practices have evolved rapidly and significantly in an attempt to keep abreast of the changes in their environment.

In order to gain some perspective of the situation, consider the fact that the 100-bed community hospital of a few years ago may today be a 500-bed metropolitan teaching-research-diagnostic-treatment center. To get a somewhat better perspective, add to this: the effects of vast technological advances in health care techniques and equipment; the ever-increasing types (and costs) of facilities and equipment deemed essential in a modern hospital; the broadened expectations of its clientele regarding the type, extent, and sophistication of the services a contemporary hospital should offer—on a 7 days per week, 24 hours per day basis; the decline in volunteer or religious order personnel available for and competent to perform necessary health care tasks and the concomitant increase both in the number of paid staff members and in prevailing wage rates; the greatly increased demand for and usage level of hospital facilities occasioned by the demise of physician house calls, the staggering accident rate on our highways, governmental programs such as Medicare and Medicaid, and the increased level of in-hospital physical examinations and diagnostic tests, dental procedures, and cosmetic surgery; and, the marked decline in the willingness of local governments or philanthropists to provide resources for expansion or replacement of buildings and equipment. An even clearer view of the situation, though by no means a complete one, is attained by considering also the fact that few patients now pay their bills for services received directly. Most charges are paid by *third-party payors*—by insurance companies or through a variety of Federal and/or state health care programs—each with its own reimbursement rules and accounting and reporting requirements. Too, major third-party payors base their payments on "reimbursable costs," as defined in insurance policies or program regulations; and the ability of hospital managers to charge "reasonable and customary" fees, that is, to establish their own fee schedules, has diminished substantially with regard to their third-party payor clientele.

No doubt it was in this context that the American Hospital Association (AHA) noted that:

THE CONTEMPORARY HOSPITAL is a highly complex organization of specialized resources, whose administration is one of the most difficult applications of the management art. Hospitals must make available on a virtually continuous basis an ever-expanding range of services. These services are provided by personnel in a diversity of occupations that require substantial investments in plant and equipment.[1]

The AHA also emphasized the importance of accounting to effective hospital management:

The social, economic, and scientific advances of the last two decades that have complicated the management task have also made accounting—as an information system—an even more vital and integral part of the management process.

The effectiveness of the management functions of establishing objectives, planning and controlling depends largely upon (1) the existence of a sound organizational structure; (2) the availability of relevant and reliable financial and statistical information related to each area of responsibility within the hospital; and (3) the ability of management to make full use of such information.[2]

## AN OVERVIEW OF HOSPITAL ACCOUNTING

Two industry professional associations—the American Hospital Association (AHA) and the Hospital Financial Management Association (HFMA)—have been dominant forces in the development and improvement of hospital financial management, accounting, and reporting. Accounting and statistical manuals, data processing services, symposiums and workshops, advisory services, and

[1] American Hospital Association, *Chart of Accounts for Hospitals* (Chicago: The Association, 1966), p. 1.

[2] *Ibid.*

recognized journals are provided for the industry on a regular basis through one or both of these associations.[3]

Private insurors and governmental agencies having jurisdiction over third-party health care payor programs also have had a significant impact on hospital accounting, though more in the area of reimbursable cost determination and statistical data requirements than in that of financial accounting per se. In addition, the American Institute of Certified Public Accountants has recently intensified its efforts in the hospital accounting and reporting area through its Committee on Health Care Institutions.

The discussion and illustrations within this chapter are based principally upon the AHA's *Chart of Accounts for Hospitals,* the most widely used and authoritative guide to generally accepted principles of hospital accounting. Though it takes exception to certain recommendations therein, the AICPA Committee on Health Care Institutions considers these AHA pronouncements to be "generally compatible" with generally accepted accounting principles.[4] Differences of opinion between the AHA and the AICPA committee (discussed later in this chapter) appear to arise largely from differing viewpoints as to the principal purposes and users of financial statements. Whereas the AICPA committee evaluated the recommendations within *Chart of Accounts for Hospitals* from the standpoint of external users and the auditor who attests to the fairness of financial statement presentations, the AHA considers the hospital *management* to be the primary statement recipient and user:

> Hospital accounting and statistical reports are prepared for a variety of uses: to submit required data to regulatory state and federal agencies; to develop cost-consciousness among hospital employees and the medical staff; to educate the general public; and to give hospital associations and health organizations helpful information about hospital activities. *The most important purpose of financial and statistical data, however, is for the use of managements in planning and controlling the affairs of their hospitals.*[5]

### Funds

The AHA chart of accounts provides for the separation of a hospital's accounts into as many as five funds: (1) Operating Fund, (2) Specific Purpose Fund, (3) Endowment Fund, (4) Plant Fund, and (5) Construction Fund. A hospital normally is to have no more than one of each of these funds. Where several funds of a given type are required they are generally handled on an intrafund "funds within a fund" basis.

---

[3] *Hospitals* is the official journal of the American Hospital Association; *Hospital Financial Management* is that of the Hospital Financial Management Association (formerly the American Association of Hospital Accountants).

[4] Committee on Health Care Institutions, American Institute of Certified Public Accountants, *Hospital Audit Guide,* (New York: The Institute, 1972) p. 4.

[5] *Chart of Accounts for Hospitals,* p. 3. (Emphasis added.)

OPERATING FUND. The Operating Fund is used to account for routine, day-to-day transactions involving expendable resources that are *not externally restricted,* that is, whose use is within the discretion of the hospital's governing body. Stated differently, all resources and transactions not accounted for in another fund are accounted for through the Operating Fund. Thus the Operating Fund is much like the General Fund of a municipality and is sometimes referred to as the "general" or "current" fund.

SPECIFIC PURPOSE FUND. The Specific Purpose Fund is established to account for expendable resources which are *externally restricted*—by third party grantors or donors, not by the governing board or administrative officers of the hospital— to use for a specified purpose or project. Typical sources of Specific Purpose Fund resources include (1) public donations for purposes such as equipment acquisition, student nurse scholarships, and provision of "free" service to indigent patients, (2) research grants, (3) restricted earnings of Endowment Funds, i.e., endowment earnings that are restricted to specific purposes or projects, and (4) investment and other income that is externally restricted as to use.

Specific Purpose Funds are similar to municipal Special Revenue (and expendable Trust) Funds, though the latter may be established by the municipal governing board as well as in response to the wishes or requirements of outsiders. *Board-restricted* assets and related liabilities of hospitals may be either (1) included within the Operating Fund on an intrafund "fund within a fund" basis, or (2) accounted for through hybrid "Board-created Specific Purpose" Funds.

ENDOWMENT FUND. The Endowment Fund is used to account for the principal (corpus) of assets given in trust to the hospital for the purpose of providing a continuing source of income for either general (unrestricted) or specified (restricted) purposes. Liabilities assumed in connection with endowments, if any, are also accounted for through this fund. Thus the Endowment Fund parallels the *nonexpendable* Trust Fund of a municipality, and a distinction must be maintained between the principal (which must be kept intact) and earnings. Where the governing board has set aside resources for similar purposes, separate "Board-created Endowment" Funds may be established.

PLANT FUND. The Plant Fund is used to account for (1) long-lived assets such as land, buildings, and equipment—and accumulated depreciation thereon, (2) long-term debt related to fixed assets, (3) assets earmarked—*either externally or internally*—for fixed asset replacements or additions, and (4) the net assets invested in—and set aside to be invested in—fixed assets by the hospital. The Plant Fund has no counterpart in contemporary municipal accounting.[6]

___

[6] Many municipalities used Plant Funds similar to those of hospitals (and colleges or universities) prior to issuance of the pronouncements of the National Committee on Municipal Accounting (now the NCGA) in the 1930s, and such funds occasionally are found in use by municipalities even today.

CONSTRUCTION FUND. A Construction Fund may be used to account for the receipt and expenditure of resources for major fixed asset acquisition or construction projects. Use of this fund is optional—such activities may be accounted for through the Plant Fund—though the AHA prefers that a Construction Fund be used where significant sums of money are involved. The Construction Fund parallels the municipal Capital Projects Fund.

COMMENTARY. Note that the overriding factor distinguishing the Operating Fund from the Specific Purpose and Endowment Funds is whether the resources are (1) *externally restricted,* termed "restricted funds," or (2) *unrestricted externally,* though possibly board-restricted, referred to as "unrestricted funds" —though both types of resources may be accounted for in the Plant and Construction Funds. The distinction between "restricted" and "unrestricted" funds, as the terms are used here, is important in hospital accounting because (1) in evaluating managerial effectiveness and efficiency, particular emphasis is placed on managerial accountability for utilization of the "unrestricted funds" within management's control, (2) additional "Board-Created Specific Purpose" and "Board-Created Endowment" Funds may be necessary in order to maintain the distinction as to the level of managerial control exercisable over resources, (3) this distinction underlies a major difference between the AHA recommendations and those of the AICPA Committee on Health Care institutions, discussed later in this chapter, and (4) as discussed below, this distinction affects the timing of revenue recognition.

### Unique Income Determination and Asset Valuation Features

Although hospital accounting is a blend of fund and commercial accounting, it conforms to commercial accounting for the most part. Several income determination and asset valuation features are peculiar to hospital accounting, however, and warrant careful attention at this point.

HOSPITAL NET INCOME REPORTED. Although hospital accounting is fund-based, it is responsibility center and "controllable cost" oriented. Further, net income of the hospital as a whole is calculated and reported. This does not mean that all hospitals are profit-seeking organizations. Rather, it reflects the predominant view (1) that hospitals are "going concerns," even if "not-for-profit," and (2) that revenues must cover all expenses (not merely *expenditures*) if the hospital's capital is to be maintained intact.[7]

Hospital revenues are classified broadly into three major categories:

1. *Nursing and Other Professional Patient Service Revenues*—the *gross* revenues, measured at regularly established standard rates, earned in the

---

[7] The AICPA Committee on Health Care Institutions prefers the title "Statement of Revenues and Expenses" to the title "Income Statement" suggested by the AHA in *Chart of Accounts for Hospitals.* The former would appear to be especially preferable for use by not-for-profit hospitals, as the latter may connote profit-seeking motivations.

several revenue-producing centers through rendering inpatient and out-patient services.

2. *Deductions from Patient Service Revenues*—the reduction in gross revenues collectible occasioned by charity services rendered, contractual adjustments arising from third-party payor agreements or regulations, policy discounts such as are often extended patients who are themselves members of the medical profession, administrative adjustments, and bad debts.

3. *Other Revenues*—all other revenues, such as general contributions, donated services and commodities, grants, cafeteria sales, vending machine commissions, medical transcript fees, and investment earnings.

Note that the first two categories above relate to patient services, the major source of revenues for most hospitals. Note also that the full normal charge for services rendered is credited to revenues in order to present the total established "market value" of those services, regardless of ultimate collectibility. Deductions arising from lesser amounts being collectible are accounted for separately for purposes of control and evaluation and in order that they will not distort gross revenue trends and evaluations. Accounting for gross revenues (charges) at full established rates also facilitates calculation and support of reimbursement claims filed with some major third party payors. Under the Medicare RCCAC (ratio of charges to Medicare patients to total patient charges, applied to cost) reimbursement formula, for example, reimbursement of allowable hospital costs (expenses) is based on the percentage that gross charges to Medicare patients is of gross charges to all patients. Thus, under the RCCAC method:

$$\frac{\text{Reimbursable Costs}}{\text{(Expenses)}} = \frac{\text{Gross charges to medicare patients}}{\text{Gross charges to all patients}} \times \frac{\text{Allowable Costs}}{\text{(Expenses)}}$$

All revenues not related to patient services (or not readily traceable thereto) are considered Other Revenues. These may be of minor consequence in some hospitals but are of major importance in those that are largely donor-supported, engage in extensive contract research, have sizable investment earnings, are heavily involved in nurse or intern training, and the like.

Expenses are likewise broadly classifiable as between (1) Patient Service Expenses and (2) Other Service Expenses. Each patient service revenue center is also a corresponding expense center, and all expenses not readily traceable to patient service revenue centers are categorized as Other Service Expenses.

The accounts of a hospital are not actually maintained according to such broad categories, of course, but consist of a series of more detailed control accounts and even more detailed subsidiary accounts. The types of revenue, deductions from revenue, and expense control accounts typically maintained may be observed from Figure 20-1; the relation of the account structure to the organizational structure may be seen in Figure 20-2.

Figure 20-1

## SUGGESTED CHART OF ACCOUNTS FOR MEDIUM-SIZE HOSPITAL

**Revenue Accounts**

*Patient Service Revenue*

Revenue from Daily Patient Services

| | |
|---|---|
| 310 | Medical and Surgical Unit A |
| 311 | Medical and Surgical Unit B |
| 312 | Medical and Surgical Unit C |
| 313 | Medical and Surgical Unit D |
| 346 | Obstetric Unit |
| 350 | Newborn Nursery |

Revenue from Other Nursing Services

| | |
|---|---|
| 360 | Operating Rooms |
| 365 | Recovery Room |
| 370 | Delivery and Labor Rooms |
| 375 | Central Services and Supply |
| 377 | Intravenous Therapy |
| 378 | Emergency Service |

Revenue from Other Professional Services

| | |
|---|---|
| 402 | Laboratory |
| 410 | Blood Bank |
| 412 | Electrocardiology |
| 421 | Radiology |
| 430 | Pharmacy |
| 435 | Anesthesiology |
| 437 | Physical Therapy |

*Deductions from Patient Service Revenue*

| | |
|---|---|
| 500 | Charity Service |
| 510 | Contractual Adjustments |
| 520 | Policy Discounts |
| 521 | Administrative Adjustments |
| 529 | Provision for Bad Debts |

*Other Revenue*

| | |
|---|---|
| 541 | General Contributions |
| 551 | Cafeteria Sales |
| 557 | Television Rentals |
| 565 | Telephone and Telegraph |
| 568 | Medical Record Transcript Fees |
| 569 | Nonpatient Sales of Drugs |
| 570 | Nonpatient Sales of Other |

Supplies

| | |
|---|---|
| 572 | Income Transfers from Specific Purpose Funds |
| 573 | Income Transfers from Endowment Funds |
| 574 | Income Transfers from Plant Funds |
| 580 | Gain on Disposal of Assets |
| 581 | Purchase Discounts |

**Expense Accounts**

*Patient Service Expense*

Nursing Services Expense

| | |
|---|---|
| 600 | Administrative Office |
| 602 | Supervision of Nursing Units |
| 610 | Medical and Surgical Nursing Unit A |
| 611 | Medical and Surgical Nursing Unit B |
| 612 | Medical and Surgical Nursing Unit C |
| 613 | Medical and Surgical Nursing Unit D |
| 646 | Obstetric Unit |
| 650 | Newborn Nursery |
| 657 | Float Nursing Personnel |
| 660 | Operating Rooms |
| 665 | Recovery Room |
| 670 | Delivery and Labor Rooms |
| 675 | Central Services and Supply |
| 677 | Intravenous Therapy |
| 678 | Emergency Service |

Other Professional Services Expense

| | |
|---|---|
| 702 | Laboratory |
| 710 | Blood Bank |
| 712 | Electrocardiology |
| 721 | Radiology |
| 730 | Pharmacy |
| 735 | Anesthesiology |
| 737 | Physical Therapy |

Figure 20-1 (cont.)

*Other Service Expense*

General Services Expense
- 800 Administrative Office
- 801 Dietary—Administrative Office
- 803 Patient Food Service
- 810 Cafeteria
- 830 Plant Operation and Maintenance
- 850 Housekeeping
- 860 Laundry and Linen
- 890 Medical Records

Fiscal Services Expense
- 900 Administrative Office
- 902 Accounting
- 920 Admitting
- 930 Cashiering
- 937 Communications
- 940 Stores

Administrative Services Expense
- 950 Administrative Executive Office
- 951 Personnel
- 955 Purchasing
- 958 Governing Board
- 959 Medical Staff
- 980 Depreciation
- 981 Insurance
- 982 Taxes
- 983 Employee Benefits
- 984 Interest
- 985 Loss on Disposal of Assets

Source: *Chart of Accounts for Hospitals,* pp. 124–26.

FUND ACCOUNTING AND REVENUE RECOGNITION. We noted earlier that although fund accounting is recommended for hospitals, all revenues recognized and expenses incurred (costs expired)—and hence the net income of the hospital as a whole—are reported in a single Statement of Net Income. Furthermore, duplication of reported revenues (such as that resulting from municipal interfund transactions) is to be avoided. Two alternative accounting approaches that achieve these objectives and are acceptable to the AHA are in fairly wide use in practice: (1) the "*single* income statement method" and (2) the "*consolidated* income statement method."

Under the "*single* income statement method" preferred by the AHA (1) *donor-restricted* resources are recorded as additions to the balances of the Specific Purpose, Endowment, Construction, or Plant Funds, as appropriate to the terms of the external restrictions thereon, and (2) *donor-unrestricted* gifts and income and *externally-unrestricted* income of all funds are recorded as revenues of the Operating Fund. Thus all revenues recognized and expenses incurred are attributed to and/or transferred to the Operating Fund. Where the "single income statement method" is followed (1) revenue and expense accounts of funds other than the Operating Fund do not enter directly into the determination of the hospital's reported net income—reported net income is based solely on the Operating Fund ledger accounts—and hence such items are often carried directly to the Fund Balance accounts of the other funds, (2) Statements of Changes in Fund Balance are prepared for other funds rather than Statements of Net Income, and (3) accounts such as "Income Transfers from Specific Purpose Fund" and "Income Transfers from Endowment Fund" may appear in the

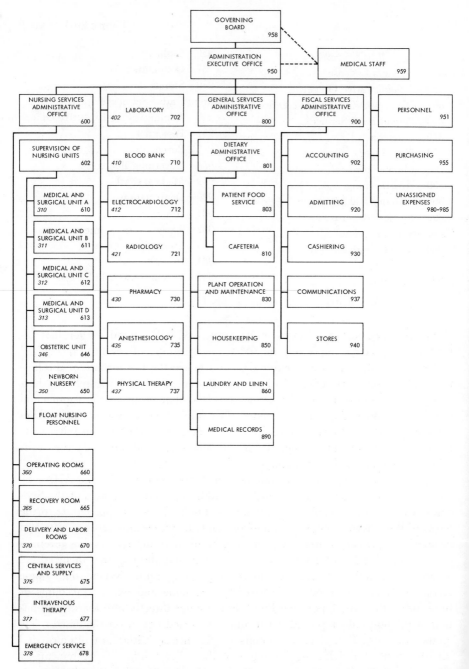

Revenue account numbers are shown at left in *italics* (*310*); Expense account numbers are shown at right (610)

Source: *Chart of Accounts for Hospitals,* p. 127. This chart is for illustrative purposes only. It should not be considered a recommended pattern of organization.

Statement of Net Income—that is, revenues of the Specific Purpose, Endowment, and Plant Funds are usually reported by *fund* source rather than *earnings* or contributions source (such as "Interest Income," "Government Grant,"
etc.). To summarize, hospital-wide revenues and *expenses* are accounted for
through the Operating Fund under the "single income statement method,"
while the other funds are accounted for on an "increases and decreases (*expenditures*) in Fund Balance" basis similar to that of a municipal expendable fund.

In simple situations, such as where the cash interest received or accrued on
investments of the Specific Purpose Fund is unrestricted, interfund attribution
and transfer entries may be avoided by recording the revenue receipt or accrual
directly in the Operating Fund. In more complex situations, such as where the
net income of an Endowment Fund is unrestricted, the revenues and expenses
must first be recorded in the Endowment Fund and its net income calculated.
This net income is then attributed to the Operating Fund by making simultaneous entries in both funds:

ENTRIES IN SPECIFIC PURPOSE FUND:

| | | |
|---|---|---|
| Revenues | 7,000 | |
|     Expenses | | 1,000 |
|     Fund Balance | | 6,000 |

To record closing of revenue and expense accounts and
computation of net income.

| | | |
|---|---|---|
| Fund Balance | 6,000 | |
|     Due to Operating Fund | | 6,000 |

To record liability to Operating Fund for net income earned.

ENTRY IN OPERATING FUND:

| | | |
|---|---|---|
| Due from Endowment Fund | 6,000 | |
|     Income Transfers from Endowment Fund | | 6,000 |

To record revenues earned by and due from Endowment Fund.

The format of the Income Statement prepared by the "single income statement
method" is illustrated in Figure 20-5.

Under the alternative *"consolidated* income statement method" (1) the
revenues and expenses of each fund are accounted for therein, and (2) a
columnar consolidating Income Statement is prepared that presents both the
reported net income of each fund and the total net income of the hospital.
Although the "consolidated income statement method" is acceptable to the
AHA only if the total column "reflects at least the same total income that
would be reported if there were only one income statement of the Operating
Fund,"[8] the methods should yield identical results if the revenue recognition
principles discussed below are followed.

[8] *Chart of Accounts for Hospitals,* pp. 20–21.

TIMING OF REVENUE RECOGNITION.    A significant feature of hospital accounting is that revenue is recognized in the period in which the related assets
(1) become available for *unrestricted* use by the governing board, or (2) are
*expended* for the donor-specified restricted purposes. Unrestricted revenues are
recognized on the accrual basis, but (1) unexpended restricted assets, such as
the principal of living trusts, are considered to be realized only in the period
in which they become unrestricted and (2) assets expended for specified purposes, such as research grants, are considered realized in the period of expenditure. Hence, where resources must be used for certain donor-specified purposes
or projects, revenue may be recognized at a point in time later than when it
would customarily be deemed to be realized in business enterprise accounting,
that is, when the related assets are *used* rather than when they become available
for use. However, where the governing board has chosen to restrict certain assets
or income therefrom and accordingly has established "Board-Created" Specific
Purpose or Endowment Funds, resulting revenues are recognized when received
or earned because they are not externally-restricted and are under the control
of management.

The rationale underlying this dual revenue recognition approach is that
restricted revenues should be matched to the related expenses of each accounting
period.

> Determination of the net income of an accounting period requires measure-
> ments of amounts of revenues, revenue deductions, and expenses associated
> with the period. . . . Unless there is a matching of accomplishment (revenue)
> with effort (expense), the reported net income of a period is a meaningless
> figure.[9]

Further, it can be argued that externally restricted resources are not truly
"earned" until they are used for their designated purpose.

In order to illustrate the effects of this dual revenue recognition practice,
assume that (1) a $50,000 cancer research grant was received by a hospital in
19A, and (2) only $15,000 was expended for this project during 19A. Appro-
priate entries in the Operating and Specific Purpose Funds during 19A in this
case can be seen on page 859.

Note in this example that although $50,000 was received (and avail-
able for the specified purpose) and credited to the Fund Balance of the Specific
Purpose Fund (1) only $15,000, the amount used for the designated purpose,
was recognized as revenue of the hospital in 19A and (2) the remaining $35,000
is included at the end of 19A in the Fund Balance account of the Specific Purpose Fund. Notice also that the only ultimate difference in effect between the
"single income statement method" and the "consolidated income statement
method" in this case is that the revenue recognized is labeled "Income Transfers from Specific Purpose Fund" in the former case and "Other Revenue" in

[9] *Ibid.*, p. 23.

| Transaction or Event | Single Income Statement Method | Consolidated Income Statement Method |
|---|---|---|
| Receipt of grant | *Specific Purpose Fund:* <br> Cash .................... 50,000 <br>    Fund Balance ........... 50,000 | *Specific Purpose Fund:* <br> Cash .................... 50,000 <br>    Fund Balance ..... 50,000 |
| Research project expense incurred (assume cash is disbursed). | *Operating Fund:* <br> Research Expense ........ 15,000 <br>    Cash .................. 15,000 | *Specific Purpose Fund:* <br> Research Expense ...... 15,000 <br>    Cash ................ 15,000 |
| Revenue and interfund liability recognized | *Specific Purpose Fund:* <br> Fund Balance ........... 15,000 <br>    Due to Operating Fund .. 15,000 <br> *Operating Fund:* <br> Due from Specific Purpose <br>   Fund ................. 15,000 <br>    Income Transfers from <br>     Specific Purpose Fund . 15,000 | *Specific Purpose Fund:* <br> Fund Balance ......... 15,000 <br>    Other Revenues ... 15,000 |
| Closing entry for Specific Purpose fund | *Specific Purpose Fund:* <br> No entry | *Specific Purpose Fund:* <br> Other Revenues ....... 15,000 <br>    Research Expense.. 15,000 |

the latter. However, had the grant receipt been credited to a deferred revenue account under the "consolidated income statement method" (and that account decreased when revenue was recognized), statements analyzing changes in the Fund Balance of the Specific Purpose Fund would *not* be comparable under the two methods. That prepared under the "consolidated income statement method" would be deficient by comparison inasmuch as the unused $35,000 grant proceeds would not be included in the Fund Balance account of the Specific Purpose Fund. Furthermore, had the research expense been initially paid from Operating Fund cash, the Specific Purpose Fund entries to properly record the revenue recognized and that fund's liability to the Operating Fund would be unduly awkward and complex. Factors such as these are no doubt among the reasons why the AHA prefers the "single income statement method."

APPRAISAL AND DEPRECIATION OF FIXED ASSETS. The AHA is emphatic in recommending that hospitals recognize depreciation:

> All assets owned by a hospital—no matter how the assets were acquired— must be included in the hospital's balance sheet. If the assets are depreciable *it would be inconsistent and confusing to recognize the assets and ignore the related depreciation.* The balance sheet valuation of the assets would be improper...and, more importantly, *the real cost of operating the hospital would be significantly understated.*
>
> It must be remembered that *depreciation of plant assets occurs whether it is recorded or not,* and regardless of the original source of the assets or the means employed to replace them. *Depreciation is an economic fact, and all hospitals should record depreciation as an operating expense.*[10] (Emphasis added)

Furthermore, the Association recommends that hospitals employ appraisal accounting procedures and that depreciation calculations and entries be based on *replacement costs:*

> Even when depreciation based on original historical cost is fully funded, there is no assurance that an adequate amount of resources will be accumulated to replace existing facilities. Price levels existing at the time of replacement, due to inflation, are likely to be well in excess of those prevailing at the time the facilities were acquired. Yet, it is clearly the responsibility of management to prevent the erosion of the hospital's capital investment and to provide for the future replacement of plant assets.
>
> It therefore is recommended that hospitals have appraisals made of plant assets by qualified appraisal firms, and that subsequent provisions for depreciation and funding be based upon the correct *replacement* costs of the plant assets as determined by the appraisal.[11]

Three criteria for the use of appraisals and replacement cost-based depreciation were set forth:

10 *Chart of Accounts for Hospitals,* pp. 22–23.
11 *Ibid.,* p. 83.

Where depreciation charges are based on current replacement costs: (1) the current replacement costs should be determined objectively by a reputable appraisal company, or by another equitable and agreed upon method; (2) the current replacement costs should be formally recorded in the accounts; and (3) full disclosure should be made in the financial statements as to the basis of valuing plant assets and of determining depreciation charges.[12]

Despite these AHA recommendations, a wide variety of asset valuation and depreciation accounting procedures may be found in practice. A few hospitals neither maintain fixed asset records nor recognize depreciation expense; some of those that have no fixed asset records record estimated depreciation charges based on some percentage of other expenses or of estimated total expenses including depreciation. *Such practices are clearly unacceptable.* A relatively large number of hospitals carry assets at original cost or, if donated, at fair market value at time of acquisition—or have entered appraisal valuations of approximate *acquisition cost* into the accounts—and record depreciation accordingly. Such practice is not only "time honored" but is in conformity with prior AHA recommendations and with current generally accepted principles of commercial accounting. Thus, inasmuch as the AHA does not require (it recommends) appraisal accounting and replacement cost-based depreciation accounting, and in view of the wide usage and acceptance of historical cost-based asset valuation and depreciation accounting generally, both cost-based and replacement cost-based procedures have found some degree of acceptance in contemporary hospital accounting.

A comprehensive analysis and evaluation of the American Hospital Association's recommendations regarding fixed asset appraisals and replacement cost-based depreciation is beyond the scope of this text. Inasmuch as the position of the AICPA Committee on Health Care Institutions is that appraisal accounting is not in conformity with generally accepted principles of accounting, and depreciation practices are varied, the illustrative entries in this chapter are based on the assumption that replacement cost appraisals are *not* formally recorded in the accounts.

LONG-TERM SECURITY INVESTMENTS. Another exception to the historical cost principle is recommended by the AHA in regard to the valuation of long-term security investments (such as stocks) held in the Endowment or Plant Funds. Although such investments traditionally have been carried at cost, or fair market value at acquisition if donated, the Association believes that periodic (quarterly, semiannual, or annual) adjustment of the investment accounts to current market values—and recognition of holding gains or losses—is now a generally accepted practice in hospitals. Note that the Association does not require such periodic revaluation, but merely recommends it. While stating that hospitals may retain historical cost valuations and deal with current market values

12 *Ibid.,* p. 15.

as supplemental information, the AHA offers these reasons for its preference for periodic revaluation of investments to market value:

1.  Cost, if used in financial reporting, serves no real "business" purpose and may even be misleading;
2.  The current market value of an investment portfolio is the true indicator of its earning power and of the stewardship responsibility of management; and
3.  The use of current market values for securities will facilitate accounting for "pooled" investments.[13]

It can be argued, of course, that disclosure of market values of long-term investment securities in the financial statements largely overcomes the first two arguments. However, the economies of pooling investments and the complexities of fairly measuring and equitably allocating investment income on other than a fair market value basis lends considerable support to the AHA position in those cases where (1) hospitals have several endowments or other sources of investment cash, and (2) investment and disinvestment transactions recur frequently. To this extent a hospital's investment management activities closely resemble those of the mutual fund (regulated investment trust) industry in which regular revaluation was found to be necessary and is now generally accepted practice. On the other hand, market value data may be used for investment pool buy-in or sell-out valuations without being formally recorded in the accounts.

The question of the propriety of periodic revaluation of investment securities and recognition of holding gains and losses has long been the topic of extensive study and debate within the accounting profession, and an in-depth analysis and evaluation of this issue is beyond the scope of this text. As in the case of fixed asset and depreciation accounting (1) the position of the AICPA Committee on Health Care Institutions is that revaluation of investments upward is not now in conformity with generally accepted accounting principles and (2) actual practices vary in this regard. Hence the illustrative entries that follow are based on the assumption that upward revaluations of long-term investments are *not* recognized in the accounts.

OTHER DISTINCTIVE FEATURES.    Two other somewhat distinctive features of hospital accounting relate to practices in regard to (1) donated services and commodities and (2) minor equipment.

The first arises because some hospitals regularly receive the services of trained religious order members, retired physicians or pharmacists, or other professionally competent personnel on a gratuity basis or for a nominal cost. To

13 *Chart of Accounts for Hospitals,* p. 14.

the extent that the value of such professional services is objectively measurable, the Association recommends that the excess of their value over their cost to the hospital be recognized by simultaneous debits and credits to the appropriate expense account and to a Donated Services (Other Revenue) revenue account, respectively. (This is *not* intented to apply to services of untrained volunteers or employees of other organizations temporarily assigned to the hospital, however, or to workers soliciting contributions to the hospital.) Likewise, the value of donated commodities should be debited to the appropriate inventory account and credited to a Donated Commodities (Other Revenue) revenue account if the commodities would otherwise have been purchased and inventoried by the hospital. The objective of these procedures is to express more accurately both the expenses incurred in rendering services and the revenues received by way of donation.

The second somewhat distinctive feature relates to minor equipment which, by definition, is (1) movable, (2) of relatively small size and minor cost, (3) subject to storeroom control (4) fairly numerous in quantity in use, and (5) apt to have a useful life of three years or less. As a matter of expediency and economy in record-keeping the AHA suggests that the *original supply* of minor equipment be inventoried at cost and amortized over a relatively short period, usually three years or less, and that *subsequent purchases* of minor equipment be charged as Supplies Expense to the departments requisitioning them.

## ILLUSTRATIVE TRANSACTIONS, ENTRIES, AND FINANCIAL STATEMENTS

Properly accounting for the varied and often complex transactions of a modern hospital requires that numerous subsidiary ledgers and other ancillary records be maintained. For example, a single Accounts and Notes Receivable–Inpatients control account will normally not suffice, though it may be used to control the following more typical types of control accounts:

Inpatient Receivables—In House
Inpatient Receivables—Discharged
Inpatient Receivables—Medicare
Inpatient Receivables—Medicaid
Inpatient Receivables—Blue Cross
Inpatient Receivables—Commercial Insurors
Inpatient Receivables—Welfare Agencies

Likewise, many of the revenue and expense accounts illustrated in Figure 20-1 would often control related subsidiary ledgers or be divided into several accounts in practice. Obviously all, or even most, of the intricacies of contemporary hospital accounting can not be discussed within the confines of this chapter.

A reasonably comprehensive case example is presented in this section of the chapter in order to illustrate (1) the common types of transactions and events that may be encountered routinely in accounting for a hospital and (2) the types of accounting entries and financial statements appropriate to record such transactions and events and present a hospital's operating results, financial position, and changes in financial position. Revenues and expenses are recorded in broad categorical accounts in the example in the interest of clarity and brevity of illustration. The reader wishing a more detailed knowledge of the multiple account classifications and numerous subsidiary ledgers and ancillary records necessitated by the complexities of modern hospital financial management is referred to a hospital accounting textbook or to *Chart of Accounts for Hospitals.*

The illustrative entries are based on the "*single* income statement method" because (1) this method is preferred by the AHA, (2) the interfund attribution and transfer procedures it entails are unusual and warrant further demonstration, and (3) in effect, both methods may be learned simultaneously through this approach. One wishing to employ the "consolidated income statement method" need only (1) ignore the interfund income attribution entries illustrated, (2) record the income of each fund therein, taking care to observe the revenue recognition principles discussed earlier, and (3) prepare a consolidating worksheet(s) as a basis for the financial statements.

Although the example is based primarily on AHA recommendations, several variances therefrom warrant mention (or repetition) at this point. As noted earlier, fixed asset and investment accounting is based on historical cost rather than on replacement cost or fair market valuations, respectively, as recommended by the AHA. In addition we choose (1) to account for unrestricted earnings in appropriately descriptive accounts, reserving use of the "Income Transfers" account to those cases in which income is recognized in a period later than the one in which it is realized, and (2) to account for interest and depreciation separately, rather than within the "Administrative Services Expense" category as suggested by the AHA. These latter variances are relatively minor, of course, and are largely matters of preference; they also are in accord with AICPA recommendations discussed later in this chapter.

### Illustrative Transactions and Entries

The case example presented here relates to Alzona Hospital, a medium size, not-for-profit, general short-term health care facility financed from patient services fees, donations, and investment earnings. The Balance Sheet of Alzona Hospital at October 1, 19A, the beginning of the fiscal year to which the example relates, is presented as Figure 20-3. The example is summarized in worksheet form in Figures 20-13 through 20-16.

## Summary of Transactions and Events

*Operating Fund:*

1. Gross charges to patients at standard established rates were as follows:

| | |
|---|---:|
| Daily patient services | $2,276,000 |
| Other nursing services | 696,000 |
| Other professional services | 1,428,000 |
| | $4,400,000 |

2. Deductions from gross revenues, exclusive of allowance for uncollectible accounts, were contractual adjustments, $280,000; and charity cases, $135,000.
3. Collections of accounts receivable totaled $3,800,000.
4. Accounts receivable written off as uncollectible during the year totaled $115,000.
5. It was estimated that $90,000 of year-end accounts receivable were uncollectible.
6. Materials and supplies, including food, purchased on account during the year totaled $600,000. A perpetual inventory system is in use.
7. Materials and supplies used were distributed among major functions as follows:

| | |
|---|---:|
| Nursing services | $170,000˙ |
| Other professional services | 50,000 |
| General services | 319,000 |
| Fiscal services | 8,000 |
| Administrative services | 3,000 |
| | $550,000 |

8. Accounts payable paid during the year were $675,000; purchase discounts of $7,000 were allowed. Cash disbursed was $668,000.
9. Salaries and wages paid during the year were for the following:

| | |
|---|---:|
| Nursing services | $1,316,000 |
| Other professional services | 828,000 |
| General services | 389,000 |
| Fiscal services | 102,000 |
| Administrative services | 65,000 |
| | $2,700,000 |

ALZONA HOSPITAL
Balance Sheet
October 1, 19A

*Assets*

Operating fund:

| | | |
|---|---|---|
| Cash | | $ 175,000 |
| Investments | | 100,000 |
| Accounts and notes receivable | $ 700,000 | |
| Less: Allowance for uncollectible receivables | 85,000 | 615,000 |
| Due from specific purpose fund | | 145,000 |
| Inventories | | 165,000 |
|     Total operating fund assets | | $1,200,000 |

Specific purpose fund:

| | | |
|---|---|---|
| Cash | | $ 20,000 |
| Investments | | 360,000 |
| Due from endowment fund | | 20,000 |
|     Total specific purpose fund assets | | $ 400,000 |

Endowment fund:

| | | |
|---|---|---|
| Cash | | $ 25,000 |
| Investments | | 475,000 |
|     Total endowment fund assets | | $ 500,000 |

Plant fund:

| | | |
|---|---|---|
| Cash | $ 25,000 | |
| Investments | 300,000 | |
| Due from operating fund | 225,000 | $ 550,000 |
| Land | $ 130,000 | |
| Land improvements | 80,000 | |
| Buildings | 5,000,000 | |
| Fixed equipment | 600,000 | |
| Major movable equipment | 90,000 | |
|     Total land, buildings, and equipment | $5,900,000 | |
| Less: Accumulated depreciation | 2,450,000 | |
|     Net land, building, and equipment | | 3,450,000 |
|     Total plant fund assets | | $4,000,000 |

Figure 20-3

*Liabilities and Capital*

Operating fund:

| | | |
|---|---:|---:|
| Accounts payable | $ 125,000 | |
| Notes payable | 150,000 | |
| Due to plant fund | 225,000 | |
| Total operating fund liabilities | | $ 500,000 |
| Operating fund balance | | 700,000 |
| Total operating fund liabilities and balance | | $1,200,000 |

Specific purpose fund:

| | |
|---|---:|
| Due to operating fund | $ 145,000 |
| Specific purpose fund balance | 255,000 |
| Total specific purpose fund liabilities and balance | $ 400,000 |

Endowment fund:

| | |
|---|---:|
| Due to specific purpose fund | $ 20,000 |
| Endowment fund balance | 480,000 |
| Total endowment fund liabilities and balance | $ 500,000 |

Plant fund:

| | | |
|---|---:|---:|
| Mortgages payable | $ 100,000 | |
| Accounts payable | 50,000 | |
| Total plant fund liabilities | | $ 150,000 |
| Plant fund balance—invested in plant | $3,300,000 | |
| Plant fund balance—reserved for plant replacement and expansion | 550,000 | |
| Total plant fund balance | | 3,850,000 |
| Total plant fund liabilities and capital | | $4,000,000 |

10. Expenses other than for salaries and materials and supplies paid during the year were chargeable as follows:

| | |
|---|---:|
| Nursing services | $ 86,000 |
| Other professional services | 79,000 |
| General services | 221,000 |
| Fiscal services | 44,000 |
| Administrative services | 327,000 |
| | $757,000 |

11. Salaries and wages accrued at year end were for the following:

| | |
|---|---:|
| Nursing services | $ 35,000 |
| Other professional services | 21,000 |
| General services | 19,000 |
| Fiscal services | 6,000 |
| Administrative services | 2,000 |
| | $ 83,000 |

12. Interest expense on Operating Fund notes payable was $8,000, of which $1,000 was accrued at year end; the principal was reduced by $20,000.

13. Interest earned during the year on Operating Fund investments was $5,000, of which $2,000 was accrued at year end.

14. Unrestricted earnings on Specific Purpose Fund investments, $24,000, received and accounted for directly in the Operating Fund.

15. Money collected as agent for special nurses for services rendered by them amounted to $48,000.

16. Of the total collected for special nurses, $45,000 was paid to them; the balance has not yet been claimed.

17. Professional services donated to the hospital were objectively valued and charged as follows:

| | |
|---|---:|
| Nursing services | $17,000 |
| Other professional services | 3,000 |
| | $20,000 |

18. Other revenues collected during the year were from the following:

| | |
|---|---:|
| Cafeteria sales | $45,000 |
| Television rentals | 30,000 |
| Medical record transcript fees | 15,000 |
| Vending machine commissions | 5,000 |
| | $95,000 |

19. General contributions received in cash, $100,000.
20. Accrued interest on Plant Fund bonds payable at year end (see transaction 29) was $40,000.

*Specific Purpose Fund:*
21. A grant of $400,000 to defray specific operating costs was received.
22. Investments made during the period were $300,000.
23. Investments maturing during the period, $150,000, had been originally purchased at par.
24. Earnings on investments, restricted to specified purposes, were $15,000.

*Endowment Fund:*
25. A benefactor gave rental properties valued at $300,000, and subject to a $100,000 mortgage, to the hospital. The corpus is to be maintained intact; earnings may be used for general operating purposes.
26. Rentals received in cash were $45,000.
27. Depreciation of rental property was $6,000.
28. Other expenses related to rental property, paid in cash, were $9,000.

*Plant Fund:*
29. Bonds were issued at par, $3,000,000, to be used to pay for a new building wing and to retire the mortgage payable. Inasmuch as the wing was being constructed under a turn-key contract, use of a separate construction fund was not considered necessary.
30. The mortgage notes were paid and the contractor was paid $2,700,000 on the $2,900,000 contract; the balance is being held pending final inspection of the new wing.
31. Major movable equipment was purchased for $18,000.

*Interfund:*
32. Specific Purpose Fund investments costing $165,000 were sold for $170,000; proceeds from gains on these investments are available for unrestricted use.
33. Cash was transferred as necessary to settle the beginning of year interfund receivables and payables.
34. A $300,000 transfer from the Specific Purpose Fund to the Operating Fund was authorized to reimburse the latter for specified expenses incurred; $200,000 of this amount was paid by the Specific Purpose Fund.
35. Endowment rental property earnings were established as a liability to the Operating Fund.
36. The Plant Fund accounts payable were paid through the Operating Fund; the latter will not be reimbursed.
37. Depreciation expense for the year was $300,000.
38. The board of directors authorized a $200,000 transfer to the Plant Fund to partially fund the depreciation expense.
39. Of the charges to General Services Expense, $5,000 was found to be for movable equipment which should have been purchased through the Plant Fund and recorded as an asset there. The Operating Fund liability to the Plant Fund was adjusted accordingly.

40. Unrestricted earnings on Plant Fund investments, $16,000, will not be transferred to the Operating Fund.
41. Fixed equipment costing $100,000, on which there was accumulated depreciation of $60,000, was sold for $30,000.
42. Restricted earnings received on Endowment Fund investments, $25,000, were recorded as a liability to the Specific Purpose Fund.

*Closing:*

43. Closing entries were made at year end.

*Entries*

*Operating Fund (Figure 20-13):*

| | | | |
|---|---|---:|---:|
| 1. | Accounts and Notes Receivable . . . . . . . . . | 4,400,000 | |
| | Revenue from Daily Patient Services | | 2,276,000 |
| | Revenue from Other Nursing Services | | 696,000 |
| | Revenue from Other Professional Services . . . . . . . . . . . . . . . . . . . . . | | 1,428,000 |
| | To record gross billings for services at established rates. | | |
| 2. | Charity Service . . . . . . . . . . . . . . . . . . . . . | 135,000 | |
| | Contractual Adjustments . . . . . . . . . . . . . . | 280,000 | |
| | Accounts and Notes Receivable . . . . . | | 415,000 |
| | To record deductions from gross revenues and receivables. | | |
| 3. | Cash . . . . . . . . . . . . . . . . . . . . . . . . . . . . . . | 3,800,000 | |
| | Accounts and Notes Receivable . . . . . | | 3,800,000 |
| | To record collections of accounts receivable. | | |
| 4. | Allowance for Uncollectible Receivables . . | 115,000 | |
| | Accounts and Notes Receivable . . . . . | | 115,000 |
| | To record write-off of accounts deemed uncollectible. | | |
| 5. | Provision for Bad Debts . . . . . . . . . . . . . . | 120,000 | |
| | Allowance for Uncollectible Receivables . . . . . . . . . . . . . . . . . . . | | 120,000 |
| | To record provision for bad debts and adjust allowance for uncollectible accounts to $90,000. | | |
| 6. | Inventories . . . . . . . . . . . . . . . . . . . . . . . . . | 600,000 | |
| | Accounts Payable . . . . . . . . . . . . . . . . | | 600,000 |
| | To record inventory purchases on account. | | |

| | | |
|---|---|---|
| 7. Nursing Services Expense .............. | 170,000 | |
| Other Professional Services Expense ..... | 50,000 | |
| General Services Expense .............. | 319,000 | |
| Fiscal Services Expense ................ | 8,000 | |
| Administrative Services Expense ........ | 3,000 | |
| Inventories....................... | | 550,000 |
| To record inventory usage. | | |
| | | |
| 8. Accounts Payable..................... | 675,000 | |
| Other Revenue................... | | 7,000 |
| Cash............................ | | 668,000 |
| To record payment of accounts payable. | | |

(Purchase discounts theoretically should be accounted for as a reduction in the cost of purchases but are customarily treated as other revenue in hospital accounting as a matter of expediency and to simplify perpetual inventory control.)

| | | |
|---|---|---|
| 9. Nursing Services Expense .............. | 1,316,000 | |
| Other Professional Services Expense ..... | 828,000 | |
| General Services Expense .............. | 389,000 | |
| Fiscal Services Expense ................ | 102,000 | |
| Administrative Services Expense ........ | 65,000 | |
| Cash ........................... | | 2,700,000 |
| To record salaries and wages paid. | | |

(A payroll account would probably be used in practice, of course, and separate checks would be drawn to recipients of insurance, tax, and other withholdings.)

| | | |
|---|---|---|
| 10. Nursing Services Expense.............. | 86,000 | |
| Other Professional Services Expense ..... | 79,000 | |
| General Services Expense .............. | 221,000 | |
| Fiscal Services Expense ................ | 44,000 | |
| Administrative Services Expense ........ | 327,000 | |
| Cash............................ | | 757,000 |
| To record expense payments. | | |
| | | |
| 11. Nursing Services Expense.............. | 35,000 | |
| Other Professional Services Expense ..... | 21,000 | |
| General Services Expense .............. | 19,000 | |
| Fiscal Services Expense ................ | 6,000 | |
| Administrative Services Expense ........ | 2,000 | |
| Accrued Salaries and Wages Payable . | | 83,000 |
| To record accrued expenses at year end. | | |
| | | |
| 12. Notes Payable........................ | 20,000 | |
| Interest Expense..................... | 8,000 | |
| Accrued Interest Payable .......... | | 1,000 |
| Cash............................ | | 27,000 |
| To record interest payment and accrual and reduction of principal of notes payable. | | |

13.  Cash .................................    3,000
     Accrued Interest Receivable ...........    2,000
         Operating Fund Investment Income..              5,000
     To record interest earned on Operating
     Fund investments.

14.  Cash .................................    24,000
     Unrestricted Specific Purpose Fund
         Investment Income .............             24,000
     To record interest earnings on Specific
     Purpose Fund investments deposited
     directly in the Operating Fund.

(Note that no entry in the Specific Purpose Fund is required in this situation. Also note that some accountants prefer to credit an Income Transfers from Specific Purpose Fund account in this situation, though the authors feel the account used is the more descriptive.)

15.  Cash .................................    48,000
         Due to Special Nurses .............             48,000
     To record fees collected as agent for spe-
     cial nurses.

(Notice that agency transactions are accounted for through the Operating Fund; hospitals normally do not establish separate Agency Funds.)

16.  Due to Special Nurses ................    45,000
         Cash ...........................             45,000
     To record payment of fees collected in
     an agency capacity to special nurses.

17.  Nursing Services Expense ..............    17,000
     Other Professional Services Expense .....    3,000
         Donated Services ................             20,000
     To record the value of donated services
     received.

18.  Cash .................................    95,000
         Other Revenues .................             95,000
     To record receipt of miscellaneous rev-
     enues.

19.  Cash .................................    100,000
         General Contributions ............             100,000
     To record receipt of unrestricted con-
     tributions.

20.  Interest Expense .....................    30,000
         Accrued Interest Payable ..........             30,000
     To record accrued interest at year end on
     bonds outstanding.

(The AHA suggests that interest payable on Plant Fund liabilities be recorded in the Plant Fund. Plant Fund debt is normally serviced through the Operating Fund; and Plant Fund cash normally is used only for fixed asset replacement and improvement, not debt service. Hence the authors prefer that the accrued interest be recorded in the Operating Fund.)

*Specific Purpose Fund (Figure 20-14):*

| | | | |
|---|---|---|---|
| 21. | Cash ............................... | 400,000 | |
| | Specific Purpose Fund Balance...... | | 400,000 |
| | To record receipt of grant to be used to defray certain operating costs. | | |

(Restricted grant proceeds are not recognized as revenue until used for their designated purpose.)

| | | | |
|---|---|---|---|
| 22. | Investments ......................... | 300,000 | |
| | Cash ............................ | | 300,000 |
| | To record investments of cash during the the period. | | |
| 23. | Cash ............................... | 150,000 | |
| | Investments ..................... | | 150,000 |
| | To record the maturity of investments originally purchased at par. | | |
| 24. | Cash ............................... | 15,000 | |
| | Specific Purpose Fund Balance...... | | 15,000 |
| | To record receipt of investment income, the use of which is restricted to specified purposes. | | |

(To repeat, restricted earnings are not recognized as revenue until used for the designated purpose.)

*Endowment Fund (Figure 20-15):*

| | | | |
|---|---|---|---|
| 25. | Rental Properties .................... | 300,000 | |
| | Mortgage Payable ............... | | 100,000 |
| | Endowment Fund Balance ......... | | 200,000 |
| | To record gift of properties, subject to mortgage assumed. The corpus is to be maintained intact; earnings are not restricted as to use. | | |
| 26. | Cash ............................... | 45,000 | |
| | Rental Revenues.................. | | 45,000 |
| | To record receipt of rentals. | | |
| 27. | Depreciation Expense ................. | 6,000 | |
| | Accumulated Depreciation ......... | | 6,000 |
| | To record depreciation of rental properties. | | |

28.  Other Rental Expenses ...............    9,000
         Cash ...........................             9,000
     To record payment of other rental ex-
     penses.

*Plant Fund (Figure 20-16):*

29.  Cash ................................3,000,000
         Bonds Payable....................         3,000,000
     To record sale of bonds at par.

(Use of a separate Construction Fund is optional in hospital accounting. The operation of a hospital Construction Fund parallels that of a municipal Capital Projects Fund and need not be illustrated here.)

30.  Buildings ...........................    2,900,000
     Mortgage Payable ...................      100,000
         Contracts Payable—Retained Per-
             centage ......................              200,000
         Cash ...........................              2,800,000
     To record payment of mortgage payable
     and building contractor, less percentage
     of contract retained pending final in-
     spection of new wing.

31.  Major Movable Equipment ............    18,000
     Plant Fund Balance—Reserved for Plant
         Replacement and Expansion ........    18,000
         Cash ...........................               18,000
         Plant Fund Balance-Invested in
             Plant........................               18,000
     To record purchase of equipment and
     reclassification of fund balance accounts.

(Alternatively, the Fund Balance accounts may be adjusted for the year's activity at year end.)
    *Interfund:*

32.  SPECIFIC PURPOSE FUND:
         Cash ..........................    170,000
             Investments ......................              165,000
             Due to Operating Fund ..........                5,000
         To record sale of investments at a gain
         and liability to Operating Fund there-
         for.

OPERATING FUND:
Due from Specific Purpose Fund ........          5,000
   Gain on Disposal of Assets .........                      5,000
To record gain on sale of Specific Pur-
pose Fund investments and receivable
therefor.

(Had the proceeds of the sale in excess of cost not been available for unrestricted use the $5,000 would have been credited to Specific Purpose Fund Balance; no entry would have been made in the Operating Fund and no revenue would have been recognized at this time.)

33.  OPERATING FUND:
Due to Plant Fund ..................          225,000
   Due from Specific Purpose Fund ....                  145,000
   Cash ...........................                      80,000
To record settlement of beginning year
interfund balances.
SPECIFIC PURPOSE FUND:
Due to Operating Fund..............          145,000
   Due from Endowment Fund .......                      20,000
   Cash ...........................                     125,000
To record settlement of beginning of year
interfund balances.
ENDOWMENT FUND:
Due to Specific Purpose Fund .........          20,000
   Cash ...........................                      20,000
To record payment of beginning of year
liability to the Specific Purpose Fund.
PLANT FUND:
Cash ..............................          225,000
   Due from Operating Fund ........                     225,000
To record receipt of beginning of year
receivable from the Operating Fund.

34.  OPERATING FUND:
Cash ..............................          200,000
Due from Specific Purpose Fund ........          100,000
   Restricted Income Transfers from
      Specific Purpose Fund ..........                 300,000
To record income transfer from Specific
Purpose Fund.
SPECIFIC PURPOSE FUND:
Specific Purpose Fund Balance..........          300,000
   Due to Operating Fund...........                     100,000
   Cash ...........................                     200,000
To record transfer to Operating Fund.

(Note that the entire transfer is recorded, even though the total was not paid immediately. This is done to effect a proper matching. The related expenses were incurred during the current period, and hence the income can now be considered "earned.")

| | | |
|---|---|---|
| 35. ENDOWMENT FUND: | | |
| Rental Revenues ..................... | 45,000 | |
| Depreciation Expense ............. | | 6,000 |
| Other Rental Expenses ........... | | 9,000 |
| Due to Operating Fund........... | | 30,000 |
| To close rental revenue and expense accounts and record liability to Operating Fund for earnings. | | |
| OPERATING FUND: | | |
| Due from Endowment Fund ........... | 30,000 | |
| Unrestricted Endowment Fund Rental Income ................ | | 30,000 |
| To record net rental income due from Endowment Fund. | | |
| | | |
| 36. OPERATING FUND: | | |
| Operating Fund Balance ............. | 50,000 | |
| Cash.......................... | | 50,000 |
| To record payment of Plant Fund Accounts payable. | | |
| PLANT FUND: | | |
| Accounts Payable.................... | 50,000 | |
| Plant Fund Balance—Invested in Plant........................ | | 50,000 |
| To record payment of accounts payable by Operating Fund and corresponding increase in Plant Fund balance. | | |
| | | |
| 37. PLANT FUND: | | |
| Plant Fund Balance—Invested in Plant .. | 300,000 | |
| Accumulated Depreciation ......... | | 300,000 |
| To record the reduction in Plant Fund equity occasioned by depreciation and the related addition to accumulated depreciation. | | |
| OPERATING FUND: | | |
| Depreciation Expense ................ | 300,000 | |
| Operating Fund Balance .......... | | 300,000 |
| To record depreciation expense for the year. | | |

(The credit to Operating Fund Balance negates the effect of depreciation expense on the postclosing balance of that account, since the loss in equity is in the Plant Fund, not the Operating Fund. Alternatively, the credit to Operating Fund Balance may be viewed as reflecting a transfer of a capital asset at book value from the Plant Fund to the Operating Fund, the value of such asset having now expired.)

38. OPERATING FUND:
    Operating Fund Balance .............. 200,000
        Due to Plant Fund ...............         200,000
        To record transfer and related liability
        to Plant Fund to partially fund deprecia-
        tion expense.
    PLANT FUND:
    Due from Operating Fund ............. 200,000
        Plant Fund Balance—Reserved for
            Plant Replacement and Expansion         200,000
        To record transfer from Operating Fund
        to partially fund depreciation.

(In order to assure the availability of money for plant asset improvement, re-placement, and expansion, most hospitals fund depreciation to the extent prac-ticable.)

39. OPERATING FUND:
    Due to Plant Fund ................... 5,000
        General Services Expense ..........         5,000
        To correct error in recording purchase
        of equipment and reduce liability to
        Plant Fund in lieu of drawing reimburse-
        ment check thereon.
    PLANT FUND:
    Major Movable Equipment ............ 5,000
    Plant Fund Balance—Reserved for
            Plant Replacement and Expansion 5,000
        Due from Operating Fund ........         5,000
        Plant Fund Balance—Invested in
            Plant.........................         5,000
        To record acquisition of equipment by
        Operating Fund expenditure, reduction
        in receivable therefrom, and to reclas-
        sify fund balance.

40. OPERATING FUND:
    Operating Fund Balance .............. 16,000
        Unrestricted Plant Fund Investment
            Income ......................         16,000
        To record revenue earned and implicit
        transfer to Plant Fund.
    PLANT FUND:
    Cash .............................. 16,000
        Plant Fund Balance—Reserved for
            Plant Replacement and
            Expansion ....................         16,000
        To record earnings on investments re-
        tained for plant replacement and expan-
        sion.

(Transactions such as this result in implicit transfers from one fund to another. Inasmuch as earnings on Plant Fund investments are not restricted, if they are retained in the Plant Fund they are in effect transferred there from the Operating Fund.)

41.  PLANT FUND:
      Cash ...............................  30,000
      Accumulated Depreciation .............  60,000
      Plant Fund Balance—Invested in Plant ..  40,000
          Fixed Equipment .................                100,000
          Plant Fund Balance—Reserved for
              Plant Replacement and Expansion             30,000
      To record sale of equipment at a $10,000
      loss and reduction—and reclassification
      of fund balance.
      OPERATING FUND:
      Loss on Disposal of Assets .............  10,000
          Operating Fund Balance ..........                10,000
      To record loss on sale of Plant Fund
      equipment.

(Note again the credit to Operating Fund Balance occasioned by recognition of an expense—or loss—in the Operating Fund where the equity of another fund is in fact reduced. As noted earlier the credit to Operating Fund Balance offsets the effect of the loss on the postclosing balance of that account. The rationale behind the above entries is made clearer by viewing it as a combination of (1) the transfer of the assets disposed of to the Operating Fund at the $40,000 book value immediately prior to sale; (2) the sale at a $10,000 loss, and (3) the transfer of the $30,000 proceeds of the sale back to the Plant Fund.)

42.  ENDOWMENT FUND:
      Cash ...............................  25,000
          Due to Specific Purpose Fund ......             25,000
          To record restricted earnings due to
          Specific Purpose Fund.
      SPECIFIC PURPOSE FUND:
      Due from Endowment Fund ...........  25,000
          Specific Purpose Fund Balance......            25,000
          To record restricted purpose earnings
          due from the Endowment Fund.

(Again, observe that no revenue has yet been recognized as a result of the above transaction, even though the earnings have been received. The revenue will be recognized in the period in which the resources are transferred from the Specific Purpose Fund to the Operating Fund or otherwise used for the specified purpose.)

*Closing:*

43. OPERATING FUND:

| | | |
|---|---|---|
| Revenue from Daily Patient Services..... | 2,276,000 | |
| Revenue from Other Nursing Services ... | 696,000 | |
| Revenue from Other Professional Services | 1,428,000 | |
| General Contributions................. | 100,000 | |
| Donated Services ..................... | 20,000 | |
| Operating Fund Investment Income .... | 5,000 | |
| Unrestricted Specific Purpose Fund Investment Income ................. | 24,000 | |
| Unrestricted Endowment Fund Rental Income.......................... | 30,000 | |
| Unrestricted Plant Fund Investment Income ......................... | 16,000 | |
| Income Transfers from Specific Purpose Fund........................... | 300,000 | |
| Gain on Disposal of Assets ............ | 5,000 | |
| Other Revenues ..................... | 102,000 | |
|     Charity Service .................. | | 135,000 |
|     Contractual Adjustments .......... | | 280,000 |
|     Provision for Bad Debts .......... | | 120,000 |
|     Nursing Services Expense .......... | | 1,624,000 |
|     Other Professional Services Expense . | | 981,000 |
|     General Services Expense .......... | | 943,000 |
|     Fiscal Services Expense ........... | | 160,000 |
|     Administrative Services Expense .... | | 397,000 |
|     Depreciation Expense ............. | | 300,000 |
|     Loss on Disposal of Assets ......... | | 10,000 |
|     Interest Expense.................. | | 38,000 |
|     Operating Fund Balance .......... | | 14,000 |
| To close accounts at year end. | | |

(Revenues and expenses of other funds are carried directly to fund balance, are closed to fund balance, or are closed in order that unrestricted income may be attributed to the Operating Fund. Thus, no closing entries are required for the Specific Purpose, Endowment, or Plant Funds.)

### Financial Statements

Three major financial statements are recommended by the AHA: (1) a Balance Sheet, (2) an Income Statement, and (3) a Statement of Changes in Fund Balance. Figure 20-4 presents the Alzona Hospital Balance Sheet at September 30, 19B prepared in the combined "pancake" format illustrated by the AHA.

An Income Statement prepared for Alzona Hospital for the year ended September 30, 19B is contained in Figure 20-5. This statement is also prepared in the AHA-suggested format though, as noted earlier, (1) the detail within the "Other Revenues" caption is slightly at variance with regard to use of

*Assets*

Operating Fund:

| | | |
|---|---:|---:|
| Cash | | $ 118,000 |
| Investments | | 100,000 |
| Accrued interest receivable | | 2,000 |
| Accounts and notes receivable | $ 770,000 | |
| Less: Allowance for uncollectible accounts | 90,000 | 680,000 |
| Inventories | | 215,000 |
| Due from Specific Purpose Fund | | 105,000 |
| Due from Endowment Fund | | 30,000 |
| Total Operating Fund assets | | $1,250,000 |

Specific Purpose Fund:

| | | |
|---|---:|---:|
| Cash | | $ 130,000 |
| Investments | | 345,000 |
| Due from Endowment Fund | | 25,000 |
| Total Specific Purpose Fund assets | | $ 500,000 |

Endowment Fund:

| | | |
|---|---:|---:|
| Cash | | $ 66,000 |
| Investments | | 475,000 |
| Rental properties | $ 300,000 | |
| Less: Accumulated depreciation | 6,000 | 294,000 |
| Total Endowment Fund assets | | $ 835,000 |

Plant Fund:

| | | |
|---|---:|---:|
| Cash | $ 478,000 | |
| Investments | 300,000 | |
| Due from Operating Fund | 195,000 | $ 973,000 |
| Land | $ 130,000 | |
| Land improvements | 80,000 | |
| Buildings | 7,900,000 | |
| Fixed equipment | 500,000 | |
| Major movable equipment | 113,000 | |
| Total land, buildings, and equipment | $8,723,000 | |
| Less: Accumulated depreciation | 2,690,000 | |
| Net land, buildings, and equipment | | 6,033,000 |
| Total Plant Fund assets | | $7,006,000 |

Figure 20-4

*Liabilities and Capital*

Operating Fund:

| | | |
|---|---:|---:|
| Accounts payable | $ 50,000 | |
| Accrued salaries and wages payable | 83,000 | |
| Accrued interest payable | 31,000 | |
| Notes payable | 130,000 | |
| Due to Plant Fund | 195,000 | |
| Due to special nurses | 3,000 | |
| Total Operating Fund liabilities | | $ 492,000 |
| Operating Fund balance (Figure 20-6) | | 758,000 |
| Total Operating Fund liabilities and balance | | $1,250,000 |

Specific Purpose Fund:

| | |
|---|---:|
| Due to Operating Fund | $ 105,000 |
| Specific Purpose Fund balance (Figure 20-6) | 395,000 |
| Total Specific Purpose Fund liabilities and balance | $ 500,000 |

Endowment Fund:

| | | |
|---|---:|---:|
| Mortgage payable | $ 100,000 | |
| Due to Operating Fund | 30,000 | |
| Due to Specific Purpose Fund | 25,000 | |
| Total Endowment Fund liabilities | | $ 155,000 |
| Endowment Fund balance (Figure 20-6) | | 608,000 |
| Total Endowment Fund liabilities and balance | | $ 835,000 |

Plant Fund:

| | | |
|---|---:|---:|
| Contracts payable-retained percentage | $ 200,000 | |
| Bonds payable | 3,000,000 | |
| Total Plant Fund liabilities | | $3,200,000 |
| Plant Fund balance-invested in plant (Figure 20-6) | $3,033,000 | |
| Plant Fund balance-reserved for replacement and expansion (Figure 20-6) | 773,000 | |
| Total Plant Fund balance | | 3,806,000 |
| Total Plant Fund liabilities and capital | | $7,006,000 |

Figure 20-5

ALZONA HOSPITAL
Income Statement
For the Year Ended September 30, 19B

| | | |
|---|---:|---:|
| Patient service revenues | | |
| Daily patient services | $2,276,000 | |
| Other nursing services | 696,000 | |
| Other professional services | 1,428,000 | |
| Gross patient service revenues | | $4,400,000 |
| Deductions from patient service revenues | | |
| Contractual adjustments | $ 280,000 | |
| Charity service | 135,000 | |
| Provision for bad debts | 120,000 | |
| Total deductions from patient service revenues | | 535,000 |
| Net patient service revenues | | $3,865,000 |
| Other revenues | | |
| General contributions | $ 100,000 | |
| Operating Fund investment income | $ 5,000 | |
| Unrestricted Specific Purpose Fund investment income | 24,000 | |
| Unrestricted Endowment Fund rental income | 30,000 | |
| Unrestricted Plant Fund investment income | 16,000 | |
| Total investment income | 75,000 | |
| Restricted income transferred from Specific Purpose Fund | 300,000 | |
| Donated services | 20,000 | |
| Gain on disposal of assets | 5,000 | |
| Other | 102,000 | |
| Total other revenues | | 602,000 |
| Total revenues | | $4,467,000 |
| Expenses | | |
| Nursing services expense | $1,624,000 | |
| Other professional services expense | 981,000 | |
| General services expense | 943,000 | |
| Fiscal services expense | 160,000 | |
| Administrative services expense | 397,000 | |
| Depreciation expense | 300,000 | |
| Interest expense | 38,000 | |
| Loss on disposal of assets | 10,000 | |
| Total expenses | | 4,453,000 |
| Net income for the year (Figure 20-6) | | $ 14,000 |

"Income Transfers" accounts and (2) depreciation and interest expenses are shown separately from Administrative Services Expense in the "Expenses" section.

Hospital income statements are most useful when prepared in comparative form and accompanied by schedules presenting detailed revenue and expense data. The income statements illustrated here are classified functionally. Other common income statement classifications—either in lieu of or supplementary to the functional classification—include patient type (inpatient, outpatient and/ or pediatric, obstetric, emergency, etc.) and broad classes or categories (e.g., administrative and general; household and property; dietary, outpatient and emergency, and professional care of patients).

A Statement of Changes in Fund Balances of Alzona Hospital for the year ended September 30, 19B appears as Figure 20-6. This statement has been prepared in a manner consistent with the assumptions of our example (1) that only limited use would be made of "Income Transfers" accounts and (2) that unrestricted income of funds other than the Operating Fund was to be attributed to the Operating Fund, not recognized in the other funds, and restricted income was to be closed to Fund Balance of the other funds. Use of separate Plant Fund columns for "Invested" and "Reserved" is optional.

An alternate Statement of Changes in Fund Balances is shown in Figure 20-7. This statement is based on the alternate assumption (not employed in our example) that net income would be recognized in each fund, closed to Fund Balance of each, and the unrestricted portion would then be transferred to the Operating Fund and the "Income Transfers" account employed there in the manner suggested by the AHA. Either approach is acceptable.

## UNSETTLED ISSUES/CONCLUDING COMMENTS

In view of the rapid change in the hospital environment in recent years and the concomitantly accelerated evolution of hospital financial management and record-keeping, it is not surprising that there are both theoretical and pragmatic differences of opinion as to what constitutes the "best" accounting and reporting practice. Some feel, for example, that separate accounting for the revenues and expenditures of each fund is sufficient and that net income need not be determined. At the other extreme are those who would abandon the fund accounting approach, combine all accounts in a single accounting entity, and account for hospitals as commercial enterprises. Some of the contemporary issues and unsettled areas between these extremes are examined briefly in this concluding section of the chapter.

### AICPA Audit Guide

As previously mentioned, the American Institute of Certified Public Accountants recently issued a *Hospital Audit Guide* for use by its membership.

Figure 20-6

ALZONA HOSPITAL
Statement of Changes in Fund Balance
For the Year Ended September 30, 19B

| | Operating Fund | Specific Purpose Fund | Endowment Fund | Plant Fund Invested | Plant Fund Reserved |
|---|---|---|---|---|---|
| Fund balances—October 1, 19A (Figure 20-3) | $700,000 | $255,000 | $480,000 | $3,300,000 | $550,000 |
| Net income (Figure 20-5) | 14,000 | | | | |
| Payment of Plant Fund accounts payable from Operating Fund | [50,000] | | | 50,000 | |
| Increase in accumulated depreciation on Plant Fund assets | 300,000 | | | [300,000] | |
| Transfer of cash from Operating to Plant Fund to partially fund depreciation | [200,000] | | | | 200,000 |
| Unrestricted plant fund investment earnings retained in Plant Fund | [16,000] | | | | 16,000 |
| Sale of fixed assets at loss—proceeds retained in Plant Fund | 10,000 | | | [40,000] | 30,000 |
| Grant—specific purpose | | 400,000 | | | |
| Restricted Specific Purpose Fund investment income | | 15,000 | | | |
| Restricted Endowment Fund investment income | | 25,000 | | | |
| Restricted income transferred to Operating Fund | | [300,000] | | | |
| Endowment received, net of mortgage assumed | | | 200,000 | | |
| Acquisition of fixed assets | | | | 23,000 | [23,000] |
| Fund balances—September 30, 19B (Figure 20-4) | $758,000 | $395,000 | $680,000 | $3,033,000 | $773,000 |

**Figure 20-7**

## ALZONA HOSPITAL
### Statement of Changes in Fund Balance
### For the Year Ended September 30, 19B (Alternate Form)

| | Operating Fund | Specific Purpose Fund | Endowment Fund | Plant Fund Invested | Plant Fund Reserved |
|---|---|---|---|---|---|
| Fund balances—October 1, 19A (Figure 20-3) | $700,000 | $255,000 | $480,000 | $3,300,000 | $550,000 |
| Net income (Figure 20-5) | 14,000 | | | | |
| Payment of Plant Fund accounts payable from Operating Fund | [50,000] | | | 50,000 | |
| Increase in accumulated depreciation on Plant Fund assets | 300,000 | | | [300,000] | |
| Transfer of cash from Operating to Plant Fund to partially fund depreciation | [200,000] | | | | 200,000 |
| Grant—specific purpose | | 400,000 | | | |
| Investment income: | | | | | |
| Unrestricted | | 24,000 | 30,000 | | 16,000 |
| Restricted | | 15,000 | 25,000 | | |
| Transfers of unrestricted income to Operating Fund | | [24,000] | [30,000] | | [16,000] |
| Transfer of restricted income from Endowment to Specific Purpose Fund | | 25,000 | [25,000] | | |
| Restricted income transferred to Operating Fund | | [300,000] | | | |
| Transfer of Plant Fund investment income back from Operating Fund (retained in Plant Fund) | [16,000] | | | | 16,000 |
| Sale of fixed assets at loss—proceeds retained in Plant Fund | 10,000 | | | [40,000] | 30,000 |
| Endowment received, net of mortgage assumed | | | 200,000 | | |
| Acquisition of fixed assets | | | | 23,000 | [23,000] |
| Fund balances—September 30, 19B (Figure 20-4) | $758,000 | $395,000 | $680,000 | $3,033,000 | $773,000 |

Developed by the Institute's Committee on Health Care Institutions and its staff, the guide contains recommendations pertaining to (1) hospital auditing and reporting standards and procedures, and (2) definitions of hospital accounting terminology. The audit guide represents the AICPA's first publication of consequence on the subject of hospital financial accounting and reporting, though it previously issued a Medicare Audit Guide, and exposure drafts were circulated for comment nationally prior to its formal issuance.

The *Hospital Audit Guide* is directed primarily to independent Certified Public Accountants conducting external audits of general purpose hospital financial statements issued to the public. Its effects on hospital accounting and reporting practices will depend upon the extent to which its recommendations find acceptance both among independent auditors and among hospital financial managers.

Members of the Committee on Health Care Institutions agreed unanimously that general purpose hospital financial reports should be prepared in accordance with generally accepted accounting principles. Thus, it concluded that authoritative statements such as the Opinions of the Accounting Principles Board and the Research Bulletins of its predecessor, and presumably statements of its successor, apply to hospitals unless they are clearly inappropriate. As noted earlier, the Committee deemed present AHA pronouncements "generally compatible" with generally accepted accounting principles and with its audit guide except with regard to (1) carrying property, plant and equipment at current replacement cost and basing fixed asset depreciation charges on current replacement cost, and (2) carrying long-term security investments at current market value.[14]

Another major departure from AHA recommendations suggested by the AICPA Committee resulted from its conviction that (1) a clear-cut distinction should be maintained in the financial statements between externally restricted and unrestricted assets, and (2) liabilities should be reported in the fund(s) or fund categories through which they will be serviced. Thus the Institute Committee suggests that a hospital's accounts be divided into two categories for reporting purposes: (1) "Unrestricted Funds" and (2) "Restricted Funds."

Included within the "Unrestricted Funds" category would be (1) all assets and liabilities carried in the Operating Fund, (2) all board-designated fund accounts, and (3) unrestricted assets set aside for plant replacement or expansion and fixed asset-related debt other than that to be serviced from restricted assets—both of which are now accounted for within the Plant Fund under AHA recommendations. Any intrafund funds within the "Unrestricted Funds" category would be reported by use of distinctively titled asset accounts, as is common in commercial accounting, rather than in separate self-balancing groups. Thus all externally unrestricted assets and most liabilities are reported within the "Unrestricted Funds" caption under the AICPA Committee's approach and

---

[14] *Hospital Audit Guide,* p. 4.

totals are presented for each; the balance sheet is classified as between current and noncurrent assets and liabilities, as is commonly done in commercial accounting and reporting, and a single "Unrestricted Funds" Fund Balance amount is reported. A "Plant Replacement and Expansion Funds" heading is included within the "Restricted Funds" category to report resources restricted to such uses. The illustrative Balance Sheet prepared by the Institute Committee is presented as Figure 20-8.

The Balance Sheet illustrated by the AICPA Committee (Figure 20-8) could be easily derived from the accounts of a system maintained according to AHA recommendations. Preparation of a Statement of Changes in Fund Balances (Figure 20-9) in the manner suggested by the Institute Committee would be a cumbersome task in the absence of a restructured fund accounting system, however, and would result in the accounts being materially at variance with the statement.

The Statement of Revenues and Expenses format (Figure 20-10) suggested by the Institute Committee also varies somewhat from that of the Income Statement illustrated in *Chart of Accounts for Hospitals*. The primary recommendation inherent in the Committee's Statement of Revenues and Expenses format is that (1) a distinction should be made between *operating* revenues and expenses and *nonoperating* revenues, expenses, gains, and losses, and (2) income or loss from operations should be clearly reported, as well as overall net income or loss. Note also that under the Institute Committee format: (1) gifts, grants, subsidies, or other income intended to defray charity service costs or similar "Deductions from Revenue" items recognized during the period are netted against such allowances and deductions before the latter are deducted from total patient service revenue to derive net patient service revenue; (2) likewise, Specific Purpose Fund income used for designated purposes and thus recognized is included as operating revenue rather than as nonoperating or other revenue; (3) the provision for depreciation is shown separately under operating expenses, and interest expense is disclosed; and (4) unrestricted gifts, earnings, and gains are included in nonoperating revenue rather than in other revenue. (Presumably a nonoperating losses category would be appropriate where such losses have been sustained.)

As noted in Chapters 13 and 14, the Statement of Changes in Financial Position came to be considered a basic statement in general purpose financial reports following issuance of APB Opinion 19. A Statement of Changes in Financial Position (prepared on a working capital basis) adapted from that presented in the *Hospital Audit Guide* is shown in Figure 20-11. Other bases (such as cash or quick assets) are also acceptable; the choice of basis is largely a matter of individual preference or opinion as to which most clearly reflects the major causes of changes in financial position in a given situation. The footnotes accompanying the AICPA Committee's illustrative statements are shown in Figure 20-12.

Figure 20-8

SAMPLE HOSPITAL
Balance Sheet
December 31, 19—
With Comparative Figures for 19—

Unrestricted Funds

| Assets | Current Year | Prior Year |
|---|---|---|
| Current: | | |
| Cash | $ 133,000 | $ 33,000 |
| Receivable (Note 3) | 1,382,000 | 1,269,000 |
| Less estimated uncollectibles and allowances | (160,000) | (105,000) |
| | 1,222,000 | 1,164,000 |
| Due from restricted funds | 215,000 | — |
| Inventories (if material, state basis) | 176,000 | 183,000 |
| Prepaid expenses | 68,000 | 73,000 |
| Total current assets | 1,814,000 | 1,453,000 |
| Other: | | |
| Cash (Note 2) | 143,000 | 40,000 |
| Investments (Notes 1 and 2) | 1,427,000 | 1,740,000 |
| Property, plant, and equipment (Notes 4 and 5) | 11,028,000 | 10,375,000 |
| Less accumulated depreciation | (3,885,000) | (3,600,000) |
| Net property, plant, and equipment | 7,143,000 | 6,775,000 |
| Total (Note 2) | $10,527,000 | $10,008,000 |

| Liabilities and Fund Balances | Current Year | Prior Year |
|---|---|---|
| Current: | | |
| Notes payable to banks | $ 227,000 | $ 300,000 |
| Current installments of long-term debt (Note 5) | 90,000 | 90,000 |
| Accounts payable | 450,000 | 463,000 |
| Accrued expenses | 150,000 | 147,000 |
| Advances from third-party payors | 300,000 | 200,000 |
| Deferred revenue | 10,000 | 10,000 |
| Total current liabilities | 1,227,000 | 1,210,000 |
| Deferred revenue—third-party reimbursement (Note 4) | 200,000 | 90,000 |
| Long-term debt (Note 5): | | |
| Housing bonds | 500,000 | 520,000 |
| Mortgage note | 1,200,000 | 1,270,000 |
| Total long-term debt | 1,700,000 | 1,790,000 |
| Fund balance | 7,400,000 | 6,918,000 |
| Total | $10,527,000 | $10,008,000 |

**Assets**

| | | |
|---|---:|---:|
| Specific purpose funds: | | |
| Cash | $ 1,260 | $ 1,000 |
| Investments (Note 1) | 200,000 | 70,000 |
| Grants receivable | 90,000 | — |
| Total specific purpose funds | $ 291,260 | $ 71,000 |
| | | |
| Plant replacement and expansion funds: | | |
| Cash | $ 10,000 | $ 450,000 |
| Investments (Note 1) | 800,000 | 290,000 |
| Pledges receivable, net of estimated uncollectible | 20,000 | 360,000 |
| Total plant replacement and expansion funds | $ 830,000 | $ 1,100,000 |
| | | |
| Endowment funds: | | |
| Cash | $ 50,000 | $ 33,000 |
| Investments (Note 1) | 6,100,000 | 3,942,000 |
| Total endowment funds | $ 6,150,000 | $ 3,975,000 |

**Liabilities and Fund Balances**

| | | |
|---|---:|---:|
| Specific purpose funds: | | |
| Due to unrestricted funds | $ 215,000 | — |
| Fund balances: | | |
| Research grants | 15,000 | 30,000 |
| Other | 61,260 | 41,000 |
| | 76,260 | 71,000 |
| Total specific purpose funds | $ 291,260 | $ 71,000 |
| | | |
| Plant replacement and expansion funds: | | |
| Fund balances: | | |
| Restricted by third-party payors | $ 380,000 | $ 150,000 |
| Other | 450,000 | 950,000 |
| Total plant replacement and expansion funds | $ 830,000 | $ 1,100,000 |
| | | |
| Endowment funds: | | |
| Fund balances: | | |
| Permanent endowment | $ 4,850,000 | $ 2,675,000 |
| Term endowment | 1,300,000 | 1,300,000 |
| Total endowment funds | $ 6,150,000 | $ 3,975,000 |

See accompanying Notes to Financial Statements (Figure 20–12).

Source: *Hospital Audit Guide*, pp. 40–41.

889

Figure 20-9

## SAMPLE HOSPITAL
### Statement of Changes in Fund Balances
### Year Ended December 31, 19—
### With Comparative Figures for 19—

|  | Current Year | Prior Year |
|---|---|---|
| *Unrestricted Funds* |  |  |
| Balance at beginning of year | $6,918,000 | $6,242,000 |
| Excess of revenues over expenses | 84,000 | 114,000 |
| Transferred from plant replacement and expansion funds to finance property, plant, and equipment expenditures | 628,000 | 762,000 |
| Transferred to plant replacement and expansion funds to reflect third-party payor revenue restricted to property, plant, and equipment replacement | (230,000) | (200,000) |
| Balance at end of year | $7,400,000* | $6,918,000 |
| *Restricted Funds* |  |  |
| Specific purpose funds: |  |  |
| Balance at beginning of year | $    71,000 | $    50,000 |
| Restricted gifts and bequests | 35,000 | 20,000 |
| Research grants | 35,000 | 45,000 |
| Income from investments | 35,260 | 39,000 |
| Gain on sale of investments | 8,000 | — |
| Transferred to: |  |  |
| Other operating revenue | (100,000) | (80,000) |
| Allowances and uncollectible accounts | (8,000) | (3,000) |
| Balance at end of year | $    76,260 | $    71,000 |
| Plant replacement and expansion funds: |  |  |
| Balance at beginning of year | $1,100,000 | $1,494,000 |
| Restricted gifts and bequests | 113,000 | 150,000 |
| Income from investments | 15,000 | 18,000 |
| Transferred to unrestricted funds (described above) | (628,000) | (762,000) |
| Transferred from unrestricted funds (described above) | 230,000 | 200,000 |
| Balance at end of year | $  830,000 | $1,100,000 |
| Endowment funds: |  |  |
| Balance at beginning of year | $3,975,000 | $2,875,000 |
| Restricted gifts and bequests | 2,000,000 | 1,000,000 |
| Net gain on sale of investments | 175,000 | 100,000 |
| Balance at end of year | $6,150,000 | $3,975,000 |

See accompanying Notes to Financial Statements (Figure 20–12).

* Composition of the balance may be shown here, on the balance sheet, or in a footnote.

Source: *Hospital Audit Guide,* p. 43.

Several other noteworthy suggestions are offered—or issues raised—either explicitly or implicitly in the *Hospital Audit Guide*. Among these are recommendations that:

1. Contributions restricted for fixed asset acquisition should be accounted for as contributed capital rather than revenue; and

**Figure 20-10**

SAMPLE HOSPITAL
Statement of Revenues and Expenses
Year Ended December 31, 19—
With Comparative Figures for 19—

|  | Current Year | Prior Year |
|---|---|---|
| Patient service revenue | $8,500,000 | $8,000,000 |
| Allowances and uncollectible accounts (after deduction of related gifts, grants, subsidies, and other income—$55,000 and $40,000) (Notes 3 and 4) | (1,777,000) | (1,700,000) |
| Net patient service revenue | 6,723,000 | 6,300,000 |
| Other operating revenue (including $100,000 and $80,000 from specific purpose funds) | 184,000 | 173,000 |
| Total operating revenue | 6,907,000 | 6,473,000 |
| Operating expenses: | | |
| Nursing services | 2,200,000 | 2,000,000 |
| Other professional services | 1,900,000 | 1,700,000 |
| General services | 2,100,000 | 2,000,000 |
| Fiscal services | 375,000 | 360,000 |
| Administrative services (including interest expense of $50,000 and $40,000) | 400,000 | 375,000 |
| Provision for depreciation | 300,000 | 250,000 |
| Total operating expenses | 7,275,000 | 6,685,000 |
| Loss from operations | (368,000) | (212,000) |
| Nonoperating revenue: | | |
| Unrestricted gifts and bequests | 228,000 | 205,000 |
| Unrestricted income from endowment funds | 170,000 | 80,000 |
| Income and gains from board-designated funds | 54,000 | 41,000 |
| Total nonoperating revenue | 452,000 | 326,000 |
| Excess of revenues over expenses | 84,000 | $ 114,000 |

See accompanying Notes to Financial Statements (Figure 20–12).
Source: *Hospital Audit Guide,* p. 42.

2. Where there are timing differences between expense reporting for financial statement purposes and for reimbursable cost calculations, the effect of such differences should be deferred in a manner similar to that employed in interperiod allocation of income taxes. For example, when financial statements are based on straight line depreciation but cost reimbursements are based on accelerated depreciation the additional revenue received

**Figure 20-11**

SAMPLE HOSPITAL
Statement of Changes in Financial Position*
(Working Capital Basis)
Year Ended December 31, 19—

*Working capital was increased by:*
Operations:

| | | |
|---|---:|---:|
| Net Income (Figure 20-10) | $ 84,000 | |
| Adjustments to reflect working capital provided: | | |
| Provision for depreciation | 300,000 | |
| Increase in deferred third party reimbursement | 110,000 | |
| Revenue restricted to fixed asset replacement, transferred to plant replacement and expansion fund | (230,000) | |
| Working capital increase from operations | | $ 264,000 |
| Other sources: | | |
| Decrease in board-designated funds | $210,000 | |
| Fixed asset expenditures financed through plant replacement and expansion funds | 628,000 | |
| Working capital increase from other sources | | 838,000 |
| | | $1,102,000 |

*Working capital was decreased by:*

| | | |
|---|---:|---:|
| Additions to property, plant, and equipment | $668,000 | |
| Reduction of long-term debt | 90,000 | |
| | | 758,000 |
| Net increase in working capital during the year | | $ 344,000 |
| Working capital, beginning of year | | 243,000 |
| Working capital, end of year | | $ 587,000 |

See accompanying Notes to Financial Statements (Figure 20–12).
Source: Adapted from *Hospital Audit Guide,* pp. 46–47

* A statement detailing the changes in working capital items should accompany, or be made part of, the Statement of Changes in Financial Position.

Figure 20-12

SAMPLE HOSPITAL
Notes to Financial Statements
December 31, 19—

NOTE 1: Investments are stated in the financial statements at cost. Cost and quoted market values at December 31, 19— are summarized as follows:

| | Cost | Quoted Market |
|---|---|---|
| Board-designated funds | $1,427,000 | $1,430,000 |
| Specific-purpose funds | 200,000 | 210,000 |
| Plant replacement and expansion funds | 800,000 | 838,000 |
| Endowment funds | 6,100,000 | 8,200,000 |

NOTE 2: Of total unrestricted assets of $10,527,000, $1,570,000 has been designated for expansion of outpatient facilities; these assets are shown as other assets because they are not expected to be expended during 19—.

NOTE 3: Revenues received under cost reimbursement agreements totaling $4,000,000 for the current year and $3,000,000 for the prior year are subject to audit and retroactive adjustment by third-party payors. Provisions for estimated retroactive adjustments under these agreements have been provided.

NOTE 4: Property, plant, and equipment is stated at cost. A summary of the accounts and the related accumulated depreciation follows:

| | Cost | Accumulated Depreciation |
|---|---|---|
| Land | $ 300,000 | $ —0— |
| Land improvements | 140,000 | 100,000 |
| Buildings | 7,088,000 | 2,885,000 |
| Fixed equipment | 2,000,000 | 800,000 |
| Movable equipment | 1,500,000 | 100,000 |
| | $11,028,000 | $3,885,000 |

Depreciation is determined on a straight-line basis for financial statement purposes. The hospital uses accelerated depreciation to determine reimbursable costs under certain third-party reimbursement agreements. Cost reimbursement revenue in the amount of $110,000 resulting from the difference in depreciation methods is deferred in the current year and will be taken into income in future years.

NOTE 5: The 3 percent housing bonds are payable in varying annual amounts to 19— and are collateralized by a mortgage on a nurses' residence carried at $800,000. The mortgage note is payable in quarterly installments of $17,500 with interest at 4 percent through 19— and is collateralized by land and buildings carried at $2,800,000.

NOTE 6: The hospital has a noncontributory pension plan covering substantially all employees. Total pension expense for the year was $48,000, which includes amortization of prior service cost over a period of 20 years. The hospital's policy is to fund pension costs accrued. The actuarially computed value of vested benefits as of December 31, 19— exceeds net assets of the pension fund and balance sheet accruals by approximately $156,000.

Source: *Hospital Audit Guide,* pp. 48–49.

Figure 20-13

## ALZONA HOSPITAL
### Operating Fund Worksheet for the year ended September 20, 19B

| | Trial Balance 10/1/19A Dr. | Trial Balance 10/1/19A Cr. | Transactions and Adjustments Dr. | Transactions and Adjustments Cr. | Pre-closing Trial Balance 9/30/B Dr. | Pre-closing Trial Balance 9/30/B Cr. | Income Statement Dr. | Income Statement Cr. | Balance Sheet Dr. | Balance Sheet Cr. |
|---|---|---|---|---|---|---|---|---|---|---|
| Cash | 175,000 | | (3) 3,800,000; (13) 3,000; (14) 24,000; (15) 48,000; (18) 95,000; (19) 100,000; (34) 200,000 | (8) 668,000; (9) 2,700,000; (10) 757,000; (12) 27,000; (16) 45,000; (33) 80,000; (36) 50,000 | 1,180,000 | | | | 118,000 | |
| Investments | 100,000 | | | | 100,000 | | | | 100,000 | |
| Accounts and Notes Receivable | 700,000 | | (1) 4,400,000 | (2) 415,000; (3) 3,800,000; (4) 115,000 | 770,000 | | | | 770,000 | |
| Allowance for Uncollectible Receivables | | 85,000 | (4) 115,000; (32) 5,000 | (5) 120,000 | | 90,000 | | | | 90,000 |
| Due from Specific Purpose Fund | 145,000 | | (34) 100,000; 5,000 | (33) 145,000 | 105,000 | | | | 105,000 | |
| Inventories | 165,000 | | (6) 600,000; (8) 675,000; (12) 20,000; (33) 225,000; (39) 5,000 | (7) 550,000; (6) 600,000 | 215,000 | | | | 215,000 | |
| Accounts Payable | | 125,000 | | | | 50,000 | | | | 50,000 |
| Notes Payable | | 150,000 | | | | 130,000 | | | | 130,000 |
| Due to Plant Fund | | 225,000 | (33) 225,000; (38) 200,000 | (38) 200,000 | | 195,000 | | | | 195,000 |
| Operating Fund Balance | | 700,000 | (36) 50,000 | (37) 300,000 | | 744,000 | | | | 744,000 |
| | 1,285,000 | 1,285,000 | | | | | | | | |
| Accrued Salaries and Wages Payable | | | (41) 16,000 | (11) 83,000 | | 83,000 | | | | 83,000 |
| Accrued Interest Payable | | | | (12) 1,000; (20) 30,000 | | 31,000 | | | | 31,000 |

| Account | Ref | | Ref | | | | |
|---|---|---|---|---|---|---|---|
| Accrued Interest Receivable | (13) | 2,000 | | | | | 2,000 |
| Due to Special Nurses | (16) | 45,000 | (15) | 48,000 | 3,000 | 3,000 | 3,000 |
| Due from Endowment Fund | (35) | 30,000 | | 30,000 | 30,000 | | 30,000 |
| **Patient Service Revenue:** | | | | | | | |
| Revenue from Daily Patient Services | (1) | 2,276,000 | | 2,276,000 | 2,276,000 | | |
| Revenue from Other Nursing Services | (1) | 696,000 | | 696,000 | 696,000 | | |
| Revenue from Other Professional Services | (1) | 1,428,000 | | 1,428,000 | 1,428,000 | | |
| **Deductions from Patient Service Revenue:** | | | | | | | |
| Charity Service | (2) | 135,000 | | 135,000 | 135,000 | | |
| Contractual Adjustments | (2) | 280,000 | | 280,000 | 280,000 | | |
| Provision for Bad Debts | (5) | 120,000 | | 120,000 | 120,000 | | |
| **Other Revenue:** | | | | | | | |
| General Contributions | (19) | 100,000 | | 100,000 | 100,000 | | |
| Donated Services | (17) | 20,000 | | 20,000 | 20,000 | | |
| Operating Fund Investment Income | (13) | 5,000 | | 5,000 | 5,000 | | |
| Unrestricted Specific Purpose Fund Investment Income | (14) | 24,000 | | 24,000 | 24,000 | | |
| Unrestricted Endowment Fund Rental Income | (35) | 30,000 | | 30,000 | 30,000 | | |
| Unrestricted Plant Fund Investment Income | (40) | 16,000 | | 16,000 | 16,000 | | |
| Restricted Income Transfers from Specific Purpose Fund | (34) | 300,000 | | 300,000 | 300,000 | | |
| Gain on Disposal of Assets | (32) | 5,000 | | 5,000 | 5,000 | | |
| Other Revenues | (8) | 7,000 | (18) | 95,000 | 102,000 | 102,000 | |
| **Patient Service Expenses:** | | | | | | | |
| Nursing Services Expense | (7) | 170,000 | | 1,624,000 | 1,624,000 | | |
| | (9) | 1,316,000 | | | | | |
| | (10) | 86,000 | | | | | |
| | (11) | 35,000 | | | | | |
| | (17) | 17,000 | | | | | |
| Other Professional Services Expense | (7) | 50,000 | | 981,000 | 981,000 | | |
| | (9) | 828,000 | | | | | |
| | (10) | 79,000 | | | | | |
| | (11) | 21,000 | | | | | |
| | (17) | 3,000 | | | | | |

## Figure 20-13 (cont.)

| | Trial Balance 10/1/19A | | | | | Pre-closing Trial Balance 9/30/B | | Income Statement | | Balance Sheet | |
|---|---|---|---|---|---|---|---|---|---|---|---|
| | Dr. | Cr. | | Dr. | Cr. | Dr. | Cr. | Dr. | Cr. | Dr. | Cr. |
| Other Service Expense: | | | | | | | | | | | |
| General Services Expense | | | (7) | 319,000 | | 943,000 | | 943,000 | | | |
| | | | (9) | 389,000 | (38) 5,000 | | | | | | |
| | | | (10) | 221,000 | | | | | | | |
| | | | (11) | 19,000 | | | | | | | |
| Fiscal Services Expense | | | (7) | 8,000 | | 160,000 | | 160,000 | | | |
| | | | (9) | 102,000 | | | | | | | |
| | | | (10) | 44,000 | | | | | | | |
| | | | (11) | 6,000 | | | | | | | |
| Administrative Services Expense | | | (7) | 3,000 | | 397,000 | | 397,000 | | | |
| | | | (9) | 65,000 | | | | | | | |
| | | | (10) | 327,000 | | | | | | | |
| | | | (11) | 2,000 | | | | | | | |
| Depreciation Expense | | | (37) | 300,000 | | 300,000 | | 300,000 | | | |
| Loss on Disposal of Assets | | | (41) | 10,000 | | 10,000 | | 10,000 | | | |
| Interest Expense | | | (12) | 8,000 | | 38,000 | | 38,000 | | | |
| | | | (20) | 30,000 | | | | | | | |
| | | | | 15,751,000 | 15,751,000 | 6,328,000 | 6,328,000 | 4,988,000 | 5,002,000 | | |
| Net Income | | | | | | | | 14,000 | | | 14,000 |
| | | | | | | | | 5,002,000 | 5,002,000 | 1,340,000 | 1,340,000 |

896

Figure 20-14

## ALZONA HOSPITAL
### Specific Purpose Fund Worksheet for the Year Ended September 30, 19B

| | Trial Balance 10/1/19A | | Transactions and Adjustments | | Trial Balance 9/30/19B | |
|---|---|---|---|---|---|---|
| | Dr. | Cr. | Dr. | Cr. | Dr. | Cr. |
| Cash | 20,000 | | (21) 400,000<br>(23) 150,000<br>(24) 15,000<br>(32) 170,000 | (22) 300,000<br>(33) 125,000<br>(34) 200,000 | 130,000 | |
| Investments | 360,000 | | (22) 300,000 | (23) 150,000<br>(32) 165,000 | 345,000 | |
| Due from Endowment Fund | 20,000 | | (42) 25,000 | (33) 20,000 | 25,000 | |
| Due to Operating Fund | | 145,000 | (33) 145,000 | (32) 5,000<br>(34) 100,000 | | 105,000 |
| Specific Purpose Fund Balance | | 255,000 | (34) 300,000 | (21) 400,000<br>(24) 15,000<br>(42) 25,000 | | 395,000 |
| | 400,000 | 400,000 | 1,505,000 | 1,505,000 | 500,000 | 500,000 |

Figure 20-15

## ALZONA HOSPITAL
### Endowment Fund Worksheet for the Year Ended September 30, 19B

| | Trial Balance 10/1/19A | | Transactions and Adjustments | | Trial Balance 9/30/19B | |
|---|---|---|---|---|---|---|
| | Dr. | Cr. | Dr. | Cr. | Dr. | Cr. |
| Cash | 25,000 | | (26) 45,000 (42) 25,000 | (28) 9,000 (33) 20,000 | 66,000 | |
| Investments | 475,000 | | | | 475,000 | |
| Due to Specific Purpose Fund | | 20,000 | (33) 20,000 | (42) 25,000 | | 25,000 |
| Endowment Fund Balance | | 480,000 | | (25) 200,000 | | 680,000 |
| | 500,000 | 500,000 | | | | |
| Rental Properties | | | (25) 300,000 | | 300,000 | |
| Mortgage Payable | | | | (25) 100,000 | | 100,000 |
| Rental Revenues | | | (35) 45,000 | (26) 45,000 | | |
| Depreciation Expense | | | (27) 6,000 | (35) 6,000 | | |
| Accumulated Depreciation | | | | (27) 6,000 | | 6,000 |
| Other Rental Expenses | | | (28) 9,000 | (35) 9,000 | | |
| Due to Operating Fund | | | | (35) 30,000 | | 30,000 |
| | | | 450,000 | 450,000 | 841,000 | 841,000 |

Figure 20-16

## ALZONA HOSPITAL
### Plant Fund Worksheet for the Year Ended September 30, 19B

| | Trial Balance 10/1/19A | | Transactions and Adjustments | | | | Trial Balance 9/30/19B | |
|---|---|---|---|---|---|---|---|---|
| | Dr. | Cr. | Dr. | | Cr. | | Dr. | Cr. |
| Cash | 25,000 | | (29) 3,000,000 (33) 225,000 (40) 16,000 (41) 30,000 | | (30) 2,800,000 (31) 18,000 | | 478,000 | |
| Investments | 300,000 | | | | | | 300,000 | |
| Due from Operating Fund | 225,000 | | (38) 200,000 | | (33) 225,000 (39) 5,000 | | 195,000 | |
| Land | 130,000 | | | | | | 130,000 | |
| Land Improvements | 80,000 | | | | | | 80,000 | |
| Buildings | 5,000,000 | | (30) 2,900,000 | | | | 7,900,000 | |
| Fixed Equipment | 600,000 | | | | (47) 100,000 | | 500,000 | |
| Major Movable Equipment | 90,000 | | (31) 18,000 (39) 5,000 | | | | 113,000 | |
| Accumulated Depreciation | | 2,450,000 | (41) 60,000 | | (37) 300,000 | | | 2,690,000 |
| Mortgage Payable | | 100,000 | (30) 100,000 | | | | | |
| Accounts Payable | | 50,000 | (36) 50,000 | | | | | |
| Plant Fund Balance—Invested in Plant | | 3,300,000 | (37) 300,000 (41) 40,000 | | (31) 18,000 (36) 50,000 (39) 5,000 | | | 3,033,000 |

Figure 20-16 (cont.)

| | Trial Balance 10/1/19A | | Transactions and Adjustments | | Trial Balance 9/30/19B | |
|---|---|---|---|---|---|---|
| | Dr. | Cr. | Dr. | Cr. | Dr. | Cr. |
| Plant Fund Balance—Reserved for Plant Replacement and Expansion | | 550,000 | (31) 18,000 (39) 5,000 | (38) 200,000 (40) 16,000 (41) 30,000 | | 773,000 |
| Bonds Payable | | | | (29) 3,000,000 | | 3,000,000 |
| Contracts Payable—Retained Percentage | | | | (30) 200,000 | | 200,000 |
| | 6,450,000 | 6,450,000 | 6,967,000 | 6,967,000 | 9,696,000 | 9,696,000 |

would be deferred, such as by crediting it to a Deferred Third Party Reimbursement account (Figure 20-8), and recognized in later periods in which more depreciation expense is recognized for financial purposes than for reimbursable cost determination.

## Other Issues and Concluding Comments

Several alternative approaches and unsettled issues in contemporary hospital accounting, both major and minor, have been discussed or alluded to in this chapter. In view of such differing viewpoints the Alzona Hospital example was based on a "middle ground" approach, that is, it was based principally on current AHA recommendations but also contained elements of the AICPA Committee viewpoint and author preference.

Other issues and questions have arisen from time to time and still others will surely arise in the future. It can be asserted pragmatically, for example, that use of terminology such as "Provision for Bad Debts" and "Provision for Depreciation" may lead some statement users to believe (erroneously) that resources have been set aside for such purposes. Obviously such accounts are intended to report expenses, not assets. Likewise, from a theoretical standpoint one can question whether the peculiarities of the hospital environment justify deferring the recognition of realized restricted revenues until the period in which the related resources are used for the specified purpose. Should such items be recognized as revenues when they become available for use rather than when they are used? Still further, it can be argued that contributions, grants, subsidies and donations —even those to defray certain specified costs or expenses—should be considered contributed capital rather than revenue and should be reflected only in the Statements of Change(s) in Fund Balance(s). (The Institute Committee took this position with regard to those restricted to plant replacement and expansion uses.) Though resolution of questions such as these is obviously beyond the scope of this chapter, they certainly provide food for thought and raise interesting research possibilities for those wishing to explore hospital accounting and reporting in more depth.

**Question 20-1.** Prepare a list of the funds recommended for use by a hospital. Opposite the funds indicate the fund or account groups recommended for municipalities by the National Committee on Governmental Accounting that are most nearly comparable in nature.

**Question 20-2.** Some of the differences of opinion between the American Hospital Association (AHA) and the AICPA Committee on Health Care Institutions noted in this chapter result from differing views with regard to the primary purposes and users of hospital financial reports. Explain.

**Question 20-3.** What is an "implicit interfund transfer"? Give an example of a hospital situation involving one.

**Question 20-4.** Name three differences between the accounting procedures of hospitals and those of municipalities.

**Question 20-5.** Why is it important to distinguish between "unrestricted" and "restricted" assets in hospital accounting? (Be sure to define these terms in your answer.)

**Question 20-6.** Contrast the positions of the American Hospital Association and the AICPA Committee on Health Care Institutions with regard both to the definition of and to the accounting and reporting significance of the terms "board restricted" and "externally restricted" as applied to assets.

**Question 20-7.** An auditor is concerned about the large amount of "Other Revenues" appearing on a hospital's Statement of Revenues and Expenses (Income Statement), as he has always tried to keep client presentations of "miscellaneous or other" revenue and expense items to a reasonable minimum. Do you agree with his concern? Why?

**Question 20-8.** What have been the principal effects of the rapidly expanded role and the significance of third party payors on hospital accounting and reporting?

**Question 20-9.** What are the advantage(s) of showing billings at standard rates and showing allowances (such as those made to hospital cost prepayment plan groups) as deductions from gross revenues rather than showing the net amount billed as revenues without disclosing the amounts of deductions?

**Question 20-10.** The following entries appeared in a hospital general journal:

| | | |
|---|---:|---:|
| 1. Depreciation Expense—Buildings (Operating Fund) ............................... | 10,000 | |
|     Accumulated Depreciation—Buildings (Plant Fund) ....................... | | 10,000 |
|     To reflect depreciation charges. | | |
| | | |
| 2. Plant Fund Balance—Invested in Plant (Plant Fund) ............................... | 10,000 | |
|     Operating Fund Balance (Operating Fund) | | 10,000 |
|     To reduce capital invested in Plant Fund by amount of depreciation charges. | | |

(a) What is wrong with these entries? (b) Prepare corrected entries. (c) What is the logic underlying the corrected entries?

**Question 20-11.** Diagnostic and analysis equipment developed by the Federal government at a cost of $1,000,000 per unit was donated to Peoples' Hospital for medical and research use. Similar equipment is available from a commercial supplier at a cost of $600,000 new or for $400,000 if used and of about the same age as that received. The hospital will use the equipment extensively, but the administrator doubts that it will be replaced when it is worn out or obsolete due to its high cost.

   a. Should the contribution be accounted for as either revenue or contributed capital by the hospital? Explain.

   b. Should depreciation be recorded and, if so, on what "cost" basis?

**Question 20-12.**
a. Should depreciation be charged on the fixed assets of a hospital if these assets have been financed from contributions but are intended to be replaced from hospital revenues?
b. Assume that the replacement of the fixed assets is intended to be financed from contributions. Should depreciation be charged on such fixed assets?

**Question 20-13.** Distinguish between the *single income statement* and *consolidated income statement* methods of hospital accounting and reporting, both as to (a) concept and procedure and (b) the effect upon reported net income.

**Question 20-14.** Both the AHA and the AICPA Committee on Health Care Institutions suggest that revenue (or contributed capital) be recognized differently where resources are "restricted." What is the difference, and is it logical?

**Question 20-15.** How do AHA and AICPA Committee on Health Care Institutions recommendations differ with respect to fixed asset, depreciation, and investment accounting? What is the apparent reason(s) underlying these differences of opinion?

**Question 20-16.** What are the primary differences between the AHA and AICPA Committee on Health Care Institutions recommendations with respect to- hospital balance sheet form, content, or classification? What is the apparent logic of each underlying these differences?

**Question 20-17.** What are the primary differences between the AHA and AICPA Committee on Health Care Institutions recommendations as to the title, form, content, or classification of hospital net income statement presentations? What is the apparent logic of each underlying these differences?

**Question 20-18.** Wisconsin City is on the modified accrual basis of accounting.
a. Is the city keeping its accounts in accordance with generally accepted principles of accounting in this respect? Explain.
b. Wisconsin City General Hospital has been organized recently and you have been retained to advise in the installation of its accounting. What basis of accounting would you recommend for the hospital? Explain.

**Question 20-19.** A county hospital derives its revenues solely from a special tax levy made for this purpose. Would the accounting procedures outlined throughout this chapter apply to such a hospital? If not, indicate the fund or funds in which the financial transactions of the hospital should be recorded.

**Problem 20-1.** (Fund worksheet from a single ledger) Community Hospital began operations in early January, 19X0, in facilities financed largely by donations from the James family. No capital expenditures were made during 19X0 and no fixed assets were retired. By action of the Board of Trustees, the administrator is responsible for funding depreciation unless excused by action of the Board. No such action has been taken.

The Edna May James Fund has been established for the special purpose of making loans to X-ray students. The Julian James Fund has been established to buy additional X-ray equipment. $10,500 in cash and $12,000 in securities were donated to form the Julian James Fund and these assets were properly combined with other cash and securities intended for plant building use.

The books were closed on December 31, 19X0. No financial statements have ever been prepared, but the list of accounts shown is in balance.

Required:
From the information contained in the following schedule of account balances and

in the data above, you are to prepare a worksheet from which a Fund Balance Sheet could be prepared at December 31, 19X0. (A formal Balance Sheet is not required.)

*Schedule of Account Balances*

| | |
|---|---:|
| Accounts payable ..................... | $ 7,000 |
| Accounts receivable ................... | 70,000 |
| Accrued interest payable ............... | 20,000 |
| Accrued salaries & wages payable ........ | 10,000 |
| Accrued taxes payable ................. | 500 |
| Accumulated depreciation—building....... | 30,000 |
| Accumulated depreciation—equipment..... | 37,500 |
| Allowance for doubtful accounts ......... | 7,800 |
| Allowance for uncollectible pledges ....... | 20,000 |
| Buildings ............................ | 1,500,000 |
| Building drive pledges receivable.......... | 115,000 |
| Capital .............................. | 2,660,400 |
| Cash—Building drive fund .............. | 73,000 |
| Cash—Edna May James ................ | 700 |
| Cash—Operating fund ................. | 41,500 |
| Cash—Payroll account.................. | 2,500 |
| Equipment .......................... | 600,000 |
| Inventory ........................... | 20,000 |
| Investments—Building drive fund ........ | 840,000 |
| Investments—Edna May James .......... | 2,000 |
| Land ............................... | 25,000 |
| Mortgage payable..................... | 500,000 |
| Petty cash .......................... | 500 |
| Prepaid expenses ..................... | 2,500 |

(FHFMA, adapted)

**Problem 20-2. Part I.** The following is a trial balance of the Operating Fund of McClusky Hospital, a general care facility, at January 1, 19X6:

| | | |
|---|---:|---:|
| Cash ............................... | $10,000 | |
| Accounts Receivable ................... | 35,000 | |
| Due from Specific Purpose Fund ........ | 3,000 | |
| Accounts Payable ..................... | | $12,000 |
| Allowance for Uncollectible Accounts .... | | 500 |
| Fund Balance......................... | | 35,500 |
| | $48,000 | $48,000 |

The following transactions took place during the year:

1. Bills rendered to patients: $500,000 for daily patient services, $400,000 for other nursing services, and $600,000 for other professional services; of these billings $10,000 is estimated to be uncollectible, $3,000 of which is attributable to expected contractual adjustments and $2,000 to expected policy discounts allowed.

2. Expenditures for salaries and wages and for materials (all paid for in cash) were as follows:

| Department | Amount |
|---|---|
| Professional care of inpatients (nursing services, etc.) | $737,000 |
| Outpatient and emergency services | 28,000 |
| Dietary services | 205,000 |
| Administrative and general | 139,000 |
| Household and property | 291,000 |

3. Accounts receivable of $1,480,000 were collected; bad debts of $4,800 were written off and contractual and policy adjustments made amounted to $2,700 and $1,900, respectively.

4. An Operating Fund billing in the amount of $10,000 was rendered to the Specific Purpose Fund for its share of the cost of recreational activities included in the expenditures above.

5. Accounts payable outstanding on January 1, 19X6 were paid.

6. The $3,000 due from the Specific Purpose Fund on January 1, 19X6, was paid to the Operating Fund.

7. Mortgage interest in the amount of $3,200 was paid.

8. The cafeteria (operated as a separate corporation) paid to the Operating Fund $20,000 representing its net income for the year.

9. The following liabilities and accruals remained unpaid at December 31, 19X6:

| | |
|---|---|
| Accounts payable (for materials and supplies used; to be charged to professional care of patients) | $ 5,000 |
| Accrued interest on mortgage | 8,000 |
| Accrued salaries and wages chargeable as follows: | |
| Administrative and general | 3,000 |
| Dietary services | 1,200 |
| Household and property maintenance | 4,800 |
| Professional care of inpatients | 13,000 |
| Outpatient and emergency services | 1,000 |

10. Annual depreciation charges:

| | |
|---|---|
| Buildings | $30,000 |
| Equipment | 50,000 |

11. Cash equal to the depreciation charges on equipment was transferred from the Operating Fund to the Plant Fund. (Single income statement approach is used.)

12. Closing entries were prepared.

Required:

Prepare a worksheet to reflect the beginning trial balance, transactions and adjustments, closing entires, and post-closing trial balance of the Operating Fund of McClusky Hospital for the year ended December 31, 19X6.

**Problem 20-2. Part II.** (Specific Purpose Fund transactions) The trial balance of the Specific Purpose Fund of McClusky Hospital at January 1, 19X6, was as follows:

| | | |
|---|---|---|
| Cash ............................ | $5,500 | |
| Due from Plant Fund .............. | 1,000 | |
| Due to Operating Fund ........... | | $3,000 |
| Fund Balance ..................... | | 3,500 |
| | $6,500 | $6,500 |

The following transactions took place during the year:

1. A donation in the amount of $25,000 was received in cash to be used for recreational purposes only.

2. The Specific Purpose Fund was billed $10,000 by the Operating Fund for its share of the cost of recreational activities.

3. Administrative expenditures (paid in cash) for the year amounted to $1,000.

4. The $3,000 liability to the Operating Fund at January 1, 19X6, was paid.

Required:

Prepare a worksheet to reflect the beginning trial balance, transactions and adjustments, and post-closing trial balance of the Specific Purpose Fund of McClusky Hospital for the year ended December 31, 19X6.

**Problem 20-2. Part III.** (Endowment Fund transactions) The trial balance of the Endowment Fund of McClusky Hospital at January 1, 19X6, was as follows:

| | | |
|---|---|---|
| Cash ................................. | $ 46,000 | |
| Investments—Certificates of Deposit ....... | 110,000 | |
| Endowment Fund—Balance A............. | | $ 81,000 |
| Endowment Fund—Balance B ........... | | 75,000 |
| | $156,000 | $156,000 |

The following transactions took place during the year:

1. A donation of $75,000 was received in cash for the purpose of establishing an Endowment Fund (hereinafter referred to as Endowment Fund C), the income from which is to be used to provide special services for patients.

2. The money was invested in bonds which were purchased at par.

3. Stocks with a market value of $100,000 were donated to the hospital for the purpose of establishing an Endowment Fund (hereinafter referred to as Endowment Fund D), the income from which is to be available for general purposes.

4. Bonds with a par value of $3,000 were sold at a loss of $300.
5. Stocks with a book value of $5,000 were sold at a profit of $500.
6. Interest income was received on certificates of deposit, $6,240. Earnings on Endowments A and B accumulate for 20 more years, at the end of which time the entire Fund Balances may be used to acquire equipment or furnishings in honor of the donors.

Required:
Prepare a worksheet to reflect the beginning balances, transactions and adjustments, and post-closing trial balance of the Endowment Fund of McClusky Hospital for the year ended December 31, 19X6.

**Problem 20-2. Part IV.**  (Plant Fund transactions) The following are the trial balances of the Plant Fund of McClusky Hospital at January 1, 19X6:

| | | |
|---|---:|---:|
| Cash..................................... | $   15,000 | |
| Investments.............................. | 6,000 | |
| Due to Specific Purpose Fund ............... | | $     1,000 |
| Land ..................................... | 90,000 | |
| Buildings................................. | 840,000 | |
| Equipment ............................... | 370,000 | |
| Mortgage Notes Payable.................... | | 160,000 |
| Allowance for Depreciation-Buildings ......... | | 10,000 |
| Allowance for Depreciation-Equipment ........ | | 30,000 |
| Fund Balance-Invested in Plant and Equipment | | 1,100,000 |
| Fund Balance-Improvements and Replacements | | 20,000 |
| | $1,321,000 | $1,321,000 |

The following transactions took place during the year:
1. The cost of constructing and equipping a major addition to the hospital was financed by a grant of $1,250,000 and borrowing on mortgage notes of $100,000. The cost is distributed as follows: land, $80,000; building, $950,000; equipment, $320,000.
2. A restricted donation of $10,000 in cash and $10,000 (market value) in stocks was received. The donation is to be used to finance improvements and replacements.
3. Dividends on stock (restricted) in the amount of $500 were received in cash.
4. Equipment costing $6,000 was purchased for cash.
5. Annual depreciation charges:

| | |
|---|---:|
| Buildings.................. | $30,000 |
| Equipment ............... | 50,000 |

(Single income statement approach)
6. Cash equal to the amount of depreciation on equipment ($50,000) was received from the Operating Fund.

Required:

Prepare a worksheet to reflect the beginning balances, transactions and adjustments, and post-closing trial balance of the Plant Fund of McClusky Hospital for the year ended December 31, 19X6.

**Problem 20-2. Part V.** (Preparation of major statements) Prepare (1) an income (revenues and expenses) statement for McClusky Hospital for the year ended December 31, 19X6, (2) a balance sheet (combined) at that date, and (3) a combined analysis of changes in Fund Balances. Follow the formats suggested by the American Hospital Association and illustrated in the Alzona Hospital example in the chapter.

**Problem 20-3. Part I.** (Single income statement method—selected entries) The following transactions and events relate to the operation of a hospital that uses the single income statement method of accounting. Prepare journal entries to reflect the effects of these transactions and events in the general ledger accounts of the appropriate fund(s). Explanations of entries may be omitted, but indicate the fund in which each is made.

a. Total billings for patient services rendered, $85,000; it was estimated that bad debt losses on these billings would be $1,000 and that contractual adjustments would amount to $6,000.

b. A transfer from the Heart Research Fund to the Operating Fund was authorized, $15,000, to defray such expenses previously recorded in the Operating Fund. The cash will be transferred later in the year.

c. An item of fixed equipment (cost, $8,000; accumulated depreciation, $5,000) was sold for $1,000. Proceeds of the sale were retained in the Plant Fund.

d. Depreciation expense on buildings was recognized, $18,000. (Depreciation is not funded regularly, but only upon special action by the governing board of the hospital.)

e. Earnings of the Endowment Fund are restricted to use for intern education. The net income of the Endowment Fund (revenues, $18,000; expenses, $4,000) was established as a liability to the appropriate fund.

f. Unrestricted income on Plant Fund investments, $3,500, was received and recorded directly in the Operating Fund.

g. An $11,000 transfer from the Operating Fund was authorized (not yet paid) to partially fund depreciation expense.

h. Of the billings for patient services rendered (see item *a* above), $1,000 was written off, $600 of which was found to relate to charity cases.

**Problem 20-3. Part II.** (Consolidated income statement method—selected entries) With reference to Problem 20-3, Part I, prepare the entries that would be *changed* if the hospital used the consolidated income statement method of accounting.

**Problem 20-4.** (Establishing Plant Fund; correcting general ledger) The Smith Medical Foundation was established in 19X0 to finance research in the field of medical science. It leased building facilities and equipment from others from the date of its foundation to December, 19X7, at which time land and buildings adaptable to its operation were purchased. It continues to lease equipment.

The Board decided to account for its plant in a separate fund, by establishment of an Operating Fund and a Plant Fund. All cash is to be handled through the Operating Fund with the Plant Fund being charged or credited with amounts applicable to it until after the close of each year. At this time settlement will be made to the extent that contributions for Plant Fund purposes received through solicitation drives planned make this possible. The plant property is to be depreciated effective January 1, 19X8, at the rate of 5 percent per annum, and depreciation is to be funded.

The assets, debts, and capital accounts as of December 31 show the following:

## SMITH MEDICAL FOUNDATION

|  | December 31 | |
| --- | --- | --- |
| *Assets* | *19X8* | *19X7* |
| Cash ............................................. | $ 42,000 | $ 36,000 |
| Investments ..................................... | 217,000 | 67,000 |
| Plant ........................................... | 96,000 | 75,000 |
| Unexpired Insurance Premiums .................... | 1,000 | |
| Plant Operations ................................ | | 1,000 |
| Total ..................................... | $356,000 | $179,000 |

| *Liabilities* | | |
| --- | --- | --- |
| Accounts Payable .............................. | $ 6,000 | $ 4,000 |
| Rents .......................................... | 3,000 | |
| Balance ........................................ | 347,000 | 175,000 |
| Total ..................................... | $356,000 | $179,000 |

Upon analysis of the Plant account you find the following:

| Date | Item | Debits | Credits |
| --- | --- | --- | --- |
| 9/30/X7 | Cash donation for purchase of plant ...... | | $100,000 |
| 12/15/X7 | Purchase of property ................... | $175,000 | |
| 1/31/X8 | Building improvements ................. | 24,000 | |
| 3/31/X8 | Building improvements ............... | 15,000 | |
| 12/31/X8 | Plant operation....................... | | 18,000 |

Debit entries in the Plant Operations account consisted of:

| | | | |
| --- | --- | --- | --- |
| 12/31/X7 | Coal, cleaning supplies, etc. ............. | $ | 1,000 |
| 2/28/X8 | Coal, cleaning supplies, etc. ............. | | 4,000 |
| 6/30/X8 | Grading and seeding of grounds ......... | | 6,000 |
| 7/31/X8 | Cleaning supplies, etc. ................. | | 1,200 |
| 12/31/X8 | Coal, cleaning supplies, etc. ............. | | 4,000 |
| 12/31/X8 | Expired insurance premiums ............ | | 1,800 |
| 12/31/X8 | Plant account ....................... | | 18,000 |

Rents consisted of $3,000 per month received in 19X8 and rent for January 19X9, which was received on December 31, 19X8. Rentals are not restricted as to use, but are considered operating revenues.

You obtain an appraisal of the land owned by the Foundation which gives a value of $75,000 at date of purchase.

Required:
(a)   Prepare journal entries setting up the Plant Fund and recording the transactions in the Fund to December 31, 19X8.
(b)   Prepare a compound entry to convert the general ledger balances at December 31, 19X8 to a corrected postclosing trial balance of the Operating Fund.
(c)   Prepare a sectional balance sheet presenting the funds as of December 31, 19X8.

**Problem 20-5.** (Worksheet to adjust balances and set up separate funds) A newly elected board of directors of Central Hospital, a not-for-profit corporation, decided that effective January 1, 1974:
(a)   the existing general ledger balances are to be properly adjusted and allocated to three separate funds (Operating Fund, John Central Endowment Fund and Plant Fund),
(b)   the totals of the John Central Endowment Fund and the Allowance For Accumulated Depreciation are to be fully invested in securities, and
(c)   all accounts are to be maintained in accordance with the principles of fund accounting. The board engaged you to determine the proper account balances for each of the funds.
The balances in the general ledger at January 1, 1974, were:

|  | Debit | Credit |
|---|---|---|
| Cash | $    50,000 |  |
| Investment in U. S. Treasury bills | 105,000 |  |
| Investment in common stock | 417,000 |  |
| Interest receivable | 4,000 |  |
| Accounts receivable | 40,000 |  |
| Inventory | 25,000 |  |
| Land | 407,000 |  |
| Building | 245,000 |  |
| Equipment | 283,000 |  |
| Allowance for accumulated depreciation |  | $   376,000 |
| Accounts payable |  | 70,000 |
| Bank loan |  | 150,000 |
| John Central Endowment Fund Balance |  | 119,500 |
| Surplus |  | 860,500 |
| Totals | $1,576,000 | $1,576,000 |

The following additional information is available:
1.   Under the terms of the will of John Central, founder of the hospital, "the principal of the bequest is to be fully invested in trust forevermore in mortgages secured by productive real estate in Central City and/or in U.S. Government securities...and the income therefrom is to be used to defray current expenses."
2.   The John Central Endowment Fund Balance account consists of the following:

| | |
|---|---:|
| Cash received in 1877 by bequest from John Central .......... | $ 81,500 |
| Net gains realized from 1932 through 1965 from the sale of real estate acquired in mortgage foreclosures ................... | 23,500 |
| Income received from 1966 through 1973 from 90-day U.S. Treasury Bill investments ................................... | 14,500 |
| Balance per general ledger on January 1, 1974 ............... | $119,500 |

3.   The Land account balance was composed of:

| | |
|---|---:|
| 1896 appraisal of land at $10,000 and building at $5,000 received by donation at that time. (The building was demolished in 1916, .. | $ 15,000 |
| Appraisal increase based on insured value in land title policies issued in 1933 ........................................... | 380,000 |
| Landscaping costs for trees planted ........................ | 12,000 |
| Balance per general ledger on January 1, 1974 ............... | $407,000 |

4.   The Building account balance was composed of:

| | |
|---|---:|
| Cost of present hospital building completed in January 1933 when the hospital commenced operations ....................... | $300,000 |
| Adjustment to record appraised value of building in 1943 ....... | (100,000) |
| Cost of elevator installed in hospital building in January 1959 ... | 45,000 |
| Balance per general ledger on January 1, 1974 ............... | $245,000 |

The estimated useful lives of the hospital building and the elevator when new were 50 years and 20 years, respectively.

5.   The hospital's equipment was inventoried on January 1, 1974. The cost of the inventory agreed with the Equipment account balance in the general ledger. The Allowance For Accumulated Depreciation account at January 1, 1974 included $158,250 applicable to equipment and that amount was approved by the board of directors as being accurate. All depreciation is computed on a straight-line basis.

6.   A bank loan was obtained to finance the cost of new operating room equipment purchased in 1970. Interest on the loan was paid to December 31, 1973.

Required:

Prepare a worksheet to present the adjustments necessary to restate the general ledger account balances properly and to distribute the adjusted balances to establish the required fund accounts at January 1, 1974. Formal journal entries are not required. Computations should be in good form and should be referenced to the worksheet adjustments which they support. In addition to trial balance columns, the following columnar headings are recommended for your worksheet:

|  | | | | John Central | | | |
|---|---|---|---|---|---|---|---|
| Adjustments | | Operating Fund | | Endowment Fund | | Plant Fund | |
| Debit | Credit | Debit | Credit | Debit | Credit | Debit | Credit |

**Problem 20-6.** (Worksheet—Fund transactions and balances from cash and other information) The Z Society, a fraternal order which operated X County Hospital for indigent members of the community, donated it on September 1, 19X5, to the Village of H, in which it is located. The gift included all of the securities in the Endowment Fund (the hospital's principal source of income), as well as the real estate, equipment and other assets. Since the village had made no appropriation for the operation and maintenance of a hospital, and no fees are charged the patients, gifts from public-spirited citizens supplemented the Endowment Fund income to provide for operating costs during the first year of its operation by the village, which coincided with the village fiscal year. No part of the principal of endowments may be used for operations. By the end of the year, preparations were under way for a drive to raise funds to enlarge and improve the plant. Since no money was collected in connection with this drive during the year under consideration, all expenditures for plant improvements were paid out of the Operating Fund, but will be reimbursed from the proceeds of the drive.

The following transactions occurred during the first year.

### Contributions and Receipts

| | | |
|---|---|---:|
| 1. | Hospital site—value .................................... | $ 25,000 |
| 2. | Hospital buildings—value .............................. | 200,000 |
| 3. | U.S. Treasury bonds contributed as endowment, principal amount ............................................. | 100,000 |
| 4. | Accrued interest on U.S. bonds at August 31, 19X5 .......... | 1,250 |
| 5. | Stocks and bonds contributed as endowments (no accrued dividends or interest)—market value .................... | 1,300,000 |
| 6. | Equipment—value ..................................... | 60,000 |
| 7. | Life insurance policies irrevocably assigned to hospital as endowments— | |

Cash value ................ $ 5,000
Face amount ............. 150,000
(The hospital is to pay the premiums on this policy; however, it may not borrow against or cancel the policy, but must await collection of the face amount upon the donor's death.)

| | | |
|---|---|---:|
| 8. | Contributions from X County for hospital operations ......... | 10,000 |
| 9. | Contributions from numerous individuals for hospital operations ........................................... | 20,000 |
| 10. | Proceeds from sponsored charity bazaar .................... | 500 |
| 11. | Interest received from U.S. Treasury bonds ................. | 2,500 |

| | |
|---|---|
| 12. Dividends from stocks .................................... | 44,000 |
| 13. Interest from bonds, other than U.S. Treasury ............. | 12,000 |
| 14. Sale of stocks included in endowments at $27,000 ........... | 52,000 |

*Disbursements*

| | | |
|---|---|---|
| 15. Building improvements ............................... | $ | 20,000 |
| 16. Equipment........................................... | | 15,000 |
| 17. Salaries............................................ | | 15,000 |
| 18. Food and dietary supplies ............................ | | 10,000 |
| 19. Medicinal supplies .................................. | | 20,000 |
| 20. Life insurance premium paid .......................... | | 2,000 |
| 21. Property insurance ................................... | | 5,000 |
| 22. Light, heat and water................................. | | 1,000 |
| 23. Expenses of charity bazaar, announcements, etc. ........... | | 15 |
| 24. Other operating expenses ............................. | | 4,000 |

*Other Information*

| | | |
|---|---|---|
| 25. Cash value of life insurance held for benefit of hospital at August 31, 19X6..................................... | $ | 6,500 |
| 26. Contributions subscribed but not collected ................. | | 5,000 |
| 27. Prepaid insurance on property at end of year............... | | 500 |
| 28. Balance in bank per bank statement of the Operating Fund at end of period....................................... | | 51,085 |

Outstanding checks amount to $3,300 and the last day's deposit of $1,200 is not included on the bank statement.

29. Upon completion of the $20,000 improvements to the hospital building it was appraised at $250,000.

30. There were no material amounts of accrued wages, inventories, or similar items at year end.

Required:

Prepare a worksheet(s) to reflect the transactions of the various funds of X County Hospital for the year ended August 30, 19X6. Your worksheet headings should appear as follows:

| *Transactions and Adjustments* *9/1/19X5–8/31/19X6* | | *Revenues and Expenses* *During 19X6* | | *Balance Sheet* *August 31, 19X6* | |
|---|---|---|---|---|---|
| *Dr.* | *Cr.* | *Dr.* | *Cr.* | *Dr.* | *Cr.* |

**Problem 20-7.** (Fund statement worksheets from single general ledger and other information) Hospital M has not previously kept its accounting records by funds, and the following balances appear in its general ledger as of January 1, 19X9:

|  | Debits | Credits |
|---|---|---|
| Cash on hand and in banks ....................... | $ 143,866 | |
| Accounts receivable—patients ..................... | 48,740 | |
| Sundry accounts receivable ....................... | 508 | |
| Inventory of supplies ........................... | 17,583 | |
| Prepaid insurance .............................. | 3,294 | |
| Stocks and bonds............................... | 3,702,010 | |
| Other investments .............................. | 225,950 | |
| Land .......................................... | 25,000 | |
| Buildings (net of $90,456 accumulated depreciation) .. | 402,305 | |
| Equipment (net of $63,500 accumulated depreciation) | 106,500 | |
| Allowance for loss on accounts receivable ........... | | $ 10,385 |
| Accounts payable .............................. | | 29,227 |
| Other current liabilities .......................... | | 38,014 |
| Bonds payable—first mortgage,* 5% ............... | | 300,000 |
| Advance payment by patients ..................... | | 6,364 |
| Balance ........................................ | | 4,291,766 |
| | $4,675,736 | $4,675,736 |

\* The mortgage is against the building, the construction of which was financed partially by bonds.

From the following information and summary of the transactions for the year ended December 31, 19X9, you are to prepare worksheets showing by appropriate funds all information needed for (a) a statement of revenues and expenses for the year and (b) a balance sheet for each fund as of December 31, 19X9. Changes in fund balances should be shown in additional columns and/or in notes to the worksheets. The single income statement method of hospital accounting is to be used.

(1)   The stocks and bonds, together with $112,150 of the cash, belong to Endowment Funds, the income of which may be used for general purposes of the hospital. An additional $12,150 of cash belongs to expendable Specific Purpose Funds. Buildings and equipment are stated net of depreciation, which has been charged to the current expenses of each year. There is no intention to provide a fund for replacement of assets; as assets are replaced, payments are made out of general cash. The other investments belong to Endowment Funds. The income from these funds may be used only for the purposes designated.

(2)   Cash income from Endowment Fund stocks and bonds amounted to $138,710. Income from other investments amounted to $11,765.

(3)   Cash donations received amounted to $41,305, all except $10,500 of which was for current use. The $10,500 was expendable only for a designated purpose.

(4)   Services billed to patients amounted to $930,480, all of which was recorded through accounts receivable—patients.

(5)   Cash collected from patients and prospective patients amounted to $925,428, of which $12,890 represented advance payments.

(6)   Cash of $1,375 was collected on sundry accounts receivable.

(7)   The allowance for loss on accounts receivable was increased by $10,000. Patients' accounts totaling $6,302 were considered to be uncollectible and were written off.

(8)   Depreciation on the buildings was $11,307; depreciation on equipment was $18,541.

(9)   The following vouchers were approved:
Storeroom supplies—$78,240; Insurance—$11,624; General operating expenses—$979,731; Maintenance—$7,488; Replacement of Equipment—$11,432; Interest on bonds—$15,000; Retirement of bonds—$10,000. Other current liabilities were credited with $505,212 of these $1,113,515 of vouchers.

(10)   The book value of equipment replaced was $2,710; it had originally cost $10,000 but was now obsolete and had no market value.

(11)   Free services rendered during the year amounted to $108,000; of this, 75 percent was for charity cases and the balance was a result of policy discounts.

(12)   Services rendered patients (see No. 4) were covered by advance payments amounting to $14,105.

(13)   Cash disbursements were made of $502,701 in payment of other current liabilities and $610,043 in payment of accounts payable. Discounts taken on accounts payable amounted to $2,305.

(14)   Storeroom supplies of $72,578 were issued for general use and $1,073 of supplies were sold to employees at cost and charged to sundry accounts receivable. Insurance expired amounted to $10,445.

(15)   Cash expenditures for Equipment from Specific Purpose Funds were $5,875.

(16)   Cash receipts for the year included unexpendable cash contributions of $50,000 (income therefrom is unrestricted), proceeds from sale of stocks and bonds of $502,164 and proceeds from sale of other investments of $52,125. There was a loss of $7,354 sustained on the sale of stocks and bonds and a $9,978 loss sustained on the sale of other investments.

(17)   Cash disbursements not vouchered consisted of $507,892 for purchase of stocks and bonds and $48,100 of the proceeds from sale of other investments which was invested in bonds.

(18)   Inventory of supplies on hand at year end, at cost, amounted to $21,500.

(AICPA, adapted)

**Problem 20-8.**   (Preparation of major statements from incomplete records) The City of Titusville built a municipal hospital on land previously owned by the city. The building was completed on March 1, 19X0. Since that date the hospital has been under the control of a superintendent. He has rendered monthly reports to the town mayor, but these reports have been on a cash basis and have not shown separation of amounts by funds. You have been employed by the city government to prepare financial statements for the ten months ending December 31, 19X0, and to do certain other work in connection with setting up an accounting system for the hospital operations. The city wants the financial statements to be on an accrual basis, to the extent such basis is appropriate, and to follow usual fund accounting practices. From the information presented below, you are to prepare statements (AHA format) showing revenues and expenses, changes in fund balances, and financial position; supporting computations or worksheet(s) should be in good form.

(1)   The total contract price of the buildings was $240,000. The contractor was paid in the following manner:

(a)   Cash of $120,000, which was a contribution by the Federal government toward the hospital cost.

(b)   Cash of $25,000 contributed by the county government toward the cost.

(c)   Hospital bonds issued by the city to the contractor in the amount of $100,000. These bonds are 5 percent bonds dated 1/1/19X0, due in ten years, interest payable semiannually. They are general obligation bonds of the city but the hospital is primarily liable for them and is to service them.

(2)  Equipment was initially obtained as follows:

(a)  Purchased by the city for cash—$35,300.

(b)  Purchased out of cash donations made by citizens for that purpose—$9,800.

(c)  Donated equipment which had an estimated value of—$11,000.

(3)  The statement of cash receipts and disbursements, exclusive of items described above, for the ten months was as follows:

Received from patients:

| | |
|---|---:|
| Rooms and meals | $105,314 |
| Laboratory and other fees | 6,170 |
| Outpatients | 4,201 |
| Miscellaneous income from meals, etc. | 515 |
| Received from estate of James Johnson, M.D. | 25,000 |
| Miscellaneous donations | 10,410 |
| Received from Beulah Jenkins | 32,500 |
| Donations from churches | 1,850 |
| Received from county for county charity patients—room and meals | 940 |
| Income from rents | 2,000 |
| Income from bonds | 2,125 |
| Total cash received | $191,025 |
| Payroll and taxes thereon paid | $ 96,200 |
| Stores and supplies purchased | 34,180 |
| Equipment purchased | 27,250 |
| Expense of operating rented property | 700 |
| Miscellaneous expenses (including bond interest of $2,500) | 4,170 |
| Total cash disbursed | $162,500 |
| Balance of cash 12/31/19X0 | $ 28,525 |

(4)  Investigation revealed the following additional information:

(a)  Patients' accounts on the books as of December 31, 19X0 amounted to $9,403 distributed as follows: For room and meals—$7,310; for laboratory and other fees—$1,095; for out-patients—$998. It is estimated that $500 of these accounts will never be collected.

(b)  As of December 31, 19X0, accrued unpaid wages amounted to $5,234; unpaid supply invoices amounted to $6,810 and accrued utilities amounted to $174. The analysis of miscellaneous expenses shows that there is $330 of prepaid insurance. Kitchen and other supplies on hand amounted to $1,760 at cost.

(c)  It has been decided to charge current income with depreciation on general hospital property at the following annual rates based on the year-end balance of the asset accounts:

Buildings ....... 2 percent

Equipment .... 10 percent and 20 percent

All equipment will take the 10 percent rate except for $18,500 of minor items of equipment, which will be depreciated at the 20 percent rate. Depreciation is to be computed for a full year and is not to be funded.

(d)   The following facts were determined in respect to the donations:

(1)   The donation from the estate of James Johnson, M.D., was received July 1, 19X0. It consisted of two houses and $25,000 in cash. The terms of the bequest provided that the cash is to be invested and that the income therefrom and from the houses is to be used for the purchase of surgical equipment. The houses had a market value of approximately $30,000, of which amount $5,000 was for the land. The estimated life of the properties from date of the gift was 25 years. (Depreciation does not reduce rental earnings available for purchase of surgical equipment.) The houses were rented and, in addition to the $2,000 of rent received, there was $150 rent receivable as of December 31, 19X0. All expenses on the houses for the year have been paid and are included in the disbursements. No purchase of surgical equipment has been approved.

(2)   The miscellaneous donations were made for general purposes of the operation of the hospital.

(3)   The Beulah Jenkins donation received June 1, 19X0, consisted of cash and of $50,000 face value of X Corporation 4¼ percent bonds. Interest dates are June 1 and December 1. The provisions of the gift were: "The amounts are to be invested by said trustees in accordance with applicable law governing trust investments and the income derived therefrom is to be used to defray or help to defray the necessary hospitalization of such indigent women as the trustees shall designate upon application by their physician." The trustees were designated in the document. These trustees have accepted their appointments but have never met or transacted any business.

(4)   The donations from churches are to apply toward purchase of an "iron lung." No order has yet been placed for such equipment.

(AICPA, adapted)

**Problem 20-9.**   (Rate determination)

a.   From the following information, compute the minimum average billed charges per day which the Peoples' Hospital must experience in order to recover the total cost of care for the year 19X8. (Submit computations in clear-cut form.)

| | | | |
|---|---|---|---:|
| 1. | Number of days of care | | 10,000 |
| 2. | Operating expenses: | Payroll | $120,000 |
| | | Supplies | 80,000 |
| | | Depreciation | 10,000 |
| | | Total | $210,000 |
| 3. | Classification of Accounts: (in days) | | |
| | Charity Cases | | 600 |
| | Contractual Cases | | 1,200 |
| | Uncollectible Accounts | | 200 |
| | Full-Pay Patients | | 8,000 |
| | Total | | 10,000 |

4.  Estimated Collections Per Day:

| | |
|---|---|
| Charity Cases | None |
| Contractual Cases | $ 14,000 |
| Uncollectible Accounts | None |
| Full-Pay Patients | Billed charges |

b.  After computing the minimum average billed charges, summarize the data and present the dollars amounts in the following form:

| | |
|---|---|
| Revenue from services to patients | $_____ |
| Deductions from revenue | $_____ |
| Net revenue from services to patients | $_____ |
| Operating expenses | $_____ |
| Net income | $_____ |

(FHFMA, adapted)

**Problem 20-10.** (Pooled investments) The Community Hospital has three Endowment Fund accounts. The investment income for the year ended December 31, 19X7, of all the funds was $11,250.

The following is a summary of the Endowment Fund principal accounts, classified by the three purposes for which held:

| | Total | Laboratory Research | Student Nurse Scholarships | Indigent Assistance |
|---|---|---|---|---|
| Balance, Jan. 1, 19X7 | $250,000 | $200,000 | $10,000 | $40,000 |
| Changes in Principal:* | | | | |
| March 1, 19X7 | 5,000 | | | 5,000 |
| May 1, 19X7 | (10,000) | (10,000) | | |
| July 1, 19X7 | 25,000 | 25,000 | | |
| December 1, 19X7 | 5,000 | | 5,000 | |
| Balance Dec. 31, 19X7 | $275,000 | $215,000 | $15,000 | $45,000 |

\* Excluding income; all were cash investments or divestments.

Required:

Assuming the investments in the Fund are pooled:

(1)  What is the average rate of return on Fund equity earned during the year ended December 31, 19X7?

(2)  What amount of income must be applied to

a.  Laboratory research?

b.  Scholarships for student nurses?

c.  Indigent assistance?

(FHFMA, adapted)

**Problem 20-11.** (Application and evaluation of rate policy) The Board of Trustees of Memorial Hospital has adopted a rate determination policy. This policy, as recorded in the minutes, reads: "The primary fiscal obligation of Memorial Hospital is to operate on a sound and conservative basis, thus assuring uninterrupted and undiminished service to the community. Toward fulfilling this obligation, it is the policy of this Board that rates charged for services rendered to patients shall be based on current costs plus five percent (5%) of current cost at an occupancy level four percent (4%) below that of the preceding year but not to exceed eighty percent (80%)."

Revenue and expense figures in summary form and related statistics for the years ended June 30, 19X2 and 19X3, and for the nine months ended March 31, 19X4, follow:

|  | Nine Months 19X4 | Fiscal Year 19X3 | Fiscal Year 19X2 |
|---|---|---|---|
| Gross revenue from services to patients | $3,104,542 | $3,795,500 | $3,396,600 |
| Allowances | $ 22,400 | $ 32,100 | $ 26,800 |
| Bad debts | 13,600 | 18,000 | 16,500 |
| Deductions from revenue | $ 36,000 | $ 50,100 | $ 43,300 |
| Net revenue from services to patients | $3,068,542 | $3,745,400 | $3,353,300 |
| Operating expenses (80% fixed) | 2,940,942 | 3,566,500 | 3,219,300 |
| Net operating income | $ 127,600 | $ 178,900 | $ 134,000 |
| Other revenue | 15,400 | 14,100 | 16,000 |
| Net income | $ 143,000 | $ 193,000 | $ 150,000 |
| Normal bed capacity | 300 | 300 | 300 |
| Patient days | 70,950 | 95,265 | 91,980 |

Required:

(a) Compute the required amount (gross revenue per patient day) for fiscal year 19X5.

(b) Evaluate the propriety of the board's rate-determination policy, citing evidence from the data above and/or Requirement (a) in support of your position.

(FHFMA, adapted)

**Problem 20-12.** (Reimbursable cost determination—alternate methods) Good Hope Hospital completed its first year of operation as a qualified institutional provider under the health insurance (HI) program for the aged and wishes to receive maximum reimbursement for its allowable costs from the government. The Hospital engaged you to assist in determining the amount of reimbursement due and furnished the following financial, statistical and other information:

1. The Hospital's charges and allowable costs for departmental inpatient services were:

| Departments | Charges for HI Program Beneficiaries | Total Charges | Total Allowable Costs |
|---|---|---|---|
| Inpatient routine services (room, board, nursing) .......................... | $425,000 | $1,275,000 | $1,350,000 |
| Inpatient ancillary service departments: | | | |
|    X-ray .............................. | 56,000 | 200,000 | 150,000 |
|    Operating room ..................... | 57,000 | 190,000 | 220,000 |
|    Laboratory ......................... | 59,000 | 236,000 | 96,000 |
|    Pharmacy .......................... | 98,000 | 294,000 | 207,000 |
|    Other.............................. | 10,000 | 80,000 | 88,000 |
|     Total ancillary .................... | 280,000 | 1,000,000 | 761,000 |
| Totals ............................. | $705,000 | $2,275,000 | $2,111,000 |

2.  For the first year the Reimbursement Settlement for Inpatient Services may be calculated at the option of the provider under either of the following apportionment methods:

(a)  *The Departmental RCC (ratio of cost centers) Method* provides for listing on a departmental basis the ratios of beneficiary inpatient charges to total inpatient charges with each departmental beneficiary inpatient charge ratio applied to the allowable total cost of the respective department.

(b)  *The Combination Method (with cost finding)* provides that the cost of routine services be apportioned on the basis of the average allowable cost per day for all inpatients applied to total inpatient days of beneficiaries. The residual part of the provider's total allowable cost attributable to ancillary (nonroutine) services is to be apportioned in the ratio of the beneficiaries' share of charges for ancillary services to the total charges for all patients for such services.

3.  Statistical and other information:

(a)  Total inpatient days for all patients ......................... 40,000

(b)  Total inpatient days applicable to HI beneficiaries (1,200 aged patients whose average length of stay was 12.5 days) ............... 15,000

(c)  A fiscal intermediary acting on behalf of the government's medicare program negotiated a fixed "allowance rate" of $45 per inpatient day subject to retroactive adjustment as a reasonable cost basis for reimbursement of covered services to the hospital under the HI program. Interim payments based on an estimated 1,000 inpatient-days per month were received during the 12-month period subject to an adjustment for the provider's actual cost experience.

Required:

(a)  Prepare schedules computing the total allowable cost of inpatient services for which the provider should receive payment under the HI program and the remaining balance due for reimbursement under each of the following methods:

1.  Departmental RCC method.

2.  Combination method (with cost finding).

(b)  Under which method should Good Hope Hospital elect to be reimbursed for its first year under the HI program assuming the election can be changed for the following year with the approval of the fiscal intermediary? Why?

(c)  Good Hope Hospital wishes to compare its charges to HI program beneficiaries with published information on national averages for charges for hospital services. Compute the following (show your computations):
1.  The average total hospital charge for an HI inpatient.
2.  The average charge per inpatient day for HI inpatients.

(AICPA)

**Problem 20-13.**  (Cost Projections) The administrator of Wright Hospital has presented you with a number of service projections for the year ending June 30, 19X2. Estimated room requirements for inpatients by type of service are:

| Type of Patient | Total Patients Expected | Average Number of Days in Hospital | | Percent of Regular Patients Selecting Types of Service | | |
|---|---|---|---|---|---|---|
| | | Regular | Medicare | Private | Semi-Private | Ward |
| Medical | 2,100 | 7 | 17 | 10% | 60% | 30% |
| Surgical | 2,400 | 10 | 15 | 15 | 75 | 10 |

Of the patients served by the hospital 10 percent are expected to be Medicare patients, all of whom are expected to select semi-private rooms. Both the number and proportion of Medicare patients have increased over the past five years. Daily rentals per patient are: $40 for a private room, $35 for a semi-private room and $25 for a ward. Operating room charges are based on man-minutes (number of minutes the operating room is in use multiplied by number of personnel assisting in the operation). The per man-minute charges are $.13 for inpatients and $.22 for outpatients. Studies for the current year show that operations on inpatients are divided as follows:

| Type of Operation | Number of Operations | Average Number of Minutes Per Operation | Average Number of Personnel Required |
|---|---|---|---|
| A | 800 | 30 | 4 |
| B | 700 | 45 | 5 |
| C | 300 | 90 | 6 |
| D | 200 | 120 | 8 |
| | 2,000 | | |

The same proportion of inpatient operations is expected for the next fiscal year and 180 outpatients are expected to use the operating room. Outpatient operations average 20 minutes and require the assistance of three persons.
The budget for the year ending June 30, 19X2, by departments, is:

General services:

| | |
|---|---:|
| Maintenance of plant | $ 50,000 |
| Operation of plant | 27,500 |
| Administration | 97,500 |
| All others | 192,000 |

Revenue producing services:

| | |
|---|---:|
| Operating room | 68,440 |
| All others | 700,000 |
| | $1,135,440 |

The following information is provided for cost allocation purposes:

| General services: | Square Feet | Salaries |
|---|---:|---:|
| Maintenance of plant .............. | 12,000 | $ 40,000 |
| Operation of plant ................ | 28,000 | 25,000 |
| Administration ................... | 10,000 | 55,000 |
| All others ...................... | 36,250 | 102,500 |
| Revenue producing services: | | |
| Operating room ................. | 17,500 | 15,000 |
| All others ..................... | 86,250 | 302,500 |
| | 190,000 | $540,000 |

Basis of allocations:
Maintenance of plant—salaries
Operation of plant—square feet
Administration—salaries
All others—8% to operating room

Required:
Prepare schedules showing the computation of:
(a) The number of patient days (number of patients multiplied by average stay in hospital) expected by type of patients and service.
(b) The total number of man-minutes expected for operating room services for inpatients and outpatients. For inpatients show the breakdown of total operating room man-minutes by type of operation.
(c) Expected gross revenue from routine services.
(d) Expected gross revenue from operating room services.
(e) Cost per man-minute for operating room services assuming that the total man-minutes computed in part "b" is 800,000 and that the step-down method of cost allocation is used (i.e., costs of the general services departments are allocated in sequence first to the general services departments that they serve and then finally to the revenue producing departments).
(AICPA, adapted)

**Problem 20-14.** (Analysis of changes in cash—cash flow) The General Medical

Institute is a not-for-profit corporation without capital stock which accounts for its activities in a single fund. Its comparative financial statements follow:

## THE GENERAL MEDICAL INSTITUTE
### Comparative Statement of Revenues and Expenses
### For the Years Ended October 31, 19X3 and 19X2

|  | 19X3 | 19X2 | Increase (Decrease) |
|---|---|---|---|
| Revenue from Services Rendered: |  |  |  |
| Services to patients | $360,000 | $304,000 | $ 56,000 |
| Less: Free services | 36,000 | 38,000 | (2,000) |
| Net revenue from services rendered ... | 324,000 | 266,000 | 58,000 |
| Operating Expenses: |  |  |  |
| Departmental expenses: |  |  |  |
| Medical services | 32,700 | 29,300 | 3,400 |
| Medicine and supplies | 14,600 | 10,500 | 4,100 |
| Nursing services | 89,900 | 76,200 | 13,700 |
| Therapy services | 34,300 | 31,300 | 3,000 |
| Dietary | 40,700 | 37,100 | 3,600 |
| Housekeeping and maintenance | 37,300 | 29,500 | 7,800 |
| Administration and other | 33,700 | 23,400 | 10,300 |
| General expenses: |  |  |  |
| Rental of leased premises (net) | — | 3,100 | (3,100) |
| Depreciation—building and equipment.. | 9,900 | 8,300 | 1,600 |
| Provision for uncollectible accounts .... | 5,400 | 3,500 | 1,900 |
| Interest expense | 6,500 | — | 6,500 |
| Loss on sale of equipment | 2,000 | — | 2,000 |
| Other | 16,200 | 6,500 | 9,700 |
| Total expenses | 323,200 | 258,700 | 64,500 |
| Excess of revenues from services rendered over expenses of patient care | 800 | 7,300 | (6,500) |
| Other Income (Expenses): |  |  |  |
| Research | (13,300) | (13,200) | (100) |
| Gain on sale of investments | 18,600 | 3,500 | 15,100 |
| Investment income | 16,500 | 13,300 | 3,200 |
| Contributions | 10,300 | 14,800 | (4,500) |
| Grant from government designated for expansion | 335,000 | — | 335,000 |
| Miscellaneous | 2,700 | 1,500 | 1,200 |
| Total other income | 369,800 | 19,900 | 349,900 |
| Excess of revenues over expenses | $370,600 | $ 27,200 | $343,400 |

## THE GENERAL MEDICAL INSTITUTE
Comparative Balance Sheets—October 31, 19X3 and 19X2

|  | 19X3 | 19X2 | Increase (Decrease) |
|---|---|---|---|
| Assets: |  |  |  |
| Cash .............................. | $ 28,600 | $ 18,500 | $ 10,100 |
| Accounts receivable—patients (net) .... | 75,500 | 55,500 | 20,000 |
| Investments (cost) .................... | 413,100 | 463,100 | (50,000) |
| Prepaid expenses .................... | 2,200 | 1,600 | 600 |
| Land, building, equipment (net)........ | 327,200 | 333,700 | (6,500) |
| Construction in progress ............. | 793,800 | — | 793,800 |
| Total assets .................... | $1,640,400 | $872,400 | $768,000 |
| Liabilities and Fund Balance: |  |  |  |
| Accounts payable—construction ........ | $ 110,800 | — | $110,800 |
| Less: Receivables from government agencies ........................ | 80,000 | — | 80,000 |
| Accounts payable—construction (net) ... | 30,800 | — | 30,800 |
| Accounts payable—current operations ... | 11,800 | $ 10,200 | 1,600 |
| Mortgage payable ................... | 365,000 | — | 365,000 |
| Total liabilities ................. | 407,600 | 10,200 | 397,400 |
| Fund balance: |  |  |  |
| Balance, November 1 .............. | 862,200 | 835,000 | 27,200 |
| Excess of revenues over expenses for year | 370,600 | 27,200 | 343,400 |
| Balance, October 31 .............. | 1,232,800 | 862,200 | 370,600 |
| Total liabilities and fund balance ... | $1,640,400 | $872,400 | $768,000 |

The audit working papers contain the following additional information:

1. Accounts Receivable—Patients are stated at the net of the Allowance for Bad Debts account, which amounted to $10,000 at October 31, 19X2, and $14,600 at October 31, 19X3. During the year bad debts totaling $800 were written off.

2. The research activities are net of research grants aggregating $10,000. Included as a research expense is depreciation of $6,600 on special research equipment.

3. During 19X3 the construction of a new building was begun. The estimated cost of the building and equipment is $1,000,000. The expansion is being financed as follows:

| | |
|---|---|
| Grant from government ................................ | $ 335,000 |
| Mortgage (Repayment to begin upon completion of building) .. | 500,000 |
| Institute available funds and issue of short-term notes payable.. | 165,000 |
| Total ........................................... | $1,000,000 |

4. New therapy equipment costing $15,000 was purchased in 19X3 and replaced therapy equipment with a book value of $5,000 which was sold for $3,000.

5. To obtain additional cash working capital, investments with a cost of $50,000 were sold during July.

Required:

Prepare a statement accounting for the increase in cash for the year ended October 31, 19X3 to be included in the annual report of The General Medical Institute. Your computations should be shown either in the body of the statement or in supporting schedules. The statement should set forth information concerning cash applied to or provided by

    1. Operations.

    2. Research activities.

    3. Acquisitions of assets.

    4. Other sources of funds.

(You may submit an appropriate worksheet solution in lieu of a formal statement.)

    (AICPA, adapted)

# 21

# Accounting for
# Colleges and Universities

The development of accounting and reporting principles for colleges and universities followed a pattern almost identical to that of municipalities. A few publications on the subject appeared during the 1910–1935 era; the first attempt at standardization, undertaken cooperatively by the various regional associations of college and university business officers, was published in 1935; there followed a series of twenty interpretive and advisory studies by the Financial Advisory Service of the American Council on Education (ACE) during the 1935–42 period.

A National Committee on the Preparation of a Manual on College and University Business Administration—formed in 1949 of representatives from the various regional business officer associations, the ACE, and the U. S. Office of Education—prepared *College and University Business Administration*. This two-volume work, published by the ACE in 1952 and 1955, respectively, was the first authoritative publication covering all areas of higher education business administration. In 1963 The Committee to Revise Volumes I and II, *College and University Business Administration* (The Committee) was formed of representatives of the National Association of College and University Business Officers

(NACUBO)[1]; the AICPA, the U. S. Office of Education, and ACE. Assisted by several special consultants, this committee prepared a one-volume revised edition of *College and University Business Administration*[2] (*CUBA*). Published in 1968 by the ACE, the revised edition of *CUBA* was described by The Committee as "a painstakingly achieved consensus of leading experts in the field."[3]

*College and University Business Administration* has found widespread acceptance in practice, and its recommendations form the basis of modern textbooks on college and university accounting. Further, although the AICPA Committee on College and University Accounting has taken exception to several practices suggested or permitted in *CUBA,* its *Audits of Colleges and Universities*[4] (an Industry Audit Guide) is based largely on them. Thus, the 1968 edition of *College and University Business Administration* is the most authoritative source of college and university accounting and reporting principles. This chapter is based principally on the recommendations in *CUBA*. Major differences between these recommendations and those of the AICPA Committee are discussed at several points in the chapter and are summarized at its conclusion.

## OVERVIEW

Many features of both municipal and hospital accounting and reporting are found in that for colleges and universities. In fact, from a pedagogic standpoint college or university accounting and reporting may be visualized as a *composite* of selected aspects of municipal accounting and reporting with selected aspects of hospital accounting and reporting. Among the features of college and university accounting shared with that for both municipalities and hospitals are (1) it is based on the fund principle and (2) the accrual basis of accounting is recommended.

FUND GROUPS. The Committee endorsed the use of the following fund groups by colleges and universities:

---

1 The various regional associations formed the National Federation of College and University Business Officers Associations in 1950, which in 1960 became the National Association of College and University Business Officers (NACUBO). NACUBO and the American Council on Education (ACE) have been instrumental in the continuing development and improvement of college and university financial management, accounting, and reporting.

2 *College and University Business Administration,* revised edition (Washington, D.C.: American Council on Education, 1968). Specifically, see Part 2, "Principles of Accounting and Reporting"; Appendix A, "The Chart of Accounts"; and Appendix B, "Illustrative Forms."

3 *Ibid.,* p. v.

4 Committee on College and University Accounting and Auditing, American Institute of Certified Public Accountants. *Audits of Colleges and Universities* (New York: The AICPA, 1973).

| Fund Group | Major Subdivision |
|---|---|
| 1. Current Funds | Unrestricted Current Funds |
| | Restricted Current Funds |
| | Auxiliary Enterprise Funds |
| 2. Loan Funds | |
| 3. Endowment and | Endowment Funds ("pure" or "true") |
|     Similar Funds | Term Endowment Funds |
| | Quasi-endowment Funds |
| 4. Annuity and Life | Annuity Funds |
|     Income Funds | Life Income Funds |
| 5. Plant Funds | Unexpended Plant Funds |
| | Funds for Renewals and Replacements |
| | Funds for Retirement of Indebtedness |
| | Investment in Plant |
| 6. Agency Funds | |

These fund groups are based on the restrictions on or the purposes of the funds. A college or university may (1) establish several separate fund entities of each type, as needed, but prepare its financial reports on a fund group basis, or (2) maintain only one fund accounting entity for each fund group and account for the subfunds on an intrafund "funds within a fund" basis. Either approach is acceptable; however, within each of the fund groups each fund must, as a minimum, have a separate account to show the balance of the fund and the results of its operations. These fund groups are discussed and illustrated more fully following a brief comparison of the major features of college or university accounting and reporting with those of municipalities and hospitals.

COMPARISON WITH MUNICIPAL ACCOUNTING AND REPORTING. College or university accounting and reporting is like that for municipalities in many respects. For example, (1) both colleges or universities and municipalities are concerned primarily with the measurement and reporting of revenues and *expenditures*— funds flows and balances—rather than with the determination of net income of the organization; (2) depreciation is *not* recorded by either except where required by law or agreement, such as to assure that the principal (corpus) of endowments or other nonexpendable trusts is maintained intact; (3) statements analyzing the changes in fund balances are the major operating statements of both colleges or universities and municipalities; (4) the current period expenditures of both may be controlled by budgets or appropriations, and statements setting forth the revenues and expenditures of a period in detail commonly include budgetary or year-to-year comparisons; (5) combined fund balance sheets are presented by both and are, in fact, the only balance sheets normally presented by colleges or universities; and (6) as noted earlier, some colleges or universities establish a separate accounting entity for each identifiable fund (subfund) within the fund groups, as do municipalities. A summary comparison of the fund structures of colleges or universities and municipalities is presented in Figure 21-2.

COMPARISON WITH HOSPITAL ACCOUNTING AND REPORTING. College or university accounting and reporting also resembles that for hospitals in many respects. For example, (1) a distinction is maintained between restricted and unrestricted resources, though the distinction is more one of "available for current expenditure" versus "not available for current expenditure" and the distinction between *externally* restricted and *internally* restricted is not as strictly maintained as it is in hospitals; (2) restricted contributions and earnings are accounted for by colleges or universities in much the same way that they are in hospitals, that is, they are recognized as revenues only in the period in which they are expended for their designated purposes; (3) the funds structures of colleges and universities are quite similar to those of hospitals, as shown in Figure 21-2; (4) though colleges or universities primarily account for funds flows and balances rather than net income, the principal operating statement of a college or university is the statement of Current Funds Revenues, Expenditures and Transfers, in which all operating revenues and expenditures recognized by the institution are reported; (5) as in hospitals, the principal operating statements of funds other than the Current Funds of colleges or universities are statements analyzing changes in the fund balances; (6) the value of donated services and facilities may be recognized by colleges or universities; (7) as in hospitals, long-term investments of college and university fund groups may be recorded either at cost or revalued periodically to fair market value, and (8) as noted earlier, colleges or universities, like hospitals, usually present a combined balance sheet rather than separate balance sheets for each fund or fund group.

SUMMARY. Many of the principal aspects of college or university accounting and reporting may be observed from the presentations in Figures 21-1 and 21-2. "Highlights of College or University Accounting and Reporting" are noted in Figure 21-1; a "Summary Comparison of Fund Structures—Colleges and Universities with Municipalities and Hospitals" appears in Figure 21-2. The reader may find it helpful to return to these figures from time to time as he studies the remainder of this chapter; they may be useful also as a review and summarization of the chapter.

Each of the fund groups commonly found in college and university accounting is discussed more fully in the following pages. These discussions are illustrated by means of a continuing case example. For simplicity of illustration we assume that "A University" is in its first year of operation, though some of the physical plant was acquired in the preceding year.

Figure 21-1

# OVERVIEW OF COLLEGE OR UNIVERSITY ACCOUNTING AND REPORTING

**FUND GROUPS**

| | Currently Available for Expenditure | | Not Currently Available for Expenditure | | | | |
|---|---|---|---|---|---|---|---|
| **Fund Groups** | Unrestricted Current Funds | Restricted Current Funds | Loan | Endowment and Similar | Annuity and Life Income | Plant | Agency |
| **Revenue Realization Rules or Conventions** | Revenues and expenditures recognized in the period earned or incurred. | Earnings, contributions, or transfers are credited to fund balances. Recognize revenue only to the extent resources are expended. | | Earnings, contributions, or transfers are credited to fund balances. Expendable earnings or other resources are transferred to Unrestricted or Restricted Current Funds, as appropriate. | | | No revenue—custodian relationship only. |
| **Principal Financial Statements** | Statement of Current Funds Revenues, Expenditures, and Transfers. Statement(s) of Changes in Fund Balances | | Statements of Changes in Fund Balances (Separate statements for each fund group) | | | | |
| | | | Balance Sheet (Combined) | | | | |

Figure 21-2

## SUMMARY COMPARISON OF FUND STRUCTURES—COLLEGES
## AND UNIVERSITIES WITH MUNICIPALITIES AND HOSPITALS

| Municipalities | Colleges and Universities | Hospitals |
|---|---|---|
| | Current: | |
| General | Unrestricted | Operating |
| Special Revenue (or *Expendable* Trust) | Restricted[a] | Specific Purpose |
| General | Auxiliary Enterprises[b] | Operating |
| | Loan | |
| *Nonexpendable* Trust | | Endowment |
| | Endowment and Similar: | |
| | Endowment (pure) | |
| | Term Endowment | |
| | Quasi-endowment[c] | ("Board-Created") Endowment |
| | Annuity and Life Income: | |
| | Annuity | |
| | Life Income | |
| | Plant: | Plant[e] |
| Capital Projects[d] | Unexpended | |
| Debt Service | For Renewals and Replacements | |
| General Fixed Assets/ General Long-term Debt | For Retirement of Indebtedness Investment in Plant | |
| Agency | Agency | |

a Restricted Current Funds revenue is considered realized, and hence is recognized as revenue, only to the extent that it has been expended for the specified purpose. Thus, the realization rule here is similar to that of a hospital Specific Purpose Fund in that (1) restricted earnings or contributions are credited to fund balance, then (2) in the period of expenditure, fund balance is debited and an appropriate revenue account is credited.

b If Auxiliary Enterprises resources are restricted, the accounting (1) is similar to that of a hospital Specific Purpose Fund if the restriction is external, and (2) is similar to that of a municipal Special Revenue Fund if the restriction is set by the college or university governing board.

c Unlike hospitals, where earnings on "Board-Created Endowment" Funds are recognized when earned, recognition of earnings of Quasi-endowment Funds of colleges and universities as revenue is deferred until the period in which they are expended for the board-designated purpose.

d Funds for renewals and replacements of municipal fixed assets may be accounted for in the General Fund or in Capital Projects, expendable Trust, or Special Revenue Funds, as appropriate to the restrictions on or purpose of these resources and their materiality.

e Plant Funds of colleges and universities are identical to those of hospitals except (1) colleges and universities do not recognize depreciation of educational and related fixed assets, and (2) hospitals may account for unexpended capital outlay project funds through a Construction Fund similar to a municipal Capital Projects Fund.

f Hospitals usually account for agency relationships in the Operating Fund rather than by setting up separate Agency Funds.

931

## CURRENT FUNDS

Current Funds, those funds that are available for current operations, may be either restricted or unrestricted. Typically they may be used either for general educational purposes or for auxiliary enterprises. A careful distinction should be maintained between *Unrestricted* Current Funds and *Restricted* Current Funds, as the accounting and reporting procedures are quite different for these two subgroups of Current Funds.

### Unrestricted Current Funds

The *Unrestricted* Current Funds subgroup includes those financial resources of the institution that are expendable for any legal and reasonable purpose agreed upon by the governing board in carrying out the primary purposes of the institution (e.g., instruction, research, public service) *and* that have not been designated *externally* (by grantors, donors, etc.) for specific purposes. Resources restricted by donors, grantors or outside agencies for specific current operating purposes are accounted for as *Restricted* Current Funds.

Unrestricted Current Funds designated by the governing board to serve as loan or quasi-endowment funds, or to be expended for plant purposes, are usually included in the Loan, Endowment, and Plant Funds, respectively. (The better practice is to designate these as "Board Designated" as is done in hospitals.) Unrestricted Current Funds designated by the governing board for specific current operating purposes should be accounted for in the *Unrestricted* Current Funds subgroup, either as formal appropriations or as general reservations of the fund balance.

### Restricted Current Funds

The *Restricted* Current Funds subgroup consists of those resources that are expendable for operating purposes but are restricted by donors, grantors, or outside agencies as to the specific purpose for which they may be expended. They are similar to Specific Purpose Funds of hospitals, and similar revenue realization conventions apply to both.

Earnings or contributions of *Restricted* Current Funds are not recognized as revenue until they are expended for their intended purpose. Amounts received or accrued usually are credited initially to a Fund Balances account. Prior to preparation of financial statements, an amount equal to that expended for the restricted purpose is deducted from the appropriate Fund Balance account and added to the appropriate Revenue account. (Alternatively, all earnings or contributions may be credited to Revenues; prior to statement preparation, an appropriate amount is added to or deducted from Revenues and deducted from or added to Fund Balances so that the amount of revenues recognized equals the expenditures during the period.)

Additions to *Restricted* Current Funds include (1) restricted gifts for specific operating purposes; (2) restricted endowment income; and (3) grants received from private organizations or governments for research, public service, or other specific purposes. Reductions of *Restricted* Current Funds balances are occasioned by: (1) expenditures charged to the funds, when corresponding amounts are transferred to revenues to "match" the revenues and expenditures; (2) refunds to donors and grantors, and (3) transfers to unrestricted revenues representing indirect cost recoveries on sponsored programs. Broadly speaking, there is no reserved-unreserved distinction here—since all the balances of these funds are reserved (restricted). The Fund Balance accounts may be titled according to restricted use or source, however, such as:

Fund Balances—Restricted Income from Endowment Funds
　　　　　　　Gifts Restricted for Operating Purposes
　　　　　　　Grants for Research, Teaching, etc.

Further, the governing board may reserve or appropriate portions of these balances for specific purposes or projects permissible under terms of the restrictions placed on them.

### "Board-Restricted" Current Funds

Some colleges and universities include "board-restricted" Current Funds in the *Restricted* Current Funds subgroup. This practice is of questionable propriety, at best, but appears to be fairly widespread, perhaps even a generally accepted alternative of *CUBA*. The authors prefer that "board-restricted" Unrestricted Current Funds be accounted for in the *Unrestricted* Current Funds subgroup. Less preferably, they may be accounted for as "Board-Restricted Current Funds." As a minimum, (1) the distinction between the balances that are externally restricted and those that are internally designated (but otherwise unrestricted) should be maintained in the accounts and disclosed in the financial statements and (2) "Board-Restricted" Funds revenue should be recognized when it is earned, that is, revenue recognition should not be deferred until the resources are expended.

### Account Classifications

The asset and liability accounts of Current Funds are usually comprised almost exclusively of current assets and current liabilities. The principal exception occurs when (1) intermediate or long-term debt has been incurred for auxiliary enterprises and (2) it is not related to fixed asset acquisition and is therefore not properly accounted for through the Plant Funds group.

Revenues and expenditures of Current Funds are usually classified by function for external reporting purposes; expenditures are classified by department and object for internal reporting and control purposes. The major functional classifications used by most colleges or universities are (1) Educational and General, (2) Student Aid, and (3) Auxiliary Enterprises. Appropriate detailed accounts would be provided, of course.

The Revenue and Expenditure functional accounts recommended in *CUBA* are presented in Figure 21-3. For ease of illustration, we use only general ledger control accounts in the illustrative entries in this chapter.

**Figure 21-3**

FUNCTIONAL CLASSIFICATIONS OF
COLLEGE AND UNIVERSITY CURRENT
FUNDS REVENUES AND EXPENDITURES

| *Revenues* | *Expenditures* |
|---|---|
| Educational and General: | Educational and General: |
|   Student Tuition and Fees |   Instruction and Departmental |
|   Governmental Appropriations |     Research |
|   Endowment Income |   Organized Activities Related to |
|   Gifts |     Educational Departments |
|   Estimated Value of Contributed |   Sponsored Research |
|     Services |   Other Separately Budgeted Research |
|   Sponsored Research |   Other Sponsored Programs |
|   Other Separately Budgeted Research |   Extension and Public Service |
|   Other Sponsored Programs |   Libraries |
|   Sales and Services of Educational |   Student Services |
|     Departments |   Operation and Maintenance of |
|   Organized Activities Related to |     Physical Plant |
|     Educational Departments |   General Administration |
|   Other Sources |   Staff Benefits |
|  |   General Institutional Expense |
| Student Aid: | Student Aid: |
|   Gifts |   (Detailed as appropriate) |
|   Endowment Income |  |
|   Governmental Appropriations |  |
|   Other |  |
| Auxiliary Enterprises: | Auxiliary Enterprises: |
|   Intercollegiate Athletics |   (Detailed as appropriate) |
|   Residence Halls |  |
|   Faculty Housing |  |
|   Food Services |  |
|   College Union |  |
|   Student Store |  |

## Budgetary Accounts—Current Funds

Budgetary accounts may be incorporated in the ledger of either Unrestricted or Restricted Current Funds in a manner similar to that used in the General Fund of a municipality. Slightly different accounts titles are commonly used by colleges or universities, as compared with municipalities, and the difference between estimated revenues and estimated expenditures is usually carried in an "Unassigned Budget Balance" or "Unallocated Budget Balance" account during the period rather than being closed to the Fund Balances account. The budgetary entry for a college or university Current Fund would appear as follows:

| | | |
|---|---|---|
| Estimated Revenues (or Unrealized Revenues) .. | 1,000,000 | |
| Appropriations (or Expenditure Allocations or Budget Allocations for Expenditures)... | | 990,000 |
| Unassigned Budget Balance (or Unallocated Budget Balance) ..................... | | 10,000 |
| To record the college or university budget. | | |

These amounts would be reversed from the accounts at year end when their purpose has been served. Inasmuch as budgetary accounting for colleges and universities so closely parallels that of a municipal General Fund, it will not be illustrated further in this chapter.

## Transactions and Entries—Unrestricted Current Funds

It is assumed for purposes of illustration that there are in use two Current Funds accounting entities: an Unrestricted Current Fund and a Restricted Current Fund, and that the operations of auxiliary enterprises are accounted for as part of the Unrestricted Current Fund. The following are some typical transactions of Unrestricted Current Funds and the entries made to record them. Transactions 10, 11, and 12 require entries not only in the Unrestricted Current Fund but also in the Plant Funds; entry 15 corresponds with entry 3 in the Restricted Current Fund illustration.

*Transactions*

1. Educational and general revenues earned during the year amounted to $2,600,000, of which $2,550,000 has been collected.
2. It is estimated that $2,000 of the accounts receivable will never be collected.
3. Other revenues of $700,000 were collected through auxiliary enterprises.
4. Total purchases for the year amounted to $600,000, of which $560,000 has been paid.
5. Materials used during the year amounted to $550,000, of which $250,000

is chargeable to educational and general activities and $300,000 to auxiliary enterprises.

6. Salaries and wages paid amounted to $2,200,000, of which $1,920,000 is chargeable to educational and general activities and $280,000 to auxiliary enterprises.

7. Legal fees, insurance expenses, interest on money borrowed for plant additions, and telephone and telegraph expenses, all chargeable to educational and general activities, amounted to $100,000 and had all been paid by the end of the year.

8. Other expenditures chargeable to auxiliary enterprises and paid for in cash totaled $10,000.

9. Student aid granted totaled $20,000.

10. Unrestricted current funds in the amount of $25,000 were used to pay an installment of the mortgage note carried as a liability in the Investment in Plant subgroup.

11. A $30,000 transfer was made from the Unrestricted Current Fund to the Unexpended Plant Fund for the purpose of financing additions to the plant.

12. Unrestricted current funds of $10,000 were spent for other plant additions.

13. In accordance with a resolution of the board of trustees of the university, $100,000 was transferred from the Unrestricted Current Fund to the Endowment and Similar Funds group for the purpose of establishing a fund which is to function as an endowment.

14. The board of trustees voted to reserve $75,000 of the Unrestricted Current Fund resources for use in making a computer use survey during the subsequent year.

15. Indirect overhead recovery on sponsored research, $8,000, was paid from the Restricted Current Fund to the Unrestricted Current Fund. (See also entry 3, Restricted Current Fund.)

16. Revenue, expenditure, and transfer accounts were closed at year end.

*Entries*

| | | | |
|---|---|---|---|
| 1. | Cash ............................... | 2,550,000 | |
| | Accounts Receivable.................. | 50,000 | |
| | Revenues-Educational and General ... | | 2,600,000 |
| | To record educational revenues earned. | | |
| | | | |
| 2. | Expenditures-Educational and General .. | 2,000 | |
| | Allowance for Uncollectible Accounts .. | | 2,000 |
| | To record provision for uncollectible accounts. | | |
| | | | |
| 3. | Cash ............................... | 700,000 | |
| | Revenues-Auxiliary Enterprises ....... | | 700,000 |
| | To record revenues of auxiliary enterprises. | | |

4. Inventory of Materials and Supplies ..... 600,000
   Cash .............................. 560,000
   Accounts Payable .................. 40,000
   To record purchases of materials and supplies.

5. Expenditures-Educational and General .. 250,000
   Expenditures-Auxiliary Enterprises ..... 300,000
   Inventory of Materials and supplies ... 550,000
   To record cost of materials and supplies used.

6. Expenditures-Educational and General .. 1,920,000
   Expenditures-Auxiliary Enterprises ..... 280,000
   Cash .............................. 2,200,000
   To record salaries and wages paid.

7. Expenditures-Educational and General .. 100,000
   Cash .............................. 100,000
   To record legal expenses, insurance expenses, interest on money borrowed for plant additions, and telephone and telegraph expenses.

8. Expenditures-Auxiliary Enterprises ..... 10,000
   Cash .............................. 10,000
   To record expenses of auxiliary enterprises other than those for materials and supplies or for salaries.

9. Expenditures-Student Aid ............. 20,000
   Cash .............................. 20,000
   To record student aid granted.

10. Transfers-Plant Funds ............... 25,000
    Cash .............................. 25,000
    To record payment of mortgage note carried as a liability in the Plant Funds.

11. Transfers-Plant Funds ............... 30,000
    Cash .............................. 30,000
    To record transfers to Plant Funds for purpose of making additions to plant.

12. Transfers-Plant Funds ............... 10,000
    Cash .............................. 10,000
    To record cost of plant additions financed from the Unrestricted Current Funds.

13. Transfers-Endowment and Similar Funds 100,000
    Cash .............................. 100,000
    To record transfer of cash to Endowment and Similar Funds group for the purpose of establishing a fund which is to function as an endowment.

14. Fund Balances-Unallocated ............    75,000
    Fund Balances-Allocated ............               75,000
    To establish a fund balance reserve for the
    estimated cost of a computer use survey to
    be made during the subsequent period.

15. Cash ..............................    8,000
    Revenues-Educational and General  ...               8,000
    To record receipt of indirect cost recovery
    on sponsored research from the Restricted
    Fund.

16. Revenues-Educational and General .....    2,608,000
    Revenues-Auxiliary Enterprises .........      700,000
    Expenditures-Educational and General               2,272,000
    Expenditures-Auxiliary Enterprises  ...               590,000
    Expenditures-Student Aid ............                20,000
    Transfers-Plant Funds  ..............                65,000
    Transfers-Endowment and Similar Funds               100,000
    Fund Balances-Unallocated ..........               261,000
    To close out revenues, expenditures, and
    transfers.

### Statement of Changes in Fund Balances—Unrestricted Current Funds

A statement analyzing the changes in fund balances of the Unrestricted Current Fund is illustrated in Figure 21-4. The excess of revenues over expenditures and transfers shown in this statement corresponds with the Fund Balances-

·Figure 21-4

A UNIVERSITY
Unrestricted Current Funds
Statement of Changes in Fund Balances
For Fiscal Year

|  | Total | Unallocated | Allocated |
|---|---|---|---|
| Balances, beginning of year* ........ | $ — | $ — | $ — |
| Additions— | | | |
| Excess of revenues over expenditures and transfers (Figure 21-6) ...... | 261,000 | 261,000 | |
| Transfers between unallocated and allocated—allocation for computer use survey ..................... | — | (75,000) | 75,000 |
| Balances, end of year .............. | $261,000 | $186,000 | $75,000 |

* The illustrative example in this chapter is for the initial year of operations of A University. Otherwise there would in all likelihood have been a beginning of year balance.

Unallocated credit in entry 16 above and with the amount shown in the statement illustrated in Figure 21-6.

It is important to note here that Current Fund transfers (whether from Unrestricted or Restricted Current Funds) are reported in the respective Statements of Changes in Fund Balances—*not* in the Statement of Current Funds Revenues, Expenditures, and Transfers—unless the governing board designates current year revenues as the source by which a transfer is to be funded. It is assumed in our example that such a designation was made by the governing board, as there were no accumulated Current Funds balances brought forward from the previous period.

### Transactions and Entries—Restricted Current Funds

The following are typical transactions of this fund group and the entries made to record them.

*Transactions*

1. Cash receipts during the year were as follows:

| | | |
|---|---:|---:|
| *Educational and General:* | | |
| Sponsored Research (grant) | $100,000 | |
| Gifts-Library Operations | 200,000 | |
| Endowment Income-Supplemental Salary | | |
| Payments* | 62,400 | $362,400 |
| *Student Aid:* | | |
| Endowment Income* | | 15,600 |
| Provision For Endowment Income | | |
| Stabilization* | | 9,700 |
| | | $387,700 |

* See also Endowment and Similar Funds, Transaction 5. The Provision for Endowment Income Stabilization is explained in that section of this chapter.

2. Expenditures were incurred as follows, of which $7,000 remained unpaid at year end:

| | | |
|---|---:|---:|
| *Educational and General:* | | |
| Sponsored Research | $ 40,000 | |
| Library Operations | 130,000 | |
| Instruction and Departmental Research | | |
| (Supplemental Salary Payments) | 50,000 | $220,000 |
| *Student Aid* | | 12,000 |
| | | $232,000 |

3. Recovery of indirect costs of $8,000, associated with the $40,000 of sponsored research expenditures, was transferred to the Unrestricted Current Fund. (See also Unrestricted Current Fund, Transaction 15.)

4. Income due from the Endowment and Similar Funds group at year end was as follows:

| | |
|---|---:|
| For Supplemental Salary Payments | $25,000 |
| For Student Aid | 5,000 |
| | $30,000 |

(See also Endowment and Similar Funds, Transaction 9.)

5. Revenue for the period was recognized and fund balances adjusted accordingly at year end.

6. Closing entries were made.

*Entries*

1. Cash .................................... 387,700
   Fund Balances—Sponsored Research....... 100,000
   Fund Balances—Library Operations ....... 200,000
   Fund Balances—Supplemental Salary
     Payments ........................... 62,400
   Fund Balances—Student Aid ........... 15,600
   Provision for Endowment Income
     Stabilization........................ 9,700
   To record resources received and establishment of provision for endowment income stabilization.

(Fund Balances subsidiary accounts usually show the sources and purposes of the resources received or accrued. Alternatively, a series of Fund Balances general ledger accounts may be used, as is done here for clarity of illustration.)

2. Expenditures—Educational and General ..... 220,000
   Expenditures—Student Aid ............... 12,000
   Accounts Payable ..................... 7,000
   Cash ................................. 225,000
   To record expenditures incurred.

3. Fund Balances—Sponsored Research......... 8,000
   Cash ................................. 8,000
   To record payment to Unrestricted Current Fund of indirect cost recovery under provisions of research grant.

4. Due from Endowment and Similar Funds .... 30,000
   Fund Balances—Supplemental Salary
     Payments........................... 25,000
   Fund Balances—Student Aid ........... 5,000
   To record resources due from endowment earnings.

    5.  Fund Balances—Sponsored Research.........   40,000
        Fund Balances—Library Operations .........  130,000
        Fund Balances—Supplemental Salary
           Payments...........................   50,000
        Fund Balances—Student Aid .............   12,000
          Revenues—Educational and General.......         220,000
          Revenues—Student Aid ................          12,000
        To recognize revenues to the extent that re-
        stricted resources were expended during the
        period.

(Compare this entry to entry 2 above. Note again that revenues are recognized only to the extent that the restricted resources are expended for the purposes or functions designated by donors, grantors, or outside agencies.)

    6.  Revenues—Educational and General.........  220,000
        Revenues—Student Aid ..................   12,000
          Expenditures—Educational and General ...         220,000
          Expenditures—Student Aid .............          12,000
        To close the Revenues and Expenditures ac-
        counts at year end.

(Obviously the entries to close the Revenue and Expenditures accounts must be in corresponding amounts in the case of Restricted Current Funds, because revenue is realized only upon expenditure of the restricted resources.)

In each case above, less resources were expended (and recognized as revenue) than were received or accrued. Had fund balances been brought forward from prior years, the opposite might have been true. Again, as in the case of Specific Purpose Funds of hospitals, the logic of the realization (revenue recognition) convention employed in Restricted Current Funds accounting— as recommended in *CUBA* and as done in most colleges and universities—is that the resources have not been earned until they have been expended for their designated purposes.

Two alternative approaches that may be found in practice warrant brief mention here. First, some colleges and universities do not observe the "revenue recognition deferral" convention with respect to Restricted Current Funds. Rather, they (1) account for the Restricted Current Funds in the same manner as the Unrestricted Current Funds during the year, and (2) at year end, they close the Revenues and Expenditures accounts to appropriately titled Fund Balance-Reserved or Fund Balance-Restricted accounts. Second, some colleges and universities account for both restricted and unrestricted resources available for current expenditures in a single Current Funds general ledger. In this case it is necessary that the fund balance accounts (and related subsidiary records) be clearly identified as between Fund Balances—Unrestricted and Fund Balances—Restricted.

The Statement of Changes in Fund Balances of A University's Restricted Current Fund for the fiscal year is presented as Figure 21-5. Note the format

Figure 21-5

A UNIVERSITY
Restricted Current Funds
Statement of Changes in Fund Balances
For Fiscal Year

| | Total | Educational and General | | | | Provision for Endowment Income Stabilization |
| | | Sponsored Research | Library Operations | Supplemental Salary Payments | Student Aid | |
|---|---|---|---|---|---|---|
| Balance, beginning of year* | $ — | $ — | $ — | $ — | $ — | $ — |
| Additions: | | | | | | |
| Sponsored research | $100,000 | $100,000 | | | | |
| Gifts | 200,000 | | $200,000 | $87,400 | $20,600 | |
| Endowment income | 117,700 | | | | | $ 9,700 |
| | $417,700 | $100,000 | $200,000 | $87,400 | $20,600 | $ 9,700 |
| Deductions†: | | | | | | |
| Expenditures (Figure 21-6) | $232,000 | $ 40,000 | $130,000 | $50,000 | $12,000 | |
| Indirect cost recoveries on sponsored programs transferred to Unrestricted Current Funds | 8,000 | 8,000 | | | | |
| | $240,000 | $ 48,000 | $130,000 | $50,000 | $12,000 | |
| Balances, end of year | $177,700 | $ 52,000 | $ 70,000 | $37,400 | $ 8,600 | $ 9,700 |

* The illustrative example in this chapter is for the initial year of operations of A University. Otherwise, there would in all likelihood have been a beginning of year balance.

† The "Deductions" section reports those amounts (1) reported simultaneously as revenues and expenditures on the Statement of Current Funds Revenues, Expenditures, and Transfers (Figure 21-6), and (2) refunds of restricted resources because of the lapsing of a governmental appropriation, because they are not needed for the restricted purpose, etc.

of this statement and that the Provision for Endowment Income Stabilization is a part of the (reserved) fund balance.

## Operating Statement—Current Funds

A Statement of Current Funds Revenues, Expenditures, and Transfers, based on the journal entries for the two Current Funds groups, is presented in Figure 21-6. It shows the total revenues from each source and the total amount spent for each major activity, both classified as to whether they pertain to unrestricted or restricted Current Funds.

To save space, detailed revenues and expenditures accounts were not used in the journal entries presented in this chapter; the most common ones (see Figure 21-3) are listed in Figure 21-6 without showing dollar amounts for them.

**Figure 21-6**

A UNIVERSITY
Statement of Current Funds Revenues,
Expenditures, and Transfers
For Fiscal Year

| | Total | Unrestricted | Restricted |
|---|---|---|---|
| Revenues[a]: | | | |
| Educational and general: | | | |
| Student tuition and fees | $ XX | $ XX | $ — |
| Governmental appropriations | XX | XX | XX |
| Endowment income | XX | XX | XX |
| Gifts | XX | XX | XX |
| Sponsored research | XX | — | XX |
| Other separately budgeted research | XX | XX | — |
| Recovery of indirect costs—sponsored programs | XX | XX | — |
| Sales and services of educational departments | XX | XX | — |
| Organized activities relating to educational departments | XX | XX | — |
| Other sources | XX | XX | — |
| Total educational and general | $2,828,000 | $2,608,000 | $220,000 |
| Student aid | 12,000 | — | 12,000 |
| Auxiliary enterprises | 700,000 | 700,000 | — |
| Total revenues | $3,540,000 | $3,308,000 | $232,000 |
| Expenditures[a]: | | | |
| Educational and general: | | | |
| Instruction and departmental research | $ XX | $ XX | $ XX |

a Reference should be made here to a detailed statement supporting this item.

**Figure 21-6 (cont.)**

| | Total | Unrestricted | Restricted |
|---|---|---|---|
| Organized activities relating to educational departments | XX | XX | XX |
| Sponsored research | XX | — | XX |
| Other separately budgeted research | XX | XX | — |
| Extension and public service | XX | XX | XX |
| Libraries | XX | XX | XX |
| Student services | XX | XX | — |
| Operation and maintenance of physical plant | XX | XX | — |
| General administration | XX | XX | — |
| Staff benefits | XX | XX | — |
| General institutional expense | XX | XX | — |
| Total educational and general | $2,492,000 | $2,272,000 | $220,000 |
| Student aid | 32,000 | 20,000 | 12,000 |
| Auxiliary enterprises (including debt service of $XX) | 590,000 | 590,000 | — |
| Total expenditures | $3,114,000 | $2,882,000 | $232,000 |
| Excess of revenues over expenditures[b] | $ 426,000 | $ 426,000 | $ — |
| Transfers[c]: | | | |
| To[d]: | | | |
| Funds functioning as endowment[a] | $100,000 | $100,000 | |
| Plant funds for: | | | |
| Additions[a] | 40,000 | 40,000 | |
| Renewals and replacements[a] | — | — | |
| Retirement of indebtedness[a] | 25,000 | 25,000 | |
| Total transfers | $ 165,000 | $ 165,000 | |
| Excess of revenues over expenditures and transfers | $ 261,000 | $ 261,000 | $ — |

[b] This amount is not presented in the format for this statement recommended by *CUBA*. It is presented here to highlight the equality of the reported revenues and expenditures of the Restricted Current Funds.

[c] Only those transfers from Current Funds to other funds that are financed from current period revenues are reported here. All other transfers from the Current Funds—and all transfers to the Current Funds from other funds—are reported in the respective Statements of Changes in Fund Balances if the recommendations in *CUBA* are followed.

[d] The "Transfers" section of this statement does *not* include transfers of Endowment and Similar Funds or Annuity and Life Income Funds earnings to the Restricted Current Funds. As noted in the chapter, these initially are added to the Restricted Current Funds balances and are reported simultaneously as both revenues and expenditures of the period in which they are expended. Transfers to the Restricted Current Fund(s) from the Unrestricted Current Fund(s) would appear in this statement.

Statements showing the details of current revenues and expenditures, and of the transfers, should be prepared in support of these major elements of the statement. For example, details of the operations of each department should be shown, and a separate statement of revenues and expenditures should be prepared for each of the auxiliary activities.

Note again that Current Fund transfers are reported here *only* if the governing board has specified that the transfers are to be funded from *current year revenues*. Furthermore, transfers to Plant Renewal and Replacement Funds financed from auxiliary enterprise revenues are reported in the expenditure section as "Provisions for Renewals and Replacements." All other transfers are reported in the appropriate Statements of Changes in Fund Balances. Clearly the recommendations in *CUBA* suggest that a "current operating" approach, as distinguished from an "all inclusive" approach, should be followed in preparing the Statement of Current Funds Revenues, Expenditures, and Transfers (Figure 21-6).

### Balance Sheet—For the University

In Figure 21-7 there is presented a balance sheet for the university at the close of fiscal year. Data from the transactions already presented for the Unrestricted Current and Restricted Current Funds are the bases of the balance sheet for the Current Funds group. The year-end balance sheets of the other funds or fund groups (after the transactions discussed later) are added to the Balance Sheets of the two types of funds already discussed.

This "pancake" form of the university-wide balance sheet is the preferred form. College and university balance sheets are often presented in columnar form to minimize the use of space. Even though like account balances of the several fund groups are placed on the same line using a columnar format, no total column is provided. This practice recognizes that assets and liabilities of the fund groups are in most cases subject to legal or donor restrictions and other obligations that may make it misleading to show totals for the university as a whole.

### LOAN FUNDS

Loan Funds are used to account for funds that may be loaned to students and, in some cases, to faculty and staff. If only the fund's income may be loaned, the principal is included in the Endowment and Similar Funds group and only the income should be included with the Loan Funds. It is desirable to classify the fund balances in appropriate ways. For example, some may come from appropriations, others from private donors, and still others from Unrestricted Current Funds set aside for this purpose by the college or university governing board. Some may be refundable to donors under specified conditions.

Figure 21-7

A UNIVERSITY
Balance Sheet
At Close of Fiscal Year

*Assets*

| | |
|---|---:|
| **Current Funds:** | |
| Unrestricted: | |
| Cash | $ 203,000 |
| Accounts receivable, less allowance for uncollectible accounts of $2,000 | 48,000 |
| Inventory of materials and supplies | 50,000 |
| Total unrestricted | $ 301,000 |
| Restricted: | |
| Cash | $ 154,700 |
| Due from endowment and similar funds | 30,000 |
| Total restricted | $ 184,700 |
| Total current funds | $ 485,700 |
| **Loan Funds:** | |
| Cash | $ 25,400 |
| Loans receivable | 49,500 |
| Investments | 25,000 |
| Total loan funds | $ 99,900 |

*Liabilities and Fund Balances*

| | |
|---|---:|
| **Current Funds:** | |
| Unrestricted: | |
| Accounts payable | $ 40,000 |
| Fund balances (Figure 21-4) | 261,000 |
| Total unrestricted | $ 301,000 |
| Restricted: | |
| Accounts payable | $ 7,000 |
| Fund balances (Figure 21-5) | 177,700 |
| Total restricted | $ 184,700 |
| Total current funds | $ 485,700 |
| **Loan Funds:** | |
| Fund balances* | $ 99,900 |
| Total loan funds | $ 99,900 |

**Endowment and Similar Funds:**

| | | |
|---|---|---|
| Assets other than fixed: | | |
| Cash | | $ 205,800 |
| Investments: | | |
| Preferred stocks, at cost (market value $625,000) | $ 500,000 | |
| Common stocks, at cost (market value, $1,215,000) | 1,065,000 | |
| Bonds, at cost (market value $465,000) | 454,700 | |
| Held in trust by others—cost, $200,000 (market value, $234,000) | — | |
| | | 2,019,700 |
| | | $2,225,500 |
| Fixed assets: | | |
| Land | | $ 100,000 |
| Buildings, less allowance for depreciation of $6,000 | | 594,000 |
| Equipment, less allowance for depreciation of $14,000 | | 136,000 |
| | | $ 830,000 |
| Total endowment and similar funds | | $3,055,500 |

**Endowment and Similar Funds:**

| | | |
|---|---|---|
| Due to restricted current funds | | $ 30,000 |
| Fund balances:* | | |
| Endowment | 2,925,500 | |
| Quasi-endowment | 100,000 | |
| | | $3,025,500 |
| Total endowment and similar funds | | $3,055,500 |

Figure 21-7 (cont.)

**Assets**

Annuity and Life Income Funds:

| | | |
|---|---:|---:|
| Cash | $ 10,000 | |
| Investments, at cost (market value, $101,000) | 100,000 | |
| Total annuity and life income funds | | $ 110,000 |

Plant Funds:

Unexpended:

| | | |
|---|---:|---:|
| Cash | $ 18,000 | |
| Investments, at cost (market value $22,100) | 20,000 | |
| Total unexpended | | $ 38,000 |

For retirement of indebtedness:

| | | |
|---|---:|---:|
| Cash | $ 25,000 | |
| Total for retirement of indebtedness | | $ 25,000 |

Investment in plant:

| | | |
|---|---:|---:|
| Land | $ 300,000 | |
| Buildings | 4,000,000 | |
| Equipment | 1,021,000 | |
| Total investment in plant | | $5,321,000 |
| Total plant funds | | $5,384,000 |

**Liabilities and Fund Balances**

Annuity and Life Income Funds:

| | |
|---|---:|
| Fund balances—annuities* | $ 110,000 |
| Total annuity and life income funds | $ 110,000 |

Plant Funds:

Unexpended:

| | |
|---|---:|
| Fund balances* | $ 38,000 |
| Total unexpended | $ 38,000 |

For retirement of indebtedness:

| | |
|---|---:|
| Fund balances* | $ 25,000 |
| Total for retirement of indebtedness | $ 25,000 |

Investment in plant:

| | | |
|---|---:|---:|
| Mortgage payable | $ 360,000 | |
| Net investment in plant* | 4,961,000 | |
| Total investment in plant | | $5,321,000 |
| Total plant funds | | $5,384,000 |

* Statements analyzing changes in the balances of each fund group should be presented in the financial report.

In the following transactions it is assumed that a Loan Fund was established to make interest-free loans and that (1) income on Fund investments is to be added to the principal of the Fund, and (2) the total assets of the Fund, both the original principal and that from earnings, may be loaned.

### Transactions

1. A donation of $100,000 was received for the purpose of making loans to students.
2. Loans in the amount of $50,000 were made.
3. The sum of $25,000 was invested in bonds. The bonds were purchased at par plus accrued interest of $100.
4. A $500 check in payment of six months' bond interest was received.
5. A student died and it was decided to write off his loan of $500 as uncollectible.

### Entries

1. Cash .................................... 100,000
      Fund Balance .........................         100,000
   To record donation received for the purpose of setting up Loan Fund.

2. Loans Receivable ....................... 50,000
      Cash .................................         50,000
   To record loans made.

3. Investments ............................ 25,000
      Accrued Interest on Investments Purchased ..   100
      Cash .................................         25,100
   To record investments and accrued interest purchased.

4. Cash .................................... 500
      Accrued Interest on Investments Purchased .         100
      Fund Balance .........................         400
   To record receipt of semiannual interest payment.

5. Fund Balance ........................... 500
      Loans Receivable .....................         500
   To write off loan as uncollectible.

## ENDOWMENT AND SIMILAR FUNDS

These Funds are used to account for assets which, at least at the moment, cannot be expended, although usually the income from them may be. Funds donated by outsiders fall into two categories: (1) Those that have been given in perpetuity and (2) Those for which the donor has specified a particular date or event after which the funds may be expended. The first are simply called "Endowment Funds,"[5] while the second are called "Term Endowment Funds."

The appropriate policy-making body of an institution may also set aside available funds for the same purposes as those donated as endowments. These, called "Quasi-Endowment Funds" or "Funds Functioning As Endowments," are of course subject to reassignment by the authority that created them.

Donors may choose to make the income from endowment-type funds available to a university but to leave the principal in the possession and control of a trustee other than the university. Such funds usually should not be included among the Endowment and Similar Funds of the university,[6] but their existence should be revealed in the financial statements by an appropriate footnote. The income from such funds is recorded as an addition to the Restricted Current Funds balance. When expended, it is reported there as Endowment Income if the trust is irrevocable; if it is a revocable trust, the income recognized should be reported there as Gifts.

## Transactions and Entries—Endowment Funds

The following transactions and entries illustrate the operation of Endowment and Similar nonexpendable Funds:

*Transactions*

1. Cash in the amount of $2,000,000 was received during the year to establish three separate endowments, as follows:

   | | |
   |---|---|
   | Endowment A (For Supplemental Salary Payments) ...... | $1,000,000 |
   | Endowment B (For Supplemental Salary Payments) ...... | 600,000 |
   | Endowment C (For Student Aid) ..................... | 400,000 |

2. It was decided to invest this money in securities that were to be pooled. The following securities were acquired at the prices indicated:

   | | |
   |---|---|
   | Preferred stocks ................. | $ 500,000 |
   | Common stocks ................. | 1,000,000 |
   | Bonds: | |
   |     Par value ..................... | 200,000 |
   |     Premiums .................... | 10,000 |

[5] These are sometimes referred to as "true" or "pure" Endowment Funds.

[6] The exception to this general rule is discussed in the concluding section of this chapter.

Bonds:

| | |
|---|---|
| Par value ...................... | 250,000 |
| Discounts ..................... | 5,000 |
| Accrued interest on investments purchased ................... | 1,000 |

3. Cash received on these investments for the year was as follows:

| | |
|---|---|
| Dividends on preferred stocks .......... | $20,000 |
| Dividends on common stocks .......... | 60,000 |
| Interest .......................... | 9,000 |

No material amounts of investment income were accrued at year end.

4. Premiums on investments in the amount of $500 and discounts in the amount of $200 were amortized at the end of the year.

5. It was decided to allow 4 percent interest to each fund on its principal and to make these credits at the end of each year. The interest income distributed in this manner at the end of the first year amounted to $78,000. The remainder of the net income from pooled investments was set aside in the Restricted Current Fund as a provision for endowment income stabilization. (See also Transaction 1, Restricted Current Fund.)

6. Common stock with a book value of $10,000 was sold for $10,500.

7. An individual donated common stock which had cost him $65,000 (hereafter referred to as Endowment Fund D). At the time of the donation the stock had a market value of $75,000. The income from these securities is available for general purposes.

8. An individual had a dormitory constructed and equipped and then turned it over to the university with the specification that the net income therefrom was to be used 1/6 for student aid and 5/6 for supplemental salary payments (hereafter referred to as Endowment Fund E). The total cost was $850,000, divided as follows:

| | |
|---|---|
| Land .................... | $100,000 |
| Building ............... | 600,000 |
| Equipment ............. | 150,000 |

9. Gross income from this enterprise (Endowment Fund E) for the current year was $170,000; and the total expenses amounted to $120,000, exclusive of depreciation of $20,000 (building, $6,000; equipment, $14,000). No receivables or payables were outstanding at year end and the net income of Endowment Fund E was established as a liability to the Restricted Current Fund. (See transaction 4, Restricted Current Fund.)

10. The sum of $100,000 was received from the Unrestricted Current Fund for the purpose of establishing an endowment in accordance with the resolution adopted by the university's Board of Trustees. (See transaction 13, Unrestricted Current Fund.)

11. An individual set up a trust (to be administered by the Village National Bank) in the amount of $200,000, the income from which was to go to the university.

*Entries*

1. Cash ............................... 2,000,000
   Endowment Fund A Balance ...... 1,000,000
   Endowment Fund B Balance........ 600,000
   Endowment Fund C Balance ...... 400,000
   To record receipt of money for the purpose of establishing three endowments.

2. Preferred Stocks ..................... 500,000
   Common Stocks ..................... 1,000,000
   Bonds ............................. 450,000
   Accrued Interest on Investments
   Purchased...................... 1,000
   Unamortized Premiums on Investments .. 10,000
   Unamortized Discounts on Investments 5,000
   Cash .......................... 1,956,000
   To record purchase of pooled investments.

3. Cash ............................... 89,000
   Income on Pooled Investments ..... 88,000
   Accrued Interest on Investments
   Purchased...................... 1,000
   To record income received as follows:

   | | | |
   |---|---|---|
   | Dividends on preferred stock | | $20,000 |
   | Dividends on common stock | | 60,000 |
   | Interest received | $9,000 | |
   | Less—Interest | | |
   | purchased | 1,000 | 8,000 |
   | | | $88,000 |

4. Unamortized Discounts on Investments .. 200
   Income on Pooled Investments ..... 300
   Unamortized Premiums on
   Investments ................... 500
   To record amortization of premiums and discounts.

5. Income on Pooled Investments ......... 87,700
   Cash .......................... 87,700
   To record payment of endowment income to the Restricted Current Fund at rate of 4 per cent per year on market value of pooled investments. Amount to be credited to the income of each Endowment Fund computed as follows:

| Fund | Fund Balance* | Percentage of Total | Income Apportioned |
|------|--------------|---------------------|--------------------|
| A | $1,000,000 | 50 | $39,000 |
| B | 600,000 | 30 | 23,400 |
| C | 400,000 | 20 | 15,600 |
| | $2,000,000 | 100% | $78,000 |

The balance of the income was transferred to the Restricted Current Fund as a provision for endowment income stabilization.

6. Cash ............................... 10,500
   Common Stock ..................... 10,000
   Endowment Fund A Balance ........ 250
   Endowment Fund B Balance......... 150
   Endowment Fund C Balance ........ 100
   To record sale of common stock at a profit of $500 and the addition of the gain to the balance of each Endowment Fund as follows:

| Fund | Fund Balance | Percentage of Total | Gain Apportioned |
|------|-------------|---------------------|------------------|
| A | $1,000,000 | 50 | $250 |
| B | 600,000 | 30 | 150 |
| C | 400,000 | 20 | 100 |
| | $2,000,000 | 100% | $500 |

7. Common Stocks ..................... 75,000
   Endowment Fund D Balance ....... 75,000
   To record donation of common stock with a market value of $75,000; the net income of Endowment D is unrestricted.

8. Land ............................... 100,000
   Building ........................... 600,000
   Equipment ......................... 150,000
   Endowment Fund E Balance ....... 850,000
   To record establishment of dormitory as endowment, net income of which is restricted to certain purposes.

9. Cash ............................... 50,000
   Allowance for Depreciation—Building 6,000
   Allowance for Depreciation—
   Equipment ..................... 14,000
   Due to Restricted Current Fund .... 30,000

* It is assumed that market values and book values of the several funds are in this case identical.

To record results of Endowment E operations for the period and liability to the
Restricted Current Fund for the net income, after depreciation, of Endowment
E.

10.  Cash ...............................        100,000
     Balance of Quasi-Endowment Funds                        100,000
     To record receipt of money from Unre-
     stricted Current Fund for purpose of set-
     ting up a fund to function as an Endow-
     ment Fund in accordance with resolution
     adopted by the university's Board of
     Trustees.

11.  No entry, or purely memorandum entry.
     (Note the balance sheet disclosure, Figure
     21-7.)

## Commentary—Endowment Funds Transactions and Entries

The following points should be noted with respect to the foregoing transactions and entries.

1. Three types of nonexpendable funds were illustrated: (1) "pure"
endowment funds, exemplified by transactions and entries nos. 1–9, (2) funds
being accounted for as endowments through action of the Board of Trustees
of the university, illustrated by transaction and entry no. 10, and (3) funds
turned over by a donor to a trustee or trustees with the stipulation that the
income therefrom is to go to the university, exemplified by transaction no. 11,
which requires no entry in the Endowment and Similar Funds group.

2. The investments of several Endowment Funds have been pooled and
premiums, discounts, and accrued interest purchases are involved and amortized.

3. Two courses of action are possible in the management and distribution
of, and accounting for, the income from pooled endowment investments. One
is to allocate to each beneficiary fund its share of the total income of the pool
for the year. The other is to set aside a portion of the total income of the pool
for the year with the expectation of stabilizing the income of the beneficiary
funds over the years. An arbitrary rate of return may be assumed as the basis
for crediting each participating fund with its share of the pool income. The
appropriate size of the provision for endowment income stabilization is a matter
of judgment by each individual institution, but the arbitrary rate of return
should not be slavishly followed when the result is an unreasonable accumulation.

In the illustrative case an arbitrary rate of return has been assumed. Entries
and transactions nos. 3 and 5 indicate that the amount earned exceeded the
amount allocated to the various funds participating in the pool; the credit
balance in the Income on Pooled Investments account is distributed to the

Restricted Current Fund. Where endowment earnings are unrestricted and in the absence of an income stabilization provision would be reported as Unrestricted Current Funds revenue, this approach may cause improper deferral of revenue recognition and is opposed vigorously by the AICPA Committee. This method was illustrated because it is unique and has been widely used by colleges and universities. It is *not* the method preferred by the authors, however.

Income stabilization may be accomplished even if all the income from the pool is distributed to the beneficiary funds. Where this is the case the total *unrestricted* income from Endowment and Similar Funds is reported as Unrestricted Current Funds revenue. The amount set aside for the provision for income stabilization is then established as a reserve and is shown in the Unrestricted Current Funds Statement of Changes in Fund Balances as a transfer to Unrestricted Current Funds Balances—Allocated from Fund Balances—Unallocated. The account, Unrestricted Current Funds Balances—Allocated, may appear in the balance sheet as a separately listed (reserved) equity balance. This method assures proper reporting of Unrestricted Current Funds revenues and, if the governing board sees fit, provides for the establishment of a fund balance reservation for endowment income stabilization. In our opinion this approach should be followed when any part of the endowment income is unrestricted.

4. Since the objective of the investment pool is the production of income, income should be computed on an accrual basis. Accordingly, both premiums and discounts on investments have been amortized in the illustrative case and any material receivables would have been accrued.

5. Since Endowment and Similar Funds are normally operated on the principles of accounting for trusts, losses or gains on the sale of pooled investments are not elements in the income calculation but are adjustments of the balances of the Endowment and Similar Funds. If the equities in pooled investments of the participating funds are maintained on a book value (cost) basis, losses or gains on the sale of pooled investments may be treated in two ways: (1) Gains may be credited and losses charged to a Reserve for Gains or Losses on Pooled Investments account, which eventually is closed out into the principal of each participating fund. (2) Gains may be credited and losses charged to the investment pool equity (and the fund principal) of each participant fund as they occur. If there are many sales of pooled securities, the first method is desirable; if there are few sales the second method may be employed.

If there are changes in the market value of pooled investments, and if the several participating funds make contributions to the pool that are not proportionate to their original investments, the book value method will not result in equitable assignments of gains or losses on the sale of investments and of income on pooled investments. Consequently The Committee (*CUBA*) endorsed the use of the market value method of accounting for the equities of the several funds and pooled investments—whether or not changes in investment market values are recorded in the accounts. Under this preferred method the initial balances of the participating funds are divided by some arbitrary value, let us say $10, that is to be assigned to a share in the pool. A fund with a $5,000 balance, then, would have 500 shares. If the market value of investments in the pool doubled, the unit value would increase to $20, but the fund with a $5,000 initial balance would still have 500 shares. A new fund being admitted to the pool would have its number of shares determined by dividing the market value of its contribution, whether in cash or investments, by $20. The number of shares then would become the basis for allocation of realized gains or losses, as well as income from the pool, among the funds.

Withdrawals of participating funds from the investment pool will be made at market value. If the market value of shares has increased, the payment to the withdrawing fund will result in a cash payment in excess of the fund balance, assuming it is carried at cost. This excess is composed of unrealized gains in the market value of investments, together with any undistributed realized gains or losses. Consequently it is appropriate to charge this share adjustment, the excess of market value over cost, to the account for (realized) gains and losses on investments.

Realized gains and losses might properly be distributed to the balances of the several funds in proportion to their numbers of shares. The same thing may be said of the share adjustments, which in effect represent a combination of realized and unrealized appreciation of the investment portfolio. In practice the account, which may be called Net Adjusted Gains and Losses, is usually accumulated, though it would be equitable to distribute it to the funds on the basis of their shares. Disclosure in the balance sheet of the nature of the account would be necessary if the amount in the account is material.

The necessity for the hybrid account, Gains and Losses on Investments—Share Adjustments (or Net Adjusted Gains and Losses), arises from the use of the cost basis in accounting for investments and fund balances. The Committee that revised *CUBA* recognized the equity of the market value method and also stated that the reported rate of return on endowment investments should be computed on the basis of the market value of the average investment during the year. Recognition in the accounts of the market value of investments, which appears to be increasing in practice, permits recognition of unrealized increments or decrements, which in turn eliminates the need for the share adjustment feature described above.[7]

6. Transaction and entry no. 7 illustrate that securities should be recorded at their market value at the date they are donated.

7. Transaction and entry no. 9 illustrate that depreciation charges must be taken into account in computing the income of an Endowment Fund that has investments in the form of fixed assets if the Fund is to remain nonexpend-

---

[7] The AICPA Committee on College and University Accounting and Auditing concluded that fair market value accounting and reporting for long-term investments is generally accepted for colleges and universities.

able. It illustrates further that it is essential to retain cash (initially) equal to depreciation charges in the Endowment Fund, and transfer only the net income to the Restricted Current Funds. If prices are rising, these depreciation charges retained, even if invested, may not provide sufficient resources to replace the fixed assets. But these charges will at least assure that the original cost is replaced and that the fund principal will, in dollar terms, remain intact. If the donor desires it, provision can be made for additional charges sufficient to replace the depreciated fixed assets. If the supplementary charges are made, the resulting credit would not be to an Allowance for Depreciation account but rather to an account representing an increase in fund balance. A donor could, of course, specify that depreciation would not be provided; if the gift is accepted, the terms of the gift must be followed.

## ANNUITY AND LIFE INCOME FUNDS

These Funds account for assets that have been given to the institution with the proviso either that the institution is required to make annuity payments to designated recipients or that the institution is required to pay the income from the assets for life to designated recipients. For example, an individual may donate cash, securities, or other assets under an agreement that he is to get a fixed or variable amount as an annuity for life but that after he dies the principal is to belong to the university. He may also place restrictions on the manner in which the principal may ultimately be used by the university.

The accounting for Annuity and Life Income Funds is like that of the Endowment and Similar Funds group. If these funds are small in amount, they may even be accounted for as a separately identified part of the Endowment and Similar Funds group. A typical transaction would be the donation of cash or securities for the establishment of an Annuity Fund. The entry to record such a transaction is:

| | | |
|---|---|---|
| Cash ........................................ | 10,000 | |
| Investments ................................ | 100,000 | |
|     Balances of Annuity Funds ................ | | 110,000 |
|     To record establishment of an annuity fund. | | |

The Balances of Annuity Funds account is a control account that would be supported by details of each Annuity Fund. There would be a similar account for Balances of Life Income Funds.

As income is earned it is reported in this Fund group; amounts awaiting distribution are reported in Undistributed Income accounts. In the case of Life Income Funds the entire amount of income is payable to the designated beneficiary. For Annuity Funds there may be differences between the Fund income and the annuity amount designated in the contract. These differences are usually accumulated in an Undistributed Income account; however material and apparently permanent earnings deficiencies or overages may be charged or credited to the Balances of Annuity Funds account. In either event the differences are a part of the fund balance.

Investments of this group may be pooled unless the pooling is prohibited by contractual agreement. (Separate investment pools should be operated for Endowment and Similar Funds and for Annuity and Life Income Funds.) As in the case of Endowment Funds, the gains or losses on sales of investments become part of the principal of the Fund. Prior to allocation to the various fund balance accounts, these gains or losses are often accumulated in a Reserve for Gains and Losses on Investment Transactions account.

Typical asset accounts would include Cash; Investments, including Real Estate and Accumulated Depreciation accounts; and Due from Other Funds. Liability and Fund Balance accounts may include Payables, Due to Other Funds, Undistributed Income—Annuity Funds, Undistributed Income—Life Income Funds, Reserve for Gains and Losses on Investment Transactions and Fund Balances accounts. As noted earlier, the fund balances should be classified as between Balances of Annuity Funds and Balances of Life Income Funds.

"Income from Investments" and "Disbursements" are control accounts that would be detailed as necessary under each agreement. Since the income of these funds is not income of the institution, incomes and disbursements would be reported in a Statement of Changes in Fund Balances rather than in a Statement of Revenues, Expenditures, and Transfers.

## PLANT FUNDS

Four separate subgroups of accounts may be used to account for the assets of Plant Funds. These subgroups are used to account for (1) assets earmarked for the acquisition of fixed assets, (2) assets earmarked for renewal and replacement of fixed assets, (3) cash and investments that have been accumulated in order to retire indebtedness that was incurred in connection with the acquisition of fixed assets, and (4) fixed assets used to carry on operations (as distinguished from fixed assets held as endowments), together with the liabilities outstanding against these assets. The accounts relating to the first group will hereafter be referred to as Unexpended Plant Funds, those relating to the second as Funds for Renewals and Replacements, those relating to the third as Funds for Retirement or Indebtedness, and those relating to the fourth as Investment in Plant. Since the Funds for Renewals and Replacements may be included in the Unexpended Plant Funds group (the first three are sometimes combined and shown as "Unexpended Funds" for reporting purposes), and in any case these first two subgroups use the same type of accounting, the following presentations assume that no separate discussion of Funds for Renewals and Replacements is necessary. The results of the transactions and entries of each fund group are shown in the Balance Sheet for that group illustrated in Figure 21-7.

## Unexpended Plant Funds

Sources of assets for the Unexpended Plant Funds subgroup are governmental appropriations, gifts, transfers from other funds, and proceeds from borrowing for plant purposes. The first three should be credited to the Fund Balances account of Unexpended Plant Funds, while the notes, bonds, or mortgages payable are shown as liabilities of this subgroup. Costs pertaining to construction projects should be charged to Construction in Progress. The balance in the Construction in Progress account may be accumulated until the project is completed, or, for reporting purposes, may be transferred to the Investment in Plant subgroup. As transfers are made from the Construction in Progress account to the Investment in Plant subgroup, corresponding liabilities or fund balances should also be transferred.

Assets for the Funds for Renewals and Replacements may come from the same sources as those for the Unexpended Plant Funds subgroup, and the accounting is similar. As noted earlier in the chapter, if provision for renewals and replacements is made from *current year* Current Funds revenues, the contributions for renewals and replacements should be reported as (1) "Transfers" in the Statement of Current Funds Revenues, Expenditures, and Transfers, except (2) if the provision is from auxiliary enterprise revenues, it is reported as an auxiliary enterprise expenditure. If provisions for renewals and replacements are made from *previously accumulated* Unrestricted Current Funds balances, the transfer of assets should be shown in the Statement of Changes in Fund Balances of the Unrestricted Current Funds.

Some typical transactions and the related entries for this group are given below. Transaction and entry no. 3 affect not only this group but also the Investment in Plant group.

### Transactions

1. A donation of preferred stocks valued at $20,000 was made by an individual for the purpose of financing additions to the plant.
2. Cash in the amount of $30,000 was transferred from the Unrestricted Current Fund to this fund for the purpose of financing additions to the plant. (See also Transaction no. 11, Unrestricted Current Fund.)
3. Equipment costing $12,000 was purchased for cash. (See also transaction no. 4 in the Investment in Plant Fund.)

### Entries

1. Investments ............................... 20,000
      Fund Balances ........................            20,000
   To record investments donated for the purpose of financing additions to plant. (The Fund Balances account controls accounts for separate funds in this group.)

*Entries*

2. Cash ...................................... 30,000
     Fund Balances ........................ 30,000
   To record receipt of cash from the Unrestricted
   Current Fund for the purpose of financing addi-
   tions to plant.

3. Fund Balances .......................... 12,000
     Cash ................................. 12,000
   To record purchase of equipment.

## Funds for Retirement of Indebtedness

Assets received from sources earmarked for the retirement of indebtedness (e.g., fees and appropriations) should be reported directly in this Fund—they should *not* be reported as Current Funds revenues. Assets received from Current Funds for payment of interest on indebtedness should be treated as expenditures in the Current Funds; principal payments should be treated as Current Fund transfers. If the provisions of debt instruments require the accumulation of sinking funds, payments made to the sinking fund involve intrafund transfers between assets of the Funds for Retirement of Indebtedness; that is, sinking fund assets remain as assets of the Funds for Retirement of Indebtedness. As principal payments are made from the Funds for Retirement of Indebtedness, the additional net investment of university funds in fixed assets should be recognized in the Net Invested in Plant account in the Investment in Plant subgroup.

The following are some typical transactions of this Fund and the related entries. Transaction no. 2 affects not only this Fund but also the Investment in Plant group.

*Transactions*

1. A donation of $15,000 was made for the purpose of paying the mortgage installment falling due during the current year.
2. The money was used for this purpose. (See also transaction no. 5 in Investment in Plant Fund.)
3. A donation of $25,000 was made for the purpose of paying the mortgage installment falling due next year.

*Entries*

1. Cash ...................................... 15,000
     Fund Balances ........................ 15,000
   To record receipt of money to pay mortgage
   installment falling due during the current year.

2. Fund Balances .......................... 15,000
     Cash ................................. 15,000
   To record payment of mortgage installment.

3.  Cash ...................................... 25,000
    Fund Balances ........................              25,000
    To record receipt of money to pay part of mort-
    gage installment falling due during the following
    year.

## Investment in Plant

The asset accounts in the Investment in Plant subgroup contain the book value of the institutional plant properties except for those in Endowment and Similar Funds. As previously discussed, no depreciation is taken on these assets. The liabilities for funds borrowed for the acquisition or construction of (completed) plant are shown here; the net equity in fixed assets is maintained in the Net Invested in Plant account, which may be kept in such detail as seems necessary. For example, separate categories might be maintained for net investment from gifts, governmental appropriations, Current Funds, or other funds.

The balances in the Investment in Plant Fund at the beginning of the period were as follows:

|  | *Debit Balances* | *Credit Balances* |
|---|---|---|
| Land | 300,000 | |
| Buildings | 4,000,000 | |
| Equipment | 1,000,000 | |
| Mortgage Payable | | 400,000 |
| Net Invested in Plant | | 4,900,000 |
| | 5,300,000 | 5,300,000 |

*Transactions*

Originating in:

1.  UNRESTRICTED CURRENT FUND (See transaction no. 10 in that Fund): Mortgage notes carried as a liability of the Investment in Plant Fund, $25,000, were paid from Unrestricted Current Funds.

2.  UNRESTRICTED CURRENT FUND (See transaction no. 12 in that Fund): Equipment was purchased for $10,000.

3.  UNEXPENDED PLANT FUND (See transaction no. 3 in that fund): Equipment Costing $12,000 was purchased for cash.

4.  RETIREMENT OF INDEBTEDNESS FUND (See transaction no. 2 in that Fund): An installment of the mortgage note in the amount of $15,000 was retired.

5.  INVESTMENT IN PLANT FUND: A piece of uninsured equipment financed from current revenues and costing $1,000 was destroyed by fire.

*Entries*

1. Mortgage Payable.......................... 25,000
     Net Invested in Plant ...................          25,000
   To record payment of mortgage principal from
   the Unrestricted Current Fund.

2. Equipment .............................. 10,000
     Net Invested in Plant ...................          10,000
   To record purchase of equipment out of the
   Unrestricted Current Fund.

3. Equipment .............................. 12,000
     Net Invested in Plant ...................          12,000
   To record purchase of equipment out of the
   Improvements and Replacements Fund.

4. Mortgage Payable.......................... 15,000
     Net Invested in Plant ...................          15,000
   To record payment of part of mortgage payable
   from the Retirement of Indebtedness Fund.

5. Net Invested in Plant ...................... 1,000
     Equipment ...........................          1,000
   To remove from this Fund the original cost of
   equipment destroyed.

## AGENCY FUNDS

A university usually serves as a depository and fiscal agent for a number of student, faculty, and staff organizations. It holds funds belonging to others. Agency liability accounts are termed "Fund Balances" in *CUBA,* as is common in Agency Funds of municipalities, and presentation of a statement analyzing the changes in the fund balances is recommended there. Only the usual asset and liability (or fund balance) accounts of Agency Funds need be maintained.

## FINANCIAL REPORTING

The primary financial statements recommended in *CUBA* for colleges and universities are:

*Combined—for all fund groups:*
Balance Sheet (Figure 21-7)
*Current Funds:*
Statement of Current Funds Revenues, Expenditures, and Transfers (Figure 21-6)
Statement of Changes in Fund Balances—Unrestricted Current Funds (Figure 21-4)

Statement of Changes in Fund Balances—Restricted Current Funds (Figure 21-5)
*For each other fund group and major subgroup:*
Statement of Changes in Fund Balances

The primary statements should be accompanied by detailed supporting schedules and footnotes appropriate to assure full disclosure and fair presentation of the operations and balances of the various fund groups and subgroups. Statements of Changes in Fund Balances of fund groups other than the Current Funds are not illustrated here in view of their simplicity and their similarity to those illustrated for the Current Funds. Likewise, summary worksheets are omitted because of the similarity of college or university accounting with that of municipalities and hospitals.

## UNSETTLED ISSUES/CONCLUDING COMMENTS

Several unsettled or controversial issues in college and university accounting have been noted in the preceding sections of this chapter. Primary among them, no doubt, is the practice of some colleges or universities of treating "board-restricted" resources as "restricted" and deferring the recognition of revenue thereon until the resources are expended. Such practice permits the manipulation of reported Current Funds revenues and, in the opinion of the authors, should not be condoned.

### AICPA Audit Guide Recommendations

Some of the conclusions of the AICPA Committee on College and University Accounting and Auditing have been mentioned in the preceding pages; others have been deferred to this point in the chapter. Some of the changes recommended by the AICPA Committee reflect suggestions made by the NACUBO; in all cases, NACUBO has agreed that the changes suggested by the AICPA Committee are generally acceptable. The major objections of the AICPA Committee to practices recommended or permitted by *CUBA,* and the AICPA Committee recommendations, are summarized below.

BASIC STATEMENTS.   The AICPA Committee illustrates the presentation of a *combined* Statement of Changes in Fund Balances (see Figure 21-8), and recommends that a Statement of Current Funds Revenues, Expenditures, and Other Changes (Figure 21-9) should replace the Statement of Current Funds Revenues, Expenditures, and Transfers (Figure 21-6). Both transfers to and from the Current Funds are included in these statements; in fact, all transfers appear on both statements. Furthermore, a detailed Statement of Changes in Current Funds Balances may be used in lieu of the two statements in presenting Current Funds operations and changes.

Figure 21-8

## SAMPLE EDUCATIONAL INSTITUTION
### Statement of Changes in Fund Balances
#### Year Ended June 30, 19—

| | Current Funds | | Loan Funds | Endowment and Similar Funds | Annuity and Life Income Funds | Plant Funds | | | |
|---|---|---|---|---|---|---|---|---|---|
| | Unrestricted | Restricted | | | | Unexpended | Renewal and Replacement | Retirement of Indebtedness | Investment in Plant |
| **Revenues and other additions:** | | | | | | | | | |
| Educational and general revenues | $5,300,000 | | | | | | | | |
| Auxiliary enterprises revenues | 2,200,000 | | | | | | | | |
| Expired term endowment revenues | 40,000 | | | | | | | | |
| Expired term endowment—restricted | | | | | | 50,000 | | | |
| Gifts and bequests—restricted | | 370,000 | 100,000 | 1,500,000 | 800,000 | 115,000 | | 65,000 | 15,000 |
| Grants and contracts—restricted | | 500,000 | | | | | | | |
| Governmental appropriations—restricted | | | | | | 50,000 | | | |
| Investment income—restricted | | 224,000 | 12,000 | 10,000 | | 5,000 | 5,000 | 5,000 | |
| Realized gains on investments—unrestricted | | | 4,000 | 10,000 | | 10,000 | 5,000 | 5,000 | |
| Realized gains on investments—restricted | | | | 109,000 | | | | | |
| Interest on loans receivable | | | 7,000 | | | | | | |
| U. S. Government advances | | | 18,000 | | | | | | |
| Expended for plant facilities (including $100,000 charged to current funds expenditures) | | | | | | | | | 1,550,000 |
| Retirement of indebtedness | | | | | | | | | 220,000 |
| Accrued interest on sale of bonds | | | | | | | | 3,000 | |
| Matured annuity and life income funds restricted to endowment | | | | 50,000 | | | | | |
| Total revenues and other additions | 7,540,000 | 1,094,000 | 141,000 | 1,679,000 | 800,000 | 230,000 | 10,000 | 78,000 | 1,785,000 |

Figure 21.9

SAMPLE 21.9. INSTITUTIONAL ...
... Funds ... Statement of ... Expenditures ...
For the Year Ended June 30, 19XX
With Comparative Figures for ...

| | Unrestricted | Restricted | Loan Funds | Endowment and Similar Funds | Annuity and Life Income Funds | Unexpended (Plant) | Renewals and Replacements | Retirement of Indebtedness | Investment in Plant | Total |
|---|---|---|---|---|---|---|---|---|---|---|
| **Expenditures and other deductions:** | | | | | | | | | | |
| Educational and general expenditures | 4,400,000 | 1,014,000 | | | | | | | | |
| Auxiliary enterprises expenditures | 1,830,000 | | | | | | | | | |
| Indirect costs recovered | | 35,000 | | | | | | | | |
| Refunded to grantors | | 20,000 | | | | | | | | |
| Loan cancellations and write-offs | | | 10,000 | | | | | | | |
| Administrative and collection costs | | | 1,000 | | | | | | | |
| Adjustment of actuarial liability for annuities payable | | | 1,000 | | 75,000 | | | | | |
| Expended for plant facilities (including noncapitalized expenditures of $50,000) | | | | | | 1,200,000 | | | | |
| Retirement of indebtedness | | | | | | | 300,000 | 220,000 | | |
| Interest on indebtedness | | | | | | | | 190,000 | | |
| Disposal of plant facilities | | | | | | | | 1,000 | 115,000 | |
| Expired term endowments ($40,000 unrestricted, $50,000 restricted to plant) | | | | 90,000 | | | | | | |
| Matured annuity and life income funds restricted to endowment | | | | | 10,000 | | | | | |
| Total expenditures and other deductions | 6,230,000 | 1,069,000 | 12,000 | 90,000 | 85,000 | 1,200,000 | 300,000 | 411,000 | 115,000 | |
| **Transfers among funds—additions/(deductions)** | | | | | | | | | | |
| Mandatory: | | | | | | | | | | |
| Principal and interest | (340,000) | | | | | | | 340,000 | | |
| Renewals and replacements | (170,000) | | | | | | 170,000 | | | |
| Loan fund matching grant | (2,000) | | 2,000 | | | | | | | |
| Unrestricted gifts allocated | (650,000) | 50,000 | 50,000 | 550,000 | | | | | | |
| Portion of unrestricted quasi-endowment funds investment gains appropriated | 40,000 | | | (40,000) | | | | | | |
| Total transfers | (1,122,000) | 52,000 | 50,000 | 510,000 | | 170,000 | (120,000) | 340,000 | | |
| Net increase/(decrease) for the year | 188,000 | 25,000 | 181,000 | 715,000 | 2,099,000 | 50,000 | 170,000 | 340,000 | 7,000 | 1,670,000 |
| Fund balance at beginning of year | 455,000 | 421,000 | 502,000 | 2,505,000 | 11,901,000 | (920,000) | 2,120,000 | 380,000 | 293,000 | 36,540,000 |
| Fund balance at end of year | $ 643,000 | 446,000 | 683,000 | 3,220,000 | 14,000,000 | (870,000) | 2,290,000 | 720,000 | 300,000 | 38,210,000 |

Source: Committee on College and University Accounting and Auditing, American Institute of Certified Public Accountants, *Audits of Colleges and Universities* (New York: The AICPA, 1973), pp. 64–65.

Figure 21-9

SAMPLE EDUCATIONAL INSTITUTION
Statement of Current Funds Revenues, Expenditures, and Other Changes
Year ended June 30, 19—
With Comparative Figures for 19—

| | Current Year | | | Prior |
| | Unrestricted | Restricted | Total | Year Total |
|---|---|---|---|---|
| **Revenues:** | | | | |
| Educational and general: | | | | |
| Student tuition and fees | $2,600,000 | | 2,600,000 | 2,300,000 |
| Governmental appropriations | 1,300,000 | | 1,300,000 | 1,300,000 |
| Governmental grants and | | | | |
| contracts | 35,000 | 425,000 | 460,000 | 595,000 |
| Gifts and private grants | 850,000 | 380,000 | 1,230,000 | 1,190,000 |
| Endowment income | 325,000 | 209,000 | 534,000 | 500,000 |
| Sales and services of educational | | | | |
| departments | 90,000 | | 90,000 | 95,000 |
| Organized activities related to | | | | |
| educational departments | 100,000 | | 100,000 | 100,000 |
| Other sources (if any) | | | | |
| Total educational and general | 5,300,000 | 1,014,000 | 6,314,000 | 6,080,000 |
| Auxiliary enterprises | 2,200,000 | | 2,200,000 | 2,100,000 |
| Expired term endowment | 40,000 | | 40,000 | |
| Total revenues | 7,540,000 | 1,014,000 | 8,554,000 | 8,180,000 |
| **Expenditures and mandatory transfers:** | | | | |
| Educational and general: | | | | |
| Instruction and departmental | | | | |
| research | 2,820,000 | 300,000 | 3,120,000 | 2,950,000 |
| Organized activities related to | | | | |
| educational departments | 140,000 | 189,000 | 329,000 | 350,000 |
| Sponsored research | | 400,000 | 400,000 | 500,000 |
| Other separately budgeted | | | | |
| research | 100,000 | | 100,000 | 150,000 |
| Other sponsored programs | | 25,000 | 25,000 | 50,000 |
| Extension and public service | 130,000 | | 130,000 | 125,000 |
| Libraries | 250,000 | | 250,000 | 225,000 |
| Student services | 200,000 | | 200,000 | 195,000 |
| Operation and maintenance of | | | | |
| plant | 220,000 | | 220,000 | 200,000 |

| | Current Year | | | Prior |
| | Unrestricted | Restricted | Total | Year Total |
|---|---|---|---|---|
| General administration | 200,000 | | 200,000 | 195,000 |
| General institutional expense | 250,000 | | 250,000 | 250,000 |
| Student aid | 90,000 | 100,000 | 190,000 | 180,000 |
| Educational and general expenditures | 4,400,000 | 1,014,000 | 5,414,000 | 5,370,000 |
| Mandatory transfers for: | | | | |
| Principal and interest | 90,000 | | 90,000 | 50,000 |
| Renewals and replacements | 100,000 | | 100,000 | 80,000 |
| Loan fund matching grant | 2,000 | | 2,000 | |
| Total educational and general | 4,592,000 | 1,014,000 | 5,606,000 | 5,500,000 |
| Auxiliary enterprises: | | | | |
| Expenditures | 1,830,000 | | 1,830,000 | 1,730,000 |
| Mandatory transfers for: | | | | |
| Principal and interest | 250,000 | | 250,000 | 250,000 |
| Renewals and replacements | 70,000 | | 70,000 | 70,000 |
| Total auxiliary enterprises | 2,150,000 | | 2,150,000 | 2,050,000 |
| Total expenditures and mandatory transfers | 6,742,000 | 1,014,000 | 7,756,000 | 7,550,000 |
| Other transfers and additions/ (deductions): | | | | |
| Excess of restricted receipts over transfers to revenues | | 45,000 | 45,000 | 40,000 |
| Refunded to grantors | | (20,000) | (20,000) | |
| Unrestricted gifts allocated to other funds | (650,000) | | (650,000) | (510,000) |
| Portion of quasi-endowment gains appropriated | 40,000 | | 40,000 | |
| Net increase (decrease) for the year | $ 188,000 | 25,000 | 213,000 | 160,000 |

Source: Committee on College and University Accounting and Auditing, American Institute of Certified Public Accountants, *Audits of Colleges and Universities* (New York: The AICPA, 1973), p. 66–67.

"OVERVIEW" TOTALS.    Combined statements may include columnar and grand totals to reflect the overall financial picture of the institution if proper disclosures are made to assure that the statements are not misleading. Thus, interfund borrowings should be disclosed in combined balance sheets or the notes thereto, and mislabeling of cross-footed totals and duplication of gross charges should be avoided in presenting the Statement of Changes in Fund Balances. The effect of this AICPA Committee recommendation apparently is to permit, if not require, that *consolidating* statements be prepared when presentation of columnar or grand totals is desired in order to present the financial status or results of financial operations of the university as a whole.

ENDOWMENT INCOME STABILIZATION RESERVE.    The AICPA Committee position is that use of such provisions in a manner that causes deferral of revenue recognition in Unrestricted Current Funds is at variance with generally accepted accounting principles. It recommends (a) that the independent auditor should qualify his opinion with respect to the fairness of presentation of material amounts included in such reserves and to material differences between unrestricted income distributed—and thus reported as unrestricted revenue—and that actually earned, and (b) that colleges and universities should not make further additions to such reserves and should make proper disposition of the balances now accumulated.

ANNUITY FUNDS/PLEDGES.    While *CUBA* requires use of actuarial methods for determining annuity liabilities on a life expectancy or term basis, it does not require that they be determined on a *present value* basis. The AICPA Committee therefore concluded that the *CUBA* recommendations are at variance with generally accepted accounting principles. The AICPA Committee also requires that (1) pledges of gifts be disclosed, and (2) if pledges are recorded as assets, that they be reported at their net estimated *present value,* after allowance for uncollectible pledges, together with disclosure of the amounts of pledges by time periods over which they are expected to be collected.

ACCOUNTING CHANGES.    Accounting Principles Board (APB) Opinion No. 20 deals with the reporting of changes in accounting principles and estimates, changes in the reporting entity, and the correction of errors in financial statements previously issued. The AICPA Committee concluded that the provisions of APB 20 apply to statements of colleges or universities except for those provisions that clearly relate only to profit-seeking organizations.

MANDATORY DEBT SERVICE PROVISIONS AND MATCHING GRANT TRANSFERS. The AICPA Committee distinguished between mandatory and nonmandatory transfers of Current Funds. Mandatory transfers for debt principal retirement, interest payments, plant renewals and replacements, loan fund principal additions, and the like, are reported with Current Funds expenditures by the AICPA Committee (see Figure 21-9). With the exception of interest payments, these are considered to be "transfers" in *CUBA.*

OTHER AICPA AUDIT GUIDE RECOMMENDATIONS.    Some of the other AICPA Committee recommendations relate to the following:

1. *Investment performance*—the total performance of the investment portfolio, based on both cost and market values, should be disclosed.
2. *Depreciation*—the expiration of capital asset costs may be reported in the

Statement of Changes of Fund Balances for the Investment in Plant subgroup of the Plant Funds, and the related depreciation or similar allowances may be reported in the Plant Funds balance sheet.

3. *Funds held in trust by others*—these may be recorded as assets if the institution has legally enforceable rights or claims which can be evaluated objectively.

4. *Provisions for Encumbrances*—these should not be treated as expenditures, a practice some have considered permissible according to the recommendations in *CUBA*.

5. *Agency Funds*—since Agency Funds contain only assets and related liabilities, there is no need for a statement analyzing the changes in the "fund balance" of Agency Funds.

### Concluding Comments

Controversy and change frustrate some persons. Others view them as positive signs that the attention of the accounting profession is increasingly being directed toward the improvement of college and university accounting and reporting. Resolution of some of these issues remains for the future, but there is little doubt that college and university accounting and reporting—indeed, that for the entire not-for-profit sector—is receiving more of the profession's attention today than ever before, and may well receive even more in the future.

Accounting and reporting concepts and practices should and must evolve continually in all fields. Through the combined efforts of many persons and organizations, that evolution appears to be accelerating in the not-for-profit sector.

**Question 21-1.** Prepare a list of the funds recommended for use by a college or university. Opposite the funds indicate the fund or account groups recommended for municipalities by the National Committee on Governmental Accounting which are most nearly comparable in nature.

**Question 21-2.** The Main City College is financed solely from a special tax levy made for this purpose. The construction of the building was financed from the sale of bonds. These bonds as well as the interest thereon are also being paid from the special tax levy referred to immediately above. Would the accounting procedure outlined in the chapter also apply to this college? If not, indicate the fund or funds in which the financial transactions of the college should be recorded.

**Question 21-3.** The American Hospital Association recommends that depreciation be taken on all fixed assets of hospitals, whereas NACUBO recommends that, with certain exceptions, no depreciation should be taken on the fixed assets of colleges. Do you think there is a better reason for charging depreciation on the fixed assets of hospitals than on the fixed assets of colleges?

**Question 21-4.** What is the purpose of charging depreciation on the fixed assets of an endowment fund? Explain.

**Question 21-5.** Each fund participating in an investment pool may be allocated its share of the pool income or an arbitaray rate of return may be assumed as the basis for distribution of the pool income. Which is the better procedure? Give reasons for your answer.

**Question 21-6.** Under what circumstances are resources expendable for operating purposes accounted for in Restricted Current Funds? At what point should contributions to Restricted Current Funds be recognized as revenue? Justify your response.

**Question 21-7.** List the funds recommended for use by a hospital down the center of a sheet of paper. To the left of the hospital funds indicate the funds or account groups recommended for municipalities by the National Committee on Governmental Accounting which are most nearly comparable in nature; to the right, do a similar comparison between hospital funds and those employed by colleges and universities. At the bottom of the page list those municipal and college or university funds and account groups for which there is no reasonably close parallel in hospital accounting.

**Question 21-8.** Name three differences between the accounting procedures of colleges and those of hospitals.

**Problem 21-1. Part I.** The trial balance of the Unrestricted Current Fund of $X$ University on September 1, 19X0, was as follows:

| | | |
|---|---:|---:|
| Cash | $155,000 | |
| Accounts Receivable | 30,000 | |
| Allowance for Uncollectible Accounts | | $ 2,000 |
| Inventory of Materials and Supplies | 25,000 | |
| Vouchers Payable | | 23,000 |
| Fund Balance | | 185,000 |
| | $210,000 | $210,000 |

The following transactions took place during the current fiscal year:

1.  Collections amounted to $2,270,000 distributed as follows: student tuition and fees, $1,930,000; gifts and grants, $170,000; organized activities relating to educational departments, $115,000; other educational and general revenues, $25,000; accounts receivable, $30,000.

2.  Receivables at end of the year, $29,000, consisting entirely of educational revenues.

3.  It is estimated that tuition receivable in the amount of $1,000 will never be collected.

4.  Revenues from auxiliary enterprises, $300,000.

5.  Materials purchased during the year for cash $500,000; on account, $50,000.

6.  Materials used amounted to $510,000 distributed as follows:

| | | |
|---|---:|---:|
| Educational and general: | | |
| General administration | $ 30,000 | |
| General expenses | 5,000 | |
| Instruction and departmental research | 305,000 | |
| Organized activities relating to educational departments | 7,000 | |
| Others | 53,000 | $400,000 |
| Auxiliary enterprises | | 110,000 |
| | | $510,000 |

7. Salaries and wages paid:

Educational and general:

| | | |
|---|---:|---:|
| General administration ............... | $ 170,000 | |
| General expenses...................... | 63,000 | |
| Instruction and departmental research .... | 1,212,000 | |
| Organized activities relating to educational departments ...................... | 80,000 | |
| Others ............,.................... | 85,000 | $1,610,000 |
| Auxiliary enterprises .................... | | 90,000 |
| | | $1,700,000 |

8. Other expenses:

Educational and general:

| | | |
|---|---:|---:|
| General administration .................... | $10,000 | |
| General expenses.......................... | 2,000 | |
| Instruction and departmental research ......... | 53,000 | |
| Organized activities relating to educational departments ..................... ....... | 3,000 | |
| Others .................................. | 7,000 | $75,000 |
| Auxiliary enterprises.......................... | | 20,000 |
| | | $95,000 |

9. Interest expenses, all chargeable to educational and general, $3,000.

10. Vouchers payable paid, $40,000.

11. A transfer of $20,000 was made from this fund to the improvements and replacements fund for the purpose of financing plant additions.

12. The board of trustees of the university passed a resolution authorizing the transfer of $150,000 to a fund which is to function as an endowment.

13. The Unrestricted Current Fund paid $20,000 for additions to the plant.

Required:

(a) Prepare journal entries.

(b) Post the opening trial balance and journal entries to "T" accounts.

**Problem 21-1. Part II.** The trial balance of the Restricted Current Fund of $X$ University on September 1, 19X0, was as follows:

| | | |
|---|---:|---:|
| Cash ......................................... | $32,000 | |
| Vouchers Payable ........................... | | $ 2,000 |
| Fund Balance .............................. | | 30,000 |
| | $32,000 | $32,000 |

The following transactions took place during the current fiscal year:

1. Cash was received from endowments, $70,000; gifts and grants, $150,000; auxiliary enterprises, $130,000; student aid, $20,000.

2. Expenditures paid in cash:

Educational and general:

| | | |
|---|---:|---:|
| General administration | $ 40,000 | |
| General expenses | 30,000 | |
| Instruction and departmental research | 125,000 | |
| Others | 20,000 | 215,000 |
| Auxiliary enterprises | | 90,000 |
| Student aid | | 20,000 |

3. Depreciation charges on auxiliary plant carried as an endowment amounted to $15,000.

4. Cash equal to the depreciation charges, namely, $15,000, was transferred from this fund to the Endowment Fund.

Required:

(a) Prepare journal entries.

(b) Post the opening trial balance and journal entries to "T" accounts.

(c) Prepare a combined balance sheet of the Unrestricted Current Fund and Restricted Current Fund as of August 31, 19X1.

(d) Prepare a combined revenues, expenditures, and transfers statement for the two Funds for the fiscal year ended August 31, 19X1.

**Problem 21-2.** The following transactions took place in the Endowment Funds of $X$ University during the fiscal year ended August 31, 19X1:

1. A cash donation of $900,000 was received to establish Endowment Fund $X$, and another donation of $600,000, also in the form of cash, was received for the purpose of establishing Endowment Fund $Y$. The income from these funds is restricted for specific purposes. It was decided to invest this money, to pool the investments of both funds, and to allow 5 percent on the book value of pooled investments at the end of the year.

2. Securities with a par value of $1,000,000 were purchased at a premium of $10,000.

3. Securities with a par value of $191,500 were acquired at a discount of $2,000; accrued interest at date of purchase amounted to $500.

4. The university trustees voted to pool the investments of Endowment Fund $Z$ with the investments of Endowment Funds $X$ and $Y$ under the same conditions as applied to the latter two Funds. The investments of Endowment Fund $Z$ at the date it joined the pool amounted to $290,000 at book value and $300,000 at market value.

5. Cash dividends received from the pooled investments during the year amounted to $70,000, and interest receipts amounted to $5,500.

6. Premiums in the amount of $500 and discounts in the amount of $100 were amortized.

7. Securities in the amount of $30,000 were sold at a profit of $2,400.

8. Each fund was credited with its share of the interest earnings for the year (see transaction no. 1).

9. Land, buildings, and equipment amounting to $800,000 were donated to the university, distributed as follows: land, $80,000; buildings, $500,000; equipment, $220,000. The donor stipulated that an endowment fund (hereafter designated as Endowment Fund N) should be established and that the income therefrom should be used for a restricted operating purpose.

10. Income from the property referred to in the preceding transaction is accounted for in Restricted Current Fund N. This Fund transferred $32,000 to Endowment Fund N, of which $10,000 represented depreciation charges on the building and $22,000 depreciation charges on equipment.

11. A trust fund in the amount of $350,000 was set up by a donor with the stipulation that the income was to go to the university to be used for general purposes.

Required:
  (a)  Prepare journal entries.
  (b)  Post to "T" accounts.
  (c)  Prepare a balance sheet of the Endowment Funds as of August 31, 19X1.

**Problem 21-3.** The following transactions took place in the loan fund of *X* University during the fiscal year ended August 31, 19X6:

1. A donation of $150,000 was received in cash for the purpose of making loans to students.

2. Cash in the amount of $50,000 was invested in bonds which were acquired at par.

3. Loans in the amount of $60,000 were made to students.

4. Interest on investments in the amount of $300 was received in cash.

5. Student loans in the amount of $1,000 were written off as uncollectible.

Required:
  (a)  Prepare journal entries.
  (b)  Post to "T" accounts.
  (c)  Prepare a balance sheet of the Loan Fund as of August 31, 19X6.

**Problem 21-4.** The trial balance of the Investment in Plant Fund of *X* University as of September 1, 19X0, was as follows:

| | | |
|---|---:|---:|
| Land ............................................ | $ 200,000 | |
| Buildings ....................................... | 3,300,000 | |
| Equipment ...................................... | 1,200,000 | |
| Mortgage Payable ............................... | | $ 250,000 |
| Investment in Plant from Donations .............. | | 800,000 |
| Investment in Plant from Current Funds ........... | | 650,000 |
| Investment in Plant from Gifts .................. | | 3,000,000 |
| | $4,700,000 | $4,700,000 |

The following transactions took place during the year:

1. A cash donation of $40,000 was received from an individual for the purpose of financing additions to the educational plant.

2. The money was invested in securities which were acquired at par.

3. Cash in the amount of $20,000 was received from the Unrestricted Current Fund for purposes of making additions and improvements to the plant.

4. Of the money received from the Unrestricted Current Fund, $10,000 was used to finance the acquisition of additional equipment.

5. Land, buildings, and equipment amounting to $800,000 were donated to the university, distributed as follows: land, $80,000; building, $500,000; equipment, $220,000. The donor stipulated that an Endowment Fund should be established (designated as endowment N in Problem 21-2).

6. The Investment in Plant Fund was reduced by the depreciation charges of $10,000 on the building and $22,000 on the equipment referred to in transactions 9 and 10 of Problem 21-2.

7. A cash donation in the amount of $75,000 was received for the purpose of paying part of the mortgage.

8. A mortgage installment of $35,000 which became due during the year was paid from the above donation.

9. An uninsured piece of equipment costing $5,000 and financed from the Unrestricted Current Fund was destroyed.

Required:
(a) Prepare journal entries for the several kinds of Plant Funds, as needed.
(b) Post the opening trial balance and entries to "T" accounts.
(c) Prepare a combined balance sheet for the Plant Funds as of August 31, 19X1.

**Problem 21-5.** From the following information relating to Prep School, prepare a work sheet showing opening balances, transactions, adjustments for the year ended June 30, 19X5, and trial balances as of June 30, 19X5, for each of the appropriate classes of funds into which the general ledger is divided.
The balances of the general ledger accounts as at July 1, 19X4, are as follows:

| | | |
|---|---:|---:|
| Cash—for general use | $ 1,000 | |
| Cash—from alumni subscriptions for new dormitory .. | 2,000 | |
| Cash—endowment | 45,000 | |
| Cash—for student loans | 1,000 | |
| Tuition receivable | 12,500 | |
| Investments—temporary investments of general cash .. | 4,000 | |
| Investments—endowment | 250,000 | |
| Stores | 15,000 | |
| Alumni subscriptions for new dormitory (due September 30, 19X3) | 8,000 | |
| Student loans receivable | 3,500 | |
| Education plant: | | |
| Financed from original and subsequent endowments | 600,000 | |
| Financed from tuition funds | 50,000 | |
| Financed from alumni subscriptions | 200,000 | |
| Financed by grant from state and local governments | 50,000 | |
| Accounts payable for supplies | | $ 3,500 |
| Unpaid expenses of alumni subscription campaign .... | | 1,000 |
| Balance | | 1,237,500 |
| | $1,242,000 | $1,242,000 |

1. Endowment investments and $40,000 of the endowment cash represent principal of Endowment Funds held under terms providing that the income therefrom shall be used only for operating expenses of the school. The balance of Endowment Fund cash represents accumulated income not transferred from the endowment to the Unrestricted Current Fund.

2. Student population was 150 students. The tuition rate was $1,000 per school year per student except for six full scholarships and three partial (one-half) scholarships.

3. 90 percent of current tuition was collected and $100 of the balance is considered uncollectible.

4. Tuition receivable of prior years was collected in the amount of $12,000 and the balance is considered uncollectible.

5. Charges for operating expenses incurred and supplies purchased during the year totaled $135,000.

6. Inventory of operating supplies at June 30, 19X5, amounted to $13,500.

7. Accounts payable for operating supplies and expenses amounted to $2,000 at June 30, 19X5.

8. All temporary investments of general cash were sold on July 1, 19X4, for $4,300 and accrued interest of $100.

9. Endowment investments having a book value of $25,000 were sold for $27,500, including accrued interest of $500.

10. Investments were purchased by the Endowment Fund trustees at a cost of $50,000.

11. Interest on Endowment Fund investments not sold during the year amounted to $20,500 for the year and was all collected in cash.

12. The endowment fund trustees transferred $22,500 to the Unrestricted Current Fund bank account.

13. As a result of the continued alumni subscription campaign, additional subscriptions in the amount of $65,000 were received for the purpose of providing a new dormitory. These subscriptions were payable one-fifth at the date of the pledge and one-fifth quarterly beginning January 15, 19X5.

14. 5% bonds in the amount of $50,000 were issued for cash on January 1, 19X5, to provide funds for immediate construction of the new dormitory. Interest was payable annually.

15. Contracts in the amount of $70,000 were let for construction of the new dormitory out of subscriptions.

16. The contract for construction of the new dormitory was 50 percent completed on June 1, 19X5, and payment for one-half of the total amount, less a retained percentage of 10 percent, was made on that date.

17. All alumni subscriptions of the current year were paid on the due dates; those due previously were also paid in full.

18. Tuition receipts amounting to $5,000 were used to build additional bleachers at the athletic stadium.

19. A riding stable costing $4,000 and financed during a previous year from tuition receipts was destroyed by fire. Insurance recovery was $4,500; the building will not be replaced.

20. Student loans amounting to $3,500 were made.

21. Student loan collections amounted to $4,000, including $200 interest.

22.   Expenses of the alumni subscription campaign were paid in full in the amount of $1,500.

(AICPA, adapted)

**Problem 21-6.**   From the following trial balance of the accounts of the University of *R* and the additional information given, prepare a balance sheet in the proper institutional form:

|  | June 30, 19X0 | |
| --- | --- | --- |
|  | Debit | Credit |
| Cash ......................................... | $    43,500 | |
| Deposit accounts ............................... | | $      2,500 |
| Income from endowment investments ............... | | 85,500 |
| Income from college operations ................... | | 100,000 |
| College operating expenses ....................... | 195,000 | |
| Interest accrued on securities purchased ........... | 500 | |
| Inventories | | |
| School supplies ............................. | 5,000 | |
| General ................................... | 3,000 | |
| Investments | | |
| Bonds ..................................... | 875,500 | |
| Mortgages ................................. | 270,000 | |
| Stocks .................................... | 990,000 | |
| Real Estate ............................... | 100,000 | |
| Mortgages payable secured by college plant.......... | | 250,000 |
| College plant | | |
| Land ...................................... | 95,000 | |
| Buildings ................................. | 1,000,000 | |
| Ground improvements ....................... | 50,000 | |
| Equipment ................................ | 160,000 | |
| Profit on sale of Endowment Fund investments ....... | | 4,000 |
| Prepaid college expenses ........................ | 2,000 | |
| Accounts receivable | | |
| Students .................................. | 3,000 | |
| Miscellaneous ............................. | 1,000 | |
| Notes receivable ............................... | 20,000 | |
| Notes payable ................................. | | 2,000 |
| Accounts payable .............................. | | 3,000 |
| Allowance for uncollectible accounts receivable ...... | | 500 |
| Accumulated depreciation of buildings held as Endowment Fund investment ....................... | | 5,500 |
| Reserve for contingencies........................ | | 5,000 |
| Excess of assets over liabilities ................... | | 3,355,500 |
| | $3,813,500 | $3,813,500 |

## Additional information

1. An analysis of the cash account shows that the cash should be divided as follows:

| | |
|---|---:|
| Current Funds | |
| Imprest cash | $ 1,000 |
| On deposit | 35,000 |
| Loan Funds | 2,000 |
| Endowment Funds | 4,000 |
| Funds subject to annuity agreements | 1,500 |
| | $43,500 |

2. All the investments were made from Endowment Funds with the exception of $25,500 in bonds purchased from funds subject to annuity agreements. The income and principal of the latter funds are to be used to make certain definite payments during the life of the annuitants. Excess of annuity payments over income has been charged to the principal of the Fund.

3. Notes receivable represent loans made to students from funds that are restricted to that purpose.

4. Memorandum records show that $11,500 of Endowment Funds are loaned temporarily to the Unrestricted Current Fund.

5. These records also show that $50,000 of Endowment Funds are invested in the college's plant in full accord with the endowment terms.

6. It was decided that the accumulated depreciation of real estate carried among the investments be funded.

(AICPA, adapted)

**Problem 21-7.** You are to prepare skeleton ledger accounts and record the following transactions of the County College for 19X0. In setting up your accounts, classify them into suitable groupings by funds to facilitate preparation of a balance sheet. You need not prepare the formal statement, but you are to prepare a trial balance of your ledger, *including all accounts used in your ledger even though they do not have a balance.* In entering the transactions in your ledger, key them to the transaction numbers given.

It is suggested that you use four columns of a 14-column sheet for the accounts of each active fund, showing the fund name and then heading the columns "Reference," "Debit," "Reference," "Credit," respectively. Only one cash account requires more than seven lines, including the account title.

## January 1

County College, which previously held no endowment funds, received five gifts as a result of an appeal for funds. The campaign closed December 31 and all gifts received are to be recorded as of January 1. Gifts were as follow:

1. From A. B. Smith, $10,000, the principal to be held intact and the income to be used for any purpose that the Board of Control of County College should indicate.

2. From C. D. Jones, $20,000, the principal to be held intact and the income to be used to endow scholarships for worthy students.

3. From E. F. Green, $30,000, the principal to be held intact and the interest to be loaned to students. All income is to be again loaned, and all losses from student loans are to be charged against income.

4. From G. H. White, $200,000. During the lifetime of the donor, semiannual payments of $2,500 were to be made to him. Upon his death, the fund was to be used to construct or purchase a residence hall for housing men students.

5. From I. J. Brown, 1,000 shares of *XYZ* stock, which had a market value on this date of $150 per share. Such shares were to be held for not more than five years and all income received thereon held intact. At any date during this period, designated by the Board of Control, all assets were to be liquidated and the proceeds used to build a student hospital.

6. The Board of Control consolidated the Smith and Jones funds as to assets into Merged Investments Account (in the proportion of their principal accounts) and purchased $25,000 Electric Power Company bonds at par. Interest rate, 4 percent. Interest dates, January 1 and July 1.

7. The cash of the Green fund was used to purchase $30,000, 5% bonds of the Steam Power Company at par and accrued interest. Interest dates, April 1 and October 1.

8. The $200,000 cash of the White fund was used to purchase $200,000, 2% U.S. Treasury notes at par. Interest dates, January 1 and July 1.

*July 1*

9. All interest has been received as stipulated on bonds owned and $4,000 dividends were received on *XYZ* stock.

10. Payment was made to G. H. White in accordance with the terms of the gift. A loan of cash was authorized from Endowment Funds to cover the overdraft created.

11. $20,000 par of Electric Power Company bonds were sold at 102. No commission was involved.

12. Loan made to M. N. Black, $300, from the Green student loan fund.

*October 1*

13. Notice was received of the death of G. H. White. There is no liability to his estate.

14. A scholarship award of $200 was made to G. P. Gray from the Jones scholarship fund.

15. $200,000 par of U. S. Treasury notes held by the White fund were sold at 101 and accrued interest. The Endowment Funds loan was repaid.

16. Interest due on bonds was received.

*December 31*

17. M. N. Black paid $100 principal and $5 interest on his student loan.

18. The Board of Control purchased a building suitable for a residence hall for $250,000, using the available funds from the G. H. White gift as part payment therefor and giving a 20-year mortgage payable for the balance.

(AICPA, adapted)

# B

## Glossary[1]

ABATEMENT. A complete or partial cancellation of a levy imposed by a governmental unit. Abatements usually apply to tax levies, special assessments, and service charges.

ACCOUNTING PERIOD. A period at the end of which and for which financial statements are prepared. See also FISCAL PERIOD.

ACCOUNTING SYSTEM. The total structure of records and procedures which discover, record, classify, and report information on the financial position and operations of a governmental unit or any of its funds, balanced account groups, and organizational components.

ACCRUAL BASIS. The basis of accounting under which revenues are recorded when earned and expenditures are recorded as soon as they result in liabilities for benefits received, notwithstanding that the receipt of the revenue or the payment of the expenditure may take place, in whole or in part, in another accounting period.

ACTIVITY. A specific and distinguishable line of work performed by one or more organizational components of a governmental unit for the purpose of accomplishing a function for which the governmental unit is responsible. For example, "Food Inspection" is an activity performed in the discharge of the "Health" function. See also FUNCTION, SUBFUNCTION, and SUBACTIVITY.

ACTIVITY CLASSIFICATION. A grouping of expenditures on the basis of specific lines of work performed by organization units. For example, sewage treatment and dis-

[1]Adapted from National Committee on Governmental Accounting, *Governmental Accounting, Auditing, and Financial Reporting* (Chicago: Municipal Finance Officers Association, 1968), pp. 151–172.

posal, garbage collection, garbage disposal, and street cleaning are activities performed in carrying out the function of sanitation, and the segregation of the expenditures made for each of these activities constitutes an activity classification.

ACTUARIAL BASIS. A basis used in computing the amount of contributions to be made periodically to a fund so that the total contributions plus the compounded earnings thereon will equal the required payments to be made out of the fund. The factors taken into account in arriving at the amount of these contributions include the length of time over which each contribution is to be held and the rate of return compounded on such contribution over its life. A Trust Fund for a public employee retirement system is an example of a fund set up on an actuarial basis.

ADVANCE FROM GOVERNMENTAL UNIT—GENERAL OBLIGATION BONDS. An account in an Enterprise or Intragovernmental Service Fund which represents the fund's liability for general obligation bonds which have been issued by a governmental unit but whose proceeds have been used to finance facilities and operations of such a fund.

ADVANCE FROM _____ FUND. A liability account used to record a long-term debt owed by one fund to another fund in the same governmental unit. See also DUE TO _____ FUND.

ADVANCE TO _____ FUND. An asset account used to record a long-term loan by one fund to another fund in the same governmental unit. See also DUE FROM _____ FUND.

ALLOCATE. To divide a lump-sum appropriation into parts which are designated for expenditure by specific organization units and/or for specific purposes, activities, or objects. See also ALLOCATION.

ALLOCATION. A part of a lump-sum appropriation which is designated for expenditure by specific organization units and/or for special purposes, activities, or objects. See also ALLOCATE.

ALLOT. To divide an appropriation into amounts which may be encumbered or expended during an allotment period. See also ALLOTMENT and ALLOTMENT PERIOD.

ALLOTMENT. A part of an appropriation which may be encumbered or expended during an allotment period. See also ALLOT and ALLOTMENT PERIOD.

ALLOTMENT PERIOD. A period of time less than one fiscal year in length during which an allotment is effective. Bi-monthly and quarterly allotment periods are most common. See also ALLOT and ALLOTMENT.

ALLOTMENT LEDGER. A subsidiary ledger which contains an account for each allotment (q.v.)[2] showing the amount allotted, expenditures, encumbrances, the net balance, and other related information. See also APPROPRIATION LEDGER.

AMORTIZATION. (1) Gradual reduction, redemption, or liquidation of the balance of an account according to a specified schedule of times and amounts. (2) Provision for the extinguishment of a debt by means of a Debt Service Fund.

ANNUITY. A series of equal money payments made at equal intervals during a designated period of time. In governmental accounting the most frequent annuities are accumulations of debt service funds for term bonds and payments to retired employees under public employee retirement systems.

[2]The letters "q.v." in parentheses mean "which see."

ANNUITY PERIOD. The designated length of time during which an amount of annuity is accumulated or paid.

APPROPRIATION. An authorization granted by a legislative body to make expenditures and to incur obligations for specific purposes.

*Note.* An appropriation is usually limited in amount and as to the time when it may be expended. See, however, INDETERMINATE APPROPRIATION.

APPROPRIATION ACCOUNT. A budgetary account set up to record specific authorizations to spend. The account is credited with original and any supplemental appropriations and is charged with expenditures and encumbrances.

APPROPRIATION BALANCE. See UNALLOTTED BALANCE OF APPROPRIATION, UNENCUMBERED ALLOTMENT, UNENCUMBERED APPROPRIATION, UNEXPENDED ALLOTMENT, and UNEXPENDED APPROPRIATION.

APPROPRIATION BILL, ORDINANCE, RESOLUTION, or ORDER. A bill (q.v.), ordinance (q.v.), resolution (q.v.), or order (q.v.) by means of which appropriations are given legal effect. It is the method by which the expenditure side of the budget (q.v.) is enacted into law by the legislative body. In many governmental jurisdictions appropriations cannot be enacted into law by resolution but only by a bill, ordinance, or order.

APPROPRIATION EXPENDITURE. An expenditure chargeable to an appropriation.

*Note:* Since virtually all expenditures of governmental units are chargeable to appropriations, the term EXPENDITURES by itself is widely and properly used.

APPROPRIATION EXPENDITURE LEDGER. See APPROPRIATION LEDGER.

APPROPRIATION LEDGER. A subsidiary ledger containing an account for each appropriation. Each account usually shows the amount originally appropriated, transfers to or from the appropriation, amounts charged against the appropriation, the net balance, and other related information. If allotments are made and a separate ledger is maintained for them, each account in the appropriation ledger usually shows the amount appropriated, transfers to or from the appropriation, the amount allotted, and the unallotted balance. See also ALLOTMENT LEDGER.

ASSESS. To value property officially for the purpose of taxation.

*Note.* The term is also sometimes used to denote the levy of taxes, but such usage is not correct because it fails to distinguish between the valuation process and the tax levy process.

ASSESSED VALUATION. A valuation set upon real estate or other property by a government as a basis for levying taxes.

ASSESSMENT. (1) The process of making the official valuation of property for purposes of taxation. (2) The valuation placed upon property as a result of this process.

ASSESSMENT ROLL. In the case of real property, the official list containing the legal description of each parcel of property and its assessed valuation. The name and address of the last known owner are usually shown.

In the case of personal property, the assessment roll is the official list containing the name and address of the owner, a description of the personal property, and its assessed value.

AUTHORITY. A governmental unit or public agency created to perform a single function or a restricted group of related activities. Usually such units are financed from service charges, fees, and tolls, but in some instances they also have taxing powers. An authority may be completely independent of other governmental units, or in some cases it may be partially dependent upon other governments for its creation, its financing, or the exercise of certain powers.

AUTHORITY BONDS. Bonds payable from the revenues of a specific authority (q.v.). Since such authorities usually have no revenue other than charges for services, their bonds are ordinarily revenue bonds (q.v.).

BOND ANTICIPATION NOTES. Short-term interest-bearing notes issued by a governmental unit in anticipation of bonds to be issued at a later date. The notes are retired from proceeds of the bond issue to which they are related. See also INTERIM BORROWING.

BOND DISCOUNT. The excess of the face value of a bond over the price for which it is acquired or sold.

*Note.* The price does not include accrued interest at the date of acquisition or sale.

BOND FUND. A fund formerly used to account for the proceeds of general obligation bond issues. Such proceeds are now accounted for in a Capital Projects Fund.

BOND ORDINANCE OR RESOLUTION. An ordinance (q.v.) or resolution (q.v.) authorizing a bond issue.

BOND PREMIUM. The excess of the price at which a bond is acquired or sold over its face value.

*Note.* The price does not include accrued interest at the date of acquisition or sale.

BONDED DEBT/BONDED INDEBTEDNESS. That portion of indebtedness represented by outstanding bonds. See GROSS BONDED DEBT and NET BONDED DEBT.

BONDS AUTHORIZED AND UNISSUED. Bonds which have been legally authorized but not issued and which can be issued and sold without further authorization.

*Note.* This term must not be confused with the term "margin of borrowing power" or "legal debt margin," either one of which represents the difference between the legal debt limit (q.v.) of a government unit and the debt outstanding against it.

BUDGET. A plan of financial operation embodying an estimate of proposed expenditures for a given period and the proposed means of financing them. Used without any modifier, the term usually indicates a financial plan for a single fiscal year.

*Note.* The term "budget" is used in two senses in practice. Sometimes it designates the financial plan presented to the appropriating body for adoption and sometimes the plan finally approved by that body. It is usually necessary to specify whether the budget under consideration is preliminary and tentative or whether it has been approved by the appropriating body. See also CURRENT BUDGET, CAPITAL BUDGET, CAPITAL PROGRAM, and LONG-TERM BUDGET.

BUDGET DOCUMENT. The instrument used by the budget-making authority to present a comprehensive financial program to the appropriating body. The budget document usually consists of three parts. The first part contains a message from the budget-making authority, together with a summary of the proposed expenditures and the means of financing them. The second consists of schedules supporting the summary. These schedules show in detail the information as to past years' actual revenues, expenditures, and other data used in making the estimates. The third part is composed of drafts of the appropriation, revenue, and borrowing measures necessary to put the budget into effect.

BUDGET MESSAGE. A general discussion of the proposed budget as presented in writing by the budget-making authority to the legislative body. The budget message should contain an explanation of the principal budget items, an outline of the governmental unit's experience during the past period and its financial status at the time of the message, and recommendations regarding the financial policy for the coming period.

BUDGETARY ACCOUNTS. Those accounts which reflect budgetary operations and condition, such as estimated revenues, appropriations, and encumbrances, as distinguished from proprietary accounts. See also PROPRIETARY ACCOUNTS.

BUDGETARY CONTROL. The control or management of a governmental unit or enterprise in accordance with an approved budget for the purpose of keeping expenditures within the limitations of available appropriations and available revenues.

CALLABLE BOND. A type of bond which permits the issuer to pay the obligation before the stated maturity date by giving notice of redemption in a manner specified in the bond contract. Synonym: Optional Bond.

CAPITAL BUDGET. A plan of proposed capital outlays and the means of financing them for the current fiscal period. It is usually a part of the current budget. If a Capital Program is in operation, it will be the first year thereof. A Capital Program is sometimes referred to as a Capital Budget. See also CAPITAL PROGRAM.

CAPITAL EXPENDITURES/CAPITAL OUTLAYS. Expenditures which result in the acquisition of or addition to fixed assets.

CAPITAL PROGRAM. A plan for capital expenditures to be incurred each year over a fixed period of years to meet capital needs arising from the long term work program or otherwise. It sets forth each project or other contemplated expenditure in which the government is to have a part and specifies the full resources estimated to be available to finance the projected expenditures.

CHARACTER. A basis for distinguishing expenditures according to the periods they are presumed to benefit. See also CHARACTER CLASSIFICATION.

CHARACTER CLASSIFICATION. A grouping of expenditures on the basis of the time periods they are presumed to benefit. The three groupings are (1) expenses, presumed to benefit the current fiscal period (but see note following EXPENSES); (2) provisions for retirement of debt, presumed to benefit prior fiscal periods primarily but also present and future periods; and (3) capital outlays, presumed to benefit the current and future fiscal periods. See also ACTIVITY, ACTIVITY CLASSIFICATION, FUNCTION, FUNCTIONAL CLASSIFICATION, OBJECT, OBJECT CLASSIFICATION, and EXPENSES.

CLEARING ACCOUNT. An account used to accumulate total charges or credits for the purpose of distributing them later among the accounts to which they are allocable or for the purpose of transferring the net differences to the proper account.

CODING. A system of numbering or otherwise designating accounts, entries, invoices, vouchers, etc., in such a manner that the symbol used reveals quickly certain required information. To illustrate the coding of accounts, the number "200" may be assigned to expenditures made by the Department of Finance and the letter "A" may be used to designate expenditures for personal services. Expenditures for personal services in the Department of Finance would then by designated, for posting and other purposes, by the code "200-A." Other examples are the numbering of monthly recurring journal entries so that the number indicates the month and the nature of the entry and the numbering of invoices or vouchers so that the number reveals the date of entry.

COMBINATION BOND. A bond issued by a governmental unit which is payable from the revenues of a governmental enterprise but which is also backed by the full faith and credit of the governmental unit.

CONTINGENT FUND. Assets or other resources set aside to provide for unforeseen expenditures or for anticipated expenditures of uncertain amount.
*Note.* The term should not be used to describe a reserve for contingencies. The

latter is set aside out of the fund balance of a fund but does not constitute a separate fund. Similarly, an appropriation for contingencies is not a contingent fund since an appropriation is not a fund.

CONTINUING APPROPRIATION. An appropriation which, once established, is automatically renewed without further legislative action, period after period, until altered or revoked.

*Note*: The term should not be confused with INDETERMINATE APPROPRIATION (q.v.).

CONTROL ACCOUNT. An account in the general ledger in which are recorded the aggregate of debit and credit postings to a number of identical or related accounts called subsidiary accounts. For example, the *Taxes Receivable* account is a control account supported by the aggregate of individual balances in individual property taxpayers' accounts.

COUPON RATE. The interest rate specified on interest coupons attached to a bond. The term is synonymous with nominal interest rate (q.v.).

COVERAGE. The ratio of net revenue available for debt service to the average annual debt service requirements of an issue of revenue bonds. See also NET REVENUE AVAILABLE FOR DEBT SERVICE.

CURRENT BUDGET. The annual budget prepared for and effective during the present fiscal year; or, in the case of some state governments, the budget for the present biennium.

CURRENT FUNDS: Funds, the resources of which are expended for operating purposes during the current fiscal period. In its usual application in plural form, it refers to general, special revenue, debt service, and enterprise funds of a governmental unit. In the singular form, the current fund is synonymous with the General Fund.

DEBENTURES OR MUNICIPAL DEBENTURES. A term used in Canada and other countries for municipal bonds.

DEBT SERVICE REQUIREMENT. The amount of money required to pay the interest on outstanding debt, serial maturities of principal for serial bonds, and required contributions to a Debt Service Fund for term bonds.

DEFERRED CHARGES/DEFERRED DEBITS. Expenditures which are not chargeable to the fiscal period in which made but are carried on the asset side of the balance sheet pending amortization or other disposition. An example is Discount on Bonds Issued.

*Note*. Deferred charges differ from prepaid expenses in that they usually extend over a long period of time (more than five years) and are not regularly recurring costs of operation.

DEFERRED CREDITS/DEFERRED INCOME. Credit balances or items which will be spread over following accounting periods either as additions to revenue or as reductions of expenses. Examples are taxes collected in advance and premiums on bonds issued.

DEFERRED SERIAL BONDS. Serial bonds (q.v.) in which the first installment does not fall due for two or more years from the date of issue.

DEFERRED SPECIAL ASSESSMENTS. Special assessments which have been levied but which are not yet due.

DEFICIENCY. A general term indicating the amount by which anything falls short of some requirement or expectation. The term should not be used without qualification.

DELINQUENT SPECIAL ASSESSMENTS. Special assessments remaining unpaid on and after the date on which a penalty for non-payment is attached.

DELINQUENT TAXES. Taxes remaining unpaid on and after the date on which a penalty for non-payment is attached. Even though the penalty may be subsequently waived and a portion of the taxes may be abated or cancelled, the unpaid balances continue to be delinquent taxes until abated, cancelled, paid, or converted into tax liens.

*Note.* The term is sometimes limited to taxes levied for the fiscal period or periods preceding the current one, but such usage is not entirely correct.

DEPOSIT WARRANT. A financial document prepared by a designated accounting or finance officer authorizing the treasurer of a governmental unit to accept for deposit sums of money collected by various departments and agencies of the governmental unit.

DIRECT DEBT. The debt which a governmental unit has incurred in its own name or assumed through the annexation of territory or consolidation with another governmental unit. See also OVERLAPPING DEBT.

DUE FROM _____ FUND. An asset account used to indicate amounts owed to a particular fund by another fund in the same governmental unit for goods sold or services rendered. This account includes only short-term obligations on open account and not long-term loans. See ADVANCE TO _____ FUND.

DUE TO _____ FUND. A liability account used to indicate amounts owed by a particular fund to another fund in the same governmental unit for goods sold or services rendered. These amounts include only short-term obligations on open account and not long-term loans. See ADVANCE FROM _____ FUND.

ENCUMBRANCES. Obligations in the form of purchase orders, contracts, or salary commitments which are chargeable to an appropriation and for which a part of the appropriation is reserved. They cease to be encumbrances when paid or when the actual liability is set up.

ENDOWMENT FUND. A fund whose principal must be maintained inviolate but whose income may be expended. An endowment fund is accounted for as a Trust Fund.

ENTERPRISE DEBT. Debt which is to be retired primarily from the earnings of publicly owned and operated enterprises. See also REVENUE BONDS.

ESTIMATED REVENUE. For revenue accounts kept on an accrual basis (q.v.), this term designates the amount of revenue estimated to accrue during a given period regardless of whether or not it is all to be collected during the period. For revenue accounts kept on a cash basis (q.v.) the term designates the amount of revenue estimated to be collected during a given period. Under the modified accrual basis (q.v.) recommended for some funds by the Committee, estimated revenues for many governmental revenues will include both cash and accrual basis revenues. See also REVENUE, REVENUE RECEIPTS, ACCRUAL BASIS, and MODIFIED ACCRUAL BASIS.

ESTIMATED REVENUE RECEIPTS. A term used synonymously with estimated revenue (q.v.) by some governmental units reporting their revenues on a cash basis. See also REVENUE and REVENUE RECEIPTS.

ESTIMATED UNCOLLECTIBLE [TYPE OF] RECEIVABLES (Credit). That portion of receivables which it is estimated will never be collected. The account is deducted from the receivable account on the balance sheet in order to arrive at the net amount of receivables expected to be collected.

EXPENDABLE FUND. A fund whose resources, including both principal and earnings, may be expended. See also NONEXPENDABLE FUND.

EXPENDITURE DISBURSEMENTS. A term sometimes used by governmental units operating on a cash basis (q.v.) as a synonym for expenditures (q.v.). It is *not* recommended terminology.

EXPENDITURES. Where the accounts are kept on the accrual basis (q.v.) or the modified accrual basis (q.v.), this term designates the cost of goods delivered or services rendered, whether paid or unpaid, including expenses, provision for debt retirement not reported as a liability of the fund from which retired, and capital outlays. Where the accounts are kept on the cash basis (q.v.), the term designates only actual cash disbursements for these purposes.
*Note.* Encumbrances are *not* expenditures.

EXPENSES. Charges incurred, whether paid or unpaid, for operation, maintenance, interest, and other charges which are presumed to benefit the current fiscal period. *Note.* Legal provisions sometimes make it necessary to treat as expenses some charges whose benefits extend over future periods. For example, purchases of materials and supplies which may be used over a period of more than one year and payments for insurance which is to be in force for a period longer than one year frequently must be charged in their entirety to the appropriation of the year in which they are incurred and classified as expenses of that year even though their benefits extend also to other periods.

FACE VALUE. As applied to securities, this term designates the amount of liability stated in the security document.

FIDELITY BOND. A written promise to indemnify against losses from theft, defalcation, and misappropriation of public funds by government officers and employees. See also SURETY BOND.

FISCAL PERIOD. Any period at the end of which a governmental unit determines its financial position and the results of its operations.

FISCAL YEAR. A twelve-month period of time to which the annual budget applies and at the end of which a governmental unit determines its financial position and the results of its operations.

FIXED CHARGES. Expenses (q.v.), the amount of which is more or less fixed. Examples are interest, insurance, and contributions to pension funds.

FLOATING DEBT. Liabilities other than bonded debt and time warrants which are payable on demand or at an early date. Examples are accounts payable, notes, and bank loans.

FORCE ACCOUNT. A method employed in the construction and/or maintenance of fixed assets whereby a governmental unit's own personnel are used instead of an outside contractor.
*Note.* This method also calls for the purchase of materials by the governmental unit and the possible use of its own equipment, but the distinguishing characteristic of the force account method is the use of the unit's own personnel.

FULL FAITH AND CREDIT. A pledge of the general taxing power for the payment of debt obligations.
*Note.* Bonds carrying such pledges are usually referred to as general obligation bonds or full faith and credit bonds.

FUNCTION. A group of related activities aimed at accomplishing a major service or regulatory program for which a governmental unit is responsible. For example, public health is a function. See also SUBFUNCTION, ACTIVITY, CHARACTER, and OBJECT.

FUNCTIONAL CLASSIFICATION. A grouping of expenditures on the basis of the principal purposes for which they are made. Examples are public safety, public health, public welfare, etc. See also ACTIVITY, CHARACTER, and OBJECT CLASSIFICATION.

FUND. An independent fiscal and accounting entity with a self-balancing set of accounts recording cash and/or other resources together with all related liabilities, obligations, reserves, and equities which are segregated for the purpose of carrying on specific activities or attaining certain objectives in accordance with special regulations, restrictions, or limitations.

FUND ACCOUNTS. All accounts necessary to set forth the financial operations and financial position of a fund.

FUND BALANCE (AVAILABLE). The excess of the assets of an expendable fund over its liabilities and reserves except in the case of funds subject to budgetary accounting where, prior to the end of a fiscal period, it represents the excess of the fund's assets and estimated revenues for the period over its liabilities, reserves, and appropriations for the period.

FUND BALANCE (TOTAL). The excess of the assets of an expendable fund, or of a nonexpendable Trust Fund, over its liabilities.

FUND BALANCE RECEIPTS. Receipts which increase the fund balance of a fund but which are not included in current revenues. Examples are taxes and accounts receivable which had previously been written off as uncollectible.

FUNDED DEFICIT. A deficit eliminated through the sale of bonds issued for that purpose. See also FUNDING BONDS.

FUND GROUP. A group of funds which are similar in purpose and character. For example, several special revenue funds constitute a fund group. See also RELATED FUNDS.

FUNDING. The conversion of floating debt or time warrants into bonded debt (q.v.).

FUNDING BONDS. Bonds issued to retire outstanding floating debt and to eliminate deficit.

FUND SURPLUS. See FUND BALANCE (AVAILABLE).

GENERAL FIXED ASSETS. Those fixed assets of a governmental unit which are not accounted for in an Enterprise, Trust, or Intragovernmental Service Fund.

GENERAL LONG-TERM DEBT. Long-term debt legally payable from general revenues and backed by the full faith and credit of a governmental unit.

GENERAL OBLIGATION BONDS. Bonds for whose payment the full faith and credit of the issuing body are pledged. More commonly, but not necessarily, general obligation bonds are considered to be those payable from taxes and other general revenues. See also FULL FAITH AND CREDIT.

GENERAL OBLIGATION SPECIAL ASSESSMENT BONDS. See SPECIAL ASSESSMENT BONDS.

GENERAL REVENUE. The revenues (q.v.) of a governmental unit other than those derived from and retained in an enterprise.

Note. If a portion of the net income in an enterprise fund is contributed to another nonenterprise fund, such as the general fund, the amounts transferred constitute general revenue of the governmental unit.

GOVERNMENTAL UNIT'S SHARE OF ASSESSMENT IMPROVEMENT COSTS. An account sometimes used in a Special Assessment Fund to designate the amount receivable from the governmental unit as its share of the cost of a special assessment improvement project.

GRANT. A contribution by one governmental unit to another unit. The contribution is usually made to aid in the support of a specified function (for example, education), but it is sometimes also for general purposes.

GROSS BONDED DEBT. The total amouut of direct debt of a governmental unit represented by outstanding bonds before deduction of any assets available and earmarked for their retirement. See also DIRECT DEBT.

IMPREST SYSTEM. A system for handling minor disbursements whereby a fixed amount of money, designated as petty cash, is set aside for this purpose. Disbursements are made from time to time as needed, a receipt or petty cash voucher being completed in each case. At certain intervals, or when the petty cash is completely expended, a report with substantiating petty cash vouchers is prepared and the petty cash fund is replenished for the amount of disbursements by a check drawn on the appropriate fund bank account. The total of petty cash on hand plus the amount of signed receipts or petty cash vouchers at any one time must equal the total amount of petty cash authorized.

INCOME. A term used in accounting for governmental enterprises to represent the excess of revenues earned over the expenses incurred on the enterprise's operations. It should not be used without an appropriate modifier, such as OPERATING, NON-OPERATING, or NET.
*Note.* The term INCOME should not be used in lieu of REVENUE (q.v.) in nonenterprise funds.

INCOME BONDS. See REVENUE BONDS.

INDEPENDENT AUDITOR. An auditor who is independent of the governmental unit or agency whose accounts are being audited.

INDETERMINATE APPROPRIATION. An appropriation which is not limited either to any definite period of time or to any definite amount, or to both time and amount.
*Note.* A distinction must be made between an indeterminate appropriation and a continuing appropriation. Whereas a continuing appropriation is indefinite only as to time, an indeterminate appropriation is indefinite as to both time and amount. Furthermore, even indeterminate appropriations which are indefinite only as to time are to be distinguished from continuing appropriations in that such indeterminate appropriations may eventually lapse. For example, an appropriation to construct a building may be made to continue in effect until the building is constructed. Once the building is completed, however, the unexpended balance of the appropriation lapses. A continuing appropriation, on the other hand, may continue forever; it can only be abolished by specific action of the legislative body.

INDUSTRIAL AID BONDS. Bonds issued by governmental units, the proceeds of which are used to construct plant facilities for private industrial concerns. Lease payments made by the industrial concern to the governmental unit are used to service the bonds. Such bonds may be in the form of general obligation bonds (q.v.) or combination bonds (q.v.) or revenue bonds (q.v.).

INTER-FUND ACCOUNTS. Accounts in which transactions between funds are reflected. See INTER-FUND TRANSFERS.

INTER-FUND LOANS. Loans made by one fund to another.

INTER-FUND TRANSFERS. Amounts transferred from one fund to another.

INTERGOVERNMENTAL REVENUE. Revenue received from other governments in the form of grants, shared revenues, or payments in lieu of taxes.

INTERIM BORROWING. (1) Short-term loans to be repaid from general revenues during the course of a fiscal year. (2) Short-term loans in anticipation of tax collections or bond issuance. See BOND ANTICIPATION NOTES and TAX ANTICIPATION NOTES.

INTERNAL AUDIT. An independent appraisal activity within a governmental unit which: (a) determines the adequacy of the system of internal control; (b) verifies and safeguards assets; (c) checks on the reliability of the accounting and reporting system; (d) ascertains compliance with established policies and procedures; and (e) appraises performance of activities and work programs.

INTERNAL CONTROL. A plan of organization under which employees' duties are so arranged and records and procedures so designed as to make it possible to exercise effective accounting control over assets, liabilities, revenues, and expenditures. Under such a system, the work of employees is subdivided so that no single employee performs a complete cycle of operations. Thus, for example, an employee handling cash would not post the accounts receivable records. Moreover, under such a system, the procedures to be followed are definitely laid down and require proper authorizations by designated officials for all actions to be taken.

JUDGMENT. An amount to be paid or collected by a governmental unit as the result of a court decision, including a condemnation award in payment for private property taken for public use.

JUDGMENT BONDS. Bonds issued to fund judgments (q.v.). See also FUNDING.

LAPSE. (Verb) As applied to appropriations, this term denotes the automatic termination of an appropriation.
*Note.* Except for indeterminate appropriations (q.v.) and continuing appropriations (q.v.), an appropriation is made for a certain period of time. At the end of this period, any unexpended or unencumbered balance thereof lapses, unless otherwise provided by law.

LEGAL OPINION. (1) The opinion of an official authorized to render it, such as an attorney general or city attorney as to legality. (2) In the case of municipal bonds, the opinion of a specialized bond attorney as to the legality of a bond issue.

LEVY. (Verb) To impose taxes, special assessments, or service charges for the support of governmental activities. (Noun) The total amount of taxes, special assessments, or service charges imposed by a governmental unit.

LOAN FUND. A fund whose principal and/or interest is loaned to individuals in accordance with the legal requirements and agreements setting up the fund. Such a fund is accounted for as a Trust Fund.

LOCAL IMPROVEMENT TAX. See SPECIAL ASSESSMENT.

LONG-TERM BUDGET. A budget prepared for a period longer than a fiscal year, or in the case of some state governments, a budget prepared for a period longer than a biennium. If the long-term budget is restricted to capital expenditures, it is called a CAPITAL PROGRAM (q.v.) or a CAPITAL IMPROVEMENT PROGRAM.

LONG-TERM DEBT. Debt with a maturity of more than one year after the date of issuance.

LUMP-SUM APPROPRIATION. An appropriation made for a stated purpose, or for a named department, without specifying further the amounts that may be spent for specific activities or for particular objects of expenditure. An example of such an appropriation would be one for the police department which does not specify the amounts to be spent for uniform patrol, traffic control, etc., or for salaries and wages, materials and supplies, travel, etc.

MODIFIED ACCRUAL BASIS. The basis of accounting under which expenditures other than accrued interest on general long-term debt are recorded at the time liabilities are incurred and revenues are recorded when received in cash, except for material and/or available revenues which should be accrued to reflect properly the taxes levied and the revenues earned.

MORTGAGE BONDS. Bonds secured by a mortgage against specified properties of a governmental unit, usually its public utilities or other enterprises. If primarily payable from enterprise revenues, they are also classed as revenue bonds. See also' REVENUE BONDS.

MUNICIPAL. In its broadest sense, an adjective which denotes the state and all subordinate units of government. In a more restricted sense, an adjective which denotes a city or town as opposed to other units of local government.

MUNICIPAL BOND. A bond issued by a state or local governmental unit.

MUNICIPAL CORPORATION. A body politic and corporate established pursuant to state authorization for the purpose of providing governmental services and regulations for its inhabitants. A municipal corporation has defined boundaries and a population, and is usually organized with the consent of its residents. It usually has a seal and may sue and be sued. Cities and towns are examples of municipal corporations. See also QUASI-MUNICIPAL CORPORATIONS.

MUNICIPAL IMPROVEMENT CERTIFICATES. Certificates issued in lieu of bonds for the financing of special improvements.
Note. As a rule, these certificates are placed in the contractor's hands for collection from the special assessment payers.

NET BONDED DEBT. Gross bonded debt (q.v.) less any cash or other assets available and earmarked for its retirement.

NET REVENUE AVAILABLE FOR DEBT SERVICE. Gross operating revenues of an enterprise less operating and maintenance expenses but exclusive of depreciation and bond interest. "Net Revenue" as thus defined is used to compute "coverage" on revenue bond issues. See also COVERAGE.
Note. Under the laws of some states and the provisions of some revenue bond indentures, net revenues used for computation of coverage are required to be on a cash basis rather than an accrual basis.

NOMINAL INTEREST RATE. The contractual interest rate shown on the face and in the body of a bond and representing the amount of interest to be paid, in contrast to the effective interest rate. See also COUPON RATE.

NONEXPENDABLE FUND. A fund, the principal and sometimes also the earnings of which may not be expended. See also ENDOWMENT FUND.

NON-EXPENDITURE DISBURSEMENTS. Disbursements which are not chargeable as expenditures; for example, a disbursement made for the purpose of paying off an account payable previously recorded on the books.

NON-REVENUE RECEIPTS. Collections, other than revenue (q.v.), such as receipts from loans where the liability is recorded in the fund in which the proceeds are placed and receipts on account of recoverable expenditures. See also REVENUE RECEIPTS.

OBJECT. As used in expenditure classification, this term applies to the article purchased or the service obtained (as distinguished from the results obtained from expenditures). Examples are personal services, contractual services, materials, and supplies. See also ACTIVITY, CHARACTER, FUNCTION, and OBJECT CLASSIFICATION.

OBJECT CLASSIFICATION. A grouping of expenditures on the basis of goods or services purchased; for example, personal services, materials, supplies, and equipment. See also FUNCTIONAL, ACTIVITY, and CHARACTER CLASSIFICATIONS.

OBJECTS OF EXPENDITURE. See OBJECT.

OBLIGATIONS. Amounts which a governmental unit may be required legally to meet out of its resources. They include not only actual liabilities but also unliquidated encumbrances. Synonymous with ENCUMBRANCES (q.v.) when used in Federal government terminology.

OPERATING BUDGET. A budget which applies to all outlays other than capital outlays. See BUDGET.

ORDER. A formal legislative enactment by the governing body of certain local government units which has the full force and effect of law. For example, county government bodies in some states pass "orders" rather than laws or ordinances.

ORDINANCE. A formal legislative enactment by the council or governing body of a municipality. If it is not in conflict with any higher form of law, such as a state statute or constitutional provision, it has the full force and effect of law within the boundaries of the municipality to which it applies.
Note. The difference between an ordinance and a resolution (q.v.) is that the latter requires less legal formality and has a lower legal status. Ordinarily, the statutes or charter will specify or imply those legislative actions which must be by ordinance and those which may be by resolution. Revenue raising measures, such as the imposition of taxes, special assessments and service charges, universally require ordinances.

OUTLAYS. Synonymous with EXPENDITURES. See also CAPITAL OUTLAYS.

OVERLAPPING DEBT. The proportionate share of the debts of local governmental units located wholly or in part within the limits of the reporting government which must be borne by property within each governmental unit.
Note. Except for special assessment debt, the amount of debt of each unit applicable to the reporting unit is arrived at by (1) determining what percentage of the total assessed value of the overlapping jurisdiction lies within the limits of the reporting unit, and (2) applying this percentage to the total debt of the overlapping jurisdiction. Special assessment debt is allocated on the basis of the ratio of assessments receivable in each jurisdiction which will be used wholly or in part to pay off the debt to total assessments receivable which will be used wholly or in part for this purpose.

PAY-AS-YOU-GO BASIS. A term used to describe the financial policy of a governmental unit which finances all of its capital outlays from current revenues rather than by borrowing. A governmental unit which pays for some improvements from current revenues and others by borrowing is said to be on a partial or modified pay-as-you-go basis.

PAY-IN WARRANT. See DEPOSIT WARRANT.

PERFORMANCE BUDGET. A budget wherein expenditures are based primarily upon measurable performance of activities and work programs. A performance budget may also incorporate other bases of expenditure classification, such as character and object, but these are given a subordinate status to activity performance.

PERPETUAL INVENTORY. A system whereby the inventory of units of property at any date may be obtained directly from the records without resorting to an actual physical count. A record is provided for each item or group of items to be inventoried and is so divided as to provide a running record of goods ordered, received, and withdrawn, and the balance on hand, in units and frequently also in value.

PREPAYMENT OF TAXES. The deposit of money with a governmental unit on condition that the amount deposited is to be applied against the tax liability of a designated taxpayer after the taxes have been levied and such liability has been established. See also TAXES COLLECTED IN ADVANCE.

PRIVATE TRUST FUND. A trust fund which will ordinarily revert to private individuals or will be used for private purposes; for example, a fund which consists of guarantee deposits.

PROGRAM BUDGET. A budget wherein expenditures are based primarily on programs of work and secondarily on character and object. A program budget is a transitional type of budget between the traditional character and object budget, on the one hand, and the performance budget, on the other. See also PERFORMANCE BUDGET and TRADITIONAL BUDGET.

PROPRIETARY ACCOUNTS. Those accounts which show actual financial position and operations, such as actual assets, liabilities, reserves, fund balances, revenues, and expenditures, as distinguished from budgetary accounts (q.v.).

PUBLIC AUTHORITY. See AUTHORITY.

PUBLIC CORPORATION. See MUNICIPAL CORPORATION and QUASI-MUNICIPAL CORPORATION.

PUBLIC TRUST FUND. A trust fund whose principal, earnings, or both, must be used for a public purpose; for example, a pension or retirement fund.

QUASI-MUNICIPAL CORPORATION. An agency established by the state primarily for the purpose of helping the state to carry out its function; for example, a county or school district.

*Note.* Some counties and other agencies ordinarily classified as quasi-municipal corporations have been granted the powers of municipal corporations by the state in which they are located. See also MUNICIPAL CORPORATIONS.

RATE BASE. The value of utility property used in computing an authorized rate of return as authorized by law or a regulatory commission.

REBATES. Abatements (q.v.) or refunds (q.v.).

RECOVERABLE EXPENDITURE. An expenditure made for or on behalf of another governmental unit, fund, or department, or for a private individual, firm, or corporation which will subsequently be recovered in cash or its equivalent.

REFUND. (Noun) An amount paid back or credit allowed because of an overcollection or on account of the return of an object sold. (Verb) To pay back or allow credit for an amount because of an over-collection or because of the return of an object sold. (Verb) To provide for the payment of a loan through cash or credit secured by a new loan.

REFUNDING BONDS. Bonds issued to retire bonds already outstanding. The refunding bonds may be sold for cash and outstanding bonds redeemed in cash, or the refunding bonds may be exchanged with holders of outstanding bonds.

REGISTERED BOND. A bond whose owner is registered with the issuing governmental unit and which cannot be sold or exchanged without a change of registration.

Such a bond may be registered as to principal and interest or as to principal only.

REGISTERED WARRANT. A warrant which is registered by the paying officer for future payment on account of present lack of funds and which is to be ·paid in the order of its registration. In some cases, such warrants are registered when issued; in others, when first presented to the paying officer by the holders. See also WARRANT.

REGULAR SERIAL BONDS. Serial bonds in which all periodic installments of principal repayment are equal in amount.

REIMBURSABLE EXPENDITURE. See RECOVERABLE EXPENDITURE.

REIMBURSEMENT. Cash or other assets received as a repayment of the cost of work or services performed or of other expenditures made for or on behalf of another governmental unit or department or for an individual, firm, or corporation.

RELATED FUNDS. Funds of a similar character which are brought together for administrative or reporting purposes; for example, Trust and Agency Funds.

REQUISITION. A written demand or request, usually from one department to the purchasing officer or to another department, for specified articles or services.

RESERVE. An account which records a portion of the fund balance which must be segregated for some future use and which is, therefore, not available for further appropriation or expenditure. A Reserve for Inventories equal in amount to the Inventory of Supplies on the balance sheet of a General Fund is an example of such a reserve.

RESERVE FOR ADVANCE TO _____ FUND. A reserve which represents the segregation of a portion of a fund balance to indicate that assets equal to the amount of the reserve are tied up in a long-term loan to another fund and are, therefore, not available for appropriation.

RESERVE FOR EMPLOYEES' CONTRIBUTIONS. A reserve in a Trust Fund for a public employee retirement system which represents the amount of accumulated contributions made by employee members plus interest earnings credited in accordance with applicable legal provisions.

RESERVE FOR EMPLOYER CONTRIBUTIONS. A reserve in a Trust Fund for a public employee retirement system which represents the amount of accumulated contributions paid by the governmental unit as employer plus interest credited in accordance with applicable legal provisions.

RESERVE FOR EMPLOYER CONTRIBUTIONS—ACTUARIAL DEFICIENCY. A reserve in a Trust Fund for a public employee retirement system which represents the amount of the actuarial deficiency in contributions made by a governmental unit as employer.

RESERVE FOR ENCUMBRANCES. A reserve representing the segregation of a portion of a fund balance to provide for unliquidated encumbrances (q.v.). See also RESERVE.

RESERVE FOR INVENTORY OF SUPPLIES. A reserve which represents the segregation of a portion of fund balance to indicate that assets equal to the amount of the reserve are tied up in inventories and are, therefore, not available for appropriation.

RESERVE FOR MEMBERSHIP ANNUITIES. A reserve in a Trust Fund for a public employee retirement system which represents the amount set aside for payment of annuities to retired members. In a joint contributory system this reserve is established at the time of employee retirement by transfers from accumulations in the *Reserve for Employees' Contributions* and the *Reserve for Employer Contributions* accounts.

RESERVE FOR REVENUE BOND CONTINGENCY. A reserve in an Enterprise Fund which represents the segregation of a portion of retained earnings equal to current assets that are restricted for meeting various contingencies as may be specified and defined in the revenue bond indenture.

RESERVE FOR REVENUE BOND DEBT SERVICE. A reserve in an Enterprise Fund which represents the segregation of a portion of retained earnings equal to current assets that are restricted to current servicing of revenue bonds in accordance with the terms of a bond indenture.

RESERVE FOR REVENUE BOND RETIREMENT. A reserve in an Enterprise Fund which represents the segregation of a portion of retained earnings equal to current assets that are restricted for future servicing of revenue bonds in accordance with the terms of a bond indenture.

RESERVE FOR UNCOLLECTED TAXES. A reserve representing the segregation of a portion of a fund balance equal to the amount of taxes receivable by a fund.

RESERVE FOR UNDISTRIBUTED INTEREST EARNINGS. An unallocated reserve in a Trust Fund for a public employee retirement system which represents interest earnings of the system that have not been distributed to other reserves such as the *Reserve for Employees' Contributions* and the *Reserve for Employer Contributions*.

RESERVE FOR VARIATIONS IN ACTUARIAL ASSUMPTIONS. An unallocated reserve in a Trust Fund for a public employee retirement system which reflects adjustments to reserves for retirement benefits in force resulting from variations in mortality, turnover, and interest experience.

RESOLUTION. A special or temporary order of a legislative body; an order of a legislative body requiring less legal formality than an ordinance or statute. See also ORDINANCE.

RESOURCES. The assets of a governmental unit, such as cash, taxes receivable, land, buildings, etc. plus contingent assets such as estimated revenues applying to the current fiscal year not accrued or collected and bonds authorized and unissued.

RESTRICTED ASSETS. Moneys or other resources, the use of which is restricted by legal or contractual requirements. The most common examples of restricted assets in governmental accounting are those arising out of revenue bond indentures in Enterprise Funds. Also called RESTRICTED FUNDS, but this terminology is not preferred.

REVENUE. For those revenues which are recorded on the accrual basis (q.v.), this term designates additions to assets which: (a) do not increase any liability; (b) do not represent the recovery of an expenditure; (c) do not represent the cancellation of certain liabilities without a corresponding increase in other liabilities or a decrease in assets; and (d) do not represent contributions of fund capital in Enterprise and Intragovernmental Service Funds. The same definition applies to those cases where revenues are recorded on the modified accrual or cash basis, except that additions would be partially or entirely to cash. See also ACCRUAL BASIS, MODIFIED ACCRUAL BASIS, and NET REVENUE AVAILABLE FOR DEBT SERVICE.

REVENUE BONDS. Bonds whose principal and interest are payable exclusively from earnings of a public enterprise. In addition to a pledge of revenues, such bonds sometimes contain a mortgage on the enterprise's property and are then known as Mortgage Revenue Bonds.

REVENUE RECEIPTS. A term used synonymously with "revenue" (q.v.) by some governmental units which account for their revenues on a "cash basis" (q.v.). See also NON-REVENUE RECEIPTS.

REVOLVING FUND. Intragovernmental Service Fund.

SCRIP. An evidence of indebtedness, usually in small denomination, secured or unsecured, interest-bearing or non-interest-bearing, stating that the governmental unit, under conditions set forth, will pay the face value of the certificate or accept it in payment of certain obligations.

SELF-SUPPORTING or SELF-LIQUIDATING DEBT. Debt obligations whose principal and interest are payable solely from the earnings of the enterprise for the construction or improvement of which they were originally issued. See also REVENUE BONDS.

SERIAL ANNUITY BONDS. Serial bonds in which the annual installments of bond principal are so arranged that the combined payments for principal and interest are approximately the same each year.

SERIAL BONDS. Bonds the principal of which is repaid in periodic installments over the life of the issue. See SERIAL ANNUITY BONDS and DEFERRED SERIAL BONDS.

SHARED REVENUE. Revenue which is levied by one governmental unit but shared, usually in proportion to the amount collected, with another unit of government or class of governments.

SHARED TAX. See SHARED REVENUE.

SINKING FUND BONDS. Bonds issued under an agreement which requires the governmental unit to set aside periodically out of its revenues a sum which, with compound earnings thereon, will be sufficient to redeem the bonds at their stated date of maturity. Sinking fund bonds are usually also term bonds (q.v.).

SPECIAL ASSESSMENT. A compulsory levy made by a local government against certain properties to defray part or all of the cost of a specific improvement or service which is presumed to be of general benefit to the public and of special benefit to such properties.

*Note.* The term should not be used without a modifier (for example, "special assessments for street paving," or "special assessments for street sprinkling") unless the intention is to have it cover both improvements and services or unless the particular use is apparent from the context.

SPECIAL ASSESSMENT BONDS. Bonds payable from the proceeds of special assessments (q.v.). If the bonds are payable only from the collections of special assessments, they are known as "special assessment bonds." If, in addition to the assessments, the full faith and credit of the governmental unit are pledged, they are known as "general obligation special assessment bonds."

SPECIAL ASSESSMENT LIENS. Claims which a governmental unit has upon properties until special assessments (q.v.) levied against them have been paid. The term normally applies to those delinquent special assessments for the collection of which legal action has been taken through the filing of claims.

SPECIAL ASSESSMENT ROLL. The official list showing the amount of special assessments (q.v.) levied against each property presumed to be benefited by an improvement or service.

SPECIAL DISTRICT. An independent unit of local government organized to perform a single governmental function or a restricted number of related functions. Special districts usually have the power to incur debt and levy taxes; however, certain types of special districts are entirely dependent upon enterprise earnings and cannot impose taxes. Examples of special districts are water districts, drainage districts, flood control districts, hospital districts, fire protection districts, transit authorities, port authorities, and electric power authorities.

SPECIAL DISTRICT BONDS. Bonds issued by a special district. See SPECIAL DISTRICT.

SPECIAL FUND. Any fund which must be devoted to some special use in accordance with specific regulations and restrictions. Generally, the term applies to all funds other than the General Fund.

SPECIAL LIEN BONDS. Special assessment bonds which are liens against particular pieces of property.

SPECIAL-SPECIAL ASSESSMENT BONDS. See SPECIAL ASSESSMENT BONDS.

STATE-COLLECTED LOCALLY-SHARED TAX. See SHARED REVENUE.

STATUTE. A written law enacted by a duly organized and constituted legislative body. See also ORDINANCE, RESOLUTION, and ORDER.

STRAIGHT SERIAL BONDS. Serial bonds (q.v.) in which the annual installments of bond principal are approximately equal.

SUBACTIVITY. A specific line of work performed in carrying out a governmental activity. For example, cleaning luminaires and replacing defective street lamps would be subactivities under the activity of Street Light Maintenance.

SUBFUNCTION. A grouping of related activities within a particular governmental function. For example, Police is a subfunction of the function Public Safety.

SURETY BOND. A written promise to pay damages or to indemnify against losses caused by the party or parties named in the document, through non-performance or through defalcation. An example is a surety bond given by a contractor or by an official handling cash or securities.

SURPLUS. See FUND BALANCE and RETAINED EARNINGS.

SUSPENSE ACCOUNT. An account which carries charges or credits temporarily pending the determination of the proper account or accounts to which they are to be posted. See also SUSPENSE FUND.

SUSPENSE FUND. A fund established to account separately for certain receipts pending the distribution or disposal thereof. Agency Fund.

TAX ANTICIPATION NOTES. Notes (sometimes called warrants) issued in anticipation of collections of taxes, usually retirable only from tax collections, and frequently only from the proceeds of the tax levy whose collection they anticipate.

TAX ANTICIPATION WARRANTS. See TAX ANTICIPATION NOTES.

TAX CERTIFICATE. A certificate issued by a governmental unit as evidence of the conditional transfer of title to tax-delinquent property from the original owner to the holder of the certificate. If the owner does not pay the amount of the tax arrearage and other charges required by law during the specified period of redemption, the holder can foreclose to obtain title. Also called tax sale certificate and tax lien certificate in some jurisdictions. See also TAX DEED.

TAX DEED. A written instrument by which title to property sold for taxes is transferred unconditionally to the purchaser. A tax deed is issued upon foreclosure of the tax lien (q.v.) obtained by the purchaser at the tax sale. The tax lien cannot be foreclosed until the expiration of the period during which the owner may redeem his property through paying the delinquent taxes and other charges. See also TAX CERTIFICATE.

TAX LEVY ORDINANCE. An ordinance (q.v.) by means of which taxes are levied.

TAX LIENS. Claims which governmental units have upon properties until taxes levied against them have been paid.
*Note.* The term is sometimes limited to those delinquent taxes for the collection of which legal action has been taken through the filing of liens.

TAX NOTES. See TAX ANTICIPATION NOTES.

TAX RATE. The amount of tax stated in terms of a unit of the tax base; for example, 25 mills per dollar of assessed valuation of taxable property.

TAX RATE LIMIT. The maximum rate at which a governmental unit may levy a tax. The limit may apply to taxes raised for a particular purpose, or to taxes imposed for all purposes, and may apply to a single government, to a class of governments, or to all governmental units operating in a particular area. Over-all tax rate limits usually restrict levies for all purposes and of all governments, state and local, having jurisdiction in a given area.

TAX ROLL. The official list showing the amount of taxes levied against each taxpayer or property. Frequently, the tax roll and the assessment roll (q.v.) are combined, but even in these cases the two can be distinguished.

TAX SUPPLEMENT. A tax levied by a local unit of government which has the same base as a similar tax levied by a higher level of government, such as a state or province. The local tax supplement is frequently administered by the higher level of government along with its own tax. A locally-imposed, state-administered sales tax is an example of a tax supplement.

TAX TITLE NOTES. Obligations secured by pledges of the governmental unit's interest in certain tax liens or tax titles.

TAXES. Compulsory charges levied by a governmental unit for the purpose of financing services performed for the common benefit.
*Note.* The term does not include specific charges made against particular persons or property for current or permanent benefits such as special assessments. Neither does the term include charges for services rendered only to those paying such charges as, for example, sewer service charges.

TAXES COLLECTED IN ADVANCE. A liability for taxes collected before the tax levy has been made or before the amount of taxpayer liability has been established.

TAXES LEVIED FOR OTHER GOVERNMENTAL UNITS. Taxes levied by the reporting governmental unit for other governmental units which, when collected, are to be paid over to these units.

TERM BONDS. Bonds the entire principal of which matures on one date. Also called sinking fund bonds (q.v.).

TIME WARRANT. A negotiable obligation of a governmental unit having a term shorter than bonds and frequently tendered to individuals and firms in exchange for contractual services, capital acquisitions, or equipment purchases.

TRADITIONAL BUDGET. A term sometimes applied to the budget of a governmental unit wherein expenditures are based entirely or primarily on objects of expenditure. See also PROGRAM BUDGET and PERFORMANCE BUDGET.

TRANSFER VOUCHER. A voucher authorizing transfers of cash or other resources between funds.

UNALLOTTED BALANCE OF APPROPRIATION. An appropriation balance available for allotment (q.v.).

UNAPPROPRIATED BUDGET SURPLUS. Where the fund balance at the close of the preceding year is not included in the annual budget, this term designates that portion of the current fiscal year's estimated revenues which has not been appropriated. Where the fund balance of the preceding year is included, this term designates the estimated fund balance at the end of the current fiscal period.

UNENCUMBERED ALLOTMENT. That portion of an allotment not yet expended or encumbered.

UNENCUMBERED APPROPRIATION. That portion of an appropriation not yet expended or encumbered.

UNEXPENDED ALLOTMENT. That portion of an allotment which has not been expended.

UNEXPENDED APPROPRIATION. That portion of an appropriation which has not been expended.

UNIT TAX LEDGER. A ledger in which is recorded the assessed value and other data on taxable properties. Where the unit tax ledger system is used, there is an individual ledger card for each piece of taxable property, and where legal provisions permit, this ledger functions in lieu of a tax roll.

UNLIQUIDATED ENCUMBRANCES. Encumbrances outstanding. See also ENCUMBRANCES.

UTILITY FUND. Enterprise Fund.

WARRANT. An order drawn by the legislative body or an officer of a governmental unit upon its treasurer directing the latter to pay a specified amount to the person named or to the bearer. It may be payable upon demand, in which case it usually circulates the same as a bank check; or it may be payable only out of certain revenues when and if received, in which case it does not circulate as freely. See also REGISTERED WARRANT and DEPOSIT WARRANT.

WORK PROGRAM. A plan of work proposed to be done during a particular period by an administrative agency in carrying out its assigned activities.

WORK UNIT. A fixed quantity which will consistently measure work effort expended in the performance of an activity or the production of a commodity.

WORKING CAPITAL FUND. Intragovernmental Service Fund.

# Index

DATE DUE